Health Psychology

Second Edition

Catherine A. Sanderson

WILEY

John Wiley & Sons, Inc.

Vice President and Executive Publisher	Jay O'Callaghan
Senior Acquisitions Editor	Robert Johnston
Associate Editor	Brittany Cheetham
Editorial Assistant	Maura Gilligan
Marketing Manager	Margaret Barrett
Media Specialist	Andre Legaspi
Photo Researcher	Sheena Goldstein
Senior Production Manager	Janis Soo
Associate Production Manager	Joyce Poh
Assistant Production Editor	Yee Lyn Song
Cover Designer	Alson Low
Cover Photo Credit	Ulrich Kerth/Getty Images, Inc.

This book was set in 11/12/ Bembo by Laserwords Private Limited and printed and bound by R.R. Donnelley. The cover was printed by R.R. Donnelley. ⊗

This book is printed on acid-free paper.

Founded in 1807, John Wiley & Sons, Inc. has been a valued source of knowledge and understanding for more than 200 years, helping people around the world meet their needs and fulfill their aspirations. Our company is built on a foundation of principles that include responsibility to the communities we serve and where we live and work. In 2008, we launched a Corporate Citizenship Initiative, a global effort to address the environmental, social, economic, and ethical challenges we face in our business. Among the issues we are addressing are carbon impact, paper specifications and procurement, ethical conduct within our business and among our vendors, and community and charitable support. For more information, please visit our website: www.wiley.com/go/citizenship.

Library of Congress Cataloging-in-Publication Data

Sanderson, Catherine Ashley, 1968–
  Health psychology / Catherine A. Sanderson.—2nd ed.
      p. cm.
    Includes bibliographical references and index.
    ISBN 978-0-470-12915-9 (hardback)
  1. Clinical health psychology.   2. Health—Psychological aspects.   3. Medicine and psychology. I. Title.
    R726.7.S26 2013
    616.89—dc23

                                                    2011047546

Printed in the United States of America

10 9 8 7 6 5 4 3 2

For Bart

PREFACE

When I agreed to write the first edition of this textbook in 2001, I was in my fourth year as an assistant professor, had a 2 1/2-year-old son, and was in my eighth month of pregnancy with my second son. As I now complete this second edition, I am struck by the large growth in this field over the past 10 years, including advances in treating illness and disease that continue to increase life expectancy, a greater understanding of the influence of genetics on health, and a growing awareness of the link between psychological states and physical well-being. I am also struck by the changes in my life over the past decade that influence the approach I bring to this material. My then-toddler turns 13 next week, and hence I write about smoking and alcohol use and motor vehicle accidents with a growing awareness of the health challenges teenagers face. I now have a daughter, and thus am increasingly aware of the pressures facing girls in terms of the thinness norm, which can lead to negative body image and disordered eating. During the past decade, I also lost my mother, who died at age 57 after a 4-month battle with ovarian cancer, and I therefore write about cancer, terminal illness, and bereavement from a highly personal perspective. On a national level, President Barack Obama is working on creating national health coverage, which will clearly have implications for health, especially for lower income people who too often lack health insurance.

I have several goals for the second edition of this book. First, one of the aspects of health psychology that I find most exciting is its basis in research, specifically in research conducted using the scientific method. I am always shocked when students refer to discussions of research methods as "the boring part" that they must suffer through before we move to the more interesting topics of alcohol and eating disorders and AIDS. Therefore, one of my major goals in this book is to show students the exciting aspects of thinking about and conducting research. Chapter 2 focuses entirely on research methods (and I promise, it is not dry or boring), and I describe specific research studies—ones chosen to be interesting to college students—in detail in each of the subsequent chapters. You'll read about a study that examines the impact of "friendship bracelets" on condom use, another study that examines whether emergency room visits are lower following the release of the latest Harry Potter book, and still another study examining whether hospice patients who get more frequent visits live longer (they do). I also include graphs of research data in every chapter to show you how research findings are typically presented and samples of actual research questionnaires so that you can see how you score on these measures (aren't you curious to know how optimistic you are and what strategies you tend to use to cope with pain?).

I also want students who read this book to actively think about and even question what I am describing. This is not a book that you should simply read and try to memorize so you can repeat back "the right answer" on an exam or homework assignment. Of course, I'd like you to read and believe what I'm writing, but I'd also like you to think critically about the information presented. I therefore include "questioning the research" queries about particular research studies in most chapters for you to try and answer—and you should be asking yourself these same types of questions throughout all the chapters. If I write that married people live longer than single people (which is true), you should think about why this may be so: Is it that being married leads people to engage in healthier behavior, or is it that people who are healthy are more likely to get married, or is it that people who are optimistic are very likely to get married and are also likely to engage in healthy behaviors? All of these are potential explanations for the link between marriage and health—and there are, of course, many others.

Third, I've added several entirely new features so that my book covers the most current findings in health psychology. I've added an entirely new chapter on injuries and injury prevention, which is particularly important because injuries are the leading cause of death for people ages 1 to 44. Sadly, the leading causes of death for adolescents and young adults—the ages of those most likely to be reading this book—are all injuries, including motor vehicle accidents, homicide, and suicide. I've also added boxes highlighting the role of development in most chapters to help students understand how psychology impacts health in different ways throughout the life span. For example, Chapter 3 examines how the price of snack foods influences children's preferences of such foods, Chapter 4 examines the influence of early stress on how people cope with stress throughout the life span, Chapter 5 examines the influence of childhood personality and adult health-related behaviors, and Chapter 7 describes the hazards of passive smoking on children's health. And because I want you to understand cultural differences in how the principles of health psychology influence behavior, I have included boxes focusing on the role of culture in most chapters. For example, Chapter 4 describes research showing that writing about negative experiences is beneficial for health in Caucasian students but not in Asian students, Chapter 5 describes how the types of social support that are most beneficial vary by culture, Chapter 6 describes the influence of culture on the risk for childhood injuries, and Chapter 11 describes the influence of culture on grief.

Fourth, I want you to learn how the topics addressed in this book have real implications for practical and real-world issues. In fact, one of the reasons, I love teaching health psychology is because the information students can learn by taking this class, and by reading this book, can make a substantial difference in their lives (and perhaps even the lives of their friends and family). This book therefore includes boxes in most chapters called "Health Psychology in the Real World," which provide a real person's experience coping with a health issue, such as deciding to test for Huntington's disease, trying to recover from an eating disorder, or the tragedy of drunk driving. And it gives you information that you can use now and for the rest of your life—information about why students often get sick right after they take final exams, strategies for managing the (tremendous) pain of childbirth, and descriptions of the stages of bereavement following the death of a loved one. I've also included numerous real-world and highly recent examples to help you make connections between what you've learned in the text and the real world, including a photo of the royal wedding between Prince William and Kate Middleton in 2011, coverage of the deadly tornados in Alabama in 2011, and coverage of the VA Tech shootings in 2007.

Finally, no matter how much information a textbook provides, it is useless if students choose not to actually read it (yes, professors are aware that students sometimes do not do all of the reading). I therefore worked to make this book interesting and exciting. It includes real-world examples, photographs, and even cartoons. A professor who reviewed the first edition of this book wrote, "This text reads like Professor Sanderson is having a conversation"—and this is exactly the tone I have tried to maintain in this updated version. Although this will be mostly a one-sided conversation, I'd love to hear what you think; please drop me an e-mail message (casanderson@amherst.edu) and tell me what you learned, what you liked, and even what you didn't like! Let the conversation begin.

Acknowledgments

Writing this book has been a tremendous undertaking, and I want to acknowledge a number of people who have provided considerable assistance at various points along the way. First, I have received considerable assistance from numerous people at Wiley, including Jay O'Callaghan (vice president and executive publisher), Robert Johnston (acquisitions editor), Steve Chasey (permissions), Sheena Goldstein (photos), Maura Gilligan (editorial assistant), Yee Lyn Song (production), Margaret Barrett (marketing), and especially Eileen McKeever and Brittany Cheetham (associate editors), who both provided and responded to multiple e-mails each day making sure I (mostly) made my deadlines and answering any and all questions.

The second edition of this book also benefitted from helpful comments from professors, who took time out of their own teaching and research responsibilities to share with me both what they liked about my plans for my revisions as well as what could be even better. This book is better thanks to the careful and constructive feedback provided by the following professors: Thomas Plante (Santa Clara University), Benita Jackson (Smith College), Luis Montesinos (Montclair State University), J. Mark McKellop (Juniata College), Dante Spetter (Harvard University), Daniel Holland (University of Arkansas at Little Rock), Astrida Kaugers (Marquette University), Linda Lin (Emmanuel College), Zaje Harrell (Michigan State University), Michael Berg (Wheaton College), and Laura Simonelli (Ohio State University).

Finally, I need to give a special thanks to my spouse (Bart) and children (Andrew, Robert, and Caroline) for letting me (at least sometimes) have quiet writing time on the weekends and evenings and allowing me to take over not only my study but also the dining room table.

CONTENTS

CHAPTER 3

Theories of Health Behavior   58

CHAPTER **4**
Stress   91

CHAPTER 5
Managing Stress: The Role of Personality and Social
Support   142

CHAPTER 8

Obesity and Eating Disorders   255

Chapter 10
Chronic Illness   344

CHAPTER 11

Terminal Illness and Bereavement   399

CHAPTER 12

Health-Care Interaction: Screening, Utilization, Adherence, and Relapse   441

CHAPTER 14

Future Directions for Health Psychology   534

CHAPTER 1

Introduction

Outline

- Peyton is a first-year student at a prestigious law school. She is taking four courses and works 10 hours a week as a paralegal to help pay her tuition. Peyton is also busy applying for summer jobs and is a writer for the law review journal. Although Peyton is under pressure, she takes a yoga class three times a week and frequently gets together with friends for dinner. She feels happy and healthy.

- Phillip is a senior in high school and smokes about a pack of cigarettes a day. Although he knows that smoking causes some types of cancer, he intends to quit smoking when he starts college next year, and he doesn't really see how smoking for just a few years is such a big deal. Most of his friends smoke, and he would feel uncomfortable being the only one at a party not smoking.

- Deirdra is 28 years old and works full time as a cashier in a drug store. She is a single mother with primary custody of her two small children—her ex-husband

1

has the children only every other weekend. Recently Deirdra has started experiencing severe migraine headaches. Sometimes they are so debilitating that she can't drive and therefore must call in sick to work. Moreover, she had been taking a few ibuprofen tablets to help ease her headache pain, but they don't seem to have much of an effect anymore.

- Annette was diagnosed with breast cancer nearly a year ago. She has undergone chemotherapy for the past year and has now lost all of her hair and generally feels tired and weak. Although Annette is married and has many close friends, she feels very isolated and alone. She is uncomfortable getting undressed in front of her husband because of her embarrassment over the changes in her body, and she doubts his assurances that he continues to find her attractive. Annette has tried to talk to her friends, but she often finds them steering the conversation to more uplifting topics.

- Dr. Weisz is interested in examining the effectiveness of different types of treatment for back pain. He recruits a pool of back-pain sufferers and obtains their informed consent to participate in an approved research study he has designed. He asks some patients to start a new exercise routine that focuses on increasing back strength and flexibility, and as a comparison, he gives other patients a pill that he tells them will reduce back pain. However, the pill provides no real medication—it is only a sugar pill that should have no physiological effect on pain. Much to his surprise, Dr. Weisz finds that patients in both groups show significant improvement over the next month.

Preview

What do all of these examples have in common? They all illustrate issues addressed by the field of health psychology, including the influence of social pressures on health-related behavior, the impact of stress on health, the impact of chronic diseases on psychological well-being, and the influence of psychological factors on the experience of pain. This chapter first introduces you to the field of health psychology, describes how this field has changed over time, and discusses how health psychology is related to other disciplines. Finally, it gives you a preview of coming attractions by describing the topics covered in each of the remaining chapters.

What Is Health Psychology?

The field of **health psychology** addresses how one's behavior can influence health, wellness, and illness in a variety of ways. Specifically, health psychology examines how psychological factors influence the experience of stress and people's physiological reactions to stress, affect the promotion and maintenance of **health**, influence coping with and treating pain and disease as well as the effects of pain and disease on psychological functioning, and affect how individuals respond to health-care recommendations as well as health-promotion messages (Table 1.1;

TABLE 1.1   *The Goals of Healthy People 2020*

In 1979, Surgeon General Julius Richmond established a set of specific goals—including decreasing rates of smoking, increasing the use of seat belts, and increasing prenatal care—that would help reduce mortality rates in the United States by 1990 (Friedrich, 2000). In 1989, these goals were revised and expanded to form the Healthy People 2000 project, which had a specific focus of improving quality of life as well as life expectancy and reducing health disparities across different groups. Researchers now examine progress toward the goals, and establish new goals every 10 years. The most recent set of goals are the Healthy People 2020 goals, which include 42 distinct categories, with specific goals under each, covering a broad range of categories. These categories and goals include the following:

Physical Activity
- Increase the proportion of adults who engage in aerobic physical activity of at least moderate intensity for at least 150 minutes/week.
- Increase the proportion of the nation's public and private schools that require daily physical education for all students.

Overweight and Obesity
- Reduce the proportion of adults who are obese.
- Reduce the proportion of children and adolescents who are considered obese.

Tobacco Use
- Reduce the initiation of tobacco use among children, adolescents, and young adults.
- Increase smoking cessation attempts by adult smokers.

Substance Abuse
- Decrease the proportion of adults reporting any use of illicit drugs during the past 30 days.
- Reduce the proportion of adolescents engaging in binge drinking during the past month.

Responsible Sexual Behavior
- Increase the proportion of sexually active persons aged 15 to 19 years who use condoms and hormonal or intrauterine contraception to both effectively prevent pregnancy and provide barrier protection against disease.
- Increase the proportion of adolescents aged 17 years and younger who have never had sexual intercourse.

Injury and Violence
- Reduce motor vehicle crash-related deaths.
- Reduce homicides.

Immunization
- Increase the proportion of children aged 19 to 35 months who receive the recommended doses of DTaP, polio, MMR, Hib, hepatitis B, varicella, and PCV vaccines.
- Increase the proportion of children and adults who are vaccinated annually against seasonal influenza.

Access to Health Care
- Increase the proportion of persons with health insurance.
- Increase the proportion of pregnant women who receive early and adequate prenatal care.

Source: www.healthpeople.gov/2020.

FIGURE 1.1   Psychological factors, including stress, personality, and social influences, impact people's physiological responses as well as their health behaviors, which in turn impact the incidence of illness and disease. However, the relationship between psychological factors and physical health is bidirectional: Physiological responses, health behaviors, and disease can also influence psychological factors.

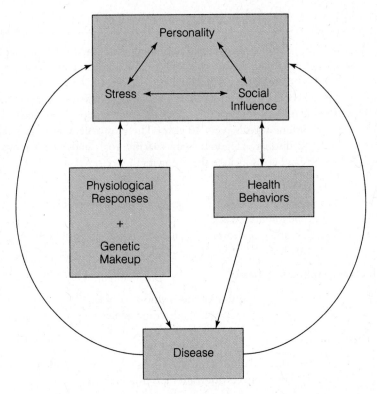

Matarazzo, 1980). As shown in Figure 1.1, these psychological factors include environmental stressors, personality factors, and social influences, which in turn influence illness and disease through their impact on physiological responses in the body as well as health-related behaviors (Adler & Matthews, 1994). Let's examine each of these factors in turn.

First, psychological factors can have a direct influence on physical health by impacting whether and how much stress a person experiences as well as the impact of stress on various physiological mechanisms in the body. Considerable research demonstrates that people who are experiencing various stressors (e.g., divorce, unemployment, taking exams, bereavement) show a weakened immune system (Cohen & Herbert, 1996; Evans & Wener, 2006; Ironson et al., 1997; Marsland, Cohen, Rabin, & Manuck, 2001; McKinnon, Weisse, Reynolds, Bowles, & Baum, 1989). In fact, after exposure to a cold virus, people who experience higher levels of stress are more likely to develop a cold than those who are experiencing less stress (Cohen, Tyrell, & Smith, 1991). Do you sometimes develop a headache when you are feeling tense? Do you sometimes feel nauseous before a "big game" or an important exam? These are all examples of how psychological factors can literally make people sick. But how, you might be wondering, can just taking an exam make you sick? Well, think about the typical behaviors of a college student during exam period. Many students stop exercising, eat more junk food, drink more caffeine, and get less sleep. In other words, the stress of exams leads people to engage in unhealthy behavior, which may ultimately lead to illness. However, people who are able to cope with stress effectively experience fewer health problems than

During periods of stress, such as college exams, many people stop engaging in health-promoting behaviors, such as exercise and healthy eating, and start engaging in unhealthy behaviors, such as pulling all-nighters and smoking cigarettes.
Source: © Beth Ambrose/iStockphoto.

those who find such experiences overwhelming. At the beginning of the chapter, you read how Peyton was experiencing a variety of challenges (e.g., applying for summer jobs, studying for law school exams, working as a paralegal) but was able to manage these stressors by taking yoga classes and spending time with friends.

Personality traits, such as optimism, hostility, and extraversion, are also associated with people's physiological responses to various situations as well as their health-related behaviors (Winett, 1995). For example, people who are high in hostility exhibit higher blood pressure and heart rate when they are in virtually any type of "competitive situation" (which could include even a game of ping-pong with a friend; Brondolo, Rieppi, Kelly, & Gerin, 2003; Miller, Smith, Turner, Guijarro, & Hallet,1996; Suls & Wan, 1993). Over time, experiencing constant high levels of physiological arousal leads to cardiovascular damage, which may explain why people who are hostile are more likely to experience heart disease (Al'absi & Bongard, 2006; Bleil, McCaffery, Muldoon, Sutton-Tyrrell, & Manuck, 2004; Boyle et al., 2004; Krantz & McCeney, 2002; Niaura et al., 2002). On the other hand, people who are high in positive emotions, such as happiness, joy, enthusiasm, and optimism, experience better health, including lower rates of getting the common cold, experiencing a stroke, and having an accident, than those with lower levels of such emotions (Cohen, Doyle, Turner, Alper, & Skoner, 2003; Cohen, Alper, Doyle, Treanor, & Turner, 2006; Peterson, Seligman, & Vaillant, 1988; Pressman & Cohen, 2005; Scheier & Carver, 1985). Personality variables also influence the types of health-related behaviors people engage in on a regular basis. People who are high in hostility, for example, may ignore doctor recommendations for treatment and thereby fail to recover—or at least they recover more slowly—from illnesses.

Second, social factors, including social support as well as social influences, are associated with individuals' physiological reactions and health-related behaviors. Individuals with high levels of social support have lower blood pressure and a more active immune system compared to those with less support (Cohen, Doyle, Skoner, Rabin, & Gwaltney, 1997; Cohen & Herbert, 1996; Pressman et al., 2005). In turn, people who have more social support may be better able to fight off minor illnesses and avoid major ones. People who have high levels of social support may also engage in more health-promoting behavior (e.g., eating nutritiously, exercising regularly), in part because their loved ones encourage such activities. Moreover, because people learn about health behaviors from watching others' behavior, the attitudes and behaviors of family members and friends also influence health-related behavior. Children who have a parent, sibling, or friend who smokes, for example, are much more likely to start smoking themselves later on. As described at the beginning of the chapter, Phillip started smoking because many of his friends smoked, and he continues to smoke as a way of coping with stress.

Third, psychological factors influence the development and treatment of pain and chronic and terminal disease (Winett, 1995). A number of psychological factors, including response to environmental stressors, personality, and internalization of social modeling, are associated with the experience of pain. As described at the beginning of the chapter, Deirdra's experience of stress led to the development of severe migraine headaches. Psychological factors are also associated with the development of some types of chronic diseases, such as coronary heart disease, cancer, and AIDS. People who are depressed have an increased risk of developing diabetes as well as experiencing a heart attack or stroke, and among those with diabetes or coronary heart disease, higher levels of depression are associated with an increased risk of mortality (see Table 1.2; Ahto, Isoaho, Puolijoki, Vahlberg, & Kivelä, 2007; Campayo et al., 2010; Katon et al., 2008; Whooley et al., 2008). As shown in Figure 1.2, individuals with higher educational attainment show lower levels of inflammation, which is associated with many diseases (Morozink, Friedman, Coe, & Ryff, 2010). One explanation for this association between educational

TABLE 1.2   *Test Yourself: Major Depression Inventory*

The following questions ask about how you have been feeling over the past 2 weeks. Please choose the answer that is closest to how you have been feeling using a scale of 0 (at no time) to 5 (all of the time).

1.   Have you felt low in spirits or sad?
2.   Have you lost interest in your daily activities?
3.   Have you felt lacking in energy and strength?
4.   Have you felt less self-confident?
5.   Have you had a bad conscience or feelings of guilt?
6.   Have you felt that life wasn't worth living?
7.   Have you had difficulty in concentrating, for example, when reading the newspaper or watching television?
8.   Have you felt subdued or slowed down?

This scale measures the degree of clinical depression, with higher scores indicating more severe depression.

Source: Bech, Rasumussen, Olsen, Noerholm, & Abildgaard, 2001.

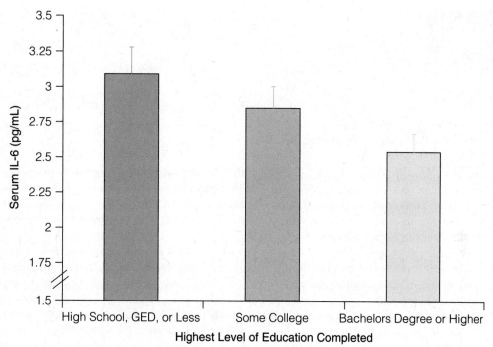

FIGURE 1.2   Higher education completed is associated with lower levels of interleukin-6, a marker of inflammation associated with cardiovascular disease, osteoporosis, and Alzheimer's disease (data from Morozink et al., 2010).

attainment and better health is that education increases people's health-related behaviors, which in turn can lead to the prevention or development of such chronic and terminal conditions. In line with this view, people with lower educational attainment are more likely to be obese and smoke (Conti & Heckman, 2010). Another explanation is that people with lower levels of education, who are more likely to be low income, tend to live in unhealthy environments (see Box 1.1: Health Psychology in the Real World).

Finally, psychological factors can also influence the effectiveness of various treatments to manage pain as well as chronic and terminal disease. Many treatments are based in psychological principles, such as reinforcement and social influence. As described at the beginning of the chapter, Dr. Weisz found that people's expectations about the effectiveness of a particular treatment can actually lead to improvements in their physical health and well-being.

Moreover, the experience of pain as well as chronic and terminal disease, not surprisingly, can influence psychological well-being. A person who is constantly in physical pain, for example, may feel depressed and anxious, avoid many social settings, and even withdraw from close family members and friends. People who experience chronic diseases, such as diabetes, cancer, and coronary heart disease, may experience similar negative emotions. For example, the beginning of the chapter described how Annette's struggle with breast cancer led her to feel awkward about engaging in intimate behavior with her husband and made her feel isolated from

Box 1.1

Health Psychology in the Real World: Ban Smoking in Public Housing

By Jonathan P. Winickoff, *Newsweek*, June 27, 2009

Ten years ago, I was the doctor for an 18-year-old with cystic fibrosis whose mother was a heavy smoker. The patient told me how she coughed, wheezed, and choked when she was at home. I became close with her; it seemed she was always in the hospital, and I couldn't help but think it was because she wanted to escape a toxic environment. Three years later, at 21, she died—more than 14 years before a person with cystic fibrosis could be expected to live at that time.

She is not the only young patient of mine to feel the effects of secondhand smoke. More must be done to address this suffering. President Obama's Family Smoking Prevention and Tobacco Control Act is a great step toward accomplishing this goal: it gives the FDA authority to regulate tobacco, especially as it pertains to minors. But change can't come fast enough for children from lower income levels, where rates of exposure to secondhand smoke are especially high—not surprising, given that poor adults smoke at higher rates. Children in densely populated public housing suffer the worst. That's ironic, since these smoke-filled environments are subsidized by the same government that spends billions of dollars on secondhand-smoke-related disease. Public-housing programs receive federal taxpayer funding from the U.S. Department of Housing and Urban Development. HUD does not prohibit local public-housing authorities from making their buildings smoke-free, but it does not require it either. It should.

Across America, landlords of privately owned multiple housing units are implementing popular smoke-free policies; taxpayers funding public accommodations should demand the same. A smoke-free designation means higher property values, and lower fire risk, insurance, and clean-up costs. But most important, it means a healthier life for children.

Some people argue that smoke-free regulation weighs against our longstanding cultural values surrounding privacy and protecting the sanctity of our homes. These values are important. But when considering them against the health of a child who has never smoked but is suffering from tobacco exposure in his own building, the choice is clear to me.

her friends. Finally, and not surprisingly, many people who are diagnosed with a terminal illness experience depression and anxiety, and survivors often experience lower levels of psychological and physical well-being.

Health psychology examines how psychological factors influence whether people take steps to identify and treat illnesses early, whether they adhere to medical recommendations, and how they respond to health-promotion messages (Winett, 1995). Behavior that involves detecting illness at an early stage as a way of reducing the illness's potential effects is called **secondary prevention** and can include checking cholesterol, performing a breast self-exam, and following an insulin-taking regimen in the case of diabetes. Secondary prevention is very important because in many cases people have more treatment options and a better likelihood of curing

Screening for diseases such as breast cancer is a highly effective way of promoting health, largely because such screening helps people find, and treat, health conditions at an earlier stage. *Source:* E Duarte/Getty Images, Inc.

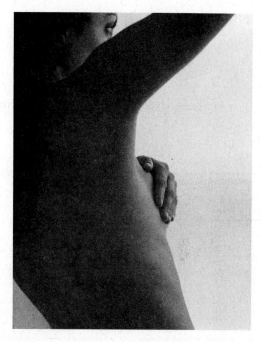

their problem if it is caught early. For example, a woman who practices regular self-exams and finds a small cancerous lump in her breast may have the option of having this lump removed in a simple operation before cancer spreads to other parts of her body. On the other hand, a woman who is found to have a lump in her breast only after the cancer has spread has unknowingly delayed treatment, decreased her treatment options, and will undergo much more difficult treatment, such as invasive surgery (possible removal of both breasts), chemotherapy, and/or radiation. However, psychological factors such as fear and anxiety influence whether someone engages in prevention and health-promotion behavior. For some people, getting tested for HIV is simply too frightening to contemplate (although in reality, ignorance is rarely bliss).

Tertiary prevention refers to actions taken to minimize or slow the damage caused by an illness or disease, such as taking medicine, engaging in regular physical therapy, and following a recommended diet (Winett, 1995). Patients with chronic conditions, such as cancer, AIDS, and heart disease, need to regularly manage their illnesses, cope with pain, and comply with medical regimens. However, some studies suggest that as many as 93% of patients fail to adhere to recommended treatments (Taylor, 1990). When sick, why do some people follow doctor recommendations and others ignore these messages? Psychological factors, including people's thoughts about their symptoms and illnesses, as well as interactions with health-care providers and the medical system in general, influence how people react to treatment plans and hence whether they recover from illness. As described in Box 1.2: Focus on Research, psychosocial factors influence how quickly people are diagnosed with cancer, how they manage this diagnosis, and even how long they live following the diagnosis (Antoni & Lutgendorf, 2007).

Box 1.2

Focus on Research: Can Writing About Feelings Help People Cope With Cancer?

Researchers in this study were interested in examining whether simply having people write about traumatic emotional experiences improved psychological and physical well-being. Early-stage breast cancer patients were randomly assigned to write over four sessions about one of three topics: their deepest thoughts and feelings regarding breast cancer, their positive thoughts and feelings regarding their experience with breast cancer, or facts about their breast cancer experience (Stanton et al., 2002). Data at the 3-month follow-up revealed that compared to those who only wrote about the facts of their illness, women who wrote about their intimate thoughts and feelings regarding the diagnosis reported significantly fewer physical symptoms. Moreover, women who wrote about either their most intimate thoughts or positive thoughts had fewer medical appointments for cancer-related morbidities. This research suggests that writing about positive feelings may lead to better health outcomes even in patients who have been diagnosed with cancer, revealing a powerful mind-body connection.

What Factors Led to the Development of Health Psychology?

Health psychology is a relatively new field. In 1973, a task force was created by the American Psychological Association (APA) to study the potential for psychology's role in health research. Although the final report of this task force in 1976 found little evidence that psychologists were examining health-related issues, the task force noted that the potential for psychological factors to influence health was clear (American Psychological Association, 1976). In turn, this report led to the creation in 1978 of a Health Psychology division, with the goal of providing "a scientific, educational, and professional organization for psychologists interested in (or working in) areas at one or another of the interfaces of medicine and psychology" (Matarazzo, 1984, p. 31). The development of this division was followed in 1982 by the creation of the *Health Psychology* journal, in which many research articles on issues in health psychology are published. This section examines various factors that led to the development of the exciting new field of health psychology.

The Nature of Illnesses Has Changed

Until the early 1900s, most people in the United States died from acute infectious diseases, such as tuberculosis, smallpox, measles, pneumonia, and typhoid fever (see Table 1.3; Grob, 1983). These diseases were caused by viruses or bacteria and were

TABLE 1.3   *The 10 Leading Causes of Death in 1900 Versus 2007*

Major Causes of Death in 1900	Major Causes of Death in 2007
1. Cardiovascular diseases (strokes, heart disease)	1. Heart disease
2. Influenza and pneumonia	2. Cancer
3. Tuberculosis	3. Stroke (cerebrovascular disease)
4. Gastritis	4. Chronic lower respiratory disease
5. Accidents	5. Accidents
6. Cancer	6. Alzheimer's disease
7. Diphtheria	7. Diabetes
8. Typhoid fever	8. Influenza and pneumonia
9. Measles	9. Nephritis (inflammation of kidneys)
10. Chronic liver disease and cirrhosis	10. Septicemia (infection in blood)

Note: In 1900, many people died from infectious diseases; today many of the leading causes of death are chronic conditions that are at least partially caused by lifestyle choices (Centers for Disease Control, 2011).

typically the result of eating or drinking contaminated water or food, interacting with infected people, or living in unhealthy conditions. Moreover, although people sought treatment for these disorders, doctors often had little knowledge or resources to treat or even manage these illnesses.

Today, in contrast, relatively few people (at least in the United States) die from the major infectious diseases that previously caused such high rates of death. What led to the decrease in the incidence of such diseases? First, changes in technology and lifestyle, such as the development of sewage-treatment plants, water purification efforts, and better overall nutrition, led to better overall hygiene. Second, because of the development of vaccines and antibiotics, very few people contract (and even fewer die from) diseases such as smallpox, tuberculosis, and polio (see Figure 1.3). Most children are vaccinated against many of the major infectious diseases, and other diseases can be effectively treated with antibiotics.

The major health problems in the United States today are caused by chronic conditions, such as cancer, cardiovascular disease, obesity, diabetes, and pulmonary diseases, which are caused at least in part by behavioral, psychosocial, and cultural factors. As shown in Table 1.3, heart disease is currently the most common cause of death in the United States.

However, the likelihood of developing heart disease is influenced by many behavioral choices—smoking, high-fat diet, physical inactivity, obesity, and alcohol use (all behavioral choices) as well as psychological variables (e.g., stress) and environmental factors (e.g., social support). Similarly, the major cause of lung cancer—which is the leading cause of cancer deaths for men and women—is cigarette smoking (Ginsberg, Kris, & Armstrong, 1993). Smoking not only contributes to heart disease and cancer but also to strokes (the third leading cause of death), chronic lower respiratory disorder (the fourth leading cause of death), pneumonia (the eighth leading cause of death), and diabetes (the seventh leading

FIGURE 1.3 As these figures clearly illustrate, rates of polio and measles decreased dramatically following the development of vaccinations (data from Matarazzo, 1982).

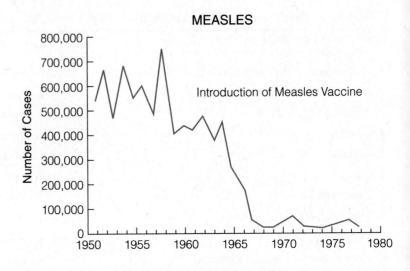

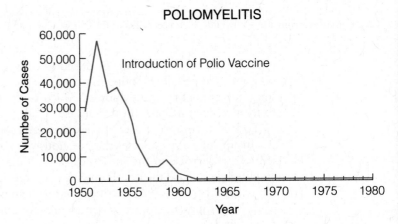

cause of death). In sum, people's own behavior contributes to many of the leading causes of death today. In fact, according to one estimate, about half of the deaths in the United States each year have preventable causes (McGinnis & Foege, 1993).

Given the role of individuals' behavior in contributing to health problems, principles of psychology can be used to try to change people's behavior, such as to increase health-promoting behavior (e.g., wearing seat belts, engaging in regular exercise, using sunscreen) and decrease health-damaging behavior (e.g., smoking, drinking and driving, eating a fatty diet). Psychological principles can be used to promote **primary prevention** behavior, namely, preventing or diminishing the severity of illnesses and diseases. Researchers in one study examined the influence of smoking and obesity on life expectancy (van Baal, Hoogenveen, de Wit, & Boshuizen, 2006). Men who smoke die on average 7.7 years sooner, and women who smoke die 6.3 years sooner. Similarly, obese men die 4.7 years earlier and obese women die 4.4 years earlier. This research provides powerful evidence that the behavioral choices people make have a major impact on how long they live.

Box 1.3

Focus on Development: The Importance of Immunizations

Although one of the major ways people can prevent disease is by getting vaccinations against contagious diseases, 29.5% of American preschool-age children do not have full immunization against currently controllable diseases (Wooten et al., 2010). Although rates of vaccination are similar across racial/ethnic groups, children who are living in poverty are less likely to be fully vaccinated. Unfortunately, when children don't get vaccinated, they can become infected with chicken pox and measles, which can lead to complications of pneumonia and even death. In 2010, 10 babies in California died from whooping cough. Although these babies were younger than 3 months, which means they were too young to have been vaccinated against this disease, they clearly came in contact with someone who wasn't vaccinated. Thus, parents have a responsibility to make sure their children have all recommended vaccinations to protect not only their children but also those with whom their children come into contact.

Yet influencing people's behavior is complex, as you will see throughout this book: Many people engage (or fail to engage in) behaviors that they know impact their health, such as smoking, getting too little sleep, not exercising, and failing to have that recommended colonoscopy. As physician John Knowles (1977) noted, "Over 99% of us are born healthy and made sick as a result of personal misbehavior and environmental conditions. The solution to the problems of ill health in modern American society involves individual responsibility, in the first instance, and social responsibility through public legislation and private volunteer efforts, in the second instance" (p. 58). Box 1.3: Focus on Development describes another example of the important role parents have in promoting health in their children by following recommended immunizations.

This shift in the pattern of illnesses from acute or infectious diseases to chronic conditions has focused attention on psychological factors related to the treatment and management of such diseases. Although many chronic conditions cannot be cured, people can often live with them for many years. Health psychologists can therefore contribute to the design of treatment programs that help people manage these illnesses, such as programs that encourage patients with heart disease to adopt healthier eating habits and to stop smoking.

The Biomedical Model Is Unable to Fully Account for Health

Another reason for the gain in popularity of health psychology is the failure of the **biomedical model** to explain many phenomena of health and illness. The biomedical model, which was formed in the 19th and 20th centuries, proposes that health problems are rooted in physical causes, such as viruses, bacteria, injuries, and

Although getting vaccinations is one of the most effective ways of preventing illness, a sizeable minority of infants in the United States are not vaccinated against all diseases for which vaccines are currently available. *Source:* © sjlocke/ iStockphoto.

biochemical imbalances (Engel, 1977; Schwartz, 1982; Wade & Halligan, 2004). This model therefore explains illness in terms of the pathology, biochemistry, and physiology of a disease: Diabetes is caused by an imbalance in blood sugar, polio is caused by exposure to a virus, and cancer is caused by genetic mutations. In turn, the biomedical model proposes that medical treatment is needed to cure or manage the physical complaint and thereby return a person to good health. The biomedical model therefore focuses on physical treatments for disease, such as a vaccine to prevent measles, medication to manage high blood pressure, and chemotherapy to delay the spread of cancer.

Although the biomedical model has led to a number of benefits for our society, including advancements in immunology, public-health policy, pathology, and surgery, increasingly evidence is showing that biological factors alone cannot account for health. First, and as described previously, psychological and behavioral factors are associated with the development of many of the leading causes of deaths such as cancer and heart disease. People who are high in neuroticism are at increased risk of developing an ulcer, chronic fatigue syndrome, or coronary heart disease (Charles, Gatz, Kato, & Pedersen, 2008; Suls & Bundle, 2005). Similarly, people who are experiencing high levels of stress—at home and/or work—are at greater risk of experiencing a heart attack (Rosengren et al., 2004). The biomedical model also fails to take into account how psychological factors, such as personality, cognitive beliefs, social support, and the relationship between the patient and the health-care practitioner, can influence development of and recovery from illness and disease. Why do placebos—drugs or treatments that influence health outcomes purely because of people's expectations of them—lead to improvement of symptoms in a sizeable portion of patients? Why do surgery patients who get more visitors leave the hospital sooner? These are just a few of the questions that the biomedical model really cannot answer.

Given the considerable evidence that the biomedical model alone can't explain physical health, researchers have turned to a **biopsychosocial model** in which the mind and body are seen as inherently connected (Ray, 2004; Suls & Rothman, 2004). The biopsychosocial model was developed in the late 1970s and posits that health is affected by both biology and social factors (Engel, 1977, 1980). In this perspective, the physical body is seen as only one aspect of a person; other aspects, such as personality, family, and society, also influence the person and his or her health. In contrast, the biomedical model, which was formed in the 19th and 20th centuries, describes health as a function only of physical attributes and sees physical health as completely separate from psychological health.

This model, which was developed by psychiatrist George Engel, views health and illness as the consequences of the complex interplay between biological factors (e.g., genetics, physiology), psychological factors (e.g., personality, cognition), and social factors (e.g., culture, community, family, media; Engel, 1977; Schwartz, 1982).

As described by Engel:

> To provide a basis for understanding the determinants of disease and arriving at rational treatments and patterns of health care, a medical model must also take into account the patient, the social context in which he lives, and the complementary system devised by society to deal with the disruptive effects of illness, that is, the physician role and the health-care system. This requires a biopsychosocial model. (p. 132)

The biopsychosocial model therefore acknowledges that biological factors can and do influence health and illness, and social, cultural, and psychological factors also exert an effect. This model is holistic in that it considers the mind and body as inherently connected. The biopsychosocial model views health as an interactive system in which biological factors (e.g., genetics, physiology) interact with psychological factors (e.g., personality, cognition) and social factors (e.g., community, family, media; Engel, 1980). The biopsychosocial model therefore contributes to the biomedical model by helping to explain the impact of psychological factors on the development and progression of chronic conditions as well as how people cope with pain, illness, and disease.

Let's take as an example a patient, Melanie, who arrives at her doctor's office complaining of recurring heart pain. A physician using the biomedical model would focus almost entirely on physical causes of such pain and would rely primarily on diagnostic tests, such as heart monitor results, temperature, pulse, and so forth, to determine the cause of this symptom. Although the physician might ask Melanie a few questions (when did you last eat? how long have you felt this pain?), the physician would base the diagnosis on the (more objective) test results. After a physical diagnosis is established, the physician prescribes a treatment regimen for the patient. In contrast, a physician using the biopsychosocial model might start by gathering personal data, such as symptoms, activities, recent behaviors, and social/family relationships. The physician might, for example, ask Melanie whether she was experiencing any particular stressors at home or work, or whether she had experienced significant life changes in the past few months (e.g., loss of job, death of a loved one). Although the physician would also use standard diagnostic tests, more emphasis would be put on eliciting psychological factors that could contribute to the symptoms. During this information-gathering phase, the physician also provides

The increasing cost of health care is one of the factors that has led to the greater interest in the field of health psychology.
Source: © The New Yorker Collection 1997 Danny Shanahan from cartoonbank.com.

"And, in our continuing effort to minimize surgical costs, I'll be hitting you over the head and tearing you open with my bare hands."

information about what is happening and why in an effort to minimize the stress on Melanie of the various medical procedures. After a diagnosis is made, the physician discusses the treatment options with Melanie, and she has a voice in selecting her own treatment plan. The physician not only works with Melanie to develop a treatment plan but also pays attention to aspects of Melanie's daily life that could influence her adherence to the plan.

Health-Care Costs Have Risen Dramatically

Health-care costs have risen sharply in the past four decades, which has caused an increasing focus on the more cost-effective approach of disease prevention. The U.S. population currently spends nearly $2.5 trillion a year on health care, which represents 17.6% of the gross domestic product (GDP; U.S. Department of Health and Human Services, 2011). In contrast, health-care costs represented only 5.1% of the GDP in 1960.

One reason for the rise in health-care costs is the increase in life expectancy that has occurred over the past 100 years. In the early 1900s, people lived to an average age of 47.3 years; today the mean life expectancy is nearly 78 years, resulting in part from the drop in infant mortality that has occurred over the past 50 years (CDC, 2011; see Figure 1.4). People today must bear the financial burden of paying for health care into their elder years, when chronic diseases requiring extended (and costly) treatments are likely to occur. Also, a wider variety of treatment options are now available to manage chronic diseases. Today, people are living with conditions that they would have died from in the past.

FIGURE 1.4 In the United States, the infant mortality rate decreased 86% between 1940 and 2006, from 47.0 infant deaths per 1,000 live births in 1940 to 6.7 in 2006. This rate includes both neonatal deaths, meaning deaths in the first 4 weeks of life, and postneonatal deaths, which occur from 28 days to 11 months after birth (Heron et al., 2009).

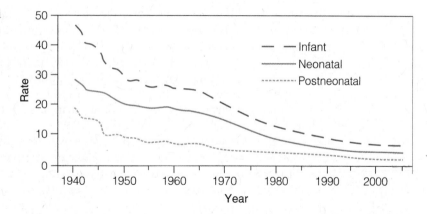

Another factor contributing to the rising cost of health care is the increasing technological advancements, such as new surgical techniques, chemotherapy, ultrasound, and genetic screening procedures, which require specialized equipment and are very expensive. Doctors are now able to perform truly remarkable procedures to save and improve lives, including transplanting organs, separating conjoined twins, and performing surgery on fetuses prior to birth. Although these treatments are partially responsible for the increase in life expectancy, they have also greatly increased the cost of health care.

Therefore, there is considerable interest in using principles of psychology to decrease such care costs. So, how can this be done? First, health psychologists try to prevent health problems from developing, for instance, by encouraging healthy

In March of 2011, Linda Lu, a 21-year-old college student, received a hand transplant at Emory University to become the 10th person in the United States to receive a complete hand transplant.
Source: John Bazemore/ASSOCIATED PRESS/AP/Wide World Photos.

eating and the use of constructive methods of managing stress. Psychological principles of persuasion, for example, are commonly used to promote condom use and to prevent smoking (Flay, 1987; Kelly et al., 1991). Similarly, persuasive messages can be used to help people detect health problems earlier, when more treatment options are available and these options are less expensive. For example, researchers have shown that describing the costs of not conducting breast self-exams is a more effective motivator to women than describing the benefits of conducting such exams (Meyerowitz & Chaiken, 1987). Psychological principles can also be used to help people manage pain and recover from illness. Holding a loved one's hand—or even looking at a photograph of that person—leads to reduced pain (Master et al., 2009), and surgical patients who receive high levels of social support show less anxiety, receive lower doses of narcotics, and are released from the hospital faster than those with lower levels of support (Krohne & Slangen, 2005). All of these psychologically based strategies for improving health can lead to decreases in health problems and/or minimize the pain and disability caused by such problems, which reduces health-care costs.

Moreover, although the development of various types of new technology has led to better overall health and longevity, it has also raised new concerns. For example, doctors now have the capacity to test fetuses for many genetic disorders, including cystic fibrosis, Down's syndrome, and sickle cell anemia. As a result, parents are sometimes faced with very difficult ethical decisions—should they abort a fetus with a life-threatening or highly disabling condition? Other advances in genetics research allow us to identify the particular gene that causes or contributes to the development of a particular disease. For example, there is a gene that causes Huntington's disease and another gene that indicates a woman is at increased risk of developing breast cancer. But what are the psychological consequences of finding out at age 20 or 25 that you are highly likely to (or in some cases, will definitely) contract a fatal disease? Health psychologists are currently conducting research on precisely these issues (and you'll learn more about their findings in Chapter 12).

The advances in medical technology also mean that, in some cases, people are now able to live with serious conditions that in the past would have killed them. For example, infants who are born 2 or 3 months premature now have a very good chance of surviving, whereas even 10 years ago, their odds were significantly worse. Similarly, people who have suffered a major accident that in earlier years would have led to certain death can sometimes be kept alive through medical means (but their quality of life must also be considered). Family members are forced to make very difficult decisions about the patients' likelihood of recovery as well as whether he or she would prefer to die than to live under such difficult circumstances. Once again, health psychologists are examining how people can best make such decisions and how to help people cope with these most challenging ethical dilemmas.

What Is the History of Health Psychology?

Although health psychology is a relatively new discipline, the idea that the mind influences the body is a very old one—in fact, historically, most cultures have recognized some type of a connection between how people think, feel, and behave and their health (Ehrenwald, 1976). Many early cultures viewed illness and disease as caused by evil spirits—and there is some evidence that early medical procedures, at least in some cases, involved such methods as drilling holes in people's skulls to "let out the evil spirits." As early as 400 B.C., Hippocrates described health as the interaction between mind and body, stating, "Health depends on a state of equilibrium among the various internal factors which govern the operation of the body and the mind; the equilibrium in turn is reached only when man lives in harmony with his environment" (Dubus, 1959, p. 114). In line with this view, Hippocrates' humoral theory described disease as caused by an imbalance in the different fluids he believed were circulating in the body: phlegm, blood, black bile, and yellow bile. Despite the faulty theory of the four humors, the emphasis on the interrelation between mind and body is clear.

However, during the 17th century, this holistic view of health changed, and for the first time, health was seen as purely caused by bodily processes. What led to this change? First, René Descartes's development of the doctrine of mind–body dualism—the view that the mind and body are two separate entities with little interaction—led to the view that the body was basically a machine. Disease was seen as resulting from the physical breakdown of the machine, and it was believed that the physician's job was to fix the machine. Second, advances in other scientific fields such as physics led to the view that science could be used to determine precise physical principles. For example, Isaac Newton's demonstration of an apple falling to the earth because of gravitational pull led other theorists to believe that all physical phenomena could be observed with such ease and explained by concrete laws. Third, various scientific advances, including Giovanni Battista Morgagni's work in autopsy, Rudolf Virchow's work in pathology, and Louis Pasteur's work in bacteriology, led to a focus on how microorganisms cause disease. All of these factors facilitated the focus on a biomedical model.

Over the past 100 years, the meaning of health has changed in several ways. Whereas health used to refer to just the absence of illness or disease, health and wellness are now seen in a much broader way. The World Health Organization (WHO) now defines health as "a state of complete physical, mental, and social well-being, and not merely the absence of disease and illness" (World Health Organization, 1964). So, people who are physiologically healthy but who are very depressed might be viewed as unhealthy under the new definition. Similarly, most college students seem healthy—generally they exercise with some regularity and exhibit few obvious signs of disease/serious illness—but can they be viewed as healthy if you look at their eating habits or, even worse, their drinking habits? By the new standard, many college students suddenly seem like they are in worse health. Along the same lines, consider someone who has no obvious signs of illness or disease but who has a mother and two aunts who have died of breast cancer. Is she healthy? In sum, researchers now see health as a continuum, ranging from a healthy level of wellness on one end and illness and even death on the other, and they have found that this continuum is viewed in different ways by different people (Antonovsky, 1987).

This change in perspective is also reflected in a relatively new focus within psychology on studying the predictors of happiness and well-being, as opposed to the predictors of depression and poor health (Seligman & Csikszentmihalyi, 2000). The newly developed field of positive psychology examines how to help people

Freud's theory about the role of unconscious conflict in leading to physical symptoms, including paralysis, sudden loss of hearing and sight, and muscle tremors, is clearly based in the theory that physical problems may represent manifestations of unconscious symptoms as opposed to a true medical disorder. *Source:* Corbis Images.

achieve physical and psychological well-being, including researching the predictors of life satisfaction, altruism, forgiveness, and hope.

Although this chapter has focused on the development of the distinct field of health psychology, several branches of medicine have also described the role of psychological factors in influencing physical health. **Psychosomatic medicine**, which developed in the 1930s, studies how emotional, social, and psychological factors influence the development and progression of illness (Lipowski, 1986). For example, researchers might study how psychological factors such as anxiety, depression, and stress might lead to physical problems such as ulcers, migraine headaches, arthritis, and asthma. The field of **medical psychology** focuses on teaching physicians how to interact with patients in a tactful and constructive way to best diagnose and manage their illness. Researchers in this discipline might examine how to handle patients who are moody or those who are reluctant to seek or follow medical care. Finally, **behavioral medicine** is an interdisciplinary field that developed in the 1970s and that focuses on the integration of behavioral and biomedical sciences. Specifically, behavioral medicine focuses on developing and applying behavioral techniques to the treatment, management, and rehabilitation of patients (Gentry, 1984). Such techniques are used widely to help people overcome various types of health-damaging behaviors. Correspondingly, the discipline of **behavioral health**, a subdiscipline of behavioral medicine, emphasizes enhancing health and preventing disease in currently healthy people (Matarazzo, 1980). Researchers in this field focus on general strategies of health promotion.

Health psychology is related not only to medical fields but also to the disciplines of sociology and anthropology. **Medical sociology** examines how social relationships influence illness, cultural and societal reactions to illness, and the organization of

Box 1.4

Focus on Culture: Health Means Different Things in Different Cultures

People in different cultures vary in how they describe health and even in the behaviors that they view as "healthy," as you'll learn throughout this book. People vary considerably, for example, in how they interpret and express physical symptoms, as well as in their willingness to rely on medical professionals as opposed to a "lay referral system" of family and friends for advice regarding medical issues (Bates, Edwards, & Anderson, 1993; Burnam, Timbers, & Hough, 1984; Landrine & Klonoff, 1994; Sanders et al., 1992). Even within a given culture, people differ in how they define health. For example, some people don't eat meat, which many physicians see as healthy because eating meat is associated with heart disease and high cholesterol. However, other people regard the vegetarian diet as a sign of unhealthy behavior because they believe there is a lack of iron and protein in the diet.

health-care services (Adler & Stone, 1979). For example, researchers in this field might examine the effects of social stress on health and illness, how attitudes and behaviors influence health and illness, and the negative consequences of labeling someone a "patient." The field of **medical anthropology** examines the differences in how health and illness are viewed by people in different cultures. Cultures, in fact, vary tremendously in how they define health, how they view disease, and, in turn, how they treat illness (see Box 1.4: Focus on Culture). Even within a single **culture**, such as the United States, people in different subcultures vary in how they view health and illness. Certain religious groups, for example, believe illnesses are caused by mental and spiritual processes, and they rely entirely on prayer and other nonmedical interventions to treat disease.

What Lies Ahead

As you know by now, Chapter 1 provides a relatively brief description of the field of health psychology as well as the factors that led to its development. Chapters 2 and 3 provide valuable background information needed for understanding and evaluating research in health psychology: Chapter 2 focuses on different research methods used within health psychology, and Chapter 3 describes various theories used in health psychology. Chapter 4 describes the impact of psychological factors on the experience and management of stress, and Chapter 5 examines how personality and social support impact how people cope with stress. Chapter 6 examines the influence of psychological factors on injuries—intentional and unintentional. Chapters 7 and 8 focus specifically on the impact of psychological factors on health-related behaviors that are often of particular interest to college students—alcohol use, smoking,

TABLE 1.4   *Information YOU Can Use*

- Stress has a negative impact on psychological and physical well-being, but coping with stress in positive ways—such as relying on social support and maintaining a positive attitude—can improve health outcomes.
- Many health problems are caused at least in part by behavior people choose to engage in, so make sure you choose to engage in health-promoting behaviors—wear a seat belt, engage in healthy eating and exercise behavior, avoid smoking and excessive alcohol use—whenever possible.
- Writing about traumatic events can help people express their feelings and, in turn, reduce physical symptoms and improve health outcomes. So, keeping a journal may in fact help you be healthy!
- Psychological factors, such as level of social support and neuroticism, influence the experience of pain, the likelihood of becoming ill, and the speed of recovery from surgery, so try to surround yourself with loved ones, and maintain a positive outlook.
- Treating health problems at an early stage is far easier than treating them later on, so make sure to engage in recommended screenings for illness, such as checking cholesterol and performing regular breast and testicular self-exams.

and eating. Chapters 9, 10, and 11 examine the bidirectional relationship between psychological factors and pain, chronic disease, and terminal illness. Issues of health-care utilization and adherence as well as the design of effective health-promotion messages are discussed in Chapters 12 and 13. Finally, Chapter 14 summarizes the main contributions of health psychology, several "hot topics" within this field, and various career options in health-related areas.

Summary

1. The field of health psychology addresses how one's behavior can influence health, wellness, and illness in a variety of different ways. Specifically, health psychology examines how psychological factors influence the experience of stress and people's physiological reactions to stress, affect the promotion and maintenance of health, influence coping with and treating pain and disease as well as the effects of pain and disease on psychological functioning, and affect how individuals respond to health care recommendations as well as health-promotion messages.

2. Psychological factors can have a direct influence on physical health by impacting whether and how much stress a person experiences as well as the impact of stress on various physiological mechanisms in the body.

3. Both personality traits and social factors are associated with people's physiological responses to various situations as well as their health-related behaviors.

4. Psychological factors influence the development and treatment of pain and chronic and terminal disease. However, the experience of pain as well as chronic and terminal diseases can influence psychological well-being.

5. Health psychology examines how psychological factors influence whether people take steps to identify and treat illnesses early, whether they adhere to medical recommendations, and how they respond to health-promotion messages. Behavior that involves detecting illness at an early stage as a way of reducing the illness's potential effects is called secondary prevention. Tertiary prevention refers to actions taken to minimize or slow the damage caused by an illness or disease.

6. A number of factors led to the development of health psychology. These include the changing

nature of illness (from infectious diseases to chronic conditions), the inability of the biomedical model to fully explain many phenomena of health and illness, and the rise in health care costs.

7. Although health psychology is a relatively new discipline, the idea that the mind influences the body is a very old one. This idea of the link between mind and body is also seen in other disciplines, such as psychosomatic medicine, medical psychology, behavioral health, medical sociology, and medical anthropology.

Key Terms

behavioral health
behavioral medicine
biomedical model
biopsychosocial model
culture

health
health psychology
medical anthropology
medical psychology
medical sociology

primary prevention
psychosomatic medicine
secondary prevention
tertiary prevention

Thought Questions

1. Your roommate has started to have frequent headaches. How would the biomedical model explain and treat his problem? How would the biopsychosocial model explain it?

2. Describe two ways that psychological factors can be effective in decreasing health-care costs.

3. Your sister has no physical health problems but is quite depressed—she has trouble getting out of bed, has a poor appetite, and finds little pleasure in spending time with friends. Your brother is a varsity athlete in high school and is in overall good physical health; however, when the team is celebrating their victory most Saturday nights, he typically gets very drunk and engages in unprotected sex. Are your siblings healthy? Why or why not?

4. Describe two distinct factors that led to the development of the field of health psychology.

5. Describe the differences among primary prevention, secondary prevention, and tertiary prevention.

CHAPTER 2

Research Methods

Outline

- Dr. Phillips works in the Student Health Center at the College of Connecticut. She has noticed that the health center is pretty quiet for most of the semester but then gets very busy during midterm week and final exam week. She is interested in examining whether students tend to get sick during exam periods, so she decides to call local drugstores to see whether their sales records indicate that they sell more cold and cough medicine during exam weeks than at other times during the semester.

- Dr. Adams is a cardiologist in San Francisco who sees many patients with coronary heart disease. In talking to his patients, he observes that most of them are very busy: They are often late for their appointments, constantly glance at their watches during office visits, and are rude to his receptionist if they are kept waiting. He decides to give his patients a survey to see whether those who are more hostile and time conscious have more severe symptoms of heart disease.

- Brandon and Brenda are student health educators at California University and are trying to decrease the amount of alcohol use on their campus. They want to determine what types of education would be most effective in accomplishing this goal, so they design two different workshops on alcohol abuse. Brenda gives one workshop to students who live in 5 dorms on the east side of campus, and Brandon gives the other workshop to students who live in 5 dorms on the west side of campus. They then plan to measure how much students who live in these 10 dorms drink during the rest of the semester to see which educational workshop was more effective.

- Dr. Ashley is a psychologist who treats patients with eating disorders. She has noticed that many of the women she sees have attended a private high school, and she wonders whether the distinct environment of a private school leads to eating disorders. To examine this question, she obtains their informed consent and then gives surveys to students at several local private and public high schools so that she can compare the rate of anorexia and bulimia at each type of school.

- Dr. Webb, who works at a large pharmaceutical company, has created a drug he thinks will help people cope with hangovers. Before he can market the drug, he must test whether it really works specifically to manage hangovers. After obtaining the necessary approval from the Institutional Review Board of his company, he puts advertisements in several liquor stores in his town to recruit people to try this drug. All people who respond are told that this is a study of new drugs, and that they may or may not receive actual medication. To half of the people who call, Dr. Webb then gives his new drug to take the next time they experience a hangover. He gives the other half a drug that is actually just a sugar pill. He then measures the number of symptoms people in each group report to see whether his drug is effective in treating hangovers.

Preview

This chapter covers a variety of topics related to conducting and evaluating research in health psychology. First, we review the steps involved in conducting research in general. We then describe five specific research methods commonly used in health psychology, with a particular focus on the strengths and weaknesses of each approach. Because health psychology addresses issues in psychology as well as in medicine, it has no distinct methodology but instead consists of research methods used in both fields. These methods include observational or naturalistic methods, surveys, experiments, quasi-experiments, and clinical studies. Part of the challenge of conducting research is choosing which method is best suited to answer a particular question (and, in fact, most questions can be answered using a variety of different methods). The chapter ends with a description of the ethical issues involved in conducting research in this field, including the specific issues involved in conducting research with animals.

What Is the Scientific Method?

Health psychology is an empirical science, and hence research in this field is based in the **scientific method** (see Figure 2.1). The general goals of scientific research are to describe a phenomenon, make predictions about it, and explain why it happens.

FIGURE 2.1   The steps in the research process.

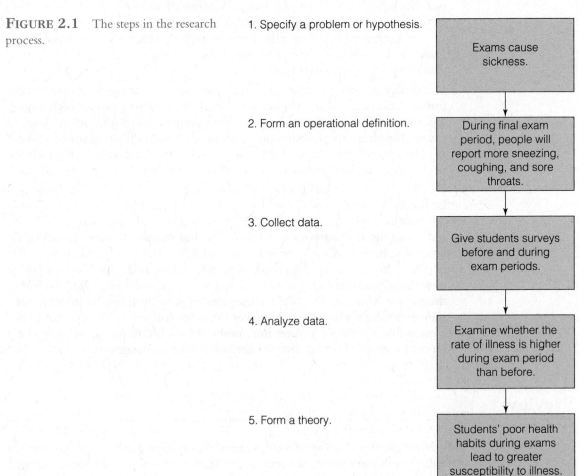

1. Specify a problem or hypothesis.

Exams cause sickness.

2. Form an operational definition.

During final exam period, people will report more sneezing, coughing, and sore throats.

3. Collect data.

Give students surveys before and during exam periods.

4. Analyze data.

Examine whether the rate of illness is higher during exam period than before.

5. Form a theory.

Students' poor health habits during exams lead to greater susceptibility to illness.

All research in health psychology as well as in other scientific fields starts with a question. Sometimes researchers form these questions based on what they observe in the world. For example, you might notice that you always seem to get a cold right after exam period. Sometimes researchers form questions based on intuition or a "gut feeling." For example, you might have a feeling that people who are happier tend to get sick less often than those who are depressed. These are both examples of a **hypothesis**, which is a testable prediction about the conditions under which an event will occur.

In other cases, researchers generate hypotheses to test a specific **theory**, an organized set of principles used to explain observed phenomena. Although hypotheses are specific predictions about the association between two events (such as exam period and illness, for example), they do not explain how or why these two events are connected. Theories provide potential explanations for particular phenomena and, therefore, generate specific ideas for future research. For example, you could have a theory that students don't take care of themselves well during exam period (e.g., they don't sleep enough and don't eat balanced meals), and these poor health behaviors in turn lead to illness. And if you had this theory, you'd be right (as you'll see in Chapter 4).

After you have formed the particular question that you will attempt to answer through experimentation, you need to form an **operational definition** of how you will study this problem. For example, you need to decide how you will classify illness (Is it sneezing and coughing? Is it a diagnosed medical health problem?) and how you will classify exam period (Is it only the time during final exams? Or the time before any test?). Researchers can define their variables in very different ways, which in turn can influence the findings, so it's important to standardize definitions.

Next, you *collect data*. Data could be collected in a number of different ways, including by observation, surveys, or experiments. For example, you could ask people about various symptoms they are experiencing at the beginning of the semester and then ask them the same questions again during exam week. Alternatively, you could track the number of students who visit the health center during the beginning of the semester and then at the end of the semester. If you are really adventurous, you could go to local stores and count how many people standing in line are buying cold medicine or go through students' trash cans and count used tissues!

After the data is collected, the next step is to *analyze the data*. This step is often one of the most exciting parts of conducting research because you get to find out the answers to your questions and write up those responses. (Although issues of data analysis are not covered in this textbook, you can learn more about different approaches to analyzing research findings by taking a statistics class.) This is my favorite part of conducting research because I get to see whether my hypothesis is right.

The next step in the research process is developing or revising a *theory* based on the findings of the research. If your data supports what you predicted in your hypothesis, you may decide to develop a theory to explain what you found. In other cases, your findings may provide additional support for a theory, which gives you confidence that the theory is accurate. However, all researchers sometimes get findings that are unexpected. When this happens, the findings may lead to a revision of the hypothesis or theory, which then of course must be tested again in another research study.

What Are Observational or Naturalistic Methods?

Observational or **naturalistic methods** are used to describe and measure people's and/or animals' behavior in everyday situations. Researchers observe behavior and record some type of systematic measurement of that behavior. The sociologist Emile Durkheim (1951) conducted naturalistic research by examining the records of people who had committed suicide between 1841 and 1872. He found that suicide was more frequent in people who were single rather than married and was more common during the week than on weekends. Through this investigation, he hypothesized that alienation from others was a predictor of suicide.

Some researchers use naturalistic or participant observation, in which they observe a group's behavior and interactions and rate them in various ways. For example, if you were interested in examining the association between obesity and activity level in children, you might observe children at a playground and, after operationally defining the variables, count the amount of physical exertion obese versus nonobese children engaged in (e.g., running, climbing, throwing). If you found that obese children were less active than nonobese children, based upon further analysis, you might conclude that there is a link between activity and obesity. Researchers can also collect naturalistic data without directly observing people's behavior. For example, in one study on the factors leading to infection with the common cold, researchers gathered and weighed used tissues as a way of measuring mucus produced by subjects (Cohen, Doyle, Skoner, Rabin, & Gwaltney, 1997).

Another type of observational approach is **archival research** in which researchers use already-recorded behavior, such as divorce rates, disease rates, and death rates. If you were interested in examining whether divorced people die younger than those who are married, you could examine obituaries and note the age of people who died as well as whether they were married. To examine the link between positive emotion and health, researchers in one study read the autobiographies of nuns and counted the number of words describing positive emotions, such as happiness, love, and pride (Danner, Snowdon, & Friesen, 2001). They then examined survival rates of these nuns when they were 75 to 95 years old. This study revealed that 55% of those who used few positive emotion words had died, as compared to 21% of those who used very many positive emotion

Counting the number of beer cans and bottles in recycling bins and trash bins is one way to examine alcohol consumption using a naturalistic method.
Source: © pryzmat/iStockphoto.

words. Similarly, at the beginning of this chapter, you read about Dr. Phillips's research on testing the link between exam time and illness through gathering drugstore records—this is a good example of archival research.

Finally, some researchers use the **case report** or **case study** to form hypotheses and theories. This research technique relies on studying one or more individuals in great depth to determine the causes of the person's behavior and to predict behavior in others who are similar. You may be familiar with Sigmund Freud's famous descriptions of his patients, such as Dora and "Little Hans," who suffered from psychological difficulties (Freud, 1963). Freud wrote detailed descriptions of his patients' experiences and dreams, and then examined these descriptions to form theories about the causes of their psychological problems.

One of the most famous examples of the use of case study to form hypotheses related to health occurred in the early 1980s, when the first documented cases of a strange new syndrome were reported in the *Morbidity and Mortality Weekly Report* (*MMWR*) of June 5, 1981 (Foege, 1983). Five young men in Los Angeles were treated for Pneumocystis carinii pneumonia, a rare type of pneumonia that typically affects those with suppressed immune systems. These previously healthy men had developed severe symptoms, including nausea, weight loss, night sweats, and general tiredness. Interestingly, all of these men were gay. At just about the same time, doctors in New York City diagnosed a rare skin cancer, Kaposi's sarcoma, in 20 gay men. Given these unusual cases affecting a particular population, a task force was created by the Centers for Disease Control (CDC) to interview all patients with these symptoms to determine what factors might have led to these illnesses. By the fall of 1981, epidemiologists determined that patients with these diseases reported having many sexual partners. Researchers then hypothesized that some type of disease was spreading in the gay population, possibly through sexual contact. Although the first cases of this strange type of pneumonia were found in gay men, doctors soon began seeing similar symptoms in other populations. Doctors in New York noticed similar symptoms in heterosexual men and women who used intravenous drugs. State health departments in New York and New Jersey also reported finding symptoms in prisoners. Nearly 1 year later, in the summer of 1982, three patients with hemophilia, a blood disorder that requires frequent blood transfusions, had developed similar symptoms. This finding finally led public-health officials to recognize that this disorder could be transmitted via blood as well as through sexual contact.

Although naturalistic or observational methods have many advantages, such approaches also have serious limitations. One problem with the observational approach is that the presence of the observer is likely to influence subjects' behavior. Specifically, people are likely to behave differently when they know they are being watched. You might, for example, load your cafeteria tray with more healthy foods if you knew that a health psychologist would be rating the nutritional content of your food as part of her study on eating behavior in college students. To avoid this issue, researchers sometimes remain in an observational environment over an extended period of time to allow people to become accustomed to them before they start to record observations. Also, observers' own biases can influence how they perceive the behavior they observe. For example, one researcher might interpret children on a playground pushing each other as normal behavior, whereas another might view such behavior as a sign of aggression or hostility. To help limit the problems of observer bias, researchers often have at least two people complete the behavior ratings independently, and then they measure how often the raters' data agrees.

FIGURE 2.2 As the number of friends increases, so does life expectancy (positive correlation). As hostility increases, the number of friends decreases (negative correlation).

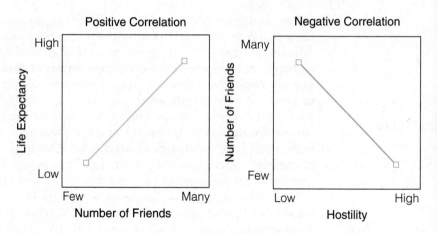

Similarly, although case studies can be very valuable in generating hypotheses and theories, their usefulness is limited because it is always possible that the person (or persons) who was studied is atypical in some way, so the information cannot be generalized to a larger population. Case studies also can be very vivid in sensory detail and can overwhelm more objective data recorded with other methods. For example, you might have a friend who became depressed following his parents' divorce, so you believe strongly that divorce causes depression even if large scientific surveys show no such association.

The most important limitation of observational methods is that while such approaches can describe behavior, they cannot explain or predict it. In other words, while they may show **correlation** between two characteristics, two behaviors, or a characteristic with a behavior, they lack the ability to determine causation. Although correlations can tell us about the strength of the association between two variables, they cannot prove that one variable causes the other. For example, if you find that people with many friends live longer than those with few friends (an example of a *positive correlation*; see Figure 2.2), you still cannot determine which of these two variables causes the other. There may be many possible explanations, and one possibility is that having friends helps buffer people from stressful events and thereby leads to fewer illnesses, and hence a longer life. However, it is also possible that people who are generally healthy have more opportunities to participate in social events, which then leads them to have more friends. Similarly, if you find that people who are more hostile have fewer friends (an example of a negative correlation), you can't tell whether people who are mean to others have trouble making friends or whether people who don't have many friends grow to be hostile over time. One study revealed that 2-year-olds whose mothers smoked during pregnancy are seven times more likely to have disruptive behavior problems than those whose mothers refrained from smoking during pregnancy (Wakschlag, Leventhal, & Pine, 2006). But is this convincing evidence that mothers' smoking itself leads to behavior problems in children?

Naturalistic or observational approaches also do not eliminate the possibility of a *third variable* that explains the observed association. For example, in men, hair loss and the death of one's spouse are positively correlated: Men who are bald are more likely to experience the death of their spouse. However, it would be inaccurate to say that balding *causes* one's spouse to die because actually both balding and becoming a widow are the result of getting older (the "third variable" in this example). Similarly, the research study proposed by Dr. Ashley at the start of this chapter can test only whether the rates of eating disorders differ in students at public versus private high schools, not whether the type of school attended leads to the development of eating disorders. This is because students are not randomly assigned to attend a particular type of school; so, a third variable, such as drive for perfection, parental pressure, or socioeconomic status, could be responsible for any differences in the rate of occurrence that she finds. Thus, while observational methods are very useful in describing the association between two variables, they do not allow researchers to determine which variable causes the other.

One study published in *The Archives of Pediatrics and Adolescent Medicine* reported that adolescents who frequently had dinner with their families reported lower levels of smoking, drinking, drug use, and depressive thoughts (Eisenberg, Olson, Neumark-Sztainer, Story, & Bearinger, 2004). These adolescents also had better grades. The media widely reported this study, and urged parents to have dinner with their kids as a way of preventing drug use and increasing grades. But let's think about whether this study demonstrates that having dinner as a family really has such a strong impact. Can you think of other explanations for this finding?

First, remember that this study shows that two things are *related* to each other, but it doesn't demonstrate that one thing—eating dinner together—*causes* less smoking and higher grades. One possibility is that parents who eat dinner with their children differ in some other way from those who don't eat dinner with their children, and that this other factor leads to this relationship. For example, maybe parents who are wealthier, or more religious, or more conscientious, spend more time with their children, and these other factors (wealth, religiosity, conscientiousness) lead to better grades and less smoking.

Another possibility is that simply spending time with children is associated with better outcomes, regardless of whether that time is during dinner specifically. In turn, research might show that parents who spend more time with their children each day, or each week, have children who have better grades and healthier behavior. In this case, it would be the amount of time that would influence these behaviors, not whether that time was during dinner.

Still another possibility is that children who engage in unhealthy behavior and show poor academic performance are less interested or willing to eat dinner with

Although adolescents who frequently eat dinner with their family have lower levels of smoking, drinking, and drug use, it isn't clear whether eating as a family causes better health or whether these two factors are simply correlated.
Source: © Catherine Yeulet/iStockphoto.

their families. Perhaps children who are "acting out" in some way refuse to eat dinner with their parents, even if their parents are home during the dinner hour. This example illustrates the principle of reverse causality, in which two factors are related in precisely the opposite direction than is hypothesized.

What Are Survey Methods?

Survey methods rely on asking people questions about their thoughts, feelings, desires, and actions and recording their answers. These questions may be asked directly by the experimenter in a face-to-face or a phone interview, or participants may complete written surveys. For example, the Experiences in Close Relationships scale is one commonly written measure that assess people's level of anxiety in their romantic relationships (Fraley, 2000; see Table 2.1). Researchers may administer this scale to subjects as well as a questionnaire assessing their health behaviors to determine whether people with high self-esteem engage in more healthy behaviors than those with low self-esteem. Similarly, the research study Dr. Adams plans to conduct to test the link between hostility and coronary heart disease uses the survey method.

Survey measures have many advantages and thus are commonly used to collect information about the link between people's attitudes and behaviors. Using surveys enables researchers to collect data from many subjects at the same time, so it is a very inexpensive way to gather data. Researchers could, for example, recruit many college students to complete a written survey on their exercise habits and illness rates to gather data on the link between physical fitness and health. Surveys also allow researchers to ask questions about a range of topics, including actions, feelings, attitudes, and thoughts, that could not be assessed simply by observing people's behavior. Finally, because surveys are often completed anonymously, researchers

TABLE 2.1   *Test Yourself: Anxious Attachment*

Please rate your agreement with each of these statements using a 1 to 7 scale, with 1 meaning "disagree strongly" and 7 meaning "agree strongly."

1. I'm afraid that I will lose my partner's love.
2. I often worry that my partner will not want to stay with me.
3. I often worry that my partner doesn't really love me.
4. I worry that romantic partners won't care about me as much as I care about them.
5. I often wish that my partner's feelings for me were as strong as my feelings for him or her.
6. I worry a lot about my relationships.
7. When my partner is out of sight, I worry that he or she might become interested in someone else.
8. When I show my feelings for romantic partners, I'm afraid they will not feel the same about me.
9. My romantic partner makes me doubt myself.
10. I find that my partners don't want to get as close as I would like.

Note: This scale measures anxious attachment in one's romantic relationships, with higher scores indicating greater levels of anxiety (Fraley, Brennan, & Waller, 2000).

do not have to be concerned about the effects of observer bias, which can be a problem with some types of studies using naturalistic observation.

Although surveys are useful, they have a number of potential problems. First, survey methods introduce the possibility of bias through the use of *leading questions*. Leading questions are those that provide some evidence of the "right answer" based on how the question is phrased. For example, experimenters should ask subjects "do you examine your breasts for cancer?" as opposed to "how often do you examine your breasts?" which implies that everyone engages in this behavior. Similarly, let's say that you want to examine the frequency of drinking and driving in college students. If you ask students, "How often have you driven an automobile after having an alcoholic drink?" you will get more accurate estimates than if you asked students, "How often have you gotten behind the wheel of your car when you have had too much to drink, thereby putting your own and others' lives in danger?" This is an extreme example, but it is not far from what actually happens in some surveys that contain leading questions.

When researchers provide different *response options*, they must be careful to phrase them in such a way as to avoid getting biased results. The provided responses give people an idea of what the "normal" or "typical" behavior is, and people often don't want to appear very different from others. (And they *really* don't want to appear worse than others.) Respondents are therefore likely to choose one of the midlevel choices as opposed to one of the more extreme (high or low) choices no matter what their actual behavior is. So, if you ask people if they smoke less than 1 cigarette a day, 1 to 2 cigarettes a day, 3 to 5 cigarettes a day, or more than 5 cigarettes a day, they will give lower estimates about their cigarette smoking than if you ask if they smoke fewer than 10, 10 to 20, 20 to 30, or more than 30 cigarettes a day. In this first example, regardless of their actual smoking behavior, people will be likely to report smoking between 1 and 5 cigarettes a day (the two midlevel choices in this set of answers), whereas in the second example, people are likely to report smoking 10 to 30 cigarettes a day, again, because these responses are the midlevel options and many respondents want to report their behavior in a way that seems to fall within the norm. Table 2.2 provides another example of how response options can influence people's reports of how much television they watch (Schwarz, Hippler, Deutsch, & Strack, 1985). In this case, only 16.2% of people

TABLE 2.2 *Reported Daily Television Watching as a Function of Response Alternatives*

Low-Frequency Alternatives	Daily Consumption Reports	High-Frequency Alternatives	Daily Consumption Reports
Up to 1/2 hour	7.4%	Up to 2 1/2 hours	62.5%
1/2 hour to 1 hour	17.7%	2 1/2 hours to 3 hours	23.4%
1 hour to 1 1/2 hours	26.5%	3 hours to 3 1/2 hours	7.8%
1 1/2 hours to 2 hours	14.7%	3 1/2 hours to 4 hours	4.7%
2 hours to 2 1/2 hours	17.7%	4 hours to 4 1/2 hours	1.6%
More than 2 1/2 hours	16.2%	More than 4 1/2 hours	0.0%

Source: Schwarz, Hippler, Deutsch, & Strack, 1985.

report watching more than 2 1/2 hours of television (the highest response option given) when it is offered as the low-frequency condition, but 37.5% of people report watching this much television when it is offered as the high-frequency condition. From this, you might see how people sometimes tailor their responses to conform to the perceived desired responses.

Although you might assume that people can accurately report on their own beliefs, attitudes, and behaviors, people are less accurate than you might think. Thus, survey methods are also limited by the possibility of *inaccurate reporting*. In some cases, people might believe they are telling the truth, but they simply may not be able to accurately recall the necessary information. For example, people may actually not remember when they last visited the dentist, when they first noticed a given symptom, or how long pain lasted. One study found that asking people to report on their sexual behavior over the past 2 weeks led to more reliable estimates than asking people to report over the past 3 months, presumably because it is easier to recall more recent behavior as well as behavior that occurred over a shorter period of time (Bogart et al., 2007). In some cases, people may simply not be very aware of their own health-related behavior. Researchers in one study found that older adults' reports of their own anxiety and depression were not highly correlated with their risk levels of coronary heart disease, whereas their spouse's reports were much more highly correlated (Smith et al., 2008). This finding suggests that people may be less accurate in reporting their own risk factors than are their spouses.

In other cases, people may be motivated to give inaccurate information. When you visit the dentist, you may overestimate the number of times you've flossed recently to avoid reporting behavior you assume might be perceived as negative. In Chapter 12, we examine cases in which people are motivated to inaccurately provide information to their health-care provider about how well they follow a prescribed medical regimen. For example, rates of adherence to medication are different when adherence is measured through self-report versus electronic

One of the problems with using self-report for conducting research is that people are at times motivated to give inaccurate answers. *Source:* Leo Cullum/cartoonbank.com. All Rights Reserved.

"What I drink and what I tell the pollsters I drink are two different things."

monitoring of how often a pill bottle is opened (Levine et al., 2006). People may be especially likely to give inaccurate information when they are asked about highly personal or sensitive attitudes or behavior. Researchers in one study examined rates of illicit drug use in a city by testing water from a sewage-treatment plant (Thompson, 2007). After all, drug users might not be willing to admit to using illegal drugs, but everyone has to urinate (which then allows researchers to measure levels of different types of drugs in a given city).

Finally, another limitation of survey methods is that they do not allow researchers to determine causality. Similar to observational or naturalistic methods, survey methods are correlational methods, so they do not enable researchers to assess the direction of the effects. For example, one highly publicized study found that people who had higher levels of education had less frequent sex (Michael, Gagnon, Laumann, & Kolata, 1994). This study does not reveal, however, whether having more education *leads* to having less sex. It may be, for example, that people who have more education also work longer hours, which allows less time to engage in sex. In this case, a third variable (number of hours worked) could be associated with both more education and less sex, and this variable leads to the association between level of education and frequency of sex. Given the limitations of both observational and survey methods in determining the causal direction of associations between variables, researchers often use experimental methods to definitely prove how two variables are associated.

What Are Experimental Methods?

In conducting an **experiment**, researchers randomly assign people to receive one or more **independent variables**, namely the factor that is being studied, to see if and how it will influence attitudes and behavior. (A particular type of drug or a particular stressful event could serve as the independent variable.) Then experimenters measure the effect of the independent variable on one or more **dependent variables**, the measured outcome of the experiment. The dependent variable could be an attitude or a behavior, such as beliefs about wearing seat belts or frequency of condom use. **Random assignment** means that every participant had an equal chance of being subjected to either of the conditions: The participants did not choose which condition they wanted, nor did the experimenter use any type of nonrandom selection process to assign people to conditions (e.g., putting the first 10 people in one condition and then the next 10 people in the second condition). Random assignment improves the likelihood that there is not a third variable causing some association between the independent and dependent variables, therefore explaining your seemingly significant findings.

Let's take a real-world example of the importance of experimental methods in drawing conclusions. As discussed in Chapter 8, losing weight is a challenge for many people, and thus many people try different dieting plans. Imagine you wanted to test whether Jenny Craig or Weight Watchers is a more effective approach to losing weight. Ideally, you could gather a representative sample of a population, obtain their informed consent, weigh them all, and then enroll half of them in the Jenny Craig diet plan and the other half in the Weight Watchers diet plan. If

FIGURE 2.3 Key
elements of experimental
design.

1. Screen participants.

2. Randomly assign participants
   to condition.

3. Give participants the treatment.

4. Measure the outcome.

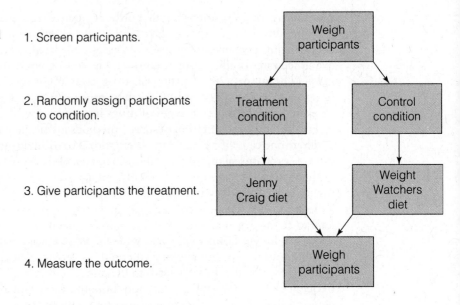

you then weigh these people again 1 month later, you could see whether those in
one group had lost more weight than those in the other group (see Figure 2.3).
Similarly, at the beginning of the chapter, you read about an experiment that
Brenda and Brandon conducted to evaluate the effectiveness of different types of
alcohol-prevention workshops. Because experiments contain multiple conditions
or groups (e.g., those who got a video or attended a workshop and those who did
not), they can show causality—that the independent variable (having the videotape
or attending the workshop) leads to the dependent variable (the loss of weight or
decrease in alcohol consumption), and not the other way around. This is therefore
an advantage experiments have over the other research methods, which show
correlation but not causation.

   Why is random assignment so important? Think about what would happen if you
ran your experiment on the effects of these different diet plans but instead of using
random assignment, you let people choose whether they'd like to receive the Jenny
Craig plan or the Weight Watchers plan. If you then find that those who received
one of these plans lost more weight than those who received the other, can you be
certain that receiving that plan caused the weight loss? No, because it is likely that
people who *chose* to enroll in a given plan differ from those who chose the other
plan. Perhaps those who chose the Weight Watchers plan, which requires people to
count and keep track of the "point allotments" for what they eat all day, are more
motivated to lose weight in general. Perhaps those who chose the Jenny Craig plan,
which requires participants to eat (and pay for) particular meals, are wealthier, and
thus have an easier time maintaining this plan over time. Perhaps those who chose
the Weight Watchers plan were all heavier to start with than those who chose the
Jenny Craig plan, which means any differences in weight loss could be a function
of the diet plan or people's initial weight. Although you can't tell whether any
of these factors influenced your findings, they are all possible. You therefore can't
tell whether the independent variable (diet plan) influenced the dependent variable

(weight loss). This is why random assignment is so important—to minimize the likelihood of a third variable influencing the results.

Despite their strengths, experiments also have some weaknesses. First, *artificial settings* can influence behavior. Because experiments typically take place in laboratory settings, the participants' attitudes and behavior can sometimes be influenced by such settings, instead of by the independent variable. For example, subjects who are asked to do an unusual procedure in the study setting may act how they think they should act, as opposed to what they would normally do in a real-life situation. In Chapter 7, you'll read about some studies in which participants are given alcohol as part of a research study to examine the impact of drinking on some type of intention or behavior. In this study design, it is certainly possible that people who are drinking in a laboratory setting—and know that drinking is being watched by researchers—will not act the same in that environment as they will in the real world. To try and overcome this potential weakness, experimenters try to design experimental procedures that are high on *experimental/psychological realism*, that is, the subjects are involved and take the experiment seriously, which in turn leads them to behave naturally and spontaneously.

Although experiments are the only research method that allows researchers to determine whether one variable *causes* another, there are some cases in which practical and/or ethical concerns make it impossible to conduct true experiments. For example, you can't randomly assign some people to get divorced or to acquire cancer to determine whether these types of major stressors lead to illness and mortality. In these cases, researchers conduct *quasi-experiments*. These are research studies in which there are distinct groups of people in different conditions, but unlike in true experiments, the people were not randomly assigned to the groups. A study that compares rate of illness in people who are divorced versus married, for example, includes an independent variable (marital status) that may impact a dependent variable (illness), but people are of course not randomly assigned to the divorced and married groups. Box 2.1: Focus on Research describes a quasi-experiment in which researchers compared life expectancy in those who were married versus those who had experienced a marital separation or divorce.

Epidemiologists, who study how disease occurs or spreads in a population, often use **quasi-experiments** (Lilienfield & Lilienfield, 1980). Epidemiologists employ two measures: **incidence**, defined as the frequency of new cases of a disease, and **prevalence**, defined as the proportion of a population that has a particular disease. These rates are measured by dividing the number of people in a given population (e.g., those at risk) by those who have the disease (to calculate the prevalence) or those who have developed the disease in a set period of time (to find the incidence). Some diseases, such as asthma, may be very prevalent (e.g., many people in a population have asthma) but have a relatively low incidence (e.g., because new cases do not occur very frequently). On the other hand, other diseases, such as the flu, may have relatively low prevalence (e.g., not many people in a given community have the flu) but have a high incidence, at least at some point during the year (e.g., flu cases are frequently diagnosed in the winter, but people do recover). After assessing the incidence and prevalence of a given disease, epidemiologists then try to examine different behaviors and lifestyles that might lead to the development of a particular disorder or disease. For example, epidemiology studies first noted the

Box 2.1

Focus on Research: The Impact of Divorce on Life Expectancy

Researchers in this study were interested in examining the impact of marital separation or divorce on early mortality (Sbarra & Nietert, 2009). To examine this question, researchers assessed data gathered starting in 1960 from a sample of more than 1,300 adults. This initial data included health and other demographic variables (age, sex, race) that could be associated with life expectancy. Researchers then examined data collected over the next 40 years to examine whether participants who had experienced marital separation or divorce experienced higher rates of mortality during that time. As predicted, people who were separated or divorced at the start of the study experienced significantly higher rates of early mortality: They were 55% more likely to die within the 41-year follow-up than those who were married, widowed, or never married. Interestingly, divorced men were particularly at risk of an early death. Moreover, this association between separation/divorce and life expectancy remained even when researchers took into account other factors associated with early mortality, including initial health status and various demographic variables. These findings suggest that being married is indeed good for your health—and longevity (we'll discuss why in more detail in Chapter 5).

relationship between smoking and lung cancer as well as the relationship between Type A behavior and coronary heart disease.

One type of epidemiological study based in quasi-experimental methods is an *ex post facto* or *case control study*. In this type of study, researchers cannot randomly assign people to various conditions or treatments but instead, they select people who differ on a particular variable of interest. This type of study is used very commonly in health psychology because many of the issues of interest in this field cannot be tested practically and ethically using experimental methods. For example, it is impossible to randomly assign women to breast-feed or bottle-feed their infants to determine the effects of breast-feeding on infant health (see Box 2.2: Focus on Development for an example of a quasi-experimental study on this topic). This type of research study is also used to test whether individuals who experience some type of naturally occurring event differ in terms of health from those who do not. In Chapter 4, you'll read about a study comparing psychological distress following the 9/11 terrorist attacks in those who lived in New York City and Washington, DC, which were targets of the attacks, versus in other parts of the country.

One type of *ex post facto* approach is a *prospective study*, which compares people with a given characteristic to people without it to see whether these groups differ in their development of a disease. These studies are prospective because they follow people over time. For example, one prospective study measured Type A behavior in a large group of men and then followed these men over time to determine whether those with higher levels of Type A behavior were more likely to develop heart disease (Rosenman et al., 1975). As predicted, men with Type A behavior were

Box 2.2

Focus on Development: The Link Between Breast-Feeding and Infant Illness

To examine the benefits of breast-feeding on health, researchers in one study compared the rates of illness in infants who were breast-fed versus bottle-fed (Chantry, Howard, & Auinger, 2006). Using data from a nationwide survey of parents of more than 2,000 children ages 6 to 24 months, researchers compared rates of pneumonia, cold, ear infections, and wheezing as a function of whether infants were breast-fed. The researchers also took into account various other factors that could influence infant health, including demographic variables, type of childcare received, and exposure to smoking. The findings revealed that babies who received only breast milk for the first 6 months of life were less likely to develop pneumonia or an ear infection. Specifically, 6.5% of bottle-fed infants developed pneumonia, compared to only 1.6% of babies who received only breast milk. Similarly, 62.7% of babies who received formula developed an ear infection, compared to 47.2% of those who were breast-fed. These findings provide compelling evidence that breast-feeding reduces the risk of infant illness.

more likely to develop heart disease. *Longitudinal studies*, in which a single group of subjects is followed over time, are a distinct type of prospective study. These studies are expensive to conduct because they require following many people over a considerable period of time. They can, however, provide valuable information about how specific variables influence health over time.

Another type of ex post facto approach is called a *retrospective study*, in which researchers examine differences in a group after a disease has occurred and attempt to look back over time to examine what previous factors might have led to the development of the disease. For example, some studies compare those who have cancer to those without cancer in terms of the experience of major life events (e.g., death of a loved one, marital discord; Sklar & Anisman, 1981). This research indicates that those with cancer have experienced more significant life events, suggesting that life stressors can lead to the development of cancer. *Cross-sectional studies*, in which researchers compare people of different ages at the same point in time, are a distinct type of retrospective study. You could, for example, compare the rate of cancer in 20-year-olds, 40-year-olds, and 60-year-olds to assess whether older people have higher rates of cancer than younger people in a cross-sectional study.

Although quasi-experimental methods can provide useful information about the effects of an independent variable on a dependent variable, they suffer from some of the same limitations as naturalistic, observational, and survey methods. First, these types of approaches do not randomly assign participants to different conditions or treatments, so they do not answer questions about correlation versus causation.

If researchers using a quasi-experiment find that students in fraternities engage in more alcohol abuse than those not in fraternities, can they be sure that fraternity life leads to more drinking, or can they conclude that those who like to drink alcohol prefer to join fraternities? Quasi-experimental approaches also do not eliminate the possibility of a third variable causing the observed association. For example, if breast-fed babies have higher IQs than bottle-fed babies, it is possible that a third variable leads to both breast-feeding and high IQ. Perhaps mothers who have a higher IQ are more likely to breast-feed, and they are also more likely to pass this high IQ on to their children. Thus, it is possible that the link between breast-feeding and high IQ is actually the result of another variable. Researchers typically try to control for potential third variables by matching participants in control and subject groups on other related variables. For example, researchers might match each woman who chose to breast-feed with a woman who had a similar IQ or income in the control group, and then compare infant IQs between these two groups. Although creating matched groups helps minimize the problem of third-variable effects, researchers obviously can match on only some, not all, variables. Quasi-experimental methods can therefore suggest associations between two or more variables, but researchers must conduct experiments to determine the precise association between the variables.

The challenges of drawing conclusions based on quasi-experimental research were clearly demonstrated over the past decade as researchers formed very different opinions about the costs and benefits of hormone-replacement therapy for women experiencing menopause. In the mid-1990s, most doctors believed that taking hormones during menopause helped reduce heart disease and osteoporosis. This belief was based largely on the results of the Nurses' Health Study, a longitudinal study showing that women who took estrogen were much less likely to develop coronary heart disease (Grodstein et al., 1996; Stampfer et al., 1991). However, in 2002, the Women's Health Initiative study was published showing that although hormone replacement therapy helped prevent osteoporosis, it was actually associated with an increased risk of heart disease, stroke, and breast cancer (Writing Group for the Women's Health Initiative Investigators, 2002).

How can these studies draw such dramatically different conclusions? One of the main problems is that these studies used different methods, which in turn led to dramatically different findings. Specifically, the Nurses' Health Study was an observational study in which women's behavior was simply measured over time. However, the women in this study may have engaged in particular behaviors other than taking hormones, which in turn led to their reduced risk of coronary heart disease. For example, perhaps the women engaged in more exercise, were more educated, or were wealthier; all of these factors could lead to a reduced risk of cardiovascular disease. On the other hand, the Women's Health Initiative study was a true experiment, in which some women received hormones and others received a placebo. Thus, the findings that women who took hormones actually experienced more health problems is particularly important because random assignment was used to make sure that women in these two groups didn't differ in any particular way. This real-world example points to the value of conducting true experiments whenever possible.

The drawbacks of relying on quasi-experimental research are clearly shown in the extremely different findings that have emerged about the effects of hormone-replacement therapy over the past 20 years. Initial research based in quasi-experimental studies pointed to largely beneficial effects, whereas research using a true experimental design pointed to largely harmful effects.

Source: © Janine Wiedel Photolibrary/Alamy.

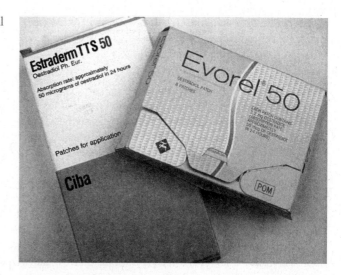

What Are Clinical Methods?

Researchers who are examining the effectiveness of different drugs or therapies on medical problems often use **clinical studies**. These methods are very similar to experiments in many ways, in that they use random assignment to condition and are often blind or even double-blind studies, meaning the participants or the participants and the experimenter are unaware of which conditions the participants are being subjected to and perhaps are unaware of the hypothesis of the study. This type of research can provide valuable information about the effectiveness—or, in some cases, lack thereof—of a particular drug or treatment. However, because these studies often involve patients who have actively sought help for a given disorder (such as cancer or depression), the practical and ethical issues involved in conducting this type of study can be complex (as described in Box 2.3: Health Psychology in the Real World).

Well-designed clinical trials must have clear *patient selection* criteria. In other words, researchers must set specific guidelines determining which participants are eligible for participation in the study. For example, if you are conducting a study on the effectiveness of a given therapy or drug on relieving back pain, you must make sure that all patients included in the study actually have back pain as defined for your study, not neck pain or joint pain.

Another issue to consider in conducting a clinical research study is whether participants have *comorbidity* and/or *concomitant treatment*. Clinical studies often involve people with comorbidity—suffering from more than one disease—which tends to add variability and make it harder to conduct a controlled experiment. For example, some people could have cardiovascular disease caused by diabetes, whereas others may only have cardiovascular disease. Similarly, people may be receiving ongoing treatment for diseases other than the one of the intended treatment they are currently participating in the study to assess. Any change in health could therefore be due to the other treatment they are receiving. Once again, random assignment helps to ensure that any findings will be caused by the effects of the intended

Box 2.3

Health Psychology in the Real World: The Ethical Challenges of Conducting Research on Cancer Treatment

By Katherine Russell Rich, *New York Times Magazine*, December 19, 1999

We all knew the treatment was a gamble. But compassion should have been a sure thing.

A friend called one morning last April to ask if I'd seen the news. The slight catch in her voice made me straighten my back, put me off, made me lie, and say I had.

I found the article quickly enough, then read with deliberate slowness, in a state approximating calm. "Breast Cancer Treatment Questioned," the headline said. Four new studies had shown that high-dose master-blaster chemo, also known as bone-marrow transplants, did almost nothing to improve the chances of women with advanced breast cancer. The next great breast-cancer cure wasn't.

But I could have told them that. Of all the women I knew who'd had a transplant, I didn't know a single one whose cancer hadn't come back. Including me.

In the weeks immediately following the report, I was sanguine, even incurious. I did not make further inquiries. I did not call the hospital and rant. Ten years of recurrent breast cancer had made me my own spin artist of disease. Of course it had been a gamble, I concluded, as quickly as if I were a spokeswoman for the hospital. Come on, the doctors never promised that the eight months of warm-up chemotherapy, followed by the four high-dose bombs, would actually work. Hadn't I signed a consent form before even getting started?

So I told my friends that the studies were irrelevant. "They're just statistics," I'd say, the paragon of cool rationality. "Maybe the treatment did help." Maybe it did: Three years later, I was still standing; the cancer's recurrence, to my adrenal gland, had been easily treated with hormones.

Or maybe I just couldn't bring myself to think about the unholy ways the transplant had leveled me—the violent, chattering fevers, the suckling weakness, the transformation into something more wormlike than human. And maybe I was still being propelled forward by the same psychic mechanism that kept me going when my red-cell count hit zero and I couldn't stand. This thing would work. It had to. Belief was all I had to go on.

The anger was slow to come, delayed, like radiation burn. But when it did, it was compressed fury, an actual physical sensation that built when I saw there wasn't anyone to aim at. Certainly not my doctors. They'd done what they thought was best, even if it meant taking me to the point of death and back four times. Four times! And for what?

In the cooling anger, the answer formed: for an experiment, that's what. I had given my body to science, had been doing that for 10 years, in fact. Most cancer patients do, for most cancer treatments are experimental. But some more so than others. It's one thing to be a medical guinea pig. It's another, in the case of the transplant, the extreme experiments, to feel like a sacrificial lamb.

Not one of the team involved in my bone-marrow transplant—not a doctor, or a social worker, or a med-tech policy maker—even informed me that it had probably been all for naught. I guess they just figured someone else would fax me the news report—if they thought about it at all. That kind of institutional arrogance is something most cancer patients encounter. (To be admitted into one program, for instance, I had to spend two hours having my vertebrae scraped in order to confirm the fact that I—a patient with a file a foot thick—did indeed have cancer.) And that arrogance flares up every six months or so, when yet another next great cure is announced. Despite the fact that 28 years after Nixon declared war on cancer, as my friend Joanne puts it, "500,000 a year still come home in a body bag."

Recently, when I was thinking about all this too late at night, I called my friend Zina, whose cancer returned six months after her bone-marrow transplant. Do you realize that procedure cost about the same as a Ferrari, I asked. If you were buying a Ferrari, you know they'd fawn all over you, she said. And if you spent 120 grand on a car and they found it didn't work, at the very least you'd get a written apology, I snorted.

We were lucky to be alive, we quickly added. But our doctors were fumbling in the dark, and until they found a better path, we were doomed to fumble along with them, like it or not. It wasn't their fault that we were sick. It wasn't even their fault that the treatment that had raised so much hope didn't end up working. But you know what? At that moment, we decided, a single expression of sorrow or regret—one indication that it mattered to them even a fraction as much as it mattered to us—would almost have changed everything. It wouldn't have altered the results. But it would have been a nod toward dignity. And that, for now, would have been change enough.

treatment and not other factors. Some clinical studies may even exclude participants with comorbidity and/or concomitant treatment to avoid the potential impact of the factors.

Finally, researchers who are conducting clinical research must be sure they have *patient cooperation*. Specifically, researchers must involve patients who will precisely follow treatment recommendations. For example, if subjects are instructed to take a particular pill every morning, they must follow the instructions because every deviation affects the accuracy of the study results. This matter of cooperation is a particularly important issue because patients often do not voluntarily disclose a lack of cooperation on their part, so the study design must encourage full cooperation as well as provide a way for participants to honestly report their conformance or nonconformance. (The issue of adherence is addressed in detail in Chapter 12.)

How Can We Evaluate Research Studies?

Thus far, you have learned about the various research techniques used in health psychology and the particular strengths and limitations of each method. However, all research studies—regardless of the method used—should be evaluated in terms of their internal and external validity. This section describes these two types of validity and explains why they are important.

Internal Validity

One way of evaluating the quality of a research study is to examine whether it is high in **internal validity**, which means that it is highly likely that the effects on the dependent variable were caused by the independent variable. For example, let's say we are conducting an experiment about the effects of a given drug on mood. We randomly assign some consenting participants to get the drug, and others to not get the drug. If the results show that those who received the drug have a better mood (as we've defined it) than those who do not receive the drug, we must be sure that this effect is caused by the independent variable (i.e., the drug). Maybe those who didn't receive the drug were disappointed that they didn't get the drug and therefore felt worse. Maybe the experimenter assumed that those who received the drug would be in a better mood and therefore was nicer to those people, affecting their responses. Perhaps those people who received the drug felt better because they were treated well by the experimenter, not because of the effects of the drug. Maybe people who received the drug talked about how great it was to receive the drug, which made those who didn't get the drug feel bad. In other words, there could be a variety of alternative explanations for the findings, which therefore weaken the internal validity of the experiment. However, if all of these effects have been eliminated or minimized in the study design, it is highly likely that the drug actually caused the improvement in mood, and therefore, the design would have high internal validity.

To increase internal validity, researchers must be sure that participants' expectations do not influence the dependent variable. Experiments often use a placebo, a treatment added to a research study as a way of controlling for the effects caused by a person's expectations. Placebos are inactive substances that should cause no psychological effects inherently; any effect that they do have, then, may be assumed to be caused by the subject's mental processes. In fact, because people who believe they are receiving a drug that will reduce their symptoms often show improvements—even if they are given only an inert sugar pill—drug companies must demonstrate that the actual drug they are marketing is more effective than a placebo pill at relieving a particular symptom. Another way to minimize the effects caused by participants' expectations about a particular treatment is to keep the participants *blind*, namely, to avoid telling them which condition they are being subjected to (e.g., whether they will experience the "real" condition or the "placebo," or control, condition). Dr. Webb's study on the effectiveness of a new drug includes a placebo condition to help prevent participant-expectancy effects. In his study, all participants received some type of pill, but no one knew whether it was real medicine or simply an inert sugar pill.

Although people commonly think of placebos as a type of inert drug (as in the preceding example), placebos can also be different types of conditions or procedures that some participants are exposed to in order to provide a comparison for participants in the test condition. For example, in some studies on HIV prevention, those in the treatment condition watch interesting videos and participate in discussions on safe sex led by trained facilitators, whereas those in the *control condition* were given a pamphlet to read by themselves. If the researchers later find that those in the treatment condition are more likely to use condoms—a behavior defined as successful adoption of this study's goals—can they determine that the increase in condom use results from the effectiveness of the information presented or from how the information was presented, with group interaction and personal attention of the facilitator? It is very likely that people learn more when they interact with the material in a fun way over a longer period of time than when they sit alone and briefly skim a brochure. So, what is a better approach to determine the efficacy of particular HIV-prevention information? You may present everyone with information in a fun group format, but some people will receive information on HIV prevention (the treatment condition) and others will receive information on smoking cessation (the control condition). This setup allows researchers to evaluate whether people who received the HIV prevention information were more likely to use condoms than those who received the smoking cessation information because both groups received their information in the same format, and therefore the effects of group interaction on learning were controlled for. Box 2.4: Focus on Research describes a clever study showing the power of the placebo effect on changes in weight, body fat, and blood pressure.

Researchers must also protect studies from experimenter-expectancy effects to increase internal validity. *Experimenter-expectancy effects* are produced when an experimenter's expectations about the results of the experiment influence his or her behavior toward the subjects and thereby ultimately do affect the results. For example, if you know which patients in a research trial are getting a real drug and which others are getting a placebo, you may treat subjects in these two conditions differently in subtle ways that influence participants' behavior and responses. You might frame questions in particular ways, based on your expectations, which then

Box 2.4

Focus on Research: The Power of Mind-Set on Health

Researchers in this study were interested in examining the effect of people's expectations on health (Crum & Langer, 2007). Eighty-four women who worked for hotels cleaning rooms were randomly assigned to one of two conditions. Women in the informed condition were told that their daily housekeeping work met the CDC's recommendations for engaging in regular exercise. They were also given specific information about the number of calories burned performing various tasks (e.g., vacuuming, changing linens, cleaning bathrooms). Finally, they were told that the type of exercise they were already doing as part of their jobs met and even exceeded the recommendations. Women in the control condition were given general information about the recommendations for engaging in regular exercise but were not told that their housekeeping work met these recommendations. Researchers also gathered physiological data from all women, including height, weight, blood pressure, and body fat. Four weeks later, all women completed self-report measures of health as well as these physiological measures again. Findings indicated that women who were informed about the benefits of their jobs for health lost an average of 2 pounds (reducing both their body fat and BMI levels) and lowered their blood pressure by an average of 10 points, whereas those in the control group showed no such changes. These findings indicate that people's mind-set, meaning how they think about their health-related behavior, influences physiological changes in the body, providing powerful evidence that how we think about something can have a real impact on our physical health.

may elicit your predicted response from subjects. For example, you might ask some people, "How much of a lessening of pain have you experienced?" (a leading question) and ask others, "Did you experience any lessening of pain?" This may happen even if you are consciously attempting to treat all participants the same. To examine the potential problems caused by experimental-expectancy effects, researchers in one study examined the safety reports of different drugs based on whether the research was funded by the manufacturer of the drug, who presumably would have a vested interest in the outcome of the drug (Nieto et al., 2007). Studies funded by pharmaceutical companies were less likely to find the adverse effects of the drug and more likely to make a favorable interpretation of any clinical effects than those receiving no funding from such companies. This finding provides compelling evidence that the preferences of researchers conducting a study may influence the results.

In fact, experimenter-expectancy effects can affect results even in studies with animals. In one clever study, an experimenter told subjects that the purpose of the trial was to replicate a well-established finding that some rats are "maze-bright," whereas others are "maze-dumb" and have more trouble learning to navigate a maze (Rosenthal & Fode, 1963). He told half of the student participants they were working with smart rats and the other half they were working with dumb rats. Each student then had to place his or her rat at the start of the runway and had to time the rat's movement through the maze. On day 1, the times for "smart" and "dumb" rats were pretty close, but over time, the "bright" rats ran faster and faster than the dumb rats (see Figure 2.4), intimating that student handler expectations and behavior somehow influenced the performance of the rats.

To protect against the biases of experimenter-expectancy effects, some experiments are conducted *double-blind*, in which neither the participants nor the

FIGURE 2.4 Students' expectancies about their rats' ability clearly influence the rats' behavior; even though there were no actual differences in the rats, "smart" rats recorded more correct responses than "dumb" rats (data from Rosenthal & Fode, 1963).

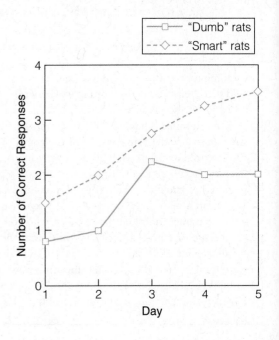

experimenter knows which participants are in which condition. In some cases, the experimenter who is interacting with the participants and collecting the data may not even know the study's hypothesis. This approach decreases the possibility of experimenter-expectancy effects influencing the data.

External Validity

External validity refers to the degree to which researchers have reasonable confidence that the same results may be obtained using the same experiment for other people and in other situations, in other words, that the experiment is repeatable. For example, magazines and television shows often feature truly amazing stories about how quickly celebrities lose pregnancy weight, and they provide helpful tips for noncelebrities on how to accomplish this goal. But the techniques provided by very wealthy celebrities—who likely are paying private chefs and personal trainers to assist with their efforts, as well as full-time nannies—may not be particularly useful for regular people. The results of these approaches probably would not be replicated widely and therefore would be considered to have low external validity.

This problem of low external validity is relatively common. For example, many studies on HIV prevention are conducted on college campuses. However, college

Just two months after giving birth, Gisele Bündchen posed for a swimsuit campaign. But the strategies she used to accomplish this weight loss would likely not be practical for many noncelebrities to use.
Source: Getty Images, Inc.

students tend to be younger and more educated than the general population, so if researchers learn that a given intervention is effective for college students, can they assume that this intervention would work in other populations? Similarly, can they assume that those individuals on a college campus who care to attend an HIV-prevention intervention are similar to those who do not come voluntarily? Findings on a self-selected sample may not generalize to other people in experiments with low external validity.

There are, fortunately, several ways of increasing external validity. First, use a *representative sample*, namely, a sample that reflects the characteristics of the target population at large. If you are interested in examining the frequency of drinking alcohol on college campuses, it would be a mistake simply to survey students who live in a fraternity or sorority house because research shows that these students drink more alcohol than those who live in residence halls or off-campus housing (Wechsler, Dowdall, Davenport, & Castillo, 1995). Instead, you might call every 10th person in the student directory to try to recruit a sample that truly represents all the students on campus (e.g., including an equal mix of males and females, athletes and nonathletes). In contrast, other studies use a *convenience sample*, namely, a sample that is selected because the members are readily accessible to the researcher (such as college sophomores who are taking a psychology course!). Using a convenience sample is not necessarily bad, but other researchers should be made aware of what sample is being used to better interpret the results. Results from a study that used only college students as participants, for example, are likely to be most accurate in predicting behavior in other college students, not the general population.

Researchers must also consider that those who take the time to participate in a study might differ from those who choose not to participate, and therefore participant responses may not generalize or be applicable to the general population (Bradburn & Sudman, 1988). For example, a study of sexual behavior was conducted by researchers at the University of Chicago (Michael et al., 1994). It included a number of questions on personal topics, such as frequency of masturbation, marital affairs, and homosexual behavior. Those participants who are relatively comfortable discussing such sensitive issues and revealing personal information to strangers were likely the ones to decide to participate in the study, knowing its topic at the screening phase; people who lack this comfort may have simply refused to participate. Individuals who are comfortable discussing such topics might also be more likely to engage in such behaviors, and thus this type of survey approach might lead to an overestimation of the frequency of these behaviors in the general population if the composition of the participant group is not considered during the interpretation of the results.

Similarly, those with particularly strong feelings about the topic of a study may be most likely to respond. Let's say you are asked to evaluate the quality of your Health Psychology course. If you really like your professor, you are probably highly motivated to complete the survey to let others know how great this class is. Similarly, if you really hated this course, you are likely to want to warn others away from this class and would complete the survey. However, if you have sort of mixed feelings about the class (you like some parts, you don't like other parts, but you don't generally feel strongly), you may not be very motivated to complete a survey at all.

Researchers can also increase external validity by making participation in the study as convenient as possible. If you recruit people to participate in a smoking cessation intervention that requires them to spend every Saturday for a month traveling to a faraway place, you are probably just involving and influencing those who are very motivated to quit, so the results may not generalize or be applicable to the average smoker (who likely lacks such extreme motivation). On the other hand, if you find that attending one 2-hour workshop helps people stop smoking, this intervention may be very generalizable to many other smokers. Many people would be willing to attend this type of program, and therefore the researchers should feel more confident that their approach could work with other people.

A third way of increasing external validity is to conduct the same study in different populations or locations. As stated previously, many studies on HIV prevention are conducted on college campuses; however, college students tend to be younger and more educated than the general population. If researchers learn that a given intervention is effective for college students, they cannot assume that this approach would work in other populations. However, if a smoking cessation program is equally effective for students in a suburban private high school, a small rural high school, and a large inner-city public high school, then researchers can be confident that the intervention would be effective for most teenagers in the general population. They might not, however, be able to determine whether this program would be effective for college students or for adults.

Finally, researchers must design studies with *high mundane realism*, that is, studies that resemble places and events that exist in the real world, in order to apply the findings from an experiment to the real world. For example, some research has examined how susceptible college students are to getting a cold during exam periods (Jemmott & Magliore, 1988). Obviously, exam periods occur several times during the academic year; therefore, findings from this type of research approach are likely to provide valuable information about how the regular college exam period impacts health. However, imagine an experiment in which students were asked questions and were given an electric shock each time they gave a wrong answer. Although getting shocked would probably be extremely stressful (as well as ethically questionable) to participants, the design setup has low mundane realism, so it may not give researchers accurate information about how stress can influence health in real-life situations. Similarly, researchers in one study examined the impact of the amount of food present on the total food consumed, which is clearly a situation with high mundane realism (just think of how much people eat in all-you-can-eat buffets; Wansink, Painter, & North, 2005). As shown in Figure 2.5, people eat far more when it is impossible to tell how much food they have consumed than when there are clear cues about the amount of food consumed.

What Is the Best Research Approach?

How do you decide which research technique to use to answer a particular question? There is no single best method, and all methods have strengths and weaknesses. Because experiments are the only technique that randomly assigns people to conditions, this approach is the best method for determining which variable definitively causes another. However, because experiments are necessarily somewhat artificial, this approach does not give as much information about what

FIGURE 2.5 Participants in this study were randomly assigned to one of two conditions: In one condition, the participants' soup bowls were continually refilled, whereas those in the other condition ate from a normal soup bowl but were allowed to eat as many bowls as they would like. Although participants consumed 73% more soup in the automatically refilling bowl condition, they did not believe they consumed more—presumably because they were relying on visual cues to determine consumption and not on their internal feelings of fullness (data from Wansink et al., 2005).

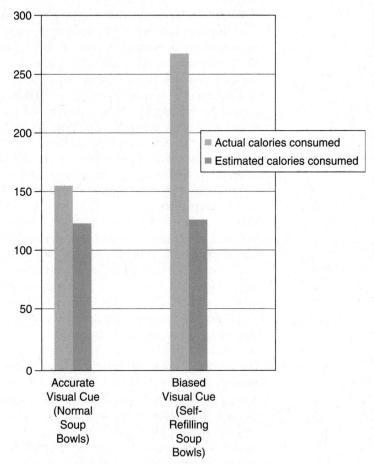

actually happens in real-life situations. On the other hand, while naturalistic observation methods provide very accurate information about what happens in the real world, they tell more about how two (or more) different variables are connected than they do about one variable causing the other. In sum, different methods are best for providing certain types of information and for answering particular questions. For example, you might use naturalistic observation or quasi-experimental methods to examine how experiencing the loss of a loved one influences life expectancy because obviously you could not answer this question using a true experimental design. On the other hand, if you are interested in examining the effectiveness of a particular type of smoking-cessation program, conducting a true experiment is probably the best approach. Finally, you can be more confident about scientific findings if researchers using different types of research methods all produce the same results. For example, and as described in Table 2.3, if researchers using a variety of different approaches all examine the link between smoking and health and reach the same conclusion, you can be confident in those results.

TABLE 2.3   *Different Research Approaches for Examining the Smoking–Health Link*

Research Method	Research Plan
Observational/Naturalistic	Examine the rate of smoking and lung cancer in a given population.
Survey	Examine people's self-reports of smoking frequency and health problems.
Experimental	Randomly assign some laboratory rats to breathe cigarette smoke and examine whether these rats are more likely to develop health problems than rats not subjected to cigarette smoke.
Quasi-Experimental	Examine rates of health problems in people who smoke versus people who do not smoke.

How Do Research Ethics Influence Scientific Studies?

Paying attention to the ethical issues involved in conducting research is now mandatory, in part because of some previous studies that were ethically questionable. For example, a study conducted in Tuskegee, Alabama, from 1934 to 1974, examined the effects of syphilis on 412 African American men. The researchers were aware that the men had syphilis, but they did not tell the subjects they were infected nor did the researchers give subjects penicillin to cure them because the researchers were interested in measuring the long-term effects of syphilis left untreated. The men were asked to return to the clinic periodically (in exchange for free hot meals) so that the researchers could conduct physical exams and blood tests. The researchers even asked local doctors to not provide treatment to these men. What did this study show? That, left untreated, syphilis causes blindness, insanity, and even death (Faden & Beauchamp, 1986). Yet, the Tuskegee experiment is considered totally unethical because, through deception, the men were left untreated and suffered greatly from the effects of the disease. This experiment has had a lasting effect on the perceptions of the health-care system in general by many African Americans. As described in Table 2.4, we now know that a number of other studies were conducted on various people, including prison inmates, pregnant women, and low-income children, who were unwittingly subjects in experiments with significant long-term health consequences.

To avoid ethically questionable studies, researchers must now follow certain procedures when conducting scientific research (see Table 2.5). First, studies must undergo an extensive *institutional review* before they are implemented. This review by a panel of experts is required by virtually all organizations in the United States, including schools, hospitals, community organizations, and so forth. These boards review whether the potential benefits of the research are justifiable in light of possible risks or harms, and they may force experimenters to make changes in the design or procedure of the research to minimize negative effects. For example, you might wonder about the effects of (falsely) telling your roommate he had cancer

TABLE 2.4   *A Sad Legacy of Unethical Research on Health*

Although the Tuskegee syphilis study has received considerable attention in recent years, other studies have also
relied on dangerous and unethical approaches. The following cases are all true examples of people's
unknowing participation in potentially life-threatening research studies.

Hazardous Oatmeal

In the 1950s, Frederick Boyce was one of about two dozen boys at the Fernald School in suburban Boston who
were fed radioactive oatmeal as part of a nutrition study. The experiment, financed by the Atomic Energy
Commission and the National Institutes of Health, was designed to show how the body absorbs various
minerals. The boys were enticed to participate with the prospect of joining a "Science Club." Letters sent to
parents by the researchers made no mention of the radiation. In fact, they suggested that the boys would
benefit from the experiment and from Science Club activities. "They get a quart of milk daily," one letter
says, "and are taken to a baseball game, to the beach, and to some outside dinners, and they enjoy it greatly."

Poison in the Womb

Emma Craft did not know that the "vitamin cocktail" her doctor gave her in 1946 contained radioactive iron.
But 47 years later, when she read newspaper reports about experiments on pregnant women at Vanderbilt
University Hospital and about children who had developed cancer, she says, "I knew in my heart that they
were writing about me and my baby." At least 820 women consumed radioactive iron as part of this study on
nutritional requirements in pregnancy. According to the report of President Bill Clinton's Advisory
Committee on Human Radiation Experiments, "There is at least some indication that the women neither
gave their consent nor were aware they were participating in an experiment."

"Elmer Allen Was No Hero"

In July 1947, when 36-year-old Elmer Allen arrived at a San Francisco hospital with an injured knee, doctors
told him that his leg would have to be amputated. Three days before the surgery, they secretly injected him
with plutonium. Like 20 other patients in hospitals around the country, Allen had unknowingly been enrolled
in an experiment financed by the Atomic Energy Commission to gather information to help protect workers
at A-bomb plants. Although the researchers understood that the injections could cause cancer, Allen was
never told that he was at risk. Nor did he know that when he was invited for "metabolism tests" and free trips
to Chicago and Rochester in 1973, the doctors were actually studying the long-term effects of radioactivity.

Source: Antonio, M. D. (1997, August 31). Atomic guinea pigs. *New York Times Magazine,* pp. 38, 41, 42.

or that he had failed out of school, but a research review panel would never allow
a study using this type of deception because of the high potential risk of harming
your unsuspecting roommate.

   Second, research studies require participants to give *informed consent*. This
consent is an individual's deliberate, voluntary decision to participate in research,
based on the researcher's description of what such participation will involve.
It is not necessary to describe every single aspect of the research to potential
participants, but they do need to hear enough to make an educated decision about
whether they would like to be involved.

   Third, patients' *confidentiality* must be protected from unauthorized disclosure;
hence, surveys often use a code number instead of the person's name to preserve
anonymity. Data also must be stored in a locked room with restricted access. Reports

TABLE 2.5   *APA Guidelines for Conducting Research With Humans: Informed Consent*

Using language that is reasonably understandable to participants, psychologists inform participants of the nature of the research; the researchers inform participants that they are free to participate or decline to participate or to withdraw from the research; the researchers explain the foreseeable consequences of declining or withdrawing; the researchers inform participants of significant factors that may be expected to influence their willingness to participate; and the researchers explain other aspects about which the prospective participants inquire.

When psychologists conduct research with individuals such as students or subordinates, psychologists take special care to protect the prospective participants from adverse consequences of declining or withdrawing from participation.

When research participation is a course requirement or opportunity for extra credit, the prospective participant is given the choice of equitable alternative activities.

Deception in Research

Psychologists do not conduct a study involving deception unless they have determined that the use of deceptive techniques is justified by the study's prospective scientific, educational, or applied value and that equally effective alternative procedures that do not use deception are not feasible.

Psychologists never deceive research participants about significant aspects that would affect their willingness to participate, such as physical risks, discomfort, or unpleasant emotional experiences.

Source: American Psychological Association, 1992.

based on the data must contain only group-level information, not descriptions of results for individual people. You would say that "most students who received the alcohol-prevention workshop drank less," instead of "most students who received the alcohol-prevention workshop drank less, except for Brad Simpson who surprisingly doubled his beer intake over the following month."

Some research studies use *deception*, in which they give false information to subjects in order to measure their responses to certain stimuli. For example, subjects may be told that they are receiving a drug, but they are actually receiving a placebo. Why would researchers do this? As we discuss in Chapter 9, people who think they are getting a drug actually have more positive results along the trial's measurement scale than those who think they are not getting a drug. Using this type of deception allows researchers to compare the effects of actually getting a particular drug to the effects of subjects simply believing they are getting a drug (e.g., comparing the efficacy of the drug to the power of positive thinking). However, deception is used only in cases in which there is no other reasonable way of studying a particular research question and in which it is extremely unlikely that physical and/or emotional harm could result.

Following participation in a research study, participants are given a *debriefing*. During this disclosure to subjects after research procedures are completed, the researcher explains the purpose of the study, answers any questions, attempts to resolve any negative feelings, and emphasizes the contributions to science of the research. This is especially important in cases in which deception has been used.

Ethical Issues Relevant to Experimentation on Animals

Although the majority of psychological research uses humans as participants, a small minority of research studies (about 7 to 9%) use animals as research subjects (Gallup & Suarez, 1985). Research is conducted with animals for both ethical and practical reasons (Miller, 1985). First, certain types of studies are impossible to conduct on humans, given ethical concerns. Researchers cannot, for example, randomly assign some pregnant women to drink alcohol in order to test the effects of this behavior on the fetus. Research with pregnant animals, however, provides convincing evidence that alcohol has negative effects on the fetus (Sutherland, McDonald, & Savage, 1997). Second, experimenters have much more control over animals' lives than over people's; hence, using animals as subjects allows researchers to come to stronger conclusions about the nature of cause and effect because many extraneous factors can be controlled for. For example, in a trial examining whether people who are under greater stress experience more illness, it is impossible to examine all of the different variables that might lead to this association, such as poor health habits, genetic factors, and lack of social support. Research with animals, however, could control for all of these variables by using genetically similar rats (e.g., rats from the same litter) and providing all rats with the same exact living environment. Researchers could then expose some rats to stress and measure whether they have higher rates of illness than nonstressed rats.

Although some animal rights activists believe that animals should never be used for research purposes, research with animals has given us important information that is helping to improve people's quality of life. Specifically, research with animals

Research by Henry Harlow in the 1960s using rhesus monkeys led to significant changes in hospital procedures to allow more sustained contact between mothers and their newborn infants.
Source: Photo Researchers, Inc.

TABLE 2.6   *APA Guidelines for Conducting Research With Animals*

- Researchers who conduct research involving animals treat them humanely.
- Psychologists trained in research methods and experienced in the care of laboratory animals supervise all procedures involving animals and are responsible for ensuring appropriate consideration for their comfort, health, and humane treatment.
- Psychologists make reasonable efforts to minimize the discomfort, infection, illness, and pain of animal subjects.
- A procedure subjecting animals to pain, stress, or deprivation is used only when an alternative procedure is unavailable and the goal is justified by its prospective scientific, educational, or applied value.
- Surgical procedures are performed under appropriate anesthesia; techniques to avoid infection and minimize pain are followed during and after surgery.
- When it is appropriate that the animal's life be terminated, it is done rapidly, with an effort to minimize pain, and in accordance with accepted procedures.

Source: APA, 1992.

has provided insight into the link between stress and health, methods of treating drug addiction and eating disorders, and strategies for helping premature infants gain weight (Miller, 1985). For example, research by Henry Harlow on the effects of deprivation of maternal touch on development in rhesus monkeys revealed the importance of developing attachments early in life, which in turn led to changes in the then standard procedure of separating newborn human infants from their mothers shortly after birth. Similarly, many people with incurable illnesses such as cancer and AIDS have benefited from drug treatments originally tested on animals.

Researchers who use animals as subjects must adhere to a set of strict guidelines regarding the animals' ethical treatment (see Table 2.6). Researchers must be

TABLE 2.7   *Information YOU Can Use*

- Breast-feeding has substantial benefits for infants' health—it is one of the best ways mothers can protect their babies from illness.
- Your mind-set, meaning how you think about your behavior, has a substantial impact on your physical health, including, at least in one study, your body fat, BMI, and blood pressure. This research provides powerful evidence of the impact of psychology on physical well-being.
- Relationships, for better or for worse, have a profound influence on psychological and physical well-being—and even on life expectancy. People who are divorced have higher rates of early mortality than those who are married, widowed, or never married.
- Although research studies may find evidence of correlation, remember that correlation is not the same as causation. Make sure to think skeptically about the scientific findings reported in the media, and carefully evaluate whether evidence truly supports the often-made causal claims about the association between different variables.
- The best way to evaluate whether a particular treatment, medication, or procedure truly impacts physical well-being is by using a true experiment. So, when you are making decisions about your own health, such as what approach to use to stop smoking or what treatment to use when diagnosed with cancer, rely most heavily on the results from experimental research (the real "gold standard" of research design).

properly trained in providing care for the animals, must justify the scientific value of the research, and must attempt to minimize stress and harm to the animals whenever possible. Moreover, Miller (1985) points out that many, many animals who are *not* used in research often suffer much more than those who are used to advance scientific research. For example, at least 20 million dogs and cats are abandoned each year in the United States, and of these, approximately half are ultimately euthanized in pounds or shelters, while many others die in painful ways (e.g., are hit by cars, starve to death). Although some people remain strongly opposed to the use of any animals in psychological research, recent studies indicate that over 70% of both psychologists and psychology majors support the use of animals in research (Plous, 1996a, 1996b).

Summary

1. Research in health psychology is based in the scientific method. This method includes forming hypotheses, developing and testing theories, and collecting and analyzing data.

2. Observational or naturalistic methods describe and/or measure behavior in everyday situations. These methods can include naturalistic or participant observation, archival research, or case reports/case studies.

3. Limitations of observational or naturalistic methods include the influence of the presence of the observer, the observer's own biases, the potential atypicality of a given circumstance, and the inability to distinguish between correlation and causation.

4. Survey methods rely on asking people questions about their feelings, thoughts, desires and/or actions, either orally (e.g., in an interview) or in writing (e.g., in a survey).

5. Survey methods have many advantages, including the ability to collect large amounts of data from multiple people in a relatively inexpensive way, asking questions about topics that could not be measured through observation (e.g., thoughts, feelings, desires), and the ability to maintain anonymity.

6. Survey methods also have limitations, including the use of leading questions, the presence of particular response options, the inaccuracy of people's responses, and the inability to distinguish between correlation and causation.

7. In using experimental methods, researchers randomly assign participants to one or more conditions (or independent variables) and measure the effect of these conditions on some outcome (the dependent variable).

8. Quasi-experiments can be used to study topics in which random assignment is not feasible. These include ex post facto, or case control, studies, as well as prospective and retrospective studies.

9. Clinical methods are used to examine the effectiveness of different drugs or therapies. These methods are very similar to experiments in many ways, although they may involve complex ethical issues.

10. Good research studies are high in internal validity, meaning that it is highly likely the effects of the study on the dependent variable were caused by the independent variable. Using a placebo and keeping participants and researchers blind to condition (and hypothesis) are techniques designed to increase internal validity.

11. Good research studies are high in external validity, meaning that the researchers have reasonable confidence that the same results would be obtained using the same experiment for other people and in other situations. Using a representative sample, making participation as convenient as possible, conducting the same study in different locations and with different populations, and designing studies with high mundane

realism are all techniques to increase external validity.

12. To avoid conducting ethically questionable studies, all research must follow particular procedures. These include undergoing institutional review, giving participants informed consent, protect participants' confidentiality, and giving participants a debriefing in cases in which the use of deception was necessary.

Key Terms

archival research
case report/case study
clinical study
correlation
dependent variable
experiment
external validity

hypothesis
incidence
independent variable
internal validity
observational or naturalistic
    methods
operational definition

prevalence
quasi-experiments
random assignment
scientific method
survey methods
theory

Thought Questions

1. You are interested in examining the association between television watching and obesity in children. How would you test this association using survey methods as compared to experimental methods?

2. Describe two ways to increase internal validity and two ways to increase external validity.

3. Your roommate, Derek, wants to know if his new hypnosis tape is actually effective in helping people to stop smoking. To test its effectiveness, he asks 10 of his close friends to participate in his experiments. He gives his five male friends the hypnosis tape and gives his five female friends a music tape. Finally, 1 week later, he asks each person how many cigarettes he or she is smoking per day. When Derek asks you for your thoughts on his study, what problems do you see?

4. You are interested in examining whether there is an association between alcohol use during pregnancy and birth defects. Describe how to examine this topic using a prospective method and a retrospective method.

5. Dr. Smith is a professor who wants to get feedback from his students on how effective he is as a teacher. He was planning to distribute an anonymous questionnaire with the midterm to get a response from all students in the course but then decided that this would be too much work. Instead, he's planning to ask students for their thoughts about the course and his teaching methods when they come in to his office for office hours. What is the problem with this approach?

CHAPTER 3

Theories of Health Behavior

Outline

- Diana knows she really should insist that her boyfriend wear a condom to protect them both from sexually transmitted diseases (STDs), but somehow she never actually makes that suggestion at the "crucial moment." She has never regularly used condoms before with other sexual partners and has never had an STD, so Diana thinks she might be invulnerable (or at least really lucky in choosing partners). Diana also heard from some friends that basically all STDs can now be cured with some type of pill or shot, and they're not such a big deal anyway. Even though she thinks she might feel more comfortable during sex if she and her partner were using a condom, Diana worries that her boyfriend might be offended by the suggestion and may even end the relationship.

- Steve has read several articles about the health benefits of regular exercise, and he is now planning to join a gym to start weight training a few times a week. He knows that he would feel good about himself if he felt more fit and strong. Steve's roommate already belongs to the local gym and thinks it is a great idea for Steve to start exercising. And Steve's parents have agreed to pay for the first year of gym membership to help him get started on his new plan.

- Hillary knows she should floss her teeth but just finds it hard to motivate herself to actually do it, particularly when she is tired at the end of a long night. Her dental hygienist suggests that she reward herself for flossing to help enhance her motivation. Hillary decides she will treat herself to a new pair of Nine West shoes every month that she flosses at least 20 times.

- Allen is a college sophomore who is currently on academic probation because of his low grades during the fall semester. Although Allen always intends to focus more effort on classes, he is living in an off-campus apartment with some friends, and they all stay up late drinking and playing cards. Some mornings Allen just can't get up for class because his head is pounding. His academic advisor pressured Allen into attending an alcohol-abuse prevention workshop, and even Allen hoped it would help him stop drinking so much. In the workshop, Allen got some advice on how to tell his roommates that he's not going to drink alcohol on weeknights anymore, and he even role-played a few practice dialogues with his friends. He began to weigh the benefits of cutting down a little on his drinking, including losing his "beer belly," having more money to spend on a spring break trip, and getting better grades.

- Maggie is 28 years old and has smoked for 10 years. During college, she mostly smoked only at parties and when she was out with friends, and she never even thought about quitting. However, Maggie got married last year, and she and her husband have recently begun talking about trying to have a baby. She knows that smoking while pregnant is very dangerous for the developing fetus, so she is trying to stop smoking. Thus far she has gone 9 days without having a single cigarette.

Preview

This chapter introduces the major theoretical perspectives used to predict and influence health-related behavior. First, we examine four continuum models of health behavior: the health belief model, the theories of reasoned action/planned behavior, learning theories, and social cognitive theory. These models all describe people's health-related behavior as the result of some combination of distinct variables, such as vulnerability, attitudes, benefits, and self-efficacy. We then examine two stage models of behavior change: the transtheoretical (stages of change) model and the precaution adoption process model. According to these models, people can be classified into distinct categories that represent their motivation to change their behavior. The six theories discussed in this chapter are often used to predict as well as to change people's health-related behavior.

What Are Continuum Theories of Health Behavior?

Continuum theories identify some set of variables that are thought to influence people's behavior and then combine those variables to predict the likelihood the person will engage in a given behavior (Weinstein, Rothman, & Sutton, 1998). Thus, these theories predict where a person is on a continuum of action likelihood. For example, the variables included in the theory might include perceived risk or vulnerability, attitudes, and self-efficacy, and these might be summed to predict whether a person will engage in a particular health-related behavior, such as smoking cigarettes, screening for cancer, or using condoms. As you will see, these theories share some common elements but also differ in terms of the specific components they use to predict behavior and how these components are combined. Before you start reading about these theories, take a minute to think about what factors influence whether or not you engage in a behavior related to health. Is it how much *not* doing the behavior scares you (e.g., the fear of getting AIDS if you don't use a condom)? Is it how much you think doing the behavior is a good idea (e.g., maybe you think exercising regularly to look fit is a good idea, but you aren't convinced that having a tetanus shot is a great benefit)? Is it how confident you feel that you could actually do the behavior (e.g., maybe you know you should give up eating those high-fat fast-food hamburgers, but you don't think you have the willpower to pass by the Golden Arches)? Is it that the negatives about doing the behavior seem more important than the positives (e.g., you know you should stop smoking, but whenever you cut back on cigarettes, you feel grouchy and nervous and start snacking all the time, which you hate)? Now read about the variables that each of these models includes, and see how well they might predict your own behavior.

Health Belief Model

The **health belief model** is one of the oldest and most widely used theories to explain people's health-related behavior. A group of social scientists originally developed this model in the 1950s to explain why people often fail to participate in programs to prevent or detect diseases (Rosenstock, 1960). For example, after the government provided free tuberculosis screening conveniently located in various neighborhoods, researchers were surprised that relatively few people took advantage of this opportunity for early detection and treatment. (Professors often feel a similar amazement when they sit waiting for students to stop by during office hours and have no visitors.) An examination of the factors that successfully led to more people using screening formed the basis of the health belief model (see Table 3.1).

The health belief model posits that the likelihood that individuals will take preventive action is a function of four types of factors (see Figure 3.1). First, individuals need to believe that they personally are **susceptible** to the condition. Perceived susceptibility can include beliefs about the general risks of engaging in a behavior (e.g., the likelihood of getting cancer if you smoke) as well as beliefs about how likely you personally would be to acquire an illness or disease. For example, you may be generally aware that tanning without sunscreen can lead to skin cancer, but if you've never used sunscreen before and have had no bad results, you might have relatively low motivation to wear sunscreen.

TABLE 3.1   *Examples of Questions Testing Components of the Health Belief Model*

Susceptibility	The possibility of getting wrinkles or age spots worries me.
Severity	It would be terrible to look older than I really am because of too much sun exposure.
Benefits	Wearing sunscreen with an SPF of at least 15 regularly when I am in the sun would reduce my chances of getting skin cancer.
Barriers	How likely is it that the cost of sunscreen would keep me from using it?

Source: Jackson & Aiken, 2000.

FIGURE 3.1   The health belief model.

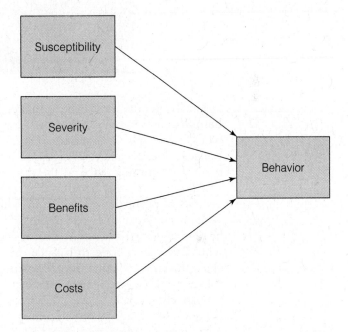

Next, individuals must believe that if they were to acquire a particular illness or disease it would have **severe** consequences. For example, if you believe that having an STD would not be particularly bad ("Hey, I'll just go get some penicillin at the campus health center"), you will be less motivated to use condoms than if you believe that having an STD would be pretty unpleasant. ("Hmm, it will hurt badly when I pee, it will be embarrassing to go to the campus health center for treatments, and I might infect someone I care about.") The evaluation of perceived severity can include the consequences we individually would face, such as pain, disability, and even death. For example, if you believe that having a baby as a teenager would hurt your chances of attending college, you will be motivated to either remain abstinent or use effective contraception if you are highly motivated to continue your education. The evaluation of severity can also include the consequences others in our social network would face if we were to experience an illness or disease. Parents who smoke, for example, may be motivated to try to stop this behavior to protect their children from the pain they would encounter if they had to cope with the death of a parent.

Although most people know that tanning leads to skin cancer, the perceived benefits of a tan can seem greater than the costs.
Source: Pictor/ImageState/Alamy Images.

Finally, people must believe that engaging in a particular behavior would have **benefits** in terms of reducing the threat of a particular illness and that these benefits would outweigh the **barriers**. The benefits of stopping smoking are pretty clear (longer life expectancy, less expense, whiter teeth, etc.), but for some people, the barriers to quitting, such as the fear of being more tense or of gaining weight, could outweigh the benefits. For example, even though I see the long-term benefits of protecting myself from skin cancer, I still sometimes go to the beach without sunscreen in an attempt to acquire a "savage tan" (perhaps from repeatedly hearing my father's mantra, "Brown fat is better than white fat"). Similarly, people who have cancer have to balance the benefits of various treatment options (e.g., chemotherapy, radiation, surgery) with the treatment option costs (e.g., losing hair, risk of death, severe illness). As described at the beginning of the chapter, Diana is relatively unlikely to use condoms because she sees the potential costs of using condoms (conflict with boyfriend) as greater than the benefits she would gain from such behavior (protection from STDs).

Although the original version of the health belief model included only the four components of severity, susceptibility, benefits, and costs, a revised version of this model also includes cues to action (Janz & Becker, 1984). **Cues to action** refers to any type of reminder about a potential health problem that could motivate behavior change. These cues can be internal, such as experiencing a health symptom, or external, such as receiving a postcard reminder to get your teeth cleaned or watching a public service announcement on television about the dangers of smoking. These cues are just the final push that it sometimes takes to get people to act. Box 3.1: Focus on Research describes the impact of reminder cues on condom use.

How good is this model at predicting what people do? Overall, the health belief model is a good predictor of whether people engage in health-related behaviors as well as whether they participate in health-screening programs (Rosenstock, 1990). For example, the health belief model can predict behavior related to dental care (Ronis, 1992), breast self-examination (Champion, 1994), condom use (Aspinwall, Kemeny, Taylor, Schneider, & Dudley, 1991), and diet (Becker, Maiman, Kirscht, Haefner, & Drachman, 1977). One study examining the predictors of HIV testing among gay, lesbian, and bisexual youth using the health belief model revealed that

Box 3.1

Focus on Research: Using "Friendship Bracelets" to Increase Condom Use

Researchers in this study were interested in testing the effectiveness of reminder cues on condom use (Dal Cin, MacDonald, Fong, Zanna, & Elton-Marshall, 2006). College students were randomly assigned to one of three interventions: a standard safe-sex intervention, a safe-sex intervention with a reminder cue, or a control intervention on drinking and driving. Both interventions consisted of a video (either stories of people living with HIV describing contracting the disease or, in the case of the control condition, a documentary about a young man killed by a drunk driver). Participants in the intervention with the reminder cue were given a "friendship bracelet" to wear at the conclusion of the intervention, were told to wear this bracelet until the end of the study period, and were told to think about the stories of the people with HIV whenever they looked at it. All participants completed a follow-up questionnaire 5 to 7 weeks later to assess the effects of these different interventions. As predicted, students in the reminder cue ("bracelet") condition were significantly more likely to report using condoms than those in the other two conditions. Specifically, participants in the reminder cue intervention reported using condoms 58% of the time in the last month, compared to 34% of those in the standard safe-sex intervention and 40% of those in the control intervention. Similarly, 55% of those in the reminder cue intervention reported using a condom the last time they had sex, compared to only 27% of those in the standard safe-sex intervention and 36% of those in the control intervention. This research provides compelling evidence that reminding people to engage in a behavior can be a valuable strategy for changing behavior.

both barriers to HIV testing and perceived susceptibility to AIDS were significant predictors of HIV testing (Maguen, Armistead, & Kalichman, 2000).

Questioning the Research 3.1

The Maguen et al. (2000) study finding that barriers to HIV testing and perceived susceptibility to AIDS were the strongest predictors of HIV testing was conducted with teenagers. Do you think these findings would be the same with older populations? Why or why not?

Although the results of studies on the health belief model have generally been favorable, researchers have raised some questions about its usefulness. First, this model does not include the component of self-efficacy, or a person's confidence that he or she can effectively engage in a behavior (Schwarzer, 1992). More recent theories, such as the theory of planned behavior and social cognitive theory, include this component, and research demonstrates that self-efficacy is a consistently strong predictor of health-related behavior. Second, while perceived barriers and perceived susceptibility tend to be the best predictors of behavior, perceived severity is not a very strong predictor of behavior (Janz & Becker, 1984) and may be a particularly poor predictor of health behavior in cases in which health problems are either hard to define in terms of severity (e.g., medical conditions with which people are unfamiliar) or are extremely severe for virtually everyone (e.g., cancer). Third, this model was originally developed to predict whether people would obtain immunizations, and it continues to be more useful in predicting one-time or limited behaviors than in predicting habitual behaviors (Kirscht, 1988). The health belief model may therefore be more useful in describing relatively simple behaviors than in describing complex behaviors.

Theories of Reasoned Action/Planned Behavior

The **theory of reasoned action** is a general psychological theory that is useful in predicting the link among attitudes, intentions, and behavior across different domains, such as voting, donating money, and choosing a career (Fishbein & Ajzen, 1975). For example, if you want to know how likely someone is to start an exercise program, you must examine the person's attitude toward exercise and intention to exercise. This theory emphasizes the role of individuals' beliefs about their social world and therefore includes components assessing individuals' beliefs about others' attitudes toward a given behavior (e.g., how do you think your friends will feel if you start an exercise program?).

This theory posits that the key determinant of people's behavior is their **intention** to engage in that behavior. For example, your intentions to brush your teeth every night are probably a very strong predictor of whether you actually do brush your teeth. In turn, according to the theory of reasoned action, intentions are determined by a person's **attitude** toward the behavior as well as the person's **subjective norms** for the behavior. Steve, described at the beginning of the chapter, has strong intentions to exercise because he has positive attitudes about exercising and believes his friends and parents are supportive of this behavior; his intentions will likely influence his subsequent behavior.

Attitudes are a person's positive or negative feelings about engaging in a particular behavior. You might have a positive attitude about eating breakfast every day but a negative attitude about avoiding your morning coffee. In turn, individuals' attitudes are a function of their beliefs about the consequences of engaging in a particular behavior as well as their evaluation of these outcomes. For example, a woman's attitudes about dieting will be formed by her beliefs about whether a diet will help her feel thinner and more attractive and her feelings about the benefits of having a thinner body (see Table 3.2).

Subjective norms refer to individuals' beliefs about whether other people would support them in engaging in a new behavior and whether they are motivated to follow the beliefs of these salient others. Who are these "other people," according to this theory? They might be family members, friends, and romantic partners. For example, an individual's intention to diet could be influenced by his beliefs

TABLE 3.2   *Sample Questions Based on the Theory of Reasoned Action*

Attitude Items	Social Norm Items
If I eat fruits and vegetables regularly, I will improve my health.	My parents would like for me to be healthier.
I would feel better about myself if I were healthier.	My friends think I should eat healthier food.

Box 3.2

Focus on Culture: The Role of Individual and Social Factors on Health

Although most of the theories predicting health-related behavior have been developed by American researchers and tested on American samples, research is now examining whether these theories are also relevant in predicting behavior in different cultures. Researchers in one study examined the role of components of both the health belief model and theories of reasoned action/planned behavior in predicting adolescents' health-related behavior in both the United States and China (Turbin et al., 2006). Researchers gathered data from 1,739 Chinese students (grades 7, 8, and 9), and 1,596 American students (also grades 7, 8, and 9) over a 1-year period to predict behavior over time. Students completed measures assessing a range of health behaviors, including eating, exercise, sleep, safety, and dental hygiene. Students also completed measures assessing the role of both individual factors (such as self-esteem, importance of health, and perceived risk) and social factors (such as family support, modeling, and peer influences) in predicting health-related behaviors. Findings revealed that in both cultures, social factors were a stronger predictor of health-related behaviors than individual factors. This research suggests that components of both the health belief model and theories of reasoned action/planned behavior are useful in predicting health-related behavior across cultures and that social factors may well have a stronger influence than individual factors on such behavior.

about whether his family and friends would be supportive of his efforts to diet as well as by whether he is motivated to engage in behaviors these people encourage. As described in Box 3.2: Focus on Culture, social factors, such as modeling, peer influence, and family support, are associated with health-related behaviors for adolescents in both America and China.

A later version of this model, the **theory of planned behavior**, added the component of **perceived behavioral control**, that is, the extent to which a person believes that he or she can successfully enact a behavior (Ajzen, 1985; see Figure 3.2). You might believe strongly that you can wear your seat belt but doubt whether you

FIGURE 3.2 Model of the theory of reasoned action/planned behavior.

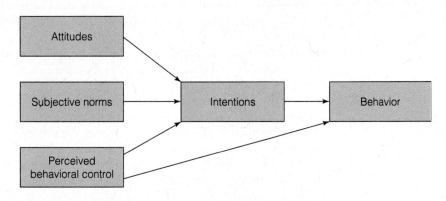

can refuse to get in a car driven by a friend who's had a few too many drinks. Perceived behavioral control is a reflection of both past experience with the behavior as well as beliefs about your ability to engage in a particular behavior in the future. For example, if you are trying to lose weight but have failed to resist eating Ben & Jerry's New York Super Fudge Chunk in the past and doubt whether your willpower is strong enough to resist eating it now, your perceived behavioral control will be low.

The theories of reasoned action and planned behavior are successful in predicting a range of different types of health behaviors, including engaging in testicular and breast self-examinations, using sunscreen, losing weight, wearing seat belts, increasing exercise frequency, smoking cigarettes, drinking alcohol, using condoms, screening for health conditions, breast-feeding, and flossing (Ajzen, Albarracín, & Hornik, 2007; Ajzen & Manstead, 2007; Albarracín, Johnson, Fishbein, & Muellerleile, 2001; Sheeran, Conner, & Norman, 2001). For example, both safe-sex norms and attitudes predict the frequency of unprotected sex (Huebner, Newilands, Rebchook, & Kegeles, 2011), and perceived behavioral control for participating in exercise predicts both exercise intentions and actual exercise behavior (Armitage, 2005). Researchers in one study examined the role of attitudes, social norms, perceived behavioral control, and intentions in predicting whether men would undergo a cancer screening in the next 12 months (Sieverding, Matterne, & Ciccarello, 2010). Attitudes, norms, and perceived behavioral control were strong predictors of intentions to undergo screening, and both social norms and intentions were particularly strong predictors of actually undergoing the screening. These studies all point to the value of these four components—attitudes, norms, perceived behavioral control, and intentions—in predicting health-related behavior.

Questioning the Research 3.2

The study by Sieverding, Matterne, & Ciccarello (2010) found that social norms were a stronger predictor than attitudes or perceived behavior control of undergoing cancer screening. Do you think social norms are generally a stronger predictor of health-related behavior, or is there something unique about screening behavior that may explain this finding?

Although the theories of reasoned action and planned behavior are widely used to predict health-related behaviors, they have some limitations. One problem with both theories is that the relevant attitudes, beliefs, and intentions toward a given behavior are typically particular to a given sample (Fishbein & Middlestadt, 1989). For example, the relevant attitudes and subjective norms toward the use of condoms in high school students may relate to their parents' attitudes toward condom use, whereas the relevant attitudes and norms in a sample of gay men may relate to their concerns about implying a lack of trust toward their partner. Another limitation of both the theory of reasoned action and the theory of planned behavior is that they fail to include the person's current or past behavior (Albarracín et al., 2001; Manstead et al., 1983). The best predictor of future behavior often is past behavior, and past behavior may influence behavior both directly and indirectly through its influence on intentions. Finally, although these theories posit that individuals'

*"I start every diet with the best intentions, but it goes
to hell as soon as I sense blood in the water."*

intentions lead directly to behavior, people often intend to do a behavior but fail to actually follow through (Sheppard, Hartwick, & Warshaw, 1988). In turn, one study found that perceived behavioral control is a stronger predictor of behavior than intentions (Johnston, Johnston, Pollard, Kinmonth, & Mant, 2004). (You can probably think of many times in which your intentions to do a behavior did not successfully lead to enacting behavior.) In sum, these theories are good, but not perfect, predictors of behavior.

One strategy that helps increase the link between intentions and behavior is to form implementation intentions, that is, a specific plan of how, where, and when to perform a behavior (Gollwitzer, 1993). For example, if you intend to exercise regularly, you will be more likely to follow through on this intention if you form such specific plans (e.g., I am going to join a gym and run on the treadmill 30 minutes right after work on Mondays, Wednesdays, and Fridays). Researchers in one study randomly selected adolescents to one of three interventions designed to prevent smoking: one focused on increasing self-efficacy for refusing cigarettes, one focused on creating specific implementation intentions regarding refusing cigarettes, and a control condition focused on creating specific implementation intentions for completing schoolwork (Connor & Higgins, 2010). Findings at the 4-year follow-up revealed that only 26.3% of those who formed implementation intentions for refusing cigarettes were smoking, compared to 34% of those who received information on self-efficacy for smoking, and 32.5% of those in the control condition. Implementation intentions are also effective for decreasing unhealthy eating (Adriaanse, de Ridder, & de Wit, 2009; Armitage, 2004; Tam, Bagozzi, & Spanjol, 2010), reducing alcohol use (Armitage, 2009), and increasing exercise (Prestwich, Perugini, & Hurling, 2010). As shown in Figure 3.3, implementation intentions may lead to improved behavior at least in part because such intentions lead to greater reliance on strategies for planning.

Learning Theories

Learning theories are based on the assumption that behavior is influenced by basic learning processes, such as association, reinforcement, and modeling (Bandura, 1977; Pavlov, 1927; Skinner, 1938; Thorndike, 1905). People learn health-related behaviors in the same way that they learn other behaviors. The three main types of learning approaches are classical conditioning, operant conditioning, and observational learning.

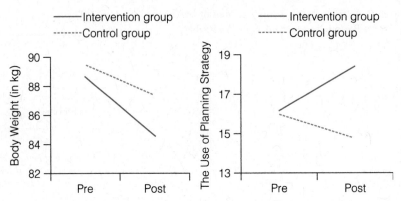

FIGURE 3.3   Researchers in this study randomly assigned overweight women attending a Weight Watchers group to the standard program or the implementation intentions program, in which in addition to participating in the regular group activities, they also made detailed plans about what types of food they would eat and exercise they would engage in during the following week. Although there were no initial differences between women in the two groups in weight or use of planning strategies, at the 2-month post-test, women in the implementation intention group had lost more weight and reported more use of planning strategies for losing weight than those in the control group (data from Luszczynska, Sobczyk, & Abraham, 2007).

Classical conditioning occurs when a previously neutral stimulus comes to evoke the same response as another stimulus with which it is paired. You may be familiar with a famous study on classical conditioning conducted by the Russian physiologist Ivan Pavlov (1927). At the start of the study, Pavlov noted that dogs normally salivate in response to the presentation of food, but they do not salivate in response to hearing a bell. For several days, he then rang a bell right before delivering food to hungry dogs. Over time, the dogs began to salivate merely at the sound of the bell before the food was presented. This research demonstrates the power of associative learning, in which dogs (and people!) understand that two events are linked.

Classical conditioning can also influence people's health-related behavior. For example, imagine that you are reclining in a seat at your dentist's office hearing the sound of a dentist's drill coming from the next room (see Figure 3.4). Even though the dentist is not anywhere near you (or your teeth), simply hearing the drill may produce feelings of arousal, anxiety, or pain because, over time, you have come to associate the noise of the drill with the pain in your mouth. Similarly, patients who have undergone chemotherapy, a treatment that often leaves people feeling nauseous and weak, sometimes develop anticipatory nausea even before they begin receiving a periodic dosage of the drugs. They may start to feel sick when they are sitting in the chair waiting for treatment or in the car as they are driving to the hospital. A study by Christine Cameron et al. (2001) demonstrated that cancer patients who had previously received either chemotherapy or radiation reported experiencing nausea or vomiting in response to smells, sights, or tastes that reminded them of their treatment. Thirty percent of the patients reported experiencing nausea in response to smells that reminded them of the treatment, and 17% reported experiencing nausea in response to sights that reminded them of the treatment.

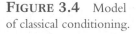

FIGURE 3.4 Model of classical conditioning.

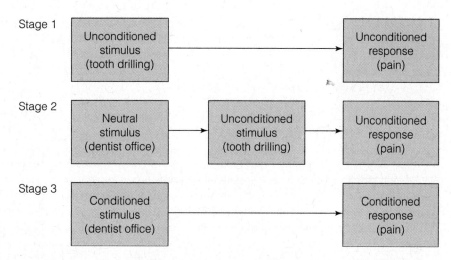

Operant conditioning refers to the idea that behaviors can be increased or decreased as a function of the consequences of engaging in them (Skinner, 1938). On the one hand, desired behaviors can be positively reinforced through rewards, which should lead to their continuation. For example, if you are trying to stick to an exercise program, you might decide to give yourself a small reward each week that you run at least 4 days. Similarly, as described at the beginning of the chapter, Hillary should be highly motivated to keep flossing so that she can buy new shoes. On the other hand, the frequency of undesirable behaviors can be decreased through punishment. For example, people who are caught driving under the influence of alcohol typically receive severe punishments, including loss of license, fines, and possibly even jail time. These negative consequences should motivate people to avoid drinking and driving.

Operant conditioning can be used to either decrease undesirable behaviors through adding a negative consequence, or increase desirable ones through adding a positive consequence. As you'll learn in Chapter 7, raising the price of cigarettes decreases smoking; in fact, estimates are that a 10% increase in price decreased the odds of teenagers' starting smoking by as much as 10% (Ross & Chaloupka, 2003). Moreover, this may be particularly true for teenagers, who typically have relatively little money to spend (and see Box 3.3: Focus on Development for an example of the use of operant conditioning approaches to increase healthy eating behavior in children). In contrast, increasing the rewards of engaging in health-promoting behaviors can also be effective. Researchers in one study asked families of obese children to give children rewards for engaging in physical activity (Epstein, Paluch, Kilanowski, & Raynor, 2004). Children who were rewarded later showed increases in physical activity and, more importantly, decreased in percent overweight.

Questioning the Research 3.3

According to learning theory, providing rewards for engaging in a behavior can increase the likelihood that someone will engage in that behavior. Can you think of any drawbacks to this approach to creating health-related behavior change?

Box 3.3

Focus on Development: Using Operant Conditioning to Improve Children's Eating and Exercise Behavior

Operant conditioning principles can help improve health-related behavior by increasing the costs of engaging in unhealthy behaviors and/or by decreasing the costs of engaging in healthy behaviors. Researchers in one study examined the effects of food costs on children's interest in different types of food options (Epstein et al., 2006). Children (ages 10 to 14) were given money and then told they could purchase portions of a healthy food (fruit or vegetable) or a less healthy food (a higher-fat snack). The price of the foods varied: Sometimes the healthy food was more expensive, and sometimes it was less expensive. Researchers then examined how the price of the different food choices influenced children's preferences. Raising the prices of both healthy and unhealthy foods decreased preference for that food, showing that decreasing the cost of healthy foods and increasing the costs of unhealthy foods may be an effective way to improve healthy eating. Unfortunately, in the real world, unhealthy foods are often much cheaper than healthy ones (think about McDonald's "value menu" with many unhealthy foods priced at just $1.00 compared to the price of many fresh fruits).

Operant conditioning approaches are most effective when people receive rewards for making small steps toward behavior change. Changing behavior is often a long and difficult process, so if people receive rewards only after they have completely adopted the behavior, they will likely experience frustration. People should therefore receive rewards simply for taking steps toward adopting the behavior. For example, if you are trying to stop smoking, you might receive a reward for cutting down the number of cigarettes you smoke each day or for delaying smoking your first cigarette each morning. After you have mastered one of these steps toward smoking cessation, you would then receive rewards only for mastering the next step.

Operant conditioning can also occur simply through **observational learning**, namely, watching someone else receive rewards or punishment for engaging in a particular behavior (Bandura, 1977, 1986). Children often form their beliefs about the consequences of various health-related behaviors by watching their parents and older siblings (Whitehead, Busch, Heller, & Costa, 1986). For example, D'Amico and Fromme (1997) examined the effects of older siblings' outcome expectancies and behavior related to health issues (e.g., drinking, sex without condoms, illicit drug use) on their younger same-gender adolescent siblings. Findings indicated that the more younger siblings believed their older siblings drank, the more the younger siblings themselves drank and the more the younger siblings believed that positive outcomes would emerge from heavy drinking. This association between younger siblings' perceptions of their older siblings' behaviors and the younger siblings' own behavior was true even though younger siblings were not particularly accurate in their beliefs about their older siblings' behavior. Second, younger siblings' beliefs about their older siblings' positive experiences with other behaviors, such as getting drunk, driving under the influence of alcohol, and having unprotected sex, led the younger adolescents to develop their own positive expectancies about engaging in these behaviors. In sum, younger siblings may learn through modeling and vicarious experience about the consequences of engaging in particular types of health-related behaviors.

Observational learning from the media—including television shows, advertisements, and movies—can also influence health-related behavior (see Box 3.4: Focus on Research: Can Watching Television Cause Teenage Pregnancy?). Researchers in one study examined the influence of a story line about teenage obesity on a popular television medical drama, *ER* (Valente et al., 2007). The presence of this story line led to changes in nutrition knowledge, attitudes, and self-reported behavior among those who watched this show. Similarly, Box 3.5: Health Psychology in the Real World describes the hazards of showing airbrushed pictures on girls' attitudes toward their own appearance. As we'll discuss in Chapter 6, television advertisements during major sporting events often include acts of unsafe behavior, which in turn could lead children to engage in more risk-taking behavior (Tamburro, Gordon, D'Apolito, & Howard, 2004), and as we'll discuss in Chapter 7, television advertisements influence children's beliefs about the effects of alcohol (Collins, Ellickson, McCaffrey, & Hambarsoomians, 2007).

Although learning theories are widely used to predict and influence behavior, these approaches have some important limitations. First, although classical conditioning can be an effective way of influencing health-related behavior, it also has some potential problems. As we examine in detail in Chapter 7, one way to help alcoholics stop drinking is to give them a drug (e.g., Antabuse) that causes them

Box 3.4

Focus on Research: Can Watching Television Cause Teenage Pregnancy?

Researchers in this study examined the link between exposure to sexual content on television and rates of teen pregnancy to examine whether such exposure may influence attitudes and behavior related to sex (Chandra et al., 2008). This study gathered data from a national longitudinal study of teenagers (ages 12 to 17) that included specific questions on whether students had watched each of 23 television programs that were popular with teenagers in the prior season. The sexual content on each of these shows was coded to assess the presence of various types of sexual behaviors (such as kissing, flirting, intercourse) as well as sexual talk (including talk about characters' sexual desires, experiences, and intentions). Researchers then examined rates of pregnancy over the next 3 years for all participants. Findings revealed that exposure to sexual content was positively associated with likelihood of experiencing a pregnancy, even when taking into account other variables that may be associated with pregnancy (such as participants' age, educational aspirations, race, and grades). Specifically, teenagers who were exposed to high levels of sexual content on television (those in the 90th percentile in terms of viewing) were twice as likely to experience a pregnancy as those with low levels of exposure (those in the 10th percentile in terms of viewing). This research provides strong evidence that watching television can have strong, and detrimental, effects on health-related behavior.

Box 3.5

Health Psychology in the Real World: The Hazards of Airbrushing

By Jessica Bennett, *Newsweek*, May 1, 2008

I reached an age, probably around 12, when *Seventeen* and *YM* became my gospel, the all-knowing mantra for the teenage life I was about to enter. I'd fork over my allowance each week to find out "how to score my dream guy" or "the secrets to a killer bod" through an immeasurable number of tip sheets and unscientific quizzes. Then I'd then curl up in my bedroom—which I wasn't coming out of much in those days—and wonder if I'd ever measure up to the oh-so-perfect models staring back at me from the page.

It may sound pathetic, but ask any woman; those early teen years are torturous, when nothing about ourselves ever seems good or pretty or perfect enough. And it doesn't stop at 16. Most women will cop to comparing themselves, at least occasionally, to the actresses and celebs of their generation that appear in magazines or advertisements. And thanks to improvements in photo retouching over the last five years, those glossy images have strayed further and further from anything resembling reality. Retouching techniques that were once used mainly to erase blemishes or stray hairs have become tools for radical human body distortion, shrinking waists and vanquishing years, turning models and actresses into leggy dolls of literally inhuman proportions.

But there's a growing backlash against this digital Barbie-fication of almost every model, actress or celebrity. Sure, anyone reading a women's magazine understands that fashion is supposed to be fantasy, but when middle-aged celebrities and teenage actresses all look as if they're about the same age and weight, people start to notice—and object. Even governments are examining the public health consequences of mass media images that look so little like the masses.

Most serious news organizations, including *Newsweek*, have strict rules against photo manipulation. But for now fashion, women's and lifestyle publications typically honor no such code. They may not admit it outright, but it's common knowledge within the industry that retouching and thinning models and celebrities is not just standard procedure, it's expected and often demanded by publicists. "We're always stretching the models' legs and slimming their thighs," a Manhattan-based photo retoucher tells *Newsweek*, speaking anonymously for fear of professional backlash. "Sometimes I feel a little like Frankenstein."

In response to the uproar over some well-publicized alterations of celebrities, though, the trade groups that represent those publications, in both Britain and the United States, say they are considering voluntary codes outlining how far art directors can go. And late last month the National Assembly of France went a step further when it approved a startling new bill that, if passed by the Senate, would make it a crime for anyone, from pro-anorexia Web sites to advertisers to editors, to publicly incite "excessive thinness" or extreme dieting. Though it's unclear how those offenses would be defined or interpreted, the law would allow judges to punish offenders by up to two years in prison and fines up to $47,000. "It's time for public action against this scourge," the bill's author told the *Washington Post*.

Whether or not magazines are actually inciting thinness, it doesn't take a genius to see that they're creating a standard of beauty that's far from what the average American reader can attain. Already models weigh about 23 percent less than the average woman, according to a 2004 SizeUSA study. We shudder to think how that disparity may have grown in the intervening four years. Retouchers today are increasingly asked by advertisers and editors to enlarge eyes, trim ears, fill in hairlines, straighten and whiten teeth and lengthen the already narrow necks, waists and legs of 18-year-old beauties—in some cases replacing hands, feet or legs altogether with the parts of "more appealing" models.

In May, *Men's Fitness* reportedly incited *thickness* in tennis star Andy Roddick by enlarging his already muscular arms to promote a story about biceps. Roddick himself mocked the photo on his personal blog; a spokesman for the magazine later told the *New York Times*, "I don't see what the big issue is here." Later, readers went crazy over the apparent slimming of "Ugly Betty" star America Ferrera on the cover of *Glamour*, despite the magazine's denials. (Irony alert: there's an entire episode of "Ugly Betty" devoted to putting "real"-looking models in magazines.) But most memorable, perhaps, were the shocking before-and-after pictures of Faith Hill on the cover of *Redbook*, revealed last July by popular femme-gossip site Jezebel and circulated around the Internet en masse. *Redbook* editor in chief Stacy Morrison defended the changes, telling the "Today" show, "In the end, they're not really photographs. They're images."

Any photographer will tell you: airbrushing has been around for decades. The problem today, of course, is how easy technology has made it to perfect those images. Buy a digital camera and it comes with retouching elements. Anyone can learn how to use Photoshop to blend and tighten and thin—people do it for their MySpace photos all the time. As actress and bikini model Elizabeth Hurley told a British newspaper recently, she *so* loves being airbrushed to look "thinner" and "younger" that she's taken to Photoshopping her own holiday photos. "Brides are airbrushing the red out of their eyes and getting rid of blemishes in their own wedding photos these days, so the technology's here to stay," says Cindi Leive, the outgoing president of the American Society of Magazine Editors (ASME) and the editor in chief of *Glamour*. "But the bottom line is that readers should not be misled."

That sounds good in theory, but it's a joke among industry insiders—and anyone with a basic knowledge of graphic design. Leive wouldn't comment on retouching as it relates to *Glamour*; a spokeswoman told *Newsweek* that Leive would answer questions for this article only on behalf of ASME. To be fair, the editors of most women's magazines would rather talk about anything but airbrushing. And in the world of fashion isn't misleading the reader, well, the point? "You have to accept that fashion is fantasy. It's wearable art," says Andrew Matusik, a New York fashion photographer and the owner of Digital Retouch, which specializes in celebrity and fashion retouching. "It's all about creating drama."

That might lead us to buy, but it's not making us any healthier. Several studies show that women feel worse about themselves after reading fashion magazines, and kids as young as six are having their photos retouched. An average girl today will see more than 77,000 advertisements by the time she's 12—and you can bet that most of those have been retouched. If that girl is like 42 percent of the population she'll want to be thinner by the time she's a third-grader, and by age 10—if she's like 81 percent of her peers—she'll be afraid of being fat, according to a 2004 global survey by the Dove Campaign for Real Beauty. "These techniques underscore the idea that the perfection portrayed in the media is unattainable by natural means," says Cynthia Bulik, a clinical psychologist and the director of the eating disorders program at the University of North Carolina at Chapel Hill.

The question is, do readers know the extent to which their favorite stars have been transformed? Last year the health ministry of Sweden put out a powerful PSA in an effort to spread the word. The spot depicted a 14-year-old girl's transformation from model to cover model. Here's what she endured: her eyebrows were reshaped and her eyelashes lengthened. Her eyes were made whiter and bluer, her teeth straighter and whiter. Her lips were plumped along with her breasts, and her blemishes were removed. Then her hair was lightened and thickened. And finally her nose was slimmed, her chin thinned, and her waist whittled away. "Those young kids looking at the magazines, they're dreaming of something that doesn't exist," says Philippe Paschkes, a Manhattan stylist and makeup artist who has worked in the industry for 30 years.

But is French-style regulation really the answer? Or should the industry be counted on to police itself? When the British edition of *GQ* was slammed in 2003 for blatantly slimming Kate Winslet on its cover, editor in chief Dylan Jones admitted, "Almost no picture that appears in *GQ*...has not been digitally altered." Five years later little has changed. Liz Hurley might be OK with that, but there are a whole lot of impressionable young kids who shouldn't be.

Observational learning, or modeling, from parents, peers, and the media is a strong predictor of smoking in teenagers.
Source: Michael A Keller/Photolibrary.

to become violently ill when they drink alcohol. The theory behind this approach is that patients will grow to associate drinking alcohol with nausea and therefore stop drinking. However, patients typically understand that the Antabuse is causing the sickness; therefore, they may simply stop taking the drug instead of avoiding alcohol. Second, operant conditioning can lead people to engage in a behavior simply to get the reward but not because of any intrinsic changes in their intentions to engage in the behavior; after the reward is withdrawn, the behavior will stop. In one study, 732 seventh-grade boys and girls were asked to use a fluoride mouthwash daily and were given small prizes for doing so (e.g., pencil, pen, yo-yo; Lund & Kegeles, 1984). Children who received rewards were more likely to use the rinse, but after the rewards were eliminated, they no longer continued to use the rinse. In sum, learning theories may be effective at changing behavior but are less effective in maintaining behavior.

Social Cognitive Theory

Social cognitive theory posits that people acquire attitudes through various sources in their immediate social network as well as by observing people presented in the media (Bandura, 1977, 1986). *Direct modeling* occurs when people observe others in their social networks engaging in particular behavior (e.g., watching my foolish father having cavities filled without pain medication), whereas *symbolic modeling* occurs when people observe people portrayed in the media, including magazines, newspapers, and on television. However, whether these attitudes lead to behavior is a function of people's beliefs about their own ability to engage (or not engage) in a particular behavior as well as their beliefs about the consequences of engaging (or not engaging) in a particular behavior. For example, when deciding whether to stop drinking alcohol, individuals might think about whether they realistically would be able to "just say no" and whether they think not drinking would have positive or negative consequences (on their health, social life, etc.). These two components of social cognitive theory are described in detail here.

Social cognitive theory includes the role of an individual's **self-efficacy**, namely, the extent to which one believes he or she can engage in a particular behavior (see Table 3.3). (This concept of self-efficacy is similar to that of perceived behavioral control, as described in the theory of planned behavior.) For example, people who strongly believe they will be able to follow through on their intentions to exercise four times a week will be more likely to successfully carry out this behavior than those who have doubts about their ability to follow through on such intentions. Self-efficacy is seen as a particularly powerful influence on health behavior because it is thought to influence people's behavior in two distinct ways (O'Leary, 1992). First, people who have a strong sense of self-efficacy for a given behavior are likely to exert considerable effort to perform the behavior. A person who has great confidence in her ability to stop smoking, for example, may try harder to resist offers of cigarettes from friends. She may also continue with her goal of quitting even if she experiences a brief lapse in judgment and smokes a cigarette on one occasion. In contrast, someone with low self-efficacy may show little resistance when confronted with tempting offers and may quickly return to regular smoking after smoking a single cigarette (Van Zundert, Ferguson, Shiffman, & Engels, 2010). Second, research shows that people with low self-efficacy have a greater physiological response to stressful situations (such as making difficult changes in their behavior), including higher heart rates and blood pressure, than those with high self-efficacy. This greater anxiety response may lead people with low self-efficacy to be less likely to even attempt to engage in behavior change than those with high self-efficacy. Finally, and perhaps most important, people with high self-efficacy show a higher correlation between knowledge and behavior: They are more likely to act on their knowledge (e.g., to eat healthy foods if they understand that healthy foods are good for them; Rimal, 2000).

Social cognitive theory also includes the component of **outcome expectancies**, an individual's beliefs about whether engaging in a particular behavior will have

TABLE 3.3   *Test Yourself: The Condom Use Self-Efficacy Scale*

This scale measures people's self-efficacy to use condoms. The questions ask about your own feelings about using condoms in specific situations. Responses are scored as follows: strongly disagree = 0, disagree = 1, undecided = 2, agree = 3, strongly agree = 4.

1. I feel confident in my ability to put a condom on myself or my partner.
2. I feel confident in my ability to suggest using condoms with a new partner.
3. I feel confident that I could remember to use a condom even after I have been drinking.
4. I feel confident that I could stop to put a condom on myself or my partner even in the heat of passion.
5. I feel confident in my ability to persuade a partner to accept using a condom when we have intercourse.
6. I feel confident in my ability to use a condom correctly.
7. I feel confident I could purchase condoms without feeling embarrassed.
8. I feel confident that I could use a condom with a partner without "breaking the mood."
9. I feel confident I could remember to carry a condom with me should I need one.
10. I feel confident I could use a condom during intercourse without reducing any sexual sensations.

Source: Brafford & Beck, 1991.

a desired outcome. For example, people who believe that eating healthy foods will make them feel good and be healthy are more likely to eat such foods than people who believe that nutritious foods taste bad and probably aren't going to help their health much anyway. As described in the section on learning theories, outcome expectancies can be learned through direct experience with a behavior, or by observing the consequence someone else experiences as a result of that behavior. You may learn, for example, that drinking alcohol leads to relaxation by watching the positive consequences your parents experience after drinking a glass of wine after a tough day at work.

Social cognitive theory is a good predictor of a variety of different types of behavior, such as smoking cessation (Baldwin et al., 2006; Borrelli & Mermelstein, 1994; Van Zundert et al., 2010), eating nutritious foods (Sheeshka, Woolcott, & MacKinnon, 1993), lowering cholesterol (Bandura, 1997), brushing and flossing teeth (Tedesco, Keffer, Davis, & Christersson, 1993), using condoms (Wulfert & Wan, 1993), losing weight (Finch et al., 2005; Linde, Rothman, Baldwin, & Jeffery, 2006), and exercising regularly (Bandura, 1997). For example, researchers in one study predicting weight loss among 349 overweight adults found that outcome expectancies regarding losing weight were associated with actual weight loss as long as 18 months later (Finch et al., 2005). Similarly, and as shown in Figure 3.5, patients with coronary heart disease who are low in self-efficacy are more likely to be hospitalized and die. These studies all suggest that social cognitive theory is a useful predictor of health-related behavior.

Questioning the Research 3.4

Although the study by Finch and colleagues revealed that outcome expectancies were associated with weight loss later on, does this finding demonstrate that such expectancies cause weight loss? (Hint: Does this finding reveal correlation or causation?). Can you think of an alternative explanation for this association?

Given the success of social cognitive theory in predicting health-related behavior, some researchers have examined how to increase and build an individual's self-efficacy for a given behavior. This work suggests that self-efficacy increases after individuals successfully achieve goals; hence, interventions should help people set attainable subgoals to guide longer-term behavior (Bandura, 1977, 1997). For example, a person who is trying to lose weight might initially fail to reach a very large goal (e.g., "lose 20 pounds") but might succeed in reaching smaller goals (e.g., "exercise for 30 minutes 3 times this week"). Simply allowing people to believe that they have high self-efficacy can be an effective approach to behavior change as well. One study on smoking cessation informed some participants that they were chosen to participate in the treatment program because they had demonstrated strong willpower and a great potential to control their own behavior, whereas others were told they were chosen at random to participate (Blittner, Goldberg, & Merbaum, 1978). After 14 weeks, 67% of those in the "self-efficacy" condition had stopped smoking compared to only 28% of those in the "random" condition (and 6% of those in the control condition), despite the fact that participants with similar senses of self-efficacy made up the study's total population.

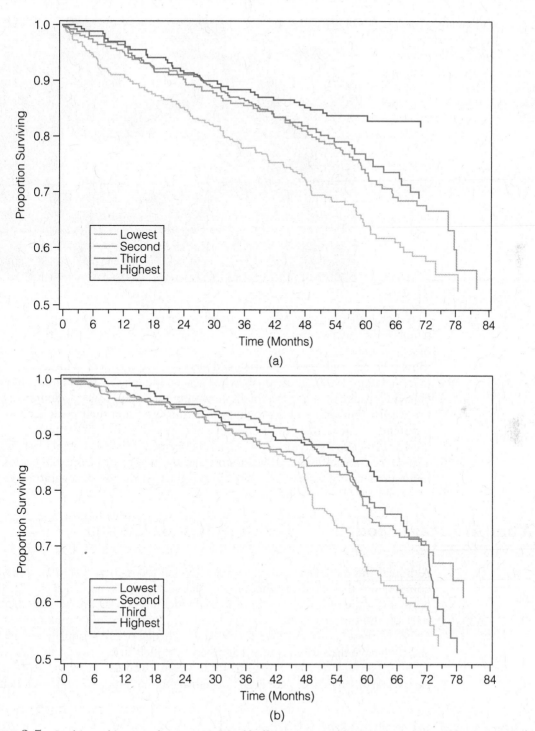

FIGURE 3.5 In this study, researchers examined self-efficacy in more than 1,000 patients with coronary heart disease, and then followed up all patients over the next 4 years. As shown in this figure, patients who were in the lowest quartile (25%) in self-efficacy were more likely to be hospitalized and to die than those who were in the highest quartile (25%) in self-efficacy (data from Sarkar, Ali, & Whooley, 2009).

A woman's sense of self-efficacy and her outcome expectations can influence her decision whether to use pain medication during childbirth.
Source: Digital Vision/Getty Images, Inc.

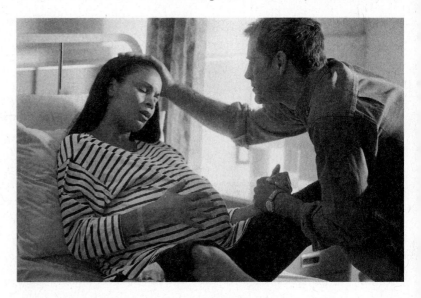

As with other theories we've discussed, social cognitive theory also has some limitations. First, interventions should be sensitive to where individuals are in their sense of self-efficacy for a behavior: "Cold turkey" approaches may be more effective with those who are high in self-efficacy and less effective for those with less confidence (Mermelstein, 1997). Individuals who lack confidence in their ability to enact a behavior change may need to focus on making small steps toward adopting a behavior to gain confidence in their ability to ultimately reach their goal. Second, some researchers believe that social cognitive theory really does not improve on other models of health behavior, such as the theory of planned behavior. For example, a study by McCaul et al. (1993) found that the theory of planned behavior was a better predictor of women's breast self-examination than social cognitive theory.

What Are Stage Models of Health Behavior Change?

Although the models described thus far have all focused on describing the various components that predict whether people engage in a particular health-related behavior, some researchers believe these models are too simple because they focus only on the outcome behavior of interest (e.g., condom use, smoking cessation). Critics of these models believe that behavior change occurs gradually and in stages, and they have therefore proposed alternative models that focus on the process that leads to behavior change. In turn, these **stage models** specify a set of ordered categories, or stages, that people go through as they attempt to change their behavior.

Transtheoretical or Stages of Change Model

According to the **transtheoretical model** (also known as the **stages of change model**), making changes in health-related behavior is a complex process, and individuals make such changes only gradually and not necessarily in a linear order (see

Figure 3.6; Prochaska, DiClemente, & Norcross, 1992). People move from one stage to another in a spiral fashion, which can include movement to new stages as well as movement back to previous stages, until they have finally completed the process of behavior change. It is likely, for example, that a person who decides to stop smoking will experience several setbacks, or relapses, as he or she attempts to quit.

The first stage in this model is **precontemplation**. Individuals who are in this stage lack an awareness of the problem behavior and have no intentions or plans to change the behavior in the foreseeable future (e.g., "I have no intention to stop smoking"). Basically, they just aren't motivated to make any change in their own behavior, and they may underestimate the benefits of change and overestimate the costs to justify their inaction. People who smoke, for example, may believe that because they exercise regularly, they will not suffer the negative health effects of smoking and that if they stop smoking, they will gain weight and hence suffer the (much worse) health consequences of obesity. They may also believe that although other people have suffered negative outcomes from the behavior, they have some unique personal invulnerability. (A friend in college once claimed that he actually drove better while intoxicated.) Individuals in this stage may also lack confidence in their ability to successfully engage in the new behavior.

Individuals who are beginning to consider making a change are in the **contemplation** stage (e.g., "I may start to think about how to quit smoking"). This stage is often characterized by a growing awareness of the costs of the negative behavior as well as of their personal susceptibility. People who are in this stage are out of the "ignorance is bliss" stage of precontemplation and are realizing that making a change would probably be a very good idea. At the start of the chapter, you read how Allen's academic problems caused him to think about cutting down on his drinking, although he is not actually taking steps (yet) to carry out this behavior. People in the contemplation stage may start seeking information on the negative effects of their behavior and strategies for changing such behavior, although they may still lack confidence in their ability to make the change. This stage is often characterized by ambivalence as well as frustration.

FIGURE 3.6 Model of stages of change.

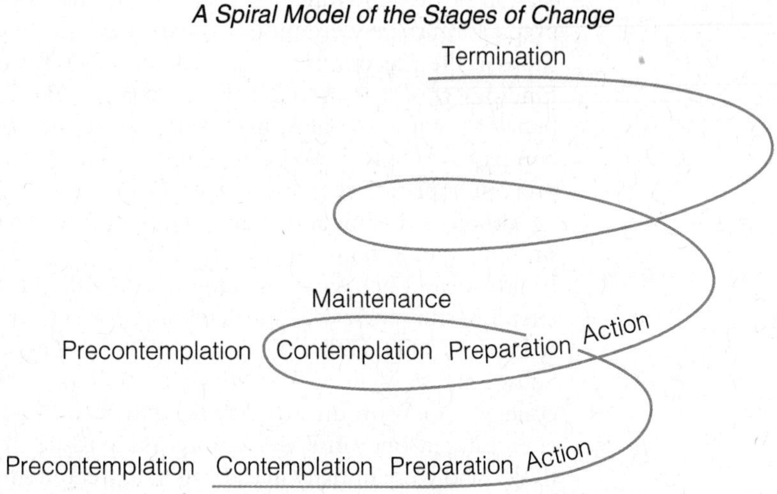

A Spiral Model of the Stages of Change

Termination

Maintenance

Precontemplation Contemplation Preparation Action

Precontemplation Contemplation Preparation Action

Individuals who have made a commitment to change their behavior are in the stage of **preparation** (e.g., "I will stop smoking within the next 30 days"). They may start making small changes in an attempt to move toward the desired end point, such as decreasing the number of cigarettes they smoke each day or trying to delay the time they have their first cigarette each day. People in this stage are preparing to ultimately change their behavior but are starting by taking a series of small steps toward the desired behavior change. Although individuals in this stage are often highly motivated to change, they may vary in how confident they are of achieving success.

The stage of **action** is reached when they are actually engaging in a new behavior ("I have stopped smoking"). The behavior change is now public, and the criterion for successfully engaging in it is high. Although the risk of relapse is strong at this stage, people often receive a lot of support from their family and friends during this stage because they have made a public commitment to changing their behavior.

Finally, the **maintenance** stage is reached when people sustain the change over time, typically 6 months ("I will continue to not smoke"). The focus in this stage is on preventing relapse. People receive less social support during this stage because they have already engaged in action, but support is still an important predictor of maintaining the new behavior.

Considerable research using the transtheoretical model has focused on its effectiveness in predicting smoking cessation (Prochaska et al., 1992; Segan, Borland, & Greenwood, 2004). One study revealed that people who are in different stages of change in terms of their smoking behavior differ in predicted ways on numerous variables, including self-efficacy for smoking cessation, perception of costs and benefits of smoking, and behavioral efforts toward quitting (DiClemente et al., 1991). Specifically, those who were in the stage of preparation had greater self-efficacy to quit than those in the stage of contemplation, who in turn had higher scores than those in the stage of precontemplation. Similarly, while those in the stage of preparation thought that the costs of smoking were greater than their benefits, those in contemplation saw the costs and benefits as equal, and those in precontemplation saw the benefits as greater than the costs. Finally, those in the preparation stage had made more lifetime and last-year quit attempts than those in either contemplation or precontemplation. At the 1-month follow-up, for example, those in the preparation stage were more likely to have made a quit attempt (56% versus 6% for those in the precontemplation stage and 24% for those in the contemplation stage). Findings at the 6-month follow-up also revealed strong differences in quitting behavior, with 80% of those in the preparation stage having made a quit attempt as compared to only 48% of those in the contemplation stage and 26% of those in the precontemplation stage (see Figure 3.7).

Although the initial research on the transtheoretical model focused on predicting smoking cessation, this model can also predict the adoption of a variety of health-related behaviors, including fruit and vegetable consumption, condom use, exercise, sunscreen use, and screening for cancer (Adams, Norman, Hovell, Sallis, & Patrick, 2009; Hellsten et al., 2008; Naar-King et al., 2006; Lippke, Zilegelmann, Schwarzer, & Velicer, 2009; Prochaska et al., 1994). For example, one study with college students found that those who were in the preparation stage in terms of exercising at one time were more likely to be exercising 1 to 3 months later than those who were initially in the stages of precontemplation or contemplation (Rosen,

FIGURE 3.7 At the 6-month follow-up, smokers who were in the stage of preparation were much more likely to report having made a quit attempt as well as currently not smoking than those who were in the stages of precontemplation or contemplation (data from DiClemente et al., 1991).

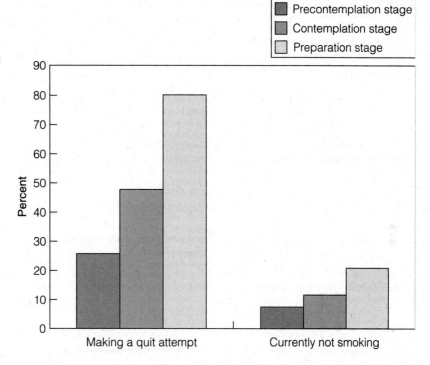

2000). This model can also predict people's decision making regarding medical issues, such as undergoing chemotherapy (Hirai, Arai, Tokoro, & Naka, 2009).

What factors influence people to move from one stage to the next? Researchers who developed this theory believe that people go through specific processes of change as they progress through the various stages (Prochaska et al., 1992). At the earliest stages, people must become aware of the problem and learn effective ways of avoiding it. For some types of health behaviors, such as smoking, people typically already have exposure to information about their negative effects, but in other cases, such as getting a regular tetanus shot, people must be educated about the benefits of engaging in the behavior. *Social liberation*, external forces that facilitate change, can also be effective in moving people along. For example, programs that prohibit smoking in particular buildings can help make the act of smoking less convenient and less comfortable. As people move along to the later stages of the models, they often examine the costs and benefits of changing their behavior. They might, for example, reflect on whether their desire to lose weight is really worth giving up late-night McDonald's trips. Perceived benefits of changing the behavior usually increase as people move from precontemplation to contemplation, and the costs of the new behavior usually decrease between the contemplation and action stages (see Table 3.4). So, behavior-change messages should help people focus on the costs of continuing the old behavior (e.g., "I have stained teeth because of all of my smoking") and the benefits of adopting the new behavior (e.g., "think about how much money I'll save by not smoking").

Finally, there are a number of strategies that help people move from the action stage to the maintenance stage, such as rewards and substituting new behaviors for

TABLE 3.4   *Test Yourself: Decisional Balance Measure for Contraceptive Use—Disease Prevention*

Please rate how important each statement is with respect to your decision whether to use contraceptives to prevent diseases. Answer each question using a scale of 1 to 5, with 1 = not important to 5 = extremely important. Items 1 to 10 measure the benefits of condom use, whereas items 11 to 20 measure the costs of condom use.

1. I would feel protected against STDs if my partner and I used condoms.
2. My partner would feel more protected against STDs if we used condoms.
3. I would feel more responsible about STDs if I used condoms.
4. Protecting myself from STDs would increase my self-esteem.
5. Using condoms to guard against the transmission of STDs builds trust.
6. Condoms are easy to use.
7. Sex would be more enjoyable if I felt protected from STDs.
8. Methods that protect you from STDs are easy to obtain.
9. Condoms are affordable.
10. If I used condoms to prevent STDs, I would gain my partner's respect.
11. My partner would find sex less exciting if a condom were used.
12. I might hurt my partner's feelings if I suggested we use a condom.
13. It is harder to insist on condom use after a commitment has been made to a partner.
14. I would hurt my partner's feelings if I suggested we use a condom when we were already using birth-control pills.
15. Methods of contraception that prevent STDs are unpleasant to use.
16. I might spoil a sexual encounter if I brought up condom use.
17. Discussing STD prevention makes my partner uncomfortable.
18. Condoms take the spontaneity out of lovemaking.
19. My partner would be angry if I refused to have sex unless a condom were used.
20. I am uncomfortable discussing STD prevention with a partner.

Source: Grimley, Riley, Bellis, & Prochaska, 1993.

the old ones. These methods might include treating oneself to dinner at a favorite restaurant after a week of not smoking or chewing gum instead of smoking. (Issues of relapse are discussed in detail in Chapter 12.) One study predicting physicians' stage of change with respect to recommending colonoscopies to their patients revealed that self-efficacy for changing their patients' behavior, beliefs about the effectiveness of colonoscopy, and negative beliefs about the challenges of explaining colonoscopy were all important predictors (Honda & Gorin, 2006).

As with all theories of health behavior, the transtheoretical, or stages of change, model has some limitations. First, although the processes of change by stage have been widely studied with respect to issues of smoking and substance abuse (DiClemente et al., 1991), some research suggests that the cognitive processes involved in leading people to stop certain behaviors (e.g., smoking) may be different from those involved in leading them to start behaviors (e.g., exercise; Rosen, 2000). Specifically, while consciousness raising and social liberation are seen as most useful during the early stages of change toward ceasing a behavior, these processes are used frequently during later stages of change toward adopting a new behavior. Second, although the transtheoretical/stages of change model describes how cognitive processes should lead people to move forward in the stages, most

The transtheoretical, or stages of change, model predicts numerous types of health-related behaviors, including exercise.
Source: © RickBL/iStockphoto.

of the research testing this model has examined people only at one point in time. However, some research indicates that people who are weighing the costs and benefits of smoking at one time are *not* more likely to move to a higher stage 1 or 2 years later (Herzog, Abrams, Emmons, Linnan, & Shadel, 1999). These researchers believe that thinking about the costs and benefits of a behavior is not a good predictor of whether people will move further toward change. Third, some researchers have questioned whether these stages are in fact distinct categories and whether they are in the correct order (Herzog, 2008; Herzog & Blagg, 2007). Relatedly, are the specific stages described in this model the right ones? As described next, the precaution adoption process model, another stage model, defines the stages of health behavior change in a different way.

Precaution Adoption Process Model

The **precaution adoption process model** is similar in some ways to the transtheoretical model—it also proposes that when individuals consider engaging in new health-related behaviors, they go through a series of stages (Weinstein, 1988). As with the transtheoretical model, people do not necessarily move directly from one stage to another but rather can move backward or forward between stages. For example, you may decide on New Year's Eve that your resolution for the upcoming year is to stop drinking alcohol, but by February 1st, you may have changed your intention to follow through with this behavior. The precaution adoption process model differs from the transtheoretical model, though, in the number of stages it proposes as well as the process by which it predicts how people progress through the stages.

As shown in Figure 3.8 and Table 3.5, the precaution adoption process model includes seven stages. In stage 1, people are not even aware of the disease or problem. For example, many adolescent girls do not get enough calcium in their

FIGURE 3.8 Precaution adoption process
model (from Weinstein, 1988).

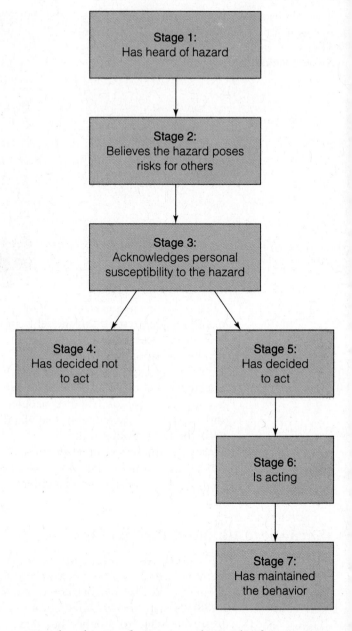

daily diet but often are unaware that this greatly increases their risk of osteoporosis
in the future. In stage 2, people are aware generally of the health risk and believe
that others might be at risk, but they do not believe that they personally are at
risk. In other words, they have an *optimistic bias* about their own level of risk.
So, you might know that wearing a seat belt can protect people in car accidents
from serious injuries, but you may believe that because you are a safe driver, you
will never experience an accident anyway. In stage 3, the decision-making stage,
people have acquired a belief in their own personal risk, but they still have not
decided to take action to protect themselves from that risk. You may know people

Many people make New Year's resolutions, yet find themselves falling short of their goals within weeks (or even days). The precaution adoption process model helps explain the challenging process of health-related behavior change.
Source: Photo by Brian Harkin/Getty Images, Inc.

who understand that lack of exercise puts them at greater risk of developing heart disease, for example, but they haven't decided whether they are going to exercise. From stage 3 people may move to stage 5, in which they decide to take action (e.g., finally do exercise), but they may also move to stage 4, in which they decide that action is unnecessary (e.g., they plan to continue being inactive, at least for the time being). In stage 6, which is similar to the stage of action in the transtheoretical

TABLE 3.5   *Examples of the Seven Stages of the Precaution Adoption Process Model*

Statement	Stage Classification
I have never seriously thought about trying to increase the amount that I currently exercise.	Stage 1
I have seriously thought about trying to increase the amount that I exercise but decided against it.	Stage 2
I have seriously thought about trying to increase the amount that I currently exercise, but I have not thought about it in the past 6 months.	Stage 3
I am seriously thinking about trying to increase the amount that I exercise some time within the next 6 months.	Stage 4
I plan to increase the amount that I exercise within the next 6 months.	Stage 5
I am currently doing things to increase the amount that I exercise.	Stage 6

(Women who were already engaging in exercise for at least 45 minutes three times a week and who reported that they had been engaging in exercise for the past 6 months were classified as stage 7.)

Source: Blalock et al., 1996.

model, people have begun to change their behavior. Finally, in stage 7, people maintain the behavior change over some period of time.

Although the precaution adoption process model is a relatively new theory of predicting health behavior, some research already provides support for it. Researchers in one study found that although few smokers are at stage 1 (probably because virtually everyone is aware of the health hazards of smoking), many are at stage 2, in which they see smoking as generally dangerous, but still possess an optimistic view of their own risk (Boney, McCoy, et al., 1992). For example, many smokers believe that compared to "typical smokers," they were less likely to suffer from smoking-related health consequences. However, smokers who had recently joined a smoking-cessation clinic were typically one or two stages further along: They recognize their own vulnerability to smoking-related health problems and have made a decision to try to quit. Similarly, Susan Blalock et al. examined the predictors of two behaviors recommended to prevent osteoporosis using the precaution adoption process model: calcium consumption and exercise (1996). Women who had never engaged in exercise had less knowledge about osteoporosis, saw fewer benefits of exercise, and had lower self-efficacy for exercise than those who were currently engaging in exercise. Second, compared with women who were currently thinking about or planning to increase their exercise frequency, those who had previously engaged in exercise (but who were no longer regularly exercising) reported lower self-efficacy, more exercise inconvenience, and fewer exercise benefits. Finally, while only 7.7% of those who had never engaged in exercise requested one of the free brochures, 22.9% of those who had previously engaged in exercise requested a brochure, and 40.2% of those who were currently exercising requested a brochure. This study provides support for the precaution adoption process model and suggests some strategies for helping women move to a further stage of behavior change. This model is also a useful predictor of engaging in home radon testing (Weinstein & Sandman, 1992), contraceptive use (Emmett & Ferguson, 1999), and mammography use (Clemow et al., 2000).

As with the other models we've discussed, the precaution adoption process model has some important implications for designing health behavior change interventions. First, individuals who are at different stages should be influenced by different types of information. When someone is deciding whether to take action (stage 3), for example, perceptions of vulnerability should predict whether he or she moves to stage 5 (decides to engage in behavior change) or stage 4 (chooses not to engage in behavior change). On the other hand, when someone has decided to engage in behavior change (stage 5), whether that person actually does so (moves to stage 6) should be influenced by obstacles and barriers to such change.

Because the precaution adoption process model is new, relatively little research has examined how useful this approach is, and, in particular, whether it is more useful than the transtheoretical model. The major difference between these two models is that the precaution adoption process model separates people into more distinct categories than the transtheoretical model does (Weinstein et al., 1998). First, the transtheoretical model groups all people who are not currently thinking about behavior change into one stage (precontemplation), whereas the precaution adoption process model separates these people into those who are unaware of a health issue (stage 1) and those who are aware of an issue but do not see themselves as personally vulnerable to it (stage 2). The precaution adoption process model also distinguishes people who have never even thought about changing their behavior (stages 1 and 2) from those who have thought about making a change but have decided against it for now (stage 4). Future research must clearly compare the effectiveness of these two stage models in predicting health behavior change.

How Should These Models Be Integrated and Extended?

Although all of the models described in this chapter view health-related behavior as caused by multiple factors, they vary in exactly which factors they include. For example, the health belief model is the only one to include the component of susceptibility, perhaps because this model (unlike most of the others) was originally developed to specifically predict health-related behavior. However, this model ignores the role of individuals' self-efficacy, which other models (theory of planned behavior, social cognitive theory) view as fundamentally important. Although research has not shown which model is the most useful in describing health-related behavior in general, it does suggest that different models may be most useful in describing particular types of behavior. Specifically, a study comparing the theory of reasoned action to the theory of planned behavior found that the component of perceived behavior control was an important predictor of behavior only for those behaviors that are under low personal control (Madden, Ellen, & Ajzen, 1992). For example, students viewed the behavior "getting a good night's sleep" as relatively outside of their control (possibly due to the challenges of getting to sleep in a college dorm), and for this behavior, having a strong belief that one could get a good night's sleep was an important predictor of behavior. On the other hand, students viewed "taking vitamin supplements" as highly under their control, and for this behavior, their personal confidence that they could take vitamins was not a strong predictor of behavior. Similarly, research generally shows that the health belief model is a better predictor of one-time or infrequent behavior, such as getting immunizations or having a mammogram, whereas other models are stronger predictors of more frequent behavior, such as quitting smoking and using condoms.

Another critique of these models is that they fail to include some factors that may be strong predictors of behavior, including race, gender, and socioeconomic status. Rosenstock (1990) has noted that all of these models focus on the individuals' own attitudes, beliefs, and self-efficacy but largely ignore broader factors that can influence health-related behavior, such as public policy, interpersonal processes, and community norms. For example, although the AIDS epidemic led to a push for monogamous, committed relationships, gay men have no option for entering legally binding relationships and often have no financial incentive to do so (e.g., health-care coverage is rarely extended to the partners of gay men; no tax benefits). Similarly, these models are largely based in studies with Whites, and often only White men; therefore, they may not consider the different values that motivate behavior among members of other ethnic groups (Cochran & Mays, 1993). For example, because the African American community places a stronger priority on interdependence and connection with extended family than does the White community, African Americans may be more influenced in terms of their health-related behavior by the attitudes of their family. Finally, socioeconomic factors can also influence whether

TABLE 3.6   *Information YOU Can Use*

- Your own outlook influences the health behaviors you do (or do not) engage in, so to make changes in your health-related behavior, focus on improving your own self-efficacy for making changes, your own attitudes toward the behavior, and your outcome expectancies regarding the behavior. People with positive attitudes toward making such changes and a strong belief in their ability to enact such changes are much more likely to follow through on their intentions.
- One of the most effective strategies for enacting behavior change is making specific plans regarding how to make such changes. So, when you are interested in making health-related behavior changes, set specific implementation intentions regarding the how, when, and where you will act.
- Health-related behaviors are heavily influenced by the media, including television, advertisements, and movies. Thus, be careful about the media influences that you—and your children—are exposed to, and make sure to limit negative media influences whenever possible.
- Health-related behaviors are often influenced by the people around you: You care about what your friends and family think about your behaviors, and you are more likely to make changes to such behavior when you have their support. So, if you are trying to make a change to your health-related behavior, such as stopping smoking or starting an exercise program, try to enlist the support of valued members of your social network, which makes behavior change more likely to occur and be maintained over time.
- Making changes in health-related behavior is a process, so you need to set specific goals that lead you toward such changes. The stage-based models you learned about in this chapter propose that initiating behavior change starts with simply thinking about such changes and then preparing to act.

people engage in health-related behaviors, but they are entirely ignored in all of these theoretical models. For example, people who have limited financial resources may be strongly motivated to eat healthy foods but simply lack the money to purchase fresh fruits and vegetables, which are often very expensive—if available at all—in many inner cities (Cochran & Mays, 1993). Similarly, people who lack transportation or health insurance may be unable to take part in regular health screenings and vaccination programs though they may want to.

Finally, although each of the distinct theories described in this chapter includes specific components and models of how these components predict behavior, the best way to predict health-related behavior may include a combination of different components from various models. For example, one study found that people's self-efficacy for engaging in exercise was a good predictor of whether constructs in the transtheoretical model successfully predicted the intention-behavior link (Rhodes & Plotnikoff, 2006). Similarly, a recent study predicting condom use found that planning, self-efficacy, and intentions were the best predictors of actual condom use one month later, again showing that constructs from different models of health behavior may be particularly useful for predicting behavior (Teng & Mak, 2011). Researchers are therefore now finding that combining different components from several models may be the best way of predicting health-related behavior (Armitage & Arden, 2008; Reynolds, Buller, Yaroch, Maloy, & Cutter, 2006).

Summary

1. Continuum theories identify some set of variables that are thought to influence people's behavior, and then combine those variables to predict the likelihood the person will engage in a given behavior.

2. The health belief model is one of the oldest and most widely used theories to predict health-related behavior. This model includes 5 components: susceptibility, severity, benefits, barriers, and cues to action.

3. The theory of reasoned action is a general psychological theory used to predict the link between attitudes and behavior. This theory posits that people's behavior is determined by their intentions regarding that behavior, and that these intentions are determined by people's attitudes and subjective norms.

4. The theory of planned behavior extended the theory of reasoned action by adding the concept of perceived behavioral control, which is thought to influence behavior both indirectly (by influencing intentions) and directly.

5. Learning theories are based on the assumption that behavior is influenced by basic learning processes, including association, reinforcement, and modeling. These theories include classical conditioning, operant conditioning, and observational learning.

6. Classical conditioning occurs when a previously neutral stimulus comes to evoke the same response as another stimulus with which it is paired.

7. Operant conditioning refers to the idea that behaviors can be increased or decreased as a function of the consequences of engaging in them. Rewarding a behavior should increase the likelihood of that behavior, whereas punishing a behavior should decrease its likelihood.

8. In the case of observational learning, watching someone else receive rewards or punishment for engaging in a particular behavior influences one's own likelihood of engaging in that behavior.

9. Social cognitive theory posits that people acquire attitudes through people in their immediate social networks as well as by observing people in the media. This theory includes the role of both self-efficacy and outcome expectancies in influencing behavior.

10. According to the transtheoretical, or stages of change, model, making changes in health-related behavior is a complex process, and individuals make such changes only gradually and not necessarily in a linear order. These stages are precontemplation, contemplation, preparation, action, and maintenance.

11. The precaution adoption process model, another stage model, proposes that when individuals consider engaging in new health-related behaviors they go through a series of seven stages. However, unlike in the transtheoretical model, people do not necessarily move directly from one stage to another but can move backward or forward between stages.

Key Terms

action	maintenance	severe
attitude	observational learning	social cognitive theory
barrier	operant conditioning	stage models
benefit	outcome expectancies	subjective norms
classical conditioning	perceived behavioral control	susceptible
contemplation	precaution adoption process	theory of planned behavior
continuum theories	model	theory of reasoned action
cues to action	precontemplation	transtheoretical (stages of
health belief model	preparation	change) model
intention	self-efficacy	

Thought Questions

1. You are in charge of creating an alcohol abuse prevention workshop at your university. Design one workshop based on the theory of planned behavior and another on the health belief model.

2. What are the similarities between the theory of planned behavior and social cognitive theory? What are their differences?

3. Describe two ways that principles of learning theory can be used to help people make changes in their health-related behavior.

4. Your friend Bill never wears his seat belt and claims that because he is a very safe driver, he has no need for such a safety device. Your roommate Jamal, on the other hand, never wore his seat belt until after his sister was injured in a car accident; he now tries to use his seat belt more regularly. According to the stages of change model, how could you help Bill and Jamal move to later stages of change?

5. What factors do you think are the most important ones to include in a model predicting whether people wear sunscreen? Are these the same or different factors that would be best to include in a model predicting the consistent use of condoms? Why or why not?

Answers to Questioning the Research

Answer 3.1 Different variables may be more or less important as predictors of behavior in different populations. Perceived susceptibility to health problems is often low in adolescents in general, and thus this belief might be a particularly strong predictor of behavior for teenagers, and less so for older adults. Barriers, on the other hand, might be an equally strong predictor of behavior across different age groups.

Answer 3.2 Although social norms were a stronger predictor of cancer screening than were attitudes or perceived behavioral control, it is not clear whether norms would also be the strongest predictor of other types of health-related behavior. Screening behavior is a short-term behavior that requires relatively little effort, whereas many other types of health-related behaviors require much more sustained effort over time. Perceived behavioral control may be an especially important predictor of these types of behavior, such as starting an exercise regimen, stopping smoking, or changing one's eating habits.

Answer 3.3 Providing rewards can encourage particular types of behaviors, but there are also drawbacks to this approach. Specifically, people may believe they are engaging in the behavior only for these extrinsic rewards and not because of any intrinsic motivation. Thus, when rewards are no longer present, it isn't clear whether such behaviors will be continued.

Answer 3.4 As with any type of nonexperimental research design, it simply isn't clear whether outcome expectancies led to weight loss or whether a third variable may explain the association between such expectancies and weight loss. Perhaps people with more social support for weight loss, greater health problems caused by their weight, or greater self-efficacy for losing weight had both more positive outcome expectancies about the benefits of losing weight and more success in losing weight.

CHAPTER 4

Stress

Outline

- Robert is a doctor in a busy and crowded emergency room. He feels overwhelmed by his long hours and the huge responsibility he has for saving people's lives. This pressure is even worse because he has no control over his work schedule—as a new doctor, Robert must cover other doctors' shifts when they can't come in, with only last-minute notice sometimes. Although Robert has always been very healthy, recently he has developed an ulcer and is experiencing frequent migraine headaches.

- Sara is a sophomore in college and is a premed major. She wants very much to be a doctor but is struggling to keep up with all of the required courses. This semester, Sara is taking chemistry and physics, and neither class is going very well. To make matters worse, even though she puts in long hours studying for her exams, whenever she takes a test, her mind simply goes blank.

- Chandler just moved to a new city and started a new job. Because he doesn't really know anyone in his new city, Chandler writes in his journal every night and calls old college friends whenever he is feeling lonely. Although he is under a lot of time pressure at his new job, Chandler knows that he needs to take some time for himself every day to relax. He therefore joins a health club with a pool so that he can swim each day after work. Chandler is enjoying the challenges of his job and looking forward to making some new friends.

- Monica just started college and already is experiencing a lot of stress. Her parents have been fighting a lot and have recently told her that they are separating. Also, she is having trouble keeping up with the reading in her English literature course and has not even started writing a paper that is due tomorrow. After being encouraged by her aunt, Monica decides to go see a therapist at the college health center to talk about her feelings about her parents' separation. She also decides that she will ask her English professor for a 1-week extension on her paper and will stop going to basketball practice until she is caught up with work.

- Elizabeth has a strong belief in the power of religion. She prays every morning, attends religious services regularly, and has a general belief that "things happen for a reason." Although Elizabeth has suffered from diabetes since she was a child, she regularly takes her medicine, watches her diet, and jogs four times a week, and hence has not experienced any really disabling effects. She feels very lucky that God is watching out for her and keeping her healthy.

Preview

Everyone has experienced **stress** (you may be feeling it as you read this chapter), and you know what people mean when they say they are "stressed." But what exactly is stress? In everyday language, stress has become a catchall term that describes the demands placed on people at school and work, such as the exam next week, being fired from a job, having a fight with a friend, or worrying about paying the credit card bill. In the field of health psychology, *stress* typically refers to either the experience of major events or the perception that one lacks the resources to cope with such events.

Stress provides a good example of the link between psychological factors and physical health (Lazarus & Folkman, 1984). This chapter examines a number of issues related to the link between stress and health. First, it describes different sources of stress and different ways of measuring stress, and then it examines two different theories about how stress influences physiological responses as well as the physical and psychological consequences of stress. Finally, this chapter describes various strategies for managing stress, including coping strategies, relaxation, and religion.

What Are the Main Sources of Stress?

Although personal relationships can be a source of support (as discussed in Chapter 5), they are also a major source of stress. In fact, one-third of the stressful events college students experience are caused by relationships (Ptacek, Smith, & Zanas, 1992), and interpersonal conflicts account for as much as 80% of the stress experienced by married couples (Bolger, Delongis, Kessler, & Schilling, 1989). These conflicts can focus on how to spend money, the balancing of work and family time, and the fair distribution of childcare and household tasks. Family issues such as an illness or divorce can also lead to stress, in part because these problems can lead to emotional and financial pressures. For example, caring for a loved one who has a chronic illness can cause financial burdens, such as the cost of in-home nursing care, and emotional problems, such as depression, anxiety, and sadness (Kiecolt-Glaser et al., 1987). Even seemingly positive events, such as marriage and the arrival of a new baby, can create stress. A couple with a new baby, for example, is likely to experience financial pressure, sleep deprivation, and challenges in balancing time, which can all lead to stress. (Chapter 10 examines the particular stresses that are caused by having a chronic illness, and Chapter 11 examines the stress associated with experiencing the loss of a loved one.)

Work pressures, including long hours, constant deadlines, and substantial responsibility, can create considerable stress (Spector, 2002). The stressful period that hits most college students at the end of the semester when they must take exams and complete term papers is a good example of this type of stress. People who have jobs that involve a responsibility for saving people's lives, such as doctors, firefighters, and air traffic controllers, often experience particularly high levels of stress because making a mistake can have dire consequences (Shouksmith & Taylor, 1997). As described at the beginning of the chapter, Robert's position as a doctor in a busy emergency room led to considerable occupational stress for him. In turn, and as we'll discuss in more detail in Chapter 12, doctors and nurses who spend more time providing direct patient care experience higher levels of stress (Rutledge et al., 2009). But even jobs without the pressure of life and death can be stressful. Other aspects of jobs that can create stress include relationships with colleagues or supervisors, lack of resources (e.g., defective equipment, few supplies), and the physical environment (e.g., noise, heat). As shown in Figure 4.1, people with longer commutes to work experience higher levels of stress (Evans & Wener, 2006).

Even positive events, such as getting married, can cause stress. *Source:* DIMITAR DILKOFF/AFP/Getty Images.

People can also experience stress from environmental pressures, such as noise, crowding, and natural disasters. People who work in noisy conditions experience increased stress (Evans, Bullinger, & Hygge, 1998), as do those who live in busy cities (Levine, 1990). Another major cause of stress caused by one's environment is poverty, which is often associated with other stressors, such as crime, overcrowded housing, pollution, and noise (Johnson et al., 1995; Myers, Kagawa-Singer, Kumanika, Lex, & Markides, 1995).

Pressures within ourselves, such as when we are torn between two different goals, is another factor that can cause stress (Lewin, 1935). For example, you

FIGURE 4.1 People with longer commutes show higher levels of cortisol, a stress hormone, in their saliva (data from Evans & Wener, 2006).

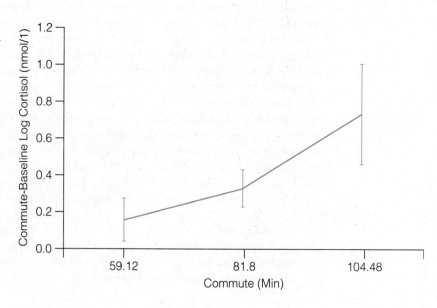

may want to take a trip with your family over spring break, but you may also want to spend time hanging out with friends. This type of conflict is called an *approach–approach conflict*, because you are torn between wanting to do two desirable things that are incompatible. In other cases, people experience *approach–avoidance* or *avoidance–avoidance conflicts*. These types of conflicts might include wanting to eat tempting foods (approach) but also wanting to lose weight (avoid), and choosing between chemotherapy (avoid) and radiation (avoid) to treat cancer.

Finally, people often experience considerable stress when they are in situations in which they lack control—this is why seemingly minor situations, such as waiting in a slow line at the post office or being stuck in a traffic jam, can be so irritating. People who have little control over their jobs, such as when, where, and how they complete their work, also experience considerable stress (Spector, 2002). For example, restaurant servers often experience high levels of stress because they must satisfy both customers and their employers, but they have very little control over their work environment (e.g., they do not prepare the food, set prices, determine how fast food is ready; Theorell et al., 1990). Physicians whose work schedule (including number of hours worked as well as when those hours are worked) is not what they prefer experience more burnout (Barnett, Gareis, & Brennan, 1999). On the other hand, although a professor's job often includes deadlines and long hours, they have a large amount of control over where and even when they do most of their work—they can write lectures and grade papers in their home or office (or even on the sidelines of their kids' soccer games!) and can choose when they'll focus on each task.

How Is Stress Measured?

Although people commonly use the term *stress* in their daily lives (e.g., "I'm feeling very stressed about my upcoming exams"), it is difficult to measure precisely how much stress a person is experiencing. This section describes the different approaches researchers have used to assess stress, including several different types of self-report inventories as well as various physiological measures.

Self-Report Inventories

Early research on stress measured stressors by asking participants to identify life events, or stressors, that require people to adapt to change, tolerate some discomfort, or deal with some threat. Specifically, researchers who use this perspective ask people to list the number of major life events they have experienced in a given period of time. One of the most commonly used approaches for measuring stress in this way is the Social Readjustment Rating Scale (SRRS), which assesses the number and type of major events that have happened in a person's life in the past year (see Table 4.1; Holmes & Rahe, 1967). It includes both negative events—getting divorced, being fired from one's job, experiencing the death of a loved one—and positive events—getting married, having a baby, receiving a promotion. Although you might expect that only negative events would cause stress, positive events can

TABLE 4.1 *Social Readjustment Rating Scale (SRRS)*

Life Event	Mean Value
1. Death of spouse	100
2. Divorce	73
3. Marital separation	65
4. Jail term	63
5. Death of a close family member	63
6. Personal injury or illness	53
7. Marriage	50
8. Fired at work	47
9. Marital reconciliation	45
10. Retirement	45
11. Major change in the health of family member	44
12. Pregnancy	40
13. Sex difficulties	39
14. Gain of a new family member	39
15. Business readjustment	39
16. Change in financial state	38
17. Death of a close friend	37
18. Changing to a different line of work	36
19. Change in the number of arguments with spouse	35
20. Mortgage over $10,000	31
21. Foreclosure on a mortgage or loan	30
22. Change in responsibilities at work	29
23. Son or daughter leaving home	29
24. Trouble with in-laws	29
25. Outstanding personal achievement	28
26. Spouse begins or stops work	26
27. Begin or end school	26
28. Change in living conditions	25
29. Revision of personal habits	24
30. Trouble with boss	23
31. Change in work hours or conditions	20
32. Change in residence	20
33. Change in schools	20

(continued)

TABLE 4.1 *(continued)*

Life Event	Mean Value
34. Change in recreation	19
35. Change in church activities	19
36. Change in social activities	18
37. Mortgage or loan for less than $10,000	17
38. Change in sleeping habits	16
39. Change in number of family get-togethers	15
40. Change in eating habits	15
41. Vacation	13
42. Christmas	12
43. Minor violation of the law	11

This scale measures the number of major life events that a person has experienced over the past few months and assigns each life event a point value that expresses the severity of the event. People who experience more stressful life events tend to have poorer health.

Source: Holmes & Rahe, 1967.

also cause stress, in part because these events cause change that most people find stressful. For example, when students start college, they may experience this change as an exciting and positive event, yet it is often accompanied by stress—stress over which classes to take, concerns about managing a heavy workload, uncertainty about living arrangements, fear of being away from home, and so on.

The SRRS scale was developed based on data from more than 5,000 patients, which revealed that significant life events seemed to precede illness (Rabkin & Struening, 1976; Rahe, Mahan, & Arthur, 1970). For example, in one of the earliest tests of this model, 2,664 male naval personnel completed a life change questionnaire 6 to 8 months prior to embarking on a navy cruise (Rahe et al., 1970). Researchers then measured the number of reported illnesses throughout their time at sea. These findings indicated that men who reported more life events experienced more reported illnesses while at sea, suggesting that the experience of these types of stressors could lead to health problems. In line with this view, those who experience more life events (both prospectively and retrospectively) are more likely to experience heart attacks, diabetes, accidents, injuries, and tuberculosis (Holmes & Masuda, 1974; Jacobs & Charles, 1980; Rabkin & Struening, 1976; Rahe & Arthur, 1978; Rahe, Biersner, Ryman, & Arthur, 1972).

Some research even points to a link between experiencing more life stressors and the development of cancer (McKenna, Zevon, Corn, & Rounds, 1999). In some cases, research suggesting a link between stress and cancer is difficult to interpret because it relies on retrospective reports of stress in which people with cancer are asked about prior stressful experiences. Studies that use this type of a research design may reveal that stress and cancer are correlated, but they can't provide evidence for whether stress in fact causes cancer. Specifically, it is possible that people with cancer report experiencing more major life events prior to the development of cancer because they are searching for an explanation for their cancer and/or are in a more negative state of mind, which leads to the recollection of more negative life events. However, studies that use a prospective design, meaning they examine reports of stress at one time and then follow participants over time to see who develops cancer, provide stronger evidence that the experience of stress can lead to cancer (see Box 4.1: Focus on Research).

However, the SRRS has been criticized for several reasons (Schroeder & Costa, 1984). First, it does not take into account the subjective experience of an event for the person. Getting divorced, for example, may be very upsetting for someone whose religion forbids divorce, whereas someone who is leaving an abusive marriage may see divorce as a welcome relief. Similarly, a pregnancy could be a very positive and exciting event for a stable married couple hoping to start a family but could be extremely negative and upsetting for a high school student. Moreover, some of the events included in this scale are objectively positive (e.g., marriage, outstanding personal achievement, vacation), whereas others are objectively negative (e.g., death of spouse, foreclosure of mortgage, jail term), and still others are ambiguous (e.g., change in job responsibilities, spouse beginning or stopping work, revision of personal habits). But experiencing positive personal events, while they may cause some stress, is typically less problematic than experiencing objectively negative events (Sarason, Johnson, & Siegel, 1978). Also, some of the items on this scale are vague, such as "change in status at work" and "son or daughter leaving home."

Box 4.1

Focus on Research: Does Stress Cause Breast Cancer?

Researchers in one study examined the relationship between stressful life experiences and the likelihood of developing breast cancer over time (Lillberg et al., 2003). More than 10,000 women completed a questionnaire assessing the life events they had experienced as well as their risk factors related to breast cancer. Fifteen years later, researchers examined the number of breast cancer cases that had developed in this population, and found 180 cases. Analyses were then conducted to examine whether women who developed breast cancer were more likely to report particular life events in the 5 years prior to completing the first survey. Findings indicated that women who had experienced more life events in the 5 years prior to completing the first questionnaire were more likely to develop breast cancer in the next 15 years. The specific life events that were associated with the greatest increase risk were divorce/separation, death of a husband, and death of a close friend or relative. The findings suggest that women who experience more highly stressful life events are at an increased risk of developing breast cancer. Because this study was conducted over time, or prospectively, it provides greater confidence that the association between life events and illness is causal and not simply correlational. However, research is still needed to examine how exactly the experience of such events increases a person's risk of developing cancer.

Because this scale assumes that change in general is stressful, regardless of whether it is positive or negative, someone who gets fired gets the same score as someone who gets promoted! Finally, some researchers have criticized this scale for focusing on stressful events that are likely to affect those in the middle or upper classes and for ignoring those that may affect people who are poor or members of minority groups (Jackson & Inglehart, 1995). Poverty and racism, for example, may be very stressful but are not included in this scale.

Although the SRRS is a widely used approach to measuring stress, some researchers have argued that many stressors come not from major life events but instead from *daily hassles*, such as losing the car keys, having difficulty paying bills, and having too many things to do (Lazarus, Kanner, & Folkman, 1980). As shown in Table 4.2, the Hassles Scale measures these types of daily life events. People report concerns about weight, health of a family member, rising prices, home maintenance, having too many things to do, money, crime, and physical appearance as the most frequent hassles they experience.

Researchers have also explored whether small uplifting events predict positive outcomes (Kanner, Coyne, Schaeffer, & Lazarus, 1981). According to this perspective, experiencing even small events that bring you pleasure, such as spending time with friends, having a good night's sleep, and reading a good book, may have beneficial effects on physical health and psychological well-being (Lazarus et al., 1980).

Both hassles and uplifts are associated with health, although in distinct ways. Hassles are a strong predictor of both psychological and physical well-being; in fact, hassles are more highly correlated with psychological and physical symptoms than are major life events (Kanner et al., 1981; Zarski, 1984). Experiencing more hassles also leads to more symptoms for those who are already suffering from an illness (Levy, Cain, Jarrett, & Heitkemper, 1997). Although the frequency of uplifts is

TABLE 4.2   *Test Yourself: The Hassles Scale*

Following is a list of experiences that many students have some time or other. Please indicate for each experience how much it has been a part of your life over the past month (1 means not at all part of your life and 4 means very much a part of your life).

1. Conflicts with boyfriend/girlfriend/spouse
2. Being let down or disappointed by friends
3. Too many things to do at once
4. Lower grades than you hoped for
5. Separation from people you care about
6. Not enough leisure time
7. Loneliness
8. Dissatisfaction with your athletic skills
9. Not enough time for sleep
10. Disliking your studies

This scale is designed to test minor hassles that are commonly experienced by many college students. Higher scores indicate more frequent hassles, whereas lower scores indicate less frequent hassles.

Source: Kohn, Lafreniere, & Gurevich, 1990.

not a particularly good predictor of physical health, people who experience more uplifts have more positive moods (Kanner et al., 1981).

Although some research suggests that measures of daily hassles (and possibly uplifts) are a better predictor of health than measures of major life events, these self-report measures have some of the same limitations we discussed previously about the SRRS. One problem is that someone who experiences a major life event is also likely to experience many daily hassles. For example, someone who gets divorced may struggle with daily financial pressures, conflicts with the ex-spouse, and increased household responsibilities. Another problem with these measures is that some scales assessing hassles and uplifts include items that refer to health-related behavior (e.g., drinking, smoking, feeling healthy). Thus, if studies find a correlation between frequency of hassles or uplifts and health, it may be due to the link between a given behavior (such as smoking) and health as opposed to the link between stress and health.

Finally, because simply asking people whether they have experienced a given life event or daily hassle does not take into account that different people evaluate such experiences in different ways, other researchers have developed a measure that assesses individuals' perceived stress (Cohen, Kamark, & Mermelstein, 1983). The Perceived Stress Scale (PSS) does not ask people whether they have experienced a particular event but simply asks how frequently they have felt stressed or upset in the past month. For example, items on this scale include, "In the past month, how often have you found that you could not cope with all the things you had to do?" and "In the past month, how often have you felt nervous and 'stressed'?" PSS predicts psychological and physical symptoms (Hewitt, Flett, & Mosher, 1992), as well as changes in the immune and endocrine systems (Harrell, Kelly, & Stutts, 1996; Maes et al., 1997).

Physiological Measures

Given the various limitations of self-report measures of stress, some researchers have instead relied on physiological measures to assess stress (Baum, Grunberg, & Singer, 1982; Uchino, Cacioppo, Malarkey, & Glaser, 1995). Because a central aspect of stress is the stimulation of the sympathetic nervous system, stress can be measured through various measures of *physiological arousal*, including heart rate, blood pressure, respiration, and changes in the skin's resistance to electrical current (galvanic skin response, or GSR).

In one of the earliest studies to experimentally test the association between the experience of stress and physiological reactions, Speisman, Lazarus, Mordkoff, and Davison (1964) manipulated people's reaction to a particularly graphic film. This film, *Subincision in the Arunta*, shows (in gruesome detail) a puberty rite in which the penises of young adolescent boys are cut with a jagged and rusty knife. Most people (particularly men) find the film quite disturbing and show a high level of physiological arousal while watching it. To examine whether people's thoughts and interpretation of the film would influence their physiological reaction, researchers accompanied the film with different narratives for different groups. While watching the film, one group heard a narration that emphasized the emotionally upsetting aspects of the ceremony, including the pain and mutilation experienced by the boys, the danger of infection, and the jaggedness of the knife. Another narration emphasized the positive aspects of the ceremony, such as the pride the boys felt in demonstrating their bravery and entering adulthood, and denied the painful aspects. A third group heard a detached and intellectual discussion of the history of the tribe and the anthropological aspects of the ceremony. Finally, a fourth group saw the film, but heard no soundtrack at all. How did the interpretation provided by the narration influence people's reactions? As predicted, those who heard about the positive aspects of the ceremony or the intellectual discussion reported feeling less upset and experienced fewer physiological reactions to the film than those who heard the pain narration. For example, skin conductance (a measure of sweating) was 20.08 micromhos for those in the trauma condition and 16.08 for those who watched the silent (control) version, but only 14.77 for those in the positive aspects condition and 13.88 for those in the intellectualized version.

Biochemical measures can be used to assess the presence of particular hormones, such as norepinephrine, epinephrine, and cortisol (Baum et al., 1982). These hormones can be detected in blood or urine tests and are reliable indicators of an individual's experience of stress. Increases in corticosteroids and catecholamines (two types of chemicals, or neurotransmitters, in the body) are found in a variety of different types of stressful situations, including in astronauts during splashdown (Kimzey, 1975), people who are doing challenging mental arithmetic (Uchino et al., 1995), people who have a long commute to work (Evans & Wener, 2006), and snake phobics who see a snake (Bandura, Taylor, Williams, Mefford, & Barchas, 1985).

Physiological measures have some limitations. First, some people find the use of physiological measures in and of themselves very stressful. If a person is nervous about having blood taken or being hooked up to a machine that is measuring sweat or heart rate, he or she will show higher levels of stress simply because of the use

Although physiological measures of stress, such as blood pressure, avoid the inherent problems associated with self-report measures of stress, interpreting the results of such tests has its own challenges.
Source: © Jonathan Ross/iStockphoto.

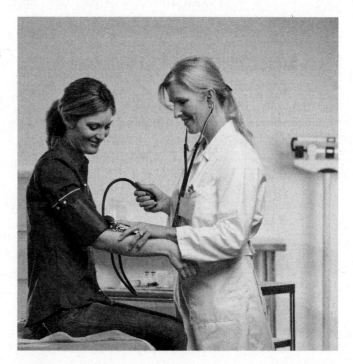

of these techniques. Second, physiological measures can be influenced by factors other than stress, including gender, weight, and physical activity level. Researchers therefore need to be aware of these complicating factors and must interpret the results accordingly. Finally, because physiological measures of stress rely on either equipment or laboratory testing, the use of these measures is very expensive and time-consuming. They also require trained technicians to perform the tests and interpret the results.

How Does Stress Influence Health?

Our understanding of how stress influences health has evolved considerably over time. This section describes two theories about how stress leads to physiological reactions, which in turn can impact physical well-being, as well as some limitations and revisions to these initial models of the stress–health relationship.

Cannon's Fight-or-Flight Response

Imagine that you are walking in a forest with some friends on a sunny afternoon. As you are talking to them, not really paying attention to where you are walking, you suddenly notice movement just in front of your right foot. You quickly glance down and see a large striped snake, coiled and seemingly ready to strike. What is your immediate physiological reaction? Like most people who are afraid of snakes, your heart will start to pound, your muscles will become tense, and you will start to sweat. In fact, you may have experienced mild forms of these reactions while reading this description of the snake.

This type of physiological reaction in response to threat, called the **fight-or-flight response**, was first described by Walter Cannon, a physiologist at Harvard Medical School in the early 1900s. According to Cannon (1932), people are normally in a state of internal physiological equilibrium or balance called *homeostasis* (Chrousos & Gold, 1992). When a person (or animal) is threatened, the immediate response is to either fight off the stressor or escape from it. To prepare for either alternative, energy is shifted from the nonessential body systems to those systems necessary to respond to the challenge. So, when someone first notices a threat (such as the snake), the person's sympathetic nervous and endocrine systems are stimulated, which causes a dramatic rise in two types of hormones: *epinephrine* (or *adrenaline*) and *norepinephrine* (*noradrenaline*). The increase in these hormone levels in the bloodstream lead to a number of other physiological responses that prepare someone to either fight off a threat (unlikely, in the case of the snake) or run from it (very likely, in the case of the snake), including increases in heart rate, blood pressure, and breathing; widening of the pupils; and movement of blood toward the muscles. Similarly, the cardiovascular system is activated, so that blood is directed to the brain and muscles. Processes that do not help fight off a threat, such as digestion and reproduction, are stopped or slowed down. This increase in some types of physiological responses and decrease in others allows the body to focus its resources where they are most needed to respond to the challenge.

General Adaptation Syndrome (GAS)

Hans Selye (1956), an endocrinologist, extended Cannon's work by describing the stages the body goes through when reacting to a stressor. He conducted a series of tests in which laboratory rats were exposed to different types of stressors, such as heat, starvation, and electric shock. Interestingly, he found that regardless of what type of stress the rats were exposed to, they developed similar physiological reactions, including enlarged adrenal glands, shrunken lymph nodes, and bleeding stomach ulcers. This observation led to the development of his **General Adaptation Syndrome** (GAS), a model to describe how stress can lead to negative health consequences over time (see Figure 4.2).

First, there is the **alarm stage**, in which the body mobilizes to fight off a threat. When a threat is perceived, the hypothalamus (a structure in the brain) activates both the sympathetic nervous system and the endocrine system. The sympathetic nervous system signals the adrenal glands (endocrine glands on the top of each kidney) to release *catecholamines*, such as epinephrine and norepinephrine. As epinephrine and norepinephrine circulate in the bloodstream, they lead to a number of physiological changes, including increases in heart rate, blood pressure, and breathing rate. These changes all help to prepare the body to react to a threat: Oxygen is brought to the muscles (to let you run or fight), pupils dilate (allowing more light to enter

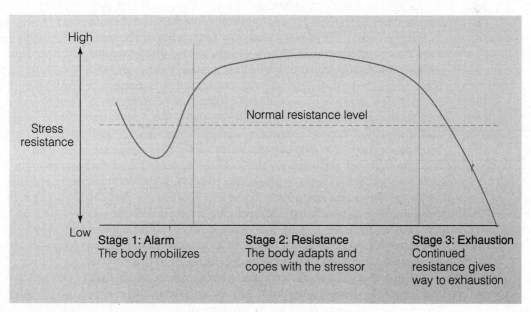

FIGURE 4.2   Model of the General Adaptation Syndrome (GAS).

to see more clearly), and palms sweat (for better gripping). This stage is similar to Cannon's fight-or-flight response. At the same time, the pituitary gland releases adrenocorticotropic hormone (ACTH), which causes the adrenal glands to produce glucocorticoids, such as cortisol. Cortisol increases the production of energy from glucose and inhibits the swelling around injuries and infections. Thus, the body has more energy to respond to threats and is protected from injuries. In this stage, the body is mobilizing all of its resources to do whatever is necessary to fight off (or escape from) the threat, and longer-term functions, such as growth, digestion, reproduction, and operation of the immune system are inhibited. (Astute readers may now be wondering why the immune system, which protects the body from illness and disease, would be inhibited during times of danger. But remember, illness and disease may kill you, but they do so slowly—the alarm stage serves to protect you from immediate threats that could kill you quickly.)

Next, there is the **resistance stage**. After the body mobilizes to fight off the initial threat, it will continue trying to respond. This stage still requires energy, so heart rate, blood pressure, and breathing are still rapid to help deliver oxygen and energy quickly throughout the body. Nonessential functions, such as digestion, growth, and reproduction, may operate but at a slower pace than normal, and no new energy is stored during this time. After all, why waste energy where it is not needed? (This is one reason why menstruation may stop in women who are under severe stress.) Although there is less of a drain on energy during this stage than during the alarm stage, the body continues to work very hard to resist the stressor on a long-term basis. If the threat is brief, the body will have enough resources to respond to the threat. However, if the threat lasts for some time, and the body stays in a state of physiological arousal for a long time, problems can begin to emerge. Essentially, the body neglects many normal physical and psychological functions during times of stress; over time, this neglect takes its toll on the body's resources.

Finally, when the threat continues for a long time, occurs repeatedly, or is very severe, the **exhaustion stage** may set in. For example, you may feel okay initially under conditions of high stress, but over time, it can be damaging to your body because all of its resources are consumed. Continuing or particularly strong stress therefore creates a situation of imbalance that results in considerable wear and tear on the body. In the exhaustion stage, the body's resources are depleted, and it becomes very susceptible to physiological damage and disease. Moreover, if epinephrine and cortisol stay at high levels over time, they can damage heart and blood vessels and suppress the immune system. These changes leave the body very susceptible to illness, such as heart disease, high blood pressure, arthritis, and colds and flu (McEwen, 1998). Stress can also lead to particularly negative health consequences in people who are suffering from chronic illnesses, who already have a weakened immune system. For example, HIV-positive men who experience the loss of a partner to AIDS (a major stressor) show signs of more rapid progression of their own AIDS illness (Kemeny et al., 1994).

According to Selye, the GAS is *nonspecific*, which means that all stressors produce the same physiological response. In other words, people will go through this three-stage process in response to any type of stressful event, including taking final exams, losing a loved one, or living in a crowded situation. In fact, although he believed positive stresses (e.g., getting married) would be less harmful than negative ones (e.g., getting divorced), both types of events are seen as causing some stress, potentially leading to the same negative physiological responses. In support of this view, research suggests that many types of stressors can lead to an increase in adrenal hormones (Baum et al., 1982).

Updates to the Fight-or-Flight and GAS Models

Although for many years researchers simply accepted Walter Cannon's observation that people respond to stress with heightened arousal (fight-or-flight response), research now suggests that people may vary in how they respond to stress as well as the impact of stress on illness (Stoney, Davis, & Mathews, 1987; Stoney, Mathews, McDonald, & Johnson, 1988). First, men tend to have higher blood pressure than women in general and also have a greater change in blood pressure during stressful situations. For example, in one study, researchers asked men and women to perform three different types of challenging tasks, including computing a series of math problems, giving a speech, and evaluating their own speech. Men showed higher blood pressure increases in each case. This greater physiological responsiveness to stress may partially explain why the rate of coronary heart disease is so much greater for men than women. Specifically, if men are constantly reacting to stress more than women, their hearts are likely to undergo much more wear and tear.

Similarly, research by Shelley Taylor et al. suggests that this reaction may not apply to everyone (Taylor et al., 2000). Because the vast majority of research on the stress response has relied on entirely male samples (and often on male rats!), it is not clear whether females show a similar response to stressful situations. Some research with humans also suggests that women prefer to affiliate with others during times of stress, whereas men prefer less social interaction. For example, when women expect that they will be given painful electric shocks, they prefer to wait with other women, whereas men often prefer to wait alone. In sum, while men do typically show the classic fight-or-flight response to stress, women may show what Taylor calls the **tend-and-befriend** response to stress, in which they seek out social support during times of stress.

Similarly, although Selye's GAS has received considerable attention in the field of health psychology, researchers have criticized it for several reasons. First, and contrary to Selye's original model proposing nonspecificity, we now know that different types of stressors are associated with different types of physiological reactions (Pacak et al., 1998). Researchers in one study exposed rats to different types of stressors, including cold, immobilization, or hemorrhage, and then measured various physiological reactions, such as level of epinephrine and norepinephrine. This research revealed that different hormones are released, depending on the specific type and intensity of emotion experienced in response to a stressor (Henry, 1990; Mason, 1975). These differences may relate to the type of threat a given stressor presents, meaning that different stressors require different responses (e.g., fighting off a physical attack requires a different reaction than staying warm).

More recent research has also updated Seyle's model by showing that the duration of the stressor influences the physiological response (Segerstrom, 2007; Segerstrom & Miller, 2004). Some stresses are acute or time-limited, meaning they are stressful for only a brief period of time. These types of stresses, such as passing a driving test, going on a blind date, and being interviewed for a job, are examples of acute stress (and the daily hassles scale described previously assesses this type of stress). The body is immensely resilient, and thus is typically able to handle such stresses with little or no impact on physical well-being. In the face of such stresses, the body turns on an **allostatic response** to meet the challenges of the demands of a given situation (McEwen, 1998, 2000; McEwen & Stellar, 1993). This response could include increases in blood pressure, the release of hormones, and the mobilization of energy mobilization, which are then discontinued when the stress is over.

However, in other cases, the stresses are chronic, meaning they continue over a long period of time. These stresses, which can include living in a dangerous neighborhood, trying to work full time while attending school, or experiencing continual discrimination based on your race, are often assessed through life events inventories. This type of long-term, cumulative stress leads the body to try to maintain a certain set point or equilibrium, which in turn can eventually lead to physiological responses that affect nearly every system in the body (Seeman, Singer, Horwitz, & McEwen, 1997). When stress becomes chronic, it suppresses immune function and increases cardiovascular hyperreactivity, which in turn increases susceptibility to disease causing negative consequences for health (Segerstrom & Miller, 2004).

Third, some researchers have argued that because Selye's theory was developed using animals, it does not address the psychological or cognitive responses that humans may have to stressful situations (Scherer, 1986). People can interpret or appraise stressors in different ways: A woman who is married and desperately trying to have a baby may react to conception differently than a woman who is single and still trying to finish college. According to the **transactional model** (also called the **relational model**), the meaning a particular event has for a person is a more important predictor of the experience of stress than the actual event (Lazarus & Folkman, 1984). Because people's cognitive interpretations of stressful events influence their reactions, people vary in how stressful they find different experiences. For example, if a couple of college students are driving and get a flat tire, the interpretations are very different. One person had no idea how to change a tire and immediately appraised the situation as a real emergency and panicked ("How much will it cost to get the car towed? How late will we be for class?"). The other person, however, calmly got the spare tire out of the trunk and within 10 minutes had replaced the bad tire. For one person, the flat tire equaled emergency. For the other, the flat tire equaled a minor inconvenience.

Lazarus and Folkman (1984) suggest that the cognitive appraisal of a stressful event includes two distinct parts. According to their transactional, or relational, model, whether people experience stress is influenced both by their initial reaction to the particular challenge and the resources they have to cope with this challenge. First, people engage in **primary appraisal** in which they assess the situation. In this stage people are interpreting the situation and what it will mean for them (e.g., "Am I in danger?"). For example, a person who is fired from his or her job may see it as a stressful event (e.g., "My family will starve") or as a positive opportunity (e.g., "Now I can explore new career options"). People then engage in **secondary appraisal** in which they assess the resources available for coping with the situation. In this stage, people examine their ability to cope with the event based on their resources (e.g., "What can I do about this?"). For example, an individual who has a working spouse may appraise the loss of a job less negatively because he or she has more financial resources to rely on than someone who is the sole wage earner in a family. In line with this view, women with chronic ongoing life stressors who experience a stressful event show high levels of cortisol (a marker of stress), whereas women with supportive environments who experience a stressful event show no such increases (Marin, Martin, Blackwell, Steltler, & Miller, 2007). The impact of a particular event may therefore have very different consequences, depending on how a person appraises it as well as the resources available for the person to cope with it.

Fourth, although all mammals experience a physiological response to stress, neuroscientist Robert Sapolsky (1994) has pointed out that not all mammals experience the negative health consequences of stress. In fact, humans seem to experience a very high rate of stress-related illnesses, including headaches, ulcers, and coronary heart disease. Sapolsky believes that humans experience more stress (and more illness) because we generate all sorts of stressful things in our heads. The physiological stress reaction characterized by Cannon's fight-or-flight response and Selye's GAS model is designed to help humans (and animals) respond to extreme, life-threatening stressors, such as occurs when you are chased by a large barking dog or when you are in combat during war. These physiological reactions may also be adaptive during other high-pressure situations, such as during a job interview or on a first date. However, we often show a physiological stress reaction to situations that are not actually life-threatening in any way. As Sapolsky (1998) writes, "Stress-related disease emerges, predominantly, out of the fact that we so often activate a physiological system that has evolved for responding to acute physical emergencies, but we turn it on for months on end, worrying about mortgages, relationships, and promotions." (p. 7). In turn, this ongoing activation of the stress response even to events that are not life threatening may lead to physiological reactions, which may help explain the high rate of stress-related illnesses, including headaches, ulcers, and coronary heart disease. This may be why, as Sapolsky cleverly writes, "zebras don't get ulcers," but humans often do.

Finally, although this section focuses on the negative physiological consequences of stress, some researchers have examined the benefits that can come from experiencing stress. Hans Selye (1974) used the term *eustress* to describe beneficial stresses. Moderate levels of stress can actually cause people to experience small amounts of arousal, providing extra energy, and can help them perform at their best. For example, athletes often want to feel somewhat excited as they compete because this feeling of "getting up for a game" can enhance their performance. In contrast, very low and very high levels of arousal can be detrimental to performance, either because they do not motivate us sufficiently (in the case of low levels) or because they create too much anxiety (in the case of high levels). In line with this view about the potential benefits of at least some stress, some research suggests that individuals who experience some adverse life events may in fact have greater physical and psychological well-being than those who experience many or very few stressors (Seery, Holman, & Silver, 2010). Researchers hypothesize that overcoming some difficult events may make people more resilient later on, and thus they are better able to handle future stressors.

Derek Jeter is often described as a "clutch player," meaning
someone who performs even better under pressure, in part
due to his home run in the bottom of the 10th inning of the
2001 World Series when the score was tied 3-3 in Game 4.
Source: TIMOTHY A. CLARY/AFP/Getty Images.

What Are the Physical Consequences of Stress?

In a nutshell, stress is damaging to your health. People who are under stress have a
greater risk of experiencing a number of illnesses and diseases, including ulcers, diabetes, colds and flu, arthritis, appendicitis, gastrointestinal disorders, herpes, asthma,
sports injuries, headaches, migraines, eczema, hives, back pain, gastrointestinal disorders, hernias, cancer, and cardiovascular disease (Glaser & Kiecolt-Glaser, 1994).
For example, stress can cause the dilation of arteries surrounding the brain and
tension in muscles in the head, neck, and shoulders, both of which may lead to
headaches (Turner & Chapman, 1982). In turn, only 7% of those who experience
low stress report experiencing frequent headache pain, as compared to 17% of
those with moderate stress, and 25% of those with high stress (Sternbach, 1986).
How exactly does stress lead to bad health? As noted previously, when a person
faces a challenge—such as taking a difficult test, walking through a dangerous
neighborhood, or giving a public speech—the body turns on an allostatic response
to adapt to this situation (McEwen, 1998; McEwen & Stellar, 1993). This physiological response includes a number of systems in the body and is shut off as soon as
the challenge ends. However, when people experience repeated stress over a long
period of time, the allostatic load builds up and can eventually lead to physiological
responses that affect nearly every system in the body (Seeman et al., 1997). The
following section examines the direct impact of such chronic stress on several
systems within the body, the interaction of these systems (as described by the field
of **psychoneuroimmunology**), and the indirect effects of stress on physiological
functioning.

Nervous System

The **nervous system**, which includes the **central nervous system** as well as the **peripheral nervous system**, controls the body's overall reaction to stress in several ways (see Figure 4.3). The central nervous system consists of the brain and spinal cord, where information processing occurs (e.g., "That's a bear—it could hurt me!"). The peripheral nervous system consists of the neural pathways that bring information to and from the brain. Specialized cells called **neurons** transmit this information, although the **neurotransmitters**, or chemical messengers, released by a particular neuron influence whether the information is transmitted (some neurotransmitters inhibit transmission, and others facilitate it). The peripheral nervous system includes the *somatic nervous system* and the *autonomic nervous system*. Both of these systems carry messages throughout the body, but they differ in the types of messages they transmit. The somatic nervous system transmits messages regarding sensation, such as touch, pressure, temperature, and pain, and messages regarding the voluntary movement of the body. In contrast, the autonomic nervous system, which consists of the *sympathetic* and *parasympathetic divisions*, carries information that is directly related to survival (for organs that are not under voluntary control).

FIGURE 4.3 Model of the nervous system.

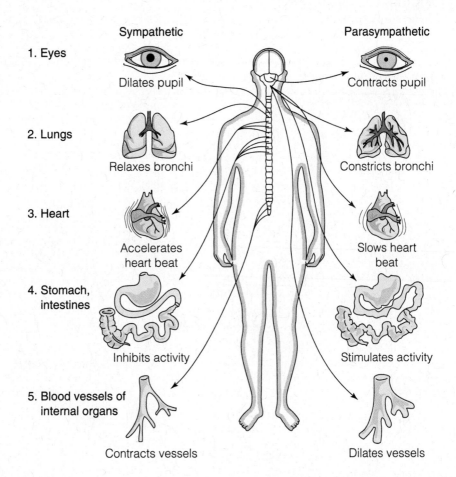

The sympathetic division mobilizes the body to react in the face of a threat, much like the response that occurs in Cannon's fight-or-flight response. This response includes increases in respiration, heart rate, and pulse; decreases in digestion and reproduction; dilation of pupils (for far vision); and movement of blood to the muscles to prepare for action. The parasympathetic division demobilizes the body to conserve energy, which includes increasing digestion; decreasing heart rate, respiration, and pulse; and constricting pupils. These physiological reactions occur because the autonomic nervous system triggers the endocrine system to react in the face of stress, as described in the next section.

Endocrine System

The **endocrine system** regulates a number of different physiological processes in the body, including physical growth, sexual arousal, metabolism, and stress response. The endocrine system works by releasing hormones from an endocrine gland, such as the pituitary, thyroid, and pancreas, into the bloodstream (see Figure 4.4).

FIGURE 4.4   Model of the endocrine system.

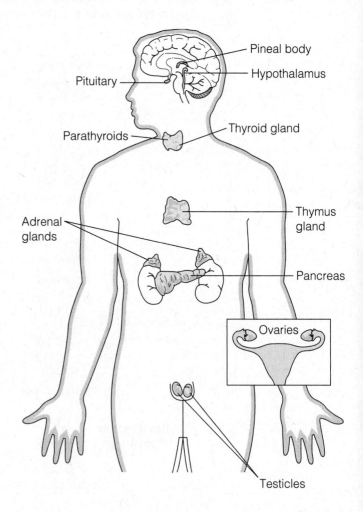

These hormones then travel through the bloodstream to influence a particular body tissue or organ. For example, when the hormone estrogen is released from a young woman's ovaries, it causes the uterus to grow in preparation for carrying an embryo, the breasts to enlarge in preparation for nursing, and the brain to increase in interest in sexual activity.

During times of stress, the sympathetic nervous system activates two core systems within the endocrine system: the **sympathetic adrenomedullary system** (SAM), which is responsible for the immediate fight-or-flight response to stress, and the **hypothalamic-pituitary-adrenal** (HPA) axis, which puts into motion a slower neuroendocrine response to stress (Chrousos & Gold, 1992; Cohen, Janicki-Deverts, & Miller, 2007). When the SAM system is activated, the hypothalamus triggers the adrenal glands to release epinephrine and norepinephrine (adrenaline and noradrenaline). These hormones act very quickly and lead to a number of physiological effects, including increased heart rate, increased blood flow, and increased sweating. The slower HPA system is also activated during times of stress. The HPA system starts by secreting corticotropin-releasing hormone (CRH), which in turn triggers the anterior pituitary gland to release adrenocorticotropic hormone (ACTH). Finally, the presence of ACTH leads the adrenal gland to release glucocorticoids, including cortisol (an important stress hormone that circulates back to the brain). As stress hormones circulate, rising levels of cortisol become a signal to the brain to shut off the fight-or-flight response, allowing the body to recover from stress. This is an important feedback system that protects the organism from the physiological harm of chronic sympathetic activation. If stress is maintained over time, the resulting high levels of cortisol can lead to damage in the hippocampus, an area of the brain involved in memory.

Several studies have demonstrated the powerful effects of stress on the endocrine system (Frankenhaeuser, 1975, 1978; Ursin, Baader, & Levine, 1978). One early study by Ursin et al. (1978), for example, examined how young military recruits reacted physiologically to the stressful situation of their first parachute-training jump. In this first stage of training, recruits climbed to the top of a 40-foot tower and then slid down a wire to the ground, which feels similar to free fall. Most people find this experience stressful, and, not surprisingly, levels of epinephrine, norepinephrine, and cortisol were significantly higher on the day of the jump than the day before. Although the type of stress experienced in this situation was obviously unique (and extreme), similar increases in stress-related hormones occur following other, more typical stressful situations, including taking oral exams, riding in a crowded commuter train car, giving a speech, and having a repetitive and low-control job (Frankenhaeuser, 1975, 1978; Sumter, Bokhors, Miers, Van Pelt, & Westenberg, 2010). Box 4.2: Focus on Development describes how stress experienced early in life may have long-term consequences on people's ability to manage stress later on.

Cardiovascular System

The primary function of the **cardiovascular system** is for the heart to generate the force necessary to pump blood to transport oxygen to and remove carbon dioxide from each cell in the body (see Figure 4.5). The blood travels initially through the larger blood vessels (such as the *aorta*), which in turn branch into

Box 4.2

Focus on Development: Why the Early Years Really Matter

Although stress is clearly associated with a variety of negative health outcomes, a growing amount of research reveals that people's biological response to stressful situations differs considerably. Interestingly, characteristics of children's early social environment—including attachment to caregivers and presence of social support—seem to partially explain such differences (Hanson & Chen, 2010; Miller & Chen, 2010). In one study, researchers examined college students' descriptions of their childhood environments, frequency of daily stress, and levels of cortisol in their saliva (a commonly used measure of stress). Students who reported having had difficult childhoods—meaning a lack of warmth from their parents and/or caregivers—showed higher levels of cortisol on days in which they experienced more stressful events. In contrast, for students who reported having had more positive childhood environments, lower levels of cortisol were found on days in which they experienced more stress. This finding suggests that having a supportive childhood environment has lasting benefits in terms of individuals' ability to manage stress in later life. Although researchers are still examining different potential explanations for this link between early life experiences and biological response to stress later on, it is clear that these early experiences lead individuals to show greater cardiovascular responsiveness and inflammation responses to stressful experiences.

smaller and smaller vessels, and eventually into capillaries. Two major measures to evaluate cardiovascular activity are *heart rate*, the number of beats per minute, and *blood pressure*, the force of blood against the artery walls.

The cardiovascular system's primary function is for the heart to pump blood, which in turn generates the force needed to both send oxygen to and remove carbon dioxide from all of the body's cells and organs (see Figure 4.5). Initially, the blood travels through the aorta and larger blood vessels. Later, the blood branches out to flow into smaller and smaller vessels, including the capillaries. Cardiovascular activity is assessed in terms of two measures: *heart rate*, meaning the number of times the heart beats per minute, and *blood pressure*, meaning the force of blood flowing against the artery walls.

The impact of stress on the cardiovascular system is well-established: People under stress show heightened cardiovascular reactivity, including high blood pressure and increased heart rate (Kamarck et al., 2004). For example, people who take a stressful math test in a psychology laboratory show faster heart rates and higher blood pressure after this stressor than before (Uchino et al., 1995), and they show a similar elevation in blood pressure when they are in stressful situations in daily life (Matthews, Owens, Allen, & Stoney, 1992). More routine types of stressors, such as interpersonal conflict, also impact the cardiovascular system: Couples with low marital satisfaction show higher heart rates during conflicts than those with greater satisfaction (Kiecolt-Glaser, Kennedy, et al., 1988; Manne & Zautra, 1989). In addition, greater adrenaline—which results from stress—causes blood to clot more rapidly, which can lead to heart attacks (Strike et al., 2006).

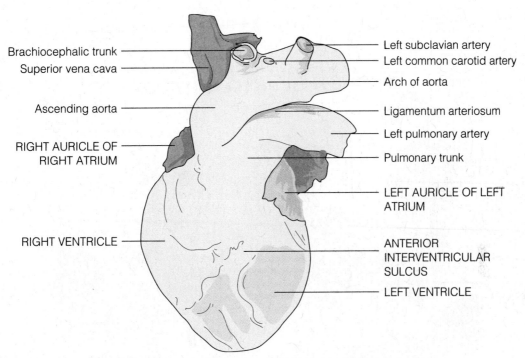

Brachiocephalic trunk
Superior vena cava

Ascending aorta

RIGHT AURICLE OF
RIGHT ATRIUM

RIGHT VENTRICLE

Left subclavian artery
Left common carotid artery
Arch of aorta

Ligamentum arteriosum
Left pulmonary artery
Pulmonary trunk

LEFT AURICLE OF LEFT
ATRIUM

ANTERIOR
INTERVENTRICULAR
SULCUS
LEFT VENTRICLE

FIGURE 4.5   Model of the cardiovascular system.

Unfortunately, prolonged periods of high blood pressure can lead to a buildup of fatty acids and glucose on blood vessel walls, which forces the heart to work even harder to pump blood through narrowing arteries. Over time, this chronic wear and tear can lead to considerable damage to the heart and arteries. Long-term, or chronic, stress can therefore have particularly negative consequences on the cardiovascular system. For example, people who provide in-home care to a spouse with Alzheimer's disease, a very stressful situation for virtually all caregivers, are at increased risk of developing coronary heart disease (von Känel et al., 2008). In fact, one large-scale study in 52 countries revealed that individuals with high rates of stress—at home and/or work—were at greater risk of experiencing a heart attack (Rosengren et al., 2004).

As discussed earlier in this chapter, lacking control in a particular situation can be very stressful and thus can also have negative health consequences. In line with this view, people who have little or no control over their work environments are more likely to experience a heart attack and other health problems than those with more control (Bosma et al., 1997; Cheng, Kawachi, Coakley, Schwartz, & Colditz, 2000). For example, men who report feeling low levels of ability to exercise control over their work lives—including scheduling their work activities and changing work activities—have higher levels of atherosclerosis, a risk factor associated with cardiovascular disease, than those who felt they had higher levels of control (Kamarck, Muldoon, Shiffman, & Sutton-Tyrrell, 2007). Employees with high job strain, meaning they experience high demands at work and low control, are more than twice as likely to die from cardiovascular-related causes than those without such strain (Kivimaki et al., 2002).

Work pressures, including long hours, heavy workload, and constant deadlines, can all create stress, which in turn can lead to increased cardiovascular activity.

Source: © 2003 David Sipress from cartoonbank.com. All Rights Reserved.

Questioning the Research 4.1

Why do employees with high job strain experience more cardiovascular events? Which factors do you think best explain this association?

The impact of ongoing stress on cardiovascular health is one potential explanation for why African Americans tend to have higher rates of hypertension and coronary heart disease than Whites. According to some researchers, feeling constantly mistreated due to discrimination and racism acts as a chronic stressor that may lead to higher blood pressure as well as damage the cardiovascular system (Clark, Anderson, Clark, & Williams, 1999; Krieger & Sidney, 1996; Krieger, Sidney, & Coakley, 1998; Mendes, Major, McCoy, & Blascovich, 2008; Merritt, Bennett, Williams, Edwards, & Sollers, 2006; Richman, Pek, Pascoe, & Bauer, 2010). To test this association among race, discrimination, and cardiovascular reactivity, researchers in one study asked both African Americans and Whites to imagine that they had been wrongly accused of shoplifting in a department store (Guyll, Matthews, & Bromberger, 2001). As predicted, both African Americans and Whites who were wrongly accused showed greater blood pressure while defending themselves. However, African Americans who attributed the false accusation to discrimination showed much higher blood pressure than those that did not make this attribution, presumably because people who perceive the world as a dangerous and racist place experience higher levels of ongoing stress than those without such a worldview. This finding suggests that the combination of experiencing a stressful event *and* attributing this event to discrimination can have negative health consequences. In line with this view, cardiovascular reactivity, including greater blood pressure, higher heart rate, and increased plaque in the arteries (an early sign of coronary heart disease), is more likely for people who have experienced past acts of discrimination, and this association is greater for African Americans than Whites (Richman, Bennett, Pek, Siegler, & Williams, 2007; Troxel, Matthews, Bromberger & Sutton-Tyrrell, 2003). Although the majority of this research has focused on the influence of ongoing stress on health in African Americans, some research reveals also that Latinos who believe they are discriminated against due to their ethnicity show higher resting blood pressure, which may lead to greater risk of cardiovascular disease (Salomon & Jagusztyn, 2008).

Immune System

The **immune system**, which is the body's major line of defense against infections and diseases, provides three levels of protection: external barriers, nonspecific responses, and specific responses (Simpson, Hurtley, & Marx, 2000). Initially, the skin serves as an external barrier to protect the body from bacteria and viruses. However, if any type of foreign material, such as a bacteria or virus, invades this barrier, the immune system begins an immediate nonspecific response (any foreign material that activates this immune response is called an *antigen*). It works to eliminate foreign, "nonself" materials, such as bacteria, viruses, and parasites, which contact or enter the body. If you get a splinter in your hand, the immune system will trigger a response to fight against this invader (in this case, wood). The blood vessels will dilate to increase blood flow to the site of the injury, which leads to warmth, redness, and swelling, and allows tissue repair to begin. A group of cells called *lymphocytes* finds and then destroys *antigens* in the bloodstream.

As shown in Figure 4.6, the body's third line of defense against foreign matter is the specific immune system, which consists of specialized types of white blood cells called lymphocytes, including B cells and T cells. These cells differ from nonspecific lymphocytes in that they find and attack only very specific antigens. The B cells, which originate in the bone marrow, control the *humoral immune response system*, in which proteins called antibodies, which bind to foreign toxins and inactivate or destroy them, are produced. The T cells, which originate in the thymus, control the *cell-mediated immune response system*, in which they bind to foreign cells to kill them. Other immune system cells include the *natural killer (NK) cells*, which detect and then destroy damaged cells, such as precancerous cells before they develop into tumors, and *macrophages*, which engulf and digest foreign cells, such as bacteria.

Although you may think of the immune system as fairly abstract, it impacts your life in a variety of ways. For example, vaccinations for diseases such as polio and chicken pox were created based on knowledge of how the immune system works. When you get a vaccination, you are actually introducing a weakened form of a

FIGURE 4.6   Model of the immune system.

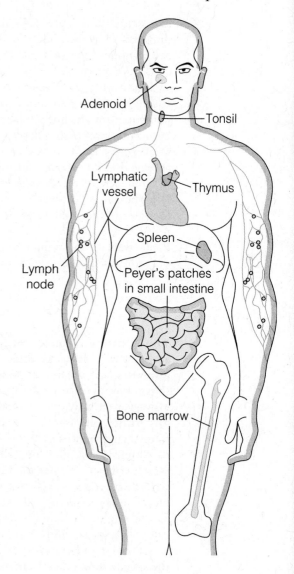

virus or bacterium into your body. The body then reacts to this threat by producing antibodies to fight it. When and if you are exposed to the actual disease, your body already has the antibodies ready to respond, and thereby protect you from illness—it is like having a head start on fighting an illness.

Considerable research with both animals and humans demonstrates that stress has a number of negative effects on the immune system (Segerstrom & Miller, 2004). Individuals who experience a variety of different types of stressors, including divorce, loneliness, unemployment, commuting, bereavement, marital conflict, and exams, have fewer B, T, and NK cells (Cohen & Herbert, 1996; Evans & Wener, 2006; Ironson et al., 1997; Kiecolt-Glaser, Page, Marucha, MacCallum, & Glaser, 1998; Kiecolt-Glaser, McGuire, Robles, & Glaser, 2002; Marsland, Cohen, Rabin, & Manuck, 2001; McKinnon, Weisse, Reynolds, Bowles, & Baum, 1989).

For example, one study by Stone, Aronson, Crain, Winslow, and Fried (1994) showed that on days in which people experienced more positive events, their bodies produced more antibodies, whereas on days with more negative events, their bodies produced fewer antibodies. Finally, the experience of stress can even influence the rate of wound healing (Kiecolt-Glaser, Marucha, Malarky, Mercado, & Glaser, 1995; Marucha, Kiecolt-Glaser, & Favayehi, 1998). In one study, dental students agreed to have small wounds placed on the roofs of their mouths during two distinct times in the semester, and researchers then measured the rate of wound healing (Marucha et al., 1998). Wound healing took 40% longer during the exam period than during summer vacation.

Although studies with humans often have difficulty showing that stress—as opposed to some third variable such as personality—causes such physiological reactions, experimental research with animals reveals such findings. For example, rats who are exposed to stressors, including noise, overcrowding, and inescapable shock, show less immune cell activity, as well as the fastest rate of tumor growth compared to those rats not under such stress (Ben-Eliyahu, Yirmiya, Liebeskind, Taylor, & Gale, 1991; Moynihan & Ader, 1996).

Because chronic stress diverts resources away from the immune system and toward more urgent physiological needs, people who experience stress over long periods of time have a greater risk of developing an infectious disease, which the body would typically be able to fight off. In a series of studies, Sheldon Cohen has recruited healthy volunteers who are willing to be exposed to a cold virus (the virus is inserted using nasal drops; Cohen, Doyle, Skoner, Rabi, & Gwaltney, 1997; Cohen, Tyrrell, & Smith, 1991). Participants are quarantined (in separate living accommodations) for a few days, complete a series of measures (such as psychological stress, social support, personality, and health status), and are then exposed to the cold virus. Researchers then examine participants daily for signs and symptoms of a cold, such as sneezing, sore throat, sinus pain, and coughing, to determine how psychosocial factors may influence who develops a cold and who is able to fight off this virus and remain healthy. Researchers in one study found that individuals who were experiencing more stress in their daily lives had a greater rate of infection with the cold, even controlling for other factors (e.g., age, gender, personality variables). Similarly, Figure 4.7 shows that people who experience longer-lasting life stressors are at greater risk of developing a cold. Although this research is conducted in a laboratory setting, studies in more real-world settings reveal similar findings. For example, one study comparing the health of caregivers of Alzheimer's patients, who are undergoing chronic stress, to a matched control group (people of a similar age but without such responsibility) found that caregivers had a weaker immune response and were more likely to develop infectious diseases (Kiecolt-Glaser, Dura, Speicher, Trask, & Glaser, 1991). This research provides strong evidence for the impact of psychological factors on physical well-being.

Another way in which the impact of stress on the immune system is seen is in the case of depression, even when the level of depression does not reach clinically significant levels (meaning a subsyndromal condition; Kiecolt-Glaser & Glaser, 2002). Individuals who have even subsyndromal levels of depression show compromised immune function, in part because even lower levels of depression can influence the cellular immune response, and thereby lead to prolonged infection and delayed wound healing.

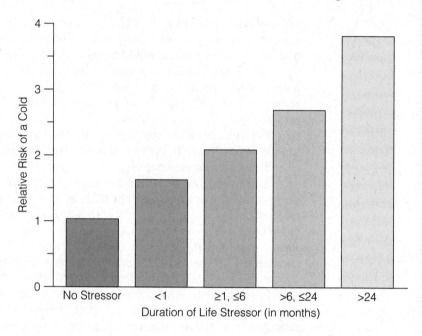

FIGURE 4.7 Sheldon Cohen et al. (1998) examined the influence of the duration of a stressor on illness by injecting people with nasal drops containing a cold virus. Individuals who experienced longer-lasting life stressors were at much greater risk of developing a cold than those who experienced shorter-term life stressors and no stressors.

Psychoneuroimmunology

So far, the impacts of stress on the nervous, endocrine, cardiovascular, and immune systems have been described as separate and distinct effects; in reality, these different body systems all interact to influence health. You may have noticed, for example, that when the endocrine system is activated, it in turn leads to cardiovascular changes, such as increases in heart rate and blood pressure. Activating the endocrine system also leads to the release of glucocorticoids, which hinder the formation of some white blood cells, including NK cells, and which kill other white blood cells (Cohen & Herbert, 1996; Jemmott & Locke, 1984; Kiecolt-Glaser & Glaser, 1986). The field of psychoneuorimmunology examines the complex connection between psychosocial factors, such as stress, and the nervous, cardiovascular, endocrine, and immune systems (Adler, 2001).

Although it is now fully accepted that the mind and body interact in complex ways to influence health, this finding was originally discovered by accident. In 1974, psychologist Robert Ader from the University of Rochester School of Medicine was working on a series of studies designed to show that rats could learn to avoid a sugar-flavored drinking water by using classical conditioning techniques (see Chapter 3 for a quick refresher on conditioning techniques). First, he gave rats a sugar-flavored water to drink, which, not surprisingly, the rats enjoyed. Then he injected the rats with an immune-suppressing drug that caused them to feel nauseous. The rats quickly learned that the drink would make them ill, hence, they developed an aversion to the taste that was associated through conditioning with the injection. However, several weeks later, Ader found that many of the rats involved in this study on taste aversion became sick and ultimately died. Testing revealed that the immune system in these rats was impaired, apparently due to the drug they had received. But amazingly, the immune system was also impaired in rats that had received only the immune-suppressing drug on one occasion and that on all future trials received only the sugar water (which obviously should have had no effect on their immune system). Apparently, the animals' immune systems associated the taste of the sugar water with the experience of immune-suppression, and hence they developed a conditioned response to this taste in later trials that led to a suppression of their immune response. Ader then conducted a series of studies with Nicholas Cohen, an immunologist, to replicate his surprising findings (1975, 1985). These studies again demonstrated that immune responses can be conditioned. These studies, which demonstrate that psychological, neural, and immunological processes interact in complex ways, led to the development of the field of psychoneuroimmunology.

Indirect Effects of Stress on Health

Although the prior sections have described the direct impact of stress on both immune and cardiovascular functioning, stress also has indirect—and negative—effects on health. For example, college students often find that they finish taking exams, and then all of a sudden get sick. In this case, what factors might lead to the link between stress and sickness? Just think of yourself during exam period: What types of things do you do to relieve your stress? If you are like most college students, during stressful times you tend to eat junk food, drink coffee and other caffeinated beverages, sleep less, and reduce (or eliminate) exercise. Thus, one explanation for this illness is that people who are experiencing stress often engage in behaviors that impact health. So, during exam times, college students may be more likely to stop exercising, eat less healthy foods, and smoke cigarettes, which, in turn, can lead to bad health outcomes.

Considerable research reveals that people who are experiencing high levels of stress are less likely to engage in health-promoting behaviors, such as exercising and getting adequate amounts of sleep, and are more likely to engage in health-impairing behaviors, such as eating less-nutritious foods and smoking cigarettes (Conway, Vickers, Ward, & Rahe, 1981; Jackson, Knight, & Rafferty, 2010; Kiecolt-Glaser & Glaser, 1988; Ogden & Mitandabari, 1997). In one study, researchers asked over 10,000 workers to complete surveys assessing their perceived level of stress and frequency of health-related behaviors (Ng & Jeffery, 2003). For both men and women, higher levels of perceived stress were associated with a higher fat diet, less frequent exercise, and cigarette smoking (interestingly, stress was not associated with alcohol intake). Similarly, people who experience more daily hassles report eating more high fat/sugar snacks, and fewer main meals and vegetables (O'Connor, Jones, Conner, McMillan, & Ferguson, 2008). Interestingly, this association between daily hassles and eating behavior was particularly strong for female participants. Perceived stress is also associated with haphazard planning (failing to plan for what one was going to eat), emotional eating (eating in response to a bad mood; Sims et al., 2008), and, not surprisingly, weight gain (Block, He, Zaslavsky, Ding, & Ayanian, 2009; Hannerz, Albertsen, Nielsen, Tuchsen, & Burr, 2004; Hunte & Williams, 2009; Vines et al., 2007). People who are experiencing stress also tend to get less sleep, which is associated with negative health outcomes (Cohen, Doyle, Alper, Janicki-Deverts, & Turner, 2009). For example, one study examined immune cell activity in a group of healthy men who were kept awake between 3 a.m. and 7 a.m.

(Irwin et al., 1994). As predicted, this type of sleep deprivation led to decreases in immune cell activity that returned only after the men had a good night's sleep. Once again, these findings suggest that the association between stress and illness may be moderated in part by unhealthy behaviors.

Questioning the Research 4.2

Many studies on the link between stress and health are based on research that assesses college students' health before and after exams. What are some limitations of this approach?

This link between psychological states, health behaviors, and health outcomes is particularly hazardous for people who are clinically depressed. Researchers in one study examined the association between depression and likelihood of experiencing a cardiovascular event, such as a stroke or heart attack, in men with coronary heart disease (Whooley et al., 2008). Depressed people were 31% more likely to experience a cardiovascular event than nondepressed people, even controlling for disease state and other risk factors. However, when researchers controlled for the level of physical activity, the association between depression and likelihood of experiencing a cardiovascular event disappeared. This finding suggests that depression has an indirect, not direct, effect on the experience of cardiovascular events, and specifically that depressed people are less likely to exercise than nondepressed people, which in turn increases the risk of a heart problem.

What Are the Psychological Consequences of Stress?

Although thus far you have seen the negative effects of stress on physical health, stress can also have negative effects on psychological health. Stress can lead to cognitive problems by impairing people's memory and attention. Have you ever misread a question on an exam and gotten the answer wrong, even though you knew the right answer? People who are under conditions of high stress often have trouble concentrating or focusing on a particular task because other thoughts continue to come into their minds (Lyubomirsky & Nolen-Hoeksema, 1995; Sarason, Sarason, Keefe, Hayes, & Shearin, 1986). For example, as you take an exam that is not going well, you may start thinking, "Everyone else seems to be nearly finished," or "If I don't do well on this test, I will get a C in this course," which in turn increases stress and makes it even harder for you to focus. As described at the beginning of this chapter, Sara experienced this type of cognitive difficulty whenever she sat down to take a final exam. Researchers in one study of work stress in physicians and nurses found that higher rates of work stress were associated with poorer memory scores (Rutledge et al., 2009). Even ongoing types of environmental stressors, such as loud noise, can lead to cognitive problems. One study examined reading and memory skills in children ages 8 to 12 who lived near a noisy airport (Hygge, Evans, & Bullinger, 2002). After the airport was shut down, the children's reading

People who experience natural disasters, such as hurricanes, earthquakes, and tornados, suffer from both psychological and physical distress (Norris & Kaniasty, 1996).
Source: Tom Pennington/Getty Images.

and memory scores improved, whereas children who lived near the new airport showed a decline in scores on these measures.

Stress also increases physiological arousal, which can lead people to make poorer decisions (Keinan, Friedland, & Ben-Porath, 1987). People who are experiencing stress are less likely to consider various options, and they tend to make more impulsive decisions. By creating a sense of urgency (e.g., "a limited time offer"), some types of sales techniques rely on this type of pressure to force people to make rushed (and often poor) decisions. Also, research with rats and monkeys has shown that long-term exposure to cortisol, a hormone released during times of stress, leads to the loss of neurons in the hippocampus, which in turn disrupts memory (Sapolsky, 1992).

Stress can lead to a variety of negative emotions, such as fear, anxiety, and sadness (Rubonis & Bickman, 1991). Routine stresses, such as constant pressure at work, can eventually lead to frustration and apathy (Maslach, 1982). This state of emotional exhaustion, or burnout, is particularly common in people who work in helping professions, such as doctors, nurses, police officers, and social workers. Posttraumatic stress disorder (PTSD), a particular type of anxiety disorder, is caused by experiencing extreme stressors, such as war, natural disasters, and assault. For example, after the 9/11 terrorist attacks, higher rates of PTSD and psychological distress were reported for those who lived in close proximity to the attacks compared to those in other parts of the country (see Table 4.3; Holman, Silver, Poulin, Andersen, Gil-Rivas, & McIntosh, 2008; Schlenger et al., 2002). One study by Gail Ironson et al. (1997) found that about one-third of people who had experienced a tremendous hurricane showed some symptoms of PTSD even several months after the storm's occurrence. In cases of extreme stress, these reactions can last for many years. For example, survivors of Nazi concentration camps sometimes report continuing anxiety and fear as long as 50 years after their internment (Valent, 2000). Interestingly, some recent research suggests that individuals' particular genetic makeup can impact the influence of natural disasters on health (Daly & MacLachlan, 2011).

TABLE 4.3   *Increased Risk of Experiencing a Heart Problem in the Three Years Following the 9/11 Terrorist Attacks*

Age	Rate of Increased Likelihood
35–49	1.91
50–64	3.30
65–79	4.59
80 and older	4.17

Source: In this study, researchers examined rates of heart problems, such as hypertension or a heart attack, in the three years following the 9/11 attacks, taking into account pre-existing risk factors, such as BMI, smoking, and cardiac problems. As shown in this table, participants were at increased risk of experiencing a heart problem during this time, and this risk increased with age (Holman, Silver, Poulin, Andersen, Gil-Rivas, & McIntosh, 2008).

Finally, stress can influence behavior in a number of ways. People who experience severe stressors may suffer from continuing behavioral problems (Kessler, Sonnega, Bromet, Hughes, & Nelson, 1995). For example, war veterans often experience severe behavioral symptoms, including sleeplessness, nightmares, and startle reactions (Sutker, Davis, Uddo, & Ditta, 1995). Stress can also lead to negative interpersonal behavior. After the devastating Hurricane Andrew hit south Florida in 1992, causing high levels of stress in the many people who experienced the destruction of their home and/or other possessions, reports of domestic violence increased dramatically (Polusny & Follette, 1995). Sexual drive is also affected by stress. It decreases in men and women during times of stress: Women are less likely to ovulate, and men are more likely to have difficulty achieving and maintaining an erection (Sapolsky, 1994).

What Are Some Strategies for Managing Stress?

People who are able to cope with stress effectively do not necessarily experience such negative stress consequences as presented in this chapter. As described by Richard Lazarus and Susan Folkman (1984), **coping** refers to an individual's efforts to manage the stressful demands of a specific situation, such as working to solve a problem, finding a new way to look at the situation, or distracting oneself from the problem. This section describes some of the strategies that help people reduce their feelings of stress and thereby experience better health, including coping styles, relaxation and mindfulness, humor, exercise, social support, and religion.

Coping Styles

One common strategy for managing challenging situations is trying to confront and change the stressor. This is called **problem-focused coping** and can include a number of different approaches, such as seeking assistance from others, taking direct action, and planning (see Table 4.4; Carver, Scheier, & Weintraub, 1989;

TABLE 4.4 *Test Yourself: How Do You Cope With Problems?*

Please answer the following questions on a scale of 1 to 4, with 1 meaning "I usually don't do this at all" and 4 meaning "I usually do this a lot."

Active Coping

I concentrate my efforts on doing something about it.

I take direct action to get around the problem.

Planning

I try to come up with a strategy about what to do.

I make a plan of action.

Suppression of Competing Activities

I put aside other activities in order to concentrate on this.

I keep myself from getting distracted by other thoughts or activities.

Restraint Coping

I force myself to wait for the right time to do something.

I hold off doing anything about it until the situation permits.

Seeking Social Support for Instrumental Reasons

I ask people who have had similar experiences what they did.

I try to get advice from someone about what to do.

Seeking Social Support for Emotional Reasons

I talk to someone about how I feel.

I try to get emotional support from friends or relatives.

Positive Reinterpretation and Growth

I look for something good in what is happening.

I learn something from the experience.

Acceptance

I learn to live with it.

I accept that this has happened and that it can't be changed.

Turning to Religion

I seek God's help.

I try to find comfort in my religion.

Focus on and Venting of Emotion

I get upset and let my emotions out.

I let my feelings out.

(continued)

TABLE 4.4 *(continued)*

Denial

I refuse to believe that it has happened.

I pretend that it hasn't really happened.

Behavioral Disengagement

I give up the attempt to get what I want.

I just give up trying to reach my goal.

Mental Disengagement

I turn to work or other substitute activities to take my mind off things.

I sleep more than usual.

Alcohol–Drug Disengagement

I drink alcohol or take drugs to think about it less.

This scale assesses 14 different strategies people sometimes use to cope with problems.

Source: Carver et al., 1989.

Folkman & Lazarus, 1980). For example, a person who is feeling stress because of too much work could ask for an extension on a paper or make an effort to stop procrastinating and finish one project each day. Strategies could include active coping (removing the stressor by dropping a class), planning how to cope with the stressor (structuring specific times for studying each day), suppressing other activities to focus on the stressor (eliminating participation in athletic events), and seeking advice or assistance with coping (talking to one's advisor about how to balance work projects). At the beginning of the chapter, you read how Monica used problem-focused coping to manage her feelings of stress by talking to a therapist about her parents' separation and asking her professor for an extension on her paper. This type of coping is often used when something constructive can be done to help solve the problem or at least make the situation better (Folkman, Lazarus, Dunkel-Schetter, DeLongis, & Gruen, 1986; Folkman & Lazarus, 1980). For example, college students are more likely to use problem-focused coping when preparing for an exam, but they are less likely to use this approach when they are nervously waiting for their grades after taking the exams (Folkman & Lazarus, 1985).

Is tackling a problem directly beneficial in terms of health? Yes: Most research suggests that people who use problem-focused coping show better adjustment (Dunkel-Schetter, Feinstein, Taylor, & Falke, 1992; Penley, Tomaka, & Wiebe, 2002). Problem-focused coping is likely to be particularly effective because it can help people solve problems. For example, if you are feeling angry about your roommate's lack of help cleaning your apartment, directly talking with her about this issue could lead to her greater assistance. Similarly, one study found that while students who procrastinate experience less stress than other students early in the semester, by the end of the semester (when procrastinating is finally catching up with them), they experience greater stress and have more symptoms of illness (Tice & Baumeister, 1997). Students who directly handle their problems by keeping up with regular course reading and assignments thereby avoid the considerable stress faced at the end of the semester by those who have ignored these responsibilities. Problem-solving coping can effectively remove stressors, which in turn can lead to beneficial health outcomes, as described in Box 4.3: Focus on Research.

More evidence for the role of resources in predicting how someone manages stress comes from work showing a link between low socioeconomic status (SES) and poor health outcomes. Specifically, considerable research reveals that individuals who are low in SES experience more negative health outcomes, including higher rates of cardiovascular disease, diabetes, arthritis, and cancer as well as higher overall mortality rates (Gallo & Matthews, 2003; Matthews, Raikkonen, Gallo, & Kuller, 2008). The link between low SES and poor health can be explained in part due to health behaviors and access to health care—in other words, people who are low in SES tend to have poorer health habits and less access to health care. However, these other factors do not fully explain this association: The association between low SES and negative health outcomes exists even when researchers take into account the frequency of specific health behaviors (Lantz et al., 1998) as well as in countries with nationally funded health care programs (Adler, Boyce, Chesney, Folkman, & Syme, 1993). According to the reserve capacity model, people with low SES experience more frequent stressful situations—by living in more crowded, noisy, and dangerous environments—and have a smaller supply of resources—tangible, interpersonal, intrapersonal—to manage stressful events. For example, people who are low in SES may be less able to borrow money for emergencies, less able to rely on stable friendship networks, and not have jobs with flexibility in work schedules. In line with this view, people who are low in SES show lower levels of optimism, self-esteem, and social support, which are associated with worse health outcomes (Matthews et al., 2008). People who are low in SES also have more difficulty quitting smoking, in part because they live in more stressful environments and receive lower levels of social support (Businelle et al., 2010). Interestingly,

Box 4.3

Focus on Research: The Influence of Problem-Focused Coping on Health

Researchers in one study examined coping styles in students as they started medical school, a typically very stressful experience, and then assessed both mental and physical health at the end of their first year (Park & Adler, 2003). Participants completed measures assessing use of both problem-focused and emotion-focused coping, depression, and health in the month prior to the start of medical school. Researchers then examined students' health at the end of the first year to assess whether the use of particular types of coping strategies was associated with particular health outcomes. Although all students showed declines in both physical and mental health over the year, presumably as a result of the chronic stress of medical school, students who used greater positive reappraisal and planful problem-solving showed less of a deterioration in physical health. This research reveals that students who use particular types of coping strategies to handle the major, and ongoing, stress of the first year of medical school experience better physical well-being.

One explanation for the link between lower socioeconomic status and poor health is that people with fewer financial resources experience greater day-to-day stress in their environments.
Source: Denis Tangney Jr/Getty Images.

even feeling low in SES—regardless of the objective SES status—is associated with worse health, including greater likelihood of becoming infected with a cold (Cohen et al., 2008).

In some cases, however, the stress can't simply be removed or eliminated, meaning that problem-focused coping can't be used to manage stress. In these cases, changing how you think about the stress can be helpful in reducing its negative effects, which is a strategy called **emotion-focused coping** (Folkman & Lazarus, 1980; Lazarus & Folkman, 1984). This type of coping can involve either *avoidance coping*, meaning denying or avoiding the problem, or *approach coping*, meaning changing how one thinks about the problem or venting about the problem to others (seeking social support). For example, someone who has a fight with a close friend could simply try to put it out of his mind as a way of avoiding feeling sad or could discuss these feelings with another person to try to make sense of the sadness.

Emotion-focused coping is often associated with negative adjustment, in part because denying or avoiding thinking about problems can actually lead to negative psychological and physical well-being (Aldwin & Revenson, 1987; Carver et al., 1993; Kelley, Lumley, & Leisen, 1997; King & Miner, 2000; Penley et al., 2002). Simply avoiding thinking about a traumatic event prevents individuals from understanding and ultimately coming to terms with the experience (Pennebaker, 1989; Wegner, 1994). One study of breast-cancer patients found that those who reported bottling up emotions instead of expressing them were more likely to experience depression and anxiety (Classen, Koopman, Angell, & Speigel, 1996). Similarly, a study by Cole, Kemeny, Taylor, Visscher, & Fahey (1996) found that among gay men who were HIV positive, those who were "in the closet" had a more rapid spread of infection—and faster death—than those who were open about their sexual orientation. The use of denial or distraction can even lead people to delay seeking medical care in response to various health symptoms, as discussed in Chapter 12. Second, deliberately trying to avoid thinking about negative events is very difficult and thus requires considerable effort (Pennebaker, 1989). Have you ever tried to *not* think about something (an ex-girlfriend, a particularly gruesome scene from a movie, a failed test) and then found that thoughts about this "forbidden" topic dominate your mind? Research by Wegner, Shortt, Blake, and Page (1990) at the University of Virginia reveals that asking people to *not* think of something can actually lead them to become preoccupied with the event. Finally, because constantly exerting effort to avoid thinking about something upsetting leads to chronic physiological arousal, relying on this coping strategy can lead to decreases in immune cell activity as well as higher blood pressure and heart rate (Petrie, Booth, & Pennebaker, 1998; Pennebaker, Hughes, & O'Heeron, 1987). For example, James Gross and Robert Levenson (1997) found that women who watched sad films and were asked to conceal their feelings while watching showed a greater cardiovascular reaction than those who were allowed to openly express their feelings.

Questioning the Research 4.3

The study by Steve Cole et al. (1996) suggests that HIV-positive gay men who are open about their sexual orientation experience better health and even live longer. But can you think of some alternative explanations for this finding?

However, avoidance coping, such as trying to withdraw from the situation and focusing on other things to take your mind off it, can be adaptive for short-term stressors (Roth & Cohen, 1986; Suls & Fletcher, 1985). In the case of short-term stressors, such as an anxiety-provoking job interview, distracting oneself can be effective. However, most work suggests that in the case of longer-term and more severe stresses, avoidance coping can be detrimental (Stanton et al., 1993). For example, women who have breast cancer and rely on avoidance coping prior to their surgery show higher levels of negative effect after their surgery than those who use other coping strategies. In this case, emotion-focused strategies such as wishful thinking (e.g., "hoped a miracle would happen") are detrimental, perhaps because their use interferes with effective cognitive processing and problem solving directed toward those decisions and/or requires significant cognitive energy, which in turn can even lead to more intensive (and intrusive) thoughts (e.g., Wegner et al., 1990).

On the other hand, approach coping, meaning changing how one thinks about a problem, can help reduce the negative effects of stress (Lazarus & Folkman, 1984). The use of *positive reappraisal*, meaning finding some beneficial aspects of even negative events, can even be effective for people who are coping with the considerable stress of managing a chronic disease (as described in Chapter 12, reappraisal is a useful way of coping with emotions in general). For example, HIV-positive men who see some positive aspects of their diagnosis, such as shifting their values and priorities, show a slower rate of progression of the disease and survive longer (Thompson, Nanni, & Levine, 1994). Researchers in one study examined whether HIV-positive men who had lost a partner or close friend were able to find some meaning in that loss, such as showing a shift in values, priorities, or perspective (Bower, Kemeny, Taylor, & Fahey, 1998). As predicted, men who found meaning showed less rapid declines in T-cell levels and lower rates of AIDS-related mortality at the 2- to 3-year follow-up, even controlling for health status at baseline, health behaviors, and other potential confounding variables. Although one possibility is that men who were in better health were more likely to see meaning in their illness than those who were in worse health at the initial baseline, this research controlled for men's baseline health, meaning they included or took into account initial health for all men when predicting later health. This approach puts greater confidence in the causal link between finding meaning and better health outcomes. These results suggest that responding in a positive way to stressful events may be associated with better immune response, which leads to better physical well-being.

Interestingly, some research suggests that simply affirming another part of one's identity can reduce stress. Researchers in one study randomly assigned participants to either a self-affirmation condition—in which they wrote about values that were important to them—or a control condition—in which they wrote about values that were not particularly important to them (Creswell et al., 2005). Next, participants completed various stressful tasks, such as giving a 5-minute speech and counting backwards by 13 from 2,083. As predicted, participants in the control condition showed significantly greater increases in cortisol—a measure of stress—than those in the self-affirmation condition. Similarly, and as shown in Figure 4.8, self-affirmation can reduce the stress of midterm exams, thereby leading to lower levels of epinephrine. The benefits of self-affirmation for reducing stress, and thereby improving health, may help explain why employed men and employed women have similar levels of illnesses, whereas women who are homemakers experience higher levels of illnesses (Weidner, Boughal, Connor, Pieper, & Mendell, 1997). Employed women also show lower levels of cholesterol than homemakers. Why do women benefit from having multiple roles? Negative experiences in one domain can be buffered by experiencing positive effects in another—days in which work projects aren't going well may be improved by spending quality time with one's family, and days full of family-related stress may be improved by accomplishing valued projects at work. In sum, for women, being employed outside the home may help buffer the effects of stressful conditions in the home, and vice versa.

On the other hand, people who have negative expectations about their illness or disease, meaning they have accepted their worsening condition and eventual death, show worse physical health—even in cases in which such expectations are realistic (Byrnes et al., 1998; Segerstrom, Taylor, Kemeny, Reed, & Visscher, 1996). In one study, researchers examined negative HIV-related expectancies in HIV-positive men, including an acceptance of their diagnosis, an awareness of the likely disease progression, and an acknowledgement that they lacked control over the disease outcome (Reed, Kemeny, Taylor, & Visscher, 1999). Follow-ups with these men over $2\frac{1}{2}$ to $3\frac{1}{2}$ years revealed that these negative expectancies about their HIV infection were associated with greater development of HIV-related symptoms (e.g., diarrhea, weight loss, high fever, night sweats), even controlling for immune measures, drug adherence, substance use, and depression. Most importantly, HIV-positive people who have accepted their condition die on average 9 months sooner than those who resist the fatality of their diagnosis—providing powerful evidence that one's attitude after receiving a diagnosis of a terminal disease influences life expectancy (Reed, Kemeny, Taylor, Wang, & Visscher, 1994).

Some of the strongest evidence for the benefits of emotion-focused coping, and in particular, even thinking about or reflecting on one's problems, comes from research on writing about emotional experiences (Campbell & Pennebaker, 2003; Langens & Schuler, 2007; Low, Stanton, & Danoff-Burg, 2006; Pennebaker & Beale, 1986; Sheese, Brown, & Graziano, 2004; Smyth, 1998). Although writing

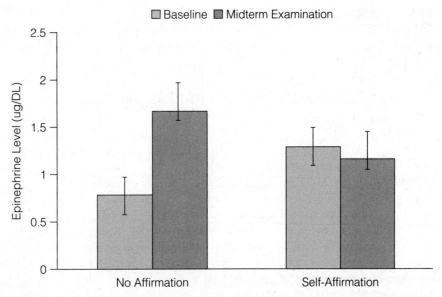

FIGURE 4.8 In this study, researchers randomly assigned students to either a self-affirmation condition—in which they wrote essays on 2 separate days about a value that was important to them and why—or a control condition—in which they wrote essays on two separate days about a value that was not important to them but was important to other students and why. Researchers measured epinephrine levels 2 weeks prior to midterms and then again during exam period. As shown in this figure, students in the self-affirmation condition did not experience the rise in epinephrine levels during exam period seen in students in the control condition (data from Sherman, Bunyan, Creswell, & Jaremka, 2009).

about traumatic events can initially lead to larger increases in blood pressure and more negative moods, individuals who write about such events show signs of better health later on, including fewer illnesses and minor health problems (e.g., headaches, acne, diarrhea). For example, and as described in Chapter 1, breast-cancer patients who write about their deepest thoughts and feelings regarding breast cancer report significantly fewer physical symptoms three months later (Stanton et al., 2002). Similarly, HIV-positive people who write about traumatic events show lower levels of the HIV virus in their blood than those who write about their activities over the past 24 hours (Petrie, Fontanilla, Thomas, Booth, & Pennebaker, 2004), and people with chronic illnesses who write about their deepest thoughts and feelings about the more stressful event they had ever undergone show better health later on than those who wrote about their plans for the day (Smyth, Stone, Hurewitz, & Kaell, 1999). Importantly, this type of written expression of emotion is especially beneficial for people who don't have supportive environments in which to confide feelings (Pennebaker & O'Heeron, 1984; Zakowski, Ramati, Morton, Johnson, & Flanigan, 2004). However, and as described in Box 4.4: Focus on Culture, the benefits of writing about one's problems may not be seen in all cultures.

Other researchers believe that both problem-focused and emotion-focused coping can be effective, depending on the situation (Forsythe & Compas, 1987; Terry & Hynes, 1998). Specifically, while problem-focused coping is very effective

Box 4.4

Focus on Culture: Writing About Problems Helps Some People But Not All

Although considerable research points to the benefits of expressive writing for health, a recent study suggests that these benefits may not be seen across all cultures. In this research, Knowles, Wearing, and Campos (2011) randomly assigned White and Asian American participants to write about their worst traumas or trivial topics over a 4-day period. They assessed physical symptoms before the writing exercise and again 1 month after the writing sessions. The researchers found that Whites who wrote about trauma reported fewer illness and depression symptoms in the second assessment, whereas these benefits were not experienced by the Asian American group. These findings suggest that people from collectivistic cultures, who focus on maintaining harmonious and cohesive relationships, may have learned to not burden others with their problems. Instead, people from collectivistic cultures may choose nonverbal measures of relieving stress. Interestingly, several such methods—yoga, tai chi, and meditation—all have origins in Asian societies. These findings indicate that the benefits of expressive writing may in fact depend on one's culture: This approach to stress reduction has health benefits for European Americans but not for Asian Americans.

in the case of stressors that you can change by actively confronting them, in cases in which you have no opportunity for improving the situation, the use of problem-focused coping may lead to feelings of frustration and disappointment (Roth & Cohen, 1986). For example, if you are struggling to come to terms with your parents' divorce, trying to use problem-focused coping will be ineffective because this situation is out of your control—you aren't going to be able to fix the problems in their relationship. On the other hand, while emotion-focused coping can be detrimental if you simply refuse to try to fix a manageable problem, this approach may be very effective when there is little that can be done to change a negative situation (Terry & Hynes, 1998). For example, emotion-focused coping is most effective in dealing with failed in vitro fertilization attempts, a situation over which couples have virtually no control. In sum, the type of coping people use must match the type of situation they are coping with for them to experience the greatest benefits. People who cope with events using the "right" type of strategy experience fewer symptoms of anxiety and depression, and subjects who cope using the "wrong" type of strategy experience more symptoms (Forsythe & Compas, 1987). In sum, because different types of situations call for different types of coping, individuals who are comfortable using a number of different coping styles have a higher likelihood of minimizing their stress in a variety of challenging situations. For example, you may need to use problem-focused coping when trying to constructively resolve a conflict with your dating partner, but you must use emotion-focused coping if your efforts to solve the problem fail, and the relationship ultimately ends.

Relaxation and Mindfulness

Yet another approach to managing stress is to change one's physiological responses to stress, which in turn can reduce its harmful effects on physical health. The *relaxation response* is a coordinated set of physiological changes that support rest and restoration, which are characterized by greater activation of the parasympathetic nervous system, leading to lower heart rate, blood pressure, and breathing rate. There are many strategies for activating the relaxation response, including imagery, hypnosis, and progressive muscle relaxation.

Progressive muscle relaxation can be an effective strategy for managing stress. In this technique, people focus on consciously tensing and then releasing each part of their body (hands, shoulders, legs, etc.) one at a time (Jacobson, 1938). This helps patients learn to distinguish states of tension from states of relaxation, thereby helping them learn how to calm themselves down in virtually any stressful situation. Progressive muscle relaxation can also be paired with *systematic desensitization*, an approach that helps people build up tolerance to a particular stressful object or event. In this technique, the person is asked to describe the specific causes of his or her anxiety and then to create a hierarchy of different stimuli associated with that anxiety. As shown in Table 4.5, these fears are ranked so that relatively low-anxiety-causing stimuli fall at the bottom of the hierarchy, and higher-anxiety-provoking stimuli set at the top of the hierarchy. The therapist then asks the patient to focus on the least-anxiety-provoking image, while encouraging the person to relax. Whenever the patient experiences anxiety, the therapist asks him or her to focus on a less-stressful stimulus. Gradually, as the patient is able to think about a low-level stimulus without feeling anxiety, the therapist continues to higher-level (more anxiety-provoking) stimuli; this process, over time, enables people to build up their tolerance to the stressful situation.

The technique of biofeedback also helps people distinguish between states of tension and relaxation but with a particular focus on how these psychological states influence their physiological reactions. Patients are attached to a monitor that shows their physiological response (heart rate, muscle tension, sweat), and they are able to learn how their thoughts and feelings influence their physiological reactions. This

TABLE 4.5   *Sample Desensitization Hierarchy for Coping With Fear of Injected Shots*

1. You are reading a magazine, and there is a photograph of someone getting a shot.
2. You are watching a television show or movie in which someone gets a shot.
3. You receive a letter from your college stating that before you return in the fall, you must have a tetanus vaccine.
4. You call the health center to make an appointment for your vaccination.
5. You leave your room on the morning of your appointment.
6. You park at the health center.
7. You sit in the line to receive your shot.
8. Your name is called by the nurse.
9. You sit in the room as the nurse wipes your arm with alcohol.
10. You watch the nurse approach with the needle.

technique is also an effective way to help people learn strategies of decreasing stress as well as the impact of stress on their physical reactions. Other relaxation strategies that are effective in decreasing physiological arousal in response to stressful situations include meditation, hypnosis, and yoga.

All of these relaxation techniques can work to reduce the negative effects of stress on psychological and physical health. For example, high school students who learn progressive muscle relaxation during their regular health class show a decrease in blood pressure (Ewart et al., 1987); medical students who are trained in relaxation techniques have better immune system functioning during exams (Kiecolt-Glaser & Glaser, 1986); people who receive a massage show higher levels of neuroendocrine and immune functioning (Rapaport, Schettler, & Bresee, 2010); and patients who are trained in biofeedback show a reduction in their symptoms associated with irritable bowel syndrome (IBS), a gastrointestinal disorder often linked to stress. Adolescents who receive training in meditation show decreases in blood pressure and heart rate compared to those who receive only health education (Barnes, Treiber, & Davis, 2001). Finally, some research suggests that training patients with severe coronary heart disease in relaxation techniques, such as meditation, can lead to a reversal in the amount of arteriosclerosis present (Ornish et al., 1998).

It feels good to relax, and it's easy to understand how relaxation—a kind of escape from real or imagined stressors—might undo the physiological and psychological symptoms of stress. The benefits are perhaps more surprising, though, when we consider the effects of simply paying attention to our thoughts, or *mindfulness*. As shown in Table 4.6, mindfulness can be described as a state of concentrated awareness in terms of what is happening in the present moment (Brown & Ryan, 2003). It consists of simply paying attention to ongoing events

Meditation, and other strategies of relaxation, can have beneficial effects on health.
Source: © Nadya Lukic/iStockphoto.

TABLE 4.6 *Test Yourself: Mindfulness Scale*

The following statements are about your everyday experience. Please indicate how frequently or infrequently you currently have each experience (1 = almost always to 6 = almost never).

1. I find it difficult to stay focused on what's happening in the present.
2. I tend to walk quickly to get where I'm going without paying attention to what I experience along the way.
3. It seems I am "running on automatic," without much awareness of what I'm doing.
4. I rush through activities without being really attentive to them.
5. I do jobs or tasks automatically, without being aware of what I'm doing.
6. I find myself listening to someone with one ear and doing something else at the same time.
7. I drive places on "automatic pilot" and then wonder why I went there.
8. I find myself doing things without paying attention.

This scale measures mindfulness, meaning how able you are to show concentrated awareness of and attention to ongoing events.

Source: Brown & Ryan, 2003.

and experiences, and thereby avoiding letting one's mind become preoccupied with other thoughts or concerns. So, while talking with a friend, you would focus intensely on this interaction, and not allow yourself to think about what you will do later on or how stressful your day has been. Training in various approaches for increasing mindfulness include meditation, breathing practices, body awareness, yoga, and tai chi.

Considerable research demonstrates that mindfulness can help reduce the harmful effects of stress on physical health. In one study, researchers examined the effectiveness of an 8-week mindfulness-based stress-reduction intervention on immune function in women recently diagnosed with breast cancer (Witek-Janusek et al., 2008). Over time, women in the mindfulness group showed increases in immune system response, such as greater NK cell activity, whereas women who were not in this group exhibited continued reductions.

How exactly does mindfulness lead to better health? More research is still needed to answer this important question (Bishop, 2002). One explanation is that receiving training in mindfulness leads to various psychological benefits, such as increased self-efficacy or social support, which in turn have beneficial effects on physical health. Another explanation is that mindfulness is simply a way of creating relaxation. Future research is needed to examine whether the beneficial effects of mindfulness training are actually due to some type of altered "mindful" consciousness.

Humor

Interestingly, having a sense of humor can lead to better physical health. In a series of studies at the University of Waterloo, Herbert Lefcourt has shown that after watching various funny videotapes, students show improvements in how well their immune system functions, including producing higher levels of NK cells and lower levels of cortisol (Lefcourt, Davidson-Katz, & Kueneman, 1990). Using humor as a coping mechanism is also associated with lower blood pressure (Lefcourt, Davidson, Prkachin, & Mills, 1997). The reason is, humor may help people cope with stressors by distracting them from their problems. For example, one study found that patients who joked and laughed prior to dental surgery experienced less anxiety during the procedure (Trice & Price-Greathouse, 1986). As Dan Shapiro (2001), a clinical psychologist and author, says, "We all have a choice as to how to respond to stressful situations. Take losing one's luggage. We can respond with humor: 'Has my luggage gone somewhere interesting? Is it having a good time?' or we can take it as a calamity."

Exercise

Another technique for coping with stressful events is exercise. Exercise improves mood and reduces anxiety and depression (McCann & Holmes, 1984). Exercise also reduces the effect of stress on cardiovascular responses, including heart rate and blood pressure, meaning that people who engage in regular exercise may experience fewer negative physiological effects of stress than those who do not regularly exercise (Forcier et al., 2006). Not surprisingly, people who exercise more frequently report fewer illnesses (Roth, Wiebe, Fillingim, & Shay, 1990). One study by Jonathon Brown (1991) examined the association between physical fitness, stress, and the number of visits to the campus health center. Students who were high in stress and low in physical fitness made the most visits, whereas those who were high in stress but also high in fitness made as few visits as those under low stress. Similarly, at the beginning of the chapter, you read how Chandler managed his job stress by swimming every day after work. So, the next time you are feeling blue, think about going for a jog—or a brisk walk— even if the thought of jogging is stressful!

Social Support

Another factor that can help people manage stress is social support. People who have support from friends and family may have more resources to cope with stressful events and may therefore see these events as less problematic. For example, if you are studying for a very important exam, your roommate's offer to bring you dinner in your room or quiz you on class material might be particularly helpful. (We discuss in detail the very important role of social support in managing stress and thereby predicting health in the next chapter).

Religion

Religion plays a very important role in the lives of many people. More than 90% of American adults consider themselves to be a part of a formal religious tradition (Kosmin & Lachman, 1993), and almost 96% believe in God or some other type of universal spirit (Becker, 2001). More than half of Americans report that prayer is an important part of their daily life, and women, African Americans, older people, and those with lower income are particularly likely to see prayer as an important coping mechanism (Princeton Religious Research Center, 1990). Although some people distinguish between *religiosity*—a formal link to religious organizations—and *spirituality*—a personal orientation toward religious beliefs—most people see these two concepts as similar (George, Larson, Koenig, & McCullough, 2000; Miller & Thoresen, 2004).

Many Americans report praying as a way of coping with stressful life events.
Source: Bob Daemmrich/The Image Works.

In turn, people who are involved in religion experience better psychological and physical health (see Table 4.7; Bergin, Masters, & Richards, 1987; Koenig, McCullough, & Larson, 2001; McFadden, 1995; Nicholson, Rose, & Bobak, 2010). For example, among those people who are caregivers for people with Alzheimer's disease or cancer (a potentially very stressful situation), those who have strong religious beliefs are less likely to experience depression (Rabins, Fitting, Eastham, & Zabora, 1990). Also, religious involvement, such as attending religious services and holding strong religious beliefs, is associated with lower levels of cancer, heart disease, stroke, and suicide (Levin, 1994; McCullough, Hoyt, Larson, Koenig, & Thoresen, 2000). People with stronger religious beliefs also have fewer complications and shorter hospital stays following heart surgery (Contrada et al., 2004).

This link between finding meaning and better health may help explain why people who have a strong religious faith have a longer life expectancy (George, Ellison, & Larson, 2002; McCullough et al., 2000). Researchers in one study examined the frequency of attending religious services in a large sample of healthy older adults, and then calculated the percent of people who had died at a 6-year follow-up (Lutgendorf, Russell, Ullrich, Harris, & Wallace, 2004). As shown in

TABLE 4.7   *The Use of Religion to Cope With Traumatic Events*

"After the flight attendant explained emergency landing procedures, we were left with our thoughts. That's when I began praying. I closed my eyes and thought, 'Dear Lord, I pray that you'll guide the pilot's hands.' I also thought that if God wanted to take my life, that it was okay with me. I was full of peace. Here I was sitting on the edge of eternity. I wasn't facing the end of my life."

"The plane smelled like a house after a fire. I was exhilarated to be alive but deeply grieved when I could see and smell death. It was like being at the doorstep of hell. I pulled my Bible out of my bag. That's all I wanted."

"I did what I needed to do to prepare to die. My thought at the time was that I wanted to be reborn into a family where I would be able to hear the teachings of Buddha. I'd done a lot of Buddhist meditation in my life, and this trained me to become one-pointed in my awareness. I was totally focused on the brace position."

These quotes are from survivors of United Flight 232, which made a crash landing in a field in Iowa on its way from Denver to Chicago on July 19, 1989. As you can see, many passengers thought about their religious beliefs during this traumatic event.

Source: Pargament, 1997.

Figure 4.9, only 14.5% of people who attended religious services regularly had died, compared to 34.4% of those who never attended religious services. Finally, and most important, religious involvement is associated with lower rates of mortality (Oxman, Freeman, & Manheimer, 1995). For example, one study with 232 patients who had open-heart surgery found that those who experienced strength and comfort from their religious beliefs were less likely to die in the 6 months following surgery.

What leads to this association between religious and/or spiritual beliefs and greater physical health (Koenig et al., 2001; Plante & Sherman, 2001; Seybold & Hill, 2001)? One explanation is that many religions directly encourage healthy behaviors, such as abstaining from smoking, alcohol/drug use, and risky sexual behaviors, which in turn leads to greater physical well-being (Gorsuch, 1995). The Mormon, Muslim, and Southern Baptist religions, for example, forbid the use of alcohol. In turn, one recent study revealed that the association between church attendance and better physical health is at least partially a function of the lower rates of substances abuse seen in those who attend church regularly (Koenig & Vaillant, 2009). Women who regularly attend religious services are also more likely to get regular mammograms and Pap smears, and to perform breast self-exam (Benjamins, 2006). Similarly, and as described at the beginning of the chapter, Elizabeth has strong religious beliefs and shows a high level of adherence to her diabetes care regimen, which helps her stay in good health. However, many of these studies control for, meaning they take into account, people's other health behaviors and still find an association between religion and health.

Another possibility is that substantial social support is provided within many religious communities, which in turn leads to greater health (and we'll talk more about the benefits of social support in the next chapter). People who are religious may have stronger and more extensive social networks. As we discuss in Chapter 5, people who are religious may belong to a church, temple, or other organization that brings them together on a regular basis with others who share their general views. One study found that 41% of community members reported they would use their clergy for help with personal problems (Pergament, 1997). In line with the view about the importance of social support, frequency of attendance at religious

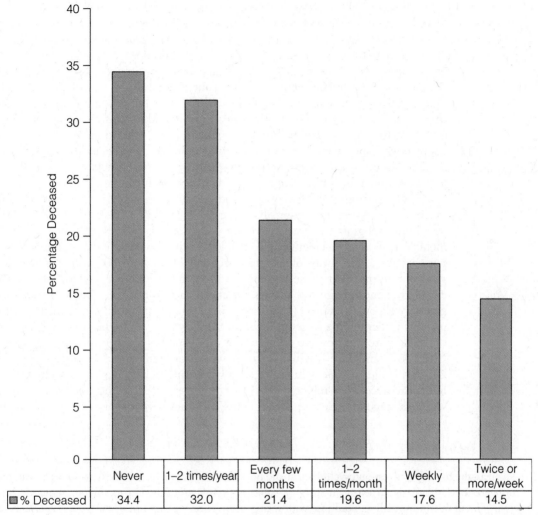

% Deceased	Never	1–2 times/year	Every few months	1–2 times/month	Weekly	Twice or more/week
% Deceased	34.4	32.0	21.4	19.6	17.6	14.5

Frequency of Religious Attendance

FIGURE 4.9 People who attend religious services more frequently show lower mortality rates, even when researchers take into account other factors that might explain this association (such as sex, social support, health behaviors, and depression) (data from Lutgendorf et al., 2004).

services is positively associated with health, whereas frequency of prayer is negatively associated with health (Nicholson et al., 2010).

Questioning the Research 4.4

The Nicholson et al. (2010) study found that attending religious services more frequently was associated with better health, whereas praying more frequently was associated with worse health. Why would these two distinct measures of religiosity be associated with health in such different ways?

A third possibility is that religion gives people a sense of meaning, which may in and of itself have beneficial effects on health (Emmons, 2005; Silberman, 2005). In one study, researchers examined changes in spirituality/religiousness following diagnosis of HIV and disease progression (as measured by T-cells and level of HIV in the blood every 6 months) over 4 years (Ironson, Stuetzle, & Fletcher, 2006). People who reported an increase in spirituality/religiousness after the diagnosis had significantly higher levels of T-cells over the 4-year period, and these results held true even after controlling for other measures (including church attendance, initial disease status, use of medication, age, gender, race, education, health behaviors, depression, hopelessness, optimism, coping strategies, and social support). In sum, these findings suggest that an increase in spirituality/religiousness, a type of emotion-focused coping, after HIV diagnosis predicts slower disease progression.

Religious commitment may also lead people to rely on more adaptive coping mechanisms (Ai, Park, Huang, Rodgers, & Tice, 2007; Pargament, 1997). Many people use religion as a way of coping with potentially stressful events, including medical problems, accidents, and problems with loved ones (Pargament, 1997). For example, one study of parents who had lost a baby to sudden infant death syndrome found that those parents who felt that religion was important to them engaged in more cognitive processing about the experience, which in turn led to greater well-being later on (McIntosh, Silver, & Wortman, 1993). Similarly, among patients undergoing a heart procedure, those who were higher in religiosity were more likely to use positive religious coping—such as seeking spiritual support and God's love and care—which in turn was associated with less distress (Ai et al., 2007). Finally, people who have strong spiritual beliefs may benefit in terms of health because their religion provides some type of meaning for even seemingly senseless tragedies. Seeing the benefits of a negative experience gives people a

TABLE 4.8   *Information YOU Can Use*

- Given all the hazards of stress on psychological and physical well-being, one of the best ways you can promote good health is to avoid stress whenever possible. So, think about the impact of your choices—the environment in which you live, your job, your relationships—on the amount of stress you experience, and try to make choices that reduce the amount of stress in your life.
- Everyone experiences some stress, but people vary considerably in how they appraise or think about particular events. You have a choice about how to interpret and experience particular events in your life, and, whenever possible, appraise events you experience as exciting challenges and not distressing stressors.
- Many of the negative effects of stress on health occur at least in part because people often fail to take care of themselves during periods of stress. Thus, during times of stress, take care of yourself—eat healthy foods, get enough sleep, maintain your exercise routine, and avoid adopting bad habits such as smoking and alcohol use.
- Think about how you choose to cope with stressful events in your life, and make sure you are using effective strategies for managing the particular situation you are in. For situations you can fix, problem-focused coping is probably the best bet, but for situations that are not solvable, emotion-focused coping can be most effective.
- Because everyone experiences some stress, it is essential that you figure out how best to cope with that stress. Think about what approaches help you manage stress, such as exercising, relaxing, social support, laughing, or religious beliefs, and try to adopt one or more of those strategies when you are experiencing stress.

chance to confront and cope with thoughts and feelings about the trauma but with a focus on its positive aspects, which can lead to greater psychological and physical well-being.

Although religiosity and spirituality are generally associated with good health, they also can have some drawbacks (Koenig et al., 2001). Some religions, such as Jehovah's Witnesses and Christian Scientists, forbid some types of medical care, including blood transfusions and immunizations. For example, Jehovah's Witnesses believe that there is no distinction in God's eyes between having a blood transfusion and drinking someone else's blood, and therefore anyone who receives a transfusion will be "turned away" from eternal salvation. People with strong religious beliefs may also delay seeking medical care or refuse life-saving medications and procedures because they believe prayer and other religious methods of managing illnesses will lead to positive outcomes. In line with this view, one study published in the *Journal of the American Medical Association* demonstrated that one reason why more African American women die from breast cancer than White women is because some of their cultural beliefs lead them to delay seeking medical care (Lannin et al., 1998). For example, African American women are much more likely than White women to believe, "If a person prays about cancer, God will heal it without medical treatments." Religious coping strategies can also be detrimental when people rely on them alone, as opposed to using a broader range of strategies (Abernethy, Chang, Seidlitz, Evinger, & Duberstein, 2002). Spouses of lung cancer patients who use moderate levels of religious coping are less depressed than those who use either lower or higher levels. In sum, religious beliefs seem to have a beneficial effect on health only when these beliefs are used in conjunction with standard medical care, not as a replacement for such care, and in conjunction with other coping mechanisms.

Summary

1. In the field of health psychology, *stress* typically refers to either the experience of major events or the perception that one lacks the resources to cope with such events.

2. The main causes of stress are personal relationships, work pressures, environmental pressures, pressures within ourselves, and situations in which we lack control.

3. Stress can be assessed through self-report inventories or physiological measures (e.g., biochemically, arousal). Each of these approaches has both strengths and weaknesses.

4. The earliest model describing the link between stress and health was Cannon's fight-or-flight response, which stated that in response to a stressful situation, the body mobilizes its resources to either fight off that stressor or escape from it.

5. The General Adaption Syndrome model describes how the body reacts to stress over time. First, there is the alarm stage in which the body initially mobilizes to fight off a stressor. Next, there is the resistance stage, in which the body continues trying to respond to the threat. Finally, there is the stage of exhaustion, in which the body's resources are depleted and thus more susceptible to illness and disease.

6. These models have now been updated in various ways to reflect current research findings. These updates include taking into account the role of individuals' appraisal of the stressor, the role of gender in influencing how people respond to stress, the influence of the type of stress on the physiological reaction, and the impact of the duration of the stressor on the physiological response.

7. Stress can have physical consequences on many systems of the body, including the nervous system, the endocrine system, the cardiovascular system, and the immune system. These different body systems can also interact to influence health, as described by the field of psychoneuroimmunology.

8. Stress can also have indirect effects on health because people who are under stress are likely to engage in more unhealthy behaviors and fewer healthy ones.

9. Stress can also have psychological consequences, including cognitive problems, negative emotions, and behavioral problems.

10. People can manage stress through using different strategies for coping with stress, which in turn can lead to better health.

11. People use a variety of different coping styles for managing stress, including problem-focused coping, in which the person tries to confront and change the stressor, and emotion-focused coping, in which the person changes how he or she thinks about the stressor.

12. Changing one's physiological response to stress, such as through using relaxation and/or mindfulness, can reduce the experience of stress and its harmful effects.

13. Other strategies for coping with stress include humor, exercise, and social support.

14. Religion, including both religiosity and spirituality, is associated with better psychological and physical health. Religion may lead to better health because religion helps people find a sense of meaning in their lives, encourages healthier behaviors, provides a source of additional social support, and leads people to use more adaptive coping mechanisms.

Key Terms

alarm stage
allostatic response
cardiovascular system
central nervous system
coping
emotion-focused coping
endocrine system
exhaustion stage
fight-or-flight response

General Adaptation Syndrome (GAS)
hypothalamic-pituitary-adrenal (HPA) system
immune system
nervous system
neurons
neurotransmitters
peripheral nervous system
primary appraisal

problem-focused coping
psychoneuroimmunology
resistance stage
secondary appraisal
stress
sympathetic adrenomedullary (SAM) system
tend-and-befriend
transactional (relational) model

Thought Questions

1. Describe two different ways that you could measure stress and the advantages and disadvantages of each method.

2. Describe the three stages of Selye's General Adaptation Syndrome (GAS), and give two critiques of this model.

3. Describe the effects of stress on the cardiovascular, endocrine, and immune systems, using specific examples from research with humans and/or animals.

4. You have recently noticed that you develop some type of minor illness, such as a sore throat or a cold,

each time you take final exams at the end of the semester. What are three specific things you could do to decrease your likelihood of getting a cold during exam week this year?

5. Although people with strong religious beliefs generally experience better psychological and physical well-being, are there some cases in which such beliefs could be detrimental to health? Why or why not?

Answers to Questioning the Research

Answer 4.1. The link between job strain and cardio-vascular events may be explained in several distinct ways. One possibility is that people who are experiencing job strain work longer hours, and thus have more sustained periods of stress—which in turn leads to cardiovascular problems—than those without such strain. Another possibility is that people with particular personality types experience both more job strain and more cardiovascular events (you'll learn more about this possibility in the next chapter). Still another possibility is that people who experience health problems, including cardiovascular concerns, are less able to concentrate at work, and thus experience more job strain. In sum, remember that correlation does not necessarily mean causation.

Answer 4.2. Many studies of the effects of stress on health are based on studies of college students who are experiencing the stress of exams. However, these studies have some substantial limitations. First, exams are predictable—you know from the beginning of the semester that they are going to happen and even when they are going to happen, whereas the most stressful events people experience lack this type of forewarning, which probably makes them even more stressful. Moreover, while exams are clearly stressful, they are not particularly life-altering like some other stressors, including death of a family member, cancer diagnosis, or divorce. These studies also rely on self-report from the college students, so it is impossible to tell whether students are giving accurate information. Many people have the belief that students engage in less healthy behavior during exam periods, so it is possible that students report that their behavior is less healthy than it actually is during exam periods or that they report engaging in healthier behavior than they really do during other times of the semester. Finally, college students by and large are a very healthy population, so stressful events may not have as much of an impact on their health as they might on less healthy people, such as senior citizens and those with chronic illnesses.

Answer 4.3. Although this study found that HIV-positive gay men who were "in the closet" had a more rapid spread of infection and earlier death, the major limitation of this study is that it shows correlation as opposed to causation. One possibility is that men who are open about their sexual orientation are more likely to be in stable, long-term relationships than those who are trying to hide their orientation. Men who are in relationships may get assistance from their partners that directly benefits their health, including reminders to take their medication, provision of healthy meals, and much-needed social support. These factors could in turn lead to better health and longevity. Another possibility is that gay men who are open about their sexual orientation are more likely to acknowledge their own risk of acquiring HIV; hence, they seek more frequent HIV testing than those who are hiding their sexual orientation. It may be that gay men who are open about their orientation simply find out that they are HIV-positive sooner than those who are still in the closet. In other words, it may not be that gay men who are open live longer with HIV, but rather they live longer *knowing* they have HIV because they get tested more frequently. Finally, gay men who are hiding their sexual orientation may be less comfortable buying condoms or asking their partners to wear condoms than those who are open about their orientation. This higher rate of unprotected sex on the part of some men could therefore lead to more exposure to HIV and other STDs that could have negative health effects, thereby leading to more illness and rapid death.

Answer 4.4. The different association with health for frequency of attending religious services versus praying may be explained by differences in what these constructs really mean for the individual. Attending religious services may be a way of gaining social support because obviously such services include numerous other people. This type of support may facilitate health in numerous ways, including people offering assistance with cooking, reminding to take medication, or offering emotional support. In contrast, praying as a strategy may have fewer tangible benefits, and could be a sign of simply relying on wishful thinking instead of taking practical steps to improve a problem.

CHAPTER 5

Managing Stress: The Role of Personality and Social Support

Outline

- Sue, a junior in college, is outgoing, energetic, and sociable; in fact, she is often described by her friends as "the life of the party." She is also full of energy—Sue is the president of the Student Government Organization, an active member in a campus volunteer organization, and the captain of the women's soccer team. Even though she is very busy with her academic and extracurricular activities, Sue is almost always happy and upbeat. Like most college students, Sue occasionally develops a cold or sore throat, but these symptoms pass quickly and rarely cause any significant disruption in her activities.

- Cindy is 28 years old and is a "rising star" in the public relations firm where she works. Cindy is very efficient at her job, in part because she works very long hours and is constantly doing many things at one time (e.g., responding to e-mail messages while talking on the phone). She tends to skip lunch, or just picks up a hamburger at a drive-through, and typically sleeps no more than 6 hours a night. Cindy is very competitive with her coworkers and prides herself on billing more hours than anyone else at her level. Although she has never experienced any health problems (and in fact plays in several local tennis tournaments each summer), Cindy has recently started experiencing migraine headaches and has developed an ulcer.

- Miles is 52 years old and is consistently in a "bad mood." Although he is a partner in a large law firm, he is very nervous whenever he must appear in court and generally feels that his job is not going very well. Miles is not married and has few close friends, in part because his anxiety tends to make others around him nervous. He also suffers from a number of recurring physical problems, including back pain, fatigue, and general achiness.

- Jason, who is 48 years old, underwent coronary heart surgery last week. Although Jason was initially nervous about having this surgery, he talked to a number of people who had experienced the procedure and became confident that the surgery would go well. In fact, Jason typically approaches upcoming events with a positive attitude—he has a strong belief that "things work out for the best." Following his surgery, Jason received many visitors in the hospital and is making great progress in his recovery. He plans to return to work within a few weeks and has started taking short walks with his wife in the evening.

- Arturo is feeling anxious because he is in the middle of a difficult exam period at school. He is having trouble sleeping and has started having headaches several times a day. However, his parents sent him a care package containing fresh fruit, and Arturo's roommate has volunteered to substitute for him at his tutoring job this week to free up time for Arturo to study. Arturo now feels more confident that he can get through the exam period, and his headaches have already disappeared.

Preview

This chapter examines how people manage stress and, in particular, how personality and social support help people cope with stress. First, we will examine how various personality traits, meaning the individual differences in people's tendencies to think, feel, and act in particular ways, influence health behavior in both positive and negative ways, as well as different explanations for the personality–health link. We will then examine the link between health and social support, including different approaches to measuring social support, the impact of social support on psychological and physical well-being, and potential explanations for the social support–health link.

What Personality Factors Are Associated With Good Health?

As soon as you meet someone for the first time, you notice what they are like. Are they friendly, outgoing, and energetic, or are they anxious, withdrawn, and fearful? If I ask you to describe your closest friends or your siblings, you can probably list a number of these types of **personality** traits. But why do people differ so much in terms of their personalities, and where do these traits come from? According to personality psychologists, at least some personality traits are strongly influenced by heredity (Eysenck, 1967, 1990). This is why identical twins who are raised apart often show very clear similarities in their personalities, whereas children who are raised together but have no genes in common (e.g., adopted children) may show little or no resemblance in terms of personality to other members of their family. Researchers believe that people inherit variations in their body chemistry that influence how sensitive they are to different types of stimulation as well as the types of moods they generally experience (Diener, 2000; Izard, Libero, Putnam, & Haynes, 1993). For example, some people may be highly sensitive to stress (which can lead them to experience more negative affect or neuroticism), others may need a high level of stimulation (which can lead them to be higher in extraversion), and still others may crave order and routine (which can lead them to be high in conscientiousness). These traits are basic characteristics of the person that are relatively stable across situations and over time. These traits are formed by people's experiences in the world, not just their biology; hence, our personalities reflect the environment in which we were raised (Sarason, Sarason, & Gurung, 1997). This section examines how four personality factors are positively associated with psychological and physical well-being: positive states, optimism, conscientiousness, and sense of control/hardiness.

Positive States

As described in Chapter 1, a growing trend in psychology is to focus on positive emotions, such as happiness, joy, enthusiasm, and contentment (Seligman & Csikszentmihalyi, 2000). These **positive states** include extraversion (feelings of energy and sociability) and positive affect (Costa & McCrae, 1980, 1992; Eysenck, 1967).

Considerable research reveals that people who are high in positive emotions experience better psychological and physical well-being (Cohen, Doyle, Turner, Alper, & Skoner, 2003; Costa & McCrae, 1980; Martin et al., 1992; Pressman & Cohen, 2005). Compared to those who are low in positive affect, people who are high in positive affect are less likely to get the common cold or experience a stroke, and have fewer accidents. Extraverts also experience better physical well-being: They have lower rates of both major and minor illnesses, including asthma, arthritis, ulcers, and even coronary heart disease (CHD; Friedman & Booth-Kewley, 1987a). For example, one study with more than 1,000 men found that those who were high in extraversion reported fewer psychological and physical symptoms (Spiro, Aldwin, Levenson, & Bosse, 1990). As described at the beginning of this chapter, Sue is busy with her academic and extracurricular pursuits, but she manages to experience high levels of psychological and physical well-being. Box 5.1: Focus on Research describes how people who are high on positive affect are less likely to develop a cold.

Box 5.1

Focus on Research: Why Positive People Are Less Likely to Get a Cold

Researchers in this study were interested in examining whether personality traits, including positive affect, protected people from becoming sick (Cohen, Alper, Doyle, Treanor, & Turner, 2006). To test this question, they recruited 193 healthy volunteers and asked them to complete measures of both positive and negative emotional style as well as their overall health. Then, using nasal drops, the researchers exposed participants to a cold virus and then quarantined them for 5 or 6 days. Researchers examined symptoms of colds, including participants' ratings of their symptoms each day as well as mucus produced (by gathering and weighing used tissues from all participants). As predicted, participants who were higher on positive affect were less likely to develop cold symptoms as assessed through either self-reported symptoms or mucus production. This association remained even when researchers considered other variables that could help explain susceptibility to colds, including age, sex, education, race, body mass, and overall health. Thus, this research provides powerful evidence that our moods may influence our likelihood of becoming sick.

Positive states are also associated with greater life expectancy. One study of more than 2,000 women found that women who are higher on extraversion and positive affect live on average 2 to 3 years longer than those who are low on these measures (Terracciano, Löckenhoff, Zonderman, Ferrucci, & Costa, 2008). Similarly, and as described in Chapter 2, nuns who included more positive words in their diaries lived considerably longer than those who used fewer positive emotion words (Danner, Snowden, & Friesen, 2001). Positive affect is even associated with lower risk of mortality in patients with diabetes, which is a leading cause of death in the United States, even controlling for other factors linked to mortality (Moskowitz, Epel, & Acree, 2008).

However, and contrary to the impression you might get from folklore and popular psychology, research does not provide support for the hypothesis that you can heal yourself from serious disease simply by having a positive mind-set. Although some research suggests that positive affect is associated with longer survival in people who are HIV positive and people with breast cancer (Levy, Lee, Bagley, & Lippman, 1988; Moskowitz, 2003), most research finds no association between positive affect and longevity in patients with serious illness, presumably because emotions are likely to have no impact on survival for those who are far along in their illness progression.

Optimism

Many researchers have examined the role of **optimism**—the expectation that good things will happen in the future, and bad things will not—in predicting behavior (see Table 5.1; Peterson, 2000; Scheier & Carver, 1993). When you take a difficult exam, do you typically believe that you did well? If so, you are probably an optimist. On the other hand, if you tend to approach different situations expecting failure or disappointment, you are probably a pessimist. Other researchers have described optimism as people's sense of hope, including their focus on pursuing their goals as well as their expectations that their goals could be achieved (Snyder et al., 1996).

TABLE 5.1   *Test Yourself: The State Hope Scale*

Please answer each item below according to the following scale: 1 = *Definitely False*; 2 = *Mostly False*; 3 = *Somewhat False*; 4 = *Slightly False*; 5 = *Slightly True*; 6 = *Somewhat True*; 7 = *Mostly True*; and 8 = *Definitely True*.

1. If I should find myself in a jam, I could think of many ways to get out of it.
2. At the present time, I am energetically pursuing my goals.
3. There are lots of ways around any problem that I am facing now.
4. Right now I see myself as being pretty successful.
5. I can think of many ways to reach my current goals.
6. At this time, I am meeting the goals that I have set for myself.

Source: Higher scores indicate greater hope, meaning a greater belief in one's ability to reach desired goals (Snyder, Sympson, Ybasco, Borders, Babyak, & Higgins, 1996).

Findings consistently indicate that holding such beliefs is associated with psychological well-being (Scheier & Carver, 1993; Taylor et al., 1992). For example, women who are optimistic and high in self-esteem are less likely to experience postpartum depression (Carver & Gaines, 1987), HIV-positive men who are optimistic are less worried about developing AIDS (Taylor et al., 1992), and people who are optimistic are less depressed following unsuccessful attempts at in vitro fertilization (Litt, Tennen, Affleck, & Klock, 1992).

Although research clearly shows that positive states are correlated with better health, one problem with interpreting the results of some studies is that researchers don't actually know if these positive states cause better health, whether better health leads to positive states, or if a third variable explains both better health and positive states. However, longitudinal research studies, which assess optimism at one time and then symptoms later on, reveal the same general findings (Scheier & Carver, 1987). For example, Charles Carver et al. (1993) interviewed women with breast cancer to assess their optimism and negative feelings at the time of diagnosis and then again 1 day before surgery, 10 days after surgery, and at 3-, 6-, and 12-month follow-up visits. As predicted, optimism at the initial diagnosis was associated with lower distress levels at each of the following dates. Similarly, college students with a negative explanatory style during their first year are more likely to experience both major and minor depression during their junior year than those who had a positive explanatory style (Alloy, Abramson, & Francis, 1999). These studies instill some confidence that having a positive outlook does in fact lead to better health.

People who have a generally optimistic view about themselves and the world also experience better physical well-being (Kivimaki et al., 2005; Scheier & Carver, 1993). People who are optimistic report having fewer infectious illnesses (e.g., colds, sore throats, flu), and fewer physical symptoms (e.g., dizziness, blurred vision, fatigue, muscle soreness; Peterson & Seligman, 1987). Researchers in one study examined data from more than 1,000 medical records of patients seen at a large medical practice over a 2-year period (Richman et al., 2005). All patients were sent a questionnaire assessing hope, and then researchers examined rates of three diseases (hypertension, diabetes, and respiratory tract infections). Patients with higher rates of hope were less likely to have received a diagnosis for any of these diseases, suggesting that positive emotions may help protect against the development of a disease. Optimists also recover more quickly from surgery and are less likely to be rehospitalized after surgery (Fitzgerald, Tennen, Affleck, & Pransky, 1993; Scheier et al., 1989, 1999). As described at the beginning of the chapter, Jason's optimism helped him make a rapid recovery following coronary heart surgery. Finally, people who are optimistic even show better health in response to potentially life-threatening stresses. In one study, women with ovarian cancer completed measures of optimism before starting chemotherapy (de Moor et al., 2006). Women with higher levels of optimism at the start of chemotherapy showed a greater decline in a marker of cancer at the end of chemotherapy.

Most important, however, having an optimistic view of oneself and the world leads to a longer life. For example, one study examined how feeling hopeless was associated with health in a sample of nearly 2,500 middle-aged men (Everson, Goldberg, Kaplan, & Cohen, 1996). Men who were high in hopelessness were

People who are high in optimism experience better overall psychological and physical well-being, including showing faster recovery following surgery.
Source: © francisblack/iStockphoto.

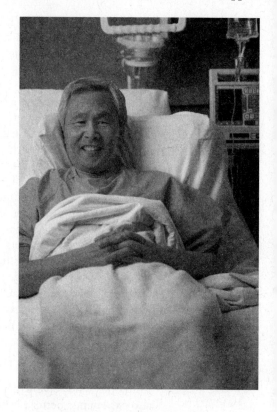

more than twice as likely to die from cancer and more than four times more likely to die from cardiovascular diseases than men who were low in hopelessness. Similarly, people who explain events in an optimistic way are less likely to die from accidental or violent causes than those without this beneficial explanatory style (Peterson, Seligman, & Vaillant, 1988). Optimism is even positively associated with life expectancy for those with very serious illnesses, including AIDS (Reed, Kemeny, Taylor, Wang, & Visscher, 1994), and cancer (Levy, Lee, Bagley, & Lippman, 1988; Schulz, Bookwala, Knapp, Scheier, & Williamson, 1996).

Although optimism is generally associated with better health, it can also have costs. Specifically, research by Neil Weinstein (1984, 1987) indicates that people who are unrealistically optimistic about their risk of various health problems may fail to protect themselves adequately from such problems. In fact, some research suggests that optimists have a higher mortality rate, perhaps because they are more careless about their health (Friedman et al., 1993; Martin et al., 2002). This is a case in which optimists' views that "it won't happen to me" can lead to risky health-related behavior, which can have serious consequences. Thus, it may be that while optimism in general is good for health, too much optimism can be bad for health. Relatedly, although optimism is generally beneficial for health, it can be associated with worse health in particularly difficult situations. Specifically, optimism is generally associated with stronger immunity, but under particularly demanding circumstances—such as when the stress continues over time—greater optimism is associated with lower levels of immune response (Segerstrom, 2006, 2007).

Conscientiousness

Conscientious people are hardworking, motivated, and persistent (Costa & McCrae, 1987). They show high levels of self-restraint (e.g., may write a term paper even when they'd rather be watching reality television) and focus intensely on their goals (e.g., may carefully choose summer internships that help them achieve their career ambitions). On the other hand, people who are low in conscientiousness are easygoing and somewhat disorganized; for example, they may have trouble deciding on a career path and meeting deadlines.

Considerable research indicates that conscientiousness is associated with better physical health and longevity (see Figure 5.1; Kern & Friedman, 2008; Martin, Friedman, & Schwartz, 2007; Terracciano et al., 2008). A meta-analysis, which combines the results of multiple studies, revealed that conscientiousness is negatively related to all risky health-related behaviors, including tobacco use, drugs, risky sex, violence, risky driving, and alcohol use, and positively associated with all health-promoting behaviors, including diet and exercise (Bogg & Roberts, 2004). Researchers in one study examined personality measures collected in more than 1,000 children in 1922 as well as follow-up data collected every few years through 1986 (Friedman et al., 1993). Findings indicated that conscientiousness was associated with better health over time. For example, a person in the top 25% on conscientiousness had only 77% of the risk of dying in a given year compared to someone in the bottom 25% on conscientiousness. Overall, children who were truthful, reliable, and hardworking tended to live about 2 years longer than those

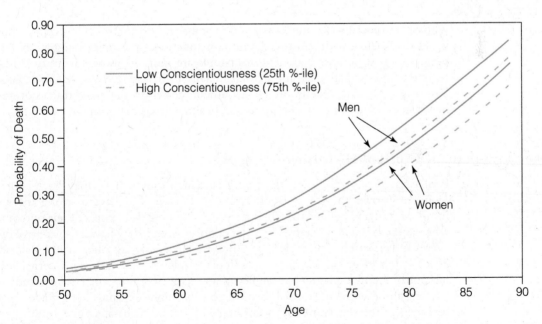

FIGURE 5.1 This study examined mortality rates in older adulthood as a function of conscientiousness. For both men and women, those in the top 25% of conscientiousness are less likely to die at a given age than those who are in the bottom 25% of conscientiousness (data from Martin, Friedman, & Schwartz, 2007).

Box 5.2

Focus on Development: The Powerful Influence of Childhood Personality on Adult Health-Related Behavior

Given the clear association between personality and patterns of general behavior at one point in time, researchers have also examined whether personality can predict patterns of health-related behavior over long periods of time. Researchers in one longitudinal study examined teachers' assessments of more than 2,000 elementary school children's personality traits (including conscientiousness, extraversion, agreeableness, openness/intellect, and emotional stability; Hampson, Goldberg, Vogt, & Dubanoski, 2006). For example, teachers were asked to indicate how a particular child ranked in terms of conscientiousness compared to their peers. Forty years later, researchers contacted these now-grown children and examined their rates of health-related behaviors. Findings indicated that childhood personality traits were associated with health later on, including all four health outcomes: smoking, alcohol use, body-mass index, and overall health. Interestingly, the link between personality in childhood and health in adulthood was stronger for women than for men. Specifically, conscientiousness was associated with less smoking and better self-related health for both men and women and was also associated with lower BMI for women. These findings provide strong evidence that childhood personality traits predict health behaviors, and in turn health outcomes, throughout one's life.

who were described as impulsive and lacking in self-control. Conscientiousness is also associated with improved immune function in people living with HIV, perhaps in part because conscientious people are more likely to adhere to medical regimens and use active coping styles (O'Cleirigh, Ironson, Weiss, & Costa, 2007). Similarly, Box 5.2: Focus on Development describes the powerful association between childhood personality traits and health-related behavior later on.

Internal Locus of Control/Hardiness

People vary considerably on the extent to which they believe they have control, or mastery, over their lives (Rotter, 1966). People who have a strong **internal locus of control** believe that their decisions and behaviors impact their outcomes, whereas those with an external locus of control believe they have little control over events and experiences in their lives (Abramson, Metalsky, & Alloy, 1989; Peterson, 2000; Peterson et al., 1998). For example, students who have an internal locus of control could explain a bad grade on an exam as due to not enough studying, whereas those with an external locus of control might explain such a grade on the trickiness of the test. Similarly, according to Suzanne Kobasa, a person most likely to stay healthy in the face of stress shows high **hardiness**, meaning a commitment to goals and activities, a sense of control over what happened to him or her, and a view of stressful events as challenging rather than threatening (Kobasa, Maddi, & Kahn, 1982). Such individuals are committed to their work and their families

TABLE 5.2   *Quotes From People Who Are High or Low in Hardiness*

High Hardiness

"I realize that setbacks are a part of the game. I've had 'em, I have them now, and I've got plenty more ahead of me. Seeing this—the big picture—puts it all in perspective, no matter how bad things get."

"I had a sense of peace inside that assured me that this loss would pass just as all of life passes.... At the funeral, I knelt in front of him and the same peace came over me. The next day I was out back chopping wood, just as three generations of family had done on this land before me."

"The key to dealing with loss is not obvious. One must take the problem, the void, the loneliness, the sorrow, and put it on the back of your neck and use it as a driving force. Don't let such problems sit out there in front of you, blocking your vision.... Use hardships in a positive way."

Low Hardiness

"I was certain I would die on the table...never wake up.... I felt sure it was the end. Then I woke up with a colostomy and figured I would have to stay inside the house the rest of my life. Now I'm afraid to go back to the doctor's and keep putting off my checkups."

"I was apprehensive all the time—he was sick for years and each day that I got out of bed, I was thinking that he was going to die. It was always in the back of my mind, always. Another fear I have is of falling. Therefore, I never go anywhere for fear I'll fall in a strange place."

"I have arthritis and every day I feel stiffer than the day before. Simple jobs around the house look so big to me and I feel fatigued oftentimes before I begin them. Sometimes I stay in bed for much longer than I should and get up feeling worse. I worry too much.... Life has never been a rose garden."

Note: These quotes illustrate differences in how people who are high in hardiness think about the potentially stressful events of their lives compared to those low in hardiness.

Source: Colerick, 1985.

and believe that what they do is important and under their own control. In fact, demanding situations can lead hardy people to perform particularly well. Table 5.2 provides some examples of perspectives of those high versus low in hardiness.

Questioning the Research 5.1

What do you think of the hardiness personality trait? Are all of its components equally important?

As discussed in Chapter 4, having a sense of control over events in one's life is an important predictor of health. Thus, not surprisingly, people who are hardy and those with an internal locus of control experience better psychological well-being (Florian, Mikulincer, & Taubman, 1995; Funk & Houston, 1987; Kobasa & Puccetti, 1983; Lakey, 1988; Peterson et al., 1988). For example, those who believe they have control suffer less depression in response to major illnesses, such as kidney failure, CHD, and cancer (Helgeson, 1992; Marks, Richardson, Graham, & Levine, 1986; Taylor, Lichtman, & Wood, 1984). Similarly, cancer patients who

Researchers in one study examined quotes from baseball players that appeared in newspaper articles describing why the team won or lost (Peterson & Seligman, 1987). Men who gave internal, stable, and global explanations for bad events lived a shorter life, as did those who offered external, unstable, and specific explanations for good events.
Source: Jason Miller/Getty Images, Inc.

have greater perceptions of control (over their illness, interpersonal relationships, and symptoms) are less depressed than those who have low perceived control (Thompson, Sobolew-Shubin, Galbraith, Schwankovsky, & Cruzen, 1993).

Feelings of control are also associated with improved physical well-being. One study examined levels of mastery—meaning a sense that you can control your outcomes—in more than 20,000 patients in the United Kingdom, and then health records over the next 6 years (Surtees, Wainwright, Luben, Khaw, & Day, 2006). Patients who were high in sense of mastery showed lower rates of mortality from all causes, including cardiovascular disease and cancer. More recent research has shown that this association is particularly strong for those at low risk of cardiovascular disease (Surtees et al., 2010). Finally, having a perception of control may be particularly important for helping people cope—and thereby stay healthy—during times of high stress. For example, Kobasa, Maddi, and Kohl (1982) conducted a study with 259 business executives to examine the associations among hardiness, stress, and level of illness. Those who were low in hardiness and who experienced many stressful life events reported experiencing high levels of illness; those who were high in hardiness remained healthy even when they experienced many stressful life events.

What Personality Factors Are Associated With Bad Health?

Although thus far we've focused on personality factors that can lead to beneficial types of health-related behavior, other personality factors are associated with poor psychological and physical health. This section examines the detrimental impact of three personality factors—neuroticism/negative affect, Type A behavior, and hostility/disagreeableness—on health.

Neuroticism/Negative Affect

Neuroticism, or **negative affect**, is a broad personality dimension that refers to the tendency of some people to experience negative emotions, such as distress, anxiety, nervousness, fear, shame, anger, and guilt, often (Watson & Clark, 1984). Although everyone experiences these feelings at times, people who are high in negative affect are in a "bad mood" frequently. They are likely to worry about upcoming events, dwell on failures and shortcomings, and have a less favorable view of themselves and others.

People who are high in neuroticism describe experiencing a greater number of physical symptoms as well as more severe and uncomfortable symptoms (Affleck, Tennen, Urrows, & Higgins, 1992; Aldwin, Levenson, Spiro, & Bosse, 1989; Lahey, 2009). For example, one study found that neuroticism was associated with reports of a number of physical symptoms, including frequency of illness, cardiovascular problems, digestive problems, and fatigue (Costa & McCrae, 1987). Similarly, college students who experience high levels of negative affect report more physical complaints, such as headaches, diarrhea, and sore throat (Watson, 1988; Watson & Pennebaker, 1989). Although cross-sectional research—meaning studies that rely on reports of personality and symptoms at the same point in time—can't distinguish between correlation and causation, other researchers have examined how negative affect is associated with psychological and physical health over time, which provides more information about the direction of the personality–health link. For example, Leventhal, Hansell, Diefenbach, Leventhal, and Glass (1996) examined negative affect in a sample of older adults (ages 62 to 73), and then followed up with the participants over 6 months. People who were higher in negative affect were more likely to report experiencing a variety of physical symptoms, including fatigue, dizziness, sleep disturbance, and energy loss.

You might have noticed that much of the research described thus far shows merely that neuroticism is associated with complaining more about physical symptoms, as opposed to actually experiencing more physical symptoms. However, research using more objective measures of health also shows such associations (Lahey, 2009; Wilson et al., 2005). People who are high in neuroticism are more likely to have a variety of health problems, including ulcers, chronic fatigue syndrome, headaches, nausea, asthma, arthritis, and even CHD (Charles, Gatz, Kato, & Pedersen, 2008; Suls & Bunde, 2005; Watson, 1988; Watson & Pennebaker, 1989). Neuroticism is also associated with longevity. A longitudinal study of more than 5,000 adults found that neuroticism is associated with greater mortality from cardiovascular disease, even controlling for age, sex, and other risk factors (such as smoking and alcohol use; Shipley, Weiss, Der, Taylor, & Deary, 2007). Similarly, among smokers with lung cancer, high neuroticism was associated with developing lung cancer at an earlier age (Augustine, Larsen, Walker, & Fisher, 2008), and cancer patients who are high on neuroticism have a 150% higher death rate than those who are low on neuroticism (Nakaya et al., 2006).

Type A Behavior

In 1956, cardiologists Meyer Friedman and Ray Rosenman were studying the association of diet and heart disease in married couples. Although women consumed as much cholesterol and fat as did their spouses (probably because couples tended to eat the same types of foods), men were much more susceptible to heart disease. One woman suggested that men's increased likelihood of heart attacks was because of the constant stress they experienced in the business world—at the time this study was conducted, many women were not involved in work outside the home. The researchers therefore interviewed 3,000 healthy middle-aged men, and then followed these men over 9 years to determine which would develop heart disease. These interviews revealed that the men varied in their personalities. While some of the men were generally easygoing, relaxed, and laid-back, others were impatient, competitive, time-conscious, and quick to anger. Friedman and Rosenman classified these two different personality types as Type B and **Type A behavior**, respectively. Moreover, of the 258 men who experienced a heart attack during the time of this study, 69% were classified as Type A, and only 31% were classified as Type B (Rosenman et al., 1975).

The Type A behavior pattern is characterized by three features (Friedman & Booth-Kewley, 1987b; Matthews, 1988). First, Type A people experience high levels of time urgency—they are irritated by and impatient with time delays and constantly try to do more than one thing at a time. If you walk and talk fast, interrupt slow speakers (or finish their sentences), race through yellow lights, and hate waiting in line, you may have a tendency toward Type A behavior. Second, Type A people have a strong competitive drive and are focused on doing better than other people in all sorts of situations (work and play). For example, Type A people engage in competitive leisure activities more than Type B people—they may prefer playing tennis (in which there is a clear winner and loser) to doing aerobics (Kelly & Houston, 1985). Finally, Type A people are prone to experiencing anger and hostility (e.g., they are more irritable when frustrated in their goal pursuit and are easily aroused to anger). Like people who are high in hostility, Type A people are quick to experience anger and may lash out at others in frustration.

Although the Friedman and Rosenman (1974) study was the first to suggest an association between Type A behavior and health, other studies have also shown this link. For example, Type A people report experiencing more minor illnesses, such as coughs, allergies, headaches, and asthma attacks, as well as more gastrointestinal problems, such as ulcers, indigestion, and nausea, than Type B people (Suls & Marco, 1990; Woods & Burns, 1984; Woods, Morgan, Day, Jefferson, & Harris, 1984). Similarly, as described at the beginning of the chapter, Cindy, who has the characteristics of a Type A personality, experiences frequent migraine headaches and has developed an ulcer. People with Type A behavior are also more likely to experience major health problems. One study found that middle-aged Type A men were more than six times as likely to experience a heart attack as Type B men (Suinn, 1975). Similarly, while only 4.5% of Type B women show signs of hypertension, 35% of Type A women show such symptoms (Rosenman & Friedman, 1961).

The Type A concept has received some support from research, but other studies suggest that there is little or no relationship between Type A behavior and CHD. Ragland and Brand (1988), for example, found that Type A people had a mortality rate of 19.2% as compared to 31.7% among Type B people! One explanation for the discrepancy in study results is that some researchers have measured Type A behavior using a self-report scale, and others have used an interview method. The structured interview is more accurate at assessing Type A behavior, in part because this behavior is more apparent during an interview than on a self-report questionnaire (Friedman & Booth-Kewley, 1987b). For example, an interviewer is likely to notice pace of speech, checking of the wristwatch, and interruptions.

Moreover, some features of the structured interview (a commonly used measure of Type A behavior) are designed to test how people react to potentially stressful situations. Thus, the interviewer is instructed to use slow and hesitating speech to see whether the person interrupts or finishes the interviewer's sentences, and to rudely interrupt the subject to challenge an answer to see how he or she responds (Chesney, Eagleston, & Rosenman, 1980; Tallmer et al., 1990).

Finally, although researchers often refer to "Type A behavior" as representing a single type of behavior, Type A behavior actually has three distinct types: impatience/speed, job involvement, and hard-driving. While the link between hostility and CHD is strong, the link between other components of Type A behavior and health is much weaker. Friedman et al. suggest that some people who are labeled Type A are simply expressive, efficient, and ambitious people who are coping well with their personal and professional lives and that these people are actually not at increased risk of experiencing health problems (Friedman, Hall, & Harris, 1985). In contrast, and as we discuss next, "real Type A people," namely, those who are tense, repressed, and hostile, are the ones most likely to experience physical problems.

Hostility/Disagreeableness

Like those who are high in neuroticism, people who are high in **hostility/disagreeableness** have more negative moods and fewer positive moods (Cook & Medley, 1954; Smith, Pope, Sanders, Allred, & O'Keefe, 1988). But this personality trait focuses specifically on people's expectations about and interactions within their interpersonal relationships. People who are hostile or disagreeable believe that others are motivated by selfish concerns and expect that other people will deliberately try to hurt them (see Table 5.3; Miller, Smith, Turner, Guijarro, & Hallet, 1996). In turn, because of their general mistrust and cynicism about other people's motivations, hostile people don't hesitate to express these feelings—they are often uncooperative, rude, argumentative, condescending, and aggressive.

TABLE 5.3   *Test Yourself: Sample Items From the Hostility–Guilt Inventory*

1. Once in a while I cannot control my urge to harm others.
2. I can't help being a little rude to people I don't like.
3. When someone makes a rule I don't like, I am tempted to break it.
4. Other people always seem to get the breaks.
5. I commonly wonder what hidden reason another person may have for doing something nice for me.
6. I can't help getting into arguments when people disagree with me.
7. Unless someone asks me in a nice way, I won't do what that person wants.
8. My motto is "Never trust strangers."
9. Whoever insults me or my family is asking for a fight.
10. If somebody annoys me, I am apt to tell him what I think of him.

This scale assesses a person's general level of hostility, including feelings of antagonism, cynicism, and aggression.

Source: Buss & Durkee, 1957.

Hostility is associated with poorer health, including higher rates of hypertension and CHD (Jorgensen, Johnson, Kolodziej, & Schreer, 1996; Miller et al., 1996; Smith, 1992). One prospective study assessed hostility in 200 healthy women and then followed these women over 10 years (Matthews, Owens, Kuller, Sutton-Tyrrell, & Jansen-McWilliams, 1998). Even controlling for variables such as smoking, women who had higher hostility scores in the earlier testing were more likely to show symptoms of cardiovascular disease 10 years later. Similarly, Niaura et al. (2002) found that older men with the highest levels of hostility were at the greatest risk of experiencing CHD. What accounts for these higher rates of cardiovascular disease symptoms? One study found that people who were high in hostility were much more likely to experience coronary artery blockage than those who were low in hostility (Iribarren et al., 2000). For example, for those with the lowest levels of hostility, only 8% showed some artery blockage as compared to 18% of those with the highest levels of hostility.

People who are high in hostility also have higher rates of mortality than those who are less hostile (Barefoot, Dodge, Peterson, Dahlstrom, & Williams, 1989). In one study, researchers examined ratings of hostility during medical school, and then subsequent health 30 years later (Barefoot, Dahlstrom, & Williams, 1983). As predicted, men who were high in hostility were five times more likely to have experienced CHD than those who were low in hostility. Specifically, 4.5% of those who were high in hostility had experienced either angina or a myocardial infarction as compared to only 1% of those who were low in hostility. Men who were high in hostility were also nearly seven times as likely to have died before the time of the follow-up than men who were low in hostility. Although this study does not indicate why men who are hostile die at younger ages than those who are not hostile, it clearly suggests that hostility matters.

Explaining the Link Between Personality and Health

Thus far, we have examined the link between many different personality variables and psychological and physical well-being. We have not discussed, however, the factors that may lead to this association. Do positive states directly enhance health, perhaps by improving health-related behaviors, coping styles, or availability of social support? Alternatively, or perhaps additionally, are the health benefits of positive states good for health because they influence how people's bodies respond physiologically to stress, thus preventing harmful processes that lead to disease? This section describes several possible pathways that may account for the association between personality and health (see Figure 5.2).

Stress

Individuals' personalities may influence how much stress they experience—or how much stress they perceive they are experiencing (Hemenover & Dienstbier, 1996). As described by Fredrickson's broaden-and-build theory, positive emotions broaden people's attention and cognition, which in turn leads to increases in physical,

FIGURE 5.2   Researchers have examined a number of different pathways that may explain the link between personality and health.

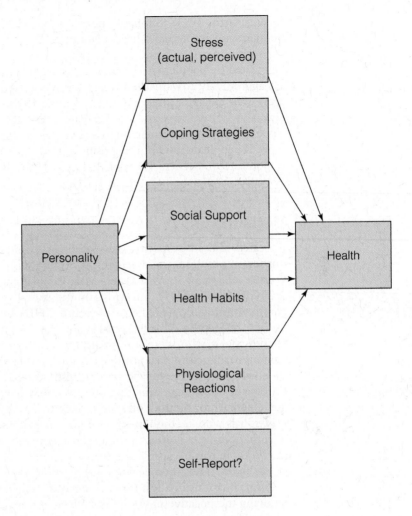

intellectual, social, and psychological resources (2001; Frederickson & Joiner, 2002). People who are high in positive emotions therefore perceive potentially stressful life events as less threatening, perhaps because they tend to focus on the positive features of the situation and thus view such events as challenging instead of anxiety-provoking (Florian et al., 1995; Hemenover, 2001). In line with this view, men who are high in optimism and diagnosed with prostate cancer show less distress, in part because they have more positive expectancies about the outcome of the diagnosis (Steginga & Occhipinti, 2006). People who experience positive emotions during times of stress are also better able to find meaning in these experiences, which leads to better health (Davis, Nolen-Hoekema, & Larson, 1998).

On the other hand, people who are high in negative emotions are likely to focus on the negative features of situations and thus perceive events as more stressful and difficult to cope with (Hemenover, 2001; Watson, 1988). People's personalities can also influence whether they create stressful situations. For example, one study found that people who were high in negative affect at one point in time experienced more stressful life events as well as greater psychological distress even 6 years later (Ormel

& Wohlfarth, 1991). Similarly, people who are high in hostility experience more frequent and severe daily hassles and major life events, and report more conflict in their jobs, marriages, and families (Smith et al., 1988). This negative pattern may be created by people who are hostile, who, because they anticipate that others will act aggressively toward them, may behave antagonistically first, which elicits the aggressive behavior they expected (Smith, 1992). People with Type A behavior may also behave in ways that increase stress; for example, when playing games, Type A people view their opponents as more competitive and hard-driving than Type B people do, and not surprisingly, they elicit more competitive and aggressive responses from others (Ortega & Pipal, 1984; Rhodewalt, Hayes, Chemers, & Wysocki, 1984; Sorensen et al., 1987).

Physiological Mechanisms

Research also suggests that personality may influence health in part through its impact on physiological mechanisms. In line with this view, individuals who have positive emotions show a faster cardiovascular recovery following stress (Tugade & Frederickson, 2004). Similarly, in one study, researchers examined increases in plasma fibrinogen (a predictor of future CHD) in response to a mental stress test in the lab (Steptoe, Wardle, & Marmot, 2005). The increase was 12 times as great in individuals who were low in happiness compared to those who were high in happiness, suggesting that positive emotions may reduce the negative impact of stress on body systems. People who are optimistic also have higher levels of T cells, even in the face of stress, suggesting that optimism may have direct physiological effects that are beneficial for fighting off illness (Segerstrom, Taylor, Kemeny, & Fahey, 1998). Individuals who are high in assorted measures of positive affect—extraversion, self-esteem, optimism—show lower cortisol increases in response to stressors (Taylor et al., 2008), in part because psychosocial resources seem to inhibit the threat responses in the brain. Thus, people who are high on positive affect may in fact reappraise stressful situations in a less threatening way, which is a pretty good mechanism for reducing the negative physiological effects of particular challenges.

This focus on the more negative aspects of situations results not only in the experience of higher levels of stress but also in greater physiological reactions to stress, including cardiovascular response and immune functioning (Scheier & Carver, 1987). Think about what happens to your body when you yell at someone—your heart rate probably increases, and, although you may not be aware of it, so does your blood pressure. People who regularly experience this higher level of physiological arousal may be at greater risk of developing cardiovascular problems because they exert so much wear and tear on their blood vessels and heart (Siegman, Anderson, Herbst, Boyle, & Wilkinson, 1992). Similarly, people who are hostile experience such high levels of physiological arousal in part because they are distrustful of others, so they are constantly on guard against slights from others. They therefore have consistently higher heart rates and blood pressure than those who are low in hostility, show more rapid cardiovascular reactions to stressful situations, and take longer for their bodies to return to normal functioning following a stressful interaction (Ewart & Jorgensen, 2004; Neumann, Waldstein, Sollers, Thayer, & Sorkin, 2004; Powch & Houston, 1996; Raikkonen, Matthews, Flory, & Owens, 1999; Smith, 1992; Suarez, Kuhn, Schanberg, Williams, & Zimmerman, 1998). Similarly, people who are Type A show a distinct physiological reaction to potentially stressful tasks, particularly those involving time urgency and competition: When they are in situations in which they feel threatened or challenged, they show greater changes in heart rate, blood pressure, and adrenaline levels than Type B people (Contrada, 1989; Lyness, 1993). These increased reactions to stress lead to wear and tear on the heart over time. Some research also suggests that people who have a pessimistic explanatory style or who are low in perceived control have weaker immune responses and poorer DNA repair (Kamen-Siegel, Rodin, Seligman, & Dwyer, 1991; Segerstrom, Taylor, Kameny, & Fahey, 1998).

Coping Strategies

Personality factors may influence the use of different coping strategies. People who are high in positive emotions are more likely to use more adaptive and functional strategies for coping with problems and less likely to use destructive coping strategies (Anderson, 1977; Carver et al., 1993; Drach-Zahavy & Somech, 2002; McCrae & Costa, 1986; Taylor et al., 1992; Williams, Wiebe, & Smith, 1992). Scheier et al. (1989) conducted a study showing that optimists recover from surgery faster than pessimists, in part because they made plans and set goals for recovery sooner and were less likely to dwell on the negative aspects of the experience. For example, pessimists tended to block out thoughts of the recovery process, whereas optimists were likely to try to get as much information as possible about what to expect and how to cope. The use of more constructive coping strategies can result in better health by leading people to experience fewer negative life events. By confronting problems earlier and more effectively, people with certain personality traits "nip problems in the bud," and thereby avoid allowing small issues to become larger ones. Researchers believe that the use of these more constructive coping styles may at least partially explain why optimists experience better health. Similarly, a study with 276 Israeli army recruits found that those who were high in hardiness were

Certain personality traits, such as hostility, negative affect/neuroticism, and Type A behavior, may lead people to both experience higher levels of stress and show a heightened physiological response to such situations.
Source: © Yula Zubritsky/iStockphoto.

more likely to use problem-focused coping and less likely to use emotion-focused coping, which in turn led to more positive psychological well-being at the end of training 4 months later (Florian et al., 1995). In contrast, people who are high in neuroticism and have an external locus of control tend to rely on maladaptive coping strategies (Hewitt & Flett, 1996). For example, one study of people who were coping with a major environmental disaster (an accident at a nuclear power plant) found that people who were high in neuroticism were more likely to use maladaptive coping mechanisms, such as self-blame, and less likely to use constructive coping strategies, such as problem solving (Costa & McCrae, 1990).

Social Support

Personality factors may influence how much social support a person has (Lepore, 1995; Smith, 1992). In line with this view, Xu and Roberts (2010) examined positive feelings in a sample of more than 6,000 adults, and then evaluated death rates over the next 28 years. Although positive feelings predicted lowered risk of all causes of mortality, this association was largely caused by social networks, meaning that people with high levels of positive emotions tend to have larger social support networks, which in turn leads to better health. In contrast, people who are hostile, neurotic, and pessimistic may have trouble forming close relationships and may experience high levels of interpersonal conflict, in part because they are likely to treat others in an antagonistic way (Sarason, Sarason, & Shearin, 1986; Smith, 1992). As described at the beginning of the chapter, because Miles's consistent anxiety makes other people uncomfortable, he has few social relationships. People who are high in hostility also have difficulty seeking and accepting social support (Houston & Vavak, 1991). For example, one study found that people who are low in hostility experience less stress when they have a friend with them while they give a difficult speech, whereas people who are high in hostility do not show any benefit from the presence of such support (Lepore, 1995).

Questioning the Research 5.2

This section discusses how personality factors such as hostility and negative affect may lead to lower levels of social support. What are some alternative explanations for this association between personality and social support?

Health Habits

Personality factors may influence individuals' health habits (Houston & Vavak, 1991; Leiker & Hailey, 1988; Seeman & Seeman, 1983). People who are high in conscientiousness, optimism, and extraversion and those who have an internal locus of control are more likely to engage in health-promoting behaviors, including taking vitamins, engaging in regular exercise and healthy eating, avoiding cigarette smoking and drugs, engaging in safer sexual behaviors, and safe driving (Blumenthal, Sanders, Wallace, Williams, & Needles, 1982; Booth-Kewley & Vickers, 1994; Korotkov, 2008; Robbins, Spence, & Clark, 1991; Scheier & Carver, 1992; Seeman & Seeman,

1983; Taylor et al., 1992; Trobst, Herbst, Masters, & Costa, 2002). In contrast, people who are high in neuroticism, hostility, and Type A behavior are more likely to smoke, abuse alcohol, eat less healthy foods, engage in unsafe sex, avoid exercise, sleep less, and drink caffeine (see Figure 5.3; Booth-Kewley & Vickers, 1994; Costa & McCrae, 1987; Folsom et al., 1985; Houston & Vavak, 1991; Korotkov, 2008; Leiker & Hailey, 1988; Miller et al., 1996; Trobst et al., 2002). For example, one study of 103 male military personnel found that neuroticism was associated with fewer wellness behaviors, less accident control behavior, and more traffic risk-taking behavior (Booth-Kewley & Vickers, 1994). This type of careless behavior may explain why people who have pessimistic explanatory styles have higher

FIGURE 5.3 People who are high in hostility drink more alcohol and are more likely to smoke cigarettes than those who are low in hostility (data from Iribarren et al., 2000).

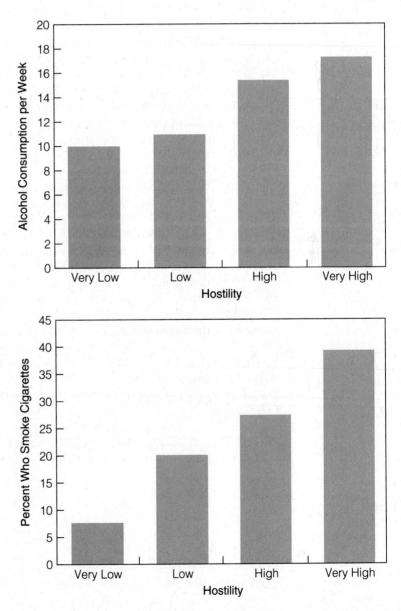

rates of death from accidents and violence but not from cancer or cardiovascular disease (Peterson et al., 1998). Personality can even predict health-related behavior over time: Children who are higher in hostility in first grade are more likely to smoke cigarettes, drink alcohol, and use marijuana during high school (Hampson, Tildesley, Andrews, Luyckx, & Mroczek, 2010), and children who are high in negative affect are more likely to be obese as adults (Pulkki-Rabach, Elovainio, Kivimäki, Raitakari, & Keltikangas-Järvinen, 2005).

Personality factors may also influence whether individuals take preventive steps to modify their behavior following illness, such as following a prescribed medical regimen or altering behaviors that produce illness (Seeman & Seeman, 1983; Wiebe & Christensen, 1997). In line with this view, conscientious people, who have the self-control to overcome potential barriers (e.g., fear) and to complete difficult, aversive, and stressful tasks (e.g., getting a mammogram, having an HIV test) tend to follow health-care advice, whereas those who are low in conscientiousness simply abandon medical regimens that are distasteful in some way (Christensen & Smith, 1995; Schwartz et al., 1999). For example, one study of patients who were undergoing dialysis found that those who were conscientious were more likely to adhere to the medical recommendations of their doctors (Christensen & Smith, 1995). Similarly, people with high levels of perceived control and optimistic expectations about their ability to overcome a particular health stressor may be more likely to adhere to diet and exercise recommendations, whereas those who believe that illnesses are caused by internal, global, and stable factors may become passive in the face of illness and may not seek or follow medical advice. In line with this view, positive affect is associated with adherence to medication in people who are HIV positive (Gonzales et al., 2004). Similarly, cardiac patients who are optimistic are more likely to take vitamins, eat low-fat foods, enroll in a rehabilitation program, successfully reduce their weight, follow a recommended diet, and start exercising (Maroto, Shepperd, & Pbert, 1996; Scheier et al., 1989).

On the other hand, hostile people and those with Type A behavior patterns may fail to adhere to medical regimens and may even react against doctors' orders to exert their independence (Lee et al., 1992; Rhodewalt & Smith, 1991). As described at the beginning of the chapter, Debbie was irritated by her physician's advice to quit smoking and believes she's the only one who should decide about her own health-related behavior. Type As may ignore early signs of a heart attack, suppress or ignore symptoms, and overexert themselves (Carver, Coleman, & Glass, 1976). They are especially likely to deny symptoms when they are focusing on a challenging task, which can lead them to delay treatment. For example, Type B people report more symptoms when they are working on a challenging task, whereas Type A people report fewer (Rhodewalt & Smith, 1991). This tendency to deny early symptoms increases a person's likelihood of dying from a heart attack.

Self-Report

Finally, the link between personality and health could be a function of self-report—in other words, personality traits may influence how focused people are on their physical health, and hence how likely they are to notice various aches, pains, and symptoms (and not just how many symptoms they notice; Watson &

Pennebaker, 1989). To test this possibility, research has included physiological tests of health, such as immune system functioning, cardiovascular fitness, and measures of cholesterol levels (Costa & McCrae, 1987; Watson & Pennebaker, 1989). This work generally suggests that there is little association between personality traits and actual physical measures of health. For example, in one study Cohen et al. (1995) asked people about their cold symptoms (e.g., runny nose, congestion) and also gathered more objective data (e.g., mucus output). Although people who were high in negative affect complained more about various health problems (e.g., headaches, chest pains, stomachaches), there was no evidence that they actually experienced more health problems (e.g., elevated blood pressure, serum lipids). Those who are high in negative affect, for example, may interpret relatively minor and normal symptoms as more painful and problematic than those people with low negative affect (Watson, 1988; Watson & Pennebaker, 1989). In line with this view, a study by Ellington and Wiebe (1999) presented subjects with a vignette describing an illness and asked them to pretend they were patients presenting these symptoms to a doctor. Students who were high in neuroticism presented more elaborate and detailed symptoms, regardless of whether the illness was low in severity (e.g., strep throat) or high in severity (e.g., acute appendicitis). In fact, research shows that people who are high in negative affect complain of all kinds of physical problems and symptoms but do not actually show evidence of increased health problems or earlier mortality—there is no evidence from biological tests that they experience more problems, visit the doctor more often, take medicine more often, or miss school/work more often.

In sum, although the model suggests that each pathway between personality and health is separate and distinct from all others, clearly these pathways could be, and probably often are, interrelated. Personality factors are likely to influence the type of coping strategy used, which influences the amount of stress experienced. Similarly, the amount of social support a person receives may impact the amount of stress he or she experiences, the coping strategies used, and even the person's health habits, any or all of which could influence health. We will now turn to examine the role of social support in helping people manage stress.

What Is Social Support?

One of the major challenges in examining the link between **social support** and health is determining how to measure social support. Different researchers have defined social support in different ways, such as the existence or quantity of social relationships, the amount of assistance individuals believe is available to them, and the amount of assistance individuals receive (House & Kahn, 1985). Is social support simply having many casual friendships? Is social support a single construct, or are there different types of social support? Is social support a reflection of what support you *think* is available or the amount of support you actually *receive*? This section examines different approaches to measuring social support, including the structure of one's social network, perceived social support available, and social support actually received.

Social Network

Some researchers have examined social support in terms of the structure of people's **social network**, that is, the number and types of social relationships (House & Kahn, 1985). These measures take into account whether a person is married or single, and whether he or she lives alone or with others, as well as the person's membership in various social organizations, such as houses of worship and clubs. The social network can also include the frequency of contact with friends and relatives.

Several large-scale surveys have assessed social support based on the existence and quantity of social relationships. For example, in a survey of people living in Alameda County, California, researchers examined four types of social ties: marriage, contacts with extended family and friends, church or temple membership, and other formal and informal group affiliations (Berkman & Syme, 1979). They created a social network index by combining these four types of social ties and then used this measure to predict mortality. Similarly, other researchers have measured different types of social relationships, such as intimate social relationships (relationships with one's spouse, friends, and family), formal nonwork organization relationships (e.g., church), and active leisure pursuits that include social contacts (e.g., attending classes; House, Robbins, & Metzner, 1982). These approaches assess the number of social relationships as well as individuals' participation in various social activities.

Questioning the Research 5.3

Note the four categories of social ties that form the social network index. What weaknesses do you see in the categories as they are set up?

Although these surveys allow researchers to discover how many relationships a person has, they do not capture the structure and complexity of social relationships. Other approaches have assessed social support in terms of the web of social relationships (as opposed to their mere existence); hence, they include not only a person's friends but also the friends of these friends. These approaches may measure other factors, such as the density of one's social relationships (the extent to which members of a network are linked to each other), durability (the duration of relationships over time), reciprocity (the extent to which support is both given and received), and dispersion (the geographic distance between network members). For example, the Social Network List (Stokes, 1983) asks people to list up to 20 people who are important to them and with whom they have contact at least once a month. As a way of assessing density, the assessor then must indicate which network members are significant in each other's lives and who has contact with each other at least once a month. Researchers have hypothesized that more-dense social networks (those in which people are very interconnected with one another) might be particularly useful in times of stress because people could better coordinate different types of support (Wortman, 1984). For example, if you needed help after surgery, nearby friends might work together to divide up various tasks they could do to help you, such as cooking, cleaning, and running errands.

Although several large-scale studies connecting social support and health have used social network measures (Berkman & Syme, 1979; House et al., 1982), their use has been criticized for several reasons. First, the mere existence of a relationship does not mean that relationship is actually supportive (Antonucci, 1990). You may have friends and relatives, for example, with whom you speak every month, but these people may not provide you with any real support. Second, assessing various characteristics of a social network (reciprocity, density, etc.) is time-consuming and may not be particularly accurate. In fact, some studies have found that individuals often do not even agree with whether they are in each other's social networks; the rate of agreement is as low as 36% in some studies (Shulman, 1976).

Perceived Social Support

Given the weaknesses of social network measures of social support, other research on the link between social support and health has focused on people's perceptions of the different types of support various relationships provide (Cohen, 1988; House, 1981; see Table 5.4 for an example of one measure assessing different types of support). Although researchers vary in how they categorize the different types of support, they generally agree on the types of support described in the following paragraphs.

TABLE 5.4   *Test Yourself: Sample Items From the Interpersonal Support Evaluation List*

Please rate whether each of the following items is true or false.

1. If I had to go out of town for a few weeks, someone I know would look after my home, such as watering the plants or taking care of the pets.
2. If I were sick and needed someone to drive me to the doctor, I would have trouble finding someone.
3. If I were sick, I would have trouble finding someone to help me with my daily chores.
4. If I needed help moving, I would be able to find someone to help me.
5. If I needed a place to stay for a week because of an emergency, such as the water or electricity being out in my home, I could easily find someone who would put me up.
6. There is at least one person I know whose advice I really trust.
7. There is no one I know who will tell me honestly how I am handling my problems.
8. When I need suggestions about how to deal with a personal problem, there is someone I can turn to.
9. There isn't anyone I feel comfortable talking to about intimate personal problems.
10. There is no one I trust to give me good advice about money matters.
11. I am usually invited to do things with others.
12. When I feel lonely, there are several people I could talk to.
13. I regularly meet or talk with my friends or members of my family.
14. I often feel left out by my circle of friends.
15. There are several different people I enjoy spending time with.

Give yourself one point for each of the following items answered true: 1, 4, 5, 6, 8, 11, 12, 13, 15, and one point for each of the following items answered false: 2, 3, 7, 9, 10, 14. Items 1 to 5 assess tangible support, items 6 to 10 assess appraisal support, and items 11 to 15 assess belongingness support.

Source: Cohen, Mermelstein, Karmarck, & Hoberman, 1985.

Emotional support, such as listening, comforting, and providing reassurance, is a particularly valuable type of social support, especially during times of stress.
Source: © Catchlight Visual Services/Alamy.

Emotional support refers to the expression of caring, concern, and empathy for a person as well as the provision of comfort, reassurance, and love to that person. Most people who are confronted with stressful life events want to be able to talk about these events with others, and having a "listening ear" can be very valuable. One study of cancer patients found that more than 90% saw emotional support as one of the most valuable types of support (Dunkel-Schetter & Wortman, 1982; Dunkel-Schetter, 1984). Similarly, college students may need emotional support to cope with the stress of a relationship breakup, a poor exam grade, or the divorce of their parents.

Belongingness support is similar to emotional support in that it too includes a focus on being able to talk to others, but this type of support refers primarily to the availability of social companionship (Cohen et al., 1985). People are interested in having others with whom they can engage in social activities, such as people with whom they can go out to dinner, see a movie, and attend a party, and this type of support is an important predictor of well-being. People who are unemployed (hence, they lose one valuable type of social integration) particularly benefit from having belongingness support, and they experience more psychological symptoms when they do not have this type of support (Cutrona & Russell, 1990).

Instrumental, or **tangible, support** refers to the provision of concrete assistance, such as financial aid, material resources, or needed services. For example, you may need instrumental support from your parents to pay for textbooks and from your friends to help carry your belongings when you move to a new apartment. Victims of natural disasters, such as hurricanes, floods, and earthquakes, particularly benefit from receiving tangible support (Kaniasty & Norris, 1995; Norris & Kaniasty, 1996).

Informational, or **appraisal, support** refers to advice and guidance about how to cope with a particular problem. For example, you may depend on your professors for informational support when you are trying to find a summer internship and depend on your friends for such support when choosing which classes to take. Victims of natural disasters, who need advice about how to organize cleanup efforts and arrange to receive government aid, also benefit from this type of support.

People also benefit from receiving **esteem**, or **validational, support**, the affirmation of self-worth. This type of support gives a person feedback that he or she is valued and respected by others. One study on long-term recovery from heart surgery found that patients who believed they received considerable esteem support from their spouses had the highest levels of emotional well-being and were the least likely to experience disruption of their everyday lives (e.g., problems with social interaction, recreation activities, sleep, walking) or symptoms of heart trouble even as long as 1 year after surgery (King, Reis, Porter, & Norsen, 1993).

Although this section has described the different types of social support that can be provided, all of these types are not interchangeable. For example, if your car breaks down and you need a ride to an appointment, getting a ride or borrowing a car will be helpful, whereas simply talking about your feelings regarding your broken car will not be very helpful. On the other hand, if you are sad following a fight with your girlfriend, it may be helpful to talk about your feelings with a close friend. According to the *matching hypothesis*, individuals benefit from receiving the type of social support that fits their particular problem (Cohen & Wills, 1985; Cutrona & Russell, 1990).

Several studies suggest that people in different situations do benefit from having different types of support. Specifically, in the case of controllable events, namely, those that can be solved or fixed, people benefit most from receiving practical types of support (Cutrona & Russell, 1990). For example, instrumental support is consistently associated with better psychological and physical well-being for new parents. Pregnancy, childbirth, and caring for an infant are challenging events that people may initially have trouble managing. However, tangible and instrumental support, such as advice on infant care, financial assistance, and assistance with childcare tasks, can help to ease this stress, and in turn benefit both the physical and mental health of the new parent. On the other hand, for uncontrollable events, such as the loss of a spouse, practical types of support will not be as effective because they will not help people solve or eliminate the stressor. Emotional support should therefore be more valuable in these cases. In support of this view, breast-cancer patients benefit from having emotional support but not from instrumental support (Helgeson & Cohen, 1996). This research all points to the importance of receiving the "right type" of support for a given problem.

Received Social Support

Although some researchers have focused on the *perceived* availability of different types of social support (i.e., how much support would be available if needed), other researchers have instead focused on assessing the amount of support that is *received* in a particular period of time. As with perceived social support, received support could also be divided into various types. For example, the Inventory of Socially Supportive Behaviors asks people to indicate how often in the past 4 weeks they have received various types of supportive behaviors, such as when someone "gave you information on how to do something" (cognitive-informational), "gave you more than $25" (tangible) or "talked with you about some interests of yours" (emotional; Barrera, Sandler, & Ramsey, 1981). As described in Box 5.3: Focus on Culture, cultures vary in the amount of support generally provided as well as in the type of support that is seen as most valuable.

Box 5.3

Focus on Culture: The Differential Presence and Benefits of Particular Types of Support

Although this section has focused on the overall benefits of social support, different cultures vary in terms of the amount of support provided as well as the impact of different types of support. Some researchers have examined whether individuals who live in countries that place a high priority on interdependence and connection with one's social group experience better health (Bond, 1991; Triandis, Bontempo, Villareal, Asai, & Luca, 1988). Countries with social norms of connection could promote better health in a variety of ways, including giving more support to elderly relatives and encouraging people to openly discuss their problems (Bond, 1991). Living in a culture that provides more social support could therefore protect people from stress, hence leading to lower rates of disease as well as longer life expectancy. For instance, the Japanese culture places a high priority on connection to one's family and social group, and, in turn, the rate of heart disease in Japan is quite low (Reed, McGee, Yano, & Feinlab, 1983). This lower rate of heart disease does not seem to be simply a function of genetics because Japanese people who live in the United States experience higher rates of heart disease than those living in Japan. The difference in rate of heart disease also cannot be explained by other likely factors, such as smoking, diet, and blood pressure. This research suggests that people who live in cultures that emphasize interdependence are generally healthier than those who live in self-focused countries, such as the United States. Interestingly, there are cultural differences in the type of social support that is most beneficial (Taylor, Welch, Kim, & Sherman, 2007). Asians and Asian Americans benefit more from thinking about implicit social support, meaning support that is provided simply through the awareness of one's connection to a broader social network, whereas European Americans benefit more from explicit support, meaning support that is provided through a direct request of assistance. This research suggests that while social support in general is valuable, the amount of support and the benefit of a particular type of support vary as a function of culture.

Although these types of measures have an advantage in that they assess actual support received and not just individuals' perceptions of the support available, they also have some disadvantages. One problem with assessing received social support is that individuals are most likely to receive support during times of need; hence, the amount of received support is often correlated with negative health symptoms (Stroebe & Stroebe, 1996). For example, individuals who are very sick may need—and may receive—more social support, but this does not mean that having this support *caused* the illness. Another problem with assessing received support is that individuals may not have needed a particular type of support during the month prior to the assessment, even though it was available. If you didn't need to borrow money from your parents in the past month, it may still have helped you simply to know that you could have received a loan if needed. Finally, and somewhat surprisingly, there is often little or no association between actual and perceived support (Lakey & Heller, 1988), and some research indicates that perceived support is a stronger predictor of well-being than received support (Cohen & Wills, 1985).

What Is the Link Between Social Support and Health?

Following the publication of these first studies, researchers became interested in examining the connection between social support and health. As it turns out, having greater social support is associated with a variety of positive health outcomes, including greater psychological well-being, greater physical well-being, faster recovery from illness, and, most important, lower rates of mortality (Stroebe & Stroebe, 1996).

Psychological Well-Being

The advantages of social support to psychological well-being are clear: Individuals with greater social support are less likely to suffer from various psychological disorders (Schwarzer & Leppin, 1992). Depressed people report having fewer friends, fewer close relationships, and less supportive family interactions than nondepressed people (Billings & Moos, 1985). Similarly, college students who perceive greater support from their families are less likely to report neurotic symptoms (Procidano & Heller, 1983). One recent study even revealed that women with breast cancer who receive more social support from their spouse show more positive emotion and less negative emotion (Gremore et al., 2011). On the other hand, women with breast cancer who have unsupportive partners report higher levels of distress (Manne, Ostroff, Winkel, Grana, & Fox, 2005), as do women who receive unwanted social support (Reynolds & Perrin, 2004).

The link between social support and psychological well-being occurs in the United States as well as in other countries. For example, one recent study with older adults in Japan and in the United States found that having strong social ties, such as a spouse or frequent contact with children, friends, neighbors, or relatives, was associated with fewer symptoms of depression in both samples (Sugisawa, Shibata, Hougham, Sugihara, & Liang, 2002).

However, studies that measure people's level of social support and psychological well-being at the same time are correlational and therefore do not tell us how these two variables are linked. Fortunately, some researchers have examined people over time, which allows them to study causal effects. For example, a study of HIV-positive gay men found that those who were satisfied with the social support they received were less likely to be depressed 1 year later than men who were not satisfied with their amount of social support (Hays, Turner, & Coates, 1992). Similarly, in a study of patients with a chronic disease, those who perceived different types of social support as readily available had less anxiety and more positive affect as long as 1 year later (Sherbourne & Hays, 1990). Another study revealed that college students who had more and higher-quality social interactions had fewer health problems and visits to the campus infirmary (Reis, Wheeler, Kernis, Spiegel, & Nezlek, 1985). Because these studies are prospective (i.e., they measure social support at one time and health at a later time), they give us some confidence that greater social support *leads* to better psychological well-being and not the reverse.

Physical Well-Being

Individuals with more social support experience better physical well-being as well as better psychological well-being (Hays et al., 1992; Holahan, Moos, Holahan, & Brennan, 1997; House, Landis, & Umberson, 1988). One study of 3,809 Japanese American men in California found that the risk of suffering from CHD was nearly twice as large for those who had the lowest levels of support compared to those with the highest amount of support (Berkman, 1985); similar findings are seen for women (Blumenthal et al., 1987). Similarly, men who receive low levels of social support are twice as likely to have high levels of prostate-specific antigen (PSA), a marker of prostate cancer, than those with high levels of support (Stone, Mezzacappa, Donatone, & Gonder, 1999). In fact, the impact on health of having low levels of support is similar in magnitude to the effect of smoking (House et al., 1988).

People with high levels of social support recover more quickly from illnesses when they do get sick. For example, those with greater social support recover more rapidly from kidney disease (Dimond, 1979), leukemia (Magni, Silvestro, Tamiello, Zanesco, & Carl, 1988) and stroke (Robertson & Suinn, 1968). For pregnant women, greater social support is associated with fewer complications during delivery, less use of anesthetics, and a shorter overall labor (Kennell, Klaus, McGrath, Robertson, & Hinckley, 1991; Sosa, Kennell, Klaus, Robertson, & Urrutia, 1980). Similarly, and as described in Box 5.4: Focus on Research, in individuals who are undergoing surgery, those who receive more social support from their spouses experience less pain, use less pain medication, show a faster recovery time from surgery, and are less likely to have to return to the hospital for complications postsurgery (Helgeson, 1991; Kulik & Mahler, 1989). Those with more social support also report experiencing fewer symptoms of angina and less functional disruption of their usual activities as long as 1 year after surgery (King et al., 1993).

Most important, greater social support is associated with lower rates of mortality (Giles, Glonek, Luszcz, & Andrews, 2005; Kaplan et al., 1988; Welin et al., 1985). The first published study on the link between social support and mortality was conducted by Berkman and Syme (1979). They collected data from a representative

Box 5.4

Focus on Research: The Effects of Social Support on Recovery From Surgery

Researchers in one study examined the link between social support and recovery from surgery (Krohne & Slangen, 2005). Prior to surgery, 84 patients (42 male, 42 female) completed measures of emotional and informational support. Following surgery, researchers assessed anxiety, amount of drugs required, and length of hospital stay. As predicted, having greater social support led to better adaptation following surgery. Patients with high levels of social support showed less anxiety, received lower doses of narcotics, and were released from the hospital 1.42 days faster than those with lower levels of support. Interestingly, women with low levels of support were much more anxious than men with low support, whereas there were no gender differences in anxiety among those high in support. This finding suggests that women found a lack of social support more concerning than did men, perhaps because women in general have higher support. These findings point to the importance of social support in general for helping people cope with the major stressor of surgery.

sample of nearly 7,000 men and women living in Alameda County, California, in 1965. Respondents completed measures of four types of social ties (marriage, contacts with extended family and friends, church membership, and other formal and informal group affiliations) and the state of their physical health. Researchers then collected mortality data from 1965 to 1974 to examine death rates as a function of social ties. Overall, people who lacked social ties were two to three times more likely to die during this period than those with social ties (see Figure 5.4). This association between support and health was true not only for the combined index of the four different types of social ties but independently for each of the separate measures of social ties. Moreover, the number of social ties predicted each of the separate causes of death, including heart disease, cancer, and circulatory disease. This study therefore provides compelling evidence about the importance of social relationships.

Considerable research supports this finding that greater social support is associated with increased longevity. In one study, researchers examined the effects of social ties, meaning connections to a broader social network, on rates of both mortality and on CHD in 28,369 male health professionals (Eng, Rimm, Fitzmaurice, & Kawachi, 2002). Over a 10-year follow-up, the risk of mortality for men with fewer social ties was significantly higher than that in more socially integrated men, even controlling for age, occupation, health behaviors, general physical condition, coronary risk factors, and dietary habits. For example, men with a moderately low number of social ties were more than twice as likely to die from accidents and suicides than men with the highest number of social connections. Researchers in another study found that emotional support (having significant intimate relationships), not social integration (simply having large social networks), was associated with lower mortality over the next decade (Rosengren, Orth-Comer, Wedel, & Wilhelmsen, 1993). Moreover, while men with many stressful life events had greater mortality

FIGURE 5.4   At every age, men and women with
the most social support are less likely to die than those
with the least social support (data from Berkman &
Syme, 1979).

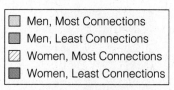

☐	Men, Most Connections
☐	Men, Least Connections
▨	Women, Most Connections
☐	Women, Least Connections

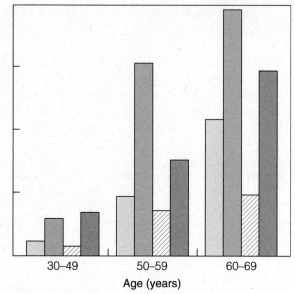

Age (years)

in general, this effect was true only for those who received low levels of emotional
support: apparently receiving high levels of emotional support buffered these men
from the negative health consequences of stressful life events. Other research has
shown similar findings with women. For example, in one study, both men and

Pregnant women who have a
supportive companion during labor
have fewer complications, shorter
labor, and less use of anesthetics.
Source: Anderson Ross/Getty Images,
Inc.

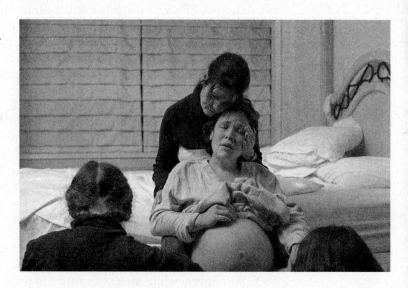

women were interviewed about their social activities and relationships, completed several biomedical measures (e.g., cholesterol, hypertension, blood glucose levels), and were followed for a 10- to 12-year period (House et al., 1982). Once again, the study results indicate that greater involvement in social activities and relationships predict longer life expectancies for both men and women. These findings help explain why married people live longer than unmarried people (Liu, 2009), why people who experience a marital separation or divorce are at greater risk of an early death (Sbarra & Nietert, 2009), and why twice as many single people die from CHD as married people (Schwarzer & Leppin, 1992).

The association between social support and life expectancy is found even in people who are critically ill (Berkman, Leo-Summers, & Horowitz, 1992; Ruberman, Weinblatt, Goldberg, & Chaudhary, 1984). One study of more than 1,000 patients with confirmed heart disease found that those with greater social support, as defined by having a spouse or close confidant, had lower rates of mortality (Williams, Barefoot, et al., 1992). Of those who were married or had a close confidant, 85% lived for at least 5 years, compared to only 50% of those without such support. Similarly, people who have cancer survive longer if they have extensive social support (Helgeson, Cohen, & Fritz, 1998; Spiegel & Kato, 1996). One study of breast-cancer patients, for example, found that participation in a weekly social support group was associated with living longer (Spiegel, Bloom, Kraemer, & Gottheil, 1989). Specifically, women who participated in this support group lived for an average of 36.6 months following the intervention versus 18.9 months for those in the control group. However, more recent research has not replicated these findings (Goodwin et al., 2001). (We talk more about the role of social support in helping people cope with chronic and terminal illness in Chapter 10).

Interestingly, giving social support may also lead to better health. One study that followed older couples over 5 years revealed that people who report providing no instrumental or emotional support to others were more than twice as likely to die over the next 5 years than those who gave such support (to friends, spouses, relatives, neighbors; Brown, Nesse, Vinokur, & Smith, 2003). This effect remained even when researchers considered other factors, such as age, health, and income, suggesting that giving support may in fact be good for your health.

How Does Social Support Lead to Better Health?

Recent research has examined the influence of social support on physiological processes that can lead to various diseases (Kennedy, Kiecolt-Glaser, & Glaser, 1990; Uchino, Cacioppo, & Kiecolt-Glaser, 1996; Uchino, Uno, & Holt-Lunstad, 1999). As a person experiences repeated stressors and their accompanying physiological reactions, his or her body may experience a state of *allostatic load*, which leads to great susceptibility to illness and disease (this phenomenon is described in more detail in Chapter 4). Social support, however, may protect against such health problems by reducing the impact of potential stressors and thereby the body's physiological response. Specifically, social support may influence individuals' appraisal of stressors,

FIGURE 5.5 Social
support may lead to
better health through a
variety of different
pathways (adapted from
Uchino et al., 1999).

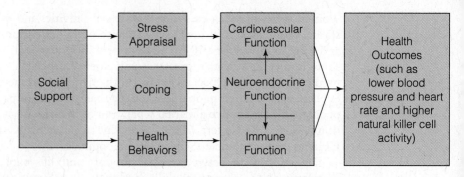

coping strategies, and health behaviors, which can all lead to physiological effects that impact health (see Figure 5.5). This section examines the impact of social support on the cardiovascular system, the immune system, and the neuroendocrine system.

Cardiovascular System

As described in Chapter 4, the cardiovascular system is responsible for transporting oxygen to and removing carbon dioxide from all the cells in the body. When the heart pumps blood, it generates the force necessary to accomplish this important transportation throughout the body. The number of times the heart beats per minute is the heart rate, one measure of cardiovascular reactivity, and the force of the blood against the artery walls is blood pressure, another such measure. The majority of research on the link between social support and physiological processes has focused on the effects of support on these two measures of cardiovascular function (Uchino et al., 1996).

The evidence overwhelmingly points to a link between social support and cardiovascular function. In fact, having low levels of social support has the same impact on mortality from cardiovascular disease as many classic risk factors, such as elevated cholesterol, tobacco use, and hypertension (Mookadam & Arthur, 2004; Uchino et al., 1996). Specifically, people who have higher levels of social support have lower heart rates and blood pressure than those without this support (Bland, Krogh, Winkelstein, & Trevisan, 1991; Linden, Chambers, Maurice, & Lenz, 1993; Unden, Orth-Gomer, & Elofsson, 1991; Whisman, 2010). For example, Unden et al. (1991) found that individuals who had high social support at work had lower mean heart rates as well as lower blood pressure. Because elevated blood pressure can be a risk factor for cardiovascular disease, this association between social support and blood pressure suggests one pathway by which greater support leads to better health. Individuals with more social support are also less reactive to stressful situations (Gerin, Pieper, Levy, & Pickering, 1992; Lepore, Mata Allen, & Evans, 1993). Researchers in one study examined whether social support can reduce cardiovascular reactivity during stressful tasks by asking female college students to complete various arithmetic tasks either alone or in the presence of a friend (Kamarck, Manuck, & Jennings, 1996). Women who had a friend with them had a significantly lower heart rate than those who completed the questionnaires alone. People who wrote about supportive relationships and then completed a stressful task in the lab showed lower heart rates and blood pressure than those who wrote about more casual acquaintances (Smith, Ruiz, & Uchino, 2004). These findings—from both correlational and experimental studies—all suggest that individuals who have more social support have better cardiovascular function.

Immune System

Again, as described in Chapter 4, the immune system helps defend the body against viruses and foreign bacteria; hence, it plays an important role in protecting us from many diseases, including HIV, cancer, and arthritis. The immune system consists of specialized types of white blood cells called lymphocytes, which include B cells, T cells, and Natural Killer (NK) cells. These cells respond to threats to the body in a variety of ways, such as by producing antibodies that bind to—and thereby inactivate—foreign cells, engulfing and destroying foreign cells, and detecting and destroying damaged cells.

People with higher levels of social support have more effective immune systems, so they are better able to fight off major and minor illnesses (Jemmott & Locke, 1984; Jemmott & Magliore, 1988; Uchino et al., 1996). Individuals who have a larger social network are even more resistant to the common cold (Cohen & Hebert, 1996). For example, Cohen, Doyle, Skoner, Rabin, & Gwaltney (1997) conducted a study in which healthy participants completed a series of questionnaires, including measures of life stressors, health practices, and the number of distinct social roles they played (e.g., parent, friend, child, sister), and were then given nasal drops that exposed them to one of two cold viruses. (As described in Chapter 2, for ethical reasons, all participants clearly were informed about this aspect of the study and agreed to undergo this exposure.) All participants were then housed together for 1 week to avoid exposure to any additional viruses, which allowed researchers to assess whether individuals with higher levels of social support had greater resistance to the cold viruses. The researchers collected several different types of data: At the end of each day, participants rated their own symptoms (sneezing, coughing, headache, etc.), and researchers collected all of the tissues used by each participant to measure the amount of mucus produced. As predicted, individuals with more social roles were less susceptible to the common cold: Those who reported having only one to three roles were four times more likely to get sick than those who reported having six or more roles. Specifically, those with more social ties reported feeling less sick and also produced less mucus. These findings suggest that individuals with more diverse social networks are less susceptible to the common cold. On the other hand, people who experience an extreme loss of social support, such as the loss of their spouse through death or divorce, typically show substantial deficits in their immune functioning (Kiecolt-Glaser, et al., 1987; Kiecolt-Glaser et al., 1988; Schleifer, Keller, Camerino, Thornton, & Stein, 1983). For example, people whose spouses have cancer (a clearly stressful situation) and who have high levels of perceived social support show greater NK cell activity, namely, a greater ability to kill off tumor cells, than those who have low levels of social support (Baron, Cutrona, Hicklin, Russell, & Lubaroff, 1990).

Social support may lead to greater immune strength, which in turn leads people to better fight off minor infections that can be life-threatening in those with chronic and terminal diseases. In line with this view, researchers in one study examined the perceived availability of emotional support in people who were HIV positive and then examined immune system strength, as reflected by CD4 counts, every 6 months for 5 years (Theorell et al., 1995). Perceived social support was associated with a significantly more rapid deterioration in T-cell count during subsequent years. Similarly, HIV-positive men who revealed low levels of social support show a faster progression to AIDS (Leserman et al., 1999). In fact, the probability of developing AIDS over a 5-year period was about two to three times as high among those below the median on social support compared with above the median on support. What types of social support are most strongly associated with physiological reactions to stress? One study of first-year college students examined antibody levels in the blood following a vaccination for influenza (see Figure 5.6; Pressman et al., 2005). Students who had a small social network size as well as those who were experiencing greater feelings of loneliness both showed lowered immune function. This demonstrates the importance of both types of social support—meaning social interactions as well as the emotional feeling of being connected to others—in promoting physical health.

Although for ethical and practical reasons most of this research is correlational, some research with animals has used more controlled, experimental studies. Such work has shown that stressful social circumstances lead to negative effects on the immune system (Moynihan & Ader, 1996). For example, monkeys who are separated from their peers have an altered lymphocyte response (Reite, Harbeck, &

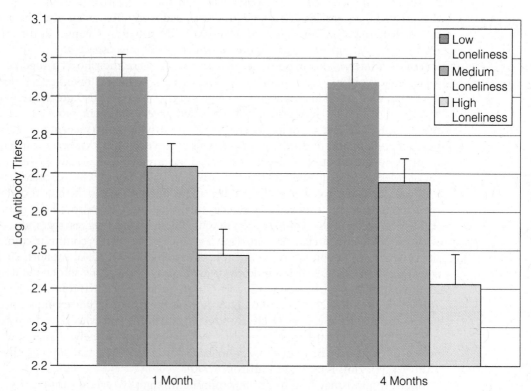

FIGURE 5.6   College freshmen who are high in loneliness show lower levels of immune response following the flu vaccination than those who are low in loneliness. In turn, lonely students are at greater risk of becoming infected with the flu (data from Pressman et al., 2005).

Hoffman, 1981). Similarly, monkey infants who are separated from their mothers show decreases in antibody production (Coe, Wiener, Rosenberg, & Levine, 1985). These studies provide additional evidence that social support impacts physiological functioning.

Neuroendocrine System

The endocrine system works by releasing hormones from various endocrine glands, such as the pituitary gland, thyroid, and pancreas, which then travel through the bloodstream to act on a particular body tissue or organ. During times of stress, the sympathetic nervous system activates two core systems within the endocrine system (Chrousos & Gold, 1992). When the *sympathetic-adrenal medullary (SAM) system* is activated, the hypothalamus triggers the adrenal glands to release epinephrine and norepinephrine, which leads to a number of cardiovascular effects (e.g., increased heart rate and blood pressure). The *hypothalamic-pituitary adrenal (HPA) system* is also activated during times of stress, which in turn leads to the release of cortisol (which decreases the effectiveness of the immune system). (These processes are described in more detail in Chapter 4.)

Social support may have a direct effect on physiology by modulating the HPA axis (DeVries, Glasper, & Detillion, 2003). A study by Seeman et al., for example, found that older adults who had more and better social relationships had lower levels of various hormones, including epinephrine, norepinephrine, and cortisol in their blood (Seeman, Berkman, Blazer, & Rowe, 1994). Similarly, Fleming, Baum, Gisriel, and Gatchel (1982) found that people who had less social support had higher levels of norepinephrine. Some experimental evidence also points to the importance of social support in influencing the neuroendocrine system (Kirschbaum, Klaver, Filipp, & Hellhammer, 1995). For example, the presence of a supportive companion during a difficult public speech leads to a lower cortisol response.

When Does Social Support Lead to Better Health?

Research indicates that social support leads to better health but has not specified whether support is always beneficial or whether it is particularly important during times of high stress. This section discussed two hypotheses that describe the link between social support and well-being in different ways.

Buffering Hypothesis

As discussed in Chapter 4, considerable research demonstrates that stress affects health (Selye, 1976). In turn, having social support may provide a buffer from the daily life stress that people experience, which in turn protects them against illness. For example, when one spouse is particularly busy at work, the other spouse may do more housework and "pick up the slack" to reduce his or her partner's responsibilities and thereby reduce the spouse's experience of stress. Similarly, as

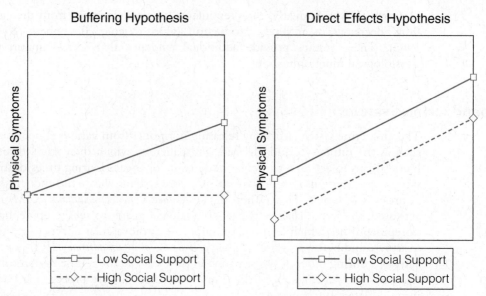

FIGURE 5.7 The buffering hypothesis suggests that social support is particularly beneficial to health during times of stress, whereas the direct effects hypothesis suggests that social support is always beneficial.

described at the beginning of this chapter, Arturo benefited during the difficult exam period from receiving a care package from his parents as well as assistance from his roommate. This hypothesis, the **buffering hypothesis**, depicted in Figure 5.7, suggests that social support leads to better health by protecting people from the negative effects of high stress (Wills, 1984).

Several research studies provide support for the buffering hypothesis by showing that the benefits of social support are greatest for people who are experiencing high levels of stress, including those involved in military combat (Solomon, Mikulincer, & Hobfoll, 1986), those with AIDS (Hays et al., 1992), those experiencing natural disasters (Fleming, Baum, Gisriel, & Gatchel, 1982; Kaniasty & Norris, 1993), and those who are unemployed (Schwarzer, Jerusalem, & Hahn, 1994). In one study by Schwarzer et al. (1994), 235 people completed questionnaires about their amount of social support, employment status, and health. Social support had only a small effect on health for those who were employed, but it had a large effect on health for those who were unemployed (and who were presumably under conditions of greater stress). In fact, those who were unemployed and who had low levels of support reported having the worst health. Similarly, a study of soldiers who fought in the Israel–Lebanon War compared those who experienced a psychological breakdown to those who did not and found that those who experienced such a breakdown received lower levels of social support from the officers in their company (Solomon et al., 1986). The soldiers may have benefited from both instrumental support, such as receiving information that helped them stay safe during intense battle conditions, as well as emotional support, such as feeling cared for and connected to others. In sum, numerous research studies suggest that social support is particularly beneficial in terms of health for people who are undergoing high levels of stress.

Other research shows that having high levels of support from one source may buffer the negative effects of a lack of support from another source. For example, mothers of critically ill children who receive low support from both their spouse and family/friends show the worst level of functioning (Rini, Jandorf, Valdimarsdottir, Brown, & Itzkowitz, 2008). However, mothers who receive low spousal support but high support from family/friends show dramatically improved coping, in line with that of women who receive high spousal support. This research suggests that support from family/friends may buffer lower levels of spousal support.

One possible explanation for how social support may buffer people from stress is that people with high levels of social support think about difficult situations more positively than those with low levels of support. People with high levels of social support know that others will be there to help them during times of need, and thus they may perceive potentially stressful events as less impactful. For example, a person who receives little support from a spouse may see the loss of employment as a very negative event posing substantial problems for the family. In contrast, a person who receives high levels of support from a spouse could interpret the loss of a job as a somewhat negative event but also as an opportunity to investigate a new career path; the loss of a job might then be perceived as less stressful.

Individuals with high levels of social support may also be able to cope more effectively with potentially stressful events. First, receiving various types of social support could help someone directly eliminate, or at least lessen, the negative effects of potentially stressful situations. For example, if your car breaks down and you can't get to work, having a friend who will drive you or loan you a car could substantially reduce your concern about your car breaking down. One research study with more than 1,000 participants found that people who were under considerable financial stress but who received high levels of tangible support were less likely to engage in heavy drinking, whereas those who received low levels of support were particularly likely to demonstrate such behavior (Peirce, Frone, Russell, & Cooper, 1996). Similarly, for adolescents with supportive friendships, uncontrollable stressors aren't linked with risky sexual risk taking, whereas for those without such friendships, they are, perhaps because simply talking to other people may help relieve stress, even if these people can't help you fix or solve the problem (Brady, Dolcini, Harper, & Pollack, 2009). These factors may help people with high levels of support experience better health.

Some research reveals that pets can provide people with valuable social support, which in turn can lead to better psychological and physical well-being. Men who are HIV positive and own a dog show lower levels of depression than those with HIV who don't have pets (Siegel, Angulo, Detels, Wesch, & Mullen, 1999). Moreover, people with pets had fewer doctor visits: those who had experienced many stressful events and did not have a pet had an average of 10.37 doctor visits during the year compared to 8.38 for pet owners (Siegel, 1990). Interestingly, the effect between pet ownership and doctor visits was true only for those who owned a dog; having a cat or a bird did not seem to produce the same beneficial effects. One study even found that pet owners who take a math test in the presence of their pet experience lower heart rates and blood pressure reactivity than those whose pets are not present (Allen, Blasovich, & Mendes, 2002)!

People with pets tend to experience better health, perhaps in part because pets can provide valuable types of social support.
Source: © Michael Krinke/ iStockphoto.

Questioning the Research 5.4

Although research generally reveals that pet owners experience better health, this research doesn't reveal why this association exists. Can you think of some explanations for why pet ownership might lead to better health?

Direct Effects Hypothesis

The buffering hypothesis suggests that social support benefits health only during times of high stress, but other researchers believe that social support benefits health regardless of the amount of stress individuals are experiencing (Wills, 1984). According to this perspective, individuals benefit from having social support during stressful and low-stress times. For example, you may be helped by having emotional support from your friends when you are under a lot of stress at exam time, but you may also be helped from having this support during low-stress times. This hypothesis, the **direct effects hypothesis**, posits that social support can help people experiencing both low levels and high levels of stress; hence, having high levels of social support is always advantageous to health.

Individuals' social relationships may also influence their attitudes and behaviors related to health (Stroebe & Stroebe, 1996). For example, significant others can encourage people to exercise, stop smoking, and eat a balanced diet. In line with this view, people who have more social connections are less likely to engage in unhealthy behaviors, such as smoking and using alcohol, and are more likely to engage in health-promoting behaviors, such as wearing a seat belt (Barrerra, Chassin, & Rogosch, 1993; Businelle et al., 2010; Maton & Zimmerman, 1992; Windle, 1992). People with more social relationships consume fewer alcoholic drinks and smoke fewer cigarettes, perhaps because larger social networks exert more pressure

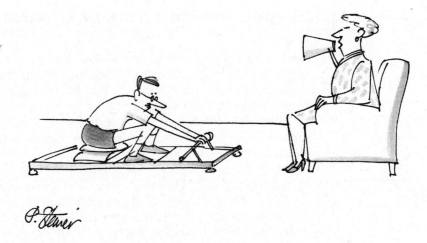

on people to stay healthy (Cohen & Lemay, 2007). In line with this view, gay men who receive high levels of social support from their partners engage in less risky sexual behavior, including extra-relationship sex and unprotected sex (Darbes & Lewis, 2005).

Significant others might also encourage people to use health-care services and follow medical regimens to help manage existing illnesses (e.g., reminding a diabetic to monitor blood sugar levels). In line with this view, individuals with high levels of social support are more likely to use health-care services (Wallston, Alagna, DeVellis, & DeVellis, 1983), adhere to medical regimens (Christensen et al., 1992; Gonzales et al., 2004; Wallston et al., 1983), self-manage chronic conditions (Brody, Kogan, Murry, Chen, & Brown, 2008), and follow recommended cancer screenings (Messina et al., 2004). One meta-analysis revealed that across different types of medical regimens, patients with cohesive families are 1.74 times more likely to adhere, whereas those from families in conflict are 1.53 times less likely to adhere (DiMatteo, 2004).

The absence of social companionship such as that provided by marriage or friendship is likely to lead to loneliness, which is associated with distress, depression, and negative physical symptoms (Peplua, 1985; Stroebe & Stroebe, 1996). To study the impact of companionship on health, Rook (1987) measured levels of stress, social support, companionship, and physical symptoms in a sample of more than 1,000 California residents. This study distinguished between social support—defined as having people to talk to about personal issues, help with household tasks, and consult when making important decisions—and social companionship—defined as having people with whom you can eat meals, visit, and engage in recreational activities. Rook's findings indicate that social support assisted people in times of stress (in line with the buffering hypothesis), and social companionship led to positive well-being regardless of stress levels (in line with the direct effects hypothesis). This work suggests that researchers must distinguish between practical types of support, such as direct help with problem solving and assistance with tasks, which may be particularly beneficial to health when people are experiencing stress, and companionate support, such as listening to people's problems and providing emotional support, which may be beneficial to health in general.

Does Social Support Benefit Men and Women Equally?

Some researchers have examined whether men or women benefit more in terms of health from having social support (Schwarzer & Leppin, 1989). On the one hand, women tend to receive more support than men (Cohen, McGowan, Fooskas, & Rose, 1984). Women typically have a broader social network and more people in whom they confide (Depner & Ingersoll, 1982). College women get more support from their friends and roommates than do men in college (Lepore, 1992). Women are also more likely than men to have a close confidant: One study found that two thirds of women report having a "best friend" compared to 25% of men (Rubin, 1986). However, these broader social networks not only provide women with more support but also give women more people they are supposed to provide support to, which in turn can cause stress (Cohen et al., 1984; Flaherty & Richman, 1989; Kessler, McLeod, & Wethington, 1985). Women are more oriented toward the needs of others (Eisenberg & Lennon, 1983; Gilligan, 1982) and are more likely than men to provide support to their aging parents, children, and friends (Kessler et al., 1985).

Women not only give and receive more social support than men, but they also tend to benefit more psychologically and physically from having social support (Antonucci & Akiyama, 1987; Schwarzer & Leppin, 1989). Women with less support are more likely to experience both depression and anxiety (Flaherty & Richman, 1989), and those who do not have a confidant are more likely to report symptoms of psychological and physical distress (Miller & Ingham, 1976). In both of the preceding studies, there was no association between social support and health for men. Similarly, one study examined level of stress, social support, and physical symptoms in a sample of 115 undergraduate men and women (Wohlgemuth & Betz, 1991). Although social support had no impact on physical symptoms for men, the amount of and satisfaction with social support was a significant predictor of symptoms for women. Finally, research also shows that women benefit more in terms of life expectancy than men from having a large social network. Findings from the Alameda County study, for example, indicated that women with few social connections had a rate of mortality 2.8 times greater than those with many social connections, whereas men with few social connections had a mortality rate only 2.3 times greater than those with many social connections (Berkman & Syme, 1979). One study found that women who were high in marital satisfaction have no increases in cortisol—a marker of stress—during the day, whereas women who are low in marital satisfaction show increases (Saxbe, Repetti, & Nishina, 2008). Men, on the other hand, show decreases in cortisol regardless of marital satisfaction.

Interestingly, although women in general benefit more from social support than men do, men benefit more from marriage (Chesney & Darbes, 1998). Although the death of a spouse is associated with increased risk of mortality for both men and women, losing a spouse is particularly impactful for men (Martikainen & Valkomen, 1996; Stroebe & Stroebe, 1983). One study examined death rates in about 8,000 people who were married or widowed (Helsing & Szklo, 1981). Although there was no difference in death rates for women who were married as compared to those who were widowed (23.2% and 24.1%, respectively), widowed men were at much greater risk of dying from various causes, including infectious diseases, accidents, and suicide, than were men whose spouse was still living (65.3% versus

51.8%, respectively). This difference in death rate for married versus widowed men was particularly large in men who were 55 years and older. However, some recent research suggests that this gap in health between married and single people may be narrowing, at least for men (Liu & Umberson, 2008).

One reason women who experience the death of a spouse have not typically suffered from the same negative health consequences as men may be that women's generally larger social networks enable them to receive more social support following the death of their spouse. For example, women are likely to have more friends available to talk with about their loss, and this emotional support can lead to better health (Stroebe & Stroebe, 1983). Moreover, men generally rely on their wives for emotional support, but women are likely to rely on their children, friends, and other family members for support (Kohen, 1983). Married men may also have relied on their wives to maintain contact with friends and family members; hence, they may feel the loss of support not only from their wives but also from their lost contact with others. Finally, because women tend to live longer than men, women who lose a spouse are likely to find a much larger support group of similar others than are men (Stroebe & Stroebe, 1983). In fact, many community-based support groups for those who have lost a spouse are focused primarily on serving the needs of women.

Another possibility is that because the woman in a married couple tends to take responsibility for much of the day-to-day functioning of the household, men who experience the death of their wife find themselves newly burdened with many household responsibilities. For example, one study of married couples found that wives reported an increase in the time they spent doing housework on days that their husbands had stressful workdays, whereas there was no association between wives' level of work stress and their husbands' participation in household tasks (Bolger, DeLongis, Kessler, & Schilling, 1989).

What Factors Lead to the Social Support–Health Link?

Multiple studies demonstrate a link between social support and health, but for ethical reasons, virtually all of this research is correlational: It is obviously impossible to randomly assign people to receive different levels of social support and then to assess the consequences of such support on well-being over time. Thus, we can tell that social support and health are correlated, but we can't tell whether having social support *causes* better health. Some researchers have therefore proposed alternatives to explain the link between social support and health.

One possible explanation for the association between social support and health is that illness leads to disruption in social support. People who are suffering from a chronic and/or debilitating illness are likely to have trouble engaging in social and recreational activities; hence, they may have difficulty making and maintaining inter-personal relationships. For example, individuals who are disabled, such as through spinal cord injury or a stroke, often report having smaller social networks than those who are of similar age but not disabled (Schulz & Decker, 1985; Schulz & Tomp-kins, 1990). People sometimes hold negative stereotypes about those who have a chronic illness and may even blame ill persons for acquiring the disease. These beliefs can lead people to avoid spending time with someone who has a chronic or terminal illness. Also having a chronic illness can cause people to feel alienated from family and friends, which thereby disrupts normal levels of social support (Dakof & Taylor, 1990; Wortman & Dunkel-Schetter, 1979). One study found that 75% of breast-cancer patients reported that people treated them differently after learning of their disease (Peters-Golden, 1982). All of these factors could lead people who are in poor physical health to experience decreases in the amount of social support they receive.

Another possible explanation for the link between social support and health is that a third variable causes this association. For example, people who are very hostile may have few friends and may also experience greater cardiovascular stress during interpersonal interactions. If researchers then found that people who have few friends have worse health, they wouldn't be able to tell if the poor health was the result of having low levels of social support or the result of having more cardiovascular reactivity, which leads to wear and tear on the heart over time. In this case, the supposed association between social support and health would simply be a reflection of hostility leading to both low levels of social support and poor health.

Although both of these alternative explanations for the link between social support and health are possible, research suggests that they are unlikely for several reasons. First, studies that follow people over time still show an association between social support and rates of mortality (House et al., 1988). For example, researchers in the Alameda County study measured social support at one point in time, and then measured death rates over the next 9 years (Berkman & Syme, 1979), and other large-scale studies that followed people over time reveal similar findings (Blazer, 1982; House et al., 1982; Kaplan et al., 1988; Ruberman et al., 1984; Williams et al., 1992). These prospective studies suggest that social support leads to well-being as opposed to the reverse.

Second, studies show a link between social support and health even when they take into account other variables, such as social class and personality, which might predict both support and health. For example, in the Alameda County study, the link between social support and mortality was found to be independent of socioeconomic status as well as other health-related behaviors, such as smoking, alcohol use, obesity, and physical inactivity (Berkman & Syme, 1979). This means that none of these other variables explains the link between social support and health. Similarly, in a study examining whether people with more social support are less susceptible to getting a cold, researchers considered a number of other variables that could explain this relationship, including smoking, poor sleep quality, alcohol abstinence, and low levels of intake of vitamin C (Cohen et al., 1997). However, the association between social support and health remained even when these other factors were considered. Nonetheless, the vast majority of research showing a link between support and health is correlational; hence, it is important to remember that this association could be interpreted in different ways.

Finally, although this section has focused on the numerous ways in which social support may lead to better health, in some cases, social support can have negative implications for psychological and physical well-being. People sometimes receive social support that is intended to be helpful but that is actually detrimental in terms of health (Dakof & Taylor, 1990; Thoits, Hohmann, Harvey, & Fletcher, 2000; Wortman & Lehman, 1985). For example, if you are depressed about a recent relationship breakup, friends may encourage you to "drown your sorrows"

TABLE 5.5 *Information YOU Can Use*

- Your outlook—including your personality, beliefs, and mood—influences your physical well-being, so try to maintain positive states, including extraversion and positive affect, whenever possible. In other words, focus on seeing the glass as half full, instead of half empty!
- People who are conscientious live longer, in part because they show amazing self-control and thus have the ability to focus on long-term goals over short-term gratification. In turn, conscientiousness is associated with better health-related behavior, including healthy eating, exercise, and adherence to medical recommendations. So, the next time you are faced with short-term temptations, try to focus on the longer-term consequences of such a choice . . . and exercise self-restraint.
- Consider getting a pet . . . and preferably a dog. Research reveals that pet owners experience better psychological and physical well-being.
- Try to form larger social networks because having more people to rely on increases the likelihood of having a particular type of support available when you need it. This might be a particularly important strategy to use when you are in new environments (e.g., starting college, moving to a new city), which may be stressful and in which you may not already have many sources of support. You should also try to maintain closer contact with old friends.
- During times of particular crisis, participate in organized social support groups that include others who are facing or have faced a similar crisis, which allows an opportunity to share feelings with others who are likely to understand and accept what you are going through. Because these groups consist of similar others, they provide not only emotional support but also tangible and informational support.

by drinking alcohol, which obviously is not a great strategy for enhancing your health. Similarly, people can give unwanted advice, discourage open discussion of the problem, and push for a too-rapid recovery following an illness or negative event (Dakof & Taylor, 1990; Dunkel-Schetter & Wortman, 1982). In fact, people who experience more problematic, or undermining, social support are at greater risk of experiencing CHD (Davis & Swan, 1999). We will talk about the impact of social support on coping with chronic illness more in Chapter 10.

Summary

1. Some personality traits—meaning individual differences in people's tendency to think, feel, and act in particular ways—are associated with good health.

2. People who are high in positive states, including extraversion and positive affect, experience better psychological and physical well-being. They are less likely to get the common cold, experience a stroke, or have an accident. They also have lower rates of major and minor illnesses, and greater life expectancy.

3. People who are optimistic, meaning those who expect good things will happen to them in the future and bad things will not, experience better health. They are less likely to experience depression, develop fewer minor and major illnesses, recover faster from surgery, and have a greater life expectancy.

4. People who are conscientiousness—meaning hardworking, motivated, and persistent—show better physical health and longevity.

5. People who have a strong internal locus of control —meaning they believe their decisions and behaviors impact the outcomes they experience—as well as those who are high in hardiness—meaning a commitment to goals and activities as well as a sense of control and a view of stressful events as challenging instead of threatening—experience better psychological and physical well-being. These traits are associated with lower levels of depression, lower rates of illness and disease, and lower rates of mortality from all causes.

6. Neuroticism, or negative affect, is associated with worse physical health. People who are high on this trait report experiencing more physical symptoms and health problems, and have a lower life expectancy.

7. Type A behavior—which is characterized by high levels of time urgency, a strong competitive drive, and higher levels of anger and hostility—is associated with worse health. People with Type A behavior report more minor and major health problems. However, more recent research suggests that the link between Type A behavior and poor health is caused largely by only one aspect of Type A behavior: hostility.

8. Hostility/disagreeableness is associated with overall poorer health. People who are high in hostility experience higher rates of minor and major illnesses and have higher rates of mortality.

9. Researchers have examined a number of explanations for the link between personality and health. These include the amount of stress experienced, the influence of personality on physiological responses, the use of different coping mechanisms, the amount of social support available, and health habits.

Researchers have also explored whether these links are in reality a function simply of self-report.

10. Researchers have measured social support in a variety of different ways. These include the structure of people's social network, the amount of perceived social support available, and the amount of social support actually received.

11. Research indicates a strong association between social support and positive health outcomes, including greater psychological well-being, greater physical well-being, faster recovery from illness, and lower rates of mortality.

12. Social support has beneficial effects on physiological processes that lead to disease. In particular, the presence of social support influences the cardiovascular system, the immune system, and the neuroendocrine system.

13. There are two alternative explanations for how social support leads to better health. The buffering hypothesis suggests that social support leads to better health by protecting people from the negative effects of high stress. In contrast, the direct effects hypothesis suggests that social support can help people experiencing both low and high levels of stress.

14. Research suggests that women in general benefit more from social support than do men. However, men benefit more from marriage—a particular type of social support—than do women.

15. Researchers have examined a number of different explanations for the link between social support and health. These include the disruption of illness on social support and the presence of a third variable that impacts both social support and health.

Key Terms

belongingness support	hardiness	neuroticism/negative affect
buffering hypothesis	hostility/disagreeableness	optimism
conscientiousness	informational support/appraisal	personality
direct effects hypothesis	support	positive states
emotional support	instrumental support/tangible	social network
esteem support/validational	support	social support
support	internal locus of control	Type A behavior

Thought Questions

1. Your roommate is a classic extravert—outgoing, sociable, and always looking for new and exciting challenges. On the other hand, his stepbrother is moody, antagonistic, and pessimistic. What might you predict about the psychological and physical well-being of each person?

2. Describe four distinct ways in which personality may influence health. Which of these pathways do you find most plausible, and why?

3. You notice that your friends who are in dating relationships seem to get sick less often than your friends who are single. Describe how both the direct effects and buffering hypotheses would explain this observation.

4. Describe two different ways that social support may influence physiological processes.

5. You are feeling overwhelmed with the amount of work you have as finals week approaches. What are two helpful things your roommate could do? What are two detrimental things he or she could do?

Answers to Questioning the Research

Answer 5.1. Although several studies have shown that the general personality trait of hardiness is associated with psychological and physical well-being, more recent research indicates that the specific components of hardiness are not all equally useful in predicting health-related behavior (Hull, Van Treuren, & Virnelli, 1987). Specifically, both commitment and control are systematically linked to health, but there is little evidence that challenge is a consistent predictor of health.

Answer 5.2. Although research shows that people who are high in negative affect experience lower marital satisfaction, this study shows only correlation, not causation. How do you think you'd grow to feel over time if you were in an unhappy and conflict-ridden marriage? It could easily lead you to feel bad about yourself and hence to experience high levels of guilt, anxiety, and depression. It may be that participating in a dysfunctional marriage *leads* to negative affect as opposed to the reverse. Another possibility is that a third variable leads to both negative affect and lower marital satisfaction. For example, people who are struggling with many negative life events, such as poverty, natural disasters, and/or major illnesses, might develop negative feelings about themselves, and, because of the pressures of their situation, they may argue more frequently with their spouses. Just remember, *correlation* does not necessarily mean *causation*.

Answer 5.3. Although this study assessed four different categories of social ties, namely marriage, contacts with extended family and friends, church or temple membership, and other formal and informal group affiliations, these do not represent the only types of social ties people could have. For example, people who are not married but who have a close relationship with a live-in partner probably experience the same benefits of social support as those who are married. These researchers also give equal weight to the four different types of social support, and thus simply count how many different types of support people have. But it is probably more important in terms of health to have close connections (e.g., with family and friends) than to have more distant contacts (e.g., casual relationships with work colleagues).

Answer 5.4. Although research suggests that owning a dog leads to better physical well-being, it is difficult to determine exactly what factors account for this relationship. One possibility is that dogs—which tend to provide unconditional love—provide high levels of emotional support, which leads to better health. Another possibility is that because dogs typically need to be walked, dog owners engage in more exercise (Brown & Rhodes, 2006), which also leads to better health. Yet another possibility is that people who walk dogs get more social support from those they encounter on these walks, and thus help people build stronger connections to people in their community. Future research is needed to examine the precise factors that determine the link between pet ownership and better health.

CHAPTER 6

Injuries

Outline

- Tabitha is excited about the new pool she is installing in her backyard. However, she is also installing a high, four-sided fence with a locked gate because she has two young kids and is well aware of the risks of drowning.

- Billy is a sophomore in college and recently crashed his car into a tree late one night after leaving a party in which he had had a few beers. Although his car was totaled, he realizes that he is lucky to be alive. Billy now intends to reduce his drinking and vows never to drink and drive again.

- Mrs. O'Connor is 77 years old and is recovering from a hip fracture in the hospital. She slipped on a rug in her house and is now afraid of returning home in fear that she will experience another fall.

- Lucy, who is a junior in high school, feels very depressed most of the time. She isn't interested in spending time with friends and often feels very sad and lonely. Sometimes Lucy thinks about killing herself.

- Ricardo is a sophomore in high school who is working very hard on his grades to make sure he can go to college. Ricardo's older brother, who was in a gang, died in a shooting in a nightclub, and Ricardo wants to make sure he avoids getting involved with this type of activity.

Preview

This chapter examines different types of injuries, the risk of injury across the life span, and strategies for preventing injuries. First, we examine different types of injury and then how the risk of injury varies across the life span. Next, this chapter describes the five leading causes of injuries: motor vehicle accidents, poisoning, suicide, falls, and homicide. Finally, we discuss different strategies for preventing injuries, including active strategies, passive strategies, and societal changes.

What Is Injury?

One of the major goals of health psychology is to prevent the development of health problems, which is a much easier and cheaper way of increasing life expectancy and life quality than treating already-established medical problems. In 2007, 182,479 Americans died from injuries, 2,855,000 persons were hospitalized for injuries, and 29,757,000 persons were treated for nonfatal injuries in U.S. hospital emergency departments (Centers for Disease Control, 2011). Injuries may lead to death as well as to continuing debilitating problems (e.g., spinal cord injuries, brain injuries) that impair life. Although injuries in general cause numerous fatalities and continuing problems, different types of injuries are caused by different factors. Specifically, psychologists divide injuries into two distinct types: unintentional injuries and intentional injuries. Let's examine each of these in turn.

Unintentional injuries are often described as "accidents" because the person who experienced the injury did not mean for it to happen. However, the leading cause of death in every age group between age 1 and 44 is unintentional injury (CDC, 2011). Many unintentional injuries are caused by car accidents, fires,

Motor vehicle accidents lead to 2.3 million people being treated in the emergency room each year for injuries and are the leading cause of death among people age 5 to 34 in the United States (CDC, 2011). *Source:* © tillsonburg/iStockphoto.

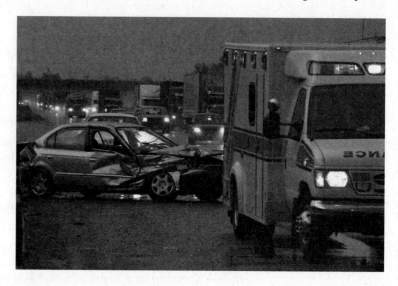

drowning, falls, poisoning, and homicide. This type of injury could include someone developing a sprained neck following a car crash, becoming paralyzed after falling from a balcony, or dying from an accidental shooting.

Although these types of injuries are called accidents, many of these injuries could be prevented (as discussed later in the chapter). For example, the number one cause of unintentional accidents in every one of these age groups is car accidents (CDC, 2011). Because many of these accidents—or at least the deaths caused by them—could be prevented through behavioral choices (putting children in car seats, wearing a seat belt, following the speed limit, and refusing to drive while intoxicated), this is a compelling example of the role that individual choice has in determining physical health.

Other types of injuries are described as **intentional injuries**, meaning the person who caused the injury meant for it to happen. This type of injury could include a school shooting in which a person deliberately kills one or more people, or a suicide, in which a person deliberately attempts to harm himself or herself.

Injuries exert a huge cost on society, not only in terms of physical health and life expectancy but also in terms of financial costs. More than 50 million Americans experience some type of injury each year, at a cost of $400 billion in medical care costs as well as loss of productivity (Corso, Finkelstein, Miller, Fiebelkorn, & Zaloshnja, 2006). As shown in Figure 6.1, many of these costs are due to motor vehicle accidents and falls.

How Does the Risk of Injury Vary Across the Life Span?

Although overall injuries are the fifth leading cause of death (following heart disease, cancer, stroke, and chronic obstructive pulmonary disease), the risk of injury, as well as death caused by injury, varies considerably across the life span (see Table 6.1; CDC, 2011). This section will examine the risk of injury across the life span, including childhood, adolescence, and adulthood.

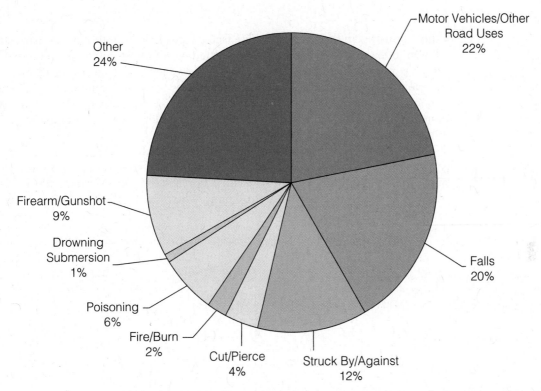

FIGURE 6.1 Data on cost of injuries from the CDC. The financial costs of injuries each year are substantial; these costs include both direct costs of medical treatment (about $80 billion a year) and indirect costs due to lost productivity (about $326 billion a year; CDC, 2011).

TABLE 6.1 *Leading Causes of Death by Age*

Birth to age 1: Congenital anomalies, short gestation, SIDS

Ages 1 to 4 years: Accidents, congenital anomalies, homicide

Ages 5 to 9 years: Accidents, malignant neoplasms, congenital anomalies

Ages 10 to 14 years: Accidents, malignant neoplasms, homicide

Ages 15 to 24 years: Accidents, homicides, suicide

Ages 25 to 34 years: Accidents, suicide, homicide

Ages 35 to 44 years: Accidents, malignant neoplasms, heart disease

Ages 45 to 54 years: Malignant neoplasms, heart disease, accidents

Ages 55 to 64 years: Malignant neoplasms, heart disease, chronic respiratory disease

Ages 65 years and over: Heart disease, malignant neoplasms, cerebrovascular disease

Although heart disease and cancer are the overall leading causes of death, more people ages 1 to 44 years die from accidents than from any other cause.

Source: CDC, 2010.

Childhood

Although infants in the first year of life face a higher likelihood of death than older children (often due to complications associated with premature birth), childhood in general is a time of relatively low mortality. However, and as shown in Figure 6.2, the leading cause of death for children from ages 1 to 14 is unintentional injury, with an estimated 5,067 children (ages 1 to 14) dying each year from unintentional injuries (CDC, 2011). In addition, close to 1,000 children 14 and younger die each year from intentional injury (homicide and suicide).

The specific types of unintentional injuries that lead to death vary considerably by age (see Table 6.2; CDC, 2011). For infants younger than 1, suffocation causes the vast majority of injury deaths. For children ages 1 to 4, the leading causes of injury-related death are drowning, which causes 28.8% of injury-related

FIGURE 6.2 Although the death rate for unintentional injuries has decreased somewhat over the past decade, unintentional injuries are still by far the leading cause of death in children ages 1 to 14 (data from CDC, 2011).

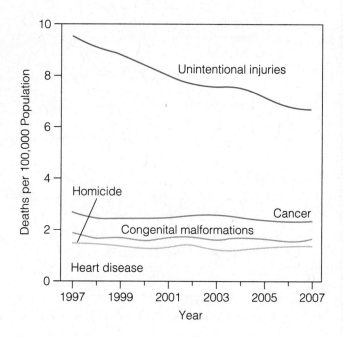

TABLE 6.2 *Leading Causes of Accidents Leading to Death in Children*

Younger than 1: Unintentional suffocation, homicide, car accident

Ages 1 to 4: Drowning, car accident, fire/burns

Ages 5 to 9: Car accident, fire/burns, drowning

Ages 10 to 14: Car accident, homicide, suicide

Although the types of causes of accidents leading to death vary by age, accidents are the leading cause of death in children age 1 to 14.

Source: CDC, 2011.

Box 6.1

Focus on Culture: The Impact of Culture on Risk for Childhood Injuries

Researchers in one study examined cultural differences in the risk of childhood injury (Vaughan, Anderson, Agran, & Winn, 2004). To examine this question, researchers interviewed 100 lower income Hispanic and 50 White mothers who had a child under the age of 5. As predicted, White mothers reported more unintentional injuries for their child than did Hispanic mothers. Among Hispanic mothers, those who preferred to speak English reported more injuries than those who preferred to speak Spanish. However, the factors that predicted the experience of injury were relatively similar for White and Hispanic women. These included the child's tendency to engage in risky behaviors, the mother's ratings of the child's level of obedience, and the presence of stressful life events. These were all more important predictors of the rate of injury than physical factors related to the home environment, such as presence of childproof locks on cabinets, presence of stairs, and presence of broken locks and doors. Finally, the predictors of childhood injury differed somewhat as a function of the degree of acculturation in Hispanic families. These findings suggest that there are both similarities and differences in terms of the influence of culture on the risk for childhood injury.

deaths, and motor vehicle accidents, which causes 27% of such deaths. For children ages 5 to 9, nearly half of all injury-related deaths are caused by motor vehicle accidents (47.3%), with a smaller number of deaths caused by fire/burns (14.1%) and drowning (12.6%). For children ages 10 to 14, over half of all injury-related deaths are caused by motor vehicle accidents (56.6%). The problem of—and some solutions for—motor vehicle accidents are discussed later in the chapter. Box 6.1: Focus on Culture describes the influence of culture on the risk of childhood injuries.

Adolescence and Young Adulthood

Injury is also one of the leading causes of deaths for adolescents and young adults (ages 15 to 24; CDC, 2011). An estimated 15,897 deaths in this age group were caused by unintentional injury, followed by homicide (5,551) and suicide (4,140). The majority of unintentional injuries are caused by motor vehicle accidents (64.6%), followed by poisoning (19.9%). (Factors leading to homicide and suicide are discussed later in the chapter).

As shown in Table 6.3, motor vehicle accidents are by far the leading cause of accidents leading to death for adolescents and young adults. Many of these accidents are a result of unsafe driving, including speeding, driving under the influence of alcohol, and driving while distracted (e.g., talking on a cell phone, texting, etc.).

Unfortunately, many people do try to text and drive, and this type of distracted driving can lead to serious, and even fatal, consequences. *Source:* Alex Gregory/cartoonbank.com. All Rights Reserved.

"This one's too hard to type on while I'm driving."

TABLE 6.3 *Leading Causes of Accidents Leading to Death in Adolescents and Young Adults*

Type of Accident	Number of Deaths
Motor vehicle	10,272
Poisoning	3,159
Drowning	630

Adulthood

Injuries are the leading cause of death in adults ages 35 to 44, but then the percentage of deaths caused by injuries decreases in older adults (CDC, 2011). Specifically, injuries are only the third leading cause of death in adults ages 45 to 54, the fourth leading cause of death in adults ages 55 to 64, and the ninth leading cause of death in those over age 65.

As shown in Table 6.4, the specific causes of injury-related deaths also change with age (CDC, 2011). In adults age 25 to 34, car accidents are the leading cause of death, followed by poisoning. In adults age 35 to 44, poisoning is the leading cause of death (44.7%), following by motor vehicle accidents (36.2%). Similarly, in adults age 45 to 54, poisoning (44.3%) and motor vehicle accidents (30.8%) are still the leading causes of injury-related deaths. In adults age 55 to 65, the leading cause is motor vehicle accidents (34.3%), followed by poisoning (25.6%) and falls (14.3%). Finally, for adults older than 64, the leading cause of death is falls, 47.9%, followed by motor vehicle accidents (17.3%).

TABLE 6.4   *Leading Causes of Injury-Related Deaths by Age in Adulthood*

Ages 25 to 34: Car accident, poisoning, homicide

Ages 35 to 44: Poisoning, car accident, suicide

Ages 45 to 54: Poisoning, car accident, suicide

Ages 55 to 64: Car accident, suicide, poisoning

Ages 65 on: Falls, car accidents, suicide

Although the leading causes of injury-related deaths vary by age, car accidents continue to claim many lives.

Source: CDC, 2011.

What Are the Leading Causes of Injuries?

This section will examine the five major causes of injury deaths: motor vehicle accidents, poisoning, suicide, falls, and homicide.

Motor Vehicle Accidents

Every year, nearly 40,000 Americans die from injuries related to motor vehicle accidents, and another 270,000 persons are hospitalized (CDC, 2011). These account for 23.0% of all injury deaths. In fact, every 12 minutes, someone dies in a car crash in the United States, and every 10 seconds, someone is injured and taken to an emergency department.

As you might imagine, the risk of motor vehicle death varies considerably by age. Motor vehicle injuries are the leading cause of death for children, with more than 1,300 children killed in car crashes each year. Motor vehicle crashes are also the leading cause of death for U.S. teens. In the United States during 2005, 1,451 children ages 14 years and younger died as occupants in motor vehicle crashes (an average of 4 deaths a day), and in 2008 alone, crashes took the lives of more than 5,800 people younger than age 20. Figure 6.3 shows the impact of age on number of fatal car crashes each year (Nell, 2002).

In addition to causing a sizeable proportion of all injury deaths, motor vehicle accidents also cause other types of lasting but not fatal problems. For example, motor vehicle accidents are responsible for nearly half of the cases of spinal cord injuries (46%), with falls and sports accidents each causing approximately 16% of the cases. Spinal cord injury is a lesion of the cord that causes permanent paralysis and loss of sensation below the level of the lesion (Zejdlik, 1983). The term *paraplegia* refers to paralysis of the lower part of the body, including the legs, whereas the term *quadriplegia* refers to paralysis of the upper and lower parts of the body, including the arms and hands. The damage is typically caused by an injury that compresses, severs, or tears the spinal cord. Most people who suffer a spinal cord injury are male (82%) and are between the ages of 16 and 30 (61%) when they suffer the injury (Hanak & Scott, 1993). More than 200,000 people in the United States today are living with spinal cord injuries.

FIGURE 6.3 The percentage of fatal car crashes caused by speeding is significantly higher in people in adolescence and early adulthood than in older adults (data from Nell, 2002).

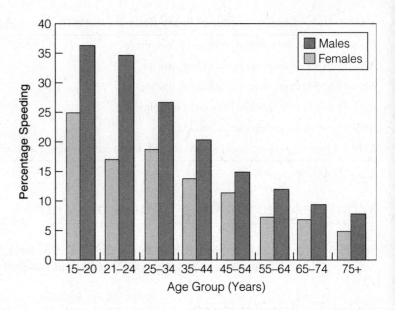

Questioning the Research 6.1

Why do you think men are more at risk of experiencing a spinal cord injury than women? What factors might explain this relationship?

People who experience a spinal cord injury face numerous physical and psychological challenges (Richards, Kewman, & Pierce, 2000; Zejdlik, 1983). First, they must focus on trying to regain as much physical functioning as possible, which can include redeveloping bladder and bowel control as well as maintaining a range of motion in their arms and legs. They may also work with physical therapists to strengthen the muscles they can control to partially compensate for their lack of control over other parts of their bodies. For example, quadriplegics may focus on improving respiration, whereas paraplegics may focus on exercises to strengthen the upper body. People with spinal cord injuries also experience significant psychological challenges and are likely to experience high levels of depression and anxiety, particularly early in their recovery. Many people report contemplating suicide or wishing that they had not survived their accident. They are often concerned about their social relationships, including whether their old friends will accept them, whether they will be a burden to their families, and whether they will be able to engage in romantic and sexual relationships.

Poisoning

Poison describes any substance that can be harmful to your health if too much of that substance is taken into your body via any mechanism (e.g., eaten, inhaled, injected, or absorbed through the skin). This can include the use of drugs for recreational purposes, as well as the use of drugs by accident, such as when a toddler mistakes a medication for candy.

Unintentional poisoning was second only to motor vehicle crashes as a cause of unintentional injury death for all ages in 2007, and, in fact, among people 35 to 54 years old, unintentional poisoning caused more deaths than motor vehicle crashes (CDC, 2011). In 2007, 29,846 (74%) of the 40,059 poisoning deaths in the United States were unintentional, meaning the person did not intend to cause themselves harm, and 3,770 (9%) were unknown in terms of their intent. Every day in the United States, nearly 82 people die as a result of unintentional poisoning, and another 1,941 are treated in emergency departments. In addition, poison control centers reported receiving calls about 2.5 million human poison exposure cases.

Most (93%) of unintentional poisoning deaths are caused by drugs. These drugs include opioid pain medications (e.g., methadone, hydrocodone, or oxycodone), cocaine, and heroin. Among those treated in emergency rooms for poisonings involving the use of prescription or over-the-counter drugs, opioid pain medications and benzodiazepines (such as Valium) were used most frequently.

Demographic factors, including gender, race, and age, are associated with the likelihood of poisoning (CDC, 2011). Men are twice as likely as women to die from poisoning. In addition, Native Americans have the highest death rates by poisoning, followed by Whites and then Blacks. The peak age of deaths by poisoning is 45 to 49 years of age.

Although mortality rates caused by poisoning among children younger than 15 are quite low because they do not abuse drugs as frequently as older people, an estimated 71,000 children visit emergency rooms each year due to medication poisonings (these numbers do not include recreational drug use; CDC, 2011). Very young children are particularly at risk of poisoning: In fact, 1 out of every 180 two year olds visits an emergency department for a medication poisoning. Over 80% of these visits occur as a result of an unsupervised child finding and consuming medicines. Medication poisonings by children are twice as common as poisonings from other household products (such as cleaning solutions and personal care products).

Suicide

Suicide is the 11th overall leading cause of death in the United States, with more than 34,000 suicides occurring each year in the United States (or 94 suicides a day; CDC, 2011). Suicides cause many more deaths each year than homicides or HIV/AIDS: On an average day, 84 people in the United States die from suicide, and close to 2,000 make an unsuccessful suicide attempt (Fine, Rousculp, Tomasek, & Horn, 1999). In 2008, 376,306 people were treated in emergency departments for self-inflicted injuries, and 163,489 people were hospitalized due to self-inflicted injury.

Suicide risk varies by age. It is the third leading cause of death in people ages 15 to 24 years and the second leading cause of death in people ages 25 to 34 (CDC, 2011). Moreover, many more people attempt suicide or consider attempting suicide. One large-scale survey of high school students revealed that 27% of girls and 15% of boys had seriously considered attempting suicide, and nearly 8% of all students had made at least one suicide attempt (Kann et al., 1998).

Suicide risk also varies by gender. During their lifetime, women attempt suicide about two to three times as often as men (CDC, 2011). Although women are more likely to attempt suicide, more men than women die from suicide: Males take their own lives at nearly four times the rate of females and represent 78.8% of all U.S. suicides. This gender difference is caused at least in part by the differences in

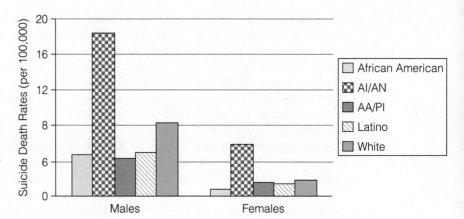

FIGURE 6.4
Although males of all races are more likely to die of suicide than females, American Indian/Native Americans have substantially higher rates of suicide than those from any other ethnicity (data from Goldston et al., 2008).

methods used—men tend to use "more effective" methods, such as firearms and hanging, whereas women are more likely to use "less effective" methods, such as poisoning (Fine et al., 1999). Firearms are the most commonly used method of suicide among males (55.7%), whereas poisoning is the most common method of suicide for females (40.2%).

Finally, there are substantial differences in rates of suicide as a function of race/ethnicity. Among American Indians/Alaska Natives ages 15 to 34, suicide is the second leading cause of death (CDC, 2011). As shown in Figure 6.4, suicide rates among American Indian/Alaskan Native adolescents and young adults ages 15 to 34 are 1.8 times higher than the national average for that age group.

Although suicide is clearly influenced by multiple factors, including substance abuse, depression, and a history of family violence, one contributing factor is access to firearms (O'Donnell, 1995). In fact, 57% of all suicides are committed by firearms, making this by far the most common method of suicide (Romero & Wintemute, 2002). People living in a house where a firearm is kept are almost five times as likely to die by suicide than people living in gun-free homes (Bailey et al., 1997; Kellerman et al., 1992; Kellerman et al., 1993; Resnick et al., 1997). Having a gun available also increases the likelihood that a suicide attempt will be successful (see Box 6.2: Focus on Research).

Questioning the Research 6.2
Although gun ownership is clearly associated with suicide, does this link necessarily show causation? Why or why not?

A suicide has a major impact on other people in the victim's life. The common experiences people have in response to other types of loss, such as anger, guilt, and sadness, are often intensified in the case of suicides. First, because suicides are not caused by natural events, these deaths are seen by survivors as deaths that were avoidable. Suicide deaths are also sudden; hence, survivors have no chance to prepare themselves. Survivors are therefore especially likely to experience feelings of blame and guilt, a sense of rejection by the victim, and difficulty in coming to terms with the death (Silverman, Range, & Overholser, 1994). Moreover, because

Box 6.2

Focus on Research: The Hazards of Owning a Firearm

This research examined the association between rates of household firearm ownership and suicide across the 50 states (Miller, Lippmann, Azrael, & Hemenway, 2007). The researchers used state-level survey data assessing household firearm ownership, mental illness, and alcohol/illicit substance use and dependence to examine the relationship between owning a gun and rates of firearm, nonfirearm, and overall suicide. The researchers took into account poverty, unemployment, mental illness, and drug and alcohol dependence and abuse. The findings revealed that residents of all ages and both sexes are more likely to die from both firearm suicides and overall suicides when they live in communities in which more households contain firearms. Interestingly, no association existed between rates of firearm ownership and rates of suicides not caused by firearms. This finding suggests that firearm ownership levels are strongly associated with higher rates of suicide at least in part because the availability of guns in a community increases the rate of successfully completed suicide.

of the stigma of suicide, survivors may be less likely to receive much-needed assistance from others.

Falls

In 2007, 23,443 persons died as the result of falls, which represented 12.8% of all injury deaths (CDC, 2011). The vast majority of fall-related deaths (96.5%) were unintentional. However, many additional people suffer fall-related injuries that do not lead to death; falls are the leading cause of injury and account for nearly 40% of

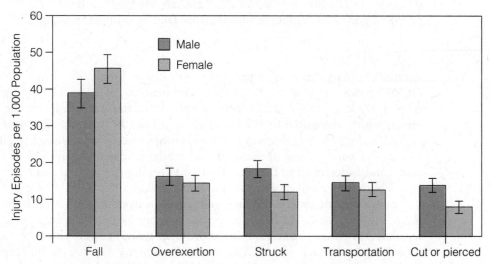

FIGURE 6.5 Falls are the overall leading cause of injury and account for more than twice as many injuries as any other cause (data from Chen, Warner, et al., 2009).

all injuries (see Figure 6.5; Chen, Warner, Fingerhut, & Makuc, 2009). About 20 to 30% of people who fall suffer moderate to severe injuries, including lacerations, fractures, or head traumas. In fact, falls are the most common cause of traumatic brain injuries (TBI). In 2000, TBI accounted for 46% of fatal falls among older adults. Many people who fall, even if they are not injured, develop a fear of falling. Sadly, this fear may cause them to limit their activities, leading to reduced mobility and loss of physical fitness, which in turn increases their actual risk of falling.

Not surprisingly, age has a substantial impact on the rate of falling as well as the likelihood of being injured or dying in a fall (CDC, 2011). Each year, one in every three adults age 65 and older falls, and among those aged 65 and older, falls are the leading cause of injury death. In addition, 2.2 million older adults are treated in emergency rooms each year for nonfatal fall injuries, and more than 581,000 of these patients were hospitalized. Although women are more likely than men to suffer a fall injury, men are more likely to die from a fall.

Falls are also the leading cause of nonfatal injuries for all children ages 0 to 19, with approximately 8,000 children every day—and 2.8 million children a year—being treated in an emergency room for a fall-related injury (CDC, 2011). For very young children, meaning those younger than age 2, many of these injuries are caused by falls from cribs, playpens, and bassinets (Yeh, Rochette, McKenzie, & Smith, 2011). An estimated 9,561 fall-related injuries occur in children younger than 2 each year, with 83.2% of these caused by a fall from a crib. Interestingly, mothers are less likely to take steps to prevent falls than to prevent other types of injuries, such as burns, drowning, and poisoning, perhaps due to a mistaken belief that fall injuries aren't particularly serious (Morrongiello & Kiriakou, 2004).

In older children, many fall-related injuries are a result of playground accidents, which can lead to fractures, internal injuries, concussions, dislocations, and amputations (Tinsworth, 2001). A study in New York City found that playgrounds in low-income areas had more maintenance-related hazards than playgrounds in high-income areas. For example, playgrounds in low-income areas had significantly more trash, rusty play equipment, and damaged fall surfaces (Suecoff, Avner, Chou, & Crain, 1999). Box 6.3: Focus on Research describes an interesting strategy for preventing injuries, including injuries from falls, in children: reading!

Homicide

Another leading causes of injury-related deaths is homicide, with an estimated 18,361 deaths per year (CDC, 2011). The majority of homicides are caused by guns. In fact, in 2007, 31,224 persons died from firearm injuries in the United States, which accounted for 17.1% of all injury deaths that year. Firearms are the second leading cause of death in every age group from 10 years to young adulthood and are the leading cause of unintentional deaths in adolescents ages 15 to 19 years. Sadly, and as described in Box 6.4: Focus on Development, child abuse and neglect causes both injury and death in far too many children.

There are both gender and race differences in likelihood of death by homicide (CDC, 2011). Males are nearly seven times more likely to die by homicide than females, and African Americans are more than twice as likely to die by homicide than Whites. In fact, one of the factors leading to the shorter life expectancy for African Americans as compared to Whites is the substantially higher rate of deaths by homicide in the African American population: At every single age range, African Americans are more likely than Whites to die from homicide, and for

Box 6.3

Focus on Research: Does Harry Potter Prevent Injuries in Children?

Researchers in this creative study compared the rate of emergency room visits by children during the weekends in which a new Harry Potter book was released and the weekends in which no new book was released (Gwilyn, Howard, Davies, & Willett, 2005). Specifically, in this study, the researchers examined emergency room visits for musculoskeletal injuries of children ages 7 to 15 to one hospital in England during the two weekends (one in June 2003 and the other in July 2005) compared to all other summer weekends during both years. The researchers also took into consideration weather conditions, which could influence children's likelihood of playing outside versus inside. As predicted, the mean attendance rate for children aged 7 to 15 years during the typical summer weekends was 67.4, whereas the attendance rate during the two weekends in which Harry Potter was released was 36.5, indicated a significant decrease in attendance. In fact, at no other point during the 3-year surveillance period was attendance that low. These findings suggest that Harry Potter books seem to protect children from traumatic injuries, presumably because children who are reading are less likely to participate in risky activities, such as in-line skating, bicycling, and riding a scooter, which can lead to injuries.

Box 6.4

Focus on Development: The Prevalence of Child Abuse and Neglect

In 2008, an estimated 772,000 American children were abused or maltreated (CDC, 2011). Of these, 71% experienced child neglect, 16% experienced physical abuse, 9% experienced sexual abuse, and 7% experienced emotional abuse. An estimated 1,740 children ages 0 to 17 died from abuse and neglect, with 80% of these deaths occurring among children younger than age 4. The rates of abuse are somewhat higher in African American children than in children from other racial backgrounds and are slightly higher for girls than for boys. Ironically, most of this abuse and neglect is caused by parents.

all age groups, African Americans are eight times more likely than Whites to be murdered. Homicide is the second leading cause of death (after accidents) in African Americans ages 1 to 4 years (boys and girls), the second leading cause of death in African American boys (ages 5 to 14 years), the leading cause of death for African American males ages 15 to 24 years, and the second leading cause of death for African American females ages 15 to 24.

Seven-year-old Nixzmary Brown was killed on January 11, 2006, by her stepfather, following a lifetime of abuse, including beatings, torture, and molestation. Her mother and stepfather were convicted of murder following her death and are now serving long prison terms. *Source:* Splash News/Newscom.

What accounts for this dramatic difference in likelihood of homicide as a function of race? One explanation is the rate of access to potentially lethal weapons in the inner cities, where African Americans are more likely than Whites to live. For example, one study found that nearly half of seventh- and eighth-grade boys living in an inner city carried knives, and 25% carried guns (Webster, Gainer, & Champion, 1993). Another factor is clearly poverty, which again is more likely to affect African Americans than Whites and increases a person's likelihood of both committing and being victimized by violence (Greenberg & Schneider, 1994).

What Are the Strategies for Preventing Injuries?

Given the tremendous life expectancy, disability, and financial costs of injuries, health psychologists have focused on developing strategies for prevention. This section will describe three distinct approaches to injury prevention: active strategies, passive strategies, and societal changes.

Active Strategies

One strategy for preventing injury is to try to motivate people to take an active role in the prevention of health problems. Using seat belts, wearing helmets, and putting children in car seats are all examples of **active strategies**—namely, those that require engaging in some type of repeated action to prevent health problems, to prevent injuries from occurring, or to decrease the harm resulting from such injuries.

Because injuries related to motor vehicle accidents are one of the leading causes of death, one very effective way to prevent health problems—and mortality—is to protect people from serious injuries while in motor vehicles (Christophersen, 1989; Williams & Lund, 1992). For example, requiring the use of seat belts in New York State alone saved an estimated 220 lives in the first 6 months of the program and prevented more than 7,000 injuries (Latimer & Lave, 1987). Unfortunately, 20% of high school students rarely or never use seat belts when they are passengers in a car (Kann et al., 1998).

Several strategies are useful for reducing children's risk of injury or death in a motor vehicle accident. For example, simply placing children in age- and size-appropriate restraint systems reduces the risk of death in cars by 71% for infants, and by 54% for toddlers ages 1 to 4 years (CDC, 2011). In fact, of the children ages 0 to 14 years who were killed in motor vehicle crashes during 2005, nearly half were unrestrained. Similarly, the National Highway Traffic Safety Administration recommends booster seats for children until they are at least 8 years of age or 4′9″ tall because booster seats reduce injury risk for children ages 4 to 7 by 59% compared to safety belts alone. For example, researchers in one study examined the injury rate in children ages 4 to 7 following a car accident as a function of whether they were in a booster seat (Durbin, Elliott, & Winston, 2003). Injuries occurred among 1.81% of all 4 to 7 year olds, including 1.95% of those in seat belts and 0.77% of those in belt-positioning booster seats. The odds of injury, taking into consideration the characteristics of the child, driver, crash, and vehicle, were 59% lower for children in booster seats than for those in seat belts alone. Moreover, children sitting in booster seats experienced no injuries to the abdomen, neck, spine, back, or lower extremities, while children in seat belts alone had injuries to all of these body regions.

Questioning the Research 6.3

Although the study by Durbin et al. (2003) found that booster seats decreased the risk of injury, are there other explanations for this association? (Hint: Does this study show correlation or causation?)

Another strategy for reducing injuries to children during car accidents is to require that all children ages 12 years and younger ride in the back seat. In fact, riding in the back seat is associated with a 40% reduction in the risk of serious injury for children younger than 16, largely because the force of a deployed airbag can injure or kill a young child even in a slow-speed, otherwise survivable crash (CDC, 2011). Researchers in one study examined the relationships of seating position and restraint status to the risk of injury among nearly 18,000 children under the age of 16 who were in passenger vehicle crashes in 15 states (Durbin, Chen, Smith, Elliott,

Placing infants in rear-facing car seats in the back of the car is one of the most effective strategies for reducing the risk of injury in a motor vehicle accident.
Source: © jenjen42/iStockphoto.

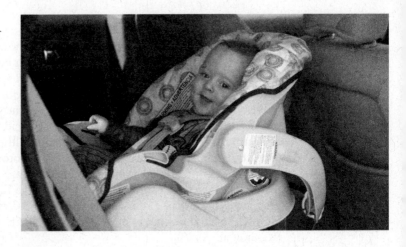

& Winston, 2005). For all age groups, unrestrained children in the front were at the highest risk of injury, and appropriately restrained children in the rear were at the lowest risk. Moreover, inappropriately restrained children were at nearly twice the risk of injury, compared with appropriately restrained children, whereas unrestrained children were at three times the risk. In addition, children in the front seat were at 40% greater risk of injury, compared with children in the rear seat. Had all children in the study population been appropriately restrained in the rear seat, 1,014 serious injuries would have been prevented. Although age-appropriate restraint—meaning car seat and/or booster seat use as well as seat belts—confers relatively more safety benefit than rear seating, the two work synergistically to provide the best protection for children in crashes.

Another common cause of car accidents is alcohol use. In 2005, 16,885 people died in alcohol-related motor vehicle crashes, accounting for 39% of all traffic-related deaths in the United States (CDC, 2011). Moreover, one out of four of all occupant deaths among children ages 0 to 14 years involve a drinking driver, and more than two thirds of these fatally injured children were riding with a drinking driver. Box 6.5: Health Psychology in the Real World describes a vivid example of the tragic results of drinking and driving.

Although wearing a helmet while biking is a very important strategy for reducing serious injuries, children are often reluctant to wear them. One survey of high school students found that of those who have ridden a bicycle, 88% rarely or never used a helmet (Kann et al., 1998). Similarly, more than 1,300 people die each year from injuries sustained while riding a bicycle, often because of collisions with cars, and 90% of those people may have lived if they had worn a helmet (Sacks, Holigreen, Smith, & Sosin, 1991). Helmet use also reduces the number of injuries to the face, head, and brain (Thompson, Rivara, & Thompson, 1996; Thompson, Nunn, Thompson, & Rivara, 1996).

The use of a helmet is particularly important for motorcycle riders. One study examining the change in motorcycle-related head injury deaths following a repeal of a Pennsylvania law requiring helmets for motorcycle riders found that head injury deaths increased 66% (Mertz & Weiss, 2008). This study points out the truth in a common emergency room expression: "What do you call motorcycle riders without helmets? Organ donors."

Box 6.5

Health Psychology in the Real World: The Very Real Tragedy of Drunk Driving

By Rob Waldron, *Newsweek*, October 30, 2003

Drunk driving isn't a new problem, but it continues to ravage our campuses. I know we can change that.

Unfortunately, I am an expert on drinking and driving. As a high-school freshman in Wayland, Mass., I suffered through the death of a classmate on my hockey team who was killed in an alcohol-related crash. Two years later I attended the funeral of another classmate who died while driving under the influence. Twelve months after that a wrestling teammate returning to Wayland from a college break totaled his car in a drunk-driving accident, partially paralyzing himself and causing permanent brain damage. His father, a town firefighter responding to a 911 call, was the one to find him on the roadside near death.

After all that, I thought I knew the worst about drunk driving. I was wrong. Three years ago my brother, Ryan, a Middlebury College senior, drove 70–100 miles an hour on a rainy rural road into a tree, ending his life. His blood-alcohol level was nearly three times the legal limit. Witnesses later recounted that he was swerving and speeding on a nearby road.

It was one of the worst accidents that officers at the crash site had ever seen. The two policemen assigned to wipe Ryan's blood and tissue off the car's broken windshield found it impossible even to talk to us about the details of what they found. According to the police report, before officers could transport Ryan to the funeral home, they had to remove a small branch that pierced his permanently flattened lips.

Ryan was last seen drinking on campus at a fraternity house that was serving vodka punch. He left the party intending to drive to his off-campus apartment three miles away to pick up a toga for yet another event. He never made it home. After his death, we found out that Ryan had developed a drinking problem while away at college. But even though he drank to excess at nearly every social function, usually three to four times a week, many of his friends never realized he was on his way to becoming an alcoholic.

It turns out that one of the staff members in the student-activities office where Ryan often came to register his fraternity's parties had suspected that he had a drinking problem. And Ryan isn't the only Middlebury student to be involved in a dangerous alcohol-related incident: in the year before his death one of Ryan's fellow students nearly died in a binge-drinking incident, saved only because the hospital pumped her stomach as she lay unconscious. Her blood-alcohol level was .425%.

What should we do about the Ryans of the world? I know that my brother was ultimately responsible for his own death, but in my view, college administrators can work harder to keep kids like Ryan from getting behind the wheel.

But many schools have been reluctant to address the problem. Why? Perhaps because taking responsibility for drinking and driving will make trustees and college presidents legally liable for college students' drunk-driving behavior. If administrators accepted this responsibility, they might ask themselves the following questions: Should we expel students who receive a D.U.I.? Has the president of our university met with the mayor to create a unified policy toward drunk driving within our town? Have we contacted organizations like M.A.D.D. and S.A.D.D. to help us implement alcohol- and driving-education programs?

On campuses like Middlebury's, where many students own cars, administrators can use more aggressive methods to combat drinking and driving. Yet after Ryan's death his university ignored my family's request to fund a Middlebury town officer to patrol the main entry into campus for out-of-control drivers on weekend evenings. This, despite the fact that the Middlebury College director of health services informed me and my family that approximately 15% of the school's freshmen were so intoxicated at some point during the last year that a classmate had to bring them to the infirmary.

Why does the problem of drunk driving persist? It's not easy to solve. College students are young and irresponsible, and drinking is part of their culture. Administrators have not wanted to abolish social houses and fraternities for fear that ending such beloved college traditions would lower alumni donations.

To college presidents, trustees and all college officials, I ask that you go home tonight and consider your love for your own son or daughter, your own brother or sister. Imagine the knock on your door at 3 a.m. when a uniformed police officer announces that your loved one has died. Then go to a mirror and look deep into your own eyes. Ask yourself the question: Have I done enough to help solve this problem?

The choice is simple. You can choose to be a leader and an agent of change on a controversial issue. Or you can continue the annual practice of authoring one of your student's eulogies. My family, in its grief, begs you to do the former.

Another leading cause of unintentional death that can be easily prevented through the use of active strategies is drowning, which is the sixth overall leading cause of unintentional injury death (CDC, 2011). In 2007, there were 3,443 fatal unintentional drownings (nonboating related) in the United States, averaging 10 deaths per day, and an additional 496 people died from drowning in boating-related incidents. Drowning is the second leading cause of death for children ages 1 to 14 years; every day, about 10 people die from unintentional drowning. Of these, 2 are children aged 14 or younger. Moreover, for every child who dies from drowning, 5 receive emergency department care for nonfatal submersion injuries, which can cause brain damage that results in long-term disabilities ranging from memory problems and learning disabilities to the permanent loss of basic functioning (i.e., permanent vegetative state).

The location of drowning varies as a function of age. Among children ages 1 to 4 years, most drownings occur in residential swimming pools. Most young children who drowned in pools were last seen in the home, had been out of sight less than 5 minutes, and were in the care of one or both parents at the time. In contrast, adolescents are more at risk of drowning in natural water settings, such as lakes, rivers, and oceans.

Sadly, many of these deaths could be avoided (Brenner & Committee on Injury, Violence, and Prevention Poisoning, 2003). Supervision by a lifeguard or designated water-watcher is important to protect young children when they are in the water, whether a pool or bathtub. Adults should not be involved in any other distracting activity (such as reading, playing cards, talking on the phone, or mowing the lawn) while supervising children. But when children are not supposed to be in the water, supervision alone isn't enough to keep them safe. Laws requiring pool fencing should be used to help prevent young children from gaining access to the pool area without caregivers' awareness. In fact, using a four-sided fence to completely enclose a pool leads to an 83% reduction in the risk of childhood drowning, compared to three-sided property-line fencing (in which children can still gain access to the pool from inside a house). Although participation in formal swimming lessons can reduce the risk of drowning by 88% among children aged 1 to 4 years, swimming lessons alone are not sufficient to protect children from drowning (Brenner et al., 2009).

Passive Strategies

Other approaches to injury prevention are passive—they do not require people to change their behavior or take any action but rather change people's environment. These **passive strategies** are often particularly effective in preventing injuries because they do not require continuing effort. For example, airbags are more effective than seat belts in reducing serious injury and death and require no active effort on the part of the passengers. Risk of death is reduced 19% for drivers (Zador & Ciccone, 1993) and 11% overall for passengers in the front seat (Braver, Ferguson, Greene, & Lund, 1997). Similarly, making cars with headlights that automatically turn on when the car is started is very inexpensive, yet leads to a reduction in crashes (Williams & Lancaster, 1995).

Societal Changes

One strategy for preventing health problems is instituting state and federal laws, such as restricting advertisements, reducing speed limits, requiring warning labels, and mandating behaviors by law (Dannenberg, Gielen, Beilenson, Wilson, & Joffe, 1993; Heishman, Kozlowski, & Henningfield, 1997; Jacobson, Wasserman, & Anderson, 1997; Kaplan, Orleans, Perkins, & Pierce, 1995). Let's take a look at each of these strategies.

One societal approach to reducing injuries and injury-related deaths is to create rules and regulations. Many states are upgrading their child-restraint laws to include provisions for the use of age-appropriate restraints through 6 to 8 years of age, with some also requiring rear seating for children, enabling the laws to be in closer alignment with best-practice recommendations (Durbin et al., 2005). Similarly, given the concerns about driving accidents caused by "driving while calling," some communities have now banned the use of handheld cell phones as well as texting while driving. Laws requiring the use of bicycle helmets, car seats, and seat belts, for example, are common and effective in reducing injuries and deaths (Dannenberg et al., 1993).

Speed limits, both national and state-wide, are another example of a strategy to reduce injuries. In 1995, the law mandating 55 as the maximum speed limit was repealed, and many states then raised their speed limits. However, estimates are that over the next decade, this increase led to a 3.2% increase in fatalities due to motor vehicle accidents, with increases of 9.1% on rural interstates and 4% on urban interstates (Friedman, Hedeker, & Richter, 2009). In turn, this change in maximum national speed limit is estimated to have caused 12,515 deaths and 36,583 injuries.

Many laws about alcohol use are designed to prevent drunk driving. Researchers in one study evaluated the existence and strength of 2 core laws and 14 expanded laws designed to control the sales of alcohol, prevent possession and consumption of alcohol, and prevent alcohol-impaired driving by those aged 20 and younger (Fell, Fisher, Voas, Blackman & Tippetts, 2008). First, laws regarding the possession and purchase account for an estimated 11.2% reduction in drunk driving. Second, making it illegal to use a false identification to purchase alcohol leads to fewer fatal crashes involving alcohol use in drivers under age 21.

Shaun White's use of a helmet helps children and
adolescents see helmet use during snowboarding
as important and not just as "uncool."
Source: Brian Bahr/Getty Images, Inc.

Similarly, laws requiring smoke detectors are designed to prevent fire deaths,
which are the fifth most common cause of unintentional injury death in the United
States (CDC, 2011). In 2009, fire departments across the country responded to
377,000 home fires, which claimed the lives of 2,565 people and injured another
13,050. Approximately half of home fire deaths occur in homes without smoke
alarms, and 40% of these occur in homes without smoke detectors. In Massachusetts,
where I live, all homes must be inspected by the local fire department for properly
working smoke detectors whenever they are sold. In fact, a property cannot change
hands without a certificate issued by the local fire department. Although the number
of fatalities and injuries caused by residential fires has declined gradually over the
past several decades, many residential fire-related deaths remain preventable: Many
of these deaths are caused by smoking.

Even simple and relatively low-cost efforts can reduce the likelihood of injuries.
Many accidents leading to death in children, such as drowning, falls, and poisonings,
could be prevented through relatively simple measures, such as putting locks on
windows, keeping chemicals in high and locked cabinets, and buying medication
with childproof caps. For example, putting woodchips under playground equipment
is a highly effective way of reducing injuries caused by falls.

Mass-media campaigns can also be an effective strategy of reducing injuries.
Several states, including Colorado, Kentucky, and New York, have implemented
community-based programs to increase booster seat use among children ages 4 to
8, including enacting community awareness campaigns and school-based programs,
airing public service announcements, posting billboards, and conducting booster
seat distribution events and car seat checkpoints. One Seattle campaign to promote
helmet use employed widespread educational messages to raise parents' awareness
about the importance of helmet use, provided a subsidy to reduce the cost
of purchasing helmets, and recruited prominent sports figures from the Seattle
Seahawks, Seattle Mariners, and the University of Washington Huskies football
team to describe how helmets are just a standard part of the sports uniform
(Bergman, Rivara, Richards, & Regers, 1990; Rivara, Thompson, & Thompson,
1994). Helmet use increased from 5 to 23% following this campaign.

Community-based efforts can successfully reduce injuries. For example, the Safe
Kids/Healthy Neighborhood Injury Prevention Program in Harlem, New York,

targeted numerous aspects of the community, including renovating playgrounds, involving children in safe and fun activities (e.g., dance, arts, sports), offering classes on injury and violence prevention, and providing safety equipment (e.g., bicycle helmets; Davidson et al., 1994). Rates of injuries declined 44% following the intervention, once again demonstrating the power of primary prevention programs in improving physical health.

Community-based interventions can also be useful in reducing injuries in older adults. Researchers in one study examined the effectiveness of providing clinicians and staff members working with elderly people in home care, outpatient rehabilitation, or senior centers with information on preventing serious fall-related injuries (Tinetti et al., 2008). Specifically, staff members in one part of Connecticut were exposed to an intervention that provided information on assessing people's risk of falling and strategies for preventing such falls, such as by reducing medication or increasing training in balance. Compared to regions in which this intervention wasn't provided, regions in which clinicians and staff members received this training reported a 9% lower rate of serious fall-related injuries and an 11% lower rate of use of medical services for fall-related injuries. This finding suggests that this type of training may be highly effective in terms of preventing falls in elderly people.

Given the substantial risk of deaths by suicide among young people, suicide prevention programs are another potentially effective strategy for reducing this type of behavior. Researchers in one study randomly assigned 2,100 high school students to participate in either a suicide intervention program, called Signs of Suicide, or a control condition (Aseltine & DeMartino, 2004). This program teaches adolescents that suicide is directly related to depression, which is a treatable mental illness, and describes the signs of depression for adolescents to recognize in themselves and others. Follow-up data 3 months later revealed that adolescents who participated in this program showed increases in knowledge and attitudes about depression and suicide and reported significantly lower rates of suicide attempts. Other research reveals that educating doctors in the signs of and effective treatments for depression and restricting access to lethal means of suicide can help to decrease rates of completed suicides as well as suicide attempts (Mann et al., 2005).

Questioning the Research 6.4

Would the Signs of Suicide program be equally useful in preventing suicides in older adults? Why or why not?

Moreover, in many cases, the costs of health promotion programs are quite low, given their potential benefits. For example, in one ambitious program to increase seat-belt use, Florida state employees were required to read and sign a sheet describing the state rules requiring seat-belt use (Rogers, Rogers, Bailey, Runkle, & Moore, 1988). They were then given stickers for their dashboards to remind them to "buckle up." Although only about 10% of workers were using their seat belts initially, this rate climbed to 52%! Moreover, this program led to a substantial decrease in the cost of accident claims, from a little over $2,000 to just under $1,000.

TABLE 6.5   *Information YOU Can Use*

- Protect yourself from motor vehicle accidents, which is the leading cause of injury-related death for adolescents and young adults. Make sure to wear a seat belt and obey the speed limit. Most importantly, don't text while driving, drive under the influence, or speed—and don't be a passenger in a car with someone who is engaging in any of these behaviors.
- Given the link between owning a firearm and both homicides and suicides, don't have a gun in your house.
- Suicide is a common cause of death for adolescents and young adults, and thus suicidal thoughts need to be taken very seriously. If you, or someone you know, is having thoughts about killing themselves, talk to an adult you trust—a teacher, parent, doctor, or religious leader—immediately.
- Drownings in both pools and natural bodies of water are common causes of death and injury, so make sure to protect yourself. Learn how to swim, and obey all water-safety guidelines, including wearing a life jacket at all times when on a boat and avoiding swimming after alcohol use.
- Fires at home cause many injuries and deaths each year and are highly preventable. Try not to smoke inside your home, and if you do smoke in your home, never smoke in bed or leave burning cigarettes unattended. Make sure to install smoke alarms, and test these smoke alarms once a month using the test button.

Summary

1. Injuries cause a substantial number of hospitalizations and deaths each year in the United States. Some of these injuries are unintentional, or accidents, meaning the person who experienced the injury did not mean for it to happen, such as occurs with car accidents, fires, and drowning. Other injuries are intentional, meaning the person who caused the injury meant for it to happen, such as occurs in the case of homicides or suicides.

2. The leading cause of death for children ages 1 to 14 is unintentional injury. Many of these injuries are caused by car accidents, drowning, and fire/burns.

3. Injury is one of the leading causes of deaths for adolescents and young adults. These deaths are often caused by motor vehicle accidents, homicides, and suicide.

4. Injuries are the leading cause of death in adults ages 35 to 44, but are less likely to cause deaths in older adults. Injuries leading to death in adulthood are often caused by car accidents, poisoning, homicide, and suicide.

5. The leading cause of injury in the United States is motor vehicle accidents. Children and teenagers are at particular risk of experiencing this type of injury.

6. Poisoning, which can include any substance that is taken into the body (e.g., drank, ate, inhaled, etc.), is the second leading cause of unintentional injury death. Many poisoning deaths are caused by drugs.

7. Suicide is one of the leading causes of injuries and deaths, especially among teenagers and young adults. Risk of attempting, and successfully competing, suicide varies as a function of age, race, and gender. One of the largest factors contributing to suicide is access to firearms.

8. Falls are another leading cause of injury and death, and are the leading cause of death for adults age 65 and older. Falls are also the leading cause of non-fatal injury in children.

9. Another leading cause of injury-related death is homicide. A majority of homicides are caused by firearms. The risk of death by firearm varies as a function of race, gender, and age.

10. Active strategies for preventing injuries from occurring, or to decrease the harm resulting from such injuries, require engaging in some type of repeated action. These strategies include using seat belts, placing children in appropriate restraint systems in cars, requiring children to sit in the backseat of cars, reducing driving under the influence, wearing helmets, and supervising children who are in any body of water (bathtubs, swimming pools, lakes).

11. Passive strategies for preventing injuries change people's environment, and may be particularly effective since they do not require continuing

effort. These strategies include requiring cars to have airbags and making cars with headlights that turn on automatically.

12. Societal changes for preventing injuries involve instituting state and federal laws to prevent or reduce injuries. These changes could include reducing speed limits, requiring warning labels on medicine bottles, and mandating behaviors by law (e.g., forbidding texting while driving, requiring smoke detectors in homes). These changes can also include community-based efforts and mass media campaigns.

Key Terms

active strategies

intentional injuries

passive strategies

unintentional injuries

Thought Questions

1. What are the age differences in terms of risk of injuries (both intentional and unintentional)?

2. What factors do you believe lead to homicides? How can health psychologists prevent such deaths?

3. Your brother is expecting his first child. What strategies would you advise him to use to prevent injuries in infants and younger children?

4. You are in charge of an orientation program for entering college students. What types of injury-prevention information do you believe would be most important for them to receive?

5. How can active strategies be used to prevent different types of injuries?

Answers to Questioning the Research

Answer 6.1. The most likely explanation for the gender difference in rate of spinal cord injury is that men tend to engage in riskier behavior in general than do women, and this includes engaging in riskier driving behavior. Specifically, men are more likely to speed when driving and to engage in driving while under the influence of alcohol.

Answer 6.2. Although owning a gun is associated with an increased risk of suicide, it is not clear that this relationship is in fact causal. After all, people who own a gun may have personality characteristics, have particular life stressors, or come from distinct backgrounds, and any of these factors could predict both gun ownership and risk of suicide (a "third variable" explanation). However, this link between gun ownership and suicide remains even when researchers take into account these other factors, providing greater confidence that owning a gun does contribute to suicides.

Answer 6.3. As is the case with examining the causes of many different types of injuries, it is difficult to determine whether factors other than booster seats contributed to the likelihood of injury. After all, parents who require their child to sit in a booster seat likely differ considerably from those who do not. In turn, there may be other differences that influence the likelihood of an injury, such as type of car driven or speed of driving.

Answer 6.4. Suicide-prevention programs that work in high school settings may also be effective in college settings, in which students also spend considerable time together and thus may recognize signs of depression easily in others. However, these programs may be harder to implement in older adults, simply because adults may have less opportunity to interact regularly with large numbers of people, and those who are depressed may be especially likely to avoid this type of social interaction.

CHAPTER 7

Smoking and Alcohol Abuse

Outline

Personality
Biological/Genetic Factors

What Are Some Strategies for Preventing Alcohol Abuse?

What Are Some Strategies for Treating Alcohol Abuse?

- Jack is 25 years old and started smoking in high school. Back then he would smoke only when he was with friends at parties and mostly when he was drinking. However, during college, Jack started smoking more frequently and smoking more cigarettes—the one or two cigarettes he used to have in an evening just didn't have the same good effects. Jack also found that smoking helped him relax during stressful times and even seemed to help his concentration when he was studying. Although he knows the health risks of smoking, Jack finds that whenever he tries to quit, he feels anxious and has trouble focusing at work.

- Annabelle is 11 years old and in sixth grade. As part of her health-education class, she has participated in several smoking-prevention programs. These programs have provided information about how cigarette companies try to trick kids into buying cigarettes, how cigarettes make your teeth turn yellow and your breath smell bad, and how many teenagers aren't interested in dating someone who smokes. Although her older sister smokes, Annabelle now thinks smoking is a pretty disgusting habit.

- Diana is 30 years old and has smoked since her sophomore year of college. She knows smoking is bad for her health and therefore has tried to stop smoking three or four times, but each time, Diana has gained weight, which then leads her back to smoking. Recently, Diana and her husband, Mark, have decided to have a baby. Because of the many negative effects that smoking can have on a developing fetus, Diana has made the decision to quit smoking. She is working with a therapist to identify the factors that lead her to crave a cigarette and has started chewing nicotine gum.

- Brad is the starting quarterback on his college football team and is a proud member of the Phi Delta Theta fraternity. However, he is now on academic probation because of his low GPA. Although he always plans to go to class, Brad finds it difficult to wake up in time for his classes when he has been out late drinking the night before. He knows that his drinking is a little out of control, but Brad believes that he is much funnier and more relaxed when he has been drinking. Also, because he's now living in the fraternity house, there is always someone around to drink with.

- Jenny is 48 years old and has had a problem with alcohol use for as long as she can remember. Although she usually drinks only on the weekends, Jenny sometimes experiences memory loss after drinking and sometimes finds herself in bed with a stranger the next morning. She has been arrested three times for driving under the influence. After her most recent arrest, Jenny lost her driver's license for 60 days and was ordered to enter an in-patient treatment program for alcohol abuse and to attend daily Alcoholics Anonymous meetings for the next 90 days.

Preview

Smoking and alcohol use are two of the most common health-compromising behaviors, and often they are used in combination (Sher, Gotham, Erickson, & Wood, 1996; Shiffman et al., 1994). These two behaviors also lead to many of the major health problems, as well as causes of death, in the United States today, including cancer, coronary heart disease, accidents/unintentional injuries, and even homicides and suicides. This chapter therefore addresses the psychological factors that influence these health-compromising behaviors. First, we examine the health consequences of smoking as well as the distinct psychological and physiological factors that lead people to start smoking as well as to continue smoking. We then examine some strategies for preventing smoking and for helping people quit smoking. Next, we examine the health consequences of alcohol abuse and the influence of biological and psychological factors on alcohol use. Finally, we examine strategies for preventing and treating alcohol abuse.

What Is the Prevalence of Smoking?

Most recent estimates suggest that 21% of American adults smoke, including a somewhat higher percentage of men than women (23.5% versus 17.9%; Centers for Disease Control, 2010). This represents about 46 million smokers in the United States alone (see Figure 7.1). Both Whites (22.1%) and African Americans (21.3%) are more likely to smoke than Hispanic Americans (14.5%), who in turn are more likely to smoke than Asian Americans (12%). Smoking is more common in people who have lower levels of education: 49.1% of adults with a GED diploma smoke, compared to only 5.6% of those with a graduate degree. Smoking is also correlated with income: 31.1% of adults who live below the poverty line smoke, compared to only 19.4% of those who live at or above it.

Most smokers acquire the habit at a relatively young age, typically before age 21 (Chen & Kandel, 1995). Approximately 60% of teenagers have smoked a cigarette before high school graduation, and more than 20% of students smoke daily. Unfortunately, among those who smoke regularly during adolescence, 70% become regular adult smokers. National statistics indicate that 17.2% of high school students are current smokers, as are 5.2% of middle school students (CDC, 2011). In fact, every day, approximately 3,450 adolescents (ages 12 to 17) smoke their first cigarette, and about 850 become daily smokers. Although most teenagers would like to quit and believe that quitting smoking would be fairly easy, only 16% of adolescents had quit smoking when they were contacted again 4 years later (Zhu, Sun, Billings, Choi, & Malarcher, 1999).

What Are the Health Consequences of Smoking?

Smoking is the leading cause of preventable mortality in the United States, causing an estimated 443,000 deaths per year in the United States alone (CDC, 2011).

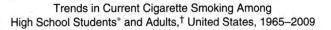

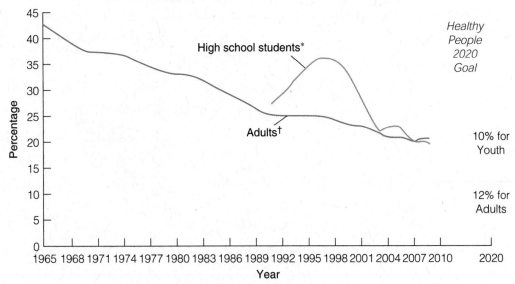

FIGURE 7.1 Although smoking rates have dropped somewhat from the mid-1960s, over 20% of adults and 17% of teenagers are current smokers (data from CDC, 2011).

In fact, more people die as a result of cigarette smoking than as a result of car accidents, HIV, suicides, and homicides combined (see Figure 7.2; Mokdad, Marks, Stroup, & Gerberding, 2004). Smoking is clearly linked with a number of types of cancer, including cancer of the lung, mouth, pharynx, esophagus, and bladder (Thun, Day-Lally, Calle, Flanders, & Heath, 1995). Smoking causes an estimated 90% of all lung cancer deaths in men and 80% of all lung cancer deaths in women (CDC, 2011). Furthermore, the risk of developing coronary heart disease and stroke, which is the leading cause of death in the United States, is twice as high for smokers than for nonsmokers (CDC, 2011). Smoking can also lead to a range of other major illnesses, such as emphysema, bronchitis, and respiratory infections, as well as relatively minor health problems, such as impotence (Mannino, Klevens, & Flanders, 1994) and the common cold (Cohen, Tyrell, Russell, Jarvis, & Smith, 1993). Even passive, or secondhand, smoking can lead to death—an estimated 3,000 lung cancer deaths each year in the United States alone are caused by passive smoking. Box 7.1: Focus on Development describes the particular hazards of passive smoking on children.

Although the health hazards of cigarette smoking are clear, other forms of tobacco, such as chewing tobacco and snuff, are also associated with negative consequences. An estimated 6.1% of high school students (and 11% of males) use smokeless tobacco (CDC, 2011). The use of smokeless tobacco is most common in White boys, especially those who are involved in organized athletics, probably because of the frequent role modeling of this behavior among professional athletes

FIGURE 7.2   Smoking causes more than 440,000 deaths each year, largely due to lung cancer, heart disease, and chronic obstructive pulmonary disease (data from CDC, 2011).

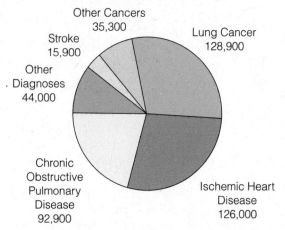

About 443,000 U.S. Deaths Attributable Each Year to Cigarette Smoking*

Other Cancers 35,300
Stroke 15,900
Other Diagnoses 44,000
Lung Cancer 128,900
Chronic Obstructive Pulmonary Disease 92,900
Ischemic Heart Disease 126,000

*Average annual number of deaths, 2000–2004, includes deaths from secondhand smoke.
Source: *MMWR* 2008;57(45):1226–1228

Box 7.1

Focus on Development: The Impact of Passive Smoking on Children

Passive smoking, or environmental tobacco smoke, is a serious problem, particularly for infants and young children. Current estimates suggest that 43% of children ages 2 months to 11 years live in a home with at least one smoker (Pirkle et al., 1996). Passive smoking is a major cause of respiratory problems in children, including pneumonia and bronchitis. In fact, an estimated 150,000 to 300,000 new cases of bronchitis and pneumonia annually are attributed to secondhand smoke in children 18 months or younger, including 75,00 to 15,000 hospitalizations (CDC, 2011). Exposure to smoke also increases a child's risk of developing asthma and increases the severity of symptoms of asthma.

Sadly, passive smoking can harm children even before they are born: Smoking by pregnant women is associated with a number of negative consequences on the fetus, including lower birthrate and miscarriage (Grunberg, Brown, & Klein, 1997). Children whose mothers smoked during pregnancy are also at increased risk of attention deficit disorders, hyperactivity, aggression, and sudden infant death syndrome (Grunberg et al., 1997; MacDorman, Cnattingius, Hoffman, Kramer, & Haglund, 1997; Wakschlag, Leventhal, Pine, Pickett, & Carter, 2006; Wakschlag, Pickett, Kasza, & Loeber, 2006). Research also suggests that maternal smoking may lead to genetic mutations in the fetus, which can in turn influence survival, birth weight, and even susceptibility to disease in both childhood and adulthood (Grant, 2005). Thus, smoking has very serious consequences not just for those who choose to smoke, but for their children.

(Tomar & Giovino, 1998). Although the risk associated with chewing tobacco is not as great as that associated with smoking, chewing tobacco is associated with oral cancer as well as cardiovascular disease (Bolinder, Alfredsson, Englund, & deFaire, 1994; Winn et al., 1981). For example, one study found that men who chewed tobacco had twice the risk of dying from coronary heart disease compared to those who did not use tobacco.

What causes the numerous health consequences of smoking? First, nicotine constricts blood vessels and increases heart rate, cardiac output, and blood pressure, so the heart becomes overworked. Cigarette smoke contains high levels of carbon monoxide, which reduces the amount of oxygen in the blood and thereby leads to arteriosclerosis (hardening of the arteries). Again, this increased buildup of plaque in the arteries forces the heart to work harder to pump blood. Also, tars, small particles of residue in smoke, contain carcinogens, or cancer-causing agents, that lead to abnormal growth of cells in the mouth, throat, and lungs. Moreover, as smoke repeatedly passes through the bronchial tubes, it disrupts the ability of the cilia (fine, hairlike structures that line the bronchial tubes) to effectively clear the lungs of foreign particles. The carcinogens therefore have consistent contact with the bronchial tubes, which is why lung cancer is one of the most common types of cancer caused by smoking.

Given the many negative health consequences of smoking, it is not surprising that an estimated 30% of smokers make a quit attempt each year (Fiore et al., 1990). However, smoking is a hard habit to break—two thirds of people who quit on their own return to smoking within 2 days, and 97% return to smoking within 6 months (Hughes et al., 1992). These rates of returning to smoking are slightly lower for people who participate in formal smoking-cessation programs, but even these programs only lead to long-term quitting in 20 to 30% of smokers (Cohen et al., 1989). Even people who are highly motivated to quit smoking have great trouble stopping. Of people who have had a laryngectomy (which is typically performed to treat throat cancer), 40% continue to smoke, as do more than 50% of those who have experienced a heart attack or surgery resulting from lung cancer (Stolerman & Jarvis, 1995).

How Do Psychological Factors Lead to the Initiation of Smoking?

As described previously, most adult smokers started smoking when they were teenagers or young adults—very few 40 and 50 year olds suddenly decide to start smoking for the first time. What leads young people to smoke their first cigarette?

First, teenagers may start to smoke as a way of trying out a new identity. Although teenagers may hold some negative views about smokers, such as they are unhealthy, foolish, and not so good at schoolwork, smokers are also viewed in some ways that might be considered positive for high school students (Aloise-Young, Hennigan, & Graham, 1996; Dinh, Sarason, Peterson, & Onstad, 1995). Specifically, smokers are seen as tough, cool, rebellious, mature, socially precocious, and more interested in the opposite sex. (Not coincidentally, advertisements for cigarettes often promote smokers as having precisely these qualities). These perceptions about smokers can lead other adolescents to consider smoking themselves to try to seem glamorous, older, or more mature. Adolescents who saw themselves as tough, liking to be with a group, consumers of alcohol, and interested in the opposite sex were more likely to think about starting to smoke (Chassin, Presson, Sherman, Corty, & Olshavsky, 1981). Similarly, one study with fifth and seventh graders who saw smokers in a positive way, viewing them as cool, good at sports, independent, and good-looking, were more likely to start smoking later (Dinh et al., 1995). In fact, the more positive an adolescent's view of smokers, the more likely he or she is to smoke.

Teenagers who smoke also seem to have distinct types of personalities (Burt, Dinh, Peterson, & Sarason, 2000; Windle & Windle, 2001). Adolescents who smoke are higher in novelty-seeking (Audrain-McGovern, Rodriguez, Tercyak, Neuner, & Moss, 2006), higher in rebelliousness and lower in achievement motivation (Brook et al., 2008; Otten, Bricker, Liu, Comstock, & Peterson, 2011), and have more tolerance for deviance (Wills, Resko, Ainette, & Mendoza, 2004a). Smoking is also associated with other risk-taking behaviors, such as alcohol and drug use, sexual activity with multiple partners, and deviant behaviors (e.g., vandalism, running away from home, graffiti; Costello, Dierker, Jones, & Rose, 2008; Emmons, Wechsler, Dowdall, & Abraham, 1998). Although adolescents who smoke may be less academically oriented and less involved in school sports, they are not antisocial—in fact, adolescents who smoke tend to be extraverted and spend considerable time socializing with friends (Stein, Newcomb, & Bentler, 1996).

Another factor that may prompt smoking in girls is a concern about weight. As we examine in Chapter 8, many girls and women, including those who are of normal weight, are concerned about body shape and size. One study of over a thousand 7th-grade to 10th-grade girls found that girls who were trying to lose weight and who had symptoms of eating disorders were much more likely to smoke than those without such concerns (French, Perry, Leon, & Fulkerson, 1994). In line with this view, college women who smoke report experiencing greater urges to smoke after seeing images of thin women than after seeing neutral images, suggesting that experiencing weight concerns may prompt the desire to smoke (Lopez, Drobes, Thompson, & Brandon, 2008).

Social factors, including modeling and peer pressure, may contribute to smoking. Most first smoking occurs in the presence of a peer, and adolescents who smoke typically have friends who smoke (Ary & Biglan, 1988; Costello et al., 2008; Mittelmark et al., 1987; Mercken, Candel, Williams, & de Vries, 2009; Otten, van Lier, & Engels, 2011; Simons-Morton, Chen, Abroms, & Haynie, 2004; Villanti, Boulay, & Juon, 2011). Exposure to tobacco-related media is associated with increased current and former smoking in both early and middle adolescence. One study of more than 50,000 middle school and high school students revealed that the largest association of current smoking was the number of friends who smoked (Evans, Powers, Hersey, & Renaud, 2006). Having more than three friends who smoke is a particularly strong predictor (Wills et al., 2004b). In fact, having friends who smoke is a stronger predictor of adolescent smoking than having a family member who smokes. How does having friends who smoke lead to smoking? One possibility is that teenagers who see smoking in a positive way choose to have friends who see more benefits to smoking, such as looking good, feeling relaxed, and being more popular (Morrell, Song, & Halpern-Felsher, 2010). In line with this view, adolescents with more than six friends who smoked report seeing more benefits of smoking over time (Morrell et al., 2010). Having friends who smoke can also encourage smoking simply by providing more access to cigarettes. One study of more than a thousand middle school and high school students found that nonsmokers receive an average of 0.16 offers of cigarettes per week as compared to 4.22 offers for smokers (Ary & Bigland, 1988).

Although social modeling by and pressures from peers are particularly powerful influences during adolescence, parents' attitudes and behaviors also influence whether teenagers smoke (Chassin, Presson, Todd, Rose, & Sherman, 1998; Villanti et al., 2011). Among those with a family history of smoking, 26.6% become adult smokers as compared to 12.5% of those whose parents did not smoke (Chassin, Presson, Rose & Sherman, 1996). Parents who started smoking earlier, smoke high amounts, and have smoked over time are especially likely to have kids who smoke (Chassin et al., 2008). On the other hand, parents who monitor behavior, have expectations for not smoking, and both discuss and punish smoking are less likely to have kids who smoke—in part because they may restrict access to friends who smoke (Chassin et al., 1998; Simons-Morton et al., 2004). In turn, children who see their parents as strongly antismoking are seven times less likely to smoke than those who see their parents as not strongly against smoking (Murray, Johnson, Luepker, & Mittelmark, 1984).

Finally, the media—including seeing actors, athletes, and rock stars smoke as well as seeing smoking in movies—also contributes to smoking, in part by portraying smoking as glamorous and cool (Dalton et al., 2003; Grunberg, Brown, & Klein, 1997; Heatherton & Sargent, 2009; Sargent, Tanski, & Gibson, 2007). This presentation of smoking as desirable occurs even in films targeted to very young children. One study even found that tobacco use (including cigarettes, cigars, and pipes) was portrayed in 56% of G-rated animated children's films, including *Bambi, Lady and the Tramp,* and *The Lion King* (Goldstein et al., 1999). More recently, research shows that 74% of movies include smoking (Sargent, Tanski, & Gibson, 2007). Unfortunately, and as described in Box 7.2: Focus on Research, exposure to smoking in movies increases adolescent smoking.

Seeing celebrities smoke in real life exerts a strong influence on smoking, especially for teenagers.
Source: NewsCom.

Box 7.2

Focus on Research: The Hazards of Smoking in Movies

Researchers in this study were interested in examining whether watching more smoking in movies was associated with more smoking in adolescents (Sargent et al., 2005). More than 6,000 adolescents across the United States were called and asked a series of questions, including what movies they had seen in the past year or two, whether they had tried a cigarette, and other measures (such as personality, education, and gender). Researchers then examined the rate of smoking occurrence in each of the movies the participants reported having seen to examine how much smoking each person had seen in movies. The researchers also took into account various other factors that could predict smoking, including age, race, personality characteristics, and parent smoking, to make sure that these variables did not explain the link between seeing smoking in movies and trying a cigarette. Findings indicated that those who watched more smoking in movies were more likely to report having tried a cigarette. Specifically, only 2% of adolescents who had seen the least amount of smoking reported having tried a cigarette compared to 22% of those who had seen smoking the most. This research provides strong evidence that teenagers who see more smoking in movies are more likely to start smoking themselves.

Exposure to smoking in movies increases teenagers' likelihood of smoking in several ways. First, after exposure to smoking in feature films, teenagers see smokers as higher in social status and develop greater intentions to smoke (Pechmann & Shih, 1999). Viewing movies with smoking also leads teenagers to have positive expectancies about smoking and to identify with smokers (Tickle, Hull, Sargent, Dalton, & Heatherton, 2006; Wills, Sargent, Stoolmiller, Gibbons, & Gerrard, 2008). In turn, compared to adolescents whose favorite stars didn't smoke in a movie (or smoked only once), adolescents whose favorite stars smoked in a movie two or more times were much more likely to have positive attitudes toward smoking and report being more likely to smoke in the future themselves (Tickle, Sargent, Dalton, Beach, & Heatheron, 2001). Finally, viewing movies with smoking leads teenagers to have more friends who smoke, which in turn increases the accessibility of cigarettes and pressure to smoke (Wills et al., 2007).

What Factors Lead to Continued Smoking?

Addiction refers to the condition in which a person has a physical and psychological dependence on a given substance, such as cigarettes, alcohol, or caffeine. Addiction is caused by repeatedly consuming the substance, which over time leads the body to adjust to the substance and to incorporate it into the "normal" functioning of the body's tissues. People who are dependent on a given substance also develop *tolerance*, in which their bodies no longer respond at the same level to a particular dose but rather need larger and larger doses to experience the same effects. They also experience unpleasant withdrawal symptoms, such as irritability, difficulty concentrating, fatigue, nausea, and weight gain, when they discontinue using the substance (Hughes & Hatsukami, 1986).

People become physically dependent on tobacco because of the nicotine they ingest. Nicotine leads to a number of physiological reactions, such as increasing alertness, blood pressure, and heart rate. However, these effects are maintained only while there is nicotine in the bloodstream—when it decays, these effects are gone. So, maybe a person starts out smoking just a couple of cigarettes when he or she feels nervous. After all, the person thinks, how much harm can a couple of cigarettes once a month really do? But the problem is that the body builds up a tolerance to nicotine and so smoking just a few cigarettes begins to have no effect. Over time, smokers need 20 or 30 or 40 cigarettes to get the same positive effects. People don't start smoking and say, "I think I'll smoke three packs a day now and see how that works"; they gradually get to that point as their tolerance for nicotine increases. Unfortunately, addiction to tobacco can happen very quickly; one study found that 10% of teenage smokers report feeling addicted within the first 2 days and 25% having done so within 30 days of first inhaling from a cigarette (DiFranza et al., 2007).

Although smoking is clearly an addiction, the precise processes that lead to nicotine addiction are unclear. This section describes the three different types of theories to explain it: nicotine-based models, affect-based models, and combined models.

Nicotine-Based Models

According to the **nicotine fixed-effect model**, nicotine stimulates reward-inducing centers in the nervous system (Leventhal & Cleary, 1980). Nicotine increases the levels of neuroregulators, such as dopamine, norepinephrine, and endogenous opioids, which lead to better memory and concentration and reduced feelings of anxiety and tension. Nicotine has a number of reinforcing physiological effects, including speeding up the heart and relaxing the skeletal muscles. These physiological effects lead to simultaneous mental alertness and physical relaxation. These positive effects are reinforcing, so people are motivated to continue smoking to experience these physiological benefits. This model is very simple—it basically proposes that smoking feels good, so people are motivated to continue the behavior.

The **nicotine regulation model** extends the fixed-effect model by predicting that smoking is rewarding only when the level of nicotine is above a certain "set point" in the body (Leventhal & Cleary, 1980). In other words, individuals need to smoke enough cigarettes to maintain a certain amount of nicotine in the bloodstream or they do not experience the physiological effects of smoking. One study by Schachter, Silverstein, Kozlowski, Herman, and Liebling (1977) provided smokers with either low- or high-nicotine cigarettes; researchers then counted how many cigarettes the smokers consumed during a 2-week period. Heavy smokers liked the high-nicotine cigarettes much more than the low-nicotine cigarettes, and they also smoked more of the low-nicotine cigarettes than the high-nicotine ones. In contrast, light smokers liked both types of cigarettes equally and showed no difference in the number of cigarettes they smoked. Moreover, many of the heavy smokers who were (unknowingly) given low-nicotine cigarettes reported feeling especially irritable and anxious. This finding suggests that the amount of nicotine does matter, at least for heavy smokers.

Although there is some evidence that smokers do try to maintain a certain level of nicotine in the body, both of these nicotine-based models have several limitations.

First, because nicotine disappears from the blood a few days after smoking ceases, quitting should not be that difficult. However, ex-smokers often continue to crave cigarettes even after they have not smoked for some time. Second, these models ignore environmental pressures that can prompt smoking, such as stress and anxiety. In fact, smokers who are undergoing stress have a much more difficult time quitting (Shiffman et al., 1996). Finally, even heavy smokers do not smoke enough to compensate for the decline in nicotine resulting from tolerance, and although nicotine-replacement methods (e.g., the patch, nicotine gum) ease some withdrawal symptoms, they do not end smokers' cravings for cigarettes.

Affect-Regulation Model

One of the earliest models predicting smoking focused on the ability of smoking to help with affect or mood regulation (Tomkins, 1966, 1968). Tomkins's **affect-regulation model** proposes that people smoke to attain positive affect or to avoid (or reduce) negative affect. Positive-affect smokers may smoke as a way of enhancing the pleasure associated with other events, such as eating a great meal or having sex (as movies so often portray). These people find smoking extremely pleasurable and smoke only when they are already feeling good. To test this theory of smoking, Howard Leventhal and Nancy Avis (1976) dipped cigarettes in vinegar (to make them taste bad) and then measured how many cigarettes people would smoke. As predicted, people who smoked primarily for its pleasure smoked significantly fewer bad-tasting cigarettes than they normally smoked, whereas those whose smoking was not motivated by pleasure smoked the same number of cigarettes they usually did.

Tomkins's affect-regulation model also proposes that people smoke as a way of coping with negative affect, including anxiety, tension, and frustration. In one of the first studies to test this model, Schachter et al. (1977) randomly assigned smokers to either a low-stress or high-stress condition. Those in the low-stress condition were told they would experience a weak electrical current that "will not be painful; it will feel like a tickle or a tingle, that's all. You will barely be able to notice it." In contrast, subjects who were in the high-stress condition were told they would receive a series of painful electrical shocks and that they would continue to increase "until you tell me that they have become so painful that you want me to stop." Researchers than counted how many cigarettes those in each group smoked as they were waiting for the shock portion of the study to begin. As predicted, those in the high-stress group smoked an average of 2.57 cigarettes compared to only 2.05 cigarettes for those in the low-stress condition. Moreover, while low-stress subjects took an average of 15.09 puffs on a cigarette, those in the high-stress condition took an average of 22.74 puffs. Thus, smokers who are experiencing more stress both smoke more cigarettes and take more puffs, indicating the use of cigarettes to manage negative emotions.

Support for the affect-regulation model is found in part by research showing a link among stress, depression, and smoking (McCaffery, Papandonatos, Stanton, Lloyd-Richardson, & Niaura, 2008; Spielberger, 1986; Wills et al., 2004a; Windle & Windle, 2001). One study followed adolescents over 8 years to assess both rates of depression and rates of smoking (Repetto, Caldwell, & Zimmerman, 2005). As shown in Figure 7.3, male adolescents who reported more depression were more

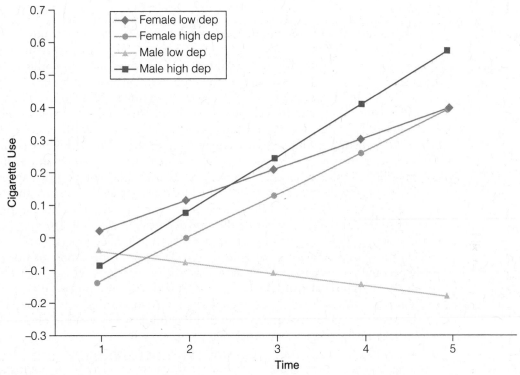

FIGURE 7.3   Although adolescent girls are more likely to start smoking over time regardless of depression, higher rates of depression are associated with increased smoking in adolescent boys (data from Repetto et al., 2005).

likely to smoke, suggesting that smoking may be a strategy for coping with negative mood. Similarly, nonsmoking adolescents whose parents experience a job loss are 87% more likely to try smoking in the next year than those whose parents don't experience this loss, suggesting that stress in the home may lead to smoking (Unger, Hamilton, & Sussman, 2004). Exposure to violence in early life is associated with alcohol abuse and/or dependence in adulthood, suggesting that adverse childhood experience may contribute to maladaptive coping patterns in adulthood (Madruga et al., 2011). As described in Chapter 4, one explanation for the link between poorer health outcomes, as well as increased rates of smoking, in people with lower incomes is the ongoing experience of greater stress (Brook, Schuster, & Zhang, 2004; Businelle et al., 2010).

Although some people may smoke occasionally to manage negative affect, over time they may become addicted to cigarettes if they come to rely on smoking as their only effective strategy for coping with unpleasant emotions. In line with this view, one large national health study found that smokers who were depressed were 40% less likely to quit than those who were not depressed (Anda et al., 1990). The first time I taught health psychology one of my students came to me during the final exam with a very important question—she was feeling very nervous and wanted permission to go outside and smoke a cigarette to calm herself down! (Although I reluctantly agreed to her request, I had to wonder what she had really learned in the course about the dangers of smoking.)

Combined Models

According to the **multiple regulation model**, the combination of physiological and psychological factors leads to addiction. This model predicts that smoking is initially used to regulate emotions (in line with Tomkins's model), but, over time, how smokers feel becomes linked with how much nicotine they have in their blood (Leventhal & Cleary, 1980). For example, an individual who is anxious may initially smoke a cigarette to feel more comfortable (the act of holding something in his or her hand, the feeling of fitting in with others, etc.). In this case, external stresses (e.g., taking a difficult exam, attending a party) lead to the desire to smoke. Over time, however, the repeated pairing of smoking and reduction in anxiety becomes linked (remember the discussion of classical conditioning in Chapter 3?). At this point, low levels of nicotine in the blood trigger feelings of anxiety (and a craving for cigarettes), even if the person is not in a stressful situation. So, people learn to smoke as a way of reducing the negative feelings that result from a drop in nicotine levels. Because smoking can be used both to reduce arousal (and thereby reduce stress) and create arousal (and thereby increase stimulation), nicotine can easily become paired with positive as well as negative states.

The **biobehavioral model** proposed by Pomerleau and Pomerleau (1989) also suggests that both psychological and physiological factors lead people to continue to smoke over time. This model proposes that nicotine has a number of physiological effects that make people feel good (e.g., improves memory and concentration, reduces anxiety and tension), which leads people to readily become dependent on smoking. Smokers then become dependent (both physically and psychologically) on using nicotine to experience these positive effects. In fact, smokers who are trying to quit often return to smoking precisely because they find it difficult to concentrate and relax without having a cigarette (and, most important, the nicotine that it provides). As described at the beginning of the chapter, Jack found that whenever he tried to stop smoking, he felt anxious and distracted at work, which in turn led him to return to smoking.

Finally, some research suggests that smoking, including the desire to smoke as well as the ease with which people become addicted to nicotine, may be at least partially based in genetics. Research indicates that about 60% of smoking behavior

Many people initially smoke to regulate their moods in some way; however, over time, the level of nicotine in the body and mood become integrally linked so that simply a drop in nicotine in the blood can trigger a negative mood, which in turn motivates smoking.
Source: Bob Daemmrich/The Image Works.

may be inherited—for example, twin studies indicate that identical twins are much more likely to be similar in their smoking behavior than fraternal twins (Heath & Madden, 1995). Moreover, genetic factors contribute not only to whether a person smokes but also the age at which smoking begins, the number of cigarettes smoked per day, and the persistence and intensity of smoking (Heath & Martin, 1993). One explanation of how genetic factors lead to smoking is that they cause personality traits (e.g., rebelliousness) that then lead to smoking. Heredity may also influence how pleasant or unpleasant someone finds tobacco. Finally, genetic factors may influence how easily and strongly someone becomes dependent on tobacco (Pomerleau, Collins, Shiffman, & Pomerleau, 1993). In line with this view, some research suggests that people who have a particular gene that is linked with dopamine release (a neurotransmitter that influences mood) are less likely to smoke (Timberlake et al., 2006).

What Are Some Strategies for Preventing Smoking?

Because most people who smoke start at an early age, efforts to prevent smoking must target adolescents before they begin smoking; these are primary prevention strategies. Although initial efforts to prevent smoking focused on the negative long-term effects of this behavior (e.g., dying of lung cancer), these approaches were basically unsuccessful for several reasons. First, many teenagers who begin to smoke are already aware of these dangers—but perceive them as not personally relevant, in part because teenagers usually intend to quit before they experience the long-term consequences. Second, even those who believe they are at risk of various health consequences may perceive the short-term benefits of smoking (e.g., looking "mature," feeling relaxed) as more important than the distant, long-term consequences. Emphasizing the long-term consequences of smoking can even backfire by making teenagers think there are no negative short-term effects. More recent smoking-prevention programs have therefore focused on providing social influence or life skills training (Flay, 1987).

Social influence programs include a number of components designed to make them effective in keeping adolescents away from smoking (Flay, 1987). First, these programs inform teenagers of the immediate physiological and social consequences of smoking, such as the financial cost of smoking, rejection by potential dating partners who don't like the smell of smoke, and having stained teeth and bad breath. In fact, emphasizing minor but short-term consequences is more effective in changing attitudes toward smoking than emphasizing the serious long-term health consequences (Pechmann, 1997)! These programs also appeal to adolescents' desire for independence by pointing out the manipulative nature of cigarette ads. The underlying message is that people who buy cigarettes are giving in to advertising slogans, whereas those who refuse to smoke are independent and self-reliant (very appealing traits to most teenagers). Third, because peers play a major role in the initiation and maintenance of smoking, these programs often emphasize that many adolescents are against smoking. Adolescents tend to overestimate the number of others who are engaging in risky behaviors, and they believe that others have more favorable perceptions of the behaviors and those who engage in them (Graham, Marks, & Hansen, 1991; Marks, Graham, & Hansen, 1992). Finally, social influence programs are typically presented by desirable role models, namely, slightly older students (e.g., high school students leading groups for junior high school students). These peer leaders demonstrate strategies for resisting peer pressure to smoke and allow participants to role-play various situations to practice their responses. For example, students might be asked to show how they would respond if someone said, "Come on, everyone is having a cigarette."

Encouragingly, some research suggests that social influence programs may reduce the rate of adolescent smoking. One study with sixth-grade students in Canada revealed that students who received a social influence program were significantly less likely to try cigarettes by the end of eighth grade than those who did not receive such a program (47% versus 60%, respectively; Best et al., 1984). Moreover, this program was even effective in helping students who were already smoking occasionally: At the 2-year follow-up, 63% of those who received this program had quit smoking as compared to only 28% of those who did not receive this program. As described at the beginning of this chapter, Annabelle's health-promotion class emphasizing the negative social and short-term physical consequences of smoking led her to form a very negative attitude toward cigarettes.

Life skills training approaches have also been used to prevent and/or reduce teenage smoking. This approach is based on the assumption that adolescents who lack self-esteem and self-confidence are at greater risk of smoking (Flay, 1987). These adolescents may turn to smoking both as a way of feeling better about themselves and because they lack the skills necessary to stand up to peer pressure influencing them to smoke. These programs may include some of the same components as social influence programs, such as information about the negative short-term consequences of smoking and the impact of media on smoking, but they also provide adolescents with general assistance in enhancing self-esteem and social competence, techniques for resisting persuasive appeals, and skills for verbal and nonverbal communication. One study by Botvin, Baker, Renick, Filazzola, & Botvin (1984) demonstrated that seventh-grade students in New York who received 15 sessions of life skills training over 4 to 6 weeks were less likely to report smoking than those who did not receive such training, even as long as 1 year later (10% versus 22%, respectively).

Although psychosocial approaches to prevent smoking may be effective, some programs have had good initial success, which then disappears as time passes (Flay et al., 1989). Moreover, because students as young as fifth grade may have already formed positive attitudes about smokers (possibly based on images in movies or television), smoking-prevention programs may need to start even earlier (Dinh et al., 1995). Students in high school are particularly likely to start smoking, and receiving a program 3 to 4 years earlier seems to have little effect. Effective programs probably need to include "booster" sessions in high school, focus attention on those who have already smoked occasionally and are therefore at high risk, and assess and provide more personal attention based on students' distinct psychological needs. It is also important to offer smoking-prevention messages to those who smoke but are not yet regular (and addicted) smokers; this is an easier time to intervene than after the habit is firmly entrenched (Ary & Biglan, 1988).

A number of mass-media approaches, including television, magazine, and billboard ads, have been used to try to prevent smoking. For example, researchers in one study examined whether adding media antismoking ads would increase the effectiveness of school-based smoking-prevention programs (Flynn et al., 1992).

To test this hypothesis, researchers compared the rate of adolescent smoking in four different communities in Vermont and Montana over 4 years. Adolescents in all four of these communities had attended at least three special antismoking classes in their schools. Researchers also ran special antismoking ads in two of the community newspapers (one in Vermont and one in Montana) for 5 months initially and then again for 1 month each year for 3 years. These ads emphasized the short-term costs of smoking, such as smelly breath and clothes, demonstrated how to refuse offers of cigarettes, and emphasized that most teenagers did not smoke. Although the smoking rates increased over time in all communities as the students got older, those who were in communities that were exposed to the ad campaigns had less smoking than in the communities that received only the school program, suggesting that adding the media components was more effective in preventing teenage smoking than simply providing school-based antismoking education. For example, 2 years after the intervention, 9.3% of students who received only the school-based program smoked as compared to 5% of those who also received media ads. These lower rates of smoking remained as long as 6 years later, indicating that media antismoking ads can be a very important tool in preventing teenage smoking.

> **Questioning the Research 7.1**
>
> Can this study really tell us whether social influence programs are effective in reducing teenage smoking? What are some limitations of this research?

Media approaches are also commonly used to prevent teenage smoking. The first national antismoking campaign, called the "truth" campaign, created edgy television, radio, and print ads that focused on exposing the tobacco industry's deceptive marketing techniques that try to lure in teenage smokers. Following this campaign, smoking prevalence among students decreased from 25.3% to 18.0% between 1999 and 2002 (Farrelly, Davis, Haviland, Messeri, & Healton, 2005). Estimates are that 22% of this decline was attributed to this campaign. Similarly, one survey of 16,000 young people ages 12 to 17 both before and after the "truth" media campaign revealed that those in markets with high levels of exposure to this campaign had more negative beliefs about tobacco industry practices and more negative attitudes about the tobacco industry (Hershey et al., 2005). In turn, they were less likely to be receptive to such advertising and had lower intentions to smoke. Chapter 13 provides more about the use of advertising and other types of persuasive messages to change health-related behavior.

Although some large-scale advertising campaigns may help prevent smoking, these approaches are largely ineffective for several reasons (Pechmann, 1997). Television networks, which don't receive money for running public-service ads, are likely to run such ads during low-viewing times (e.g., 56% occur late at night). Research also suggests that to be effective, viewers must see at least one nonsmoking ad for every four smoking ads they see. However, the U.S. tobacco industry spends about $7.12 per person in advertising each year (ads in magazines and on buses, highway billboards, event sponsorships, etc.), whereas antismoking campaigns spend well under $0.50 per person. This high rate of spending by tobacco companies helps explain why Joe Camel (a now discontinued character featured on a brand of cigarettes) was second only to Mickey Mouse in face recognition among American children (Grunberg et al., 1997).

Finally, large-scale government-based approaches, including restricting cigarette advertising and marketing, increasing cigarette prices, banning smoking in public places, and increasing enforcement of laws that deny teenagers the opportunity to buy cigarettes can also, at least in some cases, help prevent smoking (Slater, Chaloupka, Wakefield, Johnston, & O'Malley, 2007). Some of these strategies aren't particularly effective. For example, even when teenagers are unable to buy cigarettes at some stores, they go to other stores, use vending machines, or ask smokers of legal age to buy cigarettes for them. However, other approaches have been shown to be quite effective. One study of 301 Massachusetts communities revealed that teenagers who lived in towns with a strong restaurant antismoking regulation were less apt to become smokers than those who lived in towns with weak regulations (Siegel, Albers, Cheng, Hamilton, & Biener, 2008). Specifically, although smoking regulations had no impact on the likelihood of a teenager trying smoking, these laws apparently impeded teenagers' progression from experimenting with cigarettes to becoming a regular smoker. Similarly, adolescents who attend a school with strong policies prohibiting tobacco use are less likely to smoke (Lovato et al., 2010). Increasing the cost of cigarettes can be particularly effective in decreasing smoking in teenagers, probably because teenagers have relatively little disposable income (Tauras, O'Malley, & Johnston, 2001). In fact, one study found that increasing the cost of cigarettes by 10% would lead to a 10% decrease in smoking among teenagers.

On October 22, 2012, a new federal law goes into effect that requires cigarette manufacturers to display one of nine authorized graphic warnings, such as the ones pictured here. This requirement is based in part on research showing that ads focusing on young victims suffering from serious tobacco-related diseases elicited disgust and reduced intent to smoke among adolescents (Pechmann & Reibling, 2006).
Source: Ren Haijun/NewsCom.

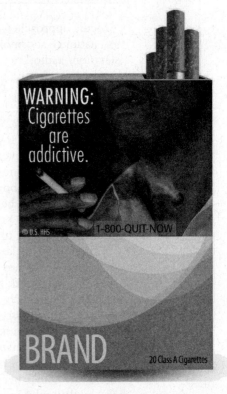

What Are Some Strategies for Quitting Smoking?

Although an estimated 30% of the smokers in the United States attempt to quit at least once each year (Fiore et al., 1990), only 19% of these attempts are effective for even a month (Hughes et al., 1992). Quitting smoking is a process—most people who successfully quit have tried to do so on repeated occasions before they are successful, and Box 7.3: Health Psychology in the Real World describes the similar challenge of quitting chewing tobacco. What predicts successful quitting? People with the following characteristics are more successful: smoke less than a pack a day (e.g., have less nicotine dependence), have fewer smoking friends, have less stress, have higher levels of education, are employed, perceive the negative effects of smoking, have intrinsic motivation, and have more positive expectations about quitting (Hertel et al., 2008; Shiffman et al., 1996). Having support from others, including family, friends, and coworkers, is also helpful (Cohen & Lichtenstein, 1990b). Not surprisingly, individuals who are higher in self-efficacy for both quitting smoking and maintaining smoking cessation are more successful in quitting (Baldwin et al., 2006; Van Zundert, Ferguson, Shiffman, & Engels, 2010). On the other hand, people who are more concerned about gaining weight following smoking cessation are, not surprisingly, less likely to successfully quit: One study found that women who were not concerned about gaining weight had a quit rate of 21% compared to 13.1% for those who were extremely concerned about gaining weight (Jeffery, Hennrikus, Lando, Murray, & Liu, 2000).

Because one of the major problems of quitting smoking is the experience of nicotine withdrawal symptoms, many approaches to smoking cessation rely on some type of **nicotine replacement** (Wetter et al., 1998). Some people use nicotine-fading strategies, such as reducing smoking by switching to low-nicotine cigarettes, and then slowly weaning themselves off of nicotine. One study found that 44% of those who gradually reduced the number of cigarettes they smoked were still abstaining 1 year later, as opposed to only 22% of those who quit "cold turkey" (Cinciripini et al., 1995). Others use nicotine-replacement strategies, such as gum and nicotine patches, which are effective in decreasing withdrawal symptoms and helping to achieve short-term and long-term success. For example, one study with 173 people who were attempting to stop smoking found that 33% of highly dependent smokers had stopped smoking even 2 years after participation in group counseling and receiving nicotine gum (Tonnesen et al., 1988). Nicotine-replacement approaches are especially effective if they are used in combination with behavioral therapy (Wetter et al., 1998) and for smokers who are highly dependent on nicotine.

Some research suggests that nicotine may be a more important factor in predicting men's smoking, whereas psychological/situational factors (e.g., the smell of cigarettes, the act of holding a cigarette) may be a more important factor in predicting women's smoking (Perkins, 1996). For example, women are less accurate than men in detecting different doses of nicotine and whether a particular substance even is nicotine. This difference in sensitivity to nicotine would help explain why women often have more trouble stopping smoking than men—the often-used nicotine replacement therapies aren't as helpful for people whose smoking is driven by psychological factors. On the other hand, research indicates that women experience much more comfort and relaxation from smoking cigarettes than men,

Box 7.3

Health Psychology in the Real World: Finally Tough Enough to Give Up Snuff

By John Hare, *Newsweek*, September 7, 2003

The brown stains on my teeth and the black and blue discoloration of my gums were signs that my affair with chewing tobacco had turned ugly. All that was left in the wake of our frequent rendezvous were empty snuff cans and a trail of putrid spit. The inside of my mouth had become so sore that almost as quickly as I put in a pinch, pain would tell me to take it out. As soon as I did, I would start obsessing about not having a chew in my mouth.

How did this come to be? What was *wrong* with me? I had tried to quit numerous times, only to succumb to the seduction of my old friend Copenhagen, in the black can with the tin lid. Those white letters were imprinted on my psyche as well as the can.

I was chewing a can of Copenhagen every day. Each failure to quit brought a new round of shame and humiliation. Some self-righteous moron would lecture me, and the pain and anger would well up inside of me like a smoldering volcano—nothing that a little pinch between the cheek and gum couldn't calm.

Twenty years earlier I had my first chaw, or wad, of tobacco. I'll never forget it. I was 16 years old, eager to try something rebellious and unique. My friend Mike had some Copenhagen, and I tried a little pinch. The particles wandering around in my mouth resulted in a grand little retching episode. You mean people actually *chew* this stuff? Boy, they must be tough.

Mike was not to be deterred. He solved the rookie chewer's inability to keep the chaw in place by wrapping it in gauze; with the messy part solved, my path to the wonders of nicotine was now clear. I achieved the wonderful nicotine rush and lightheaded euphoria on a lazy summer night in 1973—with no smoke!

So began my innocent foray into the clutches of tobacco addiction. Gradually, it crept into every aspect of my life, methodically tricking me into wanting more and more while enjoying it less and less. Somewhere along the line it went from being socially comforting, something I enjoyed sharing with other chewers, to a habit and, later, an obsession. The thrill was gone.

Several times, I gave in to pressure to quit from my friends and relatives, and vowed to kick the habit. Once I did, nothing seemed normal—my life was too entwined with my can of tobacco. It had become my security blanket. How could I concentrate without it? How could I relax? No wad after a meal? No dipping during those boring meetings? No chew after coffee or cocktails? What kind of life was that?

Then, eight years ago, I started studying addiction. This was key for me, because I was doing it for myself, not to placate my loved ones. My search led me to a book, "You Can Stop Smoking," by Jacquelyn Rogers, the founder of SmokEnders.

Although the book was written for smokers, I simply made a few adaptations for smokeless tobacco and I was ready to implement the plan. I learned how to gradually quit my habit by identifying the many triggers—like picking up a newspaper or finishing a meal—that kicked in my cravings for nicotine. Once I had identified a trigger, I'd slowly increase the time between it and the chew until, gradually, the trigger lost its power.

This knowledge and understanding gave me a feeling of control over the monster I was fighting. Little by little, I chipped away at the foundation of addiction, freeing myself from its grip.

I religiously followed the four-week plan to its conclusion. The last week went smoothly, but on "cutoff" day I came to the somewhat queasy realization that this would be the last day of a 20-year relationship. There was time for only a few more wads to chew. A feeling of ambivalence was intruding upon my quest.

These were to be the last hours, then minutes, of my nicotine habit. Tomorrow would be the first day of my new life free of the shackles of addiction. At 11:40 p.m. I put what would be my last chew of Copenhagen between my cheek and gum. The finality of it made me feel very anxious. I was *really* scared. Fear of failure was certainly there, but there was more. I was getting sentimental at losing an old friend.

To get myself back to reality, I pulled out my journal. I reviewed the many reasons I had listed for wanting to quit. At the top was "for my own freedom." Then I looked at the reasons listed in the "Why I Chew" column—they had all been scratched out. I had systematically eliminated every one.

As the clock struck midnight, I took a deep breath. I walked outside and breathed in all the summer night's sensory offerings. I removed the last chaw from my mouth, flicked it on the ground and threw the can triumphantly into the field behind my house. I felt sure I was done for good. Eight years of outwitting and ignoring my old best friend confirms that I was right. I'm free at last.

and women are more motivated to smoke by the opportunity to hold cigarettes and "bring them to their mouths." This may also be why women are more influenced than men by smoking advertisements, which promote particular social and cultural images of smoking (e.g., thinness, relaxation). Women may also have more weight issues that lead to continued smoking. The popular image of women who smoke is that they are attractive and thin—it is no accident that one of the best-selling brands for women is Virginia Slims (Grunberg, Winders, & Wewers, 1991). And research indicates that concern about weight can both lead to smoking and make smoking cessation more difficult. What's the good news for women? One recent study found that 21% of women who received cognitive-behavioral therapy (CBT) for smoking cessation that included information on possible slight weight gains had stopped smoking 1 year later, as compared to only 9% of women who received standard smoking cessation therapy (Perkins et al., 2001).

However, it is difficult to draw conclusions about whether nicotine-replacement strategies are more effective than other approaches because people may choose such strategies after other approaches have failed. In line with that view, smokers who choose the nicotine gum/patch as a strategy for quitting differ from those who don't—they are more likely to have friends who smoke, accept cigarettes from friends, and intend to smoke later on (Klesges et al., 2007). In turn, one study found that those who used the nicotine patch were 70% more likely to return to smoking than those who didn't use those products. Moreover, people who are using nicotine replacement still can experience lapses—often based on stress or bad mood or situational cues to smoking—so the replacement alone may not be effective for all people (Ferguson & Shiffman, 2010).

Aversion strategies for smoking cessation are based on principles of classical conditioning—these approaches try to reduce smoking by pairing smoking with some type of unpleasant stimulus. In the rapid-smoking technique, patients smoke rapidly and continuously to exceed their tolerance for cigarette smoke and thereby experience an unpleasant sensation (Lichtenstein & Mermelstein, 1984).

Although many people who smoke intend to quit, stopping smoking is very hard (as discussed in more detail later in this chapter).
Source: Garrett Price/cartoonbank.com. All Rights Reserved.

"Don't worry. If it turns out tobacco is harmful, we can always quit."

For example, patients may be told to take a puff every 6 seconds until they literally cannot stand it anymore. Aversion strategies may also work by pairing smoking with unpleasant or upsetting images to create negative connections. For example, people may be told to take a puff of smoke and hold it in their mouths while thinking about vomit or excrement (Kamarck & Lichtenstein, 1985). Other aversive treatments include pairing smoking with electric shocks—every time a smoker takes a drag on the cigarette a slightly painful electric shock is given. One review of the effectiveness of various smoking-cessation programs indicates that aversive strategies lead to significant increases in smoking-cessation rates (Wetter et al., 1998). Aversion strategies are especially effective for smokers who are low on physical dependence on nicotine and for those who smoke for pleasure (Zelman, Brandon, Jorenby, & Baker, 1992). The most effective strategies involve actual smoke (e.g., smoke holding), as opposed to electric shock or imagined scenes.

Self-management strategies focus on identifying those situations that lead people to smoke and then teaching people strategies to resist temptation (Lichtenstein & Mermelstein, 1984; Sussman, Sun, & Dent, 2006). In the initial stages, the emphasis is on strengthening the motivation to quit, setting a date to quit, and monitoring one's smoking patterns. After people understand the situations that lead them to want to smoke, they can then start to avoid these situations (a technique called **stimulus control**). For example, people are often tempted to smoke when they are with others who are smoking and when they are drinking alcohol (Shiffman et al., 1996). They might therefore make a decision to avoid socializing with other smokers and to avoid drinking alcohol, at least initially. Some stimulus-control methods can be very small, such as removing the ashtrays in your home and only going to nonsmoking restaurants. Even giving smokers information about the relative costs and benefits of smoking, as well as some training in strategies for quitting, can help increase intentions to resist smoking and reduce intentions to smoke (Norman, Maley, Li, & Skinner, 2008).

It is impossible to avoid all situations that prompt a cigarette craving, so people also must practice **response substitution**, or choosing another way to handle situations that lead them to want to smoke (Lichtenstein & Mermelstein, 1984). A person might go for a walk after dinner instead of smoking or chew gum whenever he or she feels like smoking. Because many smokers crave cigarettes when they are under some type of stress, self-management approaches may also include training in stress management, relaxation, and coping skills (Berkman, Dickenson, Falk, & Lieberman, 2011; Wetter et al., 1998). As described at the beginning of the chapter, Diana worked with a therapist to identify factors that led her to want a cigarette, and then she tried to avoid these situations or to cope with them in a new way. Researchers in one study provided smokers with training in a variety of quitting strategies, such as chewing gum instead of smoking, using deep-breathing methods to cope with stress, and cognitive restructuring (Stevens & Hollis, 1989). Participants were then randomly assigned to one of three follow-up conditions: a skills condition (in which they identified high-risk situations for smoking and developed and rehearsed strategies for responding to these situations), a discussion condition (in which participants described their experience related to smoking), or a no-treatment control condition. Specifically, 41.3% of those in the skills condition were not smoking at the 1-year follow-up as compared to 34.1% of those in the discussion condition and 33.3% of those who received no follow-up. This finding suggests that simply providing social support for smoking cessation is not enough—people also need ongoing training in specific coping strategies to maintain their new behavior over time.

Self-management strategies may also include providing some type of a reward for quitting smoking to increase motivation (Lichtenstein & Mermelstein, 1984; Sussman et al., 2006). One such approach is called **contingency-contracting**. In this technique, smokers give some money to a friend (or therapist), with the understanding that if they are not smoking 6 months later, they get the money back. This technique therefore uses the promise of a reward to encourage smoking cessation (an operant-conditioning approach).

Interventions that include some type of reminders and/or assistance with maintaining smoking cessation are particularly effective at helping people stop smoking. Telephone counseling, which can provide assistance with cognitive and behavioral strategies for quitting, increases smoking cessation in young adults (Glasgow et al., 2008; Lichtenstein, Zhu, & Tedeschi, 2010; Lipkus et al., 2004). Researchers in one intervention study found that 20% of those who received a self-help booklet and up to five sessions of phone counseling had quit 3 months later, compared to only 9% of those who just received the booklet (Rabius, McAlister, Geiger, Huang, & Todd, 2004). Personalized messages to promote smoking cessation are particularly effective (Webb, Simmons, & Brandon, 2005), as discussed in Chapter 13.

Questioning the Research 7.2

Although these studies have reported on the effectiveness of various strategies for helping people quit smoking, can we be sure that these approaches were in fact effective? Why or why not? (Hint: Think about how researchers are measuring the dependent variable, or outcome, in most of these studies.)

Given the widespread problem of smoking, a variety of relatively large-scale plans to decrease smoking have been attempted. One approach is to ban smoking in particular situations, such as in the workplace, in school, and on airplanes. Although these types of programs certainly help prevent the problems associated with passive smoking, smokers can just smoke more in other places to compensate. For example, one study of the effects of a workplace ban on smoking found that although there was an initial decrease of levels of nicotine in the bloodstream of smoking employees 1 week after the ban was enacted, nicotine levels were nearly back to baseline levels 6 weeks later (Gomel, Oldenburg, Lemon, Owen, & Westbrook, 1993). However, there is some evidence that providing smoking-cessation programs at work can be at least somewhat effective (Lichtenstein & Glasgow, 1992). Some efforts have been made to reach large groups of individuals in a given community by providing media information (e.g., through radio, television, newspapers) as well as extensive individual education on quitting smoking (Farquhar et al., 1990). In the Stanford Five City Project, for example, cities with this type of intensive education showed a 13% reduction in smoking over 2 to 5 years compared to rates in similar cities without such instruction. As discussed previously in terms of smoking prevention, raising cigarette prices can also help motivate quitting. In fact, one study found that more smokers reported quit attempts and were successful in abstaining from cigarettes after a tax increase in California raised cigarette prices (Reed, Anderson, Vaughn, & Burns, 2008).

What Is the Prevalence of Alcohol Use and Abuse?

Most adults drink alcohol at least occasionally—about 52% of Americans ages 18 and over are regular drinkers (having had at least 12 drinks in the past year; CDC, 2010). Rates of alcohol use also vary as a function of gender, ethnicity, and education. As you might guess, men are more likely than women to drink: 61.4% of men are regular drinkers, meaning they have at least 12 drinks in a year, compared to 43.3% of women. How is ethnicity associated with alcohol use? Drinking is more common among Caucasians (53.3% are regular drinkers) than among Hispanic Americans (42%), African Americans (39.4%), and Asian Americans (32.8%). Interestingly, although smoking is more common among people with lower levels of education, the reverse is true in terms of alcohol use. Of college graduates, 65% drink alcohol on a regular basis, compared to only 37% of those with less than a high school education. And even though alcohol use is illegal for those under age 21, large-scale national surveys reveal that 42% of high school students have drunk some alcohol in the past 30 days (CDC, 2010).

Although most people who try alcohol or drink occasionally never develop problems with alcohol abuse, about 23% engage in binge drinking (having five or

FIGURE 7.4 Binge drinking is more prevalent at all ages in men than in women and is more prevalent in younger people than in older people (data from CDC, 2010).

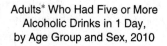

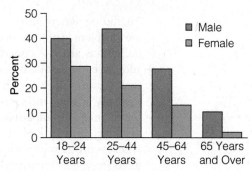

*Age 18 years and older United States;
Source: National Health interview Survey
*At least once in the past year

more drinks on the same occasion at least once in the past month; Substance Abuse and Mental Health Services Administration, 2007). As you might expect, binge drinking and heavy drinking are much more common among young people than among older adults (see Figure 7.4). This type of alcohol abuse is also much more common in men than women. For example, 30.8% of men are binge drinkers compared to only 15.1% of women. As described in Box 7.4: Focus on Culture, cultures vary considerably in terms of both alcohol regulations and consumption.

Box 7.4

Focus on Culture: The Impact of Culture on Alcohol Regulations, Consumption, and Consequences

Countries also vary considerably in their regulations involving alcohol use as well as in the prevalence of alcohol consumption. For example, the United States has a drinking age of 21, whereas many European countries have younger minimum drinking ages, such as 16 (France, Italy) or 18 (Ireland, Sweden, United Kingdom). Rates of alcohol use even among 15 and 16 year olds also vary by country, from a high of 70 to 80% (Denmark, United Kingdom) to a low of 33% (United States; Hibell et al., 2009). Drinking enough to become drunk is also somewhat more common in European countries than in the United States: Only 18% of 15 and 16 year olds in the United States report having been drunk at least once in the past month, compared to 49% of those in Denmark and 33% of those in the United Kingdom. Although alcohol regulations and rates of consumption vary by country, alcohol abuse is associated with negative consequences in all countries: Alcohol is the third largest risk factor for disease in the world (after lack of food in childhood and unsafe sex), largely due to injuries, with 2.5 million deaths each year, including 320,000 deaths of people ages 15 to 29, from alcohol-related causes (WHO, 2010).

People who are problem drinkers drink heavily on a regular basis, are psychologically dependent on alcohol, experience loss of memory while drinking, and suffer social and occupational impairments from their drinking (see Table 7.1; Mayer, 1983). They may drink often, drink alone frequently, drink during the day (including when going to work), and drive under the influence. Of those who are problem drinkers, about half are alcoholics (Davidson, 1985). **Alcoholism** is defined as alcohol consumption that is compulsive and uncontrollable, physically addictive, or habitual and that results in serious threats to a person's health and well-being. Alcoholics have a very high tolerance for alcohol, suffer blackouts or memory losses, and experience withdrawal symptoms such as delirium tremens (hallucinations, impaired motor coordination, cognitive disruption) when they stop drinking. Thus, alcoholism involves both psychological and physical dependence, whereas problem drinking involves only psychological dependence. Males are more likely to experience problems with drinking—especially White males (Chartier, Hesselbrock, & Hesselbrock, 2011).

TABLE 7.1 *Test Yourself: Are You a Problem Drinker?*

Answer yes or no to the following questions.

1. Have you found that the same amount of alcohol had less effect than before?
2. Have you found that you had to drink more than you once did to get the same effect?
3. Have you been sick or vomited after drinking?
4. Have you felt depressed, irritable, or nervous after drinking?
5. Have you found yourself sweating heavily or shaking after drinking?
6. Have you heard or seen things that weren't really there after drinking?
7. Have you taken a drink to keep yourself from shaking or feeling sick?
8. Have you ended up drinking much more than you intended to?
9. Have you found it difficult to stop drinking after you started?
10. Have you kept drinking for a longer period of time than you intended to?
11. Have you tried to cut down or stop drinking and found you couldn't do it?
12. Have you wanted to cut down or stop your drinking and found you couldn't do it?
13. Have you continued to drink even though it was a threat to your health?
14. Have you kept on drinking even though it caused you emotional problems?
15. Have you been arrested or had trouble with the police because of your drinking?
16. Have you kept drinking even though it caused you problems at home, school, or work?
17. Did a spouse or someone you lived with threaten to leave you because of your drinking?
18. Have you driven a car after having too much to drink?
19. Have you done things when drinking that could have caused you to be hurt?
20. Have you done things when drinking that could have caused someone else to be hurt?

Give yourself a point for every yes answer. What is your score? Higher scores indicate more problems with alcohol use.

Source: Dawson, Grant, & Harford, 1995.

What Are the Health Consequences of Alcohol Abuse?

Alcohol use has a number of negative health consequences. The most well known is liver damage caused when fat accumulates in the liver and blocks blood flow, which can eventually lead to cirrhosis, a buildup of scar tissue in the liver (Eckhardt et al., 1981). Alcohol abuse can also have negative effects on the brain and on neuropsychological functioning (Delin & Lee, 1992). About 10% of alcoholics are affected by Wernicke-Korsakoff syndrome; symptoms include severe memory problems, disorientation, and drowsiness (Parsons, 1977). Heavy drinking can also lead to the development of some types of cancer, including cancer of the liver, esophagus, or larynx (Levy, 1985). Excessive alcohol use by pregnant women has a number of negative effects on the growing fetus (Larroque et al., 1995). Fetal alcohol syndrome, which is caused by insufficient protein in the mother's diet, can be caused by excessive drinking during pregnancy and may result in significant problems for the fetus, including mental retardation, growth problems, and nervous system problems.

Alcohol use can also lead indirectly to a number of other health problems. Excessive alcohol use contributes to an estimated 79,000 deaths in the United States each year, as well as 1.6 million hospitalizations and 4 million emergency room visits (CDC, 2011). As described at the beginning of the chapter, Jenny's alcohol abuse led

Alcohol use is a leading cause of motor vehicle accidents and deaths.
Source: © Visual Mining/Alamy Limited.

her to repeatedly drive under the influence of alcohol and to engage in sexual activity with assorted random partners—two highly risky behaviors. Almost 30 people in the United States die each day in motor vehicle crashes that involve an alcohol-impaired driver—which amounts to one death every 48 minutes (US Department of Transportation, 2010). Alcohol use is also associated with higher rates of partial drownings, homicide, suicide, electrical shocks, and communicable diseases (CDC, 2010; Glenn, Parsons, & Stevens, 1989). Alcohol use even increases the likelihood of death while bicycling and swimming. During my first year of college, my sailing class was canceled so that a dive team could search the small pond for the body of a student who had last been seen walking home (drunk) from a fraternity party the night before; the student's body was recovered from the pond that afternoon.

Why does alcohol use lead to so many risky behaviors, with potentially detrimental health consequences, such as unsafe sex, drunk driving, and accidents? First, the physiological effects of alcohol lead to impaired information processing and reduced self-awareness (Sayette, 1999). In turn, alcohol use reduces the association between attitudes and behavior, so people are more likely to engage in extreme or excessive behaviors that are not in line with their actual beliefs (Steele & Josephs, 1990). Sometimes such uninhibited behavior might simply make you feel silly—imagine dancing on a table wearing a lampshade, for example. But in other cases, alcohol use could lead to more problematic behavior. For example, alcohol use may also lead to increased aggression (Bailey, Leonard, Cranston, & Taylor, 1983; Leonard, 1989; Subra, Muller, Begue, Bushman, & Delmas, 2010). In one study, researchers randomly assigned half of the participants to drink a high dose of alcohol and the others to drink no alcohol and then read several sentences (e.g., "she cut him off in traffic") and interpret whether the actions were done intentionally or unintentionally (Bègue, Bushman, Giancola, Subra, & Rosset, 2010). As predicted, drunk people were more likely to see acts as intentional, which helps explain why alcohol use can increase aggression—people see accidents (e.g., getting pushed in a bar) as deliberate.

Alcohol use also leads to a state called **alcohol myopia**, in which individuals under the influence of alcohol are unable to engage in the complex cognitive processing required to consider the long-term consequences of their behavior and instead base decisions primarily on the most salient and immediate cues (Steele & Josephs, 1990). For example, people who are sober may recognize that engaging in unprotected sex could have substantial long-term consequences (e.g., unintended pregnancy, transmission of STD/AIDS) and therefore refuse to have sex without a condom, whereas those who are intoxicated may act based entirely on the immediate situation (e.g., their desire to engage in sex) and may ignore the more distant consequences of this decision (see Figure 7.5; Gordon, Carey, & Carey, 1997; MacDonald, MacDonald, Zanna, & Fong, 2000; Murphy, Monahan, & Miller, 1998). To test this idea, researchers in one study randomly assigned male undergraduates to either a sober or intoxicated condition, in which they were given three alcoholic drinks (MacDonald, Zanna, & Fong, 1995). Participants than watched a 10-minute video showing two students meeting, dancing, and then going back to one of their apartments, and then answered some questions about what they would do in this situation. The findings of this study provide strong (and scary) evidence for how alcohol impairs decision making. Although both sober and intoxicated students viewed having unprotected sex in this situation as

FIGURE 7.5   Researchers in this study examined the influence of alcohol use on unprotected sex in gay men (data from Vanable et al., 2004). As shown in this figure, men who drank 4 or more drinks were more likely to engage in unprotected sex with a nonprimary partner than those who did not drink at all.

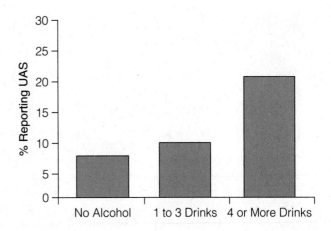

equally foolish and irresponsible, only 21% of the sober participants reported that they were even fairly likely to have sex in this situation, whereas 77% of the drunk participants did so. This study suggests that alcohol use may lead people to engage in behavior that they recognize as foolish and irresponsible. Similarly, Box 7.5: Focus on Research describes how alcohol use may impair women's likelihood of using condoms.

Questioning the Research 7.3

Although the research study by MacDonald et al. (1995) suggests that alcohol use may reduce condom use, the procedure used in this study simply asked participants to report on their expected behavior based on a hypothetical situation. Do you think these findings would be the same in the real-world behavior? Why or why not?

Alcohol myopia theory also proposes that people who are intoxicated experience **drunken self-inflation**, meaning they see themselves in an idealized way (Steele & Josephs, 1990). In one test of this hypothesis, students were asked to first rate themselves on a number of traits (friendly, intelligent, independent, sincere, etc.), then drink some alcohol, and finally to rerate themselves on the same traits (Banaji & Steele, 1989). Can you guess how drinking influenced self-ratings? As predicted, students' ratings of their most valued traits increased after drinking, particularly for those traits that they had not felt that good about previously. This drunken self-inflation unfortunately also leads people to experience *drunken invincibility*, a feeling that a person is invulnerable to the dangers he or she might normally experience (Steele & Josephs, 1990). One study by Hansen, Rayno, & Wolkenstein (1991) demonstrated that heavy drinkers view the potential negative consequences of drinking, such as being arrested for driving under the influence and doing embarrassing things, as much less serious than do light drinkers. This is why people who know that driving while intoxicated is not a good idea may believe they are able to drive "even better" when drunk. Unfortunately, college students who are unrealistically optimistic about the likelihood they will experience problems due to alcohol use are more likely to experience negative events, including missing classes,

Box 7.5

Focus on Research: Why Drinking Alcohol Interferes With Condom Use

Researchers in this study were interested in examining how alcohol use influences condom use intentions and behavior (Norris et al., 2009). Researchers randomly assigned 173 women to one of four conditions: control (participants drank orange juice), low alcohol consumption (participants drank vodka in orange juice until their blood-alcohol concentration reached .04), high alcohol consumption (participants drank vodka in orange juice until their blood-alcohol concentration reached .08), or a placebo condition (participants drank flat tonic water in orange juice that they were told was an alcoholic drink). All participants then read a story describing an interaction between a woman and man going on a date and becoming sexually intimate. Participants were then asked a series of questions about what they would do in this situation, including how likely they would be to have sex in that situation, how likely would you be to request condom use, and how likely would you be to have unprotected sex. Findings indicated that alcohol influenced women's thoughts about the situation, including their likelihood of having sex and likelihood of having unprotected sex, which in turn influenced their likelihood of requesting a condom as well as willingness to have unprotected sex. This research therefore suggests that alcohol may lead to unsafe behavior in part because intoxication influences our thoughts about potentially risky situations.

getting injured, getting in trouble with security/local police, over the next 2 years (Dillard, Midboe, & Klein, 2009).

Although we've focused thus far on all the negative consequences of alcohol abuse, there is growing evidence that alcohol use in moderation can actually have some benefits. Most research suggests that the link between alcohol use and health is a U-shaped curve—people who drink light to moderate amounts of alcohol have better health than those who drink heavily (not surprising) and those who do not drink at all (very surprising). For example, one study followed more than 2,000 people over a 10-year period and divided participants into four groups based on their drinking habits: nondrinkers, light drinkers (two or fewer drinks per day), moderate drinkers (three to five drinks per day), and heavy drinkers (six or more drinks per day; Klatsky, Friedman, & Sigelaub, 1981). Nondrinkers and moderate drinkers had a similar death rate, heavy drinkers had the highest death rate, and light drinkers had the lowest death rate (nearly half the rate of the heavy drinkers). Similarly, one study of female nurses found that those who consumed a moderate number of drinks had a lower risk of death than those who consumed no alcohol or those who consumed higher rates of alcohol (Fuchs et al., 1995). One reason drinking moderate amounts of alcohol may be beneficial is that alcohol increases the rate of high-density lipoprotein cholesterol (HDLC), which helps protect people from heart disease (Gaziano et al., 1993; Linn et al., 1993). Other research suggests that moderate alcohol use can lead to other benefits, including increased bone density (Felson, Zhang, Hannan, Kannel, & Kiel, 1995), protection from heart attacks and blood clots (Ridker, Vaughan, Stampfer, Glynn, & Hennekens, 1994), and lower rates of depression (Lipton, 1994).

How Do Psychological Factors Lead to Alcohol Abuse?

Many researchers believe that people learn to abuse alcohol the same way that they learn other behaviors, by reinforcement and modeling (Maisto, Carey, & Bradizza, 1999). This section describes several psychological theories of drinking and alcoholism, including tension-reduction theory, social learning theory, personality, and biological/genetic.

Tension-Reduction Theory

According to tension-reduction theory, people drink alcohol to cope with or regulate negative moods, including feelings of tension, anxiety, and nervousness (Cooper, Russell, Skinner, Frone, & Mudar, 1992; Greeley & Oei, 1999; Swendsen et al., 2000). In other words, a person feeling nervous or anxious may reduce the unpleasant tension by drinking alcohol; the moderation of negative affect then reinforces his or her drinking behavior. In line with this theory, rats that are exposed to social stressors (e.g., forced isolation) increase their consumption of alcohol (Roske, Baeger, Frenzel, & Oehme, 1994). Similarly, a study by Carney, Armeli, Tennen, Affleck, and O'Neil (2000) found that people who experienced more negative interpersonal events, such as conflicts with family and friends, reported more frequent alcohol use. Although this study was correlational (and therefore can't tell us whether these negative events lead to drinking), experimental research reveals similar results. For example, Hull and Young (1983) gave college students either negative or positive feedback about their IQ and then asked them to taste and rate different kinds of wine. As predicted, students who were told they had low IQ scores drank more wine, presumably in an attempt to reduce self-awareness, than those who received positive feedback.

Although tension-reduction theory was one of the first theories describing the link between psychological factors and alcohol use, overall research provides only mixed support for its usefulness in predicting drinking (Greeley & Oei, 1999). First, most evidence suggests that some people do consume alcohol to reduce tension, but many others do not. This reliance on alcohol to cope with negative events is particularly likely for men and for those who have fewer other coping skills (Cooper et al., 1992). This theory also ignores the often powerful role of people's expectations about the consequences of alcohol use, which, at least in some cases, may have a greater impact on behavior than actual alcohol use. Finally, this theory focuses only on the use of alcohol to cope with negative events (e.g., tension, stress) and thereby fails to explain the use of alcohol to celebrate positive events; people often report drinking to enhance or intensify positive emotions as well as drinking more on days with positive interpersonal events, such as being complimented and feeling cared for (Carney et al., 2000; Mohr et al., 2001).

Social Learning Theory

According to Bandura's **social learning theory** (1969), and as described in Chapter 3, children learn the norms for alcohol use by watching others, including their parents, siblings, peers, and media figures (Maisto et al., 1999). Children are likely to see people relaxing with a cocktail after a long day at the office, celebrating with a champagne toast at a wedding or graduation, and drinking beer while socializing at a party. Not surprisingly, children who have parents with lenient attitudes toward alcohol, as well as alcohol-related problems themselves, are more likely to engage in excessive drinking and to experience problems caused by alcohol (Mares, van der Vorst, Engels, & Lchtwarck-Aschoff, 2011). Even if children don't directly observe these models for alcohol use in their daily lives, television and movies provide numerous examples of the link between fun and drinking (Gibbons et al., 2010; Goldstein, Sobel, & Newman, 1999; Grube & Wallack, 1994). Alcohol use is frequently portrayed even in films marketed to children, including G-rated animated films such as *Pinocchio*, *Pocahontas*, and *Beauty and the Beast* (Goldstein et al., 1999). Moreover, exposure to drinking in movies is associated with more alcohol consumption later on, in part because exposure to alcohol use in the media leads to increases in the favorability of the adolescents' drinker prototypes, their willingness to drink, and their tendency to affiliate with friends who were drinking.

Advertisements for alcohol also model alcohol use norms and can lead to increased intentions to drink as well as alcohol consumption. Alcohol advertisements, not accidentally, typically show young, attractive people drinking in appealing settings (at parties, on the beach, etc.) and having a very good time—they don't show older adults drinking while they play shuffleboard. One study with fifth and sixth graders found that kids who had more awareness of television beer advertisements (e.g., could identify the type of beer advertised even when its name was blocked) had more favorable beliefs about the consequences of drinking and higher intentions to drink as an adult (Grube & Wallack, 1994). Sadly, greater exposure to such advertisements increases the probability of drinking in teenagers. Researchers in one study conducted in-school surveys of 1,786 South Dakota sixth graders to measure exposure to television beer advertisements, alcohol ads in magazines, in-store beer displays and beer concessions, radio-listening time, and ownership of beer promotional items, and then, a year later, they measured drinking intentions and behavior (Collins, Ellickson, McCaffrey, & Hambarsoomians, 2007). Exposure to advertising for alcohol during sixth grade predicted intentions to drink a year later as well as alcohol consumption. Specifically, sixth graders with more frequent exposure to alcohol marketing exposure were twice as likely to report drinking a year later than those with less frequent exposure.

Watching people drink also creates norms that alcohol use is appropriate and desirable. People drink more when they are part of a group than when alone, especially when they are with people who are drinking heavily (Maisto et al., 1999). They also drink more when they have friends who drink heavily. One longitudinal study with adolescents ages 10 to 15 years old revealed that friends' drinking behavior was a strong predictor of individuals' own future alcohol use, with adolescents who reported higher alcohol use in their friends showing particularly steep increases in their own alcohol use (Curran, Stice, & Chassin, 1997). Interestingly, the mere belief that other people are drinking heavily can lead people to drink more—even if this belief is wrong. A number of studies have demonstrated that college students often believe that there is too much alcohol use on campus but also believe other students like the amount of alcohol use. Moreover, the mere perception of a "heavy drinking norm" can lead students to have more positive attitudes about alcohol and even to drink more (Baer & Carney, 1993; Baer, Stacy & Larimer, 1991; Gibbons et al., 2010; Marks et al.,

1992; Prentice & Miller, 1993). Similarly, students believe that other students are more comfortable than they themselves are with smoking, drinking, and illegal drug use on campus and with media portrayals of these behaviors (Hines, Saria, & Throckmorton-Belzer, 2002).

Social learning theory also describes the role played by people's expectations about the consequences of alcohol use, which often develop even before the onset of drinking, in leading to alcohol use (Cooper, Frone, Russell, & Mudar, 1995; Goldman, Del Boca, & Darkes, 1999; Maisto et al., 1999). One study found that students who watched film clips showing desirable outcomes of drinking saw more positive expectancies for drinking than those who watched no film or a film showing negative outcomes for drinking (Kulick & Rosenberg, 2001). In fact, children as young as preschool and elementary school have expectations about the effects of alcohol, based on parental modeling as well as the portrayal of alcohol use in the media. Although these expectations are initially negative (e.g., they see alcohol as having unpleasant consequences), they get increasingly positive as children mature. As shown in Table 7.2, these expectations include the belief that alcohol use enhances social situations and interpersonal encounters in various ways, including increasing social expressiveness (e.g., "makes me more friendly") as well as "sexual prowess" (Goldman et al., 1999). As described at the beginning of the chapter, Brad sees himself as funnier and more relaxed when he is drinking, and he therefore finds it hard to stop drinking even though it is having a negative impact on his academic performance. Most important, people who have more positive

TABLE 7.2 *Test Yourself: Motives for Alcohol Use*

Please rate the following statements in terms of how frequently each of these reasons motivate you to drink alcoholic beverages (1 = never/almost never to 4 = always/almost always).

1. As a way to celebrate
2. Because it is what most of your friends do when you get together
3. To be sociable
4. Because it is customary on special occasions
5. Because it makes a social gathering more enjoyable
6. To relax
7. To forget your worries
8. Because you feel more self-confident or sure of yourself
9. Because it helps when you feel depressed or nervous
10. To cheer up when you're in a bad mood
11. Because you like the feeling
12. Because it's exciting
13. To get high
14. Because it's fun
15. Because it makes you feel good

The first five items describe social motives, the next five items describe coping motives, and the last five items describe enhancement motives. If you drink, why do you do it? Are you more motivated by social concerns, coping, or enhancement?

Source: Cooper et al., 1992.

expectations about alcohol are more likely to drink (Corbin, Iwamoto, & Fromme, 2011; Sher et al., 1996; Smith, Goldman, Greenbaum, & Christiansen, 1995; Stacy, Newcomb, & Bentler, 1991).

Personality

Many studies have examined whether certain personality traits, including neuroticism/negative affect, impulsivity/disinhibition, and extraversion/sociability, are associated with alcoholism (Sher, Trull, Bartholow, & Vieth, 1999). Support for the link between personality traits and alcoholism is primarily found in correlational studies. For example, alcoholism is associated with high rates of anxiety (Kessler et al., 1997; Kushner et al., 1996), antisocial and borderline personality disorder (Regier et al., 1990), and extraversion. However, many of these studies suffer from a major flaw: They examined people at a single point in time, so they simply can't determine whether personality traits lead to alcohol abuse, whether alcohol abuse over time leads to changes in personality traits, or whether a third variable leads to personality traits as well as alcohol abuse.

Although relatively little research has examined the link between personality traits and alcoholism over time, results from several longitudinal studies do indicate that personality traits can predict future alcohol abuse (Bates & Labouvie, 1995; Caspi et al., 1997; Chassin et al., 1996; Zucker & Gomberg, 1986). For example, adolescents who at age 18 had lower scores on harm avoidance (e.g., choosing to avoid danger, preference for safe activities) and control (measure of cautiousness and rationality) were more likely to engage in alcohol abuse at age 21 (Caspi et al., 1997). Similarly, several studies suggest that high extraversion scores are associated with alcohol problems later on, especially in women (Kilbey, Downey, & Breslau, 1998; Prescott, Neale, Corey, & Kendler, 1997). But even longitudinal studies do not tell us whether a third variable is involved. As described in the next section, biological and genetic factors may in fact influence both personality and alcoholism.

Biological/Genetic Factors

A number of researchers have examined whether certain people are born with some type of predisposition for alcohol abuse (McGue, 1999). Because studies involving children born and raised with their biological parents do not allow researchers to distinguish whether alcohol problems are the reflection of genetic factors or environmental factors, researchers usually conduct twin studies or adoption studies, which reveal a genetic influence in the development of drinking problems (Schuckit, 1985). In twin studies, they compare rates of alcohol abuse in identical twins (who share all their genes) as compared to fraternal twins (who share half their genes); in adoption studies, they compare rates of alcohol abuse in children's biological parents and adoptive parents. For example, if one member of a same-sex twin pair is an alcoholic, the risk of the other twin being alcoholic is twice as great if the twin is identical as opposed to fraternal. Similarly, adopted children with an alcoholic biological parent are four times more likely to become problem drinkers than other adoptees. A series of studies indicates that people with a particular gene are more likely to become alcoholics than those without this gene, although not everyone with this gene develops alcoholism—about 45% of alcoholics have this gene, as compared to only 26% of nonalcoholics (Cloninger, 1991). Having this gene does not mean that a person will definitely become an alcoholic, but it increases the likelihood. Interestingly, this link between genes and alcoholism is stronger for men than for women (McGue, 1999).

One reason this genetic predisposition may lead someone to have problems with alcohol is because they are less sensitive to the effects of alcohol, which then leads to overdrinking (Newlin & Thomson, 1990). Several studies have shown that men who are at high risk of developing alcoholism (based on their family history) are not as sensitive to the early effects of alcohol as those without such a history (Schuckit & Smith, 1996). For example, after consuming a set amount of alcohol, high-risk subjects report feeling less drunk and show less impairment on various tasks than low-risk subjects. People with a family history of alcoholism may also find alcohol more rewarding and less anxiety provoking than those without this predisposition (Newlin & Thomson, 1990). In other words, genetic factors may lead people to experience more positive effects of alcohol use and fewer negative consequences. Finally, some research suggests that genetic factors may influence personality, which in turn leads to alcohol abuse (McGue, 1999). As described previously, alcoholics differ from nonalcoholics in a number of ways, including impulsivity, sensation-seeking, extraversion, and neuroticism (Sher et al., 1999). Some researchers therefore believe that alcoholics are more likely to experience problems with mood regulation and then turn to alcohol in attempts to feel better.

Although many studies have shown that parents' drinking behavior predicts their children's drinking behavior, these studies usually cannot separate issues of biology (e.g., parents' drinking predicts their children's drinking because of genetic factors) and environment (e.g., children model their drinking on their parents' behavior). However, even adoption studies show that people drink more when they are raised with people who drink heavily (McGue, 1999). For example, 48% of adopted males raised in families with an alcoholic parent develop alcoholism, as compared to only 24.5% of those raised in families without alcoholic role models.

What Are Some Strategies for Preventing Alcohol Abuse?

Early-intervention programs focus on detecting people who are at risk of experiencing problems with alcohol use and then providing them with information about its dangers and strategies for decreasing alcohol use. Most programs target college students. For example, one study assigned problem drinkers to either a skills-training group, an information-only group, or a no-treatment group (Kivilan, Marlatt, Fromme, Coppel, & Williams, 1990). Those in the skills-training group received information about strategies for drinking moderately as well as training in relaxation and assertiveness skills. They were specifically given the goal of drinking just to get their blood-alcohol content (BAC) to 0.055 and were given information about how to set drinking limits to reach (but not exceed) this level (see Table 7.3 to learn how to calculate your own BAC). In contrast, those in the information-only condition received information about the effects of alcohol, the alcohol industry, and alcoholism. Findings at the 1-year follow-up indicated that those in the skills-training condition reported having only 7.6 drinks in the past

TABLE 7.3   *How to Calculate Your Estimated Blood-Alcohol Content*

Body Weight (lbs)	1	2	3	4	5	6	7	8	9	10	11	12
100	.038	.075	.113	.150	.188	.225	.263	.300	.338	.375	.413	.450
110	.034	.066	.103	.137	.172	.207	.241	.275	.309	.344	.379	.412
120	.031	.063	.094	.125	.156	.188	.219	.250	.281	.313	.344	.375
130	.029	.058	.087	.116	.145	.174	.203	.232	.261	.290	.320	.348
140	.027	.054	.080	.107	.134	.161	.188	.214	.241	.268	.295	.321
150	.025	.050	.075	.100	.125	.151	.176	.201	.226	.261	.276	.301
160	.023	.047	.070	.094	.117	.141	.164	.188	.211	.234	.258	.281
170	.022	.045	.066	.088	.110	.132	.155	.178	.200	.221	.244	.265
180	.021	.042	.063	.083	.104	.125	.146	.167	.188	.208	.228	.250
190	.020	.040	.059	.079	.099	.119	.138	.158	.179	.198	.217	.237
200	.019	.038	.056	.075	.094	.113	.131	.150	.169	.188	.206	.225
210	.018	.036	.053	.071	.090	.107	.125	.143	.161	.179	.197	.215
220	.017	.034	.051	.068	.085	.102	.119	.136	.153	.170	.188	.205
230	.016	.032	.049	.065	.081	.098	.115	.130	.147	.163	.180	.196
240	.016	.031	.047	.063	.078	.094	.109	.125	.141	.156	.172	.188

To calculate your estimated BAC, you show the estimated percentage of alcohol in the blood by the number of drinks in relation to body weight. This percentage can be estimated by doing the following:

1. Count your drinks (1 drink *equals* 1 ounce of 100-proof liquor, one 5-ounce glass of table wine, or one 12-ounce bottle of regular beer).

2. Use the chart to find the number of drinks opposite body weight, and then find the percentage of blood alcohol listed.

3. Subtract from this number the percentage of alcohol "burned up" during the time elapsed since your first drink. This figure is 0.015% per hour. (Example: 180 lb. man has 8 drinks in 4 hours equals 0.167% minus $(0.015 \times 4) = 0.107\%$.

Source: Created from NHTSA chart, with modifications.

month, as compared to 16.8 drinks for those in the information-only condition (and 15.4 drinks for those in the control condition).

Other prevention programs have focused on challenging individuals' beliefs about alcohol use. One study by Darkes and Goldman (1993) randomly assigned 218 heavy-drinking college males to one of two alcohol-abuse workshops or a no-treatment control condition. One workshop focused on the physical, social, and personal consequences of alcohol use, and the other focused on challenging individuals' expectations about the consequences of alcohol use. For example, students were given real alcohol or a placebo drink designed to taste like alcohol, and then had to guess based on their own and other people's behavior who had actually received alcohol (a very difficult task, meaning that all subjects made some errors). How effective was this approach? Only those in the expectancy condition decreased their drinking over the next month.

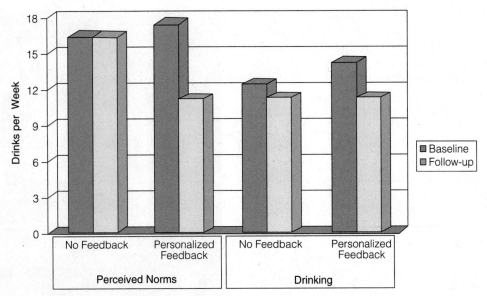

FIGURE 7.6 Students who receive information on accurate norms of alcohol use, which is often less than what students expect, report drinking fewer drinks per week 2 months later than those who do not receive this information (data from Neighbors, Lewis, Berstro, & Larimer, 2006).

Early-intervention approaches may also try to influence people's perceptions about how common drinking is among their peers (see Figure 7.6; Schroeder & Prentice, 1998). As we discussed earlier, the perception that most other people drink heavily can lead to increased alcohol abuse, even if this perception is wrong. In one study, incoming "high-risk" first-year students (those who were already heavy drinkers) met individually with a clinical psychologist who gave them personal feedback, including how much more they drank than most students, the health consequences of heavy alcohol use, and environmental risk factors for heavy drinking, such as belonging to a sorority or fraternity and having heavy-drinking friends (Marlatt et al., 1998). Although these heavy-drinking students continued to experience more alcohol-related problems than the average college student, at the end of 22 years, only 11% of those who received this feedback were judged alcohol-dependent as compared to 27% of heavy drinkers who did not receive this type of feedback. Similarly, a study by Borsari and Carey (2000) challenged students' beliefs about alcohol use as normative by giving students accurate information about the frequency (which was lower than they expected) of drinking among their peers. Students who received this intervention reported drinking an average of 11.4 drinks in the past week, as compared to 15.78 drinks for those who were in the control condition.

Questioning the Research 7.4

Although the Borsari and Carey (2000) study shows that providing information about the real frequency of drinking (which is lower than students believe) led to decreased alcohol use, can we apply the results from this study to all students with alcohol problems? Why or why not?

Although 21 is the legal age for drinking alcohol in the United States, 28.2% of youth ages 12 to 20 report consuming alcohol in the past 30 days (Chen, Yi, Williams, & Faden, 2009).
Source: © Richard Levine/Alamy.

Public policy and legal approaches to prevent alcohol abuse attempt to limit the purchase of alcohol or make such abuse seem less desirable in an effort to decrease problem drinking (Ashley & Rankin, 1988). One of the most obvious approaches is the enforcement of the drinking age, which prohibits people who are under 21 years of age from purchasing alcohol. Other approaches include limiting the number of places where and the times in which alcohol can be bought. For example, in some states, alcohol is not sold on Sundays or in grocery and convenience stores. Unfortunately, these approaches are generally ineffective in decreasing problem drinking. As you probably know, most college students are under 21, yet, often they report having little trouble gaining access to alcohol. Other drinking-prevention programs focus on promoting the negative effects of alcohol abuse. You have probably seen television and magazines ads that portray the negative consequences of drunk driving. Public policies may also place limits on alcohol advertising, including the hours in which such ads can appear on television and/or what they can portray.

What Are Some Strategies for Treating Alcohol Abuse?

Although a recent large-scale survey revealed that 75% of people who recovered from alcohol problems did so on their own, many people do need assistance in quitting drinking (Sobell, Cunningham, & Sobell, 1996). The first step for all alcoholics is **detoxification**, the drying out process in which the person withdraws from alcohol completely. This process takes about a month and can include severe symptoms, such as intense anxiety, tremors, and hallucinations (Miller & Hester, 1980). Detoxification may take place in a hospital or rehabilitation center with the use of medication in cases in which the symptoms of alcohol withdrawal are particularly severe (most often when the person has a long history of alcohol abuse), but it can sometimes take place in an outpatient setting.

Alcoholics Anonymous (AA) is the most widely known self-help program for alcohol abuse and is attended more often than any other alcohol program (Weisner, Greenfield, & Room, 1995). AA was started in the 1930s by people with drinking problems who found that sharing their problems and experiences with alcohol with others helped them remain sober. The process they used eventually evolved into 12 steps (see Table 7.4). People who are trying to stop drinking attend frequent meetings (daily, at least initially) in which members talk about their experiences with alcohol and their difficulty in quitting. The general AA philosophy is based on two principles. First, people who abuse alcohol are alcoholics and will remain that way for life, even if they never drink again. Second, taking even a single drink after being abstinent can set off an alcoholic binge; therefore, the goal is total abstinence from alcohol. Although AA claims a success rate of 75% "for those who really tried," it is difficult to systematically track its success rate given its anonymous nature (Peele, 1984). Moreover, many people who attend AA meetings in an attempt to quit drinking eventually drop out. However, some people are clearly helped by this form of therapy, with men, those with less education, and those who are highly sociable showing the greatest benefits (Miller & Hester, 1980). Also, alcoholics who regularly attend AA meetings are more likely to maintain abstinence from alcohol as long as 18 months after beginning treatment (McCrady, Epstein, & Kahler, 2004).

According to AA, loss of control occurs whenever an alcoholic consumes even a small amount of alcohol because the presence of alcohol in the bloodstream

TABLE 7.4   *The 12 Steps of Alcoholics Anonymous*

1. We admitted we were powerless over alcohol—that our lives had become unmanageable.
2. Came to believe that a power greater than ourselves could restore us to sanity.
3. Made a decision to turn our will and our lives over to the care of God as we understood Him.
4. Made a searching and fearless oral inventory of ourselves.
5. Admitted to God, to ourselves, and to another human being the exact nature of our wrongs.
6. Were entirely ready to have God remove all these defects of character.
7. Humbly ask Him to remove our shortcomings.
8. Made a list of all persons we had harmed and became willing to make amends to them all.
9. Made direct amends to such people whenever possible, except when to do so would injure them or others.
10. Continued to take personal inventory and, when we were wrong, promptly admitted it.
11. Sought through prayer and meditation to improve our conscious contact with God as we understand Him, praying only for knowledge of His will for us and the power to carry that out.
12. Having had a spiritual awakening as the result of these steps, we tried to carry this message to alcoholics and to practice these principles in all our affairs.

These 12 steps are the core of the Alcoholics Anonymous approach to drinking problems.

Source: Alcoholics Anonymous World Services, 1977.

leads to an irresistible craving for more alcohol. Thus, controlled drinking would never be possible. However, other researchers believe that problem drinkers can eventually learn to drink in moderation after they have first abstained from alcohol for some period of time. The focus on the cause of drinking influences the treatment used: Cognitive-behavioral programs may allow clients to choose their goals for modifying their drinking behavior (e.g., abstinence versus moderation), whereas other approaches (e.g., aversive treatment) do not.

Does successful treatment mean permanent abstinence from alcohol or just controlled drinking? Most research seems to support the view that controlled drinking is not usually possible—although some people may initially be able to drink in moderation, most people who have a history of alcohol abuse and who try to drink in a "controlled" way eventually return to problem drinking. However, some people are able to drink in a controlled manner. People with the best odds of managing controlled drinking are young (under 40), are socially stable (married and/or employed), have a relatively brief history of alcohol abuse and dependence (fewer than 10 years), and have not suffered severe withdrawal symptoms (Miller & Hester, 1980). The controlled drinking approach has an advantage because it may be a more realistic goal—drinkers are often unwilling to even contemplate giving up alcohol completely. And, in fact, for people in this category, problem drinking relapses are more likely to occur following total abstinence. On the other hand, for people over 40 and with high levels of physical dependence, abstainers have lower relapse rates than those who attempt controlled drinking.

Aversion strategies attempt to create associations between alcohol use and some type of stimulus, such as electric shock or nausea (Miller & Hester, 1980). As with similar types of therapy used to help people quit smoking, the theory behind this approach is that after repeated pairings of alcohol use and some unpleasant outcome, people will begin to associate drinking with negative consequences. For example, patients may be given an injection of emetine, which causes vomiting, and then are quickly given an alcoholic beverage. Patients go through several of these sessions and may also receive booster sessions after they are discharged from the hospital or clinic. One study found that approximately 63% of those who received this type of treatment remained abstinent 1 year later, although half of these then returned to drinking in the second year (Wiens & Menustik, 1983). Similarly, patients may be given Antabuse to take every day, which will then cause them to experience extreme nausea if they drink alcohol. Unfortunately, these programs are not very effective, perhaps because alcoholics can avoid the treatments in order to not experience the negative consequences. For example, patients can easily stop taking Antabuse, thereby avoid feeling sick when they drink.

Cognitive-behavioral programs view alcohol abuse as a learned behavior that can be changed using various behavioral techniques, such as self-monitoring, stimulus control, response substitution, and contingency contracting (Fletcher, 2001; Lang & Marlatt, 1982). These programs focus on helping people become aware of their expectations about the benefits of drinking, the factors that lead them to drink, and the situations that lead them to drink. Then people are trained to avoid these situations. For example, if you used to drink whenever you were hanging around with high school friends in a bar, in a cognitive-behavior program, you might be taught to suggest other activities (e.g., going to a movie, playing basketball) to substitute. Some recovered alcoholics report that they avoid any situations in which alcohol may be served, such as weddings and cocktail parties. One study with successful recovered alcoholics found that 25% had to abandon some old friends in their efforts to stop problem drinking.

Other cognitive-behavioral approaches train people to respond in new ways to tempting situations, such as bringing nonalcoholic drinks with them or eating food instead of drinking. In one study, people who were dependent on alcohol had to spend 40 minutes a day for 10 days in a "tempting situation"—holding, picking up, smelling, and thinking about drinking a desirable alcoholic drink, but they could not actually drink it (Drummond & Glautier, 1994). The goal of this training was to help people learn that they can control their urge to drink, even when they are in very tempting situations. Follow-up results show that this program was more effective than a relaxation-training condition in helping people reduce their alcohol use. Because alcoholics often use drinking as a way of coping with tension and anxiety, they might learn new methods for handling stress, such as relaxation, meditation, and exercise (Miller & Hester, 1980). For example, they could learn to hit a pillow, take a warm bath, or write in a journal whenever they feel the urge to drink as a way of coping. These approaches could also help people develop specific skills for refusing alcohol, because alcoholics are typically less skillful in and comfortable with turning down offers for drinks (Maisto et al., 1999). Telling friends that they will be the "designated driver" or that they are on medication that interacts with alcohol can be effective, for example, because they give people an "acceptable out" for not drinking and thereby reduce peer pressure to drink (see Table 7.5). Although cognitive-behavioral approaches can be effective while they are in force (e.g., contingency contracting), particularly if they train people in specific skills in drink refusal (Sobell, Sobell, & Gavin, 1995), when the reinforcement or program disappears, so might the sobriety.

Insight-oriented psychotherapy focuses on helping people understand their motivations for drinking, such as feeling negatively about themselves or coping with various problems in their lives (Miller & Hester, 1980). A therapist might then work with them to change the problems that lead them to drink, to help them gain self-esteem, to understand the factors that lead them to drink, and to learn new methods of coping with such problems. One recent study of 222 former abusive drinkers found that two thirds reported benefiting from such therapy (Fletcher,

TABLE 7.5 *How Recovered Alcoholics Handle Pressure to Drink*

1. Just say no: "No thanks." "No, thank you."
2. Simply say, "I don't drink"; "I no longer drink"; "Thanks, I don't drink."
3. Explain that you have or had a drinking problem: "No, thanks. I'm a nonpracticing alcoholic"; "I had my quota years ago."
4. Blame it on a health problem: "I have an allergy—drinking makes me break out in spots."
5. "Drinking makes me sick."
6. Ask the person to stop pushing: "Why is it so important to you that I drink?" "Because when I drink, I tend to take off my clothes and dance on the tables, and my husband doesn't like it."

These quotes are by people who have successfully overcome drinking problems.

Source: Fletcher, 2001, p. 233.

TABLE 7.6 *Information YOU Can Use*

- No one tries to become a smoker, but even a few cigarettes in high school and college can lead to a life-time of addiction. So, try to resist even occasional smoking because addiction can happen quickly.
- Because many people smoke and/or drink to reduce tension, one of the best strategies for avoiding cigarettes and excessive alcohol use is to develop other strategies for relieving the stress that we all experience at times. Therefore, think about other things you could do when you are nervous about exams or sad after a relationship breakup: Go for a run, watch a movie, or call a friend instead.
- Remember that children readily model the behavior they see in adults in their own world, so make sure to model avoiding smoking and excessive drinking in front of your kids. Also, try to restrict children's exposure to smoking and alcohol use in movies whenever possible.
- One of the single largest causes of deaths in teenagers and young adults, which includes most of the readers of this textbook, is drinking and driving. Please remember to never drink and drive or get in a car with a driver who has been drinking.
- Remember that drinking is not as prevalent as you might think it is: Many high school and college students believe that their peers drink far more than they actually do, in part because excessive drinking is likely to be more salient (and thus seem more prevalent) than not drinking or moderate drinking. Don't be fooled by how much you think others are drinking: They aren't drinking as much as you think they are (and they too, often believe that there is too much drinking).

2001). Both individual and group methods of therapy have had some modest success in treating drinking problems (Emrick & Hansen, 1983).

Although there are many different approaches to treating alcohol abuse, more than 50% of alcoholics drop out of treatment; even among those who continue, fewer than half of these remain successful over the long term (Stark, 1992). Typically, those who are older, have a higher socioeconomic status, have stable employment and social relationships, and have little or no history of other types of substance abuse are successful in stopping their alcohol abuse. Relapse issues are covered in more detail in Chapter 12.

Summary

1. Smoking and alcohol use are two of the most common health-compromising behaviors, and they are often used in combination. These two behaviors lead to many of the major health problems, and causes of death, in the United States today, including cancer, coronary heart disease, and injuries.

2. Approximately 21% of American adults smoke, with slightly higher rates among men than women. Smoking is more common among people with lower incomes and lower levels of education.

3. Smoking is the leading cause of preventable mortality in the United States. The negative health consequences of smoking are due in part to the increase in heart rate and constriction in blood vessels, which makes the heart have to work harder. In addition, carcinogens in the residue from smoke cause abnormal growth in cells and over time the consistent presence of smoke in the bronchial tubes disrupts their ability to clear the lungs of foreign particles.

4. Psychological factors, including the desire to try out a new identity, the presence of particular personality factors, social factors (e.g., modeling, peer pressure), and the presentation of smoking in the media all contribute to the initiation of smoking.

5. After someone has begun smoking, they often continue because they have developed an addiction to cigarettes and may need larger and larger amounts of nicotine in order to avoid unpleasant withdrawal

symptoms. There are many theories explaining the processes that lead to nicotine addiction, including nicotine-based models (e.g., nicotine-fixed effect model, nicotine regulation model), affect-regulation models, and combined models (e.g., multiple regulation model, biobehavioral model).

6. There are many strategies for preventing smoking, including social influences programs, life skills training approaches, mass media approaches, and large-scale government approaches.

7. Smoking is a difficult habit to quit. However, smokers who would like to quit may try a number of different strategies, including nicotine replacement, aversion strategies, and self-management strategies (e.g., stimulus control, response substitution).

8. Most adults drink alcohol at least occasionally. However, some people develop problems with alcohol use, including binge drinking and alcoholism.

9. Alcohol use has a number of negative health consequences, including liver damage, impairment of brain functioning, the development of some types of cancer, and negative effects on the growing fetus (e.g., fetal alcohol syndrome). Alcohol use can also lead indirectly to health problems, such as through driving while intoxicated. Many of these problems are due to the impairment of judgment and decision-making that can occur when under the influence of alcohol.

10. Psychological factors contribute to alcohol abuse in numerous ways. Psychological theories which help explain alcohol abuse include tension reduction theory, social learning theory, personality factors, and biology/genetics.

11. Strategies for preventing alcohol abuse may focus on detecting people who are at risk of experiencing problems with alcohol and providing them with information on its dangers and strategies for decreasing their alcohol use, challenging people's beliefs about alcohol use, changing people's perceptions about how common alcohol use is, and forming public policy and legal approaches to prevent alcohol use.

12. When a person has a serious problem with alcohol, a number of strategies can be used to treat alcohol abuse. These include attending Alcoholics Anonymous meetings, using aversion strategies, training in cognitive-behavioral techniques, and receiving insight-oriented therapy.

Key Terms

addiction
affect-regulation model
alcohol myopia theory
Alcoholics Anonymous
alcoholism
aversion strategies

biobehavioral model
contingency-contracting
detoxification
drunken self-inflation
multiple regulation model
nicotine fixed-effect model

nicotine regulation model
nicotine replacement
response substitution
social learning theory
stimulus control
tension-reduction theory

Thought Questions

1. Compare the affect-based and nicotine-based models that predict continued smoking.

2. Your friend Michael is trying to stop smoking and comes to you for advice. What are three different strategies you could suggest to him?

3. Describe two different psychological factors that can lead to alcohol abuse.

4. Describe how both aversive therapy and cognitive-behavioral therapy could be used to help people stop abusing alcohol.

5. You are a resident assistant in a dorm of first-year students and are trying to decrease your students' binge drinking. Describe two different approaches used to prevent alcohol abuse.

Answers to Questioning the Research

Answer 7.1. Social influence programs that compare rates of smoking in communities which either had or did not have exposure to a particular advertising campaign can show that there are differences in rates of smoking in different communities but often can't definitively prove that the advertising in fact *led* to any differences. After all, other factors within these communities—ease of purchasing cigarettes, cost of cigarettes, regulations regarding smoking—may also have contributed to any differences observed.

Answer 7.2. It is difficult to measure who is really a smoker and who is not. First, you must operationally define *not smoking*: Is it not having a cigarette in the last day/week/month/year? Would someone who has taken a puff or two from someone else's cigarettes but who has not smoked a whole cigarette be considered a smoker or a non-smoker? Those of you who recall some of the issues with self-report survey data from Chapter 2 may also suggest that people can lie. In fact, smokers are quite likely to misreport how much they are smoking. Smoking-prevention programs should therefore ideally include some type of physiological measure of smoking, such as a test for nicotine in saliva.

Answer 7.3. MacDonald et al. (1995) found that men who were intoxicated were less likely to report they would use a condom if they were in the situation they saw on the video, but it isn't clear whether actual condom use would be higher or lower in the real world. One possibility is that condom use would actually be higher because men would fear an unplanned pregnancy and that cue would be more salient in the presence of an actual sexual encounter than a hypothetical one. Another possibility, however, is that actual condom use would be lower because men would presumably be more sexually aroused, which in turn is often associated with lower rates of condom use.

Answer 7.4. Although the study by Borsari and Carey (2000) shows that challenging students' beliefs about how common alcohol abuse is on campus can lead to less drinking, careful readers might wonder how representative their sample is of students in general. Who would be most interested in participating in an intervention on alcohol abuse? Many intervention studies, including those on alcohol use, tend to track highly interested and motivated participants. For example, participants might have been those concerned about the amount of drinking on campus (and are already uncomfortable with it) or students who have been personally affected by problems with alcohol (such as those who have a parent with a drinking problem). But it is possible that people who have the most severe problems with alcohol use are not at all interested in getting help with their drinking; hence, they would not participate in such a research project. We therefore must be careful about how we interpret the results of these research studies—the findings may not apply to all problem drinkers.)

CHAPTER 8

Obesity and Eating Disorders

Outline

What Approaches Help Prevent Eating Disorders?
Box 8.4 Focus on Research: The Benefits of Critiquing the Thin Ideal

What Approaches Help Treat Eating Disorders?
Box 8.5 Health Psychology in the Real World: The Very Real Hazards of Disordered Eating

- Katie is 35 years old and is approximately 75 pounds over her ideal weight. Both of her parents are also overweight, and she has always been somewhat heavy. However, after the birth of her two children, Katie's weight increased even more, and she is now considered obese. Although she has tried several different diet plans, she finds it very hard to resist eating the tempting snack foods she keeps around for her children, including potato chips, Oreos, and ice cream.

- Elizabeth is a senior in college and is trying to lose 5 pounds before her planned spring break trip to Mazatlan. Although she is very focused on trying to lose weight, she tends to overeat when she is feeling nervous or stressed, which unfortunately is happening a lot now because she is in the middle of midterm exams and is also trying to apply for jobs. When Elizabeth gives in and eats something that is not on her diet—such as pizza or brownies—she has trouble restraining herself, so she really overeats.

- Bill is 54 years old, overweight, and suffering from diabetes and high blood pressure. His doctor has told him that if he doesn't lose weight, he is very likely to experience a heart attack in the next 5 years. Bill has tried a number of different diets and sometimes even manages to lose some weight, but he always seems to regain the weight within a matter of months. Because Bill is desperate to lose weight, he has just started a new weight-loss program at his office. He now exercises with a group of friends from work and has lost nearly 15 pounds in the past 3 months.

- Annie attends a private high school in New York City. Both her parents are attorneys, and they hope that she will attend a top college and perhaps even choose to go to law school one day. Although she has never been overweight, Annie has lost 15 pounds over the last few months and is hoping to lose perhaps 10 more pounds. Annie's grades in school have always been very high, but recently they have slipped some. Instead of working on her homework right after school, she now runs for 2 or 3 hours. Annie also has trouble concentrating during classes, in part because she is trying to remember exactly what she has eaten that day and about how many calories she has consumed.

- Rachel is a sophomore at college and has just started therapy to try to cope with her abnormal eating patterns. She usually eats normal meals, but whenever she is feeling anxious or depressed, she goes on huge eating binges—sometimes eating as much as a box of cookies, a bag of potato chips, a pizza, and a carton of ice cream all within just a few hours. Rachel then vomits immediately after eating to avoid gaining weight. Her therapist has asked her to keep a diary listing the times when she feels the need to binge, and together they are trying to identify some of the factors that lead to her negative feelings. Rachel has also just started taking Prozac, which is helping her feel more positive about herself.

Preview

This chapter examines how psychological factors influence eating. Obesity is very prevalent, at least in the United States, and is a significant cause of many health problems, such as cardiovascular disease and diabetes. Although eating disorders are much less common, these disorders are prevalent in the female college population and are associated with many negative health outcomes, including death. First, we examine the consequences of obesity and the role of biological/genetic factors in leading to eating. Next, we examine several different psychological factors that influence eating, as well as how psychological approaches can work to both prevent obesity in children and reduce obesity in adults. We then examine the consequences of eating disorders, such as anorexia and bulimia, and the impact of both biological/genetic and psychosocial factors in producing disordered eating. Finally, we examine strategies for preventing and treating eating disorders.

What Is Obesity?

For many years, researchers relied on the use of tables that plot normal weight ranges for people of various heights (see Table 8.1). Unfortunately, because muscle tissue and bones weigh more than fat, relying on only weight as a measure of obesity can cause some highly fit people, such as muscular athletes, to test as obese. A more accurate way to assess obesity is by calculating percentage of body fat, which can be tested by measuring a pinch of skin in several places on a person's body or (ideally) using a water-immersion technique. However, because the pinch test is not particularly accurate and the water immersion method is time-consuming and expensive, body fat measures are not widely used to determine obesity. The most common measure of obesity today is body mass index (BMI), which is calculated by dividing a person's weight (in kilograms) by the person's height (in meters) and squaring the sum (see Table 8.2). A BMI between 19 and 24 is considered ideal, between 25 and 29 is moderately overweight (about 15 to 30% over ideal weight), and greater than 30 is considered obese (about 40% over ideal weight).

Regardless of how obesity is measured, it affects a substantial number of Americans: 68% of adults are overweight, and 34% are obese (Flegal, Carroll, Ogden, & Curtin, 2010). As shown in Figure 8.1, these rates vary as a function of both gender and ethnicity: 32.2% of adult men versus 35.5% of adult women are obese, and African Americans have a higher prevalence of obesity (44.1%), than Hispanics (37.9%), who in turn have a higher prevalence of obesity than Whites (32.8%). Obesity in the United States has increased substantially over the past 30 years (see Figure 8.2). Moreover, 17% of children and adolescents, ages 2 to 19, are obese, compared to only 6% in 1980 (Centers for Disease Control, 2010). Obesity is therefore a very common problem, particularly in the United States, and seems to be increasing even further.

TABLE 8.1 *Height and Weight Tables for Women and Men*

Height and Weight Table for Women			
Height (in feet and inches)	Small Frame	Medium Frame	Large Frame
4'10''	102–111	109–121	118–131
4'11''	103–113	111–123	120–134
5'0''	104–115	113–126	122–137
5'1''	106–118	115–129	125–140
5'2''	108–121	118–132	128–143
5'3''	111–124	121–135	131–147
5'4''	114–127	124–138	134–151
5'5''	117–130	127–141	137–155
5'6''	120–133	130–144	140–159
5'7''	123–136	133–147	143–163
5'8''	126–139	136–150	146–167
5'9''	129–142	139–153	49–170
5'10''	132–145	142–156	152–173
5'11''	135–148	145–159	155–176
6'0''	138–151	148–162	158–179

Note: Weights at ages 25 to 59 years based on lowest mortality; weight in pounds according to frame (in indoor clothing weighing 3 lbs.; shoes with 1-in. heels).

Height and Weight Table for Men			
Height (in feet and inches)	Small Frame	Medium Frame	Large Frame
5'2''	128–134	131–141	138–150
5'3''	130–136	133–143	140–153
5'4''	132–138	135–145	142–156
5'5''	134–140	137–148	144–160
5'6''	136–142	139–151	146–164
5'7''	138–145	142–154	149–168
5'8''	140–148	145–157	152–172
5'9''	142–151	148–160	155–176
5'10''	144–154	151–163	158–180
5'11''	146–157	154–166	161–184
6'0''	149–160	157–170	164–188
6'1''	152–164	160–174	168–192
6'2''	155–168	164–178	172–197
6'3''	158–172	167–182	176–202
6'4''	162–176	171–187	181–207

These tables show the healthiest weights for men and women ages 25 to 59 years as a function of height.

Note: Weights at ages 25 to 59 years based on lowest mortality; weight in pounds according to frame (in indoor clothing weighing 5 lbs.; shoes with 1-in. heels).

TABLE 8.2 *Body Mass Index (BMI) Calculation Table*

BMI (kg/m²)	19	20	21	22	23	24	25	26	27	28	29	30	35	40
Height (in.)					Weight (lb.)									
58	91	96	100	105	110	115	119	124	129	134	138	143	167	191
59	94	99	104	109	114	119	124	128	133	138	143	148	173	198
60	97	102	107	112	118	123	128	133	138	143	148	153	179	204
61	100	106	111	116	122	127	132	137	143	148	153	158	185	211
62	104	109	115	120	126	131	136	142	147	153	158	164	191	218
63	107	113	118	124	130	135	141	146	152	158	163	169	197	225
64	110	116	122	128	134	140	145	151	157	163	169	174	204	232
65	114	120	126	132	138	144	150	156	162	168	174	180	210	240
66	118	124	130	136	142	148	155	161	167	173	179	186	216	247
67	121	127	134	140	146	153	159	166	172	178	185	191	223	255
68	125	131	138	144	151	158	164	171	177	184	190	197	230	262
69	128	135	142	149	155	162	169	176	182	189	196	203	236	270
70	132	139	146	153	160	167	174	181	188	195	202	207	243	278
71	136	143	150	157	165	172	179	186	193	200	208	215	250	286
72	140	147	154	162	169	177	184	191	199	206	213	221	258	294
73	144	151	159	166	174	182	189	197	204	212	219	227	265	302
74	148	155	163	171	179	186	194	202	210	218	225	233	272	311
75	152	160	168	176	184	192	200	208	216	224	232	240	279	319
76	156	164	172	180	189	197	205	213	221	230	238	246	287	328

Source: Adapted with permission from Bray, G. A., and Gray, D. S. (1988). Obesity, Part I, Pathogenesis. *Western Journal of Medicine, 149,* 429–441.

FIGURE 8.1 Although obesity rates in men do not differ as a function of ethnicity, rates of obesity are higher in African American women than in White women (data from CDC, 2011).

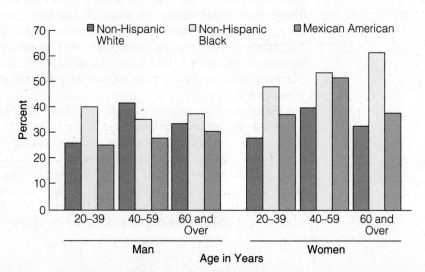

FIGURE 8.2 From 1976 to 1980 and from 2005 to 2006, the average BMI in the United States increased overall, as did the percentage of people who are the very heaviest (the far right end of the curve) (data from CDC, 2011).

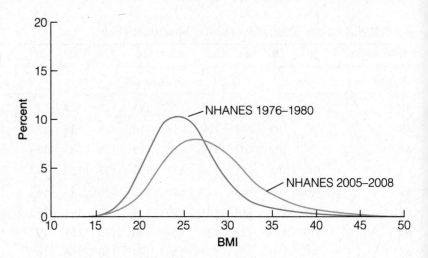

What Are the Consequences of Obesity?

Obesity is associated with a variety of negative physical consequences. People who are obese are at an increased risk of developing hypertension, kidney disease, gallbladder disease, diabetes, cardiovascular disease, and some types of cancer (Bray, 1992). In 1976, one study collected data from 115,886 women who were registered nurses ages 30 to 55 years old (Manson et al., 1990). Researchers then collected follow-up data over 8 years to examine the predictors of illness. Women who had the lowest BMI had the lowest rates of coronary heart disease, whereas those who had the highest BMI had three times the rate of coronary disease. Although women who were mildly to moderately overweight had an increased rate (80%) of coronary disease over the leanest women, even those of average weight had a rate that was approximately 30% higher. Both men and women who are overweight are at increased risk of death, and especially death caused by cardiovascular disease (Stevens et al., 1998; Yusuf et al., 2005). Being severely overweight is associated with even greater risks—in one study, death rates of very obese men and women (those with BMIs above 40) showed that they were twice as likely to die as those who were of normal weight (Bender, Trautner, Spraul, & Berger, 1998). According to a large study (more than 750,000 subjects) by the American Cancer Society, people with a BMI from 18.6 to 23.0 (for women) and from 19.9 to 22.6 (for men) had the lowest rates of coronary heart disease, diabetes, and mortality (Lew, 1985).

One of the most common health problems associated with obesity is diabetes, a chronic endocrine disorder in which the body is not able to produce or use the hormone insulin. Diabetes has increased dramatically in the United States over the past few decades and is now one of the most common chronic diseases as well as one of the leading causes of death. Type 2 diabetes (or noninsulin-dependent diabetes), which accounts for approximately 90% of diabetes cases, is most prevalent in older people and in those who are obese (Haffner, 1998). For example, 80% of people with Type 2 diabetes are obese, and a growing number of overweight children and adolescents are developing signs of diabetes (Sinha et al., 2002). In contrast, Type 1 diabetes (sometimes called insulin-dependent diabetes) typically arises in childhood or early adulthood. People with either type have high rates of cardiovascular disease and often experience other health problems, such as blindness, kidney failure, and nervous system damage that can lead to necessary amputation of various limbs.

Obese people also tend to suffer from social and psychological consequences. They tend to be rated as less likable, are at a disadvantage in dating people, get lower grades, earn less, and are generally the subject of negative social attitudes (Ryckman, Robbins, Kazcor, & Gold, 1989). One long-term study of obese women found that those who were obese made less money, completed fewer years of education, and were less likely to be married than their normal-weight peers (Gortmaker, Must, Perrin, Sobel, & Dietz, 1993). One reason why there are such negative views about obese people is that obesity is often seen as something that is within a person's control—obese people are seen as slow, lazy, sloppy, and lacking in willpower (Ryckman et al., 1989). We often have the view that if they wanted to lose weight, they could just stop eating so much, so we blame obese people for their weight. In one study, high school girls were shown a picture of a girl and read a short statement about her; they were then asked to rate how much they thought they would like her (DeJong, 1980). Some of the girls saw a picture of an overweight girl, and others saw a picture of a normal-weight girl. Of those who saw the picture of the overweight girl, some were told that her weight was a result of a medical problem with her thyroid. As predicted, the subjects who saw the normal-weight girl liked her more than those who saw the overweight girl, but those who saw the overweight girl and were told she had an acceptable reason for her weight (the thyroid condition) liked her just as much as those who saw the normal-weight girl liked the normal-weight girl. This study suggests that it is not just the weight that makes obese people seem unattractive, but the cause people attribute to the weight, such as laziness. But are obese people really different from others? No—the personality characteristics of obese and nonobese people are very similar (Poston et al., 1999).

Although this section examined the negative physical effects of obesity, some research suggests that distribution of weight on a body may be a better predictor of health than amount of weight (Wickelgren, 1998). People who have upper-body fat (e.g., "apples") are at a greater risk of experiencing major health problems, such as diabetes, hypertension, and cardiovascular disease, than those who have lower-body fat (e.g., "pears"). Some studies even suggest that weight accumulated around one's waist may be a better predictor of mortality than overall obesity (Folsom et al., 1993). For example, one study found that women with a waist-to-hip ratio of 0.88 or higher (meaning their waists were nearly as large as their hips) were three times as likely to die of coronary heart disease than those with a ratio of less than 0.72 (meaning their waists were considerably smaller than their hips; Rexrode et al., 1998). Although men are more likely than women to carry fat in the abdominals as opposed to the lower body, both men and women who have higher amounts of abdominal fat suffer similar health risks. One reason why having upper-body fat is associated with such negative health consequences is that fat cells in the abdominals are much larger than fat cells in the legs and butt; hence, abdominal fat cells are more likely to form fatty acids. In turn, high levels of fatty acids in the blood lead to higher levels of glucose in the blood as well as higher blood pressure.

How Do Genetic Factors Cause Obesity?

Considerable research indicates that genetic factors play a role in obesity. Obese people are more likely than nonobese people to have had obese parents and obese grandparents (Noble, 1997), and obese parents are more likely to have obese children. For example, about 7% of the children of normal-weight parents are obese, compared with 40% of the children in families with one obese parent, and 80% in families with two obese parents (Mayer, 1980). As described at the beginning of the chapter, Katie, who had struggled with her weight for many years, had two overweight parents. We cannot, however, attribute obesity solely to genetic factors, based upon this correlation alone. After all, parents who are obese might tend to buy and cook mostly high-fat foods or encourage their children to overeat, which may point to an environmental cause of obesity. Results from studies of adopted children provide some compelling evidence for the link between genetics and obesity, however. First, identical twins are very similar in terms of BMI regardless of whether they are raised together or apart, and identical twins are much more similar in BMI than are same-sex fraternal twins (see Figure 8.3; Grilo & Pogue-Geile, 1991). Second, there is a much stronger relationship between the adopted children's and their biological parents' weight than their adoptive parents' weight, and there is no significant correlation in weight between adopted siblings who are raised together (see Figure 8.4; Grilo & Pogue-Geile, 1991). Genetic factors appear to predict about 40 to 70% of the variation in BMI (Comuzzie & Allison, 1998).

FIGURE 8.3 BMI is highly correlated in identical twins regardless of whether they are reared together, whereas BMI is much less correlated in fraternal twins, even when they are reared together (data from Grilo & Pogue-Geile, 1991).

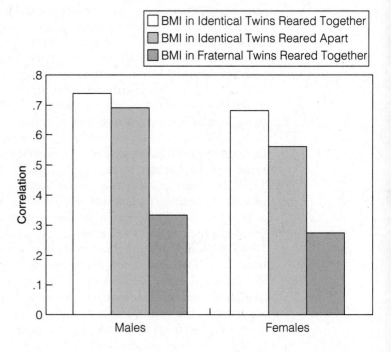

FIGURE 8.4 The weight of biological siblings is much more highly correlated than the weight of adoptive siblings or adoptive parents and children (data from Grilo & Pogue-Geile, 1991).

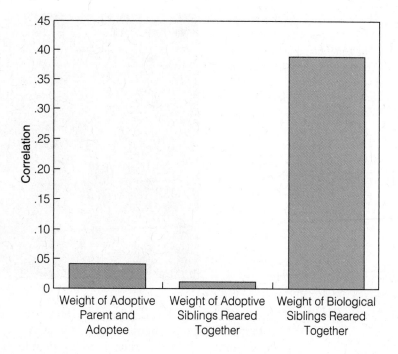

Although research on the genetic factors predicting obesity is still relatively new, recent evidence suggests that genes may influence obesity in a variety of ways. First, genes may influence how much—and even what—people want to eat. Research with mice demonstrates that a gene is responsible for directing the fat cells to release leptin, a hormone that decreases appetite and increases energy expenditure (Wang et al., 1999). In turn, when we lose weight (and lose fat cells) less leptin is released into our bloodstream, which may lead us to feel hungrier. Obese people might also have a genetic preference for energy-dense, fat-containing foods, such as chocolate, ice cream, pastries, and whipped cream (Drewnowski, 1996). Because dietary fats are the most concentrated source of energy, people who are obese might be particularly sensitive to these foods. One study found that young children's preference for fat foods was influenced not only by their own level of body fat but also their mother's level of body fat (Fisher & Birch, 1995).

Genes may also influence metabolism, the rate the body uses energy to carry out basic physiological processes, such as respiration, digestion, and blood pressure (Comuzzie & Allison, 1998). People who have a high metabolism are thought to use more energy to carry out these processes; hence, they burn off more calories. On the other hand, people with a lower metabolic rate gain more weight than people with higher metabolic rates, presumably because their bodies are not burning off as many calories (Ravussin et al., 1988). For example, in one study, normal-weight people were asked to eat an extra 1,000 calories a day for 8 weeks, and then researchers measured how much weight they gained (Levine, Eberhardt, & Jensen, 1999). Although some volunteers gained considerable amounts of weight (more than 9 pounds), others gained only small amounts (less than 1 pound). The biggest

Although obese parents are more likely to have obese children, both genetic and environmental factors clearly contribute to this association.
Source: © Raul Rodriguez/ iStockphoto.

predictor of low levels of weight gain was the incidental physical activity (not intentional exercise) people engaged in as part of daily life, such as fidgeting, sitting up straight, and flexing their muscles. People may vary in how easily they engage in activities that burn fat.

According to set-point theory, each person's body has a certain weight that it strives to maintain, much like a thermostat device (Keesey, 1995). When you eat fewer calories, your metabolism slows to keep your weight at the same level. Because people's set points may vary based on heredity, some will be heavier and some will be lighter. One way it may work is that the set point is determined by the number of fat cells a person has (Leibel, Berry, & Hirsch, 1983). Although there is little or no difference in the number of fat cells between people of normal weight and those who are slightly overweight, people who are severely obese have many more fat cells. Another possibility is that the hypothalamus influences fat stores and/or levels of glucose or insulin in the blood, which in turn influence feelings of hunger and fullness. In line with this view, research with animals demonstrates that damage to a certain part of the hypothalamus can lead to a change in weight, perhaps by allowing a new set point to be established (Keesey & Powley, 1975).

Although genes do play some role in obesity, it is clear that they do not totally predict a person's weight. First, rates of obesity in the United States have increased dramatically in recent years, which means genetics can't explain it all (Hill & Peters, 1998; Katan, Grundy, & Willett, 1997). Second, people with the same genetic background who live in different parts of the world often have very different body weights (Hodge & Zimmet, 1994). For example, Japanese people who live in Japan are thinner than those who move to Hawaii, and Japanese people who live in Hawaii are thinner than those who move to the continental United States (Curb & Marcus, 1991). These differences in weight suggest that while genetics may play some role, cultural factors, including diet and exercise, also influence weight.

How Do Psychological Factors Influence Eating (and Overeating)?

Although genetic and biological factors do influence how much we eat, they aren't the whole story. There are probably many times you have eaten even when you are not hungry, for instance. Maybe you eat when you are nervous; maybe you eat after you walk by a shop selling great-smelling cinnamon rolls in the mall; maybe you eat mindlessly while watching TV. All of these are examples of psychological factors that may lead to eating (and overeating). This section examines various psychological factors that influence eating: the internal-external hypothesis, mood regulation, restraint theory, and sociocultural factors.

Internal-External Hypothesis

One of the earliest hypotheses about why and when people eat is the **internal-external hypothesis** (Schachter, 1968). According to this view, people often fail to listen to their internal cues for eating (namely, hunger), and instead they pay attention to external cues, such as food taste, smell, and variety. Even when you are not hungry, tempting food smells and tastes can influence you to eat. For example, someone may give up eating meat for years, but still crave a hot dog with mustard when that person smells hot dogs cooking on a grill. People also eat more when they have a variety of different types of foods available (Rolls et al., 1981). Because people get tired of eating the same thing, having a diverse diet leads to more food consumption (just think about how much you eat at buffets). Similarly, rats that are given a wide variety of different foods show considerable weight gains, especially if these foods are high in fat and sugar (Sclafani & Springer, 1976). External cues can also lead people to avoid eating something they would actually enjoy. A series of studies by Rozin et al. has shown that people will refuse to eat delicious chocolate fudge if it is formed into the shape of dog poop, for example (Rozin & Fallon, 1987).

Although most people sometimes eat in response to external cues, according to Schachter's (1968) internal-external theory, people who are trying to restrain how much they eat are particularly influenced by external prompts for eating, such as TV advertisements for food, sampling a particularly good-tasting food, and even believing that it is "time to eat." For example, a normal-weight person who passes a bakery and sees tempting food will stop to buy something if he or she is hungry but will walk by if he or she has just eaten and is full. However, an obese person will find the food irresistible even if he or she has just eaten. In other words, obese people don't really pay attention to what their bodies are telling them about whether they need to eat.

In one of the earliest studies to test this theory, Schachter et al. examined whether normal-weight people are more responsive to internal cues for hunger than those who are overweight (Schachter, Goldman, & Gordon, 1968). Subjects, who were all told not to eat before coming into the lab, were randomly assigned to either the "full-stomach" condition, in which they were left in a room with a plate of sandwiches and told to eat until they were full, or the "empty-stomach" condition, in which they were not allowed to eat. Then, the subjects were brought into another room for a "cracker-rating test" in which they were asked to eat as many crackers as they would like from five unmarked boxes and to rate how much they liked each type of cracker. As predicted, the number of crackers eaten by normal-weight subjects was influenced by how hungry they were: Those with empty stomachs ate, on average, 21.89 crackers, whereas those who had eaten a meal prior to the study ate only 15.32. However, the number of crackers eaten by obese people did not differ as a function of how full they were: Obese people ate an average of 18.65 crackers when they were full and 17.89 crackers when they were hungry. This study shows that normal-weight people pay attention to their internal cues for eating (namely, how hungry they are), whereas obese people eat the same amount regardless of how hungry they might be.

In support of Schachter's externality theory, several studies have shown that obese people eat more when foods taste particularly good (Kauffman, Herman, & Polivy, 1995). In one study, Nisbett (1968) gave both normal-weight and obese subjects vanilla ice cream that was either very good (think Haagen-Dazs or Ben and Jerry's) or really bad (made with cheap vanilla and having an acrid aftertaste). When the ice cream tasted pretty bad, no one ate very much, but when the ice cream was pretty good, obese subjects ate much more than normal-weight subjects. In another study on the influence of taste on eating, six grossly obese subjects and four normal-weight subjects were placed on a hospital diet—the only thing they could eat was a bland liquid diet shake; they could have as much of the unappealing shake as they wanted at any time (Hashim & Van Itallie, 1965). Normal-weight subjects basically took in the same number of calories on the liquid diet as they did in normal life; they ate to maintain their weight (and presumably they rely on their internal cue of hunger to guide their eating). On the other hand, obese subjects consumed significantly fewer calories on this diet than they normally did, presumably because the external cues of eating were weak. The real-world implications of this study may explain why diet drinks, such as those containing aspartame, do help people lose weight (at least in the short term): It is really unappetizing to get all of your calories through a bland-tasting, textureless diet drink. All of this research suggests that obese people show a close connection between the external circumstances of eating and amount eaten, whereas for normal-weight people, the close connection is between their physiological state and amount eaten.

More recent research, however, provides little support for the internal-external theory. First, even people of normal weight are not particularly good at interpreting internal signals for hunger, such as low blood sugar and stomach pains (Rodin, 1981). People are also not very good at surmising how many calories they have consumed or how many calories their bodies need to maintain weight. Second, people at varying weight levels, including those of average weight, can be very responsive to external cues for eating particular types of foods. For example, people vary in how appealing they find snack foods, as well as how well they are able to control these desires. Not surprisingly, people who find snack foods very appealing are more likely to gain weight if they aren't good at regulating what they eat (Nederkoorn, Houben, Hofmann, Roefs, & Jansen, 2010).

Mood Regulation

Considerable research indicates that people may eat to influence how they feel (a factor psychologists describe as mood regulation). For example, people may eat to make themselves feel better when they experience stress, anxiety, or depression. As described in Chapter 4, people who experience more stress eat more high fat/sugar between-meal snacks, have less main meal and vegetable consumption (O'Connor, Jones, Conner, McMillan, & Ferguson, 2008), and show higher levels of emotional eating and haphazard planning of eating (Sims et al., 2007), which can, not surprisingly, lead to weight gain, especially for obese people (Hannerz, Albertsen, Nielsen, Tuchsen, & Burr, 2004). Researchers in one study examined weight loss over 6 months among obese women in a weight-control program (Kim, Bursac, DiLillo, White, & West, 2009). Women who experienced the lowest levels of stress lost an average of 5.2 pounds, whereas those with the highest level of stress lost an average of only 3 pounds.

Although the studies described thus far are correlational, and thus it is difficult to determine the precise way in which stress influences eating, experimental research yields similar findings. For example, Pine (1985) told subjects they would be participating in a study on how electrical stimulation influenced taste. He told some that the shock would be barely noticeable (low-anxiety condition) and others that the shocks would be painful, though not harmful (high-anxiety condition), and then he measured how many peanuts subjects ate while they waited for the shocks. As predicted, people who expected they would receive only mild shocks ate 9.02 grams of peanuts compared to 12.38 grams of peanuts for those who expected the painful shocks. This study provides additional evidence that stress indeed leads to overeating.

Interestingly, this tendency to eat more when nervous seems to be more common in women than men. One study with French high school students revealed that girls, but not boys, consumed more calories on examination days, and both boys and girls showed a tendency to eat more calories from fat on these stressful days (Michaud et al., 1990). Similarly, 62% of female college students, but only 29% of male students, report eating more when they are depressed (Rozin & Fallon, 1988). Experimental research demonstrates the same gender difference. In one study, researchers showed men and women either a relaxing video or a stressful video and then measured how much they ate (Grunberg & Straub, 1992). Men who were stressed ate about half as much as men who were not stressed, although there was no overall difference in the amount eaten for women. However, women who were stressed ate more sweet foods. This finding is in line with that from other research showing that women prefer snack foods, such as chocolate and ice cream, as comfort food, whereas men prefer hearty foods, such as steak and casseroles (Wansink, Cheney, & Chan, 2003).

Questioning the Research 8.1

Why should women show more of a tendency to eat when stressed than men? What are your hypotheses about this association?

There is rather mixed evidence, however, for the view that stress consistently leads to overeating. In fact, while some people seem to eat more when under stress, others eat less (Willenbring, Levine, & Morley, 1986). One study of female college students found that obese students ate nearly seven times as much during exam period than normal-weight students, whereas there was virtually no difference in how much obese and nonobese students ate during less stressful periods of the semester (Slochower, Kaplan, & Mann, 1981). Similarly, the study by Pine (1985) described previously found that although people who expected severe shocks generally ate more than those who expected mild shocks, obese people who expected severe shocks ate about 15.4 grams of peanuts as compared to only 9.2 for nonobese people who expected severe shocks. Other research suggests that the tendency to eat more when stressed occurs only for those who are trying to lose weight (Friedman & Brownell, 1995). For example, Baucom and Aiken (1981) found that stress leads to more eating for those who are dieting but less eating among those who are not dieting. So, all of this research suggests that some people may indeed overeat when they are experiencing stress (such as those who are obese or who are trying to lose weight), but stress does not lead everyone to overeat.

Interestingly, different moods might lead to preferences for different types of foods. Researchers in one study randomly assigned participants to one of three mood conditions: Some watched *Sweet Home Alabama* (to create a happy mood), others watched *Love Story* (to create a sad mood), and others watched no movie (Garg, Wansink, & Inman, 2007). In addition, participants were given one of two types of snacks to eat during the study: M&Ms or raisins. As shown in Figure 8.5, participants in a sad mood ate more M&Ms than participants in a happy mood, whereas those in a happy mood ate more raisins than those in a sad mood. Bad moods are particularly likely to lead people to eat more "comfort foods" when they are trying to suppress such moods, indicating that people who aren't able to regulate their moods in an adaptive way show more signs of eating as a way of coping with bad emotions (Evers, Stok, & De Ridder, 2010).

FIGURE 8.5   The type of food people eat is strongly influenced by their mood: People who are happy eat more raisins than those who are sad, but those who are sad eat more M&Ms than those who are happy (data from Garg et al., 2007).

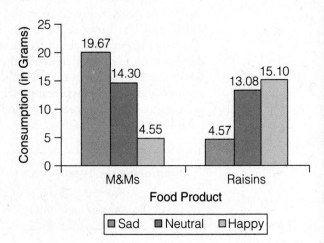

Restraint Theory

Restraint theory was developed in part to explain the sometimes mixed findings that resulted from research based in the internal-external and mood-regulation theories of obesity. According to this theory, people are generally motivated to eat as a function of internal physiological signals that cue hunger (Herman & Polivy, 1984). However, when people are trying to lose weight, they deliberately ignore these internal signals and instead use cognitive rules to limit their caloric intake. For example, dieters might develop rules about eating certain types of foods (e.g., celery, carrots, nonfat yogurt) and avoiding other types of foods (e.g., ice cream, brownies, meat).

This approach can be successful in helping people restrict their eating, but it can also backfire. Specifically, restrained eaters often develop an "all-or-nothing" mind-set about eating, which means that breaking the rules by eating small amounts of "forbidden food" can lead to overeating. For example, a person who is dieting but who gives in and eats a fattening first course at a dinner party may think, "Well, I've blown it now, so I may as well eat all I want." As described at the beginning of the chapter, Elizabeth's efforts to diet led her to overeat during times of stress. In a study by Herman and Mack (1975) subjects were told the research focused on how tasting one flavor first influences the ability to judge another flavor. Some subjects were then given two milkshakes to drink (one chocolate, one vanilla), and others were given nothing to drink (the control condition). All participants were then asked to taste and rate three different flavors of ice cream—they were told they could eat as much ice cream as necessary to rate the flavors accurately. For

Restrained eaters often divide foods into those things they are allowed to eat and those things they should not eat.
Source: © The New Yorker Collection 2001 Mike Twohy from cartoonbank.com. All Rights Reserved.

"I shouldn't, but I'm going to have the garbage."

nondieters, eating a high-calorie food decreased the amount of ice cream they ate, whereas for dieters, eating a high-calorie food led to even more eating.

Similarly, when restrained eaters feel sad or stressed, they give up the cognitive rules and can then eat excessive amounts. Heatherton et al. examined the effects of feeling sad on eating in both dieters and nondieters (Heatherton, Striepe, & Wittenberg, 1998). College women were randomly assigned to listen to either a very slow and depressing piece of music or a more neutral piece of music, and to then spend 10 minutes tasting and rating three different flavors of ice cream. As predicted, both dieting and listening to sad music influenced how much ice cream the women ate during their tasting task. First, and not surprisingly, dieters ate less than nondieters in the neutral-music condition. However, dieters ate significantly more ice cream than nondieters when they were in the sad music condition. In fact, dieters who heard the sad music ate more ice cream than dieters who were in the neutral condition and nondieters who were in either condition. Apparently, dieters use food as a way of regulating their mood; hence, they eat more ice cream when they are feeling sad.

However, some research by Lowe, Whitlow, and Bellwoar suggests that restraint theory is not always a good predictor of eating behavior (1993). The researchers believe that some people who are "restrained eaters" have developed cognitive rules that guide their eating, but they are not at the moment actively trying to lose weight (although they may have struggled with weight-loss issues in the past). In line with the predictions of restraint theory, these people should overeat under various conditions (when they are sad, when they are stressed, etc.). On the other hand, people who are actively trying to diet may also develop rules to guide their eating, but these people should not engage in the same type of "all-or-nothing" eating that nondieting restrained eaters show. In support of this view, restrained nondieters eat more after they have first had a milkshake (because they have already blown their diet anyway), whereas restrained dieters eat significantly less after having a milkshake (because they are actively trying to lose weight; Lowe et al., 1991).

Sociocultural Factors

Even subtle social factors, such as lifestyle, friends/family, and culture, can influence how much people eat. First, people eat more when they are with other people than when they are alone (De Castro & De Castro, 1989; Feunkes, De Graaf, & Van Staveren, 1995). Researchers in one study examined children's food consumption as a function of the size of the group they were in (Lumeng & Hillman, 2007). Children consumed 30% more food when eating in a group of nine children than when eating in a group of three children. People are particularly likely to eat more when eating with family and friends (De Castro, 1994). Having other people around may lead to more eating in part because meals last longer. People may also be less sensitive to internal cues for hunger when they are with other people. For example, if you are eating alone, the amount you eat is influenced by how hungry you are (e.g., if you had a late or big lunch, you eat less for dinner), whereas if you are eating with other people, you eat the same amount regardless of when you have last had a meal. Interestingly, however, most people are unaware that the presence of others impacts how much they eat. Researchers in one study measured eating in

Box 8.1

Focus on Research: Is Obesity Contagious?

Researchers in this study were interested in examining how obesity might be linked through family/friend relationships (Christakis & Fowler, 2007). To test this question, researchers examined data on weight, sex, education, and social contacts (friends, family members, neighbors) collected from more than 12,000 people over a 30-year period. This data allowed researchers to examine changes in weight over time among participants in the study as well as in their friends, family members, and neighbors. Findings indicated that obesity was linked in particular social networks, meaning that people with social contacts who are obese are more likely to become obese themselves. Specifically, a person's chances of becoming obese increased by 71% if a person had a same-sex friend who became obese during that time, by 40% if one's sibling became obese, and by 37% if one's spouse became obese. The link between obesity was not seen among neighbors or opposite-sex friends. This research suggests that obesity may in fact be "contagious," perhaps indirectly, such as through the impact of obesity leading to changes in weight-related norms, and/or directly, such as through impacting food consumption.

pairs of students, and then asked them which factors contributed to how much they ate (Vartanian, Herman, & Wansink, 2008). Most students referred to the taste of the food, how hungry they were, or their liking of the food; only 2.5% of students noted that how much their partner ate influenced what they ate. Box 8.1: Focus on Research describes the influence of our friends on obesity.

A series of fascinating studies by Wansink, van Ittersum, and Painter demonstrate that even subtle environmental factors, such as the size of the dish food is served on, influence how much we eat. In one study, guests attending an ice cream party were given either a larger or smaller bowl and ice cream scoop to serve themselves (2006). Those who received the larger bowl served themselves 31% more ice cream, and those who received the larger spoon served themselves 14.5% more. Similarly, people who serve themselves a snack mix of pretzels, nuts, and chips at a Super Bowl Party take—and consume—56% more from large bowls than small ones (Wansink & Cheney, 2005).

Cultural factors such as the availability and amount of food may also contribute to obesity (Wadden, Brownell, & Foster, 2002). The United States has the highest rates of obesity in the world but also a great abundance of fast-food restaurants featuring inexpensive and very fatty foods. Many school cafeterias now feature fast foods and soda, despite the contribution of these products to obesity. As described by Kelly Brownell, a psychologist at Yale University, "If your task was to make the American child as unhealthy as possible, could you do much better than fast food and soft drinks in the cafeteria?" (*Time*, 2002). Food is not simply readily available, but is increasingly served in larger amounts. Portions at both high-end and low-end restaurants (think "Super Size" that) in the United States have become bigger over time, which encourages overeating (Hill & Peters, 1998). The original glass Coke

Box 8.2

Focus on Development: The Long-Lasting Impact of Prenatal Tasting

Some research suggests that taste preferences are shaped even before we are born. Mennella, Jagnow, and Beauchamp conducted a very clever study in which pregnant women who were planning to breast-feed were randomly assigned to one of three groups (2001). Women in one group drank carrot juice four times a week for 3 weeks during pregnancy, women in another group drank carrot juice four times a week for 3 weeks after the baby was born, and women in the third group did not drink carrot juice. The researchers then tested how babies reacted to the taste of carrots by asking mothers to rate their babies' facial reactions and measure how much of a carrot-flavored cereal the babies ate. Babies who were exposed to the taste of carrots either through amniotic fluid or breast milk liked the taste of carrots more than babies who had no exposure to this taste, and they tended to eat more flavored cereal. This study provides compelling evidence that taste preferences may be established very early in life—in fact, even before birth.

bottles that were manufactured in the 1930s held $6^{1}/_{2}$ ounces, whereas the current "single-size" plastic Coke bottle now holds 1 liter, which is five times as much. These aspects of American culture—the abundance of food and large portion sizes—help explain why immigrants who move to the United States increase in obesity over time (Goel, McCarthy, Phillips, & Wee, 2004). Researchers in one study found that although the prevalence of obesity was 16% among immigrants and 22% among U.S.-born individuals, only 8% of immigrants who had lived in the United States for less than a year were obese compared to 19% among those living in the United States for at least 15 years. These findings suggest that exposure to American culture increases the risk of obesity.

Culture may also influence the types of foods and tastes people enjoy (Rozin, 1996). Most Americans, for example, find eating insects, snails, and dogs fairly repulsive, whereas these foods are considered delicacies in some cultures. Similarly, our food preferences are shaped by the types of flavors used in cooking, such as curry (common in India) and chili pepper (common in Mexico). Box 8.2: Focus on Development describes how cultural preferences in types of food and tastes can become established very early in life.

What Factors Help Prevent Obesity?

Preventing obesity must begin in childhood because obesity in childhood is very likely to lead to obesity in adulthood: One study examined the prevalence of adult obesity based on whether 6-month-old infants were above or below the 75th percentile for weight (Charney, Goodman, McBride, Lyon, & Pratt, 1976). Only

8% of nonobese infants became obese adults as compared to 14% of obese infants (nearly double the rate). The risk of adult obesity is even greater for children who are obese at older ages. For example, one study found that 40% of obese 7 year olds became overweight adults as compared to only 10% of nonobese 7 year olds (Stark, Atkins, Wolff, & Douglas, 1981). Fat cells develop in childhood and adolescence, and once they develop, they never disappear—they can get bigger or smaller, but they never disappear.

As described in Chapter 2, breast-feeding is one important way to decrease obesity in children. In one study, researchers at the National Institutes of Health examined data from 2,685 children ages 3 to 5 (Hediger, Overpeck, Kuczmarski, & Ruan, 2001). Children who had been breast-fed for any length of time were 16% less likely to be overweight and 37% less likely to be obese than those who were never breast-fed. One reason why breast-feeding may be so beneficial is that babies who are breast-fed learn how to regulate how much they consume because mothers have no way to gauge how much they are drinking. In contrast, bottle-fed babies are often fed a certain amount of formula periodically each day, and parents may therefore focus on getting the baby to eat the "right amount."

Questioning the Research 8.2

What other factors might explain why breast-fed babies are less likely to be obese? (Hint: Think about whether this study shows correlation or causation).

Efforts to prevent obesity can be relatively simple, such as encouraging children to exercise and eat healthy foods and modeling healthy behavior, such as using fruits as dessert, eating healthy snacks, and exercising. However, parents should never use unhealthy food as a reward for good behavior even when it is really tempting to do so. One study of 427 parents of preschool children found that 56% reported promising children a special food, such as a dessert, for finishing their dinner, and 48% reported promising children a special food for good behavior, such as cleaning their room (Stanek, Abbott, & Cramer, 1990). But what are the long-term effects of this approach? Children figure out very quickly that the "good foods" come after the "bad foods," and they in fact, show an increased desire for "forbidden" foods. In one study, 3- to 6-year-old children were at one time allowed to eat a variety of different flavors of fruit cookie bars, and at other times they were specifically told they could eat any fruit cookie bar they wanted except for one particular flavor (Fisher & Birch, 1999). Researchers then measured how much children talked about each of the kinds of cookie bars, how much they tried to obtain them, and how much they asked for them. Although there were no real differences between their interest in the different types of fruit cookie bars when they had free access, as soon as one type of cookie bar was forbidden, it became very desirable.

Another important factor in preventing obesity is limiting television watching. First, watching television is a passive activity (particularly with the advent of the remote control). So, when children come home from school (or adults come home from work) and sit in front of the television, they aren't exercising. Studies with both adults (Ching et al., 1996) and children (Andersen, Crespo, Bartlett, Cheskin,

& Pratt, 1998) have shown that people who watch a lot of television are more likely to be overweight than those who watch less television. Children from families in which the television is often on during meals also eat more salty snacks and sodas and less fruits, vegetables, and juices than those from families in which the television is rarely on (Coon, Goldberg, Rogers, & Tucker, 2001).

Second, watching television exposes children to numerous advertisements for unhealthy foods, which in turn models bad eating habits (Story & Faulkner, 1990). The average child sees more than 20,000 TV commercials in a year, and the two most common types of ads are for toys and food. Researchers in one study examined the nutritional content of 5,000 television food advertisements seen by children (Powell, Szczypka, Chaloupka, & Braunschweig, 2007). Study results showed that 97.8% and 89.4% of food-product advertisements viewed by children 2 to 11 years old and adolescents 12 to 17 years old, respectively, were high in fat, sugar, or sodium. On average, 46.1% and 49.1% of total calories among the products advertised came from sugar in the advertisements seen by these respective age groups. For example, 97.6% of cereal advertisements were for high-sugar cereals.

This constant exposure to television advertisements also leads children to develop stronger preferences for restaurants featuring unhealthy foods. More than half of 9- to 10-year-old children believe that Ronald McDonald knows what is good for children to eat (Horgen, Choate, & Brownell, 2001). Children also believe that food from McDonald's tastes better. Researchers in one study examined the effects of fast-food branding on children's taste preferences (Robinson, Borzekowski, Matheson, & Kraemer, 2007). Sixty-three children tasted 5 pairs of identical foods and beverages in packaging from McDonald's and matched but unbranded packaging and were asked to indicate if they tasted the same or if one tasted better. Overall, children preferred the tastes of foods and drinks if they thought they were from McDonald's. However, children with more television sets in their homes showed an even stronger preference for food they believed was from McDonald's. Similarly, and as shown in Table 8.3, 4- to 6-year-old children prefer snack foods featuring popular cartoon characters, such as Dora the Explorer, Shrek, or Scooby

Children who watch considerable amounts of television are at an increased risk of obesity, in part because they are exposed to many commercials for unhealthy foods and in part because they are less likely to participate in physical activity than children who watch less television.
Source: Jack Hollingsworth/Corbis Images.

TABLE 8.3   *Percentage of Children Preferring Various Snack Foods With and Without a Cartoon Character*

Food Item	Without Character	With Character
Graham crackers	12.5	87.5
Gummy fruit snacks	15	85
Baby carrots	27.5	72.5

Source: In this study, 40 4- to 6-year-old children tasted 3 pairs of identical foods (graham crackers, gummy fruit snacks, and carrots) presented in packages either with or without a popular cartoon character. Children tasted both food items in each pair and then selected which of the food items they would prefer to eat for a snack. As shown in this table, the majority of children selected the food sample with a licensed character on it for their snack (Roberto, Baik, Harris & Brownell, 2010).

Doo, to those without any character (Roberto, Baik, Harris, & Brownell, 2010). They also rate snack foods with such characters as tasting better.

How Is Obesity Treated?

It is no mystery that weight gain is at least partially a function of taking in more calories than the body burns off. Many people try to lose weight by making changes in their diet—in fact, as many as 25 to 30% of the adult American population is dieting at any one time (Bouchard, 1991). However, the amount of weight people lose on any of these diets tends to be small and temporary. These approaches don't focus on helping people make long-term changes in their dietary habits. Although it may be true that eating only grapefruit for the rest of your life would allow you to maintain a very low body weight, you would also suffer from various nutritional deficits. It is unrealistic to think that people could maintain good health on some dieting approaches.

Efforts to lose weight can also focus on increasing the number of calories expended through exercise; in fact, increasing exercise is the single best predictor of long-term weight control (Wadden, 1993). Exercise helps with weight loss in a number of ways, including increasing metabolic rate (so calories are burned at a faster rate), increasing lean body mass (which requires more calories to maintain), and suppressing appetite. Engaging in regular exercise also leads to greater physical and psychological well-being. Even moderate amounts of exercise can lead to major health benefits, including reduced risk of cardiovascular disease and diabetes (Helmrich, Ragland, Leung, & Paffenberger, 1991; Manson et al., 1992), lowered blood pressure (Kokkinos et al., 1995), and protection against osteoporosis (Greendale et al., 1995) as well as cancer (Meyerhardt et al., 2009; Wolin, Yan, Colditz, & Lee, 2009). Physical activity is even associated with increased likelihood of longer life expectancy (Sun et al., 2010). Exercise also leads to lower levels of depression and anxiety (Camacho, Roberts, Lazarus, Kaplan, & Cohen, 1991; Norvell & Belles, 1993). For example, in one study, 156 adults with clinical depression were randomly assigned to do aerobic exercise, receive drug treatment, or both (Babyak et al., 2000). Patients in all three conditions showed equivalent improvements at the 4-month and 6-month follow-up, suggesting that exercise can, at least in some cases, be as effective as drug treatment. Despite the numerous health benefits of exercise, only 35% of Americans report engaging in light to moderate physical activity at least 5 days per week, and approximately 33% of all adults report engaging in no leisure time physical activity (CDC, 2010).

First, setting proximal or short-term goals regarding exercise and eating is more effective than setting distal or long-term goals (Bandura & Simon, 1977; Marcus et al., 2000; Wadden, 1993). For example, it is better to focus on cutting calories at each meal than on eliminating a certain number of calories each week, or jogging three times a week. Researchers in one study compared a traditional intervention—focusing on information about the benefits of healthy eating—to an intervention that also included information on self-regulation (e.g., implementation intentions and strategies for accomplishing healthier eating; Stadler, Oettingen, & Gollwitzer, 2010). Findings from the 2-year follow-up revealed that self-regulation helps: Participants in the self-regulation component increased fruits and vegetables 28% more than at baseline compared to only 7% for those in the information-only intervention. This short-term approach allows people to experience small successes in reaching their larger goals and thus can help them feel more confident in their ability to achieve their weight-loss goals. Setting specific realistic goals and working toward them helps motivation stay high, and increases self-efficacy for following through on these behavior change intentions, which is particularly important because self-efficacy is one of the best predictors of whether someone engages in physical activity and adopts healthier eating habits (Anderson, Wojcik, Winett, & Williams, 2006; Fuemmeler, 2006; Kitzman-Ulrich, Wilson, Van Horn, & Lawman, 2010). Similarly, the most effective techniques emphasize gradual weight loss (1 to 2 pounds a week), as opposed to more extreme approaches. The quick and extreme plans that are often featured on magazine covers just don't work—no one can *safely* lose 10 pounds in the week before spring break without having a limb amputated.

Second, operant-conditioning approaches, in which people receive some type of reward for adhering to a diet, losing weight, or sticking to an exercise program, can also be very helpful (Jeffery, Wing, Thorson, & Burton, 1998; Wadden, 1993). For example, you could give yourself some type of reward for successfully meeting your weight-loss goals—maybe a new CD or pair of sunglasses. (Obviously, it's better to not use food as a reward to motivate yourself!) In one study, people in different businesses participated in a 3-month weight-loss challenge in which each participant was given a weight-loss goal based on his or her actual and desired weight, and the team with the greatest percentage of weight loss received a large cash prize (Brownell, Cohen, Stunkard, Felix, & Cooley, 1984). The average weight lost was 12 pounds, and only 1 of the 213 participants dropped out of the contest. Most important, a 6-month follow-up revealed that people kept off 80% of the weight they lost. Similarly, one study found that people who were given rewards (e.g., clothing, money, going to the movies) for engaging in regular exercise reported exercising an average of 2.29 times per week as compared to 1.36 for those who were not given such rewards (Noland, 1989). Operant-conditioning approaches may be especially useful for children. Researchers in one study trained parents to reward obese kids for engaging in physical activity and eating healthy foods (Epstein, Paluch, Kilanowski, & Raynor, 2004). Results indicated that these types of rewards decreased sedentary behavior (such as watching TV and playing video games) and led to a lower BMI 6 and 12 months later.

Third, monitoring exactly what, when, and where you eat can help you reduce calories (Wadden, 1993). People sometimes lack an understanding of precisely what they eat each day; therefore, they are confused when their dieting doesn't work. You may, for example, decrease the number of calories you eat at each meal, but if you consistently eat potato chips while you study or have a candy bar as a quick between-classes snack, you may not remember to count those calories. In fact, dieters tend to both underreport how much food they eat and overestimate how much they exercise (Lichtman et al., 1992). Also, people often overeat in social situations because they aren't even aware of how much they are eating. (Sadly, calories consumed while standing up still count.) After you have monitored the factors that lead to overeating, you can try to eliminate these triggers. Instead of stopping at Dunkin' Donuts for coffee and a doughnut on your way to class, you might try eating a bowl of cereal or fruit at home instead. If you eat while you watch TV, you might try eating when sitting at your dining room table with the TV off.

This type of self-monitoring is more effective if it includes regular prompts and reminders, such as mailings, signs, or phone calls, to keep people on track with the desired changes in their behavior (see Table 8.4; Andersen et al., 1998; Lombard, Lombard, & Winett, 1995; Marcus et al., 2000). In one study, signs saying, "Your heart needs exercise. Here's your chance" were posted at three locations in public areas (mall, train station, bus terminal) where escalators and stairs were both available (Brownell, Stunkard, & Albaum, 1980). The percentage of people choosing stairs increased when the sign appeared, then dropped when the sign was removed, and rose again when the sign was reinstated. Similarly, obese dieters who received reminder calls to self-monitor their eating a couple times a week didn't gain any weight during the diet-challenging 8-week holiday time (including the Thanksgiving to New Year's weeks), whereas those without these calls gained weight (Boutelle, Kirschenbaum, Baker, & Mitchell, 1999).

Other self-control approaches to weight loss focus on helping people make small changes in their behavior, or even in the way that they think about eating and weight loss (Wadden, 1993). Obese people might be encouraged to purchase healthy foods to snack on and to avoid keeping "problem foods" in the house; this way, if they overeat, they eat carrots as opposed to donuts. Similarly, people who are dieting may be advised to slow down their eating, perhaps by putting their fork

TABLE 8.4 *Percentage of Participants Meeting Recommended Eating Guidelines*

Behavior	Usual Care	Telephone Counseling
Fat consumption	12.9%	18.2%
Fiber consumption	10.4	21.8
Vegetable consumption	17.6	32.4
Fruit consumption	59.3	72.0

Participants who received a telephone-counseling intervention, followed by 18 follow-up calls over the next year, were much more likely to adhere to recommended eating guidelines than those who received only a usual-care intervention consisting of brief mailings.

Source: Eakin, Reeves, Winkler, Lawler, & Owen, 2010.

down between each bite or chewing all of their food thoroughly. These methods focus on changing people's negative or unrealistic views about weight loss (e.g., "I will never be able to lose the weight," or "I should have lost the weight by now, this isn't working"). People who have struggled with obesity for some time may view their lack of weight-loss success as a sign of personal weakness and failure, which in turn can lead them to return to unhealthy eating patterns at the first sign of trouble.

People are also more likely to follow through on their intentions to change their eating and exercise habits when these behaviors can easily fit in with their daily lives and schedules. For example, people are more likely to continue exercising when they are exercising at home as opposed to in a health club (Perri, Martin, Leermakers, Sears, & Notelovitz, 1997). Although formal exercise classes can provide social support and motivation, exercising at home is cheaper and more convenient. Similarly, people who commit to engaging in several short bouts of exercise each day (four 10-minute bouts of exercise such as climbing the stairs or walking briskly outside) are more successful at maintaining this behavior than those who attempt to engage in one longer period of exercise such as a 40-minute exercise class (Jakicic, Winters, Lang, & Wing, 1999). Even simple lifestyle changes, such as using stairs rather than escalators, walking rather than driving to work, and parking farther away from store entrances, can be as effective as more organized exercise activities in weight reduction (Andersen et al., 1999; Dunn et al., 1999; Kujala, Kaprio, Sarna, & Koskenvao, 1998; Wadden et al., 2002).

Social influence techniques, such as exercising with a friend and participating in formal weight-loss groups, can often help people successfully make changes related to diet and exercise (Duncan, & McAuley, 1993; Wadden, 1993; Wing & Jeffery, 1999). As described at the beginning of the chapter, Bill managed to lose 15 pounds after he started exercising with a group of friends from work. Group approaches are especially effective in helping people lose weight because they provide social support as well as healthy competition. For example, one study with 89 overweight men found that group contracts (receiving money based on the average group weight loss) were more effective at maintaining weight loss over 2 years than individual contracts (receiving money based on only one's own weight loss; Jeffery, Bjornson-Benson, Rosenthal, Lindquist, & Johnson, 1984). Relatedly, a study with adolescents found that having friend, parents, and siblings who support sport activities—and who watch such activities—is associated with more physical activity (Duncan, Duncan, & Strycker, 2005). Believing your parents/peers care about your sports and come watch you play is associated with more physical activity. Encouragement from others to eat a healthy diet and engage in physical activity also increases such behaviors among adults (Anderson, Wojcik, Winett, & Williams, 2006; Fuemmeler, 2006).

Large-scale interventions that integrate many of the strategies discussed previously, including education, personalized goal setting, and support for making changes, can be effective at helping participants achieve short- and long-term changes in physical activity, eating, and exercise (Ahluwalia et al., 2007; Eakin, 2007; Resnicow et al., 2005; Steptoe, Perkins-Porras, Rink, Hilton, & Cappuccio, 2004). For example, one study with overweight adults found that participation in 20 weekly group sessions to encourage dieting and engaging in exercise led to a mean weight loss of 4.4 pounds, with 69% of participants losing at least that much weight (Hollis et al., 2008). Similarly, a research study on children found that this type of broader lifestyle intervention, which focuses on diet as well as physical activity, on average leads to 8 or 9% decreases in weight, whereas those without such interventions on average show an increase of 2 to 3% (Wilfley et al., 2007). Interventions designed to decrease obesity in children are especially effective if parents are involved and supportive, including changing their own habits and/or assisting with cooking and providing healthier foods (Kitzmann et al., 2010).

Finally, in extreme cases, when obesity is a real threat to a person's health, surgical techniques can be used (Kral, 1992). One method is to wire shut a person's jaw for a certain amount of time so he or she only can drink fluids. Other surgical methods include placement of a temporary gastric band around the top of the stomach (so that the person can eat only small amounts of food before feeling full) and removal of a portion of the small intestine (which prevents food from being absorbed into the body). Although these approaches often do lead to significant weight loss, they can have unpleasant side effects, including permanent diarrhea and long-term nutritional deficits. These methods are therefore used only in cases of severe obesity that have potentially life-threatening effects.

What Are Eating Disorders?

Recent estimates indicate that nearly 3% of all teenagers ages 13 to 18 have had an eating disorder (Swanson, Crow, Le Grange, Swendsen, & Merikangas, 2011) and that 6% of adult women and 2.8% of adult men have had an eating disorder (Hudson, Hiripi, Pope, & Kessler, 2007). However, many other people experience some symptoms of disordered eating which do not meet the clinical definition of such disorders. Therefore as you read this section, you may recognize your friend, roommate, teammate, girlfriend—or even yourself.

Anorexia nervosa involves a drastic reduction in a person's food intake and an intentional loss of weight (maintaining a body weight 15% below one's normal weight based on height–weight tables, or a BMI of 17.5). This loss of weight eventually leads to amenorrhea, the absence of menstruation. People with anorexia often see themselves as heavy even when they are actually quite thin, and they have an excessive fear of gaining weight (see Table 8.5). They typically eat only very small amounts of food (e.g., a Cheerio for breakfast, a bite of an apple for lunch, lettuce for supper) and may have a variety of eating rituals that they engage in as a way of avoiding eating (e.g., cutting food into very small portions, eating very slowly). People with anorexia may also engage in strenuous exercise in an effort to lose weight. Anorexia is much more common in women than men, and tends to be most prevalent in upper-middle-class and upper-class White women (see Table 8.6). Women who participate in weight-conscious activities, including ballet, gymnastics, and modeling, are at greatest risk of developing anorexia. Although the overall prevalence of anorexia nervosa in all women in the United States is approximately 1% (only .3% for men; Hudson et al., 2007), some estimates suggest that 6 to 7% of women who attend professional schools for modeling and dance meet the criteria for having anorexia (Garner & Garfinkel, 1980).

Bulimia nervosa is characterized by recurrent episodes of binge eating followed by purging (see Tables 8.5 and 8.6). These episodes are typically triggered by some

TABLE 8.5   *Diagnostic Criteria for Eating Disorders*

Anorexia Nervosa

1. Refusal to maintain body weight at or above a minimally normal weight for age and height (e.g., weight loss leading to maintenance of body weight less than 85% of that expected)
2. Intense fear of gaining weight or becoming fat, even though underweight
3. Disturbance in the way in which one's body weight or shape is experienced, undue influence of body weight or shape on self-evaluation, or denial of the seriousness of the current low body weight
4. Amenorrhea (the absence of at least three consecutive menstrual cycles)

Bulimia Nervosa

1. Recurrent episodes of binge eating, namely, eating in a discrete period of time (e.g., within any 2-hour period) an amount of food that is definitely larger than most people would eat during a similar period of time and under similar circumstances, and feeling that one cannot stop eating or control what or how much one is eating
2. Recurrent inappropriate compensatory behavior to prevent weight gain, such as self-induced vomiting; misuse of laxatives, diuretics, enemas, or other medications; fasting; or excessive exercise
3. Binge eating and inappropriate compensatory behaviors occurring, on average, at least twice a week for 3 months
4. Self-evaluation unduly influenced by body shape and weight

These are a few criteria used to assess whether a person meets the clinical definition of anorexia nervosa and bulimia nervosa.

Source: American Psychiatric Association, 1994.

TABLE 8.6   *Test Yourself: Sample Items From Drive for Thinness and Bulimia Scales*

1. I feel extremely guilty after overeating.
2. I am terrified of gaining weight.
3. I am preoccupied with the desire to be thinner.
4. If I gain a pound, I worry that I will keep gaining.
5. I think about dieting.
6. I eat when I am upset.
7. I have gone on eating binges where I have felt that I could not stop.
8. I eat or drink in secrecy.
9. I eat moderately in front of others and stuff myself when they're gone.
10. I have the thought of trying to vomit in order to lose weight.

The first five items measure symptoms of anorexia; the second five measure symptoms of bulimia.

Source: Garner, Olmstead, & Polivy, 1983.

type of negative emotion, such as anxiety, tension, or even tiredness. During binges, bulimics rapidly consume enormous quantities of food. They typically select binge foods that are easy to swallow and vomit—fatty, sweet, high-energy foods. Bulimics then attempt to get rid of these calories, typically through vomiting or excessive exercise. This pattern of binge eating and purging occurs on a regular basis over some period of time. Bulimia is easier to hide than anorexia, in part because people with bulimia are typically normal weight. Although bulimia has a prevalence rate of approximately 1.5% in American women (.5% in American men; Hudson et al., 2007), some surveys indicate that as many as 10% of women in college show symptoms of bulimia (Becker, Grinspoon, Klibanski, & Herzog, 1999).

Although anorexia and bulimia are the most widely known disorders, the most common eating disorder is **binge eating disorder** (Hudson et al., 2007; Swanson et al., 2011). An estimated 3.5% of females and 2% of males report having binge eating disorder at some point in their lives. Not surprisingly, binge eating disorder often leads to obesity and is prevalent in up to 30% of those seeking weight-loss treatment.

Although relatively few people meet the diagnostic criteria for an eating disorder, many people, especially women, engage in some type of disordered eating. In fact, a recent study of 10,000 adolescents found that 4.4% reported having symptoms of disordered eating that did not reach clinical proportions (Swanson et al., 2011). Similarly, one study of 643 college women found that 82% engaged in some form of dieting behavior at least once daily (e.g., counting calories, eating low-calorie foods, skipping meals), 33% engaged in some form of destructive weight loss (e.g., taking laxatives, using appetite-control pills, vomiting) at least once a month, and 38% had problems with binge-eating behavior (Mintz & Betz, 1988). Fully 61% were found to have some form of unhealthy eating behavior (e.g., chronic dieting, subclinical bulimia), and only 33% were considered "normal eaters." In the larger population, an estimated 2 million women are using unhealthy strategies to lose weight, including fasting, vomiting, using diet pills, and taking laxatives (Biener & Heaton, 1995).

Eating disorders can lead to very serious, in some cases life-threatening, problems. Anorexia can cause low blood pressure, heart damage, and cardiac arrhythmia (Brownell & Fairburn, 1995). Women who recover from anorexia still may suffer with long-term problems, including bone loss (because of undernutrition and amenorrhea) and infertility (Becker et al., 1999). Bulimia can also cause a variety of medical problems. Frequent vomiting may cause tearing and bleeding in the esophagus, burning of throat and mouth by stomach acids, and damage to tooth enamel. Frequent purging can also lead to deficiencies in various nutrients, as well as anemia (an insufficient number of red blood cells), which both cause weakness and tiredness. Similarly, binge eating can cause damage to the stomach and intestines

Isabelle Caro, a French actress and model whose anorexic image appeared in a shock Italian ad campaign, died in December 2010 of anorexia. She was 28 at the time of her death.
Source: WARRIN/SIPA/NewsCom.

(Brownell & Fairburn, 1995) as well as hypoglycemia, which is a deficiency of sugar in the blood: Following a binge of sweets, the pancreas releases excessive amounts of insulin, which drives down blood sugar levels and can leave a person feeling dizzy, tired, and depressed. Most importantly, people with eating disorders have higher rates of mortality, with an estimated 4 to 6% of people with an eating disorder dying as a result of this disorder (Berkman, Lohr, & Bulik, 2007; Crow et al., 2009; Neumarker, 1997; Sullivan, 1995). Most of the deaths are a result of heart failure, organ failure, or suicide.

How Do Biological Factors Contribute to Eating Disorders?

Some research suggests that biological factors may influence the development of eating disorders (Allison & Faith, 1997; Hewitt, 1997). First, women who have a close relative who suffers from an eating disorder are two to three times more likely to experience anorexia or bulimia than are women without this link. Second, twin studies have shown that these disorders are much more likely to appear in both twins of an identical pair than in fraternal twins. For example, one study examined rates of bulimia in more than 2,000 female twins and found that genetic factors may predict bulimia in nearly 55% of cases.

Some evidence indicates that people with eating disorders have impairments in brain neurochemistry. For example, bulimics are less sensitive to serotonin, which cues feelings of fullness, than people with normal eating patterns (Sunday & Halmi, 1996). So, bulimics may eat huge amounts of food because they are unable to recognize feelings of fullness as quickly as others. On the other hand, anorexics show abnormally high levels of serotonin as well as leptin (which regulates eating; Walsh & Devlin, 1998). However, because these findings are correlational, it is not clear whether abnormal levels of serotonin produce disordered eating or perhaps are caused by disordered eating. One possibility is that these physiological changes are initially caused by irregular eating patterns but then these irregularities, once created, are maintained over time. For example, anorexics have low levels of leptin, which is secreted by fat cells, because they have such low levels of body fat. However, when anorexics increase how much they are eating, their leptin levels climb more quickly than their weight gain, making them feel full too early (hence less able to gain appropriate amounts of weight). Future research clearly must examine how biological and genetic factors can influence disordered eating.

How Do Psychological Factors Contribute to Eating Disorders?

Most research indicates that psychological factors are heavily involved in the acquisition of eating disorders. This section therefore examines how sociocultural norms, family, and personality factors can lead to disordered eating.

Sociocultural Norms

Think quickly—who is the most attractive female movie star? Without knowing who you named, she's likely very thin. Virtually all media images of women in the United States, including women in movies, on television shows, in music videos, and on the covers of magazines, show very thin women—some would say even dangerously thin: Miss America contestants have body weights 13 to 19% below the expected weight for women of their height (Wiseman, Gray, Mosimann, & Ahrens, 1992), which is one criterion for diagnosing anorexia.

The thinness norm portrayed in media is actually relatively new. Marilyn Monroe, the most revered sex symbol of the 1940s and 1950s, would be considered obese by our current standards. Movie and magazine depictions of women have become consistently thinner in the past 20 years (Silverstein, Perdue, Peterson, & Kelly, 1986). For example, between 1959 and 1978, the weight of Miss America contestants and *Playboy* centerfolds decreased significantly (Garner, Garfinkel, Schwartz, & Thompson, 1980). Similarly, over the past 20 years, women's magazines have increased the number of articles on weight-loss techniques, presumably in an attempt to "help" women reach this increasingly thin ideal (Andersen &

Box 8.3

Focus on Culture: Is the Thin Ideal Universal?

Although in the United States the thin ideal has taken hold, this preference is by no means universal. One recent study surveyed more than 7,000 people living in 10 different world regions, including the United States, Chile, Austria, Germany, Poland, Australia, China, India, and South Africa (Swami et al., 2010). All participants were asked to rate their own current and ideal figure, and women also rated the figure they believed would be most attractive to men. Finally, participants rated their own exposure to Western and local media. Findings indicated significant cross-cultural differences in ideal body shape. Participants in Eastern Europe, Scandinavia, and Western Europe generally preferred heavier figures than those in other parts of the world. In addition, less socioeconomically developed countries generally showed a stronger preference for heavier figures compared to more developed countries. This finding is in line with that from prior research showing that in societies in which food is scarce, the ideal female body type is heavy, perhaps because women who are heavier are perceived as healthy and more fertile, and heaviness can be a sign of wealth (Anderson, Crawford, Nadeau, & Lindberg, 1992). For example, in cultures with a very reliable food supply, such as the United States, 40% of people prefer a very thin female body, whereas only 17% show such preference in cultures with a fairly low reliability of food, and no cultures show such preference in cultures with a very low reliability of food. Finally, this research revealed that women in more socioeconomically developed countries have higher body dissatisfaction than those in less developed countries. Greater exposure to Western media was also associated with a stronger preference for a thinner figure, suggesting that the very thin images of women presented in typical Western media portrayals may in fact lead to greater body dissatisfaction.

DiDomenico, 1992; Garner et al., 1980). However, and as described in Box 8.3: Focus on Culture, this preference for such a thin ideal varies considerably by culture.

Even within the United States, ethnic groups vary on how much emphasis they place on the thin ideal (Halpern, Udry, Campbell, & Suchindran, 1999). Research by Wardle et al. (2004) has shown that higher socioeconomic status (SES) adolescent girls had more awareness of the thin ideal and more family/friends who are trying to lose weight. They also see a lower BMI as "fat" and are more likely to use weight-control methods, such as not eating particular foods. In fact, studies of both high school and college girls show that African Americans have a heavier ideal weight than Whites, are less preoccupied with weight and dieting, and are more satisfied with their weight (Desmond, Price, Hallinan, & Smith, 1989).

Not surprisingly, the presence of such thin women in the media often leads women of normal weight to feel too heavy. Nearly half of women of average weight are trying to lose weight (Biener & Heaton, 1995), as are 35% of normal-weight girls, and 12% of underweight girls (Schreiber et al., 1996). One study of teenage girls found that the "ideal girl" was perceived to be 5'7" tall, and 100 pounds (translating into a BMI of less than 16, which is anorexic; Nichter & Nichter, 1991). Repeated exposure to the extremely thin ideals presented by the media may also lead some women to develop more negative attitudes about their own bodies. In one study at the University of South Florida, 139 college women watched a 10-minute video of advertisements that featured either very thin women (such as those modeling weight-loss supplements, beer, and clothing) or average-weight women (such as those advertising pain relievers, household cleaning products, and insurance policies; Heinberg & Thompson, 1995). Women who already had negative views about their bodies (and hence were at greater risk of experiencing an eating disorder) increased in body dissatisfaction measures after watching the video featuring thin women (see Table 8.7).

Questioning the Research 8.3

The Heinberg and Thompson (1995) study seems to indicate that exposure to media images of very thin women can lead women to increase in body dissatisfaction. However, what are some weaknesses of this study that may limit the conclusions we can draw?

Sadly, even girls as young as 3 to 5 show signs of adopting the thin ideal (Harriger, Calgero, Witherington, & Smith, 2010). Researchers in one study asked preschool girls to select which of three body figures (one thin, one average, one fat) they would most like for their best friend. Seventy-one percent of the girls chose the thin figure, and only 7.3% chose the fat figure. Then, researchers asked the girls to play a game of Candy Land or Chutes and Ladders and to choose which of the body figures they would like to be for the game. Once again, 69% chose the thin piece, and only 11% chose the fat piece. This research suggests that this preference for the thinness norm emerges very early in life.

TABLE 8.7   *Test Yourself: Sociocultural Attitudes Toward Appearance Questionnaire*

Please read each of the following items and give the number that best reflects your agreement with the statement (1 = completely disagree, 3 = neither agree nor disagree, 5 = completely agree).

1. I tend to compare my body to TV stars' and movie stars' bodies.
2. I would like my body to look like the women/men who appear in TV shows and movies.
3. It's important for people to look attractive if they want to succeed in today's culture.
4. I often find myself comparing my physique to that of athletes pictured in magazines.
5. Music videos that show women who are in good shape make me wish that I were in better physical shape.
6. People with well-proportioned bodies look better in clothes.
7. Photographs of physically fit women/men make me wish that I had better muscle tone.
8. People find individuals who are in shape more attractive than individuals who are not in shape.
9. Attractiveness is very important if you want to get ahead in our culture.
10. I wish I looked like the women/men pictured in magazines who model underwear.

Women who compare themselves to media images of women are at increased risk of experiencing eating disorders.

Source: Cusumano & Thompson, 1997.

Given the prevalence of the thinness norm, and its clear association with femininity and attractiveness, women often believe that they must be thin to appeal to potential dating partners. In fact, both men and women rate thin women as more feminine and attractive than normal-weight or overweight women (Silverstein et al., 1986), and being thinner is often associated with greater success in dating (Paxton et al., 1991). For example, although the average high school girl is 5'3" and 126 pounds, girls of this height who weigh 110 pounds are twice as likely to be dating, and girls who weigh 140 pounds are only half as likely to be dating (Halpern et al., 1999). In turn, women often eat less in front of desirable dating partners than in front of undesirable partners, in an attempt to appear attractive (Mori, Chaiken, & Pliner, 1987). (Guys, if your date always eats well, you might need to get some better hobbies.)

Thinness in women is not only associated with greater success in dating but also in terms of general popularity with both men and women. One study with high school juniors and seniors revealed that thinner women and "average" men (not too thin, not too heavy) were seen as more popular by their peers (Wang, Houshyar, & Prinstein, 2006). Similarly, research by Crandall (1988) of women who lived in a sorority found that those who engaged in more frequent bulimic behavior were more popular than those who engaged in such behavior less frequently, presumably because engaging in this behavior indicates at least a desire to conform to the thinness norm.

Sadly, this societal focus on thinness in women can also have negative consequences on academic performance. Researchers in one study asked both men and women to participate in a study on "emotions and consumer behavior" and were asked to try on either a swimsuit or a sweater and then rate how that item made them feel (Frederickson, Roberts, Noll, Quinn, & Twenge, 1998). They were then asked to complete a brief SAT-type math test, which was supposedly part of a separate experiment given by a researcher in the education department. Although there was no difference in math scores for men, regardless of whether they had tried on the sweater or the swimsuit, women who tried on the bathing suit scored lower on the math test than those who tried a sweater. Apparently, women who wore a swimsuit felt shame about their bodies—presumably caused by societal pressures toward thinness in women—and this distraction lead them to perform more poorly on the math test. Similarly, women who exercise in front of a mirror feel worse after exercising than those who exercise without a mirror, perhaps because the presence of mirrors makes women more conscious of their concerns about their bodies (Ginis, Jung, & Gauvin, 2003).

Although most research on social pressures leading to body image dissatisfaction has focused on the prevailing thin ideal for women, some research suggests that men are also increasingly feeling pressure to conform to a similarly unrealistic body image norm (Pope, Olivardia, Gruber, & Borowiecki, 1999). However, the male ideal focuses on achieving a muscular ideal. To test the evolution of the "muscular male ideal" over time, researchers examined the measurements of the GI Joe action toy (the action toy with the longest continuous history) produced in 1973, 1975, and 1994. This review revealed a disturbing trend: The GI Joe action figure became much more muscular over time. For example, although there was no change in the height of the action figure, the biceps increased from 2.1 inches (1973) to 2.5 inches (1975) to 2.7 inches (1994). These may seem like small differences, but when translated into measurements for adult male bodies, bicep size would have increased from 12.2 inches to 16.4 inches. The latest GI Joe (the GI Joe Extreme, introduced in 1998) has biceps that translate to 26.8 inches—larger than any bodybuilder in history.

Finally, although the cultural norms in most Western societies seem to support a very thin ideal for women, these norms are not as extreme as people think. In fact, college women's ideal figure is significantly smaller than their current figure (Fallon & Rozin, 1985). In contrast, the gap between men's current and ideal figure is quite small! Women also typically believe men prefer a female figure that is thinner than men actually do. Similarly, my own research has shown that women believe other women are more supportive of the thinness norm than these women actually are (Sanderson, Darley, & Messinger, 2002). For example, women have an average BMI of 22 but believe other women have a BMI of about 20.5, and women exercise about 4 hours a week but believe other women exercise about 5.5 hours a week. Sadly, however, women who feel discrepant from the campus thinness norm—even if such a perception is inaccurate—have a greater frequency of symptoms of eating disorders, such as an extreme focus on thinness, binge eating, and purging.

Family Dynamics

Parents can influence their children's eating behaviors. First, families of women with eating disorders may also be particularly focused on weight and shape. In fact, girls who believe it is important to their parents that they are thin are more likely to be concerned about their weight and to diet than those who do not believe their parents have such preferences (Field et al., 2001). Women whose mothers are preoccupied with weight and dieting behaviors and who criticize their daughters' appearance also report more weight-loss behaviors themselves (Baker, Whisman, & Brownell, 2000; Sanftner, Crowther, Crawford, & Watts, 1996). For example, one study with 89 pairs of mothers and their teenage daughters found that girls who use extreme weight-loss methods (e.g., fasting, crash dieting, skipping meals) are very likely to have mothers who also use such methods (Benedikt, Wertheim, & Love, 1998). Although they may not be directly encouraging their daughters to engage in such behaviors, these mothers are still modeling these attitudes and behaviors. Also, while only 14% of the girls in this sample were overweight, 51% of the mothers reported that they encouraged their daughters to lose weight and 39% of the mothers wanted their daughters to be thinner. Mothers who are preoccupied with their own weight are more likely to restrict what their daughters eat and encourage them to lose weight, which in turn leads, over time, to daughters' restrained eating (Francis & Birch, 2005).

On the other hand, families who regularly have meals together tend to have children with lower rates of disordered eating behavior. Researchers in one study collected data from 4,746 adolescents to examine the association between family meal patterns and rates of disordered eating (Neumark-Sztainer, Wall, Story, & Fulkerson, 2004). Adolescents who reported more frequent family meals (as well as making eating as a family a priority, having a positive atmosphere at family meals, and having a more structured family meal environment) were less likely to engage in extreme unhealthy weight control behaviors. For example, 18.1% of girls who reported eating only one or two meals as a family engaged in extreme weight-control behaviors, such as vomiting, taking diet pills, and using laxatives/diuretics, compared to 8.8% of girls who reported eating three or four meals a week as a family. In fact, making family meals a priority, even given difficulties in scheduling, was the strongest predictor of rates of disordered eating behavior. The association between more frequent family meals and rates of disordered eating behaviors was stronger for girls than for boys.

The families of anorexics often have some distinct, potentially dysfunctional, dynamics (Kog & Vandereycken, 1985). They may appear normal, and even high achieving, from the outside, but family members have problems with engaging in open communication and managing conflict. Parents also tend to be overinvolved in their daughters' lives, and may be demanding and controlling—they often do not encourage autonomy or assertiveness in their children. One study of anorexic patients found that they typically describe their parents as setting extremely high achievement standards and as often disapproving (Waller & Hartley, 1994). Similarly, at the beginning of the chapter, you read about Annie's struggle with anorexia and the pressure for high academic achievement she felt from her parents.

The families of bulimics also often show particular characteristics, including more conflict and hostility coupled with less nurturance and support within the family group (Wonderlich, Klein, & Council, 1996). Women with bulimia may binge and purge to cope with feelings of isolation and stress, in part because they are unlikely to have supportive interpersonal relationships in their families. In one study of 21 bulimic women and 21 women without symptoms of disordered eating, participants completed measures of social interactions and social support and were then videotaped while engaging in a conflict-resolution task with a partner for 5 minutes (Grissett & Norvell, 1992). Findings revealed that bulimics felt less socially competent in a variety of ways, including in their ability to form close relationships and function well socially. They were also rated by observers as less socially effective, including worse at problem solving, less likely to be a good friend, and less skilled in social interaction.

Questioning the Research 8.4

Although several studies suggest that families with certain types of unhealthy interaction patterns (e.g., lack of support) can cause girls to develop bulimia, can you think of an alternative explanation for these findings? (Hint: Think about the difference between correlation and causation.)

Personality

Anorexics often have a distinct personality style—they are rigid, anxious, perfectionistic, and obsessed with order and cleanliness (Kaye, 1997). In fact, anorexics have high rates of diagnosis with obsessive-compulsive disorder. Anorexics hold themselves to particularly high standards; hence, they may seem like "the perfect child" to outside observers (Tiller, Schmidt, Ali, & Treasure, 1995). Often they have assimilated a very thin ideal. In one study, anorexics and normal-weight women were asked to judge the weight at which their own bodies and other women's bodies would change from "thin" to "normal" to "fat" (Smeets, 1999). Compared to women of normal weight, anorexics gave lighter weights for each of the transition points, indicating that they were setting particularly strict standards for attractiveness. These personality characteristics may not be simply a result of their current eating disorder, and hence a reflection of malnutrition, because recovered anorexics who are of normal weight show similar traits.

Women who have bulimia have quite a different set of personality characteristics than those who develop anorexia. Bulimics are often depressed and anxious, leading some researchers to believe that they use food as a way of comforting themselves. Bulimics have often struggled with weight issues for some time and may have a history of binge eating, weight fluctuation, and frequent exercise or dieting (Kendler et al., 1991). Bulimics may lack a clear sense of self-identity or have very negative self-views (Humphrey, 1986, 1988). While anorexia involves extreme levels of control, bulimics typically report feeling out of control while they are binge eating, resulting in guilt and self-contempt following such episodes. Two studies suggest that 20 to 33% of bulimics who are in treatment have made at least one serious suicide attempt (Garfinkel & Garner, 1984). Women with bulimia report higher levels of other types of destructive behaviors, including alcohol use, substance abuse, and kleptomania (compulsive stealing), than women without an eating disorder (Holderness, Brooks-Gunn, & Warren, 1994). Bulimics are also more likely to have experienced sexual abuse during childhood (Wonderlich, Wilsnack, Wilsnack, & Harris, 1996).

What Approaches Help Prevent Eating Disorders?

Because eating disorders are so prevalent and so problematic, some high schools and most colleges and universities have programs designed to prevent such problems by giving students knowledge about the hazards of disordered eating in the hopes that having such information will help prevent serious disorders. Unfortunately, research on the effectiveness of such programs has yielded somewhat mixed findings. For example, in one study by Killen et al., 967 sixth- and seventh-grade girls were randomly assigned to receive either 18 hour-long lessons on eating disorders or their regular health class (1993). The lessons included information on normal growth and development, the dangers of unhealthy dieting strategies, the influence of media images, and strategies for healthy eating and exercise. Although girls who received this intense information did have higher scores on knowledge of eating behavior than those without this program, they did not show changes in their concern about weight. Other research even points to the potential of disordered eating prevention efforts leading to unintended negative consequences. A study by Mann et al. (1997) evaluated the effectiveness of an eating disorder prevention program that was presented to 788 first-year women attending Stanford University. Contrary to expectations, women who attended this program actually had more symptoms of disordered eating 1 month after than those who did not attend the program, perhaps because the programs inadvertently taught participants strategies for engaging in unhealthy methods of weight loss. This research suggests that eating disorder prevention programs must be very careful to avoid causing unintended harm to participants.

Fortunately, some research reveals that programs focusing on healthy eating, exercise, and body image can be helpful in reducing overeating and obesity. Researchers in one study randomly assigned adolescent girls to participate in a healthy weight maintenance group or a control condition in which participants simply completed questionnaires (Stice, Presnell, Goesz, & Shaw, 2005). The healthy weight group met for three 1-hour weekly sessions, and focused on how to develop a balanced diet and engage in regular exercise and healthy eating. Findings at the 12-month follow-up revealed that the healthy weight intervention led to great decreases in bulimic symptoms compared to the control condition. In addition, and as shown in Figure 8.6, girls in the control condition were more likely than girls in the healthy weight condition to become obese over time: At the 1-year-follow-up, only 1.2% of girls in the healthy weight condition had become obese compared to 11.4% of girls in the control condition. These findings suggest participation in a healthy weight group protects girls from the increases in weight seen in those in the control condition. Encouragingly, the benefits of such an intervention can be realized using entirely computer-based approaches. Researchers in one study randomly assigned first-year college women to either a control group or a CD prevention program called Food, Food, and Attitude (Franko et al., 2005). This interactive CD presents information related to body image and healthy eating, including information on the thin ideal in the media, emotional eating, and the "freshman 15." Findings at a 3-month follow-up revealed that women

FIGURE 8.6 Although girls in the control condition show an increase in the risk of developing obesity over time, girls in the healthy weight condition show no such change in weight (data from Stice et al., 2005).

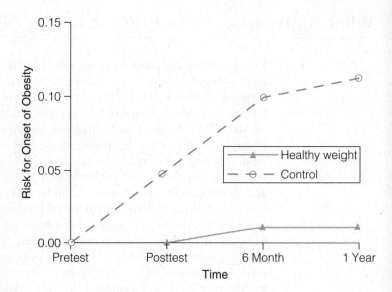

in the intervention showed improvements on all measures, including overeating and excessive exercise. Encouragingly, this type of computer-based intervention is particularly effective in terms of reducing the risk of developing eating disorders for women at high risk for developing such a disorder (Taylor, Welch, Kim, & Sherman, 2007).

Research also demonstrates that programs which help participants critique the thin ideal can help prevent eating disorders (Becker, Bull, Schaumberg, Cauble, & Franco, 2008; Stice, Chase, Stormer, & Appel, 2001; Stice, Mazotti, Weibel, & Agras, 2000; Stice, Shaw, Burton, & Wade, 2006). In one study, 148 adolescent

Intervention programs that help participants understand, and critique, the false images of thin women in the media can help reduce body dissatisfaction as well as symptoms of disordered eating. This photo shows the same woman in a natural look (on the left) and a made-up look (on the right) to illustrate the role of make-up and clothes in influencing appearance.
Source: Thomas Barwick/Getty Images, Inc.

Box 8.4

Focus on Research: The Benefits of Critiquing the Thin Ideal

To examine the effectiveness of critiquing the thin ideal on reducing disordered eating, researchers in this study randomly assigned 300 high school girls to one of two interventions (Stice, Rohde, Gau, & Shaw, 2009). The dissonance intervention, which included four separate 1 hour weekly group sessions, focused on examining the costs of the thin ideal. Participants discussed the nature, origins, and continuation of the thin ideal, wrote a letter to a hypothetical younger girl discussing the costs of this ideal, focused on positive thoughts about their own bodies, and developed strategies for coping with and countering this ideal. Participants in the control condition received an educational brochure about negative and positive body image from the National Eating Disorders Association. Researchers then examined the impact of each condition over the next year. As predicted, findings indicated that girls in the dissonance intervention reported greater decreases in idealization of the thinness norm, body dissatisfaction, dieting, and eating disorders symptoms. Moreover, 42% of those in the dissonance intervention reported clinically significant reductions in symptoms of disordered eating a year later, compared to only 24% of those in the brochure condition. This research provides strong evidence that programs which help girls critique the thin ideal may reduce rates of disordered eating.

girls (ages 13 to 20) were recruited from local high schools and universities to participate in a study on helping women improve their body image (Stice et al., 2002). Participants were then randomly assigned to a dissonance intervention group, a healthy weight control intervention group, or a waitlist control condition. Those in the dissonance group were asked to discuss how to help other women avoid body image problems. The women discussed (as a group) the nature of the thin ideal portrayed in the media, the perpetuation of this image, and the consequences of this image. They also role-played trying to convince someone not to adopt the thin ideal and wrote an essay about the costs associated with the pursuit of the thin ideal. Findings at the 3-month follow-up indicated that women who received either the dissonance-based intervention or the healthy weight control intervention reported fewer bulimic symptoms than those in the waitlist control condition. Moreover, providing strategies for improving body image and reducing excessive concern with weight using the Internet can be effective in decreasing women's extreme focus on thinness (Winzelberg et al., 2000). One study with college students found that an 8-week entirely Internet-based intervention focused on improving body satisfaction and reducing weight concerns led to increases in body image and decreases in symptoms of disordered eating. Box 8.4: Focus on Research describes the effectiveness of critiquing the thinness norm on preventing disordered eating in high school girls. Designing interventions to prevent eating disorders is discussed further in Chapter 13.

What Approaches Help Treat Eating Disorders?

Although eating disorders are obviously associated with serious health consequences, people with such disorders are often very reluctant to seek treatment (Pike & Striegel-Moore, 1997). They may feel ashamed and embarrassed to admit their behavior and may believe that the disorder will simply go away on its own at some point. While bulimics often feel out of control, depressed, and guilty about their eating habits, and hence are motivated to get better, anorexics typically feel in control and even proud of their highly restricted eating habits, and hence often resist treatment. People with anorexia may also be afraid that seeking treatment will lead them to gain weight. And in some cases, this is true—because people with anorexia often seek help (or, more often, are forced to seek help) only when they are on the verge of collapsing from starvation, tube or intravenous feeding may be used (in a hospital setting) to try to get their body weight and nutrition under control (Goldner & Birmingham, 1994). Box 8.5: Health Psychology in the Real World describes one mother's attempt to honor the memory of her daughter, who died from bulimia when she was only 19 years old, by increasing awareness of the prevalence and hazards of eating disorders.

Box 8.5

Health Psychology in the Real World: The Very Real Hazards of Disordered Eating

By Judy Avrin, January 3, 2012

"I was fourteen years old the first time I made myself throw up. If I had known that it was rapidly going to become my addiction, I would have never done it." Those are the opening lines of my daughter Melissa's college application essay. They are also the words her father read in his eulogy at Melissa's funeral when she died from a heart attack at the age of 19 following a 5 year battle with bulimia and depression.

Melissa's life was filled with great promise but she began struggling with body image issues at the age of 13. It was easy to miss the early signs of an eating disorder, in part because they are often difficult to distinguish from behaviors easily attributed to adolescence, but also because eating disorders are secretive by their very nature. They become a coping mechanism and anyone suffering from one goes to great extremes to hide the behaviors. Doctors and pediatricians often overlook the signs as well. Bulimia in particular can often take longer to detect since it does not have the extreme weight loss that is associated with anorexia. Often someone with bulimia will be within normal weight ranges as was the case with Melissa.

One of the biggest issues parents confront is the power of parental denial. Eating disorders are considered shameful, parents don't want to admit their child might have one and early symptoms are easily ignored or explained away. It was so easy to attribute the little bit of weight Melissa had lost to healthier eating and increased exercise.

Over the next 18 months as her stomach problems continued and her depression deepened, I took her to a number of doctors. I still didn't understand or fully acknowledge many of the signs of her eating disorder: food disappearing, long periods of time spent in the bathroom, her inability to make it through a school day, and pulling away from friendships. Finally, just weeks before her 16th birthday, she began treatment for bulimia at a top eating disorders program and thus began years of in- and out-patient treatment. However, critical time had been lost. What we came to learn was that the longer eating disorder behaviors continue, the more entrenched those behaviors become.

Melissa was a gifted writer and from a young age she filled notebooks with short stories, poems, song lyrics and screenplays. She dreamed of becoming a filmmaker and often made movies with her friends. That creativity continued to shine through even as depression and bulimia overwhelmed her. It was hard for her to express her feelings verbally so she used filmmaking, writing, drawing and acting as means of self-expression for the rest of her life. Ultimately, although she dreamed of a future, her body gave out before she could beat ED.

Several months after Melissa died, I finally got up the courage to read the journal she always left lying around. Afterwards I thought about sticking it in a drawer and trying to forget what she'd written, but along with words of sadness and pain, there were powerful messages of hope. I quickly realized that if the words she'd written could help someone else battling an eating disorder, I needed to figure out a way to share them. I met with a therapist I had stayed in touch with from the early years of her illness, and inspired by her journal writings and her poem "Someday..." we created a documentary, "Someday Melissa, the story of an eating disorder, loss and hope" (for more information, see www.somedaymelissa.com).

Melissa's story has traveled the globe, spurred by the power of social media, and has become an inspiration to people battling eating disorders around the world. Her story, and my ability to tell it, is helping to break through the wall of secrecy and shame surrounding eating disorders, bulimia in particular. Colleges and treatment centers are holding screenings of the film to help raise awareness. Therapists are using the film as a treatment tool with patients and their families. I continue to receive hundreds of messages but the greatest gift is when someone writes to tell me that Melissa has inspired them to fight harder for their recovery, to believe in a future, to dream of their own "Someday".

A few approaches can help in treating eating disorders. First, because family interaction patterns are thought to influence the development of disordered eating, many therapists recommend some combination of individual and family therapy in treating eating disorders, especially for anorexia (Becker et al., 1999). Anorexics need help changing their social environment and, in particular, must understand that other people do not hold themselves up to the same high standards, which is why family therapy can be helpful (Garner, Garfinkel, & Bemis, 1982). One study of patients hospitalized for anorexia showed that family therapy was more effective than individual therapy in increasing weight gain as long as 5 years later (Dare & Eisler, 1995).

Researchers in one study compared family-based treatment for adolescents with bulimia to supportive psychotherapy (Le Grange, Crosby, Rathouz, & Leventhal, 2007). Family-based therapy focuses on giving parents power to stop unhealthy binging and purging behavior, to see the disorder as separate from their child, and address how bulimia effects their child's development. Supportive psychotherapy, in contrast, focuses on helping the adolescent resolve underlying problems that may contribute to the eating disorder, and to think about how these problems affect them and what they could do about them in the future. Participants in each condition received 20 therapy sessions over 6 months of treatment. At the end of treatment, 39% of those in family therapy had stopped engaging in disordered eating behaviors, compared to only 18% of those receiving supportive therapy. These effects were generally maintained as long as 6 months after treatment, with 29% of those receiving family-based therapy showing a reduction in symptoms of bulimia compared to only 10% of those receiving supportive therapy. These findings suggest that family-based therapy may be particularly beneficial for adolescents with bulimia.

Cognitive-behavioral therapy (CBT) is another type of therapy that can be effective in treating both anorexia and bulimia (Walsh & Devlin, 1998). This type of therapy focuses on normalizing patients' eating patterns (by encouraging slow eating, regular meals), expanding their food choices (by eliminating "forbidden" foods), and changing their thoughts and attitudes about eating, food, and their bodies (by trying to avoid linking self-esteem with weight). Techniques can include monitoring the thoughts, feelings, and circumstances that lead to binge eating and purging and clarifying distorted views of eating, weight, and body shape. For example, therapists may use CBT to attempt to change faulty beliefs, such as "If I gain one pound, I'll gain a hundred," and "Any sweet is instantly converted into fat." They teach patients that media images of women are often illusions (e.g., models often have their body flaws airbrushed away) as a way of helping them develop more realistic body ideals. CBT for bulimia is especially effective when coupled with antidepressant drugs, such as Prozac. As described at the beginning of the chapter, Rachel was able to stop bingeing after working with her therapist to identify the triggers of overeating and after taking Prozac.

One study by Garner, Olmstead, and Polivy (1993) compared the effectiveness on bulimia of two types of therapy. Sixty bulimic women, ages 18 to 35 years, were randomly assigned to receive either CBT or supportive-expressive therapy over 18 weeks, with one 45- to 60-minute session each week. The CBT consisted of self-monitoring of food intake, vomiting, and binge eating, as well as monitoring feelings and thoughts surrounding eating. Supportive-expressive therapy, which views eating disorders as a symptom of larger problems, had therapists listen to and help subjects identify feelings. Both treatments were equally effective in decreasing the frequency of binge eating, but CBT was somewhat better in decreasing the frequency of vomiting (82% reduction versus 64% reduction). Although women in both groups gained some weight, those in the CBT group gained more weight (6.6 pounds versus 3.0 pounds, respectively). Finally, patients who received the CBT also had lower rates of depression, higher rates of self-esteem, and greater satisfaction with their therapy than those in the supportive-expressive therapy.

Interpersonal therapy, which focuses on the interpersonal sources of stress that lead to disordered eating, can also be effective (Agras, 1993). This type of therapy can help disordered eaters identify interpersonal problems that cause stress, such as an obsession with perfectionism (anorexics) and negative self-image (bulimics).

Although some people with eating disorders do get better, there is a relatively high rate of relapse. About half of those with anorexia or bulimia have a full recovery,

TABLE 8.8 *Information YOU Can Use*

- Pay attention to internal cues for eating—such as how hungry you are—and try to avoid relying on external factors, such as the appearance, smell, or taste of food; the size of the dishes you are using; or the presence of other people eating with you.
- If you want to lose weight, develop short-term goals for changing what you eat and increasing physical activity—and make sure to monitor your progress and reward yourself for small successes.
- Make sure to model healthy eating and exercise behavior for your children. Children form their initial attitudes toward eating and exercise from watching their parents, and these early attitudes and habits have a lasting influence.
- Don't be fooled by the very thin images of women in the media—most women are much heavier than the models and actresses portrayed in magazines, television, and movies. Also, many of the images of women seen in the media are altered in some way, so that even these photos aren't portraying accurate information about women's body shape and size.
- Eating disorders can have very serious short- and long-term consequences, yet many people who suffer from such disorders don't get help. If you, or someone you know, has an eating disorder, talk to someone you know—a parent, a professor, a counselor—to get advice on how to seek help.

about 30% have a partial recovery, and about 20% have no real improvement (Becker et al., 1999). Many anorexics continue to be underweight and may require repeat hospitalizations. Similarly, about one third of bulimics who have fully recovered experience a relapse within 2 years (Olmsted, Kaplan & Rockert, 1994). These depressing statistics suggest that recovery from eating disorders is best viewed as a process; patients and their families should not expect instant results.

Summary

1. Obesity, which is typically measured by calculating a person's body-mass index (BMI), affects a substantial number of Americans. Rates of obesity have also increased over the last 30 years.

2. Obesity is associated with a number of negative physical consequences, including increased risk of hypertension, kidney and gall bladder disease, diabetes, cardiovascular disease, and some types of cancer. Obese people may also suffer from social and psychological consequences.

3. Genetic factors play a role in obesity. Although the exact mechanisms by which genetic factors influence obesity are unclear, genes may influence how much and what types of food people prefer as well as metabolism rates.

4. Psychological factors also influence eating and overeating. Theories which explain the role of psychological factors in eating (and obesity) include the internal-external hypothesis, mood regulation theory, restraint theory, and sociocultural factors.

5. Preventing obesity should ideally begin in childhood. Strategies for preventing obesity include breast-feeding, encouraging children to exercise and eat healthy foods, and limiting television watching.

6. Obesity can be treated using a variety of different methods to reduce eating and/or increase exercise. These methods include setting short-term goals, providing rewards for meeting goals, monitoring eating, making small changes in behavior

(especially when such changes can easily fit in with one's daily habits), providing social support for such changes, and implementing large-scale interventions. In severe cases, surgical techniques can be used to treat obesity.

7. Eating disorders, including anorexia nervosa, bulimia nervosa, and binge eating disorder can lead to serious, and even life-threatening, problems.

8. Biological factors, including genetic factors and impairments in brain chemistry, may influence the development of an eating disorder.

9. Psychological factors clearly contribute to the development of eating disorders. These factors include sociocultural norms, family dynamics, and personality.

10. Eating disorders can be prevented through programs focusing on healthy eating, exercise, and body image. Programs which help participants critique the thin ideal may be especially useful.

11. Treatment for eating disorders may include some combination of individual and family therapy. Family-based therapy and cognitive-behavioral therapy are particularly effective approaches for treating eating disorders, although there is still a relatively high rate of relapse.

Key Terms

anorexia nervosa
binge eating disorder
bulimia nervosa

internal-external hypothesis
mood regulation

obesity
restraint theory

Thought Questions

1. Describe how psychological factors can influence both overeating (i.e., obesity) and undereating (i.e., anorexia).

2. Describe one physiological explanation and one psychological explanation for obesity.

3. Your roommate Jean is obese and is constantly trying, but failing, to lose weight. What two pieces of advice could you give him?

4. Describe how social, cultural, and personality factors can influence the acquisition of eating disorders.

5. Your friend Beth is a resident assistant in a dormitory of first-year students, and she thinks it would be a good idea to provide some type of eating disorder prevention program to her students. Because she knows you are in a health psychology course, she comes to you for advice on creating such a program. What would you tell her?

Answers to Questioning the Research

Answer 8.1. One possibility is that women's preference for eating when stressed—or preference for eating particular types of foods when stressed—is based on social learning. Perhaps women learn that restraining themselves from eating is normative, or expected, and thus when stressed, their typical restraint around food goes away. In contrast, men may have less of a tendency to restrain themselves from eating, so eating isn't a way to manage stress. Another possibility is that there are physiological differences in terms of what feels good to men and women from eating in general and/or from eating particular types of foods. Perhaps women do experience stronger cravings for chocolate, which result in changes in particular chemicals in the body, than do men (Yanovski, 2003).

Answer 8.2. Although one possible explanation for the link between breast-feeding and lower rates of obesity is parents' monitoring of how much babies consume—and thus less sensitivity to baby's own preference for breast-feeding mothers—other factors influence the relationship between breast-feeding and obesity. For example, mothers with a higher income and more education are more likely to breast-feed and are more likely to encourage their children to eat healthily. Also, overweight mothers are less likely to breast-feed than thin mothers, which suggests the association between breast-feeding and obesity could be due at least in part to genetic factors.

Answer 8.3. First, although this study suggests that exposure to media images of very thin women led some participants to increase in body dissatisfaction, remember that watching this video did not lead to greater dissatisfaction for all (or even most) women. Instead, only women who already had negative feelings about their bodies showed an increase in such feelings. This study therefore may indicate that women without such concerns are not really influenced by this type of exposure. Second, this study assessed women's body dissatisfaction only immediately after they viewed the tape; we cannot conclude whether seeing this video has any long-term effects.

Answer 8.4. Although this section describes the distinct features of the families of anorexics and bulimics, it is important to remember that these studies are correlational, not causational. Some of the patterning observed in these families may be a result—not a cause—of having a child with a chronic and even life-threatening illness. For example, perhaps having a daughter who is eating huge amounts of food and then vomiting or engaging in excessive exercise is very upsetting to parents, and they then distance themselves from their daughter as a way of coping with their feelings. Although this may not be a constructive approach, it may simply be too painful for them to remain close to their daughter while she is engaging in such destructive behavior. We must be very careful about how we interpret the results of correlational studies.

The Experience and Management of Pain

Outline

- Billy is 7 years old and always seems to be sick. Sometimes he says his stomach hurts, sometimes he says his leg hurts, and sometimes he says his throat hurts. His mother becomes very concerned whenever Billy is sick and must miss school. She usually stays home from work with him, lets him watch videos, and prepares his favorite foods for him.

- Antonia is 25 years old and has always been very healthy. However, for the past 6 months, she has experienced severe migraine headaches once or twice a week. Sometimes these headaches are so bad that she can't drive to work, and she is concerned that she will lose her job. Antonia doesn't know what causes her headaches, but finds that they are often worse after she's stayed up late taking care of her 3-month-old son or when she is feeling overwhelmed with her responsibilities at work.

- Melissa has just given birth to her first baby, a little boy named Matt. Although she had heard horror stories from several friends about the pain of labor, Melissa found it not so bad. She and her husband attended childbirth preparation classes, in which they learned to engage in special types of breathing. They also chose an ultrasound picture of their baby as a "focal object" on which Melissa concentrated during the most painful contractions.

- Tom has suffered from back pain for more than 10 years. He has tried many different approaches to treating his pain, including drugs, massage therapy, and even surgery. Although some of these treatments were effective for a few weeks or months, the pain always returned. However, his physician recently recommended he enter a pain clinic, in which Tom will receive training in relaxation, guided imagery, and hypnosis. His wife has also been asked to attend several sessions with other patients' family members to learn how to support Tom's therapy, in particular to understand that they must reinforce pain-free behavior while ignoring pain-related behavior.

- Brian has had problems with his knees for nearly 20 years. His doctor recently recommended a new type of drug, one he claims is the best drug he's seen developed for joint pain in some time from a company that makes many other well-performing drugs. Brian's doctor therefore strongly urged Brian to sample this new medicine. Although Brian has been taking the drug for only 3 weeks, he already feels less pain when he walks. He is thrilled with the new drug.

Preview

This chapter examines how psychological factors can influence the experience and management of pain. First, the chapter describes different types of pain as well as different theories about how people experience pain. Then we examine different ways of measuring pain, including self-report, behavioral, and physiological methods. Next, we examine how various psychological factors, such as stress, learning, cognition, and personality, can influence the experience of pain. We then review physical methods of controlling pain, including drugs, surgery, and physical stimulation, as well as psychological methods of controlling pain, such as hypnosis, relaxation, cognitive approaches, and behavior therapy. Finally, we examine the role of placebos in reducing pain.

Why Do We Care About Pain?

Pain affects more Americans than diabetes, heart disease, and cancer combined, with an estimated 76.5 million people (26% of all Americans 20 and older) experiencing chronic pain that persists for more than 24 hours in the last month (National Center for Health Statistics, 2006). More than 25% of adults report experiencing lower-back pain in the past 3 months, and 15% of adults report experiencing migraine or severe headaches in the past 3 months. Also, 46 million Americans have some form of arthritis or fibromyalgia.

However, demographic factors influence the experience of pain. Pain is more common in adults age 45 to 64 than those older or younger, is more common in Whites than in Blacks or Hispanics, and is more common in families with lower income than in those with higher income. Pain—or at least the expression of pain—is more common in women than men.

Pain imposes serious costs on both individuals and society. Approximately 8.1% of people experience severe pain that disrupts their ability to function, with headaches being the most frequent type of pain experienced (Fröhlich, Jacobi, & Wittchen, 2006). Moreover, people with pain disorder have a poorer quality of life, greater disability, and higher health-care utilization rates. Chronic lower-back pain is the leading cause of disability in Americans under 45 years old, is the second most frequent cause of visits to doctors' offices (after the common cold), causes 12% of all sick leave, and costs $16 billion a year in direct medical costs (for surgery, disability, physician/hospital visits; Arena & Blanchard, 1996; National Center for Health Statistics, 2006). Similarly, migraine headaches cost $6.5 billion to $17.2 billion annually in lost labor costs when 8.3% of those who suffer from such headaches miss work and 43.6% report reduced effectiveness at work (Holroyd & Lipchik, 1999; Schwartz, Stewart, Simon, & Lipton, 1998). In fact, the annual cost of chronic pain, including health-care expenses, lost income, and lost productivity, is $560 to $635 billion a year (Committee on Advancing Pain Research, Care, and Education, 20011). In sum, pain is a common problem for many people and has major consequences.

Although no one likes to experience pain, feeling pain is actually beneficial to long-term health and survival (Vertosick, 2000). Pain is a warning signal that your body is experiencing a problem, and it thereby motivates you to change your behavior. For example, if you touch a hot stove and burn your finger, you learn to not touch the stove again. Similarly, if you hurt your ankle, you will try to avoid putting weight on that foot, and thereby prevent further damage. People who are born with insensitivity to pain, and who therefore experience little or no sensation of pain, often suffer numerous health problems and die at a relatively young age (Manfredi et al., 1981). Because they don't experience pain, they do not have the opportunity to learn from small mistakes (e.g., they never learn that falling on pavement leads to abrasions and cuts and the potential development of infection), and hence they may suffer from constant bumps, bruises, and cuts. Their inability to feel pain also means they don't seek medical care when they should, so relatively small problems can become much larger ones (e.g., they don't see a doctor when they experience severe stomach pains, and therefore could develop a ruptured appendix). Although at times you may wish you'd never experience pain, as you can see, *not* feeling pain can have many negative consequences.

What Is Pain?

Although we all know what pain is, it can actually refer to many different sensations—a sharp pain when we step on a sliver of glass, the dull ache of a tension headache, the blistering of a sunburn, even the small but very irritating pain of a paper cut. The International Association for the Study of Pain (IASP) defines *pain* as "an unpleasant sensory and emotional experience associated with actual or potential tissue damage, or described in terms of such damage" (International Association for the Study of Pain, 1979).

Acute pain is intense but time-limited pain that is generally the result of tissue damage or disease, such as a broken bone, a cut or bruise, and the labor of childbirth (Turk, Meichenbaum, & Genest, 1983). This type of pain typically disappears over time (as the injury heals) and lasts less than 6 months. Because acute pain is intense, people suffering from it are highly motivated to seek out its causes and to treat it. Many of the pain-control techniques that we discuss later in this chapter are very effective at treating acute pain.

In contrast, **chronic pain** often begins as acute pain (in response to a specific injury or disease) but does not go away after a minimum of 6 months (Turk et al., 1983). Lower-back pain, headaches, and the pain associated with arthritis and cancer are all examples of chronic pain. Chronic pain can be divided into several different subcategories. *Recurrent acute pain* is caused by a benign, or harmless, condition and refers to pain that is sometimes intense but that also sometimes disappears. Migraine headaches are one example of this type of pain. *Intractable-benign pain* is, as its name suggests, benign but persistent. Although it may vary in intensity, it never really disappears. Lower-back pain is a particularly common type of intractable-benign pain. Finally, *progressive pain* is pain that originates from a malignant condition; hence, it is continuous and worsens over time. The pain caused by arthritis or cancer, for example, is a type of progressive pain.

Medical care professionals distinguish between acute and chronic pain because these different types of pain often have different causes and need to be treated in different ways. Acute pain generally is caused by physical damage to the body, which then improves with time as body tissues, bones, and muscles heal. In contrast, most types of chronic pain are caused at least in part by behavioral factors (although this is not necessarily true, especially for progressive pain), and this type of pain lasts long after specific tissue damage has healed. This does not mean that chronic pain is "all in your head," but rather that psychological factors may contribute in some way to physical pain. Because chronic pain is extremely resistant to treatment, it lingers for some time, leading to a number of negative consequences (Melzack & Wall, 1982). People in constant pain may feel depressed and helpless, have difficulty sleeping, and experience weight loss or weight gain. Many people with chronic pain lose their jobs, lose friends, and have dysfunctional relationships with family because they require or request constant assistance and attention and/or push people away completely.

How Do We Experience Pain?

One of the earliest theories of pain was the **specificity theory** (Melzack & Wall, 1982), which posits that there are specific sensory receptors for different types of sensations, such as pain, warmth, touch, and pressure. The classic description of this theory was presented by René Descartes in 1664, which compared the experience of pain to a bell-ringing mechanism in a church—a person on the ground floor of the church pulls a rope, and this tug of the rope travels up to the bell in the belfry at the top of the tower, causing the bell to ring. Similarly, according to specificity theory, after a person experiences an injury, a direct chain carries these messages of pain to the brain, which then sets off an "alarm"; hence, the person experiences pain.

Another early theory was the **pattern theory** (Melzack & Wall, 1982), which describes pain as resulting from the type of stimulation received by the nerve endings and theorizes that the key determination of pain is the intensity of the stimulation. A small stimulation of the nerve endings could be interpreted as touch, whereas a more substantial stimulation could be interpreted as pain. This theory explains why touching a warm heating pad feels pleasant, but touching a very hot pan in the oven feels painful.

Although both specificity and pattern theory may have some components that are correct, current evidence suggests that both of these theories have limitations. First, people can experience pain without having tissue damage (Melzack & Wall, 1988). Phantom-limb pain, which is often experienced as a severe burning or cramping, is the experience of feeling pain in a limb that has been amputated. Because the limb is nonexistent, obviously this type of pain cannot have a purely physical basis. One study found that 72% of amputees experience pain in their phantom limb 8 days after surgery, 65% have pain 6 months later, and 60% continue to have pain 2 years later. Second, people can have tissue damage and feel no pain (Fordyce, 1988). Athletes who are in the middle of a competition, for example, may experience a severe injury and yet report feeling no pain until later. In sum, lots of evidence suggests that the link between physiological stimulation and the experience of physical symptoms is indirect. Both the specificity and pattern theories fail to account for the role of psychology in the experience of pain.

The **gate control theory** of pain (Melzack & Wall, 1965, 1982, 1988), attempts to correct for the limitations of prior theories by including the role of psychological factors in the experience of pain. According to this theory, when body tissues are injured, such as when you get cut or scraped, nerve endings, or *nociceptors*, in the damaged area transmit impulses to a particular part of the dorsal horn section of the spinal cord called the *substantia gelatinosa* (see Figure 9.1). Some nerve fibers, called A-delta fibers, are small and myelinated (covered with a fatty substance that acts as insulation), so they carry information very rapidly. These fibers transmit sharp, localized, distinct pain sensations. Other nerve fibers, called C-fibers, are unmyelinated (uncoated) and transmit the sensation of diffuse, dull, or aching pain much more slowly.

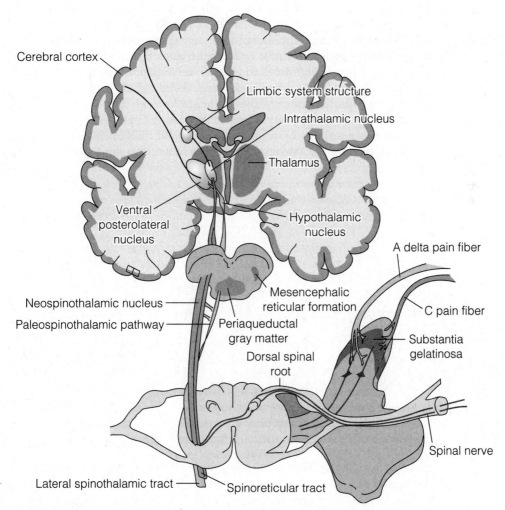

FIGURE 9.1 Pain signals are normally transmitted by nerve fibers from the point of injury to the substantia gelatinosa in the dorsal section of the spinal cord and then ultimately to the brain.

After these nerve impulses reach the substantia gelatinosa, one of two things may happen. If the sensations are sufficiently intense, the nerve impulses are sent all the way up to the brain, where they are experienced as pain—the more signals that reach the brain, the more pain the person experiences. These signals also travel to the *somatosensory cortex* of the brain, which generally allows a person to figure out exactly where on the body he or she is experiencing pain. The pain from stubbing your toe is interpreted in one part of the somatosensory cortex, whereas the pain from a paper cut on your finger is interpreted by a different area. The size of the area in the somatosensory cortex devoted to a particular region of the body determines how sensitive we are to pain experienced in that region. The area corresponding to the fingers, which are particularly sensitive, is large. On the other hand, the area corresponding to the back, which is not very sensitive, is small.

However, according to the gate control theory, not all of the pain signals carried by the nerve fibers successfully reach the brain (see Figure 9.2). Specifically, this theory posits that there is a gate in the substantia gelatinosa that either lets pain impulses travel on to the brain or blocks their progress. Any competing sensation that increases stimulation to the site of potential pain could serve to block transmission of pain sensations, or close the gate. This is why rubbing a leg cramp, scratching an itch, and putting an ice pack on a sprained ankle may all reduce pain: This type of stimulation activates the large A–beta fibers, which are responsible for modulating pain sensations by closing the gate.

The brain can also control whether the gate is open or shut by sending signals down to the spinal cord. Specifically, the *central control mechanism* influences how much information is transmitted from the brain to the spinal cord. When a person

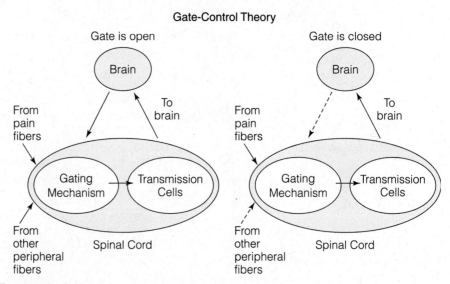

FIGURE 9.2   According to the gate control theory of pain, not all of the pain signals carried by the nerve fibers successfully reach the brain. Any competing sensation that increases stimulation to the site, such as pressure, heat, or cold, could shut the gate, thereby stopping the transmission of pain signals to the brain. Psychological factors, such as distraction and relaxation, can also send messages from the brain down to the spinal cord to shut the gate.

On November 22, 2009, Matt Stafford of the Detroit Lions threw five touchdowns in a 38-37 win over the Cleveland Browns, becoming the youngest quarterback ever to do so. But what is most amazing is that Stafford threw the final touchdown pass after suffering a separated shoulder on the previous play.
Source: © Matt Lange/Southcreek Global/Zuma Press.

feels anxious or scared, for example, the brain opens the gate and thereby increases the potential to experience pain. On the other hand, when a person is distracted or relaxed, the brain shuts the gate, thereby decreasing the potential to experience pain. This is why a person may experience something that should be very painful (e.g., an athlete who dislocates a shoulder during a game), but he or she doesn't consciously feel the pain immediately because the brain stopped the transmission of pain signals long enough for the person to "escape" (or at least finish the game). As we discuss later in the chapter, this is one of the explanations for the influence of hypnosis on pain relief—it may encourage the brain to close the gate.

Although the precise gating mechanism is not entirely understood, a portion of the midbrain, called the *periaqueductal gray*, seems to be involved in the experience of pain. Several studies, with both animals and humans, have shown that activating the periaqueductal gray area, such as through the use of mild electrical stimulation, can entirely block the experience of pain. For example, Reynolds (1969) demonstrated that following electrical stimulation of this area of the brain, rats could withstand the pain of abdominal surgery without any other type of anesthetic.

Neurochemical processes are also involved in the experience of pain (Rabin, 1999). Specifically, the neurons release chemicals called *neurotransmitters* that can increase or decrease the amount of pain experienced (see Figure 9.3). Some neurotransmitters, such as *substance P* and *glutamate*, excite the neurons that send messages about pain, therefore increasing the experience of pain. Other chemicals

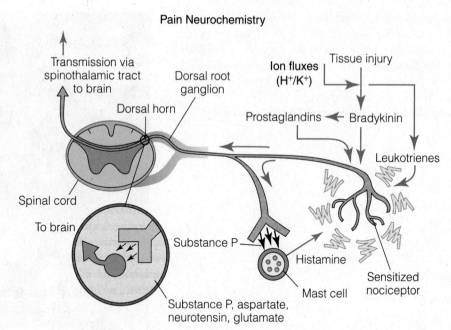

FIGURE 9.3 As shown in this figure, neurotransmitters such as *substance P* as well as other chemicals in the body, such as *bradykinin* and *prostaglandins*, excite the neurons that send messages about pain, thereby increasing the experience of pain. On the other hand, other neurotransmitters, such as *endorphins*, slow or block the transmission of nerve impulses and thereby reduce the experience of pain.

in the body, such as *bradykinin* and *prostaglandins*, are released by the body's cells when damage occurs; they, too, excite the neurons that carry information about pain as well as mobilize the body to repair the damage in a variety of ways, including causing inflammation at the site of the injury and increasing the immune system's functioning. Other neurotransmitters, such as *serotonin* and *endorphins*, work by slowing or blocking the transmission of any nerve impulses. Endorphins, for example, bind to receptors in the periaqueductal gray area of the midbrain, dramatically reducing pain. (Although endorphins are naturally produced in our bodies, opiate drugs, such as morphine, can serve a similar function in the brain, and therefore reduce pain.)

The gate control theory clearly differs from other theories in a number of ways. First, it describes pain as caused by a physiological stimulation as well as psychological factors. Specifically, it views pain as resulting partially from a person's perception or interpretation, not simply as a physiological sensation. This theory explains why the same event can be interpreted by different people as more or less painful, and why sometimes pain is not experienced immediately. This theory also describes the person as having some control over the experience of pain. Specifically, people can take concrete steps to reduce their experience of pain, such as by distracting themselves, relaxing their muscles, or using an ice pack or heating pad.

Melzack (1993) has also proposed an extension to the gate control theory that places an even stronger emphasis on the influence of the brain in the perception of pain. According to his **neuromatrix theory**, a network of neurons is distributed throughout the brain that processes the information flowing through it. Although the neuromatrix typically acts to process sensory information transmitted from the body, the neuromatrix can process experiences even in the absence of sensations. Using brain-imaging technology, researchers have learned that people who have had a limb amputated show a reorganization of how the brain processes stimulation of various body parts (Flor et al., 1995). For example, the parts of the brain that previously responded to the arm and hand may, in the case of a person who has lost that limb, now respond to facial stimulation. Moreover, the greater the reorganization, the more intense phantom limb pain is felt. This theory helps explain the phenomenon of phantom limb pain, in which the brain tells the body it is experiencing pain even in the absence of direct sensations.

How Is Pain Measured?

To assess (and hopefully ease) pain, it is important to know where it is and what it feels like. Researchers use a number of different strategies to assess pain, including self-report measures, behavioral measures, and physiological measures.

Self-Report Measures

Self-report measures of pain basically ask people to describe their pain (Turk et al., 1983). The advantage of this approach is that pain has many outward behavioral manifestations, but only the person experiencing it can tell how intense the feeling really is. In some cases professionals interview patients (and sometimes their family members) about issues related to the pain, such as when it began, the treatments they have tried, the impact it has had on the patients' professional and personal life, and how the patient typically handles it. In other cases, patients report their experience of pain by responding to a written questionnaire. For example, the West Haven-Yale Multidimensional Pain Inventory assesses the impact of pain on patients' lives, the response of others to patients' expression of pain, and the extent to which pain disrupts patients' daily lives (Kerns, Turk, & Rudy, 1985). Another type of self-report pain inventory, the McGill-Melzack Pain Questionnaire, asks people to choose various words to describe their pain, the area of the body in which they feel pain, the timing of the pain, and the intensity or strength of the pain (Melzack & Torgerson, 1971). This measure also assesses three different aspects of pain, including sensations (e.g., cramping, stabbing, aching), feelings (e.g., exhaustion, terror), and intensity (e.g., unbearable, intense, annoying). See Table 9.1 for an example of a pain self-report measure.

Although self-rating scales are easy to use and at least in some cases can capture diverse types of pain, such measures clearly have limitations. First, self-report measures of pain often require fairly high levels of verbal skills (Chapman et al., 1985). Patients must have the ability to understand and make small distinctions between types of pain, such as the difference between lacerating versus cutting, pulsing versus throbbing, and scalding versus searing. Self-report measures are

TABLE 9.1   *Test Yourself: The Pain Discomfort Scale*

Please indicate whether each of the following statements is more true or false for you using a scale of 0 (that is very untrue for me) to 4 (this is very true for me).

1.   I am scared about the pain I feel.
2.   The pain I experience is unbearable.
3.   The pain I feel is torturing me.
4.   My pain does not stop me from enjoying life.
5.   I have learned to tolerate the pain I feel.
6.   I feel helpless about my pain.
7.   My pain is a minor annoyance to me.
8.   When I feel pain I am hurting, but I am not distressed.
9.   I never let the pain in my body affect my outlook on life.
10. When I am in pain, I become almost a different person.

This scale assesses the intensity of pain and the level of distress pain causes.

Source: Jensen, Turner, Romano, & Karoly, 1991.

therefore less useful for children and people who are not fluent speakers of English (although see Figure 9.4 for a self-report measure of pain that requires few, if any, verbal skills). Most important, and as we discussed in the review of behavioral measures of pain, people sometimes misrepresent how much pain they are feeling. In some cases, people exaggerate to get sympathy or attention. For example, children learn quickly that expressing pain can lead to positive consequences (e.g., special adhesive strips, hugs and kisses, grape-flavored medicine). Similarly, professional athletes may express pain loudly immediately following a push or hit by another player in an effort to draw a foul or penalty. In other cases, people may attempt to downplay their experience of pain. One study found that male patients report

FIGURE 9.4   The Picture Scale is useful for assessing pain in children and people who have trouble with written language (from Frank, Moll, & Hort, 1982).

experiencing less pain to females than they report to males (Levine & DeSimone, 1991)! So, self-report measures can be good because they can provide information that is simply impossible to obtain through other measures, but these measures also have some weaknesses. Finally, people's memory for pain isn't perfect, and therefore asking people to recall pain experienced may not be so accurate—different people will recall pain at different levels (Stone, Schwartz, Broderick, & Shiffman, 2005).

Behavioral Measures

Behavioral pain measures assess the outward manifestations of pain, including physical symptoms (such as limping and rubbing), verbal expressions (such as sighing and groaning), and even facial expressions (such as grimacing and frowning; Craig, Prkachin, & Grunau, 1992; Keefe & Block, 1982). In some cases, these observations are made by health-care workers, and, in other cases, they are made by people familiar with the patient. For example, nurses may ask patients recovering from surgery to perform a variety of tasks, such as touching their toes, standing up, and sitting down. As an indirect measure of pain, the nurses may then rate how easily the patient performs each of these tasks.

Generally, behavioral pain measures are accurate in assessing pain. Different people seem to be able to rate pain behaviors in fairly similar ways (Keefe & Block, 1982), such as in five general clusters: guarding (abnormally stiff or rigid movement), bracing (a stationary position in which one part of the body maintains an abnormal distribution of weight), rubbing (touching, rubbing, or holding part of the body), grimacing (facial expressions such as clenching teeth and furrowing brow), and sighing (deep exhalations of breath). Behavioral approaches are an especially good way of measuring pain in children, who often are unable to accurately report on their experience of pain using self-report methods.

Although behavioral measures of pain can be very useful, judging people's pain can be hard. Researchers in one study examined the reports of pain in children undergoing painful procedures, their parents, and their nurses (Rajasagaram, Taylor, Braitberg, Pearsell, & Capp, 2009). Although there were no differences between the pain reported by children and their parents, the nurses' score was significantly lower than both the parents' and the children's scores, which may mean that children aren't receiving adequate pain medication.

Judging the amount of pain a person is experiencing is particularly difficult because people sometimes misrepresent their pain, either by pretending to feel more or less pain than they really do (Block, Kremer, & Gaylor, 1980; Romano et al., 1992). People sometimes are motivated to show they are experiencing pain as a way of getting something (or getting out of something)—you might grab your knee and walk stiffly in an attempt to avoid playing a tennis match you fear you will lose. One study found that patients often report being unable to do various activities (e.g., walking, lifting, standing), but observations by unobtrusive staff reveal patients could do more than they admitted (Kremer, Block, & Gaylor, 1981). On the other hand, sometimes people go to some lengths to (falsely) show that they are not feeling pain, perhaps to avoid undergoing an unpleasant medical procedure or to avoid appearing weak to others. Athletes who are eager to get back into a game, for example, may demonstrate to their coach that they are able to perform, even though this action causes them substantial pain.

Physiological Measures

Psychophysiological measures of pain are based on the assumption that the experience of pain should be associated in distinct ways with physiological responses, such as muscle tension, heart rate, and skin temperature (Nigl, 1984). Researchers have used a number of different physiological measures to determine whether pain is associated with such responses. For example, electromyography (EMG) can be used to measure muscle tension in patients with headaches and lower-back pain (Chapman et al., 1985). Other researchers, under the assumption that more substantial pain is associated with higher spikes in brain waves, have used electroencephalograms (EEGs) to measure electrical activity in the brain. Still other researchers have relied on autonomic nervous system responses, including increases in heart rate, blood pressure, and respiration, as a way of quantifying the amount of pain experienced.

However, most research using these measures has failed to demonstrate a consistent relationship between physiological responses and the experience of pain (Chapman et al., 1985). For example, EMG levels are sometimes higher in patients with lower-back pain, but other times they are lower. People also adapt to painful stimuli over time—a person may initially show a very rapid heart rate in response to pain, but then over time, the heart rate decreases in response to the same stimulus. There is no consistent link between the experience of pain and physiological reactions; therefore, physiological measures of pain have limited use.

How Do Psychosocial Factors Influence the Experience of Pain?

Although everyone has experienced pain, the amount of discomfort that people feel from a given injury or disease varies from person to person—one person may find that having a stomachache makes it impossible to get out of bed, whereas another person may find such pain a relatively small annoyance and continue with regular activities. In fact, people vary considerably in how much pain they can stand—some estimates are that some people can stand eight times as much pain as others (Rollman & Harris, 1987). Moreover, many pain complaints have no clear physical basis: It is estimated are that up to 85% of people seeing a doctor with a complaint of back pain have no apparent physical basis for the pain (White & Gordon, 1982). This lack of physical cause suggests that psychological factors have some role in producing such pain. This section examines several theories about how psychological factors influence the expression and/or experience of pain, including stress, learning, cognition, and mood states.

Stress

As described in Chapter 4, stress, including the stress caused by family or marital conflict, work pressures, and major life events, influences psychological and physical well-being in numerous ways (Sternbach, 1986). Pain can also be influenced by stress. For example, one study found that only 7% of those who experience low stress report experiencing frequent headache pain, as compared to 17% of those with moderate stress, and 25% of those with high stress (Sternbach, 1986). People who experience more stress on a given day not only report increases in pain on that day but also report increases in health-care use (including hospitalizations, ER visits, calls to doctors, and medication) and work absence (Gil et al., 2004). Similarly, children with recurrent abdominal pain (that has no clear physical cause) report more daily stressors, both in and out of school, than those without such pain (Walker, Garber, Smith, Van Slyke, & Claar, 2001); they also tend to describe their daily stress as more severe and report other symptoms (e.g., headache, fatigue) more often as compared to other children. Finally, stress can lead to the experience of pain over time. Researchers in one study found that patients undergoing knee surgery who were under high levels of stress experienced greater pain 1 year later (Rosenberger, Kerns, Jokl, & Ickovics, 2009). Similarly, conflicts with family members and coworkers, which clearly induce stress, are associated with the development of ulcers, a chronic and painful condition (Medalie, Stange, Zyzanski, & Goldbourt, 1992).

Questioning the Research 9.1

Does the research study by Walker et al. (2001) on the link between abdominal pain in children and stress reveal that stress causes pain? What other explanations can you think of for this association?

Researchers in one study examined the influence of a particular type of stress—worry about finances—on the experience of pain (Rios & Zautra, 2011). To test this association, 250 participants with osteoarthritis, fibromyalgia, or both completed measures of pain, level of economic hardship, and financial worries every day for 30 days. As predicted, both economic hardship and financial worries predicted more severe daily pain. Although there was no association between financial worries and the experience of pain among those who were not experiencing financial hardship, among participants with greater economic hardship, more financial worries on a given day were associated with experiencing more severe pain. These findings suggest feelings of economic stress may in fact have a direct impact on physical well-being and, in particular, on pain.

Work stress is also associated with the experience of pain. In fact, people who have low job satisfaction, poor relationships with coworkers, and stress at work are more likely to have chronic pain, as are those who perceive their work goals as conflicting with their nonwork goals (Karoly & Ruehlman, 1996). One study tested the extent to which burnout, a response to chronic exposure to stress, predicts the onset of neck, shoulder, and/or lower-back pain, in apparently healthy individuals (Melamed, 2009). Employed men and women completed measures of burnout and were then assessed for the development of pain for 3 to 5 years. During this follow-up period, 116 workers (17.8%) developed musculoskeletal pain. Workers who were experiencing symptoms of burnout were more than one and a half times as likely to develop musculoskeletal pain, even when taking into account other variables that could lead to pain (such as type of job). Similarly, researchers in another study investigated the associations between burnout and the intensity and frequency of pain (Grossi, Thomtén, Fandiño-Losada, Soares, & Sundin, 2009). Once again, the level of burnout was the most important predictor of overall pain, neck/shoulder pain, back pain, and disability, even when adjusting for other measures likely to be associated with pain. Thus, burnout seems to contribute to the development of pain as well as the disability it causes in apparently healthy individuals.

How exactly does stress lead to pain? One way stress may influence the experience of pain is that experiencing stress leads people to engage in behaviors, such as tensing their muscles, that cause pain. For example, someone who is experiencing high levels of stress might grind their teeth at night while they sleep, which in turn leads to jaw pain. So, in this case the person is experiencing real pain, but the pain was caused by a behavior, which in turn was caused by stress. Also, and as described in Chapter 4, people who experience high levels of stress may stop taking care of themselves (they may overeat or exercise less) and distance themselves from their family and friends, all of which reduces their social support and thereby increases their experience of stress and pain. Finally, stress can lead directly to physiological problems, such as dilation of arteries surrounding the brain and tension in muscles in the head, neck, and shoulders, both of which may lead to headaches (Turner & Chapman, 1982). As described at the beginning of the chapter, Antonia's stress at work and lack of sleep may have been creating considerable tension, which in turn contributed to her frequent migraines.

Learning

As we've discussed throughout this book, people acquire attitudes and behaviors by watching those around them. Children may learn how to respond to injury and disease by observing how their parents and other role models act (Bandura, 1986). One study found that teachers rated the children of chronic pain patients as displaying more illness-related behaviors, such as complaining and whining about pain, visiting the school nurse, and avoiding certain behaviors, than other children (Rickard, 1988). As described in Box 9.1: Focus on Culture, we learn about the experience of pain and the expression of pain from the culture we live in.

People may also learn to experience, or at least express, pain as a way of receiving some type of secondary gain or reinforcement (Turk, 1996). In some cases, people experiencing pain are allowed to avoid doing things they really don't want to do—a type of negative reinforcement: Perhaps you remember complaining of a stomachache on a morning you were supposed to take a test in school, hoping that your parents would let you stay home. In other cases, experiencing pain leads to very desirable consequences, such as attention and expressions of concern from others—a type of positive reinforcement. As described at the beginning of the chapter, Billy was probably motivated to continue complaining about various illnesses because he enjoyed the tender care he received from his mother (as well as missing school). One study examined the amount of pain a person complained about as a function of whether the person was told his or her spouse or a hospital clerk was listening behind a one-way mirror (Block et al., 1980). Those with spouses who were generally caring and helpful complained more when they were told that their spouse was behind the mirror, whereas those with less helpful spouses complained more when they were told a clerk was behind the mirror. Similarly, children tend to show more anxiety during medical procedures when their parents

Box 9.1

Focus on Culture: The Influence of Culture on the Experience and Expression of Pain

Cultures have very different norms about what types of experiences are painful as well as how much pain it is appropriate to express. Researchers in one study examined the expression of pain in 372 patients with chronic pain (typically back pain) from different cultural backgrounds, including Hispanics, Italians, Polish, and "old Americans," meaning those whose families had lived in the United States for some time (Bates, Edwards, & Anderson, 1993). Hispanics and Italians reported experiencing the most pain, worry, anger, and tension about their pain and also perceived their pain as interfering more with their work. In contrast, the old American and Polish patients felt they should suppress experiences of pain and were less expressive and emotional about their pain. Similarly, cross-cultural research shows that people in different countries vary in how much impairment lower-back pain causes them. Specifically, Americans report experiencing greater work and social impairment than Italians and New Zealanders, who in turn report experiencing more problems than Japanese, Mexican, and Colombian individuals (Sanders et al., 1992). These findings indicate that one's culture plays an important role in the interpretation and experience of pain.

are present than when their parents are not, presumably because children are more motivated to engage in behaviors, such as making noise and complaining, that will elicit their parents' attention when in their company (Gross, Stern, Levin, Dale, & Wojnilower, 1983; Shaw & Routh, 1982). In line with this view, one recent study even found that infants whose parents reassure them during a painful medical procedure, such as by saying "it will soon be over," show more distress (Wolff et al., 2009).

Perhaps the most obvious benefit someone might receive from experiencing pain is financial, such as a disability payment. Considerable research shows that people who receive financial benefits for experiencing pain report having more pain and find pain treatments less effective (Block et al., 1980; Fordyce, 1988; Rohling, Binder, & Langhin-Richsen-Rohling, 1995). One study reported a case in which a disabled factory worker had received $251 per week for his full-time work in a woolen mill, but began receiving $257 per week while on disability (Block et al., 1980). Can you imagine his incentive to stop feeling pain? This doesn't mean that all people who are experiencing pain—or receiving some type of benefit from the experience of such pain—are simply faking it, but it does mean that at times psychological factors can influence how much pain people feel (or how much they report feeling).

People also learn to avoid certain activities based on their fear that engaging in a particular behavior will lead to pain (Turk & Flor, 1999). For example, getting a cavity filled is typically somewhat painful, whereas simply getting your teeth cleaned is not. Someone who has had a cavity filled could then develop a general fear of

Children often show more pain when their parent is present than when they are alone or with other children, probably because parents reinforce crying with hugs, kisses, and special bandages.
Source: © Purestock/Alamy.

going to the dentist, even if he or she is not scheduled to have painful dental work done. Similarly, if you once ate an entire bag of chips and then vomited shortly afterward (because of stomach flu, not the snack consumption), you are likely to develop an association between chips and pain. Unfortunately, after a link between two behaviors is established (even in error), people's anxiety about experiencing pain again often leads them to avoid that activity completely—and they never learn that engaging in the activity would not cause the pain they anticipate. One study with patients who had lower-back pain found that 83% of them were unable to complete a series of exercises (e.g., leg lifts, bending at the waist) because of fear of pain, whereas only 5% of them were actually physically unable to complete the exercises (Council, Ahern, Follick, & Kline, 1988).

Cognition

One of the first people to demonstrate the power of cognition in the experience of pain was Dr. Henry Beecher, who treated injured soldiers during World War II. Although all of the soldiers had received surgery for severe wounds, only 49% reported experiencing "moderate" or "severe" pain, and only 32% accepted medication when it was offered (Beecher, 1959). In contrast, when Dr. Beecher later interviewed other patients in his office who had experienced similar types of surgery, 75% reported experiencing at least "moderate" pain, and 83% requested medication. According to Beecher, the cause of these differences is that the soldiers most likely compared their injuries to those of others around them who were dying; hence, they felt relatively good about their state of health, whereas those in civilian life probably compared their injuries to their own and others normal states of health, hence they felt much worse than normal. The soldiers may have also felt in some way rewarded by becoming injured, namely, getting to leave the war. The civilians, in contrast, were less likely to perceive such an obvious benefit from their surgery.

More recent research supports Dr. Beecher's findings on the impact of how people think about, or attribute the causes of, pain in how they experience pain (Keefe, Brown, Wallston, & Caldwell, 1989; Turk & Flor, 1999). Those who believe that their pain is caused by a very serious debilitating condition perceive pain as worse than those who believe the pain is caused by a more minor (and fixable) problem. For example, although chronic pain patients with cancer and chronic pain patients without cancer do not differ in self-reported pain severity, those whose pain is caused by cancer report feeling greater disability and engaging in fewer activities (Turk et al., 1998). People who blame themselves for their injury also experience more pain (Kiecolt-Glaser & Williams, 1987). On the other hand, people who perceive a clear benefit resulting from the experience of pain perceive such pain as less intense than those without such an "upside"; this may explain why people voluntarily undergo painful activities and procedures (e.g., having a navel pierced, getting a tattoo, climbing Mount Everest).

Moreover, people's beliefs about pain, and in particular their anxiety about pain, influence how much pain they report experiencing (Kent, 1985; Marvan & Cortes-Iniestra, 2001; Palermo & Drotar, 1996; Turk & Flor, 1999). Specifically, people who focus their attention on the unpleasant aspects of a procedure, who anticipate negative outcomes, and who think negative thoughts may experience or report more pain (Gil, Williams, Keefe, & Beckham, 1990; Keefe, Hauck, Egert, Rimer, & Kornguth, 1994). For example, people who are very anxious about scheduled dental procedures report experiencing more pain 3 months after the procedure than they actually felt (as reported by them immediately following the procedure). When we experience a physical problem (e.g., migraine, broken leg), our anticipation about its consequences may make the pain seem that much greater. In fact, the *anticipation* of pain can in some cases be worse than the pain itself.

In line with this view, people who tend to catastrophize—that is to think negative thoughts and feel anxious regarding pain—actually experience more pain (see Table 9.2). Catastrophizing is associated with greater bodily pain, lower quality of life, higher levels of depression, use of more pain medication, and greater work disability and absenteeism (Litt, Shafer, & Napolitano, 2004; Nijs, Van de Putte, Louckx, Truijen, & De Meirleir, 2008; Severeijns, Vlaeyen, van den Hout, & Picavet, 2004; Wolff et al., 2008). Researchers in one study examined the relationship between catastrophizing and postoperative pain outcomes (pain intensity and analgesia use) in patients undergoing elective back surgery (Papaioannou et al., 2009). As predicted, catastrophizing predicted postoperative pain intensity as well as analgesic use.

People's expectations about their ability to cope with pain also influence how much pain they experience (DeGood, 2000; Jensen, Karoly, & Harris, 1991; Turk & Flor, 1999). In fact, people's expected ability to cope with pain is a strong predictor of both the intensity and duration of pain (Bachiocco, Scesi, Morselli, & Carli, 1993) as well as the amount of disability caused by pain (Bunketorp, Lindh, Carlsson, & Stener-Victorin, 2006). Similarly, women's beliefs about their ability to go through childbirth without medication are a strong predictor of their success at doing so (Manning & Wright, 1983). Expectations about the ability to cope with pain may influence pain in part through their impact on the strategies people use to cope with pain. For example, researchers in one study examined children's beliefs about their ability to reduce their gastrointestinal pain (Walker, Smith, Garber, & Claar, 2005). Children who believed they would be unable to manage the pain

TABLE 9.2   *Test Yourself: The Pain Catastrophizing Scale*

This scale assesses the types of thoughts and feelings people have when they experience pain. Please indicate the degree to which you have these thoughts and feelings when you are experiencing pain using a scale of 0 (not at all) to 5 (all the time).

1. I worry all the time about whether the pain will end.
2. I feel I can't go on.
3. It's terrible, and I think it's never going to get any better.
4. It's awful, and I feel that it overwhelms me.
5. I feel I can't stand it anymore.
6. I become afraid that the pain will get worse.
7. I keep thinking of other painful events.
8. I anxiously want the pain to go away.
9. I can't seem to keep it out of my mind.
10. I keep thinking about how much it hurts.
11. I keep thinking about how badly I want the pain to stop.
12. There's nothing I can do to reduce the intensity of the pain.
13. I wonder whether something serious may happen.

This scale assesses the extent to which people think negative thoughts in the face of pain.

Source: Sullivan, Bishop, & Pivik, 1995.

showed passive coping—including believing that the pain was going to get worse, and that there was nothing they would be able to do about it—led to more pain symptoms, as well as more disability, depression, and symptoms 3 months later. Similarly, people who are uncertain about the nature and cause of their illness also experience greater pain, in part because illness uncertainty leads to less effective coping with pain symptoms (Johnson, Zautra, & Davis, 2006).

Although much of the research described thus far is correlational, meaning it is impossible to determine whether cognition actually causes the experience of pain, experimental research provides additional evidence that people's thoughts about pain do influence the amount of pain they feel. Researchers in one study examined the impact of threatening information on coping and pain tolerance (Jackson et al., 2005). Prior to engaging in a cold pressor test (test involves submerging a hand in a bucket of very cold ice water for as long as a person can stand it, which virtually everyone finds very painful), 121 college students were randomly assigned to one of three conditions: a threat condition in which they read an orienting passage warning them about symptoms and consequences of frostbite, a reassurance condition in which they read a passage about the safety of the cold pressor test, or a control condition in which no orienting passage was read before the experimental task. Only 15.6% of participants in the threat group completed the test to its 4-minute duration, compared with 55.6% in the reassurance group and 45.2% of those in the control group. Even though groups did not differ on the amount of pain they reported experiencing, threatened participants catastrophized more about the pain and reported less use of cognitive coping strategies (reinterpreting pain sensations, ignoring pain, diverting attention away from pain to other experiences, and using coping self-statements) than other respondents. In turn, the threatening information about the pain led people to use poorer coping strategies, which then influenced pain tolerance. Thus, thinking about pain as threatening in fact leads to less effective coping, which in turn reduces individuals' capacity to bear pain.

Interestingly, people's thoughts about pain can at times lead them to make seemingly counterintuitive decisions. Specifically, if people are asked to choose which they'd prefer, a shorter amount of pain or a longer amount of pain, virtually everyone says (not surprisingly) that they'd prefer shorter amounts of pain. However, some research suggests that in some cases, people may actually prefer a longer period of pain that includes slightly less pain at the end of the pain than shorter but consistently intense pain (Kahneman, Fredrickson, Schreiber, & Redelmeier, 1993). In one study, subjects were exposed to two unpleasant experiences: In the short trial, they held their hand in cold water for 1 minute, and in the long trial, they held their hand in cold water for 1 minute and then in *slightly* less cold water for 30 seconds. When given the choice of which trial to repeat, 69% chose to repeat the longer treatments.

Although the cold-water test is perhaps not that painful (although most people really don't enjoy it), other studies reveal similar findings for more painful procedures. For example, another study examined patients' experience of colonoscopy, a procedure in which a lighted, flexible, tubelike instrument is inserted into a person's anus and then up into their colon (Redelmeier & Kahneman, 1996). This procedure is quite painful for most people and is often carried out under conditions of mild sedation. Once again, patients' memories of the pain were influenced not by how long the procedure lasted but rather by the peak intensity of the pain they experienced and the amount of pain they experienced during the last 3 minutes of the procedure. It seems ironic that we can enhance someone's memory of a painful procedure by lengthening the procedure so that the last few minutes are more pleasant than earlier (even if they are still painful), yet given these findings, perhaps medical practitioners should concentrate more on lowering the peak intensity of pain during the last few minutes of a procedure than on reducing the overall length of a procedure. After all, people's memories of their painful experiences could increase their willingness to undergo the procedure in the future, and thereby may improve adherence to medical recommendations (as we'll discuss more in Chapter 12).

Questioning the Research 9.2

What are the ethics involved in the study by Redelmeier and Kahneman (1996) in which some patients experienced longer colonoscopies than they needed to experience? Should this experiment have been conducted? Why or why not?

Mood State

Considerable research reveals that negative emotions and, in particular, depression and anxiety, are associated with the experience of pain (Beesdo et al., 2010; Cui, Matsushima, Aso, Masuda, & Makita, 2009; Kato, Sullivan, Evengard, & Pedersen, 2006; Lee & Tsang, 2009; Sherbourne, Bunyan, Creswell, & Jaremka, 2009). First, people who are experiencing pain are more likely to report feeling anxious and/or depressed. For example, one study found that 33.7% of those in chronic pain were anxious or depressed, as compared to 10.1% of those who were not in chronic pain (Gureje, Von Korff, Simon, & Gater, 1998). Similarly, people who have chronic back pain are more likely to have an anxiety or depressive disorder (Sullivan, Reesor, Mikail, & Fisher, 1992), and people with irritable bowel syndrome (IBS), a chronically painful disease, tend to show higher rates of major depression, panic disorder, and agoraphobia (Kato, Sullivan, Evengård, & Pedersen, 2006; Walker, Katon, Jemelka, & Roy-Byrne, 1992).

Second, higher levels of anxiety and depression are associated with a greater intensity of pain (Rosemann, Laux, Szecsenyi, Wensing, & Grol, 2008). Researchers in one study examined the relationship among anxiety, depression, and pain in 102 patients with lower-back pain who were admitted to a hospital (Mok & Lee, 2008). Patients with higher levels of anxiety and depression reported experiencing more intense pain. Similarly, cancer patients who are neither anxious nor depressed show lower levels of pain than those with depression and/or anxiety (Utne, Miaskowski, Bjordal, Paul, & Rustoen, 2010).

Although much of this research is correlational, meaning it is impossible to tell the precise relationship among anxiety, depression, and pain, the bulk of evidence suggests that experiencing chronic pain tends to lead to depression, and not the reverse—in other words, people who live in chronic pain develop depression, anxiety, and anger (Magni, Moreschi, Rigatti-Luchini, & Merskey, 1994). One study followed patients with chronic lower-back pain for 6 months following treatment at an intensive rehabilitation clinic (Barnes, Gatchel, Mayer, & Barnett, 1990). Although patients with chronic pain had higher than normal scores on several measures of psychological well-being (hypochondria, neuroticism, depression) at the start of the program, these scores decreased to normal levels following treatment, which again suggests that pain is the cause of these psychological problems, not the result. Similarly, research with chronic pain patients reveals that pain led to increases over time in depression, anxiety, and anger (Feldman, Downey, & Schaffer-Neitz, 1999).

However, depression may lead to pain over time, which suggests that pain may lead to depression as well as the reverse. For example, researchers in one study evaluated the association between depressive symptoms and subsequent risk of developing severe bodily pain in patients undergoing dialysis (Yamamoto et al., 2009). Initial symptoms of depression were significantly associated with a greater likelihood of developing severe pain during the $2\frac{1}{2}$ year follow-up period. These findings suggest that the association between depression and the experience of pain probably works in both directions.

What Are Some Physical Methods of Controlling Pain?

Because the earliest theories of pain focused entirely on its physical causes, researchers concentrated on developing purely physical pain-control techniques. Physical approaches to controlling pain include more traditional methods, such as medication and surgery, as well as more recent methods, such as complementary and alternative approaches. One national survey revealed that complementary and alternative therapies were used in high frequencies with nearly 4 in 10 American adults, and 1 in 9 children, reporting using some type of complementary and alternative medicine in the past 12 months (Barnes, Bloom, & Nahin, 2008). This section reviews a number of different physical methods of controlling pain, including medication, surgery, physical therapy/exercise, and physical stimulation.

Medication

The most common way to control pain is with *analgesic drugs*, such as aspirin, acetaminophen, and ibuprofen, which reduce fever and inflammation at the site of wounds, and work to decrease pain by interfering with the transmission of pain signals (Whipple, 1987; Winters, 1985). Analgesics are very effective in reducing mild to moderate levels of pain, such as headache and arthritis pain. *Narcotics*, such as codeine and morphine, work by binding to the opiate receptors, thereby inhibiting the transmission of pain signals (Aronoff, Wagner, & Spangler, 1986). These drugs are very effective in reducing severe pain. *Local anesthetics*, such as novocaine and lidocaine, can be applied directly to the site at which pain occurs; they work by blocking nerve cells in that region from generating impulses, which is why your mouth feels numb after a shot of novocaine. Other pharmacologic methods of pain control rely on blocking the transmission of pain impulses up the spinal cord. For example, during childbirth, many women choose to have a spinal epidural, an injection of narcotics or local anesthetics in the spinal cord, which blocks the experience of pain from the point of injection down.

Although the use of drugs is effective in reducing pain, often doctors are reluctant to prescribe them (Fishman & Berger, 2000; Melzack & Wall, 1982). One reason may be that the topic of pain and pain relief typically receives little attention in medical school curricula, in part because pain is not viewed as a particularly serious problem—patients who complain of pain are often seen as "weak" or as desiring drugs because of addiction. This reluctance to prescribe medication for pain relief is also caused in part by physicians' concern that these drugs can produce dependence and addiction. In turn, even when pain-relieving drugs are prescribed, doctors often give smaller doses than is recommended by manufacturers, give medication less frequently, and stop medication earlier than is recommended. One study with cancer patients, who often experience severe pain, found that 42% were not receiving enough medication to ease their pain (Cleeland et al., 1994). Practitioners also tend to prescribe less pain relief for members of ethnic minority groups (Cleeland et al., 1994; Ng, Dimsdale, Shragg, & Deutsch, 1996).

The reluctance to prescribe drugs is especially common when patients are children, in part because both doctors and parents tend to believe that children feel less pain than adults. One study found that mothers underestimate the amount of pain their children experienced following tonsillectomy, which caused them to give their children less medication than the doctor ordered (Gedaly-Duff & Ziebarth, 1994). Similarly, for years, circumcision was practiced on infant boys without any anesthesia because of the belief that infants don't experience pain in the same way as adults (Anand & Craig, 1996). However, recent research suggests that even very young infants do experience pain; hence, ethically they should be given some type of anesthesia during painful medical procedures. Moreover, infants who do not receive pain medication during circumcision show more distress during later injections than do those who receive anesthesia, presumably because early experiences with pain make people more sensitive to pain later in their lives (Taddio, Katz, Ilersich, & Koren, 1997).

When doctors do encourage the use of medication to reduce pain, they may encounter resistance from their patients. Patients often believe they should accept the pain and save the medication for when the pain gets intense; they also may be concerned that they could become addicted to the drugs (Fishman & Berger, 2000; Ward et al., 1993). People may also refuse pain medication because of their concerns about its undesirable side effects, such as nausea, drowsiness, and mental confusion, and its high cost. In some cases, patients may fail to ask for pain medication because they dislike the method of dispensing the medicine, such as swallowing pills or getting a shot.

Surgery

In extreme cases, when other methods of pain control have failed, *surgical pain control* can be used to manage pain (Melzack & Wall, 1982). Surgical pain control typically involves severing or destroying the nerves that transmit pain signals, thereby reducing the perception of pain. This technique is especially common in the treatment of chronic back pain. In the United States, 115,000 laminectomies (in which pieces of a herniated disk are removed) and 34,000 other lumbar spine operations are performed each year (Arena & Blanchard, 1996). Surgery is much more common in the United States than in other industrialized countries: The rate of surgeries for herniated disks is four to nine times higher.

Surgical methods of pain control have very limited benefits, however. First, procedures can lead to other problems, including numbness, memory loss, and even paralysis in the region involved in the surgery. Even more problematic is that surgery sometimes provides only short-term pain relief: It may sever a particular pathway in the body that is transmitting pain signals, thereby initially eliminating or reducing pain, but because the nervous system can regenerate, and pain messages can travel to the brain in different ways, patients may begin to experience pain again weeks or months following surgery (Melzack & Wall, 1982). Surgery should be considered as a last resort when all other techniques have failed.

Physical Therapy/Exercise

Because certain types of pain are exacerbated by weak muscles, a lack of flexibility, and muscle tension, physical therapy and exercise can help reduce pain (Davies, Gibson, & Tester, 1979). People with chronic lower-back pain, for example, may experience this pain because their abdominal muscles are weak and they are overusing their back muscles to compensate. Similarly, patients with arthritis who engage in regular exercise may maintain the flexibility of their joints, and surgical patients who participate in physical therapy may restore muscle strength. This increased flexibility and muscle strength can in turn decrease the experience of pain. In turn, physicians who previously prescribed bed rest for people with back pain now urge patients with back pain to become active as soon as possible.

Several studies indicate that people who engage in regular exercise show long-term reduction in disability (Frost, Lamb, Moffett, Fairbank, & Moser, 1998). For example, researchers in one study randomly assigned patients with fibromyalgia to either a classic Yang-style tai chi or a control intervention consisting of wellness education and stretching (Wang et al., 2010). Sessions lasted 60 minutes each and took place twice a week for 12 weeks for each of the study groups. At the 6-month follow-up, patients in the tai chi group had clinically important improvements in terms of impact of fibromyalgia as well as quality of life: Scores for the tai chi group went from 62.9 to 35.1, compared to 68.0 to 58.6 for those in the control group. Scores also showed improvements in terms of physical components as well as mental components.

Both aerobic exercise and strength training can help decrease pain. Researchers in one study compared the effectiveness of four common self-management treatments on function, symptoms, and self-efficacy in women with fibromyalgia (Rooks et al., 2007). Women were randomly assigned to 16 weeks of one of four interventions: aerobic and flexibility exercise; strength training, aerobic, and flexibility exercise; a fibromyalgia self-help course; or a combination of the fibromyalgia self-help course and strength training. Participants who received any of the types of exercise (strength training, aerobic, flexibility) showed significantly greater improvements in terms of function and reduced pain than those who only received the self-help course, suggesting that exercise is an important strategy for improving functioning and decreasing pain.

In some cases, the exercise approach can be as effective as—or even more effective than—traditional methods of therapy. For example, one study of patients with lower-back pain assigned some to aerobic exercise treatment, others to behavior therapy, and a third group to aerobic exercise plus behavior therapy (Turner, Clancy, McQuade, & Cardenas, 1990). Patients in the behavior therapy condition received information about the power of social reinforcement in maintaining or reducing pain, and both they and their spouses were asked to keep track of pain behaviors and to try not to reward pain complaints but instead reward pain-free behaviors. The combined group showed the greatest benefits initially, but all three treatments seemed to be effective in reducing pain at the 1-year follow-up. Similarly, research reveals that patients with lower-back pain who engage in general physical activities to improve health show reductions in back pain and improvements in mood, whereas those who focus on completing exercises specifically designed to decrease back pain experience more pain (Hurwitz, Morgenstern, & Chiao, 2005).

> **Questioning the Research 9.3**
>
> Why should engaging in general physical exercise lead to lower rates of back pain than completing back-specific exercises? What do you believe explains this somewhat surprising finding?

Physical Stimulation

Physical stimulation or (**counterirritation**) refers to irritating body tissue to ease pain. At first, this seems counterintuitive: Why *increase* pain as a way to *reduce* it? However, the gate control theory of pain suggests that increasing pain by increasing stimulation of nerves in one region is a way to get the gate to close, thereby reducing the perception of pain (Melzack & Wall, 1982). This is why you put your finger in your mouth after you burn it on a hot stove and why you grab your foot after stubbing your toe. All of the physical stimulation methods of pain control are based on this general principle.

The **transcutaneous electrical nerve stimulation (TENS)** technique of pain reduction involves placing electrodes on the skin and administering continuous electrical stimulation (Melzack & Wall, 1982). Patients wear a small portable unit that attaches the electrodes to the skin; the degree of stimulation can be increased or decreased depending on need. This stimulation does not hurt and typically leads to a feeling of numbness in the area, which can be effective in reducing pain for some chronic conditions, such as phantom limb pain and arthritis, as well as pain following surgery.

Acupuncture, in which needles are inserted at specific points on the skin, is another type of physical stimulation technique that may help control pain. This ancient technique is widely used in Asian medicine. It is based on the idea that the body's energy flows in 14 distinct channels (Richardson & Vincent, 1986; Vincent & Richardson, 1986), and a person's health is supposedly dependent on the balance of energy flowing through them. Imbalances can be corrected by inserting tiny needles into the skin and twirling them. Acupuncture is used to treat a variety of common health problems, including nausea caused by chemotherapy and pregnancy, pain following dental surgery, painful menstruation, tennis elbow, lower-back and headache pain, and carpal tunnel syndrome (Brattberg, 1983; Helms, 1987; Richardson & Vincent, 1986). In some cases, acupuncture can even be effective in reducing pain during surgery (Melzack & Wall, 1982).

Massage therapy, a technique in which people receive deep-tissue manipulation by a trained therapist, has recently received considerable attention. Field et al. have conducted a number of studies showing that massage therapy can help reduce the experience of pain (1998). For example, in one study, 24 adults with chronic lower-back pain were randomly assigned to receive either massage therapy for 30 minutes twice a week for 5 weeks or to practice progressive muscle relaxation. By the end of the sessions, people in the massage therapy group showed significantly less

Have you ever had acupuncture? An estimated 3.1 million Americans seek this type of treatment each year (Barnes, Bloom, & Nahin, 2008).
Source: George Shelley/Corbis Images.

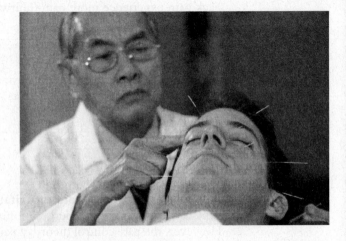

pain and anxiety, lower levels of depression, and even had greater range of motion in their backs compared to the other group. Another study with chronic migraine patients found that massage therapy led to less pain and more headache-free days as compared to those who received medication for migraines. Similar studies suggest that massage can be effective in reducing the pain of childbirth, postsurgery pain, and arthritis pain. Massage therapy also reduces physical discomfort and improves mood disturbances in women with breast cancer (Listing et al., 2009). Researchers in another study randomly assigned women with primary breast cancer into an intervention group, in which all participants received biweekly 30-minute massages, or into a control group. At the 11-week follow-up, a significantly higher reduction of physical discomfort, as well as a decrease in fatigue, was found in the intervention group compared with the control group. Some evidence even suggests that massage can lead to improvements in immune functioning and stress hormones (Hernandez-Reif, Field, Krasnegor & Theakston, 2001; Rapaport, Schettler, & Bresee, 2010).

Like massage therapy, **chiropractic therapy** focuses on manipulating the bones, muscles, and joints to improve body alignment. Between 3 and 10% of Americans visit chiropractors each year, usually with complaints of back pain (Eisenberg et al., 1993). Although the medical community is skeptical about the benefits of this approach, spinal manipulation is as effective as more traditional medical treatments for back pain (Shekelle, Adams, & Chassin, 1992).

Physical stimulation methods, such as TENS, acupuncture, and massage therapy, are not always effective in reducing pain, however, because in some cases their effects may be short lived. Massage therapy, for example, is effective in reducing ongoing pain, but this approach has no long-term effectiveness after it is discontinued (Field, 1998). Similarly, although some evidence suggests that acupuncture can be effective in reducing pain, it is not consistently more effective than other types of treatments, such as medication (Shlay et al., 1998; Taub, 1998). Moreover, physical stimulation techniques may work to reduce pain simply because they distract patients from their real pain and not because of any true physical effects. For example, people who are undergoing acupuncture may focus intensely on the feeling of the needles going into their skin and may stop concentrating on other pain. In fact, and as described in Box 9.2: Focus on Research, in some cases, the effects of these methods seem to be based largely on patients' beliefs that they will work (a placebo effect; Dowson, Lewith, & Machin, 1985). For example, one study randomly assigned patients with lower-back pain to receive TENS or sham TENS (in which no actual stimulation was given) three times a day for 4 weeks (Deyo, Walsh, & Martin, 1990). Although following treatment 47% of patients who received TENS did report significant improvements in functioning as well as reduced pain, these benefits were reported by 42% of those who received sham TENS as well.

But this is not to say that the power of physical stimulation methods is simply all in the mind. Some evidence suggests that physical stimulation methods of pain control do have some type of physical influences on pain because they work with animals, including monkeys and rats (Melzack & Wall, 1982). Moreover, in one study, 53% of patients reported experiencing less pain following acupuncture as compared to only 33% of those in a placebo group (who received fake electrical nerve stimulation), which suggests that acupuncture may lead to some type of actual physical effect on the body that reduces pain (Dowson et al., 1985). As discussed later in this chapter, if people simply believe they have control over their pain and that the pain will decrease, this can lead to physiological changes in the

Box 9.2

Focus on Research: Does Acupuncture Really Work to Reduce Pain?

Researchers were interested in examining the effectiveness of acupuncture in treating patients with migraines (Linde et al., 2007). In this study, 302 patients with migraine headaches were randomly assigned to one of three conditions: acupuncture, sham acupuncture, or waiting list control. Acupuncture and sham acupuncture were administered by specialized physicians and consisted of 12 sessions per patient over 8 weeks. Patients completed headache diaries both before and after the condition so that researchers could examine changes over time. Findings indicated that the mean number of days in which participants experienced moderate to severe headaches decreased by 2.2 for those in the acupuncture group. However, those in the sham acupuncture group experienced precisely the same decrease. In contrast, those in the waiting list control condition showed a decrease of only .8 days in which a moderate to severe headache occurred. In sum, there were no differences detected between the acupuncture and the sham acupuncture groups in terms of headaches, although both of these interventions were more effective than the waiting list control. This research indicates that some of the beneficial effects seen with acupuncture may be a reflection of people's beliefs about the effectiveness of acupuncture and not due to any specific physical properties of this treatment.

body, including the release of endorphins in the brain that do in fact inhibit the experience of pain (He, 1987).

What Are Some Psychological Methods of Controlling Pain?

Given the considerable evidence suggesting that the experience of pain is influenced by psychological factors, as well as the limitations of some of the physical methods of pain management, researchers have also examined psychological methods of controlling pain. This section reviews several different psychological methods of managing pain, including hypnosis, biofeedback, relaxation and distraction, cognition approaches, and behavioral therapy.

Hypnosis

Hypnosis refers to an altered state of consciousness or trance state that individuals can experience under the guidance of a trained therapist (Chaves, 1994). People under hypnosis may be particularly responsive to statements made by the hypnotist. Some research suggests that hypnosis can be effective in controlling pain, including the pain associated with dental work, childbirth, back pain, burns, headaches, and arthritis (Barber, 1998; Hilgard, 1975; Hilgard & Hilgard, 1983; Patterson, Everett, Burns, & Marvin, 1992; Spanos & Katsanis, 1989). For example, one study with chronic headache patients randomly assigned people to a hypnosis therapy group or a control group and found that people receiving the hypnosis therapy reported less headache pain (ter Kuile et al., 1994). Other research has examined the use of hypnosis to treat patients with burns (Askay, Patterson, Jensen, & Sharar, 2007). This study used a randomized controlled design in which the nurses and data collectors were unaware of the treatment condition to compare hypnotic analgesia with an attention-only placebo for burn pain during wound debridements. The group receiving hypnosis had a significant drop in pain compared with the control group.

> **Questioning the Research 9.4**
>
> Does the study by Askay et al. (2007) showing patients receiving hypnosis experienced less pain prove that hypnosis in fact reduces the experience of pain? What are some alternative explanations for this finding?

Research also points to the benefits of hypnosis in helping pain management among cancer patients (see Figure 9.5). Researchers in one study randomly assigned 200 breast cancer patients scheduled to undergo a breast biopsy or lumpectomy to receive a 15-minute presurgery hypnosis session or a session on empathic listening to examine whether a brief presurgery hypnosis intervention would decrease intraoperative anesthesia and analgesic use and side effects associated with breast-cancer surgery (Montgomery et al., 2007). Compared to those in the control group, patients in the hypnosis group reported less pain intensity,

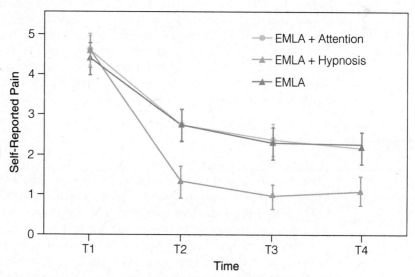

FIGURE 9.5   Researchers in this study randomly assigned 45 pediatric cancer patients to receive either an analgesic cream alone (EMLA) or in conjunction with hypnosis or additional attention from a nurse (Liossi, White, & Hatira, 2006). Patients who received the cream plus the hypnosis reported experiencing less anxiety both before and during the procedure, less pain, and less behavioral distress than those who received the analgesic cream alone or along with additional attention from the nurse.

pain unpleasantness, nausea, fatigue, discomfort, and emotional upset. Moreover, patients in the hypnosis group required less use of the pain medications propofol and lidocaine. Similarly, breast-cancer patients who participate in group therapy that includes both hypnosis and education show less of an increase over time in the intensity of pain and suffering compared to those who receive an education-only condition (Butler et al., 2009).

Although some researchers believe very strongly in the power of hypnosis in helping people cope with pain, others believe that hypnosis does not really represent a unique approach to pain relief (Spanos & Katsanis, 1989). Hypnosis may work to relieve pain simply because people believe it will work (e.g., the placebo effect) or because they want to please the experimenter (which is really a type of experimenter expectancy effect). In line with this view, people who are most susceptible to hypnosis may experience substantial pain relief, whereas those who are low in hypnotizability often show no benefits of hypnosis over a placebo (Miller, Barabasz, & Barabasz, 1991; Smith, Barabasz, & Barabasz, 1996). Hypnosis may also work to decrease pain by distracting patients and helping them relax, which in turn reduces their awareness of pain. For example, one study found that there was no difference in pain reduction between people who were hypnotized and those who were not when all participants were told that they were selected because they would be highly responsive to the pain-reduction treatment they would receive (Spanos & Katsanis, 1989). The power of suggestion may therefore be a more important predictor of pain relief than the power of hypnosis. Finally, still other research suggests that while hypnotic treatment can be effective in reducing pain, it is no more effective than cognitive-behavioral therapy (CBT; Edelson & Fitzpatrick, 1989; Stam, McGrath, & Brooke, 1984). Although there are reports of people undergoing cardiac surgery, cesarean sections, and appendectomies with no anesthesia other than hypnosis, these cases are considered anecdotal because they were not conducted using controlled, scientific methods. In sum, hypnosis probably works for some people better than or as well as other psychological methods of pain control, but there is little evidence that hypnosis itself has unique pain-relieving qualities and can thus be used in place of other methods of pain control.

Biofeedback

In **biofeedback**, people are trained, using electric monitors, to monitor and change selected physiological functions, such as their heart rate, finger temperature, muscle activity, and brain wave patterns (Arena & Blanchard, 1996). How does this process work? First, a particular biological response, such as heart rate or muscle tension, is measured, and the results are shown immediately to the patient. The patient is then asked to engage in different thoughts or behaviors in an attempt to influence that particular physiological response. They might be instructed, for example, to think relaxing thoughts or to tense their muscles and then to see how these thoughts and behaviors influence their physiological responses. By providing constant feedback on how such thoughts and behaviors influence physiological reactions, over time patients can learn to change their physiological responses by changing their thoughts or behavior. Biofeedback is an effective way to control headache pain (Turner & Chapman, 1982), back pain (Flor & Birbaumer, 1993), and hypertension (Nakao et al., 1997). For example, one study compared biofeedback to CBT and medical treatment for chronic back pain and found that biofeedback was superior to the other two approaches (Flor & Birbaumer, 1993).

Although biofeedback is an effective way of decreasing various types of pain, it has a number of drawbacks limiting its usefulness. Specifically, biofeedback is time-consuming and expensive, given the necessary equipment and time to learn the technique (Roberts, 1987). Patients must have considerable practice to learn how to influence their physiological responses, and this requires time on the part of a technician as well as access to very expensive equipment. Moreover, while biofeedback can work to reduce pain, comparison studies suggest that it is often no better than more simplistic techniques, such as relaxation (Bush, Ditto, & Feuerstein, 1985); therefore it is not widely used for managing pain.

Relaxation and Distraction

As its name implies, the relaxation approach to pain management works by helping people learn to relax, and thereby reduce their stress, anxiety, and pain (Blanchard, Appelbaum, Guarnieri, Morrill, & Dentinger, 1987). One relaxation method is called **progressive muscle relaxation**, in which patients focus on tensing and then releasing each part of their body (hands, shoulders, legs, etc.) one at a time (Jacobson, 1938). This process helps patients distinguish states of tension from states of relaxation, and therefore trains patients in ways to calm themselves in virtually any stressful situation. Similarly, in the technique of **systematic desensitization**, a person is asked to describe the specific source of his or her anxiety, and then to create a hierarchy of different stimuli (which cause increasing levels of arousal) associated with that anxiety. The therapist then asks the patient to focus on the least anxiety-provoking image: The therapist changes the focus to a less-stressful stimulus whenever the patient experiences any anxiety during the technique. Gradually, when the patient is able to think about a low-level stimulus without feeling anxiety, the therapist continues to progressively higher-level, more-anxiety-provoking stimuli; over time, this enables people to build up their tolerance to specific stressful situations. Other techniques that rely on some combination of relaxation and distraction include **guided imagery**, which pairs deep muscle relaxation with a specific pleasant image that serves to focus a patient's mind on something other than the pain (see Table 9.3), and **meditation**, in which patients relax their bodies and focus attention on a single thought, sometimes while verbalizing a single word or thought.

Finally, some techniques simply focus on trying to distract the patient to get his or her mind off the pain based on the idea that patients will not be able to concentrate on the pain because they are focusing on something else (McCaul & Marlatt, 1984). For chronic pain patients, even a simple activity such as reading a book, watching television, or listening to music can help distract them from their pain (this is why some dentist offices have televisions in the exam rooms). In line with this theory, patients with persistent pain who cope by distracting themselves experience less intense pain (Cui et al., 2009). Researchers in one study even found that people who looked at paintings they see as beautiful showed lower ratings of pain in an experimental setting compared to those who looked at paintings they found less appealing (de Tommaso, Sardaro, & Livrea, 2008). As described in Box 9.3: Focus on Research, looking at photos of a romantic partner can serve as a distraction from pain and thereby reduce the experience of pain.

TABLE 9.3   *Tension-Reducing Imagery Practice (TRIP)*

1. Decide to take a mini-TRIP by stopping all other activities and thoughts. Decide where your trip will take you (e.g., the beach, the mountains, your backyard, an abstract location or experience).

2. Take a deep breath.

3. Purse your lips and slowly exhale your first deep breath through the small opening between your lips. As you slowly exhale, say the word *relax* to yourself.

4. After this first deep breath, let your jaw relax and go slack. Future deep breaths will be taken normally.

5. Relax your jaw and then allow the feeling of relaxation to travel downward from your jaw to the rest of your body. Allow the feeling of relaxation to wash like a wave over your entire body. As the wave travels down your body, make each breath you take a deep one.

6. Begin your imagery. Make the image as rich as possible by using all of your senses. For example, if you are imagining a beach, allow yourself to see the clouds, the water, the sand, and the sky. Hear the waves, the seagulls, and the wind. Feel the sand on your feet, the sea breeze on your face, and the waves wetting your ankles. Smell the ocean mist and the sweet coconut smell of suntan oil, and taste the salt on your lips. Bring this image into your mind quickly and intensely, so that your mind is highly distracted for a brief period of time.

The mini-TRIP can be a useful way of coping with pain during relatively short medical procedures, such as injections, spinal taps, and dental procedures.

Source: Williams, 1996.

Box 9.3

Focus on Research: Can Looking at Pictures of Loved Ones Reduce Pain?

Researchers in this study examined whether simply holding a partner's hand or looking at a photograph of one's partner could reduce the experience of pain (Master et al., 2009). Women in long-term relationships underwent a series of pain events involving moderate heat. In one condition, they held a stranger's hand, in another they held their partner's hand, and in yet another they looked at a picture of their partner. As predicted, women who held their partner's hand or even looked at a photograph of their partner experienced less pain than those who held a stranger's hand. These findings suggest that bringing a photograph of a loved one to focus on during painful procedures may be a useful strategy for distracting one's self from pain, especially if the partner is unable to be with you in person. Moreover, these findings suggest that beneficial effects of social support on pain reduction may come at least in part due to the mere presence of a loved one, perhaps as a reminder of the availability of such support. In line with this view, some recent research indicates that viewing pictures of a romantic partner activates parts of the brain that are associated with the experience of reward, suggesting that this type of positive activation may have a direct influence on reducing the experience of pain in the brain (Younger, Aron, Parke, Chatterjee, & Mackey, 2010).

Relaxation and distraction techniques can be quite effective in reducing a variety of different types of pain, including pain caused by chemotherapy (Lyles Burish, Krozely, & Oldham, 1982), migraine headaches (Illacqua, 1994), lower-back problems (Carlson & Hoyle, 1993), dental procedures (Gatchel, 1980, 1986), and various medical procedures, including injections, lumbar punctures, and bone marrow aspirations (Blount et al., 1989). For example, one study found that people who listened to a tape narrating progressive muscle relaxation were able to withstand much more pain than those who did not have the help of the tape (Cogan, Cogan, Waltz, & McCue, 1987). Another study found that patients trained to meditate showed lower levels of pain and used fewer pain killers as compared to those who used traditional medical treatment (Kabat-Zinn, Lipworth, & Burney, 1985). Moreover, training in relaxation seems to provide relatively long-term relief—as long as 5 years according to some studies of chronic headache sufferers (Blanchard et al., 1987). As described in Box 9.4: Focus on Development, distraction can also help reduce the experience of pain in children (and see Figure 9.6).

There are several possible explanations for how these techniques work to decrease pain. First, they may give people power to cope with stress, which reduces pain. As discussed earlier, people who believe they can cope with pain actually feel less pain, perhaps because this expectation leads to the use of more effective pain management

Box 9.4

Focus on Development: The Impact of Watching Movies on Pain Relief in Children

Distraction can even be an effective technique to reduce pain in very young infants and children, who may have trouble using other methods of pain control (Cohen, 2002; Cohen, Blount, Cohen, Schaen, & Zaff, 1999). Cohen et al. (1999) examined two different types of strategies for controlling children's pain while receiving a series of three hepatitis B vaccinations 1 month apart. In this study, 39 fourth-graders were randomly assigned to one of three treatment conditions during each of the vaccinations, so that all children experienced each of the treatment options. Children in the distraction condition watched a movie, such as *101 Dalmatians* or *Toy Story*, while they had their shot. Children in the anesthetic condition had an anesthetic cream, which numbs the skin applied to the site of the injection. Children in the typical care condition, the control condition, were simply comforted by the nurse. After receiving all three conditions (and all three injections), the children were asked which condition was the best at helping them cope with their fear and anxiety, and which condition they preferred the next time they needed a shot. Findings from this study revealed that distraction was a very effective strategy for reducing pain and anxiety. Children showed less distress and more coping in the distraction condition, and both distraction and anesthetic were perceived by children as preferable to typical care. Specifically, 52% of the children said they would prefer distraction, whereas only 33% would select the cream, and 15% would prefer the nurse's presence. This study provides strong evidence that distraction can be an effective way of helping children cope with the pain of injections.

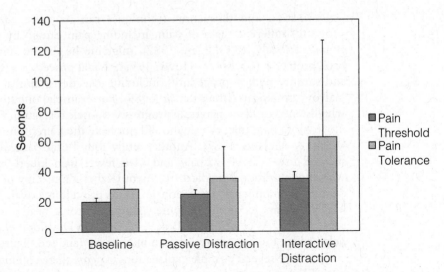

FIGURE 9.6   Children in this study were randomly assigned to the baseline condition (a control condition), a passive distraction condition (in which children watched a movie), or an interactive distraction condition (in which children played an interactive video game), and then completed a cold pressor test in which they had to keep their hands in cold water for as long as possible. Although children in both of the distraction conditions showed a higher pain threshold (number of seconds before the child reported pain) and pain tolerance (number of seconds before the child removed his/her hand), children in the interactive distraction condition tolerated the cold nearly twice as long as those in the passive distraction condition (data from Dahlquist et al., 2007).

strategies (DeGood, 2000; Jensen et al., 1991; Turk & Flor, 1999). In line with this view, research reveals that optimists generally cope with pain better than pessimists, at least in part because optimists generally cope with a painful stimulus by mentally disengaging from the pain (Geers, Wellman, Helfer, Fowler, & France, 2008). Second, relaxation may reduce muscle tension, which can then decrease the experience of pain (for headaches, back pain, ulcers; Turner & Chapman, 1982). Once again, all of these techniques may work to reduce pain primarily by giving patients the expectation that their pain will decrease, which in turn can lead to physiological changes in the body that can decrease the experience of pain. Finally, although relaxation and distraction techniques can indeed reduce the experience of pain, these strategies are probably more effective with mild and moderate pain than with severe pain (McCaul & Marlott, 1984).

Cognitive Approaches

Cognitive methods focus on helping people understand how their thoughts and feelings influence the experience of pain as well as helping people change their reactions to and perceptions of pain (Fernandez, 1986). First, helping patients see the consequences of maladaptive thoughts can be effective in reducing pain. For example, people may learn that feeling stress and anxiety could enhance pain;

therefore, they might focus on reducing these feelings as a way of decreasing the experience of pain. As described previously, people who focus their attention on the unpleasant aspects of a medical procedure, who anticipate negative outcomes, and who think negative thoughts may experience more pain (Gil et al., 1990; Keefe et al., 1994). Giving people strategies for controlling pain is another way of helping to change their thoughts about pain. Patients could, for example, focus on believing pain is manageable and having confidence in their ability to cope with it (e.g., they might think "This really isn't so bad. I can get through this."). Finally, cognitive approaches to pain control can work by helping people think about pain in new ways, a technique called *cognitive redefinition*. For example, a woman might be trained to think about the pain of labor as her baby pushing its way into the world, which puts it in a more positive light.

Many of these approaches to managing pain are used in strategies for women undergoing natural childbirth (Lamaze, 1970; Melzack & Wall, 1982). First, childbirth education classes can give couples some practical strategies for relieving pain, including positions to try during labor, massage techniques that a partner can do to help reduce pain, and special breathing exercises. These classes also provide training in relaxation and distraction. For example, couples are encouraged to choose a "focal object," such as a stuffed animal, special photo, or other personally meaningful object, to concentrate on during labor, and thus help distract women from the pain. Women are also taught to think about pain in a new way—to think about each (incredibly painful) contraction as working to bring the baby's arrival that much closer.

Cognitive techniques are effective in helping people cope with various types of pain, including headaches and back pain (Compas, Haaga, Keefe, Leitenberg, & Williams, 1998; Sanders, Shepherd, Cleghorn, & Woolford, 1994; Turner & Jensen, 1993). For example, researchers in one study randomly assigned 203 patients suffering from chronic tension headaches to receive cognitive therapy, antidepressant medication, or placebo medication (Holroyd et al., 2001). Cognitive-behavioral therapy was more effective than the placebo and as effective as the antidepressant medication in reducing headache activity, medication use, and headache-related disability. Similarly, another study compared the effectiveness of different approaches to managing pain in patients with sickle cell anemia, a rare blood disease that causes severe pain (Gil et al., 1996). Some patients received training in cognitive coping skills (relaxation, reinterpretation, calming self-statements) whereas others received more general education about their disease (they were given information about the hereditary nature of the disease, its psychological consequences, and medical treatment). As predicted, patients who received coping skills training reported lower levels of negative thinking and pain than those who received education about sickle cell anemia.

On the other hand, passive strategies, such as self-criticism (blaming oneself for the pain), overgeneralizing (believing the pain will never end and will ruin other aspects of one's life), and catastrophizing (overestimating the intensity of the pain), are associated with greater pain (Esteve, Ramírez-Maestre, & López-Martínez, 2007; Holm, Holroyd, Hursey, & Penzien, 1986; Klapow, Slater, Patterson, & Atkinson, 1995; Mercado, Carroll, Cassidy, & Cote, 2000; Ukestad & Wittrock, 1996). For example, one study examined how frequent headache sufferers would handle submerging their hand in ice water for a period of time—a very painful

TABLE 9.4 *Test Yourself: Coping Strategies Questionnaire*

Please indicate how much you engage in these types of activities when you encounter a difficult, stressful, or upsetting situation, using a scale from 1 (not at all) to 5 (very much).

1. Schedule my time better
2. Think about how I have solved similar problems
3. Analyze the problem before reacting
4. Come up with several different solutions to the problem
5. Preoccupied with aches and pains
6. Tell myself that it is not really happening to me
7. Blame myself for not knowing what to do
8. Worry about what I am going to do
9. Go out for a snack or meal
10. Watch TV
11. Try to be with other people
12. Phone a friend

Items 1 to 4 assess task coping, items 5 to 8 assess emotional coping, and items 9 to 12 assess avoidance coping.

Source: Endler & Parker, 1990.

task (Ukestad & Wittrock, 1996). Headache sufferers rated their discomfort as more severe and were more likely to rely on catastrophizing than nonheadache sufferers. Studies of patients with lower-back pain and arthritis indicate that the use of passive strategies is a stronger predictor of pain than disease-related variables, such as severity of the disease and obesity (Flor & Turk, 1988; Keefe et al., 1987). See Table 9.4 to examine which coping strategies you use.

Expressing emotion may help people cope with pain. Based on prior research demonstrating the benefits of emotional disclosure for chronically ill individuals, researchers in one study randomly assigned chronic pain patients to express their anger constructively or to write about their goals nonemotionally in a letter-writing format on two occasions (Graham, Lobel, Glass, & Lokshina, 2008). Participants in the anger expression group experienced greater improvement in terms of their control over pain, pain severity, and level of depression. These findings suggest that expressing anger may be helpful for chronic pain sufferers. On the other hand, people who try to suppress emotions may experience heightened pain intensity, perhaps in part because suppressing pain leads to increases in muscle tension as well as in blood pressure (Burns, Quartana, & Bruehl, 2007; Quartana, Burns, & Lofland, 2007). Over time, such attempts to repeatedly suppress the experience of pain can lead to long-term sensitivity to chronic pain (Elfant, Burns, & Zeichner, 2008).

Finally, some research points to the value of accepting pain as a strategy for coping with pain. For example, women with chronic pain conditions, such as osteoarthritis or fibromyalgia, who have a greater capacity to accept the experience of pain, show greater resilience (Kratz, Davis, & Zautra, 2007). Similarly, patients who are able to accept the reality of ongoing chronic pain benefit more from pain treatment interventions (Samwel, Kraaimaat, Crul, van Dongen, & Evers, 2009).

How exactly do cognitive approaches work to reduce the experience of pain? First, these approaches give people practical strategies for reducing pain. Giving women information on helpful positions they can use during labor (e.g., standing as opposed to lying down), for example, can actually help reduce the pain of labor when employed (Melzack, 1993). Second, cognitive approaches give people information about what to expect, such as the types of sensations they may experience, which can decrease anxiety and thereby reduce pain. This may be why women who attend childbirth training classes experience greater reductions in pain during labor as compared to those who don't attend classes (Melzack, Taenzer, Feldman, & Kinch, 1981).

Cognitive approaches to pain control may also work by increasing people's perceived control over the pain, which helps lessen its perceived severity (Zucker et al., 1998). As described at the beginning of the chapter, Melissa's training in cognitive techniques, such as breathing exercises and choosing a focal object, helped her to give birth without using pain medication. Similarly, one study of 141 patients with chronic pain who were enrolled in a pain program at the University of Washington found that increases in perceived control over pain were associated with decreases in depression, perceived disability, and pain intensity at the 6- and 12-month follow-ups (Jensen, Turner, & Romano, 2001). Moreover, patients who received cognitive therapy to cope with IBS showed no decreases in the frequency of daily hassles following the therapy but showed decreases in the distress such hassles caused them, suggesting that patients learned effective strategies for coping with these events (Payne & Blanchard, 1995). These findings suggest that changing patients' cognitions about pain can be an effective approach to changing perceived pain.

Finally, learning skills for managing pain may even lead to the release of pain-relieving endorphins (Bandura, O'Leary, Taylor, Gauthier, & Gossard, 1987). Bandura et al. at Stanford University were interested in examining the effectiveness of training students in perceived self-efficacy for coping with pain (1987). In this study, 72 students all first underwent a very painful procedure called the cold pressor test (as described earlier in this chapter). After completing this first test, the students were randomly assigned to one of three treatment conditions: a cognitive-coping group, a placebo-pill group, and a control group. Students in the cognitive-coping group were taught different ways to think about their pain, such as thinking about something other than the pain, thinking about the pain as completely separate from their bodies, and thinking encouraging thoughts about how well they were coping with the pain. The students in the placebo group were given an inert pill that they were told would prevent and/or alleviate their pain. All students then repeated the cold pressor test to see whether their pain tolerance had increased. Findings showed, as predicted, that those who were taught cognitive coping had a much higher pain tolerance than those in the other two conditions. Specifically, students in the cognitive-coping condition showed an increase in pain tolerance of nearly 60%, whereas those in the placebo and control conditions showed only very small increases (less than 10%).

The researchers were then interested in testing exactly how training someone in cognitive-coping skills for managing pain leads to such a remarkable increase in pain tolerance. Specifically, they were interested in examining whether this type of training increases the activation of endorphins in the body, which in turn leads to the reduction of pain. To test this part of their hypothesis, the researchers gave half of the subjects in each condition an injection of a drug called naloxone, which blocks the pain-reducing effects of endorphins, and the other half of the subjects

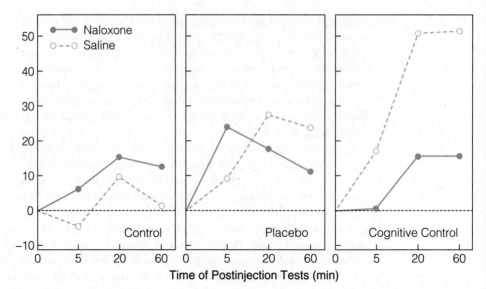

FIGURE 9.7   Although there is no difference in the change in pain tolerance as a function of whether the student received an injection of naloxone or saline for those in the control and placebo conditions, students in the cognitive-coping condition showed a much greater increase in pain tolerance if they received an injection of saline as opposed to naloxone (data from Bandura et al., 1987).

received a saline injection, which should have had no influence on the activation of endorphins. As shown in Figure 9.7, these findings showed that there was no difference in pain tolerance as a function of whether students received the naloxone or saline for those who were in the control or placebo conditions. Apparently, people in these conditions did not experience the benefits of endorphins at reducing pain, and therefore it didn't matter whether the potential effects of endorphins were blocked (in the case of those receiving the naloxone injection) or not (in the case of those receiving the saline injection). However, students in the cognitive-control condition who received saline had a much higher pain tolerance than those in this condition who received the naloxone, suggesting that participants in this condition did have higher levels of endorphins—and hence were able to withstand much more pain when these endorphins were not blocked (in the case of the saline) than when they were blocked (in the case of the naloxone). Giving someone training in cognitive techniques for controlling pain actually increases the level of endorphins in the body, which in turn reduces the feeling of pain.

Behavior Therapy

As described previously, people who are in pain often receive certain relative benefits, such as attention from others, assistance with tasks, and avoidance of undesirable activities (Turk, 1996). Operant-conditioning approaches to the reduction of pain therefore focus on eliminating the "perks" of pain (Fordyce, Brockway, Bergman, & Spengler, 1986). This approach, developed by Wilbert Fordyce, focuses on reinforcing positive behaviors (e.g., increased activity) and ignoring negative behaviors (e.g., complaints of pain). One behavior therapy technique trains family members in how to respond to a patient's complaints of pain, namely by ignoring reports of pain and disability. Research by Romano et al. (1992) demonstrated that spouses of chronic pain patients were much more likely to discourage their partners from engaging in physical tasks than those whose spouses were not chronic pain patients. For example, they were much more likely to say, "I'll do that—you rest now," and "Don't overdo it." Over time, family members are causing the patient to be dependent and may decrease patients' self-efficacy and self-esteem. Behavioral therapy programs often try to help family members understand the role they play in perpetuating pain behaviors. Behavior therapy programs also try to reduce patients' dependence on pain medication by providing drugs only at fixed intervals, as opposed to on demand, which also rewards complaints of pain. Moreover, the dose of pain medication given is gradually decreased over time without the patient knowing, so eventually he or she simply may be taking an inert substance. This approach helps reduce the patient's physical dependence on medication.

Behavioral approaches can work very well to decrease various types of chronic pain (Turner & Clancy, 1988). For example, one study examined chronic pain patients who spent 6 to 8 weeks in a hospital undergoing various types of behavior therapy (having their pain behaviors ignored, engaging in physical therapy, reducing pain-related medicines, participating in work opportunities; family members were also taught to not reinforce pain behaviors; Roberts & Reinhardt, 1980). At the end of treatment, patients were using fewer drugs, reported feeling less pain, and spent less time inactive. Another study of 148 patients with chronic back pain examined the effectiveness of an operant-conditioning program alone (they were given behavioral goals, and spouses were trained to reinforce only healthy behaviors) as compared to an operant-conditioning plus cognitive coping skills program (patients received education about the role psychological factors play in the experience and management of pain; Kole-Snijders et al., 1999). Compared to the waiting-list control condition, both operant conditioning alone and operant conditioning plus cognitive coping skills led to less negative affect, less pain behavior, and higher pain coping and pain control. Although operant-conditioning techniques can be very effective in decreasing pain, they are most effective when they are supported by cooperative family members.

Behavioral intervention may be particularly effective when combined with drug treatment. Researchers in one study examined if a combined pharmacological and behavioral intervention improves both depression and pain in primary care patients with musculoskeletal pain as well as depression (Kroenke et al., 2009). In this study, 250 patients who had lower-back, hip, or knee pain for 3 months or longer and at least moderate depression severity were randomly assigned to the intervention, which included 12 weeks of antidepressants followed by 12 weeks of a pain self-management program and then 6 months of a continuation phase of therapy, or to usual care. At the 12-month follow-up, 37.4% of the intervention patients had substantially reduced signs of depression, compared to only 16.5% of the usual care patients. In addition, 41.5% of the intervention patients experienced a reduction in pain, compared to only 17.3% of the usual care patients. These findings suggest that antidepressant therapy followed by a pain self-management program may be a particularly effective way to reduce both depression and pain.

Conclusions

This section has described separately a number of psychological methods for controlling pain. However, many pain-management programs use several techniques in combination. Pain-management programs that include multiple approaches tend to be more effective than those that include only one (Flor, Fydrich, & Turk, 1992; Murphy, 1996). As described at the beginning of the chapter, Tom's back pain decreased substantially after he entered a pain clinic, which included training in relaxation, guided imagery, and cognitive redefinition, as well as educating Tom and his wife about the consequences of rewarding pain behaviors. For example, one study with chronic headache pain patients found that education, physical therapy, stress management, and pain-management skills led to a substantial reduction in medication use (Scharff & Marcus, 1994). In fact, patients who participate in combined programs are much more likely to return to work than those who receive no treatment or only a single-treatment approach (68% versus 36%, respectively, in one study; Flor et al., 1992).

Can Placebos Decrease Pain?

A **placebo** is a treatment that affects someone even though it contains no specific medical or physical properties relevant to the condition it is supposedly treating (Liberman, 1962). In other words, placebos are psychologically inert medicines or treatments that can produce very real and even lasting effects, effects that have been demonstrated on virtually every organ system in the body and many diseases, including chest pain, arthritis, hay fever, headaches, ulcers, hypertension, postoperative pain, seasickness, and pain from the common cold (Benedetti & Amanzio, 1997). In one review involving more than 1,000 patients treated for a variety of conditions, Beecher (1955) reported an average of 35% of patients benefited from placebo treatments, with the effectiveness of placebos ranging from 15 to 58%. For example, in one study, 122 surgical patients were given either morphine or a placebo, but all were told they were getting morphine (Beecher, 1959). Of those given morphine, 67% reported some relief, but so did 42% of those given the placebo! Although one study published in the *New England Journal of Medicine* suggests that the placebo effect is not quite as strong as it is often described (Hrobjartsson & Gotzche, 2001), most evidence suggests placebos can have a substantial impact on the experience of pain, precisely because people *believe* that they will work to reduce pain.

Factors That Influence the Effectiveness of Placebos

One factor that influences the effectiveness of placebos is patients' expectations about the effects of the treatment (Skelton & Pennebaker, 1982; Stewart-Williams, 2004). In other words, patients who expect a given reaction to a placebo may look for signs that show the treatment or drug is working. For example, in one study, participants were told that they would be hearing some noise that might cause their skin temperature to change (Pennebaker & Skelton, 1981). Some subjects were told that their temperature might rise, whereas others were told it might fall although in reality the noise should have no psychological effect on temperature. As predicted, those who expected their skin temperature to rise reported feeling themselves get warmer, whereas those who expected their temperature to fall reported feeling cooler upon exposure to the stimulus. Expectations also influence other types of physiological reactions, including heart rate and amount of nasal congestion and stuffiness. In fact, one study on the role of the placebo effect in influencing people's reactions to antidepressant medication found that 75% of the effectiveness of such drugs is caused by patients' expectations that they will work, as opposed to any psychological changes in brain chemistry (Kirsch & Sapirstein, 1999).

Placebos may also work as a result of broad principles in learning, such as classical conditioning (Benedetti & Amanzio, 1997). Many of the factors that increase the effectiveness of placebos are linked with environmental cues that suggest pain relief, such as sitting in a doctor's office, receiving a pill, or feeling an injection. Over time, people may learn to associate these types of stimuli with feeling better; therefore, placebos may work simply by triggering these associations. For example, if you always take an aspirin, which reduces the pain, when you have a headache, you may experience the same reduction in pain if you take a pill that you think is aspirin but which is actually just an inert sugar pill.

Another factor that may explain the placebo effect is patients' behavior (Benedetti & Amanzio, 1997). Specifically, when people are given a pain treatment they fully expect to work, they may change their behavior in ways that in turn lead to the desired reduction of pain. For example, if you have a bad headache and take an aspirin that you fully believe will alleviate the headache, you may relax because you know the pain will soon disappear; therefore, this conscious attempt to relax may lead to a decrease in your headache pain. In sum, just the belief that the treatment will work may lead to a decrease in anxiety, which may lead directly to a reduction in pain.

Moreover, all placebo treatments are not equal in their effectiveness—some are more effective than others (Benedetti & Amanzio, 1997). Those administered

Patients' expectations about the effectiveness of a particular drug or treatment in fact have a substantial impact on whether it works.
Source: P.C. Vey/cartoonbank.com. All Rights Reserved.

"If I don't think it's going to work, will it still work?"

through injection have greater effects than those taken orally; capsules are more effective than pills; and injections are better than capsules or pills. Even the brand name of the pill can influence its effectiveness: One study showed an increase of 10% in effectiveness through the use of a known name versus an unknown name (which helps explain why people often select the higher-priced name-brand drugs over cheaper alternatives even when the chemical properties of the drugs are virtually identical). The placebo effect is also stronger when a drug is administered by a doctor in a hospital setting than when given by a family member at home. In sum, having a placebo that looks, tastes, and feels like "real medicine" is likely to increase patient confidence and thereby its effectiveness.

The behavior of the practitioner can clearly influence the effectiveness of a placebo (Gracely, Dubner, Deeter, & Wolskee, 1985; Roberts, Kewman, Mercier, & Hovell, 1993). When a placebo is administered by an enthusiastic and friendly practitioner who seems interested in and sympathetic to the patient, the placebo is more effective than when it is delivered by an angry or rejecting practitioner. For example, in one study with surgery patients, half were visited the night before their surgery by the anesthesiologist, who told them in a brusque manner that everything would be fine (Talbot, 2000). The other patients were also visited by the same anesthesiologist, who this time sat on their beds, held their hands as he talked, and was very warm and friendly. As predicted, those who saw the kind and friendly practitioner required much less pain medication and were even discharged earlier from the hospital than those who had interacted with the brusque and cold practitioner.

A practitioner's expectations about the effectiveness of the placebo can also influence responsiveness. In one study, rates ranged from 70 to 25% effective based on the attitude of the practitioner toward the placebo: One doctor always handled placebo tablets with forceps, to convey to patients that this type of drug was too powerful even to be touched by human hands. In one study, doctors were told that they would be giving their patients either a painkiller or a placebo (see Figure 9.8; Gracely et al., 1985). Although all doctors were actually giving their patients a placebo, subjects treated by the doctors who believed they were administering a painkiller actually showed a reduction in their pain. Similarly, and as described at the beginning of the chapter, Brian's knee showed remarkable improvement after he started taking a drug that was strongly recommended by his physician—this effect could be caused by the physical properties of the drug, and/or Brian's expectations about the powerful effects of this drug as described by his trusted physician. The placebo effect as well as the practitioner expectancies effect are major reasons why clinical drug trials now use double-blind procedures in which neither the patient nor the practitioner knows who is getting an active or a placebo drug.

Physiological Mechanisms That Explain the Influence of Placebos

Most importantly, placebos may lead to physiological changes in the body, which in turn inhibit the experience of pain (Bandura et al., 1987; Benedetti & Amanzio, 1997; Levine, Gordon, & Fields, 1978). Some research suggests that the endorphin system is activated when people simply believe they are receiving a painkiller, even

FIGURE 9.8 All of the patients in this study received only a placebo—an injection of a saline solution. But those whose doctors thought they might get a pain-relieving drug reported feeling significantly less pain than those whose doctors thought they would receive a pain-enhancing drug (data from Gracely et al., 1985).

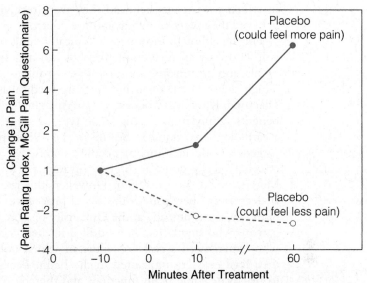

Note: Change in pain rating index between baseline (10 minutes before injection) and 10 and 60 minutes after administration of placebo.

when they are receiving a placebo (Benedetti & Amanzio, 1997). For example, researchers in one study randomly assigned dental patients to receive an injection of naloxone (which is known to reduce the effect of endorphins in providing pain relief) followed by a placebo, a placebo followed by an injection of naloxone, or simply two placebos (Levine et al., 1978). As predicted, those who got a placebo first and then naloxone reported greater pain than those who got a placebo both times, presumably because naloxone reduced the effectiveness of the endorphins (created by the placebo). Similarly, in a study with patients having their wisdom teeth removed, half were given real ultrasound therapy (known to reduce pain) during their procedure, while the others thought they were receiving this therapy but in reality the machine was unplugged (Hashish, Hai, Harvey, Feinmann, & Harris, 1988). Patients in both cases showed a decrease in pain, jaw tightness, and swelling, indicating that all of these physical effects were caused simply by the expectation that they were receiving a pain-reducing therapy. All of this evidence suggests that placebos may have both psychological and physical effects.

In line with this view, research using functional magnetic resonance imaging (fMRI) reveals that placebo analgesia—meaning the mere belief that one is receiving a pain reliever that is in reality an inert substance—leads to decreased brain activity in areas of the brain that respond to pain, including the thalamus, insula, and anterior cingulate cortex (Wager et al., 2004). In this study, researchers gave participants painful electric shocks to their wrists after applying either what they were told was an analgesic cream (which would reduce, but not eliminate, the pain) or an ineffective cream (which would serve as the control). In reality, the cream was the same in both conditions and had no properties that would reduce the experience of pain. As predicted, brain activity in areas that respond to pain was lower on trials in which participants believed they were receiving an analgesic than when they believed they were receiving an inert control.

Finally, although most people typically think of placebos as some type of medicine (a pill or an injection), placebos can also be treatments. To test the power of placebo treatments, in some cases, patients have had "placebo surgery," in which they are cut open but nothing medical is done to them (Beecher, 1959; Diamond, Kittle, & Crockett, 1960). Amazingly enough, many patients show some benefits simply from having some type of surgery. For example, Leonard Cobb, a cardiologist working in Seattle in the 1950s, performed fake surgery in which surgeons made incisions in people's chests, but did not tie off patients' arteries, as was typically done in surgery for angina at the time (Cobb, Thomas, Dillard, Merendino, & Bruce, 1959). However, this fake procedure was just as effective at decreasing chest pain as the actual procedure—which was quickly abandoned. Similarly, a recent study at the University of Toronto compared Parkinson's disease patients who simply had holes drilled in their skulls (the placebo surgery) to those who experienced a real procedure in which holes are drilled in their skulls and then fetal cells are implanted in the brain. Fetal-tissue transplantation is thought to reactivate some brain functions and thereby reverse motor problems associated with this disease. Patients who received the placebo surgery showed significant improvement in their motor functioning (although not as substantial as that shown by patients who actually received the cell implant; Talbot, 2000).

In one study, a surgeon named Bruce Moseley participated in an elaborate test of the placebo effect (Moseley et al., 2002). In this study, 180 patients with osteoarthritis of the knee were scheduled for an operation that supposedly would relieve the arthritis pain they were experiencing in that joint. Most of them were middle aged, all were former military men (treated at a Veterans Hospital), and they were told exactly what could happen: Some would have standard arthroscopic surgery, some would have their knee joint rinsed (but not scraped), and some would simply go to surgery and be anesthetized but have absolutely nothing medical done to their knees (they would simply be cut with the scalpel to create incisions and scars). To avoid experimenter expectancy effects, the study was double-blind—the surgeon went into the operating room and was then handed an envelope that told him which condition a subject was in. The patients were then assessed regularly over 2 years to determine whether "actual surgery" was indeed better than "placebo surgery" for reducing pain and increasing function (walking, climbing stairs, etc.). Results show that there were no differences in degree of pain or function among patients in the three groups at any point during the follow-up. This study was done to demonstrate, as we just discussed, that the placebo effect is most powerful when the subject really believes it, and patients strongly believe in the power of surgery. This study provides some evidence that at least in some cases, this belief alone can lead to positive results.

More recent research provides additional support for the power of "placebo surgery." Researchers in one study randomly assigned patients with painful vertebral fractures to undergo vertebroplasty, a common treatment for such fractures, or a sham procedure (Buchbinder et al., 2009). Both patients and physicians were blind in terms of condition. Although there were significant reductions in pain, as well as in physical functioning, quality of life, and perceived improvement, in both study groups at each follow-up assessment, there were no beneficial effects of

Surgery can clearly have a major impact on physical health—but is part of this effect merely caused by patients' belief in the power of surgery?
Source: Royalty-Free/Corbis Images

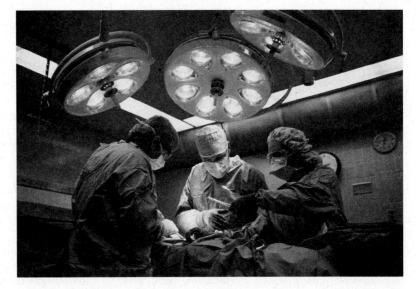

vertebroplasty as compared with a sham procedure at any of the follow-up periods. Similarly, researchers in another study randomly assigned 131 patients with vertebral fractures to undergo either vertebroplasty or, for those in the control group, a simulated procedure (Kallmes et al., 2009). One month after the procedure, both groups reported similar improvement in disability and pain scores. In sum, improvements in pain and pain-related disability associated with vertebrate fractures in patients treated with vertebroplasty were similar to those seen for patients in a control group. This research provides powerful evidence that the placebo effect can even influence people's response to surgical procedures.

TABLE 9.5   *Information YOU Can Use*

- Stress matters a lot for pain, which is why you may develop migraines or nausea during particularly stressful times. Taking steps to reduce stress in your environment—or even how you perceive potentially stressful events—can therefore help reduce pain.
- Your own thoughts, feelings, and behaviors influence how much pain you experience, which means that you can take some steps that reduce pain. Simply minimizing stress and focusing on maintaining a good mood helps decrease the experience of pain.
- Engaging in regular exercise can prevent, or at least reduce, the pain caused by headaches, back pain, and stomachache. So, think about going jogging or taking a yoga class as a way to minimize the experience of pain.
- When you are undergoing a painful experience, use psychological strategies to reduce the pain you feel. Try to relax your body, distract yourself, and/or think about pain in a new way—all of these approaches can help you feel better in the face of pain.
- Your expectations about pain relief can in fact lead to physiological changes in your body and even your brain areas that influence the experience of pain, which explains why the placebo effect is so powerful. Thus, when you take a medication or undergo a treatment to reduce pain, believing in its effectiveness can in fact improve its ability to reduce pain.

Summary

1. Pain affects more Americans than diabetes, heart disease, and cancer combined. Pain leads to serious costs for both individuals and society.

2. One type of pain is acute pain, which is intense but time-limited pain, such as occurs with a broken bruise, a cut or bruise, or childbirth. This type of pain disappears over time as the injury heals. In contrast, chronic pain may begin as acute pain but does not go away after a minimum of 6 months. This type of pain could include lower-back pain, headaches, and the pain associated with arthritis and cancer.

3. The earliest theories regarding how people experience pain included specificity theory, which suggests there are different sensory receptors for different types of sensations (including pain), and pattern theory, which suggests pain results from the type and intensity of stimulation received from the nerve ending.

4. The leading theory explaining pain is the gate control theory, which posits that when body tissues are damaged, nerve impulses travel from that area to the spinal cord. Then if the sensations are sufficiently intense, the nerve impulses will be sent all the way up to the brain. On the other hand, if the sensations are not sufficiently intense, or if there is another competing sensation that increases stimulation, a gate will block transmission of these impulses to the brain, and the experience of pain will be reduced.

5. Pain can be measured in a variety of different ways, including through self-report, behavioral measures, and physiological measures. Each of these approaches has both strengths and limitations.

6. Psychosocial factors influence the expression and/or experience of pain in numerous ways. The experience of stress leads to more pain, as does learning through direct experience and observation of others that experiencing pain (or claiming to experience pain) leads to particular benefits. Cognition, including people's attitudes, thoughts, beliefs, and expectations about pain, also influences the amount of pain felt. People's mood, and in particular the presence of depression and anxiety, is associated with the experience of pain.

7. Physical methods of controlling pain include traditional methods such as medication, surgery, physical therapy/exercise, and physical stimulation (e.g., transcutaneous electrical nerve stimulation—TENS, acupuncture, massage therapy, chiropractic therapy). The mechanisms by which these methods work to reduce pain varies, and may include both physical and psychological effects.

8. Psychological methods can also be used to control pain. These methods include hypnosis, biofeedback, relaxation and distraction (e.g., progressive muscle relaxation, systematic desensitization, guided imagery, meditation), cognitive approaches (in which people learn to think about pain in a new way), and behavior therapy (in which people and their families learn to reduce the benefits of experiencing pain).

9. The effect of placebos, meaning psychologically and physically inert medicines or treatments that can produce real and lasting effects, has been demonstrated on many different organ systems and diseases. Placebos may also work to reduce the experience of pain, at least in cases in which people believe that such an approach will work to reduce pain.

10. Several factors influence the effectiveness of placebos. These factors include patients' expectations about the effects of the treatment, the association of a treatment with environmental cues that suggest pain relief, patients' behavior, the type of treatment delivered, and the behavior and expectations of the practitioner.

11. Physiological mechanisms may help explain the influence of placebos. Placebos may activate the endorphin system, lead to decreases in brain activity (in areas which respond to pain), and lead to improvement in functioning following surgery.

Key Terms

acupuncture	biofeedback	chronic pain
acute pain	chiropractic therapy	gate control theory

guided imagery	pain	progressive muscle relaxation
hypnosis	pattern theory	specificity theory
massage therapy	physical stimulation (counter-	systematic desensitization
meditation	irritation)	transcutaneous electrical nerve
neuromatrix theory	placebo	stimulation (TENS)

Thought Questions

1. Describe two psychological methods and two physical methods of controlling pain.

2. Your roommate is having her wisdom teeth extracted next week and is very concerned about the pain she expects to experience. What are three psychological techniques for controlling pain that you could recommend to her?

3. Describe two different ways of measuring pain; include in your answer the pros and cons of each.

4. Your 3-year-old nephew is going to the doctor next week for his annual checkup, which includes a tetanus shot. What could you do to make sure this visit goes smoothly?

5. Describe three different explanations for the power of the placebo effect.

Answers to Questioning the Research

Answer 9.1. Although the study by Walker et al. (2001) shows that children who experience higher levels of stress also experience more abdominal pain, this research doesn't tell us whether stress causes pain, pain causes stress, or a third variable causes both pain and stress. This is a classic example of the challenge of distinguishing between correlation and causation. Experimental research is needed to examine the nature of this association.

Answer 9.2. Redelmeier and Kahneman (1996) exposed some patients to a longer colonoscopy than they needed to experience and thus raised important ethical issues. This study, however, like all research in health psychology was approved by an institutional review board. Several factors likely influenced the board's decision to approve this study, including the relatively brief time added to the end of the procedure (and thus minimal if any harm to the patient) and the expected benefits of finding a strategy for improving patients' experience with difficult medical procedures.

Answer 9.3. Although it may seem like doing specific back exercises would be a great way of reducing back pain, this type of intense focus on one area of the back may heighten the experience of such pain, which is why engaging in more general physical activity may in fact be better. It is also possible that doing particular back exercises serves as a reminder of the ongoing back pain, whereas engaging in more general exercise could distract from such pain.

Answer 9.4. Hypnosis led to a reduction in pain, compared to an attention-only control condition, but this study doesn't demonstrate whether hypnosis specifically led to this reduction. One possibility is that the experience of being hypnotized is relaxing, and thus patients who relax more deeply experience less pain. Another possibility is that being hypnotized is distracting, and thus patients who are distracted from what they are feeling report a reduction in pain experienced.

CHAPTER 10

Chronic Illness

Outline

- Julie is 45 years old and has suffered from arthritis in her hands for nearly 20 years. Although she has experienced some mild joint pain for many years, the pain has increased significantly in the past few months. Julie also now has trouble managing many of her daily tasks, including using a can opener, buttoning shirts, and brushing her hair. Julie's difficulty with daily functioning has led to an increasing reliance on her husband, Mike, which has put a major strain on their relationship.

- Don is 15 years old and has diabetes. His parents are very concerned about his disease and are constantly reminding him to avoid eating junk foods and to monitor his blood sugar. Although Don knows he should not eat certain foods, when he is with his friends he finds it difficult to turn down junk food. Also, because Don finds it embarrassing to monitor blood and give himself shots in front of other people, he sometimes "forgets."

- Bill, who is 60 years old, has coronary heart disease (CHD). He has always been a little overweight and has smoked since he was 17 years old. However, after experiencing his first heart attack last year, Bill became very concerned about his health and made a number of lifestyle changes. He joined a gym and walks 2 miles a day on the treadmill, has stopped smoking, and is trying to eat healthier foods.

- Betty is 58 years old and had a cancerous lump removed from her breast 2 months ago. She is now undergoing several rounds of chemotherapy to kill any cancer that possibly had spread to other parts of her body. Betty attends a weekly support group for women with breast cancer, which she thinks is very helpful. She often finds it hard to talk about her fears with her husband and children but is able to share her concerns with the other women in the group. She believes it is very comforting to be around other women who truly understand what she is feeling.

- Leslie is 32 years old and is HIV-positive. She believes she contracted HIV during her early 20s, when she was living in Boston, although she still doesn't know which of her sexual partners infected her. Leslie learned she was HIV-positive 5 years ago, when she and a new boyfriend decided to get tested together. She was initially shocked about her diagnosis, particularly because she's never really had casual sex—almost all of her sexual partners were men she was dating, and she always made sure to use condoms with new partners.

Preview

This chapter examines psychosocial factors that can influence how individuals experience and manage chronic illness. First, the chapter defines chronic illness as well as its physical, social, and psychological consequences. Next, we examine factors that influence how people cope with having a chronic illness, including the extent to which the illness interferes with daily life, type of coping used, and level of social support, as well as the role of different types of psychological interventions—education, cognitive behavioral therapy, social support—in helping people cope effectively with chronic illness. Finally, we examine how psychological factors influence the acquisition and management of three of the leading causes of death in the United States each year: cardiovascular disease, cancer, and AIDS.

What Are Chronic Diseases?

As we discussed in Chapter 1, in the early 1900s, most people died from **acute diseases**—pneumonia, tuberculosis, and typhoid fever (Grob, 1983). Many of these diseases were caused by exposure to a specific virus; acute diseases are contagious, and they kill people rather quickly. In contrast, **chronic diseases**, which cause 7 of 10 deaths in the United States, differ from acute conditions in several ways (Kung, Hoyert, Xu, & Murphy, 2008). First, chronic conditions often have multiple causes, including people's behavioral choices or lifestyles. As discussed in Chapters 7 and 8, behavioral choices regarding eating, exercising, smoking, and drinking alcohol are responsible for much of the illness, disability, and premature death related to chronic diseases. Second, chronic conditions often have a slow onset, and the disease intensity increases over time. Many people with HIV infection do not even know when they were exposed to the disease, and often they are infected for months or years before they notice any symptoms. Third, whereas acute conditions often can be cured, with medication or some other intervention, chronic conditions only can be managed—people with chronic diseases sometimes get worse and sometimes stay the same, but they can't be cured.

Chronic diseases, including heart disease, stroke, and cancer, now account for more than 50% of all deaths in the United States each year (see Table 10.1; Kung et al., 2008). Other chronic diseases also influence quality of life in numerous ways. Diabetes, which impacts 25.8 million Americans, is the leading cause of kidney failure, amputations, and new cases of blindness each year. Fifty million American adults (22% of the population) suffer from arthritis, which is the most common cause of disability. As described in Box 10.1: Focus on Culture, chronic conditions also have a major impact on life expectancy in other countries.

Not surprisingly, the prevalence of chronic conditions varies substantially by age. Most children with serious health conditions have acute conditions, whereas 88% of those over age 65 with serious health conditions have chronic conditions (Hoffman, Rice, & Sung, 1996). The number of people living with chronic illness is likely to increase as life expectancy rates continue to rise. Although 100 years

TABLE 10.1 *Number of Deaths Due to Five Leading Chronic Diseases*

Disease	Number of Deaths
Heart disease	616,067
Cancer	562,875
Stroke	135,952
Chronic lower respiratory disease	127,924
Diabetes	71,382

Chronic conditions now cause a majority of deaths in the United States each year.

Source: Centers for Disease Control, 2011.

Box 10.1

Focus on Culture: The Prevalence of Chronic Diseases Worldwide

Chronic diseases are the leading causes of death worldwide, with an estimated 17 million deaths each year due to cardiovascular disease (including heart disease and stroke), 7 million deaths due to cancer, 4 million deaths due to chronic lung diseases, and almost 1 million deaths due to diabetes (Yach, Hawkes, Gould, & Hofman, 2004). For example, India, the second most populous country, has the highest number of people with diabetes in the world, and around 2.5 million children in India die from infections such as pneumonia, diarrhea, and malaria every year. Sadly, the prevalence of chronic diseases is increasing, in part because risk factors, such as rates of smoking and obesity, continue to escalate. The development of all of these leading diseases is influenced by behavioral choices, including smoking, diet, lack of physical activity, and use of alcohol. Although many developed nations have focused considerable efforts on preventing chronic diseases, such as through instituting laws regulating tobacco or restricting alcohol and tobacco advertising, many developing countries have yet to address the problem of chronic disease.

ago relatively few people lived to age 65, because of the increase in life expectancy that has occurred in the United States over the past century, approximately one in eight Americans is now over age 65, and estimates are that people in this age group will represent 20% of the population by 2030. Because overall health generally declines as people get older, they are more likely to develop chronic conditions: The majority of older adults suffer from at least one chronic condition. Older adults also experience changes in physiological functioning, which increases their likelihood of developing an illness. For example, the responsiveness of the immune system decreases in older age, meaning that older individuals are more susceptible to mild illnesses that younger people may effectively fight off (Rabin, 2000).

What Are the Consequences of Having Chronic Illnesses?

Because chronic diseases can be managed but never cured, people with such a diagnosis face a lifetime of managing the symptoms and treatment of the disease. People diagnosed with a chronic illness therefore experience a number of consequences, including physical, social, and psychological problems.

Physical Problems

Many people with chronic diseases experience some type of physical debilitation, such as paralysis, disfigurement, incontinence, and pain (Devins & Binik, 1996; Wade & Lee, 2005). People with diabetes, for example, are at increased risk of developing heart disease, blindness, sexual dysfunction, kidney failure, and problems with circulation that can lead to amputation (Bishop, Roesler, Zimmerman, & Ballard, 1993). Symptoms of multiple sclerosis (MS), a neurological disorder, include impaired vision, weakness, tremors, incoordination, and bowel and bladder difficulties (Franklin & Nelson, 1993). Researchers in one study examined the impact of breast cancer on quality of life by comparing 5-year disease-free survivors to age-matched controls (Helgeson & Tomich, 2005). Although there were no differences between disease-free survivors and controls on many indicators of quality of life, survivors reported more difficulties with physical functioning and more physical symptoms than did women without cancer. Even chronic diseases that are not life threatening can lead to physical problems. For example, people with arthritis (a chronic, systemic, inflammatory condition causing pain and swelling of the joints) often experience constant pain from inflammation of the joints and have difficulty managing daily tasks, such as getting dressed, walking, or standing (Scott & Hochberg, 1993).

In other cases, the disease itself is not debilitating, but the treatment for it is destructive to health (Jacobson, Bovbjerg, & Reid, 1993; Jacobsen et al., 1995). An individual with kidney failure, for example, may need to undergo hemodialysis, in which his or her blood is circulated through an artificial kidney for several hours each week. Medications that are used to treat hypertension lead to a number of unpleasant side effects, such as impotence, weight gain, and drowsiness (Taylor & Aspinwall, 1993). Similarly, anticonvulsant drugs, which provide the main treatment for epilepsy, have several unpleasant side effects, such as drowsiness, nausea, mood change, and skin rash (Oles & Penry, 1987). Many of the treatments used to fight cancer, including chemotherapy, which involves administering toxic chemicals to the body in an attempt to kill the cancerous cells, and radiation, in which beams of radiation are used to destroy tissue in a particular area, have unpleasant side effects such as fatigue, diarrhea, vomiting, hair loss, loss of appetite, and nausea. For example, patients who have been treated for prostate cancer may experience long-lasting problems related to urinary, sexual, bowel, and hormonal function (Sanda et al., 2008). Although one of the most commonly used drugs to treat HIV is zidovudine (AZT), its use is associated with numerous unpleasant side effects, including anemia, headaches, itching, and even mental confusion.

Surgery, one of the most common treatments for some types of cancer, can lead to various types of disability and disfigurement of the patient, including amputation of a limb (bone cancer), removal of part or all of one or both breasts (breast

Many people find even relatively minor symptoms, such as hair loss due to chemotherapy or radiation, very upsetting.
Source: © Shelly Perry/iStockphoto.

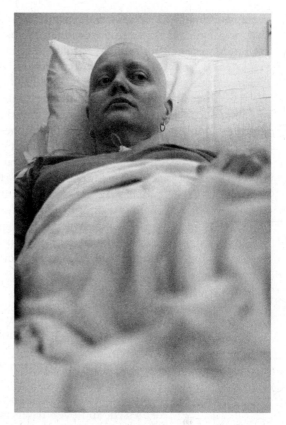

cancer), and removal of a testis (testicular cancer). Patients with colon cancer may require a colostomy, or surgical opening in the abdomen from which feces are evacuated from the body. Patients may experience feelings of shame as they are forced to handle their bodily wastes on a daily basis and may worry that others easily recognize their condition.

The physical changes caused by chronic illnesses and their treatment can also lead to sexual problems (Andersen, Woods, & Copeland, 1997; Druley, Stephens, & Coyne, 1997; Moyer, 1997). Many different kinds of cancer treatment, including treatment for breast, prostate, urinary, and colorectal cancer, can lead to changes in sexual functioning (Moyer & Salovey, 1996). One study with 116 prostate cancer patients and their partners revealed high rates of sexual dysfunction, which in many cases led to marital distress—especially if partners didn't talk about this experience (Badr & Taylor, 2009). Similarly, many people with CHD report a decrease in sexual activity, which is often caused by the fear (on the part of the patient or his/her partner) that the physical exertion of sex could lead to a heart attack (Muller, Mittleman, Maclure, Sherwood, & Tofler, 1996). However, the risk of sex triggering a heart attack is actually quite low—less than 1%.

Patients with a chronic illness often have concerns about body image, particularly if their disease or its treatment causes significant physical changes in functioning (Taylor & Aspinwall, 1993). Women who are diagnosed with breast cancer must cope with their concerns about body image, particularly if their treatment involves removal of one or both breasts (Carver et al., 1998; Moyer, 1997; Spencer et al.,

1999). These concerns are particularly salient for younger women. Encouragingly, women who undergo lumpectomies, in which only the cancerous tumor is removed from the breast, generally have fewer problems with marital and sexual adjustment than those who undergo mastectomies, in which one or both breasts are removed totally (Moyer, 1997; Taylor, Bandura, Ewart, Miller, & DeBusk, 1985).

Finally, the disease and/or treatment for the disease can lead to cognitive problems. Researchers in one study compared cognitive state in 90 breast cancer patients who had undergone chemotherapy (Weis, Poppelreuter, & Bartsch, 2009). Although the prevalence of cognitive deficits significantly decreased as time elapsed after the end of oncological therapy, 21% still displayed indications of long-term cognitive deficits. Another study compared cognitive functioning in breast-cancer patients receiving treatment to healthy controls (Collins, Mackenzie, Stewart, Bielajew, & Verma, 2009). Patients undergoing treatment showed substantially greater cognitive declines, particularly in processing speed and verbal memory, compared to healthy controls. Similarly, a sizeable percentage of breast-cancer patients show higher levels of memory loss, learning, and recall (Von Ah et al., 2009).

Social Problems

One of the most difficult aspects of coping with a chronic illness is the effect it can have on interpersonal relationships (see Box 10.2: Focus on Development; Taylor & Aspinwall, 1993; Wade & Lee, 2005). Friends may withdraw from the patient, either because of their own fears about acquiring the illness or because they cannot bear to face the physical changes in the patient. People often hold negative beliefs and biases about those with chronic illnesses, including perceiving them as helpless, depressed, and even deserving of their fate (Devins & Binik, 1996). Some people with chronic illnesses therefore report feeling shunned by others and experiencing a loss of social support—ironically, just at the time when they are most in need of such support.

People with chronic diseases therefore sometimes choose to hide their conditions from others, in part because of concerns about being pitied and/or abandoned, and may thereby withdraw from many social relationships. This approach is particularly likely in cases when people have illnesses with high levels of stigma, such as epilepsy and AIDS. People with AIDS are often worried about rejection and abandonment (Marks, Richardson, Ruiz, & Maldonado, 1992; Simoni et al., 1995). And these fears are not unreasonable—one study found that one in five women who told her partner about her HIV-positive status was abandoned. In some cases, this disclosure even leads to physical violence and abuse (Rothenberg & Paskey, 1995). One study with 266 sexually active HIV-positive people found that 41% had not disclosed their HIV status even to their sexual partners (Kalichman & Nachimson, 1999). Interestingly, people who report that religion is an important part of their lives are more likely to hide their HIV-positive status from their partners (Préau, Bouhnik, Roussiau, Lert, & Spire, 2008), as are those who are older (Emlet, 2006).

Questioning the Research 10.1
Why should religion and age influence HIV disclosure?

Box 10.2

Focus on Development: How Do Children Cope With Having a Chronic Disease?

Over the past 30 years, the prevalence of chronic conditions in children has increased dramatically (Van Cleave, Gortmaker, & Perrin, 2010). Although, in some cases, these diseases can be managed with medication and/or treatment, such as diabetes, asthma, and arthritis, in other cases, these illnesses may result in death during childhood. Cystic fibrosis and some types of cancers, for example, typically lead to death. Children with a chronic illness often have academic problems (Eiser, 1982). Potential causes include low parental/teacher expectations, missed school for medical reasons, and impairment with mental functioning caused by drugs. Social problems are also relatively common in children with severe chronic illnesses, who may become concerned about maintaining their friendships if they are frequently absent from school and worry about how other children might react if they look or act different in some way because of their illness or its treatment. The American Cancer Society and many cancer treatment centers have special programs that provide speakers for children's classes who describe why a child might look different following cancer treatment. These speakers can then let other children know what to expect when their classmate returns to school. Children with chronic illnesses are also likely to have various psychological problems, including high anxiety, negative self-concept, and feelings of interpersonal isolation. They may experience stress-related symptoms, such as bad dreams, nervousness, and depression. However, and encouragingly, children and adolescents with a chronic disease, such as asthma, dermatitis, or cancer, show better coping with everyday stressors compared to healthy controls (Hampel, Rudolph, Stachow, Lab-Lentzsch & Petermann, 2005). These results suggest that coping with a chronic illness may lead to more effective coping with everyday stressors.

Even when family members and friends want to help, they simply may not have realistic conceptions of what the patient is going through (see Table 10.2). In some cases, people with a chronic illness have family and friends with unrealistically high expectations about how patients should cope with and manage their illnesses (Hatchett, Frierd, Symister, & Wadhwa, 1997). For example, family and friends may believe that the patient could do more tasks to help around the house or that the patient's feelings of depression and anxiety are too pessimistic. One study of patients with arthritis found that those whose spouses were impatient and critical of how they were coping with their illness used less-effective coping strategies and experienced more anxiety and depression (Manne & Zautra, 1989). Moreover, 85% of people with chronic disease report experiencing unwanted attempts by family members to influence their health-related behavior, which is associated with less behavior change as well as decreases in psychological adjustment (Thorpe, Lewis, & Sterba, 2008).

In other cases, family members and friends have unrealistically low expectations about how people cope with having a chronic illness (Burish & Bradley, 1983;

TABLE 10.2 *Sample Items From the Negative Interactions Scale*

Sometimes, even when people have good intentions, they say or do something that upsets us. I am going to list some of these things. Think about the period of time since you were diagnosed up until today. How often did the following situations arise with your family or friends using the scale 1 (never) to 5 (very often)?

1. Changes the subject when I try to discuss my illness
2. Tells negative stories about other people who have cancer
3. Doesn't understand my situation
4. Avoids me
5. Appears afraid to be around me
6. Minimizes my problems
7. Seems to be hiding feelings
8. Acts uncomfortable when I talk about my illness
9. Trivializes my problems
10. Tells me I look well when I don't

This scale assesses the types of negative social interactions people with chronic diseases may encounter.

Source: Helgeson, Cohen, Schulz, & Yasko, 2000.

Hagedoorn et al., 2000; Mohr et al., 1999). They may be overly protective or indulgent, which can cause patients to feel or become dependent. For example, one study of physically disabled people found that nearly 40% had experienced emotional distress as a result of receiving unwanted help from their spouses (Newsom & Schultz, 1998). In this case, overprotection, even though well-intentioned, was associated with depression even as long as a year later. This pattern also interrupts the normal reciprocity in relationships, which can be a stressful disturbance. For example, family members might encourage the patient to simply "take it easy" and may try to discourage patients from talking about or thinking about the disease. In line with this view, researchers in one study found that wives with breast cancer whose husbands used protective buffering experienced more distress (Hinnen, Ranchor, Baas, Sanderman, & Hagedoorn, 2009). Finally, family members can offer unhelpful advice or encouragement, such as "it will turn out all right"—these sentiments are typically well meant but can raise false hopes and hence are inappropriate. So, social support is often, but not always, beneficial to patients with chronic illness.

Family members of people with chronic illnesses also may experience negative psychological reactions (Andersen, 1993). One of the major problems that families experience is dealing with the increased dependency of the ill person (Burish & Bradley, 1983). The patient may need assistance with a variety of tasks, including personal hygiene, medical care, financial responsibilities, and household chores, which can be time-consuming and emotionally upsetting for family members to accomplish. These changes in family roles can lead to great imbalances in family relationships, which increases guilt on the part of the patient and adds resentment on the part of family members (Table 10.3 presents a humorous example of the impact of chronic disease on marriage). As described at the beginning of the chapter, Julie's arthritis has made her extremely dependent on her husband, which

TABLE 10.3 *A Humorous Example of the Impact of Chronic Disease on Marital Relationships*

After her husband's checkup, a woman was called into the doctor's office. The doctor told her, "Your husband has a serious disease. There are several things you'll have to do for him, or he will surely die. Each morning fix him a healthy breakfast. Be pleasant to him. Make him a nutritious lunch for work and an especially nice meal for his dinner at night. Don't give him chores, or that will increase his stress. Don't discuss your problems with him either. Try to relax him in the evenings by wearing lingerie and giving him backrubs. Let him watch his favorite sports on TV. And, most important, make love to him several times a week and satisfy his every whim. If you do these things for the next 10 months to a year, I think he'll pull through."

On the way home, the husband asked his wife what the doctor had told her.
"You're going to die," she replied.

has put a significant strain on their relationship. One study with the caregivers of patients with cancer and MS found that those who felt the relationship was inequitable experienced more emotional exhaustion and had more feelings of anger at and detachment from the patient (Ybema, Kuijer, Hagedoorn, & Buunk, 2002). Caregivers even may suffer health problems of their own, especially if they must take care of the ill person for a long time and that person is in very poor health (Wight, LeBlanc, & Aneshensel, 1998).

Family members also suffer their own losses when a loved one is diagnosed with a chronic illness; hence, they may experience negative psychological consequences, including depression and anxiety. These feelings are particularly likely when the patient has or will have a high level of functional impairment (Fang, Manne, & Pape, 2001). For example, spouses of patients with chronic disease may experience a decrease in social activities, such as spending time with family and friends, seeing movies, and engaging in athletic activities. They may also have to give up some of their own plans and dreams, to accommodate the ill person (Manne, Alfieri, Taylor, & Dougherty, 1999).

Although most research on the social consequences of having a chronic disease has focused on the impact on the patient and the spouse, other family members, including parents, children, and siblings, are also affected. For example, one study on the effects of having a parent with cancer found that children experience a number of negative effects, including threat of losing the parent; the temporary loss of a parent because of hospitalization, side effects of treatments, or symptoms; and the disruption of normal family routines and roles (Compas et al., 1994). Parents who have a chronically ill child are, not surprisingly, also deeply influenced. Quittner et al. (1998) examined how caring for a child with cystic fibrosis (a common genetic disease that affects the lungs and pancreas and virtually always leads to death in childhood or early adulthood) influenced marital satisfaction. Compared to couples with a healthy child, couples with a child with cystic fibrosis reported having more conflict with their spouse on child-rearing practices, engaging in more childcare tasks, and having fewer positive daily interactions with their spouse. This was particularly true for women, who seemed to feel the burden of having a chronically ill child more than their husbands did. Couples with a chronically ill child also spent less time engaging in recreational activities, such as watching TV and going to the movies; couples with a sick child spent about 23% of their time engaging in recreational activities as compared to 33% of the time for those with a healthy child.

Encouragingly, some couples are able to manage the stress of chronic disease through using particular strategies of communication. In fact, couples who use positive dyadic coping, such as sharing their feelings with one another following a cancer diagnosis in one member of the couple, report better marital satisfaction, whereas those who simply withdraw from such discussion report lower marital satisfaction as well as more cancer-related distress (Badr, Carmack, Kashy, Cristofanilli, & Revenson, 2010). Similarly, researchers in another study examined different types of communication strategies couples may use to handle stressors they experience following wives' diagnosis with breast cancer (Manne et al., 2006). Couples who used mutual constructive communication experienced less distress and more relationship satisfaction for both patient and partner. On the other hand, use of demand-withdraw communication was associated with higher distress and lower relationship satisfaction for both patient and partner. Mutual avoidance was associated with more distress for patient and partner but was not associated with relationship satisfaction. Similarly, a study of couples in which one member was diagnosed with lung cancer found that engaging in relationship maintenance behaviors, such as sharing, openness, and seeking support, in the first month following diagnosis was associated with psychological and marital adjustment over time (Badr & Taylor, 2008).

People with chronic illnesses may also suffer financial problems when their symptoms or treatment affect their employment (Taylor & Aspinwall, 1993). In some cases, the symptoms of chronic illness cause people to be unable to work or at least make them unable to do certain tasks. Epileptics, for example, often have trouble holding a job because they are not allowed to drive. People who are chronically ill with life-threatening conditions, such as cancer, CHD, and AIDS, may find themselves offered less-demanding positions or passed over for promotion because employers think investing time and resources in them is a waste. These economic problems can be particularly difficult because insurance companies often do not cover all of the costs associated with health problems.

Psychological Problems

People who are diagnosed with a chronic illness often experience an initial sense of shock and disbelief (Janoff-Bulman, 1992; Moos, 1977). Receiving a diagnosis of a chronic disease is stressful for virtually all people, in part because such a diagnosis shatters people's core beliefs about a "just world," namely, that life is fair and just, and can be particularly difficult to deal with because there is "no end in sight." Researchers in one study of patients newly diagnosed with cancer found that 28% met the criteria for acute stress disorder within the first month, and 22% met the criteria for posttraumatic stress disorder (PTSD) at the 6-month follow-up (Kangas, Henry, & Bryant, 2005). Similarly, over 50% of college students with a chronic

People who are diagnosed with a chronic illness often experience intense disbelief, in part because this diagnosis challenges their worldview and thereby leads to considerable fear and uncertainty.

Source: © The New Yorker Collection 2000 Joseph Farris from the cartoonbank.com. All Rights Reserved.

"What do you mean, I have an ulcer? I give ulcers, I don't get them!"

illness experience symptoms of posttraumatic stress, although relatively few meet the criteria for PTSD (Barakat & Wodka, 2006). People who learn they have a highly disabling chronic disease, such as Parkinson's disease, cancer, or Huntington's disease, may have to put aside some plans and dreams, such as deciding not to have children or pursue a new career. Disbelief, denial, and anger are therefore common immediate reactions to receiving a diagnosis of chronic illness and are particularly common in younger people, for whom receiving such a diagnosis is especially disturbing and surprising (and see Box 10.3: Health Psychology in the Real World for a description of one woman's reaction to such a diagnosis).

Box 10.3

Health Psychology in the Real World: The Shock of a Cancer Diagnosis

By Donna Trussell, *Newsweek*, September 22, 2003

During the early summer of 2001 I felt bloated, constipated, fatigued—not my usual energetic, positive, athletic self. I had seen my personal physician several times but was always told that my symptoms probably indicated irritable-bowel syndrome, and that I should see a gastrointestinal specialist. Trying to get an appointment was like trying to get tickets to the World Series—almost impossible. Finally I was told the first available appointment was in mid-September.

I was worried. I knew something wasn't right, so in July I took the initiative and went to the emergency room. After an intern examined me, I was quickly sent for a CT scan. Soon afterward, as I was lying on the gurney in the cold of an emergency-room cubicle, he told me I had a large tumor on my ovary, which meant that I probably had ovarian cancer.

I was shocked and terribly frightened. I knew nothing about ovarian cancer. Through my tears I managed to call my significant other, who immediately said he'd cut short his vacation on Cape Cod and head home. He phoned my girlfriend, who also set off for the hospital right away. As I lay there in an emotional daze, a wonderful gynecologist held my hand and calmly answered my questions about what would happen next.

Telling my family I had cancer was the hardest thing of all. I knew they loved me and would be there for me, but I was afraid they would be despondent. But as I sat with my mother in her lovely backyard, I was comforted by her words. "You are a fighter," she said. "You will get through this." Still, I couldn't help wondering how this had happened to me. I exercised, ate well, lead a healthy life.

I didn't have much time to process what was happening. Two days later I was directed to an excellent surgeon, and within a week I had a total hysterectomy. The following month I began chemotherapy. As it turned out, I was stage 3 (out of a possible four stages, the fourth being the most advanced). If I had waited to see the gastrointestinal doctor, I might not be here today.

My story is not unique. At the hospital where I had my hysterectomy, a majority of the women who had ovarian cancer told me they had not been taken seriously by their doctors. Like me, they had been told that they were suffering from irritable-bowel syndrome or some other health problem. Their doctors never suggested that they have an ultrasound or CT scan to check out what was going on. I fear that the reluctance of many insurance companies to pay for the tests only makes doctors less likely to order them.

Early diagnosis is crucial because ovarian cancer is the most deadly form of gynecologic cancer (less than half of all patients survive past five years). It is called the "silent" cancer because there is no signature test—like the mammogram for breast cancer or the Pap smear for uterine cancer—to identify it. More than 75% of ovarian cancers go undiagnosed until the disease has reached advanced stages and is more difficult to manage. These statistics are not encouraging, but the numbers are changing with earlier detection and the availability of new, highly effective cancer drugs.

Unfortunately, the symptoms of ovarian cancer—the abdominal pressure, bloating, constipation and fatigue I experienced—seem so innocuous that they are often mistaken, even by patients, as signs of everyday ailments. Many times these symptoms are just that, but if they persist, it is wise to get an ultrasound. The test is painless and accurate.

Today ovarian cancer can be viewed as a chronic disease to be managed, just like diabetes, AIDS, or other illnesses. Psychologically, this puts a very different spin on what in the past has been considered a death sentence. Now there is real hope for those of us with ovarian cancer. We can lead healthy, productive lives while still in treatment.

For almost a year and a half, I endured long days at the Dana-Farber Cancer Institute in Boston, where I received an infusion of cancer-fighting drugs. I suffered through two rounds of treatments, lost my hair twice and struggled with fatigue, nausea, pain, depression, and fear. Then, seven months ago, I started going just once a month for two or three hours to get a newer, cutting-edge drug. Although every patient reacts differently to treatment, my cancer has been stabilized with remarkably few side effects.

My hospital roommate, a young woman with ovarian cancer, and I became each other's support system over the last two years and today remain good friends. I now have short, curly salt-and-pepper hair that my friends say makes me look like a chic SoHo artist. I am working, traveling and playing tennis. I know that my cancer will probably never be cured, but it can be managed. With the love and support of my family, my friends and my superb oncologist, I have my life back.

Many people with chronic illnesses experience depression, which is caused at least in part by the major loss of control that comes with having a chronic disease (Epping-Jordan et al., 1999; Mehnert & Koch, 2007; Spiegel, 1996; Zashikhina & Hagglof, 2007). In fact, estimates are that about 35% of individuals with disabilities suffer from depression, as compared with 12% in the nondisabled population. For example, one study of patients with MS—a disease of the central nervous system that leads to loss of function in limbs, bowel, and bladder, pain, and a loss of cognitive functioning—found that many patients felt depressed and useless (Mohr et al., 1999). Similarly, adults with asthma are at an increased likelihood of suicidal ideation and suicide attempts (Goodwin & Eaton, 2005). Researchers in one study examined the association between diabetes and depression during pregnancy and the postpartum period among a sample of low-income women (Kozhimannil, Pereira, & Harlow, 2009). Women with diabetes were nearly twice as likely to experience postpartum depression as those without diabetes.

Depression is, not surprisingly, particularly common in cases of severe and life-threatening illnesses, such as cancer, AIDS, and Alzheimer's disease (Taylor & Aspinwall, 1993). Researchers in one study found that 53.7% of patients with HIV/AIDS reported symptoms of depression, with depression particularly likely for those in worse health and with lower levels of social support (Yi et al., 2006). Moreover, 26% of the women reported attempting suicide since their HIV diagnosis, with 42% of these occurring within the first month after diagnosis and 27% within the first week (Cooperman & Simoni, 2005). Similarly, nearly half of women with breast cancer show depressive symptoms in the first year after diagnosis (Den Oudsten, Van Heck, Vander Steeg, Roukema, & De Vries, 2009), and 19.4% of breast-cancer patients meet the criteria for major depressive disorder, compared to only 8.8% of healthy women (Gandubert et al., 2009). As shown in Figure 10.1, depression can also influence life expectancy.

Anxiety, which is caused in part by the great uncertainty caused by a diagnosis of chronic disease, is another common psychological problem (Devins & Binik, 1996; Mehnert, Berg, Henrich, & Herschbach, 2009; Mehnert & Koch, 2007). One study asked patients with cancer to rate which aspects of their disease they found most stressful (Dunkel-Schetter, Feinstein, Taylor, & Falke, 1992): 41% rated fear and uncertainty about the future; 24% rated limitations in physical abilities, appearance, and lifestyle; and 12% rated managing pain as most stressful. Anxiety may be heightened when people feel overwhelmed about controlling the disease and concerned about long-term problems. They also have no idea what to expect—when symptoms will start, what symptoms will be, when they can go back to work, how people will react. One study with 80 women newly diagnosed with breast cancer found that 40% reported high levels of anxiety, which is significantly greater than in the general population (Epping-Jordan et al., 1999), and 10.4% of breast-cancer patients meet the criteria for generalized anxiety disorder (compared to only 1.6% of healthy women; Gandubert et al., 2009). Similarly, upon learning of their status, HIV-positive individuals show considerable increases in anxiety, depression, and mood disturbances, which may persist for several weeks. In some cases, experiencing the symptoms of a disease can cause great anxiety—patients with asthma, for example, often worry that they will die during an attack, which naturally heightens anxiety.

FIGURE 10.1

Patients with chronic kidney disease who are high in depression have a higher mortality rate than those who are low in depression.

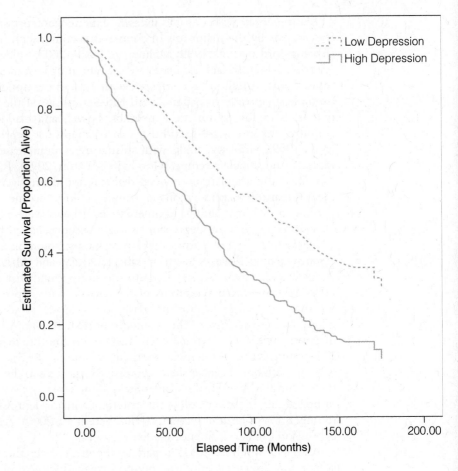

One of the biggest factors causing anxiety is a fear of reoccurrence. Researchers in one study with adult cancer survivors found that about one third of survivors continue to report worries about recurrence, worries about a second cancer, and worries that symptoms they experience may be from cancer (Deimling, Bowman, Sterns, Wagner, & Kahana, 2006). Not surprisingly, cancer-related health worries are significant predictors of both depression and anxiety. Similarly, 24% of the testicular cancer survivors reported "quite a bit" of fear of reoccurrence and 7% reported "very much" fear of reoccurrence (Skaali et al., 2009).

However, both depression and anxiety are most prevalent shortly after diagnosis, and tend to then decrease over time, as patients adjust to having such a disease (Den Oudsten et al., 2009; Stommel, Kurtz, Kurtz, Given, & Given, 2004). In fact, one study found that there were no differences in rates of depression between healthy people and those with various chronic illnesses (diabetes, arthritis, cancer, kidney disease) after the first 3 months following diagnosis (Cassileth et al., 1984).

Patients who believe they have more control over their disease also report less distress and a higher overall quality of life (Beckjord, Glinder, Langrock, & Compas, 2009). Researchers in one study assessed 101 breast-cancer patients on five occasions: 1 week after surgery, and again 1, 3, 6, and 12 months later (Bárez, Blasco, Fernández-Castro, & Viladrich, 2009). Feelings of perceived control increased over time, whereas feelings of distress decreased. In turn, women with breast cancer who were more involved in decision making regarding cancer treatment and follow-up (including surgery, radiation, chemotherapy) show improved health-related quality of life as long as 10 years after diagnosis, at least in part because involvement in such decision making increases perceptions of control (Andersen, Bowen, Morea, Stein, & Baker, 2009).

Because many chronic diseases are influenced at least in part by lifestyle choices, such as smoking, exercise, tanning, and sexual activity, people often blame themselves for developing such diseases (Burish & Bradley, 1983). For example, one study with patients with breast cancer found that 41% blamed themselves for getting the disease (Taylor, Lichtman, & Wood, 1984). Unfortunately, people who feel responsible for their illness often experience considerable guilt for the pain they are causing themselves as well as their loved ones. They may also have higher rates of depression and anxiety (Glinder & Compas, 1999). One study with breast cancer, prostate cancer, and lung cancer patients found that self-blame was associated with poorer psychological adjustment (Else-Quest, LoConte, Schiller, & Hyde, 2009).

However, it is important to note that people vary in terms of how much psychological distress they experience following a diagnosis, in part because the presence of coping resources, such as optimism, perceived control, and social support, influences such reactions (Henselmans et al., 2010; Hou, Law, Yin, & Fu, 2010). For example, researchers in one study examined psychological and physical adjustment to breast cancer over 4 years (Helgeson, Snyder, & Seltman, 2004). Many women reported high levels of adjustment throughout this time: 43% show consistent high mental functioning and 55% show consistent high physical functioning. But about 12% of women show a decline in mental functioning over time, as do about 22% of women in terms of physical functioning. The biggest change took place within the first year after diagnosis. What factors influence how much distress someone feels following a chronic disease diagnosis? Younger people, as well as those who are higher in optimism, perceived control, and social support, tend to show more positive adjustment (Helgeson et al., 2004; Henselmans et al., 2010). There are also differences as a function of marital status and gender in the experience of distress: Higher levels of distress are found among unmarried and male patients, in line with research showing that married patients cope better with cancer than unmarried patients and that women cope better than men (Goldzweig et al., 2009).

Finally, although the consequences of developing a chronic disease are primarily negative, people often experience some positive effects, such as feeling closer and more in touch with family and friends, having a greater appreciation of life, and changing life goals and priorities (see Table 10.4; Collins et al., 2001; Costanzo, Ryff, & Singer, 2009; Mohr et al., 1999; Schwartzberg, 1993; Updegraff & Taylor, 2000; Updegraff, Taylor, Kemeny, & Wyatt, 2002). In fact, 79% of breast-cancer survivors report finding some benefits of their diagnosis (Mols, Vingerhoets, Coebergh, & van de Poll-Franse, 2009). What possibly could be a benefit of having a chronic illness? People who have been diagnosed with a chronic disease may report experiencing

TABLE 10.4   *Reflection About the Benefits of Cancer By Lance Armstrong*

There are two Lance Armstrongs, pre-cancer, and post. Everybody's favorite question is "How did cancer change you?" The real question is how didn't it change me? I left my house on October 2, 1996, as one person and came home another.... The truth is that cancer was the best thing that ever happened to me. I don't know why I got the illness, but it did wonders for me, and I wouldn't want to walk away from it. Why would I want to change, even for a day, the most important and shaping event of my life?

Source: Armstrong & Jenkins, 2000.

posttraumatic growth, including relating better with others, appreciating life, and spiritual growth (Cordova, Cunningham, Carlson, & Andrykowski, 2001). For example, one study revealed that breast-cancer survivors reported experiencing posttraumatic growth in terms of relationships with others, personal strength, and appreciation of life (Mols et al., 2009). Some patients with a chronic disease report increasing in religious and/or spiritual faith. For example, 25% of adults who are diagnosed with HIV/AIDS report being more religious, 41% report being "more spiritual," and 75% report this illness has strengthened their faith (Cotton et al., 2006a, 2006b). Receiving a chronic illness diagnosis can even lead people to engage in health-promoting behavior. One study with nearly 3,000 HIV-positive people found that following their diagnosis, 43% increased their exercise, 59% improved their diet, and 49% of smokers decreased their smoking (Collins et al., 2001). Finally, receiving a diagnosis of chronic illness can encourage people to live life to the fullest and focus on achieving their dreams instead of delaying them. As writer Michael Kinsley (2001) notes, "It's like having a get-out-of-jail free card from the prison of delayed gratification. Skip the Democratic convention to go kayaking in Alaska? Absolutely. Do it now, in case you can't do it later."

Not surprisingly, people who are able to find benefits to having a chronic disease generally experience more positive mood and quality of life (Bower et al., 2005; Pakenham, 2005; Zwahlen, Hagenbuch, Carley, Jenewein, & Buchi, 2010). Adolescents with diabetes who see benefits to their disease have fewer symptoms of depression (Tran, Wiebe, Fortenberry, Butler, & Berg, 2011). Researchers in one longitudinal study investigated relations between benefit-finding domains and outcome measures in 1,757 people diagnosed with colorectal cancer (Rinaldis, Pakenham, & Lynch, 2010). Those who reported benefit-finding reported more positive affect and cancer-related quality of life, as well as less distress. In fact, breast-cancer patients who report benefit finding have lower distress and depression even 4 to 7 years later (Carver & Antoni, 2004).

However, people with chronic disease vary in the extent to which they are able to find benefits in their diagnosis. One study with breast-cancer survivors revealed that those who are married, employed, have less education, and are younger experience more posttraumatic growth (Bellizzi & Blank, 2006). The coping styles one uses to manage the diagnosis also influence the perceived benefits. For example, researchers in one study examined the predictors of the experience of cancer on posttraumatic growth in patients undergoing bone marrow transplantation (Widows, Jacobsen, Booth-Jones, & Fields, 2005). Younger people who place more reliance on positive reinterpretation and problem-solving coping strategies experience greater posttraumatic growth. Similarly, among women living with HIV/AIDS, those who use positive reappraisal coping and receive high levels of emotional support experienced higher levels of growth, whereas those who are higher in depressive affect experienced lower levels of growth (Siegel, Schrimshaw, & Pretter, 2005).

What Factors Influence How People Manage Having a Chronic Illness?

The extent of difficulty people have in coping with a chronic illness varies as a function of illness factors, personal factors, and social factors. This section examines three distinct factors that impact how well people cope with a chronic illness: illness intrusiveness, types of coping used, and level of social support.

Illness Intrusiveness

In many cases, people must make major changes in lifestyle to avoid exacerbating their conditions. These changes might include avoiding unhealthy foods, stopping smoking, and starting an exercise program. For example, patients with diabetes must limit the sugar in their diets, and patients with CHD must eat healthier foods and give up cigarettes. In some cases, people are even told to avoid certain locations and activities. People with asthma, for example, often must avoid spending time outside when pollen counts are high, and those who have experienced a heart attack may be asked to avoid stressful situations, strenuous activities, and heavy lifting. These changes can lead to anxiety, depression, and social withdrawal, particularly in cases in which managing the disease interferes with a person's daily life, including work, social, and recreational activities (Devins et al., 1990; Talbot, Nowven, Gingras, Belanger, & Audet, 1999).

People with chronic diseases must also engage in relatively complex behaviors to monitor their conditions and manage their treatment regimens (Devins & Binik, 1996). For example, diabetes is a metabolic disorder in which the body is unable to properly convert glucose (sugar) into usable energy. In normal metabolism, the body produces the hormone insulin. A person with diabetes has defective insulin production or use such that glucose cannot be readily used by the body cells, which causes glucose to accumulate in the blood, leading to hyperglycemia. A person with diabetes therefore must monitor blood glucose levels to avoid both sugar shortage and insulin shock and must administer (by injection) appropriate amounts of insulin regularly. However, many people with diabetes find this constant maintenance tedious and fail to follow their treatment regimen. As described at the beginning of this chapter, Don had particular trouble monitoring his blood sugar, following dietary recommendations, and giving himself insulin when he was with friends.

Chronic illnesses that require high levels of daily maintenance, such as diabetes, are particularly difficult to cope with.
Source: Roger Ressmeyer/Corbis Images.

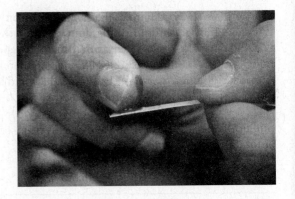

Several studies have examined the influence of patients' perceived controllability of the disease on psychological distress and well-being (Oh, 2008). For example, researchers in one study with 557 adult patients with asthma found that being confident in one's ability to control asthma symptoms was associated with better asthma control and quality of life (Lavoie et al., 2008). On the other hand, asthma patients with higher levels of both illness uncertainty and illness intrusiveness experienced more anxious and depressive symptoms and general psychological distress (Carpentier, Mullins, & Van Pelt, 2007). Perceptions of controllability of the disease also influence well-being in cancer patients, with those who view their illness as uncontrollable experiencing worse physical and mental health (Rozema, Völlink, & Lechner, 2009).

Another factor that influences the experience of having a chronic disease is the patients' continued dependence on health-care professionals and biomedical technology (Devins & Binik, 1996). Patients with severe kidney disease, for example, must undergo dialysis—a procedure in which the blood is cleaned to remove excess salts, water, and waste products—three times a week for an average of 4 to 6 hours per session. Although they may experience frustration with their disease and treatment, which can influence their feelings toward health-care workers, maintaining communication is an important part of managing their illness. Patients must also deal with medical professionals with great regularity and can experience difficulties in these relationships (e.g., understanding a physician's communications, expressing feelings, maintaining a sense of control over treatment options). One study with 97 patients with breast cancer found that 84% reported having trouble communicating with their medical team, including problems understanding physicians' instructions, expressing feelings, and asking questions (Lerman et al., 1993). Moreover, women who had more communications problems showed greater distress later. Some of these issues in patient–practitioner relationships are examined in Chapter 12.

Type of Coping Used

As discussed in Chapter 4, people cope with stressful situations in very different ways, which lead to very different outcomes. Active **problem-focused coping** strategies, which focus on dealing directly with the source of the stress, are often helpful when people are able to change the stressor in some way (Carver et al.,

1993; Felton & Revenson, 1984; Fleishman & Fogel, 1994; Macrodimitris & Endler, 2001; Patterson et al., 1996; Stanton & Snider, 1993). This type of coping can include *proactive*, or *preventive*, *coping*, in which people try to anticipate problems and then act to prevent their occurrence (Aspinwall & Taylor, 1997). For example, a person with diabetes could avoid experiencing a drop in blood sugar by regularly eating small meals to keep blood sugar at a consistent level. Another type of problem-focused coping is *combative coping*, which is used when a person must react to an unavoidable stressor.

Emotion-focused coping strategies are also used in response to stressful situations, particularly in cases in which people believe they have little or no ability to directly reduce or avoid the stressor (Carver et al., 1993; Felton & Revenson, 1984; Fleishman & Fogel, 1994; Macrodimitris & Endler, 2001; Patterson et al., 1996; Stanton & Snider, 1993). This type of coping focuses on managing the reaction to stress, although not the cause of the stress itself. Emotion-focused coping can include escape–avoidance (trying to avoid the situation) and distancing (trying to stop thinking about the problem). Both of these types of emotion-focused coping rely on avoiding the stressor—either physically or psychologically. Emotion-focused coping can also include positive reappraisal (trying to think about a negative situation in a new way) or social support. For example, some people with cancer focus on the positive aspects of having this disease (e.g., discovering what is important in life, becoming closer to family and friends; Dunkel-Schetter et al., 1992; Stanton & Snider, 1993).

Although both problem-focused and emotion-focused coping can be effective strategies for managing the stress of a chronic illness, most research suggests that directly trying to reduce a stressor is generally a more effective approach. For example, one study of 122 patients with MS found that people who relied more on problem-focused coping and less on emotion-focused coping were less depressed and felt better about their health (Pakenham, 1999). Similarly, adults with diabetes who use more direct and problem-focused coping strategies experience lower levels of anxiety and depression than those who engage in wishful thinking (e.g., wishing the situation would go away or be over) and withdrawal (e.g., sleeping more than usual, avoiding being with people; Macrodimitris & Endler, 2001). On the other hand, higher use of avoidance coping by men with cancer is associated with more interference with daily functioning, in part because avoidance of cancer-related stressors and circumstances likely contributes to declines in mood states over time (Hoyt, Thomas, Epstein, & Dirksen, 2009). However, some emotion-focused strategies, such as focusing on the positive and relying on social support, are also associated with better psychological adjustment (Stanton & Snider, 1993). For example, one study with 603 cancer patients revealed that people who coped by seeking social support and focusing on the positive experienced less depression and anxiety than those who simply wished the situation would go away, avoided being with other people, or tried to make themselves feel better by smoking, eating, or drinking (Dunkel-Schetter et al., 1992).

Findings on the impact of denial on coping with chronic illness are somewhat mixed (Havik & Maeland, 1988). On the one hand, immediately after receiving a diagnosis of chronic illness denying this reality may help people cope with the very threatening and upsetting news (Taylor & Aspinwall, 1993). Pretending to not have the disease and attempting to let it affect daily life as little as possible reduces the threat of the illness and thereby decreases anxiety, which can help people cope with the devastating news diagnosis. However, people who continue to deny the existence of their illness over time can suffer severe consequences. Patients with spinal cord injuries, for example, show greater distress when they focus on wishful thinking (e.g., imagining the accident didn't happen) as opposed to a realistic acceptance of their condition (Buckelew, Baumstark, Frank, & Hewett, 1990). This type of unrealistic optimism, such as trying to mentally "undo" an event, inhibits the person from adapting to the condition and in turn adopting new, more realistic goals and expectations about the future. Denial may also decrease people's willingness to follow medical care advice or seek prompt treatment, and can therefore lead to very negative health outcomes.

Some people with a chronic disease rely on spirituality and religion as a coping mechanism, which in some cases is associated with improved health-related quality of life as well as psychosocial functioning (Gall, Kristjansson, Charbonneau, & Florack, 2009; Wildes, Miller, de Majors, & Ramirez, 2009; Zavala, Maliski, Kwan, Fink, & Litwin, 2009). One study with breast-cancer patients found that 76% used positive religious coping—such as partnering with God or looking to God for strength, support, or guidance—"a moderate amount" or "a lot" (Hebert, Zdaniuk, Schulz, & Scheier, 2009). The use of religious coping is particularly likely to occur shortly after diagnosis, when people are gathering their coping resources (Gall, Guirguis-Younger, Charbonneau, & Florack, 2009). Even in cases in which religious beliefs do not directly affect adjustment to having a chronic disease, they may experience an enhanced sense of social support from a community with whom they share those beliefs, which in turn leads to better well-being (Howsepian & Merluzzi, 2009).

Finally, although it is often assumed that coping strategies influence psychological adjustment, it is also possible that psychological adjustment influences coping strategies. Specifically, people who feel better adjusted may find it easier to use effective strategies. In line with this view, researchers in one study examining quality of life and coping strategies in women with breast cancer over 6 months found that quality of life was a stronger predictor of coping strategies than the reverse (Danhauer, Crawford, Farmer, & Avis, 2009). This finding suggests that the link between coping strategies and quality of life may in fact work in both directions.

Level of Social Support

As described in Chapter 5, **social support** is a very important predictor of psychological and physical well-being in patients with chronic illness (Helgeson & Cohen, 1996; Taylor & Aspinwall, 1993). Studies with patients with cancer, AIDS, and CHD indicate that those who receive higher levels of social support from their family and friends experience lower levels of anxiety, depression, and anger; recover more rapidly from surgery; require less pain medication; experience fewer symptoms; and report overall better health (Alferi, Carver, Antoni, Weiss, & Duran, 2001; Ashton et al., 2005; Kulik & Mahler, 1989; Namir, Alumbaugh, Fawzy, & Wolcott, 1989; Norton et al., 2005). Patients also benefit in terms of survival from having high levels of social support (Goodwin, Hunt, Key, & Samet,

1987; Patterson et al., 1996; Reynolds & Kaplan, 1990). For example, married patients with cancer live longer following their diagnosis than patients who are single (Pistrang & Barker, 1995), and married people live longer following a heart attack (Nielsen, Faergeman, Larsen, & Foldspang, 2006). As discussed previously, receiving a diagnosis of a chronic illness is associated with various types of stress, and people who have high levels of social support are clearly better able to buffer the effects of such stress (Brown, Wallston, & Nicassio, 1989; Dunkel-Schetter et al., 1992; Rini, Jandorf, Valdimarsdottir, Brown, & Itzkowitz, 2008).

How exactly does social support lead to improved adjustment to chronic disease? One possibility is that social support is associated with better coping strategies. Women with early stage breast cancer who receive unsupportive behavior from their partner show more use of avoidant coping and, in turn, higher levels of distress (Manne, Ostroff, Winkel, Grana, & Fox, 2005). On the other hand, cancer patients who receive more social support from friends show higher levels of fighting spirit, suggesting that receiving support may lead patients to see cancer as a challenge and to take an active role in therapy and recovery (Cicero, Lo Coco, Gullo, & Lo Verso, 2009). Social support may also help patients find positive meaning in their diagnosis. In line with this view, cancer survivors who receive more emotional support in the months following the diagnosis report experiencing more positive consequences of the illness at 8 years later (Schroevers, Helgeson, Sandernnan, & Ranchor, 2010).

Another possibility is that social support provides an opportunity for patients to process information about their diagnosis. For example, patients with cancer who have high levels of social support are likely to have people with whom they can share their fears and concerns about the disease. People who can express their emotions about having cancer report less stress, anxiety, depression, and distress than those who aren't able to express these emotions (Schmidt & Andrykowski, 2004; Stanton, Kirk, Camerson, & Danoff-Burg, 2000). Similarly, prostate cancer patients who discuss treatment options with social networks prior to beginning treatment show higher levels of social support and emotional expression as well as decreases in negative affect after treatment (Christie, Meyerowitz, Giedzinska-Simons, Gross, & Agus, 2009). In sum, greater time spent talking with family and friends about treatment options may provide opportunities for patients to cope with the emotions related to their cancer diagnosis, which may improve feelings of distress over time.

Interestingly, some types of social support seem to be more effective than others (Helgeson & Cohen, 1996). Emotional support, such as the availability of people to listen, express concern, and encourage the patient to talk, consistently is found to be beneficial for people coping with a chronic illness. For example, people with cancer who feel they receive an adequate amount of emotional social support show lower distress over time. Instrumental support, such as help with chores, transportation, and assistance with childcare, is helpful, especially if it is provided by family members (as opposed to friends). This type of support is also most beneficial for people with a poor prognosis for recovery, presumably because they have more trouble managing these practical tasks. Informational support, such as giving advice and answering questions, is helpful, but only if it is given by a health-care professional—advice from friends and family members is not generally perceived as valuable (Dunkel-Schetter, 1984). Similarly, HIV-specific social support predicts less sexual risk taking in gay male couples (Darbes & Lewis, 2005).

Questioning the Research 10.2

Although considerable research shows that greater social support leads to better coping with chronic disease, can you think of an alternative explanation for this association? (Hint: Is this association really causation, or just correlation?)

How Can Psychological Interventions Help People Cope With Chronic Illness?

Given all the problems associated with having a chronic disease, how can people adjust effectively to such a diagnosis? Research suggests several different approaches that may have positive effects on patients' psychological adjustment as well as physical symptoms. These approaches include providing information and education, training in cognitive-behavioral techniques, and relying on social support groups (Meyer & Mark, 1995).

Education

One of the most common approaches to helping people adapt to a chronic disease is providing education (Taylor & Aspinwall, 1993). Patients and their families may benefit simply from learning about the disease and its treatment, in part because such knowledge enables them to feel more "in control" of the disease and its course (Helgeson & Cohen, 1996; Meyer & Mark, 1995). Education programs to help people cope with asthma, for example, teach patients about the physiology and mechanisms of breathing, as well as the common triggers for asthma attacks (Lehrer, Feldman, Giardino, Song, & Schmaling, 2002). People also are taught what occurs during an asthma attack and how medicine works to counteract the effects of an attack. Finally, they learn behavioral techniques for preventing and controlling asthma attacks. Providing this type of education decreases patients' anxiety about asthma and reduces the use of medical services. Researchers in one study examined the effectiveness of a brief self-management intervention, which emphasized the importance of planning ahead to carry out self-care behaviors, to support patients recently diagnosed with type-2 diabetes to achieve sustained improvements in their self-care behaviors (Thoolen, de Ridder, Bensing, Gorter, & Rutten, 2009). The intervention was effective in improving diet and physical activity behavior, and in fact led to significant weight loss at 12 months.

Most research suggests that education helps patients manage the psychological and physical symptoms of their disease. For example, patients with asthma who participate in an education program show fewer symptoms (Lehrer et al., 2002). Education can also be effective at reducing psychological and physical symptoms for those with cancer. At Carnegie Mellon University, Helgeson et al. (1999, 2001) randomly assigned 312 patients newly diagnosed with breast cancer to either an education group, group-discussion group, education and group-discussion group, or a control condition. Women who received information about the disease benefited in terms of psychological and physical well-being even as long as 3 years after the intervention, whereas those who participated in the discussion groups showed no such improvement. Similarly, one study with patients with cancer found that those who received detailed information (including a tour of the oncology ward, a videotaped presentation about chemotherapy, and a take-home booklet) had lower levels of nausea and vomiting, were less depressed and hostile, and experienced less disruption in their daily lives while in chemotherapy treatment compared to those who received relaxation training as well as those who received only a brief (25-minute) information session (Burish, Snyder, & Jenkins, 1991). In sum, providing education about the disease, its symptoms, and its treatment may increase patients' sense of self-efficacy and control, and thereby improve psychological and physical functioning. Interestingly, this type of intervention is particularly beneficial for men with cancer who are low in self-esteem, perhaps because these men are least confident in their own ability to manage their disease (Helgeson, Lepore, & Eton, 2006).

Educational interventions can be especially useful when they involve collaboration with health-care professionals. For example, researchers in one study examined whether coordinated care management of multiple conditions improved disease control in patients with diabetes and/or CHD (Katon et al., 2010). Patients were randomly assigned to the usual-care group or to the intervention group, in which a nurse, working with each patient's primary care physician, provided clear guidelines for managing the risk factors associated with multiple diseases. Compared to those in the control, patients in the intervention group showed greater improvement 1 year later in terms of cholesterol, blood pressure, and depression. Patients in the intervention group also reported experiencing a better overall quality of life as well as greater satisfaction with the care they received.

Cognitive-Behavioral Therapy (CBT)

Cognitive-behavioral therapy (CBT) focuses specifically on challenging individuals' irrational beliefs about their condition and giving them coping skills to handle their illness (Devins & Binik, 1996; Parker, 1995). For example, a therapist could challenge the belief held by a person with epilepsy that he or she will never get married. CBT is especially effective for helping people cope with chronic diseases with symptoms that are brought on by stress, such as asthma attacks and epileptic seizures (Lehrer et al., 2002; Parker, 1995). People with these disorders can therefore learn effective ways of reducing their anxiety and tension, which in turn will decrease their likelihood of experiencing an attack. This type of therapy also provides training in various techniques to help people handle the stress of having a chronic illness, such as progressive relaxation, meditation, biofeedback, and guided imagery.

CBT is an effective strategy for improving mental health in people with a chronic disease (Agras, Taylor, Kraemer, Southam, & Schneider, 1987; Carey & Burish, 1988; Crepaz et al., 2008). Studies with people with HIV and cancer indicate that people who receive training in stress management (including help on thinking through daily stressors in a new way, relying more on social support, and increasing assertiveness while decreasing anger) and relaxation (including progressive muscle relaxation, meditation, and guided imagery) show lower levels of anxiety, anger, and stress, and improved quality of life (Antoni et al., 2000; Cruess et al., 2000; Scott-Sheldon, Kalichman, Carey, & Fielder, 2008). For example, researchers in one study randomly assigned women with breast cancer to either a cognitive-behavioral stress management intervention program (which met for 2 hours each week for 10 weeks) or a control condition (which included a condensed version of the intervention program in a 5- to 6-hour session given on a single day; Antoni et al., 2001). The intervention program included training in relaxation techniques, expressing emotional reactions, and discussing practical strategies for coping with cancer and its treatment-related problems. Women who attended the intervention group showed a decrease in rates of depression and increases in general optimism as well as the perceived benefits of having cancer, such as bringing their families closer together and making them stronger and more patient. This intervention was especially beneficial for women who were the least optimistic at the start of the intervention. This research therefore suggests that gaining skills in managing the stress brought on by receiving a cancer diagnosis can be quite effective in reducing rates of depression and increasing rates of optimism, especially for women who are particularly devastated by their diagnosis.

Perhaps even more importantly, cognitive-behavioral interventions can improve physical well-being in patients with chronic diseases. Researchers in one study randomly assigned 67 patients with sickle cell disease to a pain coping skills intervention (e.g., relaxation, imagery, calming self-statements) or an education condition (Gil et al., 2000). At the 3-month follow-up, those who had the pain coping skills intervention reported less pain than those in the other condition. Such interventions can also help patients manage the side effects associated with treatment for their disease. For example, research with patients with cancer, who often experience nausea in anticipation of chemotherapy treatment, indicates that training in relaxation and specifically the use of *systematic desensitization* leads to a substantial decrease in nausea and vomiting (Morrow, Asbury, Hammon, & Dobkin, 1992). This type of training even leads to physiological changes 6 to 12 months later, including greater immune system functioning and higher levels of testosterone. CBT also reduces the increases in fatigue often experienced in cancer patients undergoing radiation therapy (Montgomery et al., 2009).

Even interventions that focus largely on reducing stress can lead to beneficial psychological effects. For example, researchers in one study randomly assigned women with breast cancer to the intervention (10 weekly 75-minute yoga classes) or a waitlist control group (Danhauer et al., 2009). Women who participated in the yoga classes reported improvements in mental health, depression, positive affect, fatigue, and spirituality (peace/meaning). These classes were particularly beneficial for women with higher negative affect and lower emotional well-being. Similarly, patients with cancer who engage in regular meditation (both on their own and as part of a group) show lower levels of anger, depression, and anxiety than those without such training (Speca, Carlson, Goodey, & Angen, 2000). Researchers in one study randomly assigned breast-cancer patients to a mindfulness-based stress-reduction program or a usual-care condition (Lengacher et al., 2009). Compared with usual care, subjects assigned to the stress-reduction program had lower rates of depression, anxiety, and fear of recurrence as well as higher levels of energy, physical functioning, and physical role functioning.

Patients with chronic disease benefit from interventions that reduce stress, such as meditation, yoga, and mindfulness training.
Source: © Eliza Snow/iStockphoto.

Although some of the cognitive-behavioral interventions described thus far are intensive in terms of time and money, briefer interventions can also be effective. For example, researchers in one study tested whether a 12-session, coping improvement group intervention delivered via teleconference technology could improve life quality in adults living with HIV/AIDS (Heckman et al., 2006). In line with predictions, participants who received the intervention reported fewer psychological symptoms, lower levels of life-stressor burden, increased coping self-efficacy, and less frequent use of avoidance coping. Similarly, people with chronic heart problems who receive six telephone counseling sessions to identify and address illness-related fears show improved psychological well-being (McLaughlin et al., 2005). Specifically, patients who receive such calls show a 27% improvement in depression symptoms, a 27% improvement in anxiety, and a 38% improvement in home limitations compared with controls. In sum, even relatively brief counseling can help patients adjust to chronic illness.

Social Support Groups

Social support groups, which consist of other people suffering from the same illness, are another effective way of helping people cope with chronic diseases (Devins & Binik, 1996). This approach gives people an opportunity to compare coping strategies and solutions to daily problems and provide social support to each other. They can share emotions and discuss topics such as physical problems, communication with physicians, relationships with family members, finding meaning in life, and facing death. As described at the beginning of the chapter, Betty often felt more comfortable relying on her social support group for emotional support than on her family, in part because the women in the group understood exactly what she was experiencing.

These groups may be particularly effective when participants have the opportunity to share their own successful coping strategies with others. Researchers in one study randomly assigned patients with kidney disease to either a problem-disclosure group (people described their difficulties in coping with the illness), a self-presentation group (people described the strategies they used to cope effectively with their disease), or a control group (people saw a videotape on effective coping with dialysis; Leake, Friend, & Wadhwa, 1999). At the 1-month follow-up, people in the self-presentation group had lower rates of depression and fewer physical symptoms than people in the control group or the problem disclosure group. Apparently talking about how well you are coping, as opposed to focusing on how many problems you are having, may be an effective way of helping patients with chronic disease manage their illnesses, presumably because this approach helps patients generate their own coping strategies.

Self-help groups have beneficial effects on helping people cope with diabetes, cancer, herpes, scoliosis, and genetic diseases. The best-known work on the effect of group interventions on survival with cancer patients was conducted by Spiegel, Bloom, Kraemer, and Gottheil at Stanford University (1989). In this study, 86 women with advanced breast cancer were randomly assigned to receive a weekly 90-minute group therapy session for 1 year or to receive no therapy. The patients were then followed for 10 years. Those who received the group therapy lived nearly twice as long as those in the control condition (36.6 versus 18.9 months, respectively). These results suggest that psychotherapy can help slow the progression of cancer, although it does not cure it. Some evidence suggests that participating in a social support group can improve patients' immunological response, which could help explain the longer life expectancy of those in the group therapy support group, previously mentioned (Fawzy et al., 1990).

However, a study by Canadian researchers refutes these findings (Goodwin et al., 2001). In this study, 245 women with breast cancer were randomly assigned to either a weekly supportive-expressive group therapy group, or to a control group that received no group support. Although women in the therapy group reported less pain and fewer psychological symptoms, especially for those who were depressed at the start of the study, there was no difference in length of survival. Women in both conditions lived an average of 17.5 months.

One explanation for the differences in outcomes is that the studies were carried out approximately 20 years apart (Spiegel, 2001). Medical treatment for cancer as well as techniques for detecting cancer improved dramatically between the 1970s and 1990s, which in turn led to decreases in the rate of breast-cancer deaths over time. Cancer has also become more understood and accepted during this period—patients with cancer experience lower levels of stigma and alienation, which may mean that social support groups are less beneficial. Finally, whereas now social support groups often are seen as a valued strategy for coping with chronic diseases, this acceptance was not abundant in the 1970s. Dr. David Spiegel, the author of the original study, recalls that in the 1970s, it was difficult to convince patients to attend the (presumably worthless) group therapy sessions, whereas in the 1990s, patients not assigned to receive this type of treatment were disappointed. Future research is clearly needed to examine whether, when, and for whom group therapy can work to improve physical and psychological well-being.

Support groups are especially useful for people who lack other types of social support. For example, one study with patients with cancer found that those who received low levels of emotional support from their partners benefited in terms of physical functioning from participation in a peer discussion group, but those who already had high levels of support at home showed no such change or decreases in physical functioning following participation (Helgeson et al., 2000). Although this finding was unexpected, it may be that those who participated in the group talked about their problems more at home, which in turn led to more negative interactions. It could also be that they changed their expectations about the type of support they should receive at home, and that made them sad. Similarly, women with unsupportive partners who want to express their emotional reactions to a cancer diagnosis may particularly benefit from social support interventions (Manne, Ostroff, & Winkel, 2007).

What Is Coronary Heart Disease?

Until the 20th century, **coronary heart disease** (CHD) was not a major health problem. However, heart disease is the leading cause of death for both men and women in the United States, causing 26% of deaths (Heron & Tejada-Vera, 2009). Every year, about 785,000 Americans have a first heart attack, and another 470,000 people who have already had at least one heart attack experience another attack (Lloyd-Jones et al., 2010).

Under normal conditions, the heart contracts and releases, which pumps blood throughout the body (see Figure 10.2; Smith & Pratt, 1993). The blood carries necessary oxygen to all of the cells in the body and removes carbon dioxide and other waste material from the cells. However, over time, because of diet or lifestyle, the artery walls can become clogged with a buildup of fatty substances, such as *low-density lipoprotein (LDL) cholesterol*, and other substances. (In contrast, *high-density* lipoproteins, or *HDLs,* remove LDL cholesterol from the bloodstream and thereby reduce the risk of arterial clogging.) When this buildup occurs, the area through which blood can flow decreases, and the likelihood of a blood clot increases (see Figure 10.3). This process, known as *atherosclerosis*, reduces the flow of blood and thereby deprives the heart of essential nutrients. Arteries can also lose their elasticity over time, which makes it difficult for them to expand and contract with the blood pressure. This process, known as *arteriosclerosis*, leads to a decrease in blood flow and an increase in the likelihood of a blood clot forming.

Although both atherosclerosis and arteriosclerosis can be present in the body without a person experiencing any symptoms for some time, they can eventually lead to very serious problems. First, a person may develop *angina*, a feeling of pain and tightness in the chest as the heart is deprived of oxygen. This type of attack may pass quickly but is often a sign that future cardiovascular problems will develop. In more serious cases, in which there is a complete blockage of the coronary arteries, a person may experience a *myocardial infarction*, or heart attack. Heart attacks often occur because a blood clot formed around the built-up cholesterol blocks the passage of blood to the heart. This deprivation of oxygen causes permanent damage to the heart muscles. Atherosclerosis and arteriosclerosis can lead to *strokes*. The plaque that forms on the artery wall may became detached and then travel in the bloodstream. If one of these blood clots lodges in the circulatory system so that it deprives the brain of oxygen, the person experiences a stroke, which damages neurons in the brain that can never be replaced. People who have suffered a stroke may therefore experience some type of long-term damage, such as speech impairment or difficulty in moving parts of their bodies.

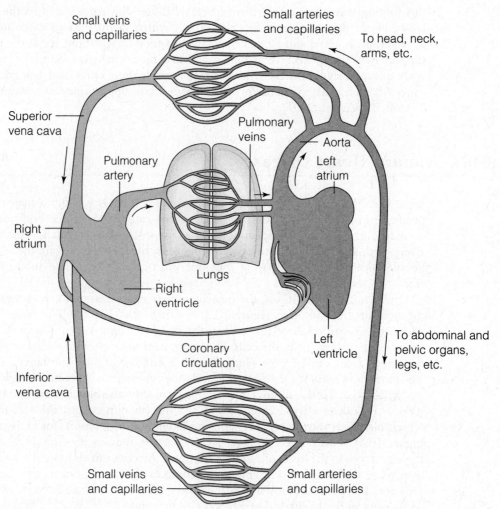

Small veins
and capillaries

Small arteries
and capillaries

To head, neck,
arms, etc.

Superior
vena cava

Pulmonary
veins

Aorta

Left
atrium

Pulmonary
artery

Right
atrium

Lungs

Right
ventricle

Left
ventricle

To abdominal and
pelvic organs,
legs, etc.

Coronary
circulation

Inferior
vena cava

Small veins
and capillaries

Small arteries
and capillaries

FIGURE 10.2   As the heart beats, blood is pumped through the body. The blood carries much-needed oxygen to all of the cells in the body and removes carbon dioxide and other waste material from the cells.

How Do Psychological Factors Influence Coronary Heart Disease?

Some of the factors associated with CHD can't be changed (Smith & Pratt, 1993). These include the demographic factors—including age and family history—that contribute to CHD (Smith & Pratt, 1993). For example, the likelihood of developing CHD increases with age, for example, presumably because over time the arteries are more likely to become clogged or hardened. People with a family history of CHD, such as a close relative who experienced a heart attack, are also at greater risk of developing this disease.

Gender is another factor associated with cardiovascular disease: Men are at greater risk of experiencing CHD than women, which is one of the reasons why men have a shorter life expectancy than women (Smith & Pratt, 1993). One possible reason for this gender difference is that testosterone, which circulates in higher

FIGURE 10.3 As cholesterol and fats build up in the arteries, the walls of the arteries become thicker and thicker, leaving little room for blood to flow. Over time, arteries can become completely blocked, which causes a heart attack.

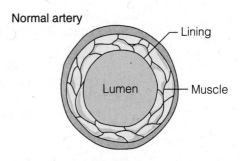

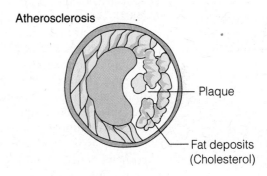

levels in men than women, is associated with aggression and competitiveness, and these behaviors may increase a person's risk of developing cardiovascular disease. However, men and women were relatively equally likely to die of heart disease until the 1920s, suggesting that hormone levels alone are unlikely to explain this gender gap (Nikiforov & Mamaev, 1998). Another possibility is that men engage in more behaviors that lead to CHD than women, including smoking, drinking alcohol, and eating high-fat foods. However, even when men and women have the same level of risky behaviors, men are still more likely than women to die of CHD (Fried et al., 1998). Although research is clearly needed to show exactly why, it is important to recognize that cardiovascular problems are not just a "male problem." In fact, CHD is the leading cause of death in women as well as men—women simply develop such problems about 15 years later than men.

There are also clear differences in the frequency of CHD as a function of race and ethnicity, with African Americans showing more risk than White and Hispanic Americans, who in turn show more risk than Asian Americans (Hayes, Greenlund, Denny, Croft, & Keenan, 2005). Heart disease death rates are also higher among African Americans than Whites (Kung et al., 2008). What causes these racial differences in CHD? Most research points to the role of socioeconomic factors. Specifically, African Americans are more likely than Whites to have low socioeconomic status (SES), and low-SES people tend to experience more risk factors for CHD, including eating a higher-fat diet, smoking, living under generally more stressful conditions, being less likely to engage in regular exercise, and having reduced access to health care (Kershaw et al., 2010; Stunkard & Sorensen, 1993). Other research suggests that African Americans may also experience more stress than Whites because they must constantly cope with racial prejudice and discrimination

(Krieger & Sidney, 1996; Krieger, Sidney, & Coakley, 1998). (The role of stress as a predictor of CHD is discussed in detail in the next section.) However, environmental factors are not the only cause of ethnic and racial differences in CHD: One recent study found that African American women were still at greater risk of experiencing a heart attack than White women even if they had similar levels of education and family income (Winkleby, Kraemer, Ahn, & Varady, 1998).

Stress

Stress, including pressure caused by work, interpersonal conflict, and financial concerns, is one factor that may contribute to CHD (Kop, Gottdiener, & Krantz, 2001). As discussed in Chapter 4, people who are under stress show accelerated heartbeat, strengthened heart contractions, and higher blood pressure. Moreover, epinephrine is released during times of stress, which decreases the time needed for blood to coagulate and causes blood vessels to constrict. Chronic stress can therefore lead to excessive wear and tear on the cardiovascular system, which over time can lead to considerable damage to the heart and arteries (Sapolsky, 1994). For example, monkeys who are at the bottom of the dominance hierarchy (hence, are continually under conditions of high stress) are very likely to develop high blood pressure as well as atherosclerosis. Similarly, people who work in jobs that have constant demands but low levels of control—such as working on an assembly line or waiting tables—are at greater risk of developing CHD than those who have less stressful jobs (Bosma, Stansfeld, & Marmot, 1998). Even relationship stress can lead to both CHD and cardiac events (Coyne et al., 2001; Matthews & Gump, 2002; Orth-Gomer et al., 2000). For example, women with CHD who experience high levels of marital conflict are three times as likely to experience a heart attack as those who are in low-conflict marriages (Orth-Gomer et al., 2000). Similarly, people who experienced chronic job strain are more likely to experience recurrent CHD, even when researchers take into account other variables associated with this disease (Aboa-Éboulé et al., 2007). Interestingly, and as described in Box 10.4: Focus on Research, environmental factors may also influence stress, and, in turn, cardiovascular health.

Some researchers have examined another type of stress that may lead to CHD—the stress of constant racial discrimination (Krieger & Sidney, 1996; Krieger et al., 1998). As described previously, African Americans have higher rates of CHD and hypertension than do Caucasian Americans, and some researchers believe that these differences are caused at least in part by the constant exposure to discrimination and racism that many African Americans encounter. In one study by Krieger et al. (1998), African American men and women who reported experiencing racial discrimination and accepting unfair treatment had significantly higher blood pressure than those who reported experiencing such discrimination but challenging unfair treatment. However, this association between accepting racial discrimination and high blood pressure was found in working-class African Americans, not among African American business professionals (Krieger & Sidney, 1996). This finding suggests that stress may be greatest among those who are trying to overcome adversity but who have limited socioeconomic resources to do so. Racial discrimination may indeed influence rates of hypertension and CHD in African Americans, but this association is also influenced by gender and SES.

Box 10.4

Focus on Research: Is Living in New York City Hazardous to Your Health?

Would you believe that living in—or even visiting—New York City could be hazardous to your health? That's exactly what some recent research by Christenfeld, Glynn, Phillips, and Shrira at the University of California at San Diego suggests (1999). These researchers examined death certificates for a 10-year period and specifically calculated the following rates of death caused by CHD: death rates for New York City residents who died in the city, New York City residents who died while traveling outside the city, and nonresidents of New York City who died while visiting the city. As predicted, people who lived in New York City had a very high death rate as a result of CHD while living in the city—in fact, their death rate from CHD was 55% higher than the national average. In contrast, New York City residents who were traveling outside of the city were 20% less likely to die from CHD than if they were in the city. Visitors to New York City experienced the same type of problems, with a death rate from CHD that is 34% higher than the national average. Is this pattern true in all cities? No. Researchers found no differences in CHD for people who lived in or visited other major cities, including Los Angeles, Chicago, Houston, Philadelphia, Dallas, San Diego, Phoenix, Detroit, San Antonio, and San Jose, as compared to the national average.

Behavioral Choices

Many behavioral choices also influence a person's risk of developing CHD. Researchers in one study examined risk factors for CHD, including smoking, physical inactivity (not exercising), and obesity in more than 23,000 men, and then evaluated these men's health over the next 15 years (Lee, Sui, & Blair, 2009). Men who didn't smoke, engaged in regular exercise, and were normal weight were 59% less likely to experience heart problems and were 69% less likely to die compared to men with all of these risk factors.

As discussed in Chapter 7, cigarette smoking influences CHD in a number of ways, including increasing the heart rate, increasing blood pressure, and constricting the blood vessels, which causes problems over time and particularly during times of stress (Smith & Pratt, 1993). Smoking also decreases the production of HDL cholesterol, which protects against heart attacks. Smoking basically increases wear and tear on the heart and accelerates atherosclerosis. In fact, a person who smokes is twice as likely to die from CHD as someone who doesn't smoke (Fried et al., 1998; Twisk, Kemper, Van Mechelen, & Post, 1997). Moreover, nonsmokers who live with smokers are about 20% more likely to develop CHD than nonsmokers who live with other nonsmokers (Werner & Pearson, 1998).

People who have *hypertension*, a condition in which their blood pressure is at a consistently high level, are at increased risk of developing CHD. Blood pressure represents the force of the blood against the artery walls, and when this pressure is too high, the artery walls can get damaged, which in turn leads to CHD. Because high blood pressure makes the heart beat more forcefully, this type of continuous wear and tear on the heart can weaken it, which also can contribute to CHD. In fact, people who have elevated blood pressure are two to four times as likely to develop CHD as those with normal blood pressure.

Although in many cases the exact cause of hypertension is unknown, considerable research suggests that diet and exercise may play a substantial role in leading to high blood pressure as well as CHD (Smith & Pratt, 1993). People who eat foods that are high in cholesterol, such as animal fats and some types of oils, are at greater risk of developing CHD than those who tend to eat foods that are low in cholesterol, such as fruits and vegetables (Stamler, Wentworth, & Neaton, 1986). Cholesterol, naturally occurring in the body as well as that introduced by diet, is transported in the bloodstream, and excessive amounts can lead to clogged or blocked arteries. A person's total cholesterol level at age 22 is a good predictor of his or her likelihood of experiencing CHD or stroke and age of death (Klag et al., 1993). People with cholesterol levels in the top 25% of the study participants are twice as likely to die of a heart attack as those with cholesterol levels in the bottom 25%. On the other hand, some types of food seem to protect people from developing CHD (Stampfer, Rimm, & Walsh, 1993). For example, women who consume high levels of vitamin E are at reduced risk of CHD (Stampfer et al., 1993), as are people who have a diet high in fiber (Katan, Grundy, & Willett, 1997). Some research even suggests that people who eat deep-sea fish regularly have a lower likelihood of experiencing a heart attack (Albert et al., 1998). Finally, people who are physically fit show faster recovery in terms of heart rate from stressful experiences (Forcier et al., 2006).

Personality

How does personality impact development of CHD? As discussed in Chapter 5, the Type A personality trait is commonly thought to predict occurrence of CHD (Friedman & Rosenman, 1959; Rosenman & Friedman, 1961; Suinn, 1975). Type A people are competitive, time-urgent, and hostile, and are more likely to experience a heart attack and to show signs of hypertension. One possibile reason for this is that Type A people show heightened levels of physiological arousal, including elevated heart rate, higher blood pressure, and increased catecholamines

Do you know what you're consuming when you eat at McDonald's (or another fast-food restaurant)? A Big Mac has 34 grams of fat and 590 calories, an order of medium-size fries has 22 grams of fat and 450 calories, and a medium Coca-Cola Classic has 0 grams of fat and 220 calories. Remember, for someone eating 2,000 calories per day (a rough average), today's nutritional guidelines recommend including 65 grams of fat per day. *Source*: Corbis Sygma.

and corticosteroids, in stressful situations (Jorgensen, Johnson, Kolodziej, & Schreer, 1996; Smith, 1992). While a Type B person might calmly sit in the car and listen to music during a traffic jam, a Type A person might experience this situation as very upsetting and arousing. Over time, this constant physiological arousal can damage the heart and blood vessels and increase the formation of blood clots, which in turn can lead to cardiovascular disease as well as heart attacks.

Although Type A is the personality variable most often associated with CHD, recent research suggests that a specific component of the Type A personality, hostility, is a particularly strong predictor (Barefoot, Dodge, Peterson, Dahlstrom, & Williams, 1989; Miller, Smith, Turner, Guijarro, & Hallet, 1996; Smith, 1992). In fact, research by Shekelle, Gale, Ostfield, and Paul (1983) reveals that men's level of hostility, but not Type A behavior, predicts their likelihood of suffering a heart attack as well as experiencing other stress-related diseases. One prospective study assessed hostility in 200 healthy women and then followed these women over 10 years (Matthews, Owens, Kuller, Sutton-Tyrrell, & Jansen-McWilliams, 1998). Even controlling for variables such as smoking, women who had higher hostility scores in the earlier test were more likely to show symptoms of cardiovascular disease 10 years later. Similarly, Williams et al. (1980) found that patients who were high in hostility had more severe heart disease than those who were low in hostility. Similarly, people who express high levels of anger, including raising their voice while arguing and yelling back when someone yells at them, are at greater risk of developing CHD (Siegman, 1993). In fact, people who frequently experience anger are three times as likely to suffer a heart attack as those who rarely experience anger (Williams et al., 2000). How does the expression of anger lead to CHD? When a person yells, his or her heart rate probably increases, and, although the person may not be aware of it, blood pressure also increases. In turn, people who regularly experience this higher level of physiological arousal may be at greater risk of developing cardiovascular problems because they have so much wear and tear on their blood vessels and heart (Siegman, Anderson, Herbst, Boyle, & Wilkinson, 1992). Physiological reactions may also explain why people who are high in hostility tend to have worse health: Hostile people have consistently higher heart rates and blood pressure than those who are low in hostility, they show extreme cardiovascular reactions to stressful situations, and they take longer to have their bodies return to normal functioning following a stressful interaction (Raikkonen, Matthews, Flory, & Owens, 1999; Smith, 1992; Suarez, Kuhn, Schanberg, Williams, & Zimmermann, 1998).

Other personality traits, including anxiety, depression, pessimism, and neuroticism, are also associated with the development of CHD (Costa & McCrae, 1987; Everson, Goldberg, Kaplan, & Cohen, 1996; Kawachi et al., 1994; Kubzansky, Cole, Kawachi, Vokonas, & Sparrow, 2006; Markovitz, Matthews, Kannel, Cobb, & D'Agostino, 1993). People who are high in anxiety are significantly more likely to develop and die from heart disease than those who are lower in anxiety (Kawachi et al., 1994; Markovitz et al., 1993). For example, men who are high in anxiety are three times more likely to die from a heart attack than those who are low in anxiety. Similarly, men who are high in hopelessness are more than four times more likely to die from cardiovascular diseases as those who are low in hopelessness (Everson et al., 1996). Finally, one study of 347 women ages 18 to 94 years revealed that neuroticism was associated with reports of a number of physical symptoms, including frequency of illness, cardiovascular problems, digestive problems, and fatigue (Costa & McCrae, 1987). However, and as you may recall from Chapter 5, some evidence suggests that people who are high in neuroticism are more likely both to interpret minor health problems as more painful and problematic and complain about health symptoms, but they do not actually experience more physical problems (Watson, 1988; Watson & Pennebaker, 1989).

Finally, although most research has focused on the negative effects of some types of emotions on CHD, some researchers have examined the benefits of positive emotions (Kubzansky & Thurston, 2007). For example, people who are higher in emotional vitality—characterized by a sense of energy, positive well-being, and effective emotion regulation—have a reduced risk of CHD. Emotional vitality may therefore help protect people against developing CHD.

How Can Psychological Interventions Help Reduce the Risk of Recurring Heart Attacks?

Because of the significant rate of CHD in the United States, many intervention programs have specifically targeted heart-attack survivors in an effort to help them change their behavior. As described at the beginning of the chapter, following his first heart attack, Bill became motivated to change his diet, stop smoking, and start exercising, all of which may decrease the likelihood of future heart problems. This is a type of secondary prevention approach to health, which focuses on reducing people's risk of experiencing another heart attack and dying of cardiovascular disease.

One type of treatment for CHD focuses on helping people change their health-related behavior (Dusseldorp, van Elderen, Maes, Meulman, & Kraaij, 1999; Smith & Pratt, 1993). Health-education programs focus on changing people's behavior, including showing them how to reduce their sodium and fat intake, lower their weight, and stop smoking. Because smoking and high-fat diets can cause the heart to operate less efficiently, making changes in these behaviors reduces the risk of CHD. Health education programs also encourage people to start exercising, which decreases the risk of cardiovascular disease in several ways, including reducing weight and improving the efficiency of the heart (Rovario, Holmes, & Holmsten, 1984). Health-education programs also provide patients with information about the medications they could take and encourage patients to follow prescribed medical regimens.

These programs can be effective in reducing CHD. People who make dietary changes show substantial reductions in cardiovascular risk factors (Brunner et al., 1997), and those who engage in regular exercise following a heart attack show lower blood pressure and lower heart rates (Rovario et al., 1984). Health-promotion programs are particularly effective at decreasing CHD risk when they also include cholesterol-lowering medication (Maher, Brown, Marcovina, Hillger, & Zhao, 1995). Lifestyle interventions can also lead to reductions in the rate of diabetes, which is often linked to CHD (Knowler et al., 2002).

The other common approach to reducing risk of CHD is through stress-management programs (Dusseldorp et al., 1999). These programs focus on training patients in techniques for managing stress, such as relaxation training. One recent study by Blumenthal et al. at Duke University (2002) found that men who participated in a weekly stress-management group for 4 months experienced fewer negative health events, including heart attacks, bypass surgery, and death, than those who simply received medicine for their condition and those who exercised. Other studies point to the availability of trained professionals as a resource in helping heart-attack survivors manage stress. For example, Frasure-Smith and Prince (1989) assigned some patients to receive regular calls from a nurse for 1 year following their heart attack. The nurse asked them whether they were experiencing stress and then either talked through the problems with the patient or referred them to another health-care professional (therapist, physician, social worker). Patients who received such follow-up contact had lower rates of mortality over the 7-year follow-up as compared to those who received standard care.

Several studies have attempted to decrease individuals' risk of CHD by teaching them techniques and methods for changing Type A cognitions, behaviors, and emotions, such as by teaching people more adaptive ways to cope with stress (Friedman et al., 1986). For example, patients might examine the triggers for their Type A behavior, and then learn cognitive and behavioral techniques to help them reduce their competitiveness, hostility, and cynicism. This type of program is very effective in reducing the risk of a second heart attack—in fact, rates of death caused by CHD were twice as high in the control group as compared to the treatment group. Similarly, other researchers have focused specifically on trying to modify anger and hostility. In one study, 22 highly hostile men with CHD were randomly assigned to a control condition (information only) or a hostility-reduction intervention, which included training in listening, problem-focused coping, and enhancing self-awareness (Gidron, Davidson, & Bata, 1999). Findings at the 2-month follow-up revealed that those in the intervention group had lower blood pressure and rates of hostility, suggesting that this might be a good way to reduce CHD.

Finally, and as shown in Figure 10.4, programs that combine health education and stress-management techniques may be effective. For example, Ornish et al. (1990, 1998) created a very intensive program in an attempt to alter behavior that was putting people at risk of CHD. This program included severe dietary restrictions (such as allowing only 10% of their calories to come from fat), assistance in smoking cessation and reducing alcohol intake, and increasing exercise, as well as training in relaxation and other stress-management techniques. Patients who participated in this program had significantly less blockage of their coronary arteries 1 year later compared to those in a control group. Moreover, findings from their 5-year follow-up indicated that patients who completed this program had fewer coronary problems. Similarly, researchers in another study randomly assigned people with CHD to one of two conditions: control group or intervention (included diet, exercise, stress management, group support; Pischke, Scherwitz, Weidner, & Ornish, 2008). Reductions in psychological distress and hostility were observed 1 year later and were maintained 5 years later. Improvements in diet, weight reduction, and stress management were observed and led to improvements in cardiovascular outcomes. Although this type of approach is clearly successful in decreasing CHD, it is very costly in terms of time, energy, and expense and is therefore not likely to be a particularly useful approach in the general population.

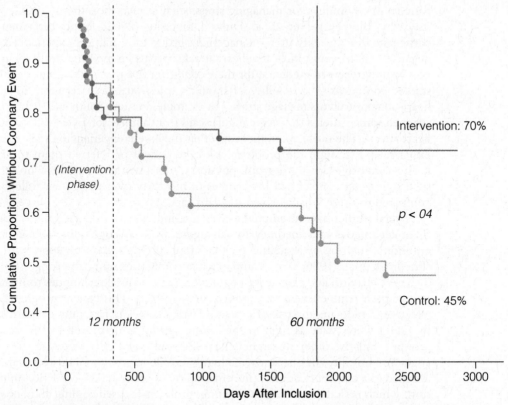

FIGURE 10.4 Patients who received an intervention focused on lifestyle changes (including smoking, diet, exercise, and stress) had lower rates of coronary events (e.g., heart attacks, bypasses, and death) than those in the standard-care condition (data from Lisspers et al., 2005).

What Is Cancer?

After heart disease, **cancer** is the leading cause of death in the United States, with an estimated 562,875 people dying from this disease each year (CDC, 2011). More than 18.6 million Americans, or 8.2% of the population, have been diagnosed with cancer. Although there are more than 200 types of cancer, the majority of cases are one of four types: carcinomas (malignancies of tissue-cells and cells lining various body organs; e.g., breast cancer, lung cancer, and skin cancer), lymphomas (cancers of the lymphatic system, such as non-Hodgkin's lymphoma and Hodgkin's disease), sarcomas (cancers of the muscles or bones), and leukemias (cancers of the blood cells or bone marrow). As shown in Figure 10.5, the five leading types of cancer in terms of mortality are cancers of the lung, prostate, breast, colon, and pancreas (Xu, Kochanek, Murphy & Tejada-Vera, 2010).

Cancer is the uncontrollable growth and spread of abnormal cells, which form tumors (Brownson, Reif, Alavanja, & Bal, 1993). Benign tumors consist of cells that are similar to the nearby cells, and they grow relatively slowly and are mostly harmless. On the other hand, malignant tumors (commonly called cancers) consist

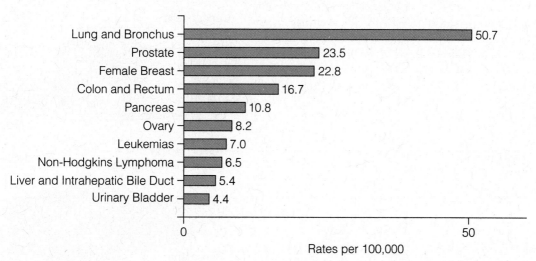

Top 10 Cancer Sites: 2007, Male and Female, United States–All Races

Lung and Bronchus 50.7
Prostate 23.5
Female Breast 22.8
Colon and Rectum 16.7
Pancreas 10.8
Ovary 8.2
Leukemias 7.0
Non-Hodgkins Lymphoma 6.5
Liver and Intrahepatic Bile Duct 5.4
Urinary Bladder 4.4

0   50

Rates per 100,000

FIGURE 10.5 Although death rates due to lung, prostate, breast, and colon cancer have declined somewhat over the past decade, lung cancer is the leading cause of cancer-related deaths (data from Xu et al., 2010).

of cells that are different from their surrounding cells and grow very rapidly. Malignant tumors often grow beyond their original location and invade other body organs (metastasize), spreading cancer throughout the body (see Figure 10.6). Tumors can cause intense pain when they put pressure on normal tissues and nerves and block the flow of fluids in the body (Melzack & Wall, 1982). If these tumors are not stopped (either by removing them with surgery or stopping their growth with radiation or chemotherapy or other therapies), they can obstruct vital organs (as in intestinal cancer), cause organs to fail (as in liver or kidney cancer), or lead to hemorrhaging or strokes.

Most cancers are caused by genetic mutations, which may gradually occur over time. Some of these mutations are simply a function of age—as cells continue to multiply, the chance of mutations occurring increases over time. This is why cancer is more common in older people than in younger people. Cancer can also be caused by *carcinogens*, any substance capable of converting normal cells into cancerous ones. Carcinogens change the cell's DNA, which in turn leads to cancer. For example, exposure to ultraviolet light while sun tanning can cause a chemical reaction in cells that alters both the components and the shape of the DNA molecule in cells. Although sometimes these changes are found and repaired by the cell, or the cell is killed before it can reproduce, other times these alterations go unnoticed and lead to cancer. In normal cells, two different types of genes act to regulate cell growth: *oncogenes* work to control cell growth and reproduction, and *suppressor genes* work to inhibit uncontrolled growth. However, when either of these types of genes is damaged by a mutation—either caused by random chance or exposure to a carcinogen—uncontrolled cell growth and reproduction can occur. For example, benzopyrene, a chemical in cigarette smoke, damages cancer suppressor genes, and may therefore lead to lung cancer (Denissenko, Pao, Tang, & Pfeifer, 1996).

FIGURE 10.6 Cancer can be caused by random and naturally occurring mutations or by carcinogens, both of which lead to changes in cells' DNA. These changes disrupt the normal functioning of both the oncogenes, which work to control cell growth and reproduction, and the suppressor genes, which work to inhibit uncontrolled growth. In turn, cancer can spread out of control.

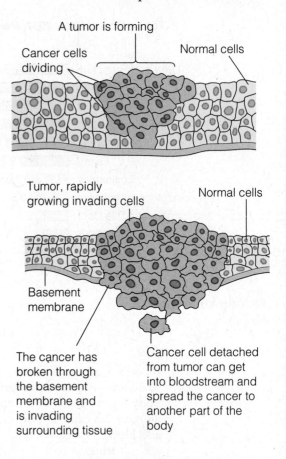

Similarly, mutations in two genes that are responsible for repairing damage to cell DNA, BRCA1 and BRCA2, are associated with an increased risk of developing breast cancer.

How Do Psychosocial Factors Influence the Development of Cancer?

Some of the factors associated with acquiring cancer are largely fixed and unchangeable. Genetic factors clearly contribute to at least some types of cancer; a woman whose mother or sister has breast cancer is at nearly twice the risk of developing breast cancer as someone without such a genetic link (Claus, Risch, & Thompson, 1993; Colditz et al., 1993). However, only 2 to 5% of breast cancers are clearly linked to genetic factors, such as the presence of BRCA1 and BRCA2, indicating other factors also contribute to the expression of such genes. People who are older are also at greater risk of developing cancer, perhaps in part because the genetic mutations that cause cancer are more likely to occur over time. However, cancer is the second leading cause of death in children ages 1 to 14 years (after accidents), so this is not simply a disease of the old.

Ethnicity is also associated with the development of cancer, with African Americans at a greater risk of developing cancer than Caucasians (Meyerowitz,

Richardson, Hudson, & Leedham, 1998). In fact, African Americans have the highest overall rate of cancer, a rate caused largely by the very high incidence of lung and prostate cancer among African American men. On the other hand, Latinos and Asian Americans in the United States have relatively low rates of cancer. African Americans probably do not have a genetic predisposition to cancer; most evidence suggests that these race differences in frequency of cancer are caused by nongenetic factors, such as knowledge, behavior, and access to health care. For example, as compared to African Americans, Caucasians know more about the risks and signs of cancer, have lower blood pressure, and eat less dietary fat (Meyerowitz et al., 1998; Winkleby, Robinson, Sundquist, & Kraemer, 1999). In addition, African Americans who are diagnosed with cancer have an overall survival rate that is lower than that seen in Caucasian and Hispanic patients (Woodward et al., 2006). Such differences may be at least in part a reflection of types of tumors seen in patients of different ethnicities, as well as a function of differences in socioeconomic factors (as will be discussed shortly).

Although demographic variables such as age and race as well as genetic factors are associated with the likelihood of developing cancer, substantial evidence points to the link between psychosocial factors and the acquisition of cancer too. This section examines three such factors.

Behavioral Choices

Lifestyle factors are a strong predictor of the development of cancer, with some evidence suggesting that 85% of all cancers could be prevented by changing people's behavior (Brownson et al., 1993). What types of things do people do that lead to cancer? Smoking is an obvious one; as described earlier, benzopyrene, a chemical in cigarette smoke, leads to lung cancer by damaging a cancer suppressor gene. In fact, 87% of lung cancer cases are attributed to cigarette smoking. Smokers are also at increased risk of developing other types of cancer, including cancer of the mouth, cancer of the bladder and pancreas, leukemia, and lymphoma. One study even found that women who smoked were 25% more likely to die of breast cancer than those who never smoked (Calle, Miracle-McMahill, Thun, & Heath, 1994). Moreover, women who started smoking before age 16 are at a much greater risk of dying from breast cancer than those who start smoking after age 20, and women who smoke more cigarettes per day have a greater likelihood of acquiring breast cancer than lighter smokers. Simply being regularly exposed to secondhand cigarette smoke increases a person's risk of developing cancer (Fielding & Phenow, 1988).

After tobacco smoke, diet is the next leading cause of cancer (American Cancer Society, 1998). Although we don't know exactly how diet influences cancer risk, there is strong evidence that what you eat—and how much you eat—influences your likelihood of getting cancer. Women who eat more high-fat foods, such as milk, cheese, and butter, have an increased likelihood of developing breast cancer (Toniolo, Ribloi, Protta, Charrel, & Coppa, 1989), and men who eat diets that are high in dietary cholesterol have twice the risk of developing lung cancer than those who eat little excess cholesterol (Shekelle, Rossof, & Stamler, 1991). Similarly, people who eat large quantities of foods that are high in animal (saturated) fat, such as red meat, are at increased risk of developing several different types of cancers, including colon, rectum, and prostate cancers (Slattery, Boucher, Caan, Potter, &

It's not just cigarettes that cause cancer—chewing tobacco is strongly associated with oral cancer (Bolinder, Alfredsson, Englund, & deFaire, 1994; Winn et al., 1981).
Source: Getty Images News and Sport Services.

Ma,. 1998). On the other hand, people who eat large quantities of fruits, vegetables, and foods high in fiber are much less likely to develop colon and rectal cancer (Slattery et al., 1998; Zhang et al., 1999), perhaps in part because these foods work to quickly rid the body of cancer-causing fats. For example, one large-scale study found that women who consumed five or more servings of fruit and vegetables each day were 23% less likely to develop breast cancer than those who ate two or fewer servings per day. Similarly, people who have diets high in *antioxidants*, such as foods containing vitamin A and vitamin C, have lower rates of lung and stomach cancer, perhaps because these vitamins help block the work of carcinogens (Hunter et al, 1993; Yong et al., 1997). In addition, patients with colon cancer who eat a diet high in meat, fat, refined grains, and dessert have a higher risk of recurrence and mortality than those who eat a diet characterized by high intakes of fruits and vegetables, poultry, and fish (Meyerhardt et al., 2007).

Questioning the Research 10.3

Do these studies really show that specific types of diet can lead to cancer? Can you think of an alternative explanation for these findings?

Other lifestyle choices also influence peoples' risk of developing cancer. Sun exposure is clearly recognized as a major cause of skin cancer, yet many people who tan regularly do not use sunscreens at all (Brownson et al., 1993; Koh et al., 1997). And even people who do use sunscreen often use a lower-than-recommended level of protection. Some patterns of sexual behavior are also associated with cancer (Brownson et al., 1993). For example, women who have multiple sexual partners, a history of STDs, and begin having sex at an early age are at increased risk of developing cervical cancer (Brownson et al., 1993). Excessive alcohol use is associated with some types of cancer, including cancers of the pancreas, esophagus, and liver (Heuch, Kvale, Jacobsen, & Bjelke, 1983).

What's the good news? Engaging in regular exercise seems to offer some protection against various types of cancer, including breast cancer (Bernstein, Henderson, Hanisch, Sullivan-Halley, & Ross, 1994; Rockhill et al., 1999; Thune, Brenn, Lund, & Gaard, 1997), prostate cancer (Lee, Paffenbarger, & Hsieh, 1992), and colon cancer (Slattery, Schumacher, Smith, West, & Abd-Elghany, 1990; White, Jacobs, & Daling, 1996). For example, one study found that young women who engaged in regular physical exercise—at least four times a week—were half as likely to develop breast cancer as those who did not engage in regular exercise (Bernstein et al., 1994). Although this study was conducted by matching women who exercised regularly to those who did not based on age, race, and whether they had children, and then comparing the rate of breast cancer in both groups, it does not definitively show that exercise decreases a woman's risk of cancer. Perhaps women who exercise regularly are generally healthier (e.g., less likely to smoke, more likely to eat healthy foods) and therefore less likely to develop cancer.

Stress

Stress, including a history of stressful life experiences as well as separation from or loss of a loved one, is associated with acquiring cancer (McKenna, Zevon, Corn, & Rounds, 1999). Studies comparing patients with cancer to those without cancer have found that those with cancer report significantly more negative life events, such as loss of loved ones and marital problems, than those without cancer. For example, children with cancer are likely to have experienced a number of life changes, such as personal injury and change in the health of a family member, in the year preceding their diagnosis (Jacobs & Charles, 1980). Although some of these studies are retrospective, and therefore it is difficult to tell whether patients' cancer diagnosis at one point leads them to look at the past in a more negative light, a recent review of many studies on the predictors of cancer demonstrated that both the experience of stressful life events and the loss of a loved one were associated with an increased likelihood of developing cancer (McKenna et al., 1999).

How exactly does stress lead to cancer? As discussed in Chapter 4, stress clearly weakens the immune system, which thereby decreases the body's ability to detect and kill abnormal cancer cells (Delahanty & Baum, 2001). Research with both humans and rats shows that stressful events, such as exams, divorce, and job loss (in humans) and rotation on a turntable, uncontrollable shocks, and flashing lights (in rats), reduces the number of immune cells in the blood. For example, people who were recently separated from their spouses have lower levels of Natural Killer (NK) cells and helper T cells (Kiecolt-Glaser & Glaser, 1989) as do people who are taking care of a terminally ill relative (Kiecolt-Glaser, Dura, Speicher, Trask, & Glaser, 1991). Stress may also reduce the body's ability to fix DNA errors, meaning that random errors that would normally be found and repaired by the body are allowed to remain instead in the body (Glaser, Thorn, Tarr, Kiecolt-Glaser, & D'Ambrosio, 1985).

Personality

Many people, including those with cancer, believe that this disease is caused at least in part by personality factors (Roberts, Newcomb, Trentham-Dietz, & Storer, 1996). A number of personality dimensions, including depression, extraversion, and difficulty expressing emotions, are often associated with the development of cancer (Dattore, Shontz, & Coyne, 1980; Persky, Kempthorne-Rawson, & Shekelle, 1987; Shaffer, Graves, Swank, & Pearson, 1987; Shaffer, Duszynski, & Thomas, 1982). In fact, some researchers describe people with such traits, namely, those who present a pleasant and cheerful face to the world, show passivity in the face of stress, and tend to suppress negative emotions, as having a "Type C," or cancer-prone, personality (McKenna et al., 1999). Many of these studies, however, have used cross-sectional designs, in which they examine people with and without cancer at a single point in time, and therefore they cannot determine whether the presence of such traits caused the cancer or vice versa. After all, it is therefore not surprising that people with cancer would show distinct types of personality traits, including a tendency to try and suppress their difficult emotions about the disease as well as depression. However, other studies using longitudinal designs have often revealed similar results. For example, Shaffer et al. (1982) examined attitudes toward family by following a group of healthy medical students, and then followed these participants to measure illness over time for 30 years. Those with impaired self-awareness, a lack of emotional expression, and feelings of self-sacrifice and self-blame were 16 times more likely to develop cancer than the others. Similarly, another study revealed that men who were depressed at one point in time were twice as likely to die from cancer 20 years later as those who were not depressed (Shekelle et al., 1981).

A meta-analysis, a combination of various studies on the link between personality and cancer, provided only moderate evidence for the role of personality traits leading to cancer (McKenna et al., 1999). First, people who rely heavily on denial and repression as a way of coping with problems are at somewhat of a greater risk of developing cancer. This type of coping pattern is associated with an overall weakened immune system, which could be one explanation for this link among denial, repression, and cancer. Second, there is limited evidence that people with a conflict-avoidant personality style are more likely to develop cancer. This type of coping is similar to that of denial and repression and may also therefore impact the immune system. Finally, current research provides no evidence that other personality dimensions, including depression/anxiety, introversion/extraversion, and expression of anger, are associated with acquiring cancer.

What Factors Predict Effective Coping With Cancer?

People who are diagnosed with a chronic illness typically experience considerable fear and uncertainty about the future, in part because many such diseases are largely uncontrollable (Dunkel-Schetter et al., 1992). In turn, one predictor of effective coping with cancer is when a person believes he or she has some control over the disease, specifically whether it spreads or reoccurs (Taylor et al., 1984). One study with 78 patients with breast cancer revealed that women who had high levels of cognitive control, namely, believing that they and their doctors could control the cancer, experienced better adjustment (e.g., less anxiety, fear, depression, anger) to their disease. Although these beliefs are largely illusions (e.g., cancer is largely uncontrollable and unpredictable), they serve a valuable role in psychological adaptation and are therefore quite functional. In fact, women who believed that both they and their doctors had control over the cancer experienced the fewest psychological problems.

People who cope with cancer using an active and engaged approach also show better psychological adjustment (Carver et al., 1993; Epping-Jordan et al., 1999; Stanton & Snider, 1993). For example, Stanton and Snider (1993) examined coping style in a sample of women who were just diagnosed with breast cancer. Those who simply wished the cancer would "go away" experienced more psychological distress than those who did not engage in such avoidant thinking. Similarly, people who cope with a cancer diagnosis by expecting positive outcomes show lower levels of anxiety and depression than those who try to avoid thinking about the disease and those who focus on negative possibilities (Carver et al., 1993; Epping-Jordan et al., 1999). One study of 101 women with breast cancer found that those who were determined to beat the disease and who expressed their feelings of anger, anxiety, and depression showed a better adjustment, including lower levels of anxiety, depression, and hostility (Classen, Koopman, Angell, & Spiegel, 1996). These findings are in line with those described in Chapter 4—people who cope with stressful events with an optimistic and active style tend to experience fewer psychological problems.

People's style of coping with cancer can even influence survival (Greer, 1991; Pettingale, Morris, Greer, & Haybittle, 1985). Specifically, those who simply "give in" and stop fighting the disease, or deny its existence, often die more rapidly than those who maintain a more aggressive and active approach. For example, one study classified women based on their response to the cancer diagnosis: stoic acceptance, helplessness/hopelessness, optimistic spirit, and denial (Pettingale et al., 1985). These patients were then followed for 10 years. Among those with stoic acceptance, 31% had died after 5 years and 75% had died after 10 years, and among those with helplessness, 80% had died after 5 years. In contrast, those with an optimistic spirit, 10% had died after 5 years and 30% after 10 years, and those who responded with denial had a 10% death rate after 5 years and a 50% death rate after 10 years. Although this study was based on a small sample of women, it certainly suggests that psychological factors may influence length of survival in patients with cancer.

What Is HIV/AIDS?

AIDS, which is caused by the human immunodeficiency virus (HIV), was first identified as a syndrome in 1981 (Foege, 1983). An estimated one million people in the United States are HIV-positive, with an estimated 56,300 Americans becoming infected each year (CDC, 2010). More than 18,000 people die of AIDS each year in the United States. In addition, an estimated 33.3 million people worldwide are living with HIV, and 1.8 million people worldwide die of AIDS each year (Joint United Nations Programme on HIV/AIDS (UNAIDS), 2010).

In the 1980s, in the early stages of the HIV epidemic, the vast majority of people with AIDS were men who had sex with men (as discussed in Chapter 2; Centers for Disease Control and Prevention, 2006). Men having sex with men is still the largest route of transmission of HIV in the United States, accounting for 53% of new HIV infections (Hall et al., 2008). However, heterosexual transmission accounts for 31% of new infections. An additional 16% of infections are caused by injection drug use.

AIDS is much more prevalent in African Americans than in Whites (Campsmith, Rhodes, Hall, & Green, 2008). Although African Americans make up only 12% of the total United States population, 46% of people living with HIV are African American. AIDS is the third leading cause of death for African American men and women between the ages of 35 and 44 years, and the ninth leading cause of death for all African Americans. This greater rate of HIV infection is caused by multiple factors, including higher rates of sexual risk behaviors and injection drug use, as well as poverty (which means less access to HIV-prevention information, safe housing, and quality health care).

HIV, which causes AIDS, is a retrovirus. Retroviruses replicate by injecting themselves into host cells and literally taking over the genetic workings of these cells. They can then produce virus particles that infect new cells. After HIV enters the bloodstream, it invades the T cells, incorporates its genetic material into the cells, and then starts destroying cells' ability to function. As discussed in Chapter 4, T cells are responsible for recognizing harmful substances in the body and for attacking such cells, in part by releasing NK cells. Although HIV is able to stay in the body in a latent and dormant state, it gradually starts replicating itself, and in the process begins destroying the T cells.

The progression from HIV to AIDS varies in time but follows a distinct pattern of four stages (McCutchan, 1990). During the first stage, which may last for a period of 1 to 8 weeks, people experience relatively mild symptoms, such as fever, headache, and sore throat. This initial stage is then followed by a latent period, in which people experience few, if any, symptoms; this stage can last as long as 10 years. During the third stage, people develop a specific group of symptoms, including night sweats, painful skin rash, swollen lymph nodes, and white spots in the mouth. Finally, as the patient's immune system begins to have trouble fighting off various infections, people may experience problems with the lungs, gastrointestinal tract, nervous system, bones, and the brain (see Figure 10.7). This stage is marked by a dramatic reduction in T cell counts—which may be 200 or less per cubic millimeter of blood compared to a rate of 1,000 in a healthy person. People infected with HIV may also experience more severe symptoms, such as shortness of breath, substantial weight loss, personality shifts, and dementia (mental confusion and memory loss). Because HIV basically destroys the immune system, people with AIDS often die of *opportunistic infections*, such as pneumonia, tuberculosis, and a type of cancer called Kaposi's sarcoma.

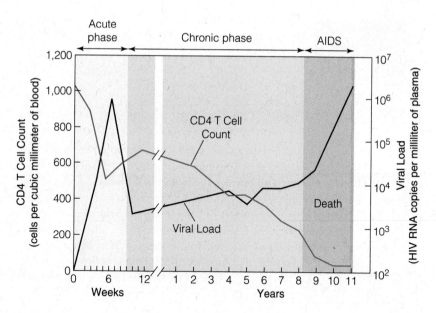

FIGURE 10.7 Although HIV may stay in its latent or dormant state for some time, eventually it spreads, which leads to a dramatic decrease in the number of T cells. People with AIDS eventually die from a series of opportunistic infections because their immune systems are mostly destroyed.

How Do Psychological Factors Predict the Acquisition of HIV?

In the United States and other Western cultures, many routes of HIV transmission occur through behavioral choices, such as the choice to engage in unprotected sex and the choice to share needles for injecting drugs. Therefore, individuals who decide to protect themselves from HIV, and follow through on these intentions, are quite safe. In fact, researchers who examined condom use in an "expert population"—prostitutes at three brothels in Nevada—found that when used correctly, condoms virtually never break, hence can provide protection against HIV transmission (Albert, Warner, Hatcher, Trussell, & Bennett, 1995). Moreover, one study with committed couples in which one partner was HIV-positive and the other was HIV-negative found that among those who consistently used condoms, none of the HIV-negative partners tested positive for HIV (de Vincenzi, 1994). So, what factors lead people to engage in unsafe sex?

According to the AIDS Risk Reduction Model (ARRM), people first must understand the threat of HIV infection and recognize that their behavior puts them at risk of acquiring this disease (Catania, Kegeles, & Coates, 1990). Information about HIV is widespread; hence, most people do understand how HIV is transmitted as well as strategies for protecting themselves from this disease (Sheeran, Abraham, & Orbell, 1999). Most people also understand that HIV is a fatal disease and that acquiring this disease would have severe negative consequences.

Despite these high levels of knowledge and perceived severity, many people do not see themselves as personally at risk of HIV infection. For example, college students tend to assume that risky people are those who dress provocatively, live in large cities, hang out in bars, and who are overly anxious for sex (Hammer, Fisher, Fitzgerald, & Fisher, 1996; Williams et al., 1992). In contrast, students overwhelmingly believe that students they know and like are not risky. Similarly,

Box 10.5

Focus on Research: The Hazards of Seeing HIV as Not Very Prevalent

Researchers in this study examined whether people's perceptions of the prevalence of HIV in their community influence rates of HIV–related behavior (Kalichman & Cain, 2005). Those in the study, 487 men and 236 women seeking care at a sexually transmitted infections (STI) clinic, completed anonymous surveys assessing their perceptions about the prevalence of HIV/AIDS and other STIs as well as their own rates of risky sexual behavior. People who estimated that fewer people in their city were infected with HIV relative to the rates in other cities reported having more sex partners, higher rates of sexual risk practices, and higher rates of STIs. Moreover, they were also less likely to have been tested for HIV. This research suggests that STI clinic patients may have a sense for the relative burden of AIDS in their city, and estimates of local disease prevalence may predict sexual risk behaviors.

one study with African American teenagers found that nearly one third believed they could avoid HIV infection simply by not having sex with "people who look like they have AIDS" (St. Lawrence, 1993), and more than 84% of women in a drug treatment program saw themselves as unlikely to contract AIDS (Kline & Strickler, 1993). Similarly, and as described in Box 10.5: Focus on Research, people who see HIV as less prevalent in their community show higher rates of risky sexual behavior. However, people who know someone who has died of HIV tend to engage in less risky behavior, presumably because this personal connection increases one's own awareness of vulnerability (Mitchell, Severtson, & Latimer, 2007).

Another factor that influences HIV protective behaviors is the perceived severity of being infected with HIV. People may, for example, believe that people can manage HIV, and thereby prevent or drastically delay death, simply by taking medications (e.g., just like people "manage" diabetes), and therefore feel comfortable engaging in risky sexual behavior. In line with this view, HIV-positive men who believe the recent advances in AIDS treatments mean they have relatively little risk of dying from HIV had the highest levels of unsafe behavior, including the most partners and the most frequent unprotected sex (Vanable, Ostrow, McKirnan, Taywaditep, & Hope, 2000). For example, researchers in one study examined rates of risky sexual behavior in gay and bisexual men in 1997 and again in 2005 (Kalichman et al., 2007). Although men reported using condoms during 82% of sex acts in 1997, this rate dropped to only 49% in 2005, in part due to advances in treating HIV which make such a diagnosis less likely to be seen as a "death sentence."

Questioning the Research 10.4

Although improvements in HIV treatment are one explanation for the decrease in rates of condom use between 1997 and 2005, are there other potential explanations for this change?

TABLE 10.5 *Test Yourself: Would You Use a Condom?*

1. If I ask to use condoms, it might make my partner not want to have sex with me.
2. If I ask to use condoms, it will look like I don't trust my partner.
3. I would feel uncomfortable buying condoms.
4. I can make sex fun or sexy when using a condom with my partner.
5. Before I decide to have sex, I will make sure we have a condom.
6. I can stop to use a condom with my main partner even if I am very sexually aroused.
7. I don't know how to use a condom.
8. I don't know how to talk to my partner about safer sex.
9. It is embarrassing to talk about condoms with a sexual partner.
10. If my partner won't let us use a condom, I won't have sex.

These items measure people's beliefs about their partner's attitudes toward condoms, their own self-efficacy for condom use, and their ability to use condoms and negotiate condom use with their partner.

Source: Rosario et al., 1999.

People also must have a strong commitment to using condoms during sex, as well as strong confidence, or self-efficacy, in their ability to do so (see Table 10.5; Catania et al., 1990). Several factors influence whether someone makes such a commitment. Their attitudes toward condoms are one factor—people who hold a negative attitude toward condoms, such as believing that condoms reduce sexual pleasure and imply a lack of trust in their partner, are less likely to engage in protected sex (Fisher, Fisher, & Rye, 1995; Kelley & Kalichman, 1998). For example, one large-scale survey of heterosexual adults found that people's beliefs about the influence of condom use on sexual pleasure were a strong predictor of whether they intended to use condoms as well as whether they actually used condoms (Albarracín et al., 2000). And even if people have positive attitudes about condoms, they still must feel confident in their ability to use them. For example, one study with 156 gay, lesbian, and bisexual adolescents found that those who weren't confident that they could suggest condom use as well as those who believed that suggesting condom use would make it seem as if they didn't trust their partner were the most likely to engage in unprotected sex (Rosario, Mahler, Hunter, & Gwadz, 1999).

People's attitudes toward condoms are also influenced by their beliefs about other people's attitudes toward condoms, including their friends and their partners (Catania et al., 1990; Fisher et al., 1995). People who believe that others in their social group are using condoms are more likely to use condoms themselves, whereas those who believe that few others use condoms are much less likely to choose to use protection. Similarly, those who feel social pressure to use condoms, namely, that other people who are important to them believe they should use condoms, are more likely to engage in safer sex. Because condom use is a behavior that involves two people, individuals' beliefs about their partner's attitudes toward condoms are a particularly strong predictor of whether they use condoms. In line with this view, partner attitudes toward condom use are a stronger predictor of condom use than more general social norms (Kashima, Gallois, & McCamish, 1993).

People also must be capable of actually using a condom at the critical moment, which is called the enactment stage (Catania et al., 1990). As discussed in Chapter 3, people's intentions do not always result in the desired behavior: People may strongly intend to use condoms but then fail to do so. A few factors influence whether people follow through on their condom-use intentions. One factor is very simple—having a condom available increases the odds that it will be used. Carrying condoms is a simple way of increasing your likelihood of engaging in protected sex. Another factor that can influence whether a condom is used is level of sexual arousal. When people feel highly sexually attracted to their partners, they are less likely to use condoms. Sexual arousal may decrease the likelihood of condom use in part because people like feeling "swept away" and overcome by passion (Galligan & Terry, 1993), which somehow doesn't fit with making the rational decision to use condoms. Condoms are often seen as destroying the magic and ruining spontaneity, which in turn decreases their use. As discussed in Chapter 7, alcohol and drug use decreases the likelihood of condom use as well (Gordon, Carey, & Carey, 1997; Leigh & Stall, 1993; MacDonald, Zanna, & Fong, 1995). For example, one study with male college students found that after drinking about five vodka tonics, students had more negative attitudes about suggesting condom use and saw condom use as interfering more with sexual pleasure (Gordon & Carey, 1996).

Another factor that influences whether condoms are used is whether the couple is in an established and committed relationship (Katz, Fortenberry, Zimet, Blythe, & Orr, 2000; Misovich, Fisher, & Fisher, 1997; Morrill, Ickovics, Golubchikov, Beren, & Rodin, 1996). Considerable research indicates that individuals who are in steady dating relationships engage in higher levels of HIV risk-related behavior than do those who are in casual dating contexts. For example, a meta-analysis of a large number of studies found that, overall, 17% of people said they always use a condom with their steady partner as compared to 30% who always use a condom with their casual partners (Sheeran et al., 1999). As described at the beginning of this chapter, Leslie was shocked to discover she was HIV-positive because she has had only a few sexual partners, and most of those were men with whom she was in a steady relationship. Similarly, an average of 52% of respondents report never using a condom with their steady partner as compared to 40% who never use a condom with casual partners. Women who are in casual sexual relationships are 11 times more likely than those in committed relationships to engage in safer sexual behaviors (Morrill et al., 1996).

Why do people in relationships tend to engage in more risky sexual behavior? One reason is that they perceive their partner as safer and hence don't feel the need to protect themselves. As described previously, people generally think those they know well and who "look normal" couldn't possibly have a disease (Hammer et al., 1996; Williams et al., 1992). Moreover, people are concerned that by suggesting condom use, they will appear promiscuous, loose, or risky themselves (Afifi, 1999). For example, you might be concerned that if you suggest using a condom, your partner will think you have a disease that you don't want to pass on. Another factor is that individuals who are in steady dating relationships worry that suggesting condom use implies a lack of monogamy or trust (Galligan & Terry, 1993). This concern about disrupting the level of intimacy in a relationship is a major factor that

People are more likely to use condoms if they are available—this doesn't mean that having a condom means people will have safer sex, but it definitely increases the odds.
Source: © Abel Mitja Varela/iStockphoto.

inhibits people from suggesting condom use in an ongoing relationship. Similarly, people are more likely to see an attractive person as less likely to have a sexually transmitted disease, presumably because they perceive partners they are attracted to as lower in risk (Blanton & Gerrard, 1997).

How Do Psychological Factors Predict the Progression of HIV?

People are now living for quite some time with HIV, and people vary considerably in the time between exposure to the virus and the development of symptoms. It is possible that psychological factors are partially responsible for these differences (Kemeny, 1994). For example, stress may increase the speed at which HIV is replicated, causing a quicker progression to AIDS. Researchers in one study examined the level of stress in men and women living with HIV/AIDS over a 6-month period (Remor, Penedo, Shen, & Schneiderman, 2007). Perceived stress was associated with a decline in CD4+ cell count over the 6-month period, even when researchers took into account other factors that may have influenced immune function (e.g., age, gender, education, income, duration of antiretroviral treatment, antiretroviral treatment and adherence, CD4+ cell count, and viral load).

Not surprisingly, people who use active-coping strategies, such as taking control of the management of their disease, disclosing their emotions regarding this diagnosis, and finding meaning in their illness, show better psychological adjustment as well as a slower rate of progression of the disease (Goodkin et al., 1992; Mulder, de Vroome, van Griensven, Antoni, & Sandfort, 1999; Reed, Kemeny, Taylor, Wang, & Visscher, 1994; Reed, Kemeny, Taylor, Visscher, 1999; Thompson, Nanni, &

Levine, 1994). For example, HIV-positive men who show higher levels of emotional disclosure and processing of trauma experience greater immunological benefits in terms of the number of NK cells, which in turn leads to survival advantages (O'Cleirigh, Ironson, Fletcher, & Schneiderman, 2008). Similarly, among men who are HIV-positive, those who find some meaning in their condition, such as shifting their values and priorities, show slower declines in their T cell levels and survive for longer periods of time (Bower, Kemeny, Taylor, & Fahey, 1998).

Although avoidance coping, such as trying to withdraw from the situation and focusing on other things, is often found to be a destructive coping technique, some research suggests that this approach can actually be beneficial for men with HIV. Specifically, HIV-positive men who use avoidance coping show a lower rate of decline of their CD4 cells and a longer progression to AIDS (Mulder et al., 1999). Similarly, HIV-positive men who refuse to accept their diagnosis actually survive 9 months longer than those who readily accept their dismal prognosis (Reed et al., 1994). This type of coping may be adaptive in the case of AIDS, especially early in illness, because there is nothing that can be done to cure it. Having an optimistic outlook may also motivate people to engage in health-promoting behaviors, such as following medical regimens and adapting a healthy lifestyle. In contrast, people who have negative expectations about their condition, such as a realistic acceptance of the disease, a belief that the disease will progress, and a belief that they have low control over its development, show a faster progression to AIDS and develop symptoms of HIV earlier than those without such beliefs (e.g., diarrhea, weight loss, high fever, night sweats; Reed et al., 1994; Reed et al., 1999). For example, one study with HIV-positive men found that those who attributed negative events to themselves had a faster rate of immune decline over the next 18 months than those without this type of attribution pattern (see Table 10.6; Segerstrom, Taylor, Kemeny, Reed, & Visscher, 1996). Similarly, women with a pessimistic outlook

TABLE 10.6 *Examples of Negative and Positive Attributions in HIV-Positive Men*

Negative

I lost a couple of friends because I am HIV-positive.

Sometimes at work I just feel isolated because I'm the only person that's gay there.

I would imagine that my T cell count would get lower because over time that's the way it goes.

Positive

To actually die of AIDS or AIDS-related complications is less likely because I think effective therapies will continue to be developed.

I've never felt much isolation because I've always benefited from having other people there . . . who share their feelings, support, and love with me.

I am less likely than other HIV-positive gay men to experience health problems related to AIDS. I think most gay men were promiscuous . . . . I just was not very promiscuous.

HIV-positive men who tend to make negative attributions show a faster decline in immune system functioning than those who tend to make positive attributions.

Source: Segerstrom et al., 1996.

show lower NK cell activity and T cell levels and, hence, are less able to fight off their HIV progression (Byrnes et al., 1998).

Another factor that influences the progression of AIDS is social support (Hays, Turner, & Coates, 1992; Kalichman, Heckman, Kochman, Sikkema, & Bergholte, 2000; Kemeny et al., 1994; Leserman, Perkins, & Evans, 1992; Leserman et al., 1999; Patterson et al., 1996; Theorell et al., 1995). People with high levels of social support report less depression and anxiety, better social adjustment, fewer physical symptoms, and a slower rate of HIV progression, including a slower decline in T cells (Pakenham, Dadds, & Terry, 1994). As described previously, HIV-positive men with large social networks live longer (Patterson et al., 1996). Social support is likely to be especially important given the stigma of AIDS and of homosexuality in general—in fact, men who hide their sexual orientation experience negative health outcomes (Cole, Kemeny, Taylor, Visscher, & Fahey, 1996). One characteristic of social support that leads to better health and longer survival is clearly that people living with HIV or AIDS who have social support engage in more positive health behaviors, including practicing safer sex, than those without such support (Heckman, Kelly, & Somlai, 1998).

Length of survival with HIV infection is also, not surprisingly, associated with strict adherence to drug regimens (Ho, 1995, 1996). As discussed in Chapter 5, personality factors may predict physical well-being in part through their impact on adherence to medical recommendations (see Figure 10.8). However, 80% of HIV care providers see treatment adherence as a major problem, and 43% of people with HIV report missing a dose of their medication in the past week (Gallant & Block, 1998). Unfortunately, even small rates of nonadherence to HIV drug regimens can lead to treatment failure (Catz, Kelly, Bogart, Benotsch, & McAuliffe, 2000). The role of psychological factors in influencing adherence to such regimens is discussed extensively in Chapter 12.

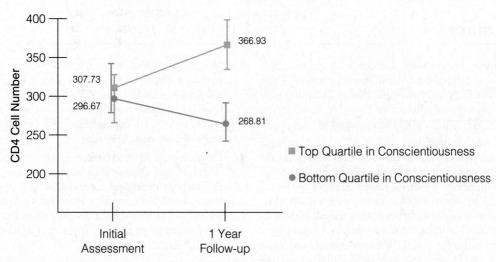

FIGURE 10.8 Participants who are high in conscientiousness show both greater increases in CD4 cell count (a marker of immune functioning) and greater decreases in the level of HIV in the blood compared to those who are low in conscientiousness (data from O'Cleirigh et al., 2007).

TABLE 10.7 *Information YOU Can Use*

- People with chronic diseases really benefit from receiving social support, both in informal ways (from family and friends) and through organized social support. Given the benefits of social support for coping with a chronic disease, seek out such support if you are diagnosed with a chronic disease, and find ways to provide such support to your loved ones with a chronic condition.
- People who can see the benefits of having a chronic disease, and find meaning in this diagnosis, experience better physical and psychological well-being. So, if you or a loved one is diagnosed with such a disease, try to focus on the positives and not just the negatives.
- Stress impacts the likelihood of developing a chronic disease and the ability to cope with such a diagnosis. Therefore, make sure to reduce the amount of stress in your life whenever possible, and take deliberate—and healthy—steps to manage the stress you experience.
- College students are at high risk for becoming infected with HIV or another sexually transmitted disease, so make sure to protect yourself. Use condoms whenever you have sex, even if the person doesn't seem risky, you are highly physically aroused, and you don't know how he or she will react to this request. Protecting yourself from such infection is just too important.
- Virtually all chronic conditions are influenced by behavioral choices, so make sure to make wise health-related decisions to protect yourself from developing such a disease: Eat a healthy diet, engage in regular physical activity, use alcohol in moderation, and, most importantly, don't smoke.

Finally, some evidence even suggests that engaging in regular exercise can help delay the progression of HIV infection (LaPerriere et al., 1990; Lox, McAuley, & Tucker, 1996; Solomon, 1991). Several studies suggest that HIV-positive people who engage in aerobic exercise interventions show fewer declines in NK cells. They also show fewer symptoms of AIDS, such as substantial weight loss.

Summary

1. Chronic diseases now account for more than 50% of the deaths in the United States each year. These diseases often have multiple causes, including people's behavioral choices or lifestyles, have a slow onset over time, and can be managed but not cured.

2. Chronic diseases are associated with a number of consequences. Physical consequences from the disease and/or its treatment include physical debilitation, sexual problems, and cognitive problems. Social problems include the impact on interpersonal relationships, such as having friends and family members withdraw, hold unrealistic expectations about what the patient is experiencing, and suffer their own losses. Psychological problems include feelings of shock and disbelief, depression, and anxiety, although these feelings tend to reduce over time.

3. Numerous factors influence how people manage having a chronic illness, including the degree of intrusiveness of the illness on their daily lives, the types of coping used (problem-focused coping, emotion-focused coping), and the level of social support provided.

4. Psychological interventions may help people cope with having a chronic disease. These interventions can include providing information and education about the disease, training in cognitive-behavioral techniques to manage the disease and its treatment, and providing social support groups for others with this disease.

5. Coronary heart disease (CHD) is now the leading cause of death for both men and women in the United States. This condition arises when the artery walls become clogged with fatty substances,

thereby decreasing the area in which blood can flow and increasing the likelihood of a clot forming. In turn, this can lead to strokes, in which a blood clot becomes lodged in the circulatory system and deprives the brain of oxygen, and heart attacks, in which a blood clot blocks the passage of blood to the heart.

6. Numerous psychological factors contribute to CHD, including demographic factors (age, race, sex), stress, behavioral choices (e.g., smoking, diet, exercise), and personality (Type A behavior, pessimism, depression, neuroticism).

7. Psychological interventions can help reduce the risk of recurring heart attacks. These interventions can focus on helping people change their health-related behavior, providing training in stress management, and teaching strategies for changing Type A-related thoughts, behaviors, and emotions.

8. Cancer, which is the uncontrollable growth and spread of abnormal cells, is the second leading cause of death in the United States. Cancer can be caused by genetic mutations or carcinogens (meaning any substance capable of converting normal cells into cancerous ones).

9. Psychosocial factors influence the development of cancer in numerous ways. These factors include demographics (age, race), behavioral choices (smoking, diet, exercise, sunscreen use), stress, and, perhaps, personality ("Type C").

10. People vary in how effectively they cope with having cancer. People who believe they have control over the disease as well as those who use an active and engaged approach show better psychological well-being, and may have longer survival.

11. AIDS, which is caused by the human immunodeficiency virus, leads to approximately 1.8 million deaths worldwide each year. After HIV enters the bloodstream, it invades the T cells (part of the immune system), and destroys the cells' ability to function, leading over time to severe problems with immune functioning.

12. Several psychological factors predict the acquisition of HIV. People may fail to protect themselves because they do not see themselves as personally at risk of becoming infected with HIV, believe that HIV can be managed, or lack confidence to insist on condom use, especially if in an ongoing relationship.

13. Psychological factors also predict the progression of HIV. People who use active-coping strategies show better psychological adjustment, as do those who use avoidance coping, have high levels of social support, adhere to drug regimens to slow the progression of HIV, and engage in regular exercise.

Key Terms

acute diseases	chronic diseases	problem-focused coping
AIDS	coronary heart disease	social support
cancer	emotion-focused coping	

Thought Questions

1. How might different psychological dimensions be associated with the experience of arthritis as compared to epilepsy?

2. Although psychological factors can clearly influence the acquisition of CHD and cancer as well as AIDS, people with AIDS are often seen as more responsible for their condition. Is this fair? Why or why not?

3. How can stress influence the acquisition and progression of two different chronic diseases?

4. Your aunt was just diagnosed with diabetes. What psychological, physical, and social consequences might she experience?

5. Describe three behaviors that people do that increase their risk of developing cancer.

Answers to Questioning the Research

Answer 10.1. Although clearly multiple factors influence whether someone reveals they are HIV-positive to a partner, both age and religion influence the likelihood of this type of disclosure. People who are older and/or more religious may feel more uncomfortable revealing they have HIV because this admission also likely means they have engaged in other behaviors (e.g., sexual behavior, HIV drug use) that may be seen negatively. These behaviors are more common, and tend to be more accepted, in younger people than in older. These behaviors may also be seen in a more negative light in some religions.

Answer 10.2. The research in this section describes the role of social support in helping people adjust well to chronic disease. However, it is possible that this association is not exactly as it appears. One possibility is that people with a chronic disease who are coping well with it find that others like to spend time with them, whereas those with such a disease who are coping less well—such as feeling very depressed and anxious—may drive away people in their support network. Another possibility is that a third variable explains both social support and adjustment to disease. Perhaps optimistic people, for example, cope well (because they are optimistic, after all), and optimistic people receive more social support. Remember to carefully evaluate research you read about—many studies in health psychology report associations that may seem to indicate causation but really only support correlation.

Answer 10.3. Although researchers have examined a number of different types of foods that may be associated with the risk of developing cancer, it is not clear whether the major link between diet and cancer is a result of eating certain types of foods and avoiding others (e.g., eating fruits and vegetables, avoiding red meat), or simply maintaining a healthy body weight. People who eat foods that are high in fat and cholesterol, for example, may indeed be more likely to develop cancer, but this could be caused by their greater body weight resulting from this type of diet. Studies that show people with a particular diet are at greater risk of developing cancer may really just indicate that people who are obese are at greater risk.

Answer 10.4. Obviously numerous societal factors changed from 1997 to 2005, which in turn may have influenced rates of condom use (in addition to improvements in treatment for HIV infection). One of the most important factors is likely the change in attitudes toward same-sex relationships, which has led, at least in some states, to the legalization of gay marriage. In turn, if same-sex relationships are now more accepted, more men may now be in monogamous relationships in which condoms aren't typically used.

CHAPTER 11

Terminal Illness and Bereavement

Outline

- Ramon is 24 years old and just found out he has an advanced stage of stomach cancer. The doctor has started him on a round of chemotherapy but has warned Ramon that the cancer may not be curable. Ramon has always been very healthy and still can't really believe he may be dying. He is angry at the doctor who diagnosed him, the other patients in the hospital who have less serious illnesses, and his friends and family who tell him "it'll all be OK."

- Julia is 55 years old and is terminally ill with breast cancer. She has been through surgery, radiation, and chemotherapy, but the cancer has now spread throughout her body, and her physician has told her that more treatment would only cause additional pain and suffering. Julia made a decision to move from the hospital to a hospice, where she can wear her own clothes and have frequent visits from close family and friends. She is finding comfort in talking to other patients and the hospice staff.

- Sally is 28 years old and is a newlywed—she and her husband Paul would have celebrated their first wedding anniversary in May. Two weeks ago, Paul was in a severe car accident. Although he received almost immediate medical care, he fell into a coma shortly after reaching the hospital and never regained consciousness; he died after a few hours. Sally planned to spend her life with him and is now completely distraught over her loss. She dwells on the final words she said to him and simply cannot bring herself to contemplate life without him.

- Phillip is 72 years old and experienced the death of his wife to heart disease 6 months ago. He was constantly surrounded by friends and family members immediately after her death and received lots of help in making funeral arrangements and settling legal affairs. However, Phillip now finds himself largely alone—he retired 5 years ago and really isn't in touch with his old colleagues, and most of the couples he and his wife spent time with rarely call to include him in social events. He doesn't like going to the grocery store or cooking for himself, so mostly he eats fast food from drive-throughs, even though his doctor has warned him to decrease the level of fat in his diet because he is at high risk of developing heart disease.

- Tiffany's brother just died from leukemia following a long illness. Tiffany grieves the loss of her only sibling, and although her friends keep inviting her to go places with them, she doesn't feel like she can relax and enjoy the same things she used to before her brother's death. Recently, her parents suggested she attend a support group for other teenagers who experienced the death of a sibling. Although she dreaded going to the meeting at first, Tiffany now finds the group very helpful. The other people in the group understand exactly what she is going through, and it feels good to be able to talk about her loss without worrying about upsetting her friends or parents.

Preview

This chapter examines how psychological issues influence the experience of dying as well as how survivors cope with death. First, we examine the leading causes of death and how the causes of death differ as a function of age, gender, and race. We then examine several different views about how terminally ill people cope with dying, including the stages of death and dying, task-based models, and the particular stages of dying in children. Next, we examine the different settings in which people die, including hospitals, nursing homes, hospice settings, and at home. We then examine the consequences of grief and bereavement as well as how survivors cope with the loss of a loved one, including the stages of mourning and factors that influence the intensity of people's grief. The final sections examine three distinct topics: how people react to different types of loss (e.g., loss of a spouse, parent, child, or sibling), children's views about death and dying, and the cutting-edge issue of assisted suicide.

When and How Do People Die?

As we discussed in Chapter 1, the leading causes of death in 1900 were acute diseases, such as pneumonia, tuberculosis, and influenza, and these diseases often killed people at very early ages. But given the technological advancements of the past 100 years, these diseases largely have been brought under control, and people now typically die from chronic conditions (see Table 11.1). Advancements have had a particularly dramatic impact on death rates for infants. As described, infant mortality has dropped from 47 deaths per 1,000 live births in 1940 to 6.7 deaths per 1,000 live births in 2006 (Heron et al., 2009). This decrease in death rates in

TABLE 11.1 *Leading Causes of Death in 2007*

Cause of Death	Number of Deaths Each Year
Heart disease	616,067
Cancer	562,875
Stroke	135,952
Chronic obstructive pulmonary disease	127,924
Accidents	123,706
Alzheimer's disease	74,632
Diabetes	71,382
Pneumonia/influenza	52,717
Nephritis, nephrotic syndrome, and nephrosis	46,448
Septicemia	34,828

As these numbers show, heart disease and cancer are responsible for the vast majority of deaths each year.
Source: CDC, 2011.

the first year of life has led to a sizeable increase in average life expectancy rates: At the start of the 20th century, people had a life expectancy of about 47.3 years, whereas the mean life expectancy now is nearly 78.

At least in the United States, the vast majority of people die from heart disease and cancer (CDC, 2011). However, the leading causes of death vary considerably by age (see Table 11.2). Although we often associate high rates of mortality with senior citizens, the highest rate of death actually occurs in children in their first year of life. The majority of infant deaths are caused by congenital anomalies, disorders caused by premature birth and low birth weight, and sudden infant death syndrome (SIDS). Congenital anomalies are also responsible for a sizeable number of deaths in children ages 1 to 4 years, but the vast majority of deaths for children in this age group are caused by accidents. Accidents, including motor vehicle accidents, falls, drowning, suffocation, and fire/burns, are also the leading cause of death for children ages 5 to 14 years. Similarly, nearly half of all deaths of teenagers and young adults are caused by motor vehicle accidents, which are often the result of high-risk behavior such as drinking and driving (Baker, O'Neill, Ginsberg, & Li, 1992). Moreover, the three leading causes of death for teenagers and young adults all involve behavioral choices as opposed to diseases, infections, or other types of "natural causes."

Although technological advancements have led to an overall increase in life expectancy, women's life expectancy is significantly longer than men's (CDC, 2011). Women in the United States live an average of 5 years longer than men (80.4 versus 75.4 years, respectively). Moreover, this gender difference in life expectancy is true in most countries, suggesting that this is not just an American phenomenon (Waldron, 1983). One possible explanation for the gender differences in life expectancy is that men tend to engage in riskier behavior in general (e.g., drinking and driving) than women, and risky behavior, in turn, leads to more accidental deaths in men than women. In line with this view, men are much more likely than women to drown, accidentally get shot, and die in car accidents. Other theories suggest that these gender differences in life expectancy are a function of

TABLE 11.2   *Leading Causes of Death by Age*

Age	Causes of Death
Birth to 1	Congenital anomalies, short gestation, SIDS
1 to 4	Accidents, congenital anomalies, homicide
5 to 9	Accidents, malignant neoplasms, congenital anomalies
10 to 14	Accidents, malignant neoplasms, homicide
15 to 24	Accidents, homicides, suicide
25 to 34	Accidents, suicide, homicide
35 to 44	Accidents, malignant neoplasms, heart disease
45 to 54	Malignant neoplasms, heart disease, accidents
55 to 64	Malignant neoplasms, heart disease, chronic respiratory disease
65 and over	Heart disease, malignant neoplasms, cerebrovascular disease

Although heart disease and cancer are the overall leading causes of death, more people ages 1 to 44 years die from accidents than any other cause.
Source: CDC, 2010.

One of the explanations for the shorter life expectancy of men as opposed to women is that men are more likely to work in dangerous occupations.
Source: Getty Images News and Sport Services.

sex roles. For example, men tend to have more stressful jobs and feel more pressure to succeed at work, which may lead to excess wear and tear on the cardiovascular system. On the other hand, women tend to get more social support, which could help them more effectively buffer the effects of stress. Third, and as we discussed in Chapter 4, men and women may differ in how they respond to stress. Men often show a greater physiological arousal than women in response to potentially stressful situations. Finally, some research indicates that sex differences in mortality are influenced by genetic factors. For example, women have two X chromosomes (which carry genes that influence the functioning of the immune system), whereas men have only one, which may explain why women seem to have greater resistance to infectious diseases than men.

There are also race differences in life expectancy as well as in the causes of death (see Figure 11.1; Arias, 2010). While a White female born in 2006 has a mean life expectancy of 80.6 years, an African American female has a life expectancy of 76.5 years. Similarly, White males have a mean life expectancy of 75.7 years, whereas an African American male born in 2006 has a mean life expectancy of 69.7 years. Socioeconomic factors are largely to blame for this dramatic difference in life expectancy among different races—African Americans are much more likely than Whites to live in poverty and to have inadequate access to health care

FIGURE 11.1
Although life expectancy has increased over the past 30 years, women still tend to outlive men, and Whites tend to outlive African Americans. However, the race gap in life expectancy is decreasing (data from CDC, 2009).

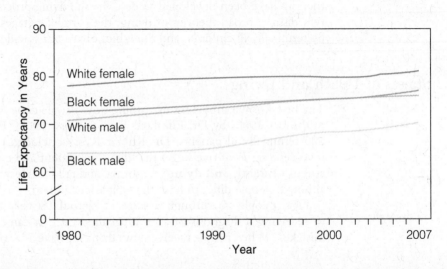

(Anderson, 1995; Bagley, Angel, Dilworth-Anderson, Liu, & Schinker, 1995; Flack et al., 1995). Also, African Americans are less likely to receive prenatal care (hence they have a higher rate of infant mortality), or to have regular vaccinations (hence they develop diseases), and they are more likely to live in dangerous situations. Sadly, one study found that African American males who lived in Harlem were less likely to reach age 65 than men living in Bangladesh, one of the poorest countries in the world (McCord & Freeman, 1990).

Although defining death seems simple in this day and age, people have measured death in different ways at different times and in different places. Listening for a heartbeat, watching the chest for breathing, or holding a mirror to a person's nose or mouth to test for exhalation, for example, are all techniques for determining death. Obviously, the technology of a given society influences the types of tests available to it. Ironically, increasing technological advances have sometimes made it more difficult to determine when death occurs. If a person shows no signs of brain waves, but the body is breathing on a respirator, is the person alive?

The current concept of death involves five guidelines that are accepted by medical professionals throughout the world (Ad Hoc Committee, 1968). First, the person is unreceptive and unresponsive to stimuli, such as touch, sound, light, and pain. Second, the person has no movement or breathing for at least 1 hour. (A person who has been on a respirator would be disconnected and then watched for 1 hour to see if he or she made any effort to breathe.) Third, the person has no reflexes, including blinking, yawning, vocalizing, and eye movements. Fourth, the person has a flat electroencephalogram (EEG) for at least 10 minutes, showing no activity in the upper brain. Fifth, the person has no circulation to or within the brain.

How Do People Cope With Dying?

Because chronic diseases are the leading causes of death today, terminally ill people are often aware that they are dying. For instance, a person may be ill for a long time, and death comes after a period of gradually declining health. Several different theories have been developed to describe the dying process. This section describes two distinct broad theories of dying, the particular stages of dying as experienced by terminally ill children, and the ethics of assisted suicide.

Stages of Death and Dying

The best-known model for explaining how people cope with dying was developed in the late 1960s by Dr. Elizabeth Kubler-Ross (1969). Based on interviews with 200 terminally ill patients, Dr. Kubler-Ross concluded that the process of dying involves a series of five stages that differ in content and emotional intensity. These **stages of death and dying** are normal and predictable ways of coping with death, although people differ in how they experience them.

First, people go through a stage of **denial**. A very common initial reaction to receiving a diagnosis of a terminal illness is, "It can't be me—this must be a mistake." When people receive news that they have a terminal illness, it is stunning, and they may experience an initial state of numbness. They simply can't face the situation and believe the prognosis is a mistake or impossible. Although this period typically doesn't last very long, this initial denial may allow the person to come to terms with the situation psychologically.

After the initial stage of numbness and denial has worn off, a common reaction is **anger**. People feel that their prognosis is unfair and may search for reasons (e.g., "Why me? What have I done?"). The person may express anger toward God, the medical staff, family members, or friends; as described at the start of this chapter, Ramon is clearly in the anger stage. Other feelings, such as rage, envy, and resentment, are also common. This stage can be hard for the family because the person's anger may be displaced, but it represents an attempt by the ill person to regain control of life.

Over time, anger transitions into **bargaining**, namely, an attempt to trade good behavior for good health. In this stage, ill persons are trying to delay the inevitable. They may start attending church regularly, take their medicine without complaint, or give generously to a charity in an attempt to make a pact for more time or bargain with God. For example, a person may try to bargain for time to reach a valued milestone, such as a child's wedding or graduation, or their own birthday or anniversary.

When bargaining fails to change the prognosis, people often experience a state of **depression**, a feeling of anticipatory grief in which the person grieves about the upcoming losses he or she will experience in death. This stage is about self-grieving, and it is important for family members and medical staff to accept the person's depression and share in the sadness. The dying person feels many losses, including that of body image, time, money, independence, social status, and relationships, and experiencing depression is a common and understandable response. This stage is often coupled with a growing realization, based on the individual's physical state, that he or she is really dying. In turn, the person may feel weak, fatigued, shameful, guilty, fearful, or have many other anxieties. This is "the worst of the worst."

The final stage of dying is **acceptance**: People finally acknowledge that death is inevitable and believe they can face it calmly. During this stage, people often cut off contact with all but a few close friends and family members in an attempt to disengage. Dr. Kubler-Ross believes that given enough time and help during the prior stages, patients can reach a stage in which they are no longer angry or depressed but rather are accepting of their fate. This stage, which Kubler-Ross describes as "quiet expectation," should not, however, be perceived as a happy stage—in contrast, this stage is more appropriately described as a time of quiet resignation, as if the patient has given up his or her struggle and is resting prior to death.

Although this perspective has received a lot of attention, it has been criticized for several reasons (Feifel, 1990; Rainey, 1988). First, Dr. Kubler-Ross didn't demonstrate "actual" stages or an orderly progression. In other words, it is not clear that people go from one stage to the next in a particular order—maybe people jump around from one phase to another, or cycle, or maybe experience stages simultaneously. In fact, all people do not go through all the stages. Some patients struggle against death (or even deny it) until the very end, whereas others seem to face death with resignation. Second, other researchers suggest that this model excludes some stages, such as anxiety, and fails to adequately describe others. The stage of denial, for example, could include a range of different reactions (e.g., "I am not ill; I am not dying; I will get better."). Third, Kubler-Ross's work focuses on only one aspect of a person's response to dying and leaves out the totality of the person's life. The experience of dying is obviously influenced by other factors, such as gender, age, race, religion, socioeconomic status, coping strategies, and social support. For example, people who are terminally ill and have strong religious views may experience less depression, in part due to their belief in an afterlife, which provides comfort (Edmondson, Park, Chaudoir, & Wortmann, 2008). Finally, although Kubler-Ross intended these stages to serve as a description of the process of dying, these stages are often seen as a prescription of how people "should" react to dying. Thus, caregivers or family members may draw the inference that terminally ill people should progress through these stages precisely and in proper order and may become concerned when the ill person is not "on schedule," which only adds unneeded stress to the situation. This model may also lead caregivers to see these stages as "the right way to die," so they think they should encourage people to "move along" to the next stage.

Task-Work Approach

According to Corr's **task-work approach** (1992) for coping with dying, people who are terminally ill focus on four distinct types of tasks. First, they must cope with physical tasks, such as managing their pain and physical symptoms, on satisfying the body's needs, and reducing distress. Second, they must focus on psychological tasks, including maintaining independence, feeling secure in the support they receive from others, and even in managing day-to-day tasks that are rewarding (e.g., taking a bath, eating a favorite food); they often need to feel in control. Third, people who are dying are concerned with social tasks, such as enhancing their interpersonal relationships, which often become limited to just a few very close persons, or interacting with hospital workers, social workers, and physicians. Finally, dying people focus on spiritual tasks, including thinking through issues of meaningfulness, hope, connectedness, and transcendence. For example, they may wonder what happens to their spirit following death and the contributions they have made in their life.

Doka (1993) describes phase-specific tasks that people with life-threatening illnesses encounter. People in the prediagnostic phase experience symptoms of their illness or disease. They may, for example, notice a lump or feel an unusual pain. After the condition is diagnosed, they are in the acute phase of the illness. In this stage, they try to understand the disease and to cope with it. After this initial focus of coming to terms with the illness, people enter the chronic phase, in which they must manage the illness and its various effects. As discussed in Chapter 10, these effects could include carrying out medical regimens, coping with feelings regarding the illness, and managing the symptoms and side effects of the illness and its treatment. In cases in which the disease can be managed, people enter the recovery phase. During this stage, they deal with their anxiety about reoccurrence of the illness as well as any lingering physical effects. However, if the illness is incurable, the person eventually enters the terminal phase in which he or she copes with managing the often increasingly difficult symptoms, preparing for death, and finding meaning in life and death.

Both of these task-based approaches offer several valuable guidelines (Kastenbaum, 2000). They view dying as a normative event within the total lifespan as opposed to an event of a very different and distinct domain. They view dying people as continuing to strive to accomplish valued goals. These task-based approaches also focus attention on a broad range of problems that dying people may encounter, not simply on the physical process of dying. This should help people pay attention to the diverse sets of needs of terminally ill patients, not just on managing their pain and/or prolonging their lives.

The value of these approaches is also seen in research showing that dying patients benefit from receiving information on psychological, social, and spiritual needs. Researchers in one study randomly assigned terminally ill patients to either a standard-care condition or a group-based intervention focused on psych-socio-spiritual needs (Miller, Chibnall, Videen, & Duckro, 2005). At the 12-month follow-up, intervention patients had fewer symptoms of depression and death-related feelings of meaninglessness as well as better spiritual well-being compared to patients who simply received standard care. This research points to the importance of addressing patients' broader needs in terms of improving the end-of-life illness experience.

Stages of Death and Dying in Children

Fatally ill children have specialized needs, including the normal developmental needs of healthy children, the special needs of children who are sick and hospitalized, and the particular needs of children who are dying (Stevens, 1997). The specific concerns of terminally ill children, however, vary by age. The youngest children, ages 3 to 5, worry primarily about separation from their parents, friends, and grandparents. They are worried that they will be left alone and are comforted by reassurance that their parents will never leave them. In contrast, children ages 5 to 9 are concerned about the ending of their life and what will happen to their body.

Adolescents have their own particular concerns about death and dying and, ironically seem to be more afraid of the process of dying than of death itself (Stevens & Dunsmore, 1996). Adolescents are very sensitive to body-image issues; hence, the physical side effects of a terminal illness can be especially upsetting at this age. Adolescents are also very focused on separating from their parents and establishing peer relationships, which can be disrupted if they are forced to spend time away from school seeking treatment and are unable to participate in many normal social activities because of their illness. They may be particularly concerned about their inability to attract a boyfriend or girlfriend, and they may worry that their peers will reject them.

Extensive observation of hospitalized children by Bluebond-Langner (1977) describes five stages that children pass through as they attempt to understand their illness. First, children are aware they have a serious illness and are concerned about feeling sick. They gradually become more sophisticated about the illness, learning names for medicines and side effects. In the second stage, they are still aware that they are ill, but are optimistic about the outcome (e.g., "I am sick, but I'll get better."). In the third stage, they learn more about the procedures and their purposes, and understand that this illness is long-term (e.g., "I'll always be sick, but I will get better."). This is followed by the fourth stage, which often comes after they have experienced several cycles of remissions and relapses. At this point, they accept that they will never get better and that they will always have this illness. Finally, in the fifth state, their declining health and observation of other dying patients leads them to realize that they will die.

Although experts disagree about whether terminally ill children should be given honest information about their condition, most believe that parents, doctors, and nurses should encourage children to talk about their fears and should try to answer questions at an age-appropriate level (Stillion & Wass, 1984). Even if children are not told directly about the nature of their illness, terminally ill children are often aware of their condition, either based on observations of other children around them or based on conversations they've overheard of family members and medical personnel. Children can also sense from their parents' nonverbal behavior that their illness is more serious than they are being told. Not surprisingly, they tend to have very high levels of anxiety. In fact, anxiety levels of terminally ill children are twice as high as those of other hospitalized children and of chronically ill, but not fatally ill, children.

The Ethics of Assisted Suicide

Over 60% of Americans believe people with a terminal illness should have the right to physician-assisted suicide (Blendon, Szalay, & Know, 1992). In 1994, Oregon became the first (and thus far, only) state to pass a law allowing physician-assisted suicide, meaning that physicians can, at a patient's request, provide a lethal dose of medicine. This type of suicide allows patients to die in a peaceful and nonviolent way and is a much less painful and faster way to die than simply refusing medical treatments (e.g., food, water, antibiotics). Researchers in one study asked 56 people from Oregon who had expressed interest in physician–assisted suicide to indicate why they had made this decision (Ganzini, Goy, & Dobscha, 2009). The most important reasons for requesting such assistance were wanting to control the circumstances of death and die at home; loss of independence; and concerns about future pain, poor quality of life, and inability to care for one's self. On the other hand, physical symptoms (e.g., pain, dyspnea, and fatigue) at the time of the interview, lack of social support, and depressed mood were rated as unimportant reasons.

Proponents of **assisted suicide** believe that people who are in severe pain and who are terminally ill should have the right to end their suffering (Kastenbaum, 1999; Sears & Stanton, 2001). They may fear losing physical and mental functioning and may fear living in an institution, particularly if they have suffered through the loss of a spouse or other caretaker. For example, in January 2002, Joan and Chester Nimitz Jr., a couple in their late 80s who lived outside Boston, chose to end their lives by taking pills (Quindlen, 2002). Chester Nimitz was suffering from congestive heart failure, constant back pain, and severe stomach problems, and Joan was blind, suffered repetitive broken bones because of severe osteoporosis, and needed round-the-clock care. They left a note in the apartment that said, "Do not dial 911 in the event we are discovered unconscious but still alive. We wish our friends and relatives to know we are leaving their company in a peaceful frame of mind."

On the other hand, opponents of assisted suicide vehemently believe that this "solution" is wrong for several reasons (Kastenbaum, 1999). First, given the many errors in diagnosis and the advancement in medical treatment, some people may wrongly make the decision to end their lives. Opponents believe that the moral issues associated with assisted suicide, including violation of the physician's oath "first, do no harm" and the potential for this procedure to be used wrongly should make assisted suicide illegal. Also, terminally ill people who want to die often suffer from clinical depression and/or inadequate pain relief. For example, one recent

Dr. Jack Kevorkian, also known as "Dr. Death," received considerable media attention in the 1990s for his involvement in the "assisted suicide" of more than 100 people. This assistance included creating a "suicide machine" that allowed severely disabled people to administer lethal drugs to themselves and giving people specific instructions on how to bring about their own deaths. In 1999, Dr. Kevorkian was found guilty of second-degree murder and sent to prison. He served 8 years before being released in 2007, with the condition that he not offer suicide advice to anyone again.
Source: © Chris Rabior/Alamy.

study conducted in Canada found that 58.8% of patients who wanted to die were depressed, as compared to only 7.7% of those who did not want to die (Chocinov et al., 1995). Similarly, while 76.5% of those in moderate or greater pain wanted to die, only 46.2% of those who did not want to die were in such severe pain. In turn, treating depression and managing pain could be a more effective approach than helping people die.

Another approach to gaining some control over one's end-of-life experience is creating an advanced care directive, or living will (see Figure 11.2). Such directives provide very clear instructions to family members, friends, and medical personnel, and thus allow people to specify their wishes about the type of care they would like to receive in the event they are incapacitated and therefore unable to make their own decisions (Kastenbaum, 1999). For example, a person may request to not be tube-fed while in a coma if there is no chance of emerging from that state. The person also designates a particular person to make medical decisions for him or her and, in particular, to make sure the wishes expressed in the living will are followed. The use of living wills therefore allows people to express their medical directives in advance of having an illness; thus, they are able to maintain control over their lives even when they have lost the ability to speak for themselves.

One problem with advance directives is that they cannot possibly provide guidance for all future medical possibilities. Researchers in one study examined how good people were at predicting the type of end-of-life treatment their loved ones would prefer (Fagerlin et al., 2001). First, students and one of their parents participated in a 15- to 30-minute discussion regarding the type of treatment they would prefer in various situations. Both parents and students then separately completed a questionnaire, which assessed the type of treatment they would want in various hypothetical situations as well as what they thought their parents would want in each situation. Unfortunately, students tended to predict their parents would want more treatment than the parents actually did prefer. For example, students often predicted that their parents would want a treatment, such as being placed on a respirator or given food and water even when in a coma, which their parents actually reported not wanting. This lack of accuracy is particularly interesting because the parents and students had very recently discussed the parents' preferences for end-of-life treatment! Moreover, students' predictions typically corresponded with their own preferences more than the actual preferences of their parents. Although this

Values History Statement

Please use this section as a guide to my values when considering the likely result of treatment.

Circle the number on the scale of 1 to 5 that most closely indicates your feelings about each of the situations described.	Much Worse Than Death: I Would Definitely Not Want Life-Sustaining Treatment	Somewhat Worse Than Death: I Would Probably Not Want Life-Sustaining Treatment	Neither Better nor Worse Than Death: I'm Not Sure Whether I Want Life-Sustaining Treatment	Somewhat Better Than Death: I Would Probably Want Life-Sustaining Treatment	Much Better Than Death: I Would Definitely Want Life-Sustaining Treatment
(a) Permanently paralyzed. You are unable to walk but can move around in a wheelchair. You can talk and interact with other people.	1	2	3	4	5
(b) Permanently unable to speak meaningfully. You are unable to speak to others. You can walk on your own, feed yourself, and take care of daily needs such as bathing and dressing yourself.	1	2	3	4	5
(c) Permanently unable to care for yourself. You are bedridden, unable to wash, feed, or dress yourself. You are totally cared for by others.	1	2	3	4	5
(d) Permanently in pain. You are in severe bodily pain that cannot be totally controlled or completely eliminated by medications.	1	2	3	4	5
(e) Permanently mildly demented. You often cannot remember things, such as where you are, nor reason clearly. You are capable of speaking, but not capable of remembering the conversations; you are capable of washing, feeding, and dressing yourself and are in no pain.	1	2	3	4	5
(f) Being in a short-term coma. You have suffered brain damage and are not conscious and are not aware of your environment in any way. You cannot feel pain. You are cared for by others. These mental impairments may be reversed in about 1 week, leaving mild forgetfulness and loss of memory as a consequence.	1	2	3	4	5

SIGNATURE OF DECLARANT

Name (print clearly) . . . . **Day/Month/Year** . . . .

Address . . . . **Date of Birth★** . . . .

★If you are under 18 years of age, you may still complete this document, though it may not have the same legal force.

WITNESS'S SIGNATURE: I declare that the above-named has signed this document in my presence. He/she has declared it to be his/her firm will, is in full capacity, and fully understands the meaning of it. I believe it to be a firm and competent statement of his/her wishes. As far as I am aware, no pressure has been brought to bear on him/her to sign such a document and I believe it to be his/her own free and considered wish. So far as I am aware, I do not stand to gain from his/her death.

Signed (Witness): . . . . Name . . . .

Address . . . .

FIGURE 11.2   This is a sample living will. If you would like to register your own living will go to www.uslivingwillregistry.com.

study was conducted entirely with a college student sample, in a follow-up study, the researchers examined accuracy in making end-of-life treatment decisions in a sample of adults who were 65 years old or older and a person they specifically chose as the one they wanted to make medical decisions for them in case they were incapacitated. This study revealed very similar findings—people tended to assume the person would want more life-saving treatment than the person actually did and again projected their own treatment preferences onto those of their loved one.

As an alternative, at Kent State University, Ditto, Druley, Moore, Danks, and Smucker (1996) suggest that people instead complete lists of "valued life activities," and then use these activities as a guide to determining whether or not to end someone's life. For example, some people would choose to sustain their lives if they could still speak and think, even if they could not move (e.g., following a paralyzing physical injury); others might choose to end their lives if they could no longer recognize family and friends (e.g., following Alzheimer's disease). These decisions are obviously very personal. Studies with both college students and elderly adults reveal that people's beliefs about whether various health impairments, such as being unable to communicate, being blind and deaf, and being confined to bed, would interfere with their ability to engage in valued life activities influence their preference for death. In other words, the more each disability is seen as interfering with their engagement in their most valued life activities, the more they would prefer death.

Where Do People Die?

Historically, most people have died in their own homes, but this trend has clearly changed during the past century—there is a growing shift from people dying at home to people dying in hospitals and nursing homes (Levy, 1983). This section describes the four main places people die: hospitals, nursing homes/extended care facilities, homes, and hospices.

Hospitals

The focus in hospitals is on curing patients, delivering technical skills and interventions, and thereby preventing death (MacLeod, 2001). In turn, hospital settings clearly provide many advantages to terminally ill patients, including highly skilled personnel, access to pain medication, and the availability of life-saving equipment.

Patients vary, however, on the extent to which they prefer receiving intensive life-prolonging care. Many people are not interested in having aggressive end-of-life care in cases when such care is likely to be futile. For example, researchers in one study conducted surveys asking people what type of care they would want in the case of a serious and life-threatening injury (Jacobs, Burns, & Bennett Jacobs, 2008). Most people would prefer simply palliative care, meaning care focused on managing pain, when doctors determine that aggressive critical care would not be beneficial in saving their lives. Interestingly, people who rely on religious coping are particularly likely to receive aggressive end-of-life treatment (Phelps et al., 2009). Researchers in one study with patients with advanced care found that people who use high levels of positive religious coping are more likely to be placed on a ventilator than those who use lower levels of religious coping (11.3% versus 3.6%). They are also more likely to receive intensive life-prolonging care during the last week of life (13.6% versus 4.2%), even when adjusting for age and race.

Questioning the Research 11.1

What factors do you think might contribute to the tendency for patients who rely on positive religious coping to receive more aggressive end-of-life care than those who rely less on this type of coping strategy?

However, hospitals often place relatively little emphasis on the care of terminally ill patients, which may represent a failure of medical techniques in curing their disease or injury (Benoliel, 1988; Rainey, 1988). In fact, one large-scale study of 9,105 adults hospitalized with a life-threatening diagnosis found that patients' care had a number of limitations, including shortcomings in communication, overuse of aggressive treatment, and insufficient pain relief (SUPPORT Principal Investigators, 1995). For example, one study found that only 47% of doctors knew when their terminally ill patients did not want to receive cardiopulmonary resuscitation (CPR). Although end-of-life discussions between physicians and their patients are generally associated with less life-prolonging measures, presumably because physicians then have a better understanding of the type of care patients do and do not want, Black patients tend to receive more life-prolonging care at the end of life than White patients (19.7% compared to 6.9%; Mack, Paulk, Viswanath, & Prigerson, 2010). This difference occurred even though Blacks and Whites have similar rates of end-of-life discussions (35.3% of Blacks, 38.4% of Whites). End-of-life discussions therefore seem to assist White patients in receiving less life-prolonging care, whereas Black patients tend to receive life-prolonging measures even when they have expressed preference to the contrary.

People who are terminally ill are also viewed and treated in particular ways by medical professionals (Maguire, 1985). Nurses and doctors who interact with dying patients may use false reassurance and distancing techniques. For example, doctors and nurses may tell the person he or she will get better soon, even when they know that this is unlikely, as a way of avoiding giving negative news. One study of physicians caring for patients with cancer found that 22.7% would not provide any estimates of survival time and would communicate a more optimistic than realistic survival time 40.3% of the time (Lamont & Christakis, 2001). In turn, patients and their families may have an inaccurate sense of their likelihood of survival and life expectancy. In line with this view, one study of parents of children with cancer found that 10.6% of parents rated their child's prognosis as very good or excellent, although their physicians had rated the child's prognosis as poor (Sung et al., 2009).

Physicians may also ignore patients' reports of psychological difficulties, such as depression and anxiety, and focus instead on patients' physical state, in part because providing intense psychological care is time-consuming and emotionally draining. Researchers in one study examined conversations between patients with lung cancer and their doctors (Morse, Edwardsen, & Gordon, 2008). Although patients expressed numerous concerns about mortality, symptoms, and treatment, physicians provided little emotional support and instead tended to shift such concerns to biomedical questions (see Box 11.1: Health Psychology in the Real

"There's no easy way I can tell you this, so I'm sending you to someone who can."

World for other examples of the lack of empathy often shown to patients). In fact, physicians responded empathically to only 10% of the concerns raised by patients. Moreover, when empathy was provided, 50% of these statements occurred in the last one-third of the encounter, whereas patients' concerns were evenly raised throughout the encounter. Physicians rarely responded empathically to the concerns raised by patients with lung cancer, and empathic responses that did occur were more frequently in the last third of the encounter. In sum, hospitals are designed to diagnose and treat disease, which is good for people with curable conditions, but not as good for those who are dying of chronic, incurable diseases.

Nursing Homes/Long-Term Care Facilities

Nursing homes and other types of long-term care facilities were developed for people who require significant assistance in caring for themselves but who do not have specific medical issues that require constant care by a physician. People with Alzheimer's disease, for example, experience memory loss and disorientation, and therefore require constant supervision but do not necessarily have acute medical needs in the early stages of this disease. Nursing-home patients are often elderly and chronically ill; therefore, they need the type of assistance that family members may be unable—or unwilling—to provide on a daily basis. Nursing-home staff members assist with routine activities of daily living, including dressing, eating, and bathing. Like hospitals, however, they are not specifically trained to help terminally ill patients cope with the process of death and dying. Nursing homes also do not generally provide intensive medical treatment—patients who need this type of care are typically transferred to a hospital.

Home

Many people want to die at home, surrounded by family; in fact, 100 years ago, most people died in their own beds. This can be more comfortable psychologically: Patients are surrounded by familiar things and familiar people. They are not forced

Box 11.1

Health Psychology in the Real World: For Cancer Patients, Empathy Goes a Long Way

By Denise Grady, *New York Times*, January 8, 2008

Four years ago, my sister found out she had two types of cancer at the same time. It was like being hit by lightning—twice.

She needed chemotherapy and radiation, a huge operation, more chemotherapy and then a smaller operation. All in all, the treatment took about a year. Thin to begin with, she lost 30 pounds. The chemo caused cracks in her fingers, dry eyes, anemia and mouth sores so painful they kept her awake at night. A lot of her hair fell out. The radiation burned her skin. Bony, red-eyed, weak and frightfully pale, she tied scarves on her head, plastered her fingers with Band-Aids and somehow toughed it out.

She saw two doctors quite often. The radiation oncologist would sling her arm around my sister's frail shoulders and walk her down the corridor as if they were old friends. The medical oncologist kept a close watch on the side effects, suggested remedies, reminded my sister she had good odds of beating the cancer and reassured her that the hair would grow back. (It did.)

People in my family aren't huggy-kissy types, but my sister greatly appreciated the warmth and concern of those two women. She trusted them completely, and their advice. Now healthy, she says their compassion played a big part in helping her get through a difficult and frightening time.

Research supports the idea that a few kind words from an oncologist—what used to be called bedside manner—can go a long way toward helping people with cancer understand their treatment, stick with it, cope better and maybe even fare better medically.

"It is absolutely the role of the oncologist" to provide a bit of emotional support, said Dr. James A. Tulsky, director of the Center for Palliative Care at Duke University Medical Center.

But in a study published last month in the Journal of Clinical Oncology, Dr. Tulsky and other researchers found that doctors and patients weren't communicating all that well about emotions.

The researchers recorded 398 conversations between 51 oncologists and 270 patients with advanced cancer. They listened for moments when patients expressed negative emotions like fear, anger or sadness, and for the doctors' replies.

A response like "I can imagine how scary this must be for you" was considered empathetic—a "continuer" that would allow patients to keep expressing their emotions. But a comment like "Give us time; we are getting there" was labeled a "terminator" that could shut the patient down.

The team found that doctors used continuers only 22 percent of the time. Male doctors were worse at it than female ones: 48 percent of the men never used continuers, as opposed to 20 percent of the women.

Surprisingly, Dr. Tulsky said, the patients didn't bring up emotions that often—in only 37 percent of the conversations.

"That's extraordinary," he said. "These are advanced cancer patients."

The reason is not clear, but he said the patients might not expect emotional support from doctors. Feelings were most often discussed when both doctor and patient were female, and younger doctors who considered themselves more "socioemotional" than "technical" gave empathetic replies more often.

One doctor who was especially good with patients, and who often consulted on very serious cases, opened discussions with new patients by saying, "Tell me what you understand about your illness," Dr.

Tulsky said. And when patients wept, this doctor would pause and wait until they were ready to continue the discussion.

By contrast, with other doctors, Dr. Tulsky said, "There were a number of times when patients brought up emotional content and it went right by the doctors."

For instance, a patient would say, "I'm scared," and the doctor would go off on a "scientific riff" about the disease, Dr. Tulsky said, adding, "We saw that a lot."

The doctors don't lack empathy, he said. They just have trouble expressing it.

"Oncologists care deeply for their patients," said Kathryn I. Pollak, the first author of the study and a social psychologist at Duke. "It's clear from listening to the tapes."

Cancer patients and oncologists have unique, intense relationships, she said, because the patients are fighting for their lives.

Even so, oncologists sometimes miss signs of distress, particularly if those signs are indirect, she said. For example, a patient may ask how big the tumors are, and the doctor may answer in millimeters—when the patient really wants to know: "Is the cancer getting worse? Am I dying?"

The good news, she and Dr. Tulsky said, is that most doctors can be taught to respond in more helpful ways. Brief, empathetic responses will suffice, the researchers said; they are not recommending extensive counseling or endless dialogue.

Patients may benefit from some coaching, too. It's perfectly reasonable, Dr. Tulsky said, to talk to an oncologist about sadness or fears about treatment, and to ask for help.

"You're vulnerable when you express your emotions," Dr. Pollak said. "But I would advise patients to be as direct as possible."

to cope with the rigid routines of hospital care, including constant monitoring by medical personnel, poor-quality meals on a set schedule, and limited visiting hours.

However, dying at home has a number of disadvantages. Home deaths obviously have some drawbacks in terms of the quality of medical care. Insurance companies often will not cover home visits by doctors and, hence, terminally ill patients may not receive adequate medication to control their pain. It can also be very difficult to transport dying patients to doctors' offices or hospitals should they need to go. Some homes also may not work well for dying people—there are issues of access for wheelchairs, appropriately equipped bathrooms, and more. Also, family members may find caring for a dying patient extremely stressful, both psychologically and physically. It can be very difficult to help that person with personal tasks, such as bathing and using a bedpan, and can be exhausting to help with virtually all of the person's needs, such as eating and dressing.

Providing home care for a terminally ill patient may be made easier if the caregivers are able to have some outside help to cope with the regular needs of the patient. In some cases, hospice programs can provide assistance to a terminally ill person who wants to stay at home (Kastenbaum, 1999). These services include visits from nurses, social workers, and chaplains. Hospice professionals also offer assistance to caregivers, including staying with patients while family members are out, reading to and caring for the dying patient, and helping families to understand and cope with the dying process.

Hospice Care

The **hospice** movement was developed by Dr. Cicely Saunders in London in the late 1960s and was specifically designed to provide better care for terminally ill patients and to provide an alternative to dying in an impersonal institution such as a hospital or nursing home (Feifel, 1990; Kastenbaum, 1999). This first hospice program in the United States was started in the mid-1970s, and in 2007, 1,045,100 patients received hospice care (Caffrey, Sengupta, Moss, Harris-Kojetin, & Valverde, 2011). Although, in some cases, hospice care is provided in a designated building, this type of care can also be provided in a particular unit or floor in a hospital or even at the patient's home. In fact, most hospice care is now provided in people's homes.

Hospice care differs from hospital care in a number of ways (Kastenbaum, 1999). First, hospice care focuses primarily on treating the symptoms of terminal illness and minimizing the patient's discomfort and pain, never on helping patients recover or prolong their lives. Patients who choose hospice care often have a limited amount of time to live—typically less than 6 months—and have illnesses or diseases, such as cancer, AIDS, or ALS (a progressive neurological condition often referred to as Lou Gehrig's disease) that cannot be cured. Second, hospice facilities allow people to personalize and control their surroundings much more than they could do in a hospital. For example, patients can wear their own clothes, have visitors at any time, and even bring in special items from home, such as a quilt, family pictures, and special mementos. Finally, hospice staff members try to provide a sense of comfort and support for the patient and his or her family. They also encourage engaging in open discussions on death and dying, and expressing feelings. Julia, described at the beginning of this chapter, made the decision to move from the hospital to a hospice care facility because she wanted the opportunity to spend more time with family and friends and to be able to openly discuss her concerns about dying. One study found that hospice patients experience less depression and anxiety, in part because they are encouraged to talk about the dying process (Hinton, 1979). In sum, hospice care focuses on providing for the patient's physical, social, psychological, and spiritual needs (see Figure 11.3).

When compared to hospital care, hospices can result in more peace of mind for patients and their families (Ganzini et al., 2002; Lynn, 2001; Viney, Walker, Robertson, Lilley, & Ewan, 1994). In one study, patients who were terminally ill

FIGURE 11.3

Hospice care provides a range of services, including physical, psychological, and spiritual, to both dying patients and their family members and friends (data from National Center for Health Statistics, 2011).

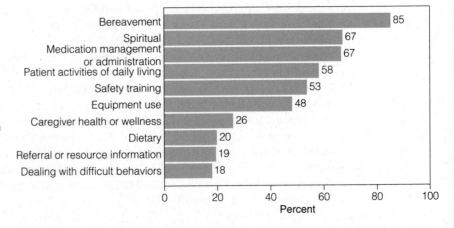

Box 11.2

Focus on Research: The Impact of Hospice Care on the End-of-Life Experience

Researchers in one study examined 332 patients with advanced cancer and their care-givers from the time they were admitted to the hospital until they died (approximately 4 months later; Wright et al., 2008). Of 332 patients, 123 (37.0%) reported having end-of-life discussions, and these discussions were not associated with higher rates of major depressive disorder or more worry. However, such discussions were associated with lower rates of ventilation (1.6% versus 11%), resuscitation (.8% versus 6.7%), and ICU admission (4.1% versus 12.4%) as well as earlier hospice enrollment (65.6% versus 44.5%). In addition, more aggressive medical care was associated with worse patient quality of life as well as higher risk of major depressive disorder in bereaved caregivers. In contrast, longer hospice stays were associated with better patient quality of life, which in turn was associated with better caregiver quality of life at follow-up. These findings suggest that end-of-life care leads to both less aggressive medical care near death and earlier hospice referrals, which in turn are associated with better overall quality of life for the patient and better adjustment to bereavement for the caregiver.

with cancer were randomly assigned to receive either conventional care or hospice care (Kane, Wales, Bernstein, Leibowitz, & Kaplan, 1984). Although there were no significant differences between hospice and hospital patients in measures of pain, symptoms, activities of daily living, or mood, hospice patients reported greater satisfaction with the care they received. Similarly, researchers in one study examined quality of life in 183 terminally ill cancer patients who were in a traditional hospital setting versus a small hospice unit on the floor of a hospital (Viney et al., 1994). Patients in the hospice unit reported better enjoyment of life and lower levels of anger than those in the general hospital unit. Moreover, hospice patients reported having more favorable interpersonal interactions and felt less lonely than hospital patients. Other research reveals that patients who died in hospice settings were less likely to complain about lack of emotional support than those who died in a nursing home, hospital, or at home without hospice services (Teno et al., 2004). In sum, terminally ill people have better overall psychological adjustment receiving care in hospice than in a general hospital unit. As described in Box 11.2: Focus on Research, patients who receive hospice care are less likely to receive aggressive medical care, which is associated with an overall increase in quality of life for both patients and their caregivers.

One of the concerns people often have about using hospice care is that this choice means giving up on treating one's illness, and thus they will die sooner. However, recent research reveals that hospice patients not only experience greater psychological well-being than patients who receive standard hospital care but also live longer. Researchers in this study randomly assigned patients with newly diagnosed lung cancer to receive either hospice care (along with standard cancer treatment) or standard cancer treatment alone (Temel et al., 2010). Patients who

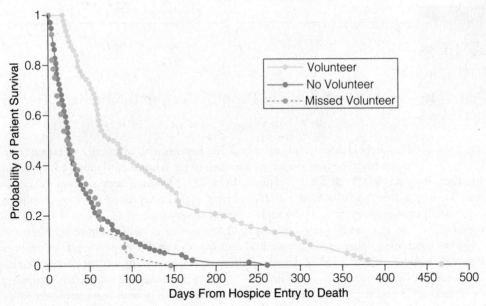

FIGURE 11.4   This study examined the impact of volunteer support on survival among 320 hospice patients. Patients either requested and received visits from a hospice volunteer, did not request or receive such visits, or requested such visits but these visits were missed (typically due to a scheduling conflict). As shown in this figure, patients who received visits from volunteers lived nearly three times as long as those without such visits (119 days versus 41 days for those who did not request a volunteer and 31.2 days for those who missed having a volunteer visit) (data from Herbst-Damm & Kulik, 2005).

received hospice care reported an overall better quality of life and were less likely to develop symptoms of depression (16% compared to 38% in the standard care condition). Although fewer patients in the hospice-care group than in the standard-care group received aggressive end-of-life care (33% compared to 54%), patients in the hospice-care condition survived an average of 11.6 months, nearly 3 months longer than those who received standard care (8.9 months). These findings suggest that hospice care can improve both psychological well-being and length of survival. Relatedly, and as shown in Figure 11.4, patients who receive visits from a hospice volunteer also show longer survival times.

Family members of hospice patients also tend to report more satisfaction and less anxiety than family members of patients in other settings (Kane et al., 1984). Researchers in one study surveyed 1,500 family members of patients who had died describing end-of-life outcomes (Teno et al., 2004). Of family members of patients who received hospice care, 73% rated the care as "excellent" compared to fewer than 50% of those dying in a hospital, nursing home, or home without such care. Family members of patients who died in hospice units are more likely to describe their loved ones as having had a "good death" than those who die on a general ward (Miyashita et al., 2008). The characteristics of a "good death" include environmental comfort, physical and psychological comfort, being respected as an individual, and having a "natural death." Moreover, these "good deaths" were more likely to include adequate pain medication and less likely to include aggressive treatments, such as chemotherapy in the last two weeks of life, as well as treatments designed to prolong life.

Perhaps most importantly, some research even suggests that people whose spouses use hospice care have lower rates of mortality. Researchers in one study compared life expectancy in nearly 60,000 widows and widowers in which their spouse had used hospice care versus not (Christakis & Iwashyna, 2003). Findings revealed that 5.4% of bereaved wives died by 18 months after the death of their husband when their deceased husband did not use hospice and 4.9% died when their deceased husband did use hospice. Similarly, whereas 13.7% of bereaved husbands died by 18 months when their deceased wife did not use hospice, 13.2% died when their deceased wife did use hospice. These findings suggest that both men and women may benefit in terms of their own life expectancy from having their spouse use hospice care, perhaps because such care focuses not only on treating the patient but also on providing care to his or her family.

What Are the Consequences of Bereavement?

Psychological problems, including depression, sadness, anger, and anxiety, are very common following the loss of a loved one (Kastenbaum, 1999; Raphael & Dobson, 2000). People who are experiencing **bereavement** may feel sad and empty and may have trouble contemplating continuing on with their lives without the deceased person. One study with HIV-positive gay men found that those whose close friends or lovers had died from AIDS in the past year were more depressed and likely to think about suicide and more likely to use sedatives, such as sleeping pills and tranquilizers, than those who were HIV-positive and had not experienced this type of loss (Martin & Dean, 1993). Not surprisingly, these feelings of anxiety and depression occur even prior to the actual death. Caregivers for patients with cancer show increased anxiety and depression over the last year of the person's life, with 15% showing moderate-severe depression and 27% showing moderate-severe anxiety (Burridge, Barnett, & Clavarino, 2009).

Grief often leads to social problems, including loneliness and isolation (Berado, 1988; Harvey & Hansen, 2000). People who suffer the loss of a friend, spouse, or child often experience a decrease in available social networks. Widows may find that they are not invited to parties or other social gatherings at which other people are all part of a couple. Similarly, parents who've lost a child may lose the network of friends who had children of the same age. Older people, in particular, may feel socially isolated as they experience the loss of friends, spouses, and siblings. Interestingly, younger widows feel more isolated socially than older widows, presumably because this type of loss is less common for younger women. Similarly, women who have lost a spouse tend to cope better than do men who have lost a spouse, again because the social support for widows tends to be greater than such support for widowers (Wisocki & Skowron, 2000).

People who are bereaved have increased rates of minor and major illnesses and even death (Berado, 1988; Martikainen & Valkonen, 1996; Raphael & Dobson, 2000; Ray, 2004; Schaefer, Quesenberry, & Wi, 1995; Wisocki & Skowron, 2000). They may experience a number of physical symptoms, such as emptiness in the abdomen, a sense of physical weakness, choking and shortness of breath, and a tightness in the chest. Researchers in one study found that the best predictors of cardiac problems, including angina, a heart attack, or sudden cardiac death, were age and living alone, with women over age 60 living alone and men over age 50 living alone especially high risk (Nielsen, Faergeman, Larsen, & Foldspang, 2006). And the impact of bereavement on mortality is not limited to those who lose a spouse but rather extends to those who lose any type of significant partner. For example, HIV-positive men who experience the loss of a partner to AIDS show signs of more rapid progression of their own AIDS illness (Kemeny et al., 1994).

Moreover, some research suggests that men in particular are at increased risk of dying following the death of their spouse. For example, one large-scale study in Finland examined death rates in the period immediately following the death of a spouse (Martikainen & Valkonen, 1996). Compared to others their age, men were 17% more likely to die in this period, whereas women were only 6% more likely to die. Similarly, researchers in another study examined the association between marital status and survival in patients with lung cancer (Saito-Nakaya et al., 2008). Although female patients with lung cancer who lost their spouse did not have higher mortality rates than those who were married, male widowed patients with lung cancer had a higher mortality rate than male married patients.

> **Questioning the Research 11.2**
>
> Can you think why men seem to be more impacted than women in terms of mortality following the loss of a spouse?

However, other research suggests that both men and women are at increased risk of dying in the year following the death of a spouse, but that the cause of a spouse's death influences individuals' likelihood of dying (Christakis & Allison, 2006). Researchers in one study examined data collected from more than 500,000 elderly people to test whether mortality after the hospitalization of a spouse varied according to the spouse's diagnosis. Interestingly, among men, 6.4% died within a year after a spouse's hospitalization for colon cancer, 6.9% after a spouse's hospitalization for stroke, 7.5% after a spouse's hospitalization for psychiatric disease, and 8.6% after a spouse's hospitalization for dementia. Among women, 3.0% died within a year after a spouse's hospitalization for colon cancer, 3.7% after a spouse's hospitalization for stroke, 5.7% after a spouse's hospitalization for psychiatric disease, and 5.0% after a spouse's hospitalization for dementia. These findings suggest that people's risk of mortality differs as a function of the cause of the spouse's death as well as by gender. Similarly, and as described in Box 11.3: Focus on Research, experiencing the loss of a spouse seems to have a larger impact on death from acute health events.

One factor that may account for these increased rates of illness and death in bereaved people is that people who are bereaved are less likely to engage in health-promoting behavior and are more likely to engage in health-damaging behavior (Berado, 1988). For example, following the loss of a spouse, people may use alcohol to try to dull their grief or may forget to eat healthy foods. Research with gay men who experienced the loss of their partner to AIDS demonstrated that rates

Box 11.3

Focus on Research: Why and When the Death of a Spouse Impacts Mortality

Researchers in this study were interested in examining the impact of the loss of a spouse on mortality (Elwert & Christakis, 2008). Data from more than 370,000 elderly couples collected over 7 years was examined to test whether the death of a spouse was generally associated with increased mortality. Researchers also examined whether particular types of deaths placed the surviving spouse at increased risk of mortality. For both men and women, the death of one's spouse was associated with an increase in mortality: 18% for men following the death of a wife and 16% for women following the death of a husband. Interestingly, although husbands generally are at more risk of dying following the loss of a spouse than are wives, different causes of deaths pose different levels of risk for the surviving spouse. Specifically, the loss of a spouse is associated with an increased risk of dying from cancer (especially colon and lung), cardiovascular disease/stroke, and accidents. However, surviving spouses are not at increased risk of dying following the death of a spouse from Alzheimer's disease or Parkinson's. These findings suggest that experiencing the death of a spouse to chronic conditions that require considerable care and management (e.g., cancer, coronary heart disease) or acute events (e.g., accidents, infections) is associated with particularly great risks to one's own health. In contrast, experiencing the loss of a spouse to chronic conditions that do not require extensive management, such as Parkinson's disease or Alzheimer's, is not associated with an increase in risk of own mortality. Given the long-term nature of these conditions, spouses may have had considerable time to adjust to the reality of the expected loss of one's spouse, which may in turn buffer some of the negative effects of being widowed. These findings suggest that although losing a spouse in general is associated with poorer health and increased mortality, the cause of a spouse's death also influences one's own mortality.

of risky sexual behavior increased dramatically in the first 4 to 6 months following their loss, although it returned to normal levels later (Mayne, Acree, Chesney, & Folkman, 1998). Similarly, bereaved people may have trouble sleeping and eating, which in turn can wear down their bodies. This explanation may work especially well to explain why men who lose their wives, who in many cases may have done most of the grocery shopping and cooking, are at such great risk of showing health problems. As described at the beginning of the chapter, Phillip felt very isolated following the death of his wife, and he lapsed into several unhealthy habits. In line with this view, research reveals that people whose spouse had died are also three times as likely to enter long-term institutional care in the month following the spouse's death than prior to the death, presumably due to a loss of social and instrumental support (Nihtilä & Martikainen, 2008).

Another factor that may explain the link between bereavement and illness is that bereavement-related stress impairs the immune system, which thereby leads to higher susceptibility to infection and disease (Kemeny et al., 1995; Raphael & Dobson, 2000; Zisook, Schuchter, Sledge, & Judd, 1994). For example, one study of former caregivers of patients with Alzheimer's disease revealed that they experienced a significant decline in their NK cell function (a measure of the immune system's ability to respond to health threats; Esterling, Kiecolt-Glaser, Bodnar, & Glaser, 1994). (This link between stress and the immune system is discussed in more detail in Chapter 4.)

Although the effects of caregiving are often seen as negative, some recent research suggests that at least in some cases, caregiving can be beneficial in terms of health. Researchers in one study examined data from a national, longitudinal study of elderly people to assess the effects of caregiving for a spouse (Brown et al., 2009). Participants were asked about the type of care they provide their spouse (e.g., eating, dressing, bathing, walking, etc.) as well as how many hours were spent giving care. Findings indicated that individuals who provided 14 or more hours of care a week to their spouse had lower rates of mortality than those who did not provide care. This is true even considering gender, self-rated health, education, and health of the spouse. These findings suggest that providing help to a loved one may in fact lead to improvements in the caregiver's health, perhaps because this type of assistance actually reduces stress.

What Factors Influence the Experience of Bereavement?

When people lose someone they care about, they experience a state of bereavement, which is accompanied by **grief**, the feelings caused by this loss, and **mourning**, the expression of these feelings. Grief and mourning are not signs of weakness or self-indulgence—they are a normal and natural human reaction to the loss of a significant person, which is intensified by our closeness to the person who has died (Berado, 1988; Feifel, 1990). This section examines factors that influence grief, the stages of mourning, and coping with bereavement.

Stages of Mourning

Bereavement begins as soon as one learns that a loved one died and typically with an initial feeling of shock (Berado, 1988). During this *reaction stage,* survivors may feel numb and show little feeling. This period allows survivors to cope initially and to handle the necessary tasks, such as planning a funeral or memorial service, notifying friends and relatives, and handling legal arrangements. However, not all survivors will be able to handle such logistics and may therefore need considerable assistance from others. At this time, people may also try to make sense of the death, especially in cases in which the loss was unanticipated (e.g., a quick-trajectory death) and inappropriate (e.g., the death of a child). They may experience anger and frustration with the person who died and others who could be seen as responsible in some way (e.g., doctors, God), and those who encourage them to accept the loss when they just aren't ready to do so. This anger may also be self-directed: Survivors may wonder what they could have done differently to prevent this death.

After this initial period of numbness, survivors enter a stage of *yearning and searching* (Berado, 1988). This stage represents a desire to return things to how they once were. Survivors may search crowds hoping to see the lost one, may expect to see the person coming up the driveway, and may wake up in the morning wondering if the person is really dead. One man whose mother was killed when he was a child recalls coming home after school and calling "Mom?" just hoping that she would answer. In this stage, people are still hoping things will return to how they were before the death and are not acknowledging or accepting the extent and finality of their loss.

After reality sets in, the survivor enters the stage of *disorganization and reorganization* (Berado, 1988), in which he or she is disappointed that the loss cannot be undone and may experience despair and depression. Survivors may have trouble enjoying old activities and, hence, have difficulty making plans and engaging in new activities. They may also struggle with forming a new identity, especially if they've lost a spouse or child—these types of deaths cause major role changes because people have to give up their previous identity as wife, husband, or parent. The plans they had made are now ruined, and it can be difficult to know how to start a "new life." Survivors may become very dependent on those who provide care for them. Their feelings in this stage are often complicated and even conflicting—it can seem like a betrayal to the dead person to give up grieving and take joy in new activities.

Finally, people enter the *reorientation and recovery stage* (Berado, 1988), in which the bereaved person is able to take part in new activities and to "rejoin" the world. He or she has accepted the changes and is now able to get life back on track. Survivors in this stage may also give the deceased a new identity, such as a place in heaven. They are still sad but are now able to move on with their own lives.

Although these stages of mourning are described as if they are a linear process, some bereaved people may experience *unresolved grief* and never return to a normal pattern of living (Berado, 1988). As described previously, people have greater difficulty adjusting to sudden and unexpected deaths; so, in these cases, adjustment may take longer. Adjustment may also take longer when coping with deaths caused by murder, especially if survivors are involved in the criminal justice system, which can prolong and even exacerbate the bereavement process (Wisocki & Skowron, 2000). People may also have difficulty resolving their grief in cases in which they had a highly conflictual relationship with the deceased person and in those in which they were excessively dependent on their relationship with that person. Researchers in one study found that people who experienced more severe stressful life events and used greater pessimistic thinking were also more likely to experience "complicated grief"—meaning intense yearning, difficulty accepting the death, excessive bitterness, numbness, emptiness, and feeling uneasy moving on and that the future is bleak—following the death of their loved one to cancer (Tomarken et al., 2008).

Influences on Grief

Different paths to death are associated with very different reactions on the part of loved ones (Rainey, 1988). On the one hand, people who have a chronic disease such as cancer, Parkinson's disease, multiple sclerosis, or Alzheimer's disease, typically experience lingering trajectory deaths: The person is ill for a long time, and death comes after a period of gradually declining health. These are usually quiet deaths, in which efforts are made to help the person remain comfortable, and do not involve last-minute heroic attempts to save them. In the past, doctors and nurses often delayed informing family members of a patient's impending death, or they told families but not the patient, in fear that it would upset the patient and perhaps cause the person to give up hope (Glaser & Strauss, 1965). However, this conspiracy of silence is usually not helpful—patients generally want to know the truth about their condition and typically appreciate knowing what to expect, including various physical symptoms and strategies for coping with pain (Rainey, 1988). Moreover, patients can pick up both verbal and nonverbal cues from doctors and family members and are very likely to hear, directly or indirectly, statements made by physicians and other hospital personnel, family members, and friends, giving them information about their prognosis (Justin, 1988). This type of open awareness—on the part of the patient and his or her family members—means that patients can make realistic plans. They may, for example, prepare a will, say good-bye to important people, make arrangements for their funeral and the custody of their children, and prepare psychologically for death (Rainey, 1988).

Lingering-trajectory deaths are often the easier for survivors to cope with because they allow people to prepare themselves for the loss of their loved one and to say their good-byes. Parents who had had a chance to say goodbye to the child experience lower levels of grief (Wijngaards-De Meij et al., 2008). However, this type of progression toward death may also pose difficulties for survivors. First, loved ones may watch the patient go through long-term pain and suffering and experience the loss of physical bodily functions and mental faculties. Friends and family members often engage in anticipatory grieving, namely, grieving small losses as they occur (e.g., loss of physical functioning, loss of ability to work); they are grieving the death but also all that is lost in the process of dying. Lingering-trajectory deaths may be draining on the physical, emotional, and financial resources of family members. Interestingly, at least in some cases, people can show improvements in health habits, such as taking their medicine, resting, and exercising, following the death of their spouse (Schulz et al., 2001). One study found that people who were the primary caregivers for their spouses and reported feeling considerable physical, mental, and/or emotional strain from this role actually had better health habits following the death of their spouse, and they did not show an increase in depression. In contrast, people who were not caregivers, or those who were caregivers but who were not experiencing strain, showed no change in health habits and increases in depression following the death of their spouse.

In contrast, **quick-trajectory deaths**, especially if they are sudden, violent, and stigmatized (e.g., AIDS, suicide), are very hard on survivors (Berado, 1988; Bradach & Jordan, 1995). Although bereaved parents have significantly worse health-related quality of life than nonbereaved parents, those whose child died in violent circumstances have particularly low levels of health-related quality of life (Song, Floyd, Seltzer, Greenberg, & Hong, 2010) and are more likely to experience complicated grief symptoms (Keesee, Currier, & Neimeyer, 2008; Meert et al., 2010). First, these deaths typically force survivors to cope with challenging practical issues. The deceased person typically has made no arrangements for his or her death, such as expressing wishes about funeral arrangements and burial preferences, writing a will, or taking care of financial issues (Becvar, 2001). Second, family members may feel a huge lack of closure—they've had no chance to say good-bye. As described at the beginning of the chapter, Sally felt completely unable to cope following the unexpected death of her husband, Paul. People may feel tremendous guilt about unresolved conflicts or things left unsaid and may dwell on the final words they said to the person, particularly if those words were unkind. Survivors of quick-trajectory deaths also don't have the opportunity to prepare themselves for a loss; hence, they can experience disbelief and intense anxiety for some time. Survivors of sudden, unexpected deaths often take considerable time to come to terms with the death and may report still actively trying to cope with it as long as 4 to 7 years later.

Coping With Bereavement

Many bereaved people have a strong need to try to make sense of the loss and may seek out any information related to the death (Raphael & Dobson, 2000; Toth, Stockton, & Browne, 2000). For example, they may go over and over the details surrounding the person's death, including the precise cause of death, the timing of the death, and whether the person experienced pain or fear. Even if these questions don't have answers, it can help the survivor recover to tell the story of their loss. Survivors have a particularly difficult time coping with deaths in which they don't have information, such as knowledge about how exactly the person died or whether their loved one suffered, and when they don't have the person's body. Researchers in one study examined grief severity among 157 parents who had experienced the death of their child (Keesee et al., 2008). Making sense of the child's death was the strongest predictor of the severity of the grief, with parents who reported having made little to no sense of their child's death experiencing a greater intensity of grief. Similarly, gay men who experienced the death of their partner to AIDS but found meaning in this loss—such as appreciating and become closer to their

Family members who lose loved ones unexpectedly, such as occurred with the 9/11 terrorist attacks, often have trouble coping with these quick-trajectory deaths.
Source: Peter C. Brandt/Getty Images, Inc.

friends, shifting their priorities, and increasing their faith—showed significantly better health than those who were not able to find such meaning (Bower, Kemeny, Taylor, & Fahey, 1998). In fact, only 3 of the 16 men who found meaning died during the follow-up period, whereas 12 of the 24 who did not find meaning had died. Similarly, adults who experience the death of a spouse and find meaning in and acceptance of the death show lower levels of anger (Kim, 2009).

Questioning the Research 11.3

What other factors might account for the finding that people who find meaning in a loved one's death experience better health?

This type of thinking about and trying to make sense of the death can be a valuable and even necessary component of working through the loss (Bower et al., 1998; Davis, Nolen-Hoeksema, & Larson, 1998; Folkman, Chesney, Collette, Boccellari, & Cooke, 1996; Folkman, Chesney, Cooke, Boccellari, & Collette, 1994; McIntosh, Silver, & Wortman 1993; Stroebe & Stroebe, 1991). Some researchers even suggest that people who fail to engage in this type of "grief work" experience poorer psychological and physical well-being. For example, one study with parents who experienced the sudden loss of their child found that those who thought frequently about the death of their child experienced more grief in the short term (3 weeks following the death) but showed greater adjustment and less distress 18 months later than those who did not do this grief work (McIntosh et al., 1993). As discussed in Chapter 4, people who try to avoid thinking about difficult thoughts show increased physiological arousal, which may in turn lead to more health problems. In line with this view, men who tried to avoid thinking about the loss of their spouse by suppressing their feelings and distracting themselves from their grief showed more maladjustment 2 years later than those who didn't use those strategies (Stroebe & Stroebe, 1991). This research suggests that confronting the loss can be a helpful coping strategy.

However, other research indicates that this type of direct confrontation and thinking about the loss is not associated with adjustment—and can even have harmful effects on psychological and physical well-being (Bonanno, Keltner, Holen, & Horowitz, 1995; Stroebe & Stroebe, 1991; Schut, van den Bout, De Keijser, & Stroebe, 1996). Research by Bonanno (2004) at Columbia University suggests that some people experience resilience in the face of a loss, meaning they show relatively stable and healthy levels of psychological and physical functioning following the upheaval of a major loss. For example, one study on coping with the loss of a spouse revealed that 46% had low levels of depression during the 18 months following the loss. Moreover, some research even suggests that people who deliberately try to avoid thinking about the loss of their spouse and exposing themselves to reminders of the loss may experience better long-term adjustment. For example, people who initially suppress or deny their sad feelings following the loss of a spouse actually show fewer symptoms of grief later on (Bonanno et al., 1995). As described in Box 11.4: Focus on Culture, grief processing is associated with more negative outcomes for Americans than for Chinese people.

Box 11.4

Focus on Culture: The Impact of Grief Processing Varies as a Function of Culture

To examine whether specific approaches to coping with grief are associated with different outcomes for people in different cultures, researchers examined grief processing in adults in both the United States and China who had experienced the death of a loved one (a child or a spouse; Bonanno, Papa, Lalande, Zhang, & Noll, 2005). Participants in both cultures completed measures of grief processing (thinking about the loved one, searching for meaning, talking about the loved one), grief avoidance (avoiding thinking about the loved one, avoiding expressing feelings about the loved one, avoiding talking about the loved one), and distress both 4 months after the loss and again 18 months later. Interestingly, both grief processing and deliberate grief avoidance early following the loss predicted greater distress for Americans 18 months following the death. However, among the participants in the People's Republic of China, neither grief processing nor deliberate avoidance was associated with distress later on. In addition, American participants who lost a child showed more distress and poorer health over time than those who lost a spouse, whereas the loss of a child and a spouse were both associated with initial poor health and distress but a similarly rapid recovery in the Chinese sample (see Figure 11.5). Similarly, Pressman and Bonanno (2007) found that Americans show more grief processing following the loss of a child than the loss of a spouse, whereas Chinese people show more grief processing following the loss of a spouse than the loss of a child. These findings suggest that individuals' cultural background influences the bereavement experience in very distinct ways.

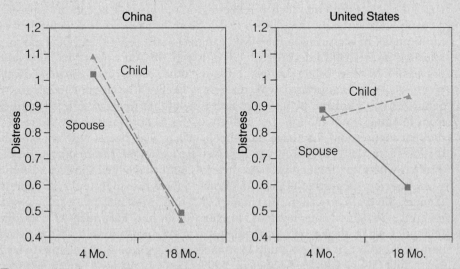

FIGURE 11.5 Both grief processing and grief avoidance 4 months after experiencing the loss of a loved one are associated with more distress 18 months later for Americans, whereas there is no association between either grief processing or avoidance and distress among Chinese people (data from Bonanno et al., 2005).

Similarly, persistently ruminating about or obsessing about one's loss without taking action to relieve such emotions can also have detrimental effects. Nolen-Hoeksema, Parker, and Larson of Yale University have conducted a number of studies on how men and women cope following the loss of a loved one (1994). In one study, Nolen-Hoeksema interviewed 253 people who had lost a loved one, such as a spouse, child, or parent, in the past month. These people were asked about the strategies they used to cope when they were feeling sad, blue, or depressed, and specifically whether they tended to rely on rumination (e.g., thinking about how hard they find concentrating, the negative consequences of their bad mood). The researchers then interviewed these people again 5 months later to see how their general coping styles influenced them over time. This study revealed that compared to men, women showed higher levels of rumination, that is, thinking about the death and the impact of the problem on their mood, and showed higher levels of depression. People who tended to ruminate more about their problems also reported experiencing more stressors, having less social support, and feeling less optimistic about their expectations for the future. Although all of these findings describe data from the first interview, other results revealed that people who ruminated more, experienced more stressors, and had less social support 1 month following their loss and higher depression scores 5 months later. Moreover, people who were more depressed 1 month after their loss were more likely to report ruminating, suggesting that initially strong depressive reactions may contribute to the tendency to ruminate, which in turn leads to even more depression. However, even taking into account these initially higher levels of depression, people who rely on rumination to cope with the death of a loved one experience higher levels of depression later on.

What accounts for these differences in terms of the effects of different types of strategies of coping with death? One explanation is that these discrepancies are caused by the type of thinking (or not thinking) people do in response to loss. Certain types of thinking, such as reflecting on the positive aspects of the deceased person's life and the meaning of his or her death, is likely to be beneficial. It may, for example, be reassuring to bereaved parents to talk about their child and to find meaning in the child's death (e.g., "This is part of God's plan," or "Our child's organs helped other babies survive."). On the other hand, ruminating and dwelling on the depression associated with the loss is likely to be detrimental (Stroebe & Schut, 2001). Similarly, people may find it helpful at times to distract themselves from thinking about the loss, but actively trying to not think about the loss (e.g., thought suppression) may have undesirable effects. The decision to not talk about the loss should also come from the bereaved person and not from others: Bereaved mothers who think frequently about their loss but believe their social environments would not be supportive of such disclosure experience high levels of depression (Lepore, Silver, Wortman, & Wayment, 1996). The most effective coping probably involves some moderate level of thinking about the loss, such as confronting memories when they arise but avoiding constant rumination about the deceased person. Researchers in one study examined coping among 219 couples who had lost a child (Wijngaards-de Meij et al., 2008). Loss-orientation—meaning focusing on the negative emotions associated with grieving and distracting oneself from the changes triggered by this loss—was predictive of negative psychological adjustment, while restoration-orientation—meaning focusing on forming new relationships and distancing oneself from the pain of the loss—was related to better adjustment.

Survivors also have a strong need to express their reactions to the death, including their feelings of anger, guilt, anxiety, helplessness, and depression, and, hence, can really benefit from the presence of social support (Kastenbaum, 1999; Raphael & Dobson, 2000; Toth et al., 2000). These feelings may be strange and intense—survivors may be angry at their loved one for getting killed, even if such a thought is totally irrational. People may feel they are going crazy, and they appreciate hearing that their reactions are normal. In fact, simply talking to other people about the loss has both psychological and physical benefits (see Box 11.5: Health Psychology in the Real World for some strategies for how to talk to people about the death of someone they love). One study of people who had lost a spouse to an accident or suicide found that those who talked to friends about the death had a smaller increase in number of illnesses following the death, whereas those who continued to ruminate about the death had more illnesses, including ulcers, headaches, and pneumonia (Pennebaker & O'Heeron, 1984). Bereaved people may also benefit from taking some type of action in response to the loss, such as planting a tree, starting a scholarship fund in the person's name, or creating a scrapbook of the person's life.

Survivors often find that friends and family are available to provide emotional and practical support immediately following the loss of a loved one, but this support typically declines over time. However, survivors often report experiencing intense pain for months, and even years, after the person's death. In fact, the intensity of a person's grief may not even be apparent immediately, when survivors often must cope with urgent matters, such as planning a funeral or memorial service, making plans for handling the body, and handling legal issues. Many survivors also experience an anniversary reaction, namely, a reaction to the death again at a later date that has some special significance (Dlin, 1985), such as an anniversary (in months or years) of the person's death, holidays, the loved one's birthday, or other special occasions.

Professional help may aid survivors in coping with their loss (Neimeyer, 2000). Some people find guided imagery helpful as grief therapy (Aiken, 1985). In this technique, bereaved individuals are taken through exercises in which they relive aspects of their relationship with the deceased: They might recall their affection for the deceased person and then replay receiving news of the death, attending the funeral, and watching the person be buried. The bereaved person is told to describe these events out loud as if they are occurring at that moment. They may also share imaginary dialogues with the deceased person, ask the person's permission to start new relationships, and ultimately say good-bye. This technique is supposed to help people come to terms with their grief and to finally make peace with the loss.

Interventions to assist family members who are experiencing bereavement may also help ease symptoms of grief. Researchers in one study randomly assigned family members of patients dying in ICUs to either typical care—meaning a conference about end-of-life options—or to an intervention designed to include more communication, including valuing what family members say, acknowledging their emotions, and eliciting questions (Lautrette et al., 2007). The family members in the enhanced communication condition also received a brochure on bereavement. Participants in the enhanced communication group had longer conferences than those in the control group (30 minutes versus 20 minutes) and spent more of the time talking (14 minutes vs. 5 minutes). Moreover, 3 months after the patient's death, those in the intervention group had fewer symptoms of depression (29% versus 56%), anxiety (45% versus 67%), and PTSD (45% versus 69%). These findings reveal

Box 11.5

Health Psychology in the Real World: What You Should—and Should Not—Say to Someone Who Is in Mourning

By Jess Decourcy, *Newsweek*, May 28, 2007

After a recent death in my family, I received a number of condolence cards that tried to talk me out of my grief. "You should be happy you have your memories," wrote one friend. "You should feel lucky you got to be with your father in the hospital." Lucky? Happy? You've got to be kidding!

Some cards made little mention of my father's death at all. Instead, they focused on the question of how I was going to distract myself from my grief. "Are you applying to grad school?" one person wrote. "How's your teaching going? Are you still renovating your apartment? Are you keeping busy?"

I was 25 when I lost my father last fall. He was only 58, and his death from bone cancer was slow and excruciating. When I cry for my father, I cry for his suffering; I cry because he worked long, grueling hours to save for a retirement he never got to enjoy. I cry because my mother is alone. I cry because I have so much of my life ahead of me, and my father will miss everything. If I marry, if I have children, he won't be there. My grief is profound: I am mourning the past, present, and future. I resent the condolence cards that hurry me through my grief, as if it were a dangerous street at night.

Why don't people say "I am sorry for your loss" anymore? Why don't people accept that after a parent's death, there will be years of grief? I am still a responsible citizen and a good teacher, despite my grief. My grief is not a handicap. People seem to worry that if they encourage me to grieve openly, I will fall apart. I won't. On the contrary, if you allow me to be sad, I will be a stronger, more effective person.

On the day of my father's funeral, we were greeted by a grinning deacon who shook our hands and chirped, "Isn't it a beautiful day? I'm so glad you have sun for your memorial!" I wanted to shake this woman. Couldn't she invoke a solemn tone for at least five seconds on the darkest morning of my life?

Our society needs to rethink the way we communicate with mourners—especially since so many people are in mourning these days. Everyone wants mourners to "snap out of it" because observing another's anguish isn't easy to do. Here's my advice: Let mourners mourn.

Before I lost my father, I was just as guilty of finding the silver lining of people's grief. If someone told me she lost her mother, I might say something like "She was sick for a very long time. It's good she's not suffering anymore." When a mourner hears nothing but these "silver linings," she begins to wonder why she can't find the good in the situation the way everyone else can. People want her to smile and agree that it's going to be OK, but she can't. Sometimes the death of a loved one becomes easier to accept with time. Sometimes it does not.

Condolences are some of the most difficult words to write or say. So it's natural that we freeze with writer's block when faced with such an immense task. As a college English teacher, I try to help students overcome writer's block by offering them structure. Writers often express themselves most freely when they know the rules of the genre in which they're writing. Here are my basic guidelines for mastering the Art of the Condolence:

1. Always begin directly and simply. "I am so sorry about your mother's death."
2. It's better to ask "How are you?" or "How are you feeling?" instead of telling someone how she should feel.

3. Never say "I can't imagine what you're going through." To me this translates as "This is too hard for me, I don't want to think about it."
4. Never give advice about how someone should get through the loss. Some mourners go to parties; others stay home with the shades drawn. Be open to the mourner's individual needs. Be open to the possibility that these needs will change day by day.
5. If you want to offer something upbeat, share a funny anecdote or memory about the deceased that might bring a smile to the mourner's face.

How do we support people in mourning? We can learn from elephants. Elephants are known to grieve in groups; they loop trunks to support the bereaved. Like elephants, we should remain connected and open to mourners' sorrow longer than a two-hour memorial service. Grieving is private, but it can be public, too. We need to stop being afraid of public mourning. We need to be open to mourners. We need to look each other in the eye, and say "I am so sorry."

that providing family members of patients who are dying in the ICU with more communication at the time of end-of-life decision making, as well as a brochure on bereavement, may lead to long-term benefits in terms of coping with the loss. Similarly, and as shown in Figure 11.6, group-based interventions for people who had lost a loved one to AIDS results in reduced grief severity (Sikkema et al., 2006).

Finally, both formal and informal grief support groups have been formed to provide support for those who have experienced similar tragedies (see Table 11.3; Raphael & Dobson, 2000). These support groups are particularly helpful because they allow people to affiliate with others in the same situation. Survivors can share their experiences, learn whether their reactions and experiences are normal, obtain guidance on coping, and discuss big questions (e.g., is life fair? is there a God?). The Widow-to-Widow Program, for example, provides people with the opportunity to

FIGURE 11.6 In this study, people who had lost a loved one to AIDS were randomly assigned to individual therapy or a group-based intervention focused on providing social support, strategies for coping, and goal setting. Participation in the intervention led to lower grief severity scores than individual therapy (data from Sikkema et al., 2006).

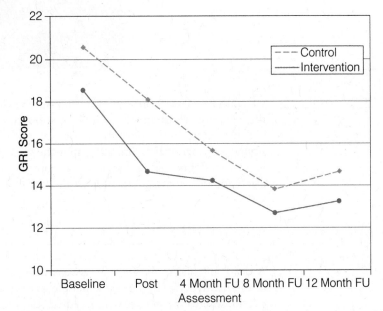

TABLE 11.3 *Survivor Support Groups*

Organization	Description
National SIDS Clearinghouse (www.sidscenter.org)	This group provides information for people affected by sudden infant death syndrome.
Parents of Murdered Children (www.pomc.com)	This group provides information for survivors of homicide.
Widowed Persons Service (www.aarp.org)	This group provides information for people who are widowed.
Mothers Against Drunk Driving (www.madd.org)	This group provides information for people who have lost someone to a drunk-driving accident.
American Association of Suicidology (www.suicidology.org)	This group provides information for survivors of suicide.
Compassionate Friends (www.compassionatefriends.org)	This group provides information for those who have lost a child.

Support groups are especially helpful when they bring together people who have all suffered the same type of loss.

Following the tragic shooting at Virginia Tech in 2007, many students attended memorial services to express their grief with others.
Source: Chip Somodevilla/Getty Images, Inc.

talk about the experience of losing a spouse with other people who have coped with this situation (Kastenbaum, 1999). As described at the beginning of the chapter, Tiffany found the support group for children who have experienced the death of a sibling very beneficial. Similarly, after the tragic shootings at Virginia Tech in 2007, several students started Facebook groups for students to share concerns, express grief, and post messages of support (Vicary & Fraley, 2010).

How Do People React to Different Types of Deaths?

A death in the family virtually always changes the types of interactions occurring in the family, and the reactions people have to death can differ depending on their relationship to the person who has died (Berado, 1988). This section examines how survivors react to different types of deaths.

Death of a Spouse

Losing a spouse is particularly devastating for virtually any married person (Field, Nichols, Holen, & Horowitz, 1999) because it deprives people of the single relationship that they may have had for a lengthy period of time, which in turn means the loss of social support, plans and dreams, and even the identity as a spouse. Many people who experience the loss of a spouse feel lonely for some time, even if they have a generally strong and supportive social network (Lichenstein, Gatz, Pederson, Berg, & McClearn, 1996). They may also experience a variety of physical symptoms, including believing they see, hear, or sense the presence of their spouse (Grimby, 1993; Lindstrom, 1995; LoConto, 1998). The loss of a spouse is particularly difficult for younger people, perhaps in part because this type of loss is less expected. Moreover, older people who have had to take care of their terminally ill spouse for some time may even feel some relief following the death (Schulz et al., 2001).

Interestingly, men and women react to and cope with the loss of their spouses in strikingly different ways (Lamme, Dykstra, & Broese Van Groenou, 1996; Stroebe, Stroebe, & Abakoumkin, 1999). Men are more likely than women to remarry, in part because women tend to outlive men and because men tend to prefer slightly younger partners than women do; hence, there are simply more eligible partners for older men than there are for older women. However, women are more likely than men to form new social relationships, such as with neighbors and other casual friends. Men also tend to suffer a greater loss of social support than do women following the death of a spouse. Men often rely on their wives for considerable social support and, therefore, are particularly devastated when she dies. Women, on the other hand, tend to rely on a broader network of people for support, including family members and friends as well as their spouse; hence, they suffer less of a decline in social support when they are widowed. This gender gap in social support is one explanation for the greater mortality risk men who have lost their spouse face as compared to women.

> **Questioning the Research 11.4**
>
> Although this research has focused on the impact of the death of a spouse, do you think the results would be the same if the study focused on people who lost long-term romantic partners who were not their spouses? Why or why not?

Death of a Parent

For adults, the death of a parent is the most common type of loss (Berado, 1988). Because these deaths are relatively common, and not so unexpected, they tend to be less traumatic than the loss of a spouse or a child. Adult children are generally able to continue with their own occupational and family responsibilities following the death of a parent, in part because there is typically some distance (emotional and physical) between adult parents and adult children.

While adult children experience relatively little disruption following the death of a parent, the death of a parent is the most significant loss a young child can encounter (Stillion & Wass, 1984; Wass & Stillion, 1988). Children are likely to express the loss of a parent through actions, such as repeating play activities that they had engaged in with their parent, and may remember parents only in terms of a few salient images. They may blame themselves for the death, feel betrayed, and believe that if the parent had loved them enough, they would not have died. The loss of a parent may also trigger new worries for children, including a fear that they too will die, and anxiety about who will take care of them. Not surprisingly, bereaved children are quite likely to suffer from psychological problems and tend to be more submissive, dependent, and introverted. For example, one study with 105 children between the ages of 2 and 17 years found that those who lost a parent showed increases in depression, sadness, irritability, crying, and other difficulties (e.g., eating, bed-wetting, school performance, sleeping; Van Eerdewegh, Bieri, Parilla, & Clayton, 1982). Similarly, adults who lost parents as children are more likely to have problems with loneliness, depression, suicide, and physical disorders such as cardiovascular disease.

The loss of a parent is particularly difficult when the death is by suicide or accident. Researchers in one study examined the effects of bereavement following a parent's death by suicide, accident, or sudden natural death (Brent, Melhem, Donohue, & Walker, 2009). Although both depression and alcohol or substance abuse 21 months after the parent's death were more common among adolescents who had lost a parent than those who had not, those who had lost a parent due to suicide or accidental death had particularly high rates of depression, and those who had lost a parent to suicide had particularly high rates of alcohol or substance abuse. In sum, children who lose a parent, especially through suicide, are vulnerable to depression and alcohol or substance abuse during the second year after the loss.

Death of a Child

Because parents expect that their children will outlive them, the death of a child is often seen as a particularly devastating type of loss—families literally can be torn apart dealing with this tragedy (Stillion & Wass, 1984). The intensity of grief following the death of a child is generally greater than that following the loss of a spouse or parent (Bass, Noelker, Townsend, & Deimling, 1990; Harvey & Hansen, 2000). Anger is a very common first reaction to learning that a child is dying. Parents may lash out at doctors, nurses, and even God. Parents may also feel anxious about the upcoming separation from their child, as well as their own eventual death (which is clearly brought home acutely in the case of a child's death). Guilt is another common reaction to learning that one's child is dying. Because parents see their role as protecting and nurturing their child, they can feel overwhelming guilt when they feel they have failed in this role. Parents often try to explain why the death happened and may feel that they are being punished (Downey, Silver, & Wortman, 1990). Parents often feel isolated and lonely. They are likely to find it difficult to continue to socialize with people who have healthy children, and they may not be able to cope with seeing other people's lives continuing normally while theirs is falling apart. All of these emotions are particularly strong when the child was initially healthy and when the death is unexpected, as in cases of an accident or suicide.

Considerable research reveals parents who lose a child experience lasting grief. For example, researchers in one study examined 261 parents whose child died in a pediatric ICU 6 months earlier (Meert et al., 2010). Parents, especially mothers, experienced a high level of complicated grief symptoms. Parental bereavement increases the risk of hospital admission for a psychiatric disorder, especially for affective disorders (Li, Laursen, Precht, Olsen, & Mortensen, 2005). Researchers in one study found that compared with parents who did not lose a child, parents who lost a child had an overall increased relative risk of a first psychiatric hospitalization for any disorder, and bereaved mothers had a higher relative risk of being hospitalized for any psychiatric disorder than bereaved fathers. Among mothers, the relative risk of being hospitalized for any psychiatric disorder was highest during the first year after the death of the child but remained significantly elevated 5 years or more after the death.

Parents can benefit from receiving particular types of support from the medical staff (Stillion & Wass, 1984). First, medical professionals must give parents clear and accurate information about the child's diagnosis, treatment, and prognosis, with a focus on relieving parents' guilt. If there is any hope that the condition will not be fatal, this possibility should be addressed to give parents some reason for optimism. They should also acknowledge the shock and despair the parents may be feeling and should encourage them to think through how they will tell others about the diagnosis (e.g., siblings, grandparents, friends). Finally, parents should be encouraged to treat the dying child as normally as possible, including maintaining consistent discipline. Parents often have a tendency, because of their guilt and grief, to indulge the terminally ill child, which can lead the child to feel confused and guilty.

Another type of commonly experienced death of a child is that of the loss of a child in utero, during birth, or shortly after birth (Davis, 1991). These deaths, often called fetal deaths, include miscarriages, stillbirths, and perinatal deaths. For many years, it was assumed such deaths cause relatively little grief to parents because they happened at such an early point in the new life. Grieving parents are often told, "You can always have another child," or "Thank goodness it happened before you really got attached to the child." But in most cases, parents start planning for and anticipating the birth of a child even at the very early stages of pregnancy. They may choose a name; buy furniture, clothes, and toys; and start imagining their lives with this baby. The death of a child, even during pregnancy, therefore typically leads to very real grieving and a sense of loss. In recent years, programs have been developed in hospitals in which parents are encouraged to see and hold their dead baby. They may have the opportunity to take photographs of the child, to give it a name, and to take some type of memento (e.g., a lock of hair, a footprint, a hospital bracelet). These practices are thought to help parents acknowledge the depth of their loss and to validate their intense feelings of grief.

Death of a Sibling

Although considerable research has examined the impact on parents of losing a child, relatively little research has examined the impact of losing a child on his or her siblings. However, the sibling relationship is a very important and unique one; hence, siblings experience many of the same emotions parents do following a child's death (Wass & Stillion, 1988), including shock, confusion, anxiety, depression, loneliness, and anger. Children may feel guilty for surviving, anxious that they will die, and responsible for their sibling's death (e.g., if the sibling had wished in a moment of anger that the child would die). The surviving child must also cope with a changed family situation, including neglect from their parents, who are focusing attention on the dying or dead child. Children often try to deny their own grief and sometimes even avoid mentioning their sibling's name, in an effort to avoid causing extreme pain to their parents. As one 12-year-old boy who recently lost a brother said, "My Dad doesn't talk about it, and my Mom cries a lot. I just stay in my room so I won't be a bother" (Wass & Stillion, 1988, p. 218). Finally, children can lose their own sense of identity if they lost their only sibling and are now no longer a sister or brother.

To help children cope with the death of a sibling, try to make them feel included, if possible, during all stages of their sibling's illness (Stillion & Wass, 1984). They should be permitted to visit their sibling in the hospital and should be allowed to attend the funeral. Although parents may try to hide their grief in an effort to protect the surviving child, it is important for adults to acknowledge their own feelings as well as to encourage children to discuss their feelings. Siblings obviously should be reassured that their own thoughts were not responsible for their sibling's condition.

How Do Children Understand Death?

What did you learn about death from your parents? If you are like most college students, the answer is probably very little. Although it happens to us all, most people are very uncomfortable with the topic of death—because it causes anxiety, thoughts of death are usually pushed out of our minds whenever possible. The topic of death is often considered taboo in our society. For example, we use euphemisms for death (e.g., she passed away, he kicked the bucket, she bought the farm), delay making wills, and put off discussions of how we'd like to be buried. In fact, one study of high school seniors found that death was never talked about in 39% of the families, and only briefly and when "absolutely necessary" in another 26% (Stillion & Wass, 1984). However, children are naturally curious about virtually everything, and their questions about death simply represent a normal part of their development (even if these questions are difficult to answer).

Many children's earliest experience with death comes through the death of a pet. Although adults may be reluctant to discuss death with children, the death of a pet can serve as a valuable learning opportunity (Wass & Stillion, 1988). Talking about death with children, and answering their questions, is often hard, but this approach lets them know that it is OK to talk about death—that death is not a "taboo topic."

Much of the knowledge about how children understand death comes from a series of studies conducted by Nagy (1948) in Budapest, Hungary, in the 1930s. She interviewed 378 children (ages 3 to 10) and asked them write down their thoughts about death (for the older children) and to make drawings about death (for the younger children). She also held discussions with the children to get them to talk about their feelings and thoughts about death. This work revealed that children's

Parents should use naturally occurring events to talk to their children about death and should give accurate information at a level the child can understand.
Source: Alan Oddie/PhotoEdit.

understanding of death evolves as they reach greater maturity and are better able to use logical as well as abstract cognitive reasoning.

First, very young children (ages 3 to 5 years) think about death in terms of separation and as something gradual and temporary, like sleeping. They may believe that someone who is dead can return to life, or that a person who is dead is just living elsewhere, as if they've moved away. In turn, they may want to know where the person is and how he or she got there. Although they may be saddened by death, as they would be by any significant separation from a loved one, they do not yet understand its finality or that it happens to everyone.

During the second stage, which starts around 5 or 6 years and lasts through about age 8, children begin to understand that death is permanent, irreversible, and final (Nagy, 1948; Stillion & Wass, 1984). However, children at this stage may still believe that death can be eluded, if one is tricky or lucky—death only happens to some people, namely, those who are bad or unlucky. In this stage, death may also be perceived as a separate person (e.g., a skeleton, a ghost, the Grim Reaper), with the idea that you can avoid this person and thereby avoid dying. Death is therefore not viewed as universal, personal, or inevitable.

By around ages 9 and 10 years, children have a view of death that is similar to that of adults; they know that everyone will die and that death is permanent (Nagy, 1948; Stillion & Wass, 1984). Children of this age can think abstractly, and they understand that death is inevitable, final, and universal.

Although Nagy's research was the first to examine how children understand death, more recent research has replicated her general findings (Speece & Brent, 1996). Speece and Brent (1996), for example, have conducted their own work on how children think about death, and their research suggests that by age 7, most children understand what they term the four key bioscientific components. These are universality (all living things die), irreversibility (things that are dead cannot be brought back to life), nonfunctionality (death involves the complete cessation of

TABLE 11.4 *Information YOU Can Use*

- Although many people avoid talking about death, it is important to think about and talk about end-of-life preferences with your loved ones so that you know what they would—and would not—want if they were to become seriously ill or injured. And these conversations are easier to have prior to a crisis situation.
- Write your own living will so that those who would be asked to make decisions on your behalf know your preferences. Would you want to be tube-fed? Placed on a ventilator? These are important decisions and your loved ones should know what you would like in such a situation.
- If you, or a loved one, are diagnosed with a terminal illness, consider using hospice care either in a hospital or home setting. Hospice care does not require giving up other forms of treatment, and it leads to better psychological and physical well-being (and even longer life expectancy) for both patients and their caregivers.
- If you experience the loss of a loved one, understand that bereavement is a process; you will eventually feel better, but it will take time. Relying on others (either formally or informally) who have experienced a similar loss can be very helpful.
- If you have a friend who has suffered the loss of a loved one, try to support them in ways that are helpful: Offer some concrete and practical help (such as preparing food for the bereaved person, assisting with funeral arrangements, or running errands), bring up the loved one's name in natural ways (people who have lost someone want the opportunity to talk about their memories of that person and often appreciate hearing stories about them), and signal your willingness to listen and help in any way (even simple statements, such as "I'm so sorry" and "Tell me how you're feeling" are appreciated).

all functions and capabilities), and causality (external and internal forces can bring about death).

So, how should parents handle the topic of death with their children? First, parents must be sensitive to children's concerns about dying and should be available to talk as the need arises (Stillion & Wass, 1984). Naturally occurring events, such as seeing a dead bird in the woods or a dead fish in an aquarium, can provide a good opportunity for parents to talk casually about death. Parents also should be prepared to provide children with accurate information in a simple and direct way. Saying, "Grandpa has died" is better than saying, "Grandpa has gone to live with the angels" or "Grandpa is sleeping."

Summary

1. The leading causes of death have changed over the last 100 years, with more people dying now from chronic conditions (e.g., heart disease, cancer) compared to acute diseases (e.g., pneumonia, tuberculosis, influenza). Life expectancy rates have also climbed, although sex and race differences in life expectancy persist.

2. The stages of death and dying theory, developed by Elizabeth Kubler-Ross, describes the process of dying as involving a series of five stages that differ in content and emotional intensity: denial, anger, bargaining, depression, acceptance. This theory has received criticism for its suggestion that these are the only stages, that these stages occur in this linear order, and that these stages are the right ones for people to experience.

3. Other approaches to describing the stages of death and dying focus on the tasks people who are dying

may encounter. The task-work model, developed by Charles Corr, describes people who are dying as focusing on four distinct types of tasks: physical, psychological, social, and spiritual. The phase-specific tasks model, developed by Kenneth Doka, describes changes in the tasks people focus on during the prediagnostic phase, chronic phase, recovery phase, and terminal phase.

4. The stages of death and dying in terminally ill children vary as a function of the age of the child, which influences their specific concerns as well as their level of awareness of their illness.

5. People have varying beliefs about the ethics of assisted suicide. Some people believe that people who are in severe pain and who are terminally ill should have the right to end their suffering. Other people believe that assisted suicide is wrong for multiple reasons, including the possibility of errors in diagnosis, the complexity of moral issues surrounding suicide, and the impact of depression on such desires.

6. Creating an advanced directive, or living will, helps patients communicate their wishes regarding end-of-life care to loved ones.

7. Although historically most people died at home, more recently deaths have typically occurred in hospitals and nursing homes. These institutions provide some advantages to terminally ill patients, including the opportunity for aggressive treatment, but may also have disadvantages, including a lack of focus on psychological issues.

8. Hospice care, which focuses on treating symptoms and managing pain but not on prolonging life, is one option for terminally ill patients. Hospice care can provide a sense of comfort and support for patients and their families. Interestingly, hospice care can also lead to longer survival.

9. Psychological problems, including depression, sadness, anger, and anxiety, are very common following the loss of a loved one. People who are experiencing bereavement may also experience social problems (e.g., loneliness, isolation) as well as increased rates of minor and major illnesses (and even death).

10. People who experience the loss of someone they care about experience a state of bereavement. The stages of bereavement include the reaction stage, yearning and searching, disorganization and reorganization, and reorientation and recovery.

11. The type of death experienced influences the nature of grief. People generally have more difficulty following quick-trajectory deaths, which occur without warning, than lingering-trajectory deaths, which are more expected.

12. People cope with bereavement in a variety of different ways, including trying to make sense of the loss, expressing their reactions to the death, relying on friends and family, and seeking professional help (either through a therapist or a support group).

13. People react in different ways depending on their relationship with the person who has died. Losing a spouse is devastating for most people, and men and women react in different ways to this loss. The death of a parent, which is the most common type of loss experienced, is easier for adult children than for young children. The death of a child is a particularly difficult type of loss, since people expect their children to outlive them. Children who lose a sibling also experience many of the same reactions as do parents who lose a child.

14. Children's understanding of death occurs gradually as they reach greater maturity and can use logical as well as abstract cognitive reasoning.

Key Terms

acceptance	denial	mourning
anger	depression	quick-trajectory deaths
assisted suicide	grief	stages of death and dying
bargaining	hospice	task-work approach
bereavement	lingering-trajectory deaths	

Thought Questions

1. Your roommate's sister just died in a car accident. What are three things you could say to her that would be helpful during this difficult time?

2. Describe the five stages of death and dying, according to Dr. Elizabeth Kubler-Ross, and two critiques of this theory.

3. What are the psychological, social, and physical consequences of bereavement?

4. Your 9-year-old child asks you why her great-grandmother has died and where she is now. What do you say?

5. What are the pros and cons of dying in a hospital versus dying in a hospice care facility? Which place of death would you prefer and why?

Answers to Questioning the Research

Answer 11.1. One possibility is that people who rely on religious coping differ from those who do not rely on such coping in a particular way, and thus a third variable explains the association between coping strategy and use of life-prolonging measures. Perhaps those who rely on religious coping are more optimistic, and thus more hopeful about the chances of overcoming a terminal disease, or perhaps they have larger social networks, and thus receive more pressure from others to continue fighting to survive. What other possible explanations for this association can you imagine?

Answer 11.2. Some research suggests that men in general benefit more from marriage than do women, which in turn may explain why the loss of a spouse is more detrimental to men's health than to women's health. Women may provide more social support to their spouses, take care of more household tasks (such as cooking and cleaning), and organize social events with family members and friends. In turn, men who experience the loss of a spouse may suffer multiple losses in terms of emotional and tangible support more than do women who experience such a loss.

Answer 11.3. People who are able to find meaning in the death of a loved one may actually be different from those who cannot, and these differences may explain the different rates of longevity between these two groups. One possibility is that people who find meaning in such a death are generally more optimistic by nature, and in turn, research shows that optimism is associated with better physical health and a longer life expectancy. Another possibility is that people who find meaning in the death of a loved one have more social support. The presence of this support, in turn, may help them see the positive side even of such a tragedy.

Answer 11.4. Although most research has focused on the impact of the death of a spouse, it is likely that people would experience similar reactions to the death of any person with whom they were intimately involved, regardless of whether they were legally married. Anyone who experiences the death of a partner who is the most important person in his or her life clearly must cope with considerable grief and bereavement. In fact, grief can be greater when a person has lost someone who is not formally recognized by others as an important part of his or her life (Berado, 1988). This type of bereavement is called *disenfranchised grief* and may be experienced by people who live together but who are not married.

CHAPTER 12

Health-Care Interaction: Screening, Utilization, Adherence, and Relapse

- Charlene was in the shower yesterday washing her hair when she felt a small lump in her neck. It was not painful and was quite small—just about the size of a pea. Charlene wondered what she should do about it and called her sister to ask for advice. Her sister recommended she see a doctor right away, but Charlene is really busy at work this week, so she decided to wait until things settle down at the office to then see a doctor.

- Peter is a 19-year-old college student and is concerned that he has an STD. He has developed a slight discharge from his penis and feels a strong burning sensation whenever he urinates. When he goes to see a doctor at the student health center, however, he is shocked to learn that the doctor is female. When she asks him to describe his problem, he suddenly loses his nerve and complains about a recurring backache.

- Bill is 62 years old and in very good health. He had his annual physical last week and passed with flying colors. His doctor did, however, suggest that he make an appointment for a colonoscopy to check for signs of colon cancer. Although this procedure is recommended for all people over age 50, Bill just sees no need for it. He feels fine and generally eats a healthy diet—and he certainly has no interest in undergoing such an embarrassing and awkward procedure. However, his doctor seemed to feel strongly that having this test was important, and Bill therefore plans to have it done.

- Larry is 58 years old and has suffered from hypertension, or high blood pressure, for the past 10 years. He is supposed to take medication daily to lower his blood pressure, but he frequently forgets. Although Larry knows the medication is probably good for him, he really doesn't feel any different whether he takes it or not, so he wonders if it is doing anything to actually help him. Plus, the medication is relatively expensive, the cost is not covered by his health insurance, and many of the side effects, including dizziness, diarrhea, muscle weakness, and frequent urination, are irritating.

- Sarah is 25 years old and has had a problem with alcohol since high school. She often finds it just impossible to wake up to go to work on the mornings after she's passed out from drinking late the night before, and she has been warned by her boss that she will be fired if she is late again. To try to stop drinking, Sarah has started working with a therapist. The therapist has asked her to make a list of the situations that prompt her to drink and the alternative ways she could handle these situations.

Preview

This chapter examines how psychological factors influence individuals' willingness to seek and follow health-care recommendations. First, we examine issues involved in screening for health-care problems, including the predictors of screening, the benefits and costs of screening, and strategies for increasing screening. Next, we examine psychological factors that influence when people seek medical care, how they interact with their health-care provider, the experience of hospitalization, and the experience of burnout in health professionals. We then examine issues in adherence to health-care regimens, including causes of nonadherence, measuring adherence, and increasing adherence. Finally, we examine issues in relapse, including theories of relapse, the influence of psychological factors on relapse, and strategies for preventing relapse.

What Is Screening?

Screening to detect illness, or even an increased likelihood of developing illness, at an early stage is an increasingly important part of health promotion (see Table 12.1). Screening behaviors, such as having your teeth cleaned to check for cavities, getting your blood pressure checked during a physical exam, and checking your breasts or testicles for signs of cancer, are secondary prevention strategies. In other words, while they do not prevent health problems from developing, by detecting a treatable

TABLE 12.1 *Screening Tests Available Today*

Diagnostic Testing: This type of testing shows whether a person has a given disease.

Neurofibromatosis

Marfan syndrome

Achondroplasia

Presymptomatic Testing: This type of testing shows whether a person is going to develop a given disease.

Huntington's disease

Hypercholesterolemia

Kidney disease

Predisposition Testing: This type of testing shows whether a person has a genetic predisposition to a given disease but not whether he or she will definitely develop the disease.

Breast cancer

Colon cancer

Alzheimer's disease

Carrier Status Testing: This type of testing shows whether a person carries a gene for a given disease and hence could pass it on to his or her children.

Tay-Sachs disease

Cystic fibrosis

Sickle-cell anemia

Duchenne muscular dystrophy

Prenatal Testing: This type of testing shows whether a fetus has a given disease.

Muscular dystrophy

Down's syndrome

disease or abnormality in its early stages, screening may enable the individual's life to be prolonged or enhanced (Harris, 1992). For example, early detection of breast and colon cancer can reduce cancer mortality as much as 30% (Kerlikowske, Grady, Rubin, Sardrock, & Ernster, 1995; Selby, Friedman, Quesenberry, & Weiss, 1992). Similarly, testicular cancer is the leading cause of cancer deaths for men ages 20 to 34 years old, in part because many cases are not diagnosed until the cancer has spread to other areas of the body (Nicholson & Harland, 1995). Estimates are that if people followed screening recommendations, cancer deaths would drop by 25 to 40% (White, Urban, & Taylor, 1993).

Advances in molecular genetics, including the mapping of disorders onto particular genes, have led to the ability to test for more than 200 inherited disorders (see Table 12.2; Croyle & Lerman, 1995; Lerman, 1997). In some cases, this testing can determine whether a person is at risk of developing a disease. For example, genetic tests are now available for breast, ovarian, and some types of colorectal cancer, as well as Huntington's disease and Alzheimer's disease (Patenaude, Guttmacher, & Collins, 2002). In other cases, genetic testing can determine whether a person carries a gene for a disorder, such as Tay-Sachs disease, cystic fibrosis, and sickle-cell anemia, which they could then transmit to their children. Couples may then use this information to determine whether they will have children or whether they might use in vitro fertilization with nongenetically related eggs or sperm to avoid passing this disease on to their children. In still other cases, testing is used to evaluate whether a fetus has various genetic conditions. The vast majority of pregnant women in the United States undergo some kind of screening, such as blood tests, ultrasound, and amniocentesis, to help evaluate the health of the fetus. Based on the results, couples can then decide to continue the pregnancy or to terminate it in cases in which the baby would not survive more than a few days or would suffer

TABLE 12.2   *When Should You Screen and for What?*

Early Cancer Detection for Men and Women

- **Colorectal cancer:** Starting at age 50, flexible sigmoidoscopy every 5 years; double contrast barium enema every 5 years; colonoscopy every 10 years; or virtual colonoscopy every 5 years.
- **Skin cancer:** Skin exam every 3 years for those ages 20 to 40; skin exam every year for those over age 40.

Early Cancer Detection for Men

- **Prostate cancer:** Starting at age 50 (or 45 for those at higher risk based on family history and demographics), men should discuss the pros and cons of prostate cancer screening to decide if testing is appropriate. Testing for prostate cancer includes the PSA blood test and digital rectal.

Early Cancer Detection for Women

- **Cervical cancer:** Yearly pelvic exam with Pap test starting at age 21 (or three years after becoming sexually active, whichever is earlier); after age 30, women who have had three normal Pap tests in a row may move to screening every 2 to 3 years.
- **Breast cancer:** Clinical breast exam by a health-care professional every 3 years for those ages 20 to 39; yearly clinical breast exam by a health-care professional and yearly mammogram for those age 40 and over.

These recommendations for screening were developed by the American Cancer Society—how many of them do you follow?

extreme, and possibly life-threatening, disability. Genetic screening will increase as more genetic tests are developed.

This section examines three topics involving screening. First, we examine the predictors of screening, including demographic factors and personality variables that influence screening as well as physician recommendations. We then examine the costs and benefits of screening, such as the ability to seek early treatment and make appropriate plans, as well as the creation of considerable anxiety and the potential for inaccurate results. Finally, we examine strategies for increasing screening, including educating people about its benefits, providing reminders, and removing barriers.

The Predictors of Screening

Demographic factors, including income and education, influence screening behavior (Jepson & Rimer, 1993; Manne et al., 2002). For example, one study found that 32% of those with only some high school education or less got screened for colorectal cancer, as compared to 78% of those with a graduate school degree (Manne et al., 2002). People who lack health insurance are, not surprisingly, less likely to have regular breast and cervical screening than those with such coverage (Rimer, Meissner, Breen, Legler, & Coyne, 2001). One's family history also predicts screening; those with a family history of breast cancer are more likely to seek screening for the genes that indicate greater risk of ovarian and breast cancer (BRCA1, BRCA2; Mellon et al., 2009).

Individual differences, such as self-efficacy, social norms, vulnerability, and perceived costs and benefits of screening, also influence who screens (see Table 12.3; Shiloh, Ben-Sinai, & Keinan, 1999; Tiro et al., 2005). People who are conscientious and high in self-efficacy for carrying out screening behavior are more likely to have mammograms (Christensen & Smith, 1995; Siegler, Feaganes, & Rimer, 1995). People who see more benefits of screening (e.g., it can lead to longer life expectancy) as well as those who see fewer costs (e.g., saves money, saves time, increases safety) are more likely to screen (Aiken, West, Woodward, & Reno,

---

TABLE 12.3   *Test Yourself: The Pros and Cons of Colorectal Cancer Screening*

1. Colon cancer tests can find growths that are not yet cancerous but that could become cancer.
2. Having colon cancer tests regularly would give me good peace of mind about my health.
3. Regular colon cancer tests will help me to live a long life.
4. Having colon cancer tests will help me avoid having a more serious cancer.
5. Colon cancer tests are a part of good health care.
6. Having a colon cancer test is very embarrassing.
7. I cannot afford to have a colon cancer test.
8. Tests for colon cancer take too much time.
9. Colon cancer tests are risky.
10. Too many things can go wrong with tests for colon cancer.

The first five items assess positive aspects of having a colon cancer test, and the next five items assess the costs or disadvantages of having a colon cancer test.

Source: Manne et al., 2002.

1994; Manne et al., 2002; McCaul, Branstetter, Schroeder, & Glasgow, 1996; Schwartz, Peshkin, Tercyak, Taylor, & Valdimarsdottir, 2005; Shepperd, Solomon, Atkins, Foster, & Frankowski, 1990). Some evidence suggests that women who are concerned about developing breast cancer are more likely to engage in screening behavior, such as mammograms and breast self-exam (BSE), than those with low concerns for developing the disease (Diefenbach, Miller, & Daly, 1999; McCaul, Branstetter et al., 1996; McCaul, Schroeder, & Reid, 1996). On the other hand, women who are at high risk for developing breast cancer, such as those with a relative who had breast cancer, are actually less likely to perform BSE and attend mammogram screenings when they are high in anxiety (Lerman, Rimer, Trock, Balshem, & Engstrom, 1990; Lerman et al., 1993). In sum, a curvilinear relationship may best predict screening: People with moderate levels of anxiety engage in more screening than those with low or high anxiety.

Practitioners' beliefs about the benefits of screening also influence screening behavior in their patients (Grady, Lemkau, McVay, & Reisine, 1992; Jepson & Rimer, 1993; Manne et al., 2002; Schwartz et al., 2005). For example, rates of HIV testing at prenatal clinics vary from 3 to 82%, and rates of mammography screening vary across communities from 22 to 70%, suggesting that practitioners' attitudes about the tests may influence how they present it as an option to patients (Bergner, Allison, Diehr, Ford, & Feigl, 1990; Meadows, Jenkinson, Catalan, & Gazzard, 1990). Women with physician referrals for screening are more likely to have both clinical breast exams and mammograms. Similarly, one study found that 89% of those with a doctor recommendation got screened for colorectal cancer, as compared to only 44% of those without such a recommendation (Manne et al., 2002). As described at the beginning of this chapter, Bill's decision to have a colonoscopy was largely a result of his doctor's strong recommendation.

Some intriguing research by Bundek, Marks, and Richardson at the University of Southern California suggests that women's beliefs about their control over various health-related behaviors influence how likely they are to follow screening recommendations (1993). Specifically, women who believed they controlled their own health outcomes were more likely to engage in screening behaviors with a high degree of personal control, such as BSE. These women agreed with statements such as, "The main thing that affects my health is what I myself do," and "I am in control of my health." In contrast, women who believed that medical professionals have control over their health outcomes were more likely to engage in screening behaviors that medical professionals have control over, such as Pap smears and clinical breast exams. These women agreed with statements such as, "Having regular contact with my physician is the best way for me to avoid illness," and "Regarding my health, I can only do what my doctor tells me to do."

The Costs and Benefits of Screening

The decision to seek screening is a complex one for many people. Screening for medical conditions—and even genetic predispositions for particular medical conditions—has both potential advantages and disadvantages (see Table 12.4). Box 12.1: Health Psychology in the Real World describes the tremendous importance of early detection of skin cancer for long-term survival.

TABLE 12.4   *Pros and Cons of BRCA1/2 Mutation Testing*

Pros

- Information for patient
- Improved cancer risk management
- Relief from uncertainty/distress
- More informed lifestyle decisions
- Information for family members

Cons

- Possibility of uninformative test results
- Loss of privacy, insurance, employment discrimination
- Psychological distress
- Unproven efficacy of management options
- Results provide a probability of developing cancer—not a certainty.

Testing to learn if one has a genetic predisposition for developing breast and ovarian cancer has both potential advantages and disadvantages (Schwartz et al., 2005). Many people who are considering undergoing this test find that talking to a genetic counselor about this decision is helpful.

Box 12.1

Health Psychology in the Real World: That Little Freckle Could Be a Time Bomb

By Susan Lennon, *Newsweek*, May 24, 2004

Perched on the edge of the examination table, I was chattering away to my dermatologist, Dr. Penny Lowenstein, as she examined my skin last December.

Uncharacteristically quiet, she pulled out a magnifier to peer at my face. "Feel anything strange above your lip?" she asked. My heart sank. Squeezing my eyes shut, I whispered, "No." My palms started to sweat when she said, "Precancerous." It was actinic keratosis, and the treatment wasn't pretty. I had to smear chemotherapy cream over the dime-size spot for the next 12 days—destroying the diseased skin, but turning it into a mass of angry red pustules along the way.

I've been through this skin-cancer thing before. A few years ago I had a basal-cell tumor. Known as "the cancer to get if you've got to have cancer," it's slow growing and it rarely spreads. That was the good news. The bad news was that it was on my forehead. Vanity took flight when I learned that, untreated, it would worm its way into my brain. A plastic surgeon dug it out, leaving me with a perpetually uplifted eyebrow.

I knew that early sunburns trigger skin cancer. When I was a kid, no one used sunscreen. I blistered from burns every summer; no one ever thought twice about it. As a teenager, I slathered myself in baby oil and roasted myself red as soon as the weather warmed. But the only concession I made after my basal-cell diagnosis was to cover my face as I sunbathed in secret. And to go for my yearly skin check.

The next year I was in for a shock. Suspicious spots were cut out and sent to a lab; a few days later I learned that I'd sprouted a dysplastic nevus—a mole that might morph into melanoma—on my neck, a squamous-cell cancer on my collarbone and a melanoma on my shoulder.

Squamous-cell carcinoma is several notches higher than basal on the Scary Cancer Scale. It grows more quickly and more deeply, and pieces can break off and lodge in inconvenient places like your lungs or liver. It seemed impossible that the skin tag on my collarbone, a teeny little bump, could have turned so monstrous.

Melanoma is the most menacing of the skin cancers. Masquerading as a freckle, it can wreak havoc without any symptoms. If it's not caught early, major organs can become riddled with the disease. It's a cancer that usually strikes people in the prime of their lives, and the five-year advanced-melanoma survival rate is grim.

Which is why I was distressed at this latest development. After umpteen precancerous moles, heaps of biopsies and four skin cancers, I scrutinize my skin like a zealot, poring over my pores, inspecting my insteps and even looking "down there." I figured that between my own vigilance and the now quarterly dermatologist visits, I was covered. I was even blase.

But when Dr. Lowenstein handed me a mirror and shone a bright light onto my face, I could barely make out three scaly spots. What I thought was a touch of dry skin was actually a time bomb.

When I told my husband, he blanched. "I can't believe it. Come into the light and let me look." Little did I know that he, too, analyzes my skin relentlessly. "So if you weren't doing these skin checks, this little thing could have killed you?"

Yup. It shook me out of my complacency. Searching the Internet for information on actinic keratosis, I found page after page on skin cancer. And I remembered how disfiguring the treatment for basal- and squamous-cell cancer was—I have enough surgery scars to call myself the Bride of Frankenstein.

Then I stumbled across the Melanoma Patients' Information Page. The "guest book" is chilling. A pregnant mom's 38-year-old husband has end-stage melanoma. A woman with three young children agonizes over two nasty therapies. Someone else writes about her own mom, 58—diagnosed in April, dead the following March.

Though teens obsessed with tanning beds have become enough of a trend to be dubbed "tanorexics," many more kids avoid skin cancer now because of prevention efforts. What about the rest of us? We know we should stay out of the sun—and I've kicked my sunbathing habit—but what about all the years we didn't? The damage is done, but we can do something about it.

Got an irregular-shaped brownish-blackish spot, or what looks like a zit but lingers and bleeds, or an itchy bump that seems a bit bigger this month? Call a skin specialist, and have yourself checked from head to toe. Catch a cancer early and you might avoid mutilating operations, brutal treatments and early death.

Not quite five years after my melanoma, I'm alive today thanks to skin self-checks and an astute dermatologist. Smaller than a pencil eraser, that freckle wanna-be could have erased my whole life.

Proponents of screening argue that this type of knowledge may help a person seek early treatment and/or engage in health-promoting behaviors (Baum, Friedman, & Zakowski, 1997; Patenaude et al., 2002). Learning he or she has high blood pressure or elevated levels of cholesterol, for example, could motivate that person to make changes in diet or increase his or her rate of exercise in an attempt to prevent developing heart disease. Similarly, some women who find out they have a genetic predisposition to breast cancer make the decision to take the drug Tamoxifen to prevent breast cancer, or they even undergo a mastectomy to avoid developing breast cancer completely (Hartmann et al., 1999; Meijers-Heijboer et al., 2001). One study found that 68% of women who learned they had the breast cancer gene had had a mammogram 1 year later as compared to 44% of those who learned they

Individuals who test positive for HIV can begin
undergoing highly active antiretroviral treatment
(HAART), which has been shown in some studies to lead
to a significant increase in life expectancy (The
Antiretroviral Therapy Cohort Collaboration, 2008).
Source: © Ulrich Doering/Alamy.

did not have this gene (Lerman et al., 2000). In line with this view, people who
learn they are HIV-positive often engage in better physical and psychological care
for themselves and appear motivated to not spread this disease to others (Coates,
Morin, & McKuskick, 1987; Coates et al., 1988; Collins et al., 2001).

Knowledge about one's genetic risk of developing a particular disease may also
help people make realistic plans for their future. If they are aware that they are likely
to develop Alzheimer's disease, for example, they may choose to not start a family or
to start a family early. They could choose to forgo a career that involves many years
of education. Moreover, in the case of diseases that progress over time, patients could
be more vigilant for symptoms of the disease and could seek more regular health
care. For example, a woman with a genetic predisposition to breast cancer could
perform BSE diligently and have very frequent mammograms in an effort to catch
signs at a very early stage. As shown in Figure 12.1, women who test positive for the
BRCA1 gene and have assistance in making a decision about whether to undergo a
mastectomy to reduce their risk of breast cancer are more likely to make a decision
(Schwartz et al., 2009). They also feel less conflict about making this important
decision as well as increased satisfaction with their choice. Finally, knowing about
genetic predisposition to a given disease can provide some peace of mind, especially
for those who are already concerned they will develop such a disorder, perhaps
based on family history, but who do not know for sure (Baum et al., 1997).

Despite the benefits of screening, this type of early detection also comes with
significant potential costs. Individuals can experience psychological harm from a
positive result (Marteau, Dundas, & Axworthy, 1997; Meissen et al., 1988; Tercyak,
Peshkin, Streisand, & Lerman, 2001; Tibben, Timman, Bannink, & Duivenvoorden, 1997). For example, people who test positive for Huntington's disease—a
progressive inherited disease that involves motor disability; a disturbance of affect,
behavior, and personality; cognitive impairment; and eventually death—typically
experience considerable anxiety, fear, and even depression. One study found that
33% of subjects reported they would consider suicide if they learned they tested
positive for this disease (Bloch, Fahy, Fox, & Hayden, 1989). Another study found
that 48% of the men who were tested for HIV but then chose to not learn the
results reported that getting a positive result would be too upsetting, and 31%
believed they would be "unable to cope" with this information (Lyter, Valdiserri,
Kingsley, Amoroso, & Rinaldo, 1987). Because most people who learn that they are
at risk of developing a serious illness experience negative reactions at least initially,

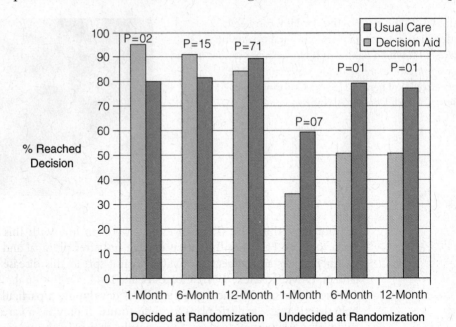

FIGURE 12.1   Researchers in this study randomly assigned women who are BRCA1 carriers and deciding whether to undergo a mastectomy to receive either standard care or a CD-ROM that included individually tailored information about women's risk of breast and ovarian cancer as well as pros and cons of different decisions. Among women who had not made a decision about what to do at the start of the study, those who received the CD-ROM were three times as likely to make a decision by the 12-month follow-up as those who received only usual care (data from Schwartz et al., 2009).

crisis intervention should be available immediately to help people deal with anxiety and fear and work through issues related to stigma, sexuality, and intimacy. These responses are particularly severe when the diagnosis is unexpected (Croyle, Smith, Botkin, Baty, & Nash, 1997).

Although some studies suggest that the anxiety that follows a positive result lessens or even disappears over time, other research indicates that anxiety stays high and can even increase (Jemmott, Sanderson, & Miller, 1995; Wiggins et al., 1992). One study of people who learned they were carriers for cystic fibrosis found that 44% reported having troubling thoughts even as long as 3 years after receiving the test results (Marteau et al., 1997). Similarly, and as described in Box 12.2, people who learn they test positive for the gene for Huntington's disease show initial decreases in anxiety, but then anxiety increases again over time (Timman, Roos, Maat-Kievit, & Tibben, 2004).

Questioning the Research 12.1

Although some research suggests that people who learn they have a positive result experience higher rates of depression initially and then return to normal levels later on, can you think of a limitation of this research? (Hint: Who chooses to get tested?)

Box 12.2

Focus on Research: The Shifting Reaction to Testing Positive for Huntington's Disease

Researchers in one study examined people's reaction to testing positive for Huntington's disease over time (Timman et al., 2004). In this study, 142 individuals who were at risk of having Huntington's disease and 104 partners completed measures of depression, hopelessness, and general health. Participants also completed these measures after learning of the test result, and again several times later (6 months, 18 months, 3 years, and 7 to 10 years). Both carriers and their partners were more distressed after the test than noncarriers and their partners, although levels of distress improved over the next 3 years, presumably as they adjusted to the diagnosis. However, at the final 7 to 10 year follow-up, both carriers and their partners again became more pessimistic, presumably because they were getting closer to the age at which symptoms would be starting. This research suggests that relatively low long-term depression and anxiety following a negative test result may be underreporting the true impact of such a result because negative emotions may actually increase over time.

Although many people choose to undergo screening, especially for genetic disorders, in an attempt to reduce the anxiety of "not knowing," screening tests do not eliminate uncertainty (Lerman, 1997). The tests for breast, ovarian, and colon cancer, as well as Alzheimer's disease, all measure whether a person has an increased likelihood of developing the disease, but do not predict whether a person will definitely get the disease. For example, for women who test positive for the gene indicating a predisposition for breast and ovarian cancer, the risk of developing breast cancer is between 56 and 85%, and the risk of ovarian cancer is between 20 and 60% (Patenaude et al., 2002). In these cases, additional genetic factors, environmental factors, or both will determine whether the person develops the disease. Moreover, even in cases in which genetic testing reveals that the person will certainly develop the disease, it will not provide information about exactly when such symptoms will develop or about how the disease will progress. And because some types of diseases have no treatment (e.g., Huntington's disease), early detection only increases the amount of time the person knows about the problem before he or she begins to experience any symptoms (Wiggins et al., 1992).

Even screening to learn if one currently has a disease, such as cancer, can in some cases provide people with information—and potentially thereby increase psychological distress—but have no benefit in terms of survival. For example, although some guidelines on early detection of prostate cancer recommend biopsy for those with a high prostate-specific antigen (PSA) score, this procedure has no impact on life expectancy (Vickers, Till, Tangen, Lilja, & Thompson, 2011). The American Cancer Society therefore does not currently recommend this type of testing, and instead recommends that men over 50 simply talk to their doctor about the advantages and disadvantages of testing for prostate cancer. Similarly, for a long time, mammograms were seen as an important part of routine health care for women ages 50 years and over, with some experts believing mammograms should begin as early as age 40

(American Cancer Society, 2011). However, in early 2002, a National Cancer Institute Panel issued a startling statement: Even for women over age 50, mammograms might make very little difference. Why? Some women have very slow-growing tumors, which are likely to be curable (by simply removing them) whenever a physician detects them during a manual exam. So, these women would not benefit from catching these tumors earlier than later, and very likely would experience a significant increase in anxiety for having to come in for follow-up mammograms (Heckman et al., 2004). Other women have very fast-growing, aggressive tumors, and, unfortunately, these tumors are so fast-growing that even when they are caught at a relatively early point, it is typically too late to make a difference in terms of survival. Therefore, these women would also not benefit from having regular mammograms. Women who have tumors that grow at a moderate rate benefit from regular mammograms because catching these tumors early is important. These women, however, represent only about 15 to 20% of breast cancer cases, meaning that the majority of women show no benefits from mammograms. These findings point to yet another tricky issue in terms of making decisions about screening.

When the results of a screening test indicate that a person does not have a particular disease, it can give a person peace of mind, a psychological benefit, but individuals can also experience psychological harm from a negative test result (Huggins et al., 1992; Lynch & Watson, 1992). In fact, people who get tested for a disease but then don't know their risk status, either because their test results were inconclusive or they chose to not learn the results, experience even more anxiety and depression than those who learn they have a positive result (Wiggins et al., 1992). A negative result may also make people more comfortable with not getting screened again, perhaps because it decreases their feelings of vulnerability, or not taking adequate precautions (e.g., "I haven't gotten AIDS thus far, so why worry about condoms now?"). One study with patients at an urban STD clinic found that rates of gonorrhea decreased 29% six months after testing for those with a positive result, but increased 106% for those who tested negative (Otten, Zaidi, Wroten, Witte, & Peterman, 1993). In other cases, people still feel susceptible to the disease, so receiving a negative test result does not even reduce uncertainty or distress (e.g., "I just haven't gotten AIDS yet"). Finally, receiving a negative test result can also make people feel guilty, especially if others in their family have tested positive (Biesecker et al., 1993). They may wonder why they were spared and feel guilty about showing their relief.

One of the most significant problems with screening is the possibility of receiving an inaccurate result, which can lead to substantial psychological and even physical consequences (Lerman & Rimer, 1995). Even a test that is 99% accurate, such as the ELISA or Western Blot tests used to determine HIV, will produce 1% false positives, meaning that in 1 of every 100 cases, the test will indicate a person has the disease, but the person really does not (Sloand, Pitt, Chiarello, & Nemo, 1991). A false positive obviously can lead to psychological distress and anxiety, which in some cases may be maintained even after the patient receives accurate results (McCormick, 1989; Skrabanek, 1988). For example, one study found that 29% of women who received false-positive results from their mammogram continued to experience moderate anxiety even 18 months later as compared to 13% of those who received a negative result (Gram, Lund, & Slenker, 1990). A false positive can also lead to unwarranted medical procedures, including surgery. In some cases, receiving a false-positive result can lead to tragic consequences—a woman who is told her fetus has life-threatening abnormalities could choose to have an abortion, for instance. On the other hand, people who receive false-negative results, meaning the person has the disease, but the test shows he or she doesn't, can experience a false sense of security (e.g., comfort with practicing unsafe sex). Receiving a false-negative test result also deprives the person of the opportunity to start treatment, a delay that can have devastating consequences in the case of illnesses such as cancer.

Finally, some of the techniques used to screen people for medical conditions can actually cause physical harm (Simon, 1977; Henifin, 1993). For example, the use of mammography to detect breast cancer exposes women to radiation, which is itself linked to cancer. Amniocentesis, a procedure in which fluid is drawn from the sack surrounding a fetus to test for abnormalities, causes miscarriage in between 1 and 200 and 1 and 400 cases. Similarly, *chorionic villus sampling*, another type of prenatal testing, which can be done at 9 to 12 weeks of pregnancy, leads to miscarriage in 1 in 100 cases. Given these consequences, health professionals generally recommend that people undergo screening only when the risk of the disorder is greater than the risk of experiencing a negative outcome of the test. For example, it is recommended that women over age 35 years, who are at increased risk of having a baby with Down's syndrome, undergo amniocentesis, but this procedure is not generally recommended for younger women (Henifen, 1993).

Strategies for Increasing Screening

Although screening can have significant benefits, many people do not follow screening recommendations (Kornguth, Keefe, & Conaway, 1996; Newcomb et al., 1991; Shepperd et al., 1990; Stevens, Hatcher, & Bruce, 1994). For example, the current guidelines from the American Cancer Society state that women should engage in a monthly breast self-exam, have a yearly clinical breast exam, and have a yearly mammogram starting at age 40. However, only 25 to 30% of women report performing BSE monthly, only one third of women report having had a clinical breast exam in the past year, and only 63% report having had a clinical exam in the past 3 years (Newcomb et al., 1991; Shepperd et al., 1990). Similarly, as of 2008 only 81% of women ages 50 years or older reported having had a mammogram in the past 2 years, and only 63% of American adults ages 50 and over have had a colon cancer screening (Centers for Disease Control and Prevention, 2010a, 2010b). So, how can we increase screening?

First, some people simply are not aware of the need to screen; so one way of increasing screening is simply to provide education about its benefits (Jepson & Rimer, 1993; Rimer, 1994; Rimer et al., 2001). Various interventions, including mass mailings, brochures, and mass-media campaigns, have been somewhat successful in increasing screening behaviors (Rimer, 1994; Rimer et al., 2001). For example, college men who read a brochure on testicular self-exam (TSE) develop more positive attitudes and greater intentions to perform TSE (Brubaker & Wickersham, 1990). Similarly, women who receive information about the benefits of mammograms are four times as likely to have a mammogram as those who do not receive such information (Champion, 1994). In cases in which the person must actually perform the screening behavior themselves, such as in the case of BSE and TSE, people also need training in exactly how to do it (Alagna & Reddy, 1984; Jones et al., 1993; Kegeles, 1985).

Celebrities Christina Applegate, Sheryl Crow, and Melissa Etheridge have been very public about their own battles with breast cancer, which in turn may well have influenced other women's decisions regarding breast cancer screening and treatment.
Source: Michael Caulfield/Stand Up To Cancer via Getty Images.

Celebrities exert a powerful influence on increasing awareness about the importance of screening. Researchers in one study examined the impact of Katie Couric's decision to have her colonoscopy shown on the *Today Show* to promote awareness of colorectal cancer on rates of colonoscopies (Katie Couric had lost her 42-year-old husband to colon cancer in 1992; Cram et al., 2003). The number of colonoscopies performed increased significantly in the month after the airing of her procedure on the *Today Show* (from 15.0 per month before this show to 18.1 per month afterwards). Moreover, this higher rate of colonoscopies performed was sustained for 9 months.

In other cases, people are aware of the need to screen, but simply forget to do so; hence, providing reminders can be an effective way of increasing screening (Craun & Deffenbacher, 1987; Mayer & Frederiksen, 1986; Strauss, Solomon, Costanza, Worden, & Foster, 1987). For example, some college campuses put instructions for breast and testicular self-exams in shower stalls in college dormitories in an effort to increase rates of screening. One study compared the rates of screening for those who were randomly assigned to one of three conditions: an educational format (provided information about breast cancer and BSE), a demonstration format (showed a demonstration of correct BSE and allowed patients to practice), and a reminder-only format (women received a monthly postcard saying "remember to practice BSE this month"; Craun & Deffenbacher, 1987). The use of the reminder was the most effective in increasing BSE frequency.

Another strategy that helps people remember to screen is asking them to form their own specific plans about the how, where, and when they will engage in screening behavior (Orbell, Hodgkins, & Sheeran, 1997; Sheeran & Orbell, 2000). Setting this type of implementation intention increases the likelihood of screening by helping people to develop specific plans for following through on their intentions. For example, Orbell et al. (1997) asked 188 college women about their intentions to perform BSE, and of these, half were asked to write down where and when they would complete this exam. At the 1-month follow-up, all of the women who made an implementation intention reported completing the exam as compared to 53% of those who did not form such a specific plan. Another study found that 92% of those who formed an implementation intention attended a cervical cancer screening as compared to 69% of those who did not.

Because the actual or perceived costs of screening, such as convenience, embarrassment, expense, and anxiety about pain, deter screening, removing these barriers is another effective way of increasing this type of health-promoting behavior (Aiken et al., 1994; Jepson & Rimer, 1993; Rimer et al., 2001). One study by Rimer et al. found that using mobile vans, similar to bloodmobiles, led to higher rates of mammograms (1992). Similarly, interventions that decrease the costs of mammography are effective at increasing screening, particularly among low-income people and those who do not have health insurance (Kiefe, McKay, Halevy, & Brody, 1994). For example, in one study with female patients at a health clinic for migrant workers, women who received a voucher for a free mammogram were 47 times more likely to have a mammogram than women who did not have such a voucher (Skaer, Robinson, Sclar, & Harding, 1996). Finally, because some people do not engage in screening because of fear of what they might find, it is important to try to reassure people that catching disease early is the best approach to maintaining health.

How Do Psychological Factors Influence Health-Care Utilization, Interaction, Hospitalization, and Burnout?

Kasl and Cobb (1966a, 1966b) distinguish three types of health-related behaviors. First, **health behavior** refers to behavior that is designed to promote a person's good health and prevent illness. This type of behavior could include exercising regularly, wearing a seatbelt, and getting immunizations to prevent disease. Second, *symptom* or **illness behavior** describes behavior that is directed toward determining one's health status after experiencing symptoms. This could include talking to other people—family and friends as well as health professionals—monitoring symptoms yourself, and reading about your health problem. One of the most common illness behaviors is doing nothing and just waiting to see if the symptom will go away on its own! Third, **sick-role behavior** describes behavior that is directed at helping people who are ill return to good health (Parsons, 1951, 1975). The sick role has certain perks, including receiving sympathy and care from others and being exempt from daily responsibilities, such as chores, work, and classes. However, the person who is sick also has the responsibility to try to get better, which can include seeking medical attention and following medical recommendations. In this section, we examine health-care utilization and patient–practitioner interaction, which are two major issues in illness behavior; the experience of hospitalization, which is one major issue in sick-role behavior; and, finally, the very real problem of burnout in medical professionals.

Health-Care Utilization

In many cases, seeking urgent care for a medical problem is very important—sometimes even a matter of life or death. For example, seeking diagnosis of cancer can make a large difference in treatment success because cancers that are caught at an early stage can be treated directly and with less-invasive procedures, whereas cancer that has metastasized (spread to other parts of the body) is much more difficult to treat. Women with breast cancer who delay seeking help less than 3 months have an 8-year survival rate of 50% as compared to 31% survival rate for those who delay treatment 6 months or more (Neale, Tilley, & Vernon, 1986). So, what factors lead people to delay seeking medical care?

First, people vary in how quickly they notice a physical experience. Some people pay more attention to their internal states than others and are more likely to notice symptoms (Pennebaker, 1982). For example, Miller, Brody, and Summerton (1988) distinguish between monitors, who actively think about and focus on the physical sensations they are feeling, and blunters, who tend to deny or ignore these sensations. People who are high in neuroticism or negative affect may also notice symptoms faster (as discussed in Chapter 5; Gramling, Clawson, & McDonald, 1996). Similarly, research demonstrates that people with hypochondriacal tendencies, those who are preoccupied with illness, are particularly likely both to set health-related goals and pay attention to illness-related information (Lecci & Cohen, 2002; Lecci, Karoly, Ruehlman, & Lanyon, 1996).

Situational and social factors also influence how and even whether we perceive various symptoms (Pennebaker, 1982). In fact, people who are bored with their jobs and socially isolated tend to notice symptoms more quickly, possibly because they have fewer distractions. In contrast, sometimes athletes suffer an injury during a game but do not notice the pain until the game is over. Similarly, the messages we get from friends, family members, and health professionals influence whether we notice as well as how we interpret health symptoms. You may have ignored an odd-shaped mole on your arm, for example, but may become concerned after a friend remarks that it could be a sign of cancer.

People's expectations about the symptoms they should experience may influence how intensely, and even whether, they feel various symptoms. For example, women who believe that most women experience severe physical symptoms prior to menstruation recall experiencing more symptoms themselves than they actually do (Marvan & Cortes-Iniestra, 2001). These expectations can be created very easily. In one study, people who were told that the inert substance they smelled was harmful reported experiencing more irritation and health symptoms than those who were told the odor was neutral or healthful (Dalton, 1999).

In some cases, these expectations can even cause various physical symptoms, such as rashes, nausea, and headaches, a phenomenon called *mass psychogenic illness*. When I teach the abnormal psychology section of my Introduction to Psychology course, an amazing thing happens each semester. As I describe the various clinical disorders (e.g., depression, schizophrenia), students all of a sudden recognize these relatively rare disorders in many of the people in their lives—their parents, siblings, friends, roommates, and sometimes even themselves all have abnormal psychological diseases. (This type of reaction is sometimes called "medical student's disease" because medical students, who study the symptoms of many serious but rare diseases, often come to believe that any relatively minor symptoms are a sign of more serious disorders; Mechanic, 1972). This type of reaction, namely hearing about a symptom and then suddenly seeing that symptom in everyone you know, can lead large numbers of people, typically in a relatively small and isolated group, to report experiencing particular symptoms. For example, students in a school may hear about a specific virus that is going around or a suspected case of food poisoning, and suddenly many will report experiencing related symptoms. Researchers believe that drawing people's attention to a particular type of symptom leads people to engage in careful (even too careful) monitoring of their bodies and to interpret various minor symptoms, such as a headache or nausea, as caused by the suspected problem.

Even after people notice a particular symptom, they do not necessarily decide that it requires medical attention. According to the self-regulatory model of illness behavior developed by Leventhal, Meyer, and Nerenz at Rutgers University (1980), people form *commonsense illness representations* about their symptoms, and these representations determine the steps the person must take, if any, to manage that illness. First, they try to *identify* the nature of their illness as well as its *cause*, based on the symptoms they are experiencing. If you are feeling pain in your stomach, you might interpret this as a stomach flu (a relatively mild condition) or appendicitis (a severe condition). But we often make wrong attributions; for example, older people often attribute symptoms such as tiredness and memory loss to aging, when these could be signs of disease (Leventhal & Prochaska, 1986). Cameron, Leventhal, and Leventhal (1995) found that people who experience a new and ambiguous symptom typically seek help relatively quickly, unless they are under conditions of stress, in which case they attribute the symptom to stress and delay seeking medical care. Third, they try to figure out the *time line* of the illness, or how long it will last. People who believe their illness is acute, temporary, and likely to disappear soon, are more likely to drop out of treatment than those who believe their illness is chronic, ongoing, and likely to continue (Meyer, Leventhal, & Gutmann, 1985). Fourth, they think about the *consequences* of their illness, including physical consequences (e.g., pain), social consequences (e.g., ability to go out with friends, play sports), and emotional consequences (e.g., loneliness, boredom). People tend to ignore symptoms that do not disrupt their daily lives much but are quite motivated to seek medical care for more disruptive symptoms. Finally, people think about whether the illness can be *treated and cured* and whether such treatment needs to be given by a doctor. If they believe that seeking a doctor won't help, they may not see a doctor or follow medical recommendations.

Safer, Tharps, Jackson, and Leventhal (1979) developed the **stages of delay model** to describe the steps people go through when deciding to get help (see Figure 12.2; Anderson, Cacioppo, & Roberts, 1995). First, even after people experience—and notice—some type of symptoms, they often show a delay in deciding whether they are ill. This type of delay is called an **appraisal delay**. For example, you might notice a small lump under your armpit, but decide it is just a clogged gland. Even after people decide they are sick, they may delay seeking professional help. **Illness delay** refers to the time between when people acknowledge they are sick and when they decide that help from a professional is required. People often believe that the symptoms will go away on their own and delay seeking medical care. For example, you may have a nagging sore throat for some time but decide that you should see a doctor only when it lasts more

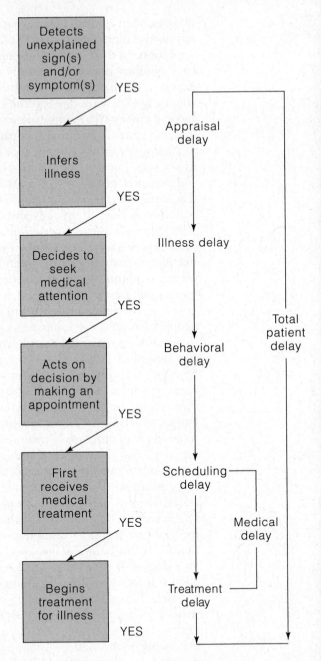

FIGURE 12.2 Even after people notice a physical symptom, they are likely to delay seeking medical attention (Anderson et al., 1995).

than a week. Even after people decide that medical care is required, they may delay making an appointment and actually going to a professional; this is called **behavioral** (or **utilization**) **delay**. **Scheduling delay** refers to the amount of time between scheduling the appointment and actually going to the appointment. (Ironically, one study of length of scheduling delay in seeing a dermatologist in a major metropolitan area found that the wait times for patients seeking a botulism injection—a cosmetic procedure—average only 8 days, whereas the wait time for patients seeking an evaluation for a mole that appears to be changing—a symptom of skin cancer—average 26 days; Resneck, Lipton & Pletcher, 2007). Finally, **treatment delay** refers to the delay between receiving medical recommendations and acting on these recommendations.

What predicts when and how long people delay? The biggest predictor of length of delay during the appraisal phase is the nature of the symptoms—delay is short when people are experiencing very strong and clear signals that there is a problem, such as severe pain and bleeding (Eifert, Hodson, Tracey, Seville, & Gunawardan, 1996; Safer et al., 1979). For example, one study found that patients who were experiencing little or no severe pain waited an average of 7.5 days before seeking medical help, whereas those who were experiencing severe pain waited an average of 2.5 days. Similarly, patients who were bleeding delayed only 1.2 days compared to 4.8 days for those who were not bleeding. People also tend to seek help quickly for symptoms that involve a "vital organ," such as the heart (Eifert et al., 1996) and when they experience new, unexpected, visible, serious/disruptive, and continuous symptoms (Prochaska, Keller, Leventhal, & Leventhal, 1987; Safer et al., 1979). On the other hand, people tend to delay seeking help for symptoms that they have had for some time (Jemmott, Croyle, & Ditto, 1988); for symptoms that others they know have (Croyle & Hunt, 1991); for symptoms that are in private body parts, such as the genital area and anus (Klonoff & Landrine, 1993); and for symptoms that cause little pain and disruption (Safer et al., 1979). As described at the beginning of this chapter, Peter's embarrassment about the discharge from his penis and pain during urination inhibited him from getting help for these symptoms from a doctor.

Unfortunately, this reluctance to seek help for symptoms that don't involve pain or disruption can lead people to delay seeking help when they have a symptom of cancer, such as a change in the color and size of a mole or a small lump under the skin, in part because cancer is not initially painful (Timko, 1987). One study by Timko (1987) of Yale University examined the factors that influenced whether women who noticed a lump in the breasts would promptly seek medical help. In this study, 134 women between the ages of 35 and 65 years completed a questionnaire that included reading a specific medical scenario and several scales measuring attitudes and intentions about seeking medical advice (see Table 12.5).

TABLE 12.5 *Scenario Used to Simulate Early Symptoms of Breast Cancer*

The scenario read as follows:

"One morning, Ann woke up and took a shower before getting dressed to leave the house. As Ann was showering, she happened to feel a hard, tiny thickening on the edge of her left nipple. The bump was quite small, smaller than the size of a pea. Ann wasn't sure there was anything unusual about the spot. Aside from this change, she hadn't noticed anything about her physical condition that was different from normal. Ann got out of the shower and thought about what she should do. She considered immediately calling a doctor for an appointment, but she thought that in this case it might be best to monitor the change herself for a while. The thickening was tiny and Ann was feeling as well as she usually did. Ann knew that women sometimes get lumps in their breast which soon disappear by themselves. She was not an alarmist, and she would closely watch the lump on her own. Ann decided she would call the doctor if the thickening persisted, grew, or changed. She felt that, for the time being, there was no risk in not calling the doctor."

This scenario was used to assess how women would respond to noticing an early symptom of breast cancer.

Participants were then asked to imagine that what happened to Ann had just happened to them and to answer the rest of the questionnaire items as if they had just noticed a lump in their breast. First, women who believed they would feel more upset about finding the lump were more likely to report seeking medical help, as were those who saw the symptom as potentially life-threatening and a sign of breast cancer were more likely to intend to seek help. Finally, this study found that women who were generally responsible in seeking regular health care were also more likely to report intending to seek help quickly.

Questioning the Research 12.2

Do people's responses about what they would do in this hypothetical situation predict what they would do if this situation really happened? Do you think the findings from this study would apply in real-world situations? Why or why not?

People's concern about the impact of the symptom can also influence the length of delay (Safer et al., 1979). For example, people who imagine severe negative consequences of being ill (e.g., can imagine themselves on the operating room table) wait an average of 1.9 days, whereas those without such imagery delay 4.4 days. Because people don't like to experience pain, they tend to avoid—if at all possible—procedures and treatments that they believe will cause pain. For example, an estimated 12 to 15% of the U.S. population never visits a dentist, in part because of fear of pain (Sokol, Sokol, & Sokol, 1985), and one study found that 77% of women who indicated they would not undergo a future mammogram rated the experience of having a mammogram as "very uncomfortable" or "intolerable" (Jackson, Lex, & Smith, 1988). People also show longer delays if they don't think the disease can be cured.

Delay can also be caused by people's desire to seek information before resorting to the medical profession (Safer et al., 1979). People often rely on a lay referral network of friends and family to provide insight about health-care symptoms and suggested treatment (Freidson, 1961). Similarly, people may choose to consult books and/or websites in an attempt to diagnose, and even treat, their health problem, and they turn to health-care professionals only if they believe medical treatment is necessary (Matthews, Siegel, Kuller, Thompson, & Varat, 1983).

Demographic factors also influence people's willingness and interest in seeking health care (Baum & Grunberg, 1991; Klonoff & Landrine, 1994). People who are very young, namely, infants and small children, often have very regular medical care: Infants, for example, typically go to the doctor at 1 month, 2 months, 4 months, 6 months, 9 months, and 12 months of age! People who are very old also tend to seek medical care frequently, often because they have chronic conditions that require regular attention. Women are more likely than men to seek help and also have greater health knowledge (Addis & Mahalik, 2003; Beier & Ackerman, 2003). Pregnancy and childbirth, which typically involve frequent medical appointments, account for some of the difference, but not all. One possibility is that women are more focused on and aware of their physical states, so they are more likely than men to notice physical symptoms (Pennebaker, 1982). Another possibility is that women are simply more willing to admit they need help, whereas men may see expressing pain as a sign of weakness.

Not surprisingly, income influences how often, and where, people seek health care (Adler, Boyce, Chesney, Folkman, & Syne, 1993; Flack et al., 1995; Kaplan & Kiel, 1993). Although people in higher socioeconomic classes have fewer health symptoms than those with lower incomes, they seek health care more often. In contrast, those in lower socioeconomic classes are less likely to seek regular preventive care (e.g., prenatal care, regular check-ups, and vaccinations), and therefore they are more likely to experience major illnesses that require care (including hospitalization). While 3.4% of those with a family income over $100,00 report being in fair or poor health, 18.1% of those with family income below $35,000 report these levels of health (U.S. Department of Health and Human Services, 2011). And when people in low socioeconomic classes seek help, it is more likely to come from emergency rooms than private doctors' offices. In some cases, patients' concern about the monetary cost of the treatment can lead to delay. In fact, patients who are very concerned about cost delay an average of 9.7 days, whereas those without such concern delay only 2.0 days (Safer et al., 1979).

Culture and religion influence how likely people are to utilize medical services (Bates, Edwards, & Anderson, 1993; Landrine & Klonoff, 1994; Sanders et al., 1992). First, people from different cultural backgrounds vary in their awareness of and attention to physical symptoms, as well as in their willingness to express such symptoms (Burnam, Timbers, & Hough, 1984). For example, Americans tend to report much more pain and impairment from back pain than do people from other countries. Cultural factors may also influence people's beliefs in the efficacy of medicine in general. For example, people from cultures that place a greater priority on using lay referral systems (e.g., family and friends) for advice about health problems may be reluctant to seek medical attention for such concerns. Similarly, people who practice certain religions, including Christian Scientists and Jehovah's Witnesses, reject the use of some or all medical treatments completely, including blood transfusions and antibiotics.

Race and ethnicity also influence people's utilization of medical care in several ways. Nearly twice as many African Americans as Whites report they are in fair or poor health, in part because minorities are much less likely than Whites to have access to regular health care (Mead et al., 2008). In turn, minorities are less likely to receive preventive treatment (e.g., immunizations) and more likely to receive treatment for medical conditions at later—and less treatable—stages (Adler et al., 1993; Adler et al., 1994; Gornick et al., 1996). Race may also influence preference for different types of medical procedures. Researchers in one study found that African Americans have lower expectations about the benefits of knee replacements than do Whites, and express a stronger preference for using natural remedies and avoiding surgery (Figaro, Russo, & Allegrante, 2004).

Research also suggests that minorities receive less-aggressive treatment for both diagnosing and treating serious illnesses, including coronary heart disease (CHD) and cancer (Fiscella, Franks, Gold, & Clancy, 2000; Schulman et al., 1999). For example, one study published in the *New England Journal of Medicine* reported that 45.7% of White patients who were hospitalized for a heart attack received cardiac catheterization within 60 days of the attack as compared to 38.4% of African American patients (Chen, Rathore, Radford, Wang, & Krumholz, 2001).

Catheterization allows doctors to determine whether blood vessels are blocked and, hence, is an important step in determining whether patients require other treatments, such as heart bypass surgery. African Americans are also less likely than White patients to be referred to a cardiologist following a report of heart symptoms or to receive angioplasty (repair of blood vessels by surgery) or bypass surgery (Crawford, McGraw, Smith, McKinlay, & Pierson, 1994); Whittle, Conigliaro, Good, & Lofgren, 1993). Similarly, Bach, Cramer, Warren, and Begg (1999) found that 64% of African American patients with lung cancer received surgery, whereas 76.7% of White patients received surgery. And sadly, this difference in rate of surgery was associated with survival rates 5 years later: 34.1% of Whites survived to this point as compared to 26.4% of African Americans.

Similarly, research reveals consistent gender differences in the likelihood of receiving particular types of medical procedures. For example, in one study, researchers examined all the cases of men and women hospitalized for CHD in Massachusetts and Maryland in a particular year (Ayanian & Epstein, 1991). They then examined the percentage undergoing various medical procedures as a function of sex. The results (at least from the point of view of women) were not encouraging: Men were overall 15 to 45% more likely than women to receive these major diagnostic and therapeutic procedures. Although women experienced symptoms that were even more disabling and severe than men's symptoms, their chest pains were addressed using less-sophisticated medical procedures for diagnosis and treatment. For example, 27.3% of the men underwent cardiac catheterization, compared to 15.4% of the women, and 12.7% of the men underwent coronary bypass surgery, compared to 5.9% of the women (Steingart et al., 1991).

What causes these dramatic gender differences in receiving potentially life-saving procedures? In part, physicians are less likely to see chest pain in women as a sign of CHD as they are in men. Specifically, physicians may be more likely to see women's physical symptoms as a sign of psychological problems, such as depression or anxiety. For example, in one study, medical students were played an audiotape of a patient complaining of symptoms typical of depression (Hall, Epstein, DeCiantis, & McNeil, 1993). When the patient was a female, the students perceived her as less seriously ill, less in need of lab tests and follow-up care, and more likely to require psychiatric evaluation than when the patient was male. Similarly, and as shown in Figure 12.3, the presence of stressful life events has no impact on the likelihood of diagnosing CHD or providing a referral to a cardiologist for male patients with symptoms of CHD, but female patients who report experiencing more stressful life events are much less likely to receive such a diagnosis or a referral (Chiaramonte & Friend, 2006).

Finally, although many people delay seeking medical help, others overuse medical care (Costa & McCrae, 1985, 1987; Larsen, 1992; Miranda, Perez-Stable, Munoz, Hargreaves, & Henke, 1991). People with *hypochondria* are very concerned about their health and interpret relatively benign symptoms as signs of more serious problems. For example, a person with hypochondria might interpret a headache as a sign of a brain tumor. In turn, these "worried well" people seek medical attention for a variety of minor problems (Wagner & Curran, 1984). Similarly, *somaticizers* develop physical symptoms in response to psychological issues and, hence, seek medical treatment for problems that have no physical cause (Miranda et al., 1991). For example, people who are constantly anxious could develop stomach pains or

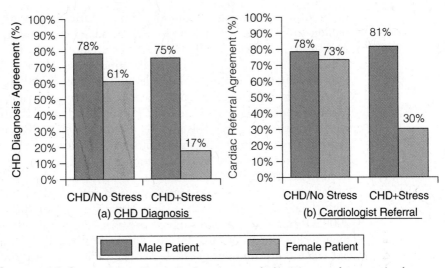

FIGURE 12.3   In this study, medical students and physicians read a scenario about a patient with symptoms of CHD and then reported their proposed diagnosis as well as whether they would make a referral to a cardiologist. Although the presence of stressful life events has no impact on the diagnosis and referral for male patients, female patients who report experiencing stressful life events are much less likely to receive a diagnosis of CHD or a referral to a cardiologist (data from Chiaramonte & Friend, 2006).

other physical problems. Several large-scale studies have shown that people who are high in neuroticism (i.e., self-consciousness, have a vulnerability to stress, and have a tendency to experience negative emotions) report experiencing many health symptoms and exaggerate the severity of these symptoms (Ellington & Weibe, 1999). Some research suggests that many people who seek medical attention frequently may be suffering from psychological problems, including anxiety and depression (Malt et al., 1997; Simon, Gater, Kisely, & Piccinelli, 1996).

Patient–Practitioner Communication

After a person has decided to see a doctor for help with a medical condition, a variety of factors regarding the patient–practitioner relationship can influence the nature of that interaction. Communication is a crucial aspect of interaction between practitioner and patient: 75% of any doctor's diagnosis is made on the basis of the patient's history (Leitzell, 1977), so patients need to be able to clearly express their symptoms (Mentzer & Snyder, 1982). Despite the importance of communication, health-care providers and patients often have difficulty communicating effectively.

First, patients can be reluctant to share certain types of highly personal information, such as sexual problems and embarrassing symptoms (Julliard et al., 2008; Mentzer & Snyder, 1982; Thompson, 1984). This concern is most common when there are differences between the doctor and patient in terms of age, gender, social class, and ethnicity (Reiff, Zakut, & Weingarten, 1999). For example, health professionals typically call patients by their first names, regardless of whether the age of the patient is greater than that of the practitioner, and this is a sign of disrespect in the African American community; hence, African American patients may be less willing to provide information as well as adhere to medical recommendations if so disrespected (Flack et al., 1995). Patients who believe they have very complex problems often aren't sure how to describe these symptoms to their doctors and thus may not share important information (Peters et al., 2009). Patients may also try to minimize how much pain they are experiencing—male patients, for example, report experiencing less pain to females than they do to males (Levine & DeSimone, 1991)! In other cases, patients may believe the doctor is able to discern their medical condition even without disclosing information. For example, they may believe that their symptoms will be evident throughout medical testing and that there is no need to describe them.

Patients also may be reluctant to share their feelings, including anxiety and fear, with their physicians, which in turn impairs good communication (Peters et al., 2009). Researchers in one study found that cancer patients are reluctant to share their feelings of emotional distress with their physicians, in part because they do not want to disturb their physicians or fear such a disclosure would have a negative impact (Okuyama et al., 2008). Moreover, breast-cancer patients who receive more helpful informational, emotional, and decision-making support from their physicians report greater trust (Arora & Gustafson, 2009).

Second, doctors often fail to allow patients to provide information about their symptoms and give patients adequate information about their diagnosis, prognosis, and recommended treatment (Ley, 1982; Marvel, Epstein, Flowers, & Beckman, 1999; Waitzkin, 1985). For example, one study of 300 patient–practitioner interactions found that in 72% of cases, physicians interrupted the patient's description of his or her symptoms, and that on average, this interruption occurred after just 23 seconds (Marvel et al., 1999)! Similarly, one recent study of more than 1,000 encounters between physicians and patients revealed that patients received complete information regarding important medical decisions in only 9% of the cases (Braddock, Edwards, Hasenberg, Laidley, & Levinson, 1999). Complete information includes specific details about different treatment options available, such as increasing the dose of one medicine or taking a new medicine, as well as the pros and cons of each option. In contrast, patients typically were told by their physician about the suggested choice (e.g., "I'd suggest you increase the dose of the atenolol you're already taking."). However, patients typically want as much information as possible about their illness (Faden, Becker, Lewis, Freeman, & Faden, 1981; Keown, Slovic, & Lichtenstein, 1984), and those who get more information are more satisfied (see Table 12.6; Hall, Roter, & Katz, 1988; Mentzer & Snyder, 1982). Interestingly, and as described in Box 12.3: Focus on Research, doctors and patients often disagree on the amount and type of information given.

What factors influence how much information is given to patients? Physicians who earn less money—and hence see fewer patients per day—tend to give more information and involve their patients more in making diagnostic and treatment decisions (Kaplan, Greenfield, Gandek, Rogers, & Ware, 1996; Waitzkin, 1985). Compared to male physicians, female physicians have longer appointments, give more information, and ask more questions (Hall, Irish, Roter, Ehrlich, & Miller, 1994; Roter, Lipkin, & Korsgaard, 1991). One meta-analysis found that female physicians engage in more patient-centered behavior, including positive talk,

TABLE 12.6   *How Much Information Would You Want? Would Your Doctor Agree?*

Type of Information	Percentage Who Think Patients Should Be Informed	
	Patients	Physicians
Name of drug	97%	92%
Common risks of normal use	89	85
Overdose information	86	76
Risks of using too little	80	52
Risks of not using at all	79	46
All possible risks of normal use	77	25
Other important uses	75	20

Patients generally want a lot of information, but physicians tend to underestimate this desire, which in turn leads to a gap between what patients want and what they get.
Source: Ley, 1982.

Box 12.3

Focus on Research: Differing Perspectives Between Patients and Physicians on Information Given

Researchers in one study examined how both physicians and their patients viewed the type of information provided and received regarding medical care in a hospital (Olson & Windish, 2010). To test such differences in perspectives, 89 patients and 43 physicians completed surveys about the experience of hospitalization and the care received/given. Findings revealed several differences between how patients and physicians viewed such care. First, although 73% of patients thought they had one main physician, only 18% correctly named who that person was, whereas 67% of physicians thought the patients knew their name and that they were the primary physician. Second, although most physicians (77%) believed that their patients knew their diagnosis, in reality, only 57% of patients were aware of the diagnosis they had received. Finally, although almost all physicians (98%) reported sometimes discussing their patients' fears and anxieties, over half (54%) of patients reported that their physicians never discussed their fears and anxieties. Thus, these findings reveal substantial differences between how patients and physicians see the care provided in a hospital, suggesting that more work needs to be done on improving patient–physician communication.

emotionally focused talk, question asking, and counseling than male physicians (Roter, Hall, & Aoki, 2002). Visits with female physicians on average last about 2 minutes longer. Although female physicians generally spend more time with patients than do male physicians, they have especially long appointments when they are seeing female patients (Hall et al., 1988).

Patient characteristics also influence the amount of information that is given: Patients who are White, female, college-educated, and from an upper-middle-class background tend to get more information, ask more questions, and have longer appointments (Epstein, Taylor, & Seage, 1985; Hall et al., 1988; Waitzkin, 1985). One study revealed that high socioeconomic status patients received an average consultation of 7.3 minutes compared to 6.3 minutes for those in the middle-status group and 5.8 minutes for those in the low-status group (Pendleton & Bochner, 1980). Finally, situational characteristics, including knowing the doctor for a longer period of time and having a serious illness, lead to getting more information.

Even when doctors do convey information to their patients, much of this information may be forgotten or misunderstood (Ley, 1982; Thompson, 1984). In fact, approximately 40% of what doctors say during a consultation is immediately forgotten. Researchers in one study examined how well people recall information they are given about their health-related risks (Croyle et al., 2006). Although 90% of participants remembered their general cardiovascular risk pretty well a month after receiving the results, only 48% were accurate in remembering their cholesterol. Not surprisingly, accuracy also declined over time. Moreover, although all participants generally remembered their health status as being better than it actually was, people at the highest level of cholesterol risk had the most optimistic recollections. Patients who are anxious are particularly susceptible to forgetting information (Charles, Goldsmith, Chambers, & Haynes, 1996), as are those who receive results from a worried doctor (Shapiro, Boggs, Melamed, & Graham, 1992).

Patients may also misinterpret the information they are given, especially if it includes complex medical jargon (Hadlow & Pitts, 1991). Patients may not understand a variety of terms commonly used by medical professionals, including *malignant, benign, void, sodium, migraine, stroke,* and *eating disorders.* Even telling a patient a test is positive or negative may be confusing to him or her—learning that the results of an HIV test is "positive" may seem like good news, but in reality it means the patient has contracted the disease. Although the use of medical jargon often is unintentional, in some cases, physicians deliberately use confusing terms as a way of avoiding giving patients potentially upsetting information. For example, a physician may say "We're worried about adreno-CA" to avoid directly mentioning the risk of lung cancer, or "This is not an entirely benign procedure" to avoid describing the pain caused by a given procedure (Klass, 1987).

Finally, people often misinterpret statistics they are given about the relative risks of various medical procedures and health risks. One study in the *Journal of the National Cancer Institute* suggests that physicians should convey health risks to patients by describing the risk in terms of individual people as opposed to an abstract risk estimate (Woloshin, Schwartz, & Welch, 2002). For example, patients think that a disease that kills 7 out of every 1,000 people is more common than one that has a death rate of 0.7%, even though these numbers represent the same odds. One study even found that medical students and residents are less accurate in interpreting the best Medicare drug plan for patients to choose when they are given too many plans to consider (Hanoch, Miron-Shatz, Cole, Himmelstein, & Federman, 2010).

Many of these problems in patient–practitioner interaction are caused by old-fashioned models of these relationships. Szasz and Hollender (1956) described three models of the patient–practitioner relationship: activity-passivity, guidance-cooperation, and mutual participation. The first model describes relationships in

Box 12.4

Focus on Culture: Attitudes Toward the Doctor–Patient Relationship Vary by Culture

Researchers in one study examined attitudes toward patient-centeredness in students attending a medical school in Singapore and compared these attitudes to those found in previous research in the United States (Lee, Seow, Luo, & Koh, 2008). In this study, 228 medical students entering their third year of medical school in Asia completed a questionnaire assessing their level of patient-centeredness, which assessed both students' focus on sharing information and caring about the patients' feelings. Female students as well as those with personal experience providing continuing care reported higher scores on both caring about patients and sharing information with patients. However, comparing these results with prior research with students attending medical school in the United States revealed that although students in both cultures had similar scores on caring about patients, American students reported higher scores on sharing information with patients than did students in Singapore. These findings suggest that Americans may be more likely to view the doctor–patient relationship as a partnership, whereas those in Asian cultures may be more likely to prefer a doctor-centered decision-making process. This distinction may be a reflection of differences in cultural norms and expectations of doctor–patient interaction in different societies.

which the doctor is entirely in control, and the patient is completely passive. This type of model is probably now best suited for describing situations in which the patient is unconscious (e.g., in surgery, in a coma), or when the patient is very young. However, this model was the common approach to medicine for much of the 1900s (Laine & Davidoff, 1996). The second model is probably still the most common model in medical practice today: The patient's thoughts and feelings are voiced, but the doctor still makes the major decisions. The third model, which is favored by those who prefer a more active involvement in their own medical care, describes a mutual interaction, in which both the patient and the practitioner share information and make decisions together. This might be the most appropriate model for describing how people manage a chronic illness, for example. However, and as described in Box 12.4: Focus on Culture, cultures vary in the attitudes they hold about the preferred nature of the doctor–patient relationship.

There are several techniques to improve patient–practitioner interaction. First, health-care providers must pay attention not just to people's physical complaints but also to their psychological concerns (Delbanco, 1992; Hall & Dornan, 1988a, 1988b). A man who is receiving treatment for prostate cancer, for example, may be more concerned about the potential side effect of impotence and its impact on his marriage than about his life expectancy. Basically, physicians must view patients as people, not just as walking medical diseases or conditions! Second, health-care providers must give straightforward explanations about the problem and its treatment, in terms that are at the appropriate level—not too complex and not too simplistic (Hall & Dornan, 1988a, 1988b; Mentzer & Snyder, 1982; Thompson,

1984; Waitzkin, 1984). Third, physicians must show better nonverbal behavior, such as maintaining eye contact, leaning toward the patient, and nodding their heads (Hall et al., 1988; LaCrosse, 1975). Physicians who engage in this type of verbal and nonverbal behavior are seen as warmer and friendlier, and in turn, their patients are more satisfied with their treatment—and are more likely to show up for future appointments (Feletti, Firman, & Sanson-Fisher, 1986; Yarnold, Michelson, Thompson, & Adams, 1998). For example, 86% of those who are pleased with their doctor's communication skills are satisfied with their medical care as compared to 25% of those who are not pleased with their doctor's communication skills (Mentzer & Snyder, 1982). They are also less likely to switch doctors—one study found that, of physicians who engaged in high levels of interactive decision making with patients, only 15% of patients changed physicians within a year, as compared to 33% of those who were least interactive with their practitioners (Kaplan et al., 1996). Patients also give more information to physicians who engage in this type of verbal and nonverbal behavior, which can help doctors make more accurate diagnoses more quickly (Hall et al., 1994; Marvel et al., 1999).

These findings all point to the importance of good physician–patient relationships for improving satisfaction with medical care. In fact, patients' trust in their physician is one of the largest predictors of their satisfaction with the outcome of their treatment (Janssen, Ommen, Ruppert, & Pfaff, 2008). Patients who believe they are treated with respect and honesty by the doctor are also more willing to both confide information and follow the doctor's recommendations (Carroll, Smith, & Hillier, 2008). Similarly, research with pregnant women with a history of problems found that provision of information, constructive communication, and good relationships predicted elevated satisfaction with health services (Lerman et al., 2007). In sum, physicians who have an ability to build rapport with their patients can foster better communication, increase empathy and compassion, and lead to the establishment of trusting relationships in which disclosure is more likely. These characteristics may be particularly important when interacting with racial and ethnic minorities, who are more likely than Whites to have lower levels of trust and satisfaction with their physician (Hunt, Gaba, & Lavizzo-Mourey, 2005). In line with this view, research with Latina patients found that they were more willing to share information if their physician demonstrated interpersonal qualities, such as compassion, caring, human interest, and kindness (Julliard et al., 2008).

Given the tremendous value of effective patient–practitioner communication, some hospitals have developed training programs that specifically focus on encouraging these types of skills (Tosteson, 1990). Researchers in one study randomly assigned 156 physicians to one of four interventions: control, physician trained (physicians received a workshop on communication skills, adherence, interpersonal difficulties, etc.), patient trained (patients received a 20-minute audio CD about planning questions for physicians and asking questions and making sure you had understanding), or both (Haskard et al., 2008). Physician training improved physicians' information giving, counseling, and communication, and increased patients' ratings of quality of care and willingness to recommend their physician to others (and this type of training was especially beneficial if both the physician and patient were trained). Similarly, researchers in one study examined whether medical students who received a communications curriculum showed improved skills in this domain (Yedidia et al., 2003). Encouragingly, students who were exposed to this curriculum showed improvements on overall communication, relationship development and maintenance, organization and time management, patient assessment, and negotiation and shared decision making. These findings provide encouraging evidence that this type of training can lead to more satisfaction with medical care and better patient outcomes.

Patients also have a role in creating more effective doctor–patient interaction—those who take an active role in their medical care receive better care (Greenfield, Kaplan, Ware, Yano, & Frank, 1988; Greenfield & Kaplan, 1985; Thompson, Nanni, & Schwankovsky, 1990). One study revealed that patients who received a 20-minute session in "assertiveness training," which focused on how to convey honest and accurate information to their physician, asked specific questions regarding medical care and negotiate these decisions and got more information from their doctor (Greenfield & Kaplan, 1985). They also report fewer health symptoms and miss fewer days of work, even 4 months later. Even having patients list the questions they have for their physician increases doctor–patient communication and patient satisfaction (Thompson et al., 1990). Most important, the patients who benefit most from being assertive are those who are the least likely to receive aggressive treatment, namely, those who are African American, poor, and in generally bad health (Krupat et al., 1999).

Finally, although most patients tend to prefer a more patient-centered style of interaction, others do prefer a more doctor-centered style, and, most important, patients are most satisfied when their physician uses the patients' preferred style. In one study by Krupat et al. (2000), people read two doctor–patient scenarios and then rated how satisfied they would have been if they were the patient in each. In one scenario, the physician exhibited a controlling, doctor-centered style: The physician focused on the biomedical meaning of the symptoms, used closed-ended questions, gave relatively little information, and maintained an air of neutrality. In the other, the physician exhibited a more open, patient-centered style: The physician used open-ended questions and showed warmth and personal interest in the patient. Although patient-centered physicians overall generated more satisfaction, people who preferred a patient-centered style (e.g., those who agreed with such statements as "the patient and doctor share responsibility for making a diagnosis") were more satisfied with a patient-oriented doctor, whereas those who preferred a more physician-centered style (e.g., those who agreed with such statements as "if doctors are truly skilled at diagnosis and treatment, the way they interact with patients is relatively unimportant") were more satisfied with doctor-centered physicians. This research suggests that physicians may need to adopt a congruent style with patient preferences to experience a good doctor–patient relationship. Training could focus on helping physicians recognize the orientations of their patients and being flexible in the interviewing style that they adopt.

The Experience of Hospitalization

Over 34 million people are admitted to the hospital each year, for an average stay of almost 5 days (CDC, 2011). The hospital is a very unique setting in that it is one of the only places (perhaps along with prison) in which a person gives up virtually every aspect of control, including normal control of one's body, the opportunity to engage in rewarding activities such as work and recreation, and the ability to

Box 12.5

Focus on Development: The Difficulties of Hospitalization on Children

Of the more than 41 million people who have surgery each year, more than 2 million are children under the age of 15 years (www.cdc.gov/nchs/fastats). All of the aspects of the hospital environment that are anxiety-producing for adults are especially upsetting for children. The procedures and treatments, particularly if they are painful or restrict patients' movement, are very difficult, and children often have no understanding of why they must undergo these procedures. They may, for example, view hospitalization as a punishment for being bad or unloved by their families. For very young children, such as those under the age of 5 years, one of the most difficult aspects of hospitalization is separation from their families. Although older children are likely to have a better understanding of why they are in the hospital, they face new issues, including concern with a loss of personal control, disruption of peer relationships, embarrassment about showing their body to others, and worry about the consequences of their illness (e.g., dying).

So, what can parents and health professionals do to help children cope with hospitalization? First, children, like adults, benefit from knowing what to expect, and hospitals should provide children and their families with information about various hospital procedures and routines (Koetting-O'Byrne, Peterson, & Saldana, 1997; Pinto & Hollandsworth, 1989). This information could include pamphlets, tours, books, videos, and even puppet shows (for very young children). The staff at Children's Medical Center in Boston, for example, worked with children's books author Margaret Rey to write the story *Curious George Goes to the Hospital*, which describes the experience of George during a brief hospitalization (Rey & Rey, 1966). One study with children who were about to undergo surgery found that those who watched a video describing the surgery experienced less anxiety and arousal than did children who did not watch this video (Pinto & Hollandsworth, 1989). Second, parents should try to spend as much time with the child as possible—some hospitals now offer parents the chance to "room-in" with the child. Training parents in how to distract their children is also effective (Bush, Melamed, Sheras, & Greenbaum, 1986). Finally, children can be trained in how to cope with their anxiety about surgery (Jay, Elliott, Katz, & Siegel, 1987; Manne et al., 1992). For example, one study found that children who received training in how to reduce their own distress during hospitalization and surgery showed reduced anxiety as well as fewer maladaptive behaviors (Zastrowny, Kirschenbaum, & Meng, 1986). Hospitals are putting this information to good use—one study of 123 pediatric hospitals in the United States found that 75% reported increasing their use of research in health psychology to assist children in coping with medical procedures (Koetting et al., 1997).

predict what will happen (Lorber, 1975; Newman, 1984; Taylor, 1979). Box 12.5: Focus on Development describes the difficulties children faced when admitted to the hospital, as well as some strategies for improving this experience.

People admitted to the hospital must live in an impersonal room (often with one or more roommates), are given typically bland food on a regimented schedule, and are subject to invasions of privacy when at virtually any moment hospital personnel enter the room (to clean, provide food, deliver medicines, check patient's vital statistics). Patients are often described by medical professionals based on their disease or illness (e.g., "the broken leg in Room 402," "the ulcer in Room 312"; Goffman, 1961), which enhances patients' feelings of depersonalization. Moreover, patients are asked a series of very personal questions ("when did you last have a bowel movement?"), forced to undergo a variety of unpleasant and sometimes painful tests, and must wear a backless gown without underwear! They may also be forced to be dependent on health-care professionals for assistance with many personal care tasks, including eating, dressing and undressing, and even going to the bathroom. Although many of the procedures and machines are likely to be unfamiliar and anxiety-provoking to patients (e.g., IV fluids, EKG machines), most patients don't get information about the procedures they are undergoing or why they are necessary (Newman, 1984).

All of this loss of control can lead to considerable stress and anxiety, which in turn can have negative immunological consequences and thereby inhibit recovery. One study found that 29% of pregnant women who had high blood pressure, an often dangerous condition during pregnancy, revealed an elevated blood pressure only when they were measured in their doctor's office (a potentially anxiety-provoking situation), a condition described as "white coat hypertension" (Bellomo et al., 1999). Moreover, women with white coat hypertension were just as likely to undergo cesarean sections (45%) as those with true high blood pressure (41%) and much more likely to undergo this procedure than those without high blood pressure (12%).

So, how do patients react to the extreme depersonalization that is common in many hospital settings? About 75% of the patients are classified as "good patients"; that is, they make few demands on the staff, ask few questions, agree to whatever is suggested, and generally give up all desire for control (Lorber, 1975; Taylor, 1979). These people take up little time of the staff and are easy to manage. However, these patients may hesitate to question wrong orders, complain about an important symptom, or otherwise provide useful information about the symptoms they are experiencing out of fear of creating a problem. These patients may experience

Simply undergoing particular medical tests can lead some people to experience considerable anxiety, which in turn can lead to increased blood pressure.
Source: David Sipress/cartoonbank.com. All Rights Reserved.

"I'm going to take your blood pressure, so try to relax and not think about what a high reading might mean for your chances of living a long, healthy life."

depression and learned helplessness, given the total lack of control, which in turn can ironically harm their recovery. As discussed in Chapter 9, some evidence even suggests that people who have less information and control over medical procedures experience more pain and take longer to recover.

On the other hand, about 25% of people are "bad patients" (Lorber, 1975; Taylor, 1979): They are younger and more educated and presumably score high in need for control; they may be demanding, questioning, and time-consuming. These patients may experience heightened anger, which leads to increased arousal. These patients may react to their loss of control by trying to regain some of it, which unfortunately can include engaging in destructive behaviors, such as smoking and not taking their medicine. Although bad patients do not experience the problems associated with giving up control, they may receive a lower quality of medical care. Specifically, medical professionals may respond less quickly to their needs, may keep them heavily sedated, and may even discharge them earlier!

One of the most threatening and anxiety-provoking aspects about hospitalization is the anticipation of surgery, in part because people often have little direct relevant experience with this situation (Contrada, Leventhal, & Anderson, 1994). Patients worry about the physical procedure (e.g., incision, anesthesia), the recovery (e.g., pain, ability to walk and eat), the resumption of normal activities (e.g., work, leisure activities), and the long-term management of their condition (e.g., the physical changes in their body, the need to diet or stop smoking following coronary heart surgery, the need to continue to take medications following an organ transplant).

However, patients who are given information about what to expect during their surgery and recovery, as well as training in how to manage these experiences, require less pain medication and leave the hospital more rapidly (Contrada et al., 1994; Janis, 1958; Johnston & Vogele, 1993; Ludwick-Rosenthal & Neufeld, 1993). As discussed in Chapter 9, this information also decreases anxiety and pain (Anderson, 1987). For example, Doering et al. (2000) demonstrated that hip replacement surgery patients who saw a videotape of a patient who had been through that procedure showed less anxiety before surgery, lower blood pressure during surgery, and less use of pain medication after surgery (see Figure 12.4). In fact, in 11 studies in which the amount of information provided was examined to predict postsurgery drug use and length of hospital stay, 10 of the studies showed that more information led to a faster recovery, with a mean decrease of 2 days in the hospital (Ley, 1982).

In addition to giving patients knowledge about what to expect (i.e., informational control), other interventions focus on giving patients cognitive control (e.g., strategies for distracting/changing thoughts), or behavioral control (e.g., strategies for reducing discomfort, such as relaxation training; Leventhal, Leventhal, Shacham, & Easterling, 1989; Manyande et al., 1995). For example, abdominal surgery patients who received training in guided imagery had lower heart rates following surgery, less pain, and requested less pain relief (Manyande et al., 1995). All of these approaches share one very important feature; they give patients a much-needed sense of control in a generally stressful environment.

Even relatively small manipulations that increase control and positive experiences have important benefits in terms of recovery from surgery. One way to enhance control is by allowing patients to control the amount and timing of pain medication they receive, as opposed to making them call for a nurse to deliver the medication or administering the medication on a set schedule (e.g., every 4 hours). But does

FIGURE 12.4   Hip replacement surgery patients who watch a videotape showing someone undergoing this surgery require lower levels of nonsteroid drugs, opioid drugs, and total pain medication after surgery than those who do not see this videotape (Doering et al., 2000).

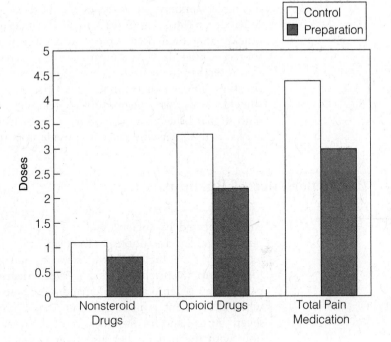

this type of control encourage patients to overmedicate themselves? No—in fact, it does just the opposite. For example, one study with patients who were recovering from a bone marrow transplant revealed that those who received a device that directly provided pain relief intravenously, who were able to control the amount and timing of pain medication administration reported lower levels of pain (and gave themselves less medicine) than those who had to ask the hospital staff for medicine (Zucker et al., 1998).

Even small changes to the hospital environment can help improve psychological and physical well-being in patients. Ulrich (1984) at the University of Delaware reviewed the records of patients in a Pennsylvania hospital for a period of about 10 years who had gallbladder surgery. Specifically, he examined a number of factors listed in the hospital records, including length of hospital stay, amount of pain medication requested and given, and nurses' notes about the patients' recovery. He also noted what room the patients were in and whether that room overlooked a group of trees or a brick wall. As predicted, patients whose hospital room had a view of trees recovered faster than those whose room looked out on a brick wall. First, patients in a room with a view stayed in the hospital for an average of 7.96 days, nearly one day shorter than those with a view of bricks (8.70 days). Patients who had a view of trees also requested less pain medication than those who had a view of bricks. Finally, the nurses' recordings on patient charts revealed an average of 3.96 negative notes per patient for those in a room with a view of bricks (e.g., "patient is upset and crying," "patient needs much encouragement") as compared to 1.13 comments per patient for those with the view of trees.

Other research reveals that patients scheduled for heart surgery who had a hospital roommate who had already undergone the same type of surgery reported feeling less anxiety, and they left the hospital sooner after surgery (Kulik, Mahler, & Moore, 1996). Those with an "experienced roommate" left the hospital more quickly after their own surgery than those whose roommate had had a different surgery—8.04 days as compared to 9.17 days, respectively. In this case, people may directly benefit from receiving support from people who have faced a similar situation. Similar others can provide a person with information about useful coping strategies as well as standards for judging one's own reaction (Thoits, 1986). Contact with similar others may also allow individuals to vent their feelings to those who are likely to understand and can provide important emotional support.

The Experience of Burnout

Many people see doctors as having a relatively easy job—they are typically well paid, respected by society, and can have very flexible schedules (e.g., play golf on Wednesday afternoons). However, and as described in Chapter 4, doctors experience very high levels of stress caused by several factors, which can lead to **burnout** (Maslach & Jackson, 1982; Siegrist et al., 2010). First, dealing with patients can be emotionally demanding. These demands can be especially difficult when the patient is in severe pain, has unsightly injuries (e.g., disfigurements, severe burns), and has little chance of recovery. Doctors may have to interact not only with the patients but also their families. Family members may have many time-consuming questions and may be anxious, upset, and angry. Moreover, no matter how good a doctor is, he or she will experience failure on a relatively consistent basis—all doctors have patients who die or who cannot be helped. This type of loss is particularly difficult when they have tried very hard to save the patient. Another aspect of the job environment that leads to stress for doctors is their relative lack of control in a hectic and time-pressured environment. Doctors rarely get to choose exactly when they work, which patients they see, or how long they spend with a particular patient. Doctors are sometimes not even able to treat patients in their preferred way without seeking—and receiving—special permission from the patient's insurance company.

How do health professionals react to this type of pressure? Sadly, sometimes they depersonalize the patients as a way of maintaining emotional distance (Maslach & Jackson, 1982; Parker & Kulik, 1995; Shinn, Rosario, Morch, & Chestnut, 1984). They may, for example, start thinking of patients in terms of their problems (e.g., "the fractured leg," "the liver cancer") as opposed to thinking of them as people; hence, they may treat patients in a cynical and callous way. One physician noted that when a patient's cancer did not respond to chemotherapy, she was described as "failing chemotherapy" (Klass, 1987). Practitioners may also develop psychological and physical problems, including CHD, alcohol and drug abuse, and depression. For example, 12% of medical students show symptoms of depression, and these symptoms increase during the first 2 years of medical school (Clark & Zeldow, 1988). One recent study of 182 medical students found that 133 had cried at least once during their clinical rotations in the hospital, and another 30 reported being on the verge of crying (Angoff, 2001). Burnout in medical professionals can have a dramatic impact on patient care: One recent study found that nurses who care for too many patients at one time experience a 23% increase in rate of burnout, which is in turn associated with a 7% increase in the rate of patient death (Aiken, Clarke, Sloan, Sochalski, & Silber, 2002)!

Although some of the causes of burnout are largely unavoidable given the stressful nature of the medical profession, giving people the opportunity to express their feelings is one way to help ameliorate the effects of this environment (Angoff, 2001). Some hospitals have developed support groups for hospital personnel, which can provide much-needed emotional support and give people the opportunity to express their feelings of frustration, exhaustion, and grief. These groups also allow medical professionals to learn they are not alone in their feelings, and to learn some strategies for coping with the difficult challenges of their profession. Moreover, physicians who are training medical students can encourage them to continue to express their feelings as opposed to denying them, as has often been the practice (Angoff, 2001). One medical student described how wonderfully a physician handled the first death of a patient for a group of students:

> "The whole team stayed outside the door while Doctor F and the intern went in to pronounce him. I was trying to fight back tears. Doctor F took us all into a room and handled it magnificently. He said let's take some time to talk about this, and said what a great guy the patient had been. He reminded us that when we had been in the patient's room, his mother looked out the window and said, "What a great day to go to God." I remember having a sense of peace."

Compare this experience to another report from a medical student:

> "It was my first surgical rotation and the first patient I found out had cancer. The patient went down for a scan. My job was to not inform the patient of the results, but as the person who knew the patient best, she kept asking me. I was avoiding her. The resident saw me cry. She gave me a lecture to not be so weak, patients die, bad things happen."

In sum, hospital environments that provide support to doctors, nurses, and medical students and acknowledge the sometimes difficult emotions that come with these jobs can help prevent some of the problems associated with burnout.

What Predicts Adherence?

Although people invest a lot of time and energy in getting diagnosed, and doctors invest considerable time in making diagnoses, many patients fail to show **adherence** to recommended medical regimens, such as taking antibiotics, making dietary changes, and having immunizations (Christensen & Ehlers, 2002; DiMatteo, 1994; DiNicola & DiMatteo, 1984; Dunbar-Jacob, Burke, & Puczynski, 1995; Kirscht & Rosenstock, 1979; Monane et al., 1996). Rates of nonadherence range from 15 to 93% (depending on the regimen), with a mean of 30%: About 50% of people do not take prescribed medications on the recommended schedule, 20 to 40% of people do not receive the recommended immunizations, and 20 to 50% of people miss scheduled appointments for medical treatment. For example, one early study on adherence revealed that only 12% of patients who were instructed to take penicillin for 10 days were actually still taking this antibiotic by the 10th day—50% had stopped by the 3rd day, 71% had stopped by the 6th day, and 82% had stopped by the 9th day (Bergman & Werner, 1963).

Nonadherence is associated with substantial costs to individuals and to society (Dunbar-Jabob et al., 1995; Kirscht & Rosenstock, 1979). Obviously, not taking one's medication, for instance, typically leads to a continuation of symptoms. Moreover, not taking medication can cause the disease to persist or even get worse. Approximately 27,600 children developed measles in 1990 alone because their parents failed to have them immunized. Individuals who do not adhere to medical recommendations show poorer outcomes, including higher mortality (Gallagher, Viscoli, & Horwitz, 1993; Horwitz et al., 1990; Irvin, Bowers, Dunn, & Wanes, 1999). For example, hypertensive patients who fail to take their recommended medication are four times as likely to be hospitalized or die as those who adhere to the treatment (Psaty, Koepsell, Wagner, LoGerfo, & Inui, 1990). Nonadherence to medication regimens and the persistence of symptoms may then lead a health-care professional to prescribe a larger dose of the drug—possibly causing an overdose—because he or she thinks the drug is having no effect at the lower dose. New diagnoses may be made based on patients' response to the treatment. Poor adherence also can lead to substantial societal costs, such as the development of drug-resistant strains of viruses (Catz, Kelly, Bogart, Benotsch, & McAuliffe, 2000; Dunbar-Jacob et al., 1995; Sumartojo, 1993) and widespread disease, with its attendant losses in productivity and quality of life.

Questioning the Research 12.3

Does adherence to medical regimens really lead to better health? Or could a third variable partially explain these findings?

Causes of Nonadherence

Nonadherence may take a variety of forms and be caused by a variety of reasons (DiNicola & DiMatteo, 1984; Epstein & Cluss, 1982; Mo & Mak, 2009). In cases of **intentional nonadherence**, patients understand the practitioner's directions but modify the regimen in some way or ignore it completely because they are unwilling to follow the recommendations. In contrast, in the case of **unintentional non-adherence**, people intend to comply, and may even believe they are complying, but for some reason they are not following instructions. These distinct types of nonadherence have different causes.

Intentional nonadherence may be caused by aspects of the treatment, including the condition being treated and the impact of the medication, as well as the patient's beliefs about the overall costs and benefits of adherence (DiNicola & DiMatteo, 1984; Le et al., 2008; Schüz et al., 2011). People show high rates of adherence to medications and treatments that relieve painful and severe conditions (Brownlee-Duffeck et al., 1987). Most cancer patients, for example, undergo recommended chemotherapy and radiation treatments in the hope that these procedures will prolong their lives. People are also more likely to comply with short-term treatments than long-term treatments, particularly those that are complex, have unpleasant side effects, and provide few clear benefits (Catz et al., 2000; Christensen, Moran, & Wiebe, 1999; Robie, 1987); at the beginning of the chapter, you read how Larry often failed to take his medication to control hypertension because of his lack of confidence in its effectiveness as well as its high cost and numerous side effects. People who see more benefits derived from following a regimen (e.g., feel better, experience less pain, live longer) are more likely to adhere to medical treatments (Brock & Wartman, 1990; Sherbourne, Hays, Ordinay, DiMatteo, & Kravitz, 1992).

However, people often show lower levels of adherence to complex treatments. For example, although the main treatment for HIV infection is *highly active antiretroviral therapy (HAART)*, this regimen involves a complicated drug-taking schedule—sometimes as many as 16 pills must be taken each day at precise times and under precise conditions (e.g., some on an empty stomach, some an hour before eating, some an hour after eating). The HAART regimen can also lead to a variety of side effects, including mental confusion, headaches, and anemia. Adherence to this regimen therefore is particularly challenging, despite its benefits in terms of reducing AIDS-related symptoms and potentially delaying death. One study found that nonadherence is nine times more likely to occur on days in which people consume alcohol, presumably because impaired cognition makes adherence to such a complex regimen even more difficult (Parsons, Rosof, & Mustanski, 2008).

Individual differences, including self-efficacy, problem-solving style, and personality, can influence whether a person complies with medical recommendations (Bond, Aiken, & Somerville, 1992; Brownlee et al., 1987; Christensen & Johnson, 2002; Goldring, Taylor, Kemeny, & Anton, 2002). In some cases, people want to comply, and even believe complying is very important, but may lack the self-efficacy to successfully carry out the behavior (e.g., to resist tempting foods, avoid alcohol while taking medication; Catz et al., 2000; DiMatteo, 1994; Senecal, Nouwen, & White, 2000). For example, HIV-positive patients who adhere to treatment recommendations have higher self-efficacy, better overall mental health, and lower feelings of stigma (Mo & Mak, 2009). People with more constructive problem-solving styles are also more likely to adhere, whereas those with more avoidant or destructive styles are less likely to adhere (Johnson, Eliot, Neilands, Morin, & Chesney, 2006; Mo & Mak, 2009). Finally, and as described in Chapter 5, personality influences adherence to medical recommendations. For example, people who are hostile show low levels of adherence, whereas people who are conscientious show high levels of adherence (Christensen, Moran, & Wiebe, 1999; Christensen & Smith, 1995). Similarly, people who are high in negative affect and depression have lower rates of adherence, in part because being in a negative mood increases the use of maladaptive coping strategies (Gonzalez et al., 2004; Johnson, Heckman, Hansen, Kochman, & Sikkema, 2009; Weaver et al., 2005).

Interestingly, adherence tends to be best when patients' characteristics or coping styles correspond with the particular demands of the medical treatment they are undergoing (Christensen & Ehlers, 2002). Specifically, and as shown in Figure 12.5, individuals with more active and internally focused coping styles tend to show higher levels of adherence when they are given treatments that emphasize self-control, whereas those with more avoidant styles of coping show higher levels of

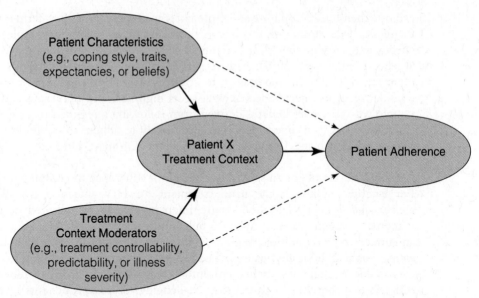

FIGURE 12.5 A model of patient X treatment interaction predicting adherence (Christensen & Johnson, 2002).

adherence when they are undergoing treatment administered by a therapist in a hospital or clinic setting. For example, one study of hemodialysis patients revealed that those who preferred active involvement in their health care showed better dietary control and adherence to fluid-intake recommendations when they were given patient-controlled dialysis at home, whereas those who preferred low levels of involvement in their own care showed better dietary control and adherence to medical recommendations when they were given staff-controlled dialysis at a hospital or clinic (Christensen, 2000). What accounts for these effects? Patients who have an active and monitoring coping style might feel out of control when given a provider-directed type of treatment, and in turn may respond to this type of situation by trying to reassert control—by deliberately disobeying medical recommendations. Similarly, patients who are high in self-efficacy and conscientiousness might be more responsive to treatments that require independence and self-reliance because these treatments would utilize their preferred coping styles and strategies. On the other hand, patients who are low in self-efficacy and high in agreeableness might prefer more passive, dependent, and possibly group-based treatments, which would encourage more (much-needed) reliance on others as well as social support (Rosenbaum & Ben-Ari Smira, 1986; Smith & Williams, 1992).

Social support from family and friends leads to increased adherence to medical recommendations; in fact, adherence is 1.74 times higher in patients with cohesive families and 1.53 times lower in patients with families in conflict (Catz et al., 2000; DiMatteo, 2004; Gonzalez et al., 2004; Weaver et al., 2005; Stanton, 1987). One study of patients with tuberculosis found that 56% of those who regularly took their medication felt their families were supportive of their taking medication as compared to 28% of those who did not regularly take their medication (Barnhoorn & Adriaanse, 1992). Similarly, people who have more supportive interpersonal relationships show more adherence to diabetic regimens (Sherbourne et al., 1992), and people who have more supportive spouses are more likely to adhere to dietary changes than those without such spousal support (Bovbjerg et al., 1995).

Demographic and cultural factors may also influence adherence (Bovbjerg et al., 1995; Catz et al., 2000; DiNicola & DiMatteo, 1984; Kirscht & Rosenstock, 1979; Stanton, 1987). People who are older tend to show higher rates of adherence than people who are younger, perhaps because younger people tend to feel more invulnerable (Lynch et al., 1992; Mo & Mak, 2009; Monane et al., 1996; Sherbourne et al., 1992; Thomas et al., 1995). There are few, if any, effects of gender on adherence. Finally, people with very low income may fail to comply simply because the recommended treatment is too costly (Robie, 1987). Patients sometimes fail to adhere because they have run out of medication and may not have enough money to buy more or because taking their medication does not fit in with their lifestyle (Hill-Briggs et al., 2005; Tucker et al., 2004). They may take medication less frequently than is recommended, skip follow-up appointments, or rely on nonprescription remedies as a way of saving money. For example, a study of mothers who did not keep their children's pediatric appointments found that the most common reasons were a lack of money, lack of transportation, or need to focus on more pressing problems (e.g., taking care of other children at home).

Another factor that is strongly related to patient cooperation is the quality of the relationship between the doctor and patient because adherence depends largely on the patient's motivation to follow the doctor's recommendation (DiNicola & DiMatteo, 1984; Dunbar-Jacob et al., 1995). Practitioners who show warmth, encourage open communication, and address their patients' concerns have more satisfied patients, who in turn are more likely to follow recommendations. One study examined more than 800 interactions between pediatricians and mothers who had brought their children in for some type of disorder (Korsch, Gozzi, & Francis, 1968). Immediately after the mother and child left the office, they were questioned about their experience. Although the majority (76%) was satisfied with the doctor's performance, nearly 20% felt they did not receive a clear statement about their baby's problem, and almost 50% were left wondering what caused the baby's problem. They also felt the visit focused only on the technical disease aspects, not their emotional concerns. In turn, this lack of information was associated with overall poor adherence with medical instructions. In fact, only 42% complied with the doctor's orders, with 38% showing partial adherence and 11% showing no adherence. Those who were satisfied with their interaction with their doctor were three times as likely to comply as those who were unsatisfied (53% for the highly satisfied versus 17% for the highly dissatisfied). Similarly, patients who feel they were involved in decision making and goal setting and treated with respect show higher levels of adherence to medical recommendations (Beach et al., 2005).

In contrast, in the case of *unintentional nonadherence*, people intend to comply, and may even believe they are complying, but for some reason they are not following instructions. As described previously, physicians often give patients very little information about their diagnosis and treatment, which in turn can lead to nonadherence (Hall et al., 1988; Ley, 1982). As described previously, physicians may spend less than a minute and a half giving information to patients (Waitzkin, 1985). Even when patients are given information about their condition, they may forget or misunderstand the instructions they are given (DiNicola & DiMatteo,

In some cases, nonadherence is caused by patients' misunderstanding of how exactly medication should be taken.
Source: © KLH49/iStockphoto.

1984). For example, one study found that patients failed to recall 56% of the instructions they had received and 48% of the treatment instructions even a short time after their appointments. Researchers in one study found that those who failed to adhere to diabetes medication typically reported forgetting to take the medication (Hill-Briggs et al., 2005).

Moreover, instructions for medical regimens are often vague; hence, patients may legitimately misunderstand exactly what they are supposed to do. In one study, patients were told to take a drug "with meals," by which the practitioner meant to imply patients should take the drug immediately after eating (Mazzullo, Cohn, Lasana, & Griner, 1974). However, 54% of the patients understood this to mean "take before meals," 33% thought it meant to "take during meals," and only 13% thought it meant to "take after meals."

In sum, adherence is predicted by a number of different factors (see Table 12.7). Adherence may be best predicted by a combination of information about the

TABLE 12.7   *Test Yourself: Adherence Determination Questionnaire*

Please answer the following questions with 1 (strongly disagree) to 5 (strongly agree).

1. The doctors and other health professionals answer all my questions.
2. The doctors and other health professionals treat me in a very friendly and courteous manner.
3. The benefits of my treatment plan outweigh any difficulty I might have in following it.
4. Following my treatment plan will help me to be healthy.
5. The kind of cancer I have is a terrible disease.
6. The chances I might develop cancer again are pretty high.
7. Members of my immediate family think I should follow my treatment plan.
8. My close friends think I should follow my treatment plan.
9. I have made a commitment to follow my treatment plan.
10. I am able to deal with any problems in following my treatment plan.

This scale assesses an individual's likelihood of adhering to his or her treatment plan.

Source: DiMatteo et al., 1993.

importance of adhering, motivation to adhere (both personal and social motivation), and behavioral skills (e.g., getting medication, managing side effects, incorporating into daily life, etc.; Fisher, Fisher, Amico, & Harman, 2006). In line with this view, one study with 100 HIV-positive patients found that adherence-related information and motivation predicted behavioral skills, which in turn predicted adherence (Starace, Massa, Amico, & Fisher, 2006).

Measuring Adherence

The most common method of measuring adherence is simply to ask the patient whether he or she has taken the required amount of medicine (Epstein & Cluss, 1982). This approach is easy, inexpensive, and sometimes the only option. However, this method has problems because patients will rarely admit that they are not complying and, hence, typically will report adherence even if it is not so. One study with diabetic children found that 53.8% of the times they reported testing their blood, they fabricated glucose levels (Wilson & Endres, 1986). Patients may also forget whether they have complied, especially if they must report on their behavior over a long period of time, such as their diet and exercise behavior over the last month. Although some studies have tried using the reports of family members to judge adherence, as a way of avoiding problems of biased or forgetful reporting, family members often base their own estimates on what the patient reports to them! Similarly, although some studies suggest reports by doctors could be useful (Epstein & Cluss, 1982), doctors generally overestimate adherence because they believe patients cooperate perfectly with their treatment recommendations.

Given the significant likelihood of inaccurate findings using self-report measures, some studies have tried assessing adherence through pill or bottle counts (Epstein & Cluss, 1982). For example, a physician could ask patients to bring in their pill bottles and could then measure whether the right number of pills is missing. Researchers in one study compared adherence data in HIV-positive patients who provided self-reports versus electronic monitoring (day, time, duration of bottle opening; Levine et al., 2006). Estimates of adherence by self-report were higher than those by electronic monitoring, especially when reporting over longer periods of time. Over the entire 6-month study period, patients estimated they had adhered 90% of the time, whereas electronic monitoring data revealed they had adhered only 67% of the time. Although this approach may clarify whether the patient accurately understands the recommended dosage, obviously people can remove pills without actually ingesting them to appear compliant. Moreover, patients may have taken the right number of pills but on the wrong schedule.

In some cases, therapeutic outcomes, such as whether the patient is getting better, are used in many cases to judge adherence (DiNicola & DiMatteo, 1984; Epstein & Cluss, 1982). If the patient is showing signs of recovering, then he or she is assumed to be complying with medical recommendations. However, this method also poses problems simply because there is not necessarily a direct correspondence between adherence and recovery: In some cases, people can show signs of recovery even when they are not complying, and, in other cases, people show no signs of recovery even when they are complying (Hays et al., 1994). For example, in one study of people with hypertension, 12% controlled the disease without complying with the regimen, and 34% complied faithfully, but the regimen was ineffective in controlling the disease (Sackett, 1979).

Researchers have also tried to use more direct measures of testing adherence (Dunbar-Jacob et al., 1995; Epstein & Cluss, 1982), including using blood, serum, or urine assays to test the concentration of the drug in the patient's body. For example, if a patient is taking penicillin, a urine test could be used to determine whether the appropriate level of penicillin is in the body. Although physiological methods are quite accurate, and they avoid the problems associated with self-report and pill counts, patients who are warned about these tests may comply only immediately before the test. For example, some smoking-cessation programs test for the presence of nicotine in saliva. But people who continue to smoke simply might not smoke in the hours before the test, and therefore appear to be not smoking, even if they usually are. Physiological measures are also relatively impractical—they are not available for all drugs, are relatively expensive, and, given individual differences in rates of metabolism, may not be entirely accurate.

Strategies for Increasing Adherence

Nonadherence is clearly irrational, a waste of time for patients and health-care professionals, and potentially dangerous. Many of the strategies for decreasing unintentional nonadherence focus on giving the patient correct information (Dunbar-Jacob et al., 1995; Ley, 1982; Thompson, 1984). In fact, simply providing clear and understandable information about the medication, its purposes, and its dosage can be very effective in preventing this type of nonadherence (see Figure 12.6). Practitioners should ask patients directly whether they have any questions. Moreover, because people sometimes forget or do not fully understand the information they receive from practitioners, providing easy-to-understand written materials, using illustrations to reinforce written materials, and even giving the patient a tape recording of the consultation can all be effective ways of increasing adherence (Ley, 1982). In fact, one study found that 91% of patients reported it was helpful to have a tape recording of their doctor visit, and patients claimed to have listened to the tape an average of 3.5 times (Butt, 1977).

Because unintentional nonadherence can also be caused by forgetting to adhere, other strategies for increasing adherence simply focus on reminding people to

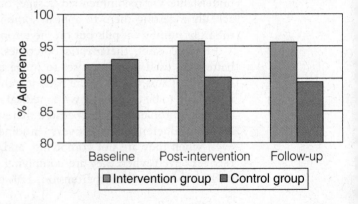

FIGURE 12.6 Researchers in this study randomly assigned HIV-positive patients to a standard-care or adherence-promoting intervention, which included tailored information about the importance of adherence and setting adherence goals and developing self-monitoring strategies. Patients in the intervention group showed an increase in adherence over time, whereas those in the control group showed a decrease (data from de Bruin et al., 2010).

engage in a particular behavior, such as taking their medication or measuring their blood pressure (Dunbar-Jacobs et al., 1995; Ley, 1982; Macharia, Leon, Rowe, Stephenson, & Haynes, 1992; Mayer & Frederiksen, 1986; Southam & Dunbar, 1986). In fact, one study found that giving patients special reminders (e.g., a sticker for their refrigerator) doubled rates of adherence to their medication regimen (Lima, Nazarian, Charney, & Lahti, 1976). Reminder calls and postcards can also be very effective in improving attendance at follow-up appointments (Kirscht & Rosentstock, 1979). Reminder techniques and cues can be especially useful with older adults. Asking patients to monitor their adherence behavior, such as by testing and recording their blood pressure (in the case of hypertensives) or blood glucose levels (in the case of diabetics), is another way of helping to remind them to adhere (Southam & Dunbar, 1986). This self-monitoring can also provide patients with increased understanding of their disease, and its management, and thereby enhance feelings of perceived control. Researchers in one study found that pediatric liver transplant recipients who received text messages reminding them to take their immunosuppressant medication substantially decreased the number of transplant rejections (Miloh et al., 2009).

The strategies for decreasing intentional nonadherence are quite different because, in these cases, people understand the medical recommendations but are simply unmotivated or unable to follow them (Dunbar-Jacobs et al., 1995; Ley, 1982). In cases in which people fail to comply because they have little concern about having or developing a particular disease, the use of fear warnings can be effective in increasing adherence (Higbee, 1969; Janis, 1967). For example, smokers who see themselves as relatively unlikely to develop lung cancer could be brought to a hospital ward filled with people dying of lung cancer to increase their level of fear arousal and motivate them to take action. Similarly, people who engage in unsafe sex and have little fear of acquiring HIV could be asked to role-play how they would respond to learning they are HIV-positive, which could increase their feelings of perceived vulnerability. In one study, mothers of obese children were randomly assigned to receive one of three communication messages—a control (no-information) message, a low-threat message, or a high-threat message (Becker, Maiman, Kirscht, Haefner, & Drachman, 1977). Children whose mothers had received either type of informational message had lost more weight than the controls at each of the four follow-up visits, and those whose mothers had received the high-threat message lost the most weight.

Another strategy for increasing adherence is to give patients some type of incentive or reward for following medical recommendations (DiNicola & DiMatteo, 1984; Hegel, Ayllon, Thiel, & Oulton, 1992; Macharia et al., 1992; Southam & Dunbar, 1986). This approach is particularly effective if patients agree to a written contract that describes specific goals they intend to meet as well as the reward they will receive if the contract is specifically carried out. These contracts are typically witnessed by others, such as physicians and family members. In some cases, rewards alone, even in the absence of a specific contract, can be effective at increasing adherence. In fact, people who receive desirable—and self-chosen—rewards, such as attending a movie or purchasing a book, show better adherence to regimens for a variety of conditions, including arthritis, diabetes, asthma, and cardiovascular disease.

Intentional nonadherence can also be caused by patients' concern that following the medical recommendations will disrupt their lives in some way, such as taking too much time or interfering with relationships (Kirscht & Rosenstock, 1979). Increasing the convenience of engaging in the recommended behavior, such as simplifying the regimens (e.g., taking a pill twice a day instead of four times a day), making bottles easier to open (especially for older patients), lowering the cost, and improving the taste of medicine can increase adherence (Robie, 1987). For example, patients who have to take one to three pills a day show an adherence rate of 77% to 88% as compared to 39% for those who have to take four pills a day (Cramer, Mattson, Prevey, Scheyer, & Ouelette, 1989). Enlisting the support of family members or friends can increase adherence (Becker, 1985; DiNicola & DiMatteo, 1984; Kirscht, Kirscht, & Rosenstock, 1981; Morisky et al., 1983). For example, one program with hypertensive patients found that 53% of those who received an exit interview and family support complied with their medical regimen at the 2-year follow-up as compared to only 40% off those in the control group (Morisky et al., 1983). Similarly, you can have buddy systems with pairs of patients. Some research suggests that patients who regularly attend group social support sessions with others who share their health issue show greater adherence (Kirscht & Rosenstock, 1979).

Given the link between depression and nonadherence, reducing depression is another strategy that can help increase adherence. Researchers in one study randomly assigned HIV-positive patients who were depressed to a usual-care intervention or a cognitive-behavioral condition that included information on both adherence and reducing depression (Safren et al., 2009). This intervention led to lower rates of depression as well as higher rates of adherence (including an improvement in adherence from 62.26% adherence to 87.61%). Similarly, the use of antidepressants increases adherence in HIV-positive people (Walkup, Wei, Sambamoorthi, & Crystal, 2008).

Finally, as described previously, patients are more likely to adhere to treatment recommendations when they like their doctor and when their doctor emphasizes the importance of adherence (DiMatteo et al., 1993; Sherbourne et al., 1992). For example, one study with more than 1,000 chronic disease patients found that those who were satisfied with the interpersonal care they received from their physicians were more likely to adhere to medical recommendations (Sherbourne et al., 1992). Patients with physicians who make strong recommendations for adherence and provide realistic information about the importance of adherence also show higher rates of adherence (Goldring et al., 2002). Another important factor influencing patient satisfaction and adherence to medical recommendations is the physician's interactional style (Krantz, Baum, & Wideman, 1980; Laine & Davidoff, 1996). Specifically, physicians who use a patient-centered style encourage an interaction between the doctor and the patient to solve the problem and seek solutions, whereas those who use a doctor-centered style (the more traditional style) are more dominant and expect the patient largely to trust their expertise and defer to their judgment. One recent study demonstrated that overweight patients whose physicians used reflexive listening and a more collaborative style in discussing weight-loss techniques lost weight over the 3-month follow-up whereas those without such a style either maintained or gained weight (Pollak et al., 2010).

FIGURE 12.7 The relapse curves for various addictions, including heroin use, smoking, and alcohol abuse, are very similar, suggesting that the relapse process across different issues shares some common points (data from Hunt et al., 1971).

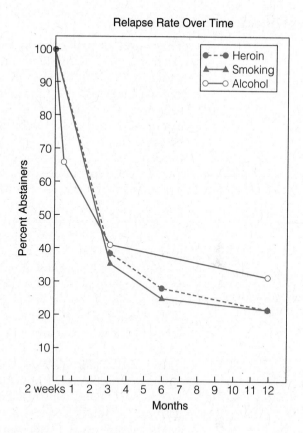

What Is Relapse?

Even when people seek medical treatment and attempt to follow recommendations, maintaining health behavior change over time is a major problem. Have you ever made a change in your health-related behavior, such as stopping smoking, starting exercising, or adopting a healthier diet, but then returned to your old—less healthy—habits after a few weeks or months (or sometimes even days)? This pattern of **relapse** is very common. For example, most people (estimates range from 50 to 80%) who quit smoking start again within a year; and one study found that less than 10% of patients were able to maintain abstinence from alcohol over a period of 2 years following participation in a treatment plan (Marlatt, 1985a). As shown in Figure 12.7, the relapse curves for alcohol use, smoking, and heroin use are very similar, with about two thirds of all relapse occurring in the first 90 days following treatment (Hunt, Barnett, & Branch, 1971; Ockene et al., 2000). This suggests that there is a common link to the process of relapse that may be similar across different types of addiction. This section examines the major theories of relapse, the influence of psychological factors on triggering relapse, and strategies for preventing relapse.

Theories of Addiction

The **moral or self-control theory** posits that people who engage in addictive behaviors, such as smoking, drinking, and gambling, have some type of moral weakness (Marlatt, 1985a). According to this theory, people who are lazy and undisciplined lack the "moral fiber" to stop engaging in these self-destructive behaviors. For example, the Temperance Movement during the 1940s and the ban of alcohol during Prohibition reflected this view advocating that people must be protected from themselves. Moreover, because any problem with addiction is a result of a lack of personal impulse control or willpower, people who engage in these behaviors in excess deserve whatever negative consequences befall them. This model holds people responsible for their own behavior and, thus, in one sense can be seen as empowering.

On the other hand, according to the **disease model**, addiction is caused primarily by internal physiological forces, such as cravings, urges, and compulsions; hence, the "addict" is unable to voluntarily control his or her behavior (Marlatt, 1985a). Alcoholics Anonymous is based on this model and posits that the alcoholic is completely powerless over the disease and that alcoholism can never be cured, only controlled. In this view, the only way for an alcoholic to stay in control is to not drink—after having one or two drinks, the alcoholic experiences a physiological addictive response that is triggered by the alcohol consumed, which leads the person to have an irresistible craving for more alcohol. The disease model of addiction has an "all or nothing" view, which means that only lifelong abstinence is effective, and hence relapse is failure. In turn, any slight deviation is seen as total failure, which of course then leads to more of the negative behavior. This can obviously lead to self-fulfilling prophecy ("I had one cigarette, I have no willpower, therefore I will return to smoking.").

According to Bandura's **social learning theory**, people who engage in addictive behaviors have acquired these habits through learning, just like they learn other habits; hence, these behaviors can be examined and changed (Marlatt, 1985a). For example, people may learn to drink or smoke based on classical conditioning (the behavior of going to a pub leads to feeling relaxed, which leads to drinking, may turn into going to a pub leads to drinking), operant conditioning (I feel more confident when I drink), observational learning or modeling (others I respect drink), and cognitive factors (drinking helps me cope with stress). This model focuses on understanding the determinants of the behavior and the consequences of the behavior. For example, many addictive behaviors are performed to reduce stress and, hence, represent maladaptive coping mechanisms. Although there may be some source of the compulsion in internal body chemistry (a physical craving), this model emphasizes the importance of the individuals' expectation that the use of a particular drug or behavior will reduce stress in determining its use.

Relapse-prevention programs are designed to teach people who are trying to make a long-term change in their behavior how to anticipate and cope with the very real problem of relapse (Marlatt, 1985b). These programs have two major goals: helping people identify high-risk situations, those that are likely triggers of relapse, and helping people learn new ways to cope with these situations (see Table 12.8). In sum, relapse-prevention programs are like fire drills; people prepare for how they will act when a fire occurs so they can act this way easily and quickly when they are suddenly faced with a fire.

TABLE 12.8 *What Would You Do?*

- You've just picked up your car from the mechanic, and the bill is twice as much as you expected it to be. As you drive home, you find that the very thing you took the car in for is still not fixed. The car stalls in rush-hour traffic. You feel angry and frustrated; you crave a cigarette.
- You're at a party with friends. People are smoking and drinking. You're having a glass of wine and intense conversation. You always used to have a cigarette with your drink. It looks good.
- While waiting at the market checkout stand, you find yourself next to the cigarette stand and you notice that the market carries your old brand of cigarettes. Boy, do those cigarettes look good—you can almost taste one.

Ex-smokers are asked to read these situations and then quickly write down exactly what they would do as a way of testing how effective their coping strategy would be.

Source: Marlatt, 1985a.

Triggers of Relapse

Many people who are trying to give up an addictive behavior find that one of the most common triggers of relapse is experiencing a particular emotional state associated with engaging in the behavior (Grilo, Shiffman, & Wing, 1989; Hodgins, El-Guebaly, & Armstrong, 1995). Negative emotional states (which account for 35% of relapses) are situations in which the individual is experiencing anger or frustration, depression, helplessness, or boredom and are likely to lead to the first lapse. "Everything was going well until I failed my statistics exam. I was feeling low and decided a cigarette would cheer me up." These states are particularly likely to lead to relapse when individuals have made extensive use of the problem behavior in the past in a given situation (e.g., "every time I have a crunch at work, I have a drink to relax"), and thereby can feel helpless when faced with similar situations without the crutch of the negative behavior. Interpersonal conflict, which accounts for 16% of relapses, is another common high-risk situation. These situations often involve a conflict in a relationship, such as with a spouse, boss, friend, or family member. Finally, social pressure situations, which account for 20% of relapses, are those in which the individual is responding to the influence of another person or group of people exerting pressure to engage in the taboo behavior. This can be direct (e.g., "you should have some champagne, this is a celebration") or indirect (e.g., all your friends are smoking while they play poker). Other high-risk states can include positive emotional states (using the drug to enhance positive feelings, making "special exceptions" for using a drug during times of celebration) and testing personal control (to see if one really is no longer addicted).

Triggers of relapse can also include particular locations, people, times of day, and life stressors (Marlatt, 1985b; Marlatt & Gordon, 1980). For example, an alcoholic may need to be aware of hanging around with certain friends, being in certain places, or feeling particular moods. Specific triggers, however, vary for different people. People with an alcohol addiction, for example, are very likely to relapse while in a bar or tavern—in one study, 63% of the relapses occurred in this type of location. On the other hand, smokers are more likely to relapse at their homes (44%) or at work (19%). Relatively few people relapse in the morning, presumably because willpower is still high, but people often have particular times of day that are

Many of the triggers for relapse are situations in which the behavior has occurred previously and in the presence of particular people who are engaging in the behavior.
Source: Royalty-Free/Corbis.

most difficult for them. Having a tough day (or week or month) can lead people to say, "I deserve a break" and hence trigger relapse (Brandon, Copeland, & Saper, 1995; Shiffman et al., 1996). In fact, one study found that exercise-adherence rates were 27% lower in those who experienced three or more life events in the past 6 months than in those who experienced none (Oman & King, 2000). The AA program uses the acronym HALT, which refers to avoiding being too hungry, angry, lonely, or tired, all of which are factors that can trigger a relapse (Fletcher, 2001).

Relapse can be precipitated by experiencing an unexpected situation with which people are unable to cope (Marlatt, 1985a). For example, a woman who is trying not to drink may deliberately go only to restaurants that do not serve alcohol. Then, a particular restaurant may be closed unexpectedly one day, so she and her friend go to the restaurant next door, which serves alcohol. When her friend orders a drink, it may be impossible for her not to also order a drink because she has not thought through how to handle this situation. Smokers may relapse because they are offered a cigarette by someone, or they find a cigarette.

Relapse can also be precipitated by making a series of very small, apparently irrelevant decisions that lead one closer and closer to temptation and eventually to relapsing (see Figure 12.8; Marlatt, 1985a). For example, an alcoholic may keep wine in the house "in case company stops by," but then finds himself unable to resist extensive use of the problem behavior in the past in a given situation.

Strategies for Preventing Relapse

First, individuals need to identify high-risk situations that may lead them to experience a craving for a particular substance (Marlatt, 1985b). As one recovered alcoholic described it, "Look for the common thread in your relapses. Break that thread." (Fletcher, 2001). These situations can be identified through self-monitoring (recording exact amounts of alcohol consumed in each situation, including time

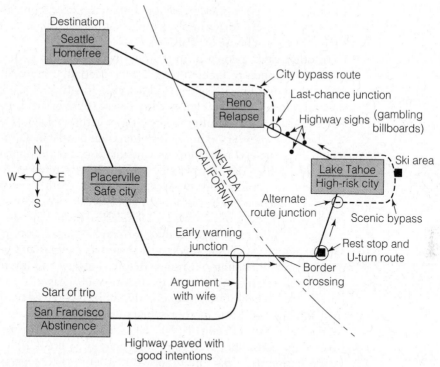

FIGURE 12.8 At each critical juncture, the gambling addict made a small decision that brought him one step closer to relapse. First, he chose to make a right and head to Lake Tahoe instead of a left heading to Placerville. Then, at the rest stop, he opted to continue on toward Lake Tahoe instead of making a U-turn and heading back toward Placerville. Third, he drove right into Reno instead of taking the city bypass route. And this series of decisions ultimately led to a weekend of gambling (Marlatt, 1985b).

of day, others present, location, mood, etc.), self-efficacy questionnaires, recall of past behaviors to determine their particular risk-prone situations, and/or direct observation. As described at the beginning of this chapter, Sarah worked with a therapist to identify the situations that prompted her alcohol use. After these high-risk situations have been identified, in some cases, people can simply remove themselves from the situation. They could, for example, avoid going to bars or being in other situations in which drinking is expected and could remove triggers for their behavior, such as ashtrays (for smokers), wine glasses, and junk food. One study with alcoholics in a hospital setting found that training in cue-exposure techniques, in which as part of therapy they were allowed to see and smell their preferred alcoholic beverage while imagining situational pressures to drink, led to much lower rates of drinking over time—only 44% of the patients who received this therapy were drinking at the 6-month follow-up, as compared to 79% of those who received traditional therapy (Monti, Rohsenow, Rubonis, & Niura, 1993). People who participated in this type of cue-exposure training learned coping skills that they could apply in real-life situations later on, which in turn likely increased their self-efficacy for refusing alcohol in tempting situations. People who are trying to make a change in their behavior should also be encouraged to choose the date carefully—dieters, for example, should not choose the week of Thanksgiving, nor should drinkers choose St. Patrick's Day!

In other cases, people need training in ways to handle high-risk situations in a new way (Cohen & Lichtenstein, 1990a; Marlatt, 1985b; Shadel & Mermelstein, 1993). For example, smokers could decide to drink coffee or chew gum during stressful times, and dieters could carry celery sticks or crackers to eat when they are bored. Because people often engage in addictive behaviors as a way of managing stress, relapse-prevention programs often train people in various stress-management techniques, such as relaxation and meditation. For example, instead of having a drink after a long day, people may learn to substitute other rewarding and positive behaviors, such as getting a massage, taking a long bath, or meditating. In this way, a negative addiction can be replaced by a positive addiction, or something else that the person enjoys and looks forward to. Similarly, because interpersonal conflict is often a trigger for relapse, people need to learn new skills for coping with these situations. One recovered alcoholic reports, "I share my feelings and get out anything that's on my mind, including old issues. Before, I always hid my feelings behind masks, and I drank to get away from all the emotional baggage. Now I make sure it doesn't pile up." (Fletcher, 2001). In one study, subjects received negative comments about their intelligence from another subject (really a confederate of the experimenters; Marlatt, Kosturn, & Lang, 1975). Subjects who had the opportunity to "retaliate" by giving electric shocks to the confederate then drank significantly less wine in a "wine-tasting test" than did those who did not get to express their anger.

Another strategy to prevent relapse is setting clear and attainable goals and creating an incentive for following through on them (Jason, Jayaraj, Blitz, Michaels, & Klett, 1990; Marlatt, 1985a). First, people should set attainable short-term goals so that they can experience quick feelings of success—a runner starts by jogging a mile or two or three, not by entering the Boston Marathon. In fact, the slogan of AA is "One day at a time." The goals should also be reasonable—not smoking for a day can quickly (although not necessarily easily) be attained, whereas "never have another cigarette for the rest of my life" is not going to be quickly accomplished. Second, people should create an incentive program that rewards them for reaching their goals and/or punishes them for not reaching their goals (Petry, Martin, Cooney, & Kranzler, 2000). Ex-smokers could, for example, plan to use the money they've saved on cigarettes to take a trip or buy new clothes. One worksite-based smoking-cessation program gave workers $10 for attending each of six group-counseling sessions, and then $1 a day for the next 180 days if they continued to not smoke. It was highly successful; 42% of participants were not smoking at the end of the program compared to 13% of those in a control group (Jason et al., 1990). Some relapse-prevention programs even ask people to set up a contract that specifies the costs of relapsing. One African American woman who was trying to stop smoking gave her therapist $50 and told her that if she smoked, the money should be donated to the Ku Klux Klan! These contracts could also specify that if a person is tempted to engage in the addictive behavior, they agree to wait at least 20 minutes before giving in. This will at least give them time to contemplate the behavior and not just act on the spur of the moment. They could also agree to only use a single "dose" at the time of relapse, for example, to have one beer, not a six-pack, or one cigarette, not a pack. This makes it easier to recover from a lapse.

> **Questioning the Research 12.4**
>
> Many of these studies examine the predictors of relapse regarding smoking cessation. But how confident should you be in these findings? (Hint: What is the relapse that is being measured?).

Social support, either from friends and family members or therapists and support groups, can play an important role in helping people maintain a new behavior (Black, Gleser, & Kooyers, 1990; Marlatt, 1985a; McBride et al., 1998; Mermelstein, Cohen, Lichtenstein, Baer, & Kamarck, 1986; Nides et al., 1995; Tsoh et al., 1997). People who are trying to change their behavior should tell people they are close to as well as people they spend a lot of time with about their intentions. These other people can be asked to support the behavior change, such as by not smoking around them or offering them unhealthy foods and by expressing confidence in the person's ability to change the behavior (Cohen & Lichtenstein, 1990b; Sorensen, Pechacek, & Pallonen, 1986). For example, one study with pregnant smokers found that those who received high levels of support from their partner were much more likely to quit than those without such support (McBride et al., 1998). However, because relapse can be precipitated by a reaction against perceived imposition of rules or regulations governing the prohibited behavior, it is important that the person himself or herself makes the decision to change the behavior. For example, people can throw off this prohibition, particularly if they believe that others (family members, friends) are forcing them to abstain. Therapists and support groups are most effective at maintaining behavior change when they continue their interaction with the patient over time, in part because such contact helps people maintain their self-efficacy for behavior change even in the face of great temptation and occasional lapses (Curry & McBride, 1994; Irvin et al., 1999; Zhu et al., 1996). Ongoing social support, brief weekly phone calls from a therapist, and even mailings all lead to much greater sustained behavior change (Brandon, Collins, Juliano, & Lazev, 2000; Perri & Nezu, 1993). For example, one study found that 14.7% of smokers who received a self-help quit kit had stopped smoking at a 12-month follow-up as compared to 19.8% of those who received the kit plus one telephone counseling session and 26.7% of those who received the kit plus up to six counseling sessions (Zhu et al., 1996).

Another strategy for preventing relapse is helping people think about their old behaviors in new ways (Marlatt, 1985a). Relapse prevention programs try to help people focus on the short-term versus the long-term consequences of engaging in the behavior (PIG, or the Problem of Immediate Gratification). The immediate consequences of engaging in an addictive behavior may be particularly strong and positive (e.g., relaxation, feel good, fit in), whereas the long-term consequences may be less salient and largely negative (e.g., have trouble with work, develop serious health problems). So, people need to be trained to focus on the delayed effects of giving in to temptation. They also need to recognize that these responses arise and subside on their own (e.g., as opposed to thinking that these cravings will gain in intensity until they give in). Learning how to externalize and label their desires is one strategy for reducing the tendency to give in to the urge (e.g., "I am experiencing an urge to smoke" instead of "I really want a cigarette"). They

TABLE 12.9   *Information YOU Can Use*

- Screening for diseases gives you valuable information that can increase your life expectancy because early detection of diseases often increases treatment options. So be sure to learn and follow recommended screenings.
- Make sure to adhere to medical regimens. Clarify any instructions about how to adhere, and develop strategies—such as creating reminders, incorporating treatment into your daily routine, and enlisting support from family and friends—that help you follow these recommendations.
- Given the importance of physician–patient interaction for increasing satisfaction with medical care as well as adherence to treatment recommendations, choose your medical-care providers carefully. Try to find a doctor who shares your beliefs about patient–physician interaction and one with whom you feel comfortable sharing information.
- If you are hospitalized, take steps to improve your psychological and physical well-being. Try to bring your own clothes and a few items from home to personalize the space. Encourage family and friends to visit to provide support. Make sure to get information about the procedures you will undergo and what to expect during your recovery.
- When trying to make behavior changes, develop strategies to help you succeed. Identify high-risk situations, and try to avoid them. Set clear and attainable goals, and mark your progress toward achieving them. Learn strategies for coping with high-risk situations so that lapses, which will occur, don't turn into relapses.

---

may also need to be trained to reevaluate their expectancies for engaging in the behavior. However, physiological cravings do matter—one study found that only 7% of smokers who were highly dependent on nicotine were still not smoking 2 years after treatment, as compared to 19% of those without such a dependency (Killen, Fortmann, Kraemer, Varady, & Newman, 1992).

Finally, relapse-prevention strategies include preparing people to see a lapse in behavior as a single, isolated incidence as opposed to a disaster that can never be undone (Marlatt, 1985a). According to the *abstinence violation effect*, if people expect they will never give in to temptation, when and if they do have a lapse in behavior, they are likely to blame it on themselves, which could lead to a total relapse (Curry, Marlatt, & Gordon, 1987; Marlatt & Gordon, 1980). For example, if a person is dieting but chooses to eat a piece of cheesecake, he or she will likely feel guilty. Then, that person will likely choose to reduce the guilt by relying on the same maladaptive coping mechanisms—eating more. Relapse-prevention programs should include exposure to some such high-risk settings to give people a chance to cope with such challenges in a controlled environment—some programs even include a "scheduled lapse." These programs also point to one potential drawback of inpatient treatment for making behavior change; namely, that patients can make great strides in their behavior change when they are in a new environment and with new people but have trouble maintaining this behavior after they return to their regular lives and the situations that triggered their old behaviors. Losing weight, for example, can be relatively easy in a special 1- or 2-week treatment program in which low-fat meals are attractively prepared and served, but much harder when you return to the rush of daily life and the temptation of fast food at every corner.

Summary

1. Screening to detect illness, or even an increased likelihood of developing illness, at an early stage is an increasingly important part of health promotion. By detecting a treatable disease or abnormality in its early stages, early detection can lead to the enhancement and prolonging of life.

2. Several factors influence whether a person chooses to engage in screening behavior. These include demographics factors (e.g., income, education), individual differences (e.g., self-efficacy, social norms, vulnerability), and practitioners' beliefs about the benefits of screening.

3. Benefits of screening include the opportunity to seek early treatment and/or engage in health-promoting behaviors and make realistic plans for the future. However, early detection can also lead to psychological harm (e.g., depression, anxiety, guilt), may not eliminate uncertainty, and may have no benefits overall in terms of survival. Screening results may also be inaccurate and screening tests may cause physical harm.

4. Strategies for increasing screening include making people aware of the need to screen and its benefits, providing reminders, asking people to form their own specific plans for engaging in screening, and removing barriers to screening.

5. Health care utilization is influenced by numerous factors, including how quickly people notice a physical experience, situational and social factors, people's expectations about symptoms, and people's beliefs about whether a symptom requires medical treatment. The stages of delay model describes the following steps people go through when deciding whether to get help: appraisal delay, illness delay, utilization or behavioral delay, scheduling delay, and treatment delay. Numerous factors influence people's willingness to seek medical care, including the nature of the symptoms and demographics (e.g., age, sex, race, culture, religion). Demographic factors may also influence the type of medical care received.

6. Patient–practitioner communication can be challenging for many reasons. Patients may be reluctant to share both information and feelings. Doctors may fail to provide patients with information, and patients may forget or misinterpret the information they are given. There are several techniques for improving patient–practitioner communication, which in turn can lead to improved satisfaction with medical care.

7. The experience of hospitalization is anxiety-provoking for many patients, in part because this environment leads to a loss of control. Providing patients with information on what to expect and strategies to increase control can lead to important benefits.

8. Doctors and other medical professionals experience high levels of burnout, in part because interacting with patients is emotionally demanding, stressful, and includes failure on a relatively consistent basis. Health professionals who have the opportunity to express their feelings may experience lower levels of stress and burnout.

9. Many people show relatively low rates of adherence with recommended medical regimens. Intentional nonadherence occurs when patients understand the practitioner's directions, but modify the regimen in some way or ignore it completely because they are unwilling to follow the recommendations. Unintentional nonadherence occurs when people intend to comply, and may even believe they are complying, but for some reason they are not following instructions.

10. The causes of intentional nonadherence include aspects of the treatment, individual differences, the match between patient and practitioner's styles, social support, demographic factors (age, culture, income), and the quality of the patient–practitioner relationship. The cause of unintentional nonadherence is typically the information given to the patient about the treatment.

11. Adherence can be measured in a variety of ways, including asking the patient, counting pills remaining in a bottle, testing therapeutic outcomes, and measuring the concentration of the drug in the patient's body. Each of these approaches has both strengths and weaknesses.

12. Strategies for increasing adherence include giving patients more information, reminding people to take medication, helping people understand the consequences of nonadherence, providing rewards for adherence, creating strategies for integrating treatment into patients' lives, and improving doctor–patient relationships.

13. Relapse occurs when people make a change in their behavior but then fail to maintain this change over time. There are several theories of addiction which explain relapse in different ways, including the moral or self-control theory, the disease model, and social learning theory.

14. Triggers of relapse include experiencing a specific emotional state, being in a particular setting (location, time of day, people), encountering an unexpected situation, and making a series of small (seemingly irrelevant) decisions.

15. Strategies for preventing relapse include identifying high-risk situations, providing training in ways to handle high-risk situations in new ways, setting clear and attainable goals, providing social support for new behaviors, helping people think about their old behaviors in new ways, and preparing people to see a lapse in their behavior as an isolated incident and not a relapse.

Key Terms

adherence
appraisal delay
behavioral (or utilization) delay
burnout
disease model
health behavior
illness behavior

illness delay
intentional nonadherence
moral theory (self-control theory)
relapse
scheduling delay
screening

sick-role behavior
social learning theory
stages of delay model
treatment delay
unintentional nonadherence

Thought Questions

1. A close friend confides in you that she is thinking about getting tested for HIV. What four things would you advise her to consider prior to getting the test?

2. Describe two symptoms that lead people to seek help for a medical problem and two symptoms that lead people to delay getting help.

3. How can we increase patient–practitioner communication in a climate of HMOs and cost-saving measures?

4. Describe two strategies that could be useful in decreasing *unintentional* nonadherence and two strategies that could be useful in decreasing *intentional* nonadherence.

5. Your brother has smoked for nearly 5 years but gave up smoking as his New Year's resolution 2 weeks ago. What four pieces of advice could you give him to help him stick with this goal?

Answers to Questioning the Research

Answer 12.1. It is important to remember that people choose whether they want to get screened for diseases—estimates are that only between 5 and 20% of those at risk for Huntington's disease and HIV infection, for example, undergo testing (Marteau, 1995). People who do not choose to get tested may be more afraid of a positive test or less prepared for the result. On the other hand, people who choose to get tested may already fear they are positive—especially if they have relatives with the disease—and testing may reduce anxiety even if it provides bad news. In contrast, a person who has no expectation of getting a positive result may be shocked. In fact, younger women who learn that their baby has Down's syndrome show greater and more sustained anxiety than older women who are already aware of their higher risk. In sum, even if some people do show few signs of depression and anxiety following testing, others may experience negative psychological effects for some time.

Answer 12.2. Whenever researchers use hypothetical situations to elicit responses, it is possible that findings in a real-world situation would differ (as you might remember from Chapter 2, this is a type of external validity). It is therefore possible that these findings showing that greater fear and concern led to greater intentions to immediately contact a physician are simply a reflection of what women report they would do following reading this hypothetical scenario but may not represent their real-life behavior in this situation.

Answer 12.3. Although it seems obvious that patients who adhere to medical recommendations would show better health than those who do not, research is mixed on whether adherence really benefits health (Haynes, McKibbon, & Kanani, 1996; Hays et al., 1994). In fact, researchers in one study found that while patients who took medicine had a lower mortality rate than those who did not, this association was true even for those who were in the placebo group; hence, they received no real physical benefits from adhering (Gallagher et al., 1993; Horwitz et al., 1990). For example, women in the placebo group who were poor adherers to the placebo medication were 2.8 times more likely to have died 2 to 3 years later than those who were good adherers.

Similarly, men who were bad adherers were 2.6 times as likely to have died than those who took the placebo medication faithfully. It is likely that patients who adhere to medical recommendations differ in numerous ways from those who don't. They may, for example, be more optimistic, more conscientious, and have more social support, all of which could lead to better health. Future research clearly needs to examine exactly how—and indeed whether—adherence truly impacts health.

Answer 12.4. One of the very tricky issues in measuring the effectiveness of different behavior-change programs is defining exactly what *success* is. Many studies suggest that long-term behavior change is relatively rare: After all, about 97% of people who quit smoking on their own return to smoking within 6 months, and even for those in formal smoking-cessation programs, only about 20 to 30% achieve long-term quitting (Cohen et al., 1989; Hughes et al., 1992). Ockene et al. (2000) therefore suggest that researchers set specific criteria for assessing relapse (e.g., smoking five or more cigarettes per day for 3 consecutive days) as compared to lapse (e.g., taking even a puff), successful change (e.g., at least 7 days of not smoking), short-term change (e.g., 6 months or more of abstinence), and long-term change (e.g., 1 year or more of abstinence). In sum, researchers must be careful in exactly how they measure success and failure of a given behavior-change program, including the length of time they track the participants, the measures used to assess behavior change, and the group to which the participants are compared. Behavior change may be more possible than we believe!

CHAPTER 13

Designing Persuasive Interventions

Outline

- Stephanie is 25 years old, and for as long as she can remember, she's spent most summer weekends at the beach. Although she's heard that tanning can lead to some types of cancer, Stephanie rarely uses sunscreen because she thinks she looks much more attractive when she has a tan. She's really not that concerned about cancer anyway—most of Stephanie's friends also don't use sunscreen, and she's heard that skin cancer can be treated easily.

- Damon is a sophomore in college and is a residential advisor in his dorm. As part of his training, he learns about the dangers of using illegal drugs, such as marijuana, cocaine, and Ecstasy, and then gives presentations to the students in his dorm to warn them away from these substances. Damon used to occasionally enjoy getting high when he was at a party, but now finds himself feeling more and more uncomfortable with that behavior.

- Bill is 45 years old and has been overweight since he was in his early 20s. He knows that his weight places him at risk of experiencing a heart attack, but he just doesn't see how he could find the time to exercise. However, Bill's doctor assures him that exercising would have substantial health benefits and suggests some specific approaches Bill could try, including using the stairs at work instead of the elevator and playing tennis with his kids on the weekend. This discussion gives Bill confidence that he could start exercising, and he decides to give it a try.

- Lucinda is 36 years old and desperately needs to have a cavity filled. Although she knows that she needs the filling, she is very anxious. Based on past experiences, Lucinda knows that she benefits from having lots of information about what to expect, and so she asks the dental hygienist to carefully describe each step of the procedure. Much to her surprise, the filling takes very little time and hardly hurts at all.

- Debbie has a summer job in a local Planned Parenthood clinic, and she has been asked to help create two different types of condom-promotion workshops for teenagers—one for males and one for females. Debbie decides that the workshop designed for boys should focus on how condoms make sex last longer and how it can therefore feel even better for both partners. On the other hand, she believes the workshop designed for girls should emphasize how to put a condom on one's partner and how to assertively insist on condom use.

Preview

This chapter examines how psychological theories and principles can be used to design persuasive communications, such as television commercials, pamphlets, and interventions, that influence people's health-related behavior. First, we examine the use of rational and emotional appeals, with a particular focus on the effectiveness of threatening messages. Next, we examine how interventions based on psychological theories, including prospect theory, learning theories, attribution theory, cognitive dissonance theory, social cognitive theory, and the theory of planned behavior, can influence health-related behaviors. Finally, we examine the benefits of receiving personally relevant messages in promoting various types of health-related behavior, including screening, managing pain and illness, and changing behavior.

Are Emotional Appeals Effective?

One of the biggest challenges facing health professionals is how to effectively persuade people to change their health-related behavior. Many health-promotion campaigns rely at least in part on mass communication, including newspapers and magazines, billboards and posters, and radio and television ads. Each of these approaches has certain advantages and disadvantages. For example, brochures can provide detailed, factual information and can be read at a person's convenience. However, brochures can be hard to deliver to the people who need the information, and people may choose to not read them at all. On the other hand, television advertising easily reaches a large audience and can be very vivid and impactful. This type of advertising is, however, expensive to produce and often provides relatively little factual information. Public-health professionals therefore must make complex decisions about the relative costs and benefits of each potential approach to delivering health-promotion information.

Some health-promotion messages simply provide the facts about a given behavior, with the hope that giving people the information will motivate change. According to this view, people who understand that smoking causes lung cancer or that unprotected sex can lead to pregnancy, for example, will be motivated to change their behavior to avoid these negative consequences. Similarly, early efforts at HIV prevention focused on providing people with straightforward information about the factors leading to the spread of HIV (e.g., unprotected sex, sharing needles). One study of 127 public-service announcements on television about AIDS revealed that 51% simply presented factual information, such as how AIDS is transmitted and the safety of donating blood (Freimuth, Hammond, Edgar, & Monohan, 1990); in the late 1980s, the surgeon general of the United States even mailed a pamphlet containing this information to every U.S. household.

Unfortunately, and as you might imagine, in most cases, information is not a sufficient motivator of behavior change. Most smokers, for example, are fully aware of the health consequences of their behavior, yet they continue to smoke. In fact, we all engage in behaviors (sometimes frequently) that we know are not great for our health (e.g., not wearing a seat belt, failing to use sunscreen, eating high-fat foods). Research studies provide additional support for the view that information alone is rarely a sufficient motivator of behavior. In one early study on health-promotion messages, Leventhal, Singer, and Jones (1965) found that none of the students who received information about the importance of having a tetanus shot actually went to the health center for the vaccination. In sum, although providing people with information about healthy behaviors does, not surprisingly, increase their knowledge about such behavior, it is rarely sufficient to lead to behavior change.

Researchers have therefore examined the use of **emotional appeals** in an attempt to change health-related behavior. This section will examine the use of emotional appeals, the drawbacks of fear-based appeals, and the strategies for increasing the effectiveness of fear-based messages.

The Use of Emotional Appeals

Some health-promotion messages provide emotional, as opposed to rational, messages about the consequences of engaging in a given behavior (Reeves, Newhagen, Maibach, Basil, & Kurz, 1991). Because people tend to seek pleasant experiences, which help them maintain positive moods, some emotion-based messages have used positive stimuli, such as appealing music and attractive people. Positive emotion-based appeals could, for example, show people enjoying themselves at a party without drinking or smoking, or a couple becoming closer through discussing condom use. Researchers in one study compared the effectiveness of different types of messages at promoting HPV vaccination acceptability among mothers of young girls (see Table 13.1; Cox, Cox, Sturm, & Zimet, 2010). Participants received a message featuring graphical statistics, nongraphical statistics, or a control message, and then rated their intentions to have their daughters vaccinated. The findings indicated that the graphic messages were the most effective: 53% of mothers in this

TABLE 13.1 *Examples of Messages Promoting HPV Vaccinations*

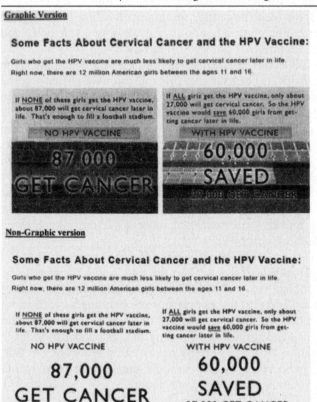

Source: Cox, Dena S.; Cox, Anthony D.; Sturm, Lynne; Zimet, Greg, "Behavioral interventions to increase HPV vaccination acceptability among mothers of young girls," *Health Psychology*, Vol 29, 1, 29–39, Jan 1, 2010, American Psychological Association, reprinted with permission. APA is not responsible for the accuracy of this translation.

Mothers who received the message showing graphical statistics about the importance of the HPV vaccine reported higher intentions to have their daughters vaccinated than those who received the nongraphical statistics (Cox et al., 2010).

TABLE 13.2   *Different Types of Emotion-Based Ads Promoting Condom Use*

- I enjoy sex, but I don't want to die for it.
- Someone I respect has been urging me to use condoms. It's the surgeon general. Believe me, I'm listening.
- Introducing condoms that let you feel good before, during, and after.
- Men could use some protection from women—and vice versa.

The first two ads are designed to elicit high fear, whereas the second two are designed to elicit low fear.

Source: Struckman-Johnson, Gilliland, Struckman-Johnson, & North, 1990.

condition stated their daughters would definitely get the vaccine, compared to 41% of those in the nongraphic condition and 37% in the control group. In line with this finding, some research suggests that attitudes that are based in how people feel about something are more predictive of behavior than attitudes that are based in what people think about something (Lawton, Conner, & McEachan, 2009).

Fear-based appeals are a particular type of emotional appeal that uses negative stimuli to create the threat of impending danger or harm caused by engaging in particular types of behavior (e.g., drug use, smoking) or failing to engage in other types of behavior (e.g., not using a condom, not wearing a seat belt), and thereby motivate behavior (Freimuth et al., 1990; Higbee, 1969; Rogers, 1975). These messages sometimes use scary verbal statements and may show graphic, even disgusting, images (see Table 13.2). For example, one television ad promoting the use of seat belts shows a young man backing his car out of the driveway on his way to pick up ice cream for his pregnant wife, but he wasn't wearing his seat belt and then was hit by a speeding car. In some other countries, such as Australia and Canada, television ads may include even more graphic images, such as dead bodies and crash survivors learning how to walk again. Fear-based messages are designed to increase people's feelings of vulnerability to various health problems and thereby motivate them to change their behavior (Janis, 1967; Leventhal, 1970). Moreover, as compared to positive messages, negative ones are thought to be more primary, easier to understand, more quickly processed, and more accurately remembered (Reeves, Lang, Thorson, & Rothschild, 1989).

Emotion-based messages are especially effective if the person is not very involved in or concerned about the message. Researchers in one study compared the effectiveness of providing college women with information regarding the risk of acquiring the hepatitis B virus, and thus the importance of obtaining a vaccination, using either narrative evidence (meaning a personal account by someone who considered themselves low risk and yet had become infected) or statistical evidence (meaning general information regarding the prevalence rate of this disease; De Wit, Das, & Vet, 2008). Those who received the narrative message reported higher levels of perceived risk and intentions to obtain vaccination.

The Drawbacks of Fear-Based Appeals

One of the earliest studies on the effectiveness of fear appeals was conducted by Leventhal and Watts (1966). Visitors to a state fair were recruited to participate in a smoking-cessation study and were randomly assigned to receive one of three smoking-cessation messages. The low-fear message consisted of a color film describing the threat of lung cancer using charts and diagrams; the medium-fear message consisted of the same film plus an additional segment documenting how a small-town newspaper editor discovered he had lung cancer; and the high-fear message consisted of the same film and additional segment plus a 10-minute color sequence showing an operation in which a lung is removed. Not surprisingly, people who watched the high-fear film showed many signs of distress, including looking away, groaning, and even crying. Researchers then gave participants the option to have a chest X-ray at a nearby booth and also sent all participants a questionnaire 5 months later to examine long-term behavior change.

This study revealed that low-fear ads versus high-fear ads have a different impact on behavior at different times. First, those in the low-fear condition were the most likely to immediately get an X-ray of their lungs at a nearby booth (53% in low fear versus 44% in medium fear, 6% in high fear). These findings clearly suggest that high-fear messages were much less effective than low or medium ones in influencing short-term behavior. However, the follow-up questionnaire revealed significant differences in the opposite direction: 57% of those in the low-fear and moderate-fear conditions reported cutting down on smoking compared to 79% of those in the high-fear condition. In sum, high-fear messages may be ineffective in the short term, as people react defensively to these upsetting and personally relevant messages, but may be effective over time.

However, more recent research suggests that fear-based appeals often just aren't effective (Des Jarlais, Friedman, Casriel, & Kott, 1987; Evans, 1988). For example, one study of Project DARE (Drug Abuse Resistance Education), a commonly used fear-based drug-prevention program for children, found that this program has little, if any, effect on preventing or reducing drug use, and it is often less effective than programs that focus simply on social skills (Ennett, Tobler, Ringwalt, & Flewelling, 1994). Similarly, a fear-arousing mass-media campaign in Australia to promote condom use led to an increase in anxiety but had little if any effect on knowledge or behavior (Rigby, Brown, Anagnostou, Ross, & Rosser, 1989; Sherr, 1990). A meta-analysis examining the effects of fear-inducing arguments about HIV revealed that such messages increased perceptions of the risk of HIV but led to decreased knowledge about HIV as well as decreased condom use (Earl & Albarracin, 2007). Similarly, and as described in Box 13.1: Focus on Development, pregnancy-prevention programs, which consist largely of fear-based messages about the hazards of engaging in premarital sex, are completely ineffective in leading to intended behaviors. Ironically, people who receive high-fear messages often report that they are very influenced but in reality show lower levels of attitude and behavior change than those who receive positive approaches (Evans, Rozelle, Lasater, Dembroski, & Allen, 1970; Janis & Feshbach, 1953).

One of the problems with fear appeals is that they create considerable anxiety, which can lead to a constriction of cognitive processing, resulting in marked interference with learning, attention, and comprehension (Janis, 1967). For example, smokers who receive a strong fear message show more tension and concern about lung cancer but less attitude change (Janis & Terwilliger, 1962), and high school students who receive a strong fear message about decayed teeth and gum disease remember fewer arguments from the message and show less attitude change than those who received a more mild argument (Janis & Feshbach, 1953). Recent research even shows that people process threatening information with more efficient

Box 13.1

Focus on Development: The Hazards of Fear-Based Approaches to Pregnancy Prevention

Some programs designed to prevent teenage pregnancy are largely based in fear appeals. These abstinence-only approaches, in which students learn only about strategies for abstaining from sexual intercourse before marriage, and not about contraceptive use, may include scary (and inaccurate) information about the long-term effects of premarital sex and the ineffectiveness of contraception. However, most research on such programs reveals that those who receive abstinence-only education are no more likely than those in a control group to abstain from sexual activity or delay the start of sexual activity, nor do such programs influence number of partners, condom use, or sexual initiation (Trenholm et al., 2008; Underhill, Montgomery, & Operario, 2007). Encouragingly, some research reveals that abstinence-only interventions that do not rely on fear-based messaging can help prevent sexual involvement in young adolescents (Jemmott, Jemmott, & Fong, 2010). Researchers in one study randomly assigned African American students in grades 6 and 7 to an abstinence-only intervention targeting reduced sexual intercourse, to a safer sex intervention targeting increased condom use only, a comprehensive intervention targeting both reducing sexual intercourse and increasing condom use, or a health-promotion control intervention. The abstinence-only intervention led to a reduction in sexual initiation. Specifically, the probability of ever having sexual intercourse by the 24-month follow-up was 33.5% in the abstinence-only intervention compared to 48.5% in the control group. Similarly, fewer abstinence-only intervention participants (20.6%) than control participants (29.0%) reported having coitus in the previous 3 months during the follow-up period. Although the abstinence-only intervention did not affect condom use, participants in the comprehensive intervention had fewer sexual partners than in the control group.

disengagement (smokers disengage from smoking-prevention messages as shown neurologically; Kessels, Ruiter, & Jansma, 2010). In line with this view, a study by Gintner, Rectanus, Accord, & Parker (1987) found that people who had a parent with hypertension and, who, hence, already see themselves as vulnerable to this problem were more than twice as likely to attend a blood pressure screening if they read a message about the benefits of acting to maintain well-being than a message that emphasized the dire consequences of hypertension. On the other hand, those without a family history of hypertension were more likely to receive screening after they received threatening information.

Moreover, because engaging in a behavior known to be risky makes people feel bad, people who receive threatening and personally relevant messages may ignore, deny, and minimize these threats (Chaiken, 1987; Freeman, Hennessy, & Marzullo, 2001; Halpern, 1994; Kunda, 1990). For example, heavy coffee drinkers are more critical of a study supposedly showing a link between caffeine consumption and disease than those who don't drink coffee, presumably because coffee drinkers really don't want to believe they are engaging in a health-damaging behavior (Liberman & Chaiken, 1992; Sherman, Nelson, & Steele, 2000). Similarly, heavy smokers evaluate their health risks as lower than light smokers, and long-term smokers evaluate their health risks as lower than short-term smokers, presumably to justify their behavior. Smokers see smoking as less risky and rate their own risk as even lower than the risk of the "typical smoker" (Halpern, 1994; McCoy et al., 1992; Strecher, Kreuter, & Kobrin, 1995).

People will even discount the risk of a particular threat when they are given clear information from medical professionals about such threats. For example, smokers who are told they have a gene that places them at greater risk of experiencing negative consequences from smoking are more likely to inaccurately recall the level of risk and to misinterpret the meaning of the result (Lipkus et al., 2004). Similarly, women who are at risk of developing breast/ovarian cancer tend to discount their risk of developing cancer, presumably as a way to manage the stress of this genetic susceptibility (Shiloh, Drori, Orr-Urtreger, & Friedman, 2009).

Another way of reducing fear is by seeing the problem as more common—a strategy of "well, if everyone else is doing it, it must not be that bad" (Croyle, Sun, & Louie, 1993; Gerrard, Gibbons, Benthin, & Hessling, 1996). For example, one study by Gerrard et al. (1996) found that teenagers who engage in various risky behaviors, such as smoking, drinking, and reckless driving, convince themselves that other teenagers are engaging in similar levels of risky behavior. Similarly, as compared to students who are told their cholesterol is at a low level, students who receive information that their cholesterol is at a somewhat risky high level perceive high cholesterol as a less serious threat, view the test as less accurate, and see high cholesterol as more common (Croyle et al., 1993).

People at high risk may even respond defensively to messages that try to change their behavior and thus deny their risk or the seriousness of the behavior. For example, college students who hear anti-drinking messages may want to drink more, and smokers who hear anti-smoking messages may show an increase in motivation to smoke. Moreover, smokers often see anti-smoking ads as biased and unconvincing, and those who see a given anti-smoking message as biased may even increase their intention to continue smoking (Rhodes, Roskos-Ewoldsen, Edison, & Bradford, 2008). Anti-smoking ads may thus backfire because smokers who see such ads simply bring to mind the people they see in their lives who support their smoking and don't process such messages. If smokers see ads as biased, they may react against them. All of this evidence suggests that fear-based appeals can have some unintended—and even dangerous—side effects.

Making Fear-Based Appeals Work

However, fear-based appeals can at times influence health-related behavior. When are such messages effective? First, messages need to create a moderate level of fear (see Figure 13.1; Janis, 1967; Janis & Feshbach, 1953; Leventhal, 1970; Witte & Allen, 2000). At very low levels of fear, the danger is not seen as very important or very severe, and hence the average person will be relatively unmotivated to seek help. On the other hand, and as described previously, at high levels of fear, people try to deny or minimize the threat to cope with their anxiety. However, at moderate levels of fear, people will be motivated to protect themselves because the threat seems relatively likely and relatively severe, but they will not be paralyzed by anxiety and hence unable to act. For example, Janis and Feshbach (1953) found

FIGURE 13.1
According to Janis (1967), medium-threat ads, which create moderate fear, are the most effective at creating attitude and behavior change. Low-threat ads don't motivate people to change, and high-threat ads lead to considerable anxiety, which in turn can reduce cognitive processing and paralyze behavior change.

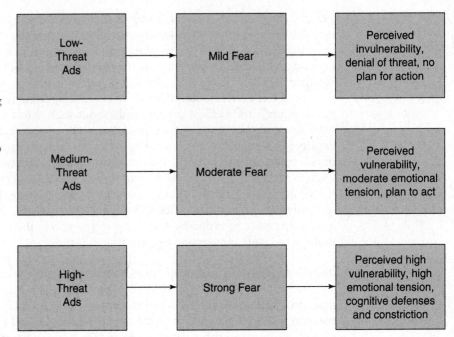

that messages that led to a moderate level of fear were the most effective in getting junior high students to engage in better dental hygiene habits.

Second, because fear appeals create considerable anxiety, people must be given a specific strategy for handling the anxiety to avoid the motivation to minimize or deny the threat (Leventhal et al., 1965; Self & Rogers, 1990; Sturges & Rogers, 1996). Students who receive highly threatening messages but who are told that they can take some specific action to manage the threat show stronger intentions to change their behavior than those who receive messages that frighten them but don't give strategies for coping (Self & Rogers, 1990). Similarly, Leventhal et al. (1965) found that 27.6% of students who received a fear message coupled with specific instructions on how to get a tetanus shot did have the vaccination as compared to 3.3% of those who received a fear message without such detailed instructions. So, fear-based drug-prevention campaigns are probably not an effective approach to attitude and behavior change, but programs that give teenagers specific techniques for managing peer pressure to use drugs without alienating friends may be quite effective. For example, the Midwestern Prevention Project, a moderately successful drug-prevention program for middle school and junior high students, provides students with information about drugs coupled with training in strategies for resisting social pressure, such as assertiveness training, modeling, and role play (MacKinnon et al., 1991). Participation in this program leads to more negative attitudes toward drugs and decreases in intentions to use drugs as well as decreased reported drug use.

Fear appeals are also effective when they focus on the short-term, as opposed to the long-term, consequences (Klohn & Rogers, 1991; Pechmann, 1997)—many people, especially teenagers, just aren't concerned about long-term consequences. Many college students say that having an unplanned pregnancy would be worse than getting HIV, presumably because pregnancy leads to an instant problem, whereas developing HIV is a much more distant problem. Similarly, people might learn that tanning can cause skin cancer but still feel that they'd like to be tan because they look healthier and more attractive (Broadstock, Borland, & Garson, 1992; Leary & Jones, 1993). As described at the beginning of the chapter, Stephanie's desire to tan—and thereby appear more attractive—was a much stronger motivator of her behavior (e.g., lack of sunscreen use) than her concern about skin cancer. In fact, Jones and Leary (1994) found that college students were more persuaded to use sunscreen after reading an essay describing the short-term negative effects of tanning on appearance (e.g., increasing wrinkles, scarring, aging) than an essay describing the long-term negative effects (e.g., the health risks of tanning, prevalence of different types of skin cancer). One study with 19 young drug sniffers (who often go on to use IV drugs) found that none gave concern about AIDS as a reason for not using IV drugs—they simply didn't want to lose control over their lives because of addiction (Des Jarlais et al., 1987).

Questioning the Research 13.1

The Jones and Leary (1994) study on the benefits of emphasizing short-term negative consequences of tanning was conducted with college students. Do you believe this type of emphasis would be equally effective in older adults? Why or why not?

Finally, fear appeals may also work when they force people to actually imagine having a particular disease or problem and thereby lead to a heightened sense of vulnerability (Janis & Mann, 1965). One public-service announcement designed to enhance people's perceived vulnerability to HIV featured an attractive Hispanic man saying the following:

"Do I look like someone who has AIDS? Of course not. I am Alejandro Paredes. I finished school. I have a good job. I help support my family. My

Messages that emphasize the short-term negative effects of tanning can be more effective in reducing tanning than those that emphasize the longer-term negative consequences.
Source: © kupicoo/iStockphoto.

kind of guy doesn't get AIDS, right? Well, I have AIDS, and I don't mind telling you it's devastating. If I had a second chance, I'd be informed. Believe me." (Freimuth et al., 1990, p. 788)

This appeal is clearly designed to increase people's vulnerability to HIV and to eliminate the use of various cognitive defenses against this information (e.g., only poor people get HIV; only people who look unhealthy have HIV). Researchers in one study examined the effectiveness of showing college students UV photographs of themselves that illustrated the damage to their skin resulting from sun exposure (Gibbons, Gerrard, Lane, Mahler, & Kulick, 2005). Students who saw these photos showed a decrease in visiting tanning booths (from 31% to 16%) whereas those who didn't see such photos reported an increase (28% to 47%). Similarly, college students who received UV photographs of their own skin showing skin damage and information about the long-term effects of such exposure (e.g., wrinkles, age spots) showed more sun protective behaviors and lighter skin 4 to 5 months later (at the end of the summer; Mahler, Kulik, Gerrard, & Gibbons, 2007). Figure 13.2 shows the effectiveness of receiving both a personalized photo and information on the hazards of photoaging on time spent tanning.

One strategy for reducing people's tendency to engage in defensive processing is to allow for some type of **self-affirmation** along with the threatening messages (Sherman & Cohen, 2002). This strategy can increase people's receptivity to messages that potentially threaten the self because buffering people's feelings of self-worth increases their ability to accept information that is seen as threatening in terms of maintaining a positive self-concept. For example, researchers in one study gave participants information about the risks of caffeine for health problems (van Koningsbruggen, Das, & Roskos-Ewoldsen, 2009). Among those who regularly

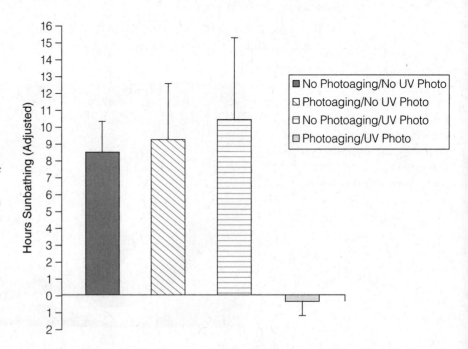

FIGURE 13.2

College students who receive information on photoaging as well as a personalized photo of their own face showing UV damage spend far fewer hours tanning than those who receive no information or those who receive only photoaging information or the photograph (data from Mahler, Kulik, Gibbons, Gerrard, & Harrell, 2010).

drank coffee, for whom these messages were highly relevant, self-affirmation led to more accessibility of the message, more positive beliefs about message quality, and more intentions to change behavior. Self-affirmation also increases people's responsiveness to messages regarding the hazards of mercury in seafood among frequent seafood eaters (Griffin & Harris, 2011), leads to higher rates of condom purchasing (Sherman et al., 2000), increases fruit and vegetable consumption (Epton & Harris, 2008), and increases ratings of risk, fear, and intention to reduce alcohol use (Harris & Napper, 2005). Box 13.2: Focus on Research describes the benefits of self-affirmation for increasing intentions to reduce smoking.

How does self-affirmation lead to changes in health-related attitudes, intentions, and behavior? One possibility is that affirming the self allows one to pay more attention to messages designed to promote behavior change. To test this idea, researchers in one study gave women an article to read that described the link between alcohol and breast cancer (Klein & Harris, 2009). Half of the women had the opportunity to self-affirm, whereas the others did not. Among women who were not self-affirmed, those who drank showed less interest in the article than those who did not drink, suggesting that women who were personally at risk

Box 13.2

Focus on Research: The Benefits of Self-Affirmation for Reducing Smoking

This research examined whether self-affirmation would reduce smokers' tendency to respond defensively to anti-smoking images and thus lead to more positive attitudes and intentions regarding smoking cessation (Harris, Mayle, Mabbott, & Napper, 2007). Young smokers were randomly assigned to either write down all of their positive characteristics (the self-affirmation condition) or perform a control task (in which they had to recall various recent events), and then saw four images intended for future use on cigarette packs. These four images were designed to be unpleasant in order to motivate smoking cessation: They included a mouth containing rotten teeth from smoking, a man on oxygen in a hospital bed, a close-up of an open thorax during a heart operation, and a photo of a young male cadaver in the morgue. Participants rated each image for threat and personal relevance. Participants viewed all images and then completed measures of intentions, self-efficacy, and perceived behavioral control for reducing cigarette consumption, negative thoughts and feelings about smoking, personal vulnerability to six smoking-related diseases, desire to quit, and plans to quit. At a 1-week follow-up, participants returned to complete measures of self-reported smoking and desire to reduce consumption. Compared to those who were not self-affirmed, self-affirmed smokers saw the images as more threatening and more personally relevant, and reported more negative thoughts and feelings about smoking as well as more intentions and self-efficacy for reducing their own cigarette consumption. Self-affirmation was particularly effective for increasing ratings on both relevance and intentions among those who smoked more. Although at the follow-up, motivation to reduce consumption remained higher in self-affirmed participants than in those in the control condition, there were no differences in reported consumption.

deliberately tried to avoid processing this threatening message. In contrast, among women who were self-affirmed, those who drank paid more attention to the article than those who did not drink.

How Effective Are Interventions Based in Psychological Theories?

Given the ineffectiveness of messages that simply provide information and the potential dangers of messages that simply use scare tactics, researchers are increasingly developing health-related behavior change messages that are based on psychological theories. This section examines how various psychological theories, including the prospect theory, the cognitive dissonance theory, the attribution theory, the learning theories, the social cognitive theory, and the theory of planned behavior, can be used to create persuasive health-related messages.

Prospect Theory

Prospect theory posits that people make very different choices when decisions are presented in different ways, such as in terms of their costs versus benefits (Tversky & Kahneman, 1981). For example, you might see condoms as more desirable when they are presented as "90% effective" than when they are presented as having a "10% failure rate." In fact, students rate a medical treatment with a 50% success rate as more effective and as one they are more likely to recommend to members of their immediate family than a treatment with a 50% failure rate (Levin, Schnittjer, & Thee, 1988), and students feel more optimistic about a person with a 90% chance of survival than a 10% chance of dying. Prospect theory also specifically states that people are more willing to take risks when they are considering the losses or costs of a particular behavior than when they are considering the gains or benefits of engaging in a behavior. For example, in a classic study on this problem, people are presented with information about the outbreak of an epidemic that is expected to kill 600 people and are asked to select one of two programs (one offering a guaranteed outcome of lives saved and the other offering a risky outcome). When the program is phrased in terms of the number of lives that will be lost, people prefer a program that provides a 33% chance of no people dying and a 66% chance of everyone dying to a solution that is certain to lead to 400 people dying and 200 people living. On the other hand, when the program is phrased in terms of the number of lives that will be saved, people prefer a program in which 200 people will be saved (and 400 people killed) to one in which there is a 33% chance of saving all 600 patients and a 66% chance of saving no one. These different preferences are based in how people tend to see the relative costs of losing something versus the relative benefits of gaining something—and people seem to experience more pain from losses than they do joy from winning. As described by the former tennis star, Jimmy Connors, "I hate to lose more than I love to win" (creativequotations.com).

TABLE 13.3   *Comparison of Sample Gain-Framed Versus Loss-Framed Persuasive Statements*

Gain Framed	Loss Framed
We will show that detecting breast cancer early can save your life.	We will show that failing to detect breast cancer early can cost you your life.
Although all women are at risk for breast cancer, there is something you can do to increase your chances of surviving it.	Although all women are at risk for breast cancer, there is something you can do that decreases your risk of dying from it.
For this reason, when you get a mammogram, you are taking advantage of the best method for detecting breast cancer early.	For this reason, when you avoid getting a mammogram, you are failing to take advantage of the best method for detecting breast cancer early.
If a cancer has not spread, it is less likely to be fatal.	If a cancer has spread, it is more likely to be fatal.
Another advantage of finding a tumor early is that you are more likely to increase your treatment options and may need less radical procedures.	Another disadvantage of failing to find a tumor early is that you may have fewer treatment options and may need more radical procedures.
The bottom line is, when you get regular mammograms, you are doing your best to detect breast cancer in its early stages.	The bottom line is, when you fail to get regular mammograms, you are not doing your best to detect breast cancer in its early stages.

These statements provide examples of gain-framed versus loss-framed persuasive statements.

Source: Banks et al., 1995.

In turn, message framing influences how persuaded people are to engage in certain health-promoting behaviors (Rothman & Salovey, 1997). According to prospect theory, people should be more persuaded to engage in behavior to detect a problem when it is framed negatively, namely, in terms of the costs of not engaging in a behavior (see Table 13.3). Engaging in detection behavior is somewhat risky because the person must risk receiving a negative outcome (e.g., learning he or she has a disease); hence, messages that emphasize the immediate costs of engaging in this type of risky behavior should encourage risk seeking. To test this hypothesis, Meyerowitz and Chaiken (1987) gave college women informational pamphlets on breast self-exam (BSE) that included either positively or negatively framed information (e.g., "Research shows that women who do BSE have an increased chance of finding a tumor in the early, more treatable stage of the disease" versus "Research shows that women who do not do BSE have a decreased chance of finding a tumor in the early, more treatable stage of the disease"). Women who were exposed to a negatively framed (loss-focused) message expressed the most positive attitudes and intentions about engaging in BSE and were more likely to report performing BSE at the 4-month follow-up.

Loss-framed messages can also influence other types of health-related behavior, including mammograms (Banks et al., 1995; Schneider et al., 2001), amniocentesis (Marteau, 1989), skin cancer detection (Rothman, Salovey, Antone, Keough, & Martin, 1993), and HIV testing (Kalichman & Coley, 1995). For example, Banks et al. (1995) found that 66.2% of women who received a loss-framed message about

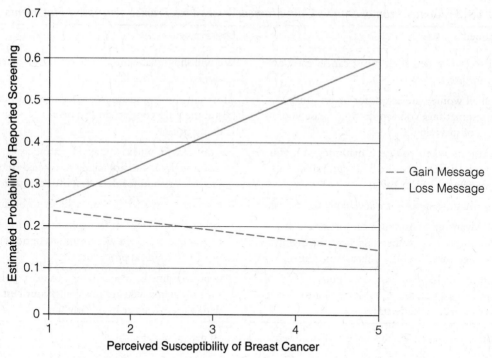

FIGURE 13.3   Women with average and higher levels of perceived susceptibility to breast cancer were more likely to report screening after a loss-framed message than a gain-framed message (data from Gallagher, Updegraff, Rothman, & Sims, 2011).

mammograms had obtained a mammogram 1 year later as compared to 51.5% of those who received a gain-framed message. Similarly, Kalichman and Coley (1995) found that 63% of women who received a negatively framed HIV video message had been tested 2 weeks later as compared to 23% of those who simply received information presented by an African American woman and 0% of those who received information presented by an African American man. In sum, and as shown in Figure 13.3, loss-framed messages are more effective than gain-framed messages at encouraging people to engage in behaviors to detect a symptom of illness.

On the other hand, prospect theory also states that gain-framed messages, those that emphasize the benefits of engaging in a behavior, should be more effective than loss-framed messages in promoting prevention behavior (e.g., use of sunscreen, condoms, and car seats; Rothman & Salovey, 1997). Because people should be more wary about taking a risk (e.g., they are risk averse) when considering gain information, they should be more willing to perform a prevention behavior after hearing a message emphasizing the benefits of engaging in a behavior than the consequences of not engaging in the behavior. Positive, gain-framed messages are indeed more effective than loss-framed ones at increasing intentions to use condoms (Kiene, Barta, Zelenski, & Cothran, 2005; Linville, Fischer, & Fischhoff, 1993) as well as to wear sunscreen (Detweiler, Bedell, Salovey, Pronin, & Rothman, 1999; Rothman, Salovey, Antone, et al., 1993). For example, 85% of students who are told that a particular brand of condoms has a 90% success rate intend to use this

TABLE 13.4 *Which Treatment Would You Choose?*

Surgery for lung cancer involves an operation on the lungs. Most patients are in the hospital for 2 or 3 weeks and have some pain around their incisions; then they spend a month or so recuperating at home. After that, they generally feel fine.

Radiation therapy for lung cancer involves the use of radiation to kill the tumor and requires coming to the hospital about 4 times a week for 6 weeks. Each treatment takes a few minutes and during the treatment, patients lie on a table as if they were having an X-ray. During the course of treatment, some patients develop nausea and vomiting, but by the end of the 6 weeks, they also generally feel fine.

Loss-Framed Wording

Of 100 people having surgery, 10 will die during treatment, 32 will have died by 1 year, and 66 will have died by 5 years. Of 100 people having radiation therapy, none will die during treatment, 23 will die by 1 year, and 78 will die by 5 years. Which treatment would you prefer?

Gain-Framed Wording

Of 100 people having surgery, 90 will live during treatment, 68 will be alive at 1 year, and 34 will be alive at 5 years. Of 100 people having radiation therapy, all will live during treatment, 77 will be alive at 1 year, and 22 will be alive at 5 years. Which treatment would you prefer?

type of condom, whereas 63% of those who learn that this brand has a 10% failure rate intend to use that type (Linville et al., 1997). Another study found that 46% of those who got the loss-framed messages about skin cancer requested free sunscreen with a sun protection factor (SPF) level of 15 as compared to 71% who received the gain-framed messages (Rothman, Salovey, Antone, et al., 1993).

Similarly, the way health practitioners describe different treatment options influences patients' preferences (Levin et al., 1988; Marteau, 1989; McNeil, Pauker, Sox, & Tversky, 1982). The decision to undergo a surgical procedure, for example, is a risk-averse or safer option because this operation should increase a person's life expectancy or relieve him or her of a given health problem (e.g., preventive behaviors). In turn, people should be more motivated to choose surgery when it is described in terms of its benefits to life expectancy as opposed to the costs in terms of life expectancy resulting from not undergoing the surgery. To test this hypothesis, physicians, patients, and medical students were given information that described the short-term and long-term consequences of having surgery versus radiation to treat lung cancer (see Table 13.4). In the short term, surgery is a riskier option than radiation because some people die on the operating table. However, in the long term, surgery prevents various health problems, and therefore it leads to longer life expectancy. As predicted, more people chose surgery when information was presented in terms of likelihood of living (a gain frame) than when information was presented in terms of likelihood of dying (a loss frame).

Cognitive Dissonance Theory

According to Festinger's (1957) cognitive dissonance theory, people are highly motivated to align their attitudes, beliefs, and behaviors, and when they engage in a behavior that is not consistent with their attitudes, they experience an unpleasant state of psychological arousal known as dissonance. Imagine, for example, that you believe very strongly in the importance of recycling and regularly encourage others to recycle their papers, bottles, and cans. Then one day, perhaps because you are feeling lazy or rushed, you toss an empty can in a trashcan instead of in a recycling bin. According to cognitive dissonance theory, you will then feel very uncomfortable because you have done something that is not in line with your pro-recycling attitude. You are now highly motivated to bring your attitudes and behavior back in line to reduce this unpleasant feeling. However, because it is very difficult, and sometimes impossible, to undo a behavior, people often try to resolve this uncomfortable feeling of arousal by changing their attitude to make it correspond with their behavior. So, perhaps after throwing the can in the trashcan, you would become less of a proponent of recycling and start to downplay its importance. Similarly, as described at the beginning of the chapter, Damon's attitudes toward drug use became more negative over time as he continued to talk to students in his dorm about their dangers. Cognitive dissonance theory is one of the most famous theories in social psychology; hence, researchers have started using this theory to help people motivate behavior change.

One of the first studies to use cognitive dissonance theory to change people's health-related behavior was conducted by Stone, Aronson, Crain, Winslow, and Fried (1994). In this study, 72 sexually active college students participated in a study on health and persuasion. All of the students were asked to write a persuasive speech about the importance of safer sex as a way of preventing HIV, and half of these students were then videotaped giving this speech (which would supposedly be shown to high school students). Finally, half of the students in each of these two conditions were asked to make a list of the times they had failed to use condoms in the past, as a way of making them feel hypocritical about their past behavior. Students who were made to publicly advocate the importance of using condoms and who were reminded of their own past failures to use condoms (which should create a feeling of dissonance) bought more condoms than those in the other conditions—in fact, 83% of the students in this condition bought condoms, whereas 33 to 50% of students in the other conditions bought condoms.

Questioning the Research 13.2

Does this study really show that creating cognitive dissonance increases condom use? (Hint: What exactly is the dependent variable?)

As described in Chapter 8, research has also used principles of cognitive dissonance theory to try to prevent eating disorders (Becker, Bull, Schaumberg, Cauble, & Franco, 2008; Stice, Mazotti, Weibel, & Agras, 2000; Stice, Presnell, & Spangler, 2002; Stice, Chase, Stormer, & Appel, 2001; Stice, Shaw, Burton, & Wade, 2006). In one study, 148 adolescent girls (ages 13 to 20) were randomly assigned to a dissonance intervention group, a healthy weight control intervention group, or a waitlist control condition (Stice et al., 2002). Participants in the dissonance group were asked to discuss how to help other women avoid body-image problems. The women discussed (as a group) the nature of the thin ideal portrayed in the media, the perpetuation of this image, and the consequences of this image. They also role played trying to convince someone not to adopt the thin ideal, and wrote an essay about the costs associated with the pursuit of the thin ideal. Findings at the 3-month follow-up indicated that women who received either the dissonance-based intervention or the healthy weight control intervention reported fewer bulimic symptoms than those in the waitlist control condition. Similarly, high school girls who participate in a dissonance intervention in which they examine the costs of the thin ideal report greater decreases in idealization of the thinness norm, body dissatisfaction, dieting, and symptoms of eating disorders a year later than those who merely receive a brochure about body image (Stice, Rohde, Gau, & Shaw, 2009). This research provides strong evidence that programs that help girls critique the thin ideal may reduce rates of disordered eating.

Attribution Theory

Attribution theory posits that people try to explain the causes of their own and others' behavior; specifically, that people perceive behavior as caused by internal factors or external factors (Kelley, 1967). In turn, behavior that is motivated by internal factors, such as an individual's desire to engage in the behavior, is expected to continue over time. For example, if you brush your teeth because you like the feeling of having clean teeth and good-smelling breath, you will probably continue to regularly brush your teeth. In fact, internal attributions for the causes of behavior are associated with the adoption of various health-related behaviors, including use of fluoride mouthwash (Lund & Kegeles, 1984), smoking cessation (Colletti & Koppel, 1979), BSE (Bundek, Marks, & Richardson, 1993), and blood pressure screening (King, 1982). On the other hand, when people engage in behavior

In one innovative approach to preventing eating disorders, participants are asked to critique the very thin idealized image of women presented in the media. This approach can be effective at leading to reductions in symptoms of disordered eating.
Source: © kevinruss/iStockphoto.

that they believe is the result of external pressures from others, they are unlikely to continue to engage in such behavior over time. So, if you brush your teeth because your parents give you a quarter each time you've brushed, you probably won't continue this teeth-cleaning routine over time. Correspondingly, external attributions for the causes of engaging in a particular behavior are associated with poorer adherence to recommendations and poorer maintenance of new behaviors.

In turn, one way to increase the persuasiveness of health messages is by trying to change the attributions people make for engaging in these behaviors (Rothman, Salovey, Turvey, & Fishkin, 1993). For example, in one study on this issue, 197 women were randomly assigned to receive one of three 20-minute tapes on mammography (Rothman, Salovey, Turvey, et al., 1993). The internal tape emphasized a woman's own responsibility to get a mammogram and detect breast cancer ("8 out of 10 lumps that you might find will not be breast cancer"; "while it is not known yet how to prevent breast cancer, the value and benefits of your finding it early are well known"). The external tape emphasized a doctor's responsibility for detecting breast cancer ("8 out of 10 lumps that a doctor might find will not be breast cancer"; "while it is not known yet how to prevent breast cancer, the value and benefits of a doctor finding it early are well known"). The information-only tape communicated information without making any particular types of attributions ("8 out of 10 lumps that are found will not be breast cancer"). Subjects' reactions and amount of knowledge learned did not differ across conditions. However, when subjects were contacted 12 months later, 57% of those in the external condition and 55% of those in the information-only condition had obtained a mammogram compared to 66% of those in the internal condition.

Learning Theories

Learning theories are based on the assumption that behavior is influenced by basic learning processes, such as association, reinforcement, and modeling (Bandura, 1977; Pavlov, 1927; Skinner, 1938; Thorndike, 1905). In turn, health-promotion interventions use a variety of techniques developed by learning theorists to help people change their behavior. For example, in the technique of operant conditioning, desired behaviors are positively reinforced through rewards, whereas undesired behaviors are punished in some way. Reinforcement should lead to the continuation of positive behaviors and the avoidance of negative behaviors. As discussed in Chapter 12, many relapse-prevention programs encourage people to give themselves rewards for maintaining a change in behavior. Programs based on operant-conditioning principles can be very effective in leading to behavior change. For example, in one study, participants were asked to set rewards for themselves for accomplishing their exercise goals (e.g., "I will get my morning cup of coffee after I've finished my 2 mile walk"; Atkins, Kaplan, Timms, Reinsch, & Lofback, 1984). Participants with these self-rewards were much more likely to continue exercising over time than those without this incentive. Similarly, in one creative health-promotion plan based on the behavioral perspective, campus police officers at a large university were asked to record the license plate numbers of vehicles with drivers wearing seat belts (Rudd & Geller, 1985). These numbers were then entered into a raffle, and 10 winners every 3 weeks were given a gift certificate to local stores. Although faculty and staff increased their seat belt use significantly during this "seat belt sweepstakes" time, students' seat belt use increased only slightly.

> **Questioning the Research 13.3**
>
> This study reveals that providing rewards for seat belt use increases use among faculty and staff but not students. Why do you think this program had a relatively small effect on students' behavior?

The preceding examples describe rewarding positive behavior, but conditioning techniques can also be used to punish negative behavior. For example, and as discussed in Chapters 7 and 12, aversion therapy is designed to eliminate unhealthy behaviors by pairing a given action, such as smoking or drinking alcohol, with a negative consequence, such as an electric shock or negative visual images (Kamarck & Lichtenstein, 1985). Over time, it is thought that this pairing should work to eliminate the undesired behavior. In line with this theory, researchers in one study paired images of snack foods with images of adverse health consequences, such as a candy bar and a fat stomach (Hollands, Prestwich, & Marteau, 2011) Participants were then asked to select a snack food, as a reward for participating in the study, from choices of fruits or other less healthy snacks (e.g., cake, candy bar). In line with the predictions of learning theories, participants who saw the pairings of snack foods and images of adverse health consequences choose healthy foods more often than those who didn't see such pairings.

Moreover, according to Bandura's social learning theory, people do not need to directly experience the rewards or costs of engaging in a particular behavior to learn about its outcomes; he believed that people could learn about such consequences through modeling (i.e., vicarious learning through observation; Bandura, 1977, 1986). As described previously, people often form their beliefs about various health-related behaviors from watching their parents' and older siblings' behavior. They can even form such beliefs from observing the behavior of someone they do not personally know, such as a famous athlete, model, or actor. In turn, many health-promotion messages portray desirable role models promoting a particular behavior. Public-service announcements on television, for example, often feature an actor urging people to avoid drug use, driving under the influence, and cigarettes. Similarly, many smoking-prevention programs for teenagers present adolescents with role models—including older students as well as media figures—describing the hazards of smoking and the benefits of refusing cigarettes (Evans et al., 1981). One study in the *Journal of the National Cancer Institute* found that many people had heard a celebrity talk about the importance of cancer screening, and about a quarter of those who heard such an announcement reported they intended to get screened (Larson, Woloshin, Schwartz, & Welch, 2005).

Although considerable research has demonstrated the effects of media images on leading to unhealthy behaviors, such as smoking and drinking, such images can also lead to health-promoting behavior. Researchers in one study examined the effects of a storyline regarding hypertension that appeared on a popular medical drama, *ER* (Valente et al., 2007). This storyline depicted an African American teenager who was found to have hypertension and therefore advised to eat more fruits and

Celebrities who promote a particular health-related behavior, such as avoiding smoking or screening for cancer, can have a substantial impact on such behavior. *Source:* Jemal Countess/WireImage/Getty Images, Inc.

vegetables and to get more exercise. Researchers then examined nationwide data on eating and exercise behavior both before and after this episode aired. Results showed that the storyline affected self-reported behavior change and had modest impacts on knowledge, attitudes, and practices. Interestingly, these effects were stronger for men than for women, possibly due to men's lower knowledge levels at baseline. Similarly, researchers in this study examined the effectiveness of the "truth" anti-smoking campaign (Hersey et al., 2005). Nationwide surveys of more than 16,000 young people ages 12 to 17 given 8 months before and 15 months after this campaign started revealed that youth in markets with higher levels of exposure to this campaign reported more negative attitudes toward and beliefs about tobacco industry practices. Box 13.3: Focus on Culture describes the benefits of a radio soap opera on promoting HIV-prevention behaviors in Tanzania.

Health-promotion interventions have also used media images in an attempt to influence behavior. For example, researchers in one study randomly assigned Caucasian women to a sun-protection program promoting image norms approving paleness (as opposed to tan skin) or a stress management control condition (Jackson & Aiken, 2006). The intervention included information on people's susceptibility and severity of skin cancer, the effectiveness of sun-protective strategies, and changing norms seen on television and in magazines showing an increasing lightness of skin tone. The image-based intervention led to increases in sun-protective knowledge, personal susceptibility to negative effects of the sun, and decreases in favorable attitudes toward tanning. Most importantly, women in this intervention reported increases in their intention to use sun-protective behaviors and decreases in their intention to tan.

Box 13.3

Focus on Culture: The Role of a Radio Program in Reducing HIV Infection

Researchers in one study examined the effects of a long-running entertainment-education radio soap opera in Tanzania on knowledge, attitudes, and adoption of HIV/AIDS preventive practices (Vaughan, Rogers, Singhal, & Swalehe, 2000). This soap opera, entitled *Twende na Wakati* ("Let's Go With the Times"), was designed to spark communication about AIDS by presenting listeners with both negative and positive role models for HIV-prevention behaviors and thereby promote HIV/AIDS prevention, family planning, and other health issues. Of those in the area in which this program was broadcast, 85% reported learning about AIDS from the soap opera. Although the radio soap opera had a relatively minimal impact on listeners' knowledge about HIV/AIDS, it led to positive effects in terms of openness to adopting HIV/AIDS-prevention practices. Specifically, after taking into account the potential effects of other national anti-AIDS programs, 12% of the people in the area in which this program was broadcast reported adopting HIV/AIDS-prevention methods, such as reducing their number of sexual partners, as the direct result of listening to the radio soap.

Finally, although media images clearly exert a strong influence on individuals' attitudes and behaviors, not all people are equally susceptible to such images. Researchers in one study examined the level exposure to tobacco and alcohol use in movies and advertising among large samples of 10 to 14 year olds (Wills et al., 2010). Although higher exposure led to more smoking and drinking as well as willingness to smoke and drink in the future, these results were seen only in those who are low in terms of level of self-control (meaning the ability to delay gratification). In sum, advertising had no influence on detrimental health behaviors among those with high levels of self-control.

Social Cognitive Theory

Bandura's social cognitive theory extends social learning theory by including the role of both self-efficacy and outcome expectancies in predicting behavior (Bandura, 1986). According to this theory, an individual's self-efficacy, the extent to which a person believes he or she can engage in a particular behavior, is a powerful predictor of whether that person actually engages in the behavior (Bandura, 1977, 1986). For example, a person's beliefs about his or her ability to exercise every day would be a strong predictor of whether the person successfully maintains a new fitness program. Although social cognitive theory was the first to include this concept of self-efficacy, many more recent theories of health behavior (e.g., theory of planned behavior, protection motivation theory) include similar constructs.

Given the important role that self-efficacy plays in predicting behavior, many health-promotion intervention programs have focused on increasing people's confidence in engaging in a given behavior. For example, McAuley, Talbot, and

Martinez (1999) gave some college women positive feedback on their fitness (e.g., told them that they were in the top 20 percentile of fitness for college-age women), whereas other women were given negative feedback (e.g., that they were in the bottom 20 percentile for fitness). When the women later participated in a 20-minute stair-climbing-machine exercise, those who received high-self-efficacy feedback reported having more positive affect, less negative affect, and less fatigue than those who received the negative feedback. Similarly, and as described at the start of this chapter, Bill decided to start an exercise program after his doctor gave him confidence that he could be successful in this pursuit.

One of the most common uses of social cognitive theory is in designing HIV-prevention programs; because one major reason for failure to use a condom is lack of confidence in discussing or implementing condom use, many HIV-prevention interventions use various techniques to increase condom use self-efficacy (Bryan, Aiken, & West, 1996; Kelly, St. Lawrence, Hood, & Brasfield, 1989). For example, Bryan et al. (1996) tried to increase condom use in 100 undergraduate women by showing them a videotape of a woman purchasing condoms at a drugstore, demonstrating the proper way to put a condom on a man, and giving each participant a condom to carry in her purse or backpack. Women who saw this tape were more likely to report carrying condoms, discussing condoms, and using condoms than those who instead received training in stress management. Similar findings about the benefits of receiving training to increase self-efficacy for condom use are found with male and female college students (Fisher, Fisher, Misovich, Kimble, & Malloy, 1996; Sanderson, 1999; Sanderson & Yopyk, 2007), gay men (Kelly et al., 1989), low-income adult STD patients (Kalichman et al., 2005; National Institute of Mental Health Multisite HIV Prevention Trial Group, 2001), African American male adolescents (Jemmott, Jemmott, & Fong, 1992), inner-city high school students (Fisher, Fisher, Bryan, & Misovich, 2002), inner-city women (Hobfoll, Jackson, Lavin, Britton, & Shepherd, 1994), and African American adult women (Carey et al., 2000).

Theory of Planned Behavior

As described in detail in Chapter 3, the theory of planned behavior describes the role of attitudes, subjective norms, and perceived behavioral control in leading to intentions, which in turn lead to behavior (Ajzen, 1985). This theory proposes that changing people's attitudes and norms will lead to changes in their intentions and behavior.

In line with this theory, considerable evidence points to the influence of norms on health-related behavior. For example, researchers in one study examined the effectiveness of an intervention designed to prevent skin cancer in college females (Abar et al., 2010). This intervention focused on providing information about the hazards of tanning (to change attitudes) as well as normative beliefs about tanning (to change subjective norms) and strategies for decreasing indoor tanning and enhancing appearance in other ways (to increase self-efficacy). Findings indicated that this intervention reduced tanning.

Intervention studies that create social influence to promote a particular type of health-related behavior are also quite effective. Researchers in one study examined the effectiveness of a social influence intervention on increasing condom use in

Box 13.4

Focus on Research: The Power of Social Norms in Increasing Condom Use

Kelly et al. (1997) created a very novel approach to HIV prevention. They asked bartenders at gay bars to identify men who seemed to be popular—those who socialized and were greeted positively by others. These men (called "opinion leaders") were then asked to participate in five weekly 2-hour group sessions in which they learned information about HIV, strategies for preventing HIV transmission, and how to talk about HIV-prevention methods. The researchers then displayed posters throughout the gay clubs that featured a traffic light logo (red, yellow, and green circles) and asked the opinion leaders to wear small lapel buttons featuring this logo whenever they were in the club. These logo buttons would then prompt discussion with these men, and in turn lead to conversations about HIV-prevention strategies. Researchers then gave surveys to all male club patrons 1 year later to measure changes in sexual behavior. The results from this study revealed that this intervention had several positive changes on patterns of sexual behavior. First, while 32% of the participants reported they had engaged in unprotected sex in the 2 months before the intervention, only 20% reported engaging in this type of behavior at the follow-up. Moreover, rates of condom use increased from 44.7% before the intervention to 66.8% at the follow-up. The researchers also collected data from men in a similar city during this time period and found no changes in their sexual behavior. For example, 27% of the participants in the other city reported engaging in unprotected sex at the first survey time, and 29% reported engaging in this behavior 1 year later. Similarly, rates of condom use remained unchanged (62 to 59%). The inclusion of data from this control city makes us more confident that the results obtained in this study were caused by the intervention and not by other factors, such as national media coverage of AIDS. This study provides evidence that social influences play an important role in health-related behavior.

sex workers (Morisky, Stein, Chiao, Ksobiech, & Malow, 2006). Female sex workers were randomly assigned to one of four conditions: manager influence, peer influence, combined manager-peer influence, or control. People in the control group reported more risk, less condom use, more negative condom attitudes, and less HIV/AIDS knowledge. The combined program was most effective at leading to positive outcomes, including more positive attitudes toward condoms and fewer STIs, more likelihood of using a condom the last time they had sex, and more knowledge of HIV. Similarly, Box 13.4: Focus on Research describes the role of a social influence in increasing condom use among gay men.

Are Personally Relevant Messages the Most Effective?

Although traditional health education messages have used a "one size fits all" approach, namely, by giving the same information to everyone, both theory and research suggest that different people respond in different ways to different types of information: As poet William Blake (Gilchrist, 1942) noted, "To generalize is to be an idiot" (Kreuter & Holt, 2001; Kreuter & Skinner, 2000; Kreuter, Strecher, & Glassman, 1999; Skinner, Campbell, Rimer, Curry, & Prochaska, 1999; Skinner, Strecher, & Hospers, 1994). According to the interactionist or "aptitude-treatment interaction" perspective, people are much more responsive to personally relevant information. Specifically, people are more likely to read, remember, comprehend, and discuss personally relevant messages, and they perceive these messages as more interesting, likeable, and in line with their attitudes (Brug, Steenhuis, van Assena, & de Vries, 1996; Campbell et al., 1994; Kalichman, Carey, & Johnson, 1996; Kreuter, Bull, Clark, & Oswald, 1999; Peterson & Marin, 1988). They also have more positive thoughts about the material, make more personal connections to the material, develop stronger intentions to change their behavior, and, most important, are more likely to be successful in their behavior change efforts. In turn, different people should find different types of health-promotion information most convincing, and should show greater behavior change in response to personally relevant messages.

Given these findings, researchers in the field of health psychology are increasingly creating different types of messages for different people. In some cases, these messages are **targeted** to a specific group of people and/or specific characteristics of a group of people. For example, teenagers might be most convinced by information about the negative effects of smoking on appearance (e.g., smelly clothes, yellow teeth, bad breath), whereas women who smoke may be most convinced by information about preventing weight gain. In sum, health-promotion messages should be most effective when they provide people with personally relevant information. In other cases, researchers have created messages that are **tailored** to an individual's particular needs and goals. A message that is created to address a specific woman's concerns about mammography (e.g., fear of pain, anxiety about learning she has cancer) is a tailored message. This section examines the benefits of receiving both types of personally relevant materials on a number of health-related behaviors, including screening, managing pain, stopping smoking, reducing alcohol consumption, engaging in safer sex, and preventing disordered eating.

Screening

Some researchers have examined whether people who receive personally tailored messages are more likely to engage in screening behaviors (Kreuter & Strecher, 1996; Rakowski et al., 1998; Skinner et al., 1994; Skinner et al., 1999). For example, Skinner et al. (1994) compared whether women who received letters from their physicians encouraging BSE that were tailored to a person's particular risk factors (e.g., age, family history) were more effective in increasing screening than standardized letters. Follow-up interviews 3 months after the letters were sent indicated that both African American and low-income women (who are at particular risk of not getting screened) were more influenced by the tailored letter than the standardized letter. Personally tailored intervention messages are also more effective than standard interventions at increasing mammography (Rakowski et al., 1998) and skin cancer exams (Manne et al., 2010). In fact, people who receive the tailored intervention promoting skin cancer exams are nearly twice as likely to have a skin exam as those who receive a generic message. Similarly, and as shown in

FIGURE 13.4 Researchers in this study examined whether matching messages promoting mammograms to women's style of coping with medical information would increase rates of screening. Specifically, this study examined the influence of individuals' preference in terms of the type of health-related information they receive: Monitors are interested in gathering information that they can process, whereas blunters prefer to avoid detailed information about their health risks. As shown in this figure, women who received a message that matched their preferred coping style were more likely to have had a mammogram 6 months later (data from Williams-Piehota, Pizarro, Schneider, Mowad, & Salovey, 2005).

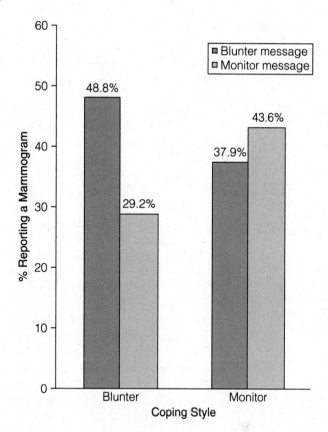

Figure 13.4, different types of messages promoting mammograms are differentially effective for particular women, depending on the level of health-related information they prefer to receive.

Other messages to promote screening specifically target a given population through the use of particular narrators, language, or music, which is a more cost-effective approach than personally tailoring messages (Kreuter & Skinner, 2000). For example, a message designed to promote mammograms could focus on the rationale for such screening for young women, who may be less likely to see themselves as at risk for developing breast cancer. In one study, Kalichman, Kelly, Hunter, Murphy, and Tyler (1993) randomly assigned 106 African American women to watch one of three videotapes on HIV risk reduction. One tape simply presented information about the importance of risk reduction delivered by a White broadcaster; another gave the same information presented by an African American woman; and a third gave the same information presented by an African American woman and included culturally relevant themes, including cultural pride, community concern, and family responsibility. Two weeks later, women who had seen either of the videos featuring African American women were more likely to have discussed AIDS with friends, request condoms at the follow-up, and have been tested for AIDS. Of the women who received the standard video, 50% requested condoms as compared to 88% and 91% of those in the other two conditions.

Managing Pain and Chronic Disease

Another contribution of research on patient–treatment matching is in managing pain—a topic that is very important to most people at one time or another. Personality researchers have shown that people vary considerably on the type of information they want to receive about medical procedures to manage their pain (see Table 13.5; Carpenter, Gatchel, & Hasegawa, 1994; Litt, Nye, & Shafer, 1995; Ludwick-Rosenthal & Neufeld, 1993). Specifically, some people prefer to manage pain by seeking detailed information about the proposed management procedure and to learn as much as possible about what to expect. Other people strongly prefer simply to not think about the procedure and to adopt an "ignorance is bliss" approach. Neither of these styles seems to be "better." What appears to be important is that people get the type of information that they want.

Many research studies provide support for the importance of matching people to treatment preferences in the management of pain and specifically suggest that different people benefit from receiving different amounts of information (Law, Logan, & Baron, 1994; Ludwick-Rosenthal & Neufeld, 1993; Miller & Mangan, 1983). Specifically, people who desire high levels of control and information about their upcoming surgical procedure show lower levels of arousal, stress, and anxiety when they receive such information than when they receive little information, whereas those who prefer to know as little as possible show the reverse pattern. For example, Law et al. (1994) found that people who desired high levels of control experienced less pain when they first saw a video of a woman seeking dental treatment and received training in coping and relaxing as compared to when they saw a neutral film (on local areas of interest) and engaged in a neutral conversation. Similarly, Lucinda, as described at the beginning of the chapter, who wanted to

TABLE 13.5   *Test Yourself: How Much Information Would You Want?*

Please rate your agreement (yes or no) with each of these statements.

1. I usually don't ask the doctor or nurse many questions about what he or she is doing during a medical exam.
2. I'd rather have doctors and nurses make the decisions about what's best than for them to give me a whole lot of choices.
3. Instead of waiting for them to tell me, I usually ask the doctor or nurse immediately after an exam about my health.
4. I usually ask the doctor or nurse lots of questions about the procedures during a medical exam.
5. It is better to trust the doctor or nurse in charge of a medical procedure than to question what he or she is doing.
6. I usually wait for the doctor or nurse to tell me the results of a medical exam rather than asking for the results immediately.
7. I'd rather be given many choices about what's best for my health than to have the doctor make the decisions for me.

This questionnaire measures people's desire to ask questions and desire to get information regarding medical decisions.

Source: Krantz, Baum, & Wideman, 1980.

receive lots of information, was much less anxious about having a cavity filled after receiving a detailed description of the procedure that would be used.

People benefit not only from receiving different amounts of information prior to medical procedures but also from receiving different types of information. For example, Litt, Kalinowski, and Shafer (1999) examined the effectiveness of different types of interventions to reduce anxiety in dental patients. Patients who were highly fearful of dental procedures in general benefited most in terms of distress (e.g., tension, nervousness, edginess) from distraction, whereas those who were fearful only in response to specific cues (e.g., sound of drill, sight of dentist) benefited most from receiving desensitization training. Another study examined how 46 patients about to undergo oral surgery handled different types of stress management interventions (Martelli, Auerbach, Alexander, & Mercuri, 1987). Some of the patients were randomly assigned to a problem-focused intervention, which provided information about the surgery, including instruments used, sequence of steps, sensations produced by the anesthesia, and instruction in the use of strategies to cognitively reanalyze information about the procedure. Others received an emotion-focused intervention, which was designed to reduce the emotion or distress associated with the surgery and included instruction on deep relaxation, distraction, and the use of calming emotion-focused statements, such as "it will soon be over." Finally, others received a mixed message, which included both types of coping strategies. The problem-focused intervention led to the lowest levels of pain and anxiety for those who wanted lots of information, whereas the emotion-focused intervention led to similarly low levels of arousal for those who wanted little information. This study shows that effectiveness in reducing stress is enhanced when treatment conditions or interventions are congruent with people's individual coping tendencies. Similarly, in another study dental patients were randomly assigned to

Although some people find visits to the dentist quite anxiety-provoking, having information can reduce the pain associated with various dental procedures. Different people, however, benefit from receiving different types of information.
Source: © The New Yorker Collection 2001 Jack Ziegler from cartoonbank.com. All Rights Reserved.

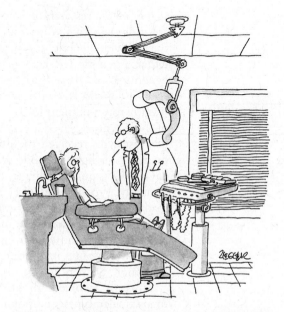

"We have adult teeth now, Debbie, and, as such, they demand adult pain."

receive either general information (information about the dental clinic's history and finances) or specific information (detailed information about the exact procedures used to extract a tooth; see Table 13.6; Auerbach, Kendall, Cuttler, & Levitt, 1976). Patients with an internal locus of control (who wanted to actively control and manipulate their environment) showed better adjustment when they received the specific information, whereas those with an external locus of control (who were less comfortable with navigating their own environment) showed better adjustment after receiving general information. This research all provides strong support for the importance of giving people what they need as a way of improving adjustment to medical procedures.

Finally, people vary in their responsiveness to different strategies for managing the stress of having a chronic disease. Researchers in one study examined the benefit of providing newly diagnosed cancer patients with a decision aid to help make decisions regarding cancer treatment (Vodermaier et al., 2011). This aid was more effective at reducing uncertainty for those who are high in health locus of control and who apparently benefit more from participating in a decision-making aid intervention. They believe they have high control over their health and thus find using this tool to make a decision helpful in terms of reducing uncertainty. Similarly, men with prostate cancer who are low in self-esteem particularly benefit from participating in a psychoeducational group (Helgeson, Lepore, & Eton, 2006). Men who are the least confident in themselves benefit the most from learning about side effects and how to cope. These findings point to the importance of tailoring interventions designed to help people who are struggling with a chronic disease.

Smoking Cessation

Considerable research on smoking-cessation programs suggests that these programs are more effective when they provide personally relevant information than when they provide generic information. For example, in one study, smokers were given either a generic letter about the reasons for stopping smoking (e.g., the general benefits of and barriers to quitting) or a personally tailored letter that addressed the specific benefits and barriers that the person had revealed during an interview in the waiting room of their doctor's office (Strecher et al., 1994). Four months later, 7.4% of those who received a generic letter had stopped smoking as compared to 20.8% of those who received the personally tailored letter. The results were even more dramatic for light to moderate smokers (those smoking fewer than 20 cigarettes a day); 30.7% quit as compared to 7.1% of those who received the generic letter. Similarly, Prochaska et al. (1993) found that smokers who received individualized manuals matched to their stage of change at the start of a smoking-cessation intervention program were more likely to have stopped smoking at the 18-month follow-up than those who simply received standardized self-help manuals. Similar results were found in a sample of 349 low-income pregnant women who smoked (Solomon, Secker-Walker, Skelly, & Flynn, 1996).

Similarly, people with different motivations for smoking also respond differently to particular types of smoking cessation interventions. For example, a study by

TABLE 13.6   *What Type of Information Would You Want Before Dental Surgery?*

General Information

This clinic was opened in 1970. At that time, 100 or more junior or senior dental students were able to provide service to the Washington, D.C., community. At present, because of continuing expansion of our facilities, there are 260 students providing services to over 5000 patients a year. Present clinical facilities include six departments that can provide for all your dental needs. These six departments, oral diagnosis and treatment planning, periodontics, endodontics, oral surgery, fixed and removable prosthodontics, and operative dentistry, cannot be maintained without your financial support. Your financial support is matched and exceeded by the federal government through the Health Professions and Loan Act. The quality of any clinic depends not only on the availability of all the needed facilities but also on the excellence of its staff. The Georgetown Dental School maintains an esteemed faculty, people who are consultants for other hospitals, participants in scientific meetings and other educational organizations, and active in their respective communities.

Specific Information

Upon your arrival in the surgery department, your diagnosis will be reviewed. Before removal, an anesthetic will be administered. This anesthetic will numb the tooth and the surrounding tissues, thus removing all pain sensations from the immediate area. After the anesthetic has taken effect, the surgical procedure will begin. The first procedure is the removal of the attachment apparatus with a molt curette. This helps to loosen the tooth. A forcep will then be placed on the tooth, and a front-to-back rocking motion will be initiated by the surgeon. This motion further helps loosen the tooth and will continue until the tooth is removed. During this procedure, you may feel considerable pressure on your tooth tissues, but you should not feel any pain. If you do feel pain, more anesthetic will be given. In some impaction cases, it will be necessary to use a mallet and a chisel. These instruments help the surgeon remove the bone surrounding the tooth. This procedure produces very little trauma and enables the surgeon to quickly remove the tooth.

Source: Auerbach, Kendall, Cuttler, & Levitt, 1976.

Zelman, Brandon, Jorenby, and Baker et al. (1992) examined the effectiveness of different types of smoking-cessation interventions (rapid smoking versus nicotine gum) for different people. In the study, 126 smokers were randomly assigned to one of two interventions, which each met six times over a 2-week period. The rapid-smoking intervention required subjects to inhale from cigarettes every 6 seconds for a 60-minute period, during which time they consumed an average of 4.7 cigarettes, and they were to refrain from smoking outside of the sessions. Those in the nicotine-gum intervention were given prescriptions for gum, and they were encouraged to use the gum whenever they wanted to. Participants were then contacted several times over a 1-year period to assess their smoking behavior. These assessments included blood testing for nicotine at the 6-month follow-up and contact with a friend or family member of the participant at the 6-month and 12-month follow-ups to verify the self-reports.

Findings from this study revealed no long-term overall differences between the effectiveness of the nicotine gum and rapid-smoking conditions, with approximately 30 to 40% of smokers in each condition abstaining from smoking at the 12-month follow-up. However, these researchers were also interested in examining whether different people responded to these interventions in different ways. Specifically, the researchers predicted that for low-craving subjects, rapid smoking would be the most effective in increasing abstinence from smoking because this type of procedure would produce disgust, whereas for those with high cravings for cigarettes, nicotine gum would be the most effective. This hypothesis was indeed confirmed: The nicotine-gum intervention was most effective when used with people who were high on physical dependence, whereas the rapid-smoking intervention was most effective when used with people who were low on physical dependence. This study provides further evidence that treatments must be matched to people's preferences and individual needs to maximize their effectiveness.

Other research indicates that even subtle factors regarding a persuasive message can impact smoking cessation in different ways for different people. For example, researchers in one study gave all smokers an identical anti-smoking message, but some smokers were told this message was produced by a health institute whereas others were told it came from a neighborhood association (Invernizzi, Falomir-Pichastor, Munoz-Rojas, & Mugny, 2003). People who identified strongly as a smoker showed more intention to quit when the message was from a neighborhood association than when it was from a health institute. Similarly, people who are high in need for cognition, a variable which assesses individuals' preference for carefully thinking through decisions, show higher rates of smoking cessation self-efficacy when they receive a tailored letter on strategies for quitting than physician-delivered information. In contrast, those who are low in need for cognition show no differences in the effectiveness of these two types of message delivery (Haug et al., 2010).

Questioning the Research 13.4

Why should written letters lead to higher rates of smoking cessation self-efficacy than messages delivered verbally by a physician, at least for some participants? What factors do you think explain this result?

Alcohol Use

As described in Chapter 7, perceived norms regarding alcohol use often influence drinking behavior, and thus one effective strategy for reducing alcohol consumption is to provide accurate information on levels of drinking on campus. For example, in one study, heavy-drinking college students were randomly assigned to receive general information or personality normative feedback about their drinking (Neighbors, Lewis, Bergstrom, & Larimer, 2006). As predicted, college students who receive information on accurate norms of alcohol use—which is often less than what students expect—report drinking fewer drinks per week 2 months later than those who do not receive this information. However, receiving personalized feedback was particularly impactful in terms of reducing the perceived alcohol-related problems among students who were high in controlled orientation, meaning they perceive pressure from their environment to conform to particular types of behaviors.

Different types of alcohol-treatment programs may also have different effects on different people. For example, an alcohol-treatment program found that people who experience strong cravings for alcohol benefit from receiving medication that reduces the cravings, whereas those who are high in verbal skills really benefit from relapse-prevention training (e.g., training in self-monitoring, stress management, modeling, role-plays; Jaffe et al., 1996). Similarly, Kadden, Cooney, Getter, and Litt (1989) found that patients who scored high in measures of psychopathology and sociopathy benefited much more from training in coping skills related to alcohol use than group-based, interactional therapy, presumably because they lack the social skills to benefit from the group experience. These findings suggest that alcohol-treatment programs need to carefully consider the factors that drive individuals' drinking in order to maximize their effectiveness.

Eating and Eating Disordered Behavior

Tailored messages can also influence eating and exercise behavior. For example, compared to patients who received general information on dietary and nutrition guidelines, participants who received an individually tailored letter (e.g., based on their beliefs about the benefits of changing their diet and their susceptibility to diet-related diseases) were more likely to remember receiving the letter, were more likely to have read all of the message, and reported eating less total fat 4 months later (Campbell et al., 1994). Tailored messages also lead to increases in fruit and vegetable consumption and recreational physical activity (Campbell et al., 2004). This type of personally relevant message may be more effective at least in part because people who get tailored messages promoting nutrition pay more attention to these than general messages (Ruiter, Kessels, Jansma, & Brug, 2006). Similarly, and as shown in Figure 13.5, messages that provide individualized feedback are particularly effective.

However, personality variables can also influence how people respond to particular messages promoting healthy eating and exercise behavior. For example, obese people who feel that their weight is outside of their control (e.g., influenced by luck, genetics) actually respond more negatively to tailored information than to generic information: They counterargue the messages that provide personally relevant strategies for taking control of their eating and exercise behavior (Holt, Clark, Kreuter, & Scharff, 2000). In contrast, obese people who believe they are in control of their weight respond more favorably to messages that provide personally relevant strategies for weight loss than to generic information.

I have also conducted two studies showing that the most effective eating disorder prevention interventions match women's distinct needs (Mutterperl & Sanderson, 2002; Sanderson & Holloway, 2003). Mutterperl and I (2002) found that college women who tend to compare their own weight and body size to that of other women on campus benefit from learning that other women on campus actually eat more and weigh more than women often believe, as described in Chapter 8. These

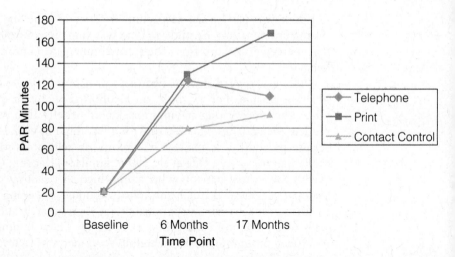

FIGURE 13.5 Adults who receive print-based individualized feedback promoting physical activity show more minutes of moderate intensity exercise 1 year later than those who receive individualized feedback on the phone or those in a control condition (data from Marcus et al., 2007).

women reported higher actual and ideal body weights as well as lower frequencies of disordered eating 5 months later than those who simply received information on "healthy eating." However, women who tend to compare themselves to more idealized images of women in the media (e.g., the cover model on *Cosmopolitan* magazine) report lower actual and ideal weights and more frequent disordered eating when they receive this information than when they receive the healthy-behaviors brochure. In turn, such information may have led these women to feel alienated from their peers, and they may have reacted to such information by redoubling their efforts to achieve the thin ideal typically portrayed in the media (hence, they showed decreases in self-reported actual and ideal weight coupled with increases in frequency of disordered eating). In another study, I found that women who already showed symptoms of eating disorders and who received messages regarding the signs, symptoms, and dangers of eating disorders presented by women who have recovered from such disorders develop an even stronger focus on achieving a very thin body (Sanderson & Holloway, 2003). Apparently, women who are struggling with eating disorders may view recovered women as role models in terms of attaining the thin ideal, and correspondingly they increase their own motivation to exercise as a way of achieving such a body. These findings provide some important information about how best to target eating disorders on college campuses—and strongly suggest that different women will benefit from receiving different types of health-promotion messages.

Finally, interventions for women who already have an eating disorder are also more effective when they take into account individuals' stage of change. Levy (1997), for example, demonstrated that women with bulimia preferred treatment that matched their current readiness for change. Specifically, women who were at the stage of precontemplation preferred a treatment group that provided only general listening support, whereas those who were in the stage of preparation preferred a group that worked on setting specific goals for decreasing the frequency of binging and purging; those who were in the stage of maintenance preferred a group that focused on how to prevent relapse. Once again, people particularly

People vary considerably in their responsiveness to different types of condom-promotion messages.
Source: © Bill Aron/PhotoEdit.

benefit from receiving health-promotion information that matches their specific needs: "One size" clearly does not "fit all."

Condom Use

Individual differences also influence people's responsiveness to different types of messages promoting safer sex behavior. For example, during graduate school, I conducted a study to examine whether different college students like and learn from different types of messages regarding condom use (Sanderson & Cantor, 1995). Specifically, we believed that some college students would prefer to receive information about condom use that focused on the technical skills related to condom use, such as how to put on a condom and how to eroticize condoms, and that others would prefer to receive information that focused on the communication skills related to condom use, such as how to discuss condom use with a sexual partner and how to insist a partner use a condom. To test this hypothesis, we randomly assigned 100 college students to receive either a technical-skills or a communication-skills small-group intervention, which included videos, activities, and discussion, and then measured their attitudes and intentions to use condoms 3 months and 12 months later. As predicted, students who were strongly focused on intimacy in their dating relationships and received the communication-skills intervention (e.g., the one that "matched" their interests) had stronger attitudes toward, self-efficacy for, and intentions regarding condom use. Those with identity goals were more responsive to interventions stressing skills in technical and hedonistic use of condoms. Most importantly, students who received a "matching" condom use intervention also reported engaging in lower levels of risky sexual behavior as long as 1 year later.

Interestingly, even the format in which information is provided can influence how different people respond to such a message. For example, researchers in one study examined how individuals in high versus low need for cognition react to a persuasive message regarding safer sexual conduct that was presented either in a written format or in a comic-strip format (Carnaghi, Cadinu, Castelli, Kiesner, & Bragantini, 2007). Compared to participants in the control group, who did not receive any information regarding safer sex, participants who received a persuasive message regarding safer sex showed increases in condom use attitude and norms. More importantly, however, participants high in need for cognition showed more positive attitudes and norms when the message was in a written, as opposed to a comic-strip, format. Participants low in need for cognition, on the other hand, reported more positive attitudes and norm in reaction to a comic strip than to a written message.

Gender, not surprisingly, also influences people's response to different types of condom-promotion messages. As you might imagine, women and men often have different concerns about using condoms; hence, condom-promotion ads may be more effective when they present different types of information to men as opposed to women (Amaro, 1995; Mays & Cochran, 1988; Marin & Marin, 1992). For example, at the beginning of the chapter, you read about Debbie's decision to design distinct condom-promotion ads for men and women. Specifically, condom-promotion ads for women might be most effective if they portrayed condom use in romantic, committed relationships, in part because women are often concerned that buying and carrying condoms makes them appear promiscuous or "loose" (Struckman-Johnson, Gilliand, Struckman-Johnson, & North, 1990). In contrast, condom-promotion ads for men, who are generally more concerned about condom use reducing their own sexual pleasure, might be more effective if they used sexually arousing content and emphasized that condoms can lengthen sex and thereby enhance both partners' experiences.

What Questions Remain?

Although many research studies on different topics have shown that different people benefit from receiving different types of information, we don't know whether people know what type of information is best for them. This question obviously has great practical importance—if people know what type of information would be best for them, health-promotion programs could simply offer a choice of messages and media (e.g., brochures, videos, intervention groups) and then ask people to choose which they prefer. If this view is correct, it would be easy to give people the "matching," and most effective, message. On the other hand, in some cases, people may not really know what type of information they would find most beneficial. A smoker, for example, may not know whether her cigarette use is triggered more by psychological factors (e.g., stress reduction) or physiological factors (e.g., nicotine cravings). In turn, if people don't know what they need, health-promotion programs would have to develop a quick way to sort people into different groups, such as through a brief questionnaire or interview. Future research is clearly needed to examine whether people do in fact know what they need or, alternatively, to develop appropriate strategies for sorting people into their "matching" group.

TABLE 13.7 *Information YOU Can Use*

- Although common sense might suggest that people would be less likely to engage in a particular health-promoting behavior if they were scared about the consequences of this behavior, fear appeals can backfire. Thus, fear-based appeals to promote behavior change need to be designed very carefully to be effective.
- Social factors, including images in the media and the norms in our environment, exert a strong influence on our health-related behavior. Try to avoid exposing yourself (or your children) to images of detrimental health-related behavior, and to seek out friends who support health-promoting behaviors.
- How you present, or frame, health-related information can have a remarkable influence on how people think about a given behavior. Framing can influence people's willingness to engage in different health-related behaviors and even people's choices regarding medical treatments.
- People are more responsive in terms of attitude and behavior change to messages that are personally relevant. Thus, whenever possible, design messages to be highly relevant for the characteristics, such as the age or gender, of the intended audience.
- One size clearly does not fit all in terms of persuading people to engage in health-related behavior. Messages need to consider the background and personality of the recipients to maximize their effectiveness.

Summary

1. Some health-promotion campaigns rely on providing detailed, factual information about a given health problem. However, this approach tends to be less effective than the use of emotional appeals.

2. Fear-based appeals are a particular type of emotional appeal that use negative stimuli in an attempt to create the threat of impending danger or harm caused by engaging in particular types of behavior (e.g., drug use, smoking) or failing to engage in other types of behavior (e.g., not using a condom, not wearing a seatbelt), and thereby attempt to motivate behavior. This approach can be especially effective if the person is not very involved in or concerned about the message.

3. Fear-based appeals may lead to increases in anxiety, but have little effect on changing behavior. These messages create considerable anxiety, which can restrict learning, attention, and comprehension. People may also defend against the fear these messages create by discounting the risk of a threat, seeing the problem as more common, or denying the seriousness of the threat.

4. Fear-based appeals can work under certain conditions. Specifically, these messages can be effective when they create a moderate level of fear, are given strategies for handling the anxiety, focus on

the short-term consequences of the behavior, and require people to actually imagine having a particular disease or condition. Self-affirmation can also increase people's willingness to process threatening messages.

5. Interventions based in prospect theory reveal that the framing of a message influences how persuaded people are to engage in different types of health-promoting behaviors. People should be more persuaded to engage in behavior to detect a problem, such as skin cancer, when it is framed negatively, namely, in terms of the costs of not engaging in a behavior. In contrast, gain-framed messages, those that emphasize the benefits of engaging in a behavior, should be more effective in promoting prevention behavior (e.g., use of sunscreen, condoms, and car seats).

6. Interventions based in cognitive dissonance theory reveal that because people want to have their attitudes and behaviors in line, requiring people to express a positive attitude toward engaging in a particular health-promoting behavior can increase their likelihood of engaging in the corresponding behavior.

7. Attribution theory posits that people try to explain the causes of their own and others' behavior. In

turn, interventions based on this theory reveal that people are more likely to engage in health-promoting behavior over time when they believe that behavior is motivated by internal, as opposed to external, factors.

8. Learning theories are based on the assumption that behavior is influenced by basic learning processes, such as association, reinforcement, and modeling. Interventions promoting health-related behaviors demonstrate that providing rewards (and/or punishments) for engaging in particular behaviors and modeling such behaviors increases their likelihood of occurring.

9. Interventions based in social cognitive theory reveal that increasing a person's self-efficacy for engaging in a particular behavior is a strong predictor of whether that person will successfully engage in that behavior.

10. Interventions based in the theory of planned behavior focus on increasing social norms for engaging in a particular behavior.

11. Research has also examined whether people benefit more from personally relevant messages. In some cases these messages are targeted to a specific group of people, and/or specific characteristics of a group of people. In other cases researchers have created messages that are tailored to an individual's particular needs and goals.

12. Personally relevant messages have been shown to improve health-related behavior across a number of domains, including screening, managing pain, stopping smoking, reducing alcohol consumption, engaging in safer sex, and preventing disordered eating.

Key Terms

emotional appeals	self-affirmation	targeted
fear-based appeals	tailored	

Thought Questions

1. What are the problems with using fear-based appeals? Can this approach ever work? When?

2. You have a summer job with your city's health department, and you are asked to design a program to reduce drug use in teenagers. Describe one potential program based on attribution theory and another one based on cognitive dissonance theory. Which one do you think would be more effective and why?

3. What is the difference between a tailored message and a targeted message?

4. As part of your community psychology class, you are asked to create two different types of television messages promoting responsible drinking in college students. What are two different approaches you could use?

5. Your younger brother is having his appendix removed and is very nervous about the procedure. You know that your brother generally reacts to stressful situations by adopting an "ignorance is bliss" attitude. What types of things will you do to help him cope before the surgery?

Answers to Questioning the Research

Answer 13.1. The Jones and Leary (1994) study found that messages emphasizing the short-term negative consequences of tanning were more effective at reducing tanning than long-term messages. However, considerable research reveals that adolescents are particularly focused on short-term outcomes, and thus, it is distinctly possible that adolescents and young adults are particularly influenced by short-term messages, and that older adults would find longer-term messages more persuasive.

Answer 13.2. Although this study seems to provide convincing evidence that students who experience cognitive dissonance change their behavior—and thereby increase their condom use—remember that the researchers measured only how many condoms students took—not whether they used them! It is possible that students who took more condoms were indeed more likely to use condoms during their next sexual encounter, but it is also possible that the effects on intentions to use condoms of creating this dissonance wore off by the time the students were next in a sexually intimate situation. Remember, intending to do a behavior sometimes but not always leads to actually doing the behavior.

Answer 13.3. One explanation for the slight improvement in frequency of seat belt use in students is their overall feelings of invulnerability. As previously noted, adolescents often feel invulnerable to various types of health problems, and therefore they may be much less responsive to health-promotion interventions than children or adults. Another factor that may inhibit seat belt use in adolescents is the desire to appear daring and rebellious (e.g., deliberately not following the law in terms of seat belt use). In turn, if this type of self-presentation motive is more valued than the possibility of winning an award, behavioral-intervention programs may have little impact on this population.

Answer 13.4. One explanation for this finding is that letters can be saved, and thus referred to over time, which thus allows for even more reinforcement (and potentially retention) of the information provided. In turn, people who are high in need for cognition may be particularly likely to both save the letter and refer to this information again. This more intensive processing of the information could thereby lead to greater smoking cessation self-efficacy.

CHAPTER 14

Future Directions for Health Psychology

Outline

- Betsy is 56 years old and in excellent health. Although Betsy smoked for 5 years in her late teens and early 20s, after receiving a strong warning from her doctor about the dangers of smoking, she quit. Quitting was very difficult, but Betsy had a strong belief that she could accomplish this goal if she just set her mind to it. She also received high levels of social support: Her husband bought gum and candy for Betsy to use whenever she felt a craving for a cigarette, and her friends promised to treat her to a weekend at a spa after she'd gone 6 months without smoking. Betsy has not had a cigarette in nearly 30 years.

- Dylan is 83 years old and in good health. He walks a mile or two each day for exercise, takes medication to control his arthritis, and eats a balanced and healthy diet. Although Dylan is in good health right now, he has already talked to his children about his desire to have minimal medical intervention if he were to become very ill. He has seen several friends spend the last years of their lives in considerable pain and with very limited mobility, and Dylan feels strongly that he would not want to be kept alive under those conditions. He has also spoken with his doctor about his preferences and hopes that his wishes to focus on quality of life, not just quantity of life, will be honored.

- Kelly is a junior in college and has a summer job working in a local day-care center. She has noticed that while most of the children are very healthy, a few children always seem to be suffering from a lingering cold or ear infection. Kelly suggested to one such child's mother that her son see a doctor, but the mother said she had only recently started a new job and hence had no health insurance for the next month. Another mother reported that she had taken the child to the doctor, but that the antibiotic prescribed was very expensive, and therefore she was giving the child only half of the recommended dose because that's all she could afford.

- Dr. Yellen is a pediatrician in a city and is on the budget committee of the local hospital. The committee is currently deciding how to spend its infant care budget and must choose between two main projects: expanding its prenatal care program to reach more low-income pregnant women or upgrading its neonatal care unit to treat premature infants. Dr. Yellen has read several studies on the importance of evaluating the relative costs and benefits of different medical-treatment options and therefore votes to expand the prenatal care program, which would in turn decrease the number of premature births.

- Mark is a psychology major and, because of his interest in health, he has always intended to go to medical school. However, after taking a course in health psychology last semester, he realized that while he is still interested in health-related issues, he would be more interested in working on preventing health problems than treating existing ones. Mark is therefore trying to find a summer job with a social-service agency and is planning to apply to graduate programs in public health.

Preview

This chapter describes how the field of health psychology has made significant contributions to the promotion of psychological and physical well-being, as well as the major challenges this field faces in the future. First, we describe the contributions of health psychology to psychological and physical well-being, including how psychological factors influence health-compromising and health-enhancing behaviors, how people cope with and manage pain as well as chronic and terminal illnesses, and how people interact with and respond to medical regimens and persuasive messages. We then review the "hot topics" in the field of health psychology, including preventing health problems, making ethical decisions, enhancing the quality of life, and reducing health-care costs. Next, we examine the challenges ahead for health psychology in the future: reducing ethnic and racial differences in health, improving women's health, and addressing international health issues. Finally, we will examine career options in health psychology as well as the pathways to such careers.

What Are the Contributions of Health Psychology?

Research in health psychology has provided a number of major contributions to the prevention and treatment of illness and disease. First, research in health psychology demonstrates that psychological factors, including how we experience and cope with stressful situations, our distinct personality traits, and the amount of social support we receive from others, influence physical health. Chapter 4 described the role of environmental pressures in creating stress, the psychological appraisal in influencing our physiological reactions to stress, and the impact of coping strategies on the experience of stress. As you read in Chapter 5, people who are optimistic and generally expect good outcomes experience better health and even live longer, whereas people who are generally hostile and expect the worst experience a number of health problems. This chapter also examined the influence of social factors on health, including the various ways that social support can benefit health (e.g., by buffering the effects of stress) and the ways that social support can sometimes damage health (e.g., by encouraging unhealthy behaviors). As described at the beginning of this chapter, the considerable social support Betsy received from her friends and husband helped her to quit smoking.

Research in health psychology has also made important contributions in the prevention of disease. Virtually all of the leading causes of death are now influenced at least in part by behavior that people choose to engage in, and in Chapters 7 and 8, we discussed how psychological factors influence health-related behaviors, such as smoking, drinking excessive amounts of alcohol, and eating a high-fat diet.

Research in health psychology has also provided important information about how to help people cope with pain and illness. As described in Chapter 9, considerable evidence suggests that the experience of pain is influenced at least in part by psychological factors, including observational learning (e.g., "How does my mother react when she must have an injection?") and reinforcement (e.g., "Do I get attention if I fall on the playground?"). Also, many pain-management treatments, such as acupuncture, meditation, and relaxation, work at least in part through psychological factors. Psychological factors also influence how people react to and cope with chronic and terminal diseases. For example, Chapter 10 discussed the influence of psychological factors on acquiring coronary heart disease (CHD), cancer, and AIDS, as well as the effectiveness of psychological therapies in managing these diseases. Chapter 11 extended this topic by focusing specifically on the role of psychological factors in influencing how a person copes with a terminal disease diagnosis as well as the nature of bereavement.

Finally, research in health psychology has examined when people seek medical treatment, whether they follow medical recommendations, and how they respond to health-promotion messages and interventions. Chapter 12 described research showing that psychological factors influence whether people get screened for various disorders and how they react to test results, when they seek health care and how they interact with their health-care provider, how they adjust to surgery, whether they adhere to medical recommendations, and whether they relapse to old patterns of behavior. Chapter 13 discussed persuasive communications and interventions based on psychological theories and principles that have already played a valuable role in changing people's health-related behavior, including encouraging screening behavior, decreasing pain, improving doctor–patient relationships, and reducing detrimental health behaviors.

What Are the Hot Topics in Health Psychology?

This section addresses four issues in the field of health psychology that are currently being debated within the field by researchers, politicians, and medical professionals: preventing health problems, making ethical medical decisions, enhancing the quality of life, and reducing health-care costs.

Preventing Health Problems

One major goal of health psychology is preventing the development of health problems, which is a much easier and cheaper way of increasing life expectancy and life quality than treating already-established medical problems (Sullivan, 1990). This is why many people take their car in for an oil change every 3,000 to 5,000 miles—they choose to pursue regular, brief, and inexpensive care for their car as a way of preventing the development of severe and costly problems. The difference between prevention and treatment is well illustrated by this example from physician John McKinlay:

> You know, sometimes it feels like this. There I am standing by the shore of a swiftly flowing river, and I hear the cry of a drowning man. So I jump into the river, put my arms around him, pull him to shore, and apply artificial respiration. Just as he begins to breathe, someone else cries for help. So I jump into the river again, reach him, pull him to shore, apply artificial respiration, and then, as he begins to breathe, there's another cry for help. So back into the river again, reaching, pulling, applying breathing, and then another yell. I'm so busy jumping in and pulling them to shore that I have no time to see who the [heck]...upstream is pushing them in. (McKinlay, 1975, p. 7)

As we've discussed throughout this book, one way to increase the quality of life is through primary prevention, meaning preventing health problems from

TABLE 14.1 *Timing of Prevention*

Level	Timing		
	Primary	Secondary	Tertiary
Individual	Self-instruction guide on HIV prevention for noninfected lower-risk individuals[a]	Screening and early intervention for hypertension[c]	Designing a very low-fat vegetarian diet for an individual with heart disease[c]
Group	Parents group to gain skills to communicate better with teens about risk behaviors[a]	Supervised exercise program for lower-SES individuals with higher risk of heart disease[c]	Cardiac rehabilitation program for groups of heart-disease patients[c]
Organization	Worksite dietary change program focusing on altering vending machine and cafeteria offerings[b]	Worksite incentive program to eliminate employee smoking[a]	Extending leave benefits so employees can care for elderly/ill parent[b]
Community	Focused media campaign to promote exercise in minority population segments[a]	Developing support networks for recently widowed individuals[c]	Providing better access for disabled individuals to all recreational facilities[b]
Institution	Enforcing laws banning the sale of cigarettes to minors[b]	Substantially increasing insurance premiums for smokers[b]	Mandating a course of treatment to facilitate recovery of stroke victims[b]

Prevention of health problems can occur at three different stages, and can be provided at many different levels.

Note: SES stands for socioeconomic status.

[a]Health promotion
[b]Health protection
[c]Preventive services
Source: Winett, 1995.

ever developing (see Table 14.1). Because people's behavioral choices and habits are responsible for most of the major causes of health problems today, some of the most important types of primary prevention strategies are avoiding smoking, eating a healthy diet, and engaging in regular exercise. Moreover, many of these health behaviors are established in late childhood and adolescence, and then persist throughout adulthood, which suggests these choices at a relatively young age could have a dramatic impact on preventing many health-related problems (Smith, Orleans, & Jenkins, 2004).

Another way to increase quality of life is to help people catch and treat health symptoms at an early point in a disease's progression—a type of secondary prevention. A report by the National Cancer Institute in 2008 revealed that the rate of cancer as well as the death rate from cancer are decreasing, largely due to decreases in the three most common types of cancers among men (lung,

FIGURE 14.1 Rates of deaths caused by cancer have dropped over the past decade due to reducing risky behaviors, increasing early detection, and improving treatment (data from Xu, Kochanek, Murphy, & Tejeda-Veia, 2010).

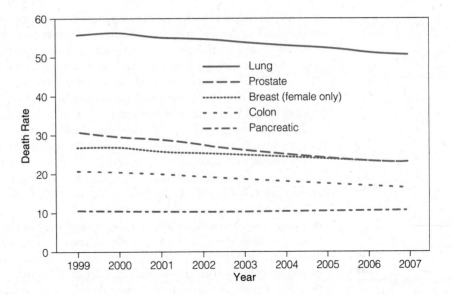

colon/rectum, and prostate) and two most common cancers among women (breast and colon/rectum; Jamal et al., 2008) (see Figure 14.1).

Finally, the most common—and expensive—approach to prevention is tertiary prevention, in which steps are taken to manage or control the effects of an already-developed illness or disease. Chemotherapy, social support groups, and surgery are all types of tertiary prevention approaches for people with cancer.

How can the development of health problems be prevented? First, attempts must be made to motivate people to take an active role in the prevention of health problems. As described in Chapter 7, cigarette smoking accounts for approximately 30% of all cancer deaths, with lung cancer accounting for 80% of the smoking-attributable cancer deaths (Jemal et al., 2008). In turn, efforts to reducing smoking could have a major impact on life expectancy. Similarly, and as described in Chapter 6, efforts to increase motor vehicle safety, through requiring seat belt use, restricting cellphone use and texting while driving, and requiring child-safety seats, can lead to a major reduction in unintentional injuries, which is the leading cause of death for people ages 1 to 44.

The most effective types of prevention programs are multifaceted and community based. An example of a widespread and successful health-promotion program occurred in San Francisco in the 1980s in response to the AIDS epidemic (Coates, 1990). This community-level HIV risk-reduction program included giving out information about risky behavior, increasing feelings of vulnerability, and modeling skills to prevent such behavior (e.g., using condoms, saying "no") and was presented through multiple organizations, including schools, churches, worksites, the health-care system, and community agencies as well as the media. This program was very successful—although before the program 60% of the gay and bisexual men in the sample engaged in high-risk behavior, only 30% reported such behavior 3 to 4 years later. A similar community-wide approach to fighting the problem of unplanned teenage pregnancy was implemented in South Carolina (Vincent, Clearie, & Schluchter, 1987). This program included school-based sex education for children in all grades with participation of parents and church leaders in various educational programs and community-wide events as well as media coverage to raise awareness of the problem. Once again, this approach was highly successful: The pregnancy rate among teenage girls ages 14 to 17 dropped from 5.4% to 2.5%—a 23.3% decrease in pregnancy rate—over the course of this intervention while it remained unchanged in surrounding communities that did not use this type of widespread prevention technique.

Another crucial strategy for preventing health problems is to improve education. Higher levels of education are consistently associated with better health, even when researchers take into account other factors (such as income; Peters, Maker, Dieckmann, Leon, & Collins, 2010). Researchers in one study examined the effect of education on health and found that individuals with more education practiced more health-protective behaviors and that education led to these behaviors through its impact on cognitive ability, numeracy, and decision-making abilities. Education teaches people how to think, which in turn leads people to think about health knowledge and their actions. For example, education explains a substantial amount of smoking behaviors and obesity (Conti & Heckman, 2010). Moreover, recent research reveals that compared to people who have completed college, those with lower levels of education, meaning a high school degree or less, have higher rates of a protein in the body, which is associated with the development of chronic diseases, including cardiovascular disease, osteoporosis, and Alzheimer's disease (Morozink, Friedman, Coe, & Ryff, 2010). This link remains even when researchers consider the effects of other variables associated with such diseases, such as age, gender, and health behaviors.

Making Ethical Medical Decisions

One of the major advances in health care over the past 20 years is clearly the development of new medical technology, such as organ transplantation, chemotherapy, and artificial hearts. Although the growing number of technological advances in health and medicine have had a major impact on life expectancy by allowing some people to live who would certainly have died, these advances lead to some tricky ethical decisions. For example, researchers are now able, at least in some cases, to extract an egg from a woman and sperm from a man and to combine the egg and sperm, and then implant the resulting embryo into the woman's uterus, thereby allowing many couples to have children who were previously considered infertile. However, physicians can screen the embryos prior to implantation, and then choose to implant only those that meet some specified set of criteria. In some cases, this poses few, if any, ethical dilemmas. A couple who is at risk of having a child with cystic fibrosis, for example, might want to implant only those embryos that do not carry this gene, and most people would probably think this selection is morally appropriate. But how about if a couple wanted to implant only those embryos that would produce babies with perfect eyesight (poor vision is another type of genetic defect), or who would be right-handed, or heterosexual. Already some couples have used this technique to have a child of their preferred sex. Experts are concerned that advancing reproductive technology will lead to an unending quest for "better babies." And even when the couple is choosing to implant embryos only on the

Advances in genetic screening can in some cases be used to prevent or treat diseases but have also created numerous challenging ethical issues for families and medical professionals.
Source: Michael S. Wirtz/KRT/Newscom.

basis of their physical health, ethical issues can still emerge. For example, in one case, a woman with a rare genetic mutation that would almost certainly lead her to develop Alzheimer's disease by age 40 sought help from fertility experts in creating a child who would not share her dismal fate. Doctors extracted eggs from the woman, fertilized those without the mutation, and then replanted these eggs into the woman's uterus. Although this child will not develop early-onset Alzheimer's, she will suffer from the loss of her mother at a relatively early age.

The increasing use of genetic screening is another example of a technological advance that leads to challenging ethical issues (Moum, 1995; Saab et al., 2004). Researchers with the Human Genome Project are now working to map the location and precise role of every gene in the human body (Watson, 1990). This information will provide health professionals with new ways to prevent, diagnosis, and treat illness and disease, but it will also raise numerous complex ethical, moral, and legal issues. Some types of screening, such as for HIV infection and cholesterol levels, are already commonly used by insurance companies to set premium rates, and genetic screening could be next. Genetic screening could also determine whether a person has a "preexisting condition," which is typically excluded from insurance. Screening can lead to discrimination in hiring and in securing health insurance. Employers obviously want healthy workers who are absent less, more productive, and less likely to quit work and/or need disability (Faden & Kass, 1993). Employers also pay less for health insurance if they hire healthy workers; hence, they are motivated to hire people who don't use a lot of health care. Would a company want to hire a worker who was certain to develop Huntington's disease within a few years? Would an insurance company charge higher rates to women with the "breast cancer gene"? How about a worker who is a carrier for a life-threatening disease, such as cystic fibrosis, and who may then have a child who needs expensive medical care (which would be covered by the employer)? Would you want to hire a diabetic or someone with a genetic predisposition for alcoholism?

Another medical issue that can lead to multiple ethical dilemmas is that of organ donation. Many more people need organs each year than organs are available, and thus health professionals, patients, and family members have proposed various

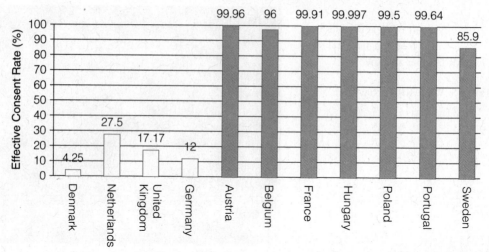

FIGURE 14.2   Countries in which people are assumed to consent to organ donation unless they have specifically opted out show a significantly higher rate of organ donation than those in which people must specifically opt in to donate their organs (data from Johnson & Goldstein, 2003).

solutions to this need. One potential strategy would be to automatically allow for useable organs to be transplanted following a person's death, as typically occurs in some other countries (see Figure 14.2). However, some people have concerns about organ donation, such as the belief that doctors will work less diligently to save someone's life if they know he or she is willing to donate their organs (O'Carroll, Foster, McGeechan, Sandford, & Ferguson, 2011). Another strategy is to allow people to sell one of their own kidneys, which could provide a benefit to the donor as well as the recipient (people have two kidneys and need only one to survive). However, a study published in the *Journal of the American Medical Association* of the impact of selling kidneys in India (where this is a legal practice) revealed that there are few lasting benefits to most donors: In fact, 86% of those who sold a kidney experienced a deterioration of their health, 75% continued to live in poverty, and 79% would not recommend selling a kidney to others (Goyal, Mehta, Schneiderman, & Sehgal, 2002). Box 14.1: Focus on Research describes the effectiveness of various different approaches to increasing organ donations.

Some medical ethicists have proposed that family members should receive some type of incentive for donating a loved one's organs to increase the number of organs available for transplantation. If the person had expressed his or her intention to donate organs, and the family chooses to follow the person's wishes, family members would receive a $10,000 federal income tax credit to apply to the deceased person's estate. This type of program would also bring publicity to the organ-donation program and thereby encourage discussion of people's wishes.

Others are firmly opposed to this proposal for a variety of reasons. First, the majority of people who could successfully donate viable organs die in relatively unusual situations, namely accidents while they are relatively young. These people are unlikely to have thought about or expressed their wishes about organ donation; hence, this incentive program would be unsuccessful in reaching them. Second, some people believe this type of incentive could encourage family members to hasten deaths,

Box 14.1

Focus on Research: Strategies for Increasing Organ Donation

Researchers in one study examined the effectiveness of different strategies for increasing organ donations (Siegel, Albers, Cheng, Hamilton, & Biener, 2008). Four different types of posters were created to prompt people to register as organ donors: counterargument (addressed common misperceptions about organ donation), emotional (emphasized the emotional impact on families who lose a loved one due to organ shortages), motivating action (designed to lead the recipient to register immediately), and dissonance (focused on reminding people of their good nature and that good people would surely donate organs). These posters were then placed in high-traffic areas in several locations—including hospitals, libraries, academic buildings—and near each of these posters was a kiosk in which participants could immediately sign up to be an organ donor. Researchers then measured the number of individuals who registered to be organ donors at each computer kiosk. Interestingly, the counterargument poster was by far the most effective at leading to registrations. This research points to the importance of examining the effectiveness of different types of health-related persuasion messages.

and potentially make people less willing to sign an organ donor card or express their wishes to family members. Finally, some people believe this type of incentive would devalue the altruism demonstrated by the person and his or her family in donating an organ, thereby making it less likely that people would choose to donate.

Finally, technology is expensive, and therefore when money is spent on technology, it takes money away from other types of health care (Butter, 1993). Health professionals must therefore decide when to use technology. For example, in 1987, the legislature of the state of Oregon had to make a decision about how to use its limited health-care budget, and specifically to choose between funding organ transplantation surgery or prenatal care. This choice is really between providing a very large effect for a small number of people (only about 30 people each year in Oregon will need an organ transplant, but for those who do, this surgery literally saves their lives) versus providing a relatively small effect for a large number of people (over 1,500 women in Oregon become pregnant and need prenatal care each year, and providing such care decreases infant mortality and birth defects). As described at the start of this chapter, Dr. Yellen's hospital committee faced the difficult decision of funding either an expanded prenatal program or upgrading its neonatal care unit—both laudable health-promotion goals, but they address very different types of health-care needs. Similarly, and as discussed in Chapter 11, because people can now be kept alive using technological means, medical professionals are forced to examine when such technology should be used and when individuals and/or their families should have the right to refuse this type of treatment. Very expensive technologies are often used to keep people alive for very short periods of time—hours or days—and sometimes in an unconscious state (Kaplan, 1991). One researcher describes this phenomenon as turning "inexpensive dying into prolonged living, usually through expensive means" (McGregor, 1989, p. 119).

And even when technological advances are used, because they are expensive and have limited availability, health professionals must decide who gets this type of treatment (Jennings, 1993; Saab et al., 2004). For example, the growth of organ transplantation procedures, coupled with a limited supply of usable organs, means that decisions must be made about who receives each available organ. These decisions are made in part based on the patient's ability to cope with the stress of such a major procedure and to follow the complex medical procedures necessary to help his or her body accept the new organ (Olbrisch, 1996). These criteria mean that very old people, who are likely to already have shorter life expectancies, and adolescents, who may have trouble following demanding medical recommendations, often are seen as poor candidates for donor organs (Olbrisch, Benedict, Ashe, & Levenson, 2002). In fact, the nation's organ-transplant network, the United Network for Organ Sharing, is considering making a change in their policy regarding kidney transplants so that younger, healthier people would receive priority over older, sicker patients for the best kidneys, instead of prioritizing those who are the sickest. The goal of this policy is to maximize the number of years saved for each kidney donation: Obviously a person who receives a transplant at age 18 is likely to live longer than someone who receives one at age 65. However, this policy would mean that older people, who might well continue to live for 20 or more years, would almost certainly die waiting for a kidney.

Ethical considerations such as fairness and justice may also influence how organs are allocated. When baseball great Mickey Mantle received a liver transplant in 1995 following the destruction of his own liver through years of alcohol abuse, some people questioned whether he was "deserving" of this organ and whether his celebrity status had shortened his waiting time. In line with these concerns, one study found that people were much more likely to offer heart transplant to someone who has never smoked than to someone who is either a current or former smoker (Sears, Marhefka, Rodrigue, & Campbell, 2000).

Enhancing the Quality of Life

One major goal of health psychology is to help people live higher-quality lives, meaning lives that are free from pain and major disability. One aspect of this goal is increasing life expectancy—which is indeed significantly higher now than it was 100 years ago. However, the increase in life expectancy has led to an increase in the number of people suffering from chronic, disabling conditions. Many diseases, such as cancer, CHD, and Alzheimer's disease, are much more prevalent with age; hence, as people live longer, they are more likely to develop such problems. Other diseases are not life-threatening but also increase in incidence with age and can decrease people's overall quality of life. For example, osteoporosis, arthritis, hearing loss, and vision problems caused by glaucoma and cataracts are all more prevalent in older people and can severely hamper a person's ability to engage in various activities. However, the ultimate goal is to allow people to maintain very good psychological and physical well-being for a long time, and then experience a relatively short period of pain and disability immediately prior to death (a compression of mortality).

This focus on quality of life, not just quantity of life, has led researchers to measure people's disability adjusted life expectancy (Kaplan & Bush, 1982). This measure calculates the number of years a person can spend free from disease and disability—their well years or health expectancy. Some researchers even propose that people should rate the quality of their overall life based on the symptoms they are experiencing, as well as the length of time they will spend experiencing these symptoms to determine their **quality-adjusted life years** (QALY; Kaplan, 1991). The quality is determined both by the severity of the symptoms (e.g., being confined to a wheelchair or experiencing considerable pain is more severe than experiencing a mild headache or spraining an ankle) and their duration (e.g., even a very painful bout of food poisoning lasts a few days at most, whereas severe cancer pain could last for years).

People's rating of their QALYs can have a substantial impact on their decisions regarding health care. For example, many people would choose to have surgery to remove a cancerous tumor, in part because this surgery can lengthen life expectancy dramatically and is associated only with a relatively brief period of low life quality during the recovery from surgery. However, many people might choose to not undergo a treatment that provides only a small increase in life expectancy and puts them in a very dependent state (e.g., being tube-fed and on a respirator). As described at the beginning of the chapter, Dylan has already talked with his children about the types of medical procedures he would and would not want and has emphasized his desire to not be kept alive under conditions of high pain, low cognitive clarity, and poor prognosis for recovery. Because doctors' estimates of their patients' preferences regarding living in various health states are not particularly accurate, it is extremely important for patients to communicate their preferences

Chronic health problems, such as Alzheimer's disease, osteoporosis, and arthritis, can severely decrease a person's overall quality of life.
Source: Bill Aron/PhotoEdit.

regarding such states to both their families and medical professionals (Elstein, Chapman, & Knight, 2005). Box 14.2: Health Psychology in the Real World describes an unusual approach to conveying one's end of life preferences.

Box 14.2

Health Psychology in the Real World: A Unique Approach to Conveying End-of-Life Preferences

By Haglund Juhl, *Newsweek,* October 13, 1997

Seventy-one may seem an odd age at which to get your first tattoo, especially for a woman. Just about the only reason I haven't gone ahead and had it done is I haven't quite figured out the wording. It will read something like this: Do Not Resuscitate. And I'll have it written right across my chest.

I've always enjoyed good health, despite a mastectomy 15 years ago. But I do have a genuine fear of becoming incapacitated by a serious accident or illness. For me, the fear has not so much to do with dying but with remaining alive and dependent on others for my care. I've always been fiercely independent—my hair has never been touched by a hairdresser, for instance. My family knows that when I die, I want to be cremated. No one could ever apply my makeup the way I do, and I'm not about to be dolled up by some undertaker. My husband attributes my idiosyncrasies to a stubborn Swedish heritage.

Maybe I am a bit peculiar. And I do admit to a touch of crotchetiness. But as far "Do Not Resuscitate" goes, I'm deadly serious.

The legal and medical communities have several systems in place that recognize my right to refuse extreme measures to keep me alive, should it come to that. Still, I remain skeptical. What if I am treated by a doctor who believes it is a physician's responsibility to apply all the heroic efforts available, despite the patient's wishes? What if my paperwork gets lost? What if my paperwork is exactly where it is supposed to be, but no one stumbles across it until after I've been resuscitated, and my oblivious body is kept alive by life support?

I don't want my children to have to make the decision to "pull the plug" on Mom. I've lived a wonderful life. I'd prefer, when the time comes, to have a wonderful death, as well.

So what to do? It occurred to me that a tattoo right across my chest would be impossible to lose or ignore. (As an artist, I truly believe a visual display is worth a thousand words.) The idea, which at first was simply a flippant remark I tossed out to amuse my painting group, has merit. Think about it: The first thing they do to you in most emergency situations is rip your shirt open to attach monitors and other gizmos of the trade. Who could miss my message?

Determined I may be, but even I cringe at the thought of all those letters being pricked a dot at a time into my bony chest. Something shorter might work; the obvious abbreviation is DNR. But that could lead to other problems. Suppose something happens to me while we're visiting our daughter in Michigan, a state where DNR stands for the Department of Natural Resources. Might I be mistaken for property of the state, just another road kill that ended up in a hospital's emergency room?

No, a shortened tattoo would leave too much to chance. As the notion continues to swirl in my mind, I envision a network much like Medic Alert. A tattoo, backed by the Do Not Resuscitate Society, should convince even the most reluctant rescue worker that I'm serious about this.

Seeing the letters, emergency-room personnel would know to contact the society at 1-800-HEYU-DNR. That call would confirm my membership and even elicit my degree of commitment:

Level 5: I really don't mean this, but I want to impress my friends with how urbane I am. Please do absolutely everything you can to revive me.

Level 4: If I probably won't die, but can be expected to live a compromised, dependent, yet relatively pain-free life, please do what you can to keep me around awhile longer.

Level 3: If it looks like I'm going to be dead by this time tomorrow, and that those next 24 hours will be extremely painful, go ahead and let me die peacefully right now.

Level 2: I mean it. If I'm going to be a vegetable, or what I define as a burden to my family, let's get this over with right now.

Level 1: Not only do I mean everything I said in Level 2, but while we're at it please help yourself to any of my usable organs so that others may enjoy a rich, full life.

"Yes, Ma'am, Mrs. Juhl is a DNR subscriber, Level 1. She asks that you please make every attempt to summon her family so they can say their goodbyes before you allow her to die with dignity."

Some people will no doubt be offended by this idea, and to them I say: Go soak your head. I don't care what you think. This is *my* life I'm talking about, and I'll decide how I want to live it.

It all boils down to mortality. If you have ever been diagnosed with a life-threatening disease, you know the issue of mortality looms large. If you're lucky, as I was, the outcome will be positive, and you'll return to good health. But then, before you know it, you're 70. Suddenly, once again, you come face to face with mortality.

While I may feel decades younger, the fact is I'm in my "golden years." Although I certainly have no interest in seeing my life end any time soon, I need to be realistic. So this is far from a death wish. If anything, it's a *life* wish.

I've always been an idea person, and my family generally offers only a pat on the head ("good dog") when I try to work up some enthusiastic support for my latest brainstorm. I'm taken seriously much less often than I should be—and that's too bad, because I've had some darn good ideas. My friends, though, think I might be on to something with this one.

Yes, you say, but history is full of people who get tattoos and live to regret them. Wouldn't something like this be irrevocable? What if you change your mind? Easy enough. Society membership would include a coupon for a free, second tattoo. It would be the universal symbol for "Do Not"—a bright red circle with a slash mark across it. Have it applied right over the top of the old tattoo, and you're back among the living.

Living as well as I can is what I intend to do until it's time for me to go to my reward.

Although communicating end-of-life preferences to loved ones and physicians should help make sure the patient's preferences are honored, these **advanced-directives**, or living wills, can also lead to problems (Ditto & Hawkins, 2005; Fried, Bradley, Towle, & Allore, 2002). First, many people, even those who are terminally ill, don't complete living wills or share their preferences with loved ones. Patients may be optimistic about the likelihood of recovery, and thus not see expressing such preferences as important. Patients and their families may also find discussing end-of-life scenarios distressing, and thus avoid the topic completely. Second, people aren't very good at assessing in the abstract what type of health state they could versus could not tolerate. Third, even when a person has completed a living will, and/or shared their preferences with family members, it can be difficult for loved ones to interpret and/or follow through on such wishes. Family members may therefore push for more aggressive care, even if this is not the expressed preference of the patient.

Reducing Health-Care Costs

One of the hottest topics in health psychology is the rapidly increasing costs of health care in the United States and how these costs can be controlled. Of the gross domestic product, 16% was spent on health care in 2008 with a total cost of $2.3 trillion (Centers for Disease Control, 2011). In contrast, other similar countries, such as Germany, Canada, and Japan, spent about 7% of their gross domestic product on health care (see Box 14.3: Focus on Culture). Overall health-care costs are about 40% more in the United States than in other countries, yet we are not a healthier country, as measured in terms of life expectancy or infant mortality (Bingamon, Frank, & Billy, 1993).

Box 14.3

Focus on Culture: How Do Other Countries Handle Health Care?

Many countries, including Canada and most European countries, view health care as a guaranteed consumer good or service; hence, health care is funded at least in part by the government. Patients can typically choose any doctor they want, and all citizens' medical bills are covered by taxes. Many countries also include prescription drug benefits and mental-health services. These benefits are not based on consumer ability to pay, as is often true in the United States. In Canada, for example, all citizens have universal health insurance, regardless of age, health status, employment—health insurance doesn't come with a job, as in the United States. These benefits are comprehensive, so people don't pay doctor or hospital bills. This system is usually complicated less with bureaucratic hurdles. The per-person expenditure on health care in the United States is $347 per year, compared to $202 in Canada (Fuchs & Hahn, 1990).

One reason costs are so much higher in the United States than in other similar countries is that physicians and hospitals in the United States spend much more on administrative costs, including advertising to recruit patients, filing for reimbursement from insurance companies, and obtaining permission to do various procedures (see Table 14.2; Woolhandler & Himmelstein, 1991). For example, the average U.S. physician's office spent about 1 hour on each insurance claim (private or Medicare), which is 20 times as long as time spent in Canada (Woolhandler & Himmelstein, 1990). Given the litigious nature of U.S. society, physicians in the United States often pay much more for malpractice insurance than do doctors in other countries. Physicians in the United States also spend more money than do Canadian physicians on "amenities" for their offices, including renting desirable office space, buying attractive furniture, and paying for interior decorating perhaps as a way of attracting patients. In contrast, Canadian physicians are more likely to attract patients by offering lower fees. U.S. physicians also rely more on technology and

TABLE 14.2 *Per Capita Cost of Health-Care Administration in the United States Versus Canada*

Cost Category	Spending Per Capita (US dollars)	
	United States	Canada
Insurance overhead	259	47
Employers' costs to manage health benefits	57	8
Hospital administration	315	103
Nursing home administration	62	29
Administrative costs of practitioners	324	107
Home-care administration	42	13

The administrative structure of the U.S. health-care system is significantly less efficient—and therefore significantly more expensive—than the Canadian health-care system.

Source: Woolhandler, Campbell, & Himmelstein, 2003.

use more medically advanced procedures (Kaplan, 1989). Finally, as compared to Canadian doctors, U.S. doctors work shorter hours, see fewer patients, perform fewer procedures, and receive higher salaries (Fuchs & Hahn, 1990)! The Canadian government keeps a tight control on fees given to physicians and on hospital budgets; hence, the fees charged for procedures as well as the income paid to physicians are lower. However, the wait for nonemergency medical procedures is often much longer in Canada than in the United States.

One obvious factor contributing to the high costs of health care is that people are living longer, so they develop more chronic, long-term diseases that require ongoing care, possibly for years. AIDS, Alzheimer's disease, CHD, and cancer are all examples of very common diseases that people may live with for many years—sometimes requiring expensive treatment (e.g., bypass surgery, drug regimens, chemotherapy, and radiation). Similarly, because of the high rate of malpractice suits in the United States, physicians must carry expensive malpractice insurance (the cost naturally is passed on to patients) and often practice "defensive medicine" in which they order every test and do every procedure to protect themselves from lawsuits (Butter, 1993).

Another factor contributing to the high cost of health care is the increasing reliance on medical technology. State-of-the-art treatment is often seen as superior to low-tech options (Butter, 1993). Technology use is also profitable for hospitals (who can charge for the equipment) and physicians (who can charge for their specialized services). In fact, rates of caesarean section are lower among women who are uninsured or are covered by Medicaid (a government program that pays health-care costs for poor people) than those who are using private insurance (Gould, Davey, & Stafford, 1989; Placek, Taffel, & Moien, 1988).

Unfortunately, this infatuation with technology has led to an overreliance on it in some cases. Some surgeries, such as coronary bypass surgery and caesarean

Although this cartoon is supposed to be funny, it describes a very real situation—people with health insurance receive more diagnostic and treatment procedures than do those without such coverage.
Source: Mike Keefe, The Denver Post.

section, are clearly beneficial to some patients but are often overused for patients that might benefit the same or more from other less-expensive procedures. In fact, one study suggested that about 20% of the pacemakers implanted in people were unwarranted (Greenspan et al., 1988). To test whether patients benefit in terms of survival from more aggressive care, researchers in one study compared the effectiveness of two different treatments for coronary artery disease: percutaneous coronary intervention versus a conservative treatment in which patients were not given any intervention (Katritsis & Ioannidis, 2005). Findings revealed no differences between patients treated in these different ways in terms of heart attacks or mortality, suggesting that the more aggressive approach may in fact not lead to any benefits. Similarly, researchers in another study examined whether implantable cardioverter-defibrillators reduce mortality in women with advanced heart failure (Ghanbari et al., 2009). Once again, there were no statistically significant decreases in mortality in women with heart failure who receive implantable cardioverter-defibrillators.

Although the research described thus far has focused on treatment for heart problems, which represent a very serious and potentially fatal disease, more aggressive treatment is also used for less serious medical conditions. For example, childbirth is usually straightforward and certainly can occur with relatively little technology intervention (for many years, women gave birth at home, often with only the assistance of a midwife). Now childbirth often includes the use of many different types of technology, including ultrasounds, epidural pain relief, and electronic fetal monitoring (Butter, 1993). This means that women today typically have a more "technologically advanced" birth but not necessarily "better" births.

As a step toward controlling the high cost of health care, a growing number of people are now enrolled in some type of managed-care system (Miller & Luft, 1994). In fact, estimates are that more than 78 million Americans now receive medical care through a **health maintenance organization (HMO)**. In this arrangement, an employer or an employee pays a set fee every month and in turn has unlimited access to medical care (at either no cost or a greatly reduced cost). In some cases, HMOs require patients to see their own staff, whereas in other systems, patients can choose from among a group of medical professionals who have agreed to accept a specified payment for their services (preferred provider organizations). HMOs assign people to a primary care physician, who manages their care and must refer patients to specialists. For a long time, most Americans received health care from a physician they paid each time they had an appointment, which is called fee-for-service care; HMOs are different from this care methodology.

One way HMOs help to decrease health-care costs is by classifying all health problems into diagnostic-related groups and then giving practitioners and hospitals a set fee for treatment of a given problem. This means that all physicians working for a given HMO have agreed to accept a set fee for their services (which is often lower than they would receive in a typical fee-for-service arrangement). HMOs also require that all of a patient's care be approved by their doctor as well as the HMO organization. Patients even need approval from their physician and/or HMO before being admitted to the hospital (another way to save HMOs money).

Unfortunately, many patients find this system less satisfying than a more traditional fee-for-service approach for several reasons (Miller & Luft, 1994). First, because HMOs have agreements with only certain specified doctors (who are willing to accept a given—often lower—payment for their services), people must choose a doctor who participates with their HMO. This means that patients may not necessarily be able to see their preferred doctor. Moreover, because all care must be approved by their physician as well as the HMO organization, patients sometimes face major obstacles in getting approval for the treatment they need. They are also less likely to be admitted to the hospital than patients on a more traditional plan, and when they are hospitalized, they are discharged faster than other patients with comparable conditions (Rogers et al., 1990). One study with a sample of 14,012 Medicare patients found that the introduction of a DRG-based payment system led to a 24% drop in length of hospital stays, although there were no differences in health outcomes or mortality (Kahn et al., 1990). Some HMO plans offer women a "bonus" for leaving the hospital within 24 hours (although state laws may allow a stay of up to 48 hours)—women who leave within 24 hours after giving birth are giving 10 hours of household and childcare help free of charge from a doula, a trained companion who provides support and assistance during childbirth and afterward. Finally, and most important, some evidence suggests that HMOs lead to worse health outcomes, especially for the chronically ill and poor people (Miller & Luft, 1994). For example, researchers in Seattle, Washington, found that for elderly patients, 54% of those in an HMO showed declines in health as compared to 28% of those in a traditional fee-for-service plan (Ware, Bayliss, Rogers, & Kosinski, 1996). Despite these problems, it is important to remember that there is little evidence overall that HMOs lead to lower quality of health care, and in fact, people in HMOs are very pleased with some aspects of their care, including waiting times for appointments and costs (Rossiter, Langwell, Wann, & Rivnyak, 1989). And while Americans want free choice of providers, complete access to medical services, no waiting, and lots of technology, they don't want to pay more for health care (Jennings, 1993; Kerrey & Hofschire, 1993).

Given the skyrocketing costs of health care, health psychologists are increasingly asked about the costs of health-promotion interventions, specifically whether these costs justify the programs (Friedman, Sobel, Myers, Caudill, & Benson, 1995; Johnson & Millstein, 2003; Kaplan, 1989; Kaplan & Groessl, 2002; Nation et al., 2003). In many cases, the costs of health-promotion programs are low, given their potential benefits. For example, the Stanford Five City Project (described in Chapter 7) provided 5 years of intensive education and training, including television and radio spots, brochures, classes, and contests, to two small cities in northern California in an effort to decrease CHD (Farquhar et al., 1990). Although the overall effects of this intervention were relatively small, the cost was only about $4 per person per year. In this case, the benefits (even if small) would probably outweigh the costs (also small). Similarly, Holtgrave and Kelly (1996) found that a 12-session, small-group HIV-prevention intervention for gay men cost about $470 per person, yet the medical costs savings of this program were substantial. Other studies indicate that giving people information about detrimental health behavior (e.g., problem drinking, smoking) and providing advice about home remedies for common health problems are inexpensive and lead to a substantial overall savings (Fries et al., 1993; Windsor et al., 1993). Even relatively expensive lifestyle interventions can be effective if they reduce costly medical procedures (e.g., Ornish et al., 1990). For example, insurance companies may prefer to pay the considerable costs of a lifestyle-change program that includes diet, exercise, meditation, and so on than the cost of a coronary artery bypass surgery. However, and as shown in Figure 14.3, the most cost-effective methods of health promotion are primary prevention strategies, such as requiring daylight-running lights on cars, using seat belts, and prohibiting teenagers from smoking (Kaplan, 2000). For example, in one ambitious program to increase seat belt use, Florida state employees were required to read and sign a

FIGURE 14.3 Tobacco restriction policies and seat belt laws are among the most cost-effective health-promotion programs, whereas surgical procedures are among the least cost-effective (data from Kaplan, 1989, 2000).

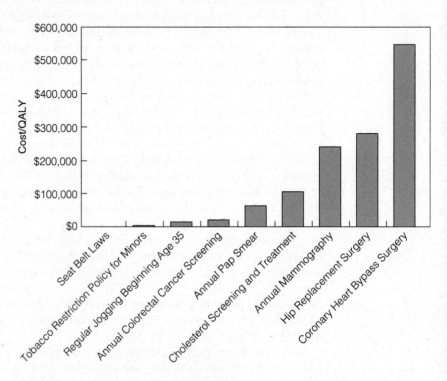

sheet describing the state rules requiring seat belt use (Rogers et al., 1988). They were then given stickers for their dashboards to remind them to "buckle up." Although only about 10% of workers were using their seat belts initially, this rate climbed to 52%! Moreover, this program led to a substantial decrease in the cost of accident claims, from a little over $2,000 to just under $1,000. Lifestyle programs to reduce the risk of diabetes, which focus on increasing physical activity and reducing weight, are more effective than drug treatment (Knowler et al., 2002).

However, in other cases, the benefits of a program in terms of health may not justify its costs (White, Urban, & Taylor, 1993). Screening programs, for example, are often found not to be as cost-effective because they involve testing many people who would never develop the disease (Moum, 1995). For example, requiring yearly mammograms is more expensive (in general and per cancer prevented) than biannual or even screenings once every 5 years, yet is more effective in reducing cancer deaths. Screening programs are also more cost-effective when they focus on those at greatest risk for the disease (Kaplan, 2000). Mammograms cost about $21,400 to produce a single year of life when used with women ages 50 to 64 years, but $105,000 per quality year lived when used in women ages 40 to 49 years. Similarly, a mass prenatal screening for cystic fibrosis could detect whether children would have this disease. However, given the tremendous costs associated with this screening, including genetic counseling, public education, and the tests themselves, it is estimated that more than $1 million would be spent to avoid a single cystic fibrosis birth (Wilfond & Fost, 1990). Because this is five times the cost of caring for a person with cystic fibrosis, this type of screening is clearly cost-ineffective. Finally, screening is especially cost-inefficient when it is used for relatively old people, who will not benefit from increased life expectancy as dramatically as younger people, and in cases in which the treatment for the condition detected leads to lower quality of life (Kaplan, 2000). For example, screening 70-year-old men for prostate cancer extends life expectancy less than 5 hours, and the treatment for prostate cancer often significantly reduces their overall enjoyment of life (Krahn et al., 1994). Once again, screening is not always the right approach to enhancing health.

Concern about high costs of health care has led to increasing acceptance of psychologists and their research by physicians and other health-care professionals for several reasons. First, principles in health psychology can be used to prevent health problems from developing, which is much more cost-effective than diagnosing and treating illness and disease (Fries, 1998; Winett, 1995). For example, preventing premature birth by ensuring pregnant women have prenatal care reduces medical costs considerably (Brown, 1985)—babies who weigh as little as 1 pound at birth can be saved, but it costs about $350,000 per baby for 4 months of care in the neonatal intensive care unit, and these babies often have ongoing struggles and disabilities. In contrast, it would cost about $600 per pregnant woman to provide prenatal care to 583 women, which substantially reduces the likelihood of premature birth (Butter, 1993). Although this type of prevention program would reduce the demand for medical services and thereby reduce health-care costs, the vast majority of funds devoted to researching health issues each year are devoted to treating illness, not preventing it (DeLeon, 2002).

Second, in many cases, psychological treatments may help people cope with and recover from medical problems but at a lower cost. Many interventions for hospitalized patients are extremely cost-effective because they help patients use less pain medication and be discharged earlier (see Chapter 12; Devine, 1992). For example, of women who are supported during labor, only 8% have a caesarean section, compared to 18% of those in the control group (Kennell, Klaus, McGrath, Robertson, & Hinkley, 1991). Patients who had a doula (a trained supportive companion to assist with labor and delivery) also had shorter labors, less use of epidural anesthesia, and were less likely to have babies that require neonatal hospitalization. This is a big cost savings. Similarly, breast-cancer patients who receive hypnosis prior to surgery cost the hospital $772.71 less per patient than those in the control group, mainly due to reduced surgical time (Montgomery et al., 2007). Psychologically based treatments can also lead to reduced costs in nonhospital settings. As described in Chapter 9, showing children a movie during vaccinations to distract from the pain is substantially cheaper than using anesthetic cream: Researchers estimated that the distraction condition would cost $421 to implement (for costs of the television, VCR, and movies) and no additional expenses, whereas providing the cream would cost $750 as an annual expense (Cohen, Blount, Cohen, Schaen, & Zaff, 1999).

Although the medical community has often resisted collaborating with psychologists (or other nonmedically trained personnel), as of July 1, 2001, the Accreditation Council for Graduate Medical Education (ACGME) required that residency programs teach skills in such collaboration, and residency programs must now demonstrate that residents have these skills prior to graduation.

What Are the Challenges for Health Psychology in the Future?

As we look to the next decade (and beyond), the field of health psychology will clearly face numerous challenges. Three of the most important, in terms of improving both the quantity and quality of life, are decreasing racial-ethnic differences in health, improving women's health, and addressing international health issues.

Decreasing Racial-Ethnic Differences in Health

Although overall life expectancy has climbed dramatically in the United States over the past 100 years, the average life span differs considerably for people in different ethnic groups: White females live an average of 4 years longer than African American females (80.6 versus to 76.5 years), and White males live an average of 6 years longer than African American males (75.7 years versus 69.7 years; Arias, 2010). In fact, compared to Whites, African Americans have higher rates of death caused by homicide, cancer, and cardiovascular disease and a higher mortality rate at every age category (Centers for Disease Control and Prevention, 2011; Flack et al., 1995; Geronimus, Bound, Waidmann, Hillemeier, & Burns, 1996). African Americans are also more likely than Whites to suffer from chronic health conditions, including stroke, cancer, heart disease, and AIDS (Kung et al., 2008; Meyerowitz, Richardson, Hudson, & Leedham, 1998). For example, although African Americans make up only 12% of the total United States population, 46% of people living with HIV are

African American (Campsmith, Rhodes, Hall, & Green, 2008). African Americans are even more likely than Whites to experience fatal job-related injuries, primarily because they are more likely to work in hazardous industries, such as construction, manufacturing, agriculture, and transportation (Loomis & Richardson, 1998).

Although most studies of ethnic differences in health have focused on differences between Whites and African Americans, studies with both Hispanics/Latinos and Native Americans generally reveal similar findings (Bagley, Angel, Dilworth-Anderson, Liu, & Schinke, 1995; Flack et al., 1995; Grossman, Krieger, Sugarman, & Forquera, 1994; Johnson et al., 1995). For example, compared to Whites, both Hispanics and Native Americans show higher rates of many diseases, including tuberculosis, diabetes, cancer, cardiovascular disease, and AIDS. Relatively little research has examined health in Asian Americans, and the existing data on health in this population suffer from several major limitations (Flack et al., 1995). However, some evidence suggests that compared to Whites, Asian Americans have higher rates of some diseases (e.g., hepatitis, tuberculosis) but lower rates of others (e.g., CHD; Johnson et al., 1995).

What leads to these dramatic differences in health and longevity? One factor is health behaviors (Johnson et al., 1995; Myers, Kagawa-Singer, Kumanika, Lex, & Markides, 1995; Yee et al., 1995). As compared to Whites, African Americans eat more high-fat foods, such as bacon, sausage, and fried foods, and eat fewer high-fiber cereals and fruits, in part because African Americans are more likely to live near fast-food restaurants but less likely to live near supermarkets (where healthier foods could be purchased; Morland, Wing, & Diez, 2002). In turn, African Americans—especially women—are more likely to be obese than Whites, and are less likely to engage in regular exercise. African Americans are also more likely to be infected with AIDS as well as other STDs than are people in other ethnic groups (Laumann & Youm, 1999; Maxwell, Bastani, & Warda, 1999). Although alcohol use and smoking rates are similar for African American and White women, African American men are more likely to engage in both of these behaviors than White men are, perhaps because of a desire to use alcohol as a means of "escaping" negative working and living conditions. It is not an accident that there are more stores selling alcoholic beverages, as well as outdoor billboard advertisements for alcohol and tobacco products, in African American and low-income neighborhoods than in more affluent ones (Moore, Williams, & Qualls, 1996; Rabow & Watts, 1984). Similarly, rates of smoking and alcohol use are higher in Native Americans than in Whites. Rates of injuries, such as those caused by drowning and fires, are significantly more common in African Americans and Native Americans than in Whites. (Ironically, some recent research suggests that African Americans are much less likely than White smokers to successfully enroll in smoking-cessation programs, although twice as many African Americans as Whites express interest in such programs; King, Cao, Southard, & Matthews, 2011). Finally, and as shown in Figure 14.4, deaths caused by homicides are much more likely in African American, Hispanic, and Native American groups than in White populations.

Minorities are also much less likely than Whites to engage in regular, preventive health care, in part because they have higher rates of unemployment and are more likely to hold low-paying jobs that do not provide health insurance (Fiscella, Franks, Gold, & Clancy, 2000; Flack et al., 1995; Johnson et al., 1995). In turn, this lack

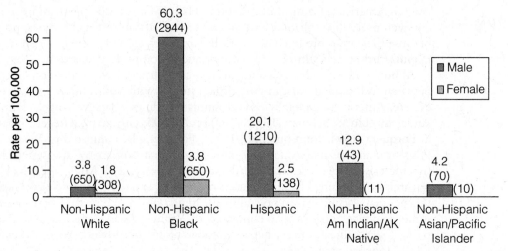

FIGURE 14.4   Rates of homicide are significantly higher for African American males than any other group; in fact, homicide is the leading cause of death for African American males ages 15 to 24 (CDC, 2011).

of regular health care increases people's risk of developing major health problems because they do not use preventive measures or catch health problems at earlier, treatable stages (Adler, Boyce, Chesney, Folkman, & Syme, 1993; Adler et al., 1994; Gornick et al., 1996). Similarly, although White women are more likely to get breast cancer than African American women, the survival rate of African American women is lower than that of White women (CDC, 2010). Moreover, members of minority groups may be less likely than Whites to rely on medical professionals for health care even when they have health insurance (Fiscella et al., 2000). Both Hispanics and Asians sometimes avoid seeking health care because of a lack of comfort with speaking English, as well as a cultural preference for both relying primarily on family members and friends for advice about physical symptoms and using alternative medical treatments (e.g., acupuncture, herbs). As described in Chapter 12, African Americans with osteoarthritis are much less likely than Whites to prefer surgery (Figaro, Russo, & Allegrante, 2004). Ethnic minorities may also have a general distrust of the medical community, based in part on prior experiments in which minority group members were used—without their knowledge or consent—in medical experiments (Jemmott & Jones, 1993; Marin & Marin, 1991). For example, and as described in Chapter 2, in the 1930s, some African American men with syphilis were left untreated so that researchers could measure the long-term effects of the disease.

Still another factor leading to ethnic differences in health is income—minorities are more likely than Whites to be poor, which in turn is associated with worse health for several reasons (Adler & Matthews, 1994; Geronimus et al., 1996). For example, in 1991, 32.7% of African Americans were living in poverty as compared to 11.3% of Whites (Flack et al., 1995). People who are poor are less likely to have access to regular health care (Anderson & Armstead, 1995; Johnson et al., 1995). People in the lowest income groups have much lower rates of immunization (26% lower among Whites, 39% lower among African Americans) than those in the highest income groups, which in turn means they have a higher risk of acquiring many preventable diseases (Gornick et al., 1996). They are also less likely to catch diseases in an early, and more treatable, stage. One study of women with annual household incomes below $15,000 found that 90% did not obtain regular mammograms, and more than 33% had never even heard of mammography (Mickey, Durski, Worden, & Danigelis, 1995). Although people who have extremely low incomes qualify for Medicaid (health coverage paid for by the government), because Medicaid reimburses health-care providers much less than they charge other patients, patients with this type of health coverage often have trouble locating a physician who will accept this low level of reimbursement. Moreover, many people who make just enough so that they don't qualify for Medicaid often have no health insurance at all, typically because the cost of this coverage simply would be too much. In fact, an estimated 48.2 million Americans under the age of 65 years, or 18% of the population, do not have health insurance (Centers for Disease Control and Prevention, 2009). And even when they do seek medical attention, people with Medicaid or no insurance receive less comprehensive medical care than those with private insurance. One study found that privately insured patients were 80% more likely to get an angiography, 40% more likely to receive bypass grafting, and 28% more likely to receive angioplasty compared to those with no insurance or those on Medicaid (Wenneker, Weissman, & Epstein, 1990). As described in Box 14.4: Focus on Development, poverty during childhood has lasting effects on health.

Although lack of access to regular health care is one explanation for the link between low income and poor health, even in countries with universal free health care, people with low income are less healthy than those with more income (Adler

Box 14.4

Focus on Development: The Long-Term Hazards of Childhood Poverty

Several studies have examined the link between childhood poverty and later health outcomes. For example, researchers in one study examined the link between duration of exposure to poverty and psychological stress in children from birth through age 13 (Evans & Kim, 2007). The more years a child had spent living in poverty, the more elevated were the child's stress reactions (e.g., cortisol levels, cardiovascular reactivity to stress). Encouragingly, however, even children who grow up in poverty may be able to overcome this disadvantage if given adequate social resources. Researchers in one study examined family income for children at age 9 and then examined smoking prevalence and body fat at age 17 (Evans & Kutcher, 2011). Adolescents who grow up in low-income households smoke more and have more body fat than those who are living in more affluent environments. However, for those living at the poverty line, those who have social capital—meaning connections with neighbors and feeling a part of the community and having support from adults—did not smoke more or have extra body weight than those who were more affluent. So, these early social resources can make up for a lack of income and buffer children from the elevated health risks they would otherwise experience.

et al., 1993). This finding indicates that factors other than the ability to pay for health care must influence the link between low income and poor health. One explanation is that poor people tend to engage in more destructive health-related behaviors, including smoking, alcohol consumption, failure to exercise, and obesity (Adler et al., 1993; Adler et al., 1994; Anderson & Armstead, 1995; Stunkard & Sorensen, 1993; Wardle, Waller, & Jarvis, 2002). For example, 41% of men and 36% of women with only a high school education or less smoke as compared to 18% of men and 17% of women with some postcollege education (Winkleby, Fortmann, & Barrett, 1990). Another explanation is that people in low socioeconomic groups experience higher levels of stress, such as overcrowded housing, homelessness, pollution, and neighborhood crime (Anderson & Armstead, 1995; Chen & Paterson, 2006; Jackson et al., 2010; Myers et al., 1995; Yee et al., 1995). As described in Chapter 4, stress can have both direct and indirect effects on health. Relatedly, people with low socioeconomic resources may have limited ability to cope with stressful life events, which in turn further heightens feelings of stress (Gallo et al., 2009). A family with little disposable income, for example, may experience a variety of negative life events as more stressful, such as needing to have a car repaired, losing a job, or having a child with a chronic medical condition.

Eliminating racial and ethnic differences in health is a difficult task, but it is a feasible goal. One step toward accomplishing this goal would be providing some type of universal health care, which would help increase access to health-care services for members of minority groups (Johnson et al., 1995). This type of coverage would lead to the prevention of health problems caused by a lack of prenatal care and immunizations. As described at the beginning of the chapter, Kelly noted that some of the children in the day-care center where she worked did not have access to regular health care or low-cost prescriptions and, hence, experienced many lingering illnesses. Focusing on prevention is another strategy for decreasing these differences, particularly because members of minority groups often engage in high rates of health-compromising behaviors. Strategies for this type of

Low-income families face a variety of stressors, including overcrowded housing, pollution, and neighborhood crime, all of which can have negative effects on health.
Source: David Butow/Corbis SABA.

prevention could include emphasizing the importance of eating a healthy diet and engaging in regular exercise, as well as avoiding smoking. Most important, reducing the drastic rate of poverty in some parts of the United States, especially in inner cities, is probably the most important means of improving health in members of minority groups. Improving the overall standard of living, by encouraging people to continue their education, providing low-cost housing and job training, and decreasing poverty, would go a long way toward reducing many of the ethnic and racial differences in health.

Focusing on the Predictors of Women's Health

For many years, research in psychology in general and health psychology in particular was based largely on samples of men (and typically samples of young, White, upper-class men who were in college; Matthews et al., 1997). This focus was caused in part by the easy access of this type of population—many researchers work in college and university settings (and many prestigious schools did not even admit women until relatively recently) and, hence, often used students who were readily available. Women may also be excluded from medical studies because of concern about the influence of hormonal changes across the menstrual cycle as well as the potential dangers to fetuses (Wenger, Speroff, & Packard, 1993). However, this exclusion of women severely limits our knowledge about the factors that influence women's health and how women respond to various psychological and medical treatments. In fact, women are even excluded from many studies of drugs that are primarily used by women, such as weight-loss pills and antidepressants (Rodin & Ickovics, 1990).

One explanation for the greater focus on men's health is that women typically have a much longer life expectancy than men; therefore, they must be healthier. However, this gender gap in life expectancy is narrowing, in part because women are increasingly engaging in health-compromising behaviors at higher rates (Rodin & Ickovics, 1990). For example, the rate of lung cancer used to be much higher in men than women, but between 1979 and 1986, the rate of lung cancer deaths climbed 44% in women and only 7% in men. In fact, lung cancer—not breast cancer—is the leading cause of cancer death for U.S. women. Moreover, women who smoke and use the birth-control pill experience a greater risk of stroke and cardiovascular disease. Women are also at a greater risk than men of acquiring HIV (Rodin & Ickovics, 1990). Although men still represent the majority of AIDS cases in the United States, the rate of new HIV infection in women is increasing dramatically, in part because women are at much greater risk of acquiring the disease during sex (Padian, Shiboski, Glass, & Vittinghoff, 1997). Similarly, Box 14.5: Focus on Research describes how people make decisions about whether to be vaccinated for HPV, a virus that causes virtually all cervical cancers (and which kills 4,000 women in the United States each year).

Women also have unique health issues and concerns (Rodin & Ickovics, 1990; Stanton, Lobel, Sears, & DeLuca, 2002). First, reproductive issues and technology, including pregnancy, infertility, abortion, contraception, prenatal screening, caesarean sections, and in vitro fertilization, impact women more directly than

---

Box 14.5

Focus on Research: Understanding the Decision to Vaccinate for HPV

Researchers in this study examined the factors that influenced people's decisions about HPV vaccinations (Cooper Robbins, Bernard, McCaffery, Brotherton, & Skinner, 2010). Focus groups at nine different schools were conducted with girls, and interviews were conducted with parents, teachers, and nurses. The issues raised during these discussions were then examined to determine the types of factors that influenced the decision to vaccinate. This analysis led to five different decision-making states:

- **Active decision—vaccinated:** People in this group held strong beliefs about the importance of prevention and had positive experiences with the medical system.
- **Passive decision—vaccinated:** People in this group chose for their daughter to be vaccinated but didn't provide a reason.
- **Passive decision—not vaccinated:** People in this group chose for their daughter not to be vaccinated but didn't provide a reason.
- **Active decision—not vaccinated:** People in this group had negative experience with the medical system, concerns about sex, and do not trust authorities.
- **Anti-vaccination:** People in this group have strong anti-vaccination beliefs.

These findings indicate that people's core health beliefs, past experiences with the medical system, and perception of media messages all influenced this decision-making process.

---

they do men. The experience of postpartum depression, for example, has recently received considerable attention because of well-publicized tragedies. Women also face unique challenges related to the experience of menstruation and menopause. Many women take the hormone estrogen, often as part of oral contraceptives prior to menopause and as hormone-replacement therapy following menopause. Although for some time researchers have thought that taking these hormones was an effective way of preventing some of the side effects of menopause, a study by the National Institutes of Health revealed that women who take estrogen and progestin to minimize the effects of menopause are at risk of experiencing major health problems (Writing Group for the Women's Health Initiative Investigators, 2002). Specifically, as compared to women in the control group who received a placebo, those who took these hormones experienced a 41% increase in strokes, a 29% increase in heart attacks, and a 26% increase in breast cancer. Finally, other diseases, such as osteoporosis and Alzheimer's disease, can occur in men and women, but are much more common in women, in part because they tend to live longer. In sum, women face particular health issues and challenges, and research must focus on examining how best to promote women's health. As described by Baum and Grunberg (1991):

> Research on health and behavior should consider men and women—not because it is discriminatory not to do so—but because it is good science. The study of women and men, of young and old, of African Americans and Caucasians, Asians, Latinos, and American Indians will all help to reveal psychosocial and biological mechanisms that are critical to understanding mortality, morbidity, and quality of life (p. 84).

Some evidence also suggests that women consistently receive lower-quality health care than men (Ayanian & Epstein, 1991; Chen, Rathore, Radford, Wang, & Krumholz, 2001; et al., 2000; Schulman et al., 1999; Steingart et al., 1991). As described in Chapter 12, women are less likely than men to receive a number of major diagnostic and therapeutic procedures, even when they are experiencing symptoms that are as severe as men's, in part because physicians are more likely to see women's physical symptoms as signs of psychological problems. Women are also less likely than men to have health insurance, primarily because they tend to have lower-paying jobs, which are less likely to provide benefits. And even when women do have health insurance, the coverage provided to men and women differs in some subtle but important ways. For example, many health insurance plans pay for Viagra (which aids men in having sex), but not for birth-control pills (which aid women in preventing pregnancy)!

Broadening the Focus to Other Cultures

Much of the research that you've read about in this book was conducted in the United States and other Western, industrialized countries. A major focus of the future in health psychology must be on conducting research in other countries, particularly because many of these countries are in desperate need of improved health care. Infectious diseases, lack of nutrition, and lack of sanitary living conditions are major causes of death in other countries, and poor countries in particular could benefit from some of the principles of health psychology.

Although major technological advances are expensive and unlikely to be of great practical help in many very poor countries, improved prenatal care, access to contraceptives, regular immunizations, and better nutrition could all lead to great increases in life expectancy (see Table 14.3). For example, more than one fifth of China's adult population is overweight, which will lead to increases in hypertension, stroke, and diabetes, and thus have substantial economic costs for this country (Popkin, 2008). Moreover, CHD is predicted to triple over the next 20 years in Latin America, the Middle East, and sub-Saharan Africa (Yach, Hawkes, Gould, & Hofman, 2004). Approximately two and a half million children die in India each year from infectious diseases, such as malaria, diarrhea, and pneumonia.

The United Nations International Children's Education Fund (UNICEF, 1991) identifies the key targets for improving international public health as birth timing and safe motherhood, breast-feeding and child growth, diarrhea and the management of respiratory infections, immunizations, home hygiene, mosquito control, and AIDS. In fact, one of the easiest ways to promote health in many developing

TABLE 14.3   *UNICEF's Key Messages for Improving International Health*

Family Planning and Reproductive Health

- Birth spacing of less than 2 years increases mortality risk for young children by 50%.
- Regular checkups during pregnancy reduce risks related to childbirth.
- Having more than four children in total increases the health risks of pregnancy and childbirth.

Breast-Feeding and Nutrition

- Breast milk alone is the best possible baby food during the first 4 to 6 months of life.
- Babies should begin breast-feeding as soon as possible after birth.
- Children between the ages of 6 months and 3 years should be weighed every month for growth monitoring.

Diarrhea and Acute Respiratory Infections

- Diarrhea can kill children through dehydration. Therefore, children with diarrhea need plenty of liquids to drink.
- If diarrhea becomes serious, trained medical attention is necessary.
- Children with coughs or colds should be kept warm and should not be exposed to smoke.

Immunization, Hygiene, and HIV

- Children not immunized are far more likely to become malnourished, suffer from disability, or die.
- Illnesses can be prevented by washing hands with soap and water.
- Any use of an unsterilized needle or syringe is dangerous.

These messages were designed by UNICEF to promote health-improving practices in many developing countries.

Source: United Nations International Children's Fund, 1991.

countries is to promote breast-feeding, which leads to significantly lower rates of diarrhea, malnutrition, and infant mortality (Chantry, Howard, & Auinger, 2006; Elder, 2001).

Some of the problems caused by malnutrition and starvation could be eliminated by reducing family size through use of contraceptives. An estimated 358,000 women die each year from pregnancy-related causes, and many others suffer serious health problems caused by (often unplanned) pregnancies (World Health Organization, 2010). Unintended pregnancies are relatively common given the high cost of and limited access to contraceptives, as well as the cultural and religious beliefs that may discourage their use. However, research in the field of family planning suggests that the media can be very helpful. In Tanzania, a country with a birthrate of six children per woman, a radio-based soap opera was created that featured popular characters communicating about the importance of using contraceptives and planning for small families (Rogers et al., 1999). This show was broadcast twice a week for 2 years, and then researchers compared the rate of contraceptive use in those who listened to the soap opera to those who did not. Although 19% of the nonlisteners used contraceptives, 64% of those who listened used contraceptives. This show also led to increased conversations between spouses about family planning—33% among nonlisteners versus 85% in listeners.

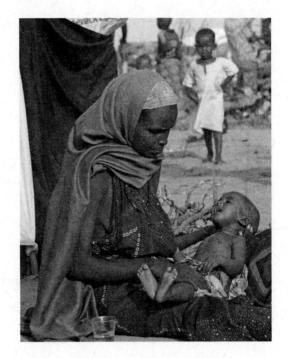

Many children in developing countries die each year from malnutrition, diarrhea, and starvation.
Source: ROBERTO SCHMIDT/AFP/Getty Images, Inc.

One international problem that health psychologists could help with is the public-health crisis in Central and Eastern Europe (Little, 1998). After the dissolution of the Soviet Union in 1989 and the shifting economic base, numerous countries, including Bulgaria, Poland, and Romania, experienced huge socioeconomic changes. Rates of unemployment, poverty, and crime increased, and the quality and availability of health services decreased. In turn, while life expectancy increased throughout much of the world during this time, death rates increased dramatically in these countries. For example, the death rate in Russia alone increased 35% from 1989 to 1993. What led to such a high death rate? Behavior choices, such as smoking and alcohol abuse (see Table 14.4), are clearly one contributor, and poor medical care—including shortage of common vaccinations and underpaid, undertrained physicians—is another. A very important problem, yet a difficult one to solve, is the presence of high levels of pollution in the air, soil, and water. Principles in health psychology can assist with many of these problems, including the prevention of health-harming behaviors and the regulation of pollution by industries, thereby improving health for many people in other countries.

Another substantial international problem is the continuing spread of HIV infection. Although rates of HIV infection have declined in some countries, including Kenya, Zimbabwe, and some countries in the Caribbean, rates of HIV infection are still increasing, in some cases at dramatic rates, in certain parts of the world. Specifically, rates of HIV infection have climbed over the past few years as much as 25% in Eastern Europe, Central Asia, and East Asia (UNAIDS, 2006). But the region most impacted by far by HIV infection is sub-Saharan Africa, with three million people becoming infected each year. In fact, 64% of new HIV infections worldwide occur in sub-Saharan Africa. Research in health psychology is clearly needed to examine how to help decrease the spread of HIV in developing countries (see Table 14.5).

TABLE 14.4 *Prevalence of Smoking Around the World*

	% Men	% Women
East Asia and Pacific	62	5
Europe and Central Asia	53	16
Latin America and Caribbean	39	22
Middle East and North Africa	38	7
South Asia	20	1
Sub-Saharan Africa	28	8
Low and middle income	49	8
High income	37	21

Although an estimated 29% of the adult population worldwide smokes, rates of smoking vary considerably by age, region of country, and income level.

Source: Jha, Ranson, Nguyen, & Yach, 2002.

TABLE 14.5 *Prevalence of AIDS Around the World*

Country	Adults and Children Estimated to Be Living With HIV
Sub-Saharan African	22,400,000
South and Southeast Asia	3,800,000
South and Central America	2,000,000
Eastern Europe and Central Asia	1,500,000
North America	1,400,000
East Asia	850,000
Western and Central Europe	850,000
Middle East and North Africa	310,000
Caribbean	240,000
Oceania	59,000

Although some countries have seen a drop in HIV infection rate, the rate continues to increase dramatically in some parts of the world.

Source: UNAIDS, 2006.

What Can You Do With a Degree in Health Psychology?

Health psychologists work on a variety of topics in a variety of settings (Belar, 1997; Enright, Resnick, DeLeon, Sciava, & Tanney, 1990). During the 1980s, the number of psychologists working in health-related fields more than doubled (Enright et al., 1990; Frank, Gluck, & Buckelew, 1990), and this trend will continue (Kaplan, 2000). Some health psychologists conduct research in academic settings and may also teach courses to undergraduate and/or graduate students. They might also do research and teach in medical, dental, and nursing schools. Other health psychologists work directly with patients to prevent and/or improve psychological and physical well-being, such as by providing diagnostic and counseling services, preparing patients for surgery and other medical procedures, and designing programs to help patients adhere to medical recommendations and cope with chronic pain. These positions often involve working in a hospital, medical school, HMO, pain and rehabilitation clinic, or independent practice. Still other health psychologists work on forming health policies and finding funding research on health-related issues, often in a government agency such as the National Institutes of Health or the Centers for Disease Control and Prevention.

What should you do if you are interested in a career in health psychology? First, you should enroll in a range of courses in psychology. The field of health psychology draws on a number of parts of the field of psychology; hence, students who are interested in this field should try to get a broad background. Taking courses in anatomy and physiology may also be beneficial, as would courses in statistics and research methods (which are required for some graduate programs). Second, many students find that getting hands-on experience in health psychology is a great way of learning more about the field, as well as a good résumé builder! You might be able to assist one of your professors with his or her research in health psychology, find a summer internship in a hospital, or volunteer with a social service agency.

After receiving an undergraduate degree in psychology, training in health psychology can involve a number of different programs. The majority of health psychologists obtain a PhD (a doctorate degree) in some type of psychology. Graduate programs in health psychology typically provide training in biology (e.g., anatomy, physiology, psychopharmacology, epidemiology, neuropsychology), the broad domains of psychology (e.g., social, developmental, personality, cognitive, neuroscience), and social factors (e.g., family, ethnicity, culture, race). They also include training in statistics and research methods. The field of *clinical health psychology* focuses on using knowledge gained in the discipline of psychology to promote and maintain physical health, including preventing and treating injury and disease, identifying causes of health problems, and improving health policy and the health-care system (Belar, 1997). Other people receive a PhD in a subfield of psychology, such as developmental, social, physiological, or clinical, but focus their coursework and research on health-related issues. For example, you might get a PhD in social-personality psychology and do research during graduate school on HIV prevention. Graduate school consists of coursework as well as training in research, which culminates in the completion of a dissertation (an original research project). Many health psychologists also choose to do postdoctoral training or an

The number of health psychologists working in hospital settings is rapidly increasing, partly because of a greater understanding of how psychological factors influence physical health.
Source: Jose Luis Pelaez/Corbis Images.

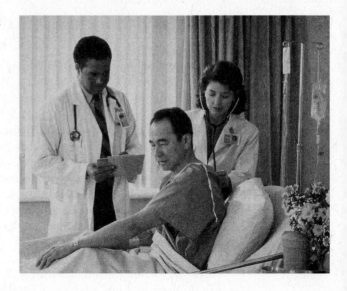

internship, often in a hospital, clinic, or university setting, for a year or two after graduate school to gain additional experience and skills.

Other people who are interested in the broad topic of health psychology choose a different training path, which could include enrolling in medical or nursing school; obtaining a master's or doctorate degree in public health; or pursuing a degree in physical therapy, occupational therapy, nutrition, or social work (see Tables 14.6 and 14.7). The specific training route you choose is determined by your major interest and career goal. Do you really like working directly with people and personally helping people make changes in their behavior or manage their pain? If so, you may want to pursue a degree in counseling or clinical psychology, social work, or nursing and work in an applied setting. Do you really like working on research projects and forming and testing different hypotheses to find the answer to a particular question? If so, you may want to pursue a degree in psychology or public health and work in a research setting. Are you primarily interested in people's physical and physiological responses and in exploring how their bodies work? In this case, you should consider pursuing a degree in medicine, physical therapy, or occupational therapy. As described at the beginning of the chapter, Mark ultimately decided to pursue a degree in public health because he realized that his primary interest was preventing large-scale public-health problems.

What Is the "Take Home" Point?

Now that you are at the end of this book—and perhaps at the end of your health psychology course—you should be asking yourself, "What exactly have I learned?" Most of all, you should have a clear understanding of the diverse ways in which psychological factors influence physical well-being: People's thoughts about various

TABLE 14.6 *Careers in Health-Related Fields*

When you think of people working as health professionals, what types of jobs come to mind? Probably doctors, nurses, and perhaps dentists. But there are many types of careers in health-related fields, and virtually all of them involve and use principles and research of health psychology in some way. Most of these careers require an undergraduate degree in the field and often some type of additional training or education for a year or two after college.

Physical therapists help people with diseases of or injuries to muscles, joints, nerves, or bones. They evaluate a patient's capabilities, including muscle strength, coordination, endurance, and range of motion, and then design a treatment to address the person's limitations. For example, a person who has experienced a major accident may need to learn how to walk again. Physical therapists may also work to increase people's mobility and decrease their pain. They may also provide training in using adaptive devices, such as crutches, canes or walkers, or prostheses (artificial limbs). They work in hospitals, nursing homes, and rehabilitation clinics.

Occupational therapists work with patients who have physical, mental, or emotional disabilities and try to help them learn the skills they need to function in a productive way. For example, they might help people learn to dress themselves, write, and prepare meals. They often work in a school, work, or community setting and may specialize in treating patients with a particular type of disability (e.g., the elderly, children, patients with spinal cord injuries). They also may evaluate a patient's capabilities and then design a treatment program.

Dietitians and *nutritionists* work on helping people create and manage healthy diets. Some people in this field work in hospitals, clinics, or nursing homes to design appealing and balanced meals. They may also work with patients and their families on making and adhering to dietary changes, especially in cases in which a person's health is seriously at risk if their diet does not change (e.g., diabetics, CHD patients).

Social workers, who work in hospitals, community agencies, clinics, and nursing homes, help individuals and their families cope with psychological and social issues. In some cases, social workers serve as therapists, such as by helping people talk about their feelings after receiving a chronic disease diagnosis. This therapy might include the patient as well as his or her family members as well. Social workers also provide important assistance with connecting people with various community services. For example, they could help a family receive temporary assistance with cooking and cleaning if the person who has provided this type of household care becomes disabled, or they could refer a chronically or terminally ill patient as well as his or her family to a local support group.

Public health researchers, who may work in academic settings, government agencies, hospitals, social service agencies, and clinics, work in a direct way to improve the health of people in a given community. They may develop and implement interventions to prevent health problems or may evaluate programs that are currently in use. For example, a public health researcher could work in a Planned Parenthood clinic to test whether its teen pregnancy prevention program is effective.

daily life situations influence whether they experience arousal; their amount and type of social support influences how long they live; their feelings of vulnerability influence their health-promoting behavior; and their need for information can influence how they respond to surgical procedures, to name a few instances. You should also have learned some things in this book that you will use in your everyday life, regardless of whether your career path takes you to a health-related field.

TABLE 14.7   *Occupational Health Psychology in Action*

Occupational health psychology focuses specifically on healthy workplaces, meaning ones in which people produce high-quality work and achieve great personal satisfaction (Quick, 1999). This field blends issues in public health, clinical psychology, organizational behavior, and industrial/organizational psychology. For example, research by occupational health psychologists suggest that people who have some control and flexibility in their jobs experience better health and satisfaction, that workers benefit from having effective ways of reducing stress (e.g., exercise, social support), and workers can be more effective when they are not concerned about family issues. These psychologists may work directly with a business and advise employers on ways to improve health (e.g., smoking-cessation interventions, exercise facilities, stress management), as described in the following two examples.

U.S. Air Force

In 1993, Joyce Adkins of the U.S. Air Force Biomedical Sciences Corps started an organizational health center at the McClellan Air Force Base in Sacramento, California (Quick, 1999). The goals of this center included improving working conditions; monitoring psychological disorders and risk factors; providing information, training, and education; and providing psychological health services to all employees. Within the first year of the project, several substantial changes were noted. First, the total cost of worker's compensation payments (given to employees who were injured) decreased 3.9%, leading to a savings of $289,099. Second, medical visits and health-care utilization for job-related injury and illness decreased by 12%—again leading to a cost savings of $150,918. Finally, there was a decrease in death rates, suggesting that perhaps 10 deaths caused by behavioral-related events were avoided. In turn, this decrease in premature mortality was associated with a tremendous savings in terms of productive years gained (e.g., recruiting, hiring, training new employees).

Johnson & Johnson

In 1978, Johnson & Johnson developed a comprehensive health-promotion program entitled Live for Life (Quick, 1999). This program included health assessments, materials promoting health-behavior change, and the development of a physical fitness program. The addition of this program led to improvements in workers' psychological and physical well-being (Bly, Jones, & Richardson, 1986). Employees showed an increase in attitudes toward commitment, working conditions, job competence, pay and benefits, and job security. These increases should lead to lower turnover and, thereby, reduce the costs associated with hiring and training new employees. The company also experienced lower health-care costs, partly because of lower rates of hospital admissions and fewer hospitalized days. Specifically, inpatient health-care costs for workers in this program were only $42 to $43 per employee as compared to $76 for those without this program.

Perhaps information you've learned in this book will motivate you to always wear your seat belt, start an exercise program, or even teach your children healthy eating behaviors. Health psychology is a field that truly matters to us all. Good health also matters to our society. As Marc Lalonde (1974), the Canadian minister of national health and welfare in the 1970s, describes:

> Good health is the bedrock on which social progress is built. A nation of healthy people can do those things that make life worthwhile, and as the level of health increases so does the potential for happiness. The Governments of the Provinces and of Canada have long recognized that good physical and mental health are necessary for the quality of life to which everyone aspires. (p. 5)

I hope this book helps you to have a life that is long in quantity and high in quality, including physical, mental, and psychological health.

Summary

1. Research in health psychology has provided a number of major contributions to the prevention and treatment of illness and disease. First, research in health psychology demonstrates that psychological factors, including how we experience and cope with stressful situations, our distinct personality traits, and the amount of social support we receive from others, influence physical health. Research in health psychology has also provided important information about how to help people cope with pain and illness, when people seek medical treatment, whether they follow medical recommendations, and how they respond to health-promotion messages and interventions.

2. One of the hot topics in the field of health psychology is preventing the development of health problems. Strategies for accomplishing this goal include motivating people to make health-promoting behavioral choices, and improving education.

3. Another hot topic in health psychology is making ethical medical decisions, including the strategies used to cope with infertility, how to best use genetic screening, how to make decisions about allocating organs for donations, and choosing how to spend limited health care dollars.

4. One major goal of health psychology is helping people live higher-quality lives, including increasing life expectancy and increasing quality-adjusted life expectancy (years spent free from disease and disability). Advanced directives, or living wills, help patients communicate their preferences regarding quality of life issues to their loved ones.

5. One of the hottest topics in health psychology is reducing health care costs, which have increased dramatically due to increases in life expectancy as well as increased reliance on medical technology. Managed care systems, such as HMOs, are one strategy for reducing medical costs, as is a focus on examining the costs per life saved for various treatments.

6. One of the challenges for health psychology in the future is decreasing racial-ethnic health differences, including differences in life expectancy and rates of chronic diseases. These differences may be reduced through access to universal health care, an increased focus on prevention, and reductions in the rate of poverty.

7. Another challenge for health psychology is focusing on the predictors of women's health. Women have unique health issues and concerns, including issues related to reproduction and menopause, and may receive lower-quality health care than men.

8. A major focus of the future in health psychology must be on conducting research in other countries, particularly because many of these countries are in desperate need of improved health care. In poor countries, small improvements related to prenatal care, access to contraceptives, regular immunizations, and better nutrition could have major benefits in terms of life expectancy.

9. Health psychologists work in a variety of settings, including academic settings (e.g., colleges and universities as well as medical, dental, and nursing schools), clinical settings (e.g., hospitals, pain clinics, HMOs, independent practice), and government settings (e.g., National Institute of Health, Centers for Disease Control and Prevention). There are a variety of different education and career pathways to working in this field.

Key Terms

advanced-directives

health maintenance organization (HMO)

quality-adjusted life years (QALY)

Thought Questions

1. Tina has a summer job with the organization MADD (Mothers Against Drunk Driving), and she has been asked to help design three different strategies for preventing injuries and deaths caused by drunk drivers. What are three distinct types of approaches to such prevention?

2. What are four explanations for the link between low socioeconomic status and poor health? Which factor do you think is the biggest contributor to this association and why?

3. Your local hospital can fund only one of the following three programs: developing technology that will allow animal organs to be used for critically ill patients in need of organ transplants, training all surgical patients in coping and behavioral strategies for managing pain, and creating a healthy eating and exercise program that will be used in gym classes at local schools. In your opinion, which of these programs should be funded and why?

4. Describe two advantages of the HMO health-care system and two disadvantages.

5. Your roommate, Mark, is taking a health psychology course right now and is really enjoying it. He comes to you for advice about what he should do if he thinks he wants a career in health psychology, and he also wants to know what a person can do with a degree in health psychology. What do you tell him?

GLOSSARY

abstinence violation effect—if people expect they will never give in to temptation, when and if they do have a lapse in behavior, they are likely to blame it on themselves, which could lead to a total relapse.

acceptance—the final stage in the stages of death or dying, in which people finally acknowledge that death is inevitable and believe they can face it calmly.

action—the stage in the transtheoretical or stages of change model in which a person is actually engaging in a new behavior.

active strategies—a strategy that requires engaging in some type of repeated action to prevent health problems, including to prevent injuries from occurring or to decrease the harm resulting from such injuries.

acupuncture—a technique in which needles are inserted in specific points on the skin in an attempt to control pain.

acute disease—a disease characterized by a relatively sudden onset of symptoms that are usually severe.

acute pain—an intense but time-limited pain that is generally the result of tissue damage or disease, such as breaking a bone, receiving a cut or bruise, and giving birth. Acute pain typically disappears over time (as the injury heals) and lasts less than 6 months.

addiction—the condition in which a person has a physical and psychological dependence on a given substance, such as cigarettes, alcohol, or caffeine. Addiction is caused by repeatedly consuming the substance, which over time leads the body to adjust to the substance and incorporate it into the "normal" functioning of the body's tissues.

adherence—the extent to which a person follows recommended treatments and health behaviors.

advanced-directives—legal documents that allow you to convey your decisions about end-of-life care ahead of time.

affect-regulation model—a model proposing that people smoke to attain positive affect or to avoid (or reduce)

negative affect. Positive affect smokers may smoke as a way of enhancing the pleasure associated with other events, such as eating a great meal or having sex, whereas negative affect smokers smoke as a way of coping with negative affect, such as reducing anxiety, tension, and frustration.

AIDS—a disease caused by the human immunodeficiency virus (HIV) in which the body's natural defense system is disabled, leaving the body unable to fight off even mild infections. Although there is no cure for AIDS, some drug regimens (such as AZT and HAART) can help prolong survival and improve the quality of life.

alarm stage—the first stage of the General Adaptation Syndrome (GAS), in which the body mobilizes to fight off a threat by activating both the sympathetic nervous system and the endocrine system.

alcohol myopia—the state in which individuals under the influence of alcohol make decisions based on salient short-term concerns while ignoring longer-term

571

consequences of their behavior. This state occurs because individuals are unable to engage in the complex cognitive processing required to consider the more distant consequences, and they instead base decisions primarily on the most salient and immediate cues. Alcohol myopia theory also describes the effects of alcohol on a person's self-evaluation. Specifically, people who are intoxicated often experience "drunken self-inflation," meaning that people who are drinking see themselves in an idealized way.

Alcoholics Anonymous (AA)—the most widely known self-help program for alcohol abuse, which is attended more often than any other alcohol program. The general AA philosophy is based on two principal views. First, people who abuse alcohol are alcoholics and will remain that way for life, even if they never drink again. Second, taking even a single drink after being abstinent can set off an alcoholic binge, and therefore the goal is total abstinence from alcohol.

alcoholism—alcohol consumption that is compulsive and uncontrollable, physically addictive, or habitual, and results in serious threats to a person's health and well-being. Alcoholics have a very high tolerance for alcohol, suffer blackouts or memory losses, and experience withdrawal symptoms such as delirium tremens (e.g., hallucinations, impaired motor coordination, cognitive disruption) when they stop drinking.

allostatic response—the body's attempt to adapt to a stressful situation. This physiological response involves a number of systems in the body and is shut off as soon as the challenge ends.

analgesic drugs—drugs, such as aspirin, acetaminophen, and ibuprofen, that reduce fever and inflammation at the site of a wound and work to decrease pain by interfering with the transmission of pain signals. Analgesics are very effective in reducing mild to moderate levels of pain, such as headache and arthritis pain.

anger—one of the stages of death and dying in which people feel that their prognosis is unfair, search for reasons why it happened, and express negative emotions, such as anger, rage, envy, and resentment.

anorexia nervosa—an eating disorder that involves a drastic reduction in people's food intake and an intentional loss of weight (maintaining a body weight 15% below one's normal weight based on height–weight tables or a BMI of 17.5).

appraisal delay—the delay from when people experience—and notice—some type of symptoms to when they decide that they are ill.

archival research—a type of observational or naturalistic method of research that uses already-recorded behavior.

arteriosclerosis—a condition in which the arteries have lost their elasticity, making it difficult for them to expand and contract. This process leads to a decrease in blood flow and an increase in the likelihood of a blood clot.

assisted suicide—helping a person to kill himself or herself, such as by providing the means to accomplish this task.

atherosclerosis—a condition that occurs when fatty substances build up in the artery walls, thereby decreasing blood flow and increasing the likelihood of a blood clot. Because the flow of blood is reduced, it can deprive the heart of essential nutrients.

attitudes—a person's positive or negative feelings about engaging in a particular behavior.

attribution theory—a theory which posits that people try to explain the causes of their own and others' behavior, and specifically that people can see behavior as caused by internal factors or external factors. In turn, behavior that is motivated by internal factors, such as an individual's desire to engage in the behavior, is expected to continue over time, whereas behavior that is the result of external pressures from others is unlikely to continue.

autonomic nervous system—one of the two parts of the peripheral nervous system. The autonomic nervous system, which consists of the sympathetic and parasympathetic divisions, carries information that is directly related to survival (e.g., organs that are not under voluntary control).

aversion strategies—strategies for behavior change that are based on principles of classical conditioning. These approaches try to reduce a behavior by pairing it with some type of unpleasant stimuli.

bargaining—a stage in the stages of death and dying in which people attempt to trade good behavior for good health, and thus delay the inevitable.

barrier—one of the components of the health belief model which describes the expected negative results of engaging in behavior change.

behavior therapy—therapy that is designed to decrease people's experience of pain by changing their behavior. For example, a person with chronic back pain might receive physical therapy to increase flexibility and/or be taught how to strengthen their abdominal muscles to put less strain on their back.

behavioral health—a subdiscipline of behavioral medicine that emphasizes enhancing health and preventing disease in currently healthy people.

behavioral medicine—the development and application of behavioral techniques for treatment, management, and rehabilitation of patients. These techniques are used widely to help people overcome various types of health-damaging behaviors, including overeating, smoking, and alcohol abuse.

belongingness support—this type of support refers to the availability of social companionship, such as having others with whom to engage in social activities (e.g., going out to dinner, seeing a movie, attending a party).

benefit—one of the components of the health belief model which describes the expected positive results of engaging in behavior change.

bereavement—the period of grief and mourning after a death.

binge drinking—having five or more drinks on the same occasion.

binge eating disorder—a disorder in which a person regularly eats an unusually large amount of food at one time, typically alone and in response to a negative mood.

biobehavioral model—a model suggesting that both psychological and physiological factors lead people to continue to smoke over time. This model proposes that nicotine has a number of physiological effects that make people feel good (e.g., improves memory and concentration, reduces anxiety and tension), which leads people to readily become dependent on smoking. Smokers then become dependent (both physically and psychologically) on using nicotine to experience these positive effects.

biofeedback—a technique in which people are trained, using electric monitors, to monitor and change selected physiological functions, such as their heart rate, finger temperature, muscle activity, and brain wave patterns. Biofeedback is an effective way of controlling headache pain, back pain, and hypertension.

biomedical model—a model formed in the 19th and 20th centuries which proposes that illnesses are caused by physical problems, such as viruses and bacteria, injuries, and biochemical imbalances. According to this perspective, physical health is completely separate from psychological health—the body is a physical entity, and the mind is a psychology/mental/spiritual entity, and that these operate completely separately.

biopsychosocial model—a model that views health as determined by individual, social, and cultural factors. It acknowledges that biological factors can and do influence health and illness, but at the same time maintains that social, cultural, and psychological factors also exert an effect. This model is holistic, in that it sees the mind and body as inherently connected and sees health as an interactive system in which biological factors (e.g., genetics, physiology) interact with psychological factors (e.g., personality, cognition) and social factors (e.g., community, family, media).

blind/double-blind—a blind study is one in which the participants do not know the hypotheses of the study or the particular conditions that are being tested. A double-blind study is one in which neither the participants nor the experimenter conducting the study know which participant is receiving which treatment.

Body Mass Index (BMI)—the most commonly used measure of obesity today. BMI is calculated by dividing a person's weight (in kilograms) by their height (in meters) squared. A BMI between 19 and 24 is seen as ideal, with 25 to 29 seen as moderately overweight (about 15 to 30% over ideal weight), and greater than 30 seen as obese (about 40% over ideal weight).

buffering hypothesis—a hypothesis which suggests that social support leads to better health by protecting people from the negative effects of high stress, and hence social support is particularly beneficial during stressful times.

bulimia nervosa—an eating disorder that is characterized by recurrent episodes of

binge eating followed by purging. These episodes are typically triggered by some type of negative emotion, such as anxiety, tension, or even being tired. During these binges, bulimics rapidly consume enormous quantities of food and then attempt to get rid of these calories, typically through either vomiting or excessive exercise. This pattern of binge eating and purging occurs on a regular basis over some period of time.

burnout—the experience of long-term exhaustion and diminished interest.

cancer—an uncontrollable growth and spread of abnormal cells, which form tumors. Benign tumors consist of cells that are relatively typical of the nearby cells and grow relatively slowly. On the other hand, malignant tumors (which are commonly called cancers) consist of cells that are different from their surrounding cells and grow very rapidly. Malignant tumors often grow beyond their original location and invade other body organs (metastasize), spreading cancer throughout the body.

cardiovascular system—a network of body systems that work to transport oxygen to and remove carbon dioxide from each cell and organ in the body. This work is accomplished through the beating of the heart, which generates the necessary force in the bloodstream.

case report/case study—a type of observational or naturalistic research which relies on studying one or more individuals in great depth.

central nervous system—a system within the body, consisting of the brain and spinal cord, where information processing occurs.

chiropractic therapy—a therapy that focuses on manipulating the bones, muscles, and joints to improve body alignment.

chronic disease—a condition that often has multiple causes, including people's behavioral choices or lifestyles, and a slow onset and increase over time. Chronic conditions can only be managed; although people with a chronic disease sometimes get worse and sometimes stay the same, they can't be cured.

chronic pain—a type of pain that may begin as acute pain (in response to a specific injury or disease) but just doesn't go away after a minimum of 6 months.

Lower-back pain, headaches, and the pain associated with arthritis and cancer are all examples of chronic pain.

classical conditioning—learning that occurs when a previously neutral stimulus comes to evoke the same response as another stimulus with which it is paired.

clinical study—a type of research that is very similar to experiments in many ways, in that it uses random assignment to condition and is often blind or even double-blind. However, because these studies often involve patients who have actively sought help for a given disorder, the practical and ethical issues involved in conducting this type of research, such as who is eligible to participate and whether they have multiple disorders, can be complex.

cognitive-behavioral strategies—strategies for coping with pain and chronic illness that include physical, cognitive, and emotional techniques. For example, cognitive-behavior strategies for regulating weight could include thinking about food in a new way and having smaller portions of food.

cognitive dissonance theory—a theory which states that people are highly motivated to have their attitudes, beliefs, and behaviors all be in line, and when they engage in a behavior that is not consistent with their attitudes, they experience an unpleasant state of psychological arousal known as dissonance. However, because it is very difficult, and sometimes impossible, to undo a behavior, people often try to resolve this uncomfortable feeling of arousal by changing their attitude to make it correspond with their behavior.

cognitive redefinition—a cognitive technique that works to help people think about pain in a new way. For example, a woman might be trained to think about the pain of labor as her baby pushing its way into the world.

commonsense illness representations—people's beliefs about the nature and cause of their health symptoms.

conscientiousness—a personality trait describing people who are hardworking, motivated, and persistent. They show high levels of self-restraint and an intense focus on their goals.

contemplation—the stage in the transtheoretical or stages of change model in which a person is beginning to consider making a change in their behavior.

contingency contracting—a behavior change technique used to give people additional motivation to change their behavior. In this technique, people who want to change their behavior give some money to a friend (or therapist), with the understanding that if they are not smoking 6 months later, they get the money back. This technique therefore uses the promise of a reward to encourage behavior change (an operant conditioning approach).

continuum theories—a set of theories that identifies some variables that are thought to influence people's behavior and then combines those variables to predict the likelihood that the person will engage in a given behavior.

controlled drinking—one view of managing alcoholism, namely by teaching people with serious drinking problems to engage in moderate amounts of drinking.

coping—expending conscious effort to solve personal and interpersonal problems, and seeking to master, minimize, reduce, or tolerate stress or conflict.

coronary heart disease (CHD)—a chronic disease in which the arteries become narrowed or clogged, due to atherosclerosis or arteriosclerosis. Coronary heart disease is the leading cause of death in the United States.

correlation—a measure of the association between two variables.

cortisol—a hormone that increases the production of energy from glucose and inhibits the swelling around injuries and infections.

counterirritation—irritating one type of body tissue to ease pain in another type of body tissue (e.g., putting your finger in your mouth after you burn it on a hot stove, rubbing your calf muscle to reduce a painful cramp). This is a type of physical stimulation.

cues to action—any type of reminder about a potential health problem that could motivate behavior change.

culture—the distinct ways that people living in different parts of the world classify and represent their experiences and think about the world.

denial—the first stage in the stages of death and dying, in which people's initial reaction to receiving a diagnosis of a terminal illness is to deny the accuracy of this information.

dependent variable—a variable that is measured as the outcome of the study. Dependent variables may be influenced by one or more independent variables.

depression—one of the stages of death and dying in which people have a feeling of anticipatory grief and grief about the upcoming losses he or she will experience in death.

detoxification—the drying out process in which an alcoholic withdraws from alcohol completely. This process takes about a month and can include severe symptoms, such as intense anxiety, tremors, and hallucinations.

direct effects hypothesis—a hypothesis that posits that social support can help people at both low and high levels of stress, so having high levels of social support is always advantageous to health.

disease model—a theory of behavior that describes addiction as caused primarily by internal physiological forces, such as cravings, urges, and compulsions, and hence the "addict" is unable to voluntarily control his/her behavior.

drunken self-inflation—the tendency for people who are intoxicated to see themselves in an idealized way.

emotion-focused coping—a type of coping that focuses on managing the emotional effects of a stressful situation. This strategy could include a number of different approaches, including simply not thinking about the problem (e.g., denial or avoidance) as well as venting about the problem to others (e.g., seeking social support).

emotional appeals—a type of persuasive message designed to elicit an emotional reaction, such as fear or happiness.

emotional support—the expression of caring, concern, and empathy toward a person as well as the provision of comfort, reassurance, and love.

endocrine system—a body system that regulates a number of different physiological processes in the body, including physical growth, sexual arousal, metabolism, and stress response. The endocrine system works by releasing hormones from an endocrine gland, such as the pituitary, thyroid, and pancreas, into the bloodstream.

endorphins—neurotransmitters that work by slowing or blocking the transmission of any nerve impulses. Endorphins bind to receptors in the periaqueductal gray area of the mid-brain, which dramatically reduces pain.

epinephrine—a hormone (also called adrenaline) that is released when the sympathetic nervous system and endocrine system are stimulated in response to stress. High levels of epinephrine in the bloodstream lead to a number of other physiological responses, including increases in heart rate, blood pressure, and breathing; a widening of the pupils; and the movement of blood toward the muscles.

esteem support/validational support—affirmation of self-worth, including feedback that a person is valued and respected by others.

euthanasia—ending the life of a person who has a painful terminal illness as a way of reducing his or her suffering.

exhaustion stage—a stage at which the body's resources are depleted and it becomes very susceptible to physiological damage and disease.

experiment—a type of study in which researchers manipulate one or more independent variables and then measure the effect of the independent variable on one or more dependent variables. Experiments include random assignment to condition and high levels of control over the participants' environment.

external validity—the degree to which there can be reasonable confidence that the same results would be obtained for other people and in other situations.

extraversion—a personality trait describing people who are outgoing, social, and assertive—they have many friends, show high levels of energy, and often take on leadership roles. People who are extraverted also tend to seek a high level of stimulation—they get bored easily, enjoy new challenges, and like to take risks.

fear-based appeals—a type of persuasive message designed to elicit fear and anxiety, which in turn may lead to attitude and behavior change.

fight-or-flight response—a response to stress in which the person tries to either fight off the stressor or escape from it (both approaches require shifting energy from the nonessential body systems to those systems necessary to respond to the challenge).

framing—the way information is presented, which can have a significant impact on decisions.

gate control theory—a theory describing the experience of pain, which states that when body tissues are injured, nerve endings, or nociceptors, in the area that is damaged transmit impulses to a particular area of the dorsal horn section of the spinal cord called the substantia gelatinosa. After these nerve impulses reach the substantia gelatinosa, one of two things can happen. If these sensations are sufficiently intense, then these signals are sent all the way up to the brain, where they are experienced as pain—the more signals that reach the brain, the more pain you experience. However, according to the gate control theory, not all of the pain signals carried by the nerve fibers will successfully reach the brain. Specifically, this theory posits that there is a gate in the substantia gelatinosa that either lets pain impulses travel to the brain, or blocks their progress, and any competing sensation that increases stimulation to the site could serve to block transmission.

General Adaptation Syndrome (GAS)—a model describing how stress can lead to negative health consequences over time.

grief—the feelings caused by bereavement following the loss of a loved one.

guided imagery—a type of relaxation method for coping with pain that pairs deep muscle relaxation with a specific type of pleasant image that serves to focus a patient's mind on something other than the pain.

hardiness—a personality variable that is associated with how a person reacts in challenging and potentially stressful situations. People who are hardy have a strong commitment to what they are doing, possess a sense of control over what is happening to them, and see stressful events as challenging rather than threatening. Hardiness is associated with better health outcomes.

health—the general condition of a person in mind, body, and spirit, usually meaning to be free from illness, injury, or pain.

health behavior—behaviors designed to promote a person's good health and prevent illness. This type of behavior could include exercising regularly, wearing a seat belt, and getting immunizations to prevent disease.

health belief model—one of the oldest and most widely used theories to explain people's health-related behavior. According to this model, the likelihood that individuals will take preventive action is a function of four types of factors: susceptibility to the disease, severity of the disease, benefits of taking action, and costs of taking action.

health psychology—a field that addresses how a person's behavior can influence health, wellness, and illness in a variety of different ways, including how psychological factors influence the experience of stress and people's physiological reactions to stress, the promotion and maintenance of health, coping with and treating pain and disease as well as the effects of pain and disease on psychological functioning, and how individuals respond to health-care recommendations as well as health-promotion messages.

health maintenance organization (HMO)—a common type of health-care plan in which an employer or an employee pays a set fee every month and in turn has unlimited access to medical care (at either no cost or a greatly reduced cost). In some cases, HMOs require patients to see their own staff, whereas in other systems patients can choose from among a group of medical professionals who have all agreed to accept a specified payment for their services (preferred provider organizations). HMOs assign people to a primary-care physician, who manages their care and must refer to specialists.

HIV (human immunodeficiency virus)—a retrovirus that causes AIDS. Retroviruses replicate by injecting themselves into host cells and literally taking over the genetic workings of these cells. They can then produce virus particles that infect new cells.

hospice—an alternative care choice for terminally ill patients that is designed to provide personal comfort and open discussion. Hospice care may be delivered within a person's home, a hospital, or a separate facility.

hostility/disagreeableness—a personality trait in which people believe that others are motivated by selfish concerns and expect that other people will deliberately try to hurt them. In turn, because of their general mistrust and cynicism about other people's motivations, hostile people don't hesitate to express these feelings—they are often uncooperative, rude, argumentative, condescending, and aggressive.

hypertension—a condition in which blood pressure is at a consistently high level. Patients are at increased risk of developing CHD.

hypnosis—an altered state of consciousness or trance state that individuals can enter under the guidance of a trained therapist. Hypnosis can be effective in controlling pain, including the pain associated with dental work, childbirth, back pain, headaches, and arthritis.

hypochondria—when a person has an excessive concern about his or her own health, which can include interpreting relatively benign symptoms as signs of more serious problems.

hypothalamic-pituitary adrenal (HPA) system—part of the endocrine system that responds during times of stress. This response starts by secreting corticotropin-releasing hormone (CRH), which in turn triggers the anterior pituitary gland to release adrenocorticotropic hormone (ACTH). Finally, the presence of ACTH leads the adrenal gland to release glucocorticoids, including cortisol.

hypothesis—a testable prediction about the conditions under which an event will occur.

illness behavior—a person's behavior that is directed toward determining his or her health status after experiencing symptoms. This could include talking to other people—family and friends as well as health professionals—personally monitoring symptoms, and reading about the health problem.

illness delay—the time required for a person to decide that help from a professional is required after realizing he or she is ill. People often believe that the symptoms will go away on their own and hence delay seeking medical care.

immune system—a body system that is the major line of defense against infection, illness, and disease. The immune system works to eliminate foreign, "non-self" materials, such as bacteria, viruses, and parasites, which contact or enter the body.

implementation intention—a specific plan of how, where, and when to perform a behavior.

incidence—the frequency of new cases of a disease.

independent variable—a variable that is measured or manipulated to determine its effect on one or more dependent variables.

informational support/appraisal support—advice and guidance about how to cope with a particular problem.

instrumental support/tangible support—the provision of concrete assistance, such as financial aid, material resources, or needed services.

intention—the specific *purpose* of doing a particular activity, including the *end* or *goal* that is aimed at, or desired to be accomplished.

intentional injuries—injuries that occur in which the person meant for it to happen.

intentional nonadherence—the condition in which patients understand the practitioner's directions but modify the regimen in some way or ignore it completely because they are not willing to follow the recommendations.

internal–external hypothesis—one of the earliest hypotheses about why and when people eat, which posits that people often fail to listen to their internal cues for eating (namely hunger) and instead pay attention to external cues, such as food taste, smell, and variety.

internal locus of control—a generalized belief people have about the extent to which events are under their own (internal) control.

internal validity—the likelihood that the effects on the dependent variable were caused by the independent variable.

lingering-trajectory deaths—deaths that occur when the person is ill for a long time, and death comes after a period of gradually declining health.

living will—a document that provides very clear instructions to family members, friends, and medical personnel about the type of treatment and procedures that a person does—or does not—want to have. The person also designates a particular person to make medical decisions for him or her, and in particular, to make sure the wishes expressed in the living will are followed. The use of living wills therefore allows people to express their medical directives in advance of having an illness, and thus maintain the ability to exercise control over their lives even when they have lost the ability to speak for themselves. This allows people to specify their own wishes about the type of care they would like to receive in the event that they are incapacitated in some way and are therefore unable to make their own decisions.

maintenance—the stage in the transtheoretical or stages of change model in which a person is sustaining the change in their behavior over time, typically 6 months.

mass psychogenic illness—a phenomenon in which people's expectations about the symptoms they should experience may influence how intensely, and even whether, they feel various symptoms. In some cases, these expectations can even cause various physical symptoms, such as rashes, nausea, and headaches.

massage therapy—a technique in which people receive deep tissue manipulation by a trained therapist. Massage can be effective in reducing various types of pain, including pain caused by childbirth, recovery from surgery, and arthritis.

medical anthropology—a field that examines differences in how health and illness are viewed by people in different cultures. Cultures in fact vary tremendously in how they define health, how they see disease, and in turn, how they treat illness.

medical psychology—a field that focuses on teaching physicians how to consider the role of the person in interacting with patients. Researchers in this tradition might examine how to handle patients who are moody or those who are reluctant to seek or follow medical care.

medical sociology—a field that examines how social relationships influence illness, cultural and societal reactions to illness, and the organization of health-care services. For example, researchers in the field of medical sociology might examine the effects of social stress on health and illness, how attitudes and behaviors influence health and illness, and the negative consequences of labeling someone a "patient."

meditation—a type of relaxation technique for coping with pain in which patients relax their bodies and focus attention on a single thought, sometimes while verbalizing a single syllable.

modeling—learning gained by watching someone else engage in a behavior.

mood regulation theory—a theory that people often use food to regulate their moods. People may eat to make themselves feel better when they experience stress, anxiety, or depression.

moral theory (self-control theory)—a theory which posits that people who engage in addictive behaviors, such as smoking, drinking, and gambling, have some type of moral weakness. According to this model, people who are lazy and undisciplined lack the "moral fiber" to stop engaging in these self-destructive behaviors.

mourning—the expression of grief following a loss.

multiple regulation model—a theory predicting smoking which states that the combination of physiological and psychological factors leads to addiction. This model predicts that smoking is initially used to regulate emotions, like the affect-regulation model, but over time, how you feel becomes linked with how much nicotine you have in your blood.

narcotics—medications, such as codeine and morphine, that work by binding to the opiate receptors and thereby inhibiting the transmission of pain signals. These drugs are very effective in reducing severe pain and can help patients cope with pain following surgery.

nervous system—the body system that is responsible for transmitting information from the brain throughout the body as well as from the body back to the brain. The nervous system consists of the central nervous system and the peripheral nervous system.

neuromatrix theory—a theory that a network of neurons is distributed throughout the brain, which processes the information that flows through it. Although the neuromatrix typically acts to process sensory information from the body, such as pain, the neuromatrix can process experiences even in the absence of sensations. This theory, which was developed by Ronald Melzack, helps explain the phenomenon of phantom limb pain in which the brain tells the body it is experiencing pain even in the absence of direct sensations.

neurons—specialized cells that transmit information to and from the brain.

neuroticism/negative affect—a personality trait that refers to the tendency to experience negative emotions, such as distress, anxiety, nervousness, fear, shame, anger, and guilt. People with this trait are likely to worry about upcoming events, dwell on failures and shortcomings, and have a less favorable view of themselves and others.

neurotransmitters—chemicals released by the brain that can increase or decrease the amount of pain experienced.

nicotine-fixed effects model—a theory of smoking which states that nicotine stimulates reward-inducing centers in the nervous system. It increases the levels of neuroregulators, such as dopamine, norepinephrine, and endogenous opioids, which leads to better memory and concentration and reduced feelings of anxiety and tension. Nicotine has a number of reinforcing physiological effects, including speeding up the heart and relaxing the skeletal muscles. These physiological effects lead to simultaneous mental alertness and relaxation. These positive effects are reinforcing, so people are motivated to continue smoking to experience these physiological benefits. This model is very simple—it basically proposes that smoking feels good, so people are motivated to continue the behavior.

nicotine-regulation model—a theory of smoking which states that smoking is rewarding only when the level of nicotine is above a certain "set point" in the body. In other words, individuals need to smoke enough cigarettes to maintain a certain amount of nicotine, or they do not experience the physiological benefits of smoking.

nicotine replacement—substances that provide nicotine in some form other than cigarettes (e.g., the patch, nicotine gum) in an attempt to ease withdrawal symptoms in smokers who are trying to stop. They do not end smokers' cravings for cigarettes but may reduce such cravings.

norepinephrine—a hormone (also called noradrenaline) that is released when the sympathetic nervous system and endocrine system are stimulated in response to stress. High levels of norepinephrine in the bloodstream lead to a number of other physiological responses, including increases in heart rate, blood pressure, and breathing; a widening of the pupils; and the movement of blood toward the muscles.

obesity—the state of being 40% or more over one's ideal weight. The most commonly used measure of obesity is Body Mass Index (BMI), which is calculated by dividing a person's weight (in kilograms) by their height (in meters) squared. A BMI between 19 and 24 is seen as ideal, with 25 to 29 seen as moderately overweight (about 15 to 30% over ideal weight), and greater than 30 seen as obese (about 40% over ideal weight).

observational learning—learning gained by watching someone else engage in a behavior.

observational or naturalistic methods—a type of research used to describe and measure people's and/or animals' behavior in everyday situations. In this approach, researchers observe behavior and record some type of systematic measurement of that behavior.

operant conditioning—the theory that behaviors can be increased or decreased as a function of the positive as well as negative consequences of engaging in them.

operational definition—the specific way in which variables to be examined in a research study are measured.

optimism—a personality trait that refers to the expectation that good things will happen in the future whereas bad things will not. This personality trait is associated with better health outcomes.

outcome expectancies—an individuals' beliefs about whether engaging in a particular behavior will have a desired outcome.

pain—an unpleasant sensory and emotional experience associated with actual or potential tissue damage.

Parkinson's disease—a progressive disorder that is most common in people over 60 years old. This disease is not usually fatal, but it leads to uncontrollable tremors in the limbs, muscle rigidity, and a shuffling gait. Drug treatment can ease some of the symptoms, although this medication has several undesirable side effects.

passive strategies—an approach to injury prevention that involves changing people's environment instead of requiring people to change their behavior or take any action.

pattern theory—a theory that describes pain as resulting from the type of stimulation received by the nerve endings and states that the key determination of pain is the intensity of the stimulation. A small stimulation of the nerve endings could be interpreted as touch, whereas a more substantial stimulation could be interpreted as pain. This theory explains why touching a warm heating pad feels pleasant, but touching a very hot pan in the oven feels painful.

perceived behavioral control—the extent to which people believe they can successfully enact a behavior. This concept is similar to self-efficacy and is one of the components of the theory of planned behavior.

peripheral nervous system—a part of the nervous system consisting of the neural pathways that bring information to and from the brain, including the somatic nervous system and the autonomic nervous system.

personality—the particular combination of emotional, attitudinal, and behavioral response patterns of an individual.

phantom limb pain—the experience of feeling pain in a limb that is no longer there. Phantom limb pain is often described as a severe burning or cramping.

physical stimulation (counterirritation)—the irritation of one type of body tissue to ease pain in another type of body tissue (e.g., putting your finger in your mouth after you burn it on a hot stove; rubbing your calf muscle to reduce a painful cramp).

placebo—a treatment that affects someone even though it contains no specific medical or physical properties relevant to the condition it is supposedly treating. In other words, placebos are psychologically inert medicines or treatments that can produce very real, and even lasting, effects. The effects of placebos have been demonstrated on virtually every organ system in the body and on many diseases, including chest pain, arthritis, hay fever, headaches, ulcers, hypertension, postoperative pain, seasickness, and pain from the common cold.

positive psychology—a newly developed field within psychology that examines how to help people achieve healthy physical and psychological well-being, including the predictors of life satisfaction, altruism, forgiveness, and hope.

positive states—emotions, such as happiness, joy, enthusiasm and contentment, as well as personality traits such as extraversion (feelings of energy and sociability) and positive affect.

posttraumatic stress disorder (PTSD)—a particular type of anxiety disorder caused by experiencing extreme stressors, such as war, natural disasters, and assault.

precaution adoption process model—a model of behavior change which proposes that when individuals consider engaging in new health-related behaviors, they go through a series of seven stages.

precontemplation—the stage in the transtheoretical or stages of change model in which a person lacks awareness of the problems associated with their behavior and has no intentions or plans to change the behavior in the foreseeable future.

preparation—the stage in the transtheoretical or stages of change model in which a person has made a commitment to change their behavior and is taking small steps toward that new behavior.

prevalence—the proportion of a population that has a particular disease.

primary appraisal—an appraisal in which people assess the situation. In this stage, people are interpreting the situation and what it will mean for them (e.g., "am I in danger?").

primary prevention—the prevention of illnesses and diseases either by increasing health-promoting behavior (e.g., wearing seat belts, engaging in regular exercise, using sunscreen) and/or by decreasing health-damaging behavior (e.g., smoking, drinking and driving, eating a fatty diet).

problem-focused coping—a common strategy for managing challenging situations by trying to confront and change the stressor, which can include seeking assistance from others, taking direct action, and planning.

progressive muscle relaxation—a technique in which people focus on tensing and then releasing each part of their body (e.g., hands, shoulders, legs, etc.) one at a time. This process helps patients distinguish states of tension from states of relaxation and therefore trains patients in ways to calm themselves down in virtually any stressful situation.

prospect theory—a theory which posits that people make very different choices when decisions are presented in different ways, such as in terms of their costs versus benefits. Moreover, according to this theory, people are more willing to take risks when they are considering the losses or costs of a particular behavior than when they are considering the gains or benefits of engaging in a behavior.

psychoneuroimmunology—a field that examines the complex connection between psychosocial factors, such as stress and the nervous, cardiovascular, endocrine, and immune systems.

psychosomatic medicine—a field that examines how emotional, social, and psychological factors influence the development and progression of illness. For example, researchers might study how psychological factors, such as anxiety, depression, and stress, might lead to physical problems, such as ulcers, migraine headaches, arthritis, and asthma.

quality-adjusted life years (QALY)—a measure of the number of years a person would likely live following the treatment multiplied by the quality of each of those years. The quality is determined both by the severity of the symptoms (e.g., being confined to a wheelchair or experiencing considerable pain is more severe than experiencing a mild headache or spraining your ankle) and their duration (e.g., even a very painful bout of food poisoning lasts a few days at most, whereas severe cancer pain could last for years).

quasi-experiment—a type of research study in which distinct groups of people serve as the independent variable, but unlike in true experiments, the people are not randomly assigned to the groups.

quick-trajectory deaths—deaths in which the loss is sudden and unexpected.

random assignment—a procedure used in experiments to make sure that every person has an equal chance of being in any of the conditions. Random assignment improves the quality of research studies.

relapse—a return to an old pattern of behavior after beginning to change it.

resistance stage—the second stage of the General Adaptation Syndrome (GAS), in which the body continues to try to respond to the initial threat by maintaining high levels of heart rate, blood pressure, and breathing to help deliver oxygen and energy quickly throughout the body, but by slowing nonessential functions, such as digestion, growth, and reproduction.

response substitution—a strategy for managing situations that prompt a craving for a particular behavior by choosing another way of handling the situation.

restraint theory—a theory of eating which states that people are generally motivated to eat as a function of internal physiological signals that cue hunger. However, when people are trying to lose weight, they deliberately ignore these internal signals and instead use cognitive rules to limit their caloric intake.

scheduling delay—a type of delay that occurs when people fail to make an appointment for medical care after they have decided they are in need of assistance.

scientific method—a method based on gathering empirical and measurable evidence that consists of systematic observation, measurement, and experiment, and the formulation, testing, and modification of hypotheses.

screening—behaviors designed to detect an illness or disease at an early stage.

secondary appraisal—a type of appraisal in which people assess the resources available for coping with the situation. In this stage, people examine their ability to cope with the event based on their resources (e.g., "what can I do about this?").

secondary prevention—the detection of illness at an early stage, as a way of reducing its effects, such as checking cholesterol, performing a breast self-exam, and following insulin-taking regimens (in the case of a diabetic). Secondary prevention is very important because, in many cases, people have more treatment options and a better likelihood of curing their problem if it is caught early.

self-affirmation—a strategy designed to increase people's receptivity to messages that potentially threaten the self by buffering feelings of self-worth.

self-efficacy—a person's confidence that he or she can effectively engage in a given behavior. Self-efficacy is one of the components of the theory of planned behavior.

set-point theory—a theory stating that each person's body has a certain weight that it strives to maintain, much like a thermostat device. When you eat fewer calories, your metabolism slows to keep your weight at the same level. Because people's set points may vary, based on heredity, some will be heavier, and some will be lighter.

severe—one of the parts of the health belief model indicating the degree of seriousness of a particular condition.

sick role behavior—behavior that is directed at helping people who are ill return to good health. The sick role has certain perks, including receiving sympathy and care from others and being exempt from daily responsibilities, such as chores, work, and classes. However, the person who is sick also has the responsibility for trying to get better, which can include seeking medical attention and following medical recommendations.

social cognitive theory—a theory which posits that people's behavior is a result of their beliefs, expectancies, and confidence. According to this view, behavior is routed in people's thoughts, which can include their beliefs about their own ability to engage (or not engage) in a particular behavior as well as their beliefs about the consequences of engaging (or not engaging) in a particular behavior.

social learning theory—a theory stating that people do not need to directly experience the rewards or costs of engaging in a particular behavior to learn about their outcomes but rather could learn about such consequences through observational learning or modeling.

social network—a measure of social support in terms of the structure of people's social relationships, namely, the number and types of such relationships.

social support—the individual belief that a person is cared for and loved, esteemed and valued, and belongs to a network of communication and mutual obligations.

somatic nervous system—a part of the nervous system that transmits messages regarding sensation, such as touch, pressure, temperature, and pain, as well as messages regarding the voluntary movement of the body.

specificity theory—a theory of pain which states that there are specific sensory receptors for different types of sensations, such as pain, warmth, touch, and pressure. When a person experiences an injury, a direct chain carries these messages of pain to the brain, which then sets off an "alarm," and hence the person experiences pain.

stages of death and dying—a well-known five stages model for explaining how people cope with dying that was developed in the late 1960 s by Dr. Elizabeth Kubler-Ross.

stages of delay model—a model that describes the steps people go through when deciding to get medical help.

stage models—theories that specify a set of ordered categories, or stages, that people go through as they attempt to change their behavior.

stimulus control—a self-management strategy for behavior change that focuses on identifying those situations that lead people to engage in a given behavior (e.g., smoking, drinking, overeating, etc.) and then avoiding these situations.

stress—a state of challenge or threat that disrupts the normal rhythm and balance of a person's life.

stroke—a condition in which a blood clot lodges in the circulatory system and deprives the brain of oxygen. Strokes occur when the plaque that forms on the artery wall becomes detached, travels in the blood, and lodges in the circulatory system.

subjective norms—individuals' beliefs about whether other people would support them in engaging in a new behavior and whether they are motivated to follow the beliefs of these salient others, including family members, friends, and romantic partners. Subjective norms are one of the components of the theory of reasoned action and the theory of planned behavior.

survey methods—a type of study that relies on asking people questions about their thoughts, feelings, desires, and action. These questions could be asked directly by the experimenter in an interview either in person or on the phone, or participants could complete written surveys.

susceptible—one of the parts of the health belief model indicating the degree of vulnerability a person has to a particular condition.

sympathetic-adrenal medullary (SAM) system—a part of the endocrine system that responds during times of stress. When this system is activated, the hypothalamus triggers the adrenal glands to release epinephrine and norepinephrine. These hormones act very quickly and lead to a number of physiological effects, including increased heart rate, increased blood flow, and increased sweating.

sympathetic system—a part of the nervous system that works to mobilize the body to react in the face of a threat, much like the response that occurs in Cannon's "fight-or-flight" response. This response includes increases in respiration, heart rate, and pulse; decreases in digestion and reproduction; dilating pupils (for far vision); and moving of blood to the muscles to prepare for action.

systematic desensitization—a technique in which a person is asked to describe the specific source of their anxiety and then to create a hierarchy of different stimuli (that cause increasing levels of arousal) associated with that anxiety. The therapist then asks the patient to focus on the least anxiety-provoking image and changes the focus to a less-stressful stimulus whenever the patient experiences any anxiety. Gradually, as the patient is able to think about a low-level stimulus without feeling anxiety, the therapist continues to higher level (e.g., more anxiety-provoking) stimuli, which, over time, enables people to build up their tolerance to the stressful situation.

tailored—a message that is created to match an individual's particular needs and goals.

tangible support—the provision of concrete assistance, such as financial aid, material resources, or needed services.

targeted—a message that is created to match a specific group of people, and/or specific characteristics of a group of people.

task-work approach—a model developed by Charles Corr that describes coping with dying as focusing on four distinct types of tasks: physical, psychological, social, and spiritual.

tend-and-befriend—a pattern shown by women in which the preference is to affiliate with others during times of stress.

tension reduction theory—a theory of alcohol use which posits that people drink to cope with or regulate negative moods, including tension, anxiety, and nervousness.

tertiary prevention—actions taken to minimize or slow the damage caused by an illness or disease, such as taking medicine, engaging in regular physical therapy, and following a recommended diet.

theory—an organized set of principles used to explain observed phenomena.

theory of planned behavior—a theory of health behavior that extends the theory of reasoned action by adding the component of perceived behavioral control. This theory describes behavior as a result of intentions and perceived behavior control, and sees intentions as determined by people's attitudes toward the behavior, subjective norms for the behavior, and perceived behavioral control over the behavior.

theory of reasoned action—a theory of health behavior which posits that the key determinant of people's behavior is their intention to engage in that behavior, and that intentions are determined by people's attitudes toward the behavior as well as their subjective norms for the behavior.

tolerance—the situation in which people's bodies no longer respond at the same level to a particular dose of a given substance (e.g., alcohol, tobacco) but rather need larger and larger doses to experience the same effects. They also experience unpleasant withdrawal symptoms, such as irritability, difficulty concentrating, fatigue, nausea, and weight gain, when they discontinue using the substance.

transactional model (relational model)—a model which posits that the meaning a particular event has for a person is a more important predictor of the experience of stress than the actual event.

transcutaneous electrical nerve stimulation (TENS)—a technique of pain reduction that involves placing a small portable unit that attaches electrodes to the skin and gives continuous (but not painful) electrical stimulation.

transtheoretical/stages of change theory—a continuum model of health behavior change that describes making changes in health-related behavior as a complex process in which individuals make such changes only gradually and not necessarily in a linear order. Instead, people move from one stage to another in a spiral fashion, which can include movement to new stages as well as movement back to previous stages, until they have finally completed the process of behavior change. The five stages of this model are precontemplation, contemplation, preparation, action, and maintenance.

treatment delay—a type of medical delay that occurs when people delay receiving medical recommendations.

Type A behavior—a personality trait that refers to three distinct types of behavior,

namely time urgency, competitive drive, and anger/hostility. Type A people experience high levels of time urgency—they are irritated by and impatient with time delays and constantly try to do more than one thing at a time. Second, Type A people have a strong competitive drive and are focused on doing better than other people in all sorts of situations (work and play). Finally, Type A people are prone to experiencing anger and hostility (e.g., more irritable when frustrated in their goal pursuit, easily aroused to anger). Like people who are high in hostility, Type A people are quick to experience anger and may lash out at others in frustration.

unintentional injuries—injuries that the person did not mean to happen.

unintentional nonadherence—the condition in which a person intends to comply, and may even believe he or she is complying, but for some reason is not following instructions.

utilization (behavioral) delay—a delay in the time it takes people to decide to actually get help from a professional after they realize they are ill and in need of medical help.

withdrawal—the unpleasant physical and psychological symptoms that people experience when they stop using a particular substance (e.g., tobacco, alcohol) on which they are dependent.

REFERENCES

Abar, B. W., Turrisi, R., Hillhouse, J., Loken, E., Stapleton, J., & Gunn, H. (2010). Preventing skin cancer in college females: Heterogeneous effects over time. *Health Psychology, 29,* 574–582.

Abernethy, A. D., Chang, H. T., Seidlitz, L., Evinger, J. S., & Duberstein, P. R. (2002). Religious coping and depression among spouses of people with lung cancer. *Psychosomatics, 43,* 456–463.

Aboa-Éboulé, C., Brisson, C., Maunsell, E., Mâsse, B., Bourbonnais, R., Vézina, M., . . . Dagenais, G. R. (2007). Job strain and risk of acute recurrent coronary heart disease events. *Journal of the American Medical Association, 298,* 1652–1660.

Abramson, L. Y., Metalsky, G. I., & Alloy, L. B. (1989). Hopelessness and depression: A theory-based subtype of depression. *Psychological Review, 96,* 358–372.

Adams, M. A., Norman, G. J., Hovell, M. F., Sallis, J. F., & Patrick, K. (2009). Reconceptualizing decisional balance in an adolescent sun protection intervention: Mediating effects and theoretical interpretations. *Health Psychology, 28,* 217–225.

Addis, M., & Mahalik, J. (2003). Men, masculinity, and the contexts of help seeking. *American Psychologist, 58,* 5–14.

Ader, R., & Cohen, N. (1975). Behaviorally conditioned immunosuppression. *Psychosomatic Medicine, 37,* 333–340.

Ader, R., & Cohen, N. (1985). CNS-immune system interactions: Conditioning phenomena. *Behavioral and Brain Sciences, 8,* 379–394.

Ad Hoc Committee of the Harvard Medical School to Examine the Definition of Brain Death. (1968). A definition of irreversible coma. *Journal of the American Medical Association, 205,* 337–340.

Adler, N. E., Boyce, W. T., Chesney, M. A., Cohen, S., Folkman, S., Kahn, R. L., & Syme, S. L. (1994). Socioeconomic status and health: The challenge of the gradient. *American Psychologist, 49,* 15–24.

Adler, N. E., Boyce W. T., Chesney M. A., Folkman S., & Syme S. L. (1993). Socioeconomic inequalities in health: No easy solution. *Journal of the American Medical Association, 269,* 3140–3145.

Adler, N., & Matthews, K. (1994). Health psychology: Why do some people get sick and some stay well? *Annual Review of Psychology, 45,* 229–259.

Adler, N. E., & Stone, G. C. (1979). Social science perspectives on the health system. In G. C. Stone, F. Cohen, & N. E. Adler (Eds.), *Health psychology—A handbook: Theories, applications, and challenges of a psychological approach to the health care system* (pp. 19–46). San Francisco, CA: Jossey-Bass.

Adler, R. (2001). Psychoneuroimmunology. *Current Directions in Psychological Science, 10,* 94–98.

Adriaanse, M. A., de Ridder, D. T. D., & De Wit, J. B. F. (2009). Finding the critical cue: Implementation intentions to change one's diet work best when tailored to personally relevant reasons for unhealthy eating. *Personality and Social Psychology Bulletin, 35,* 60–71.

Affleck, G., Tennen, H., Urrows, S., & Higgins, P. (1992). Neuroticism and the pain-mood relation in rheumatoid arthritis: Insights from a prospective daily study. *Journal of Consulting and Clinical Psychology, 60,* 119–126.

Afifi, W. A. (1999). Harming the ones we love: Relational attachment and perceived consequences as predictors of safe-sex behavior. *Journal of Sex Research, 36,* 198–206.

Agras, W. S. (1993). Short-term psychological treatments for binge eating. In C. G. Fairburn & G. T. Wilson (Eds.), *Binge eating: Nature, assessment, and treatment* (pp. 270–286). New York, NY: Guilford Press.

Agras, W. S., Taylor, C. B., Kraemer, H. C., Southam, M. A., & Schneider, J. A. (1987). Relaxation training for essential hypertension at the worksite: II. The poorly controlled hypertensive. *Psychosomatic Medicine, 49,* 264–273.

Ahluwalia, J. S., Nollen, N., Kaur, H., James, A. S., Mayo, M. S., & Resnicow, K. (2007). Pathway to health: Cluster-randomized trial to increase fruit and vegetable consumption among smokers in public housing. *Health Psychology, 26,* 214–221.

Ahto, M., Isoaho, R., Puolijoki, H., Vahlberg, T., & Kivelä, S.-L. (2007). Stronger symptoms of depression predict high coronary heart disease mortality in older men and women. *International Journal of Geriatric Psychiatry, 22,* 757–763.

Ai, A. L., Park, C. L., Huang, B., Rodgers, W., & Tice, T. N. (2007). Psychosocial mediation of religious coping styles: a study of short-term psychological distress following cardiac surgery. *Personality & Social Psychology Bulletin, 33,* 867–882.

Aiken, L. H., Clarke, S. P., Sloane, D. M., Sochalski, J., & Silber, J. H. (2002). Hospital nurse staffing and patient mortality, nurse burnout, and job dissatisfaction. *Journal of the American Medical Association, 288,* 1987–1993.

Aiken, L. R. (1985). *Dying, death, and bereavement.* Boston, MA: Allyn and Bacon.

Aiken, L. S., West, S. G., Woodward, C. K., & Reno, R. R. (1994). Health beliefs and compliance with mammography-screening recommendations in asymptomatic women. *Health Psychology, 13,* 122–129.

Ajzen, I. (1985). From intentions to actions: A theory of planned behavior. In J. Kuhl & J. Beckman (Eds.), *Action control: From cognition to behavior* (pp. 11–39). Berlin, Germany: Springer.

Ajzen, I., Albarracín, D., & Hornik, R. (Eds.) (2007). *Prediction and change of health behavior: Applying the reasoned action approach.* Mahwah, NJ: Erlbaum.

Ajzen, I., & Manstead, A. S. R. (2007). Changing health-related behaviors: An approach based on the theory of planned behavior. In K. van den Bos, M. Hewstone, J. de Wit, H. Schut & M. Stroebe (Eds.), *The scope of social psychology: Theory and applications* (pp. 43–63). New York: Psychology Press.

Al'Absi, M., & Bongard, S. (2006). Neuroendocrine and behavioral mechanisms mediating the relationship between anger expression and cardiovascular risk: assessment considerations and improvements. *Journal of Behavioral Medicine, 29,* 573–591.

Alagna, S. W., & Reddy, D. M. (1984). Predictors of proficient technique and successful lesion detection in breast self-examination. *Health Psychology, 3,* 113–127.

Albarracín, D., Johnson, B. T., Fishbein, M., & Muellerleile, P. A. (2001). Theories of reasoned action and planned behavior as models of condom use: A meta-analysis. *Psychological Bulletin, 127,* 142–161.

Albarracin, D., McNatt, P. S., Williams, W. R., Hoxworth, J., Zenlumer, J., Ho, R. M.,... Iatesta, M. (2000). Structure of outcome beliefs in condom use. *Health Psychology, 19,* 458–468.

Albert, A. E., Warner, D. L., Hatcher, R. A., Trussell, J., & Bennett, C. (1995). Condom use among female commercial sex workers in Nevada's legal brothels. *American Journal of Public Health, 85,* 1514–1520.

Albert, C. M., Hennekens, C. H., O'Donnell, C. J., Ajani, U. A., Carey, V. J., Willett, W. C.,.... Manson, J. E. (1998). Fish consumption and risk of sudden cardiac death. *Journal of the American Medical Association, 279,* 23–28.

Alcoholics Anonymous World Services. (1977). *Alcoholics anonymous: The twelve steps and twelve traditions* (3rd ed.). New York, NY: Author.

Aldwin, C. M., Levenson, M. R., Spiro, A., III., & Bosse, R. (1989). Does emotionality predict stress? Findings from the Normative Aging Study. *Journal of Personality and Social Psychology, 56,* 618–624.

Aldwin, C., & Revenson, T. A. (1987). Does coping help? A reexamination of the relation between coping and mental health. *Journal of Personality and Social Psychology, 53,* 337–348.

Alferi, S. M., Carver, C. S., Antoni, M. H., Weiss, S., & Duran, R. E. (2001). An exploratory study of social support, distress, and life disruption among low-income Hispanic women under treatment for early stage breast cancer. *Health Psychology, 20,* 41–46.

Allen, K., Blasovich, J., & Mendes, W. B. (2002). Cardiovascular reactivity and the presence of pets, friends, and spouses: The truth about cats and dogs. *Psychosomatic Medicine, 64,* 727–739.

Allison, D. B., & Faith, M. S. (1997). Issues in mapping genes for eating disorders. *Psychopharmacology Bulletin, 33,* 359–368.

Alloy, L. B., Abramson, L. Y., & Francis, E. L. (1999). Do negative cognitive styles confer vulnerability to depression? *Current Directions in Psychological Science, 8,* 128–132.

Aloise-Young, P. A., Hennigan, K. M., & Graham, J. W. (1996). Role of the self-image and smoker stereotype in smoking onset during early adolescence: A longitudinal study. *Health Psychology, 15,* 494–497.

Amaro, H. (1995). Love, sex, and power: Considering women's realities in HIV prevention. *American Psychologist, 50,* 437–447.

American Cancer Society. (1998). Cancer facts & figures—1998. Atlanta, GA: Author.

American Cancer Society. (2011). Cancer Facts & Figures 2011. Atlanta, GA: Author.

American Psychiatric Association. (1994). *Diagnostic and Statistical Manual of Mental Disorders* (4th ed.). Washington, DC: Author.

American Psychological Association. Task Force on Health Research. (1976). Contributions of psychology to health research: Patterns, problems, and potentials. *American Psychologist, 31,* 263–274.

American Psychological Association. (1992). Ethical principles of psychologists and code of conduct. *American Psychologist, 47,* 1597–1611.

Anand, K. J., & Craig, K. D. (1996). New perspectives on the definition of pain. *Pain, 67,* 3–6.

Anda, R. F., Williamson, D. R., Escobedo, L. G., Mast, E. E., Giovino, G. A., & Remington, P. L. (1990). Depression and the dynamics of smoking. *Journal of the American Medical Association, 264,* 1541–1545.

Andersen, A. E., & DiDomenico, L. (1992). Diet vs. shape content of popular male and female magazines: A dose-response relationship to the incidence of eating disorders? *International Journal of Eating Disorders, 11,* 283–287.

Andersen, B. L. (1993). Cancer. In C. Niven & D. Carroll (Eds.), *The health psychology of women* (pp. 75–89). Chur, Switzerland: Harwood Academic.

Andersen, B. L., Cacioppo, J. T., & Roberts, D. C. (1995). Delay in seeking a cancer diagnosis: Delay stages and psychophysiological comparison processes. *British Journal of Social Psychology, 34,* 33–52.

Andersen, B. L., Woods, X. A., & Copeland, L. J. (1997). Sexual self-schema and sexual morbidity among gynecologic cancer survivors. *Journal of Consulting and Clinical Psychology, 65,* 1–9.

Andersen, M. R., Bowen, D. J., Morea, J., Stein, K. D., & Baker, F. (2009). Involvement in decision-making and breast cancer survivor quality of life. *Health Psychology, 28,* 29–37.

Andersen, R. E., Crespo, C. J., Bartlett, S. J., Cheskin, L. J., & Pratt, M. (1998). Relationship of physical activity and television watching with body weight and level of fatness among children: Results from the third National Health and Nutrition Examination Survey. *Journal of the American Medical Association, 279*, 938–942.

Andersen, R. E., Wadden T. A., Bartlett S. J., Zemel B., Verde T. J., & Franckowiak S. C. (1999). Effects of lifestyle activity vs. structured aerobic exercise in obese women: A randomized trial. *Journal of the American Medical Association, 281*, 335–340.

Anderson, C. R. (1977). Locus of control, coping behaviors and performance in a stress setting: A longitudinal study. *Journal of Applied Psychology, 62*, 446–451.

Anderson, E. A. (1987). Preoperative preparation for cardiac surgery facilitates recovery, reduces psychological distress, and reduces the incidence of acute postoperative hypertension. *Journal of Consulting and Clinical Psychology, 55*, 513–520.

Anderson, E. S., Wojcik, J. R., Winett, R. A., & Williams, D. M. (2006). Socialcognitive determinants of physical activity: The influence of social support, self-efficacy, outcome expectations, and self-regulation among participants in a church-based health promotion study. *Health Psychology, 25*, 510–520.

Anderson, J. L., Crawford, C. B., Nadeau, J., & Lindberg, T. (1992). Was the Duchess of Windsor right? A cross-cultural review of the socioecology of ideals of female body shape. *Ethology and Sociobiology, 13*, 197–227.

Anderson, N. B. (1995). Behavioral and sociocultural perspectives on ethnicity and health. *Health Psychology, 14*, 589–591.

Anderson, N. B., & Armstead, C. A. (1995). Toward understanding the association of socioeconomic status and health: A new challenge for the biopsychosocial approach. *Psychosomatic Medicine, 57*, 213–225.

Angoff, N. R. (2001). Crying in the curriculum. *Journal of the American Medical Association, 286*, 1017–1018.

Antoni, M. H., Cruess, D. G., Cruess, S., Lutgendorf, S., Kumar, M., Ironson, G., ... Schneiderman, N. (2000). Cognitive-behavioral stress management intervention effects on anxiety, 24-hour urinary norepinephrine output, and T-cytotoxic/suppressor cells over time among symptomatic HIV-infected gay men. *Journal of Consulting and Clinical Psychology, 68*, 31–45.

Antoni, M. H., Lehman, J. M., Kilbourn, K. M., Boyers, A. E., Culver, J. L., Alferi, S. M., ... Carver, C. S. (2001). Cognitive-behavioral stress management intervention decreases the prevalence of depression and enhances benefit finding among women under treatment for early-stage breast cancer. *Health Psychology, 20*, 20–32.

Antoni, M. H., & Lutgendorf, S. (2007). Psychosocial factors and disease progression in cancer. *Current Directions in Psychological Science, 16*, 42–46.

Antonio, M. D. (1997, August 31). Atomic guinea pigs. *New York Times Magazine, 38*, 41–42.

Antonovsky, A. (1987). *Unraveling the mystery of health: How people manage stress and stay well.* San Francisco, CA: Jossey-Bass.

Antonucci, T. C. (1990). Social support and social relationships. In R. H. Binstock & L. K. George (Eds.), *Handbook of aging and the social sciences* (3rd ed., pp. 205–226). Orlando, FL: Academic Press.

Antonucci, T. C., & Akiyama, H. (1987). An examination of sex differences in social support among older men and women. *Sex Roles, 17*, 737–749.

Arena, J. G., & Blanchard, E. B. (1996). Biofeedback and relaxation therapy for chronic pain disorders. In R. J. Gatchel & D. C. Turk (Eds.), *Psychological approaches to pain management: A practitioner's handbook* (pp. 179–230). New York, NY: Guilford Press.

Arias, E. (2010). United States life tables, 2006. *National Vital Statistics Reports, 58(21)*. Hyattsville, MD: National Center for Health Statistics.

Armitage, C. J. (2004). Evidence that implementation intentions reduce dietary fat intake: A randomized trial. *Health Psychology, 23*, 319–323.

Armitage, C. J. (2005). Can the theory of planned behaviour predict the maintenance of physical activity? *Health Psychology, 24*, 235–245.

Armitage, C. J. (2009). Effectiveness of experimenter-provided and self-generated implementation intentions to reduce alcohol consumption in a sample of the general population: A randomized exploratory trial. *Health Psychology, 28*, 545–553.

Armitage, C. J., & Arden, M. A. (2008). How useful are the stages of change for targeting interventions? Randomized test of a brief intervention to reduce smoking. *Health Psychology, 27*, 789–798.

Armstrong, L., & Jenkins, S. (2000). *It's not about the bike: My journey back to life.* New York, NY: Putnam.

Aronoff, G. M., Wagner, J. M., & Spangler, A. S. (1986). Chemical interventions for pain. *Journal of Consulting and Clinical Psychology, 54*, 769–775.

Arora, N. K., & Gustafson, D. H. J. (2008). Perceived helpfulness of physicians' communication behavior and breast cancer patients' level of trust over time. Journal of General Internal Medicine, 24, 252–255.

Ary, D. V., & Biglan, A. (1988). Longitudinal changes in adolescent smoking behavior: Onset and cessation. *Journal of Behavioral Medicine, 11*, 361–382.

Aseltine, R. H. Jr., & DeMartino, R. (2004). An outcome evaluation of the SOS suicide prevention program. *American Journal of Public Health, 94*, 446–451.

Ashley, M. J., & Rankin, J. G. (1988). A public health approach to the prevention of alcohol-related problems. *Annual Review of Public Health, 9*, 233–271.

Ashton, E., Vosvick, M., Chesney, M., Gore-Felton, C., Koopman, C., O'Shea, K., ... Spiegel, D. (2005). Social support and maladaptive coping as predictors of the change in physical health symptoms among persons living with HIV/AIDS. *AIDS Patient Care and STDs, 19*, 587–598.

Askay, S. W., Patterson, D. R., Jensen, M. P., & Sharar, S. R. (2007). A randomized controlled trial of hypnosis for burn wound care. *Rehabilitation Psychology, 52*, 247–253.

Aspinwall, L. G., Kemeny, M. E., Taylor, S. E., Schneider, S. G., & Dudley, J. P. (1991). Psychosocial predictors of gay men's AIDS risk-reduction behavior. *Health Psychology, 10*, 432–444.

Aspinwall, L. G., & Taylor, S. E. (1997). A stitch in time: Self-regulation and proactive coping. *Psychological Bulletin, 21*, 417–436.

Atkins, C. J., Kaplan, R. M., Timms, R. M., Reinsch, S., & Lofback, K. (1984). Behavioral exercise programs in the management of chronic obstructive pulmonary disease. *Journal of Consulting and Clinical Psychology, 52*, 591–603.

Audrain-McGovern, J., Rodriguez, D., Tercyak, K. P., Neuner, G., & Moss, H. B. (2006). The impact of self-control indices on peer smoking and adolescent smoking progression. *Journal of Pediatric Psychology, 31*, 139–151.

Auerbach, S. M., Kendall, P. C., Cuttler, H., & Levitt, N. R. (1976). Anxiety, locus of control, type of preparatory information, and adjustment to dental surgery. *Journal of Consulting and Clinical Psychology, 44*, 809–818.

Augustine, A. A., Larsen, R. J., Walker, M. S., & Fisher, E. B. (2008). Personality predictors of the time course for lung cancer onset. *Journal of Research in Personality, 42*, 1448–1455.

Avrin, J. (2012). The very real hazards of disordered eating. Personal communication.

Ayanian, J. Z., & Epstein, A. M. (1991). Differences in the use of procedures between women and men hospitalized for coronary heart disease. *New England Journal of Medicine, 325*, 221–225.

Babyak, M., Blumenthal, J. A., Herman, S., Rhatri, P., Doraiswamy, M., Moore, K., . . . Krishnan, K. R. (2000). Exercise treatment for major depression: Maintenance of therapeutic benefit at 10 months. *Psychosomatic Medicine, 62*, 633–638.

Bach, P. B., Cramer, L. D., Warren, J. L., & Begg, C. B. (1999). Racial differences in the treatment of early-stage lung cancer. *New England Journal of Medicine, 341*, 1198–1205.

Bachiocco, V., Scesi, M., Morselli, A. M., & Carli, G. (1993). Individual pain history and familial pain tolerance models: Relationships to post-surgical pain. *Clinical Journal of Pain, 9*, 266–271.

Badr, H., Carmack, C. L., Kashy, D. A., Cristofanilli, M., & Revenson, T. A. (2010). Dyadic coping in metastatic breast cancer. *Health Psychology, 29*, 169–180.

Badr, H., & Taylor, C. L. (2008). Effects of relationship maintenance on psychological distress and dyadic adjustment among couples coping with lung cancer. *Health Psychology, 27*, 616–627.

Badr, H., & Taylor, C. L. (2009). Sexual dysfunction and spousal communication in couples coping with prostate cancer. *Psycho-Oncology, 18*, 735–746.

Baer, J. S., & Carney, M. M. (1993). Biases in the perceptions of the consequences of alcohol use among college students. *Journal of Studies on Alcohol, 54*, 54–60.

Baer, J. S., Stacy, A., & Larimer, M. (1991). Biases in the perception of drinking norms among college students. *Journal of Studies on Alcohol, 52*, 580–586.

Bagley, S. P., Angel, R., Dilworth-Anderson, P., Liu, W., & Schinke, S. (1995). Adaptive health behaviors among ethnic minorities. *Health Psychology, 14*, 632–640.

Bailey, D. S., Leonard, K. E., Cranston, J. W., & Taylor, S. P. (1983). Effects of alcohol and self-awareness on human physical aggression. *Personality and Social Psychology Bulletin, 9*, 289–295.

Bailey, J. E., Kellermann, A. L., Somes, G. W., Banton, J. G., Rivara, F. P., & Rushforth, N. P. (1997). Risk factors for violent death of women in the home. *Archives of Internal Medicine, 157*, 777–782.

Baker, C. W., Whisman, M. A., & Brownell, K. D. (2000). Studying intergenerational transmission of eating attitudes and behaviors: Methodological and conceptual questions. *Health Psychology, 19*, 376–381.

Baker, S. P., O'Neill, B., Ginsburg, M. J., & Li, G. (1992). *The injury fact book.* New York, NY: Oxford University Press.

Baldwin, A. S., Rothman, A. J., Hertel, A. W., Linde, J. A., Jeffery, R. W., Finch, E. A., & Lando, H. A. (2006). Specifying the determinants of the initiation and maintenance of behavior change: An examination of self-efficacy, satisfaction, and smoking cessation. *Health Psychology, 25*, 626–634.

Banaji, M. R., & Steele, C. M. (1989). The social cognition of alcohol use. *Social Cognition, 7*, 137–151.

Bandura, A. (1969). Social learning of moral judgments. *Journal of Personality and Social Psychology, 11*, 275–279.

Bandura, A. (1977). Self-efficacy: Toward a unifying theory of behavioral change. *Psychological Review, 84*, 191–215.

Bandura, A. (1986). *Social foundations of thought and action: A social cognitive theory.* Englewood Cliffs, NJ: Prentice Hall.

Bandura, A. (1997). *Self-efficacy: The exercise of control.* New York, NY: Freeman.

Bandura, A., O'Leary, A., Taylor, C. B., Gauthier, J., & Gossard, D. (1987). Perceived self-efficacy and pain control: Opioid and nonopioid mechanisms. *Journal of Personality and Social Psychology, 53*, 563–571.

Bandura, A., & Simon, K. M. (1977). The role of proximal intentions in self-regulation of refractory behavior. *Cognitive Therapy and Research, 1*, 177–193.

Bandura, A., Taylor, C. B., Williams, S. L., Mefford, I. N., & Barchas, J. D. (1985). Catecholamine secretion as a function of perceived coping self-efficacy. *Journal of Consulting and Clinical Psychology, 53*, 406–414.

Banks, S. M., Salovey, P., Greener, S., Rothman, A. J., Moyer, A., Beauvais, J., & Epel, E. (1995). The effects of message framing on mammography utilization. *Health Psychology, 14*, 178–184.

Barakat, L. P., & Wodka, W. (2006). Posttraumatic stress symptoms in college students with a chronic illness. *Social Behavior and Personality, 34*, 999–1006.

Barber, J. (1998). When hypnosis causes trouble. *International Journal of Clinical & Experimental Hypnosis, 46*, 157–170.

Barefoot, J. C., Dahlstrom, W. G., & Williams, R. B. (1983). Hostility, CHD incidence, and total mortality: A 25-year follow-up study of 255 physicians. *Psychosomatic Medicine, 45*, 59–63.

Barefoot, J. C., Dodge, K., Peterson, B., Dahlstrom, W. G., & Williams, R. (1989). The Cook-Medley Hostility Scale: Item content and the ability to predict survival. *Psychosomatic Medicine, 51*, 46–57.

Bárez, M., Blasco, T., Fernández-Castro, J., & Viladrich, C. (2009). Perceived control and psychological distress in women with breast cancer: A longitudinal study. *Journal of Behavioral Medicine, 32*, 187–196.

Barnes, D., Gatchel, R. J., Mayer, T. G., & Barnett, J. (1990). Changes in MMPI profiles of chronic low back pain patients following successful treatment. *Journal of Spinal Disorders, 3*, 353–355.

Barnes, P. M., Bloom, B., & Nahin, R. L. (2008). Complementary and alternative medicine use among adults and children: United States, 2007. *National Health Statistics Reports; No 12.* Hyattsville, MD: National Center for Health Statistics.

Barnes, V. A., Treiber, F., & Davis, H. (2001). Impact of Transcendental Meditation on cardiovascular function at rest and during acute stress in adolescents with high normal blood pressure. *Journal of Psychosomatic Research, 51*, 597–605.

Barnett, R. C., Gareis, K., & Brennan, R. T. (1999). Fit as a mediator of the relationship between work hours and burnout. *Journal of Occupational Health Psychology, 4*, 307–317.

Barnhoorn, F., & Adriaanse, H. (1992). In search of factors responsible for noncompliance among tuberculosis patients in Wardha District, India. *Social Science & Medicine, 34*, 291–306.

Baron, R. S., Cutrona, C. E., Hicklin, D., Russell, D. W., & Lubaroff, D. (1990). Social support and immune function among spouses of cancer patients. *Journal of Personality and Social Psychology, 59*, 344–352.

Barrerra, M., Chassin, L., & Rogosch, F. (1993). Effects of social support and conflict on adolescent children of alcoholic and nonalcoholic fathers. *Journal of Personality and Social Psychology, 64*, 602–612.

Barrerra, M., Jr., Sandler, I., & Ramsey, T. (1981). Preliminary development of a scale of social support: Studies on college students. *American Journal of Community Psychology, 9*, 435–447.

Bass, D. M., Noelker, L. S., Townsend, A. L., & Deimling, G. T. (1990). Losing an aged relative: Perceptual differences between spouses and adult children. *Omega, 21*, 21–40.

Bates, M. E., & Labouvie, E. W. (1995). Personality-environment constellations and alcohol use: A process-oriented study of intraindividual change during adolescence. *Psychology of Addictive Behaviors, 9*, 23–35.

Bates, M. S., Edwards, W. T., & Anderson, K. O. (1993). Ethnocultural influences on variation in chronic pain perception. *Pain, 52*, 101–112.

Baucom, D. H., & Aiken, P. A. (1981). Effect of depressed mood on eating among obese and nonobese dieting and nondieting persons. *Journal of Personality and Social Psychology, 47,* 577–585.

Baum, A., Friedman, A. L., & Zakowski, S. G. (1997). Stress and genetic testing for disease risk. *Health Psychology, 16,* 8–19.

Baum, A., & Grunberg, N. E. (1991). Gender, stress, and health. *Health Psychology, 10,* 80–85.

Baum, A., Grunberg, N. E., & Singer, J. E. (1982). The use of psychological and neuroendocrinological measurements in the study of stress. *Health Psychology, 1,* 217–236.

Beach, M. C., Sugarman, J., Johnson, R. L., Arbelaez, J. J., Duggan, P. S., & Cooper, L. A. (2005). Do patients treated with dignity report higher satisfaction, adherence, and receipt of preventive care? *Annals of Family Medicine, 3,* 331–338.

Bech, P., Rasmussen, N., Olsen, L. R., Noerholm, V., & Abildgaard, W. (2001). The sensitivity and specificity of the Major Depression Inventory, using the Present State Examination as the index of diagnostic validity. *Journal of Affective Disorders, 66,* 159–164.

Becker, A. E., Grinspoon, S. K., Klibanski, A., & Herzog, D. B. (1999). Current concepts: Eating disorders. *New England Journal of Medicine, 340,* 1092–1098.

Becker, C. B., Bull, S., Schaumberg, K., Cauble, A., & Franco, A. (2008). Effectiveness of peer-led eating disorders prevention: A replication trial. *Journal of Consulting and Clinical Psychology, 76,* 347–354.

Becker, D. M. (2001). Public health and religion. In N. Schneiderman et al. (Eds.), *Integrating behavioral and social sciences with public health* (pp. 351–368). Washington, DC: American Psychological Association.

Becker, M. H. (1985). Patient adherence to prescribed therapies. *Medical Care, 23,* 539–555.

Becker, M. H., Maiman, L. A., Kirscht, J. P., Haefner, D. P., & Drachman, R. H. (1977). The health belief model and prediction of dietary compliance: A field experiment. *Journal of Health and Social Behavior, 18,* 348–366.

Beckjord, E. B., Glinder, J., Langrock, A., & Compas, B. E. (2009). Measuring multiple dimensions of perceived control in women with newly diagnosed breast cancer. *Psychology & Health, 24,* 423–438.

Becvar, D. S. (2001). *In the presence of grief: Helping family members resolve death, dying, and bereavement issues.* New York, NY: Guilford Press.

Beecher, H. K. (1955). The powerful placebo. *Journal of the American Medical Association, 159,* 1602–1606.

Beecher, H. K. (1959). *Measurement of subjective responses.* New York, NY: Oxford University Press.

Beesdo, K., Jacobi, F., Hoyer, J., Low, N. C., Höfler, M., & Wittchen, H. U. (2010). Pain associated with specific anxiety and depressive disorders in a nationally representative population sample. *Social Psychiatry and Psychiatric Epidemiology, 45,* 89–104.

Bègue, L., Bushman, B. J., Giancola, P. R., Subra, B., & Rosset, E. (2010). "There is no such thing as an accident," especially when people are drunk. *Personality and Social Psychology Bulletin, 36,* 1301–1304.

Beier, M. E., & Ackerman, P. L. (2003). Determinants of health knowledge: An investigation of age, gender, abilities, personality, and interests. *Journal of Personality and Social Psychology, 84,* 439–447.

Belar, C. D. (1997). Clinical health psychology: A specialty for the 21st century. *Health Psychology, 16,* 411–416.

Bellizzi, K. M., & Blank, T. O. (2006). Understanding the dynamics of post-traumatic growth in breast cancer survivors. *Health Psychology, 25,* 47–56.

Bellomo, G., Narducci P. L., Rondoni F., Pastorelli G., Stangoni G., Angeli G., & Verdecchia, P. (1999). Prognostic value of 24-hour blood pressure in pregnancy. *Journal of the American Medical Association, 282,* 1447–1452.

Bender, R., Trautner, C., Spraul, M., & Berger, M. (1998). Assessment of excess mortality in obesity. *American Journal of Epidemiology, 147,* 42–48.

Benedetti, F., & Amanzio, M. (1997). The neurobiology of placebo analgesia: From endogenous opioids to cholecystokinin. *Progress in Neurobiology, 52,* 109–125.

Benedikt, R., Wertheim, E., & Love, A. (1998). Eating attitudes and weight-loss attempts in female adolescents and their mothers. *Journal of Youth and Adolescence, 27,* 43–57.

Ben-Eliyahu, S., Yirmiya, R., Liebeskind, J. C., Taylor, A. N., & Gale, R. P. (1991). Stress increases metastatic spread of a mammary tumor in rats: Evidence for mediation by the immune system. *Brain, Behavior, and Immunity, 5,* 193–205.

Benjamins, M. R. (2006). Religious influences on preventive health care use in a nationally representative sample of middle-age women. *Journal of Behavioral Medicine, 29,* 1–16.

Bennett, J. (2008, May 1). Picture perfect. *Newsweek.*

Benoliel, J. Q. (1988). Institutional dying: A convergence of cultural values, technology, and social organization. In H. Wass, F. M. Berado, & R. A. Neimeyer (Eds.), *Dying: Facing the facts* (2nd ed., pp. 159–184). New York, NY: Hemisphere.

Berado, D. H. (1988). Bereavement and mourning. In H. Wass, F. M., Berado, & R. A. Neimeyer (Eds.), *Dying: Facing the facts* (2nd ed., pp. 279–300). New York, NY: Hemisphere.

Bergin, A. E., Masters, K. S., & Richards, P. S. (1987). Religiousness and mental health reconsidered: A study of an intrinsically religious sample. *Journal of Counseling Psychology, 34,* 197–204.

Bergman, A. B., Rivara, F. P., Richards, D. D., & Rogers, L. W. (1990). The Seattle Children's Bicycle Helmet Campaign. *American Journal of Diseases of Children, 144,* 727–731.

Bergman, A. B., & Werner, R. J. (1963). Failure of children to receive penicillin by mouth. *New England Journal of Medicine, 268,* 1334–1338.

Bergner, M., Allison, C. J., Diehr, P., Ford, L. G., & Feigl, P. (1990). Early detection and control of cancer in clinical practice. *Archives of Internal Medicine, 150,* 431–436.

Berkman, E. T., Dickenson, J., Falk, E. B., & Lieberman, M. D. (2011). Using SMS text messaging to assess moderators of smoking reduction: Validating a new tool for ecological measurement of health behaviors. *Health Psychology, 30,* 186–194.

Berkman, L. F. (1985). The relationship of social networks and social support to morbidity and mortality. In S. Cohen & L. Syme (Eds.), *Social support and health* (pp. 243–262). New York, NY: Academic Press.

Berkman, L. F. (1986). Social networks, support, and health: Taking the next step forward. *American Journal of Epidemiology, 123,* 559–562.

Berkman, L. F., Leo-Summers, L., & Horowitz, R. I. (1992). Emotional support and survival after myocardial infarction. *Annals of Internal Medicine, 17,* 1003–1009.

Berkman, L. F., & Syme, S. L. (1979). Social networks, host resistance, and mortality: A nine-year follow-up study of Alameda County residents. *American Journal of Epidemiology, 109,* 186–204.

Berkman, N. D., Lohr, K. N., & Bulik, C. M. (2007). Outcomes of eating disorders: A systematic review of the literature. *International Journal of Eating Disorders, 40,* 293–309.

Bernstein, L., Henderson, B. E., Hanisch, R., Sullivan-Halley, J., & Ross, R. K. (1994). Physical exercise and reduced risk of breast cancer in young women. *Journal of the National Cancer Institute, 86,* 1403–1408.

Best, J. A., Flay, B. R., Towson, S. M. J., Ryan, K. B., Perry, C. L., Brown, K. S., . . . d'Avernas, J. R. (1984). Smoking prevention and the concept of risk. *Journal of Applied Social Psychology, 14,* 257–273.

Biener, L., & Heaton, A. (1995). Women dieters of normal weight: Their motives, goals, and risks. *American Journal of Public Health, 85,* 714–717.

Biesecker, B. B., Boehnke, M., Calzone, K., Markel, D. S., Garber, J. E., Collins, F. S., & Weber, B. L. (1993). Genetic counseling for families with inherited susceptibility to breast and ovarian cancer. *Journal of the American Medical Association, 269,* 1970–1974.

Billings, A. G., & Moos, R. H. (1985). Life stressors and social resources affect posttreatment outcomes among depressed patients. *Journal of Abnormal Psychology, 94,* 140–153.

Bingamon, J., Frank, R. G., & Billy, C. L. (1993). Combining a global health budget with a market-driven delivery system: Can it be done? *American Psychologist, 48,* 270–276.

Bishop, D. B., Roesler, J. S., Zimmerman, B. R., & Ballard, D. J. (1993). Diabetes. In R. C. Brownson, P. L., Remington, & J. R. Davis (Eds.), *Chronic disease epidemiology and control* (pp. 221–240). Washington, DC: American Public Health Association.

Bishop, S. R. (2002). What do we really know about Mindfulness-Based Stress Reduction? *Psychosomatic Medicine, 64,* 71–83.

Black, D. R., Gleser, L. J., & Kooyers, K. J. (1990). A meta-analytic evaluation of couples weight-loss programs. *Health Psychology, 9,* 330–347.

Blalock, S. J., DeVellis, R. F., Giorgino, K. B., DeVellis, B. M., Gold, D. T., Dooley, M. A., . . . Smith, S. L. (1996). Osteoporosis prevention in premenopausal women: Using a stage model approach to examine the predictors of behavior. *Health Psychology, 15,* 84–93.

Blanchard, E. B., Appelbaum, K. A., Guarnieri, P., Morrill, B., & Dentinger, M. P. (1987). Five year prospective follow-up on the treatment of chronic headache with biofeedback and/or relaxation. *Headache, 27,* 580–583.

Bland, S. H., Krogh, V., Winkelstein, W., & Trevisan, M. (1991). Social network and blood pressure: A population study. *Psychosomatic Medicine, 53,* 598–607.

Blanton, H., & Gerrard, M. (1997). Effect of sexual motivation on men's risk perception for sexually transmitted disease: There must be 50 ways to justify a lover. *Health Psychology, 16,* 374–379.

Blazer, D. (1982). Social support and mortality in an elderly community population. *American Journal of Epidemiology, 116,* 684–694.

Bleil, M. E., McCaffery, J. M., Muldoon, M. F., Sutton-Tyrrell, K., & Manuck, S. B. (2004). Anger-related personality traits and carotid artery atherosclerosis in untreated hypertensive men. *Psychosomatic Medicine, 66,* 633–639.

Blendon, R. J., Szalay, U. S., & Knox, R. A. (1992). Should physicians aid their patients in dying? The public perspective. *Journal of the American Medical Association, 267,* 2658–2662.

Blittner, M., Goldberg, J., & Merbaum, M. (1978). Cognitive self-control factors in the reduction of smoking behavior. *Behavior Therapy, 9,* 553–561.

Bloch, M., Fahy, M., Fox, S., & Hayden, M. R. (1989). Predictive testing for Huntington disease: II. Demographic characteristics, lifestyle patterns, attitudes, and psychosocial assessments of the first fifty-one test candidates. *Journal of Medical Genetics, 32,* 217–224.

Block, A. R., Kremer, E. F., & Gaylor, M. (1980). Behavioral treatment of chronic pain: The spouse as a discriminative cue for pain behavior. *Pain, 9,* 243–252.

Block, J. P., He, Y., Zaslavsky, A. M., Ding, L., & Ayanian, J. Z. (2009). Psychosocial stress and change in weight among US adults. *American Journal of Epidemiology, 170,* 181–192.

Blount, R. L., Corbin, S. M., Sturges, J. W., Wolfe, V. V., Prater, J. M., & James, L. D. (1989). The relationship between adults' behavior and child coping and distress during BMA/LP procedures: A sequential analysis. *Behavior Therapy, 20,* 585–601.

Bluebond-Langner, M. (1977). Meanings of death to children. In H. Feifel (Ed.), *New meanings of death* (pp. 47–66). New York, NY: McGraw-Hill.

Blumenthal, J. A., Babyak, M., Wei, J., O'Connor, C., Waugh, R., Eisenstein, E., . . . Reed, G. (2002). Usefulness of psychosocial treatment of mental stress-induced myocardial ischemia in men. *American Journal of Cardiology, 89,* 164–168.

Blumenthal, J. A., Burg, M., Barefoot, J., Williams, R. B., Haney, T., & Zimet, G. (1987). Social support, Type A behavior, and coronary artery disease. *Psychosomatic Medicine, 49,* 331–340.

Blumenthal, J. A., Sanders, W., Wallace, A. G., Williams, R. B., & Needles, T. L. (1982). Physiological and psychological variables predict compliance to prescribed exercise therapy in patients recovering from myocardial infarction. *Psychosomatic Medicine, 44,* 519–527.

Bly, J. L., Jones, R. C., & Richardson, J. E. (1986). Impact of worksite health promotion on health care costs and utlization. *Journal of the American Medical Association, 256,* 3235–3240.

Bogart, L., Walt L., Pavlovic, J., Ober, A., Brown, N., & Kalichman, S. C. (2007). Cognitive strategies affecting recall of sexual behavior among high-risk men and women. *Health Psychology, 26,* 787–793.

Bogg, T., & Roberts, B. W. (2004). Conscientiousness and health-related behaviors: A meta-analysis of the leading behavioral contributors to mortality. *Psychological Bulletin, 130,* 887–919.

Bolger, N., DeLongis, A., Kessler, R. C., & Schilling, E. A. (1989). Effects of daily stress on negative mood. *Journal of Personality and Social Psychology, 57,* 808–818.

Bolinder, G., Alfredsson, L., Englund, A., & deFaire, U. (1994). Smokeless tobacco use and increased cardiovascular mortality among Swedish construction workers. *American Journal of Public Health, 84,* 399–404.

Bonanno, G. A. (2004). Loss, trauma, and human resilience: Have we underestimated the human capacity to thrive after extremely adverse events? *American Psychologist, 59,* 20–28.

Bonanno, G. A., Keltner, D., Holen, A., & Horowitz, M. J. (1995). When avoiding unpleasant emotions might not be such a bad thing: Verbal-autonomic response dissociation and midlife conjugal bereavement. *Journal of Personality and Social Psychology, 69,* 975–989.

Bonanno, G. A., Papa, A., Lalande, K., Zhang, N., & Noll, J. G. (2005). Grief processing and deliberate grief avoidance: A prospective comparison of bereaved spouses and parents in the United States and China. *Journal of Consulting and Clinical Psychology, 73,* 86–98.

Bond, G. G., Aiken, L. S., & Somerville, S. C. (1992). The health belief model and adolescents with insulin-dependent diabetes mellitus. *Health Psychology, 11,* 190–198.

Bond, M. H. (1991). Chinese values and health: A cultural-level examination. *Psychology and Health, 5,* 137–152.

Boney McCoy, S., Gibbons, F. X., Reis, T. J., Gerrard, M., Luus, C. A. E., & Von Wald Sufka, A. (1992). Perceptions of smoking risk as a function of smoking status. *Journal of Behavioral Medicine, 15,* 469–488.

Booth-Kewley, S., & Vickers, R. R., Jr. (1994). Associations between major domains of personality and health behavior. *Journal of Personality, 62,* 281–298.

Borrelli, B., & Mermelstein, R. (1994). Goal setting and behavior change in a smoking cessation program. *Cognitive Therapy and Research, 18,* 69–82.

Borsari, B., & Carey, K. B. (2000). Effects of a brief motivational intervention with college students. *Journal of Consulting and Clinical Psychology, 68,* 728–733.

Bosma, H., Marmot, M. G., Hemingway, H., Nicholson, A. C., Brunner E., & Stansfeld, S. A. (1997). Low job control and risk of coronary heart disease in Whitehall II (prospective cohort) study. *British Medical Journal, 314,* 558–565.

Bosma, H., Stansfeld, S. A., & Marmot, M. G. (1998). Job control, personal characteristics, and heart disease. *Journal of Occupational Health Psychology, 3,* 402–409.

Botvin, G. J., Baker, E., Renick, N., Filazzola, A. D., & Botvin, E. M. (1984). A cognitive-behavioral approach to substance abuse prevention. *Addictive Behaviors, 9*, 137–147.

Bouchard, C. (1991). Is weight fluctuation a risk factor? *New England Journal of Medicine, 324*, 1887–1889.

Boutelle, K. N., Kirschenbaum, D. S., Baker, R. C., & Mitchell, M. E. (1999). How can obese weight controllers minimize weight gain during the high risk holiday season? By self-monitoring very consistently. *Health Psychology, 18*, 364–368.

Bovbjerg, V. E., McCann, B. S., Brief, D. J., Follette, W. C., Retzlaff, B. H., Dowdy, A. A.,...Knopp, R. H. (1995). Spouse support and long-term adherence to lipid-lowering diets. *American Journal of Epidemiology, 141*, 451–460.

Bower, J. E., Kemeny, M. E., Taylor, S. E., & Fahey, J. L. (1998). Cognitive processing, discovery of meaning, CD4 decline, and AIDS-related mortality among bereaved HIV-seropositive men. *Journal of Consulting and Clinical Psychology, 66*, 979–986.

Bower, J. E., Meyerowitz, B. E., Desmond, K. A., Bernaards, C. A., Rowland, J. H., & Ganz, P. A. (2005). Perceptions of positive meaning and vulnerability following breast cancer: Predictors and outcomes among long-term breast cancer survivors. *Annals of Behavioral Medicine, 29*, 236–245.

Boyle, S. H., Williams, R. B., Mark, D. B., Brummett, B. H., Siegler, I. C., Helms, M. J., & Barefoot, J. C. (2004). Hostility as a predictor of survival in patients with coronary artery disease. *Psychosomatic Medicine, 66*, 629–632.

Bradach, K. M., & Jordan, J. R. (1995). Long-term effects of a family history of traumatic death on adolescent individuation. *Death Studies, 19*, 315–336.

Bradburn, N. M., & Sudman, S. (1988). *Polls and surveys: Understanding what they tell us.* San Francisco, CA: Jossey-Bass.

Braddock, C. H., III, Edwards, K. A., Hasenberg, N. M., Laidley, T. L., & Levinson, W. (1999). Informed decision making in outpatient practice: Time to get back to basics. *Journal of the American Medical Association, 282*, 2313–2320.

Brady, S. S., Dolcini, M., M., Harper, G. W., & Pollack, L. M. (2009). Supportive friendships moderate the association between stressful life events and sexual risk taking among African American adolescents. *Health Psychology, 28*, 238–248.

Brafford, L. J., & Beck, K. H. (1991). Development and validation of a condom self-efficacy scale for college students. *Journal of American College Health, 29*, 219–225.

Brandon, T. H., Collins, B. N., Juliano, L. M., & Lazev, A. B. (2000). Preventing relapse among former smokers: A comparison of minimal interventions through telephone and mail. *Journal of Consulting and Clinical Psychology, 68*, 103–113.

Brandon, T. H., Copeland, A. L., & Saper, Z. L. (1995). Programmed therapeutic messages as a smoking treatment adjunct: Reducing the impact of negative affect. *Health Psychology, 14*, 41–47.

Brattberg, G. (1983). Acupuncture therapy for tennis elbow. *Pain, 16*, 285–288.

Braver, E. R., Ferguson, S. A., Greene, M. A., & Lund, A. K. (1997). Reductions in deaths in frontal crashes among right front passengers in vehicles equipped with passenger air bags. *Journal of the American Medical Association, 278*, 1437–1439.

Bray, G. A. (1992). Pathophysiology of obesity. *American Journal of Clinical Nutrition, 55*, 488S–494S.

Bray, G. A. & Gray, D. S. (1988). Obesity: Part I, pathogenesis. *Western Journal of Medicine, 149*, 429–441.

Brenner, R. A., & Committee on Injury, Violence, and Poison Prevention. (2003). Prevention of drowning in infants, children, and adolescents. *Pediatrics, 112*, 440–445.

Brenner, R. A., Taneja, G. S., Haynie, D. L., Trumble, A. C., Qian, C., Klinger, R. M., & Klebanoff, M. A. (2009). Association between swimming lessons and drowning in childhood: A case-controls. *Archives of Pediatric and Adolescent Medicine, 163*, 203–210.

Brent, D., Melhem, N., Donohoe, M. B., & Walker, M. (2009). The incidence and course of depression in bereaved youth 21 months after the loss of a parent to suicide, accident, or sudden natural death. *The American Journal of Psychiatry, 166*, 786–794.

Broadstock, M., Borland, R., & Gason, R. (1992). Effects of suntan on judgements of healthiness and attractiveness by adolescents. *Journal of Applied Social Psychology, 22*, 157–172.

Brock, D. W., & Wartman, S. A. (1990). When competent patients make irrational choices. *New England Journal of Medicine, 322*, 1595–1599.

Brody, G. H., Kogan, S. M., Murry, V. M., Chen, Y.-F., & Brown, A. C. (2008). Psychological functioning, support for self-management, and glycemic control among rural African American adults with diabetes mellitus Type 2. *Health Psychology, 27*, S83–S90.

Brondolo, E., Rieppi, R., Kelly, K. P., & Gerin, W. (2003). Perceived racism and blood pressure: A review of the literature and conceptual and methodological critique. *Annals of Behavioral Medicine, 25*, 55–65.

Brook, D. W., Brook, J. S.. Zhang, C., Whiteman, M., Cohen, P., & Finch, S. J. (2008). Developmental trajectories of cigarette smoking from adolescence to the early thirties: Personality and behavioral risk factors. *Nicotine & Tobacco Research, 10*, 1283–1291.

Brook, J., Schuster, E., & Zhang, C. (2004). Cigarette smoking and depressive symptoms: A longitudinal study of adolescents and young adults. *Psychological Reports, 95*, 159–166.

Brown, G. K., Wallston, K. A., & Nicassio, P. M. (1989). Social support and depression in rheumatoid arthritis: A one year prospective study. *Journal of Applied Social Psychology, 19*, 1164–1181.

Brown, J. D. (1991). Staying fit and staying well: Physical fitness as a moderator of life stress. *Journal of Personality and Social Psychology, 60*, 555–561.

Brown, K. W., & Ryan, R. M. (2003). The benefits of being present: Mindfulness and its role in psychological well-being. *Journal of Personality and Social Psychology, 84*, 822–848.

Brown, S. G., & Rhodes, R. E. (2006). Relationships among dog ownership and leisure-time walking in Western Canadian adults. *American Journal of Preventive Medicine, 30*, 121–136.

Brown, S. L., Nesse, R., Vinokur, A. D., & Smith, D. M. (2003). Providing support may be more beneficial than receiving it: Results from a prospective study of mortality. *Psychological Science, 14*, 320–327.

Brown, S. L., Smith, D. M., Schulz, R., Kabeto, M. U., Ubel, P. A., Poulin, M.,...Langa, K. M. (2009). Caregiving behavior is associated with decreased mortality risk. *Psychological Science, 20*, 488–494.

Brown, S. S. (1985). Can low birth-weight be prevented? *Family Planning Perspectives, 17*, 112–118.

Brownell, K. D., Cohen, R. Y., Stunkard, A. J., Felix, M. R. J., & Cooley, N. B. (1984). Weight loss competitions at the work site: Impact on weight, morale and cost-effectiveness. *American Journal of Public Health, 74*, 1283–1285.

Brownell, K. D., & Fairburn, C. G. (1995). *Eating disorders and obesity: A comprehensive handbook.* New York, NY: Guilford Press.

Brownell, K. D., Stunkard, A. J., & Albaum, J. M. (1980). Evaluation and modification of exercise patterns in the natural environment. *American Journal of Psychiatry, 137*, 1540–1545.

Brownell, K. D., & Wadden, T. A. (1992). Etiology and treatment of obesity: Understanding a serious, prevalent, and refractory disorder. *Journal of Consulting and Clinical Psychology, 60*, 505–517.

Brownlee-Duffeck, M., Peterson, L., Simonds, J. F., Goldstein, D., Kilo, C., & Hoette, S. (1987). The role of health beliefs in the regimen adherence and metabolic control of adolescents and adults with diabetes mellitus. *Journal of Consulting and Clinical Psychology, 55*, 139–144.

Brownson, R. C., Reif, J. S., Alavanja, M. C. R., & Bal, D. G. (1993). Cancer. In R. C. Brownson, P. L., Remington, & J. R. Davis (Eds.), *Chronic disease epidemiology and control* (pp. 137–167). Washington, DC: American Public Health Association.

Brubaker, R. G., & Wickersham, D. (1990). Encouraging the practice of testicular self-examination: A field application of the theory of reasoned action. *Health Psychology, 9*, 154–163.

Brug, J., Steenhuis, I., van Assema, P., & de Vries, H. (1996). The impact of computer-tailored nutrition information. *Preventive Medicine, 25*, 236–242.

Brunner, E., White, I., Thorogood, M., Bristow, A., Curle, D., & Marmot, M. (1997). Can dietary interventions change diet and cardiovascular risk factors? A meta-analysis of randomized controlled trials. *American Journal of Public Health, 87*, 1415–1422.

Bryan, A. D., Aiken, L. S., & West, S. G. (1996). Increasing condom use: Evaluation of a theory-based intervention to prevent sexually transmitted diseases in young women. *Health Psychology, 15*, 371–382.

Buchbinder, R., Osborne, R. H., Ebeling, P. R., Wark, J. D., Mitchell, P., Wriedt, C., . . . Murph, B. (2009). A randomized trial of vertebroplasty for painful osteoporotic vertebral fractures. *New England Journal of Medicine, 361*, 557–568.

Buckelew, S. P., Baumstark, K. E., Frank, R. G., & Hewett, J. E. (1990). Adjustment following spinal cord injury. *Rehabilitation Psychology, 35*, 101–109.

Bundek, N. I., Marks, G., & Richardson, J. L. (1993). Role of health locus of control beliefs in cancer screening of elderly Hispanic women. *Health Psychology, 12*, 193–199.

Bunketorp, L., Lindh, M., Carlsson, J., & Stener-Victorin, E. (2006). The perception of pain and pain-related cognitions in subacute whiplash-associated disorders: Its influence on prolonged disability. *Disability and Rehabilitation, 28*, 271–279.

Burish, T. G., & Bradley, L. A. (1983). Coping with chronic disease: Definitions and issues. In T. G. Burish & L. A. Bradley (Eds.), *Coping with chronic disease: Research and applications* (pp. 3–12). New York, NY: Academic Press.

Burish, T. G., Snyder, S. L., & Jenkins, R. A. (1991). Preparing patients for cancer chemotherapy: Effect of coping preparation and relaxation interventions. *Journal of Consulting and Clinical Psychology, 59*, 518–525.

Burnam, M. A., Timbers, D. M., & Hough, R. L. (1984). Two measures of psychological distress among Mexican Americans, Mexicans, and Anglos. *Journal of Health and Social Behavior, 25*, 24–33.

Burns, J. W., Quartana, P. J., & Bruehl, S. (2007). Anger management style moderates effects of emotion suppression during initial stress on pain and cardiovascular responses during subsequent pain-induction. *Annals of Behavioral Medicine, 34*, 154–165.

Burridge, L. H., Barnett, A. G., & Clavarino, A. M. (2009). The impact of perceived stage of cancer on carers' anxiety and depression during the patients' final year of life. *Psycho-Oncology, 18*, 615–623.

Burt, R. D., Dinh, K. T., Peterson, A. V., & Sarason, I. G. (2000). Predicting adolescent smoking: A prospective study of personality variables. *Preventive Medicine, 30*, 115–125.

Bush, C., Ditto, B., & Feuerstein, M. (1985). A controlled evaluation of paraspinal EMG biofeedback in the treatment of chronic low back pain. *Health Psychology, 4*, 307–321.

Bush, J. P., Melamed, B. G., Sheras, P. L., & Greenbaum, P. E. (1986). Mother–child patterns of coping with anticipatory medical stress. *Health Psychology, 5*, 137–157.

Businelle, M. S., Kendzor, D. E., Reitzel, L. R., Costello, T. J., Cofta-Woerpel, L., Li, Y., . . . Wetter, D. W. (2010). Mechanisms linking socioeconomic status to smoking cessation: A structural equation modeling approach. *Health Psychology, 29*, 262–273.

Buss, A. H., & Durkee, A. (1957). An inventory for assessing different kinds of hostility. *Journal of Consulting Psychology, 21*, 343–349.

Butler, L. D., Koopman, C., Neri, E., Giese-Davis, J., Palesh, O., Thorne-Yocam, K., . . . Spiegel, D. (2009). Effects of supportive-expressive group therapy on pain in women with metastatic breast cancer. *Health Psychology, 28*, 579–587.

Butt, H. R. (1977). A method for better physician–patient communication. *Annals of Internal Medicine, 86*, 478–480.

Butter, I. H. (1993). Premature adoption and routinization of medical technology: Illustrations from childbirth technology. *Journal of Social Issues, 49*, 11–34.

Byrnes, D. M., Antoni, M. H., Goodhin, K., Efanto-Potter, J., Asthane, A., Simon, T., . . .

Fletcher, M. (1998). Stressful events, pessimism, natural killer cell cytotoxicity, and cytotoxic/suppressor T cells in HIV+ black women at risk for cervical cancer. *Psychosomatic Medicine, 60*, 714–722.

Caffrey, C., Sengupta, M., Moss, A., Harris-Kojetin, L., & Valverde, R. (2011). Home health care and discharged hospice care patients: United States, 2000 and 2007. *National Health Statistics Reports, 38*, 1–2.

Calle, E. E., Miracle-McMahill, H. L., Thun, M. J., & Health, C. W. (1994). Cigarette smoking and risk of fatal breast cancer. *American Journal of Epidemiology, 139*, 1001–1007.

Camacho, T. C., Roberts, R. E., Lazarus, N. B., Kaplan, G. A., & Cohen, R. D. (1991). Physical activity and depression: Evidence from the Alameda County study. *American Journal of Epidemiology, 134*, 220–231.

Cameron, C. L., Cella, D., Herndon, J. E., III, Kornblith, A. B., Zuckerman, E., Henderson, E., . . . Holland, J. C. (2001). Persistent symptoms among survivors of Hodgkin's disease: An explanatory model based on classical conditioning. *Health Psychology, 20*, 71–75.

Cameron, L., Leventhal, E. A., & Leventhal, H. (1995). Seeking medical care in response to symptoms and life stress. *Psychosomatic Medicine, 57*, 37–47.

Campayo, A., de Jonge, P., Roy, J. F., Saz, P., de la Cámara, C., Quintanilla, M. A., . . . Lobo, A. (2010). Depressive disorder and incident diabetes mellitus: The effect of characteristics of depression. *American Journal of Psychiatry, 167*, 580–588.

Campbell, M., Carbone, E., Honess-Morreale, L., Heisler-Mackinnon, J., Demissie, S. L., & Farrell, D. (2004). Randomized trial of a tailored nutrition education CD-ROM program for women receiving food assistance. *Journal of Nutrition Education and Behavior, 36*, 58–66.

Campbell, M. K., DeVellis, B. M., Strecher, V. J., Ammerman, A. S., DeVellis, R. F., & Sandler, R. S. (1994). Improving dietary behavior: The effectiveness of tailored messages in primary care settings. *American Journal of Public Health, 84*, 783–787.

Campbell, R. S., & Pennebaker, J. W. (2003). The secret life of pronouns: Flexibility in writing style and physical health. *Psychological Science, 14*, 60–65.

Campsmith, M. L., Rhodes, P., Hall, H. I., & Green, G. (2008). HIV Prevalence Estimates—United States, 2006. *Morbidity and Mortality Weekly Report, 57*, 1073–1076.

Cannon, W. B. (1932). *The wisdom of the body.* New York, NY: Norton.

Carey, M. P., Braaten, L. S., Maisto, S. A., Gleason, J. R., Forsyth, A. D., Durant, L. E., & Jaworski, B. C. (2000). Using information, motivational enhancement, and skills training to reduce the risk of HIV infection for low-income urban women: A second randomized clinical trial. *Health Psychology, 19*, 3–11.

Carey, M. P., & Burish, T. G. (1988). Etiology and treatment of the psychological side effects associated with cancer chemotherapy: A critical review and discussion. *Psychological Bulletin, 104*, 307–325.

Carlson, C. R., & Hoyle, R. H. (1993). Efficacy of abbreviated muscle relaxation training: A quantitative review of behavior medicine research. *Journal of Consulting and Clinical Psychology, 61*, 1059–1067.

Carnaghi, A., Cadinu, M., Castelli, L., Kiesner, J., & Bragantini, C. (2007). The best way to tell you to use a condom: The interplay between message format and individuals' level of need for cognition. *AIDS-Care, 19*, 432–440.

Carney, M. A., Armeli, S., Tennen, H., Affleck, G., & O'Neil, T. P. (2000). Positive and negative daily events, perceived stress, and alcohol use: A diary study. *Journal of Consulting and Clinical Psychology, 68*, 788–798.

Carpenter, D. J., Gatchel, R. J., & Hasegawa, T. (1994). Effectiveness of a videotaped behavioral intervention for dental anxiety: The role of gender and need for information. *Behavioral Medicine, 20*, 123–132.

Carpentier, M. Y., Mullins, L. L., & Van Pelt, J. C. (2007). Psychological, academic, and work functioning in college students with childhood-onset asthma. *Journal of Asthma. 44*, 119–124.

Carroll, J., Smith. H., & Hillier, S. (2008). When will older patients follow doctors' recommendations? Interpersonal treatment, outcome favorability, and perceived age differences. *Journal of Applied Social Psychology, 38*, 1127–1146.

Carver, C. S., & Antoni, M. H. (2004). Finding benefit in breast cancer during the year after diagnosis predicts better adjustment 5 to 8 years after diagnosis. *Health Psychology, 26*, 595–598.

Carver, C. S., Coleman, A. E., & Glass, D. C. (1976). The coronary-prone behavior pattern and the suppression of fatigue on a treadmill test. *Journal of Personality and Social Psychology, 33*, 460–466.

Carver, C. S., & Gaines, J. G. (1987). Optimism, pessimism, and postpartum depression. *Cognitive Therapy and Research, 11*, 449–462.

Carver, C. S., Pozo, C., Harris, S. D., Noriega, V., Scheier, M. F., Robinson, D. S., ... Clark, K. S. (1993). How coping mediates the effect of optimism on distress: A study of women with early stage breast cancer. *Journal of Personality and Social Psychology, 65*, 375–390.

Carver, C. S., Pozo-Kaderman, C., Price, A. A., Noriega, V., Harris, S. D., Dehagopion, R. P., ... Moffatt, F. L., Jr. (1998). Concern about aspects of body image and adjustment to early stage breast cancer. *Psychosomatic Medicine, 60*, 168–174.

Carver, C. S., Scheier, M. F., & Weintraub, J. K. (1989). Assessing coping strategies: A theoretically based approach. *Journal of Personality and Social Psychology, 56*, 267–283.

Caspi, A., Begg, D., Dickson, N., Harrington, H., Langley, J., Moffitt, T. E., & Silva, P. A. (1997). Personality differences predict health-risk behaviors in young adulthood: Evidence from a longitudinal study. *Journal of Personality and Social Psychology, 73*, 1052–1063.

Cassileth, B. R., Lusk, E. J., Strouse, T. B., Miller, D. S., Brown, L. L., Cross, P. A., & Tenaglia, A. N. (1984). Psychosocial status in chronic illness: A comparative analysis of six diagnostic groups. *New England Journal of Medicine, 311*, 506–511.

Catania, J. A., Kegeles, S. M., & Coates, T. J. (1990). Towards an understanding of risk behavior: An AIDS reduction model (ARRM). *Health Education Quarterly, 17*, 53–72.

Catz, S. L., Kelly, J. A., Bogart, L. M., Benotsch, E. G., & McAuliffe, T. L. (2000). Patterns, correlates, and barriers to medication adherence among persons prescribed new treatments for HIV disease. *Health Psychology, 19*, 124–133.

Centers for Disease Control and Prevention. (2006). Epidemiology of HIV/AIDS-United States, 1981–2005. *Morbidity and Mortality Weekly Report, 55*, 589–592.

Centers for Disease Control and Prevention. (2009, April). FastStats: Health Insurance Coverage. Retrieved September 17, 2011 from http://www.cdc.gov/nchs/fastats/hinsure.htm.

Centers for Disease Control and Prevention. (2010). Vital Signs: Colorectal Cancer Screening Among Adults Aged 50–75 Years-United States, 2008. *Morbidity and Mortality Weekly Report, 59*, 1–5.

Centers for Disease Control and Prevention. (2010). Vital Signs: Breast Cancer Screening Among Women Aged 50–75 Years-United States, 2008. *Morbidity and Mortality Weekly Report, 59*, 6–9.

Centers for Disease Control and Prevention. (2010, June). NCHS Health E-Stat: Prevalence of Obesity Among Children and Adolescents: United States, Trends 1963-1965 Through 2007-2008. Retrieved September 14, 2011 from http://www.cdc.gov/nchs/data/hestat/obesity_child_07_08/obesity_child_07_08.htm.

Centers for Disease Control and Prevention. (2010, July). HIV in the United States. Retrieved September 17, 2011 from http://www.cdc.gov/hiv/resources/factsheets/us.htm.

Centers for Disease Control and Prevention. (2010, September). Vital Signs: Current Cigarette Smoking Among Adults Aged ≥18 Years-United States, 2009. *Morbidity and Mortality Weekly Report, 59*, 1135–1140. Retrieved September 10, 2011, from http://www.cdc.gov/mmwr/preview/mmwrhtml/mm5935a3.htm?s_cid=mm5935a3_w.

Centers for Disease Control and Prevention. (2010, September). Injury Prevention and Control—Data & Statistics: Ten Leading Causes of Death and Injury. Retrieved September 15, 2011 from http://www.cdc.gov/injury/wisqars/LeadingCauses.html.

Centers for Disease Control and Prevention. (2010, October). FastStats: Exercise or Physical Activity. Retrieved September 14, 2011 from http://www.cdc.gov/nchs/fastats/exercise.htm.

Centers for Disease Control and Prevention. (2010, December). CDC Features: Adults Having Five or More Alcoholic Beverages in 1 Day. Retrieved September 10, 1011 from http://www.cdc.gov/features/ds5drinks1day/.

Centers for Disease Control and Prevention. (2011). CDC Health Disparities and Inequalities Report-United States, 2011. *Morbidity and Mortality Weekly Report, 60* (Supplement).

Centers for Disease Control and Prevention. (2011, February). FastStats: Health Expenditures. Retrieved September 15, 2011 from http://www.cdc.gov/nchs/fastats/hexpense.htm.

Centers for Disesae Control and Prevention. (2011, February). FastStats: Hospital Utilization. Retrieved September 17, 2011 from http://www.cdc.gov/nchs/fastats/hospital.htm.

Centers for Disease Control and Prevention. (2011, May). FastStats: Life Expectancy. Retrieved September 14, 2011 from http://www.cdc.gov/nchs/fastats/lifexpec.htm.

Centers for Disease Control and Prevention. (2011, June). Injury Prevention and Control. Retrieved September 13, 2011 from http://www.cdc.gov/injury/overview/data.html.

Centers for Disease Control and Prevention. (2011, July). Lung cancer: Risk factors. Retrieved September 10, 2011 from http://www.cdc.gov/cancer/lung/basic_info/risk_factors.htm.

Centers for Disease Control and Prevention. (2011, August). Alcohol and public health. Retrieved September 10, 2011 from http://www.cdc.gov/alcohol/index.htm.

Centers for Disease Control and Prevention. (2011, August). CDC Features: Rates for New

Cancer Cases and Deaths by Race/Ethnicity and Sex. Retrieved September 17, 2011 from http://www.cdc.gov/Features/dsCancerDisparities/.

Centers for Disease Control and Prevention. (2011, September). FastStats: Leading Causes of Death. Retrieved September 14, 2011 from http://www.cdc.gov/nchs/fastats/lcod.htm.

Chaiken, S. (1987). The heuristic model of persuasion. In M. P. Zanna, J. M. Olson, & C. P. Herman (Eds.), *Social influence: The Ontario symposium* (Vol. 5, pp. 3–39). Hillsdale, NJ: Erlbaum.

Champion, V. L. (1994). Strategies to increase mammography utilization. *Medical Care, 32*, 118–129.

Chandra, A., Martino S. C., Collins, R. L., Elliott, M. N., Berry, S. H., Kanouse, D. E., & Miu, A. (2008). Does watching sex on television predict teen pregnancy? Findings from a national longitudinal survey of youth. *Pediatrics, 122*, 1047–1054.

Chantry, C. J., Howard, C. R., & Auinger, P. (2006). Full breastfeeding duration and associated decrease in respiratory tract infection in US children. *Pediatrics, 117*, 425–432.

Chapman, C. R., Casey, K. L., Dubner, R., Foley, K. M., Gracely, R. H., & Reading, A. E. (1985). Pain measurement: An overview. *Pain, 22*, 1–31.

Chapman, H. A., Hobfoll, S. E., & Ritter, C. (1997). Partners' stress underestimation lead to woman's distress: A study of pregnant inner-city women. *Journal of Personality and Social Psychology, 73*, 418–425.

Charles, C., Goldsmith, L. J., Chambers, L., & Haynes, R. B. (1996). Provider-patient communication among elderly and nonelderly patients in Canadian hospitals: A national survey. *Health Communication, 8*, 281–302.

Charles, S. T., Gatz, M., Kato, K., & Pedersen, N. L. (2008). Physical health 25 years later: The predictive ability of neuroticism. *Health Psychology, 27*, 369–378.

Charney, E., Goodman, H. C., McBride, M., Lyon, B., & Pratt, R. (1976). Childhood antecedents of adult obesity: Do chubby infants become obese adults? *New England Journal of Medicine, 295*, 6–9.

Chartier, K. G., Hesselbrock, M. N., & Hesselbrock, V. M. (2011). Alcohol problems in young adults transitioning from adolescence to adulthood: The association with race and gender. *Addictive Behaviors, 36*, 167–174.

Chassin, L., Presson, C. C., Rose, J. S., & Sherman, S. J. (1996). The natural history of cigarette smoking from adolescence to adulthood: Demographic predictors of continuity and change. *Health Psychology, 15*, 478–484.

Chassin, L., Presson, C. C., Seo, D., Sherman, S., Macy, J., Wirth, R., & Curran, P. (2008). Multiple trajectories of cigarette smoking and the intergenerational transmission of smoking: A multigenerational, longitudinal study of a Midwestern community sample. *Health Psychology, 27*, 819–827.

Chassin, L., Presson, C. C., Sherman, S. J., Corty, E., & Olshavsky, R. W. (1981). Self-images and cigarette smoking in adolescence. *Personality and Social Psychology Bulletin, 7*, 670–676.

Chassin, L., Presson, C. C., Todd, M., Rose, J. S., & Sherman, S. J. (1998). Maternal socialization of adolescent smoking: The intergenerational transmission of parenting and smoking. *Developmental Psychology, 34*, 1189–1201.

Chatters, L. M., & Taylor, R. J. (1993). Intergenerational support: The provision of assistance to parents by adult children. In J. S. Jackson, L. M. Chatters, & R. J. Taylor (Eds.), *Aging in Black America* (pp. 69–83). Newbury Park, CA: Sage.

Chaves, J. F. (1994). Recent advances in the application of hypnosis to pain management. *American Journal of Clinical Hypnosis, 37*, 117–129.

Chen, C. M., Yi, H., Williams, G. D., & Faden, V. B. (2009). Surveillance report #86, trends in underage drinking in the United States, 1991–2007. Bethesda, MD: National Institute on Alcohol Abuse and Alcoholism.

Chen, E., & Paterson, L. Q. (2006). Neighborhood, family, and subjective socioeconomic status: How do they relate to adolescent health? *Health Psychology, 25*, 704–714.

Chen, J., Rathore, S. S., Radford, M. J., Wang, Y., & Krumholz, H. M. (2001). Racial differences in the use of cardiac catheterization after acute myocardial infarction. *New England Journal of Medicine, 344*, 1443–1449.

Chen, K., & Kandel, D. B. (1995). The natural history of drug use from adolescence to the mid-thirties in a general population sample. *American Journal of Public Health, 85*, 41–47.

Chen, L. H., Warner, M., Fingerhut, L., & Makuc, D. (2009). Injury episodes and circumstances: National Health Interview Survey, 1997–2007. *Vital Health Statistics, 10*(241), 1–55.

Cheng, Y., Kawachi, I., Coakley, E. H., Schwartz, J., & Colditz, G. (2000). Association between psychosocial work characteristics and health functioning in American women: Prospective study. *British Medical Journal, 320*, 1432–1436.

Chesney, M., & Darbes, L. (1998). Social support and heart disease in women: Implications for intervention. In K. Orth-Gomer, M. Chesney, & N. K. Wenger (Eds.), *Women, stress, and heart disease* (pp. 165–182). Mahwah, NJ: Erlbaum.

Chesney, M. A., Eagleston, J. R., & Rosenman, R. H. (1980). The Type A structured interview: A behavioral assessment in the rough. *Journal of Behavioral Assessment, 2*, 252–272.

Chiaramonte, G. R. & Friend, R. (2006). Medical students' and residents' gender bias in the diagnosis, treatment, and interpretation of CHD symptoms. *Health Psychology, 25*, 255–266.

Ching, P. L. Y. H., Willett, W. C., Rimm, E. B., Colditz, G. A., Gortmaker, S. L., & Stampfer, M. J. (1996). Activity level and risk of overweight in male health professionals. *American Journal of Public Health, 86*, 25–30.

Chochinov, H. M., Wilson, K. G., Enns, M., Mowchun, N., Lander, S., Levitt, M., & Clinch, J. J. (1995). Desire for death in the terminally ill. *American Journal of Psychiatry, 152*, 1185–1191.

Christakis, N. A., & Allison, P. D. (2006). Mortality after the hospitalization of a spouse. *New England Journal of Medicine, 354*, 719–730.

Christakis, N. A., & Fowler, J. H. (2007). The spread of obesity in a large social network over 32 years. *New England Journal of Medicine, 357*, 370–379.

Christakis, N. A., & Iwashyna, T. J. (2003). The health impact on families of health care: A matched cohort study of hospice use by decedents and mortality outcomes in surviving, widowed spouses. *Social Science and Medicine, 57*, 465–475.

Christenfeld, N., Glynn, L. M., Phillips, D. P., & Shrira, I. (1999). Exposure to New York City as a risk factor for heart attack mortality. *Psychosomatic Medicine, 61*, 740–743.

Christensen, A. J. (2000). Patient-by-treatment context interaction in chronic disease: A conceptual framework for the study of patient adherence. *Psychosomatic Medicine, 62*, 435–443.

Christensen, A. J., & Ehlers, S. L. (2002). Psychological factors in end-stage renal disease: An emerging context for behavioral medicine research. *Journal of Consulting and Clinical Psychology, 70*, 712–724.

Christensen, A. J., & Johnson, J. A. (2002). Patient adherence with medical treatment regimens: An interactive approach. *Current Directions in Psychological Science, 11*, 94–97.

Christensen, A. J., Moran, P. J., & Wiebe, J. S. (1999). Assessment of irrational health beliefs: Relation to health practices and medical regimen adherence. *Health Psychology, 18*, 169–176.

Christensen, A. J., & Smith, T. W. (1995). Personality and patient adherence: Correlates of the five-factor model in renal dialysis. *Journal of Behavioral Medicine, 18*, 305–313.

Christensen, A. J., Smith, T. W., Turner, C. W., Holman, J. M., Jr., Gregory, M. C., & Rich, M. A. (1992). Family support, physical impairment, and adherence in hemodialysis: An investigation of main and buffering effects. *Journal of Behavioral Medicine, 15*, 313–326.

Christie, K. M., Meyerowitz, B.E., Giedzinska-Simons, A., Gross, M., & Agus, D.B. (2009). Predictors of affect following treatment decision-making for prostate cancer: Conversations, cognitive processing, and coping. *Psycho-Oncology, 18*, 508–514.

Christophersen, E. R. (1989). Injury control. *American Psychologist, 44*, 237–241.

Chrousos, G. P. (1998). Stressors, stress, and neuroendocrine intregration of the adaptive response. *Annals of the New York Academy of Sciences, 851*, 311–335.

Chrousos, G. P., & Gold, P. W. (1992). The concepts of stress and stress system disorders. Overview of physical and behavioral homeostasis. *Journal of the American Medical Association, 267*, 1244–1252.

Cicero, V., Lo Coco, G., Gullo, S., & Lo Verso, G. (2009). The role of attachment dimensions and perceived social support in predicting adjustment to cancer. *Psycho-Oncology, 18*, 1045–1052.

Cinciripini, P. M., Lapitsky, L., Seay, S., Wallfisch, A., Kitchens, K., & VanVunakis, H. (1995). The effects of smoking schedules on cessation outcome: Can we improve on common methods of gradual and abrupt nicotine withdrawal? *Journal of Consulting and Clinical Psychology, 63*, 388–399.

Clark, D. C., & Zeldow, P. B. (1988). Vicissitudes of depressed mood during four years of medical school. *Journal of the American Medical Association, 260*, 2521–2528.

Clark, R., Anderson, N. B., Clark, V. R., & Williams, D. R. (1999). Racism as a stressor for African Americans: A biopsychosocial model. *American Psychologist, 54*, 805–816.

Classen, C., Koopman, C., Angell, K., & Speigel, D. (1996). Coping styles associated with psychological adjustment to advanced breast cancer. *Health Psychology, 15*, 434–437.

Claus, E. B., Risch, N., & Thompson, W. D. (1993). Autosomal dominant inheritance of early onset breast cancer: Implications for risk prediction. *Cancer, 73*, 643–651.

Cleeland, C. S., Gonin, R., Hatfield, A. K., Edmonson, J. H., Blum, R. H., Stewart, J. A., & Pandya, K. J. (1994). Pain and its treatment in outpatients with metastatic cancer. *New England Journal of Medicine, 330*, 592–596.

Clemow, L., Costanza, M. E., Haddad, W. P., Luckmann, R., White, M. J., Klaus, D., & Stoddard, A. M. (2000). Underutilizers of mammography screening today: Characteristics of women planning, undecided about, and not planning a mammogram. *Annals of Behavioral Medicine, 22*, 80–88.

Cloninger, C. R. (1991). D2 dopamine receptor gene is associated but not linked with alcoholism. *Journal of the American Medical Association, 266*, 1833–1834.

Coates, T. (1990). Strategies for modifying sexual behavior for primary and secondary prevention of HIV disease. *Journal of Consulting and Clinical Psychology, 58*, 57–69.

Coates, T. J., Morin, S. F., & McKusick, L. (1987). Behavioral conseqences of AIDS antibody testing among gay men. *Journal of the American Medical Association, 258*, 1989.

Coates, T. J., Stall, R. D., Kegeles, S. M., Lo, B., Morin, S. F., & McKusick, L. (1988). AIDS antibody testing. Will it stop the AIDS epidemic? Will it help people infected with HIV? *American Psychologist, 43*, 859–864.

Cobb, L. A., Thomas, G. I., Dillard, D. H., Merendino, K. A., & Bruce, R. A. (1959). An evaluation of internal mammary artery ligation by double blind technique. *New England Journal of Medicine, 260*, 1115–1118.

Cochran, S. D., & Mays, V. M. (1993). Applying social psychological models to predicting HIV-related sexual risk behaviors among African Americans. *Journal of Black Psychology, 19*, 142–154.

Coe, C. L., Wiener, S. G., Rosenberg, L. T., & Levine, S. (1985). Endocrine and immune responses to separation and maternal loss in non-human primates. In M. Reite & T. Field (Eds.), *The Psychobiology of Attachment and Separation* (pp. 163–199). Orlando, FL: Academic Press.

Cogan, R., Cogan, D., Waltz, W., & McCue, M. (1987). Effects of laughter and relaxation on discomfort thresholds. *Journal of Behavioral Medicine, 10*, 139–144.

Cohen, L. (2002). Reducing infant immunization distress through distraction. *Health Psychology, 21*, 207–211.

Cohen, L., Blount, R. L., Cohen, R. J., Schaen, E. R., & Zaff, J. F. (1999). Comparative study of distraction versus topical anesthesia for pediatric pain management during immunizations. *Health Psychology, 18*, 591–598.

Cohen, L. H., McGowan, J., Fooskas, S., & Rose, S. (1984). Positive life events and social support and the relationship between life stress and psychological disorder. *American Journal of Community Psychology, 12*, 567–587.

Cohen, S. (1988). Psychosocial models of the role of social support in the etiology of physical disease. *Health Psychology, 7*, 269–297.

Cohen, S., Alper, C. M., Doyle, W. J., Adler, N., Treanor, J. J., & Turner, R. B. (2008). Objective and subjective socioeconomic status and susceptibility to the common cold. *Health Psychology, 27*, 268–274.

Cohen, S., Alper, C. M., Doyle, W. J., Treanor, J. J., & Turner, R. B. (2006). Positive emotional style predicts resistance to illness after experimental exposure to rhinovirus or influenza A virus. *Psychosomatic Medicine, 68*, 809–815.

Cohen, S., Doyle, W. J., Alper, C. M., Janicki-Deverts, D., & Turner, R. B. (2009). Sleep habits and susceptibility to the common cold. *Archives of Internal Medicine, 12*, 62–67.

Cohen, S., Doyle, W. J., Skoner, D. P., Fireman, P., Gwaltney, J., & Newsom, J. (1995). State and trait negative affect as predictors of objective and subjective symptoms of respiratory viral infections. *Journal of Personality and Social Psychology, 68*, 159–169.

Cohen, S., Doyle, W. J., Skoner, D. P., Rabin, B. S., & Gwaltney, J. M. (1997). Social ties and susceptibility to the common cold. *Journal of the American Medical Association, 277*, 1940–1944.

Cohen, S., Doyle, W. J., Turner, R. B., Alper, C. M., & Skoner, D. P. (2003). Sociability and susceptibility to the common cold. *Psychological Science, 14*, 389–395.

Cohen, S., Frank, E., Doyle, W. J., Skoner, D. P., Rabin, B. S., & Gwaltney, J. M., Jr. (1998). Types of stressors that increase susceptibility to the common cold in adults. *Health Psychology, 17*, 214–223.

Cohen, S., & Herbert, T. B. (1996). Health psychology: Psychological factors and physical disease from the perspective of human psychoneuroimmunology. *Annual Review of Psychology, 47*, 113–132.

Cohen, S., Janicki-Deverts, D., & Miller, G. E. (2007). Psychological stress and disease. *Journal of the American Medical Association, 298*, 1685–1687.

Cohen, S., Kamarck, T., & Mermelstein, R. (1983). A global measure of perceived stress. *Journal of Health and Social Behavior, 24*, 385–396.

Cohen, S., & Lemay, E. (2007). Why would social networks be linked to affect and health practices? *Health Psychology, 26*, 410–417.

Cohen, S., & Lichtenstein, E. (1990a). Partner behaviors that support quitting smoking. *Journal of Consulting and Clinical Psychology, 58*, 304–309.

Cohen, S., & Lichtenstein, E. (1990b). Perceived stress, quitting smoking, and smoking relapse. *Health Psychology, 9*, 466–478.

Cohen, S., Lichtenstein, E., Prochaska, J. O., Rossi, J., Gritz, E. R., Carr, C. R., . . . Ossip-Klein, D. (1989). Debunking myths about self-quitting: Evidence from 10 prospective studies of persons who attempt to quit smoking by themselves. *American Psychologist, 44,* 1355–1365.

Cohen, S., Mermelstein, R., Karmarck, T., & Hoberman, H. M. (1985). Measuring the functional components of social support. In I. G. Sarason & B. R. Sarason (Eds.), *Social support: Theory, research, and applications* (pp. 73–94). The Hague, Netherlands: Martinus Nijhoff.

Cohen, S., Sherrod, D. R., & Clark, M. S. (1986). Social skills and the stress-protective role of social support. *Journal of Personality and Social Psychology, 50,* 963–973.

Cohen, S., Tyrell, D. A. J., Russell, M. A. H., Jarvis, M. J., & Smith, A. P. (1993). Smoking, alcohol consumption, and susceptibility to the common cold. *American Journal of Public Health, 83,* 1277–1283.

Cohen, S., Tyrrell, D. A. J., & Smith, A. P. (1991). Psychological stress in humans and susceptibility to the common cold. *New England Journal of Medicine, 325,* 606–612.

Cohen, S., & Wills, T. A. (1985). Stress, social support, and the buffering hypothesis. *Psychological Bulletin, 98,* 310–357.

Colditz, G. A., Willett, W. C., Hunter, D. J., Stampfer, M. J., Manson, J. E., Hennekens, C. H., & Rosner, B. A. (1993). Family history, age, and risk of breast cancer: Prospective data from the Nurses' Health Study. *Journal of the American Medical Association, 270,* 338–343.

Cole, S. W., Kemeny, M. E., Taylor, S. E., Visscher, B. R., & Fahey, J. L. (1996). Accelerated course of human immunodeficiency virus infection in gay men who conceal their homosexual identity. *Psychosomatic Medicine, 58,* 219–231.

Colerick, E. J. (1985). Stamina in later life. *Social Science and Medicine, 21,* 997–1006.

Colletti, G., & Kopel, S. A. (1979). Maintaining behavior changes: An investigation of three maintenance strategies and the relationship of self-attribution to the long-term reduction of cigarette smoking. *Journal of Consulting and Clinical Psychology, 11,* 25–33.

Collins, B., Mackenzie, J., Stewart, A., Bielajew, C., & Verma, S. (2009). Cognitive effects of chemotherapy in post-menopausal breast cancer patients 1 year after treatment. *Psycho-Oncology, 18,* 134–143.

Collins, R. L., Kanouse, D. E., Gifford, A. L., Senterfitt, J. W., Schuster, M. A., McCaffrey, D. F., . . . Wenger, N. S. (2001). Changes in health-promoting behavior following diagnosis with HIV: Prevalence and correlates in a national probability sample. *Health Psychology, 20,* 351–360.

Collins, R., Ellickson, P., McCaffrey, D., & Hambarsoomians, K. (2007). Early adolescent exposure to alcohol advertising and its relationship to underage drinking. *Journal of Adolescent Health, 40,* 527–534.

Committee on Advancing Pain Research, Care, and Education. (2011). *Relieving pain in America: A blueprint for transforming prevention, care, education, and research.* Washington, DC: The National Academies Press.

Compas, B. E., Haaga, D. A., Keefe, F. J., Leitenberg, H., & Williams, D. A. (1998). Sampling of empirically supported psychological treatments from health psychology: Smoking, chronic pain, cancer, and bulimia nervosa. *Journal of Consulting and Clinical Psychology, 66,* 89–112.

Compas, B. E., Worsham, N. L., Epping-Jordan, J. E., Grant, K. E., Mireault, G., Howell, D. C., & Malcarne, V. L. (1994). When mom or dad has cancer: Markers of psychological distress in cancer patients, spouses, and children. *Health Psychology, 13,* 507–515.

Comuzzie, A. G., & Allison, D. B. (1998). The search for human obesity genes. *Science, 280,* 1374–1377.

Connell, C. M., & D'Augelli, A. R. (1990). The contribution of personality characteristics to the relationship between social support and perceived physical health. *Health Psychology, 9,* 192–207.

Conner, M., & Higgins, A.R. (2010). Long-term effects of implementation intentions on prevention of smoking uptake among adolescents: A cluster randomized controlled trial. *Health Psychology, 29,* 529–538.

Conti, G., & Heckman, J.J. (2010). Understanding the early origins of the education–health gradient: A framework that can also be applied to analyze gene–environment interactions. *Perspectives on Psychological Science, 5,* 585–605.

Contrada, R. (1989). Type A behavior, personality hardiness, and cardiovascular responses to stress. *Journal of Personality and Social Psychology, 57,* 895–903.

Contrada, R. J., Goyal, T. M., Cather, C., Rafalson, L., Idler, E. L., & Krause, T. J. (2004). Psychosocial factors in outcomes of heart surgery: The impact of religious involvement and depressive symptoms. *Health Psychology, 23,* 227–238.

Contrada, R. J., Leventhal, E. A., & Anderson, J. R. (1994). Psychological preparation for surgery: Marshalling individual and social resources to optimize self-regulation. In S. Maes, H. Leventhal, & M. Johnston (Eds.), *International review of health psychology* (Vol. 3, pp. 219–266). New York, NY: Wiley.

Conway, T. L., Vickers, R. R., Ward, H. D., & Rahe, R. H. (1981). Occupational stress and variation in cigarette, coffee, and alcohol consumption. *Journal of Health and Social Behavior, 22,* 155–165.

Cook, W. W., & Medley, D. M. (1954). Proposed hostility and pharisaic-virtue scales for the MMPI. *Journal of Applied Psychology, 38,* 414–418.

Coon, K. A., Goldberg, J., Rogers, B. L., & Tucker, K. L. (2001). Relationships between use of television during meals and children's food consumption patterns. *Pediatrics, 107,* E7.

Cooper, M. L., Frone, M. R., Russell, M., & Mudar, P. (1995). Drinking to regulate positive and negative emotions: A motivational model of alcohol use. *Journal of Personality and Social Psychology, 69,* 960–1005.

Cooper, M. L., Russell, M., Skinner, J. B., Frone, M. R., & Mudar, P. (1992). Stress and alcohol use: Moderating effects of gender, coping, and alcohol expectancies. *Journal of Abnormal Psychology, 101,* 139–152.

Cooper Robbins, S. C., Bernard, D., McCaffery, K., Brotherton, J. M., & Skinner, S. R. (2010). "I just signed": Factors influencing decision-making for school-based HPV vaccination of adolescent girls. *Health Psychology, 29,* 618–625.

Cooperman, N. A., & Simoni, J. M. (2005). Suicidal ideation and attempted suicide among women living with HIV/AIDS. *Journal of Behavioral Medicine, 28,* 149–156.

Corbin, W. R., Iwamoto, D. K., & Fromme, K. (2011). A comprehensive longitudinal test of the acquired preparedness model for alcohol use and related problems. *Journal of Studies on Alcohol and Drugs, 72,* 602–610.

Cordova, M. J., Cunningham, L. L. C., Carlson, C. R., & Andrykowski, M. A. (2001). Post-traumatic growth following breast cancer: A controlled comparison study. *Health Psychology, 20,* 176–185.

Corr, C. A. (1992). A task-based approach to coping with dying. *Omega, 24,* 81–94.

Corso, P., Finkelstein, E., Miller, T., Fiebelkorn, I., & Zaloshnja, E. (2006). Incidence and lifetime costs of injuries in the United States. *Injury Prevention, 12,* 212–218.

Costa, P. T., Jr., & McCrae, R. R. (1980). Influence of extraversion and neuroticism on subjective well-being: Happy and unhappy people. *Journal of Personality and Social Psychology, 38,* 668–678.

Costa, P. T., Jr. & McCrae, R. R. (1985). Hypochondriasis, neuroticism, and aging. When are somatic complaints unfounded? *American Psychologist, 40,* 19–28.

Costa, P. T., Jr., & McCrae, R. R. (1987). Neuroticism, somatic complaints, and disease: Is the bark worse than the bite? *Journal of Personality, 55,* 299–316.

Costa, P. T., Jr., & McCrae, R. R. (1990). Personality: Another "hidden factor" in stress research. *Psychological Inquiry, 1,* 22–24.

Costa, P. T., Jr., & McCrae, R. R. (1992). Four ways five factors are basic. *Personality and Individual Differences, 13,* 653–665.

Costanzo, E. S., Ryff, C. D., & Singer, B. H. (2009). Psychosocial adjustment among cancer survivors: Findings from a national survey of health and well-being. *Journal of Health Psychology, 28,* 147–156.

Costello, D., Dierker, L. C., Jones, B. L., & Rose, J. S. (2008). Trajectories of smoking from adolescence to early adulthood and their psychosocial risk factors. *Health Psychology, 27,* 811–818.

Cotton, S., Puchalski, C.M., Sherman, S.N., Mrus, J.M., Peterman, A.H., Feinberg, J., ... Tsevat, J. (2006a). Spirituality and religion in patients with HIV/AIDS. *Journal of General Internal Medicine, 21,* S5–S13.

Cotton, S., Tsevat, J., Szaflarski, M., Kudel, I., Sherman, S.N., Feinberg, J., ... Holmes, W.C. (2006b). Changes in religiousness and spirituality attributed to HIV/AIDS: Are there sex and race differences? *Journal of General Internal Medicine, 21,* S14–S20.

Council, J. R., Ahern, D. K., Follick, M. J., & Kline, C. L. (1988). Expectancies and functional impairment in chronic low back pain. *Pain, 33,* 323–331.

Cox, D. S., Cox, A. D., Sturm, L., & Zimet, G. (2010). Behavioral interventions to increase HPV vaccination acceptability among mothers of young girls. *Health Psychology, 29,* 29–39.

Coyne, J. C., Rohrbaugh, M. J., Shoham, V., Sonnega, J. S., Nicklas, J. M., Cranford, J. A. (2001). Prognostic importance of marital quality for survival of congestive heart failure. *American Journal of Cardiology, 88,* 526–529.

Craig, K. D., Prkachin, K. M., & Grunau, R. V. E. (1992). The facial expression of pain. In D. C. Turk & R. Melzack (Eds.), *Handbook of pain assessment* (pp. 257–276). New York, NY: Guilford Press.

Cram, P., Fendrick, A. M., Inadomi, J., Cowen, M. E., Carpenter, D., & Vijan, S. (2003). The impact of a celebrity promotional campaign on the use of colon cancer screening: The Katie Curic effect. *Archives of Internal Medicine, 163,* 1601–1605.

Cramer, J. A., Mattson, R. H., Prevey, M. L., Scheyer, R. D., & Ouellette, V. L. (1989). How often is medication taken as prescribed? *Journal of the American Medical Association, 261,* 3273–3277.

Crandall, C. S. (1988). Social contagion of binge eating. *Journal of Personality and Social Psychology, 55,* 588–598.

Craun, A. M., & Deffenbacher, J. L. (1987). The effects of information, behavioral rehearsal, and prompting on breast self-exam. *Journal of Behavioral Medicine, 10,* 351–366.

Crawford, S. L., McGraw, S. A., Smith, K. W., McKinlay, J. B., & Pierson, J. E. (1994). Do Blacks and Whites differ in their use of health care for symptoms of coronary heart disease? *American Journal of Public Health, 84,* 957–964.

Crepaz, N., Passin, W. F., Herbst, J. H., Rama, S. M., Malow, R. M., Purcell, D. W., ... HIV/AIDS Prevention Research Synthesis Team. (2008). Meta-analysis of cognitive-behavioral interventions on HIV-positive persons' mental health and immune functioning. *Health Psychology, 27,* 4–14.

Creswell, J. D., Welch, W. T., Taylor, S. E., Sherman, D. K., Greunewald, T. L., & Mann, T. (2005). Affirmation of personal values buffers neuroendocrine and psychological stress responses. *Psychological Science, 16,* 846–851.

Crow, S. J., Peterson, C. B., Swanson, S. A., Raymond, N. C., Specker, S., Eckert, E. D., & Mitchell, J. E. (2009). Increased mortality in bulimia nervosa and other eating disorders. *The American Journal of Psychiatry, 166,* 1342–1346.

Croyle, R. T., & Hunt, J. R. (1991). Coping with health threat: Social influence processes in reactions to medical test results. *Journal of Personality and Social Psychology, 60,* 382–389.

Croyle, R. T., & Lerman, C. (1995). Psychological impact of genetic testing. In R. T. Croyle (Ed.), *Psychosocial effects of screening for disease prevention and detection* (pp. 11–38). New York, NY: Oxford University Press.

Croyle, R. T., Loftus, E. F., Barger, S. D., Sun, Y-C., Hart, M., & Getting, J. (2006). How well do people recall risk factor test results? Accuracy and bias among cholesterol screening participants. *Health Psychology, 25,* 425–432.

Croyle, R. T., Smith, K. R., Botkin, J. R., Baty, B., & Nash, J. (1997). Psychological responses to BRCA1 mutation testing: Preliminary findings. *Health Psychology, 16,* 63–72.

Croyle, R. T., Sun, Y., & Louie, D. H. (1993). Psychological minimization of cholesterol test results: Moderators of appraisal in college students and community residents. *Health Psychology, 12,* 503–507.

Cruess, D. G., Antoni, M. H., Schneiderman, N., Ironson, G., McCabe, P., Fernandez, J. B., ... Kumas, M. (2000). Cognitive-behavioral stress management increases free testosterone and decreases psychological distress in HIV seropositive men. *Health Psychology, 19,* 12–20.

Crum, A., & Langer, E. (2007). Mindset matters: Exercise as a placebo. *Psychological Science, 18,* 2.

Cui, J., Matsushima, E., Aso, K., Masuda, A., & Makita, K. (2009). Psychological features and coping styles in patients with chronic pain. *Psychiatry and Clinical Neurosciences, 63,* 147–152.

Cunningham, M. R., & Barbee, A. P. (2000). Social support. In C. Hendrick & S. S. Hendrick (Eds.), *Close relationships: A sourcebook* (pp. 273–285). Thousand Oaks, CA: Sage.

Curb, J. D., & Marcus, E. B. (1991). Body fat and obesity in Japanese Americans. *American Journal of Clinical Nutrition, 53,* 1552S–1555S.

Curran, P. J., Stice, E., & Chassin, L. (1997). The relation between adolescent alcohol use and peer alcohol use: A longitudinal random coefficients model. *Journal of Consulting and Clinical Psychology, 65,* 130–140.

Curry, S., Marlatt, G. A., & Gordon, J. R. (1987). Abstinence violation effect: Validation of an attributional construct with smoking cessation. *Journal of Consulting and Clinical Psychology, 55,* 145–149.

Curry, S. J., & McBride, C. M. (1994). Relapse prevention for smoking cessation: Review and evaluation of concept and interventions. *Annual Review of Public Health, 15,* 345–366.

Cusumano, D. L., & Thompson, J. K. (1997). Body image and body shape ideals in magazines: Exposure, awareness and internalization. *Sex Roles, 37,* 701–721.

Cutrona, C. E., & Russell, D. W. (1990). Type of social support and specific stress: Toward a theory of optimal matching. In B. R. Sarason, I. G. Sarason, & G. R. Pierce (Eds.), *Social support: An interactional view* (pp. 319–366). New York, NY: Wiley.

Dahlquist, L. M., McKenna, K. D., Jones, K. K., Dillinger, L., Weiss, K. E., & Ackerman, C.S. (2007). Active and passive distraction using a head-mounted display helmet: Effects on cold pressor pain in children. *Health Psychology, 26,* 794–801.

Dakof, G. A., & Taylor, S. E. (1990). Victims' perceptions of social support: What is helpful from whom? *Journal of Personality and Social Psychology, 58,* 80–89.

Dal Cin, S., MacDonald, T. K., Fong, G. T., Zanna, M. P., & Elton-Marshall, T. E. (2006). Remembering the message: Using a reminder cue to increase condom use following a safer sex intervention. *Health Psychology, 25,* 438–443.

Dalton, M. A., Sargent, J. D., Beach, M. L., Titus-Ernstoff, L., Gibson, J. J., Ahrens, M. B., ... Heatherton, T. F. (2003). Effect of viewing smoking in movies on adolescent smoking initiation: A cohort study. *Lancet, 362,* 281–285.

Dalton, P. (1999). Cognitive influences on health symptoms from acute chemical exposure. *Health Psychology, 18*, 579–590.

Daly, M., & MacLachlan, M. (2011). Heredity links natural hazards and human health: Apolipoprotein E gene moderates self-rated health in earthquake survivors. *Health Psychology, 30*, 228–235.

D'Amico, E. J., & Fromme, K. (1997). Health risk behaviors of adolescent and young adult siblings. *Health Psychology, 16*, 426–432.

Danhauer, S. C., Crawford, S. L., Farmer, D. F., & Avis, N. E. (2009). A longitudinal investigation of coping strategies and quality of life among younger women with breast cancer. *Journal of Behavioral Medicine, 32*, 371–379.

Dannenberg, A. L., Gielen, A. C., Beilenson, P. L., Wilson, D. H., & Joffe, A. (1993). Bicycle helmet laws and educational campaigns: An evaluation of strategies to increase children's helmet use. *American Journal of Public Health, 83*, 667–674.

Danner, D. D., Snowden, D. A., & Friesen, W. V. (2001). Positive emotions in early life and longevity: Findings from the nun study. *Journal of Personality and Social Psychology, 80*, 804–813.

Darbes, L. A., & Lewis, M. A. (2005). HIV-specific social support predicts HIV risk behavior in gay male couples. *Health Psychology, 24*, 617–622.

Dare, C., & Eisler, I. (1995). Family therapy and eating disorders. In K. D. Brownell & C. G. Fairburn (Eds.), *Eating disorders and obesity: A comprehensive handbook* (pp. 318–323). New York, NY: Guilford Press.

Darkes, J., & Goldman, M. S. (1993). Expectancy challenge and drinking reduction: Experimental evidence for a mediational process. *Journal of Consulting and Clinical Psychology, 61*, 344–353.

Dattore, P. J., Shontz, F. C., & Coyne, L. (1980). Premorbid personality differentiation of cancer and non-cancer groups: A list of the hypotheses of cancer proneness. *Journal of Consulting and Clinical Psychology, 48*, 388–394.

Davidson, L. L., Durkin, M. S., Kuhn, L., O'Connor, P., Barlow, B., & Heagarty, M. C. (1994). The impact of the Safe Kids/Healthy Neighborhoods Injury Prevention Program in Harlem, 1988–1991. *American Journal of Public Health, 84*, 580–586.

Davidson, R. S. (1985). Behavioral medicine and alcoholism. In N. Schneiderman & J. T. Tapp (Eds.), *Behavioral medicine: The biopsychosocial approach* (pp. 379–404). Hillsdale, NJ: Erlbaum.

Davies, J. E., Gibson, T., & Tester, L. (1979). The value of exercises in the treatment of low back pain. *Rheumatology and Rehabilitation, 18*, 243–247.

Davis, C.G., Nolen-Hoeksema, S., & Larson, J. (1998). Making sense of loss and growing from the experience: Two construals of meaning. *Journal of Personality and Social Psychology, 75*, 561–574.

Davis, D. L. (1991). *Empty cradle, broken heart: Surviving the death of your baby*. Golden, CO: Fulcrum.

Davis, M. C., & Swan, P. D. (1999). Association of negative and positive social ties with fibrinogen levels in young women. *Health Psychology, 18*, 121–139.

Davis, R. C., Smith, B. E., & Nickles, L. B. (1998). The deterrent effect of prosecuting domestic violence misdemeanors. *Crime and Delinquency, 44*, 434–443.

Dawson, D. A., Grant, B. F., & Harford, T. C. (1995). Variation in the association of alcohol consumption with five DSM-IV alcohol problem domains. *Alcoholism: Clinical and Experimental Research, 19*, 66–74.

de Bruin, M., Hospers, H. J., van Breukelen, G. J. P., Kok, G., Koevoets, W. M., & Prins, J. M. (2010). Electronic monitoring-based counseling to enhance adherence among HIV-infected patients: a randomized controlled trial. *Health Psychology, 29*, 421–428.

De Castro, J. M. (1994). Family and friends produce greater social facilitation of food intake than other companions. *Physiology & Behavior, 56*, 445–455.

De Castro, J. M., & De Castro, E. S. (1989). Spontaneous meal patterns of humans: Influence of the presence of other people. *American Journal of Clinical Nutrition, 50*, 237–247.

Decourcy, J. (2007, May 28). "I'm sorry" shouldn't be the hardest words. *Newsweek*.

DeGood, D. E. (2000). Relationship of pain-coping strategies to adjustment and functioning. In R. J. Gatchel & J. N. Weisberg (Eds.), *Personality characteristics of patients with pain* (pp. 129–164). Washington, DC: American Psychological Association.

Deimling, G. T., Bowman, K. F., Sterns, S., Wagner, L. J., & Kahana, B. (2006). Cancer-related health worries and psychological distress among older adult, long-term cancer survivors. *Psycho-Oncology, 15*, 306–320.

DeJong, W. (1980). The stigma of obesity: The consequences of naive assumptions concerning the causes of physical deviance. *Journal of Health and Social Behavior, 21*, 75–87.

Delahanty, D. L., & Baum, A. (2001). Stress and breast cancer. In A. Baum, T. A. Revenson, & J. E. Singer (Eds.), *Handbook of Health Psychology* (pp. 747–756). Mahwah, NJ: Erlbaum.

Delbanco, T. L. (1992). Enriching the doctor–patient relationship by inviting the patient's perspective. *Annals of Internal Medicine, 116*, 414–418.

DeLeon, P. H. (2002). Presidential reflections: Past and future. *American Psychologist, 57*, 425–430.

Delin, C. R., & Lee, T. H. (1992). Drinking and the brain: Current evidence. *Alcohol & Alcoholism, 27*, 117–126.

de Moor, J. S., de Moor, C. A., Basen-Engquist, K., Kudelka, A., Bevers, M. W., & Cohen, L. (2006). Optimism, distress, health-related quality of life, and change in cancer antigen 125 among patients with ovarian cancer undergoing chemotherapy. *Psychosomatic Medicine, 68*, 555–562.

Denissenko, M. E., Pao, A., Tang, M., & Pfeifer, G. P. (1996). Preferential formation of benzoapyrene adducts at lung cancer mutational hotspots in P53. *Science, 274*, 430–432.

Den Oudsten, B. L., Van Heck, G. L., Van der Steeg, A. F., Roukema, J. A., & De Vries, J. (2009). Predictors of depressive symptoms 12 months after surgical treatment of early-stage breast cancer. *Psycho-Oncology, 18*, 1230–1237.

Depner, C., & Ingersoll, B. (1982). Employment status and social support: The experience of mature women. In M. Szinovacz (Ed.), *Women's retirement: Policy implications of recent research* (pp. 61–76). Beverly Hills, CA: Sage.

Des Jarlais, D. C., Friedman, S. R., Casriel, C., & Kott, A. (1987). AIDS and preventing initiation into intravenous (IV) drug use. *Psychology and Health, 1*, 179–194.

Desmond, S. M., Price, J. H., Hallinan, C., & Smith, D. (1989). Black and White adolescents' perceptions of their ideal weight. *Journal of School Health, 59*, 353–358.

de Tommaso, M., Sardaro, M., & Livrea, P. (2008). Aesthetic value of paintings affects pain thresholds. *Consciousness and Cognition, 17*, 1152–1162.

Detweiler, J. B., Bedell, B. T., Salovey, P., Pronin, E., & Rothman, A. J. (1999). Message framing and sunscreen use: Gain-framed messages motivate beach-goers. *Health Psychology, 18*, 189–196.

de Vincenzi, I. (1994). A longitudinal study of human immunodeficiency virus transmission by heterosexual partners. *New England Journal of Medicine, 331*, 341–346.

Devine, E. C. (1992). Effects of psychoeducational care for adult surgical patients: A meta-analysis of 191 studies. *Patient Education and Counseling, 19*, 129–142.

Devins, G. M., & Binik, Y. M. (1996). Faciliating coping with chronic physical illness. In M. Zeidner & N. S. Endler (Eds.), *Handbook of coping: Theory, research, applications* (pp. 640–696). New York, NY: Wiley.

Devins, G. M., Mandin, H., Hons, R. B., Burgess, E. D., Klassen, J., Taub, K., . . . Buchle, S. (1990). Illness intrusiveness and quality of life in end-stage renal disease: Comparison and stability across treatment modalities. *Health Psychology, 9*, 117–142.

DeVries, A .C., Glasper, E. R. & Detillion, C. E. (2003). Social modulations of stress responses. *Hormones and Behavior, 79*, 399–407.

De Wit, J. B. F., Das, E., & Vet, R. (2008). What works best: Objective statistics or a personal testimonial? An assessment of the persuasive effects of different types of message evidence on risk perception. *Health Psychology, 27*, 110–115.

Deyo, R. A. (1991). Fads in the treatment of low back pain. *New England Journal of Medicine, 325*, 1039–1040.

Deyo, R. A., Walsh, N. E., & Martin, D. (1990). A controlled trial of transcutaneous electrical nerve stimulation (TENS) and exercise for chronic low back pain. *New England Journal of Medicine, 322*, 1627–1634.

Diamond, E. G., Kittle, C. F., & Crockett, J. F. (1960). Comparision of internal mammary artery ligation and sham operation for angina pectoris. *American Journal of Cardiology, 5*, 483–486.

DiClemente, C. C., Prochaska, J. O., Fairhurst, S. K., Velicer, W. F., Velasquez, M. M., & Rossi, J. S. (1991). The process of smoking cessation: An analysis of precontemplation, contemplation, and preparation stages of change. *Journal of Consulting and Clinical Psychology, 59*, 295–304.

Diefenbach, M. A., Miller, S. M., & Daly, M. B. (1999). Specific worry about breast cancer predicts mammography use in women at risk for breast and ovarian cancer. *Health Psychology, 18*, 532–536.

Diener, E. (2000). Subjective well-being: The science of happiness and a proposal for a national index. *American Psychologist, 55*, 34–43.

DiFranza, J. R., Savageau, J. A., Fletcher, K., O'Loughlin, J., Pbert, L., Ockene, J. K., .. Wellman R. J. (2007). Symptoms of tobacco dependence after brief intermittent use: The development and assessment of nicotine dependence in youth–2 study. *Archives of Pediatric and Adolescent Medicine, 161*, 704–710.

Dillard, A. J., Midboe, A. M., & Klein, W. M. (2009). The dark side of optimism: Unrealistic optimism about problems with alcohol predicts subsequent negative event experiences. *Personality and Social Psychology Bulletin, 35*, 1540–1550.

DiMatteo, M. R. (1994). Enhancing patient adherence to medical recommendations. *Journal of the American Medical Association, 271*, 79–83.

DiMatteo, M. R. (2004). Social support and patient adherence to medical treatment: A meta-analysis. *Health Psychology, 23*, 207–218

DiMatteo, M. R., Hays, R. D., Gritz, E. R., Bartoni, R., Crane, L., Elashoff, R., . . . Marcus, A. (1993). Patient adherence to cancer control regimens: Scale development and initial validation. *Psychological Assessment, 5*, 102–112.

Dimond, M. (1979). Social support and adaptation to chronic illness: The case of maintenance hemodialysis. *Research in Nursing and Health, 2*, 101–108.

Dinh, K. T., Sarason, I. G., Peterson, A. V., & Onstad, L. E. (1995). Children's perception of smokers and nonsmokers: A longitudinal study. *Health Psychology, 14*, 32–40.

DiNicola, D. D., & DeMatteo, M. R. (1984). Practitioners, patients, and compliance with medical regimens: A social psychological perspective. In A. Baum, S. E. Taylor, & J. E. Singer (Eds.), *Handbook of psychology and health: Vol. 4. Social psychological aspects of health* (pp. 55–84). Hillsdale, NJ: Erlbaum.

Ditto, P. H., Druley, J. A., Moore, K. A., Danks, H. J., & Smucker, W. D. (1996). Fates worse than death: The role of valued life activities in health-state evaluations. *Health Psychology, 15*, 332–343.

Ditto, P. H., & Hawkins, N. A. (2005). Cancer decision making near the end of life. *Health Psychology, 24*, S63–S70.

Dlin, B. (1985). Psychobiology and treatment of anniversary reactions. *Psychosomatics, 26*, 505–520.

Doering, S., Katzlberger, F., Rumpold, G., Roessler, S., Hofstoetter, B., Schatz, D. S., . . . Schuessler, G. (2000). Videotape preparation of patients before hip replacement surgery reduces stress. *Psychosomatic Medicine, 62*, 365–373.

Doka, K. J. (1993). *Living with life-threatening illness.* Lexington, MA: Lexington Books.

Downey, G., Silver, R. C., & Wortman, C. B. (1990). Reconsidering the attribution-adjustment relationship following a major negative event: Coping with the loss of a child. *Journal of Personality and Social Psychology, 59*, 925–940.

Dowson, D. I., Lewith, G. T., & Machin, C. (1985). The effects of acupuncture versus placebo in the treatment of headache. *Pain, 21*, 35–42.

Drach-Zahavy, A., & Somech, A. (2002). Coping with health problems: The distinctive relationships of hope sub-scales with constructive thinking and resource allocation. *Personality & Individual Differences, 33*, 103–117.

Dressler, W. (1985). Extended family relationships, social support, and mental health in a southern

Black community. *Journal of Health and Social Behavior, 26*, 39–48.

Drewnowski, A. (1996). The behavioral phenotype in human obesity. In E. D. Capaldi (Ed.), *Why we eat what we eat: The psychology of eating* (pp. 291–308). Washington, DC: American Psychological Association.

Druley, J. A., Stephens, M. A., & Coyne, J. C. (1997). Emotional and physical intimacy in coping with lupus: Women's dilemmas of disclosure and approach. *Health Psychology, 16*, 506–514.

Drummond, D. C., & Glautier, S. (1994). A controlled trial of cue exposure treatment in alcohol dependence. *Journal of Consulting and Clinical Psychology, 62*, 809–817.

Dubus, R. (1959). *The mirage of health.* New York, NY: Harper.

Dunbar-Jabob, J., Burke, L. E., & Puczynski, S. (1995). Clinical assessment and management of adherence to medical regimens. In P. M. Nicassio & T. M. Smith (Eds.), *Managing chronic illness: A biopsychosocial perspective* (pp. 313–349). Washington, DC: American Psychological Association.

Duncan, S. C., Duncan, T. E., & Strycker, L. A. (2005). Sources and types of social support in youth physical activity. *Health Psychology, 24*, 3–10.

Duncan, T. E., & McAuley, E. (1993). Social support and efficacy cognitions in exercise adherence: A latent growth curve analysis. *Journal of Behavioral Medicine, 16*, 199–218.

Dunkel-Schetter, C. (1984). Social support and cancer: Findings based on patient interviews and their implications. *Journal of Social Issues, 40*, 77–98.

Dunkel-Schetter, C., Feinstein, L. G., Taylor, S. E., & Falke, R. L. (1992). Patterns of coping with cancer. *Health Psychology, 11*, 79–87.

Dunkel-Schetter, C., & Wortman, C. (1982). The interpersonal dynamics of cancer: Problems in social relationships and their impact on the patient. In H. S. Friedman & M. R. DiMatteo (Eds.), *Interpersonal issues in health care* (pp. 69–100). New York, NY: Academic Press.

Dunn, A. L., Marcus, B. H., Kampert, J. B., Garcia, M. E., Kohl, H. W., III, & Blair, S. N. (1999). Comparison of lifestyle and structured interventions to increase physical activity and cardiorespiratory fitness. *Journal of the American Medical Association, 281*, 327–334.

Durbin, D. R., Chen, I., Smith, R., Elliott, M. R., & Winston, F. K. (2005). Effects of seating position and appropriate restraint use on the risk of injury to children in motor vehicle crashes. *Pediatrics, 115*, e305–309.

Durbin, D. R., Elliott, M. R., & Winston, F. (2003). Belt-positioning booster seats and reduction in risk of injury among children in vehicle crashes. *Journal of the American Medical Association, 289*, 2835–2840.

Durkheim, E. (1951). *Suicide*. New York, NY: Free Press.

Dusseldorp, E., van Elderen, T., Maes, S., Meulman, J., & Kraaij, V. (1999). A meta-analysis of psychoeducational programs for coronary heart disease patients. *Health Psychology, 18*, 506–519.

Eakin, E. G., Bull, S. S., Riley, K. M., Reeves, M. M., McLaughlin, P., & Gutierrez, S. (2007). Resources for health: A primary-care-based diet and physical activity intervention targeting urban Latinos with multiple chronic conditions. *Health Psychology, 26*, 392–400.

Eakin, E., Reeves, M., Winkler, E., Lawler, S., & Owen, N. (2010). Maintenance of physical activity and dietary change following a telephone-delivered intervention. *Health Psychology, 29*, 566–573.

Earl, A., & Albarracin, D. (2007). Nature, decay, and spiraling of the effects of fear-inducing arguments and HIV counseling and testing: A meta-analysis of the short and long-term outcomes of HIV-prevention interventions. *Health Psychology, 26*, 496–506.

Eckhardt, M. J., Harford, T. C., Kaelber, C. T., Parker, E. S., Rosenthal, L. S., Ryback, R. S., ... Warren, K. R. (1981). Health hazards associated with alcohol consumption. *Journal of the American Medical Association, 246*, 648–666.

Edelson, J., & Fitzpatrick, J. L. (1989). A comparison of cognitive-behavioral and hypnotic treatments of chronic pain. *Journal of Clinical Psychology, 45*, 316–323.

Edmondson, D., Park, C. L., Chaudoir, S. R., & Wortmann, J. (2008). Death without God: Religious struggle, death concerns, and depression in the terminally ill. *Psychological Science, 19*, 628–632.

Ehrenwald, J. (1976). *The history of psychotherapy: From healing magic to encounter*. New York, NY: Aronson.

Eifert, G. H., Hodson, S. E., Tracey, D. R., Seville, J. L., & Gunawardane, K. (1996). Heart-focused anxiety, illness beliefs, and behavioral impairment: Comparing healthy heart-anxious patients with cardiac and surgical inpatients. *Journal of Behavioral Medicine, 19*, 385–399.

Eisenberg, D. M., Kessler, R. C., Foster, C., Norlock, F. E., Calkins, D. R., & Delbanco, T. L. (1993). Unconventional medicine in the United States: Prevalence, costs, and patterns of use. *New England Journal of Medicine, 328*, 246–252.

Eisenberg, M. E., Olson, R. E., Neumark-Sztainer, D., Story, M., & Bearinger, L. H. (2004). Correlations between family meals and psychosocial well-being among adolescents. *Archives of Pediatrics and Adolescent Medicine, 158*, 792–796.

Eisenberg, N., & Lennon, R. (1983). Sex differences in empathy and related capacities. *Psychological Bulletin, 94*, 100–131.

Eiser, C. (1982). The effects of chronic illness on children and their families. In J. R. Eiser (Ed.), *Social psychology and behavioral medicine* (pp. 459–481). New York, NY: Wiley.

Elder, J. P. (2001). *Behavior change and public health in the developing world*. Thousand Oaks, CA: Sage.

Elfant, E., Burns, J. W. & Zeichner, A. (2008). Repressive coping style and suppression of pain-related thoughts: Effects on responses to acute pain induction. *Cognition & Emotion, 22*, 671–696.

Ellington, L., & Wiebe, D. J. (1999). Neuroticism, symptom presentation, and medical decision making. *Health Psychology, 18*, 634–643.

Else-Quest, N. M., LoConte, N. K., Schiller, J. H., & Hyde, J. S. (2009). Perceived stigma self-blame, and adjustment in lung, breast, and prostate cancer patients. *Psychology & Health, 24*, 949–964.

Elstein, A. S., Chapman, G. B., & Knight, S. J. (2005). Patients' values and clinical substituted judgments: The case of localized prostate cancer. *Health Psychology, 24*, S85–92.

Elwert, F., & Christakis, N. A. (2008). Variation in the effect of widowhood on mortality by the causes of death of both spouses. *American Journal of Public Health, 98*, 2092–2098.

Emlet, C. A. (2006). A comparison of HIV-stigma and disclosure patterns between older and younger adults living with HIV/AIDS. *AIDS Patient Care and STDs, 20*, 350–358.

Emmett, C., & Ferguson, E. (1999). Oral contraceptive pill use, decisional balance, risk perception and knowledge: An exploratory study. *Journal of Reproductive and Infant Psychology, 17*, 327–343.

Emmons, K. M., Wechsler, H., Dowdall, G., & Abraham, M. (1998). Predictors of smoking among U.S. college students. *American Journal of Public Health, 88*, 104–107.

Emmons, R. A. (2005). Striving for the sacred: Personal goals, life meaning, and religion. *Journal of Social Issues, 61*, 731–746.

Emrick, C. D., & Hansen, J. (1983). Assertions regarding effectiveness of treatment for alcoholism: Fact or fantasy? *American Psychologist, 38*, 1078–1088.

Endler, N. S., & Parker, J. D. A. (1990). Multidimensional assessment of coping: A critical evaluation. *Journal of Personality and Social Psychology, 58*, 844–854.

Eng, P. M., Rimm, E. B., Fitzmaurice, G., & Kawachi, I. (2002). Social ties and change in social ties in relation to subsequent total and cause-specific mortality and coronary heart disease incidence in men. *American Journal of Epidemiology, 155*, 700–709.

Engel, G. L. (1977). The need for a new medical model: A challenge for biomedicine. *Science, 196*, 129–136.

Engel, G. L. (1980). The clinical application of the biopsychosocial model. *American Journal of Psychiatry, 137*, 535–544.

Ennett, S. T., Tobler, N. S., Ringwalt, C. L., & Flewelling, R. L. (1994). How effective is drug resistance education? A meta-analysis of Project DARE outcome evaluations. *American Journal of Public Health, 84*, 1394–1401.

Enright, M. F., Resnick, R., DeLeon, P. H., Sciara, A. D., & Tanney, F. (1990). The practice of psychology in hospital settings. *American Psychologist, 45*, 1059–1065.

Epping-Jordan, J. E., Compas, B. E., Osowiecki, D. M., Oppedisano, G., Gerhardt, C., Prine, K., & Krag, D. N. (1999). Psychological adjustment in breast cancer: Processes of emotional distress. *Health Psychology, 18*, 315–326.

Epstein, A. M., Taylor, W. C., & Seage, G. R. (1985). Effects of patients' socioeconomic status and physicians' training and practice on patient–doctor communication. *American Journal of Medicine, 78*, 101–106.

Epstein, L. H., & Cluss, P. A. (1982). A behavioral medicine perspective on adherence to long-term medical regimens. *Journal of Consulting and Clinical Psychology, 50*, 950–971.

Epstein, L. H., Handley, E. A., Dearing, K. K., Cho, D. D., Roemmich, J. N., Paluch, ... Spring, B. (2006). Purchases of food in youth: Influence of price and income. *Psychological Science, 17*, 82–89.

Epstein, L. H., Paluch, R. A., Kilanowski, C. K., & Raynor, H. A. (2004). The effect of reinforcement or stimulus control to reduce sedentary behavior in the treatment of pediatric obesity. *Health Psychology, 23*, 371–380.

Epton, T., & Harris, P. R. (2008). Self-affirmation promotes health behavior change. *Health Psychology, 27*, 746–752.

Esterling, B. A., Kiecolt-Glaser, J. K., Bodnar, J. C., & Glaser, R. (1994). Chronic stress, social support, and persistent alterations in the natural killer cell response to cytokines in older adults. *Health Psychology, 13*, 291–298.

Esteve, R., Ramirez-Maestre, C., & Lopez-Martinez, A. E. (2007). Adjustment to chronic pain: The role of pain acceptance, coping strategies, and pain-related cognitions. *Annals of Behavioral Medicine, 33,* 179–188.

Evans, G. W., Bullinger, M., & Hygge, S. (1998). Chronic noise exposure and physiological response: A prospective study of children living under environmental stress. *Psychological Science, 9,* 75–77.

Evans, G. W., & Kim, P. (2007). Childhood poverty and health. *Psychological Science. 18,* 953–957.

Evans, G. W., & Kutcher, R. (2011). Loosening the link between childhood poverty and adolescent smoking and obesity: The protective effects of social capital. *Psychological Science, 22,* 3–7.

Evans, G. W., & Wener, R.E. (2006). Rail commuting duration and passenger stress. *Health Psychology, 25,* 408–412.

Evans, R. I. (1988). Health promotion—science or ideology? *Health Psychology, 7,* 203–219.

Evans, R. I., Rozelle, R. M., Lasater, T. M., Dembroski, T. M., & Allen, B. P. (1970). Fear arousal, persuasion, and actual versus implied behavior change: New perspective utilizing a real-life dental hygiene program. *Journal of Personality and Social Psychology, 16,* 220–227.

Evans, R. I., Rozelle, R. M., Maxwell, S. E., Raines, B. E., Dill, C. A., Guthrie, T. J., . . . Hill, P. C. (1981). Social modeling films to deter smoking in adolescents: Results of a three year field investigation. *Journal of Applied Psychology, 66,* 399–414.

Evans, W. D., Powers, A., Hersey, J., & Renaud, J. (2006). The influence of social environment and social image on adolescent smoking. *Health Psychology, 25,* 26–33.

Evers, C., Stok, F. M., & De Ridder, D. T. D. (2010). Feeding your feelings: Emotion regulation strategies and emotional eating. *Personality and Social Psychology Bulletin, 36,* 792–804.

Everson, S. A., Goldberg, D. E., Kaplan, G. A., & Cohen, R. D. (1996). Hopelessness and risk of mortality and incidence of myocardial infarction and cancer. *Psychosomatic Medicine, 58,* 103–121.

Ewart, C. K., Harris, W. L., Iwata, M. M., Coates, T. J., Bullock, R., & Simon, B. (1987). Feasibility and effectiveness of school-based relaxation in lowering blood pressure. *Health Psychology, 6,* 399–416.

Ewart, C. K., & Jorgensen, R.S. (2004). Agonistic interpersonal striving: Social-cognitive mechanism of cardiovascular risk in youth? *Health Psychology, 23,* 75–85.

Eysenck, H. J. (1967). *The biological basis of personality.* Springfield, IL: Thomas.

Eysenck, H. J. (1990). Biological dimensions of personality. In L. A. Pervin (Ed.), *Handbook of personality theory and research* (pp. 244–276). New York, NY: Guilford Press.

Faden, R. R., & Beauchamp, T. L. (1986). *A history and theory of informed consent.* New York, NY: Oxford University Press.

Faden, R. R., Becker, C., Lewis, C., Freeman, J., & Faden, A. I. (1981). Disclosure of information to patients in medical care. *Medical Care, 19,* 718–733.

Faden, R. R., & Kass, N. E. (1993). Genetic screening techonology: Ethical issues in access to tests by employers and health insurance companies. *Journal of Social Issues, 49,* 75–88.

Fagerlin, A., Ditto, P. H., Danks, J. H., Houts, R. M., & Smucker, W. D. (2001). Projection in surrogate decisions about life-sustaining medical treatment. *Health Psychology, 20,* 166–175.

Fallon, A. E., & Rozin, P. (1985). Sex differences in perception of desirable body shape. *Journal of Abnormal Psychology, 94,* 102–105.

Fang, C. Y., Manne, S. L., & Pape, S. J. (2001). Functional impairment, marital quality, and patient psychological distress as predictors of psychological distress among cancer patients' spouses. *Health Psychology, 20,* 452–457.

Farnsworth, E. (2007, June 1). Starvation of the spirit. *Newsweek.*

Farquhar, J. W., Fortmann, S. P., Flora, J. A., Taylor, C. B., Haskell, W. L., Williams, P. T., . . . Wood, P. D. (1990). Effects of community-wide education on cardiovascular disease risk factors: The Stanford Five-City Project. *Journal of the American Medical Association, 264,* 359–364.

Farrelly, M. C., Davis, K. C., Haviland, M. L., Messeri, P., & Healton, C. G. (2005). Evidence of a dose- response relationship between "truth" anti-smoking ads and youth smoking prevalence. *American Journal of Public Health, 95,* 425–431.

Fawzy, F. I., Cousins, N., Fawzy, N. W., Kemeny, M. E., Elashoff, R., & Morton, D. (1990). A structured psychiatric intervention for cancer patients: I. Changes over time in methods of coping and affective disturbance. *Archives of General Psychiatry, 47,* 720–725.

Feifel, H. (1990). Psychology and death: Meaningful rediscovery. *American Psychologist, 45,* 537–543.

Feldman, S. I., Downey, G., & Schaffer-Neitz, R. (1999). Pain, negative mood, and perceived support in chronic pain patients: A daily diary study of people with reflex sympathetic dystrophy syndrome. *Journal of Consulting and Clinical Psychology, 67,* 776–785.

Feletti, G., Firman, D., & Sanson-Fisher, R. (1986). Patient satisfaction with primary-care consultations. *Journal of Behavioral Medicine, 9,* 389–399.

Fell, J. C., Fisher, D. A., Voas, R. B., Blackman, K., & Tippetts, A. S. (2008). The relationship of underage drinking laws to reductions in drinking drivers in fatal crashes in the United States. *Accident Analysis & Prevention, 40,* 1430–1440.

Felson, D. T., Zhang, Y., Hannan, M. T., Kannel, W. B., & Kiel, D. P. (1995). Alcohol intake and bone mineral density in elderly men and women: The Framingham Study. *American Journal of Epidemiology, 142,* 485–492.

Felton, B. J., & Revenson, T. A. (1984). Coping with chronic illness: A study of illness controllability and the influence of coping strategies on psychological adjustment. *Journal of Consulting and Clinical Psychology, 52,* 343–353.

Ferguson, S. G., & Shiffman, S. (2010). Effect of high-dose nicotine patch on the characteristics of lapse episodes. *Health Psychology, 29,* 358–366.

Fernandez, E. (1986). A classification system of cognitive coping strategies for pain. *Pain, 26,* 141–151.

Fernandez, E., & Turk, D. C. (1992). Sensory and affective components of pain: Separation and synthesis. *Psychological Bulletin, 112,* 205–217.

Festinger, L. (1957). *A theory of cognitive dissonance.* Stanford, CA: Stanford University Press.

Feunkes, G. I. J., De Graaf, C., & Van Staveren, W. A. (1995). Social facilitation of food intake is mediated by meal duration. *Physiology and Behavior, 58,* 551–558.

Field, A. E., Camargo, C. A. Jr., Taylor, C. B., Berkey, C. S., Roberts, S. B., & Colditz, G. A (2001). Peer, parent, and media influences on the development of weight concerns and frequent dieting among preadolescent and adolescent girls and boys. *Pediatrics, 107,* 54–60.

Field, N. P., Nichols, C., Holen, A., & Horowitz, M. J. (1999). The relation of continuing attachment to adjustment in conjugal bereavement. *Journal of Consulting and Clinical Psychology, 67,* 212–218.

Field, T. M. (1998). Massage therapy effects. *American Psychologist, 53,* 1270–1281.

Fielding, J. E., & Phenow, K. J. (1988). Health effects of involuntary smoking. *New England Journal of Medicine, 319,* 1452–1460.

Figaro, M. K., Russo, P. W., & Allegrante, J. P. (2004). Preferences for arthritis care among urban African Americans: "I don't want to be cut". *Health Psychology, 23,* 324–329.

Finch, E. A., Linde, J. A., Jeffery, R. W., Rothman, A. J., King, C. M., & Levy, R. L. (2005). The effects of outcome expectations and satisfaction on weight loss and maintenance: Correlational and experimental analyses—a randomized trial. *Health Psychology, 24,* 608–616.

Fine, P. R., Rousculp, M. D., Tomasek, A. D., & Horn, W. S. (1999). Intentional injury. In J. M. Raczynski & R. J. DiClemente (Eds.), *Handbook of health promotion and disease prevention* (pp. 287–308). New York, NY: Plenum.

Fiore, M. C., Novotny, T. E., Pierce, J. P., Giovino, G. A., Hatziandreu, E. J., Newcomb, P. A., . . . Davis, R. M. (1990). Methods used to quit smoking in the United States: Do cessation programs help? *Journal of the American Medical Association, 263,* 2760–2765.

Fiscella, K., Franks, P., Gold, M. R., & Clancy, C. M. (2000). Inequality in quality: Addressing socioeconomic, racial, and ethnic disparities in health care. *Journal of the American Medical Association, 283,* 2579–2584.

Fishbein, M., & Ajzen, I. (1975). *Belief, attitude, intention, and behavior.* Reading, MA: Addison-Wesley.

Fishbein, M., & Middlestadt, S. E. (1989). Using the theory of reasoned action as a framework for understanding and changing AIDS-related behaviors. In V. M. Mays, G. W. Albee, & S. Schneider (Eds.), *Primary prevention of AIDS: Psychological approaches* (pp. 93–110). Newbury Park, CA: Sage.

Fisher, J. D., Fisher, W. A., Amico, R., & Harman, J. J. (2006). An information-motivation-behavioral skills model of adherence to antiretroviral therapy. *Health Psychology, 25,* 462–473.

Fisher, J. D., Fisher, W. A., Bryan, A. D., & Misovich, S. J. (2002). Information-motivation-behavioral skills model-based HIV risk behavior change intervention for inner-city high school youth. *Health Psychology, 21,* 177–186.

Fisher, J. D., Fisher, W. A., Misovich, S. J., Kimble, D. L., & Malloy, T. E. (1996). Changing AIDS risk behavior: Effects of an intervention emphasizing AIDS risk reduction information, motivation, and behavioral skills in a college student population. *Health Psychology, 15,* 114–123.

Fisher, J. O., & Birch, L. L. (1995). Fat preferences and fat consumption of 3- to 5-year-old children are related to parental adiposity. *Journal of the American Dietetic Association, 95,* 759–764.

Fisher, J. O., & Birch, L. L. (1999). Restricting access to palatable foods affects children's behavioral response, food selection, and intake. *American Journal of Clinical Nutrition, 69,* 1264–1272.

Fisher, W. A., Fisher, J. D., & Rye, B. J. (1995). Understanding and promoting AIDS-preventive behavior: Insights from the theory of reasoned action. *Health Psychology, 14,* 255–264.

Fishman, S., & Berger, L. (2000). *The war on pain: How breakthroughs in the new field of pain medicine are turning the tide against suffering.* New York, NY: HarperCollins.

Fitzgerald, T. E., Tennen, H., Affleck, G., & Pransky, G. S. (1993). The relative importance of dispositional optimism and control appraisals in quality of life after coronary artery bypass surgery. *Journal of Behavioral Medicine, 16,* 25–43.

Flack, J. M., Amaro, H., Jenkins, W., Kunitz, S., Levy, J., Mixon, M., & Yu, E. (1995). Epidemiology of minority health. *Health Psychology, 14,* 592–600.

Flaherty, J., & Richman, J. (1989). Gender differences in the perception and utilization of social support: Theoretical perspectives and an empirical test. *Social Science and Medicine, 28,* 1221–1228.

Flay, B. R. (1987). Social psychological approaches to smoking prevention: Review and recommendations. In W. B. Ward (Ed.), *Advances in health education and promotion* (Vol. 2, pp. 121–180). Greenwich, CT: JAI Press.

Flay, B. R., Koepke, D., Thomson, S. J., Santi, S., Best, A., & Brown, S. (1989). Six-year follow-up of the first Waterloo school smoking cessation trait. *American Journal of Public Health, 79,* 1371–1376.

Flegal, K. M., Carroll, M. D., Ogden, C. L., & Curtin, L. R. (2010). Prevalence and trends in obesity among US adults, 1999-2008. *Journal of the American Medical Association, 303,* 235–241.

Fleishman, J. A., & Fogel, B. (1994). Coping and depressive symptoms among people with AIDS. *Health Psychology, 13,* 156–169.

Fleming, R., Baum, A., Gisriel, M. M., & Gatchel, R. J. (1982). Mediating influences of social support on stress at Three Mile Island. *Journal of Human Stress, 8,* 14–22.

Fletcher, A. M. (2001). *Sober for good.* New York, NY: Houghton-Mifflin.

Flor, H., & Birbaumer, N. (1993). Comparison of the efficacy of electromyographic biofeedback, cognitive-behavioral therapy, and conservative medical interventions in the treatment of chronic musculoskeletal pain. *Journal of Consulting and Clinical Psychology, 61,* 653–658.

Flor, H., Elbert, T., Knecht, S., Wienbruch, C., Pantev, C., Birbaumer, N., . . . Taub, E. (1995). Phantom-limb pain as a perceptual correlate of cortical reorganization following arm amputation. *Nature, 375,* 482–484.

Flor, H., Fydrich, T., & Turk, D. C. (1992). Efficacy of multidisciplinary pain treatment centers: A meta-analytic review. *Pain, 49,* 221–230.

Flor, H., & Turk, C. D. (1988). Chronic back pain and rheumatoid arthritis: Predicting pain

and disability from cognitive variables. *Journal of Behavioral Medicine, 11,* 251–265.

Florian, V., Mikulincer, M., & Taubman, O. (1995). Does hardiness contribute to mental health during a stressful real-life situation? The roles of appraisal and coping. *Journal of Personality and Social Psychology, 68,* 687–695.

Flynn, B. S., Worden, J. K., Secker-Walker, R. H., Badger, G. J., Geller, B. M., & Costanza, M. C. (1992). Prevention of cigarette smoking through mass media intervention and school programs. *American Journal of Public Health, 82,* 827–834.

Foege, W. (1983). The national pattern of AIDS. In K. M. Cahill (Ed.), *The AIDS epidemic* (pp. 1–17). New York, NY: St. Martin's Press.

Folkman, S., Chesney, M. A., Collette, L., Boccellari, A., & Cooke, M. (1996). Post-bereavement depressive mood and its prebereavement predictors in HIV+ and HIV- gay men. *Journal of Personality and Social Psychology, 70,* 336–348.

Folkman, S., Chesney, M. A., Cooke, M., Boccellari, A., & Collette, L. (1994). Caregiver burden in HIV-positive and HIV-negative partners of men with AIDS. *Journal of Consulting and Clinical Psychology, 62,* 746–756.

Folkman, S., & Lazarus, R. S. (1980). An analysis of coping in a middle-aged community sample. *Journal of Health and Social Behavior, 21,* 219–239.

Folkman, S., & Lazarus, R. S. (1985). If it changes it must be a process: Study of emotion and coping during three stages of a college examination. *Journal of Personality and Social Psychology, 48,* 150–170.

Folkman, S., Lazarus, R. S., Dunkel-Schetter, C., DeLongis, A., & Gruen, R. J. (1986). Dynamics of a stressful encounter: Cognitive appraisal, coping, and encounter outcomes. *Journal of Personality and Social Psychology, 50,* 992–1003.

Folsom, A. R., Hughes, J. R., Buehler, J., Mittlemark, M. B., Jacobs, D. R., Jr., & Grimm, R. H., Jr. (1985). Do Type A men drink more frequently than Type B men? Findings in the Multiple Risk Factor Intervention Trial (MRFIT). *Journal of Behavioral Medicine, 8,* 227–236.

Folsom, A. R., Kaye, S. A., Sellers, T. A., Hong, C. P., Cerhan, J. D., Potter, J. D., & Prineas, R. J. (1993). Body fat distribution and 5-year risk of death in older women. *Journal of the American Medical Association, 269,* 483–487.

Forcier, K., Stroud, L.R., Papandonatos, G.D., Hitsman, B., Reiches, M., Krishnamoorthy, J., & Niaura, R. (2006). Links between physical fitness and cardiovascular reactivity and recovery to psychological stressors: A meta-analysis. *Health Psychology, 25,* 723–739.

Fordyce, W. E. (1988). Pain and suffering: A reappraisal. *American Psychologist, 43,* 276–283.

Fordyce, W. E., Brockway, J. A., Bergman, J. A., & Spengler, D. (1986). Acute back pain: A control-group comparison of behavioral vs. traditional management methods. *Journal of Behavioral Medicine, 9*, 127–140.

Forsythe, C. J., & Compas, B. E. (1987). Interaction of coping appraisals of stressful events and coping: Testing the goodness of fit hypothesis. *Cognitive Therapy and Research, 11*, 473–485.

Fraley, R. C., Waller, N. G., & Brennan, K. A. (2000). An item–response theory analysis of self–report measures of adult attachment. *Journal of Personality and Social Psychology, 78*, 350–365.

Francis, L. A., & Birch, L. L. (2005). Maternal influence on daughters' restrained eating behavior. *Health Psychology, 24*, 548–554.

Frank, A. J. M., Moll, J. M. H., & Hort, J. F. (1982). A comparison of three ways of measuring pain. *Rheumatology and Rehabilitation, 21*, 211–217.

Frank, R. G., Gluck, J. P., & Buckelew, S. P. (1990). Rehabilitation: Psychology's greatest opportunity. *American Psychologist, 45*, 757–761.

Frankenhaeuser, M. (1975). Sympathetic-adrenomedullary activity behavior and the psychosocial environment. In P. H. Venables & M. J. Christie (Eds.), *Research in psychophysiology* (pp. 71–94). New York, NY: Wiley.

Frankenhaeuser, M. (1978). Psychoneuroendocrine approaches to the study of emotion as related to stress and coping. *Nebraska Symposium on Motivation, 26*, 123–162.

Franklin, G. M., & Nelson, L. M. (1993). Chronic neurologic disorders. In R. C. Brownson, P. L., Remington, & J. R. Davis (Eds.), *Chronic disease epidemiology and control* (pp. 307–335). Washington, DC: American Public Health Association.

Franko, D.L., Mintz, L.B., Villapiano, M., Green, T.C., Mainelli, D., Folensbee, L., ... Budman, S.H. (2005). Food, mood, and attitude: Reducing risk for eating disorders in college women. *Health Psychology, 24*, 567–578.

Frasure-Smith, N., & Prince, R. (1989). Long-term follow-up of the Ischemic Heart Disease Life Stress Monitoring Program. *Psychosomatic Medicine, 51*, 485–513.

Fredrickson, B. L. (2001). The role of positive emotions in positive psychology: The broaden-and-build theory of positive emotions. *American Psychologist, 56*, 218–226.

Fredrickson, B., & Joiner, T. (2002). Positive emotions trigger upward spirals toward emotional well-being. *Psychological Science, 13*, 172–175.

Frederickson, B. L., Roberts, T.-A., Noll, S. M., Quinn, D. M., & Twenge, J. M. (1998). That swimsuit becomes you: Sex differences in objectification, restrained eating, and math performance. *Journal of Personality and Social Psychology, 75*, 269–284.

Freeman, M. A., Hennessy, E. V., & Marzullo, D. M. (2001). Defensive evaluation of anti-smoking messages among college-age smokers: The role of possible selves. *Health Psychology, 20*, 424–433.

Freidson, E. (1961). *Patients' views of medical practice.* New York, NY: Russell Sage.

Freimuth, V. S., Hammond, S. L., Edgar, T., & Monohan, J. L. (1990). Reaching those at risk: A content-analytic study of AIDS PSAs. *Communication Research, 17*, 775–791.

French, S. A., Perry, C. L., Leon, G. R., & Fulkerson, J. A. (1994). Weight concerns, dieting behavior and smoking initiation among adolescent: A prospective study. *American Journal of Public Health, 84*, 1818–1820.

Freud, S. (1963). *Dora: An analysis of a case of hysteria.* New York, NY: Macmillan.

Fried, L. P., Kronmal, R. A., Newman, A. B., Bild, D. E., Mittelmark, M. B., Polak, J. F., ... Gardin, J. M. (1998). Risk factors for 5-year mortality in older adults: The Cardiovascular Health Study. *Journal of the American Medical Association, 279*, 585–592.

Fried, T. R., Bradley, E. H., Towle, V. R., & Allore, H. (2002). Understanding the treatment preferences of seriously ill patients. *New England Journal of Medicine, 346*, 1061–1066.

Friedman, H. S., & Booth-Kewley, S. (1987a). The "disease-prone personality": A meta-analytic view of the construct. *American Psychologist, 42*, 539–555.

Friedman, H. S., & Booth-Kewley, S. (1987b). Personality, Type A behavior, and coronary heart disease: The role of emotional expression. *Journal of Personality and Social Psychology, 53*, 783–792.

Friedman, H. S., Hall, J. A., & Harris, M. J. (1985). Type A behavior, nonverbal expressive style, and health. *Journal of Personality and Social Psychology, 48*, 1299–1315.

Friedman, H. S., Tucker, J. S., Tomlinson-Keasey, C., Schwartz, J. E., Wingard, D. L., & Criqui, M. H. (1993). Does childhood personality predict longevity? *Journal of Personality and Social Psychology, 65*, 176–185.

Friedman, L. S., Hedeker, D., & Richter, E. D. (2009). Long-term effects of repealing the national maximum speed limit in the United States. *American Journal of Public Health, 99*, 1626–1631.

Friedman, M., & Rosenman, R. H. (1959). Association of specific overt pattern with blood and cardiovascular findings. *Journal of the American Medical Association, 169*, 1286–1296.

Friedman, M., & Rosenman, R. H. (1974). *Type A behavior and your heart.* New York, NY: Knopf.

Friedman, M., Thoresen, C. D., Gill, J. J., Ulme, D., Powell, L. H., Price, V. A., ... Dixon, T. (1986). Alteration of Type A behavior and its effects on cardiac recurrences in post myocardial infarction patients: Summary results of the recurrent coronary prevention project. *American Heart Journal, 112*, 653–665.

Friedman, M. A., & Brownell, K. D. (1995). Psychological correlates of obesity: Moving to the next research generation. *Psychological Bulletin, 117*, 3–20.

Friedman, R., Sobel, D., Myers, P., Caudill, M., & Benson, H. (1995). Behavioral medicine, clinical health psychology, and cost offset. *Health Psychology, 14*, 509–518.

Friedrich, M. J. (2000). More healthy people in the 21st century? *Journal of the American Medical Association, 283*, 37–38.

Fries, J. F. (1998). Reducing the need and demand for medical services. *Psychosomatic Medicine, 60*, 140–142.

Fries, J. F., Koop, C. E., Beadle, C. E., Cooper, T. P., England, M. J., Greaves, R. F., ... Wright, D. (1993). Reducing health care costs by reducing the need and demand for medical services. The Health Project Consortium. *New England Journal of Medicine, 329*, 321–325.

Fröhlich, C., Jacobi, F., & Wittchen, H. U. (2006). DSM-IV pain disorder in the general population: an exploration of the structure and threshold of medically unexplained pain symptoms. *European Archives of Psychiatry and Clinical Neuroscience, 256*, 187–196.

Frost, H., Lamb, S., Moffett, J., Fairbank, J., & Moser, J. (1998). A fitness programme for patients with chronic low-back pain: 2 year follow-up of a randomized controlled trial. *Pain, 75*, 273–279.

Fuchs, C. S., Stampfer, M. J., Colditz, C. A., Giovannucci, E. L., Manson, J. E., Kawachi, I., ... Rosner, B. (1995). Alcohol consumption and mortality among women. *New England Journal of Medicine, 332*, 1245–1250.

Fuchs, V. R., & Hahn, J. S. (1990). How does Canada do it? A comparison of expenditures for physicians' services in the United States and Canada. *New England Journal of Medicine, 323*, 884–890.

Fuemmeler, B. F. (2006). Psychosocial mediation of fruit and vegetable consumption in the body and soul effectiveness trial. *Health Psychology, 25*, 474–483.

Funk, S. C., & Houston, B. K. (1987). A critical analysis of the Hardiness scale's validity and utility. *Journal of Personality and Social Psychology, 53*, 572–578.

Gall, T. L., Guirguis-Younger, M., Charbonneau, C., & Florack, P. (2009). The trajectory of religious coping across time in response to the diagnosis of breast cancer, *Psycho-Oncology, 18,* 1165–1178.

Gall, T. L., Kristjansson, E., Charbonneau, C., & Florack, P. (2009). A longitudinal study on the role of spirituality in response to the diagnosis and treatment of breast cancer, *Journal of Behavioral Medicine, 32,* 174–186.

Gallagher, E. J., Viscoli, C. M., & Horwitz, R. I. (1993). The relationship of treatment adherence to the risk of death after myocardial infarction in women. *Journal of the American Medical Association, 270,* 742–743.

Gallagher, K. M., Updegraff, J. A., Rothman, A. J., & Sims, L. (2011). Perceived susceptibility to breast cancer moderates the effect of gain- and loss-framed messages on use of screening mammography. *Health Psychology, 30,* 145–152.

Gallant, J. E., & Block, D. S. (1998). Adherence to antiretroviral regimens in HIV-infected patients: Results of a survey among physicians and patients. *Journal of the International Association of Physicians in AIDS Care, 4,* 32–35.

Galligan, R. F., & Terry, D. J. (1993). Romantic ideals, fear of negative implications, and the practice of safe sex. *Journal of Applied Social Psychology, 23,* 1685–1711.

Gallo, L. C., de Los Monteros, K. E., Allison, M., Roux, A. D., Polak, J. F., Watson, K. E., & Morales, L. S. (2009). Do socioeconomic gradients in subclinical atherosclerosis vary according to acculturation level? Analyses of Mexican-Americans in the multi-ethnic study of atherosclerosis. *Psychosomatic Medicine, 71,* 756–762.

Gallo, L. C., & Matthews, K. A. (2003). Understanding the association between socioeconomic status and health: Do negative emotions play a role? *Psychological Bulletin, 129,* 10–51.

Gallup, G. G., & Suarez, S. D. (1985). Animal research versus the care and maintenance of pets: The names have been changed but the results remain the same. *American Psychologist, 45,* 1104–1111.

Gandubert, C., Carrière, I., Escot, C., Soulier, M., Hermès, A., Boulet, P., ... Chaudieu, I. (2009). Onset and relapse of psychiatric disorders following early breast cancer: A case-control study. *Psycho-Oncology, 18,* 1029–1037.

Ganzini, L., Goy, E. R., & Dobscha, S. K. (2009). Oregonians' reasons for requesting physician aid in dying. *Archives of Internal Medicine, 169,* 489–492.

Ganzini, L., Harvath, T. A., Jackson, A., Goy, E. R., Miller, L. L., & Delorit, M. (2002).

Experiences of Oregon nurses and social workers with hospice patients who requested assistance with suicide. *New England Journal of Medicine, 347,* 582–588.

Garfinkel, P. E., & Garner, D. M. (1984). Bulimia in anorexia nervosa. In R. C. Hawkins, W. J. Fremouw, & P. F. Clement (Eds.), *The binge-purge syndrome: Diagnosis, treatment and research* (pp. 27–46). New York, NY: Springer.

Garg, N., Wansink, B., & Inman, J. J. (2007). The influence of incidental affect on consumer's food intake. *Journal of Marketing, 71,* 194–206

Garner, D. M., & Garfinkel, P. E. (1980). Sociocultural factors in the development of anorexia nervosa. *Psychological Medicine, 10,* 647–656.

Garner, D. M., Garfinkel, P. E., & Bemis, K. M. (1982). A multidimensional psychotherapy for anorexia nervosa. *International Journal of Eating Disorders, 1,* 3–46.

Garner, D. M., Garfinkel, P. E., Schwartz, D., & Thompson, M. (1980). Cultural expectations of thinness in women. *Psychological Reports, 47,* 483–491.

Garner, D. M., Olmstead, M. A., & Polivy, J. (1983). Development and validation of a multidimensional eating disorder inventory for anorexia nervosa and bulimia. *International Journal of Eating Disorders, 2,* 12–34.

Garner, D. M., Rockert, W., Davis, R., Garner, M. V., Olmsted, M. P., & Eagle, M. (1993). A comparison between cognitive-behavioral and supportive-expressive therapy for bulimia nervosa. *American Journal of Psychiatry, 150,* 37–46.

Gatchel, R. J. (1980). Effectiveness of procedures for reducing dental fear: Group-administered desensitization and group education and discussion. *Journal of the American Dental Association, 101,* 634–637.

Gatchel, R. J. (1986). Impact of a video taped fear reduction program on people who avoid dental treatment. *Journal of the American Dental Association, 123,* 37–41.

Gaziano, J. M., Buring, J. E., Breslow, J. L., Gold-haber, S. Z., Rosner, B., Van-Denburgh, M., ... Hennekens, C. H. (1993). Moderate alcohol intake, increased levels of high-density lipoprotein and its subfractions, and decreased risk of myocardial infarction. *New England Journal of Medicine, 329,* 1829–1834.

Gedaly-Duff, V., & Ziebarth, D. (1994). Mothers' management of adenoid-tonsillectomy pain in 4- to 8-year-olds: A preliminary study. *Pain, 57,* 293–299.

Geers, A. L., Wellman, J. A., Helfer, S. G., Fowler, S. L., & France, C. R. (2008). Dispositional optimism and thoughts of well-being determine

sensitivity to an experimental pain task. *Annals of Behavioral Medicine, 36,* 304–313.

Gentry, W. D. (1984). Behavioral medicine: A new research paradigm. In W. D. Gentry (Ed.), *Handbook of behavioral medicine* (pp. 1–13). New York, NY: Guilford Press.

George, L. K., Ellison, C. G., & Larson, D. B. (2002). Explaining the relationships between religious involvement and health. *Psychological Inquiry, 13,* 190–200.

George, L. K., Larson, D. B., Koenig, H. G., & McCullough, M. E. (2000). Spirituality and health: What we know, what we need to know. *Journal of Social and Clinical Psychology, 19,* 102–116.

Gerin, W., Pieper, C., Levy, R., & Pickering, T. G. (1992). Social support in social interaction: A moderator of cardiovascular reactivity. *Psychosomatic Medicine, 54,* 324–336.

Geronimus, A. T., Bound, J., Waidmann, T. A., Hillemeier, M. M., & Burns, P. B. (1996). Excess mortality among Blacks and Whites in the United States. *New England Journal of Medicine, 335,* 1552–1558.

Gerrard, M., Gibbons, F. X., Benthin, A. C., & Hessling, R. M. (1996). A longitudinal study of the reciprocal nature of risk behaviors and cognitions in adolescents: What you do shapes what you think, and vice versa. *Health Psychology, 15,* 344–354.

Ghanbari, H., Dalloul, G., Hasan, R., Daccarett, M., Saba, S., David, S., & Machado, C. (2009). Effectiveness of implantable cardioverter-defibrillators for the primary prevention of sudden cardiac death in women with advanced heart failure: A meta-analysis of randomized controlled trials. *Archives of Internal Medicine, 69,* 1500–1506.

Gibbons F. X., Etcheverry, P.E., Stock, M.L., Gerrard, M., Weng, C.-Y., Kiviniemi, M., & Hara, R.E. (2010). Exploring the link between racial discrimination and substance use: What mediates? What buffers? *Journal of Personality and Social Psychology, 99,* 785–801.

Gibbons, F. X., Gerrard, M., Lane, D. J., Mahler, H. I., & Kulik, J. A. (2005). Using UV photography to reduce use of tanning booths: A test of cognitive mediation. *Health Psychology, 24,* 358–363.

Gidron, Y., Davidson, K., & Bata, I. (1999). The short-term effects of a hostility-reduction intervention on male coronary heart disease patients. *Health Psychology, 18,* 416–420.

Gil, K. M., Carson, J. W., Porter, L. S., Scipio, C., Bediako, S. M., & Orringer, E. (2004). Daily mood and stress predict pain, health care use, and work activity in African American adults with sickle cell disease. *Health Psychology, 23,* 267–274.

Gil, K. M., Carson, J. W., Sedway, J. A., Porter, L. S., Schaeffer, J. J. W., & Orringer, E. (2000). Follow-up of coping skills training in adults with sickle cell disease: Analysis of daily pain and coping practice diaries. *Health Psychology, 19,* 85–90.

Gil, K. M., Williams, D. A., Keefe, F. J., & Beckham, J. C. (1990). The relationship of negative thoughts to pain and psychological distress. *Behavior Therapy, 21,* 349–362.

Gil, K. M., Wilson, J. J., Edens, J. L., Webster, A. A., Abrams, M. A., Orringer, E., ...Janal, M. N (1996). Effects of cognitive coping skills training on coping strategies and experimental pain sensitivity in African American adults with sickle cell disease. *Health Psychology, 15,* 3–10.

Gilchrist, A. (1942). *Life of William Blake.* London, England: JM Dent.

Giles, L. C., Glonek, G. F. V., Luszcz, M. A., & Andrews, G. R. (2005). Effect of social networks on 10 year survival in very old Australians: The Australian longitudinal study of aging. *Journal of Epidemiology and Community Health, 59,* 574–579.

Gilligan, C. (1982). *In a different voice.* Cambridge, MA: Harvard University Press.

Ginis, K. A. M., Jung, M. E., & Gauvin, L. (2003). To see or not to see: Effects of exercising in mirrored environments on sedentary women's feeling states and self-efficacy. *Health Psychology, 22,* 354–361.

Ginsberg, R. J., Kris, M. G., & Armstrong, J. G. (1993). Cancer of the lung. In V. T. DeVita, Jr., S. Hellman, & S. A. Rosenberg (Eds.), *Cancer: Principles and practice of oncology* (pp. 673–758). Philadelphia, PA: Lippincott.

Gintner, G., Rectanus, E., Accord, K., & Parker, B. (1987). Parental history of hypertension and screening attendance: Effects of wellness appeal versus threat appeal. *Health Psychology, 6,* 431–444.

Glaser, B., & Strauss, A. (1965). *Awareness of dying.* Chicago, IL: Aldine.

Glaser, R., & Kiecolt-Glaser, J. K. (1994). *Handbook of stress and immunity.* San Diego, CA: Academic Press.

Glaser, R., Thorne, B. E., Tarr, K. L., Kiecolt-Glaser, J. K., & D'Ambrosio, S. M. (1985). Effects of stress on methyltransferase synthesis: An important DNA repair enzyme. *Health Psychology, 4,* 403–412.

Glasgow, R. E., Estabrooks, P. A., Marcus, A. C., Smith, T. L., Gaglio, B., Levinson, A. H., & Tong, S. (2008). Evaluating initial reach and robustness of a practical randomized trial of smoking reduction. *Health Psychology, 27,* 780–788.

Glenn, S. W., Parsons, O. A., & Stevens, L. (1989). Effects of alcohol abuse and familial alcoholism on physical health in men and women. *Health Psychology, 8,* 325–341.

Glinder, J. G., & Compas, B. E. (1999). Self-blame attributions in women with newly diagnosed breast cancer: A prospective study of psychological adjustment. *Health Psychology, 18,* 475–481.

Goel, M. S., McCarthy, E. P., Phillips, R. S., & Wee, C. C. (2004). Obesity among US immigrant subgroups by duration of residence. *Journal of the American Medical Association, 292,* 2860–2867.

Goffman, E. (1961). *Asylums.* Garden City, NY: Doubleday.

Goldman, M. S., Del Boca, F. K., & Darkes, J. (1999). Alcohol expectancy theory: The application of cognitive neuroscience. In K. E. Leonard & H. T. Blane (Eds.), *Psychological theories of drinking and alcoholism* (2nd ed., pp. 203–246). New York, NY: Guilford Press.

Goldner, E. M., & Birmingham, C. L. (1994). Anorexia nervosa: Methods of treatment. In L. Alexander-Mott & D. B. Lumsden (Eds.), *Understanding eating disorders: Anorexia nervosa, bulimia nervosa, and obesity* (pp. 135–157). Washington, DC: Taylor & Francis.

Goldring, A. B., Taylor, S. E., Kemeny, M. E., & Anton, P. A. (2002). Impact of health beliefs, quality of life, and the physician-patient relationship on the treatment intentions of inflammatory bowel disease patients. *Health Psychology, 21,* 219–228.

Goldstein, A. O., Sobel, R. A., & Newman, G. R. (1999). Tobacco and alcohol use in G-rated children's animated films. *Journal of the American Medical Association, 281,* 1131–1136.

Goldston, D. B., Molock, S. D., Whitbeck, L. B., Murakami, J. L., Zayas, L. H., & Hall, G. C. (2008). Cultural considerations in adolescent suicide prevention and psychosocial treatment. *American Psychologist, 63,* 14–31.

Goldzweig, G., Andritsch, E., Hubert, A., Walach, N., Perry, S., Brenner, B., & Baider, L. (2009). How relevant is marital status and gender variables in coping with colorectal cancer? A sample of middle-aged and older cancer survivors. *Psycho-Oncology, 18,* 866–874.

Gollwitzer, P. M. (1993). Goal achievement: The role of intentions. *European Review of Social Psychology, 4,* 141–185.

Gomel, M., Oldenburg, B., Lemon, J., Owen, N., & Westbrook, F. (1993). Pilot study of the effects of a workplace smoking ban on indices of smoking, cigarette craving, stress and other health behaviours. *Psychology and Health, 8,* 223–229.

Gonzalez, J. S., Penedo, F.J., Antoni, M.H., Durán, R. E., McPherson-Baker, S., Ironson, G., ...Schneiderman, N. (2004). Social support, positive states of mind, and HIV treatment adherence in men and women living with HIV/AIDS. *Health Psychology, 23,* 413–418.

Goodkin, K., Blaney, N. T., Feaster, D., Fletcher, M. A., Baun, M. K., Montero-Atienza, E., ...Eisdorfer, C. (1992). Active coping style is associated with natural killer cell cytotoxicity in asymptomatic HIV-1 seropositive homosexual men. *Journal of Psychosomatic Research, 36,* 635–650.

Goodwin, J. S., Hunt, W. C., Key, C. R., & Samet, J. M. (1987). The effect of marital status on stage, treatment, and survival of cancer patients. *Journal of the American Medical Association, 258,* 3125–3130.

Goodwin, P. J., Leszcz, M., Ennis, M., Koopmans, J., Vincent, L., Guther, H., ... Hunter, J. (2001). The effect of group psychosocial support on survival in metastatic breast cancer. *New England Journal of Medicine, 345,* 1719–1726.

Goodwin, R. D., & Eaton, W. W. (2005). Asthma, suicidal ideation, and suicide attempts: Findings from the Baltimore epidemiologic catchment area follow-up. *American Journal of Public Health, 95,* 717–772.

Gordon, C. M., & Carey, M. P. (1996). Alcohol's effects on requisites for sexual risk reduction in men: An initial experimental investigation. *Health Psychology, 15,* 56–60.

Gordon, C. M., Carey, M. P., & Carey, K. B. (1997). Effects of a drinking event on behavioral skills and condom attitudes in men: Implications for HIV risk from a controlled experiment. *Health Psychology, 16,* 490–495.

Gornick, M. E., Eggers, P. W., Reilly, T. W., Mentnech, R. M., Fitterman, L. K., Kucken, L. E., Vladeck, B. C. (1996). Effects of race and income on mortality and use of services among medicare beneficiaries. *New England Journal of Medicine, 335,* 791–799.

Gorsuch, R. L. (1995). Religious aspects of substance abuse and recovery. *Journal of Social Issues, 51,* 65–83.

Gortmaker, S. L., Must, A., Perrin, J. M., Sobol, A. M., & Dietz, W. H. (1993). Social and economic consequences of overweight in adolescence and young adulthood. *New England Journal of Medicine, 329,* 1008–1012.

Gould, J. B., Davey, B., & Stafford, R. (1989). Socioeconomic differences in rates of cesarean section. *New England Journal of Medicine, 321,* 233–239.

Goyal, M., Mehta, R. L., Schneiderman, L. J., & Sehgal, A. R. (2002). Economic and health consequences of selling a kidney in India. *Journal of the American Medical Association, 288*, 1589–1593.

Gracely, R. H., Dubner, R., Deeter, W. R., & Wolskee, P. J. (1985). Clinicians' expectations influence placebo analgesia. *Lancet, 1*, 43.

Grady, D. (2008, January 8). For cancer patients, empathy goes a long way. *New York Times.*

Grady, K. E., Lemkau, J. P., McVay, J. M., & Reisine, S. T. (1992). The importance of physician encouragement in breast cancer screening of older women. *Preventive Medicine, 21*, 766–780.

Graham, J. E., Lobel, M., Glass, P., & Lokshina, I. (2008). Effects of written anger expression in chronic pain patients: Making meaning from pain. *Journal of Behavioral Medicine, 31*, 201–212.

Graham, J. W., Marks, G., & Hansen, W. B. (1991). Social influence processes affecting adolescent substance use. *Journal of Applied Psychology, 76*, 291–298.

Gram, I. T., Lund, E., & Slenker, S. E. (1990). Quality of life following a false positive mammogram. *British Journal of Cancer, 62*, 1018–1022.

Gramling, S. E., Clawson, E. P., & McDonald, M. K. (1996). Perceptual and cognitive abnormality model of hypochondriasis: Amplification and physiological reactivity in women. *Psychosomatic Medicine, 58*, 423–431.

Grant, S. G. (2005). Qualitatively and quantitatively similar effects of active and passive maternal tobacco smoke exposure on *in utero* mutagenesis at the *HPRT* locus. *BMC Pediatrics, 5*, 20.

Greeley, J., & Oei, T. (1999). Alcohol and tension reduction. In K. E. Leonard & H. T. Blane (Eds.), *Psychological theories of drinking and alcoholism* (2nd ed., pp. 14–53). New York, NY: Guilford Press.

Greenberg, M. R., & Schneider, D. (1994). Violence in American cities: Young Black males is the answer, but what was the question? *Social Science and Medicine, 39*, 179–187.

Greendale, G. A., Barrett-Connor, E., Edelstein, S., Ingles, S., & Haile, R. (1995). Lifetime leisure exercise and osteoporosis: The Rancho Bernardo Study. *American Journal of Epidemiology, 141*, 951–959.

Greenfield, S., & Kaplan, S. H. (1985). Expanding patient involvment in care: Effects on patient outcomes. *Annals of Internal Medicine, 102*, 520–528.

Greenfield, S., Kaplan, S. H., Ware, J. E., Jr., Yano, E. M., & Frank, H. J. (1988). Patients' participation in medical care: Effects on blood sugar control and quality of life in diabetes. *Journal of General Internal Medicine, 3*, 448–457.

Greenspan, A. M., Kay, H. R., Berger, B. C., Greenberg, R. M., Greenspon, A. J., & Gaughan M. J. (1988). Incidence of unwarranted implementation of permanent cardiac pacemakers in a large medical population. *New England Journal of Medicine, 318*, 158–163.

Greer, S. (1991). Psychological response to cancer and survival. *Psychological Medicine, 21*, 43–49.

Gremore, T. M., Baucom, D. H., Porter, L. S., Kirby, J. S., Atkins, D. C., & Keefe, F. J. (2011). Stress buffering effects of daily spousal support on women's daily emotional and physical experiences in the context of breast cancer concerns. *Health Psychology, 30*, 20–30.

Griffin, D. W., & Harris, P. R. (2011). Calibrating the response to health warnings: Limiting both overreaction and underreaction with self-affirmation. *Psychological Science, 22*, 572–578.

Grilo, C. M., & Pogue-Geile, M. (1991). The nature of environmental influences in weight and obesity: A behavior genetic analysis. *Psychological Bulletin, 110*, 520–537.

Grilo, C. M., Shiffman, S., & Wing, R. R. (1989). Relapse crises and coping among dieters. *Journal of Consulting and Clinical Psychology, 57*, 488–495.

Grimby, A. (1993). Bereavement among elderly people: Grief reactions, post-bereavement hallucinations and quality of life. *Acta Psychiatrica Scandinavica, 87*, 72–80.

Grimley, D. M., Riley, G. E., Bellis, J. M., & Prochaska, J. O. (1993). Assessing the stages of change and decision-making for contraceptive use for the prevention of pregnancy, sexually transmitted diseases, and acquired immunodeficiency syndrome. *Health Education Quarterly, 20*, 455–470.

Grissett, N. I., & Norvell, N. K. (1992). Perceived social support, social skills, and quality of relationships in bulimic women. *Journal of Consulting and Clinical Psychology, 60*, 293–299.

Grob, G. N. (1983). Disease and environment in American history. In D. Mechanic (Ed.), *Handbook of health, health care, and the health professions* (pp. 3–22). New York, NY: Free Press.

Grodstein, F., Stampfer, M. J., Manson, J. E., Colditz, G. A., Willett, W. C., Rosner, B., . . . Hennekens, C. H. (1996). Postmenopausal estrogen and progestin use and the risk of cardiovascular disease. *New England Journal of Medicine, 335*, 453–461.

Gross, A. M., Stern, R. M., Levin, R. B., Dale, J., & Wojnilower, D. A. (1983). The effect of mother-child separation on the behavior of children experiencing a diagnostic procedure. *Journal of Consulting and Clinical Psychology, 51*, 783–785.

Grossi, G., Thomtén, J., Fandino-Losada, A., Soares, J. J. F., & Sundin, O. (2009). Does burnout predict changes in pain experiences among women living in Sweden? A longitudinal study. *Stress and Health, 25*, 297–311.

Gross, J. J., & Levenson, R. W. (1997). Hiding feelings: The acute effects of inhibiting negative and positive emotion. *Journal of Abnormal Psychology, 106*, 95–103.

Grossman, D. C., Krieger, J. W., Sugarman, J. R., & Forquera, R. A. (1994). Health status of urban American Indians and Alaska Natives: A population-based study. *Journal of the American Medical Association, 271*, 845–850.

Grube, J. W., & Wallack, L. (1994). Television beer advertising and drinking knowledge, beliefs, and intentions among schoolchildren. *American Journal of Public Health, 84*, 254–259.

Grunberg, N. E., Brown, K. J., & Klein, L. C. (1997). Tobacco smoking. In A. Baum, S. Newman, J. Weinman, R. West, & C. McManus (Eds.), *Cambridge handbook of psychology, health and medicine* (pp. 606–611). Cambridge, England: Cambridge University Press.

Grunberg, N. E., & Straub, R. O. (1992). The role of gender and taste class in the effects of stress on eating. *Health Psychology, 11*, 97–100.

Grunberg, N. E., Winders, S. E., & Wewers, M. E. (1991). Gender differences in tobacco use. *Health Psychology, 10*, 143–153.

Gureje, O., Von Korff, M., Simon, G. E., & Gater, R. (1998). Persistent pain and well-being: A World Health Organization study in primary care. *Journal of the American Medical Association, 280*, 147–151.

Guyll, M., Matthews, K. A., & Bromberger, J. T. (2001). Discrimination and unfair treatment: Relationship to cardiovascular reactivity among African American and European American women. *Health Psychology, 20*, 315–325.

Gwilyn, S., Howard, D. P. J., Davies, N., & Willett, K. (2005). Harry Potter casts a spell on accident prone children. *British Medical Journal, 331*, 1505–1506.

Hadlow, J., & Pitts, M. (1991). The understanding of common health terms by doctors, nurses, and patients. *Social Science and Medicine, 32*, 193–196.

Haffner, S. M. (1998). Epidemiology of type 2 diabetes: Risk factors. *Diabetes Care, 21*, C3–6.

Hagedoorn, M., Kuijer, R. G., Buunk, B. P., DeJong, G. M., Wobbes, T., & Sanderman, R. (2000). Marital satisfaction in patients with cancer: Does support from intimate partners benefit those who need it the most? *Health Psychology, 19*, 274–382.

Haglund Juhl, M. (1997, October 13). A tattoo in time. *Newsweek.*

Hall, H. I., Song, R., Rhodes, P., Prejean, J., An, Q., Lee, L M., …. Janssen, R. S. (2008). Estimation of HIV Incidence in the US. *Journal of the American Medical Association, 300,* 520–529.

Hall, J. A., & Dornan, M. C. (1988a). Meta-analysis of satisfaction with medical care: Description of research done in and analysis of overall satisafction levels. *Social Science and Medicine, 26,* 637–644.

Hall, J. A., & Dornan, M. C. (1988b). What patients like about their medical care and how often they are asked: A meta-analysis of the satisfaction literature. *Social Science and Medicine, 27,* 935–939.

Hall, J. A., Epstein, A. M., DeCiantis, M. L., & McNeil, B. J. (1993). Physicians' liking for their patients: More evidence for the role of affect in medical care. *Health Psychology, 12,* 140–146.

Hall, J. A., Irish, J. T., Roter, D. L., Ehrlich, C. M., & Miller, L. H. (1994). Gender in medical encounters: An analysis of physician and patient communication in a primary care setting. *Health Psychology, 13,* 384–392.

Hall, J. A., Roter, D. L., & Katz, N. R. (1988). Meta-analysis of correlates of provider behavior in medical encounters. *Medical Care, 26,* 657–675.

Halpern, C. T., Udry, J. R., Campbell, B., & Suchindran, C. (1999). Effects of body fat on weight concerns, dieting, and sexual activity: A longitudinal analysis of Black and White adolescent girls. *Developmental Psychology, 35,* 721–736.

Halpern, M. (1994). Effect of smoking characteristics on cognitive dissonance in current and former smokers. *Addictive Behaviors, 19,* 209–217.

Hammer, J. C., Fisher, J. D., Fitzgerald, J. F., & Fisher, W. A. (1996). When two heads aren't better than one: AIDS risk behavior in college-age couples. *Journal of Applied Social Psychology, 26,* 375–397.

Hampel, P., Rudolph, H., Stachow, R., Lab-Lentzsch, A., & Petermann, F. (2005). Coping among children and adolescents with chronic illness. *Anxiety, Stress, and Coping, 18,* 145–155.

Hampson, S. E., Goldberg, L. R., Vogt, T. M., & Dubanoski, J. P. (2006). Forty years on: Teachers' assessments of children's personality traits predict self-reported health behaviors and outcomes at midlife. *Health Psychology, 25,* 57–64.

Hampson, S. E., Tildesley, E., Andrews, J. A., Luyckx, K., & Mroczek, D. K. (2010). The relation of change in hostility and sociability during childhood to substance use in mid adolescence. *Journal of Research in Personality, 44,* 103–114.

Hanak, M., & Scott, A. (1993). *Spinal cord injury: An illustrated guide for health care professionals* (2nd ed.). New York, NY: Springer.

Hannerz, H., Albertsen, K., Nielsen, M.L., Tuchsen, F., & Burr, H. (2004). Occupational factors and 5-year weight change among men in a Danish national cohort. *Health Psychology, 23,* 283–288.

Hanoch, Y., Miron-Shatz, T., Cole, H., Himmelstein, M., & Federman, A.D. (2010). Choice, numeracy, and physicians-in-training performance: The case of Medicare Part D. *Health Psychology, 29,* 454–459.

Hansen, W. B., Raynor, A. E., & Wolkenstein, B. H. (1991). Perceived personal immunity to the consequences of drinking alcohol: The relationship between behavior and perception. *Journal of Behavioral Medicine, 14,* 205–224.

Hanson, M. D., & Chen, E. (2010). Daily stress, cortisol, and sleep: The moderating role of childhood psychosocial environments. *Health Psychology, 29,* 394–402.

Hare, J. (2003, September 7). My turn: Finally tough enough to give up the snuff. *Newsweek.*

Harrell, E. H., Kelly, K., & Stutts, W. A. (1996). Situational determinants of correlations between serum cortisol and self-reported stress measures. *Psychology: A Journal of Human Behavior, 33,* 22–25.

Harriger, J. A., Calogero, R. M., Witherington, D. C., & Smith J. E. (2010). Body size stereotyping and internalization of the thin-ideal in preschool-age girls. *Sex Roles, 63,* 609–620.

Harris, J. R. (1992). Breast cancer (first of three parts). *New England Journal of Medicine, 327,* 319–328.

Harris, P. R., Mayle, K., Mabbott, L., & Napper, L. (2007). Self-affirmation reduces smokers' defensiveness to graphic on-pack cigarette warning labels. *Health Psychology, 26,* 437–446.

Harris, P. R., & Napper, L. (2005). Self-affirmation and the biased processing of threatening health-risk information. *Personality and Social Psychology Bulletin, 31,* 1250–1263.

Hartmann, L. C., Schaid, D. J., Woods, J. E., Crotty, T. P., Myers, J. L., Arnold, P. G., … Jenkins, R. B. (1999). Efficacy of bilateral prophylactic mastectomy in women with a family history of breast cancer. *New England Journal of Medicine, 340,* 77–84.

Harvey, J. H., & Hansen, A. M. (2000). Loss and bereavement in close romantic relationships. In J. H. Harvey & A. M. Hansen (Eds.), *Close relationships* (pp. 359–370). Thousand Oaks, CA: Sage.

Hashim, S., & Van Itallie, T. (1965). Studies in normal and obese subjects with a monitored food dispensing device. *Annals of the New York Academy of Science, 131,* 654–661.

Hashish, I., Hai, H. K., Harvey, W., Feinmann, C., & Harris, M. (1988). Reduction of postoperative pain and swelling by ultrasound treatment: A placebo effect. *Pain, 33,* 303–311.

Haskard, K. B., Williams, S. L., DiMatteo, M. R., Rosenthal, R., White, M. K., & Goldstein, M. G. (2008). Physician and patient communication training in primary care: Effects on participation and satisfaction. *Health Psychology, 27,* 513–522.

Hatchett, L., Friend, R., Symister, P., & Wadhwa, N. (1997). Interpersonal expectations, social support, and adjustment to chronic illness. *Journal of Personality and Social Psychology, 73,* 560–573.

Haug, S., Meyer, C., Ulbricht, S., Gross, B., Rumpf, H.-J., & John, U. (2010). Need for cognition as a predictor and a moderator of outcome in a tailored letters smoking cessation intervention. *Health Psychology, 29,* 367–373.

Havik, O. E., & Maeland, J. G. (1988). Verbal denial and outcome in myocardial infarction patients. *Journal of Psychosomatic Research, 32,* 145–157.

Hayes, D.J., Greenlund, K.J., Denny, C.H., Croft, J..B., & Keenan, N.L. (2005). Racial/ethnic and socioeconomic disparities in multiple risk factors for heart disease and stroke-United States, 2003. *Morbidity and Mortality Weekly Report, 54,* 113–117.

Haynes, R. B., McKibbon, K. A., & Kanani, R. (1996). Systematic review of randomized trials of interventions to assist patients to follow prescriptions for medications. *Lancet, 348,* 383–386.

Hays, R. B., Turner, H., & Coates, T. J. (1992). Social support, AIDS-related symptoms, and depression among gay men. *Journal of Consulting and Clinical Psychology, 60,* 463–469.

Hays, R. D., Kravitz, R. L., Mazel, R. M., Sherbourne, C. D., DiMatteo, M. R., Rogers, W. H., & Greenfield, S. (1994). The impact of patient adherence on health outcomes for patients with chronic disease in the Medical Outcomes Study. *Journal of Behavioral Medicine, 17,* 347–360.

He, L. F. (1987). Involvement of endogenous opioid peptides in acupuncture analgesia. *Pain, 31,* 99–121.

Heath, A. C., & Madden, P. G. (1995). Genetic influences on smoking behavior. In J. R. Turner, L. R. Cardon, & J. K. Hewitt (Eds.), *Behavior genetic approaches in behavioral medicine* (pp. 37–48). New York, NY: Plenum.

Heath, A. C., & Martin, N. G. (1993). Genetic models for the natural history of smoking: Evidence for a genetic influence on smoking persistence. *Addictive Behaviors, 18,* 19–34.

Heatherton, T. F. & Sargent, J.D. (2009). Does watching smoking in movies promote teenage smoking? *Current Directions in Psychological Science, 18,* 63–67.

Heatherton, T. F., Striepe, M., & Wittenberg, L. (1998). Emotional distress and disinhibited eating: The role of stress. *Personality and Social Psychology Bulletin, 24*, 301–313.

Hebert, R., Zdaniuk, B., Schulz, R., & Scheier, M. F. (2009). Positive and negative religious coping and well-being in women with breast cancer. *Journal of Palliative Medicine, 12*, 537–545.

Heckman, B. D., Fisher, E. B., Mones, B., Merbaum, M., Ristvedt, S. & Bishop, C. (2004). Coping and anxiety in women recalled for additional diagnostic procedures following an abnormal screening mammogram. *Health Psychology, 23*, 1, 42–48.

Heckman, T. D., Kelly, J. A., & Somlai, A. M. (1998). Predictors of continued high-risk sexual behavior in a community sample of persons living with HIV/AIDS. *AIDS and Behavior, 2*, 127–135.

Heckman, T. G., Barcikowski, R., Ogles, B., Suhr, J., Carlson, B., Holroyd, K., & Garske, J. (2006). A telephone-delivered coping improvement group intervention for middle-aged and older adults living with HIV/AIDS. *Annals of Behavioral Medicine, 32*, 27–38.

Hediger, M. L., Overpeck, M. D., Kuczmarski, R. J., & Ruan, W. J. (2001). Association between infant breastfeeding and overweight in young children. *Journal of the American Medical Association, 285*, 2453–2460.

Hegel, M. T., Ayllon, T., Thiel, G., & Oulton, B. (1992). Improving adherence to fluid restrictions in male hemodialysis patients: A comparison of cognitive and behavioral approaches. *Health Psychology, 11*, 324–330.

Heinberg, L. J., & Thompson, J. K. (1995). Body image and televised images of thinness and attractiveness: A controlled laboratory experiment. *Journal of Social and Clinical Psychology, 14*, 325–338.

Heishman, S. J., Kozlowski, L. T., & Henningfield, J. E. (1997). Nicotine addiction: Implications for public health policy. *Journal of Social Issues, 53*, 13–33.

Helgeson, V. S. (1991). The effects of masculinity and social support on recovery from myocardial infarction. *Psychosomatic Medicine, 53*, 621–633.

Helgeson, V. S. (1992). Moderators of the relation between perceived control and adjustment to chronic illness. *Journal of Personality and Social Psychology, 63*, 652–666.

Helgeson, V. S., & Cohen, S. (1996). Social support and adjustment to cancer: Reconciling descriptive, correlational, and intervention research. *Health Psychology, 15*, 135–148.

Helgeson, V. S., Cohen, S., & Fritz, H. L. (1998). Social ties and cancer. In J. C. Holland (Ed.), *Psychooncology* (pp. 99–109). New York, NY: Oxford University Press.

Helgeson, V. S., Cohen, S., Schulz, R., & Yasko, J. (1999). Education and peer discussion group interventions and adjustment to breast cancer. *Archives of General Psychiatry, 56*, 340–347.

Helgeson, V. S., Cohen, S., Schulz, R., & Yasko, J. (2000). Group support interventions for women with breast cancer: Who benefits from what? *Health Psychology, 19*, 107–114.

Helgeson, V. S., Cohen, S., Schulz, R., & Yasko, J. (2001). Long-term effects of educational and peer discussion group interventions on adjustment to breast cancer. *Health Psychology, 20*, 387–392.

Helgeson, V. S., Lepore, S. J., & Eton, D. T. (2006). Who benefits: Moderators of the benefits of a psychoeducational intervention for men with prostate cancer. *Health Psychology, 25*, 348–354.

Helgeson, V. S., Snyder, P. R., & Seltman, H. (2004). Psychological and physical adjustment to breast cancer over 4 years: Identifying distinct trajectories of change. *Health Psychology, 23*, 3–15.

Helgeson, V. S., & Tomich, P. L. (2005). Surviving cancer: A comparison of 5-year disease-free breast cancer survivors with healthy women. *Psycho-Oncology, 14*, 307–317.

Hellsten, L-A., Nigg, C., Norman, G., Burbank, P., Braun, L., Breger, R., . . . Wang, T., (2008). Accumulation of behavioral validation evidence for physical activity stage of change. *Health Psychology, 27*, S43–S53.

Helmrich, S. P., Ragland, D. R., Leung, R. W., & Paffenbarger, R. S. (1991). Physical activity and reduced occurrence of non-insulin-dependent diabetes mellitus. *New England Journal of Medicine, 325*, 147–152.

Helms, J. M. (1987). Acupuncture for the management of primary dysmenorrhea. *Obstetrics and Gynecology, 69*, 51–56.

Helsing, K., & Szklo, M. (1981). Mortality after bereavement. *American Journal of Epidemiology, 114*, 41–52.

Hemenover, S. H. (2001). Self-reported processing bias and naturally occurring mood: Mediators between personality and stress appraisals. *Personality and Social Psychology Bulletin, 27*, 387–394.

Hemenover, S. H., & Dienstbier, R. A. (1996). Prediction of stress appraisals from mastery, extraversion, neuroticism, and general appraisal tendencies. *Motivation and Emotion, 20*, 299–318.

Henifin, M. S. (1993). New reproductive technologies: Equity and access to reproductive health care. *Journal of Social Issues, 49*, 62–74.

Henry, J. P. (1990). The arousal of emotions: Hormones, behavior, and health. *Advances, 6*, 59–62.

Henselmans, I., Helgeson, V. S., Seltman, H., de Vries, J., Sanderman, R., & Ranchor, A. V. (2010). Identification and prediction of distress trajectories in the first year after a breast cancer diagnosis. *Health Psychology, 29*, 160–168.

Herbst-Damm, K., & Kulik, J. (2005). Volunteer support, marital status, and the survival times of terminally ill patients. *Health Psychology, 24*, 225–229.

Herman, C. P., & Mack, D. (1975). Restrained and unrestrained eating. *Journal of Personality, 43*, 647–660.

Herman, C. P., & Polivy, J. (1984). A boundary model for the regulation of eating. In A. J. Stunkard & E. Stellar (Eds.), *Eating and its disorders* (pp. 141–156). New York, NY: Raven.

Hernandez-Reif, M., Field, T., Krasnegor, J., Theakston, T. (2001) Low back pain is reduced and range of motion increased after massage therapy. *International Journal of Neuroscience, 106*, 131–145.

Heron, M., & Tejada-Vera, B. (2009). Deaths: Leading causes for 2005. *National Vital Statistics Report, 5*, 1–97.

Hershey, J. C., Niederdeppe, J., Evans, W. D., Nonnemaker, J., Blahut, S., Holden, D., . . . Haviland, M. L. (2005). The theory of "truth": How counterindustry campaigns affect smoking behavior among teens. *Health Psychology, 24*, 22–31.

Hertel, A.W., Finch, E. A., Kelly, K. M., King, C., Lando, H., Linde, J. A., . . . Rothman, A. J. (2008). The impact of expectations and satisfaction on the initiation and maintenance of smoking cessation: An experimental test. *Health Psychology, 27*, S197–206.

Herzog, T. A. (2008). Analyzing the transtheoretical model using the framework of Weinstein, Rothman, and Sutton (1998): The example of smoking cessation. *Health Psychology, 27*, 548–556.

Herzog, T. A., Abrams, D. B., Emmons, K. M., Linnan, L. A., & Shadel, W. G. (1999). Do processes of change predict smoking stage movements? A prospective analysis of the transtheoretical model. *Health Psychology, 18*, 369–375.

Herzog, T. A., & Blagg, C. O. (2007). Are most precontemplators contemplating smoking cessation? Assessing the validity of the stages of change. *Health Psychology, 26*, 222–231.

Heuch, I., Kvale, G., Jacobsen, B. K., & Bjelke, E. (1983). Use of alcohol, tobacco and coffee, and risk of pancreatic cancer. *British Journal of Cancer, 48*, 637–643.

Hewitt, J. K. (1997). Behavior genetics and eating disorders. *Psychopharmacology, 33*, 355–358.

Hewitt, J. L., & Flett, G. L. (1996). Personality traits and the coping process. In M. Zeidner & N. S. Endler (Eds.), *Handbook of coping: theory, research, applications* (pp. 410–433). New York, NY: Wiley.

Hewitt, P. L., Flett, G. L., & Mosher, S. W. (1992). The Perceived Stress Scale: Factor structure and relation to depression symptoms in a psychiatric sample. *Journal of Psychopathology and Behavioral Assessment, 14*, 247–257.

Hibell, B., Guttormsson, U., Ahlstrom, S., Balakiereva, O., Bjarnason, T., et al. (2009). The 2007 ESPAD Report: Substance use among students in 35 European countries. Stockholm: The Swedish Council for Information on Alcohol and Other Drugs. Retrieved on September 10, 2011, from http://www.espad.org/espad-reports.

Higbee, K. L. (1969). Fifteen years of fear arousal: Research on threat appeals: 1953–1966. *Psychological Bulletin, 72*, 426–444.

Hilgard, E. R. (1975). The alleviation of pain by hypnosis. *Pain, 1*, 213–231.

Hilgard, E. R., & Hilgard, J. R. (1983). *Hypnosis in the relief of pain*. Los Altos, CA: Kaufman.

Hill, J., & Peters, J. (1998). Environmental contributions to the obesity epidemic. *Science, 280*, 1371–1374.

Hill-Briggs, F., Gary, T. L., Bone, L. R., Hill, M. N., Levine, D. M., & Brancati, F. L. (2005). Medication adherence and diabetes control in urban African Americans with type 2 diabetes. *Health Psychology, 24*, 349–357.

Hines, D., Saris, R. N., & Throckmorton-Belzer, L. (2002). Pluralistic ignorance and health risk behaviors: Do college students misperceive social approval for risky behaviors on campus and in media? *Journal of Applied Social Psychology, 32*, 1–21.

Hinnen, C., Ranchor, A. V., Baas, P. C., Sanderman, R., & Hagedoorn, M. (2009). Partner support and distress in women with breast cancer: The role of patients' awareness of support and mastery. *Psychology and Health, 4*, 439–455.

Hinton, J. (1979). Comparison of places and policies for terminal care. *Lancet, 1*, 29–32.

Hirai, K., Arai, H., Tokoro, A., & Naka, N. (2009). Self-efficacy, psychological adjustment and decisional-balance regarding decision making for outpatient chemotherapy in Japanese advanced lung cancer. *Psychology and Health, 24*, 149–160.

Ho, D. D. (1995). Time to hit HIV, early and hard. *New England Journal of Medicine, 333*, 450–451.

Ho, D. D. (1996). Therapy of HIV infections: Problems and prospects. *Bulletin of the New York Academy of Medicine, 73*, 37–45.

Hobfoll, S. E., Jackson, A. P., Lavin, J., Britton, P. J., & Shepherd, J. B. (1994). Reducing inner-city women's AIDS risk activities: A study of single, pregnant women. *Health Psychology, 13*, 397–405.

Hodge, A. M., & Zimmet, P. Z. (1994). The epidemiology of obesity. In I. D. Caterson (Ed.), *Bailliere's clinical endocrinology and metabolism: International practice and research* (pp. 577–599). London, England: Bailliere Tindall.

Hodgins, D. C., El-Guebaly, N., & Armstrong, S. (1995). Propsective and retrospective reports of mood states before relapse to substance abuse. *Journal of Consulting and Clinical Psychology, 63*, 400–407.

Hoffman, C., Rice, D., & Sung, H.-Y. (1996). Persons with chronic conditions: Their prevalence and costs. *Journal of the American Medical Association, 276*, 1437–1479.

Holahan, C. J., Moos, R. H., Holahan, C. K., & Brennan, P. L. (1997). Social context, coping strategies, and depressive symptoms: An expanded model with cardiac patients. *Journal of Personality and Social Psychology, 72*, 918–928.

Holderness, C. C., Brooks-Gunn, J., & Warren, M. P. (1994). Co-morbidity of eating disorders and substance abuse: Review of the literature. *International Journal of Eating Disorders, 16*, 1–34.

Hollands, G. J., Prestwich, A., & Marteau, T. M. (2001). Using aversive images to enhance healthy food choices and implicit attitudes: An experimental test of evaluative conditioning. *Health Psychology, 30*, 195–203.

Hollis, J. F., Gullion, C. M., Stevens, V. J., Brantley, P. J., Appel, L. J., Ard, J. D., . . . Weight Loss Trail Reearch Group. (2008). Weight loss during the intensive intervention phase of the weight-loss maintenance trial. *American Journal of Preventive Medicine, 35*, 118–126.

Holman, E. A., Silver, R. C., Poulin, M., Andersen, J., Gil-Rivas, V., & McIntosh, D. N. (2008). Terrorism, acute stress, and cardiovascular health: A 3-year national study following the September 11th attacks. *Archives of General Psychiatry, 65*, 7–80.

Holm, J., Holroyd, K., Hursey, K., & Penzien, D. (1986). The role of stress in recurrent tension headache. *Headache, 26*, 160–167.

Holmes, T. H., & Masuda, M. (1974). Life change and illness susceptibility. In B. S. Dohrenwend & B. P. Dohrenwend (Eds.), *Stressful life events: Their nature and effects* (pp. 45–72). New York, NY: Wiley.

Holmes, T. H., & Rahe, R. H. (1967). The Social Readjustment Rating Scale. *Journal of Psychosomatic Research, 11*, 213–218.

Holroyd, K. A., & Lipchik, G. L. (1999). Psychological management of recurrent headache disorders: Progress and prospects. In R. J. Gatchel & D. C. Turk (Eds.), *Psychological factors in pain: Critical perspectives* (pp. 193–212). New York, NY: Guilford Press.

Holroyd, K. A., O'Donnell, F. J., Stensland, M., Lipchik, G. L., Cordingley, G. E., & Carlson, B. W. (2001). Management of chronic tension-type headache with tricyclic antidepressant medication, stress management therapy, and their combination: A randomized controlled trial. *Journal of the American Medical Association, 285*, 2208–2215.

Holt, C. L., Clark, E. M., Kreuter, M. W., & Scharff, D. P. (2000). Does locus of control moderate the effects of tailored health education materials? *Health Education Research, 15*, 393–403.

Holtgrave, D. R., & Kelly, J. A. (1996). Preventing HIV/AIDS among high risk urban women: The cost-effectiveness of a behavioral group intervention. *American Journal of Public Health, 86*, 1442–1445.

Honda, K., & Gorin, S. S. (2006). A model of stage of change to recommend colonoscopy among urban primary care physicians. *Health Psychology, 25*, 65–73.

Horgen, K. B., Choate, M., & Brownell, K. D. (2001). Television food advertising: Targeting children in a toxic environment. In D. G. Singer & J. L. Singer (Eds.), *Handbook of children and the media* (pp. 447–461). Thousand Oaks, CA: Sage.

Horwitz, R. I., Viscoli, C. M., Berkman, L., Donaldson, R. M., Horwitz, S. M., Murray, C. J., . . . Sindelar, J. (1990). Treatment adherence and risk of death after myocardial infarction. *Lancet, 336*, 542–545.

Hou, W. K., Law, C. C., Yin, J., & Fu, Y. T. (2010). Resource loss, resource gain, and psychological resilience and dysfunction in the year following cancer diagnosis: A growth mixture modeling approach. *Health Psychology, 29*, 484–495.

House, J. S. (1981). *Work stress and social support*. Reading, MA: Addison-Wesley.

House, J. S., & Kahn, R. L. (1985). Measures and concepts of social support. In S. Cohen & S. L. Syme (Eds.), *Social support and health* (pp. 83–108). New York, NY: Academic Press.

House, J. S., Landis, K. R., & Umberson, D. (1988). Social relationships and health. *Science, 241*, 540–545.

House, J. S., Robbins, C., & Metzner, H. L. (1982). The association of social relationships and activities with mortality: Prospective evidence from the Tecumseh Community Health Study. *American Journal of Epidemiology, 116*, 123–140.

Houston, B., & Vavak, C. (1991). Cynical hostility: Developmental factors, psychosocial correlates and health behaviors. *Health Psychology, 10*, 9–17.

Howsepian, B. A., & Merluzzi, T. V. (2009). Religious beliefs, self-efficacy, and adjustment to cancer. *Psycho-Oncology, 18*, 1069–1079.

Hoyt, M., Thomas, K., Epstein, D., & Dirksen, S. (2009). Coping style and sleep quality in men with cancer. *Annals of Behavioral Medicine, 31*, 88–93.

Hrobjartsson, A., & Gotzche, P. C. (2001). Is the placebo effect powerless? An analysis of clinical trials comparing placebo with no treatment. *New England Journal of Medicine, 344*, 1594–1602.

Hudson, J. I., Hiripi, E., Pope, H. G. Jr., & Kessler, R. C. (2007). The prevalence and correlates of eating disorders in the National Comorbidity Survey Replication. *Biological Psychiatry, 61*, 348–358.

Huebner, D. M., Neilands, T., Rebchook, G. M., & Kegeles, S. M. (2011). Sorting through chickens and eggs: A longitudinal examination of the associations between attitudes, norms, and sexual risk behavior. *Health Psychology, 30*, 110–118.

Huggins, M., Bloch, M., Wiggins, S., Adam, S., Suchowersky, O., Trew, M., ... Thompson, L. P. (1992). Predictive testing for Huntington's disease in Canada: Adverse effects and unexpected results in those receiving a decreased risk. *American Journal of Medical Genetics, 42*, 508–515.

Hughes, J. R., Gulliver, S. B., Fenwick, J. W., Valliere, W. A., Cruser, K., Pepper, S., ... Flynn, B. S. (1992). Smoking cessation among self-quitters. *Health Psychology, 11*, 331–334.

Hughes, J. R., & Hatsukami, N. D. (1986). Signs and symptoms of tobacco withdrawal. *Archives of General Psychiatry, 43*, 289–294.

Hull, J. G., Van Treuren, R. R., & Virnelli, S. (1987). Hardiness and health: A critique and alternative approach. *Journal of Personality and Social Psychology, 53*, 518–530.

Hull, J. G., & Young, R. D. (1983). Self-consciousness, self-esteem, and success-failure as determinants of alcohol consumption in male social drinkers. *Journal of Personality and Social Psychology, 44*, 1097–1109.

Humphrey, L. L. (1986). Structural analysis of parent-child relationships in eating disorders. *Journal of Abnormal Psychology, 95*, 395–402.

Humphrey, L. L. (1988). Relationships within subtypes of anorexic, bulimic, and normal families.

Journal of the American Academy of Child and Adolescent Psychiatry, 27, 544–551.

Hunt, K. A., Gaba, A., & Lavizzo-Mourey, R. (2005). Racial and ethnic disparities and perceptions of health care: Does health plan type matter? *Health Services Research, 40*, 551–576.

Hunt, W. A., Barnett, L. W., & Branch, L. G. (1971). Relapse rates in addiction programs. *Journal of Clinical Psychology, 27*, 455–456.

Hunte, H. E. R., & Williams, D. R. (2009). The association between perceived discrimination and obesity in a population-based multiracial and multiethnic adult sample. *American Journal of Public Health, 99*, 1285–1292.

Hunter, D. J., Manson, J. E., Colditz, G. A., Stampfer, M. J., Rosner, B., Hennekens, C. H., ... Willett, W. C. (1993). A prospective study of the intake of vitamins C, E, and A and the risk of breast cancer. *New England Journal of Medicine, 329*, 234–240.

Hurwitz, E. L., Morgenstern, H., & Chiao, C. (2005). Effects of recreational physical activity and back exercises on low back pain and psychological distress: Findings from the UCLA Low Back Pain Study. *American Journal of Public Health, 95*, 1817–1824.

Hygge, S., Evans, G. W., & Bullinger, M. (2002). A prospective study of some effects of aircraft noise on cognitive performance in schoolchildren. *Psychological Science, 13*, 469–474.

Illacqua, G. E. (1994). Migraine headaches: Coping efficacy of guided imagery training. *Headache, 34*, 99–102.

International Association for the Study of Pain. (1979). Pain terms: A list with definitions and a note on usage. *Pain, 6*, 249–252.

Invernizzi, F., Falomir-Pichastor, J. M., Munoz-Rojas, D., & Mugny, G. (2003). Social influence in personally relevant contexts: The respect attributed to the source as a factor increasing smokers' intention to quit smoking. *Journal of Applied Social Psychology, 33*, 1818–1836.

Iribarren, C., Sidney, S., Bild, D. E., Liu, K., Markovitz, J. H., Roseman, J. M., & Matthews, K. (2000). Association of hostility with coronary artery calcification in young adults: The CARDIA Study. *Journal of the American Medical Association, 283*, 2546–2551.

Ironson, G., Stuetzle, R., & Fletcher, M. A. (2006). An increase in religiousness/spirituality occurs after HIV diagnosis and predicts slower disease progression over 4 years in people with HIV. *Journal of General Internal Medicine, 21*, S62–S68.

Ironson, G., Wynings, C., Schneiderman, N., Baum, A., Rodriguez, M., Greenwood, D., ... Fletcher, M. A. (1997). Posttraumatic stress symptoms, intrusive thoughts, loss, and

immune function after Hurricane Andrew. *Psychosomatic Medicine, 59*, 128–141.

Irvin, J. E., Bowers, C. A., Dunn, M. E., & Wang, M. C. (1999). Efficacy of relapse prevention: A meta-analytic review. *Journal of Consulting and Clinical Psychology, 67*, 563–570.

Irwin, M., Mascovich, M., Gillin, C., Willoughby, R., Pike, J., & Smith, T. L. (1994). Partial sleep deprivation reduces natural killer cell activity in humans. *Psychosomatic Medicine, 56*, 493–498.

Izard, C. E., Libero, D. Z., Putnam, P., & Haynes, O. M. (1993). Stability of emotion experiences and their relations to traits of personality. *Journal of Personality and Social Psychology, 64*, 847–860.

Jackson, J. S., & Inglehart, M. R. (1995). Reverberation theory: Stress and racism in hierarchically structured communities. In S. E. Hobfoff & M. W. De Vries (Eds.), *Extreme stress and communities: Impact and intervention* (pp. 353–373). Dordrecht, Netherlands: Kluwer Academic Publishers.

Jackson, J. S., Knight, K. M., & Rafferty, J. A. (2010). Race and unhealthy behaviors: Chronic stress, the HPA axis, and physical and mental health disparities over the life course. *American Journal of Public Health, 100*, 933–939.

Jackson, K. M., & Aiken, L. S. (2000). A psychosocial model of sun protection and sunbathing in young women: The impact of health beliefs, attitudes, norms, and self-efficacy for sun protection. *Health Psychology, 19*, 469–478.

Jackson, K. M., & Aiken, L. S. (2006). Evaluation of a multi-component appearance-based sun-protective intervention for young women: Uncovering the mechanisms of program efficacy. *Health Psychology, 25*, 34–46.

Jackson, T., Pope, L., Fritch, A., Iezzi, T., Chen, H. & Nagasaka, T. (2005) The impact of threatening information about pain on coping and pain tolerance. *British Journal of Health Psychology, 10*, 441–451.

Jackson, V. P., Lex, A. M., & Smith, D. J. (1988). Patient discomfort during screen-film mammography. *Radiation, 168*, 421–423.

Jacobs, L. M., Burns, K., & Bennett Jacobs, B. (2008). Trauma death: Views of the public and trauma professionals on death and dying from injuries. *Archives of Surgery, 143*, 730–735.

Jacobs, T. J., & Charles, E. (1980). Life events and the occurrence of cancer in children. *Psychosomatic Medicine, 42*, 11–24.

Jacobsen, P. B., Bovbjerg, D. H., & Redd, W. H. (1993). Anticipatory anxiety in women receiving chemotherapy for breast cancer. *Health Psychology, 12*, 469–475.

Jacobsen, P. B., Bovbjerg, D. H., Schwartz, M. D., Hudis, C. A., Gilewski, T. A., & Norton, L. (1995). Conditioned emotional distress in women receiving chemotherapy for breast cancer. *Journal of Consulting and Clinical Psychology, 63,* 108–114.

Jacobson, E. (1938). *Progressive relaxation: A physiological and clinical investigation of muscle states and their significance in psychology and medical practice* (2nd ed.). Chicago, IL: University of Chicago Press.

Jacobson, P. D., Wasserman, J., & Anderson, J. R. (1997). Historical overview of tobacco legislation and regulation. *Journal of Social Issues, 53,* 75–95.

Jaffe, A. J., Rounsaville, B., Chang, G., Schottenfeld, R. S., Meyer, R. E., & O'Malley, S. S. (1996). Naltrexone, relapse prevention, and supportive therapy with alcoholics: An analysis of patient treatment matching. *Journal of Consulting and Clinical Psychology, 64,* 1044–1053.

Jakicic, J. M., Winters, C., Lang, W., & Wing, R. R. (1999). Effects of intermittent exercise and use of home exercise equipment on adherence, weight loss, and fitness in overweight women: A randomized trial. *Journal of the American Medical Association, 282,* 1554–1560.

Janis, I. L. (1958). *Psychological stress.* New York, NY: Wiley.

Janis, I. L. (1967). Effects of fear arousal on attitude change: Recent developments in theory and experimental research. In L. Berkowitz (Ed.), *Advances in experimental social psychology* (Vol. 3, pp. 166–224). San Diego, CA: Academic Press.

Janis, I. L., & Feshbach, S. (1953). Effects of fear-arousing communications. *Journal of Abnormal and Social Psychology, 48,* 78–92.

Janis, I. L., & Mann, L. (1965). Effectiveness of emotional role-playing in modifying smoking habits and attitudes. *Journal of Experimental Research in Personality, 1,* 84–90.

Janis, I. L., & Terwilliger, R. (1962). An experimental study of psychological resistance to fear-arousing communications. *Journal of Abnormal and Social Psychology, 65,* 403–410.

Janoff-Bulman, R. (1992). *Shattered assumptions: Towards a new psychology of trauma.* New York, NY: Free Press.

Janssen, C., Ommen, O., Ruppert, G., & Pfaff, H. (2008). Patient- and hospital-related determinants on subjective evaluation of medical treatment outcome of severely injured patients. *Journal of Public Health, 16,* 53–60.

Janz, N. K., & Becker, M. H. (1984). The health belief model: A decade later. *Health Education Quarterly, 11,* 1–47.

Jason, L. A., Jayaraj, S., Blitz, C. C., Michaels, M. H., & Klett, L. E. (1990). Incentives and competition at a worksite smoking cessation intervention. *American Journal of Public Health, 80,* 205–206.

Jay, S. M., Elliott, C. H., Katz, E., & Siegel, S. E. (1987). Cognitive-behavioral and pharmacologic interventions for childrens' distress during painful medical procedures. *Journal of Consulting and Clinical Psychology, 55,* 860–865.

Jeffery, R. W., Bjornson-Benson, W. M., Rosenthal, B. W., Lindquist, R. A., & Johnson, S. L. (1984). Behavioral treatment of obesity with monetary contracting: Two-year follow-up. *Addictive Behaviors, 9,* 311–313.

Jeffery, R. W., Hennrikus, D. J., Lando, H. A., Murray, D. M., & Liu, J. W. (2000). Reconciling conflicting findings regarding postcessation weight concerns and success in smoking cessation. *Health Psychology, 19,* 242–246.

Jeffery, R. W., Wing, R. R., Thorson, C., & Burton, L. R. (1998). Use of personal trainers and financial incentives to increase exercise in a behavioral weight-loss program. *Journal of Consulting and Clinical Psychology, 66,* 777–783.

Jemal, A., Siegel, R., Ward, E., Hao, Y., Xu, J., Murray, T., & Thun, M.J. (2008). Cancer statistics, 2008. *CA: A Cancer Journal for Clinicians, 58,* 71–96.

Jemmott, J. B., III, Croyle, R. T., & Ditto, P. H. (1988). Commonsense epidemiology: Self-based judgments from laypersons and physicians. *Health Psychology, 7,* 55–73.

Jemmott, J. B., III, Jemmott, L. S., & Fong, G. T. (1992). Reductions in HIV risk-associated behaviors among Black male adolescents: Effects of an AIDS prevention intervention. *American Journal of Public Health, 82,* 372–377.

Jemmott, J. B., III, Jemmott, L. S., & Fong, G. T. (2010). Efficacy of a theory-based abstinence-only intervention over 24 months: A randomized controlled trial with young adolescents. *Archives of Pediatrics and Adolescent Medicine, 164,* 152–159.

Jemmott, J. B. III, & Jones, J. M. (1993). Social psychology and AIDS among ethnic minority individuals: Risk behaviors and strategies for changing them. In J. B. Pryor & G. D. Reeder (Eds.), *The Social Psychology of HIV Infection* (pp. 183–224). Hillsdale, NJ: Erlbaum.

Jemmott, J. B., III, & Locke, S. E. (1984). Psychosocial factors, immunologic mediation, and human susceptibility to infectious disease: How much do we know? *Psychological Bulletin, 95,* 78–108.

Jemmott, J. B., III, & Magliore, K. (1988). Academic stress, social support, and secretory immunoglobulin A. *Journal of Personality and Social Psychology, 55,* 803–810.

Jemmott, J. B., III, Sanderson, C. A., & Miller, S. M. (1995). Changes in psychological distress and HIV risk-associated behavior: Consequences of HIV antibody testing. In R. T. Croyle (Ed.), *Psychosocial effects of screening for disease prevention and detection* (pp. 82–125). New York, NY: Oxford University Press.

Jennings, B. (1993). Health policy in a new key: Setting democratic priorities. *Journal of Social Issues, 49,* 169–184.

Jensen, M. P., Karoly, P., & Harris, P. (1991). Assessing the affective component of chronic pain: Development of the Pain Discomfort Scale. *Journal of Psychosomatic Research, 35,* 149–154.

Jensen, M. P., Turner, J. A., Romano, J. M., & Karoly, P. (1991). Coping with chronic pain: A critical review of the literature. *Pain, 47,* 249–283.

Jensen, M. P., Turner, J. A., & Romano, J. M. (2001). Change in beliefs, catastrophizing, and coping are associated with improvement in multidisciplinary pain treatment. *Journal of Consulting and Clinical Psychology, 69,* 655–662.

Jepson, C., & Rimer, B. K. (1993). Determinants of mammography intentions among prior screenees and nonscreenees. *Journal of Applied Social Psychology, 23,* 40–51.

Jha, P., Ranson, M. K., Nguyen, S. N., & Yach, D. (2002). Estimates of global and regional smoking prevalence in 1995, by age and sex. *American Journal of Public Health, 92,* 1002–1006.

Johnson, C. J., Heckman, T. G., Hansen, N. B., Kochman, A., & Sikkema, K.J. (2009). Adherence to antiretroviral medication in older adults living with HIV/AIDS: A comparison of alternative models. *AIDS Care, 21,* 541–551.

Johnson, E. J. & Goldstein, D. G. (2003). Do defaults save lives? *Science, 302,* 1338–1339.

Johnson, K. W., Anderson, N. B., Bastida, E., Kramer, B.J., Williams, D., & Wong, M. (1995). Macrosocial and environmental influences on minority health. *Health Psychology, 14,* 601–612.

Johnson, L., Zautra, A., & Davis, M. (2006). The role of illness uncertainty on coping with fibromyalgia symptoms. *Health Psychology, 25,* 696–703.

Johnson, M. O., Elliott, T. R., Neilands, T. B., Morin, S. F., & Chesney, M. A. (2006). A social problem solving model of adherence to HIV medications. *Health Psychology, 25,* 355–363.

Johnson, S. B., & Millstein, S. G. (2003). Prevention opportunities in health care settings. *American Psychologist, 58,* 475–481.

Johnston, D. W., Johnston, M., Pollard, B., Kinmonth, A.-L., & Mant, D. (2004). Motivation is not enough: Prediction of risk behavior following diagnosis of coronary heart disease from the theory of planned behavior. *Health Psychology, 23,* 533–538.

Johnston, M., & Vogele, C. (1993). Benefits of psychological preparation for surgery: A meta-analysis. *Annals of Behavioral Medicine, 15,* 245–256.

Joint United Nations Programme on HIV/AIDS (UNAIDS). N (2010). *Global Report: UNAIDS Report on the Global AIDS Epidemic 2010.* Geneva, Switzerland: UNAIDS. Retrieved September 17, 2011 from http://www.unaids .org/globalreport/global_report.htm.

Jones, J. A., Eckhardt, L. E., Mayer, J. A., Bartholomew, S., Malcarne, V. L., Hovell, M. F., & Elder, J. P. (1993). The effects of an instructional audiotape on breast self-examination proficiency. *Journal of Behavioral Medicine, 16,* 225–235.

Jones, J. L., & Leary, M. R. (1994). Effects of appearance-based admonitions against sun exposure on tanning intentions in young adults. *Health Psychology, 13,* 86–90.

Jorgensen, R. S., Johnson, B. T., Kolodziej, M. E., & Schreer, G. E. (1996). Elevated blood pressure and personality: A meta-analytic review. *Psychological Bulletin, 120,* 293–320.

Julliard, K., Vivar, J., Delgado, C., Cruz, E., Kabak, J., & Sabers, H. (2008). What Latina patients don't tell their doctors: A qualitative study. *Annals of Family Medicine, 6,* 543–549.

Justin, R. G. (1988). Adult and adolescent attitudes toward death. *Adolescence, 23,* 429–435.

Kabat-Zinn, J., Lipworth, L., & Burney, R. (1985). The clinical use of mindfulness meditation for the self-regulation of chronic pain. *Journal of Behavioral Medicine, 8,* 163–190.

Kadden, R. M., Cooney, N. L., Getter, H., & Litt, M. D. (1989). Matching alcoholics to coping skills or interactional therapies: Post-treatment results. *Journal of Consulting and Clinical Psychology, 57,* 698–704.

Kahn, K. L., Keeler, E. B., Sherwood, M. J., Rogers, W. H., Draper, D., Bentow, S. S., . . . Brook, R. H. (1990). Comparing outcomes of care before and after implementation of the DRG-based prospective payment system. *Journal of the American Medical Association, 264,* 1984–1988.

Kahneman, D., Fredrickson, B. L., Schreiber, C. A., & Redelmeier, D. A. (1993). When more pain is preferred to less: Adding a better end. *Psychological Science, 4,* 401–405.

Kalichman, S. C., & Cain, D. (2005). Perceptions of local HIV/AIDS prevalence and risks for HIV/AIDS and other sexually transmitted infections: Preliminary study of intuitive epidemiology. *Annals of Behavioral Medicine, 29,* 100–105.

Kalichman, S. C., Cain, D., Weinhardt, L., Benotsch, E., Presser, K., Zweben, A., . . . Swain, G. R. (2005). Experimental components analysis of brief theory-based HIV/AIDS risk-reduction counseling for sexually transmitted infection patients. *Health Psychology, 24,* 198–208.

Kalichman, S. C., Carey, M. P., & Johnson, B. T. (1996). Prevention of sexually transmitted HIV infection: A meta-analytic review of the behavioral outcome literature. *Annals of Behavioral Medicine, 18,* 6–15.

Kalichman, S. C., & Coley, B. (1995). Context framing to enhance HIV-antibody-testing messages targeted to African American women. *Health Psychology, 14,* 247–254.

Kalichman, S. C., Eaton, L., Cain, D., Cherry, C., Fuhrel, A., Kaufman, M., & Pope, H. (2007). Changes in HIV treatment beliefs and sexual risk behaviors among gay and bisexual men, 1997 to 2005. *Health Psychology, 26,* 650–656.

Kalichman, S. C., Heckman, T., Kochman, A., Sikkema, K., & Bergholte, J. (2000). Depression and thoughts of suicide among middle-aged and older persons living with HIV-AIDS. *Psychiatric Services, 51,* 903–907.

Kalichman, S. C., Kelly, J. A., Hunter, T. L., Murphy, D. A., & Tyler, R. (1993). Culturally tailored HIV-AIDS risk-reduction messages targeted to African American urban women: Impact on risk sensitization and risk reduction. *Journal of Consulting and Clinical Psychology, 61,* 291–295.

Kalichman, S. C., & Nachimson, D. (1999). Self-efficacy and disclosure of HIV-positive serostatus to sex partners. *Health Psychology, 18,* 281–287.

Kalichman, S. C., Russell, R. L., Hunter, T. L., & Sarwer, D. B. (1993). Earvin "Magic" Johnson's HIV serostatus disclosure: Effects on men's perceptions of AIDS. *Journal of Consulting and Clinical Psychology, 61,* 887–891.

Kallmes, D. F., Comstock, B. A., Heagerty, P. J., Turner, J. A., Wilson, D. J., Diamond, T. H., . . . Jarvik, J. G. (2009). A randomized trial of vertebroplasty for osteoporotic spinal fractures. *New England Journal of Medicine, 361,* 569–579.

Kamarck, T. W., & Lichtenstein, E. (1985). Currents trends in clinic-based smoking control. *Annals of Behavioral Medicine, 7,* 19–23.

Kamarck, T. W., Manuck, S. B., & Jennings, J. R. (1996). Social support reduces cardiovascular reactivity to psychological challenge: A laboratory model. *Psychosomatic Medicine, 52,* 42–58.

Kamarck, T. W., Muldoon, M. F., Shiffman, S. S., & Sutton-Tyrrell, K. (2007). Experiences of demand and control during daily life are predictors of carotid atherosclerotic progression among healthy men. *Health Psychology, 26,* 324–332.

Kamarck, T. W., Muldoon, M. F., Shiffman, S. S.; Sutton-Tyrrell, K., Gwaltney, C. & Janicki, D. L. (2004). Experiences of demand and control in daily life as correlates of subclinical carotid atherosclerosis in a healthy older sample. *Health Psychology, 23,* 24–32.

Kamen-Siegel, L., Rodin, J., Seligman, M. E. P., & Dwyer, J. (1991). Explanatory style and cell-mediated immunity in elderly men and women. *Health Psychology, 10,* 229–235.

Kane, R. I., Wales, J., Bernstein, L., Leibowtiz, A., & Kaplan, S. (1984). A randomized controlled trial of hospice care. *Lancet, 1,* 890–894.

Kangas, M., Henry, J. L., & Bryant, R. A. (2005). Predictors of posttraumatic stress disorder following cancer. *Health Psychology, 24,* 579–585.

Kaniasty, K., & Norris, F. H. (1993). A test of the support deterioration model in the context of natural disaster. *Journal of Personality and Social Psychology, 64,* 395–408.

Kaniasty, K., & Norris, F. H. (1995). Mobilization and deterioration of social support following natural disasters. *Current Directions in Psychological Science, 4,* 94–98.

Kann, L., Kincher, S. A., Williams, B. I., Ross, J. G., Lowry, R., Hill, C. V., . . . Kolbe, L. J. (1998). Youth Risk Behavioral Survelliance–United States, 1997. *Morbidity and Morality Weekly Report, 47,* No. SS-3.

Kanner, A. D., Coyne, J. C., Schaeffer, C., & Lazarus, R. S. (1981). Comparison of two modes of stress measurement: Daily hassles and uplifts versus major life events. *Journal of Behavioral Medicine, 4,* 1–39.

Kaplan, G. A., & Kiel, J. E. (1993). Socioeconomic factors and cardiovascular disease: A review of the literature. *Circulation, 88,* 1973–1998.

Kaplan, G. A., Salonen, J. T., Cohen, R. D., Brand, R. J., Syme, S. L., & Puska, P. (1988). Social connections and mortality from all causes and from cardiovascular disease: Prospective evidence from Eastern Finland. *American Journal of Epidemiology, 128,* 370–380.

Kaplan, G. A., Strawbridge, W. J., Cohen, R. D., & Hungerford, L. R. (1996). Natural history of leisure-time physical activity and its correlates: Association with mortality from all causes and cardiovascular disease over 28 years. *American Journal of Epidemiology, 144,* 793–797.

Kaplan, R. M. (1989). Health outcome models for policy analysis. *Health Psychology, 9,* 723–735.

Kaplan, R. M. (1991). Health-related quality of life in patient decision making. *Journal of Social Issues, 47,* 69–90.

Kaplan, R. M. (2000). Two pathways to prevention. *American Psychologist, 55,* 382–396.

Kaplan, R. M., & Bush, J. W. (1982). Health-related quality of life measurement for evaluation research and policy analysis. *Health Psychology, 1,* 61–80.

Kaplan, R. M., & Groesll, E. J. (2002). Applications of cost-effectiveness methodologies in behavioral medicine. *Journal of Consulting and Clinical Psychology, 70,* 482–493.

Kaplan, R. M., Orleans, C. T., Perkins, K. A., & Pierce, J. P. (1995). Marshaling the evidence for greater regulation and control of tobacco products: A call for action. *Annals of Behavioral Medicine, 17,* 3–14.

Kaplan, S. H., Greenfield, S., Gandek, B., Rogers, W. H., & Ware, J. E., Jr. (1996). Characteristics of physicans with participatory decision-making styles. *Annals of Internal Medicine, 124,* 497–504.

Karoly, P., & Ruehlman, L. S. (1996). Motivational implications of pain: Chronicity, psychological distress, and work goal construal in a national sample of adults. *Health Psychology, 15,* 383–390.

Kashima, Y., Gallois, C., & McCamish, M. (1993). The theory of reasoned action and cooperative behaviour: It takes two to use a condom. *British Journal of Social Psychology, 32,* 227–239.

Kasl, S. V., & Cobb, S. (1966a). Health behavior, illness behavior, and sick role behavior I. Health and illness behavior. *Archives of Environmental Health, 12,* 246–266.

Kasl, S. V., & Cobb, S. (1966b). Health behavior, illness behavior, and sick role behavior II. Sick role behavior. *Archives of Environmental Health, 12,* 531–541.

Kastenbaum, R. (1999). Dying and bereavement. In J. C. Cavanaugh & S. K. Whitbourne (Eds.), *Gerontology: An interdisciplinary perspective* (pp. 155–185). New York, NY: Oxford University Press.

Kastenbaum, R. (2000). *The psychology of death* (3rd ed.). New York, NY: Springer.

Katan, M. B., Grundy, S. M., & Willett, W. C. (1997). Beyond low fat diets. *New England Journal of Medicine, 337,* 563–567.

Kato, K., Sullivan, P.F., Evengård, B., & Pedersen, N.L. (2006). Chronic widespread pain and its comorbidities: A population-based study. *Archives of Internal Medicine, 166,* 1649–1654.

Katon, W., Fan, M. Y., Unutzer, J., Taylor, J., Pincus, H., & Schoenbaum, M. (2008). Depression and diabetes: A potentially lethal combination. *Journal of General Internal Medicine, 23,* 1571–1575.

Katon, W. J., Lin, E. H. B., Von Korff, M., Ciechanowski, P., Ludman, E. J., Young, B., . . . McCulloch, D. (2010). Collaborative care for patients with depression and chronic illnesses. *New England Journal of Medicine, 363,* 2611–2620.

Katritsis, D. G., & Ioannidis, J. P. (2005). Percutaneous coronary intervention versus conservative therapy in nonacute coronary artery disease: A meta-analysis. *Circulation, 111,* 2906–2912.

Katz, B. P., Fortenberry, J. D., Zimet, G. D., Blythe, M., & Orr, D. P. (2000). Partner-specific relationship characteristics and condom use among young people with sexually transmitted diseases. *Journal of Sex Research, 37,* 69–75.

Kauffman, N. A., Herman, C. P., & Polivy, J. (1995). Hunger-induced finickiness in humans. *Appetite, 24,* 203–218.

Kawachi, I., Colditz, G. A., Stampfer, M. J., Willett, W. C., Manson, J. E., Rosner, B., . . . Hennekens, C. H. (1994). Smoking cessation and time course of decreased risks of coronary heart disease in middle-aged women. *Archives of Internal Medicine, 154,* 169–175.

Kaye, W. H. (1997). Anorexia nervosa, obsessional behavior, and serotonin. *Psychopharmacology Bulletin, 33,* 335–344.

Keefe, F. J., & Block, A. R. (1982). Development of an observation method for assessing pain behavior in chronic low back pain patients. *Behavior Therapy, 13,* 363–375.

Keefe, F. J., Brown, G. K., Wallston, K. A., & Caldwell, D. S. (1989). Coping with rheumatoid arthritis pain: Catastrophizing as a maladaptive strategy. *Pain, 37,* 51–56.

Keefe, F. J., Caldwell, D. S., Queen, K. T., Gil, K. M., Martinez, S., Crissor, J. E., . . . Nunley, J. (1987). Pain coping strategies in osteoarthritis patients. *Journal of Consulting and Clinical Psychology, 55,* 208–212.

Keefe, F. J., Hauck, E. R., Egert, J., Rimer, B., & Kornguth, P. (1994). Mammography pain and discomfort: A cognitive-behavioral perspective. *Pain, 56,* 247–260.

Keesee, N. J., Currier, J. M., & Neimeyer, R. A. (2008). Predictors of grief following the death of one's child: The contribution of finding meaning. *Journal of Clinical Psychology, 64,* 1145–1163.

Keesey, R. E. (1995). A set-point model of weight regulation. In K. D. Brownell & C. G. Fairburn (Eds.), *Eating disorders and obesity* (pp. 46–50). New York, NY: Guilford Press.

Keesey, R. E., & Powley, T. L. (1975). Hypothalamic regulation of body weight. *American Scientist, 63,* 558–565.

Kegeles, S. S. (1985). Education for breast self-examination: Why, who, what, and how? *Preventive Medicine, 14,* 702–720.

Keinan, G., Friedland, N., & Ben-Porath, Y. (1987). Decision making under stress: Scanning of alternatives under physical threat. *Acta Psychologica, 64,* 219–228.

Kellerman, A. L., Rivara, F. P., Rushforth, N. B., Banton, J. G., Reay, D. T., Francisco, J. T., . . . Somes, G. (1993). Gun ownership as a risk factor for homicide in the home. *New England Journal of Medicine, 329,* 1084–1091.

Kellermann, A. L., Rivara, R. P., Somes, G., Reay, D. T., Francisco, J., Banton, J. G., . . . Hackman, B. B. (1992). Suicide in the home in relation to gun ownership. *New England Journal of Medicine, 327,* 467–472.

Kelley, H. H. (1967). Attribution theory in social psychology. In D. Levine (Ed.), *Nebraska symposium on motivation* (pp. 192–238). Lincoln: University of Nebraska Press.

Kelley, J. E., Lumley, M. A., & Leisen, J. C. C. (1997). Health effects of emotional disclosure in rheumatoid arthritis patients. *Health Psychology, 16,* 331–340.

Kelly, J. A., & Kalichman, S. C. (1998). Reinforcement value of unsafe sex as a predictor of condom use and continued HIV/AIDS risk behavior among gay and bisexual men. *Health Psychology, 17,* 328–335.

Kelly, J. A., Murphy, D. A., Sikkem, K. J., McAuliffe, T. L., Roffman, R. A., Solomon, L. J., . . . Kalichman, S. C. (1997). Randomized, controlled, community-level HIV-prevention intervention for sexual-risk behaviour among homosexual men in U. S. cities. *Lancet, 350,* 1500–1505.

Kelly, J. A., St. Lawrence, J. S., Diaz, Y. E., Stevenson, L. Y., Hauth, A. C., Brasfield, T. L., . . . Andrew, M. E. (1991). HIV risk behavior reduction following intervention with key opinion leaders of population: An experimental analysis. *American Journal of Public Health, 81,* 168–171.

Kelly, J. A., St. Lawrence, J. S., Hood, H. V., & Brasfield, T. L. (1989). Behavioral intention to reduce AIDS risk activities. *Journal of Consulting and Clinical Psychology, 57,* 60–67.

Kelly, K. E., & Houston, B. K. (1985). Type A behavior in employed women: Relation to work, marital, and leisure variables, social support, stress, tension, and health. *Journal of Personality and Social Psychology, 48,* 1067–1079.

Kemeny, M. E. (1994). Stressful events, psychological responses, and progression of HIV infection. In R. Glaser & J. Kiecolt-Glaser (Eds.), *Handbook of human stress and immunity* (pp. 245–266). New York, NY: Academic Press.

Kemeny, M. E., Weiner, H., Duran, R., Taylor, S. E., Visscher, B., & Fahey, J. L. (1995). Immune system changes following the death of a partner in HIV positive gay men. *Psychosomatic Medicine, 57,* 549–554.

Kemeny, M. E., Weiner, H., Taylor, S. E., Schneider, S., Visscher, B., & Fahey, J. L. (1994). Repeated bereavement, depressed mood, and immune parameters in HIV seropositive and seronegative gay men. *Health Psychology, 13,* 14–24.

Kendler, K. S., MacClean, C., Neale, M. C., Kessler, R., Heath, A. C., & Eaves, L. (1991). The genetic epidemiology of bulimia nervosa. *American Journal of Psychiatry, 148,* 1627–1637.

Kennedy, S., Kiecolt-Glaser, J. K., & Glaser, R. (1990). Social support, stress, and the immune system. In B. R. Sarason, I. G. Sarason, & G. R. Pierce (Eds.), *Social support: An interactional view* (pp. 253–266). New York, NY: Wiley.

Kennell, J., Klaus, M., McGrath, S., Robertson, S., & Hinkley, C. (1991). Continuous emotional support during labor in a U.S. hospital. *Journal of the American Medical Association, 265,* 2197–2201.

Kent, G. (1985). Memory of dental pain. *Pain, 21,* 187–194.

Keown, C., Slovic, P., & Lichtenstein, S. (1984). Attitudes of physicians, pharmacists, and laypersons toward seriousness and need for disclosure of prescription drug side effects. *Health Psychology, 3,* 1–12.

Kerlikowske, K., Grady, D., Rubin, S. M., Sandrock, C., & Ernster, V. L. (1995). Efficacy of screening mammography: A meta-analysis. *Journal of the American Medical Association, 273,* 149–154.

Kern, M. L., & Friedman, H. S. (2008). Do conscientious individuals live longer? A quantitative review. *Health Psychology, 27,* 505–512.

Kerns, R. D., Turk, D. C., & Rudy, T. E. (1985). The West Haven-Yale Multidimensional Pain Inventory. *Pain, 23,* 345–356.

Kerrey, B., & Hofschire, P. J. (1993). Hidden problems in current health-care financing and potential changes. *American Psychologist, 48,* 261–264.

Kershaw, K. N., Mezuk, B., Abdou, C. M., Rafferty, J. A., & Jackson, J. S. (2010). Socioeconomic position, health behaviors, and C-reactive protein: A moderated-mediation analysis. *Health Psychology, 29,* 307–316.

Kessels, L. T., Ruiter, R. A., & Jansma, B. M. (2010). Increased attention but more efficient disengagement: Neuroscientific evidence for defensive processing of threatening health information. *Health Psychology, 29,* 346–354.

Kessler, R., McLeod, J., & Wethington, E. (1985). The costs of caring: A perspective on the relationship between sex and psychological distress. In I. G. Sarason & B. R. Sarason (Eds.), *Social support: Theory, research, and applications* (pp. 4951–506). The Hague, Netherlands: Martinus Nijhoff.

Kessler, R. C., Crum, R. M., Warner, L. A., Nelson, C. B., Schulenberg, J., & Anthony, J. C. (1997). Lifetime co-occurrence of DSMIII-R alcohol abuse and dependence with other psychiatric disorders in the National Comorbidity Survey. *Archives of General Psychiatry, 54,* 313–321.

Kessler, R. C., Sonnega, A., Bromet, E., Hughes, M., & Nelson, C. B. (1995). Post-traumatic stress disorder in the National Comorbidity Survey. *Archives of General Psychiatry, 52,* 1048–1060.

Kiecolt-Glaser, J. K., Dura, J. R., Speicher, C. E., Trask, O. J., & Glaser, R. (1991). Spousal caregivers of dementia victims: Longitudinal changes in immunity and health. *Psychosomatic Medicine, 53,* 345–362.

Kiecolt-Glaser, J. K., & Glaser, R. (1986). Psychological influences on immunity. *Psychosomatics, 27,* 621–624.

Kiecolt-Glaser, J. K., & Glaser, R. (1988). Methodological issues in behavioral immunology research with humans. *Brain, Behavior, and Immunity, 2,* 67–78.

Kiecolt-Glaser, J. K., & Glaser, R. (1989). Psychoneuroimmunology: Past, present, and future. *Health Psychology, 8,* 677–682.

Kiecolt-Glaser, J. K., & Glaser, R. (2002). Depression and immune function: Central pathways to morbidity and mortality. *Journal of Psychosomatic Research, 53,* 873–876.

Kiecolt-Glaser, J. K., Glaser, R., Shuttleworth, E. C., Dyer, C. S., Ogrocki, P., & Speicher, C. E. (1987). Chronic stress and immunity in family caregivers of Alzheimer's disease victims. *Psychosomatic Medicine, 49,* 523–535.

Kiecolt-Glaser, J. K., Kennedy, S., Malkoff, S., Fisher, L., Speicher, C. E., & Glaser, R. (1988). Marital discord and immunity in males. *Psychosomatic Medicine, 50,* 213–229.

Kiecolt-Glaser, J. K., Marucha, P. T., Malarky, W. B., Mercado, A. M., & Glaser, R. (1995). Slowing of wound healing by psychological stress. *Lancet, 346,* 1194–1196.

Kiecolt-Glaser, J. K., McGuire, L., Robles, T. F., & Glaser, R. (2002). Psychoneuroimmunology: Psychological influences on immune function and health. *Journal of Consulting and Clinical Psychology, 70,* 537–547.

Kiecolt-Glaser, J. K., Page, G. G., Marucha, P.T., MacCallum, R. C., & Glaser, R. (1998). Psychological influences on surgical recovery. Perspectives from psychoneuroimmunology. *American Psychologist, 53,* 1209–1218.

Kiecolt-Glaser, J. K., & Williams, D. A. (1987). Self-blame, compliance, and distress among burn patients. *Journal of Personality and Social Psychology, 53,* 187–193.

Kiefe, C. L., McKay, S. V., Halevy, A., & Brody, B. A. (1994). Is cost a barrier to screening mammography for low-income women receiving Medicare benefits? A randomized trial. *Archives of Internal Medicine, 154,* 1217–1224.

Kiene, S. M., Barta, W. D., Zelenski, J. M., & Cothran, D. L. (2005). Why are you bringing up condoms now? The effect of message content on framing effects of condom use messages. *Health Psychology, 24,* 321–326.

Kilbey, M. M., Downey, K., & Breslau, N. (1998). Predicting the emergence and persistence of alcohol dependence in young adults: The role of expectancy and other risk factors. *Experimental and Clinical Psychopathology, 5,* 149–156.

Killen, J. D., Fortmann, S. P., Kraemer, H. C., Varady, A., & Newman, B. (1992). Who will relapse? Symptoms of nicotine dependence predict long-term relapse after smoking cessation. *Journal of Consulting and Clinical Psychology, 60,* 797–801.

Killen, J. D., Taylor, C. B., Hammer, L. D., Litt, I., Wilson, D. M., Rich, T., . . . Varady, A. (1993). An attempt to modify unhealthful eating attitudes and weight regulation practices of young adolescent girls. *International Journal of Eating Disorders, 13,* 369–384.

Kim, K. H., Bursac, Z., DiLillo, V., White, D., & West, D. S. (2009). Stress, race and body weight. *Health Psychology, 28,* 131–135.

Kim, S.H. (2009). The influence of finding meaning and worldview of accepting death on anger among bereaved older spouses. *Aging & Mental Health, 13,* 38–45.

Kimzey, S. L. (1975). The effects of extended spaceflight on hematologic and immunologic systems. *Journal of the American Medical Women's Association, 30,* 218–232.

King, A. C., Cao, D., Southard, C. C., & Matthews, A. K. (2011). Racial differences in eligibility determination and enrollment in a smoking cessation clinical trial. *Health Psychology, 30,* 40–48.

King, J. B. (1982). The impact of patients' perceptions of high blood pressure on attendance at screening: An extension of the health belief model. *Social Science and Medicine, 16,* 1079–1992.

King, K. B., Reis, H. T., Porter, L. A., & Norsen, L. H. (1993). Social support and long-term recovery from coronary artery surgery: Effects on patients and spouses. *Health Psychology, 12,* 56–63.

King, L. A., & Miner, K. N. (2000). Writing about the perceived benefits of traumatic events: Implications for physical health. *Personality and Social Psychology Bulletin, 26,* 220–230.

Kinsley, M. (2001, December 17). A defense of denial. *Time.*

Kirsch, I., & Sapirstein, G. (1999). Listening to Prozac but hearing placebo: A meta-analysis of antidepressant medications. In I. Kirsch (Ed.), *How expectancies shape experience* (pp. 303–320). Washington, DC: American Psychological Association.

Kirschbaum, C., Klauer, T., Filipp, S., & Hellhammer, D. H. (1995). Sex-specific effects of social support on cortisol and subjective responses to acute psychological stress. *Psychosomatic Medicine, 57*, 23–31.

Kirscht, J. P. (1988). The health belief model and predictions of health actions. In D. S. Gochman (Ed.), *Health behavior: Emerging research perspectives* (pp. 27–42). New York, NY: Plenum.

Kirscht, J. P., Kirscht, J. L., & Rosenstock, I. M. (1981). A test of interventions to increase adherence to hypertensive medical regimens. *Health Education Quarterly, 8*, 261–272.

Kirscht, J. P. & Rosenstock, I. M. (1979). Patients' problems in following recommendations of health experts. In G. C. Stone, F. Cohen, & N. E. Adler (Eds.), *Health psychology: A handbook* (pp. 198–215). San Francisco, CA: Jossey-Bass.

Kitzman-Ulrich, H., Wilson, D. K., Van Horn, M. L., & Lawman, H. G. (2010). Relationship of body mass index and psychosocial factors on physical activity in underserved adolescent boys and girls. *Health Psychology, 29*, 506–513.

Kitzmann, K. M., Dalton, W. T., Stanley, C. M., Beech, B. M., Reeves, T. P., Buscemi, J., . . . , Midgett, E. L. (2010). Lifestyle interventions for youth who are overweight: A meta-analytic review. *Health Psychology, 29*, 91–101.

Kivilan, D. R., Marlatt, G. A., Fromme, K., Coppel, D. B., & Williams, E. (1990). Secondary prevention with college drinkers: Evaluation of an alcohol skills training program. *Journal of Consulting and Clinical Psychology, 58*, 805–810.

Kivimäki, M., Leino-Arjas, P., Luukkonen, R., Riihimaki, H., Vahtera, J., & Kirjonen, J. (2002). Work stress and risk of cardiovascular mortality: Prospective cohort of industrial employees. *British Medical Journal, 325*, 857.

Kivimäki, M., Vahtera, J., Elovainio, M., Helenius, H., Singh-Manoux, A., & Penti, J. (2005). Optimism and pessimism as predictors of change in health after death or onset of severe illness in family. *Health Psychology, 24*, 413–421.

Klag, M. J., Ford, D. E., Mead, L. A., He, J., Whelton, P. K., Liang, K. Y., & Levine, D. M. (1993). Serum cholesterol in young men and subsequent cardiovascular disease. *New England Journal of Medicine, 328*, 313–318.

Klapow, J., Slater, M., Patterson, T., & Atkinson, J. (1995). Psychological factors discriminate multidimensional clinical groups of chronic low back-pain patients. *Pain, 62*, 349–355.

Klass, P. (1987). *A not entirely benign procedure: Four years as a medical student.* New York, NY: Putnam.

Klatsky, A. L., Friedman, G. D., & Sigelaub, A. B. (1981). Alcohol and mortality: A ten-year Kaiser-Permanente experience. *Annals of Internal Medicine, 94*, 139–145.

Klein, W. M., & Harris, P. R. (2009). Self-affirmation enhances attentional bias toward threatening components of a persuasive message. *Psychological Science, 20*, 1463–1467.

Klesges, R. C., Klesges, L. M., Vander Weg, M. W., DeBon, M. Poston, W. S. C., Ebbert, J., . . . Haddock, C. K. (2007). Characteristics of Air Force personnel who choose pharmacological aids for smoking cessation following an involuntary tobacco ban and tobacco control program. *Health Psychology, 26*, 588–589.

Kline, A., & Strickler, J. (1993). Perceptions of risk for AIDS among women in drug treatment. *Health Psychology, 12*, 313–323.

Klohn, L. S., & Rogers, R. W. (1991). Dimensions of the severity of a health threat: The persuasive effects of visibility, time of onset, and rate of onset on young women's intentions to prevent osteoporosis. *Health Psychology, 10*, 323–329.

Klonoff, E. A., & Landrine, H. (1993). Cognitive representations of bodily parts and products: Implications for health behavior. *Journal of Behavioral Medicine, 16*, 497–508.

Klonoff, E. A., & Landrine, H. (1994). Culture and gender diversity in commonsense beliefs about the causes of six illnesses. *Journal of Behavioral Medicine, 17*, 407–418.

Knowler, W. C., Barrett-Conner, E., Fowler, S. E., Hammon, R. F., Lachin, J. M., Walker, E. A., & Nathan, D. M. (2002). Reduction in the incidence of type 2 diabetes with lifestyle intervention or metformin. *New England Journal of Medicine, 346*, 393–403.

Knowles, E. D., Wearing, J. R., & Campos, B. (2011). Culture and the health benefits of expressive writing. *Social Psychological and Personality Science, 2*, 408–415.

Knowles, J. H. (1977). The responsibility of the individual. In J. H. Knowles (Ed.), *Doing better and feeling worse: Health in the United States* (pp. 57–80). New York, NY: Norton.

Kobasa, S. C., Maddi, S. R., & Kahn, S. (1982). Hardiness and health: A prospective study. *Journal of Personality and Social Psychology, 42*, 168–177.

Kobasa, S. C., & Puccetti, M. C. (1983). Personality and social resources in stress resistance. *Journal of Personality and Social Psychology, 45*, 839–850.

Koenig, H. G., McCullough, M. E., & Larson, D. B. (2001). *Handbook of religion and health.* New York, NY: Oxford University Press.

Koenig, L. B., & Vaillant, G. E. (2009). A prospective study of church attendance and health over the lifespan. *Health Psychology, 28*, 117–124.

Koetting-O'Byrne, K., Peterson, L., & Saldana, L. (1997). Survey of pediatric hospitals' preparation programs: Evidence of the impact of health psychology research. *Health Psychology, 16*, 147–154.

Kog, E., & Vandereycken, W. (1985). Family characteristics of anorexia nervosa and bulimia: A review of the research literature. *Clinical Psychology Review, 5*, 159–180.

Koh, H. K., Bak, S. M., Geller, A. C., Mangione, T. W., Hingson, R. W., Levenson, S. M., . . . Howland, J. (1997). Sunbathing habits and sunscreen use among White adults: Results of a national survey. *American Journal of Public Health, 87*, 1214–1217.

Kohen, J. A. (1983). Old but not alone: Informal social supports among the elderly by marital status and sex. *Gerontologist, 23*, 57–63.

Kohn, P. M., Lafreniere, K., & Gurevich, M. (1990). The inventory of college students' recent life experiences: A decontaminated hassles scale for a special population. *Journal of Behavioral Medicine, 13*, 619–630.

Kokkinos, P. F., Narayan, P., Colleran, J. A., Pittaras, A., Notargiacomo, A., Reda, D., & Papademetriou, V. (1995). Effects of regular exercise on blood pressure and left ventricular hypertrophy in African-American men with severe hypertension. *New England Journal of Medicine, 333*, 1462–1467.

Kole-Snijders, A. M. J., Vlaeyen, J. W., Goossens, M. E., Rutten-van Molken, M. P., Heuts, P. H., van Breukelen, G., & van Eek, H. (1999). Chronic low-back pain: What does cognitive coping skills training add to operant behavioral treatment? Results of a randomized clinical trial. *Journal of Consulting and Clinical Psychology, 67*, 931–944.

Kop, W. J., Gottdiener, J. S., & Krantz, D. S. (2001). Stress and silent ischemia. In A. Baum, T. A. Revenson, & J. E. Singer (Eds.), *Handbook of health psychology* (pp. 669–682). Mahwah, NJ: Erlbaum.

Kornguth, P. J., Keefe, F. J., & Conaway, M. R. (1996). Pain during mammography: Characteristics and relationship to demographic and medical variables. *Pain, 66*, 187–194.

Korotkov, D. (2008). Does personality moderate the relationship between stress and health behavior? Expanding the nomological network of the five factor model. *Journal of Research in Personality, 42*, 1418–1426.

Korsch, B. M., Gozzi, E. K., & Francis, V. (1968). Gaps in doctor-patient communications: 1. Doctor-patient interaction and patient satisfaction. *Paediatrics, 42*, 855–871.

Kosmin, B. A., & Lachman, S. P. (1993). *One nation under God: Religion in contemporary American society.* New York, NY: Harmony Books.

Kozhimannil, K. B., Pereira, M. A., & Harlow. B. L. (2009). Association between diabetes and perinatal depression among low-income mothers. *Journal of the American Medical Association, 301*, 842–847.

Krahn, M. D., Mahoney, J. E., Eckman, M. H., Trachtenberg, J., Pauker, S. G., & Detsky, A. S. (1994). Screening for prostate cancer: A decision analytic view. *Journal of the American Medical Association, 272*, 773–780.

Kral, J. G. (1992). Overview of surgical techniques for treating obesity. *American Journal of Clinical Nutrition, 55*, 552S–555S.

Krantz, D. S., Baum, A., & Wideman, M. V. (1980). Assessment for preferences for self-treatment and information in health care. *Journal of Personality and Social Psychology, 39*, 977–990.

Krantz, D. S., & McCeney, M. K. (2002). Effects of psychological and social factors on organic disease: A critical assessment of research on coronary heart disease. *Annual Review of Psychology, 53*, 341–369.

Kratz, A., Davis, M., & Zautra, A. (2007). Pain acceptance moderates the relation between pain and negative affect in female osteoarthritis and fibromyalgia patients. *Annals of Behavioral Medicine, 33*, 291–301.

Kremer, E. F., Block, A., & Gaylor, M. S. (1981). Behavioral approaches to treatment of chronic pain: The inaccuracy of patient self-report measures. *Archives of Physical Medicine and Rehabilitation, 62*, 188–191.

Kreuter, M. W., Bull, F. C., Clark, E. M., & Oswald, D. L. (1999). Understanding how people process health information: A comparison of tailored and nontailored weight-loss materials. *Health Psychology, 18*, 487–494.

Kreuter, M. W., & Holt, C. L. (2001). How do people process health information? Applications in an age of individualized communication. *Current Directions in Psychological Science, 10*, 206–209.

Kreuter, M. W., & Skinner, C. S. (2000). Tailoring: What's in a name? *Health Education Research, 15*, 1–3.

Kreuter, M. W., & Strecher, V. J. (1996). Do tailored behavior change messages enhance the effectiveness of health risk appraisal? Results from a randomized trial. *Health Education Research: Theory and Practice, 11*, 97–105.

Kreuter, M. W., Strecher, V. J., & Glassman, B. (1999). One size does not fit all: The case for tailoring print materials. *Annals of Behavioral Medicine, 21*, 276–283.

Krieger, N., & Sidney, S. (1996). Racial discrimination and blood pressure: The CARDIA study of young Black and White adults. *American Journal of Public Health, 86*, 1370–1378.

Krieger, N., Sidney, S., & Coakley, E. (1998). Racial discrimination and skin color in the CARDIA study: Implications for public health research. *American Journal of Public Health, 88*, 1308–1313.

Kroenke, K., Bair, M. J., Damush, T. M., Wu, J., Hoke, S., Sutherland, J., & Tu, W. (2009). Optimized antidepressant therapy and pain self-management in primary care patients with depression and musculoskeletal pain: A randomized controlled trial. *Journal of the American Medical Association, 301*, 2099–2110.

Krohne, H. W., & Slangen, K. E. (2005). Influence of social support on adaptation to surgery. *Health Psychology, 24*, 101–105.

Krupat, E., Irish, J. T., Kasten, L. E., Freund, K. M., Burns, R. B., Moskowitz, M. A., & McKinlay, J. B. (1999). Patient assertiveness and physician decision-making among older breast cancer patients. *Social Science & Medicine, 49*, 449–457.

Krupat, E., Rosenkranz, S. L., Yeager, C. M., Barnard, K., Putnam, S. M., & Inui, T. S. (2000). The practice orientations of physicians and patients: The effect of doctor-patient congruence on satisfaction. *Patient Education and Counseling, 39*, 49–59.

Kubler-Ross, E. (1969). *On death and dying.* London, England: MacMillan.

Kubzansky, L. D., Cole, S. R., Kawachi, I., Vokonas, P., & Sparrow, D. (2006). Shared and unique contributions of anger, anxiety, and depression to coronary heart disease: A prospective study in the normative aging study. *Annals of Behavioral Medicine, 31*, 21–29.

Kubzansky, L. D., & Thurston, R. C. (2007). Emotional vitality and incident coronary heart disease: Benefits of healthy psychological functioning. *Archives of General Psychiatry, 64*, 1393–1401.

Kujala, U. M., Kaprio, J., Sarna, S., & Koskenvuo, M. (1998). Relationship of leisure-time physical activity and mortality: The Finnish Twin Cohort. *Journal of the American Medical Association, 279*, 440–444.

Kulick, A. D., & Rosenberg, H. (2001). Influence of positive and negative film portrayals of drinking on older adolescents' alcohol outcome expectancies. *Journal of Applied Social Psychology, 31*, 1492–1499.

Kulik, J. A., & Mahler, H. I. M. (1989). Social support and recovery from surgery. *Health Psychology, 8*, 221–238.

Kulik, J. A., Mahler, H. I. M., & Moore, P. J. (1996). Social comparison and affiliation under threat: Effects on recovery from major surgery.

Journal of Personality and Social Psychology, 71, 967–979.

Kunda, Z. (1990). The case for motivated reasoning. *Psychological Bulletin, 108*, 480–498.

Kung, H. C., Hoyert, D. L., Xu, J., & Murphy, S. L. (2008). Deaths: Final data for 2005. *National Vital Statistics Report, 56*, 1–120.

Kushner, M. G., Mackenzie, T. B., Fiszdon, J., Valentiner, D. P., Foa, E., Anderson, N., & Wangensteen, D. (1996). The effects of alcohol consumption on laboratory-induced pain and state anxiety. *Archives of General Psychiatry, 53*, 264–270.

LaCrosse, M. B. (1975). Nonverbal behaviour and perceived counsellor attractiveness and persuasiveness. *Journal of Counseling Psychology, 22*, 563–566.

Lahey, B. B. (2009). Public health significance of neuroticism. *American Psychologist, 64*, 241–256.

Laine, C., & Davidoff, F. (1996). Patient-centered medicine: A professional evolution. *Journal of the American Medical Association, 275*, 152–156.

Lakey, B. (1988). Self-esteem, control beliefs and cognitive problem solving as risk factors in the development of subsequent dysphoria. *Cognitive Therapy and Research, 12*, 409–412.

Lakey, B., & Heller, K. (1988). Social support from a friend, perceived support, and social problem solving. *American Journal of Community Psychology, 16*, 811–824.

Lalonde, M. (1974). *A new perspective on the health of Canadians.* Ottawa: Government of Canada.

Lamaze, F. (1970). *Painless childbirth: Psychoprophylactic method.* Chicago, IL: Regnery.

Lamme, S., Dykstra, P. A., & Brose Van Groenou, M. I. (1996). Rebuilding the network: New relationships in widowhood. *Personal Relationships, 3*, 337–349.

Lamont, E. B., & Christakis, N. A. (2001). Prognostic disclosure to patients with cancer near the end of life. *Annals of Internal Medicine, 133*, 1096–1105.

Landrine, H., & Klonoff, E. A. (1994). Cultural diversity in causal attributions for illness: The role of the supernatural. *Journal of Behavioral Medicine, 17*, 181–193.

Lang, A. R., & Marlatt, G. A. (1982). Problem drinking: A social learning perspective. In R. J. Gatchel, A. Baum, & J. E. Singer (Eds.), *Handbook of psychology and health* (pp. 121–169). Hillsdale, NJ: Erlbaum.

Langens, T. A., & Schuler, J. (2007). Effects of written emotional expression: The role of positive expectancies. *Health Psychology, 26*, 174–182.

Lannin, D. R., Mathews, H. F., Mitchell, J., Swanson, M. S., Swanson, F. H., & Edwards, M. S. (1998). Influence of socioeconomic and cultural factors on racial differences in late-stage presentation of breast cancer. *Journal of the American Medical Association, 279,* 1801–1807.

Lantz, P. M., House, J. S., Lepkowski, J. M., Williams, D. R., Mero, R. P., & Chen, J. (1998). Socioeconomic factors, health behaviors, and mortality: Results from a nationally representative prospective study of US adults. *Journal of the American Medical Association, 279,* 1703–1708.

LaPerriere, A. R., Antoni, M. H., Schneiderman, N., Ironson, A., Klimas, N., Caralis, P., & Fletcher, M. A. (1990). Exercise intervention attenuates emotional distress and natural killer cell decrements following notification of positive serologic status for HIV-1. *Applied Psychophysiology and Biofeedback, 15,* 229–242.

Larroque, B., Kaminski, M., Dehaene, P., Subtil, D., Delfosse, M.-J., & Querleu, D. (1995). Moderate prenatal alcohol exposure and psychomotor development at preschool age. *American Journal of Public Health, 85,* 1654–1661.

Larsen, R. J. (1992). Neuroticism and selective encoding and recall of symptoms: Evidence from a combined concurrent-retrospective study. *Journal of Personality and Social Psychology, 62,* 480–488.

Larson, R. J., Woloshin, S., Schwartz, L. M., & Welch, H. G. (2005). Celebrity endorsements of cancer screening. *Journal of the National Cancer Institute, 97,* 693–695.

Latimer, E. A., & Lave, L. B. (1987). Initial effects of the New York State auto safety belt law. *American Journal of Public Health, 77,* 183–186.

Laumann, E. O., & Youm, Y. (1999). Racial/ethnic group differences in the prevalence of sexually transmitted diseases in the United States: A network explanation. *Sexually Transmitted Diseases, 26,* 250–261.

Lautrette, A., Darmon, M., Megarbane, B., Joly, L. M., Chevret, S., Adrie, C., ... Azoulay, E. (2007). A communication strategy and brochure for relatives of patients dying in the ICU. *New England Journal of Medicine, 356,* 469–478.

Lavoie, K. L., Bouchard, A., Joseph, M., Campbell, T. S., Favreau, H., & Bacon S. L. (2008). Association of asthma self-efficacy to asthma control and quality of life. *Annals of Behavioral Medicine, 36,* 100–106.

Law, A., Logan, H., & Baron, R. S. (1994). Desire for control, felt control, and stress inoculation training during dental treatment. *Journal of Personality and Social Psychology, 67,* 929–936.

Lawton, R. J., Conner, M. T., & McEachan, R. R. C. (2009). Desire or reason: Predicting health behaviors from affective and cognitive attitudes. *Health Psychology, 28,* 56–65.

Lazarus, R. S., & Folkman, S. (1984). *Stress, appraisal, and coping.* New York, NY: Guilford Press.

Lazarus, R. S., Kanner, A., & Folkman, S. (1980). Emotions: A cognitive-phenomenological analysis. In R. Plutchik & H. Hellerman (Eds.), *Theories of emotion* (pp. 189–217). New York, NY: Academic Press.

Le, T. T., Bilderback, A., Bender, B., Wamboldt, F. S., Turner, C. F., Rand, C. S., & Bartlett, S. J. (2008). Do asthma medication beliefs mediate the relationship between minority status and adherence to therapy? *Journal of Asthma, 45,* 33–37.

Leake, R., Friend, R., & Wadhwa, N. (1999). Improving adjustment to chronic illness through strategic self-presentation: An experimental study on a renal dialysis unit. *Health Psychology, 18,* 54–62.

Leary, M. R., & Jones, J. L. (1993). The social psychology of tanning and sunscreen use: Self-presentational motives as a predictor of health risk. *Journal of Applied Social Psychology, 23,* 1390–1406.

Lecci, L., & Cohen, D. J. (2002). Perceptual consequences of an illness–concern induction and its relation to hypochondriacal tendencies. *Health Psychology, 21,* 147–156.

Lecci, L., Karoly, P., Ruehlman, L. S., & Lanyon, R. I. (1996). Goal-relevant dimensions of hypochondriacal tendencies and their relation to symptom manifestation and psychological distress. *Journal of Abnormal Psychology, 105,* 42–52.

Lee, C-D., Sui, X., & Blair, S. N. (2009). Combined effects of cardiorespiratory fitness, not smoking, and normal waist girth on morbidity and mortality in men. *Archives of Internal Medicine, 169,* 2096–2101.

Lee, D., Mendes de Leon, C., Jenkins, C., Croog, S., Levine, S., & Sudilovsky, A. (1992). Relation of hostility to medical adherence, symptom complaints, and blood pressure reduction in a clinical field trial of antihypertensive medication. *Journal of Psychosomatic Research, 36,* 181–190.

Lee, I.-M., Paffenbarger, R. S., Jr., & Hsieh, C.-C. (1992). Physical activity and risk of prostatic cancer among college alumni. *American Journal of Epidemiology, 135,* 169–179.

Lee, K. H., Seow, A., Luo, N., & Koh, D. (2008). Attitudes towards the doctor–patient relationship: A prospective study in an Asian medical school. *Medical Education, 42,* 1092–1099.

Lee, S., & Tsang, A. (2009). A population-based study of depression and three kinds of frequent pain conditions and depression in Hong Kong. *Pain Medicine, 10,* 155–163.

Lefcourt, H. M., Davidson, K., Prkachin, K. M., & Mills, D. E. (1997). Humor as a stress moderator in the prediction of blood pressure obtained during five stressful tasks. *Journal of Research in Personality, 31,* 523–542.

Lefcourt, H. M., Davidson-Katz, K., & Kueneman, K. (1990). Humor and immune-system functioning. *Humor, 3,* 305–321.

Le Grange, D., Crosby, R. D., Rathouz, P. J., & Leventhal, B. L. (2007). A randomized controlled comparison of family-based treatment and supportive psychotherapy for adolescent bulimia nervosa. *Archives of General Psychiatry, 64,* 1049–1056.

Lehrer, P., Feldman, J., Giardino, N., Song, H.-S., & Schmaling, K. (2002). Psychological aspects of asthma. *Journal of Consulting and Clinical Psychology, 70,* 691–711.

Leibel, R. L., Berry, E. M., & Hirsch, J. (1983). Biochemistry and development of adipose tissue in man. In H. L. Conn, E. A. DeFelice, & P. Kuo (Eds.), *Health and obesity* (pp. 21–48). New York, NY: Raven Press.

Leigh, B. C., & Stall, R. (1993). Substance use and risky sexual behavior for exposure to HIV: Issues in methodology, interpretation, and prevention. *American Psychologist, 10,* 1035–1045.

Leiker, M., & Hailey, B. J. (1988). A link between hostility and disease: Poor health habits? *Behavioral Medicine, 3,* 129–133.

Leitzell, J. D. (1977). Patient and physician: Is either objective? *New England Journal of Medicine, 296,* 1070.

Lengacher, C. A., Johnson-Mallard, V., Post-White, J., Moscoso, M. S., Jacobsen, P. B., Klein, T. W., ... Kip, K. E. (2009). Randomized controlled trial of mindfulness-based stress reduction (MBSR) for survivors of breast cancer. *Psycho-Oncology, 18,* 1261–1272.

Lennon, S. (2004, May 24). That little freckle could be a time bomb. *Newsweek.*

Leonard, K. E. (1989). The impact of explicit aggressive and implicit nonaggressive cues on aggression in intoxicated and sober males. *Personality and Social Psychology Bulletin, 15,* 390–400.

Lepore, S. J. (1992). Social conflict, social support, and psychological distress: Evidence of cross-domain buffering effects. *Journal of Personality and Social Psychology, 63,* 857–867.

Lepore, S. J. (1995). Cynicism, social support, and cardiovascular reactivity. *Health Psychology, 14,* 210–216.

Lepore, S. J., Mata Allen, K. A., & Evans, G. W. (1993). Social support lowers cardiovascular reactivity to an acute stressor. *Psychosomatic Medicine, 55,* 518–524.

Lepore, S. J., Silver, R. C., Wortman, C. B., & Wayment, H. A. (1996). Social constraints, intrusive thoughts, and depressive symptoms among bereaved mothers. *Journal of Personality and Social Psychology, 70,* 271–282.

Lerman, C. (1997). Psychological aspects of genetic testing: Introduction to the special issue. *Health Psychology, 16,* 3–7.

Lerman, C., Daly, M., Walsh, W. P., Resch, N., Seay, J., Barsevick, A., . . . Birenbaum, L. (1993). Communication between patients with breast cancer and health care providers. *Cancer, 72,* 2612–2620.

Lerman, C., Hughes, C., Croyle, R. T., Main, D., Durham, C., Snyder, C., . . . Lynch, H. T. (2000). Prophylactic surgery decisions and surveillance practices one year following BRCA1/2 testing. *Preventive Medicine, 31,* 75–80.

Lerman, C., & Rimer, B. K. (1995). Psychosocial impact of cancer screening. In R. T. Croyle (Ed.), *Psychosocial effects of screening for disease prevention and detection* (pp. 65–81). New York, NY: Oxford University Press.

Lerman, C., Rimer, B., Trock, B., Balshem, A., & Engstrom, P. F. (1990). Factors associated with repeat adherence to breast cancer screening. *Preventive Medicine, 19,* 279–290.

Lerman, S. F., Shahar, G., Czarkowski, K. A., Kurshan, N., Magriples, U., Mayes, L. C., & Epperson, C. N. (2007). Predictors of satisfaction with obstetric care in high-risk pregnancy: The importance of patient-provider relationship. *Journal of Clinical Psychology in Medical Settings, 14,* 330–334.

Leserman, J., Jackson, E. D., Petitto, J. M., Golden, R. N., Silva, S. G., Perkins, D. O., . . . , Evans, D. L. (1999). Progression to AIDS: The effects of stress, depressive symptoms, and social support. *Psychosomatic Medicine, 61,* 397–406.

Leserman, J., Perkins, D. O., & Evans, D. L. (1992). Coping with the threat of AIDS: The role of social support. *American Journal of Psychiatry, 149,* 1514–1520.

Leventhal, E. A., Hansell, S., Diefenbach, M., Leventhal, H., & Glass, D. C. (1996). Negative affect and self-report of physical symptoms: Two longitudinal studies of older adults. *Health Psychology, 15,* 193–199.

Leventhal, E. A., Leventhal, H., Shacham, S., & Easterling, D. V. (1989). Active coping reduces reports of pain from childbirth. *Journal of Consulting and Clinical Psychology, 57,* 365–371.

Leventhal, E. A., & Prochaska, T. R. (1986). Age, symptom interpretation, and health behavior. *Journal of the American Geriatrics Society, 34,* 185–191.

Leventhal, H. (1970). Findings and theory in the study of fear communications. In L. Berkowitz (Ed.), *Advances in experimental social psychology* (Vol. 5, pp. 119–185). San Diego, CA: Academic Press.

Leventhal, H., & Avis, N. (1976). Pleasure, addiction, and habit: Factors in verbal report or factors in smoking behavior? *Journal of Abnormal Psychology, 85,* 478–488.

Leventhal, H., & Cleary, P. (1980). The smoking problem: A review of the research and theory in behavioral risk modification. *Psychological Bulletin, 88,* 370–405.

Leventhal, H., Meyer, D., & Nerenz, D. (1980). The common-sense representation of illness danger. In S. Rachman (Ed.), *Medical psychology* (pp. 7–30). New York, NY: Pergamon.

Leventhal, H., Singer, R., & Jones, S. (1965). Effects of fear and specificity of recommendation upon attitudes and behavior. *Journal of Personality and Social Psychology, 2,* 20–29.

Leventhal, H., & Watts, J. C. (1966). Sources of resistance to fear-arousing communications on smoking and lung cancer. *Journal of Personality, 34,* 155–175.

Levin, I. P., Schnittjer, S. K., & Thee, S. L. (1988). Information framing effects in social and personal decisions. *Journal of Experimental Psychology, 24,* 520–529.

Levin, J. S. (1994). Investigating the epidemiologic effects of religious experience: Findings, explanations, and barriers. In S. Levin (Ed.), *Religion in aging and health* (pp. 3–17). Thousand Oaks, CA: Sage.

Levine, A. J., Hinkin, C. H., Marion, S., Keuning, A., Castellon, S. A., Lam, M. N., . . . Durvasula, R. S. (2006). Adherence to antiretroviral medications in HIV: Differences in data collected via self-report and electronic monitoring. *Health Psychology, 25,* 329–335.

Levine, F. M., & DeSimone, L. L. (1991). The effects of experimenter gender on pain report in male and female subjects. *Pain, 44,* 69–72.

Levine, J. A., Eberhardt, N. L., & Jensen, M. D. (1999). The role of non-exercise activity thermogenesis in resistance to fat gain in humans. *Science, 283,* 212–214.

Levine, J. D., Gordon, N. C., & Fields, H. L. (1978). The mechanism of placebo analgesia. *Lancet, 2,* 654–657.

Levine, R. V. (1990). The pace of life. *American Scientist, 79,* 450–459.

Levy, B. R., Slade, M. D., Kunkel, S. R., & Kasl, S. V. (2002). Longevity increased by positive self-perceptions of aging. *Journal of Personality and Social Psychology, 83,* 261–270.

Levy, R. K. (1997). The transtheoretical model of change: An application to bulimia nervosa. *Psychotherapy, 34,* 278–285.

Levy, R. L., Cain, K. C., Jarrett, M., & Heitkemper, M. M. (1997). The relationship between stress and gastrointestinal symptoms in women with irritable bowel syndrome. *Journal of Behavioral Medicine, 20,* 177–194.

Levy, S. M. (1983). The process of death and dying: Behavioral and social factors. In T. G. Burish & L. A. Bradley (Eds.), *Coping with chronic disease: Research and applications* (pp. 425–446). New York, NY: Academic Press.

Levy, S. M. (1985). *Behavior and cancer: Lifestyle and psychosocial factors in the initiation and progression of cancer.* San Francisco, CA: Jossey-Bass.

Levy, S. M., Lee, J., Bagley, C., & Lippman, M. (1988). Survival hazards analysis in first recurrent breast cancer patients: Seven-year follow-up. *Psychosomatic Medicine, 50,* 520–528.

Lew, E. A. (1985). Mortality and weight: Insured lives and the American Cancer Society studies. *Annals of Internal Medicine, 103,* 1024–1029.

Lewin, K. (1935). *A dynamic theory of personality.* New York, NY: McGraw-Hill.

Ley, P. (1982). Giving information to patients. In J. R. Eiser (Ed.), *Social psychology and behavioral science* (pp. 339–373). New York, NY: Wiley.

Li, J., Laursen, T. M., Precht, D. H., Olsen, J., & Mortensen, P. B. (2005). Hospitalization for mental illness among parents after the death of a child. *New England Journal of Medicine, 352,* 1190–1196.

Liberman, A., & Chaiken, S. (1992). Defensive processing of personally relevant health messages. *Personality and Social Psychology Bulletin, 18,* 669–679.

Liberman, R. (1962). An analysis of the placebo phenomenon. *Journal of Chronic Diseases, 15,* 761–783.

Lichtenstein, E., & Glasgow, R. E. (1992). Smoking cessation: What have we learned over the past decade? *Journal of Consulting and Clinical Psychology, 60,* 518–527.

Lichtenstein, E., & Mermelstein, R. J. (1984). Review of approaches to smoking treatment: Behavior modification strategies. In J. D. Matarazzo, S. M. Weiss, J. A. Herd, N. E. Miller, & S. M. Weiss (Eds.), *Behavioral health: A handbook of health enhancement and disease prevention* (pp. 695–712). New York, NY: Wiley.

Lichtenstein, E., Zhu, S. H., & Tedeschi, G. J. (2010). Smoking cessation quitlines: an under-recognized intervention success story. *American Psychologist, 65,* 252–261.

context of men's cancer screening intention and behavior? Application of an extended theory of planned behavior. *Health Psychology, 29*, 72–81.

Sikkema, K. J., Hansen, N. B., Ghebremichael, M., Kochman, A., Tarakeshwar, N., Meade, C. S., & Zhang, H. (2006). A randomized controlled trial of a coping group intervention for adults with HIV who are AIDS bereaved: Longitudinal effects on grief. *Health Psychology, 25*, 563–570.

Silberman, I. (2005). Religion as a meaning system: Implications for the new millennium. *Journal of Social Issues, 61*, 641–663.

Silverman, E., Range, L., & Overholser, J. (1994). Bereavement from suicide as compared to other forms of bereavement. *Omega, 30*, 41–51.

Silverstein, B., Perdue, L., Peterson, B., & Kelly, E. (1986). The role of the mass media in promoting a thin standard of bodily attractiveness for women. *Sex Roles, 14*, 519–532.

Simon, G., Gater, R., Kisely, S., & Piccinelli, M. (1996). Somatic symptoms of distress: An international primary care study. *Psychosomatic Medicine, 58*, 481–488.

Simon, N. (1977). Breast cancer induced by radiation. *Journal of the American Medical Association, 237*, 789–790.

Simoni, J., Mason, H., Marks, G., Ruiz, M., Reed, D., & Richardson, J. (1995). Women's self-disclosure of HIV infection: Rates, reasons, and reactions. *Journal of Consulting and Clinical Psychology, 63*, 474–478.

Simons-Morton, B. G., Chen, R., Abroms, R., & Haynie, D. L. (2004). Latent growth curve analyses of peer and parent influences on smoking progression among early adolescents. *Health Psychology, 23*, 612–621.

Simpson, S., Hurtley, S. M., & Marx, J. (2000). Immune cell networks. *Science, 290*, 79.

Sims, R., Gordon, S., Garcia, W., Clark, E., Monye, D., Callender, C., & Campbell, A. (2008). Perceived stress and eating behaviors in a community-based sample of African Americans. *Eating Behaviors, 9*, 137–142.

Sinha, R., Fisch, G., Teague, R., Tamborlane, W. V., Banyas, B., Allen, K., . . . Caprio, S. (2002). Prevalence of impaired glucose tolerance among children and adolescents with marked obesity. *New England Journal of Medicine, 346*, 802–810.

Skaali, T., Fossa, S., Bremnes, R., Dahl, O., Haaland, C. F., Hauge, E. R., . . . Dahl, A. A. (2009). Fear of recurrence in long-term testicular cancer survivors. *Psycho-Oncology, 18*, 580–588.

Skaer, T. L., Robinson, L. M., Sclar, D. A., & Harding, G. H. (1996). Financial incentives and the use of mammography among Hispanic migrants to the United States. *Health Care for Women International, 17*, 281–291.

Skelton, J. A., & Pennebaker, J. W. (1982). The psychology of physical symptoms and sensations. In G. S. Sanders & J. Suls (Eds.), *Social psychology of health and illness* (pp. 99–128). Hillsdale, NJ: Erlbaum.

Skinner, B. F. (1938). *The behavior of organisms.* New York, NY: Appleton.

Skinner, C. S., Campbell, M. K., Rimer, B. K., Curry, S., & Prochaska, J. O. (1999). How effective is tailored print communication? *Annals of Behavioral Medicine, 21*, 290–298.

Skinner, C. S., Strecher, V. J., & Hospers, H. (1994). Physician's recommendations for mammography: Do tailored messages make a difference? *American Journal of Public Health, 84*, 43–49.

Sklar, L. S., & Anisman, H. (1981). Stress and cancer. *Psychological Bulletin, 89*, 369–406.

Skrabanek, P. (1988). The physician's responsibility to the patient. *Lancet, 1*, 1155–1157.

Slater, S. J., Chaloupka, F. J., Wakefield, M., Johnston, L. D., & O'Malley, P. M. (2007). The impact of retail cigarette marketing practices on youth smoking uptake. *Archives of Pediatric and Adolescent Medicine, 161*, 440–445.

Slattery, M. L., Boucher, K. M., Caan, B. J., Potter, J. D., & Ma, K.-N. (1998). Eating patterns and risk of colon cancer. *American Journal of Epidemiology, 148*, 4–16.

Slattery, M. L., Schumacher, M. C., Smith, K. R., West, D. W., & Abd-Elghany, N. (1990). Physical activity, diet, and risk of colon cancer in Utah. *American Journal of Epidemiology, 128*, 989–999.

Sloand, E. M., Pitt, E., Chiarello, R. J., & Nemo, G. J. (1991). HIV testing: State of the art. *Journal of the American Medical Association, 266*, 2861–2866.

Slochower, J., Kaplan, S. P., & Mann, L. (1981). The effects of life stress and weight on mood and eating. *Appetite, 2*, 115–125.

Smeets, M. A. M. (1999). Body size categorization in anorexia nervosa using a morphing instrument. *International Journal of Eating Disorders, 25*, 451–455.

Smith, C. A., & Pratt, M. (1993). Cardiovascular disease. In R. C. Brownson, P. L. Remington, & J. R. Davis (Eds.), *Chronic disease epidemiology and control* (pp. 83–107). Washington, DC: American Public Health Association.

Smith, G. T., Goldman, M. S., Greenbaum, P. E., & Christiansen, B. A. (1995). Expectancy for social facilitation from drinking: The divergent paths of high-expectancy and low-expectancy adolescents. *Journal of Abnormal Psychology, 104*, 32–40.

Smith, J. T., Barabasz, Z., & Barabasz, M. (1996). Comparision of hypnosis and distraction in severly ill children undergoing painful medical procedures. *Journal of Counseling Psychology, 43*, 187–195.

Smith, T. W. (1992). Hostility and health: Current status of a psychosomatic hypothesis. *Health Psychology, 11*, 139–150.

Smith, T. W., Orleans, C. T., & Jenkins, C. D. (2004). Prevention and health promotion: Decades of progress, new challenges, and an emerging agenda. *Health Psychology, 23*, 126–131.

Smith, T. W., Pope, M. K., Sanders, J. D., Allred, K. D., & O'Keefe, J. L. (1988). Cynical hostility at home and work. *Journal of Research in Personality, 22*, 525–548.

Smith, T. W., Ruiz, J. M., & Uchino, B. N. (2004). Mental activation of supportive ties, hostility, and cardiovascular reactivity to laboratory stress in young men and women. *Health Psychology, 23*, 476–485.

Smith, T. W., Uchino, B. N., Berg, C. A., Florsheim, P., Pearce, G., Hawkins, M., . . . Yoon, H-C. (2008). Associations of self-reports versus spouse ratings of negative affectivity, dominance, and affiliation with coronary artery disease: Where should we look and who should we ask when studying personality and health? *Health Psychology, 27*, 676–684.

Smith, T. W., & Williams, P. G. (1992). Personality and health: Advantages and limitations of the five-factor model. *Journal of Personality, 60*, 395–423.

Smyth, J. M. (1998). Written emotional expression: Effect sizes, outcome types, and moderating variables. *Journal of Consulting and Clinical Psychology, 66*, 174–184.

Smyth, J. M., Stone, A. A., Hurewitz, A., & Kaell, A. (1999). Effects of writing about stressful experiences on symptom reduction in patients with asthma or rheumatoid arthritis: A randomized trial. *Journal of the American Medical Association, 281*, 1304–1309.

Snyder, C. R., Sympson, S. C., Ybasco, F. C., Borders, T. F., Babyak, M. A., & Higgins, R. L. (1996). Development and validation of the State Hope Scale. *Journal of Personality and Social Psychology, 70*, 321–335.

Sobell, L. C., Cunningham, J. A., & Sobell, M. B. (1996). Recovery from alcohol problems with and without treatment: Prevalence in two population surveys. *American Journal of Public Health, 86*, 966–972.

Sobell, M. B., Sobell, L. C., & Gavin, D. R. (1995). Portraying alcohol treatment outcomes: Different yardsticks of success. *Behavior Therapy, 26*, 643–669.

Sokol, D., Sokol, J., & Sokol, C. (1985). A review of nonintrusive therapies used to deal with anxiety and pain in the dental office. *Journal of the American Dental Association, 110,* 217–222.

Solomon, G. F. (1991). Psychosocial factors, exercise, and immunity: Athletes, elderly persons, and AIDs patients. *International Journal of Sports Medicine, 12,* S50–S52.

Solomon, L. J., Secker-Walker, R. H., Skelly, J. M., & Flynn, B. S. (1996). Stages of change in smoking during pregnancy in low-income women. *Journal of Behavioral Medicine, 19,* 333–344.

Solomon, Z., Mikulincer, M., & Hobfoll, S. E. (1986). Effects of social support and battle intensity on loneliness and breakdown during combat. *Journal of Personality and Social Psychology, 51,* 1269–1276.

Song, J., Floyd, F. J., Seltzer, M. M., Greenberg. J. S., & Hong, J. (2010). Long-term effects of child death on parents' health-related quality of life: A dyadic analysis. *Family Relations, 59,* 269–282.

Sorensen, G., Jacobs, D. R., Pirie, P., Folsom, A., Luepker, R., & Gillum, R. (1987). Relationships among Type A behavior, employment experiences, and gender: The Minnesota Heart Survey. *Journal of Behavioral Medicine, 10,* 323–336.

Sorensen, G., Pechacek, T., & Pallonen, U. (1986). Occupational and worksite norms and attitudes about smoking cessation. *American Journal of Public Health, 76,* 544–549.

Sosa, R., Kennell, J., Klaus, M., Robertson, S., & Urrutia, J. (1980). The effect of a supportive companion on perionatal problems, length of labor, and mother–infant interaction. *New England Journal of Medicine, 303,* 597–600.

Southam, M. A., & Dunbar, J. (1986). Facilitating patient compliance with medical interventions. In K. A. Holroyd & T. L. Creer (Eds.), *Self-management of chronic disease: Handbook of clinical interventions and research* (pp. 163–187). New York, NY: Academic Press.

Spanos, N. P., & Katsanis, J. (1989). Effects of instructional set on attributions of nonvolition during hypnotic and nonhypnotic analgesia. *Journal of Personality and Social Psychology, 56,* 182–188.

Speca, M., Carlson, L. E., Goodey, E., & Angen, M. (2000). A randomized, wait-list controlled clinical trial: The effect of a mindfulness meditation-based stress reduction program on mood and symptoms of stress in cancer outpatients. *Psychosomatic Medicine, 62,* 613–622.

Spector, P. E. (2002). Employee control and occupational stress. *Current Directions in Psychological Science, 11,* 133–136.

Speece, M. W., & Brent, S. B. (1996). The development of children's understanding of death. In C. A. Corr & D. M. Corr (Eds.), *Handbook of childhood death and bereavement* (pp. 29–50). New York, NY: Springer.

Speisman, J. C., Lazarus, R. S., Mordkoff, A., & Davison, L. (1964). Experimental reduction of stress based on ego-defense theory. *Journal of Abnormal and Social Psychology, 68,* 367–380.

Spencer, S. M., Lehman, J. M., Wynings, C., Arena, P., Carver, C. S., Antoni, M. H., ... Love, N. (1999). Concerns about breast cancer and relations to psychosocial well-being in a multiethnic sample of early-stage patients. *Health Psychology, 18,* 159–168.

Spiegel, D. (1996). Cancer and depression. *British Journal of Psychiatry, 168,* 109–116.

Spiegel, D. (2001). Mind matters—Group therapy and survival in breast cancer. *New England Journal of Medicine, 345,* 1767–1768.

Spiegel, D., Bloom, J. R., Kraemer, H. C., & Gottheil, E. (1989). Effect of psychosocial treatment on survival of patients with metastatic breast cancer. *Lancet, 2,* 888–891.

Spiegel, D., & Kato, P. (1996). Psychosocial influences on cancer incidence and progression. *Harvard Review of Psychiatry, 4,* 10–26.

Spielberger, C. D. (1986). Psychological determinants of smoking behavior. In R. D. Tollison (Ed.), *Smoking and society: Toward a more balanced assessment* (pp. 89–134). Lexington, MA: D. C. Heath.

Spiro, A., Aldwin, C. M., Levenson, M. R., & Bosse, R. (1990). Longitudinal findings from the Normative Aging Study: II. Do emotionality and extraversion predict symptom change? *Journals of Gerontology, 45,* 136–144.

Stacy, A. W., Newcomb, M. D., & Bentler, P. M. (1991). Personality, problem drinking, and drunk driving: Mediating, moderating, and direct-effect models. *Journal of Personality & Social Psychology, 60,* 795–811.

Stadler, G., Oettingen, G., & Gollwitzer, P. M. (2010). Intervention effects of information and self-regulation on eating fruits and vegetables over two years. *Health Psychology, 29,* 274–283.

Stam, H. J., McGrath, P. A., & Brooke, R. I. (1984). The effects of a cognitive-behavioral treatment program on temporo-mandibular pain and dysfunction syndrome. *Psychosomatic Medicine, 46,* 534–545.

Stamler, J., Wentworth, D., & Neaton, J. D. (1986). Is relationship between serum cholesterol and risk of premature death from coronary heart disease continuous and graded? Findings in 356, 222 primary screenees of the Multiple Risk Factor Intervention Trial (MRFIT). *Journal of the American Medical Association, 256,* 2823–2828.

Stampfer, M. J., Colditz, G. A., Willett, W. C., Manson, J. E., Rosner, B., Speizer, F. E., & Hennekens, C. H. (1991). A prospective study of postmenopausal estrogen therapy and cardiovascular diseases: Ten-year follow-up from the Nurses' Health Study. *New England Journal of Medicine, 325,* 756–762.

Stampfer, M. J., Rimm, E. B., & Walsh, D. C. (1993). Commentary: Alcohol, the heart, and public policy. *American Journal of Public Health, 83,* 801–804.

Stanek, K., Abbott, D., & Cramer, S. (1990). Diet quality and the eating environment of preschool children. *Journal of the American Dietetic Association, 90,* 1582–1584.

Stanton, A. L. (1987). Determinants of adherence to medical regimens by hypertensive patients. *Journal of Behavioral Medicine, 10,* 377–394.

Stanton, A. L., Danoff-Burg, S., Sworowski, L. A., Collins, C. A., Branstetter, A. D., Rodriguez-Hanley, ... Austenfeld, J. L. (2002). Randomized, controlled trial of written emotional expression and benefit finding in breast cancer patients. *Journal of Clinical Oncology, 20,* 4160–4168.

Stanton, A. L., Kirk, S. B., Camerson, C. L., & Danoff-Burg, S. (2000). Coping through emotional approach: Scale construction and validation. *Journal of Personality and Social Psychology, 78,* 1150–1169.

Stanton, A. L., Lobel, M., Sears, S., & DeLuca, R. S. (2002). Psychosocial aspects of selected issues in women's reproductive health: Current status and future directions. *Journal of Consulting and Clinical Psychology, 70,* 751–770.

Stanton, A. L., & Snider, P. R. (1993). Coping with a breast cancer diagnosis: A prospective study. *Health Psychology, 12,* 16–23.

Starace, F., Massa, A., Amico, K. R., & Fisher, J. D. (2006). Adherence to antiretroviral therapy: An empirical test of the Information-Motivation-Behavioral Skills model. *Health Psychology, 25,* 153–162.

Stark, M. J. (1992). Dropping out of substance abuse treatment: A clinically oriented review. *Clinical Psychology Review, 12,* 93–116.

Stark, O., Atkins, E., Wolff, O. H., & Douglas, J. W. B. (1981). Longitudinal study of obesity in the National Survey of Health and Development. *British Medical Journal, 283,* 13–17.

Steele, C. M., & Josephs, R. A. (1990). Alcohol myopia: Its prized and dangerous effects. *American Psychologist, 45,* 921–933.

Steginga, S. K., & Occhipinti, S. (2006). Dispositional optimism as a predictor of men's decision-related distress after localized prostate cancer. *Health Psychology, 25*, 135–143.

Stein, J., Newcomb, M., & Bentler, P. (1996). Initiation and maintenance of tobacco smoking: Changing personality correlates in adolescence and young adulthood. *Journal of Applied Social Psychology, 26*, 160–187.

Steingart, R. M., Packer, M., Hamm, P., Coglianese, M. E., Gersh, B., Geltman, E. M., . . . the Survival and Ventricular Enlargement Investigators (1991). Sex differences in the management of coronary artery disease. *The New England Journal of Medicine, 325*, 226–230.

Steptoe, A., Perkins-Porras, L., Rink, E., Hilton, S., & Cappuccio, F. P. (2004). Psychological and social predictors of changes in fruit and vegetable consumption over 12 months following behavioral and nutrition education counseling. *Health Psychology, 23*, 574–581.

Steptoe, A., Wardle, J., & Marmot, M. (2005). Positive affect and health-related neuroendocrine, cardiovascular, and inflammatory processes. *Proceedings of the National Academy of Sciences of the United States, 102*, 6508–6512.

Sternbach, R. A. (1974). *Pain patients: Traits and treatment.* New York, NY: Academic Press.

Sternbach, R. A. (1986). Pain and "hassles" in the United States: Findings of the Nuprin pain report. *Pain, 27*, 69–80.

Stevens, J., Cai, J., Pamuk, E. R., Williamson, D. F., Thun, M., & Wood, J. L. (1998). The effect of age on the association between body-mass index and mortality. *New England Journal of Medicine, 338*, 1–7.

Stevens, M. M. (1997). Psychological adaptation of the dying child. In D. Doyle, G. W. C. Hanks, & N. MacDonald (Eds.), *Oxford textbook of palliative medicine* (pp. 1046–1055). New York, NY: Oxford University Press.

Stevens, M. M., & Dunsmore, J. C. (1996). Adolescents who are living with a life-threatening illness. In C. A. Corr & D. E. Balk (Eds.), *Handbook of adolescent death and bereavement* (pp. 107–135). New York, NY: Springer.

Stevens, V. M., Hatcher, J. W., & Bruce, B. K. (1994). How compliant is compliant? Evaluating adherence with breast self-exam positions. *Journal of Behavioral Medicine, 17*, 523–535.

Stevens, V. J., & Hollis, J. F. (1989). Preventing smoking relapse, using an individually tailored skills-training technique. *Journal of Consulting and Clinical Psychology, 57*, 420–424.

Stewart-Williams, S. (2004). The placebo puzzle: Putting together the pieces. *Health Psychology, 23*, 198–206.

Stice, E., Chase, A., Stormer, S., & Appel, A. (2001). A randomized trial of a dissonance-based eating disorder prevention program. *International Journal of Eating Disorders, 29*, 247–262.

Stice, E., Mazotti, L., Weibel, D., & Agras, W. S. (2000). Dissonance prevention program decreases thin-ideal internalization, body dissatisfaction, dieting, negative affect, and bulimic symptoms: A preliminary experiment. *International Journal of Eating Disorders, 27*, 206–217.

Stice, E., Presnell, K., Groesz, L., & Shaw, H. (2005). Effects of a weight maintenance diet on bulimic pathology: An experimental test of the dietary restraint theory. *Health Psychology, 24*, 402–412.

Stice, E., Presnell, K., & Spangler, D. (2002). Risk factors for binge eating onset: A prospective investigation. *Health Psychology, 21*, 131–138.

Stice, E., Rohde, P., Gau, J., & Shaw, H. (2009). An effectiveness trial of a dissonance-based eating disorder prevention program for high-risk adolescent girls. *Journal of Consulting and Clinical Psychology, 77*, 825–834.

Stice, E., Shaw, H., Burton, E., & Wade, E. (2006). Dissonance and healthy weight eating disorder prevention programs: A randomized efficacy trial. *Journal of Consulting and Clinical Psychology, 74*, 263–275.

Stillion, J., & Wass, H. (1984). Children and death. In E. S. Shneidman (Ed.), *Death: Current perspectives* (pp. 225–246). Palo Alto, CA: Mayfield.

St. Lawrence, J. (1993). African-American adolescents' knowledge, health-related attitudes, sexual behavior, and contraceptive decisions: Implications for the prevention of adolescent infection. *Journal of Consulting and Clinical Psychology, 61*, 104–112.

Stokes, J. P. (1983). Predicting satisfaction with social support from social network structure. *American Journal of Community Psychology, 11*, 141–152.

Stolberg, S. G. (1999, April 25). Sham surgery returns as a research tool. *New York Times*, p. 3.

Stolerman, I. P., & Jarvis, M. J. (1995). The scientific case that nicotine is addictive. *Psychopharmacology, 117*, 2–10.

Stommel, M., Kurtz, M. E., Kurtz, J. C., Given, C. W., & Given, B. A. (2004). A longitudinal analysis of the course of depressive symptomatology in geriatric patients with cancer of the breast, colon, lung, or prostate. *Health Psychology, 23*, 564–573.

Stone, A. A., Mezzacappa, E. S., Donatone, B. A., & Gonder, M. (1999). Psychosocial stress and social support are associated with prostate-specific antigen levels in men: Results from a community screening program. *Health Psychology, 18*, 482–486.

Stone, A. A., Schwartz, J. E., Broderick, J. E., & Shiffman, S. S. (2005). Variability of momentary pain predicts recall of weekly pain: A consequence of the peak (or salience) memory heuristic. *Personality and Social Psychology Bulletin, 31*, 1340–1346.

Stone, J., Aronson, E., Crain, A. L., Winslow, M. P., & Fried, C. (1994). Inducing hypocrisy as a means of encouraging young adults to use condoms. *Personality and Social Psychology Bulletin, 20*, 116–128.

Stoney, C. M., Davis, M. C., & Mathews, K. A. (1987). Sex differences in physiological responses to stress and coronary heart disease: A causal link? *Psychophysiology, 24*, 127–131.

Stoney, C. M., Mathews, K. A., McDonald, R. H., & Johnson, C. A. (1988). Sex differences in acute stress response: Lipid, lipoprotein, cardiovascular and neuroendocrine adjustments. *Psychophysiology, 25*, 645–656.

Story, M., & Faulkner, P. (1990). The prime time diet: Eating behavior and food messages in television program content commercials. *American Journal of Public Health, 80*, 738–740.

Strauss, L. M., Solomon, L. J., Costanza, M. C., Worden, J. K., & Foster, R. S. (1987). Breast self-examination practices and attitudes of women with and without a history of breast cancer. *Journal of Behavioral Medicine, 10*, 337–350.

Strecher, V. J., Kreuter, M. W., Den Boer, D.-J., Kobrin, S., Hospers, H. J., & Skinner, C. S. (1994). The effects of computer tailored smoking cessation messages in family practice settings. *Journal of Family Practice, 39*, 262–270.

Strecher, V. J., Kreuter, M. W., & Kobrin, S. C. (1995). Do cigarette smokers have unrealistic perceptions of their heart attack, cancer, and stroke risks? *Journal of Behavioral Medicine, 18*, 45–54.

Strike, P. C., Magid, K., Whitehead, D. L., Brydon, L., Bhattacharyya, M. R., & Steptoe, A. (2006). Pathophysiological processes underlying emotional triggering of acute cardiac events. *Proceedings of the National Academy of Sciences of the United States of America, 103*, 4322–4327.

Stroebe, M. S., & Schut, H. (2001). Models of coping with bereavement: A review. In M. S. Stroebe, R. O. Hansson, W. Stroebe, & H. Schut (Eds.), *Handbook of bereavement research: Consequences, coping, and care* (pp. 375–403). Washington, DC: American Psychological Association.

Stroebe, M. S., & Stroebe, W. (1983). Who suffers more? Sex differences in health risks of the widowed. *Psychological Bulletin, 93*, 279–301.

Stroebe, M. S., & Stroebe, W. (1991). Does "grief work" work? *Journal of Consulting and Clinical Psychology, 59*, 479–482.

Stroebe, W., & Stroebe, M. S. (1996). The social psychology of social support. In E. T. Higgins & A. W. Kruglanski (Eds.), *Social psychology: Handbook of basic principles* (pp. 597–621). New York, NY: Guilford Press.

Stroebe, W., Stroebe, M. S., & Abakoumkin, G. (1999). Does differential social support cause sex differences in bereavement outcome? *Journal of Community and Applied Social Psychology, 9*, 1–12.

Struckman-Johnson, C. J., Gilliland, R. C., Struckman-Johnson, D. L., & North, T. C. (1990). The effects of fear of AIDS and gender on responses to fear-arousing condom advertisements. *Journal of Applied Social Psychology, 20*, 1396–1410.

Stunkard, A. J., & Sorensen, T. I. (1993). Obesity and socioeconomic status—a complex relationship. *New England Journal of Medicine, 329*, 1036–1037.

Sturges, J. W., & Rogers, R. W. (1996). Preventive health psychology from a developmental perspective: An extension of protection motivation theory. *Health Psychology, 15*, 158–166.

Suarez, E. C., Kuhn, C. M., Schanberg, S. M., Williams, R. B., Jr., & Zimmerman, E. A. (1998). Neuroendocrine, cardiovascular, and emotional responses of hostile men: The role of interpersonal challenge. *Psychosomatic Medicine, 60*, 78–88.

Subra, B., Muller, D., Bègue, L., Bushman, B. J., & Delmas, F. (2010). Automatic effects of alcohol and aggressive cues on aggressive thoughts and behaviors. *Personality and Social Psychology Bulletin, 36*, 1052–1057.

Substance Abuse and Mental Health Services Administration, Office of Applied Studies. (August 2, 2007). *The NSDUH report: Gender differences in alcohol use and alcohol dependence or abuse: 2004 and 2005.* Rockville, MD.

Suecoff, S. A., Avner, J. R., Chou, K. J., & Crain, E. F. (1999). A comparison of New York City playground hazards in high- and low–income areas. *Archives of Pediatrics & Adolescent Medicine, 153*, 363–366.

Sugisawa, H., Shibata, H., Hougham, G. W., Sugihara, Y., & Liang, J. (2002). The impact of social ties on depressive symptoms in U.S. and Japanese elderly. *Journal of Social Issues, 58*, 785–804.

Suinn, R. M. (1975). The cardiac stress management program for Type A patients. *Cardiac Rehabilitation, 5*, 13–15.

Suinn, R. M. (2001). The terrible twos—anger and anxiety: Hazardous to your health. *American Psychologist, 56*, 27–36.

Sullivan, L. (1990). Sounding board: Healthy People 2000. *New England Journal of Medicine, 323*, 1065–1067.

Sullivan, M. J. L., Bishop, S. R., & Pivik, J. (1995). The Pain Catastrophizing Scale: Development and validation. *Psychological Assessment, 7*, 524–532.

Sullivan, M. J. L., Reesor, K., Mikail, S., & Fisher, R. (1992). The treatment of depression in chronic low back pain: Review and recommendations. *Pain, 50*, 5–13.

Sullivan, P. F. (1995). Mortality in anorexia nervosa. *The American Journal of Psychiatry, 152*, 1073–1074.

Suls, J., & Bunde, J. (2005). Anger, anxiety, and depression as risk factors for cardiovascular disease: The problems and implications of overlapping affective dispositions. *Psychological Bulletin, 131*, 260–300.

Suls, J., & Fletcher, B. (1985). The relative efficacy of avoidant and non-avoidant coping strategies: A meta-analysis. *Health Psychology, 4*, 249–288.

Suls, J., & Marco, C. A. (1990). Relationship between JAS- and FTAS-Type A behavior and non-CHD illness: A prospective study controlling for negative affectivity. *Health Psychology, 9*, 479–492.

Suls, J., & Rothman, A. J. (2004). Evolution of the psychosocial model: Implications for the future of health psychology. *Health Psychology, 23*, 119–125.

Suls, J., & Wan, C. K. (1993). The relationship between trait hostility and cardiovascular reactivity: A quantitative review and analysis. *Psychophysiology, 30*, 615–626.

Sumartojo, E. (1993). When tuberculosis treatment fails: A social behavioral account of patient adherence. *American Review of Respiratory Disorders, 147*, 1311–1320.

Sumter, S. R., Bokhorst, C. L., Miers, A. C., Van Pelt, J., & Westenberg, P. M. (2010). Age and puberty differences in stress responses during a public speaking task: Do adolescents grow more sensitive to social evaluation? *Psychoneuroendocrinology, 35*, 1510–1516.

Sun, Q., Townsend, M. K., Okereke, O. I., Franco, O. H., Hu, F. B., & Grodstein, F. (2010). Physical activity at midlife in relation to successful survival in women at age 70 years or older. *Archives of Internal Medicine, 170*, 194–201.

Sunday, S. R., & Halmi, K. A. (1996). Micro- and macroanalyses of meal patterns in anorexia and bulimia nervosa. *Appetite, 26*, 21–36.

Sung, L., Klaassen, R. J., Dix, D., Pritchard, S., Yanofsky, R., Ethier, M.-C., & Klassen, A. (2009). Parental optimism in poor prognosis pediatric cancers. *Psycho-Oncology, 18*, 783–788.

SUPPORT Principal Investigators. (1995). A controlled trial to improve care for seriously ill hospitalized patients: The Study to Understand Prognoses and Preferences for Outcomes and Risks of Treatments (SUPPORT). *Journal of the American Medical Association, 274*, 1591–1598.

Surtees, P. G., Wainwright, N. W. J., Luben, R., Khaw, K.-T., & Day, N. E. (2006). Mastery, sense of coherence and mortality: Evidence of independent associations from the EPIC-Norfolk prospective cohort study. *Health Psychology, 25*, 102–110.

Surtees, P. G., Wainwright, N. W. J., Luben, R., Wareham, N. J., Bingham, S. A., & Khaw, K.-T. (2010). Mastery is associated with cardiovascular disease mortality in men and women at apparently low risk. *Health Psychology, 29*, 412–420.

Sussman, S. Y., Sun, P., & Dent, C. W. (2006). A meta-analysis of teen cigarette smoking cessation. *Health Psychology, 25*, 549–557.

Sutherland, R. J., McDonald, R. J., & Savage, D. D. (1997). Prenatal exposure to moderate levels of ethanol can have long-lasting effects on hippocampal synaptic plasticity in adult offspring. *Hippocampus, 7*, 232–238.

Sutker, P. B., Davis, M. J., Uddo, M., & Ditta, S. R. (1995). War zone stress, personal resources, and PTSD in Persian Gulf War returnees. *Journal of Abnormal Psychology, 104*, 444–452.

Swami, V., Frederick, D. A., Aavik, T., Alcalay, L., Jüri Allik, J., Anderson, D., . . . Zivcic-Becirevic, I. (2010). The attractive female body weight and female body dissatisfaction in 26 countries across 10 world regions: Results of the international body project I. *Personality and Social Psychology Bulletin, 36*, 309–325.

Swanson, S. A., Crow, S. J., Le Grange, D., Swendsen, J., & Merikangas, K. R. (2011). Prevalence and correlates of eating disorders in adolescents: Results from the national comorbidity survey replication adolescent supplement. *Archives of General Psychiatry, 68*, 714–723.

Swendsen, J. D., Tennen, H., Carney, M. A., Affleck, G., Willard, A., & Hromi, A. (2000). Mood and alcohol consumption: An experience sampling test of the self-medication hypothesis. *Journal of Abnormal Psychology, 109*, 198–204.

Szasz, T. S., & Hollender, M. H. (1956). A contribution to the philosophy of medicine. *Archives of Internal Medicine, 97*, 585–592.

Taddio, A., Katz, J., Ilersich, A. L., & Koren, G. (1997). Effects of neonatal circumcision on pain response during subsequent routine vaccination. *Lancet, 349*, 599–603.

Talbot, F., Nouwen, A., Gingras, J., Belanger, A., & Audet, J. (1999). Relations of diabetes intrusiveness and personal control to symptoms of depression among adults with diabetes. *Health Psychology, 18*, 537–542.

Talbot, M. (2000, January 9). The placebo prescription. *The New York Times Magazine.*

Tallmer, J., Scherwitz, L., Chesney, M., Hecker, M., Hunkeler, E., Serwitz, J., & Hughes, G. (1990). Selection, training, and quality control of Type A interviews in a prospective study of young adults. *Journal of Behavioral Medicine, 13*, 449–466.

Tam, L., Bagozzi, R. P., & Spanjol, J. (2010). When planning is not enough: The self-regulatory effect of implementation intentions on changing snacking habits. *Health Psychology, 29*, 284–292.

Tamburro, R. F., Gordon, P. L., D'Apolito, J. P., & Howard, S. C. (2004). Unsafe and violent behavior in commercials aired during televised major sporting events. *Pediatrics, 114*, 694–698.

Taub, A. (1998). Thumbs down on accupuncture. *Science, 279*, 159.

Tauras, J. A., O'Malley, P. M., & Johnston, L. D. (2001). *Effects of price and access laws on teenage smoking initiation: A national longitudinal analysis (National Bureau of Economic Research Working Paper 8331)*. Cambridge, MA: NBER.

Taylor, C. B., Bandura, A., Ewart, C. K., Miller, N. H., & DeBusk, R. F. (1985). Exercise testing to enhance wives' confidence in their husbands' cardiac capability soon after clinically uncomplicated acute myocardial infarction. *American Journal of Cardiology, 55*, 635–638.

Taylor, S. E. (1979). Hospital patient behavior: Reactance, helplessness, or control? *Journal of Social Issues, 35*, 156–184.

Taylor, S. E. (1990). Health psychology: The science and the field. *American Psychologist, 45*, 40–50.

Taylor, S. E., & Aspinwall, L. G. (1993). Coping with chronic illness. In L. Goldberger & S. Breznitz (Eds.), *Handbook of stress: Theoretical and clinical aspects* (pp. 511–531). New York, NY: Free Press.

Taylor, S. E., Burklund, L. J., Eisenberger, N. I., Lehman, B. J., Hilmert, C. J., & Lieberman, M. D. (2008). Neural bases of moderation of cortisol stress responses by psychosocial resources. *Journal of Personality and Social Psychology, 95*, 197–211.

Taylor, S. E., Kemeny, M. E., Aspinwall, L. G., Schneider, S. G., Rodriguez, R., & Herbert, M. (1992). Optimism, coping, psychological distress, and high-risk sexual behavior among men at risk for acquired immunodeficiency syndrome (AIDS). *Journal of Personality and Social Psychology, 63*, 460–470.

Taylor, S. E., Klein, L. C., Lewis, B. P., Gruenewald, T. L., Gurung, R. A. R., & Updegraff, J. A. (2000). Biobehavioral responses to stress in females: Tend-and-befriend, not fight-or-flight. *Psychological Review, 107*, 411–429.

Taylor, S. E., Lichtman, R. R., & Wood, J. V. (1984). Attributions, beliefs about control, and adjustment to breast cancer. *Journal of Personality and Social Psychology, 46*, 489–502.

Taylor, S. E., Welch, W., Kim, H. S., & Sherman, D. K. (2007). Cultural differences in the impact of social support on psychological and biological stress responses. *Psychological Science, 18*, 831–837.

Tedesco, L. A., Keffer, M. A., Davis, E. L., & Christersson, L. A. (1993). Self-efficacy and reasoned action: Predicting oral health status and behaviour at one, three, and six month intervals. *Psychology and Health, 8*, 105–121.

Temel, J. S., Greer, J. A. Muzikansky, A., Gallagher, E. R., Admane, S., Jackson, V. A., ... Lynch, T. J. (2010). Early palliative care for patients with metastatic non–small-cell lung cancer. *New England Journal of Medicine, 363*, 733–742.

Teng, Y., & Mak, W. W. S. (2011). The role of planning and self-efficacy in condom use among men who have sex with men: An application of the Health Action Process Approach model. *Health Psychology, 30*, 119–128.

Teno, J. M., Clarridge, B. R., Casey, V., Welch, L. C., Wetle, T., Shield, R., & Mor, V. (2004). Family perspectives on end-of-life care at the last place of care. *Journal of the American Medical Association, 291*, 88–93.

Ter Kuile, M. M., Spinhoven, P., Linssen, A. C., Zitman, F. G., Van Dyck, R., & Rooijmans, H. G. (1994). Autogenic training and cognitive self-hypnosis for the treatment of recurrent headaches in three different subject groups. *Pain, 58*, 331–340.

Tercyak, K. P., Peshkin, B. N., Streisand, R., & Lerman, C. (2001). Psychological issues among children of hereditary breast cancer gene (BRCA1/2) testing participants. *Psycho-Oncology, 10*, 336–346.

Terracciano, A., Löckenhoff, C. E., Zonderman, A. B., Ferrucci, L., & Costa, P. T., Jr. (2008). Personality predictors of longevity: Activity, emotional stability, and conscientiousness. *Psychosomatic Medicine, 70*, 621–627.

Terry, D. J., & Hynes, G. J. (1998). Adjustment to a low-control situation: Reexamining the role of coping responses. *Journal of Personality and Social Psychology, 74*, 1078–1092.

The Antiretroviral Therapy Cohort Collaboration. (2008). Life expectancy of individuals on combination antiretroviral therapy in high-income countries: A collaborative analysis of 14 cohort studies. *Lancet, 372*, 293–299.

Theorell, T., Ahlberg-Hulten, G., Sigala, F., Perski, A., Soderholm, M., Kallner, A., & Eneroth, P. (1990). A psychosocial and biomedical comparison between men in sex contrasting service occupations. *Work and Stress, 4*, 51–63.

Theorell, T., Blomkvist, V., Jonsson, H., Schulman, S., Berntorp, E., & Stigendal, L. (1995). Social support and the development of immune function in human immunodeficiency virus infection. *Psychosomatic Medicine, 57*, 32–36.

Thoits, P. A. (1986). Social support as coping assistance. *Journal of Consulting and Clinical Psychology, 54*, 416–423.

Thoits, P. A., Hohmann, A. A., Harvey, M. R., & Fletcher, B. (2000). Similar other support for men undergoing coronary artery bypass surgery. *Health Psychology, 19*, 264–273.

Thomas, W., White, C. M., Mah, J., Geisser, M. S., Church, T. R., & Mandel, J. S. (1995). Longitudinal compliance with annual screening for fecal occult blood. *American Journal of Epidemiology, 142*, 176–182.

Thompson, C. (2007, December 9). Community urinalysis. *New York Times.*

Thompson, D. C., Nunn, M. E., Thompson, R. S., & Rivara, F. P. (1996). Effectiveness of bicycle safety helmets in preventing serious facial injury. *Journal of the American Medical Association, 276*, 1994–1995.

Thompson, D. C., Rivara, F. P., & Thompson, R. S. (1996). Effectiveness of bicycle safety helmets in preventing head injuries: A case-control study. *Journal of the American Medical Association, 276*, 1968–1973.

Thompson, J. (1984). Communicating with patients. In R. Fitzpatrick, J. Hinton, S. Newman, G. Scrambler, & J. Thompson (Eds.), *The experience of illness* (pp. 87–108). New York, NY: Tavistock.

Thompson, S. C., Nanni, C., & Levine, A. (1994). Primary versus secondary and central versus consequence-related control in HIV-positive men. *Journal of Personality and Social Psychology, 67*, 540–547.

Thompson, S. C., Nanni, C., & Schwankovsky, L. (1990). Patient-oriented interventions to improve communication in a medical visit. *Health Psychology, 9*, 390–404.

Thompson, S. C., Sobolew-Shubin, A., Galbraith, M., Schwankovsky, L., & Cruzen, D. (1993). Maintaining perceptions of control: Finding perceived control in low-control circumstances.

Journal of Personality and Social Psychology, 64, 293–304.

Thoolen, B. J., de Ridder, D., Bensing, J., Gorter, K., & Rutten, G. (2009). Beyond good intentions: The role of proactive coping in achieving sustained behavioural change in the context of diabetes management. *Psychology & Health, 24,* 237–254.

Thorndike, E. L. (1905). *The elements of psychology.* New York, NY: Seiler.

Thorpe, C. T., Lewis, M. A., & Sterba, K. R. (2008). Reactions to health-related social control in young adults with type 1 diabetes. *Journal of Behavioral Medicine, 31,* 93–103.

Thun, M. J., Day-Lally, C. A., Calle, E. E., Flanders, W. D., & Heath, C. W. (1995). Excess mortality among cigarette smokers: Changes in a 20-year interval. *American Journal of Public Health, 85,* 1223–1230.

Thune, I., Brenn, T., Lund, E., & Gaard, M. (1997). Physical activity and the risk of breast cancer. *New England Journal of Medicine, 336,* 1269–1275.

Tibben, A., Timman, R., Bannink, E. C., & Duivenvoorden, H. J. (1997). Three-year follow-up after presymptomatic testing for Huntington's disease in tested individuals and partners. *Health Psychology, 16,* 20–35.

Tice, D. M., & Baumeister, R. F. (1997). Longitudinal study of procrastination, performance, stress, and health: The cost and benefits of dawdling. *Psychological Science, 8,* 454–458.

Tickle, J. J., Hull, J. G., Sargent, J. D., Dalton, M. A., & Heatherton, T. F. (2006). A structural equation model of social influences and exposure to media smoking on adolescent smoking. *Basic and Applied Social Psychology, 28,* 117–129.

Tickle, J. J., Sargent, J. D., Dalton, M. A., Beach, M. L., & Heatherton, T. F. (2001). Favourite movie stars, their tobacco use in contemporary movies and its association with adolescent smoking. *Tobacco Control, 10,* 16–22.

Tiller, J., Schmidt, U., Ali, S., & Treasure, J. (1995). Patterns of punitiveness in women with eating disorders. *International Journal of Eating Disorders, 17,* 365–371.

Timberlake, D. S., Haberstick, B. C., Lessem, J. M., Smolen, A., Ehringer, M., Hewitt, J. K., & Hopfer, C. (2006). An association between the DAT1 polymorphism and smoking behavior in young adults from the national longitudinal study of adolescent health. *Health Psychology, 25,* 190–197.

Timko, C. (1987). Seeking medical care for a breast cancer symptom: Determinants of intentions to engage in prompt or delay behavior. *Health Psychology, 6,* 305–328.

Timman, R., Roos, R., Maat-Kievit, A., & Tibben, A. (2004). Adverse effects of predictive testing for Huntington Disease underestimated: Long-term effects 7–10 years after the test. *Health Psychology, 23,* 189–197.

Timmer, S. G., Veroff, J., & Hatchett, S. (1996). Family ties and marital happiness: The differential experiences of Black and White newlywed couples. *Journal of Social and Personal Relationships, 13,* 335–359.

Tinetti, M. E., Baker, D. I., King, M., Gottschalk, M., Murphy, T. E., Acampora, D., ... Allore, H. G. (2008). Effect of dissemination of evidence in reducing injuries from falls. *New England Journal of Medicine, 359,* 252–261.

Tinsworth, D., & McDonald, J. (2001). *Special Study: Injuries and deaths associated with children's playground equipment.* Washington, DC: U.S. Consumer Product Safety Commission.

Tiro, J. A., Diamond, P. M., Perz, C. A., Fernandez, M., Rakowski, W., DiClemente, C. C., & Vernon, S. W. (2005). Validation of scales measuring attitudes and norms related to mammography screening in women veterans. *Health Psychology, 24,* 555–566.

Tomar, S. L., & Giovino, G. A. (1998). Incidence and predictors of smokeless tobacco use among U.S. youth. *American Journal of Public Health, 88,* 20–26.

Tomarken, A., Holland, J., Schachter, S., Vanderwerker, L., Zuckerman, E., Nelson, C., . . . Prigerso, H. (2008). Factors of complicated grief pre-death in caregivers of cancer patients. *Psycho-Oncology, 17,* 105–111.

Tomkins, S. S. (1966). Psychological model of smoking behavior. *American Journal of Public Health, 56* (suppl.), 17–20.

Tomkins, S. S. (1968). A modified model of smoking behavior. In E. F. Borgatta & R. Evans (Eds.), *Smoking, health and behavior* (pp. 165–186). Chicago, IL: Aldine.

Toniolo, P., Ribloi, E., Protta, F., Charrel, M., & Coppa, A. P. (1989). Calorie-providing nutrients and risk of breast cancer. *Journal of the National Cancer Institute, 81,* 278–286.

Tonnesen, P., Fryd, V., Hansen, M., Helsted, J., Gunnersen, A. B., Forchammer, H., & Stockner, M. (1988). Effect of nicotine chewing gum in combination with group counseling on the cessation of smoking. *New England Journal of Medicine, 318,* 15–18.

Tosteson, D. C. (1990). New pathways in general medical education. *New England Journal of Medicine, 322,* 234–238.

Toth, P. L., Stockton, R., & Browne, R. (2000). College student grief and loss. In J. H. Harvey

& E. D. Miller (Eds.), *Loss and trauma* (pp. 237–248). Philadelphia, PA: Brunner-Rutledge.

Tran, V., Wiebe, D. J., Fortenberry, K. T., Butler, J. M., & Berg, C. A. (2011). Benefit finding, affective reactions to diabetes stress, and diabetes management among early adolescents. *Health Psychology, 30,* 212–219.

Trenholm, C., Devaney, B., Fortson, K., Clark, M., Bridgespan, L. Q., & Wheeler, J. (2008). Impacts of abstinence education on teen sexual activity, risk of pregnancy, and risk of sexually transmitted diseases. *Journal of Policy Analysis and Management, 27,* 255–276.

Triandis, H. C., Bontempo, R., Villareal, M. J., Asai, M., & Lucca, N. (1988). Individualism and collectivism: Cross-cultural perspectives on self-ingroup relationships. *Journal of Personality and Social Psychology, 54,* 323–338.

Trice, A. D., & Price-Greathouse, J. (1986). Joking under the drill: A validity study of the CHS. *Journal of Social Behavior and Personality, 1,* 265–266.

Trobst, K. K., Herbst, J. H., Masters, H. L., & Costa, P. T. (2002). Personality pathways to unsafe sex: Personality, condom use, and HIV risk behaviors. *Journal of Research in Personality, 36,* 117–133.

Troxel, W. M., Matthews, K. M., Bromberger, J. T., & Sutton-Tyrrell, K. (2003). Chronic stress burden, discrimination, and subclinical cardiovascular disease in African American and Caucasian women. *Health Psychology, 22,* 300–309.

Trussell, D. (2003, September 22). The disease is silent. We don't have to be. *Newsweek* .

Tsoh, J. Y., McClure, J. B., Skaar, K. L., Wetter, D. W., Cinciripini, P. M., Prokhorovet, A. V., . . . Gritz, E (1997). Smoking cessation 2: Components of effective intervention. *Behavioral Medicine, 23,* 15–27.

Tucker, J. S., Orlando, M., Burnam, M. A., Sherbourne, C. D., Kung, F.-Y., & Gifford, A. L. (2004). Psychosocial mediators of antiretroviral nonadherence in HIV-positive adults with substance use and mental health problems. *Health Psychology, 23,* 363–370.

Tugade, M. M., & Fredrickson, B. L. (2004). Resilient individuals use positive emotions to bounce back from negative emotional experiences. *Journal of Personality and Social Psychology, 86,* 320–333.

Turbin, M. S., Jessor, R., Costa, F. M., Dong, Q., Zhang, H., & Wang, C. (2006). Protective and risk factors in health-enhancing behavior among adolescents in China and the United States: Does social context matter? *Health Psychology, 25,* 445–454.

Turk, D. C. (1996). Biopsychosocial perspective on chronic pain. In R. J. Gatchel & D. C. Turk

(Eds.), *Psychological approaches to pain management: A practitioner's handbook* (pp. 3–32). New York, NY: Guilford Press.

Turk, D. C., & Flor, H. (1999). Chronic pain: A biobehavioral perspective. In R. J. Gatchel & D. C. Turk (Eds.), *Psychosocial factors in pain: Critical perspectives* (pp. 18–34). New York, NY: Guilford Press.

Turk, D. C., Meichenbaum, D., & Genest, M. (1983). *Pain and behavioral medicine: A cognitive-behavioral perspective*. New York, NY: Guilford Press.

Turk, D. C., Sist, T. C., Okifuji, A., Miner, M. F., Florio, G., Harrison, P.,...Zevon, M. A. (1998). Adaptation to metastatic cancer pain, regional/local cancer pain, and non-cancer pain: Role of psychological and behavioral factors. *Pain, 74,* 247–256.

Turk-Charles, S., Gatz, M., Kato, K., & Pedersen, N. L. (2008). Physical health 25 years later: The predictive ability of neuroticism. *Health Psychology, 27,* 369–378.

Turner, J. A., & Chapman, C. R. (1982). Psychological interventions for chronic pain: A critical review. I: Relaxation training and biofeedback. *Pain, 12,* 1–21.

Turner, J. A., & Clancy, S. (1988). Comparison of operant behavioral and cognitive-behavioral group treatment for chronic low back pain. *Journal of Consulting and Clinical Psychology, 56,* 261–266.

Turner, J. A., Clancy, S., McQuade, K. J., & Cardenas, D. D. (1990). Effectiveness of behavioral therapy for chronic low back pain: A component analysis. *Journal of Consulting and Clinical Psychology, 58,* 573–579.

Turner, J. A., & Jensen, M. P. (1993). Efficacy of cognitive therapy for chronic low back pain. *Pain, 52,* 169–177.

Tversky, A., & Kahneman, D. (1981, January 30). The framing of decisions and the psychology of choice. *Science, 211,* 453–458.

Twisk, J. W. R., Kemper, H. C. G., van Mechelen, W., & Post, G. B. (1997). Tracking of risk factors for coronary heart disease over a 14-year period: A comparison between lifestyle and biologic risk factors with data from the Amsterdam Growth and Health Study. *American Journal of Epidemiology, 145,* 688–696.

Uchino, B. N., Cacioppo, J. T., & Kiecolt-Glaser, K. B. (1996). The relationships between social support and physiological processes: A review with emphasis on underlying mechanisms and implications for health. *Psychological Bulletin, 119,* 488–531.

Uchino, B. N., Cacioppo, J. T., Malarkey, W., & Glaser, R. (1995). Individual differences in cardiac sympathetic control predict endocrine and immune responses to acute psychological stress. *Journal of Personality and Social Psychology, 69,* 736–743.

Uchino, B. N., Uno, D., & Holt-Lunstad, J. (1999). Social support, physiological processes, and health. *Current Directions in Psychological Science, 8,* 145–148.

Ukestad, L. K., & Wittrock, D. A. (1996). Pain perception and coping in female tension headache sufferers and headache-free controls. *Health Psychology, 15,* 65–68.

Ulrich, R. S. (1984). View through a window may influence recovery from surgery. *Science, 224,* 420–421.

UNAIDS. (2006). *AIDS epidemic update: December 2006.* Geneva, Switzerland: UNAIDS.

Unden, A., Orth-Gomer, K., & Elofsson, S. (1991). Cardiovascular effects of social support in the work place: Twenty-four hour ECG monitoring of men and women. *Psychosomatic Medicine, 53,* 50.

Underhill, K., Operario, D., & Montgomery, P. (2007). Systematic review of abstinence-plus HIV prevention programs in high-income countries. *PLoS Medicine* 4(9): e275.

Unger, J. B., Hamilton, J. E., & Sussman, S. (2004). A family member's job loss as a risk factor for smoking among adolescents. *Health Psychology, 23,* 308–313.

United Nations International Children's Eduction Fund (UNICEF). (1991). *Facts for life.* New York, NY: Author.

United States Department of Health & Human Services. (2011). *Centers for medicare & medicaid services: National health expenditure data.* Retrieved September 14, 2011 from https://www.cms.gov/NationalHealthExpend Data/25_NHE_Fact_sheet.asp.

United States Department of Health & Human Services. (2011). *Summary health statistics for the U. S. population: National health interview survey, 2010.* Retrieved on September 17, 2011 from http://www.cdc.gov/nchs/nhis.htm.

United States Department of Transportation, National Highway Traffic Safety Administration. (2010). *Traffic safety facts 2009: Alcohol-impaired driving.* Washington, DC.

Updegraff, J. A., & Taylor, S. E. (2000). From vulnerability to growth: Positive and negative effects of stressful life events. In J. H. Harvey & E. D. Miller (Eds.), *Loss and trauma: general and close relationship perspectives* (pp. 3–28). Philadelphia, PA: Brunner-Routledge.

Updegraff, J. A., Taylor, S. E., Kemeny, M. E., & Wyatt, G. E. (2002). Positive and negative effects of HIV infection in women with low socioeconomic resources. *Personality and Social Psychology Bulletin, 28,* 382–394.

Ursin, H., Baade, E., & Levine, S. (1978). *Psychobiology of stress: A study of coping men.* New York, NY: Academic Press.

Utne, I., Miaskowski, C., Bjordal, K., Paul, S. M., & Rustoen, T. (2010). The relationships between mood disturbances and pain, hope, and quality of life in hospitalized cancer patients with pain on regularly scheduled opioid analgesic. *Journal of Palliative Medicine, 13,* 311–318.

Valent, P. (2000). Stress effects of the Holocaust. In G. Fink (Ed.), *Encyclopedia of stress* (pp. 390–395). San Diego, CA: Academic Press.

Valente, T. W., Murphy, S., Huang, G., Gusek, J., Greene, J., & Beck, V. (2007). Evaluating a minor storyline on ER about teen obesity, hypertension, and 5 a day. *Journal of Health Communication, 12,* 551–566.

Van Baal, P. H., Hoogenveen, R. T., De Wit, G. A., & Boshuizen, H. C. (2006). Estimating health-adjusted life expectancy conditional on risk factors: Results for smoking and obesity. *Population Health Metrics, 4,* 14.

Van Cleave, J., Gortmaker, S. L., & Perrin, J. M. (2010). Dynamics of obesity and chronic health conditions among children and youth. *Journal of the American Medical Association, 303,* 623–630.

Van Eerdewegh, M. M., Bieri, M. D., Parilla, R. H., & Clayton, P. J. (1982). The bereaved child. *American Journal of Psychiatry, 140,* 23–29.

Van Koningsbruggen, G. M., Das, E., & Roskos-Ewoldsen, D. R. (2009). How self-affirmation reduces defensive processing of threatening health information: Evidence at the implicit level. *Health Psychology, 28,* 563–568.

Van Zundert, R. M. P., Ferguson, S. G., Shiffman, S., & Engels, R. C. M. E. (2010). Dynamic effects of self-efficacy on smoking lapses and relapse among adolescents. *Health Psychology, 29,* 246–254.

Vanable, P. A., McKirnan, D. J., Buchbinder, S. P., Bartholow, B. N., Douglas, J. M., Jr., Judson, F. N., & MacQueen, K. M. (2004). Alcohol use and high-risk sexual behavior among men who have sex with men: The effects of consumption level and partner type. *Health Psychology, 23,* 525–532.

Vanable, P. A., Ostrow, D. G., McKirnan, D. J., Taywaditep, K. J., & Hope, B. A. (2000). Impact of combination therapies on HIV risk perceptions and sexual risk among HIV-positive and HIV-negative gay and bisexual men. *Health Psychology, 19,* 134–145.

Vartanian, L. R., Herman, C. P., & Wansink, B. (2008). Are we aware of the external factors that influence our food intake? *Health Psychology, 27*, 533–538.

Vaughan, E., Anderson, C., Agran, P., & Winn, D. (2004). Cultural differences in young children's vulnerability to injuries: A risk and protection perspective. *Health Psychology, 23*, 289–298.

Vaughan, P. W., Rogers, E. M., Singhal, A., & Swalehe, R. M. (2000). Entertainment-education and HIV/AIDS prevention: A field experiment in Tanzania. *Journal of Health Communication, 5*, 81–100.

Vertosick, F. T., Jr. (2000). *Why we hurt: The natural history of pain.* New York, NY: Harcourt.

Vicary, A., & Fraley, R. (2010). Student reactions to the shootings at Virginia Tech and Northern Illinois University: Does sharing grief and support over the Internet affect recovery? *Personality and Social Psychology Bulletin, 36*, 1555–1563.

Vickers, A. J., Till, C., Tangen, C. M., Lilja, H., & Thompson, I. M. (2011). An empirical evaluation of guidelines on prostate-specific antigen velocity in prostate cancer detection. *Journal of the National Cancer Institute, 103*, 462–469.

Villanti, A., Boulay, M., & Juon, H. S. (2011). Peer, parent and media influences on adolescent smoking by developmental stage. *Addictive Behaviors, 36*, 133–136.

Vincent, M., Clearie, A. F., & Schluchter, M. D. (1987). Reducing adolescent pregnancy through school and community-based education. *Journal of the American Medical Association, 257*, 3382–3386.

Vines, A. I., Baird, D. D., Stevens, J., Hertz-Picciotto, I., Light, K. C., & McNeilly, M. (2007). Associations of abdominal fat with perceived racism and passive emotional responses to racism in African American women. *American Journal of Public Health, 97*, 526–530.

Viney, L. L., Walker, B. M., Robertson, T., Lilley, B., & Ewan, C. (1994). Dying in palliative care units and in hospital: A comparison of quality of life of terminal cancer patients. *Journal of Consulting and Clinical Psychology, 62*, 157–164.

Vodermaier, A., Caspari, C., Wang, L., Koehm, J., Ditsch, N., & Untch, M. (2011). How and for whom are decision aids effective? Long-term psychological outcome of a randomized controlled trial in women with newly diagnosed breast cancer. *Health Psychology, 30*, 12–19.

Von Ah, D., Harvison, K. W., Monahan, P. O., Moser, L. R., Zhao, Q., Carpenter, J. S., . . . Unverzagt, F. W. (2009). Cognitive function in breast cancer survivors compared to healthy age- and education-matched women. *The Clinical Neuropsychologist, 23*, 661–674.

Von Känel, R., von Känela, R., Mausbach, B. T., Patterson, T. L., Dimsdale, J. E., Aschbacher, K., . . . , Grant, I. (2008). Increased Framingham coronary heart disease risk score in dementia caregivers relative to non-caregiving controls. *Gerontology, 54*, 131–137.

Wadden, T. A. (1993). The treatment of obesity: An overview. In A. J. Stunkard & T. A. Wadden (Eds.), *Obesity: Theory and therapy* (2nd ed., 197–217). New York, NY: Raven.

Wadden, T. A., Brownell, K. D., & Foster, G. D. (2002). Obesity: Responding to the global epidemic. *Journal of Consulting and Clinical Psychology, 70*, 510–525.

Wade, D. T., & Halligan, P. W. (2004). Do biomedical models of illness make for good healthcare systems? *British Medical Journal, 329*, 1398–1401.

Wade, T. D., & Lee, C. (2005). The impact of breast cancer on the lives of middle-aged women: Results from the Australian Longitudinal Study of Women's Health. *Health Psychology, 24*, 246–251.

Wager, T. D., Rilling, J., Smith, E. E., Sokolik, A., Casey, K., Kosslyn, S. M., . . . Cohen, J. D. (2004). Placebo-induced changes in fMRI in the anticipation and experience of pain. *Science, 303*, 1162–1167.

Wagner, P. J., & Curran, P. (1984). Health beliefs and physician identified "worried well." *Health Psychology, 3*, 459–474.

Waitzkin, H. (1984). Doctor–patient communication. *Journal of the American Medical Association, 252*, 2441–2446.

Waitzkin, H. (1985). Information giving in medical care. *Journal of Health and Social Behavior, 26*, 81–101.

Wakschlag, L., Leventhal, B., Pine, D., Pickett, K. & Carter, A. (2006). Elucidating early mechanisms of developmental psychopathology: The case of prenatal smoking and disruptive behavior. *Child Development, 77*, 893–906.

Wakschlag, L., Pickett, K., Kasza, K., & Loeber, R. (2006). Is maternal smoking during pregnancy associated with a developmental pattern of conduct problems in young boys? *Journal of the American Academy of Child and Adolescent Psychiatry, 45*, 461–467.

Waldron, I. (1983). Sex differences in illness incidence, prognosis and mortality: Issues and evidence. *Social Science and Medicine, 17*, 1107–1123.

Waldron, R. (2003, October 30). Students are dying; colleges can do more. *Newsweek.*

Walker, E. A., Katon, W. J., Jemelka, R. P., & Roy-Bryne, P. P. (1992). Comorbidity of gastrointestinal complaints, depression, and anxiety in the Epidemiologic Catchment Area (ECA) Study. *American Journal of Medicine, 92*, 26S–30S.

Walker, L. S., Garber, J., Smith, C. A., Van Slyke, D. A., & Claar, R. L. (2001). The relation of daily stressors to somatic and emotional symptoms in children with and without recurrent abdominal pain. *Journal of Consulting and Clinical Psychology, 69*, 85–91.

Walker, L. S., Smith, C. A., Garber, J., & Claar, R. L. (2005). Testing a model of pain appraisal and coping in children with chronic abdominal pain. *Health Psychology, 24*, 364–374.

Walkup, J., Wei, W., Sambamoorthi, U., & Crystal, S. (2008). Antidepressant treatment and adherence to combination antiretroviral therapy among patients with AIDS and diagnosed depression. *Psychiatric Quarterly, 79*, 43–53.

Waller, G., & Hartley, P. (1994). Perceived parental style and eating psychopathology. *European Eating Disorders Reveiw, 2*, 76–92.

Wallston, B. S., Alagna, S. W., DeVellis, B. M., & DeVellis, R. F. (1983). Social support and physical illness. *Health Psychology, 2*, 367–391.

Walsh, B. T., & Devlin, M. J. (1998). Eating disorders: Progress and problems. *Science, 280*, 1387–1390.

Wang, C., Schmid, C. H., Rones, R., Kalish, R., Yinh, J., Goldenberg, D. L. . . . McAlindon, T. (2010). A randomized trial of tai chi for fibromyalgia. *New England Journal of Medicine, 363*, 743–754.

Wang, S. S., Houshyar, S., & Prinstein, M. J. (2006). Adolescent girls' and boys' weight-related behaviors and cognitions: Associations with reputation- and preference-based peer status. *Health Psychology, 25*, 658–663.

Wang, T., Hartzell, D. L., Rose, B. S., Flatt, W. P., Hulsey, M. G., Menon, N. K., . . . Baile, C. A. (1999). Metabolic responses to intracerebroventricular leptin and restricted feeding. *Physiology and Behavior, 65*, 839–848.

Wansink, B., & Cheney, M. M. (2005). Super bowls: Serving bowl size and food consumption. *Journal of the American Medical Association, 293*, 1727–1728.

Wansink, B., Cheney, M. M., & Chan, N. (2003). Exploring comfort food preferences across gender and age. *Physiology and Behavior, 79*, 739–747.

Wansink, B., Painter, J. E., & North, J. (2005). Bottomless bowls: Why visual cues of portion size may influence intake. *Obesity Research, 13*, 93–100.

Wansink, B., van Ittersum, K., & Painter, J. E. (2006). Ice cream illusions: Bowl size, spoon size, and serving size. *American Journal of Preventive Medicine, 145*, 240–243.

Ward, S. E., Goldberg, N., Miller-McCauley, V., Mueller, C., Nolane, A., Pawlik-Plank, D., . . . Weissman, D. E. (1993). Patient-related barriers to management of cancer pain. *Pain, 52,* 319–324.

Wardle, J., Haase, A. M., Steptoe, A., Nillapun, M., Jonwutiwes, K., & Bellisle, F. (2004). Gender differences in food choice: The contribution of health beliefs and dieting. *Annals of Behavioral Medicine, 27,* 107–116.

Wardle, J., Waller, J., & Jarvis, M. J. (2002). Sex differences in the association of socioeconomic status with obesity. *American Journal of Public Health, 92,* 1299–1304.

Ware, J. E., Jr., Bayliss, M. S., Rogers, W. H., & Kosinski, M. (1996). Differences in four-year health outcomes for elderly and poor, chronically ill patients in HMO and fee-for-service systems: Results from the Medical Outcomes Study. *Journal of the American Medical Association, 276,* 1039–1047.

Wass, H., & Stillion, J. M. (1988). Death in the lives of children and adolescents. In H. Wass, F. M. Berado, & R. A. Neimeyer (Eds.), *Dying: Facing the facts* (2nd ed., pp. 201–228). New York, NY: Hemisphere.

Watson, D. (1988). Intraindividual and interindividual analyses of positive and negative affect: Their relation to health complaints, perceived stress, and daily activities. *Journal of Personality and Social Psychology, 54,* 1020–1030.

Watson, D., & Clark, L. A. (1984). Negative affectivity: The disposition to experience aversive emotional states. *Psychological Bulletin, 96,* 465–490.

Watson, D., & Pennebaker, J. W. (1989). Health complaints, stress, and distress: Exploring the central role of negative affectivity. *Psychological Review, 96,* 234–254.

Watson, J. D. (1990). The human genome project: Past, present, and future. *Science, 248,* 44–49.

Weaver, K. E., Llabre, M. M., Durán, R. E., Antoni, M. H., Ironson, G., Penedo, F. J., & Schneiderman, N. (2005). A stress and coping model of medication adherence and viral load in HIV-positive men and women on highly active antiretroviral therapy (HAART). *Health Psychology, 24,* 385–392.

Webb, M. S., Simmons Nath, V., & Brandon, T. H. (2005). Tailored interventions for motivating smoking cessation: Using placebo-tailoring to examine the influence of expectancies and personalization. *Health Psychology, 24,* 179–188.

Webster, D. W., Gainer, P. S., & Champion, H. P. (1993). Weapon carrying among inner-city junior high school students: Defensive behavior vs. aggressive delinquency. *American Journal of Public Health, 83,* 1604–1608.

Wechsler, H., Dowdall, G. W., Davenport, A., & Castillo, S. (1995). Correlates of college student binge drinking. *American Journal of Public Health, 85,* 921–926.

Wegner, D. M. (1994). Ironic processes of mental control. *Psychological Review, 101,* 34–52.

Wegner, D. M., Shortt, J. W., Blake, A. W., & Page, M. S. (1990). The suppression of exciting thoughts. *Journal of Personality and Social Psychology, 58,* 409–418.

Weidner, G., Boughal, T., Connor, S. L., Pieper, C., & Mendell, N. R. (1997). Relationship of job strain to standard coronary risk factors and psychological characteristics in women and men of the family heart study. *Health Psychology, 16,* 239–247.

Weinstein, N. D. (1984). Why it won't happen to me: Perceptions of risk factors and susceptibility. *Health Psychology, 3,* 431–457.

Weinstein, N. D. (1987). Unrealistic optimism about susceptibility to health problems: Conclusions from a community-wide sample. *Journal of Behavioral Medicine, 10,* 481–500.

Weinstein, N. D. (1988). The precaution adoption process. *Health Psychology, 7,* 355–386.

Weinstein, N. D., Rothman, A. J., & Sutton, S. R. (1998). Stage theories of health behavior: Conceptual and methodological issues. *Health Psychology, 17,* 290–299.

Weinstein, N. D., & Sandman, P. M. (1992). A model of the precaution adoption process: Evidence from home radon testing. *Health Psychology, 11,* 170–180.

Weis, J., Poppelreuter, M., & Bartsch, H. H. (2009). Cognitive deficits as long-term side-effects of adjuvant therapy in breast cancer patients: 'Subjective' complaints and 'objective' neuropsychological test results. *Psycho-Oncology, 18,* 775–782.

Weisner, C., Greenfield, T., & Room, R. (1995). Trends in the treatment of alcohol problems in the U.S. general population, 1979–1990. *American Journal of Public Health, 85,* 55–60.

Welin, L., Tibblin, G., Svardsudd, K., Tibblin, B., Ander-Peciva, S., Larsson, B., & Wilhelmsen, L. (1985). Prospective study of social influences on mortality. *Lancet, 1,* 915–918.

Wenger, N. K., Speroff, L., & Packard, B. (1993). Cardiovascular health and disease in women. *New England Journal of Medicine, 329,* 247–256.

Wenneker, M. B., Weissman, J. S., & Epstein, A. M. (1990). The association of payer with utilization of cardiac procedures in Massachusetts. *Journal of the American Medical Association, 264,* 1255–1260.

Werner, R. M., & Pearson, T. A. (1998). What's so passive about passive smoking? Secondhand smoke as a cause of atherosclerotic disease. *Journal of the American Medical Association, 179,* 157–158.

Wetter, D. W., Fiore, M. C., Gritz, E. R., Lando, H. A., Stitzer, M. L., Hasselblad, V., & Baker, T. B. (1998). The agency for health care policy and research smoking cessation clinical practice guideline: Findings and implications for psychologists. *American Psychologist, 53,* 657–669.

Whipple, B. (1987). Methods of pain control: Review of research and literature. *IMAGE: Journal of Nursing Scholarship, 19,* 142–146.

Whisman, M. A. (2010). Loneliness and the metabolic syndrome in a population-based sample of middle-aged and older adults. *Health Psychology, 29,* 550–554.

White, A. A., III, & Gordon, S. L. (1982). Synopsis: Workshop on idiopathic low-back pain. *Spine, 13,* 1407–1410.

White, E., Jacobs, E. J., & Daling, J. R. (1996). Physical activity in relation to colon cancer in middle-aged men and women. *American Journal of Epidemiology, 144,* 42–50.

White, E., Urban, N., & Taylor, V. (1993). Mammography utilization, public health impact, and cost-effectiveness in the United States. *Annual Review of Public Health, 14,* 605–633.

Whitehead, W. E., Busch, C. M., Heller, B. R., & Costa, P. T. (1986). Social learning influences on menstrual symptoms and illness behavior. *Health Psychology, 5,* 13–23.

Whittle, J., Conigliaro, J., Good, C. B., & Lofgren, R. P. (1993). Racial differences in the use of invasive cardiovascular procedures in the Department of Veterans Affairs medical system. *New England Journal of Medicine, 329,* 621–627.

Whooley, M. A., de Jonge, P., Vittinghoff, E., Otte, C., Moos, R., Carney, R. M., . . . Browne, W. S. (2008). Depressive symptoms, health behaviors, and risk of cardiovascular events in patients with coronary heart disease. *Journal of the American Medical Association, 300,* 2379–2388.

Wickelgren, I. (1998). Do "apples" fare worse than "pears"? *Science, 280,* 1365.

Widows, M., Jacobsen, P., Booth-Jones, M., & Fields, K. (2005). Predictors of post traumatic growth following bone marrow transplantation for cancer. *Health Psychology, 24,* 266–273.

Wiebe, J. S., & Christensen, A. J. (1997). Health beliefs, personality, and adherence in hemodialysis patients: An interactional perspective. *Annals of Behavioral Medicine, 19,* 31–35.

Wiens, A. N., & Menustik, C. E. (1983). Treatment outcome and patient characteristics in an aversion therapy program for alcoholism. *American Psychologist, 38,* 1089–1096.

Wiggins, S., Whyte, P., Huggins, M., Adam, S., Theilmann, J., Bloch, M., ... Hayden, M. R. (1992). The psychological consequences of predictive testing for Huntington's disease. *New England Journal of Medicine, 327,* 1401–1405.

Wight, R. G., LeBlanc, A. J., & Aneshensel, C. S. (1998). AIDS caregiving and health among midlife and older women. *Health Psychology, 17,* 130–137.

Wijngaards-de Meij, L., Stroebe, M. S., Schut, H. A. W., Stroebe, W., Van den Bout, J., van der Heijden, P. G. J., & Dijkstra, I. C. (2008). Neuroticism and attachment insecurity as predictors of bereavement outcome. *Journal of Research in Personality, 41,* 498–505.

Wildes, K. A., Miller, A. R., de Majors, S. S., & Ramirez, A. G. (2009). The religiosity/spirituality of Latina breast cancer survivors and influence on health-related quality of life. *Psycho-Oncology, 18,* 831–840.

Wilfley, D. E., Stein, R. I., Saelens, B. E., Mockus, D. S., Matt, G. E., Hayden-Wade, H. A., ... Epstein, L. H. (2007). Efficacy of maintenance treatment approaches for childhood overweight: A randomized controlled trial. *Journal of the American Medical Association, 298,* 1661–1673.

Wilfond, B. S., & Fost, N. (1990). The cystic fibrosis gene: Medical and social implications for heterozygote detection. *Journal of the American Medical Association, 263,* 2777–2783.

Willenbring, M. L., Levine, A. S., & Morley, J. E. (1986). Stress induced eating and food preferences in humans: A pilot study. *International Journal of Eating Disorders, 5,* 855–864.

Williams, A. F., & Lancaster, K. A. (1995). The prospects of daytime running lights for reducing vehicle crashes in the United States. *Public Health Reports, 110,* 233–239.

Williams, A. F., & Lund, A. K. (1992). Injury control: What psychologists can contribute. *American Psychologist, 47,* 1036–1039.

Williams, D. A. (1996). Acute pain management. In R. J. Gatchel & D. C. Turk (Eds.), *Psychological aapproaches to pain management: A practitioner's handbook* (pp. 55–77). New York, NY: Guilford Press.

Williams, J. E., Paton, C. C., Siegler, I. C., Eigenbrot, M. L., Nieto, F. J., & Tyroler, H. A. (2000). Clinical investigation and reports: Anger proneness predicts coronary heart disease risk: Prospective analysis from the Atherosclerosis Risk in Communities (ARIC) Study. *Circulation, 101,* 2034–2039.

Williams, P. G., Wiebe, D. J., & Smith, T. W. (1992). Coping processes as mediators of the relationship between hardiness and health. *Journal of Behavioral Medicine, 15,* 237–255.

Williams, R. B., Barefoot, J. C., Califf, R. M., Haney, T. L., Saunders, W. B., Pryor, D. B., ... Mark, D. B. (1992). Prognostic importance of social and economic resources among medically treated patients with angiographically documented coronary artery disease. *Journal of the American Medical Association, 267,* 520–524.

Williams, R. B., Jr., Haney, T. L., Lee, K. L., Kong, Y., Blumenthal, J. A., & Whalen, R. E. (1980). Type A behavior, hostility, and coronary arteriosclerosis. *Psychosomatic Medicine, 42,* 539–549.

Williams, S. S., Kimble, D. L., Covell, N. H., Weiss, L. H., Newton, K. J., Fisher, J. D., & Fisher, W. A. (1992). College students use implicit personality theory instead of safer sex. *Journal of Applied Social Psychology, 22,* 921–933.

Williams-Piehota, P., Pizarro, J., Schneider, T. R., Mowad, L., & Salovey, P. (2005). Matching health messages to monitor-blunter coping styles to motivate screening mammography. *Health Psychology, 24,* 58–67.

Wills, T. A. (1984). Supportive functions of interpersonal relationships. In S. Cohen & L. Syme (Eds.), *Social support and health* (pp. 61–82). New York, NY: Academic Press.

Wills, T. A., Gibbons, F. X., Sargent, J. D., Gerrard, M., Lee, H.-R., & Dal Cin, S. (2010). Good self-control moderates the effect of mass media on adolescent tobacco and alcohol use: Tests with studies of children and adolescents. *Health Psychology, 29,* 539–549.

Wills, T. A., Resko, J. A., Ainette, M. G., & Mendoza, D. (2004a). Smoking onset in adolescence: A person-centered analysis. *Health Psychology, 23,* 158–167.

Wills, T. A., Resko, J. A., Ainette, M. G., & Mendoza, D. (2004b). Role of parent support and peer support in adolescent substance use: A test of mediated effects. *Psychology of Addictive Behaviors, 18,* 122–134.

Wills, T. A., Sargent, J. D., Stoolmiller, M., Gibbons, F. X., & Gerrard, M. (2008). Movie smoking exposure and smoking onset: A longitudinal study of mediation processes in a representative sample of U.S. adolescents. *Psychology of Addictive Behaviors, 22,* 269–277.

Wills, T. A., Sargent, J. D., Stoolmiller, M., Gibbons, F. X., Worth, K. A., & Dal Cin, S. (2007). Movie exposure to smoking cues and adolescent smoking onset: A test for mediation through peer affiliations with adolescents in Northern New England. *Health Psychology, 26,* 769–776.

Wilson, D. P., & Endres, R. K. (1986). Compliance with blood glucose monitoring in children with type 1 diabetes mellitus. *Journal of Pediatrics, 108,* 1022–1024.

Wilson, R. S., Krueger, K. R., Gu, L., Bienias, J. L., Mendes de Leon, C. F., & Evans, D. A. (2005). Neuroticism, extraversion, and mortality in a defined population of older persons. *Psychosomatic Medicine, 67,* 841–845.

Windle, M. (1992). A longitudinal study of stress buffering for adolescent problem behaviors. *Developmental Psychology, 28,* 522–530.

Windle, M., & Windle, R. C. (2001). Depressive symptoms and cigarette smoking among middle adolescents: Prospective associations and intrapersonal and interpersonal influences. *Journal of Consulting and Clinical Psychology, 69,* 215–226.

Windsor, R. A., Lowe, J. B., Perkins, L. L., Smith-Yoder, D., Artz, L., Crawford, M., ... Boyd, N. R., Jr. (1993). Health education for pregnant smokers: Its behavioral impact and cost benefit. *American Journal of Public Health, 83,* 201–206.

Winett, R. A. (1995). A framework for health promotion and disease prevention. *American Psychologist, 50,* 341–350.

Wing, R. R., & Jeffery, R. W. (1999). Benefits of recruiting participants with friends and increasing social support for weight loss and maintenance. *Journal of Consulting and Clinical Psychology, 67,* 132–138.

Winickoff, J. P., Friebely, J., Tanski, S. E., Sherrod, C., Matt, G. E., Hovell, M. F., & McMillen, R. C. (2009). Beliefs about the health effects of "thirdhand" smoke and home smoking bans. *Pediatrics, 123,* 74–79.

Winkleby, M. A., Fortmann, S., & Barrett, D. (1990). Social class disparities in risk factors for disease: Eight-year prevalence patterns by level of education. *Preventive Medicine, 19,* 1–12.

Winkleby, M. A., Kraemer, H. C., Ahn, D. K., & Varady, A. N. (1998). Ethnic and socioeconomic differences in cardiovascular disease risk factors. *Journal of the American Medical Association, 280,* 356–362.

Winkleby, M. A., Robinson, T. N., Sundquist, J., & Kraemer, H. C. (1999). Ethnic variation in cardiovascular disease risk factors among children and young adults: Findings from the Third National Health and Nutrition Examination Survey, 1988–1994. *Journal of the American Medical Association, 281,* 1006–1013.

Winn, D. M., Blot, W. J., Shy, C. M., Pickle, I. W., Toledo, A., & Frameni, J. F. (1981). Snuff dipping and oral cancer among women in the Southeastern United States. *New England Journal of Medicine, 304,* 745–749.

Winters, R. (1985). Behavioral approaches to pain. In N. Schneiderman & J. T. Tapp (Eds.),

Behavioral medicine: The biopsychosocial approach (pp. 565–587). Hillsdale, NJ: Erlbaum.

Winzelberg, A. J., Eppstein, D., Eldredge, K. L., Wilfley, D., Dasmahapatra, R., Dev, P., & Taylor, C. B. (2000). Effectiveness of an Internet-based program for reducing risk factors for eating disorders. *Journal of Consulting and Clinical Psychology, 68,* 346–350.

Wiseman, C. V., Gray, J. J., Mosimann, J. E., & Ahrens, A. H. (1992). Cultural expectations of thinness in women: An update. *International Journal of Eating Disorders, 11,* 85–89.

Wisocki, P. A., & Skowron, J. (2000). The effects of gender and culture on adjustment to widowhood. In R. M. Eisler & M. Hersen (Eds.), *Handbook of gender, culture, and health* (pp. 429–447). Mahwah, NJ: Erlbaum.

Witek-Janusek, L., Albuquerque, K., Chroniak, K. R., Chroniak, C., Durazo-Arvizu, R., & Mathews, H. L. (2008). Effect of mindfulness based stress reduction on immune function, quality of life and coping in women newly diagnosed with early stage breast cancer. *Brain, Behavior, and Immunity, 22,* 969–981.

Witte, K., & Allen, M. (2000). A meta-analysis of fear appeals: Implications for effective public health campaigns. *Health Education & Behavior, 27,* 591–615.

Wohlgemuth, E., & Betz, N. E. (1991). Gender as a moderator of the relationships of stress and social support to physical health in college students. *Journal of Counseling Psychology, 38,* 367–374.

Wolff, B., Burns, J. W., Quartana, P. J., Lofland, K., Bruehl, S., & Chung, O. Y. (2008). Pain catastrophizing, physiological indexes, and chronic pain severity: Tests of mediation and moderation models. *Journal of Behavioral Medicine, 31,* 105–114.

Wolff, N. J., Darlington, A.-S. E., Hunfeld, J. A. M., Verhulst, F. C., Jaddoe, V. W. V., Moll, H. A., . . . Tiemeier, H. (2009). The association of parent behaviors, chronic pain, and psychological problems with venipuncture distress in infants: The Generation R study. *Health Psychology, 28,* 605–613.

Wolin, K. Y., Yan, Y., Colditz, G. A., & Lee, I. M. (2009). Physical activity and colon cancer prevention: A meta-analysis. *British Journal of Cancer, 100,* 611–616.

Woloshin, S., Schwartz, L. M., & Welch, H. G. (2002). Risk charts: Putting cancer in context. *Journal of the National Cancer Institute, 94,* 799–804.

Wonderlich, S., Klein, M. H., & Council, J. R. (1996). Relationship of social perceptions and self-concept in bulimia nervosa. *Journal of Consulting and Clinical Psychology, 64,* 1231–1237.

Wonderlich, S. A., Wilsnack, R. W., Wilsnack, S. C., & Harris, T. R. (1996). Childhood sexual abuse and bulimic behavior in a nationally representative sample. *American Journal of Public Health, 86,* 1082–1086.

Woods, P. J., & Burns, J. (1984). Type A behavior and illness in general. *Journal of Behavioral Medicine, 7,* 277–286.

Woods, P. J., Morgan, B. T., Day, B. W., Jefferson, T., & Harris, C. (1984). Findings on a relationship between Type A behavior and headaches. *Journal of Behavioral Medicine, 7,* 277–285.

Woodward, W. A., Huang, E. H., McNeese, M. D., Perkins, G. H., Tucker, S. L., Strom, E. A., . . . Buchholz, T. A. (2006). African-American race is associated with a poorer overall survival rate for breast cancer patients treated with mastectomy and Doxorubicin-based chemotherapy. *Cancer, 107,* 2662–2668.

Woolhandler, S., Campbell, T., & Himmelstein, D. U. (1993). Costs of health care administration in the United States and Canada. *New England Journal of Medicine, 349,* 768–775.

Woolhandler, S., & Himmelstein, D. U. (1991). The deteriorating administrative efficiency of the U.S. health care system. *New England Journal of Medicine, 324,* 1253–1258.

Wooten, K. G., Kolasa, M., Singleton, J. A., & Shefer, A. (2010). National, state, and local area vaccination coverage among children aged 19–35 months—United States, 2009. *Morbidity and Mortality Weekly Report, 59*(36), 1171–1177.

World Health Organization. (1964). *Basic documents* (15th ed., p. 1). Geneva, Switzerland: Author.

World Health Organization. (2010). *Global strategy to reduce the harmful use of alcohol.* Geneva, Switzerland: Author.

World Health Organization. (2010). *Media center: Maternal mortality.* Retrieved September 17, 2011 from http://www.who.int/mediacentre/factsheets/fs348/en/index.html.

Wortman, C. B. (1984). Social support and cancer: Conceptual and methodological issues. *Cancer, 53,* 2339–2360.

Wortman, C. B., & Dunkel-Schetter, C. (1979). Interpersonal relationships and cancer: A theoretical analysis. *Journal of Social Issues, 35,* 120–155.

Wortman, C. B., & Lehman, D. (1985). Reactions to victims of life crises: Support attempts that fail. In I. G. Sarason & B. R. Sarason (Eds.), *Social support: Theory, research, and application* (pp. 463–489). The Hague, Netherlands: Martinus Nijhoff.

Wright, A. A., Zhang, B., Ray, A., Mack, J. W., Trice, E., Balboni, T., . . . Prigerson, H. G.

(2008). Associations between end-of-life discussions, patient mental health, medical care near death, and caregiver bereavement adjustment. *Journal of the American Medical Association, 300,* 1665–1673.

Writing Group for the Women's Health Initiative Investigators (2002). Risks and benefits of estrogen plus progestin in healthy postmenopausal women: Principal results from the Women's Health Initiative Randomized Controlled Trial. *Journal of the American Medical Association, 288,* 321–333.

Wulfert, E., & Wan, C. K. (1993). Condom use: A self-efficacy model. *Health Psychology, 12,* 346–353.

Xu, J., Kochanek, K. D., Murphy, S. L., & Tejada-Vera, B. (2010). Deaths: Final data for 2007. *National Vital Statistics Reports, 58,* 1–136.

Xu, J., & Roberts, R. E. (2010). The power of positive emotions: It's a matter of life or death: Subjective well-being and longevity over 28 years in a general population. *Health Psychology, 29,* 9–19.

Yach, D., Hawkes, C., Gould, C. L., & Hofman, K. J. (2004). The global burden of chronic diseases: Overcoming impediments to prevention and control. *Journal of the American Medical Association, 291,* 2616–2622.

Yamamoto, Y., Hayashino, Y., Akiba, T., Akizawa, T., Asano, Y., Saito, A., . . . Fukuhara, S. (2009). Depressive symptoms predict the subsequent risk of bodily pain in dialysis patients: Japan Dialysis Outcomes and Practice Patterns Study. *Pain Medicine, 10,* 883–889.

Yanovski, S. Z. (2003). Binge eating disorder and obesity in 2003: Could treating an eating disorder have a positive effect on the obesity epidemic? *International Journal of Eating Disorders, 34,* S117–S120.

Yarnold, P. R., Michelson, E. A., Thompson, D. A., & Adams, S. L. (1998). Predicting patient satisfaction: A study of two emergency departments. *Journal of Behavioral Medicine, 21,* 545–563.

Ybema, J. F., Kuijer, R. G., Hagedoorn, M., & Buunk, M. P. (2002). Caregiver burnout among intimate partners of patients with a severe illness: An equity perspective. *Personal Relationships, 9,* 73–88.

Yedidia, M. J., Gillespie, C. C., Kachur, E., Schwartz, M. D., Ockene, J., Chepaitis, A. E., . . . Lipkin, M. J. (2003). Effect of communications training on medical student performance. *Journal of the American Medical Association, 290,* 1157–1165.

Yee, B. W. K., Castro, F. G., Hammond, W. R., John, R., Wyatt, G. E., & Yurg, B. R. (1995).

Panel IV: Risk-taking and abusive behaviors among ethnic minorities. *Health Psychology, 14,* 622–631.

Yeh, E. S., Rochette, L. M., McKenzie, L. B., & Smith, G. A. (2011). Injuries associated with cribs, playpens, and bassinets among young children in the U.S., 1990–2008. *Pediatrics, 127,* 479–486.

Yi, M. S., Mrus, J. M., Wade, T. J., Ho, M. L., Hornung, R. W., Cotton, S., . . . Tsevat, J. (2006). Religion, spirituality, and depressive symptoms in patients with HIV/AIDS. *Journal of General Internal Medicine, 2,* S21–S27.

Yong, L.-C., Brown, C. C., Schatzkin, A., Dresser, C. M., Slesinshi, M. J., Cox, C. S., & Taylor, P. R. (1997). Intake of vitamins E, C, and A and risk of lung cancer: The NHANES I Epidemiologic Followup Study. *American Journal of Epidemiology, 146,* 231–243.

Younger, J., Aron, A., Parke, S., Chatterjee, N., & Mackey, S. (2010). Viewing pictures of a romantic partner reduces experimental pain: Involvement of neural reward systems. *PLoS ONE 5(10),* e13309.

Yusuf, S., Hawken, S., Ounpuu, S., Dans, T., Avezum, A., Lanas, F., . . . INTERHEART Study Investigators. (2005). Effect of potentially modifiable risk factors associated with myocardial infarction in 52 countries (the INTERHEART study): Case-control study. *Lancet, 364,* 937–952.

Zador, P. L., & Ciccone, M. A. (1993). Automobile driver fatalities in frontal impacts: Air bags compared with manual belts. *American Journal of Public Health, 83,* 661–666.

Zakowski, S. G., Ramati, A., Morton, C., Johnson, P., & Flanigan, R. (2004). Written emotional disclosure buffers the effects of social constraints on distress among cancer patients. *Health Psychology, 23,* 555–563.

Zarski, J. J. (1984). Hassles and health: A replication. *Health Psychology, 3,* 243–251.

Zashikhina, A., & Hagglof, B. (2007). Mental health in adolescents with chronic physical illness versus controls in Northern Russia. *Acta Paediatrica, 96,* 890–896.

Zastrowny, T. R., Kirschenbaum, D. S., & Meng, A. L. (1986). Coping skills training for children: Effects on distress before, during, and after hospitalization for surgery. *Health Psychology, 5,* 231–247.

Zavala, M. W., Maliski, S. L., Kwan, L., Fink, A., & Litwin, M. S. (2009). Spirituality and quality of life in low-income men with metastatic prostate cancer. *Psycho-Oncology, 18,* 753–761.

Zejdlik, C. M. (1983). *Management of spinal cord injury.* Monterey, CA: Wadsworth.

Zelman, D. C., Brandon, T. H., Jorenby, D. E., & Baker, T. B. (1992). Measures of affect and nicotine dependence predict differential response to smoking cessation treatments. *Journal of Consulting and Clinical Psychology, 60,* 943–952.

Zhang, S., Hunter, D. J., Forman, M. R., Rosner, B. A., Speizer, F. F., Colditz, G. A., . . . Willett, W. C. (1999). Dietary carotenoids and vitamins A, C, and E and risk of breast cancer. *Journal of the National Cancer Institute, 91,* 547–556.

Zhu, S.-H., Sun, J., Billings, S. C., Choi, W. S., & Malarcher, A. (1999). Predictors of smoking cessation in U.S. adolescents. *American Journal of Preventive Medicine, 16,* 202–207.

Zhu, S.-Y., Stretch, V., Balabanis, M., Rosbrook, B., Sadler, G., & Pierce, J. P. (1996). Telephone counseling for smoking cessation: Effects of single-session and multiple-session interventions. *Journal of Consulting and Clinical Psychology, 64,* 202–211.

Zisook, S., Schuchter, S. R., Sledge, P. A., & Judd, L. L. (1994). The spectrum of depressive phenomena after spousal bereavement. *Journal of Clinical Psychiatry, 55,* 29–36.

Zucker, R. A., & Gomberg, E. S. L. (1986). Etiology of alcoholism reconsidered: The case for a biopsychosocial process. *American Psychologist, 41,* 783–793.

Zucker, T. P., Flesche, C. W., Germing, U., Schroter, S., Willers, R., Wolf, H. H., & Heyll, A. (1998). Patient-controlled versus staff-controlled analgesia with pethidine after allogenic bone marrow transplantation. *Pain, 75,* 305–312.

Zwahlen, D., Hagenbuch, N., Carley, M. I., Jenewein, J., & Buchi, S. (2010). Posttraumatic growth in cancer patients and partners—effects of role, gender and the dyad on couples' posttraumatic growth experience. *Psycho-Oncology, 19,* 12–20.

AUTHOR INDEX

SUBJECT INDEX